THE ECONOMICS OF THOMAS ROBERT MALTHUS

STUDIES IN CLASSICAL POLITICAL ECONOMY / IV

SAMUEL HOLLANDER

The economics of Thomas Robert Malthus

UNIVERSITY OF TORONTO PRESS
Toronto Buffalo London

Toronto Buffalo London
Printed in Canada

ISBN 0-8020-0790-2 (cloth)

Printed on acid-free paper

Canadian Cataloguing in Publication Data

Hollander, Samuel, 1937–
The economics of Thomas Robert Malthus

(Studies in classical political economy ; 4)
Includes bibliographical references and index.
ISBN 0-8020-0790-2

1. Malthus, T.R. (Thomas Robert). 1766–1834.
2. Economics – Great Britain – History. I. Title.
II. Series.

HB863.H64 1997 330.15′3 C96-931581-3

University of Toronto Press acknowledges the financial assistance to its publishing program of the Canada Council and the Ontario Arts Council.

This book has been published with the help of a grant from the Humanities and Social Sciences Federation of Canada, using funds provided by the Social Sciences and Humanities Research Council of Canada.

The illustration on the jacket and title page is a reproduction of a proof engraving of Malthus in the papers of Piero Sraffa, housed in the Trinity College Library, Cambridge. It appears here by kind permission of the Master and Fellows of Trinity College.

TO PERLETTE

CONTENTS

III / Employment, aggregate demand, and money

PREFACE

This book is the fourth in my series Studies in Classical Political Economy, the first three volumes of which treat, respectively, the economics of Adam Smith (1973), David Ricardo (1979), and John Stuart Mill (1985). In the last two of those studies, and also in my text *Classical Economics* (1987), I approached Malthus's economics as the foil that set off Ricardo and Mill rather than in its own right. In this work I reverse the perspective, especially with regard to the Malthus–Ricardo link, and attempt to do full justice to Malthus, with reference to demography; economic growth; aggregate demand; value and distribution; money, banking, and trade; and the theory of policy. The study culminates in a drawing-together of the whole from the perspective of methodology.

A general objective here is to evaluate Lord Keynes's famous statement of the dichotomy between Ricardian and Malthusian method: 'In economic discussions Ricardo was the abstract and *a priori* theorist, Malthus the inductive and intuitive investigator who hated to stray too far from what he could test by reference to the facts and his own intuitions'; but 'it was Ricardo's more fascinating intellectual construction which was victorious, and Ricardo who, by turning his back so completely on Malthus's ideas, constrained the subject for a full hundred years in an artificial groove.' Isolating the source of the theoretical differences between Ricardo and Malthus by referring to their formally stated methodological predilections (in this manner) proves unconvincing; all in all, it emerges that, on the broad grounds of method, the contestants were far closer than is generally supposed.

Defining Malthus's relation to certain of his predecessors is a further general concern in this work. Malthus was by no means obeisant to Adam Smith; yet the roots of many of his views can be found in the

Wealth of Nations, including aspects of his position on aggregate demand. An unravelling of the complex web of ideas involving Smith, Malthus, and Ricardo is of particular intellectual interest, considering Lord Robbins's observation that Malthus's role in building up the classical system 'is a matter likely to arouse much more controversy than the answer to a similar question in the case of the other great classical economists.' Most significant, a physiocratic or quasi-physiocratic dimension to Malthus's work hitherto underestimated by scholars emerges. As well, an unexpected 'Sraffian' dimension – the corn-profit model – is shown to be present. These results may have major implications for nineteenth- and twentieth-century historiography.

This study addresses the relation between Malthusian theory and the available empirical data. The results prove particularly significant with respect to demography and growth theory, revealing the illegitimacy of the textbook perspective that characterizes Malthus as a social-welfare pessimist. The common notion of Malthus as spokesman of the landowning classes is also shown to be a fallacy. A fundamentally important discovery that throws much light on this issue relates to Malthus's ultimate abandonment of agricultural protectionism. With it, he in effect turned away from the physiocratic orientation and threw in his lot with the Ricardians, for it was his support of the 1815 Corn Bill that had struck so discordant a note from a 'classical' economist.

A further undertaking of this work is to evaluate the standard charges against Malthus of inconsistency, and even intellectual dishonesty. Here, these charges are shown to be seriously exaggerated. The implications of his theology are also investigated and shown to be unobtrusive, despite appearances, as far as concerns his positive economics and policy recommendations.

The methodological approach followed is that of the earlier volumes in this series. I adopt a combination of what the late George Stigler refers to as 'scientific exegesis,' which seeks that interpretation which maximizes the number of major theoretical conclusions that follow from alternative readings of the text, and 'personal exegesis,' which seeks that interpretation which best satisfies the writer's style (in the broadest sense of the term), method, and objective. Thus, in the interpretative process, allowance is made for both the logical and the biographical. I take issue with those historians of economics who believe that the researcher must pretend to lack knowledge of the future beyond the period under study in order to avoid the danger of anachronistic readings. Of course, we must avoid superimposing on an early writer reference frameworks that were developed only subsequently. But such a constraint does not require that we avoid modern vocabulary and categories in tracing the filiation of ideas. One is writing, after all, for modern readers. There is also a sophisticated form of anachronism that entails denying the presence in an early writer's work of modern concepts merely because they are expressed differently.

Tracing the filiation of ideas requires common sense and good judgment, not a pretence at innocent ignorance.

I should state at the outset my own personal attitude towards Malthus. Despite all the trouble he has caused me, I remain an admirer. I admire, above all, his courageous, politically incorrect recommendation for the control of population growth, against the official views of the church and military of the day, and despite his own status as priest of the Church of England. Had he lived today he would surely have been hauled before some college committee for his Travel Diaries. And who cannot like a man who penned this on his way up the River Elbe to Hamburg: 'The master of our boat ... hailed his wife from the shore & brought forwards two or three of the groups to see us pass. It is difficult to judge of the happiness of a people through a telescope, which by the by we used to bring them near to us, but, influenced perhaps by the fineness of the evening & the beauty of the scene, we could not help fancying from the air of neatness & cheerfulness that seemed generally to prevail among the cottages, that the inhabitants were happy' (1966, 31). Finally, I greatly admire his abandonment of agricultural protectionism. It is only a pity that Ricardo did not live to witness it.

Critics lamented that the earlier volumes in this series grew in size exponentially. I have taken their complaint to heart; this book is no longer than my *Mill*. And to help readers (and me) negotiate the material, I have inserted an unusually generous set of cross-references.

ACKNOWLEDGMENTS

I commenced this study during the academic year 1987–8 while visiting the Hebrew University, Jerusalem, and continued my preliminary researches at the University of Auckland, New Zealand, where I was a University of Auckland Foundation Visitor. I am most grateful to those institutions for providing admirable facilities. It is customary for an author to acknowledge individuals who have provided advice and criticism while, at the same time, retaining responsibility for remaining errors and defects; I shall abide by this commendable practice – while also taking credit for at least some of the positive features of this work – and express my warmest appreciation to a large number of friends and colleagues who have helped me one way or another. Even if they have forgotten, I have not. My thanks go to: R.D.C. Black; Giovanni Caravale; Lila Costabile; Tim Davis; Robert Dorfman; Walter Eltis; Tony Endres; Stanley Engerman; the late Robert Fenn; the late Barry Gordon; Arnold Heertje; Jim Irwin; Tom Kompas; Cigdem Kurdas; Heinz Kurz; Sergio Nistico; Sandra Peart; J.-P. Platteau; Bette Polkinghorn; Pier-Luigi Porta; John Pullen; Kevin Reilly; Annalisa Rosselli; Paul Samuelson; Brenda Spotton; Ian Steedman; the late George Stigler; and Masazumi Wakatabe. My intellectual obligations to David Levy and A.M.C. Waterman are very great indeed; I cannot find adequate words to express my appreciation for their careful reading of my manuscript, and their tolerance even when we differ. Kelly Baxter, Rafael Gomez, Agnes Kruchio, Alexandra Mackay, Raphael Solomon, Andrew Tepperman, Antonella Vergati, and Lata Narayanaswamy provided efficient research assistance. I'm grateful to Margaret Cronan for preparing the indexes.

My thanks also go to Leanne Pander and Dianne Gutscher, of the Bowdoin College Library; Jill Richardson, of the War Memorial Library, Jesus College, Cambridge; Angela Whitelegge, of the Goldsmith's Library, University of London; Jonathan Smith, of Trinity College Library, Cambridge; to the staff at John Murray, London, for access to their archives; and to the library staff at the British Library, the London School of Economics, New College Edinburgh, the National Library of Scotland, the University Library Cambridge, and the Public Archives, Matlock, Derbyshire. I am much indebted to the late Professor Kenneth Bourne of the London School of Economics for his permission to see and refer to some of Malthus's letters.

It is a pleasure to express appreciation for the generous assistance provided by Gerald Schwartz of the Onex Corporation, Toronto; by the Social Sciences and Humanities Research Council of Canada; and by the Acting Dean of Arts and Science, the Vice-President of Research and International Relations, and the Humanities and Social Sciences Committee at the University of Toronto. In regard to research funding, as well as moral support, I owe a substantial debt to the initiatives taken by my friend Ian Mirlin.

I wish to thank the Derbyshire Record Office, Matlock, for permission to reproduce extracts from Malthus's correspondence in their collection; the Master and Fellows of Trinity College, Cambridge, for permission to cite from a letter Malthus wrote to Whewell, held in the Whewell Papers; New College, Edinburgh, for permission to cite from material in the Thomas Chalmers Collection; the British Library for permission to cite from the Macvey Napier and Arthur Young papers.

THE ECONOMICS OF THOMAS ROBERT MALTHUS

INTRODUCTION

This book I think of as a natural partner to my *Economics of David Ricardo* (1979). It should have been written next in sequence, though for various reasons I chose to turn first to *The Economics of John Stuart Mill* (1985). My mode of interpretation is the same as in those earlier volumes: I keep very close to the text as a means to the end of discerning 'authorial intent.' My procedure is not simple-minded. It does not preclude an interest in 'rhetoric' and other literary devices designed to persuade readers (the 'arithmetic' and 'geometric' ratios provide a prime instance). And it does not preclude 'inconsistency,' though to rely too soon on that as an escape route mitigates against the requirement to take the text seriously. But consistency, even as a working hypothesis, does not mean that a particular theory is developed *ab initio*; not only must we recognize that a writer may change his opinion over time, but we must also allow for periods when a position is in the course of development, and therefore not yet fully defined or firmly established in his mind. Nor does consistency mean that the writer cannot have more than one theory simultaneously, or make more than one particular assumption about some variable or functional relation; different purposes may call for different assumptions and different models, depending on the context. While allowing for the foregoing situations, I exclude inconsistency or error – always in relation to the writer's frame of reference, not some other – except as a last resort. Some varieties of inconsistency, however, may not be serious; a writer may introduce a definition and not keep to it on every single occasion. Such carelessness is common enough even among those who are otherwise consistent in their substantive model-building.

The topics covered include those discussed in the earlier works – particularly value, distribution, growth, and money. Value measurement receives special attention – more than is usual in most commentaries – and the population issue and the problem of aggregate demand – both treated from theoretical, empirical, and policy perspectives – figure large.

The organization of a vast mass of material proved difficult in the extreme. Over a period of some three decades, Malthus wrote a flow of works that he subjected to continual alteration. I have attempted to take account of the modifications. For the *Essay on Population*, I have used the originals for the third (1806), fourth (1807), and fifth (1817) versions, and the Wrigley–Souden edition of Malthus's *Works* for the first (1798), second (1803), and sixth (1826).[1] (For an evaluation of this edition, see Hollander, 1991a.) Because of the centrality of the *Essay* in social history with respect to economic development and demography, and in order to keep a firm handle on the chronological development of Malthus's position, I have kept the discussion of that work in these spheres within part I, which is designated 'Early explorations ...' Part I also takes account of Malthus's famous correspondence with Ricardo, both before and after the appearance of his pamphlets of 1814–15, again with respect to growth and development. (For those pamphlets, I rely on the Wrigley–Souden edition; and, for the correspondence, on Sraffa's edition of Ricardo's *Works*.)

I use the term 'early explorations in growth and development' in order to draw some kind of dividing line between the last major revision to the *Essay*, occurring in 1817, and the *Principles* of 1820. Unfortunately, the *Principles* is far from a polished statement of position; although its revision was set in hand almost immediately after it appeared in print, the preparation of a second edition remained unfinished at Malthus's death. But at least it does contain an effort to convey essentials. Again, my concern is to trace changes in Malthus's position over time in the *Principles* itself, and between the *Principles* and the *Essay on Population* and the 1814–15 pamphlets. The Cambridge edition of the *Principles*, edited by John Pullen, has proven invaluable.

One outcome of this study – perhaps it will prove *the* major outcome – is the discernment of a possible backward link between the Physiocrats and Malthus, partly mediated via Adam Smith, and a forward link to Sraffa in so far as Malthus developed explicitly a corn-profit model. (His Sraffian-style value theory was earlier discerned by Costabile, 1983.) A by-product of the exercise is the strong confirmation of Ricardo as an economist fully in the 'scarcity' tradition. For it is Ricardo who insisted, against Malthus, on treating corn precisely as any other product in terms of independent demand and supply functions, and who rejected the superior productivity attrib-

1 As a typical example of the tinkering: In the 1803 edition, Malthus wrote: 'Upon the whole ... our commerce has not done much for our agriculture; but ... our agriculture has done a great deal for our commerce.' In 1806 this is modified: 'Our commerce has not done so much for our agriculture as our agriculture has for our commerce.' In 1807, he fiddled some more: 'It must be allowed ... upon the whole, that our commerce has not done more for our agriculture, than our agriculture for our commerce.'

uted to agricultural activity. How far Malthus retained his physiocratic orientation will greatly preoccupy us here. In the end he surrendered much of it, and with it went his agricultural protectionism. Ricardo had won a great posthumous victory. It is Ricardo, too, who is shown to have priority over Malthus for the simultaneous decline in real-wage and profit rates in a growing economy subject to land scarcity, as portrayed in Samuelson's 'canonical' classical growth model (1978). Neither recognized Adam Smith's contribution.

I have designed the concluding chapter as a summary statement of the main results of my analysis viewed from a methodological standpoint. There I consider the commonly raised charges of inherent inconsistency, and even intellectual dishonesty, to be found in the literature on Malthus. The reader who seeks a preview might even start with that last chapter. Here I shall briefly summarize some reactions to Malthusian method in order to set the stage.

Keynes wrote of the Ricardo–Malthus friendship that it 'will live in history on account of its having given rise to the most important literary correspondence in the whole development of Political Economy' (1933, 137). This still remains true. It was something of a love–hate relationship for Ricardo. He took Malthus very seriously – why else the lengthy correspondence and his *Notes* on Malthus's *Principles* and *Measure of Value*? But he was frustrated. He complained in 1815 of the excessive complexity, even incoherence, of Malthus's position as it emerged in the essays of 1814–15: 'The whole appears to me a labyrinth of difficulties; one is no sooner got over than another presents itself, and so in endless succession' (17 April 1815; 1951–73, VI, 214). A year later, he looked forward to finding in the prospective fifth edition of the *Essay on Population* 'a regular and connected statement of your opinions on what I deem the most difficult, and perhaps the most important topic of Political Economy, namely the progress of a country in wealth and the laws by which the increasing produce is distributed' (23 February 1816; VII, 24). Before the appearance of the *Principles* (when already familiar with parts of the manuscript), he expressed the hope of finding there a statement of Malthus's general system: 'I wish to have an opportunity of judging of your system as a whole, and therefore shall be glad when it comes in its printed form' (20 August 1818; 284); but this proved premature, for shortly after he suggested to James Mill that the delay reflected 'doubts which [Malthus] cannot help entertaining of the correctness of his opinions. So much for Polit. Econ.' (28 December 1818; 379–80).

Apart from his difficulties in pinning Malthus down, Ricardo complained that Malthus misunderstood and misrepresented him: 'I am glad,' he wrote to Trower, 'that you speak with approbation of the spirit in which I carry on the contest with Mr. Malthus – I always wish him to see what I have against his opinions before I publish them, that I may be sure that I have not misunderstood him, and therefore not misrepresented him. He certainly has not done the same to me, and has, I am sure without intending it, misrepresented me in many important particulars' (2 March 1821; VIII, 349). Several conspicuous instances of 'misrepresentation' caused Ricardo distress, and we shall see that on one occasion he protested: 'This is disingenuous.'

Ricardo, in all this, took for granted that Malthus's (failed) procedure was of the hypothetico-deductive variety. Francis Horner, too, emphasized the 'speculative' dimension of Malthus's economics – and a related love of 'paradox': 'Malthus has been a day or two in town; and gave me a little of his society, enough to enable me to judge of him; and I am happy to say, that a more philosophic candour, calm love of truth, and ingenious turn for speculation in his important branch, I have seldom met with. It is quite delightful to find, how closely he has taught himself to examine the circumstances of the lower classes of society, and what a scientific turn he gives the subject. There is a new speculation of his, about the importance of the people being fed dear, which I wish you were here to discuss; it has the look of a paradox, and, like most of his views, is revolting to the common belief; but I have not yet detected the fallacy, if there is one' (to Lord Webb Seymour, 6 July 1807; in Horner, 1853, I, 433–4). Horner went yet further, complaining to John Murray of Malthus's drawing deductions from inadequately formulated axioms: 'I think in this review [of Newenham] you will find the defect to which I have already alluded, and which affects all Malthus's writings; a want of precision in the statement of his principles, and distinct perspicuity in upholding the consequences which he traces from them' (27 October 1808; 463–4). This is, in fact, close to a charge against Malthus of practising the 'Ricardian Vice.'

Horner was not alone. John Weyland (1816) objected strongly to a procedure defining the 'natural tendency of population to increase' or the *maximum* conceivable geometric rate, and then considering the 'checks' that constrain the actual behind the maximum rate. Researchers would do better 'if, instead of blindly acquiescing in these *assumed* data, they proceed to inquire into the degree in which the principle of population *naturally and really* operates in the several stages of society. They will find this to be very distinct from its assumed "possible" operation, and in most cases to be very far from having a necessary tendency "to push the number of people beyond the point at which food can be acquired from them"' (20). This is to turn all Malthus's formal objections against Ricardo 180 degrees against himself.

There were other severe critics, Robert Torrens among them.[2] Torrens

2 At age seventeen and heavily influenced by James Mill, J.S. Mill responded to Malthus's 1824 critique of the New School in unpleasant terms: 'If Mr. Malthus excels in any thing, it is not certainly in smoothing the road to knowledge; and if any truths are contained in the works to which we have alluded' – *The Measure of Value* and the *Principles* – 'they must be of the number of truths which lie hidden in the bottom of a well' (1825a/1967, IV, 28). 'If, indeed, it be a merit to puzzle what is plain, to render intricate that which is simple, obscure that which is clear, and difficult that which is easy, it would be hard to find in the whole circle of Political Economists, one with whose merits he might not vie' (43).

lists a litany of sins – lack of originality; weakness in logical deduction; inconsistency, particularly in policy matters. For Torrens had 'looked in vain for a development of principles before undiscovered, or for consistent deductions from those already established. It is a singular fact, and one which it is not improper to impress upon the public, that, in the leading questions of economical science, Mr. Malthus scarcely ever embraced a principle, which he did not subsequently abandon' (1815, viii–ix). But although Malthus's works 'cannot, perhaps, in any instance, be safely consulted for practical authorities, they may always be advantageously referred to as furnishing materials for speculation, and suggesting hints for inquiry' (xi–xii). A rather condescending allowance. So, too, is the observation that the lack of system – at least, of faulty system – itself protected Malthus against conspicuous error, though the inductivist 'spirit' of Malthus's work is more warmly received: 'The spirit, too, in which his essays are written, forms a pleasing contrast to that which pervades the publications of certain economists, patrician and plebeian, who, having lost themselves in the labyrinth of erroneous theory, with disdainful pertinacity reject the clue of facts' (xii). Torrens later described Malthus's *Principles* as 'a chaos of original but unconnected elements,' contrasting with Ricardo's, which went too far in the opposite direction, 'possess[ing] a regularity and simplicity beyond what exists in nature' (1821, v). Though he now allowed Malthus a degree of originality, he dismissed Malthus on gluts as 'vague, fallacious, and inconsistent throughout' (385).

Torrens implicitly ascribed to Malthus a 'Baconian' procedure, though he was scarcely enthusiastic. But there is also the very positive perspective of the so-called inductivists to which we now turn. The charges against Malthus for *lack* of 'system,' deficient deduction, and inconsistency were seen in a very different light in some quarters.

Malthus is often said to have been party to the concerted attack on Ricardo launched by Cambridge inductivists, represented in economics by Richard Jones. The matter is complex since pinning down what the inductivist method consisted of is difficult. In fact, Jones puffed out a smokescreen, for he never abandoned the deductive method he so harshly condemned, adopting indeed some of its least defensible traits (see Hollander, 1985, I: 36–46). That he failed to lay out an effective alternative troubled his co-worker William Whewell, as is clear from a letter to Jones in February 1831: 'How can you expect to lay down rules and describe an extensive method with no examples to guide and substantiate your speculations? You may say a number of fine things and give rules that look wise and arguments that look pretty, but you have no security that these devices are at all accurate or applicable' (Todhunter, 1876, II, 115–16). But an impression of a distinct inductivist alternative was created by Jones, and Jones excluded Malthus as well as Adam Smith from his general indictment of the British economists (1831, v–vi).

Keynes in our century carried on the favourable Jones tradition. His famous biographical essay – surely the most cited evaluation in the literature – gives Malthus excellent press on methodological grounds: 'In economic discussions Ricardo was the abstract and *a priori* theorist, Malthus the inductive and intuitive investigator who hated to stray too far from what he could test by reference to the facts and his own intuitions' (1933, 135). The *High Price of Provisions* (1800) indicated 'that Malthus was already disposed to a certain line of approach in handling practical economic problems which he was to develop later in his correspondence with Ricardo, – a method which to me is most sympathetic, and, as I think, more likely to lead to right conclusions than the alternative approach of Ricardo. But it was Ricardo's more fascinating intellectual construction which was victorious, and Ricardo who, by turning his back so completely on Malthus's ideas, constrained the subject for a full hundred years in an artificial groove' (122). The charge against Ricardo for holding economics back for a century is asserted by Keynes repeatedly, always with a valid 'Malthusian' alternative in mind:

> According to Malthus's good common-sense notions prices and profits are primarily determined by something which he described, though none too clearly, as 'effective demand.' Ricardo favoured a much more rigid approach, went behind 'effective demand' to the underlying conditions of money on the one hand and real costs and the real division of the product on the other, conceived these fundamental factors as automatically working themselves out in a unique and unequivocal way, and looked on Malthus's method as very superficial. But Ricardo, in the course of simplifying the many successive stages of his highly abstract argument, departed, necessarily and more than he himself was aware, away from the actual facts; whereas Malthus, by taking up the tale much nearer its conclusion, had a firmer hold on what may be expected to happen in the real world. Ricardo is the father of such things as the Quantity Theory of Money and the Purchasing Power Parity of the Exchanges. When one has painfully escaped from the intellectual domination of these pseudo-arithmetical doctrines, one is able, perhaps for the first time for a hundred years, to comprehend the real significance of the vaguer intuitions of Malthus. (122–3)

The Ricardo–Malthus correspondence revealed 'the seeds of economic theory, and also the divergent lines – so divergent at the outset that the destination can scarcely be recognised as the same until it is reached – along which the subject can be developed. Ricardo is investigating the theory of the *distribution* of the product in conditions of equilibrium, and Malthus is concerned with what determines the *volume* of output day by day in the real world. Malthus is dealing with the monetary economy in which we happen to live; Ricardo with the abstraction of a neutral money economy' (138). 'One cannot rise from a perusal of this correspondence without a feeling that the almost total obliteration of Malthus's line of approach and the complete domination of Ricardo's for a period of a hundred years has been a disaster to the progress of economics. Time after time in these letters Malthus is talking plain sense, the force of which Ricardo with his head in the clouds wholly fails to comprehend. Time after time a crushing refutation by Malthus is met by a mind so completely closed that Ricardo does not even see what Malthus is saying ...' (141). 'If only Malthus, instead of Ricardo,' Keynes lamented, 'had been the parent stem from which nineteenth-century economics had proceeded, what a much wiser and richer place the world would be to-day! We have laboriously to re-discover and force through the obscuring envelopes of our misguided education what should never have ceased to be obvious. I have long claimed Robert Malthus as the first of the Cambridge economists ...' (144–5).

In more recent commentary we find the same sharp contrasts drawn between Ricardian and Malthusian method. Myint, for example, emphasizes Malthus's concern with the short-run, contrasting with the long-run, normal equilibrium of Ricardo (1948, 35). Neil de Marchi and R.P. Sturges describe Malthus as 'the insistent realist, countering Ricardo's "strong cases" with reference to specific historical experience, and calling attention to what happens during the "intervals" ignored by Ricardo's long-run equilibrium analysis' (1973, 379). Hutchison points to the Introduction to the *Principles*, where 'Malthus did something to uphold the empirical–historical method of Adam Smith' (1978, 55). Pullen refers to 'the importance of observed facts in political economy [which] reflects the empirical side of Malthus's own methodology, and reminds us that he was a professor of history as well as political economy' (1989, xlvii). Pullen also puts great weight on the distinctiveness of Malthus's method implicit in his celebrated 'doctrine of proportions,' even relating this orientation to his character (1982). Hodgson (1993) classifies Malthus, together with Veblen, as adopting an open-ended evolutionary perspective. And among the old institutionists, John Commons was greatly enamoured: 'He was the first scientific evolutionist, indeed the first scientific economist, in that he derived his theory, not from assumptions, like Smith's reversal of the historic process, but from investigation of the process itself' (1934, 246).

As for the *Essay on Population*, it is allowed, even by those who draw sharp contrasts between Malthusian and Ricardian methodology in favour of the former, that the 1798 version was too much of the extreme deductive variety. Whewell took this view: 'A good deal of the Malthus's population is a beginning of such a process [genuine induction] excluding of course his anticipatory thesis, the only thing usually talked of' (Todhunter, 1876, II,115–16). Marshall contrasted the first and later editions: 'In the first edition ... Malthus gave his argument without any detailed statement of facts ... In the second edition, 1803, he based himself on so wide and careful a statement of facts as to claim a place among the founders of historical economics' (1820, 179n). Keynes expressed much the same opinion: 'The first essay is not only *a priori* and philosophical in method, but it is bold and rhetorical in style with much *bravura* of language and sentiment; whereas in the later editions political philosophy gives way to political economy, general principles are overlaid by the inductive verifications of a pioneer in sociological history, and the brilliance and high spirits of a young man writing in the last years of the Directory disappear' (1933, 117). Again: 'Malthus's transition from the *a priori* methods of Cambridge – whether Paley, the Mathematical Tripos, or the Unitarians – to the inductive arguments of the later editions was assisted by a tour which he undertook in search of materials' in 1799 and 1802 (120–1). And Hutchison assures his readers that 'Malthus had, of course, matured, methodologically, as contrasted with the dogmatic, *a priori* deductivism of his first *Essay*, which was on somewhat Millian–Ricardian lines' (1978, 56n).

This general consensus seems now to be under revision. Malthusian theory has been increasingly subjected to 'rational reconstruction' in mathematical terms. The old view of Malthus as a 'hopelessly muddled thinker ... has been turned on its head in recent years and his reputation as a theoretician is deservedly higher than at any time this century' (Rutherford, 1987, 175). Much of what follows in this book points to the untenability of any notion that a sharply differentiated methodology distinguishes Malthus from Ricardo. We establish, in particular, a penchant of Malthus's for 'long-run' analysis carried even further in some conspicuous respects than by Ricardo. And though it is true enough that Malthus failed to develop a full-fledged 'system,' this was certainly his ideal.

I/EARLY EXPLORATIONS IN GROWTH AND DEVELOPMENT THEORY

ONE

The *Essay on Population*, 1798–1807

I INTRODUCTION

Malthus's intentions in his celebrated 'arithmetic ratio' of food increase and 'geometric ratio' of population increase remain in dispute. It has long been a matter of debate whether this formulation reflected the principle of diminishing returns. We have Cannan's insistence upon the absence of the law in any meaningful sense: 'that law remained practically unknown till near the close of the Great War. Malthus may, perhaps, display some inkling of it here and there in the first edition. In the second he certainly uses one of the principal ideas on which it is based as an incidental and subsidiary argument. In the later editions its existence is frequently recognized. But to imagine that the *Essay on the Principle of Population* was ever based on the law of diminishing returns is to confuse Malthusianism as expounded by J.S. Mill with Malthusianism as expounded by Malthus' (1917, 113–14). From Cannan's standpoint the geometric and arithmetic ratios do *not* reflect the law: 'The question of population with Malthus was not, as it is with us, a question of the density of population and productiveness of industry, but a question about the comparative rapidity of the increase of population and of the increase of the annual produce of food' (108). 'Overpopulation,' in the sense that, if population were smaller, average product would be higher, was not the issue.

This general position is also found in Schumpeter's *History*, where it is expressed in harsh terms: 'As presented in the first edition, [the theory] clearly was intended to mean that population was actually and inevitably increasing faster than subsistence and that this was the reason for the misery observed. The geometrical and arithmetical ratios of these increases, to which Malthus like earlier writers seems to have attached considerable importance, as well as his other attempts at mathematical precision, are nothing but faulty expressions of this view which can be passed by here in the remark that there is of course no point whatever in trying to formulate independent "laws" for the behavior of two interdependent quantities. The performance as a whole is deplorable in technique and little short of foolish in substance ...' (1954, 579). Schumpeter cites Cannan to the effect that the *Essay* (the second edition as well as the first) 'falls to the ground as an argument, and remains only a chaos of facts collected to illustrate the effect of laws which do not exist.' Moreover, he (like Cannan) distinguishes Malthus from J.S. Mill in that the latter 'put the law of population into a relation to the "law" of diminishing returns from land – which ... was entirely absent from Malthus' *Essay* ...' (581).

J.S. Mill himself attributed diminishing returns to Malthus and discounted the significance of the ratios, as such: 'I ask, then, is it true, or not, that if their numbers [agricultural labourers] were fewer they would obtain higher wages? This is the question, and no other: and it is idle to divert attention from it, by attacking any incidental position of Malthus or some other writer, and pretending that to refute it, is to disprove the principle of population. Some, for instance, have achieved an easy victory over a passing remark of Mr. Malthus, hazarded chiefly by way of illustration, that the increase of food may perhaps be assumed to take place in an arithmetical ratio, while population increases in a geometrical: when every candid reader knows that Mr. Malthus laid no stress on this unlucky attempt to give numerical precision to things which do not admit of it, and every person capable of reasoning must see that it is wholly superfluous to his argument' (1848/1965, II, 353). Subsequently, W.S. Jevons understood the ratios themselves as referring to diminishing returns: 'It is a mistake to suppose that [the arithmetic series] can be altogether true or that Malthus can really have meant it to be accurate. I take it to be merely a rough way of saying that food cannot be increased much without a great increase of difficulty; or, in other words, that the increase of food is not proportional to the increase of labour' (1972–81, VI, 57). And Alfred Marshall (1920, 179n) took a similar view. He cited Malthus's rule for food production, which he read as holding good upon the assumption of a population doubling every twenty-five years: 'Let us then take this for our rule, though certainly far beyond the truth; and allow that [by great exertion] the whole produce of the Island might be increased every twenty-five years, by a quantity of subsistence equal to what it at present produces' (1798/1986, *1*, 12).[1] Marshall was a little critical of Malthus's 'habit' of speaking of production as capable of increasing in an arithmetic ratio, but took it to entail no more than a convenient way of expressing the maximum any reason-

1 Marshall actually cites the third edition. The words in square brackets here ('by great exertion') appear in the first edition.

able critic would require. More important: 'What [Malthus] meant, stated in modern language, was that the tendency of diminishing return, which is assumed throughout this argument, would begin to operate sharply after the produce of the island had been doubled. Doubled labour might give double produce; but quadrupled labour would hardly treble it: octupled labour would not quadruple it.'

The Marshallian view has been reiterated more recently by Lionel Robbins: 'I do not think that [Cannan] was right. Admittedly, the mere comparison of geometrical and arithmetical potentialities of increase does not of itself necessarily involve this relationship [the law of diminishing returns]. But the idea underlying the comparison is of the same order of conceptions; and it is surely no mere coincidence that in another connection Malthus [1815] was one of the first to formulate the so-called law' (1970, 60). 'Surely it is odd to contend in the light of the essay on Rent,' Robbins noted in another context, 'that not the least suspicion of it had crossed his mind at the time when his main population theory was developed' (88).

In some modern formulations the link between the ratios and diminishing returns is said to be implicit only, but yet specific enough to be formulated mathematically. Thus Stigler: 'Malthus' ratios implicitly assumed sharply diminishing returns, for his numbers define the production function

$$L = 2^{P-1}$$

where L is labor (proportional to population) and P is produce' (1965, 163; see also Lloyd, 1969). Written in this form, population is formally treated as a function of output – we shall see that this is indeed characteristic of Malthus's formulation; but it would be more familiar to us if rewritten as

$$P = \frac{\log L}{\log 2} + 1$$

such that, as population rises to achieve levels of 1, 2, 4, 8, 16 ..., so in consequence produce grows to achieve levels of 1, 2, 3, 4, 5, ..., implying a sharply concave total-production curve.

This perspective has been adopted by Waterman (1987), who bases a mathematical interpretation of aspects of the growth pattern implicit in the first *Essay* on the premise that 'the putatively "arithmetical" increase of the "means of subsistence" is conditional upon a "geometrical" increase in population' (260; also 1991, 264, and 1992, 205–6).[2] The passage upon

2 If $\frac{d\ln N}{dt} = n$, then $\frac{dF}{dt} = h$, where N is labour per period, and F is food per period. This is modified subsequently to relate output to doses of labour and capital: 'It was Malthus's central contribution to argue that if successive "doses" of the composite

which this view is based falls within the context used by Marshall: 'In the next twenty-five years [i.e., period 2], it is impossible to suppose that produce could be quadrupled. It would be contrary to all our knowledge of the qualities of the land. The very utmost that we can conceive, is, that the increase in the second twenty-five years might equal present produce. Let us then take this for our rule, though certainly far beyond the truth ... [This] ratio of increase is evidently arithmetical. It may be fairly said, therefore, that the means of subsistence increase in an arithmetical ratio' (1798/1986, *1*, 12; see also 68).

I myself am on record as ascribing to the view that 'the key to the first essay is to be found in the principle of diminishing returns' (Hollander, 1986, 190n). But a close rereading of the *Essay* indicates that the matter is far more complex than I ever imagined. There is good reason for the extraordinary disparity between the interpretations we have reviewed.

* * *

Our study of the first *Essay* in this chapter proceeds as follows. Section II takes up the issue of the geometric and arithmetic ratios. The evidence seems overwhelmingly to favour the Cannan–Schumpeter position. There is little justification for reading into the ratios a tight functional dependency of the type envisaged by Stigler and Waterman, or even the less formal dependency envisaged by Marshall and Robbins. The point, we shall show in section III, which takes up an application of the contrasting ratios to Godwin's idealistic scheme, is that quadrupled labour *might* yield quadrupled product if appropriate preparatory investments are made in land improvement or other forms of real-capital accumulation before the higher rate of application of labour is undertaken. And the fact that average product would not necessarily fall with increased population density is immaterial to the polemical purpose of the essay, which is satisfied by demonstrating the necessity for a reduction of the population growth rate below its maximum potential. This conclusion is supported by the discussion of the Poor Law institution (section IV).

To deny that the *ratios* turn on the principle of diminishing returns is not, however, to deny the presence of that principle in the *Essay*. This indeed is a major source of difficulty in interpretation, for the possibility must be faced that concepts found within the confines of a single essay were not necessarily intended to be combined into a single whole by the author. In sections V and VI, we show that the principle of diminishing

---

factor are applied to the vector or "profile" of land at a geometrically increasing rate, then output will increase only arithmetically' (261). On this matter see below, p. 24.

For a mathematical critique of the Stigler–Waterman perspectives on Malthus's production function, see Pullen and Baldry, 1988.

returns does manifest itself, indeed conspicuously so, in the first *Essay*. Here, indeed, we find the origin of Malthus's formal growth model involving a declining path of real wages in consequence of a decelerating rate of growth of labour demand. On this view, while Malthus's ratios constitute a wholly polemical device with little analytical content, there is much worthwhile economics elsewhere in the *Essay*. Still lacking is an explicit analysis of the profit rate and its secular course. Moreover, it is not a simple application to land of labour and capital that is involved, but application entailing land 'improvement.'

In section VII we consider Malthus's analysis in 1798 of the contemporary British situation. The 'model' here applied is *not* the land-scarcity version – that related specifically to the case of new colonies. Rather, the picture is one of very slow growth of population and food, proceeding for centuries at roughly constant real wages and driven by periodic bursts of new technology. The analysis of the British case is undertaken with an eye to explaining what Malthus considered to be the surprisingly *slow* growth of population; that is, there is no question of excessive population growth, as Schumpeter has it.

The implications for population growth of the distribution of activity between agriculture and manufactures is the topic of section VIII, particularly a criticism of Adam Smith for identifying increased aggregate labour demand with increased national 'revenue or stock' rather than with expanded agricultural output. Section IX considers a celebrated discussion of wage oscillations during the course of growth, and its relation to the growth model. At this point we take leave of the first *Essay*.

In sections X and XI, the 1803 and 1806 versions of the *Essay* are taken up, again with particular reference to the role accorded to diminishing returns. The first of these two sections documents a reinforcement and refinement of the technical apparatus involving a decline in average agricultural product per capita with increased population density, and a falling real wage towards subsistence and correspondingly reduced population growth. The common opinion that the formulation of this diminishing-returns principle constitutes a novelty introduced to counter references by James Anderson (1801) to a form of increasing returns is questioned in the light of the earlier statements of 1798. Also, as in 1798, the major concern remains the impossibility of food increasing at a rate comparable to that of population growth *when unchecked*, necessitating reduction of the latter below its maximum potential – a proposition that is consistent with *constant* average productivity upon increase in population density, provided sufficient time is allowed prior to the increased application. None the less, the existence of the more formal case based on reduced productivity should not be downplayed. Contemporary application is another matter entirely. The picture of British growth given in 1803 contrasts radically with that of 1798 – and with the more formal growth model – for it involves *acceleration* of food supply and population growth.

Section XI considers an appendix of 1806 designed to correct misconceptions regarding the *Essay.* The emphasis is wholly on the proposition that land scarcity constrains the population growth rate below its maximum, without, however, having recourse to the diminishing-returns concept involving falling per-capita output with increased population density. Modifications made in the 1803 and 1806 editions to the original account of wage oscillations are the subject of section XII.

The reader is asked to bear in mind the technical orientation of this chapter; the *Essay* is placed in a broader intellectual context in chapters 18 and 19. Moreover, there is this difference between the first and later versions: In 1798, population economics was incidental to a concern to justify private-property institutions against Jacobinism, whereas, in 1803 and thereafter, it came into its own.

II THE 'GEOMETRICAL' AND 'ARITHMETICAL' RATIOS[3]

On the basis of the two celebrated postulates (indeed, 'laws of nature') – 'that food is necessary to the existence of man' and 'that the passion between the sexes is necessary, and will remain nearly in its present state' (1798/1986, *1*, 8) – Malthus asserts 'that the power of population is indefinitely greater than the power of the earth to produce subsistence for man' (9) with obvious consequences: 'Population when unchecked, increases in

3 Malthus made no claims to priority for the formal ratios. By 1798 they had a pedigree. See on this Rashid, 1988, 62; Hartwick, 1988; and Schumpeter, 1954, 254f.

As for the 'principle' of population itself, Malthus paid tribute to a variety of authors in a retrospective account in 1803: 'The only authors from whose writings I had deduced the principle, which formed the main argument of the *Essay*, were Hume, Wallace, Adam Smith, and Dr. Price; and my object was to apply it, to try the truth of those speculations on the perfectibility of man and society, which at that time [1798] excited a considerable portion of the public attention' (1986, *2*, i).

Waterman has made the case that 'virtually the whole of Malthus's population theory is to be found in Paley's brief exposition ... including strong hints of Malthus's own phraseology. Nature has provided for "an indefinite multiplication" of the human, as of all other species. Under favourable conditions, population doubles in twenty (not twenty-five) years. There is a "tendency" to continual increase; but this is countered by "checks" to population. It is "the constitution of the sexes" that affords the stimulus to population, provided males do not indulge in "irregular gratifications." Marriage is the chief cause of population, but "men will not marry" unless they can expect "that mode of subsistence to which each class ... is accustomed." And when living standards rise (and remain high for long enough), there is a ratchet effect upon the socially-determined "subsistence" requirement: for "habitual superfluities become actual wants"' (1996b). See also Waterman on Paley's discussion of the preventive check 'which is almost certainly the chief source of Malthus's concept.' In considering this case, it is perhaps noteworthy that Malthus neglected to mention Paley among writers to whom he was *originally* indebted for the 'principle of population' or among those of whom he became aware after 1798 (see 1986, *2*, ii). There is a further problem: Waterman allows that Paley lacked a theory of *production*, though such a theory is crucial to Malthusian population analysis.

a geometrical ratio. Subsistence only in an arithmetical ratio. A slight acquaintance with numbers will shew the immensity of the first power in comparison of the second. By the law of our nature, which makes food necessary to the life of man, the effects of these two unequal powers must be kept equal. This implies a strong and constantly operating check on population from the difficulty of subsistence. This difficulty must fall somewhere; and must necessarily be severely felt by a large portion of mankind.'[4] Malthus extends his notion of a high *potential* of human population growth to the animal and vegetable worlds, and points out that these too are in actuality constrained. In this passage the constraints on population growth reflect lack of space as well as of food: 'Through the animal and vegetable kingdoms, nature has scattered the seeds of life abroad with the most profuse and liberal hand. She has been comparatively sparing in the room and the nourishment necessary to rear them.'

Various elaborations in the second chapter of the *Essay* involve a doubling of population every twenty-five years as maximum growth rate, or approximately 3 per cent annually, drawn from contemporary American data. Even this, Malthus allowed, fell short of the situation, 'where the means of subsistence were so abundant, that no part of the society could have any fears about providing amply for a family, the power of population being left to assert itself unchecked' (11). In such an ideal situation 'the increase of the human species evidently would be much greater than any increase that has been hitherto known.' For no state had ever existed 'where the manners were so pure and simple, and the means of subsistence so abundant, that no check whatever has existed to early marriage ... in no state that we have known, has the power of population been left to assert itself with perfect freedom.' Although the American data illustrate a growth rate falling short of the maximum theoretically conceivable, Malthus nevertheless took it as his 'rule' because it had been experienced in actuality: 'This ratio of increase, though short of the utmost power of population, yet as the result of actual experience, we will take as our rule; and say, that population, when unchecked, goes on doubling itself every twenty five years, or increases in a geometrical ratio' (12).

Malthus then turns to a completely different geographical location to illustrate his arithmetic rate of food expansion – namely, Britain. Here he takes as his 'rule' equal increments of output every twenty-five years, setting out from the 'present state of cultivation,' albeit a growth rate 'far beyond the truth,' assuming as it does 'the best possible policy ... the breaking up more land, and ... great encouragements to agriculture.' The arithmetic

4 It emerges that 'misery' includes the *fear* of low standards and the necessity for delayed marriage as well as low standards as such (see section VII, below, on the 'preventive' vs the 'positive' check). It may be helpful to perceive of 'unchecked' populaton growth as the rate generated in communistic schemes proposing *inter alia* the abolition of the family unit, thereby reducing the private marginal cost of producing offspring to *zero*. On this perspective, see section III, below, and also chapter 18: IV.

rate of increase per twenty-five-year period is, in short, an *overestimate*, again adopted for the sake of argument: 'In the next twenty five years, it is impossible to suppose that the produce could be quadrupled. It would be contrary to all our knowledge of the qualities of land. The very utmost that we can conceive, is, that the increase in the second twenty five years might equal the present produce. Let us then take this for our rule, though certainly far from the truth; and allow that by great exertion, the whole produce of the Island might be increased every twenty five years, by a quantity of subsistence equal to what it at present produces. The most enthusiastic speculator cannot suppose a greater increase than this. In a few centuries it would make every acre of land in the Island like a garden.'

This 'ratio of increase,' Malthus declares with a straight face, 'is evidently arithmetical,' just as the posited U.S. population growth rate is evidently geometrical. But clearly nothing depends upon the arithmetic versus geometric dimensions *per se.* It adds nothing to point out that a (supposed) doubling of population every twenty-five years constitutes a geometric rate of growth, and an expansion of food supplies by equal increments during the same period constitutes an arithmetic rate of growth. In any event, food supplies could never, in practice, Malthus allowed, grow at the specific arithmetic rate posited; and population growth, in contrast, would, if truly 'unrestricted,' exceed the posited geometric rate. What matters is that an (overestimated) *maximum* growth rate of British or world food supply falls short of an (underestimated) *maximum* growth rate of population.[5]

Malthus next combines the two rates. Assuming that, in 1800, an output of X units of food 'is equal to support' 7 million – the initial situation – it follows that, by 1850, a food output of 3X will suffice for only 21 million, leaving 7 million 'unprovided for,' and so forth (see table 1.1). To generalize (and avoid the issue of emigration), Malthus applies his rules to the world as a whole.[6] In 2,000 years (by A.D. 3800) 'the difference would be almost incalculable, though the produce in that time would have increased to an immense extent' (13).

5 Even a geometric rate, of course, may imply a small absolute population increase, and an arithmetic rate large absolute increases of food over periods which are reasonable to consider.

6 He assumes that 'the restraints to population [are] universally removed' and that 'the subsistence for man that the earth affords [is] increased every twenty-five years by a quantity equal to what the whole world at present produces' (13). The latter assumption is said to imply that 'the power of production in the earth [is] absolutely unlimited, and its rate of increase much greater than we can conceive that any possible exertions of mankind could make it.' This rule yields the following result:

	1800	2025	2100
Population	1	512	4,096
Food	1	10	13

TABLE 1.1 Summary of Geometric and Arithmetic Ratios

	1800	1825	1850	1875	1900	1925
Population (m)	7	14	28	56	112	224
Food supply	X	2X	3X	4X	5X	6X
'Equal to support of' (m)	7	14	21	28	35	42
'Unprovided for' (m)	0	0	7	28	77	182
[% unprovided for]	0	0	25	50	68	81

It is unconvincing to argue that, by all this, Malthus intended to define, even crudely, a *technical* relation between population growth (as 'cause') and agricultural output (as 'effect'), such that *if* population grows at a geometric rate, *then* food supply grows at an arithmetic rate. The two rates – one an underestimate deriving from the American case, the other an overestimate of British and world potentials – are allowed for the sake of argument; but how technically the arithmetic growth rate of food production would be achieved is simply not entered into, except in such loose suggestions as implied by the reference to 'great encouragements to agriculture' (above, p. 19). (Change in the workforce is, presumably, at play, but as one among various unidentified variables.) Thus, in his universalist example, according to which in 2,000 years the difference between population and food would be 'incalculable,' the conclusion is that the population growth rate would in fact necessarily be kept down to the food growth rate, with the latter *still assumed to proceed at the arithmetic pace*: 'No limits whatever are placed to the production of the earth; they may increase forever and be greater than any assignable power; yet still the power of population being a power of a superior order, the increase of the human species can only be kept commensurate to the increase of the means of subsistence, by the strong law of necessity acting as a check upon the greater power.' There is no hint here that cutting the population growth rate will play back on the rate of food supply; the latter is assumed *given*, and the former has to come into line with it. And even if we are meant to take for granted some reduction in the food growth rate, there is no indication whatsoever regarding the precise technical relation entailed.

Bringing the rates together, as Malthus does so conspicuously, is a polemical device designed to emphasize that – except in the special case of North America – actual population growth is constrained to the lower rate imposed by the growth of food supply, leading on to an analysis of the operative 'checks' over time and space; and to a warning against the artificial encouragement of population growth beyond the rate of growth of food.[7] The combination of the two rates does not seem to have the

7 On this perspective see also Rashid, 1988, 61.

analytical implication that, with population growing at a 'geometric ratio,' food will (in consequence) grow only at an 'arithmetic ratio.'

III THE CRITIQUE OF WILLIAM GODWIN

In analysing the proposals in Godwin's *Enquiry Concerning Political Justice* (2d ed., 1796), Malthus takes the likely population growth rate to be a doubling per twenty-five-year period, or 3 per cent annually – again an underestimate.[8] The estimate for the food supply is, as before, taken to be equal increments per twenty-five-year period, starting from the current British base. It is a deliberate overestimate, which, like the underplaying of population growth, is adopted to weigh the case against himself, and so avoid any charge of exaggeration. The Godwin system would entail 'extraordinary encouragements of population' with 'every cause of depopulation ... removed,' so that 'the numbers would necessarily increase faster than in any society that has ever yet been known' (1798/1986, *1*, 68). These encouragements include the absence of war, of 'unwholesome trades and manufactures,' of 'pestilent cities,' and of 'drinking, gaming and debauchery'; clean and roomy housing, spaced well apart; 'equality'; and the absence of 'luxury,' that is, of a manufacturing or a service sector. Also assumed are schemes ensuring the 'amicable' sharing of agricultural tasks and the distribution of output 'according to wants' (66–7). Abolition of marriage is contemplated. While there would still be a natural inclination for men and women to continue to live in individual partnerships, it 'would be of little consequence ... how many children a woman had, or to whom they belonged. Provisions and assistance would spontaneously flow from the quarter in which they abounded, to the quarter that was deficient.' As for education, 'every man would be ready to furnish instruction to the rising generation according to his capacity.'

Under such conditions – which include the abolition of the *private* cost of a family, that is, a zero private marginal cost of producing offspring – it might actually be expected that population would double itself in periods of less than fifteen years, though, as mentioned, Malthus accepts a twenty-five-year period, since such had been experienced in the northern states as a whole.[9] With the assumptions listed above – Malthus reiterates especially an equal distribution of property and the devotion of *all* labour to agriculture – output of food would certainly rise, but at a slower rate than would population: 'To meet the demand of a population increasing so rapidly' at least one-half of each labourer's time would be required to

8 This at least is the rate allowed initially, for the whole point of the argument is that such a rate could not long be maintained.

9 England, being 'naturally healthier,' might be expected to achieve an even higher population growth rate in the absence of any checks.

be devoted to agriculture (rather than a half-hour per day, as maintained by Godwin). Even so, 'with such, or much greater exertions, a person who is acquainted with the nature of the soil in this country, and who reflects on the fertility of the lands already in cultivation, and the barrenness of those that are not cultivated, will be very much disposed to doubt, whether the whole average produce could possibly be doubled in twenty five years from the present period' (68). An outside possibility of doubling food output in the first period is allowed if a meat diet is abandoned and grazing land ploughed up; but even this outcome is improbable since 'the soil of England will not produce much without dressing; and cattle seem to be necessary to make that species of manure, which best suits the land ...' But assuming that a doubling of (a largely vegetable) food supply *could* be achieved, that is, a supply sufficient to 'support in health' a population of 14 million, a second doubling to meet the (supposedly given) requirements of 28 million was inconceivable; even increasing food supplies in the second period by an equal increment was unlikely – again the arithmetic increase starting from the current base was an outside or extreme hypothesis taking account of both the *intensive* and the *extensive* margins of expansion: 'During the next period of doubling, where will the food be found to satisfy the importunate demands of the increasing numbers? Where is the fresh land to turn up? Where is the dressing necessary to improve that which is already in cultivation? There is no person with the smallest knowledge of land, but would say, that it was impossible that the average produce of the country could be increased during the second twenty five years by a quantity equal to what it at present yields' (69). As in the general case, by the end of the second period (1850) there would be 7 million 'unprovided for' out of 28 million, and within fifty years the initially established system of 'just laws' and 'benevolence' would end in 'violence, oppression, falsehood, misery, hateful vice, and distress' (70).[10]

10 The polemical nature of the entire exercise is confirmed by the very fact that the posited 'geometrical' growth rate – the twenty-five-year period of progression – could not long be maintained: 'I am sufficiently aware that the redundant 28 million, or 77 million, that I have mentioned, could never have existed ...' (70). Indeed, Malthus cited Godwin himself to the effect that 'population is perpetually kept down to the level of the means of subsistence,' a reference to the 'degree of misery, the necessary and inevitable result of the laws of nature ...' The full case against the idealists is that excessive population growth under communism will be checked by the collapse of living standards, a collapse which generates social chaos and leads to the abandonment of the experiment: 'It seems highly probable ... that an administration of property, not very different from that which prevails in civilized States at present, would be established, as the best, though inadequate remedy, for the evils which were pressing on the society' (72). Similarly with regard to the marriage institution: The initial abandonment thereof – and community assurance that children would be provided for – would generate a rate of population increase that could not conceivably be met by food supplies. A restitution of individual responsibility for children is predicted as a check to population growth.

The remark that, with one-half of each worker's time 'or much greater exertions,' an equal increment of produce per twenty-five-year period could scarcely be imagined is subsequently reinforced by the assertion that, even were 'the *whole* attention and labour' of society devoted to agriculture, the constraint on food supply would apply, and this notwithstanding 'every other encouragement' conceivable: 'The powers of the earth would be absolutely inadequate to produce food for the population that would inevitably ensue; ... even, if the whole attention and labour of the society were directed to this sole point, and if, by the most perfect security of property, and every other encouragement that could be thought of, the greatest possible increase of produce were yearly obtained; yet still, the increase of food would by no means keep pace with the much more rapid increase of population' (72).

What emerges in all this for the production function? It is a feature of the argument that the constraints imposed on the growth rate of food derive not only from *scarce land,*[11] but also from *scarce real capital*: 'the soil of England will not produce much without dressing'; 'where is the dressing necessary to improve that which is already in cultivation.' This fact is important, having in mind an interesting observation by Waterman regarding Malthus's 'production function': 'Seed-corn, cottages, barns, horses, wagons, ploughs, and tools are required by an expanding population employed on the land. Malthus must be assuming that new entrants to the work-force come equipped with these goods, else it could be argued against him that falling average product was caused by (remediable) capital-scarcity and hence his polemic would fail. I therefore take it that Samuelson [1978, 1415–16] is correct in stating that "the classicists in effect assume that output is produced by a production function involving land input and a *dose* of labour-*cum*-capital input." It was Malthus's central contribution to argue that if successive "doses" of the composite factor are applied to the vector or "profile" of land at a geometrically increasing rate, then output will increase only arithmetically' (1987, 261; see also 1991, 266). But this is *not* the case, at least in the first *Essay,* which is explicit that capital scarcity plays a key role in constraining the growth of food supply. As for Malthus's polemical purpose, this can be easily appreciated, provided we read it as relating specifically to temporal rates of change. Thus conceivably capital scarcity *is* remediable, but only if sufficient time is allowed. Should the population growth rate be appropriately reduced, it might then be possible to achieve a proportionate advance of food, thus

---

On the 'stability' of the system, the re-establishment of private-property institutions after their abandonment, see Waterman, 1991, ch. 2.

11 In the sense of limited fertility – 'the fertility of the lands already in cultivation, and the barrenness of those that are not cultivated' – and in an absolute sense – 'where is the fresh land to turn up?'

avoiding any fall in output per capita.[12] That average product would not necessarily fall with increased population density is immaterial to the polemical purpose, which is satisfied merely by demonstrating the requirement for a reduction of the population growth rate below its maximum potential.

In the general account it had appeared that Malthus merely 'superimposed' the ratios, as it were, treating them as independent; a variation in the growth rate of population would then leave the arithmetic food increase unchanged (see above, pp. 21–2). In the critique of Godwin, the matter is a little more complex. I have in mind an extension of the polemic, involving a fifteen-year rather than a twenty-five-year geometric increase of population in the event that Godwin's scheme were established 'in its utmost perfection,' which allows – always as an outside possibility, for the sake of argument – food-supply increases by equal absolute increments from the initial base in the shorter period (1798/1986, *1*, 75). An increase in the population growth rate thus raises the food growth rate, with the scheme collapsing, as before, by the end of the second period: 'If then we were to take the period of doubling at fifteen, instead of twenty five years; and reflect upon the labour necessary to double the produce in so short a time, even if we allow it possible; we may venture to pronounce with certainty, that ... not thirty years could elapse, before its utter destruction from the simple principle of population.'

Although it is implied that an increase in the population growth rate has an impact on the growth of food supplies, this extension does not establish any strict functional relation between growth of population at a geometric rate (as an independent variable) and growth of food at an arithmetic rate (as a dependent variable). Malthus was rather engaged in an exercise involving erasure of the comparative ratios applied to a twenty-five-year period and their replacement by the same ratios applied to a fifteen-year period, with the outcome that the scheme collapses within thirty rather than fifty years. The extension sheds no new light on Malthus's conception of the production function. To reiterate the point: The device of geometric–arithmetic ratios used in the polemic against the idealists does not *necessarily* turn on a declining product per capita with increasing population density.

IV APPLICATION TO THE POOR LAWS

The discussion of the Poor Laws is relevant to the nature of the production function. Summing up their impact, Malthus writes of 'the first obvious

12 A passage in the 1803 edition (1986, *3*, 488–9) relating to a 'plan' to check population growth and allow preliminary investment in land preparation points directly to this conclusion; see also 458, on capital scarcity as an impediment to agricultural expansion (below, p. 56).

tendency [which] is to increase population without increasing the food for its support,' a reference to the encouragement given by money grants to imprudent marriages (1798/1986, *1*, 33). This puts upward pressure on food prices to the detriment of those who are not supported, leading them also to require support. The Poor Laws thus 'in some measure create the poor which they maintain.'[13]

What is the reason for the zero (or negligible) response of food to net increases in demand? Malthus expands on this matter in an allusion to marginal extensions in 'old' countries: 'It should be remembered always, that there is an essential difference between food, and those wrought commodities, the raw materials of which are in great plenty. A demand for these last will not fail to create them in as great a quantity as they are wanted. The demand for food has by no means the same creative power. In a country where all the fertile spots have been seized, high offers are necessary to encourage the farmer to lay his dressing on land, from which he cannot expect a profitable return for some years. And before the prospect of advantage is sufficiently great to encourage this sort of agricultural enterprise, and while the new produce is rising, great distresses may be suffered from the want of it. The demand for an increased quantity of subsistence is, with few exceptions, constant every where, yet we see how slowly it is answered in all countries that have been long occupied' (35).

In this passage we seem to have what was to be the basic difference between manufactured and agricultural products so characteristic of nineteenth-century classicism. Yet the matter is far from clear. Diminishing returns of a secular order would imply that, at larger population sizes – or because of permanent increases in the demand for food for whatever reason – per-capita output falls, and food prices rise. Yet this is *not* Malthus's conclusion. The 'distress' is temporary, lasting only 'while the new produce is rising.' It may be fair, therefore, to attribute to him a form of *short-term* diminishing productivity, whereas if enough time is allowed for land preparation and the like, constant productivity will be the rule; what is involved is investment to overcome rising real costs. This is precisely the conclusion reached in our analysis of the geometric and arithmetic ratios as applied to Godwin's scheme.[14]

13 Apart from money-wage supplements, there is also the matter of support in workhouses. Food grants to inmates would reduce the amount available outside, putting upward pressure on prices.

Similarly, Malthus wrote of Pitt's Poor Law proposal that it 'possesses in a high degree the great and radical defect of all systems of the kind, that, of tending to increase population without increasing the means for its support, and thus to depress the condition of those who are not supported by parishes, and consequently, to create more poor' (36).

14 Malthus leaves the final impression that *ultimately* food-supply constraints can be over

V DIMINISHING RETURNS AND LAND SCARCITY–BASED GROWTH THEORY

Malthus's arithmetic growth rate implies that there are no absolute limits to agricultural production: 'If the subsistence of man that the earth affords was to be increased every twenty five years by a quantity equal to what the whole world at present produces; this would allow the power of production in the earth to be absolutely unlimited, and its rate of increase much greater than we can conceive that any possible exertions of mankind could make it ... No limits are placed to the productions of the earth; they may increase for ever and be greater than any assignable quantity ...' (1798/1986, *I*, 13). Similarly: 'All this time we are supposing the produce of the earth absolutely unlimited, and the yearly increase greater than the boldest speculator can imagine' (70). This points away from diminishing returns, at least any version of the principle that implies a maximum total output.[15] (The arithmetic rate of increase implies, of course, a declining percentage increase. Malthus does not seem to concern himself with this characteristic.) But if we have in mind that the arithmetic increase is an outside estimate assumed for the sake of argument – a maximum Malthus did not believe could be achieved – the door may be left open for absolute limits, though such allowance was not needed for Malthus's response to the utopians, which relates entirely to comparative rates of change.[16] For even were the growth rate of food to be greater under Godwin's scheme than under private property (as Malthus believed would be the case, as we show later, in chapter 18, p. 910), the difference between birth rate – in a system where the private marginal cost of a family is zero – and food supply would be sufficient to establish his case.

Our next task is to take account of passages where the notion of an absolute limit to food supplies *is* explicitly recognized. It is in these contexts that there emerges most clearly the notion that, as population density

---

come. This is a weaker conclusion than the one reached earlier in the chapter – namely, that the impact of the Poor Laws on food supplies would be negligible. These perspectives might be partly reconciled if we assume *ongoing* artificially stimulated population growth; then there would be a 'permanant' lag in food supplies.

We must exercise caution in another respect. Malthus did not believe that the Poor Law institution, as it was organized in practice, had much stimulated population growth (see below, p. 36).

15 But Waterman (1991, 267–8), in his rational reconstruction of Malthus, insists on the compatibility of diminishing returns and the absence of 'limits,' that is, a positive slope to the total product curve whatever the magnitude of the variable factor, the marginal product approaching the x-axis asymptotically.

16 Even in this context, however, there are to be found loose allusions to an ultimate maximum to food supply. Thus: 'I have already pointed out the error of supposing that no distress and difficulty would arise from an overcharged population before the earth absolutely refused to produce any more' (66).

rises, so per-capita output and the real wage fall, ultimately leading to stationariness of population. One such statement will be found in a letter to Godwin written shortly after the appearance of the *Essay*: 'Could we suppose any country by the most extraordinary exertions, to arrive at the *ne plus ultra* of subsistence and population, in one or two centuries we have reason to think that the pressure of population in its utmost weight would be felt in frequent famines and pestilences, and particularly in the small recompense of labour; for I think you yourself must allow that under the present form of society the real recompense of labour depends upon the increase of the funds for its maintenance; and, when these funds are completely stationary and have continued so some time, this recompense will naturally be the least possible' (20 August 1798; cited in Bonar, 1926, iv). We consider from this perspective – it is a Smithian perspective, in fact – a series of chapters in the first *Essay* dealing with aspects of the population problem in 'civilized nations' as a whole, in England, and in North America.

Chapter IV of the *Essay* (1798) commences with a declaration relating absolute population size to absolute food supplies: 'The reason that the greater part of Europe is more populous now than it was in former times, is, that the industry of the inhabitants has made these countries produce a greater quantity of human subsistence. For, I conceive, that, it may be laid down as a position not to be controverted, that, taking a sufficient extent of territory to include within it exportation and importation; and allowing some variation for the prevalence of luxury, or of frugal habits; that population constantly bears a regular proportion to the food the earth is made to produce' (1798/1986, *1*, 23–4). Malthus next proceeds to a contemporary debate regarding 'the populousness of ancient nations,' remarking that the argument would be resolved 'could it be clearly ascertained that the average [i.e., *total*, extracting from seasonal or other fluctuations] produce of the countries in question, taken altogether, is greater now than it was in the time of Julius Caesar.' That contemporary China has an 'immense' population is indicated by the facts of a very great food output and a very low per-capita income: 'When we are assured that China is the most fertile country in the world; that almost all the land is in tillage; and that a great part of it bears two crops a year; and further that the people live very frugally, we may infer with certainty, that the population must be immense ...'[17]

This theme is elaborated in a criticism of Hume's *Essay on the Popu-*

17 Malthus did not commit himself to Adam Smith's view that the Chinese population was stationary, only that 'it certainly seems very little probable that the population of China is fast increasing' (25). Evidence of this was derived from the supposition that 'every acre of land has been so long in cultivation that we can hardly conceive there is any great yearly addition to the average [i.e., total] produce.'

lousness of Ancient and Modern Nations, where Malthus insists on the need to distinguish between growth rates and absolute size of population. Specifically, he rejects Hume's theme that the record of early marriage and low celibacy in ancient times indicates a large absolute population, and that of high celibacy and late marriage in modern nations a smaller population: 'If I find that at a certain period in ancient history, the encouragements to have a family were great, that early marriages were consequently very prevalent, and that few persons remained single, I should infer with certainty that population was rapidly increasing, but by no means that it was then actually very great; rather, indeed, the contrary, that it was then thin, and that there was room and food for a much greater number. On the other hand, if I find that at this period the difficulties attending a family were very great; that, consequently, few early marriages took place, and that a great number of both sexes remained single, I infer with certainty that population was at a stand; and, probably, because the actual population was very great in proportion to the fertility of the land, and that there was scarcely room and food for more' (24–5).

We have here the twofold notion that population growth depends on the magnitude of *per-capita* income, which in turn is governed by the population/land ratio. The latter relationship is suggested by the reference to 'room and food for a much greater number' at low *absolute* population sizes (always relative to land),[18] and to situations of very great *absolute* populations, where there is 'scarcely room and food for more,' implying low per-capita income. In the limit, population is 'at a stand'; conversely, it is presumably a high per-capita income at low absolute populations that provides the great 'encouragements to have a family.'

The related notions of reduced per-capita output at higher absolute population sizes (with a minimum to earnings and a corresponding maximum to population size) and of a *deceleration* of population growth with increase in population density are applied in an analysis of North American development (Chapter VI). There, because of high per-capita income in consequence of low population density, the growth rate of population was extremely high, which is to say that the 'checks' are removed: 'It has been universally remarked, that all new colonies settled in healthy countries, where there was plenty of room and food, have constantly increased with astonishing rapidity in their population ... the European settlements in the new world bear ample testimony to the truth of [the] remarks ... A plenty of rich land, to be had for little or nothing, is so powerful a cause of population, as to overcome all other obstacles ...' (39). There follows an important statement describing the effect initially on per-capita output, and secondari-

18 There is, however, an important qualification. Populations were sometimes stationary in 'thinly inhabited' countries (25) because of low per-capita income, reflecting what we would call the 'poverty trap' (see below, p. 54).

ly on the population growth rate, of a reduction in absolute population size: 'Whatever was the original number of British emigrants that increased so fast in the North American colonies; let us ask, why does not an equal number produce an equal increase, in the same time, in Great Britain? The great and obvious cause to be assigned, is, the want of room and food, or, in other words, misery; and that this is a much more powerful cause even than vice, appears sufficiently evident from the rapidity with which even old states recover the desolations of war, pestilence, or the accidents of nature. They are then for a short time placed a little in the situation of new states; and the effect is always answerable to what might be expected. If the industry of the inhabitants be not destroyed by fear or tyranny, subsistence will soon increase beyond the wants of the reduced numbers; and the invariable consequence will be, that population which before, perhaps, was nearly stationary, will begin immediately to increase' (41–2).[19]

The high rate of population increase of the United States could be maintained over time in so far as food supplies were able to keep up, as had indeed been the case: 'on account of the extreme cheapness of good land, a capital could not be more advantageously employed than in agriculture ...' (40); having in mind also the impact on agriculture of favourable institutions, the result was a population increase 'without parallel in history.'[20] In local areas where diversions of labour to manufacturing and commerce were avoided ('the inhabitants applied themselves solely to agriculture, and luxury was not known'), the increase in the food growth rate was such as to permit the 'extraordinary' rate of population increase of doubling in fifteen years (41).

19 An important technical issue might be addressed at this point. Having in mind the later full-fledged Malthusian analysis of the growth process, there is a missing step in the account so far. For the growth rate of population turns, not directly on per-capita output, but on the *wage*, which is determined in the first instance by the growth rate of labour demand (identifiable for simplicity with the growth rate of 'food' (g_K). It is g_K that is the governing force, for it varies with the magnitude of per-capita income: the higher the latter, the higher at each given wage will be *the profit rate*, and therefore g_K and the greater the stimulus to population growth (g_L). It remains true that high (low) population growth is linked to high (low) per-capita income, and high (low) per-capita income to low (high) population density, but the first connection is mediated via the labour market; the higher per-capita income at a *given* wage, the higher the profit rate, and therefore the higher g_K. It is this that puts upward pressure on the wage and encourages population growth. Although the labour market is not always formally discussed, we must suppose that such a market was presumed to exist in analyses of capitalist economies. That this is so emerges clearly in the North American analysis (see below, p. 34) with its discussion of a falling wage path. However, even there we find no discussion of the profit rate and its trend.

20 Malthus emphasized the positive effect of good laws and institutions on food expansion: internal free trade; 'liberty and equality'; 'alienation and division of property'; the legal requirement to develop land rather than leave it uncultivated; and a small tax burden.

But in arguing thus, Malthus feared he had been led into a damaging concession. For apparently food supplies *can* increase at a rate equivalent to the geometric rate attributed to American population. His answer – which unfortunately still insists formally on the geometric and arithmetic ratios – may be the first clear distinction in the literature between stocks and flows:

In instances of this kind, the powers of the earth appear to be fully equal to answer all the demands for food that can be made upon it by man. But we should be led into an error, if we were thence to suppose that population and food ever really increase in the same ratio. The one is still geometrical and the other an arithmetical ratio, that is, one increases by multiplication, and the other by addition. Where there are few people, and a great quantity of fertile land, the power of the earth to afford a yearly increase of food may be compared to a great reservoir of water, supplied by a moderate stream. The faster population increases, the more help will be got to draw off the water, and consequently an increasing quantity will be taken every year. But the sooner, undoubtedly, will the reservoir be exhausted, and the streams only remain. When acre has been added to acre, till all the fertile land is occupied, the yearly increase of food will depend upon the amelioration of the land already in possession; and even this moderate stream will be gradually diminishing. But population, could it be supplied with food, would go on with unexhausted vigour, and the increase of one period would furnish the power of a greater increase the next, and this without any limit. (41n)[21]

At low population/land ratios, the growth rate of food keeps up with the (maximum) growth rate of population. Once the land constraint is activated (when 'all fertile land is occupied') – how soon this occurs depends on how fast population is growing – the rate of growth of food falls, with increasing fractions of the (growing) labour supply diverted to 'ameliorate' land already in use.[22] The deceleration of the food growth rate evidently plays back on population growth, for only if population can be appropriately supplied with food can it 'go on with unexhausted vigour.'

To insist that food proceeds at an arithmetic rate ('by addition'), as Malthus does at the outset of the passage, implies constant absolute increments per period, whereas nothing in the account justifies this: Initially, the rate of increase of food is 'geometric' on a par with that of population, and subsequently it slackens, though little can be said regarding its precise course. (Quite possibly the absolute increases per period actually

21 This passage is cited by Bonar (1926, xx) as constituting the 'germ' of the diminishing-returns principle. So, too, is the passage on 1986, *1*, 68 (cited above, p. 23) but, as explained, that account provides inadequate proof.

22 This formulation confirms that the application of the variable factor incorporates land improvement; there is no sharp distinction between diminishing returns, given technology, and changes in technology.

decline.) And it is self-contradictory to insist on the geometric rate for population when at the same time it is allowed – this in fact is the object of the whole exercise – that the growth rate of population is increasingly constrained *below its potential.* Malthus was grasping at straws by devising his simile in defence of the geometric and arithmetic ratios. He must have thought they were important to his case, but in this he seems to have been carried away. (But see Waterman, 1992, 205–6, for a more positive representation to the effect that, for Malthus, the ratios are activated only once land scarcity is encountered.)

* * *

In Chapter VII, Malthus goes farther in formulating a model of growth along the lines thus far outlined. It is highly suggestive of what, later on, he came to state with impressive precision – namely, the land scarcity based growth model. The argument, in the context of a comparison of British demographic data for two periods (Elizabethan to the mid-seventeenth century compared with late-seventeenth to mid-eighteenth century): 'Dr. Price thinks that the registers in the former period are not to be depended upon; but, probably, in this instance, they do not give incorrect proportions. At least, there are many reasons for expecting to find a greater excess of births above the burials in the former period than in the latter. In the natural progress of the population of any country, more good land will, *ceteris paribus*, be taken into cultivation in the earlier stages of it than in the later. And a greater proportional yearly increase of produce will invariably be followed by a greater proportional increase of population' (46–7).[23] It is not made absolutely clear whether 'good land' is at all 'available' to be taken up at later stages of development, or whether the fraction of total land newly taken into cultivation that is 'good' declines. But, in either case, the passage alludes to an increasing scarcity (in some sense) of 'good' land, that is, *to a decline in quality of land at the extensive margin*, and to a more rapid increase in food production in early than in later stages of development, a differential evidently related to the increasing land scarcity. The more rapid rate of food production at early stages will be 'invariably followed' by a similarly rapid rate of population growth; and by implication (the context makes clear this was Malthus's intention), the subsequently

23 Malthus elaborated thus: 'I say *ceteris paribus*, because the increase of the produce of any country will always very greatly depend on the spirit of industry that prevails, and the ways in which it is directed. The knowledge and habits of the people and other temporary causes, particularly the degree of civil liberty and equality existing at the time, must always have great influence in existing and directing this spirit.' This qualification is in line with the introduction into his discussion of North American expansion of the legal and institutional framework: see above, note 20.

decelerating growth rate of food production will be followed by a deceleration of population growth.

VI THE DOWNWARD WAGE PATH

Now if, in fact, the population growth rate (g_L) decelerates in line with that of food (g_F), then with $g_F = 0$, population growth, too, will cease. Such is the stationary state. Malthus, it is true, also alludes to the 'forcing' of population: 'The only true criterion of a real and permanent increase in the population, of any country, is the increase of the means of subsistence,' but in China 'the people have been habituated by degrees to live almost upon the smallest possible quantity of food. There must have been periods in such countries when population increased permanently without an increase in the means of subsistence' (1798/1986, *1*, 49). But the major European states (England and France) were not subject to this problem of excessive population growth.[24] The data regarding birth and death rates indicated that 'population has accommodated itself, very nearly to the average produce of each country,' so that periodic plagues 'to repress what is redundant' are not a feature of the recent record (47). In short: 'The discouragements to marriage, the consequent vicious habits, war, luxury, the silent though certain depopulation of large towns, and the close habitations and insufficient food of many of the poor, prevent population from increasing beyond the means of subsistence.' It is the low real wage which discourages population growth and ensures that it stays in line with the declining growth rate of food in the course of regular secular expansion. (Malthus is here assuming private property; under communism, the zero private marginal cost of a family precludes such adjustment, even if living standards are low.) Similarly, an acceleration of food production, by raising real wages, will encourage an appropriate population increase: 'The true reason [for workers refusing to increase their numbers in the face of institutional encouragements of various kinds] is, that the demand for a greater population is made without preparing the funds necessary to support it. Increase the demand for agricultural labour by promoting cultivation, and with it

24 There are instances of European populations increasing in greater proportion than food supplies, but these, too, are special cases. Prussia, Lithuania, Pomerania, Brandenburgh, and Magdeburgh illustrated the 'periodical though irregular returns of sickly seasons' (45), characterized by high death rates and low birth rates, unrelated to the question of land scarcity: 'Is it not probable, that in this case, the number of inhabitants had increased faster than the food and the accommodation necessary to preserve them in health? ... These causes may produce such an effect, though the country, absolutely considered, may not be extremely crowded and populous' (44). Yet Malthus also observed of Brandenburgh and Magdeburgh, notwithstanding their occasional sickly seasons, that they are 'increasing rather fast for old states' and takes this fact as proof that 'cultivation must have been improving, and marriages, consequently encouraged.'

consequently increase the produce of the country, and ameliorate the condition of the labourers, and no apprehensions whatever need be entertained of the proportional increase of population' (50).[25]

What now of the course of real wages in the normal course of secular development? Evidently they are at their lowest in the stationary state – setting aside the possibility of 'forced' reductions – and by implication they must tend downwards over time. But we can be more explicit than that, for Malthus brings in the North American case – characterized by plentiful land resources – where 'the reward of labour is at present so liberal' (49), adding that 'it might be expected, that in the progress of the population of America, the labourers will in time be much less liberally rewarded.' (As we shall shortly see, Malthus later indicates that the decline was already under way.)

No *formal* reason is given for the prospective decline, though it is evidently related to the increasing effect of land scarcity. Malthus merely asserts: 'The numbers will in this case permanently increase, without a proportional increase in the means of subsistence.' Here one must be cautious. Since excessive population growth had been represented as a *special case* relating to 'forced' expansion of population, as in China, or to miscalculation, as in Germany, the population pressure expected in the American case must be of an *equilibrating* nature; for example, should the decline in the food growth rate cease, there will be a lag during which the wage falls, bringing population growth into line but no further secular pressure exerted by $g_L > g_F$. And, because as g_F falls, g_L comes into line, the 'permanent increase' in numbers 'without a proportional increase in the means of subsistence' must refer to the *falling average product* rather than differential growth rates.

Caution is in order also regarding a related passage in the same chapter: 'The happiness of a country ... [depends] upon the rapidity with which it is increasing, upon the degree in which the yearly increase in food approaches to the yearly increase of an unrestricted population' (51). This should not be read to imply that population growth is in fact usually 'unrestricted' – we know that there are scarcely any such cases. Rather, the higher the real wage, the higher will be g_L (up to some maximum, the 'unrestricted' rate); and the wage will rise as g_F rises towards the level of an unrestricted population growth. Should g_F be lower – and we know Malthus believed it almost invariably will be – then the real wage will be lower; but in either case actual g_L will (presumably after a lag) accommodate itself to g_F.

25 Read literally, the notion of a 'proportional' increase of population suggests a horizontal secular population-growth-rate curve, at least till the maximum doubling in twenty-five years. But, as we shall see in what follows, the texts in the main imply an upward-sloping curve.

Our interpretation is confirmed by a subsequent critique of Richard Price regarding stages of civilization as they affect population growth. Malthus there makes a further explicit statement regarding the downward course of real wages, its ultimate 'cause' and its impact on population growth, with special reference to the North American case: '[Price] does not seem to be aware, that the happiness of the Americans, depended much less upon their peculiar degree of civilization, than upon the peculiarity of their situation, as new colonies, upon their having a great plenty of fertile uncultivated land ... The superior degree of civil liberty which prevailed in America, contributed, without doubt, its share to promote the industry, happiness, and population of these states: but even civil liberty, all powerful as it is, will not create land. The Americans may be said, perhaps, to enjoy a greater degree of civil liberty, now they are an independent people, than while they were in subjection to England; but we may be perfectly sure, that population will not long continue to increase with the same rapidity as it did then. A person who contemplated the happy state of the lower classes of people in America twenty years ago, would naturally wish to retain them forever in that state. [But] ... the situation of new colonies, well governed, is a bloom of youth that no efforts can arrest ... the best directed exertions, though they may alleviate, can never remove the pressure of want' (120–1). Here then, once again, is the 'prediction' of a continuation of the declining American real wage already under way for some two decades. Also clearly expressed is the negative effect – the equilibrating effect – of the declining real wage on population growth. The emphasis is upon the abatement of population growth in consequence of the falling wage. This wage decline is evidently attributed to a deceleration in labour demand, which in turn reflects that in food production. The increasing impact of land scarcity is conspicuous and apparently mediated via the labour market.

The diminishing-returns model used to interpret the American case is subject to limitations. First, almost nothing is said of the profit rate; in particular, the downward trend in the profit rate characteristic of later versions of the *Essay* (and even to be found in the *Wealth of Nations*) plays no part.[26] Second, the emphasis is on the average rather than the marginal product.

VII THE ENGLISH CASE

We turn now to 'the principal states of modern Europe.' These were

26 The closest one comes to a discussion of the implications of wage movements for the profit rate is on page 16, where 'farmers and capitalists' are described as 'growing rich from the real cheapness of labour' (cited below, p. 44). But the context relates to *oscillatory* movements, not the *secular* trend.

characterized by *slow* population growth: 'In examining the principal states of modern Europe, we shall find, that though they have increased very considerably in population since they were nations of shepherds, yet that, at present, their progress is but slow; and instead of doubling their numbers every twenty-five years, they require three or four hundred years, or more, for that purpose. Some, indeed, may be absolutely stationary, and others even retrograde. The cause of this slow progress in population cannot be traced to a decay of the passion between the sexes. We have sufficient reason to think that this natural propensity exists still in undiminished vigour. Why then do not its effects appear in a rapid increase of the human species?' (1798/1986, *1*, 26).[27] The answer – England is taken as representative – turns on the operations of the 'preventive' and 'positive' checks: 'A foresight of the difficulties attending the rearing of a family, acts as a preventive check; and the actual distress of some of the lower classes, by which they are disabled from giving the proper food and attention to their children, acts as a positive check to the natural increase of population.' The *preventive* check is thus defined in terms of 'prudential' population control; and this, as we show later, in chapter 18: IV, V, entails 'vice.' (A *formal* allowance for 'moral restraint' is introduced in 1803.) The *positive* check, entails 'misery.'

As for the contemporary operation of the positive check, Malthus concedes that it is 'not so obvious to common view' as the preventive check (29), and he relies on impressionistic evidence to indicate its prevalence, which is said to be less in the country than in the towns. Even the Poor Laws are said, despite all the previous warnings, to have had a relatively small impact on population growth because of the precise manner of their administration: 'Notwithstanding then, the institution of the poor-laws in England, I think it will be allowed, that considering the state of the lower classes altogether, both in the towns and in the country, the distresses which they suffer from the want of proper and sufficient food, from hard labour and unwholesome habitations, must operate as a constant check to incipient population' (38).

Evidently the contemporary low standards are not accounted for by 'excessive' population growth – as mentioned, even the Poor Laws had not much speeded up population growth; Malthus's intention was not (as Schumpeter presumed it to be) to convey the message that 'population was actually and inevitably increasing faster than subsistence and that this was the reason for the misery observed' (above, p. 13). Rather, such an out-

27 Malthus refers to the Price–Howlett debate regarding population (110–11). Price believed population had actually fallen and, while Malthus disagreed, he saw Price as closer to the truth in that population growth was 'very slow.' He then refers to population growth as 'very slow, in comparison with the increase of wealth,' which is not quite the same thing.

come would result from the extension of the Poor Laws or the adoption of communistic-type proposals such as Condorcet's or Godwin's, particularly considering the absence of a positive private cost of maintaining a family. As for actual British and European conditions, it is precisely very *slow* population growth for which he was attempting to account. Malthus's position reflects his generalization that the course of population can be deduced from that of food production: 'If the effectual funds for the maintenance of labour are increasing, that is, if the territory can maintain, as well as the stock employ, a greater number of labourers, this additional number will quickly spring up' (110). Correspondingly, population growth would be slow should the expansion of cereal production be slow, activating the various checks – 'positive' and 'preventive,' the former deriving from *actual* low living standards, that is, entailing 'misery,' and the latter from the effort to avoid a deterioration, and entailing 'vice.'[28]

The 'proof' that the slow rate of increase of population in contemporary Europe could be explained by the various checks enumerated is taken up in Chapter VI of the *Essay* (1798). The new colonies of North America (which enjoyed 'plenty of room and food') had experienced the comparatively rapid increase that had 'invariably taken place, wherever these causes had been in any considerable degree removed' (38); 'these facts seem to shew that population increases exactly in the proportion that the two great checks to it, misery and vice, are removed ...' (41). That an equal absolute population in Britain did not produce 'an equal increase [of population] in the same time' as in the United States was precisely because of 'the great and obvious cause, the want of room and food, or, in other words misery,' or a low per-capita income.[29]

In the context of a comparison with the United States, land scarcity is thus represented as the ultimate cause of low standards in the British case.

28 Malthus frequently extends his categories of 'vice' and 'misery' to include forces acting upon the birth and death rates independently of actual or prospective living conditions. For example: 'The unwholesomeness of towns, to which some persons are necessarily driven from the nature of their trades, must be considered as a species of misery; and even the slightest check to marriage from a prospect of the difficulty of maintaining a family, may be fairly classed under the same head' (41). The effect on marriage falls within the formal definition of the preventive check; but unwholesome towns (and, in other contexts, war) cannot be said technically to constitute one of the positive checks since they are unrelated to the wage level.

29 Malthus's extension of his constraints to include housing as well as food silently complicates the model. For an early allusion to poor accommodation in 1798, see note 24, above. Further references are made to overcrowding as well as malnutrition in discussions of the mortality rate in 1803 and thereafter: 'crowded houses and insufficient and unwholesome food' were 'the natural consequence of an increase of population faster than the accommodations of a country with respect to habitation and food will allow' (1986, *3*, 308).

We recall also the application of reasoning derived from growth based on land scarcity to account for the supposedly higher British population growth rate *circa* 1600–50 compared with *circa* 1680–1750 (see above, p. 32). Yet, for all that, Malthus did not perceive Britain as densely populated; Britain in his day is expressly described as 'thinly inhabited,' or at least 'not extremely crowded and populous' (44). Presumably, then, the comparison with the United States must be understood in a relative sense.[30] The rationale – the increasing-land-scarcity rationale – offered for declining per-capita income in the period ending in the mid-eighteenth as compared with the seventeenth century does, however, pose a problem. For it is not the only account given of British development. I refer to a striking declaration regarding the determinants of 'happiness' applied to England: 'The happiness of a country does not depend, absolutely, upon its poverty, or its riches, upon its youth, or its age, upon its being thinly, or fully inhabited, but upon the rapidity with which it is increasing, upon the degree in which the yearly increase of food approaches to the yearly increase of an unrestricted population.[31] This approximation is always the nearest in new colonies, where the knowledge and industry of an old State, operate on the fertile unappropriated land of a new one. In other cases, the youth or the age of a State is not in this respect of very great importance. It is probable, that the food of Great Britain is divided in as great plenty to the inhabitants, at the present period, as it was two thousand, three thousand, or four thousand years ago. And there is reason to believe that the poor and thinly inhabited tracts of the Scotch Highlands, are as much distressed by an overcharged population, as the rich and populous province of Flanders' (51). To say, as Malthus does here, that a country's population/land ratio is *irrelevant* to the pace of growth of food supplies and the magnitude of real wages implies that the actual and prospective American growth pattern constituted a unique case. As for Britain, living standards had remained at low and roughly constant levels for ages, with population increasing in response to expansions in food supply, which, one is given to understand, reflect the 'natural progress of civilization' – the internal generation of novel technologies or higher motivation and the like.[32] In the absence of

30 There is also the absence in the American case of institutions and policy hostile to agriculture.

31 In his unpublished pamphlet of 1796 (*The Crisis*), Malthus had taken issue with Paley (1785), specifically regarding the appropriate index of 'happiness'; see below, chapter 19: VI.

32 In the 1803 edition also Malthus spelled out that growth of the food supply had reflected 'gradual' improvement so that the corresponding growth rate of population was far below the maximum potential rate: 'This increase [of population] ... will merely follow the slow augmentation of produce from the gradual improvement of agriculture; and population will still be checked by the difficulty of procuring subsistence' (1986, *3*, 448).

such forms of progress, there would be, apparently, no scope for growth at all. A stationary state is possible even where population is 'thin.'[33]

The analysis of British historical demography in terms of a downward trend in population growth owing to increasing land scarcity does not conform with the alternative just given. But the fact is that Malthus had proposed the analysis based on land scarcity circumspectly and with reservation (above, note 23). This treatment of the demographic data, important though it is from a theoretical perspective, should not therefore be weighed too heavily in attempting to isolate Malthus's considered vision of English development. Our conclusion is confirmed by examination of Malthus's fuller analysis, from which it emerges that an agricultural-growth model tracing the implications of increasing land scarcity under pressure of rising population would be too simple for the more complex English case. In the English case net capital accumulation in the manufacturing sector, and therefore manufacturing output, had proceeded apace, with little positive effect upon the wages fund and labour demand. To this complexity we turn next.

VIII THE DISTRIBUTION OF ACTIVITY BETWEEN AGRICULTURE AND MANUFACTURING

Our concern here is with the implications of the distribution of activity between agriculture and manufacturing for population growth. The key issues are found in 1798 in the course of a criticism of Adam Smith's analysis of labour demand. Malthus warned against hoarding as a threat to output and employment (1798/1986, *1*, 104–5) – the context is a reaction to Godwin – adopting Smith's position that a country 'grows rich by parsimony,' since the savings process involves a transfer of revenue 'from the maintenance of labour that is generally unproductive ... [to] the maintenance of what realizes itself in valuable commodities' (100). But Smith had erred by identifying 'every increase of the revenue or stock of a society with an increase of these [real-wage] funds' (108). That identification was valid only from the perspective of the individual employer, whose (real) demand for labour indeed turned on his surplus stock or revenue. It was invalid from the perspective of society: 'It will not be a real and effectual demand for the maintenance of an additional number of labourers, unless the whole, or at least a great part of this increase of the stock or revenue of the society, be convertible into a proportional quantity of provisions; and it will not be so convertible, where the increase has arisen merely from the produce of labour, and not from the produce of

33 See also note 18, above. Rashid has criticized Malthus on the empirical grounds that in Ireland 'the prime Malthusian variable, the land–labor ratio, has little relation with poverty' (1981, 66). He has failed to see that this perspective is Malthus's own.

land. A distinction will in this case occur, between the number of hands which the stock of society could employ, and the number which its territory can maintain.' It followed that net capital accumulation in the manufacturing sector, and therefore manufacturing output, might proceed apace with no positive effect upon the wages fund and labour demand: 'Dr. Adam Smith defines the wealth of a nation to consist in the annual produce of its land and labour. This definition includes manufactured produce, as well as the produce of the land. Now supposing a nation, for a course of years, was to add what it saved from its yearly revenue, to its manufacturing capital solely, and not to its capital employed upon the land, it is evident, that it might grow richer according to the above definition, without a power of supporting a greater number of labourers, and therefore, without an increase in the real funds for the maintenance of labour.' The effect of capital accumulation would be on money wages and food prices, not on real wages: 'There would, notwithstanding, be a demand for labour, from the power which each manufacturer would possess, or at least think he possessed, of extending his old stock in trade, or of setting up new works. This demand would of course raise the price of labour; but if the yearly stock of provisions in the country was not increasing, this rise would soon turn out to be merely nominal, as the price of provisions must necessarily rise with it.' Similarly: 'A great accession of work from manufactures, though it may raise the price of labour even more than an increasing demand for agricultural labour; yet, as in this case, the quantity of food in the country may not be proportionably increasing, the advantage to the poor will be but temporary, as the price of provisions must necessarily rise in proportion to the price of labour' (106).[34]

Food supplies might actually *fall* as the increasing demand for manufacturing labour attracts workers from the farms, although this outcome is set aside by the supposition that such a transfer would be 'compensated by improvements in the instruments of agriculture' (108). This allowance for new technology is not made merely to simplify the argument; technical change is represented as part and parcel of the 'normal' growth patterns. This view emerges immediately in a reference to manufactures: 'Improvement in manufacturing machinery would of course take place,' contributing (together with the higher manufacturing workforce drawn from agriculture) to an expansion of manufacturing output. And this without 'giving the labouring poor a greater command over the necessaries and conveniences of life' – indeed, even causing a net deterioration in well-being because of unhealthy conditions in the manufacturing centres and 'the greater uncertainty of manufacturing labour' (109).

34 To some extent the expansion of manufacturing reflected mercantilist interferences which attracted 'the very best land,' even 'land that would bear good crops of corn.' But pressure of demand for meat is also said to be 'a natural and inevitable consequence of the general progress of civilization' (112), a Smithian perspective.

The positive effect on food supplies of rising food prices is minimized, for transfers of capital into agriculture would occur but slowly, especially since the rise had been *preceded* by an increase in money wages, which acts as a depressant.[35] Food imports are also played down, for 'very high' food prices would be required 'to make an [appreciable] importation and distribution answer in large countries.' All in all, the expectation is of unchanged (even reduced) food supplies in consequence of non-agricultural expansion.

Various references in the *Essay* to contemporary English development make sense only when read with the foregoing in mind. Thus England is said to be 'one of the most flourishing states of Europe' and yet its population 'increases slowly' (26). Its 'flourishing' nature cannot consist in rapid increases in food supply, for then, on Malthus's own account, one would expect *rapid* population growth, which is not the case. This is further confirmed by an application to the consequences for labour of development since 1688. From the rapid expansion of domestic and foreign trade and of the value of national output, which reflected manufacturing progress, labourers had not benefited: 'though the wealth of the nation has been advancing with a quick pace, the effectual funds for the maintenance of labourers have been increasing very slowly ... The increasing wealth of the nation has had little or no tendency to better the condition of the labouring poor. They have not, I believe, a greater command of the necessaries and conveniences of life; and a much greater proportion of them, than at the period of the revolution, is employed in manufactures, and crowded together in close and unwholesome rooms' (110).[36] There had, however, been some net expansion of food (cereal) supplies, and consequently some growth of population: 'That the produce of the land has been decreasing, or even that it has been absolutely stationary during the last century, few will be disposed to believe' (111). *But this very moderate expansion was the outcome of 'improved husbandry,' not a growing agricultural workforce,* as we shall show later, in chapter 15: II. (Malthus actually asserts that the numbers in the agricultural workforce had fallen absolutely as a

35 Here an impact on the profit rate is implied.

36 This emerges, too, in a discussion of the preventive check as it applies to 'the sons of tradesmen and farmers' in England: 'These are exhorted not to marry, and generally find it necessary to pursue this advice, till they are settled in some business, or farm, that may enable them to support a family. These events may not, perhaps, occur till they are far advanced in life. The scarcity of farms is a very general complaint in England. And the competition in every kind of business is so great that it is not possible that all would be successful' (27). (The reference to a 'scarcity of farms' probably alludes, not to land scarcity as such in the technical sense, but to institutional impediments to land transfer. Contrast the American case, with its system of 'alienation and division of property,' absence of primogeniture, and illegality of land hoarding.) The passage confirms the notion of England as a 'flourishing' state – but it is flourishing with respect to capital accumulation generally, not in agriculture.

result of reorganization and labour-displacing technology.) The net population expansion must, therefore, have been employed almost wholly in manufactures. The small increase in wage goods, coupled with the instability of manufacturing (and also the immobility of labour owing to the Poor Law institution), suggested that living standards were no higher than a century before.[37]

IX THE OSCILLATORY PROCESS

The precedence of food over population is a frequent theme of the first *Essay*. For example, 'the only true criterion of a real and permanent increase in the population, of any country, is the increase of the means of subsistence' – apart from special cases where population is 'forced' despite the absence of a prior increase of food (cited above, p. 33). It is suggested also by the generalization that 'population constantly bears a regular proportion to the food the earth is made to produce' (above, p. 28), or that 'a greater proportional yearly increase of produce will invariably be followed by a greater proportional increase of population' (above, p. 32); or that 'if the effectual funds for the maintenance of labour are increasing ... [the] additional number [of labourers] will quickly spring up' (above, p. 37).[38]

Notwithstanding these generalizations regarding the precedence of food supply over population expansion, Chapter II of the first *Essay* introduces an analysis – one that has recently attracted attention and various attempts at 'rational reconstruction' – in which the expansion of population and that of food supply occur in interlocked steps. This analysis makes no mention of the geometric and arithmetic growth rates of population and food, respectively. Nothing in fact is said regarding *rates* of growth; it is the process of absolute expansion that is at issue. It is here that we would expect to encounter a notion of diminishing returns, but it is absent.

The 'population principle' in this context takes the form in 1798 – though not in later editions – of the simple assertion that 'in all societies, even those that are most vicious [see below, chapter 18: IV], the tendency to a virtuous attachment [to one woman] is so strong, that there is a constant effort towards an increase of population' (1798/1986, *1*, 14).[39]

37 For a discussion of Malthus on 'immiserizing growth,' see Gilbert, 1980.

38 As a further example: 'the increasing produce of a country, and the increasing demand for labour ... ameliorate the condition of the labourer, as greatly to encourage marriage' (45). On the other hand, a few sentences earlier it is from 'a *prospect* of increasing plenty in any country, [that] the weight that represses population is in some degree removed' (emphasis added), which is not quite the same as an actual increase of food.

39 In subsequent editions the generalization reads: 'There are few states in which there is

This increase occurs whenever food supplies have grown relative to population to ensure the 'easy support' of labour:

> We will suppose the means of subsistence in any country just equal to the easy support of its inhabitants. The constant effort towards population, which is found to act even in the most vicious societies, increases the number of people before the means of subsistence are increased. The food therefore which before supported seven [1803: eleven] millions must now be divided among seven millions and a half or eight millions [1803: eleven millions and a half]. The poor consequently must live much worse, and many of them be reduced to severe distress. The number of labourers also being above the proportion of the work in the market, the price of labour must tend toward a decrease [1803: tend to fall]; while the price of provisions would at the same time tend to rise. The labourer therefore must work harder [1803: do more work] to earn the same as he did before. During this season of distress, the discouragements to marriage, and the difficulty of rearing a family are so great that the population is at a stand [1803: that population is nearly at a stand; 1817: the progress of population is retarded]. In the meantime, the cheapness of labour, the plenty of labourers, and the necessity of an increased industry amongst them, encourage cultivators to employ more labourers upon their land; to turn up fresh soil, and to manure and improve more completely what is already in tillage; till ultimately the means of subsistence become [1803: may become] in the same proportion to the population as at the period from which we set out. The situation of the labourer being then again tolerably comfortable, the restraints to population are in some degree loosened; and [1803: and after a short period] the same retrograde and progressive movements with respect to happiness are repeated. (14–15)[40]

In this account, agricultural expansion is as much dependent upon the prior expansion of population as population growth is upon the prior expansion of agriculture; more intensive and extensive cultivation is undertaken only in response to reduced corn wages. But the striking feature of the account is the *secular constancy* of product per capita: 'The means of subsistence become in the same proportion to the population as at the period from which we set out.' The stimulus to expansion generated by falling corn wages apparently peters out as the downward movement slackens and is then reversed, but the end result is a larger aggregate food supply proportionate to the initially increased population.

---

not a constant effort in the population to increase beyond the means of subsistence.' In all editions Malthus continued: 'This constant effort as constantly tends to subject the lower classes of society to distress, and to prevent any permanent amelioration of their condition' (see 1986, *2*, 17).

40 The variations between editions are taken up below, in section XII.

The oscillatory pattern, Malthus admitted, was not easy to discern statistically: 'This sort of oscillation will not be remarked by superficial observers; and it may be difficult even for the most penetrating mind to calculate its periods. Yet that in all old states some such vibration does exist; though from various transverse causes, in a much less marked, and in a much more irregular measure than I have described it, no reflecting man who considers the subject deeply can well doubt. Many reasons occur why this oscillation has been less obvious, and less decidedly confirmed by experience, than might naturally be expected' (15).[41] Concealing the oscillatory pattern is 'the difference between the nominal and real price of labour' (16). For the money wage is pretty constant. Still the real wage falls as the price of corn rises under pressure of (temporary) scarcity; the correction, which involves expansion of food supplies, is ultimately achieved, capitalist farmers being enriched 'from the real cheapness of labour' and reacting by expanding capital (food output) and the demand for labour: 'It very rarely happens that the nominal price of labour universally falls; but we well know that it frequently remains the same, while the nominal price of provisions has been gradually increasing. This is, in effect, a real fall in the price of labour; and during this period, the condition of the lower orders of the community must be growing worse and worse. But the farmers and capitalists are growing rich from the real cheapness of labour. Their increased capitals enable them to employ a greater number of men. Work therefore may be plentiful; and the price of labour would consequently rise.' Ultimately, the money wage rises under pressure of increasing labour demand, though this, too, is impeded somewhat by employer combinations and parish laws.[42]

The oscillatory process was not apparently intended to cancel the precedence accorded food over population. Rather, the purpose of the exercise was to bring out 'the manner in which the constant check upon population acts.' Some formulations are worthy of James Mill: 'That population cannot increase without the means of subsistence, is a proposition so evident that it needs no illustration' (17). In brief, the sort of population growth which, by depressing the corn wage, stimulates agricultural expansion in the oscillatory process, must be contrasted with the 'forcing' of population described in the account of China, where 'population increased permanently, without an increase in the means of subsistence' (49).[43]

There remains the relevance of oscillations for the British case. While

41 For later modifications to this passage, see below, p. 63.

42 Complicating features include the systems of money-wage supplements. As the account of Chapter V has it: 'The food of a country that has been long occupied, if it be increasing, increases slowly and regularly, and cannot be made to answer any sudden demands; but variations in the distribution of the money of a society are not infrequently occurring, and are undoubtedly among the causes that occasion the continual variations which we observe in the price of provisions' (32–3).

43 The oscillations also must be contrasted with the special cases of excessive population growth characterizing various German states (above, note 24).

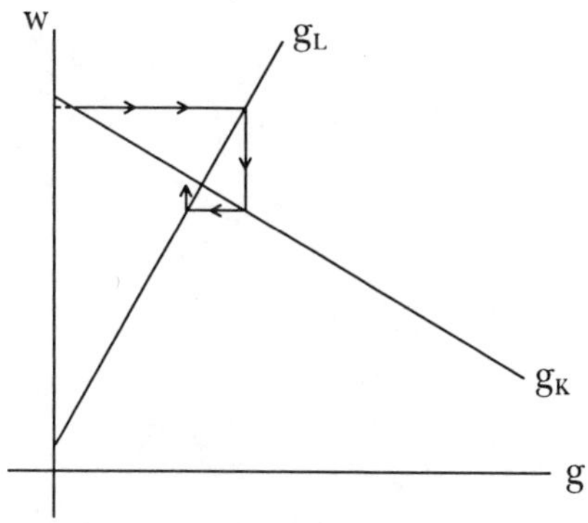

FIGURE 1.1 The equilibrium wage and the equilibrium growth rate of 'the real funds for the maintenance of labour' (corn) are determined by the intersection of g_L – the relation between the corn wage and population growth – and g_K, the capital (food) growth rate.

Malthus stressed the actuality of the phenomenon, his account of British development does *not* in fact seem to accord with the oscillatory pattern. What small expansion of domestic food supplies (corn) occurred is said to have been achieved despite a *declining* agricultural workforce by means of new technology, rather than under pressure of (temporarily) falling real wages (sections VII and VIII, above).[44]

* * *

Various interpretations have been offered for the wage oscillations. Eltis (1984, 117) reads Malthus as describing fluctuations of the corn wage about an equilibrium wage, and corresponding fluctuations of the *growth rate of food* about an equilibrium rate – a stable cobweb solution – as in figure 1.1. This interpretation turns on differential *growth rates* of food and population, whereas the passage itself refers to *absolute* population expansion before food is provided followed by absolute food expansion with population temporarily constant. This may not be too problematic if we understand the passage as stating a matter of general principle that might be extended.[45] More serious is the fact that the oscillations – and their corn-wage counterparts – do not, according to the text, peter out at some 'equilibrium' rate. Eltis has, I believe, read too much into the passage.

That the corn wage is represented as fluctuating about a *constant* level in the course of population growth should be kept in mind in evaluating

44 It may be pertinent that, in the 1803 edition, the applicability of the oscillatory process to 'all old states' is altered to 'the generality of old states' (see below, p. 63).

45 In 1817 Malthus himself refers to the passage in terms of population 'increasing at certain periods *faster than food*' (see below, chapter 5: VIII). This contrast helps evaluate the respective positions adopted by Waterman (1987) and Dooley (1988) in their debate as to whether Malthus intended a 'zigzag' path (Waterman) or *continuous* capital accumulation and population growth, each variable subject to a lagged reaction to change in its respective return (Dooley).

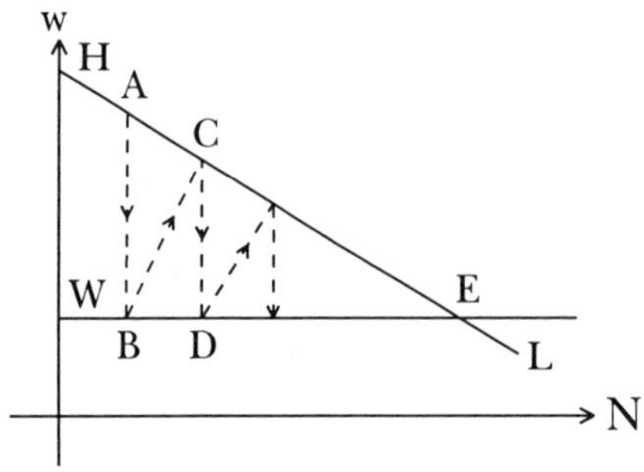

FIGURE 1.2 WE represents a subsistence-wage path such that population growth would cease at that wage. HE represents the maximum corn wage compatible with the mininum profit rate, or that profit rate at which net accumulation is zero. The wage oscillates on the path to final equilibrium at E (Waterman, 1987, 258, 264, 266). If some growth of capital occurs before population growth ceases, points such as B, D would lie on a curve above WE (but approaching E).

a representation of the Malthusian oscillatory perspective by Waterman (1987; 1991, 52); Waterman rejects the 'dynamic cobweb' about a steady-state equilibrium attributed to Malthus.[46] There is rather a gravitation of the corn wage towards the stationary state that occurs by way of fluctuations, entailing 'a concertina-like edging towards stationary equilibrium. First population grows, forcing wages down and raising the rate of profit. Then population stops and capital grows, raising wages and forcing down the rate of profit. And so on' (1987, 259, 269; also 1991, 52; see figure 1.2).

On Waterman's account, population growth occurs only when wages are at their maximum (on HE) – this is his reading of the initial supposition that 'the means of subsistence [are] just equal to the easy support of its inhabitants ...' (1987, 264); and capital (food supply) growth occurs only when wages are at their minimum (WE), or the profit rate at its maximum. On an *average*, both the corn wage and the profit rate decline to their respective permanent minima in the stationary state. This seems an extreme reading. The main problem is the fact that the oscillatory account makes no mention of increasing land scarcity. There does exist in the first *Essay* a land scarcity–based model which is applied to the American case (above, section VI). But this entails a *declining* secular corn wage, whereas the oscillatory process is conspicuous for *constancy* (on an average) of the corn wage. This land scarcity–based model, one might add, makes no mention of the trend path of the profit rate (it is a partial formulation only) in contrast to the oscillatory model, where fluctuations in the profit rate do make an appearance.

46 He objects to Eltis's view on the grounds that the g_K or capital-growth curve (identifiable with wage goods and constituting labour demand) shifts inwards under pressure of increasingly scarce land, generating a *decline* of the 'maximum wage' towards the subsistence level (1987, 267).

Waterman in effect is proposing that we superimpose Malthus's oscillations onto a *full-fledged* land-based growth model, though such a model does not yet exist in the first *Essay*, and though the average path of corn wages, in any event, differs between the two accounts. There is, in fact, some evidence that Malthus did not intend such superposition, although one cannot be sure. For he *limits* the applicability of his oscillations: 'in all *old* states some such vibration does exist' (1798/1986, *1*, 15 cited above, p. 44; emphasis added), a constraint which might well reflect the fact that the increase of American food supplies and population were so continuously high as to render oscillations inconsequential.[47]

X DIMINISHING RETURNS AND GROWTH, 1803

We consider now textual evidence of 1803 regarding land scarcity reflected in diminishing returns, as ultimate rationale for deceleration of food production, and consequently of population growth. Although our concern here is not primarily with the empirical dimension, we shall find that it inevitably intrudes.

We have, in 1803, the same perspective as in 1798 regarding the American case involving the dual linkages: (1) of per-capita output to population density, and (2) of population growth to per-capita output, the latter mediated via the labour market and turning on capital accumulation in agriculture or the growth rate of food supplies (1798/1986, *1*, 39f.; 1803/1986, *2*, 304f.). There is little doubt that the notion of diminishing returns – in the guise of a decline in per-capita output with increases in the population/land ratio – was central to the analysis. There is also in both editions reference to the 'expectation' (indeed, a trend actually under way) that 'in the progress of the population of America, the labourers will in time be much less liberally rewarded,' that is, a falling real-wage path (*1*, 49; *2*, 313). And in both, there is lacking any formal discussion of the profit rate and its trend.

We call attention now to a reformulation in 1803 of the criticism of David Hume's position that absolute population size had declined over the ages.[48] (For the original account in 1798, see above, pp. 28–9.) The prevalence of 'checks' to marriage could not be taken as *a priori* evidence of a low population; rather, the contrary:

> no cause, physical or moral, unless it operate in an excessive and unusual manner, will have any considerable and permanent effect on the population, except in as far as it influences the production and distribution of the means of subsistence.

47 On this see also Dooley, 1988.
48 Malthus also had in mind Wallace, 1753, 80.

In the controversy concerning the populousness of ancient and modern nations this point has not been sufficiently attended to; and physical and moral causes have been brought forward on both sides, from which no just inference in favour of either party could be drawn. It seems to have escaped the attention of both writers, that *the more productive and populous a country is in its actual state, the less probably will be its power of obtaining a further increase of produce*, and consequently the more checks must necessarily be called into action, to keep the population down to the level of this stationary or slowly increasing produce. From finding such checks, therefore, in ancient or modern nations, no inference can be drawn against the absolute populousness of either ... When the difficulties attending the rearing a family are very great, and consequently many persons of both sexes remain single, we may naturally enough infer that population is stationary, but by no means that it is not absolutely great; *because the difficulty of rearing a family may arise from the very circumstance of a great absolute population, and the consequent fullness of all the channels to a livelihood*; though the same difficulty may undoubtedly exist in a thinly peopled country, which is yet stationary in its population. (*2*, 151–2; emphasis added)

The notion of reduced per-capita output, and accordingly of population growth at higher absolute population size (with allusion to the limiting stationary state), is formulated already in 1798, and indeed directed against Hume, who had pointed to strong encouragement of marriage and procreation as a sign of high absolute population, and to the converse in the case where checks are strong. The reformulation of 1803 adds precision by its reference to the declining 'power of obtaining a further increase of produce' at higher absolute population and aggregate food output, for this seems to entail diminishing returns – indeed, diminishing *marginal* returns. This is an open possibility, but we must also allow that the reference may be to a declining *growth rate* of produce with absolute increase in population density. Yet even in the latter case, the last section of our extract does bring out clearly enough the notion of reduced per-capita income at high population/land ratios.[49]

While this particular formulation adds precision to the discussion of 1798, the case is reversed in another context. In the first *Essay* there is found a brief statement of the land scarcity–based growth model, including deceleration of food production owing to diminishing returns at the extensive margin accompanied by (or rather 'followed by') a corresponding decline of population growth (above, p. 32). This formulation is absent in 1803 (cf. *1*, 47; *2*, 248). The context suggests why. The issue in 1798 is the accuracy of the village and market-town 'registers,' particularly the accuracy of the registers for the earlier period, which indicated a higher excess of

49 But it also qualifies that notion by allowing for cases where per-capita income is low despite low population density. On this qualification, see below, pp. 54–5.

births over deaths than subsequently. Richard Price (1792)[50] had questioned the early data, but Malthus argued tentatively in their favour and provided a possible rationale – namely, the encouragement given population growth by relatively good land resources, and, by implication, the deceleration of population growth with increasing land scarcity manifested in diminishing returns at the extensive margin. Now, by 1803, Malthus was newly aware of the fact of *accelerating* population growth, attributing it to 'the more rapid progress of commerce and agriculture' (*2*, 238).[51] He came to question the accuracy of the registers (his main concern in 1803 is actually to compare the early and later years of the eighteenth-century), so that the theoretical rationale originally offered in support of a decelerating growth rate was no longer relevant. That fact does not, however, necessarily touch on the validity of the model itself.

The 1817 version, we shall find (chapter 5: III), explains with admirable clarity that the deceleration of population growth imposed by land scarcity and exercised by declining corn wages might be avoided by working-class constraints on procreation. This alternative is to be found already in the 1803 essay, though less formally expressed, in a reference to the hope that labour should acquire 'the habit of proportioning the supplies of labour to a stationary or even decreasing demand, without an increase of misery and mortality' (*3*, 567).

* * *

There is, we conclude, clear recognition in 1798 and 1803 of the notion of falling average product with rising population density, with a maximum to population size when the wage is reduced to subsistence, an outcome, it is intimated in 1803, that might be avoided by deliberate population constraint.

We consider next further textual evidence often alluded to in the secondary literature. One conspicuous passage involves the 'reservoir' analogy of 1798, originally introduced to refute the notion that, in the American case, food supplies must have been growing at a geometric rate since they keep pace with population growth (*1*, 41n; above, p. 31). (Actually, the refutation was merely nominal; Malthus had effectively conceded that food does grow geometrically as long as a 'reservoir' of untapped land is available.) In the second edition, the 'reservoir' analogy is absent, and with it is abandoned even the formal attempt to show that subsistence never increases at a geometric rate (cf. Cannan, 1917, 111). But Malthus retains the notion of 'the yearly increase of food' as a diminishing *stream*,

50 Malthus used the fifth (1792) edition of Price's *Reversionary Payments*; see James, in Malthus, 1803/1989, II, 325.

51 See, for an elaboration, chapter 16, below, on the 'population problem.'

assuming in effect the reservoir of 'fertile land' to be emptied. The last three sentences in the following passage are exactly as in the 1798 edition, though now given a conspicuous place in the first chapter: 'It may safely be pronounced, therefore, that population, when unchecked, goes on doubling itself every twenty five years, or increases in a geometrical ratio. The rate according to which the productions of the earth may be supposed to increase, it will not be so easy to determine. Of this, however, we may be perfectly certain, that the ratio of their increase must be totally of a different nature from the ratio of the increase of population. A thousand millions are just as easily doubled every twenty five years by the power of population as a thousand. But the food to support the increase from the greater number will by no means be obtained with the same facility. Man is necessarily confined in room. When acre has been added to acre till all the fertile land is occupied, the yearly increase of food must depend upon the amelioration of the land already in possession. This is a stream, which, from the nature of all soils, instead of increasing, must be gradually diminishing. But population, could it be supplied with food, would go on with unexhausted vigour; and the increase of one period would furnish the power of a greater increase the next, and this without any limit' (2, 10–11). This famous passage refers explicitly to alternative *annual rates of increase.* It asserts that the maximum growth rate of food declines with increasing paucity of agricultural resources,[52] whereas maximum potential population growth remains constant. But it does not necessarily imply diminishing returns in the sense of falling average (let alone marginal) product at higher population/land ratios; for conceivably a reduction in the time period over which given absolute increases in food are attempted, that is, a reduction of the food growth rate below its maximum, would avoid falling per-capita output. This latter possibility is precluded if we read the passage in the light of the texts discussed above that *do* involve falling productivity with increased population density. Whether we are justified in so doing is an open question. It remains true (as in the 1798 case) that the polemical object of the essay would in any event be assured in terms of the more general argument entailing a constraint on population growth despite constant average product.

In the elaboration that follows, Malthus refers to the *length of time* required to 'improve the minds' and 'direct the industry' of various races as an indication of the constraints on the global growth rate of food supplies. He takes Europe (especially Britain) as the best case for his illustration of the theme:

Europe is by no means so fully peopled as it might be. In Europe there is the fairest chance that human industry may receive its best direction. The science of

52 This possibly reflects nothing more than the *arithmetic ratio,* which of course entails a falling percentage annual increase.

agriculture has been much studied in England and Scotland; and there is still a great portion of uncultivated land in these countries. Let us consider at what rate the produce of this island might be supposed to increase under circumstances the most favourable to improvement.

If it be allowed that by the best possible policy, and great encouragements to agriculture, the average produce of the island could be doubled in the first twenty five years, it will be allowing, probably, a greater increase than could with reason be expected.

In the next twenty years, it is impossible to suppose that the produce could be quadrupled. It would be contrary to all our knowledge of the properties of land. The improvement of the barren parts would be a work of time and labours and it must be evident to those who have the slightest acquaintance with agricultural subjects, that in proportion as cultivation extended, the additions that could yearly be made to the former average produce must be gradually and regularly diminishing. That we may be the better able to compare the increase of population and food, let us make a supposition, which, without pretending to accuracy, is clearly more favourable to the power of production in the earth, than any experience we have had of its qualities will warrant.

Let us suppose that the yearly additions which might be made to the former average produce, instead of decreasing, which they certainly would do, were to remain the same; and that the produce of this island might be increased every twenty five years, by a quantity equal to what it at present produces: the most enthusiastic speculator cannot suppose a greater increase than this. In a few centuries it would make every acre of land in the island like a garden. (*2*, 11–12)

When compared with the equivalent passage of 1798 (cf. *1*, 11–12; cited above, p. 19), we find here: (1) added confirmation (the first paragraph) that 'a great portion of uncultivated land' and high technology characterized the British economy; (2) added reference to the 'time and labours' required by 'improvement of the barren parts';[53] and (3) an insertion regarding the '*gradually and regularly' diminishing yearly additions 'to the former average produce.*'

Again, too much should not be made of this latter modification as a *new* allusion to the law of diminishing returns. In the first place, the text simply reiterates what had appeared already in 1798 (see above, section III): 'a person who is acquainted with the nature of the soil in this country, and who reflects on the fertility of the lands already in cultivation, and the

53 In the 1806 appendix, Malthus introduced an analogy with the preparation of a farm by proper management before added stock could be effectively supported; similarly, without appropriate preparation of the land, an expansion of population would generate unacceptably low standards, but, with it, the same expansion might be accommodated under more favourable conditions (1806, II, 508–9, 517–18). See also Malthus 1824b/1986, *4*, 180–1, 195.

barrenness of those that are not cultivated, will be very much disposed to doubt, whether the whole average produce could possibly be doubled in twenty five years from the present period ... Difficult, however, as it might be, to double the average produce of the island in twenty five years, let us suppose it effected ... During the next period of doubling [of population], where will the food be found to satisfy the importunate demands of the increasing numbers. Where is the fresh land to turn up? Where is the dressing necessary to improve that which is already in cultivation? There is no person with the smallest knowledge of land, but would say, that it is impossible that the average produce of the country could be increased during the second twenty five years by a quantity equal to what it at present yields' (*1*, 68–9; for the identical 1803 statement see *3*, 333–4). To assert in 1803 that 'the additions that could yearly be made to the former average produce must be gradually and regularly diminishing' is only to make explicit what is already very clear in 1798. But, as is true of the 1798 statement, the notion of diminishing *yearly* additions to the former average produce is not necessarily identifiable with 'diminishing returns.'[54]

Cannan, who was critical of the idea that the *Essay* turns on diminishing returns, conceded (1917, 115) that there is in 1803 a 'rudimentary' allowance for the true law in the rejection of Anderson's proposition (in Malthus's paraphrase) 'that every increase of population tends to increase relative plenty and *vice versa*': 'But when an accidental depopulation takes place in a country which was before populous and industrious, and in the habit of exporting corn, if the remaining inhabitants be left at liberty to exert, and do exert, their industry in the same direction as before, it is a strange idea to entertain, that they would then be unable to supply themselves with corn in the same plenty; particularly as the diminished numbers would of course cultivate principally the more fertile parts of their territory, and not be obliged, as in their more populous state, to apply to ungrateful soils ... [If] absolute populousness were necessary to relative plenty, as some agriculturalists have supposed, it would be impossible for new colonies to increase with the same rapidity as old states' (1803/1986, *3*, 452).[55]

Cannan, with this passage in mind, warned readers not to exaggerate the implications of a 'casual' and 'subsidiary' use of one of the principal

54 In both editions we also have the rhetorical question regarding a doubling at fifteen years – Where is 'the labour needed to double the produce in so short a time'? (1986, *1*, 75; *3*, 339) – implying the possibility of a doubled produce with doubled population, assuming a longer period. For the same motion in the third edition, see 1806, II, 120.

55 Jacob Hollander argued – as do others more recently – that, whereas in 1798 there is 'no explicit statement of a law of diminishing returns,' Malthus in 1803 responded to James Anderson's allusions to *increasing returns* by inserting a long note in reply and intimating in the text 'a law of diminishing returns in unmistakable terms' (1903, 4–5).

ideas on which the law of diminishing returns is based. The main population principle, he believed, still turned, as in 1798, on the geometric and arithmetic ratios. Now it is certainly the case that the primary concern of the passage is the growth rate of food relative to that of population, rather than produce per capita, as such. This is suggested by the reference to new colonies at the close of the passage, and more clearly by a footnote attached thereto which alludes to Anderson's position in the *Calm Investigation* (1801) and adds: '[Anderson] concludes his proofs by observing that, if the facts which he had thus brought forward and connected do not serve to remove the fears of those, who doubt *the possibility of this country producing abundance to sustain its increasing population (were it to augment in a ratio greatly more progressive than it has yet done)* he should doubt whether they could be convinced of it, were one even to rise from the dead to tell them so ... I agree with Mr. Anderson however, entirely, respecting the importance of directing a greater part of the national industry to agriculture; but, from the circumstance of its being possible for a country with a certain direction of its industry always to export corn, although it may be very populous, he has been led into *the strange error of supposing, that an agricultural economy could support an unchecked population*' (emphasis added).[56] The main issue for Malthus, as is so usual, is the limited capacity of food to increase when compared with maximum population growth (even should agriculture be artificially encouraged), imposing checks on the population growth rate. At the same time we cannot neglect the fact that, as a rationale for the relatively slow growth of food supply in a populous country, recourse *is* had to the principle of diminishing returns – higher (lower) average product at lower (higher) population size. We need not be quite as reticent as Cannan in recognizing elements of the land scarcity–based growth model in the early essays. It would, however, be unjustified to put great weight on the passage as a novelty stimulated by the appearance of Anderson's pamphlet, considering the similar passage of 1798 regarding the rapidity with which even 'old states' recover from war and natural disaster (*1*, 41–2; above, p. 30).[57]

A criticism of Lord Kames in the final chapter of Book III, on 'sources of the prevailing errors on the subject of population,' is also pertinent. The point at issue is the generalization attributed to Kames (close to

56 On this note, and more generally for a discussion of Anderson's possible influence on Malthus, including the formulation of diminishing returns in Anderson (1777), see Prendergast, 1987.

57 However, while this latter passage provides a statement – actually repeated in 1803 (1986, *2*, 307) – of higher average product at lower population size (and also of population increase in response), Malthus did not formally generalize to conclude that ongoing *expansion* of population (in the normal circumstances of old states) runs into diminishing returns; the cases of absolute population decrease and increase are not necessarily symmetrical.

Anderson's) that 'an increase of population in any state, not cultivated to the utmost, will tend rather to augment than to diminish relative plenty of the whole society' – that average produce rises – so that countries with the highest population densities may yet have the 'greatest plenty' and greatest corn-export capacity (*3*, 448). Following Sir James Steuart, Malthus accepted no more than that a 'well-conducted' agricultural economy yields a *surplus* available for the support of 'free hands'; provided the latter 'do not increase as to reach the limit of the number which can be supported by the surplus produce, the whole population of the country may continue for ages increasing with the improving state of agriculture, and yet always be able to export corn.' However, this population increase will 'after a certain period' fall short of the 'natural and unrestricted increase of population,' and 'will merely follow the slow augmentation of produce from the general improvement of agriculture; ... population will still be checked by the difficulty of procuring subsistence.' There is here a loosely expressed idea of deceleration of agricultural, and therefore of population, growth in the fall below the 'unrestricted' increase allowed at some early period of development. But the deceleration is not a steady one towards ultimate stationariness; in fact, 'the gradual improvement of agriculture' can apparently continue endlessly.[58]

* * *

The often-encountered qualification to the general rule of declining per-capita output with increase in population density requires attention. Thus, in 1798, there is the sharp contrast between new colonies where wages (and product per capita) initially exceed subsistence by a large margin, and other low-density economies with *low* productivity: 'There are many thinly inhabited states that are yet stationary in their population' (*1*, 25). Similarly, in 1803, it is observed that low wages may characterize cases of low as well as high density: 'the difficulty of rearing a family may arise from the very circumstance of a great absolute population, and the consequent fullness of all the channels to a livelihood; though the same difficulty may undoubtedly exist in a thinly peopled country, which is yet stationary in population' (*2*, 151–2).

In making the qualification regarding low wages – or, perhaps more meaningfully, low per-capita output – at low population density, Malthus is writing as a development economist: 'It has appeared, I think, clearly in the review of different societies given in the former part of this work, that those countries, the inhabitants of which were sunk in the most barbarous ignorance, or oppressed by the most cruel tyranny, however low they might be [in] actual population, were very populous in proportion to their means

58 This perspective is actually in line with the vision of English growth given in 1798.

of subsistence' (*3*, 453). Malthus is, therefore, careful to specify in his discussion of a decline in population owing to war or natural disaster that 'the remaining inhabitants [are] left at liberty to exert, and do exert, their industry in the same direction as before' (above, p. 52) or, in 1798, that 'the industry of the inhabitants be not destroyed by fear or tyranny' (above, p. 30). Only then can an *increase* in average product result. In other cases of depopulation, this will not be the outcome: 'In the numerous instances of depopulation which occur in history, the causes may always be traced to the want of industry or the ill direction of that industry, arising from violence, bad government, ignorance, etc. which first occasions a want of food, and of course depopulation follows' (451). Whether or not a lower population implies a higher average product thus depends on a variety of circumstances; it may be taken for granted only if we are assured that the labour force has the characteristics (and the knowledge base) typical of 'advanced' economies.

All this suggests that we must be careful in our deductions from the remarkable declaration (obviously directed against Paley), already made in 1798, that 'the happiness of a country does not depend, absolutely, upon its poverty, or its riches, upon its youth, or its age, upon its being thinly, or fully inhabited' (*1*, 51; above, p. 38). Such extremely long comparisons involve entirely different social organizations and behavioural characteristics. It remains true, however, that per-capita output in contemporary Britain, relatively densely populated, was seen in 1798 to be *no lower* than in the past: 'It is probable, that the food of Great Britain, is divided in as great plenty to the inhabitants, at the present period, as it was two thousand, three thousand, or four thousand years ago.' In 1803 this view is actually modified to allow for *rising* per-capita output despite rising density – a probable division 'in more liberal shares' (*2*, 314). Malthus doubtless was allowing for new technology and organizational change in making these statements regarding the effects of population expansion. It would be an error to insist strongly on the modern notion of a given production function, and shifts thereof; where diminishing productivity is introduced, it may well be with consideration made for new technology. But there is no emphasis on the phenomenon of falling productivity in this sense when it comes to the account of contemporary Britain. Indeed, we are faced with an apparent *empirical* refutation of the *theoretical* structure.

The proposition that the growth rate of population is necessarily constrained below its maximum potential by a sort of short-run form of diminishing returns surmountable *in time* by appropriate land improvement – the proposition serving the original polemical purpose of the *Essay* – remains firm. It is nicely confirmed in a discussion of a 'plan' to check population growth to allow preliminary investment in land preparation: '[An] objection that may be made to this plan is, the diminution of population that it would cause. It is to be considered, however, that this diminution is merely relative; and when once this relative diminution has been effected, by keeping the population stationary, while the supply of food had increased, it might then start afresh, and continue increasing for ages, with the increase of food, maintaining always the same relative proportion to it. I can easily conceive that this country, with a proper direction of the national industry, might, in the course of some centuries, contain two or three times its present population, and yet every man in the kingdom be much better fed and clothed than at present. While the springs of industry continue in vigour, and a sufficient part of that industry is directed to agriculture, we need be under no apprehensions of a deficient population' (*3*, 488–9). And the problem of capital shortage figures large in an explanation of 'the appearance of uncultivated lands': 'The great obstacle to the amelioration of land is the difficulty, the expense, and sometimes the impossibility of procuring a sufficient quantity of dressing' (458).[59]

XI THE 1806 DEFENCE

An appendix of 1806 was devised to correct specific misinterpretations of the *Essay* and to summarize its central message. We shall consider it for allusions to the issues that have preoccupied us, especially evidence of recognition of the diminishing-returns principle in the analysis of a growing economy.

The argument commences with a reiteration of the denial that food per-capita *necessarily* varies inversely with the population/land ratio: 'It is an utter misconception of my argument to infer that I am an enemy to population. I am only an enemy to vice and misery, and consequently to that unfavourable proportion between population and food, which produces these evils. But this unfavourable proportion has no necessary connection with the quantity of absolute population which a country may contain. On the contrary, it is more frequently found in countries that are thinly peopled, than those which are populous' (1806, II, 507–8). This formulation appears to deny outright diminishing productivity as the norm, and even to imply increasing productivity. But caution is in order. We have here an 'empirical' (rather than a 'theoretical') statement which may well allow for shifts in the production function, reflecting not only altered technology, but also changes in social and legal organization, work ethic, and so forth. It remains possible, allowance made for the earlier formulations involving absolute reduction in population size which (in a context evidently holding these variables constant) without question emphasize higher per-capita product (above, p. 55), that Malthus did not *exclude* a 'law' of diminishing returns. Whether he would have taken such a law seriously is quite another matter; what can reasonably be held constant

59 Awareness of the contrast between the extensive and intensive margins is also apparent in this context.

upon contraction of population size may be wholly inappropriate in the case of expansion. With serious uncertainty such as this, it may be safer to avoid committing ourselves too far. We can say for certain only that there is no formal statement in the appendix of falling per-capita output with increase in population density.

A second passage relevant for us relates to the question of absolute limits to food production. Malthus points out that the implication of the arithmetic ratio that 'the produce of the earth [is] unlimited' was 'certainly going too far' (II, 517), and was introduced to avoid dispute by weighing the case against himself. Here he amplifies his true position – that there *does* exist an absolute limit, albeit 'indefinite': 'The power of the earth to produce subsistence is certainly not unlimited, but it is strictly speaking indefinite, that is, its limits are not defined, and the time will probably never arrive when we shall be able to say, that no further labour or ingenuity of man could make further additions to it. But the power of obtaining an additional quantity of food from the earth by proper management, and in a certain time, has the most remote relation imaginable to the power of keeping pace with an unrestricted increase of population' (517–18). The important point for us is that even allowing for the possibility of continued absolute increase in output did not dilute the central message, that food supply cannot expand at a rate equivalent to *unrestricted* population growth and, thus, that the latter is necessarily constrained.

The 'chief object' of the essay was, in fact, not to provide a 'proof' of the differential ratios. These are represented as self-evidently true: 'The first of these propositions I considered as proved as soon as the American increase was related, and the second proposition as soon as it was enunciated' (520n). Malthus's concern was rather 'what effects these laws, which I considered as established in the first six pages had produced, and were likely to produce on society.' The wholly rhetorical purpose of the arithmetic–geometric contrast is hereby confirmed. And he complained of readers who, while accepting 'the different ratios of increase on which all [his] principal conclusions are founded,' yet claimed 'that no difficulty or distress could arise from population, till the productions of the earth could not be further increased' (517). There emerges here by implication a notion of *deceleration* of the food growth rate as the 'limit,' albeit 'indefinite,' is approached. (Needless to say, deceleration is implied by the very definition of an arithmetic rate, a fact that Malthus rarely seems to emphasize.) But that was evidently not Malthus's concern, which remained the simple fact of an excess of 'unrestricted' growth of population over the maximum conceivable growth rate of food.

Since the principle is then applied in a developmental context to New Holland (Australia), the implications for the English case are uncertain: 'The knowledge and industry, which would enable the natives of New Holland to make the best use of the natural resources of their country, must ... come to them gradually and slowly ...; but the passions which prompt to the increase of population are always in full vigour, and are ready to produce their full effect even in a state of the most helpless ignorance and barbarism' (518). The passage is characteristically ambiguous. It may imply that a given increase in the growth rate of food (from an initial stationary state) – or perhaps an acceleration – would be swamped by an *actually excessive* growth rate of population; or less strongly, that any release of the constraints on population growth would generate a rate of increase equal to that of food. Malthus proceeds to observe that, although in actuality the population/land ratio was *lower* in New Holland than in China, yet 'misery and vice' were almost as severe, again illustrating the fact that low absolute population size relative to land might yet entail high pressure of population: 'It will readily be allowed, that the reason why New Holland, in proportion to its natural powers, is not so populous as China, is the want of those human institutions which protect property and encourage industry; but the misery and vice which prevail almost equally in both countries, from the tendency of population to increase faster than the means of subsistence, form a distinct consideration, and arise from a distinct cause. They arise from the incomplete discipline of the human passions ...' Once again we have apparently the formal notion that population is actually increasing faster than food. But the fact is that China certainly, and New Holland possibly, are represented as *stationary states*, with population in both cases held at constant levels by low real earnings. Thus, *excessive growth of population is not in fact the issue.* Presumably, then, the passage refers to the mere fact of low food per capita; that is, given the 'incomplete discipline of the human passions,' constancy of population is assured only at low standards.

Consider next a revealing statement of the differential 'ratios of increase.' The context is a rejection of the notion that the poor have a 'right' to support: 'If it appear, as it must appear on these ratios being allowed, that it is not possible for the industry of man to produce on a limited territory sufficient food for all that would be born, if every person were to marry at the time when he was first prompted to it by inclination [at puberty], it follows, irresistibly, that all cannot have the *right* to support' (519). Similarly, there is reference to the 'physical impossibility of relieving this progressive population.' It is then *land scarcity* in some general sense that precludes a rate of growth of food equivalent to the maximum growth rate of population, the rate which would apply, assuming an open-ended guarantee of support. Nothing, however, is said regarding a *deceleration* of food production and a widening of the differential over time.[60] Clearly, the high growth rate of the American population is made possible by the

60 Except by implication in the remark which follows that the case for a right to support considers 'that the American increase of population is a miracle, and does not arise from the greater facility of obtaining the means of subsistence' (520).

high growth rate of food, and would only be maintained, given the special and temporary confluence of circumstances characterizing new colonies. Moreover, as mentioned above, though the notion of a deceleration of food production is inherent in the very concept of an arithmetic ratio, none of this is made explicit in the 1806 appendix; Malthus's concern is with the simple fact of a differential between the 'ratios,' not a widening thereof over time as the (undefined) limit is approached.

We come next to an application of the principle of population to current policy. A reform program designed to raise per-capita wages cannot succeed unless accompanied by a fall in natality to compensate for the expected reduced death rate: 'The following proposition may be said to be capable of mathematical demonstration. In a country, the resources of which will not permanently admit of an increase of population more rapid than the existing rate, no improvement in the condition of the people, which would tend to diminish mortality, could *possibly* take place without being accompanied by a smaller proportion of births, supposing of course no particular increase of emigration ... In this country it has appeared that, according to the returns of the Population Act in 1801, the proportion of births to deaths was about 4 to 3. This proportion with a mortality of 1 in 40 would double the population in $83\frac{1}{2}$ years; and as we cannot suppose that the country could admit of more than a quadrupled population in the next 166 years, we may safely say that its resources will not allow of a permanent rate of increase greater than that which was then taking place. But if this be granted, it follows as a direct conclusion, that if Mr. Young's plan, or any other, really succeeded in bettering the condition of the poor, and enabling them to rear more of their children, the vacancies in cottages in proportion to the number of expectants would happen slower than at present, and the age of marriage must inevitably be later' (534–5).[61] Here we have allusion to a maximum conceivable 'permanent' growth rate of population predicated (apparently) upon a presumption regarding the maximum conceivable growth rate of food. It is interesting to note that the notion of an 'arithmetic ratio' is entirely abandoned.[62] We must take seriously Malthus's repeated claim that it was

61 For Young's plan see Young, 1801, 1804. He proposed that cottages and three or four acres of land be provided for a specific number of families.

62 Allowing the celebrated equal increments per twenty-five years for food production, we would have (assuming, for simplicity, a base for food of 11 million bushels):

1800	1825	1850	1875	[1883]	1900	1925	1950	[1966]	1975
11	22	33	44	*ca* 48	55	66	77	[*ca* 80]	88

If population growth keeps in line (assuming the same base level), it would be approximately 48 million in 1883, and 80 million in 1966, the latter just over *seven* times the 1800 figure, not the *four* times 'in the next 166 years' alluded to in the text.

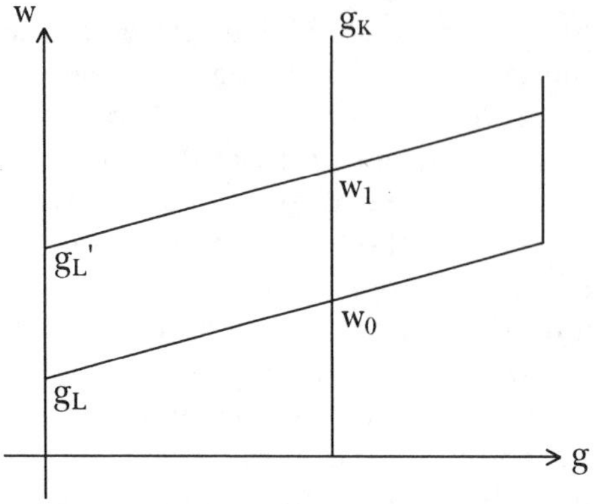

FIGURE 1.3 Diagrammatically, we have a population growth rate (g_L) which rises with the real wage (w) at least, we must assume, until some maximum; the food growth rate (g_k) is assumed to be given. A reform policy designed to raise w from w_0 to w_1 can be successfully undertaken only if the average age of marriage is delayed, which entails an increase in the preventive check (forced on labourers by lack of house space) represented as an inward shift of g_L to g_L'.

adopted merely for argument's sake – to weigh the case against himself – whereas in fact he envisaged a much slower growth rate of food, and therefore of population. Again, in this application, *nothing is said of a prospective deceleration (inward shift) of* g_F, *reflecting the impact of land scarcity*; all we have is an allowance (as an outside possibility) for a 'permanent rate of increase [no] greater' than that pertaining at the first census taking. (On this case, see figure 1.3.)

Here, too, there is further confirmation of 'the increased healthiness observed of late years,' an allusion to a falling mortality rate, which 'could not possibly have taken place without [the] accompanying circumstance' of delayed marriage: 'Two or three years in the average age of marriage, by lengthening each generation, and tending, in a small degree, both to diminish the prolifickness of marriages, and the number of born living to be married, may make a considerable difference in the rate of increase, and be adequate to allow for a considerably diminished mortality' (536–7). The delay in marriage itself is described as 'the natural consequence of that prudence and respectability generated by a better government' (since 1688), placing England ahead of France in that respect. The technical point is that an exogenous decrease in mortality (this is apparently what Malthus had in mind here) *without* a compensatory delay of marriage would raise the population growth rate relative to that of food (in effect the g_L curve shifts *outwards*), driving down the real wage, thereby effacing the initial improvement in health and bringing g_L back into line with g_F at a lower wage. An earlier observation regarding the effect of inoculation confirms the above interpretation: 'if the resources of the country would not permanently admit of a greatly accelerated rate of increase in the population (and whether they would or not, must depend upon other causes besides the number of lives saved by the vaccine inoculation), one of two things would happen, either an increased mortality of some other diseases, or a diminution in the proportion of births' (514). Malthus's support for the vaccine turned on the expectation of a compensatory reduction in mortality.[63]

With an eye to contemporary experience, Malthus reiterated that a falling birth *rate* is consistent with ongoing population increase: 'It should always be recollected that a diminished *proportion* of births may take place under a constant annual increase of the absolute number. This is in fact exactly what has happened in England and Scotland during the last forty years' (550n). And here he observes that a program involving reduced mortality and natality acts positively upon the growth rate of food itself by raising the 'efficient population,'[64] setting in motion a sort of virtuous circle. This generalization is the basis for a warning against 'former prejudices' which entailed *direct* encouragement of births: 'If it be really true, that without a diminished proportion of births we cannot attain *permanent* improvement in the health and happiness of the mass of the people, and cannot secure that description of population, which, by containing a larger share of adults, is best calculated to create fresh resources, and consequently to encourage a continued increase of efficient population; it is surely of the highest importance that this should be known, that, if we take no steps directly to promote this effect, we should not, under the influence of the former prejudices on this subject, endeavour to counteract it' (550–1).

In none of this is there any allusion, even tangential, to an actual or prospective decelerating growth rate of food; if anything, *acceleration* would be closer to the truth. In a note attached to the foregoing, Malthus actually refers to 'the almost constant demand for labour, which prevails in every prosperous country,' and maintains that 'there is no man, who has the slightest feeling for the happiness of the most numerous class of society, or has even just views of policy on the subject, who would not rather choose that the requisite population should be obtained by such a price of labour, combined with such habits, as would occasion a very small mortality, than from a great proportion of births of which comparatively few would reach manhood.' His choice is for g_L' rather than g_L in figure 1.3.

* * *

Between 1798 and 1803, as we know (above, p. 49), Malthus became aware

63 In the event of reduced mortality resulting from higher real wages, the improved state could be maintained without a compensatory delay of marriage since it must be attributed to a prior shift outwards of g_K.

64 Cf. 509 for the sense of 'efficient population,' as participants in the workforce.

of the fact of *accelerating* population growth supported by accelerating agricultural production. The empirical picture was transformed. But the 1798 criticism of Smith, as far as concerns the principle that national income might expand without benefit to labour (above, pp. 39–40), was repeated in 1803 (1986, *3*, 694–5) and again in 1806 (II, 189–98). The 1806 edition, however, adds the qualification that expanded demand for manufacturing labour 'would probably entice some from private service' as well as from agriculture, though, as in 1798, it is assumed that food supplies are maintained 'by improvements in the instruments or mode of culture' (191–2). There is also an added explanatory note which raises the possibility that, even given the food supply, expanded manufacturing output might yet raise the real wage, though not food per capita: 'My intention is ... to show that the funds for the maintenance of labour do not increase exactly in proportion to the increase in the produce of the land and labour of a country, but with the same increase of produce may be more or less favourable to the labourer, according as the increase has arisen principally from agriculture and manufactures. On the supposition of a physical impossibility of increasing the food of a country it is evident, that by improvements in machinery it might grow yearly richer in the exchangeable value of its manufacturing produce, but *the labourer though he might be better clothed and lodged, would not be better fed*' (emphasis added). The demand for labour is thus identified with the food supply, but this does not gainsay that the wage basket may be a mixed one, so that labour benefits from non-agricultural growth.[65] This perspective apparently reflects the position that it is the *corn* wage alone that matters as far as concerns population growth.

A further modification in 1806 again reflects altered contemporary circumstances. In the original version (1986, *1*, 110; above, p. 41), British experience since 1688 is used to illustrate the argument that even rapid expansion of 'the annual produce' might be of no advantage at all to labour. Recent changes dictated a modification in 1806: 'During the last ten or twelve years it cannot be doubted, that the annual produce of the land and labour of England has very rapidly increased, and in consequence the nominal wages of labour have greatly increased; but the real recompense of the labourer, though increased, has not increased in proportion' (II, 202). This is a far weaker application of the principle under consideration.

65 In the first edition, the manufacturing component, while recognized, is played down rather more: 'It seems in many respects improper, to exclude the clothing and lodging of a whole people from any part of their revenue. Much of it may, indeed, be of very trivial and unimportant value, in comparison with the food of the country; yet still it may be fairly considered as a part of its revenue' (1986, *1*, 115).

XII FOOD AND POPULATION: THE ORDER OF PRECEDENCE AND THE OSCILLATORY PROCESS, 1803, 1806/7

The original statement in 1798 of the 'oscillatory' process (see above, p. 43) is modified in various subtle ways in the second edition (1986, *2*, 17–18). Apart from the more realistic figures selected for population size (11 instead of 7 million), there is the replacement of *constant* population at the corn-wage trough – 'population is at a stand' – by a population that is 'nearly at a stand,' which allows for *ongoing* expansion throughout. (This might seem inconsequential were it not for a further modification in 1817 to the effect that 'the progress of population is retarded,' which confirms ongoing expansion, albeit at a slackened pace.) Finally, the long-run constancy of the corn wage on an average is rendered less certain by the introduction of the one word 'may.' (On this latter modification and its possible relation to the polemic against Godwin, see Waterman, 1987, 268–9; 1991, 138.)

The difficulty impeding empirical observation of the cycles (above, p. 44) is also restated. In 1803, it reads as follows: 'This sort of oscillation will not probably be obvious to common view; and it may be difficult even for the most attentive observer to calculate its periods. Yet that *in the generality of old states* some such vibration [1817: alternation of this kind] does exist though in a much less marked, and in a much more irregular manner, than I have described it, no reflecting man, who considers the subject deeply, can well doubt' (18; emphasis added). The applicability of the oscillatory process to 'the generality of old states' replaces the universal applicability – 'all old states' – of 1798. As we have already noted, it is not clear that Malthus applied the model to Britain itself, given the weight placed on new technology in his accounts (see above, p. 45).

We come now to a modification of 1806 to the original proposition in 1798 regarding the fall in the corn wage during the oscillatory process – steady money wages but a rising corn price – which raises the profit rate and stimulates accumulation and employment (above, p. 44). This is now supplemented by reference to the check to population growth attributable to the reduced real wage. Downward stickiness of the money wage remains prominent: 'This is, in effect, a real fall in the price of labour; and, during this period, the condition of the lower classes of the community must be gradually growing worse. But the farmers and capitalists are growing rich from the real cheapness of labour. Their increasing capitals enable them to employ a greater number of men; and, as the population had probably suffered some check from the greater difficulty of supporting a family, the demand for labour, after a certain period, would be great in proportion to the supply, and its price would of course rise, if left to find its natural level; and thus the wages of labour, and consequently the condition of the lower classes of society, might have progressive and retrograde movements, though the price of labour might never nominally fall' (1806, I, 27).

* * *

So much for the 'oscillatory' process laid out early in the *Essay*. There is also the insistence on the precedence of food over population growth (see above, p. 43, for the 1798 version). In 1803 a considerable part of a new chapter, 'Of the Principal Sources of the Prevailing Errors on the Subject of Population' (Book III, ch. 11), is devoted to the issue of 'precedence.'[66] Here, Malthus commended de Mirabeau for admitting the error of 'considering population as the source of revenue' (on which matter see chapter 8, below), and questioned Sir James Steuart's position that population growth generates agricultural expansion: 'That an increase of population, when it follows in its natural order, is both a positive good in itself, and absolutely necessary to a further increase in the annual produce of the land and labour of any country, I should be the last to deny. The only question is, what is the order of its progress? In this point Sir James Steuart, who has in general explained this subject so well, appears to me to have fallen into an error. He determines, that multiplication is the efficient cause of agriculture, and not agriculture of multiplication' (1986, *3*, 454–5).[67] For his own part he insisted that cases could be cited of population increase that are non-sustainable because there had been no agricultural response, whereas there were none of agricultural expansion which had not been followed by population growth: 'And we know, that multiplication has in numberless instances taken place, which has produced no effect upon agriculture, and has merely been followed by an increase of diseases; but perhaps there is no instance, where a permanent increase of agriculture has not effected a permanent increase of population somewhere or other. Consequently, agriculture may with more propriety be termed the efficient cause of population, than population of agriculture; though they certainly react upon each other, and are mutually necessary to each other's support. This indeed seems to be the hinge on which the subject turns; and all the prejudices respecting population have, perhaps, arisen from a mistake about the order of precedence' (455).

But all this is too general, especially considering the allowance of a

66 This chapter is renamed 'General Observations' in 1817 (Book III, ch. 14), and various substantive additions are inserted, as we shall see.

67 The first sentence of this passage is ambiguous. It might refer to an increase in population as necessary for food expansion from the perspective of a larger workforce or from that of higher demand. But the general context of the debate would suggest the latter.

In a note attached to this attribution, Malthus allows that Steuart had in mind 'principally the multiplication of those persons, who have some valuable consideration to give for the products of agriculture' – that is, not population growth, as such – but, he points out, in that case Steuart 'seems to admit the incorrectness of the general proposition.'

'mutual' relation. A more specific, if formal, sense of the precedence accorded food is the excess of *per-capita food supply over subsistence* as a condition for population growth: 'These products, in their actual state, must be beyond the lowest wants of the existing population, before any permanent increase can possibly be supported.' At the same time, the stimulus to agricultural *expansion* is said to include the prospect of acquiring manufactures via exchange: 'But though it may be allowed, that the increase of people, beyond what could easily subsist on the natural fruits of the earth, first prompted man to till the ground; and that the view of maintaining a family, or of obtaining some valuable consideration in exchange for the products of agriculture, still operates as the principal stimulus to cultivation ...'

In all this it is still not made adequately clear what precise interaction between agriculture and population – recognizing *agricultural* precedence but also allowing prospects of increased exchange against manufactures as a motive to agricultural expansion – operates in practice. Some indications of the process emerge at the outset of the chapter. The context is a corn-exporting country wherein the domestic food supply cannot be said to determine population size; what is relevant is the *state of employment*: 'It is in the nature of agriculture, particularly when well conducted, to produce support for a considerable number above that which it employs; and consequently if these members of the society, or, as Sir James Steuart calls them, the free hands, do not increase so as to reach the limit of the number which can be supported by the surplus produce, the whole population may continue for ages increasing with the improving state of agriculture, and yet always be able to export corn ... *The precise measure of the population in a country thus circumstanced will not indeed be the quantity of food, because part of it is exported, but the quantity of employment*' (448–9; emphasis added). Now it is the 'state of employment' – more precisely its rate of change – that by acting upon the real wage governs labour's demand for food and also (by implication) its domestic supply: 'The state of this employment however will necessarily regulate the wages of labour, on which depends the power of the lower classes of people to procure food; and according as the employment of the country is increasing, whether slowly or rapidly, these wages will be such, as either to check or encourage early marriages; such, as to enable a labourer to support only two or three, or as many as five or six children' (449). This statement, while still not wholly unambiguous regarding the order of 'precedence,' suggests that increased purchasing power on the part of the *existing* population – itself reflecting the state of employment opportunities mediated via the real wage – assures an increase in the domestic food supply, and thus the ability to maintain *larger* families. While, therefore, food takes formal precedence over population in the sense suggested above, its increase *is a response to higher demand*; and population growth is a prerequisite for expansion of demand, since, were labourers to choose to devote increased purchasing power to 'luxuries' rather than the maintenance of larger families, there would be no stimulus to agricultural expansion. On this view there is much less to distinguish Malthus from Steuart than appears at first glance; and also Malthus from Ricardo at a subsequent period, considering Ricardo's insistence that population increase backed by increase in purchasing power and acting on the demand for food provides the stimulus for agricultural expansion (1951–73, I, 406–7).

If Malthus's argument applied only to a corn-exporting country, it would be much constrained. But subsequently we encounter in a general context the same distinction between 'the check [to population growth] from want of employment,' identified with restrictions on marriage and birth rates, and 'the check from want of food,' identified with the death rate: 'The quantity of employment in any country will not of course vary from year to year, in the same manner as the quantity of produce must necessarily do, from the variation of the seasons; and consequently the check from want of employment will be much more steady in its operation, and be much more favourable to the lower classes of people, than the check from the immediate want of food. The first will be the preventive check; the second the positive check. When the demand for labour is either stationary, or increasing very slowly, people not seeing any employment open by which they can support a family, or the wages of common labour being inadequate to this purpose, will of course be deterred from marrying. But if a demand for labour continue increasing with some rapidity, although the supply of food be uncertain, on account of variable seasons and a dependence on other countries, the population will evidently go on, till it is positively checked by famine or the diseases arising from severe want' (1986, *3*, 451).

Labour demand is here clearly *not identified* with the rate of growth of food supplies; the food constraint is said to act unambiguously only in the case of a 'permanently declining population.' But precisely what determines the level of employment is left open. And so, too, is the relation between the two sets of determinants of population growth. These omissions raise a serious problem. It is a major argument against Adam Smith (already established in 1798) that the real demand for labour will be unaffected should capital accumulation – in effect, employment opportunities – expand in the manufacturing sector (above, p. 39). In that context any possible response of food supplies to increased demand on the part of labour is played down. Malthus now seems to be saying that increased employment opportunities – he does not specify that they must occur in agriculture – will, by generating higher real wages, encourage population expansion, and an elastic response of food supplies to the increased demand.[68]

68 The significance of a manufacturing sector is elaborated elsewhere in the 1803 version

XIII SUMMARY AND CONCLUSION

The first *Essay* approaches the American case in terms of initially plentiful naturally productive land (a low population/land ratio),[69] but prospective increasing land scarcity, manifestations of which were actually evident in a decline in the real wage and a deceleration of population growth. In this context, then, we find the embryonic growth model, based on diminishing returns, though still lacking formal analysis of the falling profit rate.

In the English case, real wages were, by contrast, 'initially' low because of an 'initially' low level of knowledge; here a more or less regular flow of new technology allows for expansion of population. There did not exist the same opportunities at early stages of development, flowing from excellent natural resources, as in the United States, but increasing land scarcity is not the issue. If at any time the system runs into some form of diminishing returns, as one might expect, expansion yet occurs in consequence of new technology.

Malthus's general 'vision' of English development was evidently not one of rapid population growth in the face of land scarcity. On the contrary, population growth had been very slow.[70] Population trends were a matter of contemporary debate, but from the (supposed) course of population could be deduced that of food production, since population growth was governed by that of food: 'If the effectual funds for the maintenance of labour are increasing, that is, if the territory can maintain, as well as the stock employ, a greater number of labourers, this additional number will quickly spring up' (see above, p. 37).[71] Moreover, the slow growth of

with an eye to the impact of industrial instability acting as a *check* to population growth: 'we all know how subject particular manufactures are to fail, from the caprice of taste, or the accident of war. The weavers of Spitalfields were plunged into the most severe distress by the fashion of muslins instead of silks; and numbers of the workmen in Sheffield and Birmingham were, for a time, thrown out of employment, from the adoption of shoestrings and covered buttons, instead of buckles and metal buttons. Our manufactures, taken in the mass, have increased with great rapidity, but, in particular places, they have failed, and the parishes, where this has happened, are invariably loaded with a crowd of poor, in the most distressed and miserable condition ... The cause of this sudden check to population, was the commencement of the war, and the failure of commercial credit, which occurred about this time; and such a check could not have taken place, in so sudden a manner, without being occasioned by the most severe distress' (1986, *3*, 695). The data provided by Aikin (1795) suggested a fall in the birth rate and rise in the death rate in 1794, compared with 1792, in Manchester and Rochdale.

69 And also with recourse to 'the knowledge and industry' of European states (above, p. 38).

70 Price believed population had actually fallen (above, note 27).

71 Here, Malthus neglected the population lag behind food increase; elsewhere (as on 107–8) he chose to focus upon it.

population is not explained by proximity to the stationary state, for England illustrated a country 'not extremely crowded and populous' and, in the absence of faulty policies favouring manufacturing, 'might undoubtedly have been much more populous than at present, and yet not be more incumbered by its population' (1986, *I*, 118). *Rather, despite the significantly increased potential for expansion created by agricultural reorganization and new technology, the food supply appropriate for working-class consumption had been growing slowly because of diversions of capital to satisfy rising upper-class demands.*[72]

On one occasion (41–2; see above, p. 30), Malthus refers to a hypothetical fall in population size, which would generate a rise in per-capita output and (by implication) in real wages and a rapid correction of the population loss.[73] That food supply per capita, and therefore the real wage, would rise upon an absolute fall in population size is taken for granted as the outcome of a fall in the population/land ratio. But it is one thing to maintain that, in consequence of a flow of new technology, an *increase* in population will not imply diminishing productivity, and quite another to assert that a *decrease* in population will imply increasing productivity. In the analysis of England, the historical path had in fact been one of *constant* per-capita output; and the projections, as far as concerns policy, do not turn at all on deceleration and ultimate stationariness. If there is an ultimate limit to growth (see above, p. 27), it is not made use of in this application.

The reason seems to be that Malthus's concern when he wrote his first *Essay* was not with a population growth rate actually exceeding that of food supplies; on the contrary, the English concern should be to *increase* the growth rate of population. But it was to be done responsibly, avoiding direct encouragement of the birth rate; for that route – extensions of the Poor Laws and the anti-property proposals of Condorcet and Godwin – promised disaster by giving free reign to *the ever-existing potential of population to expand faster than food supplies.* The sensible approach was to raise the growth rate of agricultural output and rely on population growth to respond to higher real wages; population growth could look after itself. And though there were limits to what could be achieved by this program, deriving from the constrained possibilities for agricultural growth in an 'old settled' country, there is no notion that the higher real wages that were attainable would be effaced by excessive increases in labour supply.

72 These diversions were not merely a question of mercantilist interference . The higher price of meat, under pressure of demand, is said to be 'a natural and inevitable consequence of the general progress of civilization' (see above, note 34).

73 Were the English population cut by 2 million, or the French by 6 million, one would expect the excess of the birth rate over the death rate to rise, causing an increase in the rate of population growth in consequence of the real-wage increase (47–8).

Without the institutional encouragement of population, labour supply would rise at most at a rate *corresponding* to that of labour demand, as is implied by the fact that the higher standards hoped for are not represented as merely temporary.

Taking this view points away from the standard interpretation of the principle of population, such as Schumpeter's, turning on *excessive* population pressure. Excess population growth is a matter of potentialities, not actualities. As Senior was later to suggest, it is partly the ambiguous term 'tendency' that engendered the standard misconceptions (see below, chapter 18: IX); the *Essay on Population* presents a far less pessimistic picture than seems to be the case at first glance.

The primary analytical contribution of the 1803 version is a somewhat sharper formulation of the land scarcity–based growth model, involving falling corn wages, and some indication of what in 1817 is greatly developed, as we show later, in chapter 5 – namely, the potential role of prudential population control in maintaining the corn wages. But there is still lacking, in all early versions of the *Essay*, any great concern with the profit rate, as such, and its secular course.

TWO

The Malthus–Ricardo correspondence, 1813–1814

I INTRODUCTION

As I show in section II, below, when the Ricardo–Malthus correspondence opens in 1813 – an exchange initiated by Ricardo in a response to Malthus's review of one of Ricardo's monetary contributions entailing Say's Law of Markets – we find Malthus denying any effect on the profit rate deriving from the conditions of agricultural productivity. Land scarcity exerts its effect on the real wage, not on the profit rate. Profits are *insulated* from decline and depend, rather, on 'the state of capital compared with the demand for it,' countering the Law of Markets. It is argued, in fact, that agricultural protection and domestic expansion of farming may actually *stimulate* the profit rate. This linkage, first stated in July 1814, works by way of a negative effect on manufacturing capital and output, which reverses the downward pressure of prices and profits characterizing regular secular expansion or Smithian 'competition of capital.'

Under pressure from Ricardo, Malthus came to accept an effect of agricultural productivity on profits. The concession applied only in the *limit* – a high level of productivity assuring a high agricultural profit rate and generating a high rate of capital accumulation, population, and final demand for manufactures – and conversely in the 'ultimate' or stationary state (see section III, below). We have, then, the manufacturing profit rate kept in line with the agricultural rate by way of the *indirect* consequence of land-scarcity conditions on population, and therefore on the demand for final goods. As for intermediate periods, the war decades 1793–1813 illustrated high (agricultural) profits owing to pressure of *demand for corn* emanating from a prosperous manufacturing sector.

Under further pressure from Ricardo, Malthus was obliged to concede an effect on the profit rate of increasing land scarcity over the full secular path – at least as a 'tendency.' But he still held back, since the appropriate preconditions need not be fulfilled. This case had a parallel with the downward 'tendency' of the real wage – which is, significantly, actually represented as a 'more *directly* necessary consequence' of increasing land scarcity. In the course of this account, it becomes clear that Malthus failed to appreciate that a declining real-wage trend as a result of increasing land scarcity *cannot* insulate the profit rate from the same downward pressure – that the burden or incidence of diminishing returns is on both labour and capital.

Characteristic of Malthus's position is the insistence, against Ricardo, on a supplementary force depressing the profit rate owing to accumulation, as such. This theme – elaborated below, in section IV – is the counterpart to Smith's increasing competition of capitals. A letter of 29 December 1814 clarifies, first, that the aggregate-demand problem relates specifically to manufacturing, not to agriculture; in effect, Malthus applied the Law of Markets to 'necessaries,' whereby an increase in corn supply is assumed to be accompanied by an increase in demand – a central feature of the surplus versus scarcity perspective, discussed later, in chapter 8.[1] Second, the letter makes clear that population growth – governed by land-scarcity conditions – impinges on the profit rate via its effect on the demand for manufactures. The model is one where food *precedes* population growth, increased food supply generating its own demand; whereas the increase of demand for manufactures on the part of labourers 'precedes' supply.

From these principles it followed that the discovery of new land areas permits renewed or increased population growth, and consequently increased demand for manufactures. Here, Malthus proceeds along the Smithian path, in that Smith had perceived the consequence of new land discoveries to be comparable to that of new markets – as relaxing the downward pressure on manufacturing profits by attracting capital from industry (cf. 1776/1937, 93). But if an increase in the land area acts on population growth, it seems logical to suppose that it does so by raising demand for labour, *implying a prior effect on the profit rate.* (That the profit rate does initially rise in agriculture is indicated by the fact that capital flows *from* industry and 'old' land *to* the new areas.) If this is so, agricultural productivity must play directly on the agricultural profit rate, with the manufacturing rate coming into line as manufacturing output declines in spite of increased demand emanating from population expansion.

Related issues arise in the analysis of the standard 'classical' secular

1 The rule is reconfirmed in August–September 1816 (below, chapter 4, p. 151f.). However, we frequently find deviations from the rule, and generalization to agriculture of the excess-supply problem – or at least grey areas. This is not surprising, since all depends on the population response to increase in food supply, and therefore on the time period involved.

problem – the simultaneous decline of the real wage and profit rates with increasing land scarcity. Ricardo provided a clear formulation of the shared incidence of diminishing returns between labour and capital as early as December 1814 and in an earlier, implicit, statement in October, and he has priority over Malthus for this fundamental insight. Malthus, for his part, maintained – or was doubtful about the issue – that the profit rate might be *insulated* by the fall in the corn wage.

II DIRECT EFFECT OF AGRICULTURAL PRODUCTIVITY ON PROFIT RATE DENIED: THE STIMULATORY EFFECT OF AGRICULTURAL PROTECTION

The diminishing-returns principle emerges clearly in Malthus's letter to Francis Horner of 16 June 1813. While corn-import restrictions would encourage the expansion of agricultural output – a proposition actually *rejected* by Horner following Adam Smith's analysis – such a policy was objectionable on efficiency grounds. The argument is placed in a dynamic context entailing diminishing returns (letter cited in Tucker, 1954, 331–2; see, below, chapter 17, p. 820). None the less, in his correspondence with Ricardo during the summer of 1813, Malthus denied that agricultural-productivity conditions had dictated movements in the *profit rate* during the preceding war years.

Malthus had argued – in lost correspondence and probably in personal discussion – that (in Ricardo's paraphrase) 'the opening of new markets or extending the old' – as in the war decades 1793–1813 – 'prove[s] a general increase of profits [and a] material growth of prosperity,' Ricardo maintaining for his part that the increased profit rate was to be accounted for by 'decided improvements of agriculture' which rendered the facts 'perfectly reconcileable to my theory ... My conclusion is that there has been a rapid increase of Capital which has been prevented from shewing itself in a low rate of interest by new facilities in the production of food' (letters to Malthus of 10 and 17 August 1813; in Ricardo, 1951–73, VI, 93, 94–5). Malthus's position is that of Adam Smith, whereby the acquisition of 'new branches of trade' (as well as new territory) 'may sometimes raise the profits of stock ... even in a country fast advancing in the acquisition of riches' by reducing the pressure exerted by 'competition of capitals' (1776/1937, 93).

Ricardo reported Malthus's position again, in a letter to Trower, the following spring.[2] Both agreed that the profit rate 'rises only when the means of employment for Capital bears a greater proportion than before to the Capital itself, and falls when the Capital bears a greater proportion

2 Malthus's position was expressed, apart from correspondence, in a non-extant paper critical of an early draft, also wanting, of Ricardo's *Essay on Profits* (see Trower to Ricardo, 2 March 1814; 1951–73, VI, 102).

to the arena, as Mr. Malthus has called it, for its employment' (8 March 1814; 1951–73, VI, 103).[3] The disputed question related to the determinants of that proportion. Malthus, according to Ricardo, 'thinks that the arena for the employment of Capital may increase, and consequently profits and interest may rise, altho' there should be no new facilities, either by importation, or improved tillage, for the production of food; – that the profits of the farmer no more regulate the profits of other trades, than the profits of other trades regulate the profits of the farmer, and consequently if new markets are discovered, in which we can obtain a greater quantity of foreign commodities in exchange for our commodities, than before the discovery of such markets, profits will increase and interest will rise. In such a state of things the rate of interest would rise as well as the profits of the farmer, he thinks even if more Capital were employed on the land' (104).

In this summary, Ricardo suggests that Malthus did not deny a potential effect on the general profit rate from agricultural-productivity conditions, but, instead, insisted on a supplementary force: 'Nothing, I say, can increase the profits permanently on trade, with the same or an increased Capital, but a really cheaper mode of obtaining food. A cheaper mode of obtaining food will undoubtedly increase profits says Mr. Malthus but there are many other circumstances which may also increase profits with an increase of Capital. The discovery of a new market where there will be a great demand for our manufactures is one' (104–5). But it is not certain that Ricardo captured precisely Malthus's position. For Malthus himself wrote to Ricardo shortly after, in a letter dated 6 July 1814, denying that reduced agricultural productivity lowers the profit rate: '[You] must mean that it is the *rate* of production, not the absolute quantity of produce which determines profits. But even this rate of production, or more definitely speaking, the proportion of production to consumption necessary to such production, seems to be determined by the quantity of accumulated capital compared with the demand for the products of capital, and not by the mere difficulty and expence of procuring corn. If it is necessary to employ a hundred days labour instead of fifty, in order to produce a certain quantity of corn, there seems to be no reason whatever that the person who possesses an accumulation sufficient to make the necessary advances should have a less remuneration for his capital' (111).[4] In fact, Malthus closes by specifying that the incidence of reduced agricultural productivity

3 According to Sraffa (editorial note, 103n), the phrase itself first appears in print in the 1817 *Additions to the Fourth and Former Editions of 'An Essay on the Principle of Population'*: 'This country, from the extent of its lands, and its rich colonial possessions, has a large *arena* for the employment of an increasing capital.' See also *Principles*, 1820, 331.

4 The reference to a 'rate of production' and its amplification indicate that Malthus attributed to Ricardo a *physical* or corn-ratio profit calculation, which was not in fact Ricardo's position (see below, notes 15 and 24).

will fall *on labour alone* in the form of reduced corn wages – presumably the corn-price increase is not fully compensated by the money-wage increase[5] – and not at all on capital: 'The effects of a great difficulty in procuring corn would in my opinion be, a diminution of capital, a diminution of produce, and a diminution in the real wages of labour, or their price in corn; but not a diminution of profits.'[6]

Malthus was, therefore, suggesting that profits may be completely insulated from diminishing returns.[7] He allowed only that if an 'abundance of capital' should, fortuitously, accompany higher corn costs the profit rate might fall, the 'prime mover' involving, not agricultural productivity, but the relation between 'capital' and *demand*: 'unquestionably low profits might accompany a great difficulty of procuring corn, if at the same time that this difficulty existed there was a great abundance of capital. In short all will in my opinion depend upon the state of capital compared with the demand for it. *This will be the prime mover, and it is this which will determine the profits which a capital employed in agriculture shall yield, whether the land be naturally rich or naturally poor, much worked or little worked*' (emphasis added).[8] This statement does not, unfortunately, indicate whether 'the state of capital compared with the demand for it' extends to the agricultural sector itself or applies to the manufacturing sector specifically. We shall have to pay close attention to this issue.

That Malthus did not expect an 'abundance of capital' to accompany increased costs can be inferred from Ricardo's formulation of 26 June 1814, which indicates that Malthus perceived agricultural protection as reducing aggregate output *more* than aggregate demand, thereby *raising* the rate of return.[9] The *elevating* effect on the profit rate of corn-import

5 See letter of 5 August, 117–18; cited below, p. 75.

6 This statement reiterates a position specified in the non-extant correspondence that protective Corn Laws would *not* depress the return on capital. This is clear from Ricardo's reply to that earlier letter: 'I cannot partake of your doubts respecting the effects of restrictions on the importation of corn, in tending to lower the rate of interest ... I never was more convinced of any proposition in Polit:Economy than that restriction on importation of corn in an importing country has a tendency to lower profits' (26 June; 108–9).

7 My interpretation assumes that Malthus was allowing for expansion of domestic agriculture onto marginal land in consequence of protection, considering the reference to 'a hundred days labour, instead of fifty, in order to produce a certain quantity of corn.'

8 Malthus specifies the significance of *expected* or *future* demand as the relevant consideration: 'The demand for capital depends, not upon the abundance of *present* product, but upon the demand for the future products of capital, or the power of producing something by means of capital which shall be more in demand than the produce actually employed. And in this question that great element of effective demand, – the desire to consume in those who possess revenue, must always have great influence. I think you overlook it too much' (111–12).

9 Ricardo for his part expressed the contrary view based on the Law of Markets: 'I cannot partake of your doubts respecting the effects of restriction on the importation of corn ... With the same Capital there would be less production, and less demand. Demand

restriction is spelled out in Malthus's reply on 6 July. It involves the effect of rising money wages – the money wage rises presumably with the increase in the corn price – in reducing the labour commanded by monied capital (its 'real value'), and thus supposedly in reducing output relative to aggregate demand: 'You have not yet removed my doubts on the effects of Restrictions upon the *profits of stock* and *interest* of money ... You observe that in the case supposed, there would be less production and less demand with the *same* capital; but surely there would be *much less capital.* There would be a smaller quantity both of corn, and of all other commodities, and every monied accumulation would command less labour and less produce. The question then seems to be whether production or demand would decrease the fastest? and as in my opinion the dearness of labour [money wages] would have more effect in diminishing capital than in diminishing revenue, particularly, rents, I do not see why the usual effects of a diminution of capital should not take place' (110).

A subsequent letter to Ricardo reiterates forcefully that the agricultural profit rate is not the determining rate but, on the contrary, is governed by the 'general' rate, implying a rate determined outside agriculture. Since there is little doubt that, in what follows, the expressions 'variations in the rate of produce on land' and 'some increase of difficulty in procuring corn' imply extensions to marginal land, the proposition is that *reduced real wages will swamp any negative effect on profits of diminishing returns*: 'The more I reflect on the subject, the more firmly I feel convinced, that *it is the state of capital, or the general profits of stock and interest of money, which determines the particular profit upon the land*; and that it is not the particular profits or rate of produce upon the land which determines the general profits of stock and the interest of money. A slight fall in the real price of labour, which according to general principles ought to take place on any diminution of capital, or what comes to the same thing, a rise in the price of produce without a *proportionate* rise of labour, a most natural and frequent occurrence, will allow of great variations in the rate of produce on land, and easily make up for some increase of difficulty in procuring corn' (5 August 1814, 117–18; emphasis added, 'proportionate' italicized in original). In this formulation the fall in the real wage is not attributed directly to land scarcity.[10] Rather, it reflects the '*diminution of capital*'; and this latter is identified with the apparent effect of higher money wages on manufacturing.

To summarize a complex argument: (1) The increase in the corn price with agricultural protection and domestic extensions necessitates a rise in

has no other limits but the want of power of paying for the commodities demanded. Everything which tends to diminish production tends to diminish this power' (108).

10 But this latter attribution – more in line with the *Essay on Population* – does emerge later in the correspondence (below, p. 86).

the *money* wage, which rise entails a reduction in the labour commanded by 'monied' capital; (2) this so-called reduction in capital carries with it a fall in the *real* wage applicable to all sectors; (3) and it is this real-wage decline which allows a higher profit rate in agriculture despite higher labour costs of production, along with the higher profit rate supposedly generated in manufacturing upon the reduction of (aggregate) capital, and therefore of supply relative to demand. By implication at least, the agricultural profit rate would decline with reduced agricultural productivity were it not for the fall in the real wage emanating from manufacturing. *We are evidently far removed from the mature model wherein the incidence of diminishing returns is upon both the profit and the wage rates.*

For Malthus, reduced capital was a *necessary* accompaniment of agricultural protection.[11] This point is further clarified in a letter of 5 August. As in the formulation of 6 July, here he had in mind the reduction in 'labour commanded' by money capital in consequence of the rise in money wages: 'You seem to think that there is no necessary connection between restrictions upon importation, and a reduction of capital. I think on the contrary that there is an absolutely necessary connection, and that it is precisely owing to this connection that profits do not fall. If the capitalist in the Cotton or Woollen manufacture be obliged to pay more for the labour which he employs, owing to restriction upon importation, he will not be able to work up the same quantity of goods with his capital; the goods will in consequence rise in price, and his profits, from the general scarcity of capital, will be increased' (5 August; 116–17).[12] The

11 Ricardo insisted, against the statement by Malthus of 6 July (110–11), that the *possibility* of a reduced capital had to be kept apart from the impact of protection and agricultural extension. Ricardo's case runs thus: 'It appears to me that you have changed the proposition on which we first appeared to differ. The proposition advanced by you, if I recollect right, was that restrictions on the importation of corn would not lower the rate of profits and interest, – but now you add or rather your argument leads to the conclusion, "if the consequence of such restriction be a great reduction of Capital." So amended I should not object to the proposition, – but I think it material that causes should be kept distinct, and their due effects ascribed to each. Restrictions on the trade of corn, if capital suffers no diminution, will occasion a fall in the rate of profits and interest. A reduction of capital independently of restrictions on importation of corn will have a tendency to raise profits and interest, – but there is no necessary connection between these two operating causes, as they may at the same time be acting together or entirely in opposite direction' (25 July; 113–14).

12 Malthus's elaboration elicited a lengthy reaction from Ricardo in a letter dated 11 August. The following are the salient points: (1) Capital contraction is a 'probable' not a 'necessary' consequence of corn-import restriction. The context suggests that a fall in 'capital' for Ricardo is not a matter of reduced labour command by monied capital, reflecting a higher money wage, as it is for Malthus, but a contraction of the real stock of capital goods. One effect of such contraction, should it occur, will be to 'diminish the work to be done, and consequently ... the wages of labour' – presumably the *real* wage – and 'the demand for food.' This negative effect on agricultural activity would have to

focus here is on excess demand, specifically in *manufacturing*. But this may have been by way of illustration only. We cannot yet exclude the possibility that the pressure on profits flowing from the aggregate supply–demand relation extends also to agriculture itself.

* * *

Malthus's initial position of 1813, whereby extended trade raises the general profit rate, is at odds with the Law of Markets. Similarly, the proposition of 6 July 1814, that an increase in the money wage reduces capital to a greater degree than it reduces 'revenue,' implies divergence between aggregate demand and supply. The latter formulation continues by rejecting Ricardo's position that demand is limited by production; were that so, there should be no observed increase in the profit rate following cases of capital loss: 'I can by no means agree with you [108] in thinking that every thing which diminishes produce, tends to diminish the power of paying for the commodities wanted, or as you intimate, to diminish the effective demand. If this were true, why do profits rise at the commencement of a war when stock is destroyed? or why do not profits invariably increase with the increase of capital, as *produce* unquestionably does' (110–11).

Ricardo responded to the challenge by conceding a temporary lag in aggregate demand behind variations in capital and output, but insisting that productivity considerations governed the profit rate *in the long run* (25 July; 114).[13] Malthus leapt on the concession: 'You say yourself most justly that profits will augment under a diminution of capital and product, *if demand tho' diminished* does not diminish *so rapidly* as capital and produce; but this is exactly what happens in all cases of diminution of capital, and shews that what you say in another place cannot be quite correct namely,

---

be set against the *expansion* of agriculture induced by protection. Whether the (agricultural) profit rate rises or falls will depend on the relative force of the contracting and expanding pressures (119). (2) Ricardo next tackles the effect on the manufacturing sector of retrograde capital. This turns on the rise in *money* wages, the profit margin depending on the extent sales prices rise along with money-wage costs. (This point Ricardo was later to retract.) The profit rate falls in the event that consumer demand (and the rise in prices) is constrained. The expectation is that the manufacturing profit rate will *ultimately* fall in the case of a retrograde capital, since 'in the long run effective demand cannot augment or continue stationary with a diminishing capital' (120).

13 More strongly, agricultural-productivity variation would actually correct any *short-run* divergence between demand and supply: 'It appears to me that the difficulty and expence of procuring corn will necessarily regulate the demand for the products of capital, for the demand must essentially depend on the price at which they can be afforded, and the prices of all commodities must increase if the price of corn be increased.' Here, Ricardo allows for a general rise in prices with the price of corn, a relationship later withdrawn. At this stage, his objection to Smith's analysis, whereby higher wages result in higher manufacturing prices, was not yet formalized.

"that effective demand cannot augment or long continue stationary with a diminishing capital." The whole amount of demand will from advanced prices diminish of course, but the *proportion of demand* to the *supply* which is always the main point in question, as determining prices and profits, may continue to increase as it does in all countries the capital of which is retrograde. In such countries the effective demand compared with the supply is permanently great, and the profits of stock very high' (5 August; 118).

Ricardo also could not fathom this linkage of 'the production to the consumption necessary to such production' to aggregate demand rather than to agricultural productivity – Malthus's assertion (above, p. 73) that 'there seems to be no reason whatever' for the agricultural profit rate to fall, supposing a halving of labour productivity.[14] In response, Malthus reiterated his insistence on the relative 'abundance' of capital as the determinant of the profit rate, such that the profit rate actually *rises* with reduced agricultural productivity: 'If the nominal price of corn be doubled, and the nominal amount of capital employed be not quite doubled which you seem to allow might be the case, instead of saying "how is it possible to conceive that the rate of profits will not be diminished" I should say how is it possible to conceive that it should not be increased? *In no case of production, is the produce exactly of the same nature as the capital advanced. Consequently we can never properly refer to a material rate of produce, independent of demand, and of the abundance or scarcity of capital*' (117; emphasis added). This striking statement, designed to enforce the case against Say's Law, involves the agricultural sector, though till this point this had been in some doubt (above, pp. 74, 77). Still we are faced with the question of whether Malthus intended deliberately thus to extend the range of his objections to the Law of Markets or whether we are dealing with a special case imposed by Ricardo's specific frame of reference.[15]

14 Ricardo's objection runs thus: 'The capitalist "who may find it necessary to employ a hundred days labour instead of fifty in order to produce a certain quantity of corn" cannot retain the same share for himself unless the labourers who are employed for a hundred days will be satisfied with the same quantity of corn for their subsistence that the labourers employed for fifty had before. If you suppose the price of corn doubled, the capital to be employed estimated in money will probably be also nearly doubled, – or at any rate will be greatly augmented and if his monied income is to arise from the sale of the corn which remains to him after defraying the charges of production how is it possible to conceive the rate of his profits will not be diminished?' (25 July; 114–15).

15 Ricardo responded to Malthus's objection that since, 'in no case of production, is the produce exactly of the same nature as the capital advanced,' a 'material rate of produce, independent of demand, and of the abundance or scarcity of capital' was ruled out, by insisting that societies *do* 'estimate their profits by the material production' in contrast with individuals *who are subject to money illusion.* Much has been made by commentators of Malthus's ascribing to Ricardo the notion of a 'material rate of produce.' But clearly Ricardo did not intend the homogeneity of input and output; he had in mind, rather, 'materiality,' in the specific sense of an avoidance of money illusion: 'Individuals do not estimate their profits by the material production, but nations invari-

We have already considered one aspect of Ricardo's reply of 11 August (above, note 12). There the effect of a retrograde capital on the *manufacturing* profit rate turned on the magnitude of manufacturing-price increases relative to money-wage costs. A rise in the profit rate could occur, Ricardo conceded, should consumer spending be maintained adequately, though this was impossible *in the long run* (120). But, though a positive long-run effect on the profit rate of a reduced capital acting *via the maintenance of consumer spending* is denied, an effect is allowed acting *via productivity*: 'I maintain, as I think you have done, that consumption as compared with production is always greatest where Capital is most accumulated. Diminish the capital of England one half, and you will undoubtedly augment profits, but it will not be in consequence of a greater proportion of demand but of a greater proportion of production, demand as compared with production could hardly fail to diminish' (121).[16] From the context, it is clear that the reference to a 'greater proportion of production' cannot refer to production relative to demand; it can only refer to productivity considerations – output relative to costs. For his part, Malthus forcefully rejected the accompanying proposition that consumer spending would fall relative to output in the event of a halving of the capital stock – that 'demand as compared with production could hardly fail to diminish': 'Precisely the reverse would I think take place. You do not certainly take sufficiently into your consideration the natural desires of man, which are after all the foundation of all demand. When corn is scarce there is a greater demand for corn than for labour, for produce, than for population' (19 August; 123).[17]

---

ably do. If we had precisely the same amount of commodities of all descriptions in the year 1815 that we now have in 1814 as a nation we should be no richer, but if money had sunk in value they would be represented by a greater quantity of money, and individuals would be apt to *think* themselves richer' (11 August; 121).

16 The high consumption where 'Capital is most accumulated' reflects the depressing effect on saving of a low profit rate, a relationship Ricardo claimed Malthus also adopted – namely, that 'the temptation to save from revenue to augment capital is always in proportion to the rate of profits, and if from accumulation of capital profits and interest should fall very low indeed, at that point accumulation would nearly stop, because it would be almost without an object.'

Ricardo, therefore, rejected Malthus's gloss (see above, p. 78) on the relative increase in demand in the case of a retrograde capital: 'You say, what I did not before understand you to admit, "that the whole amount of demand will from advanced prices diminish of course, but the proportion of demand to supply, which is always the main point in question, as determining prices and profits, may continue to increase, *as it does in all countries the capital of which is retrograde*" but I do not agree even to this explanation.'

17 The question arises here whether the focus is upon the short-run consequences of protection in reduced corn output and a higher market price, rather than an increase in cost price. From the formulation (above, p. 74), it appears that the scarcity of corn is the consequence of higher costs or of 'a great difficulty in procuring corn.'

This notion of a relative increase in aggregate demand with contraction of capital and output is much elaborated in Malthus's next letter (11 September).[18] He set out by insisting that the phenomenon of permanently high profits in the event of a 'scanty capital,' formally alluded to by Ricardo, in fact entailed 'a comparative excess of demand over supply,' reflecting a high *will* to consume or high potential demand:[19] 'I think you would allow that when capital is scanty compared with the means of employing it, from whatever cause arising, whether from insecurity of property, or extravagant habits, profits will be high not only temporarily but permanently. And I cannot help being of opinion that these high profits always indicate a comparative excess of demand above supply, even though the demand and supply should *appear* to be precisely equal. Effectual demand consists of two elements the *power* and the *will* to purchase. The power to purchase may perhaps be represented correctly by the produce of the country whether small or great; but the will to purchase will always be the greatest, the smaller is the produce compared with the population, and the more scantily the wants of the society are supplied. When capital is abundant it is not easy to find new objects sufficiently in demand. When capital is scarce nothing is more easy. In a country abundant in capital the value of the whole produce cannot increase with rapidity from the insufficiency of demand. In a country with little comparative capital the value of the yearly produce may very rapidly increase from the greatness of demand' (131–2). The letter continues with a formal rejection of James Mill's 1808 version of the Law of Markets – directed against Spence's *Britain Independent of Commerce* (1807) – and charges that Ricardo was trapped by that perspective: 'In short I by no means think that the power to purchase necessarily involves a proportionate will to purchase; and I cannot agree with Mr. Mill in an ingenious position which he lays down in his answer to Mr. Spence, that in reference to a nation, supply

18 It was in reply to Ricardo's letter of 30 August. Here Ricardo had allowed that profits might be permanently high in consequence of 'bad government and the consequent insecurity of property' or from a low savings disposition – despite productive land resources – but *not* because 'demand for produce is great compared with the supply' (128). 'It would surely be incorrect to say that the cause of the high profits was the greater proportion of demand for produce, when in both countries, the supply would be, or might be, precisely equal to the demand, and no more' (129). Similarly, the American profit rate exceeded the British because of highly productive land, although 'the proportion of supply to demand is greater in the former country' – alluding by this, however, to *the excess of output over consumption*, a different conception from Malthus's: 'I think it must necessarily be so in all countries which are most rapidly increasing in riches, for from whence do riches come but from production preponderating over consumption.'

19 The formulation enables us, by extension, to appreciate the earlier cryptic comment regarding the case of 'scarce corn' when there is 'a greater demand ... for produce, than for population.'

can never exceed demand. A nation must certainly have the power of purchasing all that it produces, but I can easily conceive it not to have the will: and if we were to grow next year half as much corn again as usual, a great part of it would be wasted, and the same would be true if all commodities of all kinds were increased one half. It would be impossible that they should yield the expence of production. You have never I think taken sufficiently into consideration the wants and tastes of mankind. It is not merely the proportion of commodities to each other but their proportion to the wants and tastes of mankind that determines prices' (132). A sudden increase *in either agricultural or manufacturing output* would be cleared only at a loss because of lack of 'will' to purchase. In the converse case – the specific case at hand – a scarcity of commodities would be accompanied by a high 'will' to purchase, and accordingly a high profit rate. Here at least the opposition to the Law of Markets applies to *all* sectors, including farming.[20]

Ricardo's reply insists on agricultural productivity as the major force acting on profits – at least in the long run or 'permanently.' There was merely formal or definitional agreement between the correspondents regarding the general proposition that profits turn on the magnitude of capital relative to 'the means of employing it' (16 September; 133). As for the matter of aggregate demand, Ricardo now provides a systematic defence of the Law of Markets in a growth context. He identifies consumption and investment expenditure as far as concerns their effect on aggregate demand; the fall in the profit rate during the course of growth dissuades investors but is counteracted by 'an increased inclination for luxuries of all description' (133–4). The 'activity' of demand in conditions of capital scarcity, insisted upon by Malthus, was more apparent than real, reflecting the low price of corn at relatively early stages of development. The rapid growth rate of annual output in such economies did not indicate 'greatness of demand' in the sense of a high *will* to purchase, but, rather, a relatively great *power* to purchase, by which Ricardo intended either the residual purchasing power available for other products in the event of a low corn price or the low general level of prices in such a case, since at this stage he still took the Smithian view that general prices are governed by the corn price (134). He considered Malthus's case involving a sudden increase of corn output irrelevant, though he agreed that corn – as any other individual product suddenly doubled in supply – would be in excess. The pertinent question related to the effect of an increase *in general income*; and he insisted that the recipient would increase his expenditure in proportion, if not on consumption, then on investment goods (134–5).

A fortnight earlier, Ricardo had been optimistic that general agreement

20 Malthus does not, however, stay with this position (see below, p. 92).

could be reached: 'I think if we could talk together we should not very much differ on the question which has lately engaged us, our principal difference is about the permanence of the effects' (30 August; 128). Malthus had been equally hopeful: 'I agree with you in thinking that we should not probably differ much on our present subject of discussion, if we could talk it well over' (11 September; 131). But quite clearly the two could not have been farther apart.

III EFFECT OF AGRICULTURAL PRODUCTIVITY CONCEDED AND THE 'TEMPORARY' EFFECT OF MANUFACTURING PROSPERITY

Malthus's reply on 9 October 1814 allows a qualified role for land scarcity in profit-rate determination, a major concession considering his earlier rejection of any such role. His objection to Ricardo turns formally on 'practical' issues, namely, insistence on deviations of the profit rate from trends that result from new technology – he refers to manufacturing as well as agriculture – and to higher corn prices, assuming a lag in costs: 'You seem to think that the state of production from the land, compared with the means necessary to make it produce, is almost the sole cause which regulates the profits of stock, and the means of advantageously employing capital. After what I have written on the subject of food and population I can hardly be supposed not to allow a very great effect to so very great a cause. But unless it could be shewn that no improvements were ever to take place either in agriculture or manufactures, and that upon a rise in the price of raw produce, new leases would be immediately granted, new taxes levied, and that the price of labour and of every other commodity both foreign and domestic would rise without delay exactly in proportion, the doctrine is evidently not correct in practice. And as these contemporaneous effects are in my opinion not only improbable but impossible, it would be quite useless to lay much stress upon it even as a theoretical groundwork' (1951–73, VI, 139–40).[21] This statement might be understood as conveying the message that, in the *Essay on Population*, Malthus himself had recognized the effect of land scarcity on the profit rate. But the editions of 1798, 1803, 1806, and 1807 contain no such explicit account, as we saw in chapter 1, above. Possibly the statement reflects a new realization that the author of the *Essay* could not deny such an impact.[22]

As mentioned, the concession is qualified. The essential point is that, because the specified preconditions are not generally satisfied, agricultural

21 Costs include wages, taxes, and *rent*, indicating an absence of the concept of the zero-rent margin.

22 It is unclear from this whether Malthus allows that Ricardo also adopted the falling real-wage trend. His specific concern is with the profit-rate trend.

productivity can be said to determine only the *limits* to the profit rate – a high level at early stages of development encouraging rapid capital accumulation, population growth, and high demand, and a low stationary-state level ultimately, with reverse manifestations – but not the entire pattern. Furthermore, the manufacturing rate is said to come into line with those limiting rates via the *indirect* effect of land-scarcity conditions on population growth, and thus on demand conditions: 'It appears to me that nearly all which can be safely advanced respecting the dependence of profits on the state of the land is, that *the facility of acquiring food, and particularly the possession of a great quantity of good land is the main cause of high profits, and of a rapid increase of capital population and demand, and that the difficulty of acquiring food is the main cause of low profits, and the ultimate check to the indefinite extension of capital population and demand*' (140; emphasis added).

Although it is not made explicit that it is specifically demand pressure exerted by labourers in the *manufacturing* sector that is intended, one suspects that it is, since the availability of food *precedes* population growth. This argument is confirmed on 29 December 1814 (below, p. 92.). But all that refers to the limits. In 'the interval between the two extremes, considerable variations may take place; and ... practically no country was ever in such a state as not to admit of increase of profits on the land, for a period of some duration, from the advanced price of raw produce.' An increase between 1793 and 1813 illustrated the sense in which the profit rate – the context relates solely to agriculture – can rise 'from the advanced price of raw produce':[23] 'The Profits of stock, or the means of employing capital advantageously may be said to be accurately equal to the price of produce, *minus* the expence of production. And consequently whenever the price of produce keeps a head of the price of production the profits of stock must rise. And this has unquestionably been the case on the land in this country during the last 20 years. It is not the *quantity* of produce compared with the expence of production that determines profits, (which I think is your proposition) but the exchangeable value or money price of that produce, compared with the money expence of production. And the exchangeable value of produce is not of course always proportioned to its quantity' (140–1).[24] The deviation between the money price of corn and money costs was seen to reflect the pressure of demand for corn, for the passage continues with the generalization that the (agricultural) rate is lower in 'poor' or low-density countries compared with 'middling' countries – experiencing 'an increasing commerce' – than Ricardo's real-cost approach suggested: 'In stating the cause of high profits you seem to me to consider

23 The course of labour productivity is not specified. All we are told is that corn prices increased during the war period *relative* to costs, which is consistent with an absolute increase in costs, but also with technological improvement precluding any such increase.

24 On the attribution to Ricardo of a *material* profit rate, see above, notes 4 and 15.

almost exclusively the expence of production without attending sufficiently to the price of produce, and greatly to under rate the wants and tastes of mankind in affecting prices, and consequently in affecting the means of profitably employing capital' (141).

There then follows a reiteration of the main general proposition at the very outset of the 1813 correspondence (above, p. 72) that extended trade raises aggregate value by acting on the '*will* to purchase,' a perspective which controverted Mill's Law of Markets: 'What is it I would ask that enables the foreign merchant to sell the tea sugar and tobacco which he imports at a higher price than the manufactures which he has sent out in exchange for them. Solely their being better suited to the wants and tastes of society. There is no greater power to purchase them, but there is a greater will. And the *final cause* of the wealth which the country derives from these commodities, and of the means of profitably employing capital in their importation, is the existence of a taste for them. It is in considering merely of the proportions of commodities to one another, and not of their proportions to the wants and tastes of mankind that the error of Mr. Mill, in my opinion, consists.'

Here also Malthus makes (to my knowledge) his first formal statement of the problem of sustainable growth[25] in the course of a rejection of Ricardo's identification of investment and consumption in their impact on demand; 'accumulation' *as such* depresses the profit rate by *lowering* prices relative to costs: 'I cannot by any means agree with you in your observation that "the desire of accumulation will occasion demand just as *effectually* as a desire to consume" and that "consumption and accumulation equally promote demand." I confess indeed that I know no other cause for the fall of profits which I believe you will allow generally takes place from accumulation than that the price of produce falls compared with the expence of production, or in other words that the *effective* demand is diminished' (141–2). Here he appeals to Smith's authority: 'For this is how I understand the term effective demand, and this I think is the interpretation of it given by Adam Smith. And according to this interpretation, that is upon the supposition that a greater effective demand means a greater excess of the price of produce above the expence of production, you would surely allow that the effective demand would always be greatest when the quantity of capital was comparatively the smallest, or the profits of stock highest' (142). Ricardo's distinction (above, p. 81) between a hypothetical increase in any *one* product which could doubtless be cleared only at a loss, and an expansion of national income which would not encounter a comparable problem, Malthus denied: 'The true question relative to Mr. Mill's proposition is not whether a man would like to spend half as much again; but whether you can furnish to persons of the same incomes a great additional

25 The proposition is not formally restricted to any specific sector.

quantity of commodities without lowering their price so much compared with the price of production as to destroy the effective demand for such a supply, and consequently to check its continuance to the same extent.' An increase in *aggregate* output would be cleared only at unprofitable prices – unless, one has been given to understand, it is accompanied or preceded by expanded commerce.[26]

26 One notes the presumption of a common acceptance of a downward trend in the profit rate; the issue is its cause. At this point, just when it appears that Malthus has diverted attention from the impact of land scarcity on the profit rate to focus, rather, on an inability to absorb increasing aggregate output at constant prices, we encounter a cryptic summary statement that calls attention to the differential *cost* conditions of agriculture and manufacturing: 'The principal difficulties on the present question appear to me to arise from the very different effects of an increase, or diminution of capital on the land, and in manufactures and commerce; particularly with regard to price, occasioned by the different nature of the instruments employed, one set naturally growing worse, and the other generally growing better' (142).

A brief word here on Ricardo's reaction. Ricardo readily allowed temporary variations in the profit rate, notwithstanding a downward trend (23 October; 145–6). Clarity of thought required that alternative causes of a rising corn price be sharply distinguished. There is, first, the rise in the corn price, reflecting secular expansion in the face of increasingly scarce land, which (via the money wage) depresses the profit rate: 'A rise in the price of raw produce may be occasioned by a gradual accumulation of capital which by creating new demands for labour may give a stimulus to population and consequently promote the cultivation or improvement of inferior lands, – but this will not cause profits to rise but to fall, because not only will the rate of [money] wages rise, but more labourers will be employed without affording a proportional return of raw produce. The whole value of the wages paid will be greater compared with the whole value of the raw produce obtained' (146). This, of course, constitutes the main growth model – all in price terms – with one difference: that, at this stage, Ricardo alludes to two depressing forces at play, whereas he came to realize that the fall in productivity is, in fact, reflected in the money wage.

There are also corn-price increases reflecting seasonal reductions in corn output and temporary inflation, and these act to 'disturb' the secular trend. Ricardo sums up by listing a variety of disturbing causes or alterations in the *ceteris paribus* conditions assumed by statements of the regular growth process (147).

The contention that his land-based growth model could not account for the relatively low profit rate 'often' observed in low-density economies, and conversely, in the case of high-density economies, Ricardo rejected on the grounds that, in the first category, it would be found that real wages were 'enormously' high (and constituted a major source of savings), and should in part be treated as profits, and, in the second, that they were 'too low,' apparently *artificially* repressed: 'You observe that in rich countries profits are often much higher, and in poor countries much lower than according to my theory, to which I reply that profits are very much reduced in the poor country by enormous wages; – the wages themselves may be considered as part of the profits of stock, – and are frequently the foundation of new capital. In rich countries wages are low, too low for the comforts of the labourers; – too large a portion of the gross produce is retained by the owner of stock, and is reckoned as profit.' This passage implies that, in the event of less extreme magnitudes of the real wage – and with appropriate classification of 'profits' – *the declining profit trend would be apparent, notwithstanding the downward trend of wages. Shortly after, he explicitly argued the case that the increasing incidence of diminishing returns is necessarily shared by both capitalists and labourers* (below, note 35).

In taking this line Malthus was complicating matters in Smithian fashion by adding a second secular force playing on the profit rate to that exerted by increasing land scarcity. But a qualification is in order, for it emerges later that, for Malthus alone, increasing competition of capitals emanating from the supply side might be avoided (below, p. 91). Moreover, only for Malthus does the effect of land scarcity on the manufacturing rate work its way *indirectly* by playing on population growth, and thus on demand (as we have seen), at least regarding the *limits* imposed by agricultural conditions.

* * *

On 23 November, Malthus again asserted that 'I have never that I recollect doubted or denied the general *tendency* of the accumulation of capital upon the land to diminish profits' (152). This is a questionable disclaimer since, in the earlier correspondence, he had questioned this tendency. His allowance now apparently extends beyond the limits *to the whole secular path.* None the less, 'the acknowledgment of this obvious truth' was 'very different from the general position that the state of the land *regulates* profits.' He drew a parallel with the 'certain' fact of a downward trend in the real wage, but the inappropriateness of saying that land-scarcity conditions 'regulate' the real wage, and this because of the need for supplementary conditions to assure the appropriate wage decline – a high rate of capital accumulation in cases of low density and (by implication) a lower rate in cases of higher density: 'Nothing can be more certain, for instance, than that the state of the land is the main cause of high wages, or the most scanty wages, according as it is fertile and abundant, or comparatively poor and scarce. But still it would be most incorrect to say that the state of the land *regulates* wages; because there are numerous instances where land is fertile and abundant, and yet wages are very low and the population stationary or retrograde. The reason of this is, that tho' fertile land and a great plenty of it are the main cause of high wages of labour, yet they are not the sole or regulating cause, and without the accumulation of capital, which may be prevented by extravagant habits or a bad government, are inefficient to produce such high wages.' The impact of increasing land scarcity on the real wage in particular is reiterated with rather more force later in the same letter: 'The diminution of wages is a more directly necessary consequence of a difficulty in obtaining food, than the diminution of profits, as wages are the great regulator of the progress of population' (155).

It is unclear from all this whether Malthus was fully aware of the implication of his allowing at least a 'tendency' towards a reduced profit rate with increasing land scarcity, and also a fall in the real wage – namely, that the wage reduction *cannot* insulate the profit rate from decline. *For he also represents 'the constant tendency' to a fall in real wages – not merely a temporary fall – as acting positively on the profit rate,* along with the 'prosperous or adverse states of commerce and manufactures': 'In the same manner though the state of the land, – whether it is fresh and fertile, or comparatively at its utmost stretch of exertion, be the main cause of high profits, and of the final fall and almost ultimate extinction of profits, yet as the state of the land is by no means the sole cause which determines profits, but as they are powerfully influenced by the varying demands for produce occasioned by the prosperous or adverse state of commerce and manufactures, and the constant tendency to a fall in the wages of labour, it neither accords with theory or experience to call the state of the land the *regulator* of general profits' (152).[27] This passage asserts that the falling real wage contributes to *insulate* the profit rate from decline (cf. Peach, 1988, 113–14). Malthus has lapsed into serious contradiction, since in the immediately preceding sentences he had explicitly alluded to downward trend paths in *both* variables. He has fallen into a common error, failing to ask *why* the wage declines with increasing land scarcity unless it is under pressure from a decelerating labour demand, itself attributable to a falling profit rate.

* * *

The relation between sectors is given further attention in the letter of 23 November. Here the profit rate in agriculture is said to rise in the event of 'prosperous' manufacturing or commerce because capital is attracted to those buoyant sectors *from* agriculture; it is then those sectors that 'take the lead': 'The question is whether agriculture always takes the lead in the determination? and I should certainly say that it did not. When a new foreign commerce is opened, and new objects greatly in demand are brought into the market, the profits of such commerce must be higher than usual; and you allow that in this case capital may be taken from the land. But to allow this is at once to allow that the profits of foreign commerce determine in this case the profits on the land and that whichever is the highest will take the lead of the other' (153).[28] Yet Malthus's case did not actually require the 'withdrawal of capital from the land' in the event of a 'new foreign commerce' – the argument was designed to trap Ricardo. It would operate even with an expanded demand for agricultural produce, reflecting 'a greater value of commodities to be exchanged for raw produce,' which directly raises the agricultural profit rate and positively stimulates accumulation and land 'improvement': 'Without however

27 Here one again notes that profits are explained by demand pressure in manufacturing and commerce, not in agriculture.

28 Ricardo could not fathom the attribution made to him: 'I do not recollect ever having allowed that an extension of foreign commerce will take capital from the land, unless we were an exporting country as far as regards corn, in which case my proposition would be true – namely, 'that the rate of profits can never permanently rise unless capital be withdrawn from the land' (18 December; 163).

supposing capital to be taken from the land, the throwing of new objects of desire into the market will increase the value of the whole mass of commodities in the country, estimated either in money, or in corn and labour, and there will in consequence be a greater value of commodities to be exchanged for the raw produce. This increase in the value of raw produce must raise the profits of farming for a period of some duration; and it is in fact during these periods (with the exception of the first start as in America) that capital is most rapidly accumulated upon the land and the greatest improvements are made.'[29]

It is only *temporary* deviations from the downward trend that are insisted upon – in *all* sectors, including agriculture – a deviation that might last 'for 20 years perhaps,' an obvious reference to actual experience in 1793–1813: 'With regard to the actual duration of such a period, it must of course depend upon various circumstances, particularly upon the extent and duration of the commerce, and the continued improvements made in manufacturing machinery. And without meaning to deny that a foreign commerce however prosperous is more easily saturated with capital than a large extent of fresh land, yet both theory and experience shew that a period of comparatively high profits, (for 20 years perhaps), may take place contemporaneously in agriculture manufactures and foreign commerce, after a period of comparatively low profits' (153–4).[30] But that Malthus takes seriously the operation of the downward profit-rate trend itself is evident, for there follows once again a reference to an ultimate *limit* imposed by land scarcity; also significant is the agreement with Ricardo that 'permanently' high profits – an exceptional case – would be accompanied by a low corn price: 'These periods I consider are of great importance to nations, and not to be undervalued, because as the progress of population and capital cannot be absolutely unlimited, the further you proceed the nearer you must approach the limit. *Permanent* high profits cannot take place but under the greatest national misfortunes – a premature but permanent and effective check to accumulation or a great and irrecoverable loss of capital, and I entirely agree with you that they would be accompanied with low instead of high prices, at least with regard to agricultural products' (154).[31]

Responding to Ricardo's appeal for more precision regarding the *causes* of corn-price increase (above, note 26), Malthus again insisted on the stimulatory effect of increases in the corn price, *not the result of diminishing*

29 This position is consistent with that of 9 October (above, p. 82).

30 The reference to a twenty-year deviation from trend reiterates what had been said earlier in the correspondence (above, p. 83).

31 Recognition that permanently high profits entail a *low* corn price implies that the normal course of expansion will entail a rise in the corn price. This had been established earlier (see above, pp. 75–6), but then Malthus had *denied* the impact of land scarcity on the profit rate.

returns but of pressure of demand, which – for some twenty years – counteract the falling profit-rate trend:

It is of great importance as you justly observe to ascertain the causes which may occasion a rise in the price of raw produce, and in enumerating them I cannot help thinking that you have too much overlooked those natural and necessary, – not accidental causes, which in every rich and populous country make a bushel of corn command a much greater quantity of manufactured and foreign produce, and generally of labour, than in a poor, country; and which owing to circumstances which counterbalance the principle you lay down, diminish rather than increase in rich and highly cultivated countries, the proportion of the whole population employed upon the land. My conclusion therefore on the whole is this, that tho I should allow without the least hesitation and quite as a matter of course, the *tendency* of an accumulation of capital on the land as well as in every other employment, to lower profits, yet I should say that this tendency was at times so counterbalanced by other causes naturally accompanying the progress of improvement, that a period when the profits on land were 8 per cent, might often be followed by a period of 20 years perhaps, when they were 10 or 12 per cent, and this, without the removal of capital from the land but while the progress of cultivation was going on *and during these periods the state of manufactures and commerce would regulate the profits on land.* (154–5; emphasis added, 'tendency' italicized in the original)

There emerges from all this: (1) a firm attachment to increasing land scarcity as the (or at least *one*) source of a falling general profit-rate trend; and (2) insistence on periods of some two decades, illustrated by the war years, where the lead role is played by the manufacturing sector, reversing the profit trend by raising the demand for corn. As for (1), the linkage with the manufacturing sector is left unexplained; but it may be inferred – and this is later confirmed (below, p. 93) – that the mechanism involving population growth and demand (alluded to originally with respect to the *limits* [above, pp. 82–3]) is now extended. As for (2), the 'temporary' counteracting pressures raising the relative corn price are represented as 'natural and necessary, – not accidental causes' or 'causes naturally accompanying the progress of improvement.' Although the immediately preceding paragraphs had dealt largely with the consequences of new commercial opportunities, the current formulations seem not to refer to that sort of disturbance, though we cannot be sure.[32] Mention had also been made of 'continued improvements made in manufacturing machinery' (above,

32 For it is unclear why new commercial opportunities would be regarded as 'natural and necessary' rather than 'accidental.' Second, though they would stimulate demand for corn, why would they raise the corn price *relative* to manufacturing prices? And, third, why would they 'diminish ... the proportion of the whole population employed on the land'?

p. 88), and these fit in rather better in that they act to raise the relative corn price by reducing those of manufactures, and also because, by attracting labour, they 'diminish rather than increase in rich and highly cultivated countries the proportion of the whole population employed on the land.'

IV THE PROFIT-RATE TREND ELABORATED

As we have seen, it is specifically during '*temporary*' – though not '*accidental*' – periods that the state of manufactures and commerce would regulate the profits on land. Whether new commercial opportunities or new industrial technology is intended, the leading sector is evidently manufacturing, an increasing profit rate in that sector extending to agriculture by way of demand for farm produce. By implication, the *secular* trend itself is dictated by the agricultural rate, the manufacturing rate coming into line.[33] How is this achieved? To deal with this problem, we must recall the impact on the trend itself of Smithian 'competition of capitals' – the problem of sustainable growth. This supplementary secular force is encountered in the letter of 9 October (above, p. 82), and again in the present letter of 23 November, which refers to a tendency 'of an accumulation of capital on the land *as well as in every other employment,* to lower profits' (above, p. 89; emphasis added). The issue of non-sustainable expansion of capacity because of inadequate markets is elaborated in what follows: 'Accumulation of *produce* is not accumulation of *capital,* unless what is accumulated is worth more than it cost, and if you were at once to employ all our soldiers sailors and menial servants in productive labour, the price of produce would fall more than ten per cent, and the encouragement to employ the same quantity of capital would cease ... I am of the opinion that a positive fall of price is a very common effect of the employment of more capital, *and will always take place when produce is increased by the employment of an unusual quantity of capital,* before the wants and tastes of mankind and their power of purchasing have been increased in proportion' (1951–73, VI, 155–6; emphasis added, 'produce' and 'capital' italicized in original). One notes the reference to an expansion of 'produce,' a term which often designates *corn.* But the argument is, in fact, quite general, as is clarified by the text covered by our ellipses. To appreciate that text, we must recall that Malthus had earlier queried 'whether you can furnish to persons of the same incomes a great additional quantity of commodities' without downward pressure on prices relative to costs (above, pp. 84–5).[34] Malthus

33 We set aside the trend path of real wages, which, like that of the profit rate, is treated as tending downwards with increasing land scarcity but, inconsistently, also envisaged as *insulating* the profit rate from land-scarcity pressures (above, p. 87).

34 Ricardo's position was that an expansion of output implies an expansion of income, and a corresponding expansion of demand (above, p. 81).

now reiterates: 'I think I am right in what I said about the *same incomes.* In fact unless the commodities produced are new and more desirable, or cheaper, the producers will certainly be left to consume what they have produced them selves. Others will neither have the power nor the will to consume more' (155). In brief, inappropriately expanded *physical output* will not entail *expansion of income,* and this because of lack of markets.[35]

We are in Adam Smith's world. Though increasing land scarcity is allowed as a force depressing the profit rate, expansion of aggregate supply also subjects the profit rate to downward pressure. Smith's 'increasing competition of capitals,' therefore, retains its validity, with this major difference: that, for Smith, ongoing accumulation *necessarily* forces down prices and profits, whereas Malthus suggests this outcome only with accumulation of 'an *unusual* quantity of capital ...' The qualification allows that the problem could, under appropriate conditions, be avoided – conditions ensuring a *prior* increase in 'the power of purchasing' derived from *demand-side* considerations. (Throughout the rest of the correspondence, this qualification is neglected; it takes on major significance only in *formal* discussion of the aggregate-demand issue, on which see chapter 11, below.)

35 In his reply Ricardo insisted that 'permanent' variation in the profit rate turns *solely* on inverse variation in the real cost of producing wage goods. In the absence of land scarcity, there would be no downward pressure on profits: 'If with every accumulation of capital we could tack on a piece of fresh fertile land to our Island, profits would never fall' (18 December; 162). Ricardo allowed that reduced costs of *manufactured* wage goods would raise the profit rate, and formally satisfied his position that the profit rate cannot rise unless capital is withdrawn from the land, by remarking that capital in agriculture would indeed be reduced, since agricultural capital, including wages, has to be revalued downwards: 'I admit at the same time that commerce, or machinery, may produce an abundance and cheapness of commodities, and if they affect the prices of those commodities on which the wages of labour are expended they will so far raise profits; – but then it will be true that less capital will be employed on the land, for the wages paid for labour form a part of that capital.'

This formulation accords the strategic role to the *money* wage rate in profit-rate determination. In fact, Ricardo's letter of 18 December 1814 contains all the main elements entering into the growth model of his *Principles,* for it proceeds explictly to indicate that the burden of diminishing returns is shared between capitalists and labourers: 'A diminution of the proportion of produce, in consequence of the accumulation of capital, does not fall wholly on the owner of stock, but is shared with him by the labourers. *The whole amount of wages paid will be greater, but the portion paid to each man, will in all probability, be somewhat diminished*' (162–3; emphasis added).

Ricardo now drew on J.B. Say's version of the Law of Markets to reinforce his opposition to the notion that accumulation, as such, depresses the profit rate. Expansion of output and income generates an expansion of the market, provided, of course, that the specific commodities produced are '*properly selected*' (163–4). Malthus's requirement for a *prior* increase in value – that 'without ... supposing capital to be taken from the land, the throwing of new objects of desire into the market will increase the value of the whole mass of commodities in the country, estimated either in money, or in corn and labour' (see above, pp. 87–8) – made no sense from Ricardo's perspective.

Furthermore, the two forces are not represented as independent of each other, as we have seen with respect to the limits, but involve the depressing effect of increasing land scarcity on demand by way of decelerating population growth (above, p. 83). It will soon become clear that Malthus extends this relation to the whole growth path.

In his next letter, dated 29 December 1814, Malthus again reiterates that expansion of (manufacturing) output with accumulation depresses profits: 'I had remarked the passage you mention in Mr. Says work, and think it well done, though I cannot quite agree with him' (168). But he did not condemn Say outright, *for now the Law of Markets is allowed when restricted to 'necessaries'*: 'I think the source of his error is, that he does not properly distinguish between the necessaries of life and other commodities, – the former create their own demand the latter not.' In this case we are a major step closer to an answer to our problem (above, pp. 78, 81) of whether excess supply could apply to agriculture as well as manufactures.[36] It would not, however, be justified to give the present declaration a reading precluding, under all circumstances, pressure on profits from an excess supply of 'necessaries.' Since the mechanism works by way of population expansion, much will depend on the time period supposed, and would certainly be inapplicable in the treatment of, say, seasonal variation.

Malthus also reverts to the forces at play counteracting land-scarcity effects. He again allows that upward movement of the corn price relative to costs – under pressure of demand emanating from 'a prosperous commerce' – and accordingly, of the agricultural profit rate, would not be 'permanent,' but insists that they might last for some two or three decades. During this period 'the profits of commerce will take the lead': 'We should explain what we mean by *permanently*. Of course I never mean to say that the high price of raw produce compared with the price of production, occasioned, (in my opinion) by a prosperous commerce, can be really *permanent.* It is the nature of all such means of employing capital to become less and less advantageous. And all that I contend for is that a period of some duration may occur (20 years for instance) when the profits of commerce will take the lead, and regulate the profits of agriculture' (167). He asked Ricardo to account for a thirty-year period of *falling* corn prices, and yet low profits, and the twenty war years of *rising* corn prices, and yet high profits: 'You say that profits depend entirely upon the low price of Corn? What was the reason that from 1720 to 1750 the interest of money and the profits of stock fell very considerably and were very low at the same time that the

36 The former create their own demand by way of population expansion – a Smithian conception. Cf. Smith, 1776/1937, 475–6, regarding the impact of a corn-export bounty in reducing domestic corn output, and consequently reducing 'the whole market and consumption of corn'; and 146: 'As men, like other animals, naturally multiply in proportion to the means of subsistence, food is always, more or less in demand.' This distinguished pedigree suggests that Malthus was now making explicit a position held earlier in the correspondence, though until now left unstated.

price of corn was gradually becoming cheaper; while from 1793 to 1812 the interest of money and the profits of stock were high, at the same time that the price of corn was becoming peculiarly dear' (168).

Rising corn prices between 1793 and 1812 are thus ascribed to a 'prosperous commerce,' *not* to diminishing returns, settling any remaining doubts on that score. It is from this direction that Malthus pushed home his challenge. He rejected Ricardo's denial that foreign commerce increases the value of aggregate output: 'I have certainly always thought that in the exchange of the tin of Cornwall for the deals of Norway, both countries had the value of the whole mass of their commodities decidedly increased; and this increase of value has always appeared to me to be the consequence of all profitable exchanges both external and internal.'[37] Setting aside the *temporary* countervailing effect on the profit rate exerted by a 'prosperous commerce,' agricultural profits 'take the lead.'

The linkage between the agricultural and the manufacturing rate of profits during the regular course of growth is not formally attended to. But a comment on Ricardo's hypothetical case of an addition of 'fresh fertile land' (above, note 35) is most pertinent to the issue and confirms the interpretation given earlier (above, p. 89). Malthus could not accept the role of money wages in Ricardo's argument; for him *the positive effect on profits of a relaxation of land scarcity would work via population growth and increased demand for manufactures*: 'I quite agree with you that a piece of fertile land added to the country upon every increase of capital would prevent the fall of profits, but more in my opinion from *its increasing the demand for manufactures* by increasing the number of people than by its preventing the rise of wages, an effect which it would probably not have' (168–9; emphasis added).[38]

V CONCLUDING REMARKS

Did Malthus at this stage positively exclude a *direct* effect on the agricul-

37 He also suggested that Ricardo reconsider the case of an increase in the foreign demand for domestic corn; for here the agricultural profit rate would rise, despite agricultural expansion. Ricardo had implied in passing (18 December; 1951–73, VI, 163) that an increase in trade involving expanded *corn exports* would indeed raise the agricultural profit rate but entail a *contraction* of agricultural capital. Malthus objected: 'I do not think that a prosperous commerce would have an effect very essentially different from a great foreign demand for our raw produce. But supposing a great foreign demand for our raw produce, would not the profits of capital employed in agriculture be increased, although certainly more rather than less capital would be employed upon the land. The instruments of production compared with the price of produce would be cheaper, but it could not with any propriety be said that capital was withdrawn from the land.' Ricardo's logic for this latter case is indeed difficult to fathom, though in his reply early in the New Year he seems to reverse himself.

38 For an elaboration of this case, allowing for a transfer of resources from manufacturing, see below, chapter 4, p. 130.

tural profit rate generated by the relaxation of land-scarcity conditions, that is, one *not* operating by way of population and demand? The alteration in those conditions affects population growth via the (corn) wage, and for this to occur there *must,* one supposes, be some prior impact on the profit rate, and thus on accumulation and the demand for labour. It seems unlikely, therefore, that he intended to rule out a direct effect on the agricultural rate, though he certainly rejected Ricardo's precise mechanism.

With the Law of Markets at hand, Ricardo was left with land scarcity alone as the source of secular profit-rate decline. Here we note his satisfaction on reading Malthus's concession that the effect exerted by increased commerce was a temporary one: 'I thought you maintained, that the high or low profits on commerce were totally independent of the amount of capital which might be employed on the land; consequently that high profits might continue as long as commerce was prosperous, whether that was for 20 or for 100 years. I now understand you to say, that the profits of commerce may take the lead, and may regulate the profits of agriculture for a period of some duration, possibly for 20 years. I have always allowed that under certain circumstances profits on agriculture might be diverted from their regular course for short periods, so that we only appear to differ with respect to the duration of such profits; instead of 20 years I should limit it to about 4 or 5' (13 January; 170). Despite the conciliatory tone of this passage, the two approaches differed in fundamental respects; the debate was evidently not one concerning the meaning of 'temporary.' If, for Ricardo, a variety of forces could influence the profit rate 'temporarily,' it was by relationships peculiar to his model alone, acting via the money wage. When Malthus allows for 'temporary' variations of the general profit rate attributable to events in manufacturing and commerce, he has in mind demand pressures ruled out by the Law of Markets approach.

THREE

The *Inquiry into Rent* (1815)

I INTRODUCTION

On 29 December 1814, Malthus informed Ricardo that he was busy on his *Inquiry into Rent* and hoped to publish it before Parliament met (Ricardo, 1951–73, VI, 167). The pamphlet – in part based on notes, some of which had been written as far back as 1807[1] – was published in February, and Ricardo had read it in print by 6 February 1815 (172). This chapter deals with the theory of growth as it emerges in the *Inquiry*.[2] Other aspects of the pamphlet are taken up in chapter 8.

In section II, we consider the function of diminishing returns in 'separating out' rent proper from profits (and wages), that is, in generating a return to land ownership. Rent proper emerges with the setting in of a decline in the wage and profit rates, for this decline acts to reduce production 'costs' relative to the 'corn price.' Malthus seems, then, to have at last abandoned the erroneous notion that a fall in the corn wage can insulate the profit rate, though we shall see that there still remains some doubt regarding this matter. A difficulty with the analysis is the intrusion of

1 This is explained in the 'Advertisement' to the pamphlet: 'The following Tract contains the substance of some notes on Rent, which, with others on different subjects relating to political economy I have collected in the course of my professional duties at the East India College. It has been my intention, at some time or other, to put them in a form for publication; and the very near connection of the subject of the present inquiry, with the topics immediately under discussion, has induced me to hasten its appearance at the present moment' (1815b/1986, 7, 115).

2 Much of the pamphlet is absorbed into the *Principles*. For convenience I include in the citations given below variations from the later versions (1820, 1836).

micro-economic terms in the treatment of an essentially macro-economic problem. A further problem relates to sectoral interdependence. The initial analysis appears to entail an agricultural model, with the declining trend of the profit rate explained by increasing land scarcity. But there is subsequent allowance for a negative effect on the general profit rate of capital accumulation in *manufacturing* (the Smithian conception), which decline appears to be accorded the lead, allowing expansion onto inferior marginal land, or at the intensive margin, at a reduced agricultural profit rate. The attractive possibility must be entertained that the initial formulation constitutes a brief statement of main trends, whereas the extension provides the fuller picture. This particular solution to sectoral interdependence in the analysis of the trend, however, is not that of the early correspondence (see chapter 2, above), which treats agriculture as the lead sector and involves an effect of increasing land scarcity on the manufacturing rate via growth of population and demand for manufactures. (We shall see in chapter 4, below, that this perspective reappears in later correspondence.)

Section III investigates the role accorded absolute increase in the corn price, reflecting higher input coefficients at the higher outputs called forth by increasing demand. It is unclear whether this formulation was introduced as an alternative statement of the growth process viewed from a different perspective; since there is no formal discussion of their intended relationship, the impression is one of compartmentalized formulations.

Section IV spells out two forms of stationariness – the end-point of a 'regular' growth process and the 'premature' cessation of growth owing to institutional or sociological obstacles. In section V we turn from the growth process, as such, to the direct effect on rent of expanding foreign demand for domestic corn, or the indirect effect on rent of expanding sales of manufactures and new manufacturing technology. The discussion elaborates on the theme of a stimulating impact of manufacturing activity on agricultural profits, a major preoccupation of the earlier correspondence. Ricardo's reaction to the *Inquiry* and his exchange with Malthus are the subject-matter of section VI.

II AN AGRICULTURAL-GROWTH MODEL AND AN EXTENSION

After establishing the 'source' of rent in a 'most inestimable quality in the soil, which God bestowed on man – the quality of being able to maintain more persons than are necessary to work it' (1815b/1986, 7, 122), Malthus clarified that, within that designation, he intended 'the whole fund for the support of those who are not directly employed upon the land,' thus including farmers' profits. (One may perhaps presume that an extraction is made to allow for farmers' subsistence consumption.) Profits were a surplus – since 'they are in no respect proportioned (as intimated by the

Economists) to the wants and necessities of the owners of capital,'[3] – but yet had to be separated out from rent, narrowly defined, since 'they take a different course in the progress of society.' In the course of the argument, wages too – or rather, part of wages – are included within the 'surplus' category. What follows provides us with elements of a Malthusian growth model.

The essential proposition is that rent proper emerges with manifestations of diminishing returns, assuming ongoing growth of capital and labour, the fall in agricultural productivity depressing the profit rate, which together with reductions in the corn-wage rate ensures a payment for land services, as such:

> In the early periods of society, or more remarkably perhaps [1836: In the settlement of a new colony], when the knowledge and capital of an old society are employed upon fresh and fertile land, this surplus produce, this bountiful gift of Providence [1820: the surplus produce of the soil], shews itself chiefly in extraordinary high profits, and extraordinary high wages [1836: in high profits, and high wages], and appears but little in the shape of rent. While fertile land is in abundance, and may be had by whoever asks for it, nobody of course will pay a rent to a landlord. But it is not consistent with the laws of nature and the limits and quality of the earth, that this state of things should continue. Diversities of soil and situation must necessarily exist in all countries. All land cannot be the most fertile: all situations cannot be the nearest to navigable rivers and markets. But the accumulation of capital beyond the means of employing it [1836: with the same returns] on land of the greatest natural fertility, and the greatest advantage of situation [1820: the most advantageously situated], must necessarily lower profits; while the tendency of population to increase beyond the means of subsistence must, after a certain time, lower [1836: while the rapid increase of population will tend to lower] the wages of labour. (123; 1820, 150–1; 1836, 149)

The foregoing account can be read as ascribing the reduction in the profit and corn-wage rates to the reduced productivity of 'inferior' land, the incidence of diminishing returns at the extensive margin falling on both capital and labour. (The intensive margin is also alluded to, though less conspicuously; see 132; cf. 1820, 183; 1836, 177.) In this case Malthus would at last have adopted the Ricardian position that the falling wage cannot insulate the profit rate, a matter left in some doubt in the earlier correspondence. But there are complexities. For one thing, there is an apparent reference at the close of the formulation to *excessive* population growth, contrasting with the later full-fledged statement of the growth

3 Cf. 142n: 'I have hinted before, in a note, that profits may, without impropriety, be called a surplus. But, whether surplus or not, they are the most important source of wealth, as they are, beyond all question, the main source of accumulation.'

model in which the corn-wage rate falls, despite reduction in the population growth rate as well as the capital (food) growth rate, and the profit-rate decline is attributed to a rise in *proportional* wages, which itself reflects diminishing returns. However, a summary of position is more in line with the mature account, attributing *both* the wage- and the profit-rate reductions to land scarcity: 'Rent then has been traced to the same common nature with that general surplus from the land, which is the result of certain qualities of the soil and its products; and it has been found to commence its separation from profits, as soon as profits and wages fall, owing to the comparative scarcity of fertile land in the natural progress of a country towards wealth and population' (125).[4]

A further complexity in the passage is its reference to 'accumulation of capital beyond the means of employing it on land of the greatest natural fertility ...' which might suggest downward pressure on the profit rate prior to extension of cultivation onto inferior land (a form of diminishing returns at the intensive margin), which pressure – together with similar downward pressure on the wage – *motivates* the extension. Such motivation is, in fact, stated explicitly thus: 'When capital has [1820: further] accumulated, and labour [1836: corn wages] fallen on the most [1820: more] eligible lands of a country, other lands less favourably circumstanced with respect to fertility or situation, may [1820: might] be occupied with advantage. The expenses of cultivation, including profits [1836: The quantity of produce required to replace wages and profits] having fallen, poorer land, or land more distant from markets [1820: rivers and markets], though yielding at first no rent, may [1820: might] fully repay these expenses, and fully answer to the cultivator. And again, when either the profits of stock or the wages [1836: corn wages] of labour, or both have still further fallen, land still poorer, or still less favourably situated, may [1820: might] be taken into cultivation' (125; 1820, 153–4; 1836, 152–3).[5] Even so, it remains true that the lower marginal product on inferior land suffices only to accommodate a lower profit rate and lower corn wage.

We have, therefore, at the outset of 1815, the essentials of the classical land scarcity–based (single-sector) growth model with its secular downward trend of the

4 The *Principles* reads: 'It has been found to commence its separation from profits and wages, as soon as they begin to fall from the scarcity of fertile land whether occasioned by the natural progress of a country towards wealth and population, or by the premature and unnecessary monopoly of the soil' (1820, 160; 1836, 157).

At this juncture in the 1815 pamphlet we can perhaps see the break between earlier notes and more recently written material (see Jacob Hollander, 1903). The text continues: 'Having examined the nature and origin of rent, it remains for us to consider the laws by which it is governed, and by which its increase or decrease is regulated.'

5 The variations for the second edition strengthen the notion of a pure corn model, though this line is not consistently carried through in the Rent chapter (see below, chapter 10, p. 498).

profit and wage rates. This simple fact raises the matter of precedence. In laying out the model, Malthus says nothing about its origins. We have found that, in his early correspondence with Ricardo, Malthus initially denied a *direct* effect of land scarcity on the agricultural profit rate, claiming that the fall in the wage insulates the profit rate from decline. It is only in October and November 1814 that, *under pressure from Ricardo,* he came to concede a direct effect, though there remained hints that he had not completely abandoned the notion of 'insulation' (see above, chapter 2, p. 87). But Ricardo, on 23 October, strongly implied the principle that the incidence of diminishing returns is shared between capital and labour and, on 18 December, explicitly stated the principle (above, chapter 2, notes 26 and 35). It is my impression that Ricardo has precedence, leaving his mark on Malthus, who then absorbed the notion into the *Rent* pamphlet. It is relevant that, subsequently, Malthus himself claimed precedence only for the declining wage in consequence of land scarcity – allowing Ricardo priority for the declining profit rate (see below, chapter 4, pp. 168–9). But there is evidence from later correspondence with Ricardo (below, p. 111) that Malthus was still not sure of himself. And we should also take into account in evaluating the 'debt' to Ricardo that the model thus far outlined does not constitute the entire picture; it represents a simple case that requires revision to allow for a manufacturing sector.

* * *

Thus far the case has been stated in corn terms. In a continuation of the main argument, it is a matter of reduced '*expenses*' – a lower corn wage and profit rate – *relative to the 'value' of corn*: 'The expense of production will thus be diminished, but the value of the produce, that is, the quantity of labour, and of the other products of labour besides corn which it can command, instead of diminishing, will be increased. There will be an increasing number of people demanding subsistence, and ready to offer their services in any way in which they can be useful. The exchangeable value of food will, therefore, be in excess above the cost of production, including in this cost the full profits of the stock employed upon the land, according to the actual rate of profits, at the time being. And this excess is rent' (123).[6] But what precisely did Malthus believe happens to the

6 The 'excess' must refer to a *total* or *average* dimension, if we presume that Malthus adopts the notion of a rent-free margin. The last sentence, in fact, reads thus in the *Principles* (1820): 'The exchangeable value of food will therefore be in excess above the cost of production, on all the more fertile lands; and this excess is that portion of the general surplus derived from land which has been peculiarly denominated rent' (1820, 150–1). But, strangely, the second edition reworks the entire passage, detracting attention from the intramarginal surplus: 'The costs of production in corn wages and profits will thus be diminished; but the value of the produce, that is, the quantity of labour

absolute corn price with extensions to increasingly inferior land, and the corresponding fall in the corn wage and profit rate envisaged as reduced 'expenses'? Formally, the corn price is said to rise *relative to labour* (and manufactures) – the corn wage falls in effect; but this is difficult to appreciate, since the reduction in expenses includes the fall in the corn wage; that is, the increase in corn command over labour is already taken into account. In the *Principles* reference is made at this point to 'the tendency of an abundance of food to increase population, [which] is necessary both to give a value to the surplus of necessaries which the cultivators can obtain on the first land cultivated; and also to create a demand for more food than can be procured from the richest lands' (1820, 151; 1836, 150), alluding to 'that quality peculiar to the necessaries of life' – a form of Say's Law applied to food, introduced in 1815 – 'of being able to create their own demand, or to raise up a number of demanders in proportion to the quantity of necessaries produced' (119; 1820, 139–40; 1836, 140). *But all this does not amount to the claim that the absolute corn price will tend to rise.* In fact, in elaborating the process of expansion to increasingly unproductive land with falling labour and capital 'expenses' – at least in 1815 and 1820 – all that is insisted upon is an assurance against an (absolute) reduction of the corn price, and this is provided by the increasing demand for corn emanating from the non-agricultural sector (the sector supported by the agricultural surplus): '*And, at every step it is clear, that if the price of produce does not fall, the rents of land will rise. And the price of produce will not fall,* as long as the industry and ingenuity of the labouring classes, assisted by the capitals of those not employed upon the land, can find something to give in exchange to the cultivators and landlords, which will stimulate them to continue undiminished their agricultural exertions, and maintain their increasing excess [1820: their excess] of produce' (125; 1820, 154; emphasis added).[7]

To assert that 'expenses' *fall*, in the sense of falling profits per cent and wages per capita, is meaningful at the aggregate level but unhelpful within an industry framework. It is scarcely surprising that the notion of a corn price – appropriate for partial-equilibrium analysis – should have proven difficult to incorporate.[8] On the other hand, Say's Law applied to food makes no sense at the industry level of analysis, which of course requires independence of supply and demand.

---

which it can command, instead of diminishing, will have a tendency to increase. There will be an increasing number of people demanding subsistence, and ready to offer their services in any way in which they can be useful. The value of food will be in excess above the value of the labour and profits which are the condition of its supply; and this excess is that portion of the general surplus derived from land which has been peculiarly denominated rent' (150).

7 The second version of the *Principles* is truncated, ending with 'at every step of this kind it is clear, that the rent of land must rise' (153).

8 The second version of the *Principles* avoids the problem.

* * *

Malthus's opening statement of the separating-out of rents narrowly defined (above, p. 97) appears to attribute the declining profit rate directly to diminishing agricultural returns, and to account for the decline *within the confines of the agricultural sector.*[9] Yet, on the same page of the *Inquiry*, there is also a reference to 'such an accumulation ... as decidedly to lower the *general* profits of stock, and, consequently, the expenses of cultivation, so as make it answer to cultivate poorer land.' Here the fall in the profit rate appears to be determined *outside agriculture*, stimulating agricultural expansion at the extensive margin with a *resultant* depression of the agricultural profit rate: 'Nor is it possible that these rents should permanently remain as parts of the profits of stock, or of the wages of labour. If such an accumulation were to take place, as decidedly to lower the *general* profits of stock, and, consequently, the expenses of cultivation, so as to make it answer to cultivate poorer land; the cultivators of the richer land, if they paid no rent, would cease to be mere farmers, or persons living upon the profits of agricultural stock. They would unite the characters of farmers and landlords – a union by no means uncommon; but which does not alter, in any degree, the nature of rent, or its essential separation from profits. If the *general* profits of stock were 20 per cent and particular portions of land would yield 30 per cent on the capital employed, 10 per cent of the 30 would obviously be rent, by whomsoever received' (123–4; emphasis added).[10] This is admittedly, by itself, not too much to go on. But the reference in 1815 to 'the actual rate of profits, at the time being' in the

9 This applies whether we interpret the contention that 'the accumulation of capital beyond the means of employing it on land of the greatest natural fertility, and the greatest advantage of situation, must necessarily lower profits': (1) as a reference to downward pressure on the profit rate of activity on good land, which fall *stimulates* expansion onto poorer land; or (2) as the decline in the profit rate *resulting from* the extensions of poorer land (see above, p. 98).

10 There is also the 'inevitable' reduction of the corn-wage rate. Malthus was led, therefore, to the 'incontrovertible truth ... that as a nation reaches any considerable degree of wealth, and any considerable fullness of population which of course cannot take place without a great fall in both the profits of stock and the wages of labour, the separation of rents, as a kind of fixture upon lands of a certain quality, is a law as invariable as the action of the principle of gravity' (125; 1820, 155; 1836, 153). Ricardo's *Note 64* on the *Principles* protests: 'Who denies this? I have expressly affirmed it' (1951–73, II, 127). But, for Malthus, this truth confirmed the fallacy of the notion that rent is a socially nefarious transfer payment: 'rents are neither a mere nominal value, nor a value unnecessarily and injuriously transferred from one set of people to another; but a most real and essential [1836: most important] part of the whole value of the national property [1836: of the annual produce, necessarily resulting from its continued increase], and placed by the laws of nature where they are, on the land, by whomsoever possessed, [1820: whether by few or many,] whether [by] the landlord, the crown, or the actual cultivator.'

analysis of rent (above, p. 99) points in the same direction.[11] And in an elaboration of the 'main causes' that affect rent by reducing expenses, we apparently have (as the first cause) *capital accumulation, as such,* depressing the profit rate, which suggests Smithian 'competition of capitals':[12] 'In tracing more particularly the laws which govern the rise and fall of rents, the main causes which diminish the expenses of cultivation, or reduce the costs of the instruments of production, compared with the price of produce [1836: which practically tend to increase the difference between the price of produce, and the expenses of cultivation including ordinary profits], require to be more specifically enumerated. The principal of these seem to be four: – *1st, Such an accumulation of capital* [1836: compared with the means of employing it,] *as will lower the profits of stock*; 2dly, such an increase of population as will lower the wages [1836: corn wages] of labour; 3dly, such agricultural improvements, or such increase of exertions as will diminish the number of labourers necessary to produce a given effect; and 4thly, such an increase in the price [1836: *price*] of agricultural produce, from increased demand, as, without nominally lowering the expense of production, will increase the difference between this expense and the price of produce [1836: as, while it probably raises the money price of labour, or occasions a fall in the value of money, is nevertheless, accompanied by a diminution either temporary or permanent, of the money outgoings of the farmer, compared with his money returns]' (125–6; 1820, 160–1; 1836, 157–8; emphasis added).[13] What happens to the *direct* depressing effects

11 The *Principles* reworks the passage in a manner reinforcing the internal (agricultural) profit rate. The text of 1820 sets off, as in 1815: 'Nor is it possible that rents should permanently remain as parts of the profits of stock, or of the wages of labour' (1820, 152). This is modified in 1836: 'Nor is it possible that in a country increasing in wealth and population, the whole produce could continue to be divided only between the capitalists and labours, as the profits of capital and the wages of labour' (1836, 151). But neither version makes mention of a *general* profit rate: 'If profits and [1836: corn] wages were not to fall, then, without particular improvements in cultivation, none but the very richest lands could be brought into use. The fall of profits and wages which practically takes place, undoubtedly transfers a portion of produce to the landlord .... If the profits of stock [1836: capital] on the inferior land taken into cultivation were thirty per cent and portions of the old land would yield forty per cent, ten per cent of the forty would obviously be rent by whomsoever received' (1820, 152–3; 1836, 151–2).

A thoroughgoing reformulation of the 1815 pamphlet was, however, not undertaken. There is reference in the *Principles* to an excess of the food price over expenses, including the profit rate 'according to the actual rate of profits, at the time being,' which possibly suggests reference to a return external to agriculture. What follows in our text is common to all three versions. And we refer in chapter 10: XI, below, to a determining profit rate to which the agricultural return must conform.

12 Ricardo was to complain of the version appearing in the *Principles*: 'It is here inferred that a fall of profits is a necessary consequence of an accumulation of capital. No mistake can be greater' (*Note 71*; 1951–73, II, 132).

13 In summarizing, 'the accumulation of capital' is again referred to as if independent of agriculture: 'We see then that a progressive rise of rents seems to be necessarily con-

of land scarcity on the profit rate is left unstated. But since profit-rate equality is the rule, a downward trend in the profit rate in *manufactures* would allow marginal agricultural investments, keeping the agricultural rate in line. We must then face the strong possibility that the earlier, agricultural, analysis was provided by way of introduction, but does not yield the whole picture.

III ON THE RISING REAL COSTS OF MARGINAL EXTENSIONS: AN ALTERNATIVE PERSPECTIVE

As we have seen, the original analysis of growth in the *Inquiry* does not use the diminishing-returns principle in the Ricardian manner, to generate a secular upward trend in the corn price, reflecting rising *real* costs. On the contrary, the (absolute) corn price might remain *constant* in the face of falling 'expenses,' thus generating rent on intramarginal units of output (above, p. 100). However, in a fuller account of diminishing returns later in the essay, the order of events does involve expansion of food supply at higher real cost: 'We should consider the soil as a present to man of a great number of machines, all susceptible of continued improvement by the application of capital to them, but yet of very different original qualities and powers. This great inequality in the powers of the machinery employed in procuring [1836: obtaining] raw produce, forms one of the most remarkable features [1836: forms the most remarkable feature] which distinguishes the machinery of the land from the machinery employed in manufactures' (1815b/1986, 7, 133; 1820, 184; 1836, 178). What follows treats manufacturing as a constant-cost industry, subject to periodic improvement and downward shifts of long-run supply price, that price reflecting productivity conditions of the most efficient firm. By contrast: 'The most fertile [1836: and best situated] lands of a country, those which, like the best machinery in manufactures, yield the greatest products with the least labour and capital [1836: least expenditure], are never found sufficient [1820, 1836: owing to the second main cause of rent before stated,] to supply the effective [1836: effectual] demand of an increasing population. The price of raw produce, therefore, naturally rises till it becomes sufficiently high to pay [1836: answers to pay] the cost of raising it with inferior machines, and by a more expensive process; and, as there cannot

nected with the progressive cultivation of new land, and the progressive improvement of the old; and that this rise is the natural and necessary consequence of the operation of four causes, which are the most certain indications of increasing prosperity and wealth – namely, the accumulation of capital, the increase of population, improvements in agriculture, and the high [1820: market] price [1836: a rising market price] of raw produce, occasioned by the extension of our manufactures and commerce [1820: occasioned either by a great demand for it in foreign countries, or by the extension of commerce and manufactures]' (130; 1820, 178; 1836, 173).

be two prices for corn of the same quality, all the other machines, the working of which requires less capital [1836: expenditure] compared with the produce, must yield rents in proportion to their goodness' (133–4; 1820, 185; 1836, 179). In an extension involving differential growth rates between economies, the source of pressure on agriculture is traced to expansion of manufacturing capital, also implying population growth *prior to*, and responsible for, expansion of food: 'Let us now suppose one [economy] very greatly to increase in capital and manufacturing skill above the rest, and to become in consequence much more rich and populous [1836: to become much more rich and populous without increased skill in agriculture]. I should say, that this great comparative increase of riches could not possibly [1836: could not] take place, without a great comparative advance in the price of raw produce [1836: a great comparative increase in the prices of corn and labour]; and that such advance of price [1836: increase of prices] would, under the circumstances supposed, be the natural sign and absolutely necessary consequence [1836: and necessary consequence], of the increased wealth and population of the country in question' (136; 1820, 195; 1836, 187).

These formulations suggest a response of food supply to the prior expansion of population and demand, though this conflicts with the application of the Law of Markets – supply generates its own demand – to agricultural produce: 'that quality peculiar to the necessaries of life of being able, when properly distributed, to create their own demand, or to raise up a number of demanders in proportion to the quantity of necessaries produced' (above, p. 100). And, in fact, the variation in the *Principles* which refers to 'the second main cause of rent before stated' is precisely an allusion to that application. This wholly inappropriate concept, involving the *interdependence* of demand and supply, undermines the quality of the analysis purporting to trace out the implications of an upward-sloping supply curve in the face of outward shifts of demand.

Fortunately, various conspicuous elaborations are, so to speak, 'neutral' on this matter and avoid the problem. Thus, setting aside currency 'irregularities' and other 'temporary and accidental circumstances,' 'the cause of the high comparative money price of corn' is said in 1815 to be 'its high comparative real price, or the greater quantity of capital and labour which must be employed to produce it: and ... the reason why the real price of corn is higher and continually rising in countries which are already rich, and still advancing in prosperity and population, is to be found in the necessity of resorting constantly to poorer land – to machines which require a greater expenditure to work them – and which consequently occasion each fresh addition to the raw produce of the country to be purchased at a greater cost – in short, it is to be found in the important truth that corn, in a *progressive country*, is sold at the price necessary to yield the actual supply; and ... as this supply becomes more and more difficult, the price rises in proportion' (135).[14] The 1820 version is in substance the same (1820, 194). But the 1836 version – apart from replacing 'capital and labour' by 'labour, and other conditions of supply' – incorporates an allowance for technical progress: 'The reason why the price of corn would be high and tend to rise in countries already rich, and still advancing in prosperity and population, would be to be found in the necessity of resorting to poorer land, without proportional improvements in agriculture ...' (1836, 186).

This representation of diminishing agricultural productivity as a strong *empirical* principle is also to be found shortly afterwards in all versions, including that of 1815: 'With regard to improvements in agriculture, which in similar soils is the great cause which retards the advance of price compared with the advance of produce [1836: ... of price under an increase of produce]: although they are sometimes very [1820: most] powerful [1820: and of very considerable duration], they are rarely found sufficient [1820: they cannot finally be sufficient] to balance the necessity of applying to poorer land [1836: we know from experience that they have not been sufficient to balance the effects of applying to poorer land], or inferior machines. [1836: Added – Corn is obtained with less labour in the United States of America than in any European country.] In this respect, raw produce is essentially different from manufactures' (137; 1820, 197; 1836, 188). So powerful is the latter tendency that manufacturing prices in the 'richest' countries are generally lowest, despite the higher corn price and money wage rate: 'The real price of manufactures [1820: The cost of manufactures; 1836: The elementary cost of manufactures]; the quantity of labour and capital [1836: labour and other conditions of supply] necessary to produce a given quantity of them, is almost constantly diminishing [1820: has a constant tendency to diminish]; while the quantity of labour and capital [1836: labour and other conditions of supply] necessary to procure the last addition that has been made to the raw produce of a rich and advancing country, is almost constantly increasing [1820: has a constant tendency to increase]. We see in consequence, [1820: from the

14 To this passage is attached a note in 1815 alone asserting that (1) given capital and population (i.e., no growth) and assuming (2) *all land to be of the same quality*, the cost-pricing principle breaks down. (The intensive margin is here neglected.) But, even so, Malthus insisted that the usual case does entail a gradation of land qualities, and thus an upward-rising supply curve generating differential rents: 'It will be observed, that I have said in a *progressive country*: that is, in a country which requires yearly employment of a greater capital on the land, to support an increasing population. If there were no question about fresh capital, or an increase of people, and all the land were good, it would not then be true that corn must be sold at its necessary price. The actual price might be diminished; and if the rents of land were diminished in proportion, the cultivation might go on as before, and the same quantity be produced. It very rarely happens, however, that all the lands of a country actually occupied are good, and yield a good neat rent.'

combined operation of the two causes, which have been stated in this section,] that in spite of continued improvements in agriculture, the money price of corn is *ceteris paribus* [1820: the money price of corn is generally; 1836: the price of corn is generally] the highest in the richest countries, while in spite of this high price of corn, and consequent high price of labour [1836: while notwithstanding the high prices of corn and labour] the money price of manufactures still continues [1836: the prices of many manufactures still continue] lower than in poor countries' (137; 1820, 197; 1836, 188–9).[15]

Malthus closes with a criticism of Adam Smith for denying that high corn prices – Smith's index of a low value of the precious metals – are any indication of comparative national wealth: 'I cannot then agree with Adam Smith, in thinking that the low value of gold and silver is no proof of the wealth and flourishing state of the country, where it takes place. Nothing of course can be inferred from it, taken absolutely, except the abundance of the mines [1836: as such high prices may depend upon the abundance of the mines]; but taken relatively, or in comparison with the state of other countries, much may be inferred from it [1836: but taken relatively to other commodities and in comparison with the state of other countries at no great distance, and connected with each other, much may be inferred from it] ...' (137; 1820, 197–8; 1836, 189).[16] The 1815 essay remarks that it 'is not of course meant to be asserted, that the high price of raw pro-

15 The more elaborate version of the *Principles* is clearer if spelled out as follows: 'The cost of manufactures [1836: The elementary cost of manufactures]; the quantity of labour and capital [1836: labour and other conditions of supply] necessary to produce a given quantity of them, has a constant tendency to diminish; while the quantity of labour and capital [1836: labour and other conditions of supply] necessary to procure the last addition that has been made to the raw produce of a rich and advancing country, has a constant tendency to increase]. We see in consequence, from the combined operation of the two causes, which have been stated in this section, that in spite of continued improvements in agriculture, the money price of corn is generally [1836: the price of corn is generally] the highest in the richest countries, while in spite of this high price of corn, and consequent high price of labour [1836: while notwithstanding the high prices of corn and labour] the money price of manufactures still continues [1836: the prices of many manufactures still continue] lower than in poor countries' (1820, 197; 1836, 188–9).

16 The elaboration runs thus in the 1815 version: 'If we are to measure the value of the precious metals in different countries, and at different periods in the same country, by the price of corn and labour, which appears to me to be the nearest practical approximation that can be adopted (and in fact corn is the measure used by Adam Smith himself) it appears to me to follow, that in countries which have a frequent commercial intercourse with each other, which are nearly at the same distance from the mines, and are not essentially different in soil; there is no more certain sign, or more necessary consequence of superiority of wealth, than the low value of the precious metals, or the high price of raw produce.' The formulations of the *Principles* are similar. See also 134; 1820, 192–3; 1836, 184–5, for the charge that Smith failed to recognize rising real corn costs in a growing economy.

duce is, separately taken, advantageous to the consumer; but it is the necessary concomitant of superior and increasing wealth, and that one of these cannot be had without the other' (138).[17]

IV TWO CLASSES OF STATIONARY STATE

Two categories of stationariness emerge in the *Inquiry* (and later in the *Principles*): premature stationariness, and the end-point of a full-fledged growth process, the latter being of particular relevance for the argument to this point. An instance of the first appears early in the essay in a gloss on the regular model, and involves a case of zero net accumulation for various institutional and sociological reasons, notwithstanding the availability of good land. Here the decline in the corn wage is inevitable, its rapidity depending upon the degree of prudence practised. Ultimately the fall will be such as to bring population growth to a halt; and while the profit rate remains high, rents also rise, with the unavoidable fall in the wage: 'We observe ... that in all those countries, such as Poland, where, from the want of accumulation, the profits of stock remain high, and the progress of cultivation either proceeds very slowly, or is entirely stopped, the wages of labour are extremely low. And this cheapness of labour, by diminishing the expenses of cultivation, as far as labour is concerned, counteracts the effects of the high profits of stock, and generally leaves a larger rent to the landlord than in those countries, such as America, where, by a rapid accumulation of stock, which can still find advantageous employment, and a great demand for labour, which is accompanied by an adequate increase of produce and population, profits cannot be low, and labour for some considerable time remains very high' (1815b/1986, 7, 124). A similar case is taken up near the close of the pamphlet, as reinforcement for the proposition that a high corn price need not be detrimental to labour – rather, the contrary. Correspondingly, a *low* corn price need not be advantageous, should it lack a stimulus for expanding labour demand: 'instances every where abound of a very low money price of labour, totally failing to produce an increasing demand for it. And among the labouring classes of different countries, none certainly are so wretched as those, where the demand for labour, and the population are stationary, and yet the prices of provisions extremely low, compared with manufactures and foreign commodities. However low they may be, it is certain, that under such circumstances, no more will fall to the share of the labourer than is necessary just to maintain the actual population; and his condition will be depressed, not only by the stationary demand for labour, but by the

17 All this is relevant to a later claim by Malthus that he had priority over Ricardo for the analysis of the so-called cost of obtaining the precious metals (see below, chapter 14, pp. 714, 735).

additional evil of being able to command but a small portion of manufactures or foreign commodities, with the little surplus which he may possess' (139–40). In this account of a stationary economy, it is confirmed that growth of labour supply responds to the *corn* wage. Whether the precise confluence of circumstances does or does not permit the purchase of other wage goods is immaterial from the perspective of population growth.

Apart from cases of premature stagnation, there is also the stationary state in the usual sense of 'the ultimate check to the indefinite progress of a country in wealth and population,' for it is conceded that the rising corn price that results from diminishing returns has a limit. It is a matter of a reduced probability of 'future rapid progress' under conditions of high corn prices and correspondingly high money wages: 'At the same time it should be observed, that the high price of corn, occasioned by the difficulty of procuring it, may be considered as the ultimate check to the indefinite progress of a country in wealth and population. And, although the actual progress of countries be subject to great variations in their rate of movement, both from external and internal causes, and it would be rash to say that a state which is well peopled and proceeding rather slowly at present, may not proceed rapidly forty years hence; yet it must be owned, that the chances of a future rapid progress are diminished by the high price of corn and labour, compared with other countries' (140).[18] Unfortunately, there is little elaboration here of the actual path of the profit and real-wage rates.

V THE EFFECT OF EXOGENOUS INCREASE IN THE CORN PRICE

We turn now to an elaboration of the fourth 'cause' acting on rent – namely, 'such an increase in the price of agricultural produce, from increased demand, as, without nominally lowering the expense of production, will increase the difference between this expense and the price of produce' (above, p. 102). The analysis does not entail the growth model, as such, but is indirectly relevant to it, dealing in part with reversals of the downward trend of the agricultural profit rate as a result of pressures emanating in the *commercial and manufacturing sectors,* a major preoccupation of the correspondence of 1813–14 (see above, chapter 2).

The main issue is expressed thus in 1815 (and also in the *Principles*) and entails an increasing foreign demand for domestic corn: 'If a great and continued demand should arise among surrounding nations for the raw produce of a particular country, the price of this produce would of course rise considerably; and the expenses of cultivation rising only slowly and gradually to the same proportion, the price of produce might for a long time keep so much a head as to give a prodigious stimulus to improve-

18 In a letter of 1 October 1815, Malthus steps back: 'Surely with regard to money prices, we have attributed too much to difficulty of production' (see below, chapter 4, p. 142).

ment, and encourage the employment of much capital in bringing fresh land under cultivation, and rendering the old much more productive' (1815b/1986, 7, 126; cf. 1820, 167; 1836, 162–3).[19] A second case entails higher demand for corn, attributable, not to foreign purchases, but (indirectly) to the export of domestic manufactures: 'Nor would the effect be essentially different in a country which continued to feed its own people, if instead of a [foreign] demand for its raw produce, there was the same increasing demand for its manufactures. These manufactures, if from such a demand the value of their amount in foreign countries was greatly to increase, would bring back a great increase of value in return, which increase of value could not fail to increase the value of the raw produce. The demand for agricultural as well as manufactured produce would be augmented; and a considerable stimulus, though not perhaps to the same extent as in the last case, would be given to every kind of improvement on the land' (126; cf. 1820, 170; 1836, 166).

A stimulus to agriculture might originate in a prosperous manufacturing sector. In the case of new industrial technology and organization – 'the introduction of new machinery, and a more judicious division of labour in manufactures' – for 'not only that the quantity of manufactures is very greatly increased, but that the value of the whole mass is augmented, from the great extension of the demand for them both abroad and at home, occasioned by their cheapness. We see, in consequence, that in all rich manufacturing and commercial countries, the value of manufactured and commercial products bears a very high proportion to the raw products; whereas, in comparatively poor countries, without much internal trade and foreign commerce, the value of their raw produce constitutes almost the whole of their wealth' (126–7; cf. 1820, 170–1; 1836, 166–7).[20]

The effect on wages of the disturbance is then considered. A proportional rise of the money wage along with the corn price is said to be a 'very rare case' (127). But, even then, a lag in other of the farmer's outgoings ensures an increase in the price–costs differential: 'Even when the price of labour does really rise in proportion to the price of produce, which is a very rare case, and can only happen when the demand for labour precedes, or is at least quite contemporary with the demand for produce; it is so impossible that all the other outgoings in which capital is expended, should rise precisely in the same proportion, and at the same time, such

19 It is uncertain whether by 'expenses of cultivation' is intended real input, or money wages, or both. The last is probable.

20 A note here refers to Colquhoun: 'According to the calculations of Mr. Colquhoun, the value of our trade, foreign and domestic, and of our manufactures, exclusive of raw materials, is nearly equal to the gross value derived from the land. In no other large country probably is this the case. – Treatise on the Wealth, Power, and Resources of the British Empire, p. 96.' In 1815 Malthus added that 'the whole annual produce is estimated at about 430 millions, and the produce of agriculture at about 216 millions.'

as compositions [*sic*] for tithes, parish rates, taxes, manure, and the fixed capital accumulated under the former low prices, that a period of some continuance can scarcely fail to occur, when the difference between the price of produce and the cost of production is increased' (127; cf. 1820, 171–2; 1836, 167).

Even should the *immediate* effect of the disturbances be 'great temporary profits' (that had been the main concern of the correspondence), the ultimate – or permanent – effect is to increase rent (the main concern of the pamphlet). The formulation reads as follows in 1815, though the message is the same in all versions: 'In some of these cases, the increase in the price of agricultural produce, compared with the cost of the instruments of production, appears from what has been said to be only temporary and in these instances it will often give a considerable stimulus to cultivation, by an increase of agricultural profits, without shewing itself much in the shape of rent. It hardly ever fails, however, to increase rent ultimately. The increased capital, which is employed in consequence of the opportunity of making great temporary profits, can seldom or ever be entirely removed from the land, at the expiration of the current leases; and, on the renewal of these leases, the landlord feels the benefit of it in the increase of his rents.'

A summary formulation of the 'causes' playing on rent that follows confirms that the analysis of the war period did not entail the standard growth model involving increasing land scarcity, but rather the effects: (1) of new agricultural technology, and (2) of higher demand for corn emanating from an expanding manufacturing sector – so much insisted upon in the correspondence of 1813 with Ricardo (128; 1820, 173–4; 1836, 169; see below, chapter 15, p. 756).

VI REACTIONS BY RICARDO

During the first week of February 1815, Ricardo read Malthus's *Inquiry*. The theory of differential rent met with his approval: 'It is no praise to say that all the leading principles in it meet with my perfect assent' (6 February; 1951–73, VI, 172–4). Yet, while agreeing on broad principle, he pointed out certain applications of the theory that Malthus had failed to make, or about which Malthus had expressed uncertainty. Since 'rents are always withdrawn from the profits of stock' – are never a new creation – the importation of cheap foreign corn results in a social advantage measured by the price differential alone,[21] there being no need to correct, in Malthus's manner, for the loss of rents; the taxation of 'necessaries or raw

21 Cf. the *Essay on Profits* (1815): 'Would it be wise at a great expense to use some of the worst of these machines, when at a less expense we would hire the very best from our neighbours' (1951–73, IV, 34).

produce' cannot fall on the landlord, since 'the last portion of land cultivated, yields nothing more than the profits of stock'; land improvements (which raise output for a given outlay or reduce the outlay for a given output) will benefit the landlord only in so far as the farmer brings poorer land into cultivation but in themselves are advantageous only to the farmer.

Malthus had also neglected to consider 'the relations of rent with the profits of Stock and the wages of labour'; and 'by treating of the joint effect of the two latter on rent,' he had 'not made the subject so clear as it might have been.' In reply, Malthus explained that, had he proceeded by distinguishing profits and wages in their separate relationships with rent, he 'should have been too much detained by the question of profits about which we differ, and which certainly deserves a separate discussion' (12 February; 176). This response suggests that Malthus – despite the apparent adoption in the *Inquiry* of the Ricardian notion that the falling corn wage cannot insulate the profit rate (above, p. 99) – could not have been very confident of himself. The excuse must, in fact, colour the entire reading of the *Inquiry* as far as concerns profit-rate analysis.

Malthus held his ground, however, regarding the proposition that improvements in agricultural practice and equipment tend to raise rents; rents, though 'a part of the wealth already created,' were still a 'creation' of wealth (174–5). Here, appealing to recent Scottish experience, he had in mind the higher value of land owing to investments made during the preceding lease: 'when the machines [i.e., lands] were returned to their owners very much increased in value, it could hardly be said to be at the expense of the general profits of stock, which could not be much influenced by these particular instances confined to particular spots. Profits naturally find a level, and when the benefits of a particular employment of capital continue much greater than usual, either monopoly or rent must be concerned' (175).[22] Ricardo, for his part, insisted that the higher rents received by Scottish farmers arose 'not from improvements in agriculture, but from poorer land being taken into cultivation' (13 February; 177). Rents would increase from 'monopoly' pressure only in the event of an absolute inelasticity of land supply in the face of a rising demand; in the less extreme case, the corn price is determined by (marginal) costs. In all this Ricardo drew on Malthus's *Inquiry* itself, complaining of a failure to draw out the obvious implications of the differential-rent principle in usual cases: 'The effects of monopoly cannot I think be felt till no more land can

22 But concerning the effects of taxes on necessaries, he conceded some error: 'With regard to the tax *being thrown off* on the Landlord I did not certainly express myself as I meant' (176). Yet he also added that there were taxes which fell on land: 'I think however that there are often cases where taxes are thrown off on the landlord, and I meant to say that those which had not already been thrown off on the consumer would then be thrown off on the landlord.'

be advantageously cultivated. You have yourself said, and I very much admire the passage, that the last portion of capital employed on the land yields only the common profits of stock, and does not afford any rent. If so corn like every thing else is regulated in its price by the cost of production, and every other portion of capital employed on the land is reduced to the same level of profits only because no more capital can be employed with more advantage, and all which it any where yields more is rent and not profit' (177).[23]

VII SUMMARY AND CONCLUSION

We have isolated two perspectives in the *Inquiry* on the trend path of the profit rate, one agricultural, with the falling profit rate and corn-wage rate explained internally, the other entailing manufacturing as the lead sector, with the manufacturing rate falling under pressure of accumulation, carrying the agricultural rate with it by making possible expansion onto poorer land at a depressed profit rate. Conceivably Malthus intended a single model, the initial formulation constituting an incomplete statement designed as convenient summary of the global trends. The idea, emerging in the early correspondence, of agriculture as lead sector indirectly governing the manufacturing profit rate via population growth and demand is absent from the *Inquiry*. (The correspondence of 1815 and 1816, discussed in chapter 4, below, does, however, elaborate further on this matter.)

The analysis of trend in the *Inquiry* (in its simple or complex form) lacks a true price-theoretic structure. Yet we have also encountered an explanation of agricultural expansion from the perspective of demand, specifically a rising secular demand for corn in the face of an upward-sloping agricultural supply curve. But what are we to make of the emphasis placed on positively rising corn prices (and money wages) during the process of growth, considering the original statement (above, p. 100) which requires only that the (absolute) corn price does not decline? The original formulation entails a 'macro' level, of analysis, where rent emerges in consequence of *declining* corn costs in the sense of declining profit and wage rates; the alternative is more appropriate for the 'micro' level where relative prices are governed by relative costs in the sense of relative labour and capital coefficients, and where demand for corn comes into the picture as *independent* of supply, reflecting the idea of shifting demand in the face of rising supply price. Unfortunately, we have seen that even here – at least, in a gloss made in the *Principles* on one of the formulations of 1815 (above, p. 104) – the dependence of demand for corn on supply emerges.

23 See also a complaint in December 1818 that Malthus had abandoned the entire notion of no-rent output (below, chapter 4, pp. 170–1).

Setting aside this latter complexity, the two models might perhaps be said to reflect alternative perspectives of the *same* construct. There need be no conflict or inconsistency in one respect. For it would be quite in order to express the basic growth model in real or corn terms, and also to obtain many of the same results in terms involving relative values. But this relationship exists only in principle. It is difficult to avoid an impression that two unintegrated perspectives are involved in Malthus's formulations.[24]

24 Conceivably the duality reflects disparate times of composition (see above, p. 95).

FOUR

The Malthus–Ricardo correspondence, 1815–1819

I INTRODUCTION

We consider next the Malthus–Ricardo exchange immediately following the appearance of the latter's *Essay on Profits* (1815). In July 1814, it will be recalled, Malthus had proposed that agricultural protection and domestic expansion of farming may actually *stimulate* the profit rate. This linkage involves the contraction of manufacturing capital and output, which reverses the downward pressure of prices and profits, characterizing regular secular expansion, or Smithian 'competition of capital' (above, chapter 2: II). This sequence is absent from the *Inquiry on Rent*. But in the reaction to Ricardo's own *Essay*, a new case for a positive effect of agricultural expansion on the profit rate – it is shared with Torrens – is developed (section II, below). It turns on the increased *corn surplus* (in one modification, the increased *money surplus*), which, by creating increased purchasing power available for expenditure on manufactured goods, stimulates the general profit rate. As we show in section III, the downward profit rate characterizing regular expansion is said to occur under pressure of increasing *manufacturing* supply, and this *despite*, not because of, higher *relative* corn prices. Nevertheless, the notion of agriculture as 'lead' sector is shown, despite everything, to be implicit in the argument. As for agricultural expansion generated by higher foreign demand for domestic corn or agricultural protection – expansion which entails *absolute* increases in the corn price – the contention is that downward pressure on the profit rate would be avoided, though the corn wage must decline.

One other theme is developed in section III. The discovery of new land areas had been said in late 1814 to permit renewed or increased population growth, and consequently increased demand for manufactures (above, chapter 2, p. 93). This *indirect* effect of land-scarcity conditions on the profit rate, working by way of population growth and demand, is supplemented in the correspondence related to Ricardo's *Essay* by the notion that 'competition of capitals' in manufacturing would be relaxed by the transfer of capital to the new land. But again, throughout we find an implicit (perhaps unintended) allowance for a direct effect of agricultural productivity.

In section IV various advantages attributed to a high (relative) corn price are spelled out. As usual the contemporary Corn Laws are of prime relevance.

Section V traces Malthus's further formal attempts to undermine the Ricardian emphasis on agricultural productivity in the analysis of distribution. Malthus insisted, as in the correspondence of 1814, that the high profit rate coinciding with easy land-supply conditions at early stages of development reflected the fact that, at those stages, population growth, and therefore demand, was high relative to capital and commodity supply. But a direct effect seems at least implicit in the argument – why is population growth initially high if not because of the effect of a high profit rate on accumulation, and thus the corn wage? It is confirmed, too, that Malthus ascribed to secularly increasing land scarcity a negative effect on food supply, and thus on population, the latter constraining demand for manufactures and depressing the general profit rate. And again, a direct effect seems implicit, though Malthus declined to emphasize it.

The inverse wage–profit relation is elaborated in section VI. Here we encounter our old question of the ability of a falling corn wage to insulate the profit rate from decline. As we have seen, Ricardo has priority for the shared incidence of diminishing returns as early as December 1814 (above, chapter 2: IV); and Malthus was still not quite clear about this issue in the correspondence related to Ricardo's *Essay on Profits*, and this despite his own allowance in the *Inquiry into Rent* (above, chapter 3: II). But, by December 1815, he had apparently been persuaded, though there remain doubts regarding the role allowed market pressures in the secular decline of the real wage.

In section VII we attempt to isolate the source of the contrasting positions on the major issues addressed thus far. Section VIII concerns first reactions in correspondence to Ricardo's *Principles* on these same issues. A strong and, at first sight, definitive statement asserting that the profit rate depends 'entirely upon the competition of capital' and 'not on the state of the land' should not, we argue, be taken literally; it reflects the focus of attention on contemporary fluctuations of the profit rate.

In section IX we relate Malthus's struggles with the manuscript of his own *Principles*, especially with respect to the inverse wage–profit relation. In this context we find that a role is accorded increasing land scarcity in forcing down the corn wage (a process involving an upward trend in the corn price relative to a constant money wage). Unfortunately, the secular course of the agricultural profit rate is left unclear; we have only an allowance for a downward trend in the manufacturing rate. For all that, it is unlikely that Malthus denied the relevance of land scarcity in secular profit-rate analysis, especially considering the allowances in the *Principles* itself and the 1817 *Essay on Regulation* (see below, chapter 5). But what we have called the 'indirect' effects of increasing land scarcity operating on the manufacturing rate via deceleration of population growth and demand makes no appearance; this particular theme of the earlier correspondence had apparently been abandoned or forgotten.

A caution is in order: It is to be kept in mind that Ricardo and Malthus are presuming a world with a *commodity* money.

II AGRICULTURAL EXPANSION AND PROFIT-RATE INCREASE

At a meeting in London (see Malthus to Ricardo, 10 March 1815; in Ricardo, 1951–73, VI, 182), Malthus objected to the table in Ricardo's *Essay on Profits* for neglecting to consider that an increase in the corn price of manufactures reduces total production costs in *corn terms*, given the presence of manufactured goods within 'capital,' including its wages component. This perspective, involving a falling *corn* wage, pointed away from Ricardo's theory of profit-rate determination, and – so Malthus maintained – supported his own allowance for an effect on profits of *demand* considerations, in this case a rising demand for manufactures emanating from agriculture during the course of expansion: 'I confess I think that the kind of calculation which I mentioned to you in Town, shews in what manner profits on land may rise decidedly, from the alteration in the relative value of corn, and therefore shews that *general profits may be determined by the general supply of stock compared with the means of employing it, and not merely by the stock employed on the land.* Nor can I yet satisfy myself either from theory or experience that profits depend solely on the price of corn. I am struck by your persevering conviction, but I cannot see the subject in the same light; and it appears to me that experience is clearly against it' (10 March; 182–3, emphasis added). Again: 'Pray think once more on the effect of a rise in the relative price of corn, upon the whole surplus derived from land already in cultivation. It appears to me I confess, as clear as possible that it must be increased. The expenses estimated in Corn will be less, owing to the power of purchasing with a less quantity of corn, the same quantity of fixed capital, and of the circulating capital of tea, sugar, clothes &c: for the labourers; *and consequently more clear surplus will remain in the shape of rent and profits together, (no matter which) for home demand.* Pray tell me whether any objection to this strikes you ... Let me know as soon as you can, your opinion on the effects of a rise in the relative value of corn, *upon rents and profits united*' (12 March; 185–6; emphasis added).[1] In a letter to Francis Horner the issue is spelled out further: 'On the supposition which

1 Malthus does not specify *why* the relative price of corn rises, though, if he was keeping to Ricardo's framework in the *Essay*, it would presumably reflect diminishing returns.

is generally allowed, that in a rich and progressive country, corn naturally rises compared with manufactured and foreign commodities, will it not follow that, as the real capital of the farmer which is advanced does not consist merely in raw produce, but in ploughs, wagons, threshing machines &c: and in the tea, sugar, clothes &c: &c: used by his labourers, if with a less quantity of raw produce he can purchase the same quantity of these commodities, *a greater quantity of raw produce will remain for the farmer and landlord, and afford a greater surplus from the land for the maintainance and encouragement of the manufacturing and mercantile classes* ... Out of this increased produce the farmer will either receive proportionably increased profits, or will divide them with the landlord and thus a rise in the price of corn appears to increase the productiveness of all the capital previously employed on the land' (14 March; 187, emphasis added).[2] Malthus reiterated that the matter had profound implications for the source of rising aggregate demand for manufactures: 'This proposition appears to me to involve consequences so very important with regard to home demand, that I should like much to know whether you see any error in the premises or conclusion.' Had Ricardo worked in terms of 'the actual materials of which capital consists' or in money terms, rather than corn, he would have been led to recognize the impact of a *relative* rise in the price of corn (187–8).[3]

2 Illustrative data are drawn from physiocratic literature, and probably these data reflect the sort of calculation mentioned to Ricardo at their London meeting: 'The Economists calculate that one third of the raw produce obtained by the farmer is advanced to the sterile classes. On this supposition let the produce of an acre be represented by 8 of which $\frac{1}{4}$ goes to the landlord, and $\frac{3}{4}$ are received by the farmer, that is, 2 go to the landlord, and 6 to the farmer, out of which latter sum the farmer expends one third or 2 in the commodities above mentioned. The farmer therefore retains 4 for his raw produce-expenditure, and profits; that is, he retains the value of the half of the gross produce. Let us now suppose the price of corn to double, while the price of manufactured and foreign commodities rises only one fourth. The whole produce will then be represented by 16 of which $\frac{1}{4}$, as before, or 4, go to the land and only $2\frac{1}{2}$ instead of 4 go to the expenditure in manufactured and foreign commodities; the consequence of which will be, that $9\frac{1}{2}$ out of 16 will remain to the farmer instead of 4 out of 8, that is about $\frac{3}{5}$ instead of $\frac{1}{2}$.'

Torrens, in his *Essay on the External Corn Trade*, which also appeared in February 1815, had argued similarly that, following an increase in the corn price, 'the farmer and the landowner receiving a greater sum of the produce of their ground will have a greater sum to give for other articles. The money demand for other commodities being thus increased the capitalist will be indemnified by increased money price for the increased money wages which the rise in corn obliged him to advance' (1815, 82).

3 Ricardo conceded that the consequences of a rise in the corn price, as such, would indeed be reduced total costs in corn terms, and consequently an increase in the corn surplus and in the corn rate of surplus: 'I cannot hesitate in agreeing with you that if from a rise in the relative value of corn less is paid [in terms of corn] for fixed capital and wages, – more of the produce must remain for the landlord and farmer together, – this is indeed self-evident, but is really not the matter in dispute between us' (14 March; 189). Beyond this allowance he refused to go, given the cost determination of prices: 'If no more labourers were employed and the price of corn rose your proposi-

The effect of agricultural expansion on the demand for manufactures and the profit rate in manufacturing arises from higher agricultural *rent and profit combined.* But it is implicit in the argument that the rise in the manufacturing rate would carry the agricultural rate with it since there cannot be two profit rates in the system (see also below, p. 124). (The text of the letter of 10 March itself suggests this: 'General profits may be determined by the general supply of stock compared with the means of employing it, and not merely by the stock employed on the land.') If this is so, the agricultural profit rate would be *insulated* from secular decline despite recourse to poorer land. Indeed, such recourse, by depressing corn costs, including the corn wage, actually puts *upward pressure* on the profit rate.

In his next letter Malthus hit upon Ricardo's failure to emphasize *marginal* costs: 'You seem to forget what I think you had formerly allowed, that it is only the last 500,000 quarters of corn that have been added to the mass, which require for their production a greater quantity of capital' (15 March; 190–1). On intramarginal output, since real costs do not rise, the corn surplus necessarily grows: 'You distinctly allow that if no more labour and capital be employed, the productive power of that labour and capital, or the surplus of rents and profits, will increase, owing to an increase in the relative price of corn. Consequently when a rise in the price of corn takes place from an increasing population, or restrictions upon importation, all the capital previously employed upon the land will become more productive, and it is only the new capital that will be less so; that is you will have the capital which produces the previous ten millions of quarters of wheat, yield a greater material surplus, while it is only the last additions to the mass which require more labour' (191). And here the implication of all this for his own version of profit-rate determination is again spelled out; *the higher agricultural surplus provides the source for increased expenditure on*

---

tion could not be disputed, but the cause of the rise of the price of corn is solely on account of the increased expence of production.' Accordingly, he rejected Malthus's contentions, since any such rise in the price of corn necessarily implied an increase in total labour and fixed capital costs (in terms of corn) relative to the absolute increase in the surplus; and he insisted again on the falling profit rate: 'You will see by what I have said that a rise in the price of corn is always in my opinion accompanied by a less material surplus produce, but it may be of equal value as compared with other things. Of this produce the landlord gets so large a share that in spite of the rise of produce the situation of the farmer is constantly getting worse' (190).

Ricardo's position is formally consistent with the tabular formulation of his *Essay*, according to which – despite an increase in the corn surplus or 'total produce in quarters of wheat, after paying the cost of production' – the ratio of the corn surplus to corn costs declines steadily (1951–73, IV, 17).

Ricardo, in his letter, accepted Malthus's contention that the *corn wage rate* declines during secular expansion: 'Observe that I do not question that each individual labourer might receive a less corn price of labour because I believe that would be the case' (VI, 189).

manufactures: 'Under these circumstances it is quite clear to me that a rise in the relative value of corn, will occasion the whole mass of corn to be raised at a less corn-expenditure; and consequently will leave a larger surplus for the maintenance and encouragement of the mercantile and manufacturing classes. This, if true, is a most important principle and deserves to be thoroughly considered.'

In an amplification of his argument, Malthus focused on the *motive* for agricultural expansion. In Ricardo's table, on his reading, extensions to poorer land were the consequence of a falling profit rate. In such a case, he pointed out, *there would be no rise at all in the corn price.*[4] The experience of the preceding two decades suggested to him an alternative sequence: 'Observe, that, if poor land be brought under cultivation merely by the fall of profits as in your table [1951–73, IV, 17], this effect of course will not follow, and in this case indeed corn will not necessarily rise, although there will be a rise of rent. But if poor land be brought under cultivation by a rise of prices as has been the case during the last 20 years, it appears to me that the whole capital on the land must have become more and more productive. This seems to be confirmed by the circumstance of a much smaller proportion of the population being employed on the land than formerly. Pray tell me where you think I am wrong. The conclusion half startles me. If I am right it will establish the effect of the high price of corn on home demand' (191–2). The higher price of corn to which Malthus here refers thus reflects the *increased demand for corn* emanating from expanded commerce and manufactures so much emphasized in the 1814 correspondence in discussion of the same two decades, 1793–1814. It is the *playback* such a corn-price increase exerts – by raising agricultural 'productivity' (the corn surplus), and consequently the 'home demand' for manufactures – that he found so new and 'startling.'[5]

4 The rationale presumably reflects the position that the profit rate constitutes a cost item, and its decline roughly cancels the effect of reduced marginal productivity.

5 Malthus's perspective seemed paradoxical to Ricardo. It implied that, notwithstanding diminishing returns, population expansion generated a *rising* ratio of corn output to corn expenses or, alternatively expressed, that despite diminishing (average) returns, and a rising corn price in consequence, the ratio of corn output to corn input increases: 'If this be true the principle of population is false, because the more you increase the people the greater surplus of abundance will appear' (17 March; 192). In all this Ricardo continues to argue in terms of average-cost pricing, relying on the proposition that diminishing returns ensure that average costs *must* increase. Indeed, while 'it is only the last portion of capital employed on the land which will be attended with an increased corn expence ... unless it renders the whole produce together at an increased expence the price of produce will not rise' (193). He did not question Malthus's ascription of expansion to marginal land in the table to a lower profit rate, but asserted that such expansion none the less necessarily entails a higher cost price of corn, such increase ensuring (via the money wage) a general fall in the profit rate – the celebrated inverse wage–profit relation: 'It can never happen I think that profits can fall, and encourage the cultivation of poor land in the manner assumed in my table, without a

Malthus's letter of 19 March elaborates further on the supposedly stimulatory effect of agricultural expansion. It insisted first on something akin to true marginal additions: 'What would be the real process. Not such a jump as from ten million to fifteen [quarters of corn]; but from ten million to ten million and a half' (195). Ongoing population growth (or protection) raises the demand and price of corn, given the initial supply,[6] reducing the per-capita corn wage. It is this corn-wage reduction[7] that allows a larger corn surplus, which is available 'for the maintenance and encouragement of the manufacturing classes': 'And I maintain that if half a million more quarters of corn were wanting either from the natural increase of population, or from restrictions upon importation, that the effect would be first a rise of price, which rise of price would increase the productiveness of all the capital previously employed, and awarding only 14 bushels instead of two quarters to precisely the same number of men would leave a greater portion of the ten millions of quarters for the maintenance and encouragement of the manufacturing classes.'

Malthus's case is not limited to a short-run or intermediate effect on the corn surplus of a reduced corn wage owing to the higher *demand-induced* corn price. The reduction of the corn wage, he proceeds, stimulates agricultural expansion. But even following such expansion and taking account of the higher real costs of marginal output, there will still be a *net* expansion of the corn surplus because of the relative smallness of the additional output compared with intramarginal units: 'In the mean time this increased cheapness in the instruments of production would occasion more poor land to be brought under cultivation, and more men to be employed upon the land; but still so as to leave a larger surplus for the manufacturing and mercantile classes, as it is impossible to suppose that the increased corn expences upon the new land should equal the diminished corn expences upon the old land.' To emphasize that a higher corn surplus remains on *intra*marginal lands, the principle of *marginal*-cost pricing is reiterated: 'The natural price of corn depends entirely upon the

rise in the price of corn' (194). Again, the inverse wage–profit relation in terms of the money wage is formulated: 'It is by the rise of the price of corn that all other profits are regulated to agricultural profits. If the price of corn remained low money wages would not rise and general profits could not fall.' Finally, Ricardo could not fathom Malthus's appeal to empirical evidence of higher agricultural productivity: 'If it be true that capital has become more and more productive on the land, it can I think only be accounted for on the supposition that great improvements have taken place in agriculture, and that wages have been kept moderate by the improvements in those manufactures which supply the poor with the necessaries on which a part of their wages are expended.' Only true technical progress could account for the supposed phenomenon.

6 The higher demand for corn thus need not reflect an initial expansion of manufactures and commerce such as was envisaged earlier.

7 From the earlier letters, we may suppose a corresponding reduction in other constituents of capital measured in corn.

price of the last additions, and it does not matter whether with regard to the old land, a capital yields 50 per cent (rent and profit together) or 20 per cent. In either case the price of corn on such land has nothing to do with the cost of production.' The letter closes with a rejection of Ricardo's contention (see above, note 5) that his position undermined the population principle: 'I am not alarmed at what you say about the principle of population, as I can conceive that the addition of another labourer on the land would not pay his expences, although not more than $\frac{1}{4}$ of the population were employed upon the land. No pressure can destroy rents. This you know is what I have always maintained' (195–6). The rising corn surplus or higher agricultural productivity did not, in brief, imply the absence of an equilibrium position, as Ricardo implied.

Ricardo reacted strongly. He allowed a rising absolute corn surplus – rent and profits combined – but he again denied that this surplus rises relative to corn costs, for this would imply *increasing* returns and undermine the population principle: 'If this be true there is no check to the increase of population, and food can be increased in a ratio exceeding that at which mankind increase' (21 March; 196–7). Ricardo's challenge proved effective. Malthus was obliged to modify his formulation in his reply of 24 March. Before coming to the modification, he insisted on specifying the limits to his 'principle': 'I think you push my principle much too far; and do not recollect the limitations to which it must necessarily be subject' (199). The corn/manufactures price ratio (P_c/P_m) lagged behind the corn-price increase because manufacturing prices also rose to some extent: 'All depends upon the relation between corn and other commodities, and as labour and corn enter into the price of all commodities, the difference between corn and other commodities cannot possibly increase in any proportion to the increase in the money price of corn.'[8] The constrained rise in the relative price of corn nevertheless altered the *distribution* of the corn output 'on the old land'; and since it did not raise aggregate food supplies from that land, there was no conflict with the population principle: 'There is no more food produced, on the old land. It is only that there is a difference in the distribution of it, and a larger share of the raw produce remains for profit and rent, chiefly of course the latter. Before, – the farmer to pay his money wages and purchase his fixed capital, was obliged to sell more corn: – Now, he can do this with less, and will have

8 Malthus emphasized an equilibrating process which diminishes the price differential: 'It is of course quite impossible to suppose that the relative value of corn to other commodities can continue regularly increasing in proportion to any additional number of men which we may chose to suppose employed upon the land. There will be in fact a constant reaction to prevent such increasing difference. The increased profits of agriculture [he refers to total surplus], and diminished profits of other employments will increase the quantity of raw produce compared with other commodities, and this joined to the increased money price of corn, will be continually raising the money price of commodities, and bring them again nearer to a level' (200).

a larger remainder, but the same quantity of corn, neither more nor less, is distributed to the public, and as we dont suppose the people to live worse, precisely the same number are supported from the old land.'

Malthus's restatement, however, entailed a major modification to the original formulations. His discovery no longer turned on a higher *physical*, but rather on a higher *money*, surplus from the 'old land' area: 'I have been wrong however in supposing as I did at one time that a greater *quantity* of raw produce would be set free from the old land for the use and encouragement of the manufacturing and mercantile classes. While the same number of men are employed on the old land without a greater production, and living as well, this cannot be the case' (201; emphasis added).[9] We set out the argument. First, we have the admitted effect on productivity – in corn terms – of diminishing returns with population expansion and increased demand: 'On the new land brought into cultivation in consequence of [increasing] demand, more men are employed in proportion to the quantity of corn produced, and as the same number of men as before are employed to obtain the old produce, there will be a greater number of men employed in proportion to the whole produce' (200). None the less, 'if the new produce be inconsiderable compared with the old, it appears to me quite certain that the increased corn expenditure of the former will be more than counterbalanced, by the diminished corn expenditure of the latter; and owing to the increased value of corn, *the whole money cost of production on the land will bear a less proportion to the money value of the whole produce.* On the other hand, if the new produce is so large, as to require 2 millions of labourers to obtain it, the increased corn expenditure owing to the additional number of persons employed, will more than counterbalance the diminished corn expenditure arising from the increased relative value of corn' (emphasis added).[10]

Taking for granted expansion of output on new land – and working in money terms – Malthus proceeded to reiterate the stimulus afforded demand for manufactures. This increased demand acts to counteract

9 It emerges later in the same letter that the supposition that people do not 'live worse' or live 'as well' does not imply *a given corn wage*, for the corn wage actually declines – reflecting an increased corn price and given money wage; it must then refer to a given fixed-proportions commodity wage: 'I think further that the increased price of corn is in the order of things rather a cause than a consequence of more men being employed. The price rises first from increased demand, and this rise, by increasing the value of produce compared with the instruments of production determines what poor lands can be cultivated. *No greater number of men can be employed at the same [money] wages till the [corn] price rises*' (200–1; emphasis added). But this is difficult to reconcile with the *denial* of a higher physical (corn) surplus on the 'old' land.

10 This exposition still fails to clarify the effect of any fall in the corn price from its intermediate (high) level to its lower long-run cost level – the latter higher, of course, than the starting price.

downward pressures on manufacturing profits.[11] The net result is striking – rising general profits along with a rising corn price, albeit not likely 'of long continuance': 'In fact, while that capital the produce of which relatively rises in value becomes more productive [agriculture], those capitals the produce of which relatively falls in value will become less productive, or yield less profits. But then the greatly increased *money* value of the corn in the country arising both from its increased quantity and increased price cannot fail to occasion such an increased demand for manufactured and foreign products as to encourage the growth of them and to render improvements in machinery particularly advantageous. *Under such circumstances general profits may rise with rising prices of corn, and fall with falling prices, as we find from experience, though such periods are not likely to be of long continuance*' (201; emphasis added). Malthus closed by expressing his own surprise at the result, which he conceded still needed deeper thought: 'The subject is very curious, and the principle when properly matured will I think throw some light on it.'

Ricardo complained in reply that his correspondent made too cavalier a transfer from a proposition regarding an increasing ratio of *corn* surplus to *corn* costs to a very different proposition regarding an increasing *money* surplus relative to *money* costs. The latter proposition alone was acceptable since, allowance made for rent, the profit rate might still decline; but the ratio of *corn* surplus to *corn* costs must necessarily decline in consequence of diminishing returns (27 March; 204).[12]

Malthus's response of 2 April is confusing. He had expressly conceded on 24 March an error in originally supposing 'that a greater quantity of raw produce would be set free *from the old land* for the rise and encouragement' of manufacturing. Yet, in his new reply, he seems to step back from this

11 Presumably these include the increasing P_c/P_m ratio; and also perhaps increasing 'competition of capitals.'

12 Ricardo agreed that the increase in P_c/P_m with extensions to marginal land alters the 'distribution of the produce from the old land,' but arrived at a very different conclusion from Malthus's. For the increase in P_c/P_m forces manufacturing profits *down*, which – apparently assuming that the agricultural profit rate falls *pari passu* – generates rising rents in agriculture: 'I agree with you that a rise in the price of corn occasions a different distribution of the produce from the old land. It does this by lowering profits. Instead of a manufacturer having it in his power to maintain a servant or mechanic who may contribute to his enjoyment, that power will be transferred to the landlord and this will arise from the lower corn value of manufactured goods. Indeed I see no limit to the fall of the corn value of goods but the impossibility of manufacturing them with any the least return of profit, and this will not happen till the landlord has appropriated to himself in the form of rent nearly the whole surplus produce of the land. It appears to me that the progress of wealth, whilst it encourages accumulation, has a natural tendency to produce this effect and is as certain as the principle of gravitation' (203–4). The problem here is that the process of profit-rate decline is said to work via the rise in P_c/P_m (the manufacturing profit rate governing the agricultural rate), not via the money-wage rate, as Ricardo had argued on 17 March (194), and indeed proceeds to argue again even in the present letter of 27 March (204–5).

position. *He also restates his case in corn terms,* again seemingly reneging on his earlier modified formulation. In this reformulation the declining corn wage (now expressed per family) remains conspicuous: 'You understood my proposition as going farther than I intended, at first; and now perhaps not quite far enough. Although I suppose no more corn to be produced by the same number of labourers on the old land, and no less corn actually to be consumed by them, yet I still think the corn expences are diminished compared with the corn profits. Each family on the land instead of receiving 8 quarters a year receives now only 7. In both cases it actually consumes 4, and spends the remainder in manufactures and foreign commodities. In the latter case, owing to the increased relative value of corn, the remainder 3 is as effectual as 4 was before. And not only a greater money value, but a greater quantity of raw produce will remain to the farmer and landlord' (207). On this version, too, the consequences for profit-rate theory were profound. *Increased demand for manufactures can reverse the downward trend in the manufacturing profit rate otherwise expected with accumulation.*

The reformulation commences by pointing out that the increase in corn surplus creates a *potential* for a higher agricultural rate – 'ample room for an increase of profits upon the land' – which might be prevented by the fall in the profit rate in manufactures, implying that this fall dictates the breakdown of the surplus between rent and profits presumably because there cannot be two profit rates in the system (above, p. 118). This showed manufacturing to be the lead sector as far as concerns the profit rate: 'I own I think it affects your theory essentially; because it shews that there is ample room for an increase of profits upon the land; and if this increase of profit be prevented from taking place, it can only be owing to the diminished profits in manufactures, and *consequently it would appear that manufacturing profits determined the profits upon the land, and not the profits upon the land, manufacturing profits*' (emphasis added). The apparent discovery that any fall in the manufacturing profit rate might itself be prevented by the higher demand emanating from agriculture, implied – though this is left unstated – prevention of a fall in the *agricultural* rate: 'I cannot however help thinking that the increasing demand for manufactured commodities must prevent the profits upon them from falling for any length of time. If five coats be now necessary to purchase the same quantity of corn as could be purchased formerly by four, will it not to a certainty follow, that the whole quantity of corn in the country will exchange for a greater number of coats than before; and consequently that there will be both the power and will to purchase with the raw produce of the country, a greater quantity of manufactured and foreign commodities' (207–8). Malthus could not hide his enthusiasm: 'This is a most important and vital question as it appears to me, and I wish you to give me your opinion upon it.' And conversely: 'If the value of the whole raw produce falls compared with manufactured and foreign produce does not such fall necessarily involve a diminution of demand for manufactured and foreign produce?'

Ricardo's contention (above, note 12) that there was 'no limit' to the fall in the command of manufactures over corn short of the manufacturing profit rate reaching its minimum, Malthus denied on the grounds stated earlier (above, p. 121), that the relative corn/manufacturing price could not diverge too far, considering that corn and labour entered into manufacturing costs: 'Surely you don't seem to be sufficiently aware of the necessary limits to the separation in the price of manufactured commodities and raw produce' (208). He further objected that, since wage costs relating to the *last* man employed cannot exceed the 'value' of marginal output, it was illegitimate to presume *arbitrarily* any degree of falling productivity: 'If 400 yards of cloth require ten persons to produce them, and a hundred quarters of corn (last added) require ten persons, each at a profit of ten per cent (the last of course without rent) is it physically possible that the labour employed in producing the 100 quarters of corn should be increased so much as one third, while the people continue to eat the same quantity of corn as before. Of course I presume that no person will employ an additional labourer upon his land, whose wages are more than the value of what he adds to the former produce. Upon this supposition which is unquestionably the true one, when the profits on land are only ten per cent and no rent, the limits to the number of persons which can be employed with advantage on the land are a good deal confined. And such suppositions as you made in a former letter are not admissible. We cannot say for instance "Suppose now the 100 quarters of corn in the progress of society to require for their production 25 men instead of ten." The thing is physically impossible consistently with giving the labourers the same quantity of food, which we have all along taken for granted.'[13]

* * *

Ricardo concentrated in his reply on Malthus's notion that an increase in the corn surplus on old land (in real and money terms), acting on the demand for manufactures, threatened the declining profit-rate theorem involving extensions to marginal land: 'You think that my theory of a diminishing rate of profit, in consequence of being obliged to cultivate poorer lands, is affected by my admission that there will be a greater quantity of surplus produce and a greater money value from the old land' (4 April; 209).[14] He responded with two arguments. First, Malthus had failed to distinguish between rent and profits: 'This would be true, if any part of either the additional quantity or additional value, belonged to the owner of stock. You however expressly say that this additional value or

13 As remarked earlier (note 9) Malthus assumes (and now also attributes to Ricardo) a *constant* fixed-proportions wage basket. The *corn wage declines*, though labourers obtain 'the same quantity of food.'

14 For Ricardo's agreement – indeed, insistence – that the *absolute* corn surplus rises on old land with extensions, see VI, 196–7 (cited above, p. 121). He denied the proposition that the *ratio* of surplus to costs rises.

quantity "will remain to the farmer and landlord" [207]. Before my theory is affected it must be shewn that the whole will not remain with the landlord, as if the farmer gets no share of it his rate of profits cannot be raised.' Now in fact, Malthus had distinguished rent and profit in agriculture when he asserted an increase in the agricultural profit rate in line with that in manufacturing.

Second – here Ricardo reverted to the Law of Markets – the fact that an increase in P_c/P_m assured 'both the power and will to purchase with the raw produce of the country, a greater quantity of manufactured and foreign commodities' (Malthus, 208), was irrelevant for the profit rate. Expansion would proceed with a continuously rising P_c/P_m accompanied by rising demand for manufactures and yet with a *declining* profit rate because of increasing land scarcity. This formulation reflects nicely the essential contrast in perspective – Ricardo's consistent appeal to land scarcity in contrast to Malthus's attempt to allow for *two* forces and devise a model to define their relationship.

Ricardo next pointed out that Malthus's case was self-contradictory; the fall in the corn wage, taken for granted thus far, was ruled out by Malthus's acceptance of the (Smithian) view that manufacturing prices (including those of manufactured wage goods) rise with the corn price: 'You, I think, agree with Mr. Torrens that a rise in the price of corn will be followed by a rise in the price of home commodities; – but your theory requires that there should be no rise in the price of those commodities on which the wages of labour are expended, for if they rose in the same proportion as corn, there could be no fall in the corn wages of labour. Is it not however very improbable that all manufactures should rise at home and yet that those on which labour [the wages of] are expended should not rise? Is not the price of soap, candles &c.[a], though foreign commodities, necessarily affected by the rise in the price of those home goods which are given in exchange for them' (17 April; 212–13). Ricardo himself dismissed the whole case. As in his later *Principles*, manufacturing prices rise slightly, and only to compensate for any increase in raw materials' costs (cf. 9 March; 179). The higher corn price, therefore, necessarily depresses manufacturing profits by forcing money costs up relative to money revenue; and the agricultural rate had to keep in line: 'Mr. Torrens theory however on this part of the subject appears to me defective, as I think that the price of commodities will be very slightly affected either by a rise or fall in the price of corn. If so every rise in the price of corn must affect profits on manufactures, and it is impossible that agricultural profits can materially deviate from them' (213).[15] He closed on a note of evident frustration: 'The whole appears to me a labyrinth of difficulties ... Let me intreat you to give

15 He also objected: 'Your theory supposes too what is impossible that the demand for manufactures will increase in the same proportion as the demand for corn at the very time that more men are employed on the land to obtain a less proportion of produce' (214).

my simple doctrine fair consideration, and you must allow that it accounts for all the phenomena in an easy, natural manner.'

Malthus replied on 18 April, again charging Ricardo with arbitrariness in his specific illustration.[16] There is some justification for the charge, but the correspondents were evidently talking past each other. For Ricardo the higher corn price reflects higher *costs*, presupposing a specific labour requirement on land to produce an additional 80 quarters, rather than (as Malthus has it) a higher demand price for the original quantity; and, for Ricardo, it is these higher costs which govern the general profit rate via the money wage, whereas, *for Malthus, the profit rate determined outside the agricultural sector, governs – as he now explains – the extent of any increase of labour on land*: 'Do you not perceive that the conclusion you have drawn from your calculation depends entirely upon the arbitrary assumption that the next portion of land taken into cultivation will require $8\frac{1}{2}$ men to produce 80 quarters of corn ... I suppose in this case the rise in the price of corn to be occasioned by demand, and to be its market price. What additional quantity of labour will be employed on new land will depend entirely upon circumstances – upon the causes which determine the general rate [of] profits' (18 April; 216).

Agricultural extensions are here said to be governed by the *general return on capital*, whereas in the previous month they had been attributed to a *falling corn wage* resulting from increased, demand-determined, corn prices (above, note 9; also p. 120). Possibly these can be reconciled. An expansion may be induced by the initial rise in the corn price, or fall in the corn wage; but exactly how far it goes depends on the general profit rate.

As is usual for him, Malthus also insists on true *marginal* extensions. The ellipses in the passage just quotes refer to Ricardo's new table, Malthus questioning the extent of the profit-rate decline with agricultural extension supposed by Ricardo, and even hints at the possibility of an increase: 'But as you have distinctly allowed that, on account of the rise of price occasioned by demand, from £4 to £4.10s, the profits on the old land will rise from 25 to 32 per cent, surely there is land that may be brought into cultivation at all the intermediate gradations of profit from 32 per cent to 25, and 19.7 and nothing can be so improbable as that if the last land yielded 32 the next taken into cultivation should yield only 19.7.'[17] If – and when – the notion of a higher surplus and higher demand for manufactures with secular expansion was abandoned remains an open question.

16 Ricardo had meanwhile devised a fresh arithmetic illustration to justify the proposition in the letter of 27 March 1815, 204 (above, p. 123).

17 *Temporarily* the profit rate rises from 25 to 32 per cent; but if new land can be brought in at some rate above 25 per cent, the final result itself will entail an actual *increase* in the profit rate.

III AN EVALUATION OF THE *ESSAY ON PROFITS*

Apart from the foregoing reaction to Ricardo's specific illustration, there is a general evaluation of the *Essay on Profits* itself. Malthus commended the model as such, but criticized its application to cases not covered by its assumptions: 'I think your theory simple just and consistent as far as it goes; but I think you wrong in the application of it, that is, you expect similar results when the premises are essentially different' (18 April; 216). Alternative causes of rising P_c/P_m are distinguished in the elaboration that follows.

1 / P_c/P_m rises with *a declining absolute* P_m, the latter associated with the falling profit rate *in the manufacturing sector* presumed to accompany capital accumulation. (Here it is accumulation, as such, that depresses the profit rate, not *excessive* accumulation; contrast above, chapter 3: II). This rise in the *relative* corn price was not the cause of a falling profit rate; on the contrary, it 'tended' to raise it, though this counteracting force was swamped: 'The source of this error, as it appears to me, is, that because a relative rise in the price of corn (or rather perhaps fall in the price of manufactures) always accompanies an accumulation of stock and fall of profits, you assume such rise in the price of corn as the *cause* when in fact the whole operation of this rise as far as relates to the land, goes the other way, and tends to raise rather than to lower profits, although of course when the rise is absolutely occasioned by the fall of profits, such fall must overcome the tendency, and all the advantage derived from it will go, as you justly observe to the Landlord' (216–17). Though Malthus neglected to specify *how* a rise in the relative corn price tends to raise the profit rate, he probably intended the earlier notion, whereby such rise increases the agricultural surplus, and therefore the demand for and prices of manufactures. This positive effect on the profit rate is swamped, evidently because the P_c/P_m increase now assumed entails a *fall* in manufacturing prices and profit rate. The latter dictates the fall in the agricultural rate, so that the increased surplus is to the advantage of the *landlords*.

This analysis seems to accord the manufacturing profit rate precedence in the growth process. Yet this impression is belied by an application of the argument – in reverse, so to speak – to Ricardo's table. The *high* profit rate at early stages of the growth process reflected, Malthus argued, a small degree of competition of capital, especially in the manufacturing sector, manifested in high absolute manufacturing prices; *the low relative corn price* considered in itself tends to *lower* the profit rate, although this is swamped by the reverse force: 'Now the error you appear to me to fall into is, that, of applying your neat simple and ingenious table to a state of things not contemplated in it, and to which it does not apply. The high profits of stock which appear in the early periods of your table are owing, not to the low relative price of corn (which in fact has a contrary tendency) but to the small quantity of capital in the country compared with the means of employing it, and *particularly to the small quantity of capital employed in manufactures, which unless furnished very sparingly could never bring such high profits as could be obtained from the land*' (217; emphasis added). The reference in the closing sentence to an initially high agricultural profit rate with which the manufacturing rate must coincide suggests that the role of prime mover is after all played by agriculture, though unfortunately the 'high profits as could be obtained from the land' are not explicitly accounted for.[18]

2 / There is also a rise in P_c/P_m with an *absolute increase in* P_c *resulting from increased demand for corn*, such increase stimulating agricultural expansion *without putting downward secular pressure on the profit rate*: 'But there are other causes of a relative rise in the price of corn besides the fall of profits, such as a foreign demand for it, a greater home demand occasioned by restrictions on importation, and a prosperous foreign trade, by which we can at once import a great abundance and a great value of foreign commodities. These are causes (particularly the two former) of a rise in the relative price of corn in no respect necessarily connected with a fall of profits, and under the influence of these causes fresh land may be taken into cultivation, at various profits (to refer to your instance) from 32 to 26 [*sic*] per cent.' The manufacturing rate would in this case rise, with higher demand presumably emanating in the buoyant agricultural sector: 'With regard to manufactures in this case, if they did not rise immediately from increased demand, some of the capital vested in them would go to the land till the level was restored.' This is the phenomenon that so much excited Malthus earlier in his letter. It confirms the position that the profit rate does not tend downwards with agricultural expansion, *when such expansion is induced by an initial (absolute) rise in the corn price (or fall in the corn wage)*.[19]

That an increased market price of corn resulting from, say, agricultural protection or other sources of higher demand for domestic produce can, by raising P_c/P_m, allow expansion to poorer land *without depressing – even increasing – the profit rate* is, of course, a supremely important contention, considering the contemporary Corn Law debate (see also above, chapter 2: II). The position that ongoing agricultural accumulation, when attributable to an initial demand increase, can proceed with a constant profit rate, though with the corn wage declining (the decline implicit in the absolute increase in the corn price),[20] confirms what had emerged much earlier: 'The diminution of wages is a more directly necessary consequence of

18 The same issues arose earlier regarding the consequence of new land areas (above, chapter 2: IV).

19 As on 19 and 24 March (above, p. 120 and note 9) where we have agricultural extensions stimulated by a falling corn wage resulting from a rising corn price.

20 Actually the commodity wage would fall less than the corn wage, considering the higher purchasing power of corn. Conceivably, the commodity wage remains constant.

difficulty in obtaining food, than the diminution of profits ...' (23 November 1814; 155; see above, chapter 2, p. 86).

It followed from all this that the low profit rate at later stages of development could not be reversed by a low *absolute* P_c; only a low *relative* P_c 'occasioned by scantiness of capital and high profits' would do the trick: 'But this state of things [an initially high agricultural profit rate] cannot surely be brought back by a low price of corn not occasioned by scantiness of capital and high profits, and if it be not preceded by these causes, its effects will be to lower not to raise the profits of agriculture' (217). Accordingly, 'a large tract of new land added to this Island' would put upward pressure on the profit rate by reducing the pressure of manufacturing supply, in effect reversing the high competition of capitals. The rise in manufacturing cost prices – incorporating the higher profit rate – entails a *relatively* low corn price, and this latter should be seen as the 'consequence,' not the cause, of the high profit rate: 'A large tract of rich land added to the Island, would indeed restore the state contemplated in your table. Before any fall of [the absolute corn] price had taken place, capital would be removing fast both from the old land and from manufactures. There would be a real want of stock compared with the means of profitably employing it; *manufactures would rise considerably in price, from higher profits,* and corn not rising, on account of the abundance of rich land, the relative price of corn would become low; but as a *consequence* (remark) not as a *cause* of high profits' (217–18; emphasis added, 'consequence' and 'cause' italicized in original).[21] The main object of the analysis is to preclude a rise in the absolute corn price in the secular process. Yet, as before, the argument *implies* that the profit rate in agriculture does (in some unexplained fashion) rise initially with the additional new tract – why else is capital attracted from industry? – the manufacturing rate then coming into line.[22] Again, Malthus seems to have been led astray; on his own terms, agricultural-productivity conditions do play directly on the general profit rate.[23]

Should there occur an *absolute* reduction in P_c because of reduced demand, as with easier corn importation, matters would be very different.

21 The higher profit rate in agriculture is balanced by the supposed increase in productivity.

22 The notion that 'manufactures would rise considerably in price, from higher profits ...' is tricky. Manufactures, one would suppose, rise in price from the contraction in output, generating higher profits by way of reduced competition of capitals. Conceivably the mode of expression reflects a confusion between industry as a whole and individual industries.

23 The present analysis of the consequences of a new tract of land says nothing of its effect in raising population and demand for manufactures (compare above, chapter 2, p. 93). But this does not mean that Malthus had abandoned that notion; it re-emerges subsequently (below, section V).

The agricultural profit rate would then fall, and with the expulsion of capital to manufacturing, so would the manufacturing rate: 'The case would be quite different if you begin by a fall in the price of corn, not occasioned by [manufacturing] high profits, such as the opening of the ports or the stoppage of a foreign demand for corn. Capital would in this case be expelled from the land slowly by low profits, instead of removing with alacrity for high profits. Manufactures would be overloaded with capital instead of being very scantily furnished with it; and nothing I conceive but the immediate vicinity of such a country could under such circumstances so increase the prices of manufactures as to occasion generally high profits' (218).[24]

A summary statement describes the downward trend in the profit rate over the course of 'regular progress' involving reduced manufacturing and constant corn prices, rather than Ricardo's constant manufacturing and rising corn prices: 'In your table, by the by, putting the affair of mining out of the question which it is difficult to estimate, I should say that the regular progress would be a fall in the price of manufactures from lower profits, and a stationary price of corn, rather than a rising price of corn, and a stationary one of manufactures. And this I think accords best with experience, but it is of no great consequence which, except perhaps, as it might serve to distinguish [an absolute] rise occasioned by demand from a [relative] rise by a fall of profits.' This summary statement, which emphasizes the fall in the profit rate as reflecting increased competition of capitals in manufacturing and lower manufacturing prices and profits, says nothing of the agricultural rate, leaving an impression that the latter must (somehow) come into line – a movement that compensates for any reduction in agricultural productivity, thereby assuring a constant corn price. Yet, as already mentioned, the immediately preceding texts *imply* a decline in the agricultural rate as a direct consequence of increasing land scarcity, with a fall in the manufacturing sector occurring *pari passu* as a consequence of increasing competition of capitals.[25]

* * *

Ricardo's reply reiterates his totally different view of the effect of a new tract of land. 'You agree with me that if a large tract of rich land were added to the Island it would restore the state contemplated in my table

24 The reason why, in this case, agricultural profits fall is left unstated. In fact, if expansion can proceed under the stimulus of higher demand at an unchanged profit rate, one might suppose contraction could proceed similarly. However, various cost rigidities could account for the decline.

25 In each case the fall of profits is considered as entering into costs, resulting in a net fall in the manufacturing price (assuming constant industrial productivity), and a constant corn price (assuming diminishing agricultural productivity).

[the original high profit rate]. Though we agree in the conclusion we differ materially in our opinion of the means by which it would be brought about' (21 April; 220). Whereas Malthus argued for *rising* manufacturing prices – manufacturing output falling as resources are attracted to the 'new tract' of land – Ricardo (basing himself on zero demand elasticity for corn) argued that given food requirements could now be satisfied at lower cost, *releasing resources to manufactures.* The result of higher manufacturing output for Ricardo is not reduced prices but constant prices: 'The price of manufactures would continue nearly stationary whilst the price of corn would fall. Is not this the natural consequence of more capital being employed on manufactures and less on agriculture?' (221). Moreover, manufacturing profits would rise with the fall in the price of corn, given roughly constant manufacturing prices.[26]

There is a parting shot regarding the case of an additional tract. Ricardo attempted to undermine Malthus's analysis (above, p. 130) by observing that, if the manufacturing price level is dictated by the corn price, as it is on Malthus's Smithian principles, it could not rise with an unchanged corn price: 'Have you not, too, uniformly supported the opinion that a fall in the price of corn will occasion a fall in the price of commodities? If they act on each other as you think but to which I do not agree, how can manufactures rise in price with a stationary price of corn? I should have thought that on your principles such an effect would be deemed impossible.'

Malthus, in a reply dated 23 April 1815, insisted that if, in the case of an added tract of land, resources flowed from agriculture to manufacturing (as Ricardo had it), there must occur a *fall* of the profit rate, assuming a given population: 'We do indeed differ materially as to the mode by [which] a large additional tract of rich land would bring things back to the state contemplated in the early parts of your table. If as you suppose more capital would go to manufactures, from the impossibility of employing it with advantage on the land, no two cases could well have less resemblance' (222). More generally, 'nothing certainly but the continued absorption of fresh capital on the land, to supply the wants of a rapidly increasing

26 The case is based on a *cost* theory of price: 'It appears to me that my table is applicable to all cases in which the relative price of corn rises from more labour being required to produce it, and under no other circumstances can there be a rise, however great the demand may be, unless commodities fall in value from less labour being required for their production' (220). However, Ricardo still must justify his position that manufacturing prices remain constant despite an increased supply. This might be done by taking account of the release of purchasing power from the food budget for expenditure on manufactures. A second problem relates to the precise manner whereby a reduced corn price acts to raise manufacturing profits. For the effect to work by way of a lower money wage, the possibility of population adjustment must be allowed, whereas the case at hand explicitly assumes a given population.

[manufacturing] population could put a manufacturing country into the state of America. If any cause were to stop the rapid increase of population, the profits of stock would almost immediately fall.'[27]

Malthus also hit upon the apparent problem in Ricardo's account that manufacturing prices remain constant despite expansion of output: 'Under the circumstances that you suppose it is contrary to every principle of supply and demand that your manufactures should keep up their price. At the old prices and in such quantities it is not in the nature of things that there should be a demand for them.' This is an invalid criticism if allowance is made for the transfer of expenditure from the food to the manufactures budget (above, note 24). As for Ricardo's parting shot regarding the impossibility (on Malthus's Smithian principles) of manufacturing prices rising with supposedly constant corn price, Malthus replied: 'Surely I have always maintained that when corn rises, though other commodities would rise they would not rise in proportion. I do not see then why it should be contrary to my principles, as you intimate, that manufactures should rise in price from the comparative scarcity of capital, and consequent high profits; while the same scarcity of capital should not raise the price of corn, on account of the superior fertility of the land employed.'[28]

Malthus appreciated that profit-rate variations occur for Ricardo by way of inverse movements of the money wage. This emerges in an important summary statement of his own contrasting position regarding the 'natural progress of accumulation.' The statement might have come directly from the *Wealth of Nations* – it reflected the 'usual doctrines of political economy' – and reiterates the falling profit-rate theorem in terms of increasing competition of capitals: 'You ask whether the natural consequence of employing more capital in manufactures, is not their *stationary* price. I should say that according to the usual doctrines of political Economy, it would be on the contrary a fall in their price, from a fall of profits. The more I consider the subject, the more I am inclined to think that in the natural progress of accumulation the fall in the profits of stock employed in manufactures is occasioned rather by the fall in their price owing to the abundant supply occasioned by such accumulation, than to the rise in the price of wages' (222–3).[29] Though this statement pertains to the manufacturing sector, it does not explicitly exclude a downward trend in the agricultural rate with increasing land scarcity. Earlier statements leave an *impression* that the industrial sector takes the lead; at the same time it is clear that, on Malthus's own terms, agricultural productivity does exert

27 The idea here is apparently that capital is drawn *from* manufacturing, thus preventing the fall in the profit rate attributable to Smithian accumulation.

28 This merely restates what had been said earlier – 'on account of the abundance of rich land' (above, p. 130) – and the same rationale applies.

29 The pressure on the profit rate is represented here as the norm rather than a consequence specifically of *excessive* accumulation.

a direct impact on the profit rate (above, pp. 129, 130). One surmises that the campaign to undermine the role Ricardo accorded a higher absolute corn price and money wage was carried too far.

IV ON THE ADVANTAGES OF A HIGH CORN PRICE

The advantages attached to high corn prices (above, sections II and III) are elaborated further in the correspondence. These advantages, Malthus explained, pertained only if the high price is not 'solely' attributable to diminishing returns: 'I saw Lord King last night. He speaks of having heard of very general distress among farmers and shopkeepers all over the country. I confess I feel more and more convinced of the unavoidable evils attending a general fall of prices, and of the unobserved advantages attending the high prices of corn and labour (when not arising solely from diff^y of production). I mentioned the subject to Lord K. but we had not time to discuss it. He said he would consider it, and that the view which I took of the effect of such prices on foreign commerce appeared to him to be quite new' (19 June 1815; 1951–73, VI, 231). Ricardo's reply [30] elucidated from Malthus what 'advantages' were here intended. He listed various possible causes of 'a high relative price of corn' other than higher real costs: 'Division of labour in manufactures; machinery; Demand for corn abroad; Restrictions on importations; Prosperous foreign commerce &c.' (16 July; 236). 'None of these,' he proceeds, 'involve diminished profits.' Malthus goes further: 'I certainly do not mean to consider a difficulty of producing as desirable in itself; but I think that a high price of corn when not occasioned by such difficulty is a decided advantage, and that it is at all times the best remedy for that difficulty of producing food, which in the progress of society is absolutely unavoidable.' The 'remedy,' which refers to the stimulus

30 For his own part, Ricardo envisaged two 'causes' of a rise of prices. First, depreciation, which by redistributing income in favour of the savings class would augment 'riches' at the expense of 'happiness' since the 'advantage' was achieved by reducing real wages and the real income of those on fixed incomes (27 June; VI, 233). He could see no advantages at all flowing from corn-price increases owing to 'difficulty of producing' – the second possible cause. And he thought Malthus agreed. If this were the case, he proceeds, Malthus was inconsistent: 'This opinion is however a little at variance with that which you have long been supporting, for you have said that the high price of corn and labour in this country at this time was an advantage, although it is universally allowed that that high price is mainly owing to difficulty of production' (234). The latter assertion confirms that (at least for Ricardo) contemporary high corn prices reflected diminishing returns.

Ricardo did not deny that temporary reductions in prices were damaging, but insisted that fluctuations were irrelevant for the question of secular 'prosperity': 'The farmers and shopkeepers may suffer very general distress from a sudden and general fall of prices, but I hold that this would be no criterion by which to judge of the general or permanent prosperity of a country.'

given agricultural extension in the face of diminishing productivity and without pressure on the profit rate, is in line with the important letter of 18 April (217; above p. 129).[31] Recent contemporary trends reflected such a confluence of circumstances since high corn prices were *not* mainly attributable to land scarcity: 'In our own case I believe that a great part of our high bullion prices is attributable to other causes, besides the barrenness of the land to be taken into cultivation.' As for the 'decided advantage,' without such a sequence of events over the two decades from 1794 to 1814 – involving high corn prices (and money wages) *relative to trading partners* with wartime trade restrictions – Britain would have been unable 'to subsidize Europe, and make such extraordinary exertions.'

This matter is elaborated in the next letter, which clarifies that the trading advantages flowing from 'high' corn prices (and money wages) pertained only when they were high relative to those of trading partners, which necessitated absolutely low domestic manufacturing prices. A situation of high *absolute* money wages and corn prices owing to land scarcity was incompatible with a permanent international differential: 'I do not, I confess, see how it is possible to resist the conclusion, that, if the nominal price of your corn and labour be double that of surrounding nations, in every million's worth of goods you exchange, or every million of subsidy you grant, you are able to command twice as much foreign labour, as if your corn and labour were of the same price with your neighbour's. But of course this state of things is not affected by the mere difficulty of producing corn. I do not indeed see how it is possible that the necessity of much more labour in the production of corn can ever have the effect of filling a country with the precious metals, and of enabling it to circulate all its commodities at a high price. A high permanent price of corn and labour *compared with other countries*, can only be caused in my opinion by great facility of production in manufactures, or in some peculiar natural products, and is therefore really the consequence of facility, rather than of difficulty of production. Without some such peculiar advantages, difficulty of production, or taxes on labour, would not permanently raise prices, relative to other countries' (26 August; 255–6).[32]

It is a striking fact that Malthus played down positive increases in the real cost of producing corn in contemporary conditions; *diminishing returns are not represented as a significant current issue.* Corn-import restriction had,

31 There is was explained that an absolute increase in P_c under pressure of demand, by raising P_c/P_m stimulates agricultural expansion and allows it to proceed without a reduction in the profit rate, and that a relative increase in P_c resulting from an absolute fall in P_m counteracts, though cannot prevent, the decline in the general profit rate.

32 This is an early statement of the proposition often identified with Senior regarding the maintenance in equilibrium of a higher level of money prices by way of high export efficiency.

on the other hand, checked the decline in manufacturing prices and, by implication, the profit rate – presumably by attracting resources *from* the manufacturing sector: 'In our own case, I conceive that the restrictions upon importation have increased in a slight, but only in a slight degree the difficulty of producing corn, while by preventing the home competition from lowering to a very much greater extent the prices of our exportable commodities, it has rendered our manufacturing labour vastly more productive than it would have been otherwise, and greatly overbalanced the trifling disadvantage that has been felt in a very slight increase of the difficulty of raising corn' (256).[33] In summary: 'You see therefore that I attribute the power of granting subsidies in this case to a general *facility* rather than difficulty of production; and I am very far from agreeing with you in thinking, that the high relative [corn] prices, with regard to other countries arise solely from the real difficulty of production.'[34]

The effect of high corn prices on labour's well-being was also taken into account, by drawing on the proposition – the physiocratic proposition – that workers benefit from an increase in the money wage roughly in proportion to the higher corn price, considering the mixed wage basket: 'If the wages of labour are mainly determined by the price of food, I do not see why an increase of money prices should diminish happiness. It will injure some undoubtedly, but will benefit a much greater number' (236). This proposition is applied even when the higher corn price reflects increased real costs: 'And it is consolatory to reflect that even when it arises from difficulty of production, the high relative value of corn constantly counterbalances in a considerable degree the evil of reduced corn wages.'[35]

V RESTATEMENT OF OBJECTIONS TO RICARDO'S 'NEW VIEW'

The correspondents met in London shortly after the letter of 23 April (cf. Ricardo, 1951–73, VI, 221, 224). They then discussed the case for a free

33 The reference to 'more productive' manufacturing sector is possibly an allusion to the maintenance of the terms of trade in favour of Britain's manufactures.

34 To this Malthus added: 'They may indeed, and do arise from the high price of the materials of capital, but by no means always from the greater quantity of labour required.' This is mysterious.

35 Malthus's closing remark implies *some* fall in the commodity basket. Other statements are ambiguous.

Ricardo reiterated in reply that increases in the corn price reflecting land scarcity are an unmitigated disadvantage: 'A really high price of corn is always an evil; in this opinion I think you would concur because it is always occasioned by difficulty of production. I know of no other cause and you allow difficulty of production not to be desirable in itself' (30 July; 241). As for absolute increase in the bullion price of corn, there were admittedly a variety of possible causes, but none generated any advantage. (See also note 43, below, on the alleged advantages of a high corn price.)

corn trade, having in mind Torrens's *Essay on the External Corn Trade.*[36] In his next letter (5 May 1815), Malthus agreed with Torrens's conclusion that there would be a *negative* effect on the profit rate, despite domestic agricultural contraction and the abandonment of least-productive land, a conclusion he had already reached earlier (above, p. 131). The argument now turns on the relative fixity of money wages and other cost items in the face of falling corn prices: 'When it is considered that a fall in the price of corn would not occasion an equal fall in labour, and still less of an equal fall in the other advances of the farmer, such as timber, bricks, leather, &c: &c: I own it appears to me quite impossible that the profits of capital employed on the land should not diminish, notwithstanding a very great reduction of the cultivation, particularly as some of these advances of the farmer cannot fall very much, on account of the demand and difficulty of supply occasioned by a full population, and the necessary and permanent rise of price occasioned by taxation. Under these circumstances I really think that a fall in rent profits and [money] wages at the same time would be compatible, though I should consider it as a great national misfortune' (223–4).[37]

All this is scarcely definitive. But the correspondents had also discussed in London a more general issue: the implications for distribution of increased 'facility of production.' For Malthus – *who here assumes a given population* – the outcome would be an increase in the real wage, not the profit rate (as it is for Ricardo), a result that could only be prevented by higher wage-goods prices, which are not to be expected in the circumstances supposed: 'I am convinced that the effects of the facility of production supposed, would go exclusively to wages not profits; indeed I cannot help thinking that you are fundamentally wrong in measuring the rate of profits by the facility of production. For what in fact is meant by facility of production? It is that a days labour instead of producing two measures of corn, cloth and cotton will produce four. And what is the natural consequence of this facility? why, that four measures of corn, cloth and cotton are worth only the price of a days labour; and nothing can prevent this

36 On Torrens see Sraffa's editorial note: 'The case supposed by Torrens is that of "a free external corn trade." He claims to have shown, first, that "in the present circumstances of these countries, an unrestrained corn trade would lower the price of corn, and bring down the monopoly rents occasioned by the war"; secondly, that "a reduction in the value of corn reduces wages"; and thirdly, "that the low natural price of subsistence heightens the productive powers of industry; that these heightened powers accelerate the accumulation of stock; and that this accumulation lowers the rate of profit." Thus, he concludes, "a free external trade in corn ... would effect a reduction in rents, wages, and profits"' (*Essay on the External Corn Trade,* 298); subsequent pages describe the beneficial effects of this reduction' (Ricardo, 1951–73, VI, 223n).

37 The same theme as far as concerns the profit rate turning on the sluggishness of cost reduction had been expressed as early as the second edition of the *Essay on Population*; and in the correspondence of October 1814.

consequence, but a scarcity of capital compared with the means of imploying it profitably. But the means of imploying capital profitably can never coexist with an abundant capital and produce and a *stationary* population, on account of the necessary effect of such a state of things in increasing the real price of labour' (224).[38]

The conclusion reached is that 'facility of production[39] ... *mainly affects the real wages of labour, and not the rate of profits*' (emphasis added). That this conclusion includes the effect on profits of productivity improvement in agriculture is confirmed by the proposition that – always assuming constant population – profits might actually decline, *notwithstanding highly productive land,* at early stages of development, with low prices but high real wages: 'if at any one time in the early periods of society *population were to be stopped* and accumulation were to go on, profits would fall extremely low although at the same time the labour of one man might be able to produce the food for ten or twenty. In this case everything would be in abundance and cheap except labour; and probably labourers would only work $\frac{1}{4}$ of their time and yet live luxuriously' (225; emphasis added). Again, 'profits do not depend upon facility of production.' That profits were admittedly 'often high when the facility of production is great' reflected the circumstance that 'capital is often scarce, and generally so indeed, at the time that land is most productive.' This affirmation reiterates the conclusion reached in the analysis of Ricardo's table (above, pp. 128–9) indeed much earlier regarding the 'limits' to the profit rate – see above, chapter 2: III). Now Malthus had there explicitly specified the *manufacturing* sector as particularly subject to the competition-of-capitals phenomenon; and this is probably his intention at the present juncture, although he expressed himself more generally.[40]

But all this is still not definitive from a secular perspective since it relates to a hypothetical case of continuous accumulation, given population. It is in fact allowed that technical progress would act to raise the profit rate, *should it be accompanied by increasing population, and therefore demand*: 'The rate of profits depends upon the scanty or abundant supply of capital compared with the means of employing it profitably. And these means will upon the common principles of supply and demand be increased either by a diminution of capital, or by an extension of the market for it, by the opening of new channels of trade *and by improvements in agriculture and manufactures, when accompanied as is almost invariably the case,*

38 In the earlier letters the effect on the real wage occurs via the change in commodity prices, not directly in the labour market. Presumably this remains Malthus's position, albeit that this last sentence *might* be read as involving the labour market directly.

39 He adds that this facility extends to 'the materials of capital ... which tends therefore to make the other materials of capital besides labour as plentiful as the commodities produced for consumption.'

40 The application of Say's Law to agriculture was first made on 29 December 1814 (above, chapter 2, p. 92).

by an increase of population and demand' (emphasis added).[41] The proposition that increased agricultural productivity raises the profit rate, provided we allow for population expansion and increased demand, accords with the analysis in earlier correspondence of the effect of a new tract of land (above, chapter 2, p. 93). The earlier analysis had entailed the influence of increased land supply on population growth and, consequently, on the *demand for manufactures.* That demand for manufactures is now intended is confirmed in a reaction to Ricardo's principle of 'demand depending entirely on the power of production'; this principle, which for Ricardo reflects the Law of Markets and does not require population expansion, is given an entirely different gloss: 'The principle of demand depending entirely on the power of production is true as long as each sort of commodity is in the proper proportions, and above all, *food so as to keep up demand [for manufactures] by a progressive population.* But the principle is not true when population cannot be made to increase proportionally. If it be supposed stationary, capital may very easily increase beyond the powers of employing it productively' (emphasis added).[42]

* * *

Malthus raised an explosive issue in his letter of 26 August 1815: 'In a country without land what determines the profits of stock?' (256). His object here was evidently to undermine Ricardo's position – as he mistakenly understood it – that the general profit rate is *determined* in the agricultural sector solely by productivity considerations.[43] His next letter (1 October)[44] contrasts Ricardo's 'New View' of profit-rate determination

41 An earlier analysis of technical progress (above, chapter 2: III) allowed a positive effect on the profit rate; but that had specified manufacturing, not agricultural, improvements.

42 See below, p. 154, for a very similar formulation on 8 September 1816, where demand for manufactures is clearly intended.

43 Ricardo then returns to the alleged advantages of a high corn price. His reply of 10 September is important in clarifying his firm opposition to Torrens's (Smithian) view that high corn prices are reflected in high manufacturing prices: 'If I agreed with Mr. Torrens that such high prices [for raw produce] were accompanied with a rise in the prices of commodities, – and if I thought that such rise would not preclude the usual exchanges with foreign countries, I should of course agree with you that with such general high prices we should command a greater quantity of foreign commodities in exchange for a given quantity of ours, – but I cannot admit in the first place that commodities would rise because corn rose, and secondly if they did so rise there are but very few which we could sell in equal quantity at the advanced price to foreigners, and if we sold less to them we could buy less of them and thus would our general commerce suffer. I can see great advantages attending low general prices but none in high prices. On this subject we are not likely to agree' (269).

44 The set of letters from 19 June on had not focused *specifically* on the profit rate. The new set beginning with the letter of 1 October does.

with the valid Smithian perspective: 'The more I consider our old subject, the less I find I can agree with you in the new view which you have taken of capital as depending with respect to profits, on facility of production rather than as was formerly supposed on quantity and competition' (289). The 'error' was that 'because a small quantity of capital compared with the means of employing it is always accompanied with facility of production, you attribute the high profits which are yielded in this case, to the latter cause instead of the former; although it is quite certain that great facility of production, accompanied by *abundant* capital compared with the demand, could only shew itself in increased rents and wages, and could not possibly appear in the shape of profits' (289–90). Similarly, there were cases entailing highly productive land but low profits, and *also* low wages sufficient only 'to support a stationary population,' in which event the advantage flowed entirely to rent.[45] And the 'error' is traced to a failure to distinguish 'productiveness of industry,' or the *physical* productivity of labour, from 'productiveness of capital,' or the *value return on capital* dependent on demand-side considerations. Only in the limit imposed by land scarcity (the stationary state) does the former govern the profit rate: 'You appear to me to overlook a most important distinction between productiveness of industry and productiveness of capital. *They are in fact very different, and do not necessarily go together except perhaps in the last capital that can be employed on the land, where the productiveness of industry finally limits the productiveness of capital.* In manufactures they have very little indeed to do with each other; and in land except in the case above mentioned, they seldom increase and decrease in the same proportion. I have no doubt, it frequently happens that with regard to the last capital employed upon the land in two countries, the soil of one may be such as to yield ten fold, and the soil of the other only eight fold, and yet the capital on the latter, from

45 Malthus illustrates from Tahiti: 'In Otaheite where perhaps the facility of production is the greatest of any country we know, there is scarcely any capital wanted, and almost the whole of the produce goes to rent and wages. Universally where land is limited in quantity, the facility of production upon it, will go mainly to rent; and the soil of a country might be of such fertility as to yield 60 fold instead of 8 or 10, and yet the profits of stock be only 6 per cent, and the wages of labour both nominally and really low; – only just sufficient, in short, to support a stationary population.' The low requirement for capital reflects the contribution of 'spontaneous fruits of the earth,' as is made clear in a subsequent letter: 'You have rather misapprehended my illustration from Otaheite [see Ricardo to Malthus, 7 October; 292]. I did not mean, that from want of skill their capital yielded but little, though their soil was extremely fertile; but that from the nature of their products, consisting chiefly of the spontaneous fruits of the earth, scarcely any advances in the shape of capital were necessary, and consequently that all the richness of their soil must go to rent and labour, but chiefly to rent' (11 October; 296).

the greater demand for corn, and the greater relative price, may yield a higher per centage profit' (290; emphasis added).[46]

Despite the reformulation all of this merely restates what had been maintained as early as 9 October 1814 (above, chapter 2, p. 82),[47] and again on 18 April and 5 May 1815 (above, pp. 128–9, 137–9). In every instance, Malthus assumes special cases to make his point. Thus, in the event of highly productive land, a high profit rate would be precluded should there be a constraint on 'demand' – usually involving constant population – relative to capital. It is in the special case that the manufacturing profit rate is kept low, forcing the agricultural rate below its maximum potential, as given by the state of agricultural productivity. But this does not touch on the 'true' growth process, where initially the high profit rate available in agriculture – implicitly directly attributable to high productivity – ensures rapid accumulation and population growth, and thus high demand *for manufactures*, compared with the small quantity of capital as yet invested in that sector, thus keeping the manufacturing sector in line with agriculture.[48] At the other limit – in the final stationary state – population growth ceases, and demand is low relative to the stock of manufacturing capital, again keeping the manufacturing profit rate in line with the (low) agricultural rate. Setting aside movements below the maximum potential profit rate defined by agricultural productivity, agriculture emerges as the lead sector over the secular path and not only at the limits, carrying the manufacturing rate with it *via* aggregate demand. All this is confirmed in the correspondence that follows, as we shall presently see (below, pp. 146–7, 155).

The objections to Ricardo's 'New View' are also applied to that version

46 By 'industry' Malthus intended *labour*: 'When you speak of difficulty or facility or production, do you mean to refer to industry or capital. If you refer to capital, of course difficulty or facility of production must be synonimous with low, or high profits, and our difference is merely verbal. If you refer to industry or labour, the difference is real, and I am not I fear likely to see the subject in the same light with you. Pray give me a definition of productiveness in your next' (290–1).

However, a subsequent letter seems ambiguous in this regard: 'I am rather surprised that you do not see the distinction between productiveness of industry and productiveness of capital which I still think most important. They often go together but by no means always. The machine which does the work of five people, yields often no more profit than the commonest instrument' (11 October; 296).

47 There Malthus refers also to the *initial* as well as the *final* limit.

48 In one of his earlier versions of 'the small quantity of capital ... compared with the means of employing it,' Malthus has specified 'particularly ... the small quantity of capital *employed in manufactures*' (above, p. 129; emphasis added). The present statement is not thus restricted formally, implying that his acceptance of Say's Law in the case of necessaries (above, chapter 2: IV) is not always applied strictly. Indeed at the close of the passage just cited in our text, the divergence of the profit rate from land productivity explicitly refers to demand pressure for *corn*.

which relates the profit rate to the corn price: 'Your doctrine that high profits depend upon the low money price of corn appears to me still more objectionable and still more uniformly contradicted by experience, than the dependance of profits upon facility of production' (291).[49] There was no one-to-one relation between the corn price and agricultural productivity. For the price of corn would be high despite productive land should a high profit rate – this itself a profit rate determined *outside* the farm sector – 'counterbalance' the high productivity; and conversely, in the case of low productivity: 'Facility of production on land does not always *necessarily* occasion a cheap money price, the high profits often counterbalancing such facility; and in a similar manner low profits will often counterbalance in price, difficulty of production. For a hundred and fifty years after the reign of Edward the third, corn continued to fall, and so it did from 1640 to 1750 – profits falling at the same time.'

Treatment of the profit rate as a *cost item* in agriculture to be combined with the labour coefficient raised the possibility of constancy of the (absolute) corn price during secular expansion, notwithstanding diminishing returns.[50] To this is attached a denial that the corn price of manufactures would rise 'very greatly' with diminishing returns; since the cost of raw materials increases along with that of corn, manufacturing prices could not get far out of line: 'By the by surely we have been both wrong in thinking that in the progressive cultivation of poor land, the price of corn compared with manufactures would very greatly rise. I much question whether the natural and necessary rise of the raw material will not in general be nearly in proportion to the additional labour employed on the land. In wool, leather, and flax, I have little doubt that this is the case.' Why this theme is stated as a novelty is unclear, since it had emerged earlier (above, p. 121). Possibly only a quantitative re-evaluation was intended.

The Ricardian notion that a secular increase in the corn price – at least one reflecting higher real costs – will result in higher money wages is also questioned. Here the argument seems to be that increased money wages must be maintained by an inflow of the precious metals, which would not necessarily be forthcoming: 'Is it possible that a difficulty in the production of corn, should, without the operation of any other peculiar cause, make the precious metals abundant and cheap in a country, and greatly raise the price of labour compared with other states. Surely with regard to money prices, we have attributed too much to difficulty of production.'[51] Implicit in this comment is the Smithian notion that the

49 To Ricardo these are scarcely separate versions. The profit rate varies with agricultural productivity via the money wage, reflecting the price of corn.

50 This is the same position as that of 18 April; above, p. 131.

51 This passage contains an implicit allusion to the cost of obtaining the precious metals (see below, chapter 14).

price level is affected by money wages, which, of course, is *not* Ricardo's position.

In reply to Ricardo's reaction to his analysis of the consequences of increased agricultural productivity,[52] Malthus reiterated that where, as in the Tahiti case (above, note 45), capital advances were *unnecessary*, the 'richness of the soil' would be to the advantage of landowners – a wholly irrelevant proposition; more pertinently, he responded to Ricardo's demand–supply approach to rent by insisting on applying that principle to *capital*, his object being to force an admission that the profit rate might be low because of inadequate commodity demand, and accordingly demand for capital, though agricultural productivity may be high: 'I have always distinctly allowed, and ever shall allow in future that any causes which tend to make land less in demand will lower rents. I only want to make you allow, according to the same great principle of supply and demand, that any causes which tend to make *capital* less in demand, will lower *profits*; but you appear to me to except profits from the laws which operate upon all other commodities, and will not allow that they will be low for the same reasons that the rents of land and the wages of labour are low' (11 October; 296).[53] Most important is a confirmation that his case for a positive effect of increased productivity on *rent* rather than profits, assumed popula-

52 Ricardo denied the attribution to him of a sole concern with *natural* fertility; a low profit rate in Tahiti despite highly productive land was explicable, allowance made for 'skill, machinery, and labour' (7 October; 292). He was 'astonished' by Malthus's assertion that 'universally, where land is limited in quantity, the facility of production upon it, will go mainly to rent, and the soil of a country might be of such fertility as to yield 60 fold instead of 8 or 10 and yet the profits of stock be only 6 pc.' and the wages of labour both nominally and really low' (cited note 45, above). Understanding the exercise as involving an increase in agricultural productivity, he insisted *on demand–supply principles*: 'Land like every thing else rises or falls in proportion to the demand for it; every improvement which shall enable you to raise the same quantity of produce on a less quantity of land, or which is the same thing, a larger quantity of produce on the same quantity of land can not increase the demand for land, and therefore can not raise rent ... I ask whether it be possible that $\frac{3}{4}$ of the land of a country can be suffered to pass from a state of tillage to a state of nature without occasioning a fall in rents? If land is less in demand must not the rent of it fall? If you say no, there is no truth in the proposition that value depends upon the proportion between supply and demand' (293).

53 He proceeds along the same line by introducing another special case involving constant and high marginal product up to some limit, at which limit the profit and wage rates would be 'very low' and rent very high: 'You are astonished that I maintain that when land is limited in quantity, the facility of production upon it will go mainly to rent and that though it might yield 60 fold instead of ten, profits might be only 8 per cent. Now I would ask distinctly what would happen with respect to profits in a country limited to 100,000 acres all of the richest conceivable quality, yet peopled and capital'd up to the utmost limits of its produce. Would not both the profits of stock and the wages of labour be very low, although the quantity of produce yielded by a given capital *including rent* might be 100 per cent' (296–7).

tion increase – implying a corresponding increase in the demand for corn: 'I believe I mentioned to you some farms in Scotland the value of the produce of which compared with the capital employed is 56 per cent: and I have very little doubt that the whole landed produce of great Britain is much above twenty per cent on the whole of the labour and capital employed upon the soil, and yet the common profits of farming stock and of other stock in general are not more than ten per cent. Are not these instances of the benefit derived by rents from the fertility of our soil, and our skill in agriculture; and if both were greatly to improve, would not rents very greatly rise, *as soon at least as the population had reached the limits of the more abundant produce which would be in a short time comparatively.* Fertility is in fact the essence of high rents, and low rents are the necessary result of barrenness however scarce corn may be. If land will support no more than those who work upon it, there can be no rent' (297; emphasis added).[54] All this leaves open the consequences of secularly declining agricultural productivity *for the profit rate.*

* * *

In maintaining a fall in rent with higher agricultural productivity, Ricardo had focused on the short run, assuming given population, as he himself insisted in his reply of 17 October: 'But I ask if by any miracle the produce of that land could at once be doubled would rents then continue as high as before, or could they possibly rise? *We are speaking of the immediate not the ultimate effects.* The improvements in skill and machinery may in 1000 years go to the Landlord but for 900 they will remain with the tenant' (302; emphasis added).[55] Regarding Malthus's insistence upon the demand–supply principle as it related to capital and its return, Ricardo emphasized that he too made full allowance, but that in the absence of land scarcity there were no checks to the 'demand for capital,' that is, to investment. His allowance for the demand–supply principle as it applied to capital was evidently not Malthus's: 'our difference is still very serious' (301). The elaboration provides us with one of the clearest formulations of Ricardian growth theory in which the Law of Markets precludes the notion of declining (marginal) efficiency of capital as a result of Smithian 'increasing competition of capital,' and in which capital and population growth are

54 The case was alluded to in the letter of 12 February and Ricardo's reply of 13 February, above, chapter 3: VI. (The remark 'however scarce corn may be' is problematic.)

55 Ricardo accepted Malthus's special case: 'Fertility is as you justly observe the essence of high rents, and low rents are the necessary result of barrenness however scarce corn may be. I agree with you too that in a country limited to 100,000 acres all of the richest conceivable [quality], yet peopled and capital'd up to the utmost limits of its produce, the profits of stock and the wages of labour would both be very low, although the quantity of produce yielded by a given capital *including rent* might be 100 pc.', ...' (301–2).

both checked by increasing land scarcity, implying *declining real wage and profit rates acting upon the growth rates of the variable factors.*[56]

Malthus agreed 'that in the progress of cultivation there is a regular tendency to a diminution in the productiveness of industry on the land, in the same manner as there is a regular tendency to a diminution in the real wages of labour' (16 October; 303). This formulation places 'productiveness of industry' on a par with the real (corn) wage, suggesting thereby *the profit rate* and its 'regular' downward trend path (along with the corn wage) with diminishing agricultural returns. Now 'productiveness of industry' had earlier been defined as physical productivity (above, p. 140) and its impact on the profit rate was allowed only in the *limit.* Does the new formulation amount to a major concession? On balance, I would say not. Even in the earlier context it is implicit that agricultural productivity imposes a maximum profit rate – a declining maximum – over the trend; the concern had been to insist on the possibility of variations of the profit rate occurring below this maximum. This is precisely the tack now taken – just as it had been much earlier, when Malthus was forced to the same concession (above, chapter 2: III): 'It is quite erroneous I think to infer that the profits of stock may not, as will the wages of labour, rise for periods of some duration during the course of this progress. In fact, profits on the land will always rise, when population increases faster than capital, independently of improvement &c.' (303–4). In terms of the sort of argument developed to this point, if the profit rate does rise as 'population increases faster than capital,' it must be because demand increases faster than supply, counteracting increasing competition of capitals, not because of temporary downward pressure on the real wage in the labour market, as for Ricardo.[57]

56 As usual he insists that his mechanism operates via the effect of rising corn prices on the money wage: 'I most distinctly allow that any causes which tend to make capital less in demand will lower profits, but I contend that there are no causes which will for any length of time make capital less in demand, however abundant it may become, but a comparatively high price of food and labour; – that profits do not *necessarily* fall with the increase of the quantity of capital because the demand for capital is infinite and is governed by the same law as population itself. They are both checked by the rise in the price of food, and the consequent increase in the value of labour. If there were no such rise what could prevent population and capital from increasing without limit? I acknowledge the effects of the great principle of supply and demand in every instance, but in this it appears to me that the demand will enlarge at the same rate as the supply, if there be no difficulty on the score of food and raw produce.'

57 Ricardo readily allowed *temporary variations* in the profit rate: 'That profits may rise on the land if population increases faster than capital, I am not disposed to deny, but this will be a partial rise of profits on a particular trade, for a limited time, and is very different from a general rise of profits on trade in general' (17 October; 305). It is unclear why such variations are said to be *partial* – for Ricardo, differentials between capital and population growth rates should apply to all sectors – except that Malthus was focusing on agriculture *per se.*

The influence exerted by increasing land scarcity on the entire secular trend of the profit rate – presumably the maximum potential rate – is confirmed in a letter of 30 October. This letter contains the important statement that Malthus had 'always allowed that the progress of capital and population, while they can go on together, uninterrupted by the difficulty of procuring subsistence, is absolutely unlimited; but I most distinctly deny that the demand for capital is unlimited, with a limited population; and this appears to me to be the proposition that you maintain';[58] or again: 'I cannot help thinking that your doctrine of the indefinite demand for capital without reference to a proportionate increase of population, is an assumption, directly in the teeth of the great principle of Supply and demand, and *uniformly* contradicted by experience' (319).[59] This position seems to neglect the standard insistence on the depressing force on profits flowing from inadequate aggregate demand – Smith's increasing competition of capitals – unless we understand it (as we must) as referring to the assurance of expansion of aggregate demand generated by an increasing population.[60] And since the only constraint on population growth and

58 Actually, Ricardo had also maintained this notion of an 'indefinite demand for capital' in the context of a proportionate increase of capital and population, and had allowed a falling profit rate, assuming more rapid accumulation than population growth. But that decline is unrelated to inadequacy of aggregate demand; that is, it occurs despite an unlimited demand for capital, understanding the latter as a reference to the Law of Markets.

59 On 19 June 1815, Malthus had set in motion a renewed spate of correspondence by alluding to the 'unavoidable evils attending a general fall of prices' (above, p. 134). He reverted to this same issue on 16 October, having in mind reports 'that all home trade was most exceedingly slack' (303), in a formal rejection of the Law of Markets: 'Is it possible for above half the national income to fall very greatly in price, without affecting the demand and the other half. I confess I feel no doubt that the main cause of the present slackness of trade is the diminished incomes of the Landlords and Farmers. The actual produce of a country will always be sold, and the loss of the sellers will be the gain of the buyers; but it makes an infinite difference to a country whether its produce is sold at a price which will encourage production, or discourage it. During the period of a fall of prices it appears to me that all sorts of productions are prodigiously discouraged; and that at the end of 7 or 8 years of falling prices, or 7 or 8 years of rising prices, the state of a country will be most essentially different in point of wealth.'

Ricardo went so far in his reply as to deny the putative facts of excess aggregate supply: 'It is dangerous to listen to reports respecting briskness or slackness of trade. It is I believe certain that the revenue has been uncommonly productive the last quarter which is no indication of diminished trade. As you allow that the loss of the sellers is the gain of the buyers, you appear to me to attribute effects much too great to the fall of raw produce which has lately taken place. – It does not follow that because prices are low production will be discouraged. If money were to fall very much in value whilst a country was making great advances in prosperity would not production be encouraged notwithstanding a fall of prices?' (17 October; 304–5).

60 Even so, the precise process intended is not spelled out. Does such increase in demand relate to increased demand for manufactures; or is it increased demand for corn, which by absorbing capital into agriculture prevents a reduction in the manufacturing rate that would otherwise occur? Here the analysis regarding an added tract of land is pertinent; above, p. 130; also chapter 2: IV.

demand alluded to is that imposed by land-scarcity conditions, *we have here the fundamental contention that the pressure on the profit rate deriving from 'competition of capitals' is itself dependent on increasing land scarcity.*

* * *

Malthus then turns from the secular issue to apply himself once again to Ricardo's position that an increase in agricultural productivity reduces land rent in the case of a *given* population, and that such constancy of population pertained over long periods (above, p. 144). For Malthus, since population increase was a relatively rapid matter, it could be taken for granted that, in practice, agricultural improvements raise *rent*, not the profit rate: 'What can you possibly mean by the improvement in farming going to the Landlord in a thousand years? Few of these improvements have doubled the produce, and five and twenty or fifty years would proportion the population to them, and *double the rents*, while profits would be left as they were before notwithstanding this increased facility of production. When before the revolutionary war, the rate of interest was below 4 per cent and profits in proportion, might it not be said that almost all previous improvements in machinery had gone to the land' (318–19). The criticism is then extended to increased capital productivity. And this is the main point of the challenge. Ricardo's allowance that the profit rate declines in the event of capital accumulation faster than population increases – *a fortiori* so, given population – relates specifically to the upward pressure on the wage *in the labour market.* The object now was to force Ricardo to recognize an effect on profits of increased aggregate output – generated by new technology – *in commodity markets* in the face of sluggish population growth, and therefore sluggish demand, thereby, of course, undermining the Law of Markets:

You seem to argue quite upon different principles in reference to land and profits. You say that the demand for capital will enlarge at the same rate as the supply; and yet think that a moderate supply of land or what is equivalent to it, of produce, will have an effect for a very considerable time in lowering rents ... You say that if half the land will yield the same produce rents will fall? Upon the same principle, if half the capital will yield the same produce, why should not profits fall? Where could the remaining half find employment? You will say perhaps that though some difficulty might be found at first, yet after a time the demand would be proportioned to the supply; that is you ask for an interval with regard to profits, and yet with regard to rents you say 'we are speaking of *immediate*, not ultimate effects.' You allow that profits may rise on the land if population increases faster than produce, and fall, if produce increases faster than population, but surely in every case where a great facility of production suddenly takes place, produce may be said to increase faster than population. Without an increase of population in this case profits must fall; and after a proportionate increase of population, the facility of production will go to the land. I am still firmly of opinion therefore that 'Universally where land is limited in quantity the facility of production upon it will go mainly to rent.'

The letter of 30 October pushes home the challenge with a reiteration of the earlier contrast (see above, pp. 140, 145) between 'productiveness of industry' (a physical variable) and 'productiveness of capital' (a value variable identified with or governing the return on capital): 'The rent of land depends upon its productiveness, combined with the demand for it. Given the productiveness the rent varies as the demand; and given the demand the rent varies as the productiveness. In the same manner profits, depend upon the productiveness of industry, and the demand for capital. To neglect the consideration of *demand* in either case, is equally erroneous. I am quite surprised that you [do] not see the difference between the productiveness of industry, and of capital. You may as well say that a capital machine which every body might have for little or nothing would necessarily yield high profits' (319–20).[61] The same point is again repeated a fortnight later: 'Our great difference arises from your not sufficiently considering demand; and not allowing the very marked distinction there is, between the productiveness of industry and the productiveness of capital. What do you think of land which yields sixty fold, instead of ten, without any purchasers for the produce? Would the profits be in the one case six times greater than in the other?' (13 November; 323).[62]

61 Ricardo had already insisted on 7 October that 'productiveness of capital' varied *pari passu* with 'productiveness of industry': 'I do not clearly see the distinction which you think important between productiveness of industry and productiveness of capital. Every machine which abridges labour adds to the productiveness of industry, but it adds also to the productiveness of capital. England with machinery and with a given capital will obtain a greater real net produce, than Othaeite with the same capital, without machinery, whether it be in manufactures or in the produce of the soil. It will do so because it employs much fewer hands to obtain the same produce. Industry is more productive, so is Capital. It appears to me that one is a necessary consequence of the other' (294). Accordingly, the secular decline in the former has as its consequence a secular decline in the latter, *a proposition rejected by Malthus*: 'the opinion which I have advanced and which you are combating is that in the progress of society, independently of all improvements in skill and machinery, the produce of industry constantly diminishes as far as the land is concerned, and consequently capital becomes less productive.' This fall in the 'productivity of capital' accounts for the falling secular return on capital: 'this diminution of produce is beneficial to all owners of land ... at the expense of manufacturers, amongst which I include farmers, first by rendering the commodities which they manufacture of less exchange value than they before were for corn, and secondly by raising the cost of production by raising the price of labour.' This formulation is confusing. To identify farmers as manufactures and then to refer to a falling profit rate with a rising P_c/P_m is contradictory.

62 These formulations appear to contravene the principle that an increase in the supply of corn ensures an equivalent increase in demand. But this is scarcely surprising, given the depression extending to agriculture which was evidently on Malthus's mind.

The aggregate-demand issue is again raised by Malthus in a query of 6 August 1816 regarding the manner in which trade expansion can raise the general profit rate: 'what are the causes which occasion an increase of demand without a diminution of price, that is, what is the nature of that demand which increases price, and can it be general? I think it can, and that a new value thrown into the market always tends to create such a demand' (1951–73, VII, 53). The question entails the contrast between *increase in quantity demanded* in response to a price reduction, and *increase in demand* which raises price. But it extends beyond the pricing of individual goods to goods-in-general.[63]

63 The reply by Ricardo turns on Law of Markets reasoning, from which perspective a general expansion in demand – in contrast to that of an individual commodity – implies a corresponding general expansion in supply, in which case there would be no tendency for overall price variation, setting aside that induced by relative money-supply changes (9 August; 58). Malthus's reaction is that an expansion of commodities might *not* meet with a corresponding demand. But it is a garbled response, for it supposes an increased demand for luxury services and/or for leisure, implying a reduction in demand for output, though in such a case there surely would occur a corresponding reduction in supply: 'With regard to demand in general I cannot help thinking that in all our discussions, – bullion, as well as corn – &c: you have greatly underrated the effect of the wants and tastes of mankind, on which, after all every exertion of human industry depends; and so far is it from being true that they may be considered as always ready for the supply, they are really very difficult to generate. Two alternatives are always ready to check their growth as far as the employment of capital is concerned. Among the higher classes the luxury of menial service, and among the lower classes the luxury of idleness, may always be preferred to commodities, and if this were to take place when labour and capital were thrown out of employment in equal proportions, would not capital become more abundant than labour, and profits fall?' (8 September; 70).

The final two clauses are incomprehensible: What disturbance is assumed at play to throw capital and labour 'out of employment'? (It is apparently not the contraction in demand *per se*). Second, why should this render capital 'more abundant than labour'?

One other matter was raised by Ricardo at this juncture in the correspondence – his problems relating to value theory. He had noted Torrens's agreement that an increase in the money-wage rate leaves general prices unaffected (23 February 1816; 24); and Malthus objected on 28 April to Ricardo's adoption of a labour theory (below, note 69). In a letter by Ricardo to Malthus of 5 October, however, we read of new difficulties: 'I have been very much impeded by the question of price and value, my former ideas on those points not being correct. My present view may be equally faulty, for it leads to conclusions at variance with all my preconceived opinions. I shall continue to work, if only for my own satisfaction, till I have given my theory a consistent form' (71–2). As Sraffa has suggested, his 'present view' probably refers to the possibility that a rise of wages might generate a *fall* of prices (72n, and Ricardo to James Mill, 14 October; 82). But it remains true that by December he was able to reiterate the key principles (already specified on 10 September 1815) that the corn price did not govern general prices; as he wrote to McCulloch: 'Your system proceeds upon the supposition that the price of corn regulates the price of all other things, and that when corn rises or falls, commodities also rise or fall, – but this I hold to be an erroneous system, although you have great authorities in your favour, no less than Adam Smith, Mr. Malthus and M. Say' (4 December; 105).

* * *

At the close of 1815 Malthus returned to the attack, summarizing his differences with Ricardo thus: 'I think the principal difference between us relating to the subjects we have last discussed, is, your opinion that General Profits never fall from a general fall of prices compared with labour, but from a general rise of labour compared with prices. I own, I can see no reason for this opinion' (22 December 1815; VI, 341–2). The statement captures Malthus's own insistence on the consequences for profits of *absolutely falling commodity prices.* It formally leaves open whether or not the principle applies only to manufactures, but the contrast drawn between the two systems seems to focus on manufacturing. And it catches Ricardo's position in so far as that entails the effect on the general profit rate of rising money wages.

Malthus repeated his denial of any upward trend in *money* wages in the course of expansion to increasingly unproductive land (cf. above, p. 142), while taking for granted a secular decline in the *corn* wage. His logic is twofold. First, the (absolute) increase in the corn price would be 'very small,'[64] and, since the corn wage falls, there was no reason to expect any compensatory rise of money wages. But, second, an increase in the money wage was, in any event, precluded on monetary grounds. Though these monetary grounds had been stated earlier, Malthus apparently allowed too much during a personal encounter: 'I believe I assented in par[ting][65] to the proposition that in the successive cultivation of poorer land, the price of labour would rise as well as the price of corn. When however the rise in the price of corn is occasioned solely and exclusively by the necessity of cultivating poorer land I am now convinced that the rise must be very small, and as the real price of labour must fall, I see no reason why the nominal price of labour should rise. How can such a country purchase the

64 He does not say why. But see above, pp. 131, 142, regarding an approximate constancy of cost price with lower agricultural productivity compensated by a fall in the general profit rate.

65 Sraffa suggests that the first sentence might read: 'I believe I assented in part ...' In a reply dated 2 January 1816, Ricardo complained that Malthus had misrepresented his position by suggesting that money wages rise *relative* to general prices, a formulation which allows for the latter rising to some degree. In fact, for Ricardo, general prices are *constant,* corn and wages alone rising: 'As for the difference between us on Profits of which you speak in your letter, – you have not I think stated it correctly. You say that my opinion is 'that General Profits never fall from a general fall of prices compared with labour, but from a general rise of labour compared with prices.' I will not acknowledge this to be my proposition. I think that corn and labour are the variable commodities, and that other things neither rise nor fall but from difficulty or facility of production, or from some cause particularly affecting the value of money, – and that no alteration of price proceeding from these causes affect general profits; allowing always some effect for cheapness of the raw material' (1951–73, VII, 3).

precious metals so as to occasion a general rise in the price of labour. Of course I suppose that it has no peculiar advantage in manufacture. If it had, its corn and labour might both rise from a different cause. This, if true, would make an alteration in your view of Profits' (342).[66] Shortly thereafter, Malthus again questioned whether the money wage will rise at all in the course of secular expansion, *since the commodity wage falls*: 'Can you give me a good reason why the money price of labour should rise because it is necessary to cultivate poorer land, and the *real* price of labour must fall' (8 January 1816; 1951–73, VII, 8). He then summarized his own position: 'In the progress of cultivation, independently of any causes but such progress, it appears to me that the money price of corn will rise, but not much, the money price of labour remain stationary nearly, and the money price of manufactured good[s] fall from the fall of profits' (9).[67]

Ricardo, it is clear from his next letter, attributed to Malthus the view that the lower corn wage immunizes the profit rate against a fall with increasing land scarcity (10 January 1816; 10).[68] But this follows only on Ricardo's own terms, whereby the profit rate moves inversely with the *money* wage. These terms are not those of Malthus, who insisted on a falling profit rate – as well as a falling corn-wage rate – during the course of growth, *despite constancy of the money wage.* The problem is that Malthus failed to specify whether agricultural extensions *per se* are at all responsible for the falling profit rate – in agriculture and generally – and if so, by what process.

We are taken a step forward towards solving our dilemma by the important letter of 6 August 1816.[69] Here Malthus formally minimized the em-

66 Here we encounter an allusion to the theorem regarding the cost of obtaining money. See also note 51, above.

67 On this formulation, the *corn* wage falls secularly, though it is not clear that the *commodity* wage falls, allowance made for manufactured wage goods. (But see above, note 35.)

68 Ricardo had no difficulty in justifying the consistency of a rising money wage with agricultural extensions, notwithstanding the real wage decline, admitting at the same time that to prove that this must be so would require a book: 'I cannot think it inconsistent to suppose that the money price of labour may rise when it is necessary to cultivate poorer land, whilst the real price may at the same time fall. Two opposite causes are influencing the price of labour [:] one the enhanced price of some of the things on which wages are expended, – the other the fewer enjoyments which the labourer will have the power to commend, – you think they may balance each then, or rather that the latter will prevail. I on the contrary think the former the more powerful in its effects. I must write a book to convince you.' Ricardo here asserts that the two positions differ in the relative weights accorded diminishing agricultural productivity relative to the lower real wage. For his own part, the fall in productivity *necessarily* outweighed that of the real wage, forcing up the money wage; for Malthus this was not the case.

69 In the meantime, Ricardo had raised the problem of the measure of value, considering the need to strengthen his argument that general prices remain constant in the face of a rising corn price (7 and 23 February; 20, 24). In response to his admission that 'obstacles almost invincibly oppose themselves to my progress, and I find the greatest

pirical relevance of direct effects on the profit rate emanating from changing agricultural productivity: '*By the by the more I think on the subject the more I feel convinced that the rate of the profits of stock depends mainly on the demand and supply of stock compared with the demand and supply of labour, and very little (directly) on facility or difficulty of production, properly so called.* By facility or difficulty of production I mean the greater or less quantity of produce that can be obtained by a given quantity of labour, and by no means the quantity of any sort of produce which must be given for labour, which merely expresses the exchangeable value of that produce compared with labour, and has nothing to do with facility or difficulty of production. If a piece of land worked by 10 labourers and producing 110 quarters of corn, should afterwards produce 165 quarters with the same quantity of labour, might not the rate of profits continue the same, and the only difference be that the labourers would be paid 15 quarters instead of ten. Does not the different *rate* of profit in America and Poland in land of nearly the same quality shew that profits depend on the proportion of capital to labour, and not on facility of production' (6 August; 52, emphasis added). By his expression 'the demand and supply of stock, compared with the demand and supply of labour,' Malthus did not intend pressure on the profit rate exerted in Ricardian fashion *via* the labour market, but rather his own aggregate demand–supply perspective, demand turning on population expansion, as is explicitly confirmed in the letters that follow.[70] But

difficulty to avoid confusion in the most simple of my statements' (24 April; 28), Malthus gave a rather self-righteous response: 'I cannot help thinking that the reason why with your clear head, you find a difficulty in your progress is that you are got a little into a wrong track. On the subject of determining all prices by labour, and excluding capital from the operation of the great principle of supply and demand, I think you must have swerved a little from the right course. But on this point of course you differ from me' (28 April; 30). The assertion that Ricardo had 'excluded' capital from treatment in terms of supply–demand is an old charge which Ricardo had denied, though the two were at cross purposes on this issue (above, p. 144). As for the allusion to Ricardo's *labour theory of value,* nowhere thus far had the matter been phrased in the earlier correspondence in precisely this way, though it may have been in the frequent encounters between the two during this period.

70 This is the sense of an alternative expression used earlier: 'The rate of profits depends upon the scanty or abundant supply of capital compared with the means of employing it profitably' (see above, p. 138). What is intended there is the determination of commodity prices and profits by aggregate output relative to demand, the latter emanating from population. Malthus is now writing to confirm his position, though he expresses it somewhat differently. Unfortunately, at the very close of the passage given in our text, there is reference to profits depending on 'the proportion of capital to labour,' which, if taken literally rather than as shorthand, does suggest the Ricardian labour-market mechanism.

A second issue relating to value theory is raised by Malthus in his letter of 6 August, but we postpone its examination until we have considered Ricardo's response to the passage treating the profit rate.

Ricardo in his reply formally accepted this proposition, provided that 'by those words you [Malthus] mean the rise or fall of wages. That is my identical proposition' (9 August; 57).[71] The two were as much at cross purposes as they had been in October 1815.

Malthus recognized Ricardo's formal allowance that, with appropriate labour-market conditions, a profit-rate increase might not result from the abandonment of poor land, and tried to force Ricardo to relinquish the principle (a principle that Ricardo did *not* in fact maintain) that agricultural productivity alone governed the profit rate: 'If, as you say, you have no difficulty in agreeing with me that the rate of profits depends mainly upon the demand and supply of stock compared with the demand and supply of labour it is surely allowing that the profits of stock depend upon competition, and not on facility of production; and it will clearly follow that when land is thrown out of cultivation, the profits of stock will not necessarily rise on the remainder, if capital and labour continue still in the same proportion to each other' (8 September; 68–9). But, as for the regular growth process, he himself emphasized the *indirect* role of increasing land scarcity in profit-rate determination – involving *the depression of population growth relative to that of capital, implying output expansion in the face of relatively static demand*: 'Of course I should be the very last to deny that the difficulty

71 Proceeding, however, on his own terms, Ricardo distinguished between rising money wages as a result of labour-market pressures (reflecting rising commodity wages) and rising money wages as a result of falling agricultural productivity. The latter force had 'an incessant operation,' whereas the former did not, so that there was no reason in a secular context to envisage rising commodity wages as a force depressing the profit rate. We are now wholly in the world of Ricardo's *Principles*.

We are given an early glimpse of the methodological principles governing Ricardo's emphasis on agricultural productivity: 'Now if labour rises, no matter from what cause, profits will fall; – but there are two causes which raise the wages of labour, one the demand for labourers being great in proportion to the supply – the other that the food and necessaries of the labourer are difficult of production, or require a great deal of labour to produce them. The more I reflect on the subject the more I am convinced that the latter cause has an incessant operation ... The proportion between labour and capital will undoubtedly affect profits, because it will affect wages, but it is not the only element in the consideration of the subject of profits; – there are other causes which also affect wages' (57–8).

As for the illustration used by Malthus involving a *rise* in agricultural productivity and *constant* profit rate with increasing commodity wages, Ricardo denied the likelihood of a proportional real wage increase: 'It is very seldom that the whole additional produce obtained with the same quantity of labour falls to the lot of the labourers who produce it' (57). (This principle may be applied to the case of falling productivity.) But even if the real wage should absorb the supposed productivity rise, the profit rate would *rise*, in consequence of the abandonment of marginal land: 'but if it should, I should yet contend that the rate of profits would fall [should read: rise] because the price of corn would fall with such an increased facility of production, – capital would be withdrawn from the land, rents would fall and profits rise.' This argument implies given population and demand for corn.

of procuring food has an incessant operation; but to shew that the mode in which it operates is chiefly by checking food and population without *proportionately* checking other sorts of commodities, I would ask whether, if population were miraculously stopped while the most fertile land remained uncultivated, profits would not fall upon the supposition of an increase of capital still going on, owing to the further accumulation of materials and machinery and the employment of a greater *proportion* of the stationary population in productive labour' (69).

It is obviously capital accumulation in manufacturing that is at stake here, driving down the profit rate in the face of a demand that fails to rise proportionately with supply because of the constraint imposed on population growth. The question still remains: Which is the lead sector? For the possibility that Malthus regarded agriculture as the lead sector cannot be precluded; after all, the constraint on population growth and demand emanates from that sector; and that constraint, which has to be explained, implies a *direct* effect of increasing land scarcity on the agricultural profit rate.[72]

Malthus was frustrated: 'I really think that you have sometimes conceeded these points; but such concessions seem quite at variance with your general doctrine respecting profits, which the longer I consider it, appears to me more and more erroneous.' And he pushed home his perspective. In the event of highly productive land but *plentiful* capital relative to population and demand, the profit rate could not be 'very high'; and conversely, high profits under such conditions reflected capital scarcity 'compared with population and demand' – an expression that confirms a concern with aggregate-demand pressure relative to supply, demand emanating from the labour force, rather than Ricardo's direct labour-market pressures: 'The nature of every species of capital may be illustrated by a machine the value of which, however great its powers of production will only be determined by the price necessary to supply it. Upon the same principle in the most fertile soil if nothing is wanted but to plough and sow, and the trifling advances necessary for this purpose are in great abundance compared with the population, is it possible to conceive that the rate of profits should be very high? and does it not follow as I have always said that the productiveness of industry, or the facility of production, is totally different from the productiveness of capital, or the rate of profits [see above, p. 140]. *The only reason why profits on land are generally high in the early periods of society is, because labour is so well paid that population increases faster than capital, and capital is in consequence scarce compared with population and demand*' (69–70; emphasis added).

As is so often the case (above, p. 141), Malthus introduces a special case

72 The analysis in terms of the deceleration of the stimulus to population growth seems to conflict with Malthus's earlier emphasis on a rising corn surplus with increasing land scarcity, which implies a positive stimulus (above, sections II and III).

involving some constraint on population growth and demand, despite highly productive land. But the formulation does bring to a head the key issues. The very circumstance that labour is so well paid in corn at early stages, when land is highly productive (such that the population growth rate, and thus 'demand,' is high), implies that the agricultural profit rate must initially be high to ensure the appropriate growth rate of real (corn) demand for labour. In this case, despite Malthus's ambiguities and apparent assertions to the contrary, his own model entails a *direct* effect of agricultural productivity on the agricultural profit rate. The logic of his own formulations dictates therefore: (1) that the agricultural profit rate *is* governed by productivity conditions; (2) that the manufacturing rate is governed by the aggregate supply–demand conditions, the latter entailing the impact of land supply on population growth. We have a *dual* theory in which the manufacturing rate is kept up to the rate available in agriculture via the pressure of demand.[73]

Approaching the issue, as always, in terms of direct labour-market pressure, Ricardo had no difficulty in agreeing that accumulation in the face of given population must depress the profit rate. This allowance was fully compatible with the inverse wage–profit relation. As he had already pointed out in his previous letter, two distinct forces might act to raise the *money* wage – labour-market pressures which increase the wage basket, and higher costs of 'necessaries' (5 October; 72).[74] But their agreement was a mere formality, since Malthus intended a wholly different process – at least with respect to manufacturing – involving the aggregate demand–supply dimension, *with land scarcity operating on the manufacturing profit rate by way of its effect on population growth, and thus on the demand for manufactures.*

A little earlier in the same letter, Ricardo had written of his hope to see in print Malthus's 'matured opinions on the progress of rent, profits, and wages, and in what manner they are affected by the increasing difficulty of procuring food, by the increase of capital, and the improvement of machinery' (71). To a despondent remark that he had little hope of reaching agreement, Malthus responded more cheerfully, again pushing Ricardo to abandon agricultural productivity as the key to profit-rate determination: 'I am sorry to find that you are hopeless about our agreeing on the subject of labour profits &c. I had some idea that we were approaching, as it appeared to me that by allowing that profits depend upon the demand and supply of labour, you in fact allow that they depend

73 This applies to the secular growth path. It is not precluded that the manufacturing rate can take the lead, forcing the agricultural rate below its potential (see above, p. 145).

74 He at the same time questioned the likelihood of population growth falling far short of that of capital: 'You must however allow that this is an extraordinary case, and out of the common course of events, for the tendency of the population to increase is, in our state of society, more than equal to that of the capital to increase.'

upon competition. Will it not be true in all cases that rent will depend upon the demand compared with the supply of good land, wages on the demand compared with the supply of labour, and profits on the demand compared with the supply of capital. By an increased demand for capital I always mean, such prices of commodities compared with the expences of production as will yield increased profits' (9 October; 77).[75]

This letter closes with an important remark that helps us appreciate Malthus's campaign to divert attention from agricultural productivity: 'If under any facility of production, an increase of capital faster than the increase of labour will lower profits, can it possibly be said that profits depend on facility of production and that the throwing poor land out of cultivation must nessarily raise them.' As on so many previous occasions, agricultural protection is the underlying issue – whether the abandonment of marginal land areas 'necessarily' raises the profit rate or extensions lower it (above, chapter 2: II; and this chapter, Sections III and IV).

VI ON THE WAGE–PROFIT RELATION

We now revert to the letters of early May 1815 and the wage–profit relationship as it there emerges. Ricardo objected to Malthus's predictions relating to a free corn trade (above, p. 137): 'It cannot ... be true that rent, profits and wages can all *really* fall at the same time' (1951–73, VI, 8 May; 226). As for the determination of the real wage, all depended on demand for labour out

75 Ricardo answered by reiterating yet again his case that the money-wage rate was played upon by *two* forces: the market process determining the real wage, and the cost of producing wage goods. Accordingly it was wholly conceivable to envisage a low profit rate despite highly productive land and low corn prices; such would be the case with high commodity wages, owing to a market turned in labour's favour. He concluded: 'All I mean to contend for is that profits depend on wages, wages under common circumstances, on the price of food, and necessaries, and the price of food and necessaries on the fertility of the last cultivated land' (11 October; 78). As for Malthus's expression of distribution in demand–supply terms, there was only limited *formal* agreement: 'In all cases it is perhaps true that rent will depend upon the demand compared with the supply of good land, and wages on the demand compared with the supply of labour, if it be allowed that the price of necessaries influence the demand and supply of labour' (as was to be fully explained in the *Principles*). But the case of capital created difficulty: 'I do not quite understand the expression that profits depend on the demand compared with the supply of capital.' Ricardo here considered a case of two identical economies differing only in their land resources, and suggested that the profit rate would then differ: 'What would you say of two countries in which there are precisely equal capitals, – where wages are also equal, and where the population is precisely in the same number. Would the demand compared with the supply of capital be the same in both? If you say they would I ask whether their rate of profits would be the same under any other supposition but that of their land being exactly of the same degree of fertility? To me it appears quite probable that the ordinary and usual rate of profits might in one be 20 and in the other only 15 pc.^t or in any other proportions' (79).

of capital relative to labour supply; accordingly, increased productivity had no immediate impact on wages such as Malthus had asserted (above, p. 138), and was relevant only if translated into capital accumulation and demand for labour. A rise in the real wage reflecting upward pressure in the labour market would indeed be at the expense of profits; but should the upward movement be accompanied by technical progress in agriculture, a reduction in the profit rate might be avoided. Ricardo also took issue with Malthus's proposition 'that the means of imploying capital profitably can never co-exist with an abundant capital and produce and a stationary population, on account of the necessary effect of such a state of things in increasing the real price of labour' (226–7). *A rising profit rate was, in fact, consistent with a rising commodity wage, assuming technical progress*: 'The rise of wages [is] by no means a necessary effect of an abundant capital and produce, for it may be accompanied with new facilities in procuring corn, and then wages even if they should rise would not lessen profits, they will only keep them lower than they otherwise would be.'[76] If *rising* real wages and profit rates are consistent, assuming increasing productivity, then presumably *falling* real wage and profit rates are consistent, assuming diminishing returns. This implication of Ricardo's last letter of 8 May 1815 reflects the position of 23 October 1814 (above, chapter 2, note 26) and, in particular – considering the explictness of the formulation – that of 18 December 1814 (above, chapter 2, note 35).

As for Malthus, matters are far more complex. His letters of 6 July and 5 August 1814 imply that a reduction in the real wage can insulate the profit rate from falling with reduced agricultural productivity (above, chapter 2: II). By 23 November 1814 the matter *seemed* to have been resolved by acceptance of land scarcity as the source of a downward tendency, both of the profit rate and of the real wage, but unfortunately the falling real wage was inconsistently regarded as capable of insulating the profit rate from decline (above, chapter 2, pp. 86–7). Further remarks in the letter of 12 February 1815 indicate uncertainty regarding the theory of profit-rate determination (above, chapter 3: VI); while those of 12 and 14 March and 18 April revert to the insulation of the profit rate (above, pp.

76 Ricardo closed his letter, and this stage of the debate, by *formally* accepting Malthus's summary of profit-rate determination, but indicating the substantive and profound differences between the two accounts: 'It is true that the rate of profits depends upon the scanty or abundant supply of capital compared with the means of employing it profitably, – and these means will as you say upon the common principles of supply and demand be increased either by a diminution of capital or by an extension of the market for it. Our enquiry is in fact what the causes are of an extension of the market and I hold that the most powerful and the only one which operates permanently, is a reduction in the relative value of food. You appear to me to concede a little respecting demand being regulated by the power of production, - but you are yet very far from yielding all that I demand' (228–9).

118, 129). His letter of 5 May asserts that 'facility of production ... mainly affects the real wages of labour, and not the rate of profits' (above, p. 138), though that assertion assumes constant population, and does not immediately address the full secular case. In December 1815, we have seen, he questioned the logic of a rising *money* wage with diminishing return, given a fall in the corn wage, but clearly he did allow a simultaneous fall in the wage and profit rates (above, p. 151).

A letter of 13 October 1816 attends formally to Ricardo's inverse wage–profit theorem, representing it as a mere 'truism' when expressed in terms of the proportionate shares in given output, but invalid when wages are expressed either in *money* or in *commodity* terms: 'To say that profits depend upon wages appears to me I confess, a very vague proposition, as in fact they may be extremely different with either the same money wages of labour, or the same real wages of labour, although it is unquestionably true, or rather a mere truism, to say that given the production, and supposing it to consist of wages and profits, the higher is the amount of one, the lower must be the amount of the other' (13 October 1816; 1951–73, VII, 79–80). There is a major difference of opinion here, or perhaps incomprehension on Malthus's part.[77] For Ricardo, the same *commodity* wage was consistent with different profit rates, since all depends on the productivity level supposed, the magnitude of the *money* wage incorporating both the commodity wage and the productivity dimension (the price of necessaries); accordingly, given the money wage, the profit rate is specified. And Ricardo's response of 14 October summarizes with admirable clarity his distribution theorem with its use of *money* as a proportions-measuring device.[78]

77 In any event, Malthus proceeds to repeat his own position: 'The real question is, what is the main cause which determines the rate of profits under all the varying degrees of productiveness? and I have no hesitation in answering distinctly that it is the proportion which capital bears to labour; or the plenty or scarcity of capital compared with the plenty or scarcity of labour.' And in reply to Ricardo's query (above, note 75), there is the clarification that 'what I mean by the demand for capital is a scarcity of capital compared with labour.' These formulations taken literally seems to focus on the *real wage* as the direct determinant of the profit rate. But this cannot be the case, both because it would conflict with what is said at the outset of the very same letter and because, as we have seen over and again, it is the aggregate supply–demand relation that he had in mind, aggregate demand depending on population growth.

The definition of 'demand for capital' is not the same as that given on 9 October (above, p. 156). And the formal statement of profit-rate determination also differs, for he had then stated that 'profits [depend] on the demand compared with the supply of capital.'

78 Supposing a case of *rising* productivity (and setting aside rent), the result will be a decrease in the money wage – notwithstanding an increase in the commodity wage – and an inverse variation in the profit rate: 'The money wages of labour are I apprehend generally regulated by facility of production. With an abundant production too I think that a less proportion of the whole will be given to the landlords, and more will remain

Ricardo proceeded to an elaboration of the proportions-measuring property of his *money*, contrasting his position with that of Malthus, whom he understood as denying both: (1) that the profit rate varied with proportionate wages – which is overstated since Malthus had stated it to be a truism not an error; and (2) that the money wage measured proportions: 'The difference between us is this. I say, that with every facility of difficulty of production, of the quantity of necessaries, that is to be divided between profits and wages, different proportions will be given to each, and that money will accurately shew those proportions. You appear to me to think that profits do not depend on the division of the produce, and that money wages may as often rise with facility of production as fall' (81). As for Malthus's summary proposition regarding profit-rate determination: 'You state the real question fairly [;] it is "what is the main cause which determines the rate of profits under all the varying degrees of productiveness?" You do not appear to me to solve the question when you answer "that it is the proportion which capital bears to labour."' His objection turns on the observation that the profit rate is *low* where either the real wage is low or the capital-labour ratio *least*: 'In a rich country where profits are low and where a great portion of produce is paid to the landlords for rent the proportion of labour to capital will be the greatest, and yet according to your theory it should be the least. You will not I think deny that in a country where labour is high a manufacturer would employ more capital to produce the same commodities than what he would do in a country where wages are low, and there also would profits be low, – that is to say profits are high where capital bears a large proportion to labour and low where labour bears a large proportion to capital' (81–2).

We certainly have here ample confirmation of Ricardo's position, whereby with economic growth both the profit and the real-wage rates decline. Ricardo, it is true, was using the term 'proportion of capital to labour' in a different sense from Malthus's, conceiving capital as inclusive of wage outlays, with the very formal or definitional outcome of a low profit rate where the capital/labour ratio is low, 'capital' incorporating (low) wages. This is far removed from Malthus's perspective, in which wages would be low in a 'rich' country subject to land scarcity, generating low population

for the other two classes of capitalists and labourers, – but of this increased quantity a greater proportion will be given to Capitalists, and a less proportion to labourers. Now though what you call the real wages of labour, (but which I think a wrong term,) will increase the money wages will fall. But this will not be the case with profits, what you would call real profits would increase but so would also money profit. Under the circumstances then that I have supposed the rate of profits would rise though money wages would fall' (14 October; 80–1). If we reverse the case and suppose falling productivity, we have here all the standard growth propositions of the *Principles* – *a falling commodity wage but a rising money wage and a falling profit rate.*

growth, and in turn low demand for output and for capital, thereby depressing the profit rate. For all that, we know that for both there is a downward trend in the factor returns. We should, however, keep in mind that, in Malthus's case, it has not been possible to state with certainty that the fall in the real wage is dictated by market pressures affecting the basket as a whole. At times he proceeds consistently with the notion of a given fixed-proportions basket but a declining *corn* wage (above, notes 9, 13, 20, 35, 67).[79]

VII THE SOURCE OF THE CONTRASTING POSITIONS

We have reached the last of the extant letters before the publication of the fifth (1817) edition of Malthus's *Essay on Population*,[80] and of Ricardo's *Principles*, published 19 April 1817. This is an appropriate point to step back and consider the source of their differences until this juncture.

There is, first, the methodological difference suggested in Ricardo's famous declaration that Malthus's concern was with 'the immediate and temporary effects of particular changes,' while his own was with 'the permanent state of things which will result from them' (24 January 1817; 1951–73, VII, 120). Malthus accepted this perspective, taking the opportunity to condemn what has since come to be termed the 'Ricardian Vice': 'I agree with you that one cause of our difference in opinion is that which you mention. I certainly am disposed to refer frequently to things as they are, as the only way of making one's writings practically useful to society, and I think also the only way of being secure from falling into the errors of the taylors of Laputa, and by a slight mistake at the outset arrive at conclusions the most distant from the truth' (26 January; 121–2). Malthus refers, in particular, to the circumstance that 'progress' proceeds typically in *irregular* fashion: 'Besides I really think that the progress of society consists of irregular movements, and that to omit the consideration of causes which for eight or ten years will give a great *stimulus* to production and population, or a great *check* to them, is to omit the causes of the wealth and poverty of nations – the grand object of all enquiries in Political Economy. A writer may, to be sure, make any hypothesis he pleases; but if he supposes what is not at all true practically, he precludes himself from drawing any practical inferences from his hypothesis ... We see in all the countries around us, and in our own particularly, periods of greater and less prosperity, and sometimes of adversity, but *never* the uniform progress which you seem alone to contemplate' (122).[81]

79 On Ricardo's position see my exchange with Gibbard (Gibbard, 1994; Hollander, 1994b).

80 Cf. letter of 26 January 1817: 'I am busy about my new edition which is after all to be three volumes' (1951–73, VII, 123–4). The Preface is dated 7 June 1817.

81 Cf. above, p. 145, regarding 16 October 1815; also chapter 2: III.

The criticism is illustrated by Ricardo's *Essay on Profit*, which supposes 'the real wages of labour constant; but as they vary with every alteration in the prices of commodities, (while they remain nominally the same) and are in reality as variable as profits, there is no chance of your inferences being just as applied to the actual state of things.' Since for Malthus the 'real' wage refers to the commodity wage, and the 'nominal' wage to the money wage, we have here the notion *that growth proceeds with money wages constant.* This notion – which had been expressed late in 1815 (above, p. 150) – sets the Malthusian perception of expansion in opposition to Ricardo's, with its upward tendency to the money wage. This particular criticism of Ricardo does not, however, make a case for a falling *secular* real wage in contrast to Ricardo's fixed wage, but only for *fluctuations* in the real wage (brought about by fluctuations in the corn price relative to a stable money wage). This is not to say that Malthus rejected the downward trend path on principle; only that he insists on taking account also of fluctuations. Methodological preferences of this order can take us only so far, since the striking outcome of our analysis relates to the differing results obtained by the correspondents even when focusing on the *same* range of problems.

The key to our problem will be found in the circumstance that, where Malthus denies an effect of agricultural productivity on the profit rate, he is presuming a situation which in some way freezes secular expansion and imposes a constraint on the expansion of demand. Thus to demonstrate the possible coincidence of high agricultural productivity and a low profit rate at early stages, he imposes constancy of population; this constrains growth of demand for manufacturers, depressing the manufacturing rate, which in turn carries the agricultural rate with it (above, pp. 141, 155). Similarly, his denial of a positive influence on the profit rate of exogenous improvements in agricultural technology or the discovery of fertile land turns on *constant* population, and thus unchanged demand for manufactures (above, p. 137). Malthus himself indeed pointed to his rejection of Say's Law as his 'more specific and fundamental' difference with Ricardo: 'You seem to think that the wants and tastes of mankind are always ready for the supply; while I am most decidedly of opinion that few things are more difficult, than to inspire new tastes and wants, particularly out of old materials; that one of the great elements of demand is the value that people set upon commodities, and that the more completely the supply is suited to the demand the higher will this value be, and the more day's labour will it exchange for, or give the power of commanding. The advantage of foreign commerce consists in a great degree in its tendency to increase this value and the disadvantage of a fall in the money price of any class of commodity which is not made up by a proportionate increase of their quantity, arises from the diminution of the sum of values thus occasioned, or the smaller quantity of labour that these values can command. I am quite of opinion that *practically* the actual check to produce and population arises more from want of stimulus than want of power to produce' (122–3). And more generally, Malthus's rejection of Say's Law is central to his perspective on secular expansion. It explains the linkage between the agricultural profit rate and the general rate, by dictating the manner in which land scarcity impinges on the general rate – namely, via population growth, and thus demand for manufactures.

What, though, of the *direct* consequences of land scarcity for the agricultural profit rate? The evidence from the correspondence shows that Ricardo has priority over Malthus for the falling wage- and profit-rate paths with diminishing returns. Malthus himself later accorded priority to Ricardo for the falling profit rate with diminishing returns, claiming priority for his *Essay on Population* as far as concerns the falling wage, though he did insist also on an *implicit* decline in the profit rate appearing in the *Essay* (see below, pp. 168–9). The *logic* of his own case indeed dictates a fall in the profit rate directly attributable to diminishing returns (above, pp. 141, 146–7, 155). Yet, in the correspondence, he accepted the notion with unease, and only under constant prodding from Ricardo. This hesitancy requires explanation.

There is, first, a matter of overstatement. In his quest to oblige Ricardo to admit the possibility of excess commodity supply, he was carried away, leaving a false impression that agricultural productivity generated no direct effects. By the same token, he set up a straw man when he represented Ricardo's position as relating the profit rate *uniquely* to agricultural productivity. But this was a misrepresentation. Even if we remain within the confines of a single-sector corn model of growth, we have – assuming given savings and demographic propensities – agricultural productivity dictating the rates of capital accumulation and population growth, yielding simultaneously (via demand and supply in the labour market) the wage and profit rates and their trend paths. Unfortunately, Malthus – supposing a blind attachment on Ricardo's part to agricultural productivity, and constrained to deny the extreme version – went too far in his protestations. A related source of misunderstanding flows from the eagerness to emphasize short-run deviations from the trend mentioned earlier – deviations lasting two decades are often referred to, usually with the Napoleonic period in mind. Belief that Ricardo entirely neglected such deviations seems to have led him to bend the rod too far in the other direction and exaggerate his own objections to the role of agricultural productivity in profit-rate determination.

There is a further element to consider – namely, an apparently temporary diversion of attention emphasizing *the lead role of manufacturing* in determining the agricultural profit rate. This perspective Malthus raised in 1815 as an analytical novelty in response to Ricardo's *Essay on Profits.* It entails the positive effect on total surplus (rent and profits combined) of an increase in the corn price of manufactures (P_c/P_m) with rising corn costs 'in a rich and progressive country' (above, p. 117). The higher surplus in turn raises demand for manufactures, preventing the fall in the manufacturing rate of profit that would otherwise occur with accumulation; since two profit rates are excluded, this fixes the agricultural rate and accounts for the division of the surplus between rent and profits. The determination of the manufacturing rate via demand emanating from a higher agricultural surplus and the playback onto agriculture, which accounts for the breakdown of the surplus between landlord and capitalists, forces the conclusion that, in early 1815 – despite the *Inquiry* – Malthus was not yet firmly committed to the notion of a direct effect of changes in secular land-scarcity conditions on the agricultural profit rate.

The analysis was also applied to a rise in the corn price of manufactures attributable to an *initial* increase in the demand for corn. Here, and in fact throughout the correspondence, there emerges the issue of *agricultural protection*. At the outset of the correspondence, Malthus maintained that the Corn Laws would *raise* the profit rate (above, chapter 2: II), and the analysis suggested to Malthus by Ricardo's *Essay* provided new support for that case. The argument for protection related in part to the resultant increase in the demand for home corn, which assures a high (short-run) corn price, thus stimulating expansion with no fall in the profit rate – conversely, in the event of the opening of the ports; and in part to the secular effect of domestic agricultural expansion in drawing capital from manufactures, thus reducing the 'competition of capital' (above, pp. 130, 136).

This perspective, entailing a complex interconnection between the two sectors, with the manufacturing profit rate dictating the agricultural profit rate, though itself played upon by agricultural cost conditions, seems to have been weakened, as far as it concerns the *secular* path, by a concession that the benefits of a high corn price pertained when this price is not 'solely' attributable to increased difficulty of production (above, p. 134). And its relevance for *agricultural protection* – an initial high corn price via increased demand for corn – was undermined by the recognition that, since materials' costs rise along with corn, any increase in the corn price of manufactures is severely constrained (above, pp. 121, 142).

VIII FIRST REACTIONS TO RICARDO'S *PRINCIPLES*[82]

Ricardo's *Principles* appeared on 19 April 1817.[83] On 17 August, Malthus gave his summary opinion (1951–73, VII, 176). Agricultural productivity as

82 I set aside the temporal sequence, postponing discussion of the 1817 version of the *Essay on Population* until chapter 5.

83 Malthus had access to the manuscript in March (cf. Ricardo, 1951–73, VII, 139, 143, 145).

determinant of profits held good as a 'limiting case,' but was unhelpful 'practically,' a theme stated as early as October 1814 (above, chapter 2: III). As for the labour 'measure' of exchange value – actually, labour as determinant of exchange value is intended here – that was false 'in theory or fact': 'I have read over your book again with much gratification. There is much collateral matter in which I quite agree with you. I also quite agree with you that the difficulty of procuring subsistence is the necessarily limiting cause with regard to profits, but I still cannot agree with you that labour alone in the sense you understand it is either in theory or fact the best measure of exchangeable value; or that the state of the land practically determines the existing rate of profits in different countries. Pray do you allow that in different countries, where profits are different, your theory of value does not hold good. I dont feel quite sure.' Ricardo in reply conceded readily the latter point: 'I certainly allow that my theory of value does not hold good in different countries when profits are different' (4 September; 186), referring Malthus to the comparative-cost principle (1951–73, I, 133).

In this same letter Ricardo wrote of the current upturn in activity (VII, 185–6);[84] and on 10 October he reiterated his optimistic prognosis (192). Malthus leaped on those observations regarding contemporary circumstances to raise various issues relating to their respective growth models. For one thing, the coincidence of low profits and low wages – the challenge implies Malthus referred to low *money* wages – pointed away from Ricardo's position: 'We have both of us, as you observe, always been confident in the resources of the country, and there is certainly now every appearance that our views will be justified by the result. The present state of things however perhaps tends to contradict one of your opinions respecting profits. Labour has certainly fallen, and though I have no doubt it will rise again gradually and is in fact now rising; yet it must be allowed that now while it is low, profits and interest are also low' (12 October; 193). To this Ricardo replied that, while the interest rate was indeed low, this did not signify a low profit rate in the going (disequilibrium) circumstances: 'Although interest is undoubtedly ultimately regulated by profits, rising when they are high, and falling when they are low, yet there are considerable intervals during which a low rate of interest is compatible with a high rate of profit, and this generally occurs when capital is moving from the employments of war to those of peace' (21 October; 199). Ricardo thus defended his theory involving *full employment* by reference to

84 He doubted 'whether we have even during the late distresses ceased to advance as a nation in wealth, but at present I think no one can doubt that we are again making forward strides in prosperity, – a bad harvest does not perhaps very much check the progress of wealth, but it materially interferes with the general happiness.'

data derived from a disequilibrium state. Malthus (quite rightly) rejected this defence, which implied that on *average* the profit rate was high, since profits had been generally low in the postwar period: 'It is impossible I think to doubt that profits have been low, as well as interest during the last two or three years. What destroyed so much agricultural capital, but low profits or rather no profits? and what occasioned so much distress among merchants and manufacturers but a want of demand and fall of prices?' (3 December; 214).

Malthus's express concern was with an approach to profit-rate determination that was of some practical relevance; and the focus was to be on 'variations in general prices' since they were 'unquestionably much more common, than variations in value arising from different quantities of labour imployed in producing corn,' though these general price movements were governed by movements in the corn price: 'Such variations of prices, or of the circulating [*sic* – circulating medium?] if you please, begin in my opinion perpetually with a rise in the price of corn, and proceed successively, and not immediately, to other commodities. This has certainly been the case with us, during the last 25 years.' Considering his interpretation elsewhere of the postwar depression, Malthus probably intended an impact on manufacturing prices of rising corn prices acting via *demand* for manufactures rather than via manufacturing *costs.*[85] He went further and denied the occurrence of any increase in the real cost of corn over the preceding eight or nine decades or that real-cost increases could account for recent corn-price increases (214–15).[86] 'Surely,' he concluded, 'it would be most unsafe and incorrect to draw any conclusions respecting the rate of profits from the assumption that [general] prices remain the same, in the midst of continual variations in the circulating medium which you yourself acknowledge.'

In conclusion, Malthus summarized his own position on profit-rate determination: 'The question I put to you in my last letter[87] was intended

85 Subsequently higher aggregate agricultural revenues and expenditure are explicitly attributed to poor harvests (below, p. 166).

86 See on this below, chapter 15: V.

87 The query of 12 October was the following: 'Capital is wholly employed in the purchase of materials and machinery, and the maintenance of labour. If from any cause whatever, materials machinery and the maintenance of the labourer, and his wages, fall considerably in money value, is it *possible* that the same amount of monied capital can be employed in the country?' (193). To this Ricardo replied: 'I answer that it is *possible* but by no means probable. Suppose the mines were to produce a diminished quantity of the precious metals, at the same time that materials and machinery were greatly increased in quantity; might not the increased aggregate quantity of materials and machinery be of a greater money value than before, altho each particular portion should be at a less? Might we not by importation appropriate to ourselves a larger proportion of the mass of money distributed amongst all the countries of the world? I cannot doubt the *possibility* of the case' (21 October; 200).

to imply the absolute incompatibility of an abundant capital with high profits; and to shew that profits depend *entirely* upon the competition of capital, or the state of capital compared with labour, and not on the state of the land. The high relative price of labour is an effect, and not an original cause' (215; emphasis added). By 'competition of capital' – a Smithian phrase – Malthus alludes to reduced general prices with excess commodity supply, which entails a rise in the real wage (presumably of those employed); that is the sense of his allusion to a 'high relative price of labour [as] an effect.'[88] This statement formally precludes any effect on the profit rate emanating from agriculture, even in *limiting* cases. But Malthus was not in fact concerned here with the growth process, as such; it is probably safe to say that this strong assertion reflects his position on contemporary movements of the profit rate, and not on matters of principle relating to secular matters. (We shall see, in fact, that the notion of the relevance of agricultural productivity, at least in the 'limit,' is reiterated later in the correspondence.)

Malthus had also maintained on 12 October that Ricardo failed to draw the correct conclusion from his valid observation that a scanty harvest 'does not perhaps very much check the progress of wealth' (cited above, note 84). That circumstance, Malthus insisted, pointed to his own view that an increase in *aggregate* value – such as is generated by a poor harvest – acts to stimulate growth: 'I quite agree with you in what you said in your previous letter on the effects of a scanty harvest upon the progress of national wealth; but I draw from it an inference favourable to my hypothesis that an increase of the value of the general [agricultural] produce determined by the supply and the demand, is the great stimulus to industry and future production and will often more than counteract, in reference to general and future wealth, the evils of a dearth to individuals, if it does not go too far. Abundance without increase of value, (which you contemplate as the result of foreign trade) would, it appears to me, necessarily lead to a stagnation of demand and of industry. If the value of the national produce however abundant will not command more labour this year than the last, the demand for labour must be stationary and the new labourers coming into the market must be unemployed' (193–4). This response is in line with the general case that expansion of aggregate value, as by extended trade, is stimulating (see below, chapter 13).

Ricardo's reply in this regard was, in fact, conciliatory. He claimed to be in substantial agreement since all hinged on the stimulus to industry generated by the low real wages characteristic of a period of poor harvest (200–1). Needless to say, the agreement was not a substantive one since Malthus was referring to an effect on industry acting from the demand, not

88 Cf. the statement of 22 December 1815 (above, p. 150) regarding general profits falling 'from a general fall of prices compared with labour.'

the cost, side. It is regrettable that Ricardo did not take up the challenge of 3 December relating to the *fact* of low profits. His letter of 16 December makes no substantive contribution to the debate.

Mention should be made, finally, of an important letter by Malthus that shows his more general difference with Ricardo. In a letter of 21 October 1818, he pointed to the Law of Markets as the major 'practical' difference between them, and traced Ricardo's position to a failure to recognize the role of 'value' as stimulus to wealth or output: 'I am inclined to think that where we shall most essentially differ in our practical conclusions is on the point where Say and Mill are distinctly with you. Your conclusions however naturally follow from your original definition of value in exchange and your too decided separation of wealth and value, which I have always thought fundamentally wrong. You have quite overlooked the consideration of *value* as the prime power of industry and the grand stimulus to production' (312). Once again we find confirmation that Malthus envisaged his own major contribution to lie in the role accorded aggregate-demand considerations.

IX A SUMMING-UP ON THE TREND PATHS OF THE FACTOR RETURNS

Malthus struggled with the manuscript of his own *Principles*, in part held back by difficulties raised in discussion with Ricardo. One involved Ricardo's inverse wage–profit relation, turning on the money wage. Malthus hit upon a special case where (by construction) the money wage is *necessarily constant* during the expansion process: 'Under these circumstances I should like to know from you how the profits of stock would be *regulated*. They could not evidently be regulated by the rise in money wages of labour, because labour would not alter in money value' (10 September 1819; 1951–73, VIII, 65).[89] The preface to his query implies the operation of increasing competition of capitals reducing *manufacturing* prices: 'The money price of labour could never permanently either rise or fall; and the accumulation of capital in all cases where capital was used and the same quantity of labour employed, would shew itself in a fall of prices owing to the diminished rate of profits.'[90] Only the corn price would rise 'on account of the increased quantity of labour required; but the rise would be inconsiderable, and strictly limited by the diminution of *corn* wages which the labourer could bear.' The 'inconsiderable' increase in the cost price reflects the partial compensation provided by a reduced profit rate. And

89 The special case involves a given quantity of silver 'picked up [without capital] by a days search on the sea shore,' money then always costing and commanding the same quantity of labour (see below, chapter 7). But throughout the earlier correspondence Malthus had argued for constancy of the money wage expressed in *real-world* money.

90 This formulation is troublesome since it is left open why the rate of profit falls. One would have expected that fall to be attributable to the fall of manufacturing prices, not the reverse.

the 'limit' to the process governs the approach to stationariness: 'I am strongly disposed to think that a rise of money wages, supposing money always to retain its value, is by no means absolutely necessary in the progress of cultivation to its extreme limits. It is only necessary that corn should rise to such a point, as with fixed money wages will put a stop to the further increase of population.'[91]

The decline in the corn wage – governed by land-scarcity conditions – thus provides the immediate key to the deceleration and ultimate cessation of population growth. (See chapter 5, below, for the analysis in the 1817 version of the *Essay on Population.*) Unfortunately, the course of the *profit rate* is neglected, except for its decline in the manufacturing sector. Possibly it is taken for granted that this is the rate to which agriculture adjusts since there cannot exist two rates in the economy (though precisely how, in that case, the equalization occurs is an open question); or Malthus was perhaps silently assuming a fall of the agricultural rate, directly related to deteriorating productivity, to which the manufacturing rate conforms. It is the second reading that may be preferable: (1) because so much of the correspondence to this point at least implies a direct effect of land-scarcity conditions on the agricultural rate; (2) because such an effect is spelled out in the 1817 *Essay on Population* – though in a model limited to agriculture (see below, chapter 5); and (3) because the *Principles*, at this time under preparation for publication, adopts such an effect. There we find a parallel between 'the laws which regulate the rate of profits and the progress of capital' and those 'which regulate the rate of wages and the progress of population,' and the attribution to Ricardo of priority for the theorem regarding a *falling profit rate* with increasing land scarcity; and priority to himself (in the *Essay on Population*) for the *falling real wage* owing to the same cause: 'Mr. Ricardo has very clearly shown that the rate of profits must diminish, and the progress of accumulation be finally stopped, under the most favourable circumstances, by the increasing difficulty of

91 The *actual* behaviour of the money wage is a separate issue. Malthus, in fact, continues by allowing an increase in the money wage during the growth process, but this reflects a fall in 'the value of money': 'In general when money wages rise, which is one of the commonest events in the progress of wealth, I am inclined to think, it may be fairly concluded that the value of money has fallen. According to my measure of value indeed I should say at once that money had fallen if it would command less labour; and according to your theory it could only command less labour and yet retain the same value, from the accidental circumstance of capital being employed in the production of it.'

In a subsequent letter to McCulloch, Ricardo complained of Malthus's loose use of his measure: 'Mr. M. adopts a measure of value very different from mine, but he no where adheres to it. Sometimes when he speaks of the rise of commodities he means their rise in money, at other times their rise in labour' (2 May 1820, 180; see also 13 June, 193). The above passage provides us with an example of Malthus's imprecision and looseness.

procuring the food of the labourer. I, in like manner, endeavoured to show in my *Essay on the principle of population*, that, under circumstances the most favourable to cultivation which could possibly be supposed to operate in the actual state of the earth, the [1836: real] wages of the labourer would [1836: gradually] become more scanty, and the progress of population be finally stopped by the increasing difficulty of procuring the means of subsistence' (1820, 370–1; 1836, 327). Even so, it is important to recognize that nothing is said of the *indirect* consequence of increasing land scarcity involving decelerating population growth and demand for manufactures that figure so conspicuously in the earlier correspondence.

It is unclear from this whether Malthus allowed that Ricardo also adopted the falling real-wage trend. His specific concern was with the profit-rate trend, regarding the analysis of which he found Ricardo wanting for his neglect of *other* possible causes of decline: 'But Mr. Ricardo has not been satisfied with proving the position just stated. He has not been satisfied with showing that the difficulty of procuring the food of the labourere is the only *absolutely necessary* cause of the fall of profits, in which I am ready fully and entirely to agree with him: but he has gone on to say, that there is *no other cause* of the fall of profits in the actual state of thing that has any degree of permanence. [1836, note: By this expression I mean such a degree of permanence as to be called the ordinary rates of profits.]' (1820, 371; 1836, 327).

* * *

Ricardo had little trouble dealing with the artificial case Malthus had devised. According to his *general* theory, the profit rate varies inversely with the proportional share of wages, even if the money wage (held constant for Malthus's supposition) failed as a proportions-measuring device. More specifically, he agreed that the corn price might rise because of diminishing returns, and the corn wage therefore decline; but he insisted that, none the less, *proportional* wages must rise: 'The supposition you make of half an ounce of silver being picked up on the sea shore by a day's labour, is you will confess an extravagant one. Under such circumstances silver could not as you say rise or fall, neither could labour, but corn could or rather might. Profits I think would still depend on the proportions of produce allotted to the capitalist and the labourer. – The whole produce would be less, which would cause its price to rise, but of the quantity produced the labourer would get a larger proportion than before. This larger proportion would nevertheless be a less quantity than before, and would be of the same money value. In the case you suppose the rise of money wages does not appear to be necessary in the progress of cultivation to its extreme limits, but the reason is that you have excluded the use of capital entirely in the production of your medium of value' (21 September

1819; 1951–73, VIII, 21).[92] Regarding this response to his query, in terms of proportionate wages, Malthus briefly noted: 'Your answer to my query was as I expected, and I agree with you' (14 October; 108).

This is potentially important, for it suggests that Malthus *accepted the inverse wage–profit relation as a theorem regarding proportions.*[93] But there are problems. Ricardo himself was uncertain regarding Malthus's position on the relation of the profit rate to labour's proportionate share in the product to be divided between labour and capital: 'The truth of this doctrine I deem to be absolutely demonstrable, yet I think that Mr. Malthus does not fully admit it' (letter to McCulloch, 13 June 1820; 195). This is scarcely surprising since on 22 December 1818, he had reported (to James Mill) a major change of position by Malthus on rent – rejection of the notion of no-rent land and, *with it, the notion that cost price excludes rent.*

92 Ricardo adds that it is no 'accident' that money is produced by labour and capital rather than by labour alone: 'You know I agree with you that money is a more variable commodity than is generally imagined, and therefore I think that many of the variations in the price of commodities may be fairly attributed to an alteration in the value of money. It is difficult to conceive that in a great, and civilized country any commodity of importance could be produced with equal advantage without the employment of capital.'

93 His immediate concern, however, related more specifically to the technology entailed in producing the monetary commodity: 'You observe that my supposition is an extravagant one. It is so. But perhaps it is safer to reject capital and profits entirely, than to apply them in any given way, under the certainty that scarcely any other commodity can reasonably be supposed to have required in its production exactly the same quantity of fixed and circulating capital employed for exactly the same time. On any supposition you can make respecting the capital employed in the production of the precious metals, it is scarcely possible that all your calculations should not be necessarily and fundamentally erroneous.'

Ricardo's response to this (9 November) is the celebrated insistance that his 'calculations' (his numerical calculations) were designed to 'elucidate a principle'; he did not doubt they were 'erroneous.' In this specific case, the principle was the proportionality theorem, governed by the real (labour) cost of producing wage goods: 'With respect to my calculations, I have only this to say in defence of them, that I never brought them forward for any practical use, but merely to elucidate a principle. It is no answer to my theory to say that "it is scarcely possible that all my calculations should not be necessarily and fundamentally erroneous," for that I do not deny, but still it is true that the proportion of produce in agriculture or manufactures, retained by the capitalist who sets the labourers to work, will depend on the quantity of labour necessary to provide for the maintenance and support of the labourers' (130).

In a letter to McCulloch the following May, Ricardo rehearses his own position, but utilizing *Malthus's* special money thus: 'If produced by labour only – if half an ounce of silver could be picked up on the sea shore by a day's labour, the natural price of labour would be always half an ounce of silver, it could neither rise nor fall. Corn might however be produced with more difficulty, and by the rise of its price, the wages of the labourer would be less adequate to procure him comforts and conveniences. In this case I should say wages would rise, because I always measure the rise of every thing by the quantity of labour necessary to produce it, and the wages though less in quantity would require more labour to produce them' (2 May 1820; 179).

Ricardo himself protested that his case stood firm, given the formulation in terms of the *intensive* margin: '[Malthus] read to me some more of his intended publication. He has altered his opinion you know about there being land in every country which pays no rent, and appears like M Say to think that when that is proved, my doctrine of rent not entering into price is overthrown – they neither of them advert to the other principle which cannot be touched, of capital being employed on land, already in cultivation, which pays no rent. I have entered my protest against his omitting the consideration of this important fact' (1951–73, VII, 372). And again to Mill on 28 December: 'Is it not wonderful that after Malthus publication on rent (1814), after acknowledging the same principles as I contend for, he should now agree with Say, and contend that there is no corn grown in any country which does not pay a rent? – he says that he committed an error in saying otherwise, and that I have followed him in it, and by the conclusions which I draw from it, have proved the incorrectness of the principle' (379).[94]

* * *

One further substantive matter was raised by Malthus on 14 October 1819. On his reading of Ricardo's theory of profits, the contraction of agriculture upon the relaxing of corn-import restrictions generates a higher profit rate by way of the effect of a lower money wage *in the manufacturing sector*, given manufacturing prices. The profit rate in agriculture merely *comes into line.* For this interpretation he sought confirmation, though it is unclear what he might have had in mind in raising this issue: 'Pray just tell me whether, when land is thrown out of cultivation from the importation of foreign corn, you consider the new rate of profits as determined by the state of the land, or the stationary prices of manufactured and mercantile products compared with the fall of wages. According to your view of the subject, will not capital be withdrawn from the land, till the last capital yields the profit obtained by the fall of wages in manufactures, on the supposition of the price of such manufactures remaining stationary' (1951–73, VIII, 108). Ricardo readily confirmed the reading, thus providing a striking indication that, for him, profits are *not* determined in the agricultural sector: 'You ask me "whether when land is thrown out of cultivation from the importation of foreign corn, I consider the new rate of profits as determined by the state of the land, or the stationary prices of manufactured and mercantile

94 Ricardo complained that de Sismondi (1819) made the same error: 'In his attacks on me he is not candid but misrepresents me in several instances. – He as well as Say attempts to refute the doctrine of rent, because there is no land they say which does not pay rent' (Ricardo to James Mill, 6 September 1819; VIII, 57). See also the same complaint made directly to Say (11 January 1820; 149–50).

products compared with the fall of wages." You have correctly anticipated my answer: "Capital will" I think "be withdrawn from the land, till the last capital yields the profit obtained (by the fall of wages) in manufactures, on the supposition of the price of such manufactures remaining stationary"' (9 November; 130). Unfortunately, there is no (extant) response to this letter, which seems to be the last prior to the appearance of Malthus's *Principles.*

As for Malthus himself, we have seen that, while he accorded a role for increasing land scarcity in forcing down the corn wage (a process involving an upward trend in the corn price relative to a constant money wage), the secular course of the agricultural profit rate is left unclear. (Only the downward trend in the manufacturing rate is explicit.) We have argued, however, that Malthus presumably did not deny land scarcity as a relevant consideration in secular profit-rate analysis, especially considering the analysis in the *Principles* itself, where the direct effect of agricultural productivity is reinforced with a vengeance, Malthus adopting a Sraffa-like *corn-profit model* to explain the profit rate to which the manufacturing rate must accord (see below, chapter 10). But what in our discussion of the early correspondence we have called the 'indirect' effects of increasing land scarcity operating on the manufacturing rate via deceleration of population growth and demand makes no appearance. The same is true of the 1817 *Essay* (see below, chapter 5). An important exploratory theme had been abandoned or forgotten.

FIVE

The *Essay on Population* revised (1817)

I INTRODUCTION

The 1817 edition of the *Essay on Population* contains a considerably sharpened analysis of the land-based growth model – the 'canonical' classical model (Samuelson, 1978) – with particular reference to the falling trend paths of the corn-wage and the profit rates. This contrasts with earlier versions of the *Essay*, where only the declining wage is allowed. The 1817 version abandons the hesitancy documented above, in chapter 4, to allow a *direct* effect on the profit rate emanating from land-productivity conditions, and has nothing to say about the *indirect* effect involving an impact on population growth and demand for *manufactures*.

Much of relevance for us is to be found in a triptych of chapters in Book III: 'Of the Agricultural System' (ch. 8), 'Of the Commercial System' (ch. 9), and 'Of Systems of Agriculture and Commerce Combined' (ch. 10), a complex that replaces two chapters dealing with 'agricultural and commercial systems' in earlier editions.[1] Section II, below, considers

1 The preparation of the edition of 1817 was set in motion much earlier. On 1 October 1815, Malthus wrote to Ricardo: 'I am now thinking about a new edition of the Essay which Murray wishes to have finished before anything else is done. I am now casting the chapters about the agricultural and commercial systems, and making them apply more directly to the main subject; but am greatly puzzled about what to do with the chapter on the bounty, the greatest part of which I still think quite correct, and am unwilling therefore to throw it out, lest it should give rise to charges of a change of opinion which I do not feel. My real change of opinion is very *partial* indeed' (Ricardo, 1951–73, VI, 289). On the new edition see also above, chapter 4, note 80.

checks to growth in 'agricultural systems' – systems without practical land constraints – of a sociological or institutional nature, including capital scarcity; checks to growth in 'commercial systems' entailing a concept akin to Smithian 'competition of capitals' applicable specifically to manufactures; and checks to growth in a much-championed 'mixed system' such as Britain's. Here the Smithian problem is avoided, and any checks reflect increasing land scarcity alone. Of particular interest is the allowance, despite a falling corn wage, for the possibility of an unchanged *commodity* basket in consequence of the higher corn price of manufactured wage goods.

Sections III and IV lay out the formal growth model with a particular eye to prudential population control, both exogenous and endogenous to the growth process, the latter relating to the influence on behaviour of the rising corn price of manufactures. (For an elaboration of the notion of 'prudence' see below, chapter 18: IV.) Disturbances to the *ceteris paribus* conditions on which the falling trend paths of the factor returns are predicated are dealt with in section V.

Section VI considers Malthus's response in an appendix of 1817 to criticisms by John Weyland (1816). This provides another opportunity to consider the methodological underpinnings to Malthus's position on economic growth and the problem of population, with particular reference to the consequences of urbanization. The complexities introduced by allowance for a growing manufacturing sector are examined further in section VII.

In section VIII we take up a matter that had preoccupied Malthus from the outset (see above, chapter 1): the order of precedence of food supply and population growth and the so-called oscillatory process. The chapter closes with a statement of some interpretive problems.

II CHECKS TO GROWTH IN 'AGRICULTURAL,' 'COMMERCIAL,' AND 'MIXED' SYSTEMS

In Book III, Chapter 8, 'Of the Agricultural System' (1817), Malthus refers to the common view that, since agriculture produces subsistence beyond the needs of the cultivators, the population of an economy 'could never be checked from the want of the means of subsistence' (1817, II, 381). This he denied – population growth may cease, notwithstanding available land resources and high profits: 'The increase of such a country is not immediately checked, either by the want of power to produce, or even by the deficiency of the actual produce of the soil compared with the population.' This should not be read as a denial of limits to growth emanating from land scarcity, for some such ultimate check is implied by what follows regarding the United States. Rather, his concern is specifically to elucidate various 'immediate checks' sometimes encountered independent of land scarcity: 'if we examine the condition of [the] labouring classes [in agricultural systems], we shall find that the real wages of their labour are such as essentially to check and regulate their increase, by checking and regulating their command over the means of subsistence' (381–2). Such a check may apply even with available agricultural resources in the sense of a high actual (and potential) surplus over the wage.[2]

The analysis commences by reference, for contrast, to the American case: 'In a country where there is an abundance of good land, where there are no difficulties in the way of its purchase and distribution, and where there is an easy foreign vent for raw produce, both the profits of stock and the wages of labour will be high. These high profits and high wages, if habits of economy pretty generally prevail, will furnish the means of a rapid accumulation of capital and a great and continued demand for labour, while the rapid increase of population which will ensue will maintain undiminished the demand for produce, and check the fall of profits. If the extent of territory be considerable, and the population comparatively inconsiderable, the land may remain understocked both with capital and people for some length of time, notwithstanding a rapid increase of both; and it is under these circumstances of the agricultural system that labour is able to command the greatest portion of the necessaries of life, and that the condition of the labouring classes of society is the best' (382–3). Here we have allusion to high profit and wage rates, out of which savings are made at a rapid pace, assuring a constant growth rate of labour demand at a high level. One notes the ultimate dependency of this set of conditions on a low population/land ratio (allowance made for land quality). By strong implication, should this ratio deteriorate – should diminishing returns set in – both the profit and the wage rates (and the capital and population growth rates) will decline.

This version of the 'mature' growth model contains two complexities. The first is the assumption of an open economy entailing the export of corn – 'an easy foreign vent for raw produce.' The second complexity is the notion (emerging also in correspondence) that rapid population growth 'checks' – though apparently cannot prevent – the fall of profits by maintaining a high 'demand for produce,' a term usually reserved for food rather than manufactures. For the downward profit-rate trend in the absence of this counter-force, no *formal* rationale is offered; the negative effect on the profit rate of increasing land scarcity seems to be taken for granted as self-evident.[3]

The discussion of the American case is intended as a prologue by way of

2 This is not a new theme, but it is much developed in the new chapter.

3 The high real wage characterizing the American case must be qualified by the relatively low command by labour over foreign manufactured goods. Thus the real differential between contemporary American and English earnings is played down. And, in fact, the picture of real English wages is remarkably buoyant; one contemporary observer 'could not help wondering where the poor of England and their dwellings were concealed' (387).

contrast to the main analysis – namely, states of stationariness (or near-stationariness), notwithstanding available land resources and high profit rates. These are the consequence of *capital scarcity*: 'The instances where, under the agricultural system, the condition of the lower classes of society is very wretched, are more frequent. When the accumulation of capital stops, whatever may be the cause, the population, before it comes to a stand, will always be pressed on as near to the limits of the actual means of subsistence, as the habits of the lower classes of the society will allow; that is, the real wages of labour will sink, till they are only just sufficient to maintain a stationary population' (391). The passage proceeds to the key proposition that the degree of prudential restraint is affected by forces *endogenous* to the system, particularly the ratio of corn to manufacturing prices: 'Should this happen, as it frequently does, while land is still in abundance and capital scarce, the profits of stock will naturally be high; but corn will be very cheap, owing to the goodness and plenty of the land, and the stationary demand for it, notwithstanding the high profits of stock; while these high profits, together with the usual want of skill and proper division of labour, which attend a scanty capital, will render all domestic manufactured commodities comparatively very dear. This state of things will naturally be unfavourable to the generation of those habits of prudential restraint which most frequently arise from the custom of enjoying conveniences and comforts, and it is to be expected that the population will not stop till the wages of labour, estimated even in food, are very low' (391–2).

Slow population growth could not be attributed, as some maintained, to the mere fact of an agriculturally based economy; the 'premature check to the capital and the demand for labour, which occurs in some of the countries of Europe, while land continues in considerable plenty' – Poland, parts of Russia, Siberia, and European Turkey – was 'not occasioned by the particular direction of their industry [to agriculture], but by the vices of the government and the structure of the society, which prevent its full and fair development in that direction' (394). The moral is to examine the sociological and institutional considerations governing savings decisions; for 'the quantity of food permanently awarded to the labourer may be such as not to allow of an increase of population; and their state, in respect to their being progressive, stationary or declining, will depend upon other causes than that of directing their attention principally to agriculture' (400–1).

* * *

The chapter 'Of the Agricultural System' thus contests a presumption that such an economy could never encounter checks to population growth; checks existed even in cases of *low* population density. In the companion chapter, 'Of the Commercial System' (1817) – which reinforces a briefly mentioned theme of 1803 regarding the significance of *domestic* agriculture for the maintenance of a healthy manufacturing sector (1986, *3*, 673) – Malthus rejects the position that population growth in an economy based on manufacturing and commerce might proceed unchecked until the lands of agriculturally based trading partners were 'fully cultivated' (1817, II, 402). In fact, there were several sources of premature deceleration and ultimate stationariness. The first relates to 'foreign competition': 'It is unreasonable ... to expect that any one country, merely by the force of skill and capital, should remain in possession of markets uninterrupted by foreign competition. But, when a powerful foreign competition takes place, the exportable commodities of the country in question must soon fall to prices which will essentially reduce profits; and the fall of profits will diminish both the power and the will to save. Under these circumstances the accumulation of capital will be slow, and the demand for labour proportionably slow, till it comes nearly to a stand' (403–4). The fall in profits is here unrelated to increasing land scarcity; the ratio P_c/P_m indeed rises, but because of an absolute reduction in P_m, not an absolute increase in P_c. It is an important part of the argument that savings are positively stimulated by the return on capital, $S = f(r)$, reflecting both the motive and the ability to save; moreover, as r falls to some minimum, net savings, and accordingly net growth of labour demand, ceases, and with it net population growth. Here are the ingredients of the 'canonical' growth model, but in a context involving an open economy engaged in the export of manufactures in exchange for food.

The theme of an undermining of the manufacturing nation's competitive edge emerges again subsequently in the brief chapter. Specialization patterns are not graven in stone, and the declining profit rate in the foreign (agricultural) economy, for which no formal rationale is provided, is said to act as motive for diversification abroad to the detriment of the manufacturing nation: 'It is generally an accidental and temporary, not a natural and permanent, division of labour, which constitutes one state the manufacturer and the carrier of others. While, in these landed nations, agricultural profits continue very high, it may fully answer to them to pay others as their manufacturers and carriers; but when the profits on land fall, or the tenures on which it can be held are not such as to encourage the investment of an accumulating capital, the owner of this capital will naturally look towards commerce and manufactures for its employment; and, according to the just reasoning of Adam Smith and the Economists, finding at home both the materials of manufactures, the means of subsistence, and the power of carrying on their own trade with foreign countries, they will probable be able to conduct the business of manufacturing and carrying for themselves at a cheaper rates than if they allowed it to continue in the hands of others ... And thus, in the natural progress of national improvement, and without the competition of superior skill and capital, a purely commercial state must be undersold and driven out of the markets by those who possess the advantage of land' (411–12).

The possibility of an agricultural economy attaining stationariness, notwithstanding a high profit rate and good land resources, in consequence of indolence and ill-governance is a theme we have already encountered (above, pp. 174–6). In our present context, Malthus adds that, should foreign agricultural development be thus halted, the growth rate of the domestic manufacturing economy (including population growth) would be threatened, a threat manifested in deteriorating terms of trade: 'Unless ... an increase of wealth and demand were produced in the surrounding countries, the increasing ingenuity and exertions of the manufacturing and commercial state would be lost in continually falling prices. It would not only be obliged, as its skill and capital increased, to give a larger quantity of manufactured produce for the raw product which it received in return; but it might be unable, even with the temptation of reduced prices, to stimulate its customers to such purchases as would allow of an increasing importation of food and raw materials; and without such an increasing importation, it is quite obvious that the population must become stationary' (409–10). The chapter closes with a caution that a check to corn imports into a 'manufacturing and commercial nation' for any of the foregoing reasons would reduce the population growth rate in 'nearly the same proportion' (398). The final formulation is important for its account of a *stationary state* at which real wages are reduced to 'subsistence' (defined in cultural terms): 'Universally it may be observed, that if, from any cause or causes whatever, the funds for the maintenance of labour in any country cease to be progressive, the effective demand for labour will also cease to be progressive; and wages will be reduced to that sum, which, under the existing prices of provisions, and the existing habits of the people, will just keep up, and no more than keep up, a stationary population ... [As] long as it is unable to make yearly additions to its imports of food, it will evidently be unable to furnish the means of support to an increasing population; and it will necessarily experience this inability, when, from the state of its commercial transactions, the funds for the maintenance of its labour become stationary, or begin to decline' (418–19). This passage says nothing about the level of the domestic profit rate in an economy based on food imports.

In addition to prospective foreign competition putting downward pressure on the profit rate of a manufacturing economy, there is also increasing *domestic* competition. The argument commences with reference to a new invention in a particular industry (cotton provided a conspicuous contemporary example) which reduces costs and raises profits initially, only to be followed by an inflow of new capital which, by raising supply, forces profits back to the general level (404). There follows an implicit extension of the argument to the economy as a whole, emphasizing a *general* fall in the profit rate (and the wage rate) until ultimate stationariness of capital (and population) is attained: 'In the cotton trade of this country, which has extended itself so wonderfully during the last twenty-five years [written in 1816], very little effect has hitherto been produced by foreign competition. The very great fall which has taken place in the prices of cotton goods has been almost exclusively owing to domestic competition; and this competition has so glutted both the home and foreign markets, that the present capitals employed in the trade, notwithstanding the very peculiar advantages which they possess from the saving of labour, have ceased to possess any advantage whatever in the general rate of their profits ... [A] country, such as we are considering, engaged principally in manufactures ... would ... find its rate of profits diminished by an increase of capital, and no ingenuity in machinery [which was not continually progressive] could save it, after a certain period, from low profits and low wages, and their natural consequences, a check to population' (405–7; 1826/1986, *3*, 395–6; bracketed phrase added in 1826). The precise logic for a falling general profit rate with increased competition, as distinct from a reduction of the profits of a *single industry* towards a going general level, is not spelled out in the above extract. But the perspective is certainly that of Adam Smith's 'competition of capitals' (1776/1937, 87).

In the chapter on commercial systems, no emphasis is placed on diminishing agricultural returns. The phenomenon is raised, only to be deliberately played down as a relevant concern: 'It would come to the same thing, whether this inability to obtain an increasing quantity of food were occasioned by the advancing money price of corn, or the falling money price of manufactures. In either case the effect would be the same; and it is certain that this effect might take place in either way, from increasing competition and accumulation in the manufacturing nation, and the want of them in the agricultural, long before any essential increase of difficulty had occurred in the production of corn' (1817, II, 410).

* * *

The third chapter of the trio – 'Of Systems of Agriculture and Commerce Combined' (1817) – is of prime importance in the growth context.[4] Here Malthus argues the case 'that it is the union of the agricultural and commercial systems, and not either of them taken separately, that is calculated to produce the greatest national prosperity' (441). The model is designed for the British case.

From a historical-development perspective, the successful transfer from feudalism required a flourishing manufacturing sector. This generalization actually appears in the earlier chapter, 'Of the Agricultural System,' in an allusion to Poland (395). This perspective is then elaborated in the third

4 A mixed economy exists 'where the resources in land, and the capitals employed in commerce and manufactures, are both considerable, and neither preponderating greatly over the other' (420).

chapter of the trio in a formal account of the growth process in mixed systems. Reference is made to the 'ready market at home' for agricultural produce which 'is peculiarly favourable to the progressive increase of capital,' and thus labour demand, and also to the high command of corn over manufactured goods (owing to falling prices of the latter), which enhances labour's condition: 'Under these circumstances, it is scarcely possible that it should ever experience that premature stagnation in the demand for labour, and the produce of the soil, which at times has marked the history of most of the nations of Europe. In a country in which manufactures and commerce flourish, the produce of the soil will always find a ready market at home; and such a market is peculiarly favourable to the progressive increase of capital. But the progressive increase of capital, and [1826: particularly of the quantity and value] of the funds for the maintenance of labour, is the great cause of a demand for labour, and of high corn wages, while the high relative price of corn, occasioned by the improved machinery and extended capital employed in manufactures, together with the prosperity of foreign commerce, enables the labourer to exchange any given portion of his earnings in corn for a large proportion both of domestic and foreign conveniences and luxuries' (421–2; 1986, *3*, 401–2). A further feature of the account relates to an ultimate 'slackening' of effective demand for labour generating *reduced corn wages and a deceleration of population growth.* Yet the *real* wage (allowance made for a mixed wage basket and the high P_c/P_m ratio) is maintained. 'Even when the effective demand for labour begins to slacken, and the corn wages to be reduced, still the high relative value of corn keeps up comparatively the condition of the labouring classes; and though their increase is checked, yet a very considerable body of them may still be well lodged and well cloathed, and able to indulge themselves in the conveniences and luxuries of foreign produce. Nor can they ever be reduced to the miserable condition of the people in those countries, where, at the same time that the demand for labour is stationary, the value of corn, compared with manufactures and foreign commodities, is extremely low.' As we shall see, it is increasing land scarcity that plays the causal role in the deceleration process, though at this stage nothing is said explicitly of an absolute increase in corn prices.

A mixed system, unlike a purely manufacturing economy, is protected against the potentially severe consequence of increasing foreign competition in export markets – namely, actual retrogression – though there would be some slackening of the growth rate: 'A country which raises its own food cannot by any sort of foreign competition be reduced at once to a necessarily declining population .... The great and most important of all trades, the domestic trade carried on between the towns and the country, will remain comparatively undisturbed. It may indeed be checked in the rate of its progress for a time by the want of the same stimulus; but there is no reason for its becoming retrograde; and there is no doubt that the capital thrown out of employment by the loss of foreign trade will not lie idle. It will find some channel in which it can be employed with advantage, though not with the same advantage as before; and will be able to maintain an increasing population, though not increasing at the same rate as under the stimulus of a prosperous trade' (423–4).

The existence of an agricultural sector also reduces the danger of increasing domestic competition in manufacturing. While the corn/manufacturing price ratio rises – and here there *is* specific allusion to diminishing returns – the *aggregate* value (command over corn) of manufactures will not decline: 'In a state merely manufacturing and commercial, home competition and abundance of capital may so reduce the price of manufactured compared with raw produce, that the increased capital employed in manufactures may not procure in exchange an increased quantity of food. In a country where there are resources in land this cannot happen; and though from improvements in machinery and *the decreasing fertility of the new land taken into cultivation*, a greater quantity of manufactures will be given for raw produce, yet the mass of manufactures can never fall in value, owing to a competition of capital in this species of industry, unaccompanied by a correspondent competition of capital on land' (424–5; emphasis added).

Now contemporary Britain provided the pre-eminent instance of a 'combined' system as distinct from one 'engaged principally in manufactures' which 'would sooner find its rate of profits diminished by an increase of capital' (396). In the non-diversified case, as we have seen, 'no ingenuity of machinery could save it, after a certain period, from low profits and low wages, and their natural consequences, a check to population.' By contrast, new technology in British cotton manufacture had generated a surplus sufficient to finance rapid accumulation over the preceding quarter-century; and while the profit rate in cotton had been reduced to the general level, that level itself had been maintained. The existence of plentiful land as well as the expansion of markets had prevented the depressant influence otherwise exerted on the profit and wage rates by expansion of manufactures. We are in a wholly Smithian world (1776/1937, 93) where two countervailing forces work against the fall in the profit rate – the acquisition of new territory and new markets: 'The high temporary profits of the [cotton] trade have occasioned a great accumulation of capital, and consequently a great demand for labour; while the extending markets abroad and the new values thrown into the market at home, have created such a demand for the products of every species of industry, agricultural and colonial, as well as commercial and manufacturing, as to prevent a fall of profits. This country, from the extent of its lands, and its rich colonial possessions, has a large *arena* for the employment of an increasing capital; and the general rate of its profits are not, as it appears, very easily and rapidly reduced by accumulation' (1817, II, 406–7).

It would seem that increasing Smithian 'competition of capitals' can be avoided (certainly alleviated) by *balanced growth*. This is also suggested by what follows. An economy 'with resources in land' can expand regardless of 'the state and progress of other countries' in agricultural development: 'When its manufacturing capital becomes redundant, and manufactured commodities are too cheap, it will have no occasion to wait for the increasing raw products of its neighbours. The transfer of its own redundant capital to its own land will raise fresh products, against which its manufactures may be exchanged, and by the double operation of diminishing comparatively the supply, and increasing the demand, enhance their price. A similar operation, when raw produce is too abundant, will restore the level between the profits of agriculture and manufactures. And upon the same principle the stock of the country will be distributed through its various distant provinces, according to the advantages presented by each situation for the employment, either of agriculture or manufacturing capital' (426–7). A closed but diversified economy might indeed proceed *without limit*, albeit at a slower pace than if it could engage in foreign commerce: 'A country, in which in this manner agriculture, manufactures, and commerce, and all the different parts of a large territory, act and react upon each other in turn, might evidently go on increasing in riches and strength, although surrounded by Bishop Berkely's wall of brass. Such a country would naturally make the most of its foreign commerce, whatever might be the actual state of it; and its increase or decrease would be the addition or removal of a powerful stimulus to its own produce; but still the increase of this produce, to a very considerable extent, would be independent of foreign countries; and though it might be retarded by a failure of foreign commerce, it could not either be stopped or be made retrograde' (427). And we even find (in the course of a recommendation that Britain avoid a 'preponderance' of manufacturing in the light of potential American industrial competition) a notion of, in effect, limitless expansion: 'The countries which thus unite great landed resources with a prosperous state of commerce and manufactures, and in which the commercial part of the population never essentially exceeds the agricultural part, are eminently secure from sudden reverses. Their increasing wealth seems to be out of the reach of all common accidents; and there is no reason to say that they might not go on increasing in riches and population for hundreds, nay almost thousands of years' (429–30).

III LAND SCARCITY, THE FACTOR RETURNS, AND PRUDENTIAL POPULATION CONTROL

The suggestion of limitless growth in a diversified economy discussed above, in section II, was, however, qualified. We have already encountered a brief reference to 'the decreasing fertility of the new land taken into cultivation' (above, p. 181), and Malthus proceeded to specify a variety of 'limits,' all based on diminishing returns, though without any suggestion that such limits had any immediate relevance. All this is clarified in the following summary statement in the chapter on combined systems, which alludes to a limit to population at which the subsistence wage absorbs the marginal product: 'We must not however imagine that there is no limit to this progress though it is distant, and has certainly not been attained by any large landed nation yet known. We have already seen that the limit to the population of commercial nations is the period when, from the actual state of foreign markets, they are unable regularly to import an increasing quantity of food. And the limit to the population of a nation which raises the whole of its food on its own territory is, when the land has been so fully occupied and worked, that the employment of another labourer on it will not on an average raise an additional quantity of food sufficient to support a family of such a size as will admit of an increase of population' (1817, II, 430). This is immediately corrected; the population limit is lowered to ensure that the marginal product suffices to cover profits and also a wage higher than the minimum food requirements of a stationary population: 'This is evidently the extreme practical limit to the progress of population, which no nation has ever yet reached, nor, indeed, ever will; since no allowance has been here made either for other necessaries besides food, or for the profits of stock, both of which, however low, must always be something not inconsiderable' (430–1). (This is possibly an allusion to China, which elsewhere is treated as a stationary state.)

A correction in the other direction is conceded. In the case of a non-profit system involving the 'forced direction of the national industry,' a transfer of labour to agriculture might occur until the maximum food supply is achieved – the point of zero marginal product. The economic principles are formulated with remarkable clarity:

Yet even this limit is very far short of what the earth is capable of producing, if all were employed upon it who were not employed in the production of other necessaries [manufactures]; that is, if soldiers, sailors, menial servants and all the artificers of luxuries, were made to labour upon the land. They would not indeed produce the support of a family, and ultimately not even of themselves; but till the earth absolutely refused to yield any more, they would continue to add something to the common stock; and by increasing the means of subsistence, would afford the means of supporting an increasing population. The whole people of a country might thus be employed during their whole time in the production of mere necessaries, and no leisure be left for other pursuits of any kind. But this state of things could only be effected by the forced direction of the national industry into one channel by public authority. Upon the principle of private property, which it may be fairly presumed will always prevail in society, it could never happen. With a view to the individual interest either of a landlord or farmer, no labourer can ever be employed on the soil, who does not produce more than the value of his wages; and if these wages be not on an average sufficient to maintain a wife, and rear two children to the age of marriage, it is evident that both the population and produce must come to a stand. Consequently, at the most extreme practical limit of population, the state of the land must be such as to enable the last employed labourers to produce the maintenance of as many, probably, as four persons. (431–2)

The 'practical limits of population,' assuming private property and profit maximization, therefore 'must be always very far short of the utmost power of the earth to produce food' (433).[5]

At this juncture we find an impressive statement of the process of expansion towards the so-called practical limits. It is a process entailing deceleration of capital and population in consequence of the increasing exhaustion of 'cultivable land,' and declining wage and profit rates until their respective minima are attained, at which point capital and population growth cease. In this formulation of the growth model, Malthus also spells out the conditions – including that of unchanged technology – that have to be satisfied for a 'regular' deceleration of population growth and of the wage and the profit rates; for in practice a steady pattern was not to be expected:

It is also of great importance to recollect that long before this practical limit is attained in any country the rate of the increase of population will gradually diminish. When the capital of a country becomes stationary from bad government, indolence, extravagance, or a sudden shock to commerce, it is just possible that the check to population may in some degree be sudden, though in that case it cannot take place without a considerable convulsion. But when the capital of a country comes to a stop from the continued progress of accumulation and the exhaustion of the cultivable land, both the profits of stock and the wages of labour must have been gradually diminishing for a long period, till they are both ultimately so low as to afford no further encouragement to an increase of stock, and no further means for the support of an increasing population. If we could suppose that the capital employed upon the land was at all times as great as could possibly be applied with the same profit, and there were no agricultural improvements to save labour, it is obvious that, as accumulation proceeded, profits and wages would regularly fall, and the diminished rate in the progress of population would be quite regular. But practically this can never happen; and various causes, both natural and artificial, will concur to prevent this regularity, and occasion great variations at different times in the rate at which the population proceeds towards its final limit. (433–5)

5 Cf: 'There is, however, a limit which, if the capital and population of a country continue increasing, they must ultimately reach, and cannot pass; and ... this limit, upon the principle of private property, must be far short of the utmost power of the earth to produce food' (441–2).

Malthus further emphasized that the approach to stationariness of capital and population, setting aside disturbing causes, is a very slow one: 'But, notwithstanding these causes of irregularity in the progress of capital and population, it is quite certain that they cannot reach their necessary practical limit but by a very gradual process. Before the accumulation of capital comes to a stop from *necessity*, the profits of stock must for a long time have been so low as to afford scarcely any encouragement to an excess of saving above expenditure; and before the progress of population is finally stopped, the real wages of labour must have been gradually diminishing, till, under the existing habits of the people, they could only support such families as would just keep up, and no more than keep up, the actual population' (440–1).

* * *

These themes are elaborated in the chapter – it appears with variations in all editions except the first – 'Of Increasing Wealth, as It Affects the Condition of the Poor' (1817, Book III, ch. 13). The context is Malthus's long-standing objection to Adam Smith's notion that the demand for labour varies with 'wealth' (i.e., national income or 'annual produce'). Expanding national income might take the form of manufactured luxuries alone, and thus fail entirely to stimulate population growth. This, however, is a limiting case; the normal case entails only a lag of population growth behind the increase of 'wealth': 'In the usual progress of improvement the increase of wealth and capital is rarely accompanied with a proportionately increased power of supporting an additional number of labourers' (1817, III, 4). This lag parallels that of agriculture behind general activity – a lag noted by Smith – which is attributed primarily to land scarcity. The principle is applied to the period since Elizabeth I: 'The best land would naturally be the first occupied. This land, even with that sort of indolent cultivation and great waste of labour which particularly marked the feudal times, would be capable of supporting a considerable population; and on the increase of capital, the increased taste for conveniences and luxuries, combined with the decreasing power of production in the new land to be taken into cultivation, would naturally and necessarily direct the greatest part of this new capital to commerce and manufactures, and occasion a more rapid increase of wealth than of population' (6). The position that the (agricultural) wage fund does not necessarily increase with the increase of wealth, and rarely in proportion to it, was already developed in the earlier editions, including the diminishing-returns rationale (cf. a similar statement in 1798, above, chapter 1, pp. 32–3). But in 1817 Malthus put greater weight on the land-scarcity phenomenon, taking Smith to task for an undue emphasis upon *faulty institutions* in his analysis of stationariness of population, 'wealth,' and agriculture in the Chinese case: 'In all these cases, it is not on account of any undue preference given to commerce and manufactures, compared with agriculture, that the effect just described takes place, but merely because the powers of the earth in the production of food have narrower limits than the skill and tastes of mankind in giving value to raw materials, and consequently in the approach towards the limits of subsistence there is naturally more room, and consequently more encouragement, for the increase of the one species of wealth than of the other' (9–10).[6] In arguing thus, Malthus was revising his position, since in 1803 (1986, *3*, 674) and in 1806 (1806, II, 214–15) he too had offered an institutional rationalization for the observed lag in agricultural activity in the British case.[7]

A further proposition weakens the dependency of working-class welfare on food supply – thus relaxing the criticism of Smith – by recognizing 'that the condition of the lower classes of society does not depend exclusively upon the *increase* of the funds for the maintenance of labour, or the power of supporting a *greater* number of labourers' (1817, III, 2–3; emphasis added). That the wage basket is mixed had long been recognized, but the full argument of 1817 provides the basis for one of the most important statements of the growth process in the classical literature: 'But the condition of the lower classes of society certainly does not depend exclusively upon the increase of the funds for the maintenance of labour, or the means of supporting more labourers. That these means form always a very powerful ingredient in the condition of the poor, and the main ingredient in the increase of population, is unquestionable. But, in the first place, the comforts of the lower classes of society do not depend solely upon food, nor even upon strict necessaries; and they cannot be considered as in a good state unless they have the command of some conveniences and even luxuries. Secondly, the tendency in population fully to keep pace with the means of subsistence must in general prevent the increase of these means from having a great and permanent effect in improving the condition of the poor. And, thirdly, the cause which has the most lasting effect in improving the situation of the lower classes of society depends chiefly upon

6 The 1817 account of 'increasing wealth as it affects the condition of the poor' also differs from that of 1798 (1986, *1*, 107–8), 1803 (1986, *3*, 694), and 1806 (1806, II, 190) in its removal of the notion of upward wage movement as a result of *deviations* between the growth rates of population and food. It contains now merely a reference to Smith's position that, as the wage fund rises, so wages rise (1817, III, 2).

7 It is, however, unlikely that this justification for the lag of agricultural behind industrial investment, and of food supply relative to total output, applied to *contemporary* Britain since, as will emerge shortly, an outstanding feature of that account is increasing returns in agriculture, reflecting new technology. Even in the discussion of potential Chinese manufacturing the point of earlier editions – for example, 1798 (1986, *1*, 108–9), 1803 (1986, *3*, 694) – is reiterated that, despite the likely transfer of labour from agriculture, it could be taken for granted that agricultural output would remain unchanged in consequence of new technology (1817, III, 8–9; also 1806, II, 204 and 191–2).

the conduct and prudence of the individuals themselves, and is therefore not immediately and necessarily connected with an increase in the means of subsistence' (10–11). The first qualification identifies demand for labour (or employment capacity) with food advances – at least food advances constitute the 'main ingredient' – yet envisages the real wage basket as including 'conveniences and even luxuries.'[8] The second alludes to a highly elastic labour-growth supply such that, as the growth rate of food increases, the response of population prevents any 'great [positive] effect' on the (corn) wage. This version, which turns on 'the tendency in population *fully to keep pace with* the means of subsistence,' differs from a notion of tendency given at the outset of the essay – namely, 'to increase beyond the means of subsistence' (1817, I, 5). But the third sets the 'tendency' (in either sense) aside, *by recognizing the possibility of deceleration of population growth relative to that of food so as to assure rising corn wages, irrespective of the actual growth rate of food.* Conceivably the wage may even rise as a result of such self-imposed prudential control, despite decelerating (even zero) growth of food.

The textual amplification spells out further the elements of a growth model based on diminishing returns as population density rises, with an ultimate limit to food (and thus to population size). Increasing land scarcity accounts for the necessary deceleration of food supply in a growing economy, and the consequentially necessary deceleration of population growth.[9] Whether the corn wage declines or not turns on labour-supply conditions. In the absence of *increasing* prudential control, the corn wage necessarily declines, for it is this decline that acts to impede population growth. With increasing prudential control, however, any decline in corn wages can be avoided: 'A diminished power of supporting children is an absolutely unavoidable consequence of the progress of a country towards the utmost limits of its population. If we allow that the power of a given quantity of territory to produce food has some limit, we must allow that as this limit is approached, and the increase of population becomes slower and slower, the power of supporting children will be less and less, till finally, when the increase of produce stops, it becomes only sufficient to

8 On this view, labour demand is defined in corn terms, and together with labour supply determines the corn wage. But labour supply is governed in part by non-corn considerations. By 1817, Malthus had become increasingly impressed by the significance of the manufacturing component in the wage basket: 'The merchants and manufacturers who so loudly clammer for cheap corn and low money wages think only of selling their commodities abroad, and often forget that they have to find a market for their returns at home, which they can never do to any great extent, when the money wages of the working classes, and monied incomes in general are low' (1817, III, 422–3n).

9 It is not a full model because there is no firm discussion of the labour-demand growth curve. It decelerates but it is not clear whether or not it is interest-elastic at any given stage.

maintain, on an average, families of such a size as will not allow of a further addition of numbers. This state of things is generally accompanied by a fall in the *corn* price of labour; but should this effect be prevented by the prevalence of prudential habits among the lower classes of society, still the result just described must take place; and though, from the powerful operation of the preventive check to increase, the wages of labour estimated even in corn might not be low, yet it is obvious that in this case the power of supporting children would rather be nominal than real; and the moment this power began to be exercised to its apparent extent, it would cease to exist' (1817, III, 12–13).[10]

The story does not end here as far as concerns labour's welfare. For a fall in the corn wage will be compensated, at least in part, by rising corn command over manufactures, as real corn costs rise absolutely and manufacturing costs fall absolutely. Thus, while the population growth rate must be negatively affected by increasing land scarcity, the wage basket defined inclusively may actually *rise*: 'in the natural progress of cultivation and wealth, the production of an additional quantity of corn will require more labour, while, at the same time, from the accumulation and better distribution of capital, the continual improvements made in machinery, and the facilities opened to foreign commerce, manufactures and foreign commodities will be produced or purchased with less labour; and consequently a given quantity of corn will command a much greater quantity of manufactures and foreign commodities than while the country was poor. Although, therefore, the labourer may earn less corn than before, the superior value which every portion which he does not consume in kind will have in the purchase of conveniences, may more than counterbalance this diminution. He will not indeed have the same power of maintaining a large family; but with a small family he may be better lodged and clothed, and better able to command the decencies and comforts of life' (22–3). Having in mind 'the high relative price of corn, occasioned by the improved machinery and extended capital employed in manufactures, together with the prosperity of foreign commerce' (1817, II, 422), it followed that 'even when the effective demand for labour begins to slacken, and the corn wages to be reduced, still the high relative value of corn keeps up comparatively the

10 The alternative outcomes are in fact already apparent, though less formally expressed, as early as 1803: 'If the lower classes of people had acquired the habit of proportioning the supplies of labour to a stationary or even decreasing demand, without an increase of misery and mortality, as at present, we might even venture to indulge a hope that at some future period the processes for abridging human labour, the progress of which has of late years been so rapid, might ultimately supply all the wants of the most wealthy society with less personal labour than at present; and if they did not diminish the severity of individual exertion, might, at least, diminish the number of those employed in severe toil' (1986, *3*, 567).

condition of the labouring classes; and though their increase is checked, yet a very considerable body of them may still be well lodged and well clothed, and able to indulge themselves in the conveniences and luxuries of foreign produce. Nor can they ever be reduced to the miserable condition of the poor in those countries where, at the same time that the demand for labour is stationary, the value of corn, compared with manufactures and foreign commodities, is extremely low.'[11] Of course, this improvement will *a fortiori* pertain should the corn wage be maintained by increasing prudential control in the face of decelerating food supplies.

An appendix explains precisely what is entailed in practice. The context is a proposal by Arthur Young (1812) 'so to adjust the wages of day labour as to make them at all times equivalent to the purchase of a peck of wheat' (1817, III, 419). Malthus objected to the plan that 'in its general operation, and supposing no change of habits among the labouring classes, it would be tantamount to saying that, under all circumstances, whether the affairs of the country were prosperous or adverse; whether its resources in land were still great, or nearly exhausted; the population ought to increase exactly at the same rate, a conclusion which involves an impossibility' (420).[12] Here we have an appeal to the standard model; the corn-wage path *must* fall to ensure the appropriate deceleration in the population-growth rate. But allow for prudential population control and the picture is transformed; constancy of the corn wage might be achieved despite an increasing labour/land ratio: 'If, however, this adjustment, instead of being enforced by law, were produced by the increasing operation of the prudential check to marriage, the effect would be totally different, and in the highest degree beneficial to society. A gradual change in the habits of the labouring classes would then effect the necessary retardation in the rate of increase, and would proportion the supply of labour to the effective demand, as society continued to advance, not only without the pressure of a diminishing quantity of food, but under the enjoyment of an increased quantity of conveniences and comforts; and in the progress of cultivation and wealth, the condition of the lower classes of society would be in a state of constant improvement' (420–1). According to the closing proposition,

11 Cf. a statement of 1815 favouring a high corn price from labour's perspective, even when it reflects land scarcity (see above, chapter 4: IV).

12 For a similar formulation, in the context of 'the poor-laws as a general system,' cf. 1817, II, 350. The argument Malthus opposed implied 'that the funds for the maintenance of labour in this country are not only infinite, but not subject to variation; and that, whether the resources of a country be rapidly progressive, slowly progressive, stationary or declining, the power of giving full employment and good wages to the labouring classes must always remain exactly the same, – a conclusion which contradicts the plainest and most obvious principles of supply and demand, and involves the absurd position that a definite quantity of territory can maintain an infinite population.' In earlier editions the message is the same but expressed in much less formal terms; cf. 1806, II, 188.

constant corn wages are consistent with increasing real wages, including 'conveniences and comforts.' Here again Malthus is alluding to the notion that an increase in the *relative* price of corn to those of manufactures – owing to absolute increase in the former and absolute decrease in the latter – allows an increase in the general purchasing power of a given corn wage, a theme running through the *Essay.*

An outstanding statement of the basic growth model, spelling out with brilliant clarity the prospect of stationariness at 'high' wages, will be found in a letter to Senior of 23 March 1829, and is cited here for convenience: 'If the population of Great Britain were to go on increasing for two hundred years at the rate at which it increased during the twenty years between the census of 1800 and that of 1820, it would be sixteen times as great as at present. It is not easy to believe that this is possible. A retardation in the rate of increase seems to be absolutely inevitable. And the question is, whether we are entitled from past experience to expect that this will take place without some diminution of corn wages, and some increased difficulty of maintaining a family. At all events, it is quite certain, that no desire, however great, of increasing our subsistence can keep us out of the reach of the most miserable poverty, if we do not, at the same time, exercise the most efficient power we possess of restraining the progress of population by prudential habits' (in Senior, 1829, 70). Even in the stationary state, labour might enjoy good wages: 'The rate at which social improvements proceeds, does not depend exclusively upon the rate at which subsistence can be made to increase faster than population. I look forward to the possibility, and even the probability of the labouring classes of society being altogether in a better situation then they are now, when the means of a further increase of food shall be nearly exhausted, and both subsistence and population shall have come nearly to a stand. But, it is obvious, that if this improvement should be accomplished, it cannot be by exertions to increase food, but by the moral restraint which will diminish the misery and vice constantly occasioned by the tendency of population to press against subsistence.' And in his *Encyclopaedia Britannica* contribution 'Population' (1824), Malthus cited his own *Principles* (1820) regarding the two alternative reaction patterns: 'From high wages, or the power of commanding a large portion of the necessities of life, two very different results may follow; one, that of a rapid increase of population, in which case, the high wages are chiefly spent in the maintenance of large and frequent families; and the other, that of a decided improvement in the modes of subsistence, and the conveniences and comforts enjoyed, without a proportionate acceleration in the rate of increase' (1986, *4*, 205).

IV PRUDENCE ENDOGENIZED

We now come to a potent relationship that sets at nought any notion of

Malthus as 'dismal scientist.'[13] Malthus does not treat increasing prudential control – in effect, the timing of marriage – solely as a matter of exogenous change in habits (stimulated perhaps by education or propaganda program). Rather it is *endogenous to the growth process.* Already in 1803 there is brief reference to the possibility that rising wages stimulate improved prudential control by way of more sophisticated tastes: 'Nothing is more difficult than to lay down rules on these subjects that do not admit of exceptions. Generally speaking, it might be taken for granted that an increased facility in the means of gaining a livelihood, either from a great previous mortality or from improving cultivation and trade, would produce a greater proportion of annual marriages; but this effect might not perhaps follow. Supposing the people to have been before in a very depressed state, and much of the mortality to have arisen from the want of foresight which usually accompanies such a state, it is possible that the sudden improvement of their condition might give them more of a decent and proper pride' (1986, *2*, 196). The improved degree of prudence in turn would reduce the mortality rate: 'The proportional number of marriages might remain nearly the same, but they would all rear more of their children, and the additional population that was wanted would be supplied by a diminished mortality, instead of an increased number of births' (196–7).

The 1817 formulation goes a step farther, finding a role for rising P_c/P_m in the process of changing taste patterns. From 'experience' Malthus drew a relationship linking a taste for manufactured wage goods to diminishing returns on land, the upward pressure on the corn price itself encouraging inward shifts of the labour-growth curve which check, and possibly prevent, reductions in the corn wage: 'it seems to be proved by experience, that the lower classes of society seldom acquire a decided taste for conveniences and comforts till they become plentiful compared with food, which they never do till food has become in some degree scarce. If the labourer can obtain the full support of himself and family by two or three days' labour; and if, to furnish himself with conveniences and comforts, he must work three or four days more, he will generally think the sacrifice too great compared with the objects to be obtained, which are not strictly necessary to him, and will therefore often prefer the luxury of idleness to the luxury of improved lodging and clothing ... On the other hand, if the main part of the labourer's time be occupied in procuring food, habits of industry are necessarily generated, and the remaining time, which is but inconsiderable compared with the commodities it will purchase, is seldom grudged. It is under these circumstances, particularly when combined with a good government, that the lower classes of society are most likely to acquire a decided taste for the conveniences and comforts of life; and this taste may

13 I use this term loosely. It apparently originated with Carlyle, who applied it against economists who opposed slavery (Carlyle, 1849).

be such as even to prevent, after a certain period, a further fall in the corn price of labour' (1817, III, 23–4).[14] In this case of constant corn wages, the beneficial effect on labour's welfare exerted by land scarcity may be a potent one indeed, even 'in individual cases, where large families occur': 'But if the corn price of labour continues tolerably high while the relative value of commodities compared with corn falls very considerably, the labourer is placed in a most favourable situation. Owing to his decided taste for conveniences and comforts, the good corn wages of labour will not generally lead to early marriages; yet in individual cases, where large families occur, there will be the means of supporting them independently, by the sacrifice of the accustomed conveniences and comforts; and thus the poorest of the lower classes will rarely be stinted in food, while the great mass of them will not only have sufficient means of subsistence, but be able to command no inconsiderable quantity of those conveniences and comforts, which, at the same time that they gratify a natural or acquired want, tend unquestionably to improve the mind and elevate the character' (24–5).

A general summary allows for the maintenance of good conditions in a slowly growing economy, and conversely possibly poor conditions with rapid growth. All depends on the population-growth function: 'Strictly speaking, the good or bad condition of the poor is not *necessarily* connected with any particular stage in the progress of society to its full complement of wealth. A rapid increase of wealth indeed, whether it consists principally in additions to the means of subsistence or to the stock of conveniences and comforts, will always, *caeteris paribus*, have a favourable effect on the poor; but the influence even of this cause is greatly modified and altered by other circumstances, and nothing but the union of individual prudence with the skill and industry which produce wealth can permanently secure to the lower classes of society that share of it which it is on every account so desirable that they should possess' (25–6).[15] Here we have a rejection of the Smithian view that with capital growing only slowly, real wages *must* be low.

There is a further complexity. In so far as the wage basket includes

14 Wrigley refers to this mechanism when he writes of Malthus's 'most subtle' point (in Malthus, 1986, *1*, 25), but finds it first in the *Principles* (1820).

15 The argument is applied in a comparison between countries, the same corn wage being consistent with different population-growth rates, depending on the comparative state of prudential habits: 'In the case also of the prevalence of prudential habits, and a decided taste for the conveniences and comforts of life, as, according to the supposition, these habits and tastes do not operate as an encouragement to early marriages, and are not in fact spent almost entirely in the purchase of corn, it is quite consistent with the general principles laid down, that the population should not proceed at the same rate as is usual, *caeteris paribus*, in other countries, where the corn wage of labour are equally high' (34).

manufactured goods, a manufacturing sector must be allowed for in a full exposition of the formal model. This is particularly so if we recall that a rising proportion of manufacturing activity in the total is attributed to the peculiar constraints on agriculture (above, p. 185). There is some indication, too, that population-growth rates differ between sectors *ceteris paribus*. Thus a feature of 'the natural and regular progress of the country to a state of great wealth and population' – in addition to the 'diminished power of supporting children' – is 'the employment of a larger proportion of the population in occupations less favourable to health, and more exposed to fluctuations of demand and unsteadiness of wages' (12).[16] To this extent there is a higher death rate in manufactures than in agriculture, especially a higher infant-death rate. The implications of this differential will be taken up in a discussion of Malthus's response to criticisms by Weyland (below, section VII).

V CHANGES IN *CETERIS PARIBUS* CONDITIONS

Various impediments to 'regular' growth are considered by Malthus. The first entails a minimum-scale and total-cost threshold appropriate for major land investments, and capital scarcity which impedes such investment, even when profitable under alternative tenure conditions: 'In the first place, land is practically almost always understocked with capital. This arises partly, from the usual tenures on which farms are held, which, by discouraging the transfer of capital from commerce and manufactures, leaves it principally to be generated on the land; and partly, from the very nature of much of the soil of almost all large countries, which is such that the employment of a small capital upon it may be little productive, while the employment of a large capital in draining, or in changing the character of the soil by a sufficient quantity of natural and artificial manures, may be productive in a high degree; and partly also, from the circumstance that after every fall of profits and wages there will often be room for the employment of a much greater capital upon the land than is at the command of those, who, by being in the actual occupation of farms, can alone so employ it' (1817, II, 435). In addition, there is technical change proper: 'Secondly; improvement in agriculture. If new and superior modes of cultivation be invented, by which not only the land is better managed, but is worked with less labour, it is obvious that inferior land may be cultivated at higher profits than could be obtained from richer land before; and an

16 Cf.: 'It must be allowed then, that in the natural and usual progress of wealth, the means of marrying early and supporting a family are diminished, and a greater proportion of the population is engaged in employments less favourable to health and morals, and more subject to fluctuations in the price of labour, than the population employed in agriculture' (20).

improved system of culture, with the use of better instruments, may for a long period more than counterbalance the tendency of an extended cultivation and a great increase of capital to yield smaller proportionate returns' (435–6). In land improvement and in technical progress, we thus have forces counterbalancing diminishing returns, perhaps 'for a long period,' and reversing or at least checking the trend paths of the key variables. The formulation treats technical change as a *disturbing cause*, while the 'tendency' is governed by increasing land scarcity in what was to become the orthodox classical fashion.[17]

A third source of variation in 'the rate at which population proceeds to its final limit' is technical progress *in manufacturing*. Such technical progress, by raising the corn command over manufactures, counteracts the 'tendency' towards a decline in the corn surplus over outlay, and may even allow an increase in the profit rate: '[It] is well known that, from the principle of home competition and the consequent great increase of quantity, the prices of ... manufactures will greatly fall; and, as far as they include the necessaries and accustomed conveniences of labourers and farmers, they must tend to diminish that portion of the value of the whole produce which is consumed necessarily on the land, and leave a larger remainder. From this larger remainder may be drawn a higher rate of profits, notwithstanding the increase of capital and extension of cultivation' (436–7). The same applies to improvements in the terms of trade favouring agriculture: 'If from a prosperous foreign commerce our labour and domestic commodities rise considerably in price, while foreign commodities are advanced comparatively very little, an event which is very common, it is evident that the farmer or labourer will be able to obtain the tea, sugar, cottons, linens, leather, tallow, timber, &c., which he stands in need of, for a smaller quantity of corn or labour than before; and this increased power of purchasing foreign commodities will have precisely the same effect, in allowing the means of an extended cultivation without a fall of profits, as the improvements in manufactures just referred to' (437). In all this we apparently revert to an 'agricultural model' (albeit, as it were, with a manufacturing attachment). The relation between the agricultural and manufacturing rates of profit is left an open question.

A fifth disturbance is enumerated – 'a temporary increase in the relative price of raw produce from increased demand.' Here Malthus refers to the lag in money wages and manufacturing prices behind the price of corn: 'Allowing, what is certainly not true, that a rise in the price of raw produce, will after a certain number of years, occasion a proportionate rise in labour and other commodities, yet, during the time that the price of raw

17 Elsewhere 'diminishing returns' *incorporates* new technology (see above, chapter 3: III regarding the *Inquiry into Rent* and the *Principles*), thus entailing an empirical rather than a strictly analytical relation.

produce takes the lead, it is obvious that the profits of cultivation may increase under an extended agriculture, and a continued accumulation of capital. And these intervals, it should be observed, must be of infinite importance in the progress of the wealth of a landed nation, particularly with reference to the causes of deficient capital upon the land before mentioned. If the land for the most part generates the new capital which is employed in extending its cultivation; and if the employment of a considerable capital for a certain period will often put land in such a state, that it can be cultivated afterwards at comparatively little expense; a period of high agricultural profits, though it may last only eight or ten years, may often be the means of giving to a country what is equivalent to a fresh quantity of land' (437–9). One notices in the passage the introductory acceptance – but only for argument's sake – of the Smithian notion of an ultimately *proportional* rise of the wage and general prices following a corn-price increase. Second, an important note limits the entire proposition to increases in the corn price *not* attributable to diminishing returns: 'A rise, which is occasioned exclusively by the increased quantity of labour which may be required in the progress of society to raise a given quantity of corn on the last land taken into cultivation, must, of course, be peculiar to raw produce, and will not be communicated to those commodities, in the production of which there is no increase of labour.' Malthus is here formulating the Ricardian position.

Contemporary Britain illustrated the main themes. There the 'tendency' for the wage and profit rates to decline had been reversed, despite massive expansion of capital and population, as we later show in chapter 15: V.

VI THE RESPONSE TO WEYLAND: IMPLICATIONS FOR THE GROWTH MODEL

John Weyland (1816) took issue with Malthus's general procedure, which emphasizes the 'natural tendency of population to increase' or the *maximum* conceivable geometric rate, and then considers the 'checks' which supposedly constrain the actual behind the maximum rate: 'the origin of what are conceived to be the mistakes and false reasonings, with respect to the principle of population, appears to be the assumption of a tendency to increase in the human species, the quickest that can be proved possible in any *particular* state of society, as that which is natural and theoretically possible in *all*; and the characterising of every cause which tends to prevent such quickest possible rate, as *checks* to the natural and spontaneous tendency of population to increase; but as checks evidently insufficient to stem the progress of an overwhelming torrent' (17). A difference of 'principle' was involved. Researchers would do better 'if, instead of blindly acquiescing in these *assumed* data, they proceed to inquire into the degree in which the principle of population *naturally and really* operates in the several stages of society. They will find this to be very distinct from its assumed "possible" operation, and in most cases to be very far from having a necessary tendency "to push the number of people beyond the point at which food can be acquired for them"' (20).

Weyland's own substantive position was that, in the absence of 'grossly impolitic laws, or pernicious customs' stimulating population growth artificially or depressing agricultural productivity artificially, population had 'a *natural* tendency to keep *within the powers* of the soil to afford it subsistence in every gradation, through which society passes' (21); or, alternatively expressed, 'that every step which a country takes towards the end of its resources is accompanied by a corresponding abatement in the tendency of its population to increase' (124); or again: 'that population does actually advance, though with abated rapidity, as the power of supplying with food becomes more scanty and precarious' (157). This perspective, he maintained, 'exclude[d] the *necessity* of "vice, misery", or such a modification of "moral restraint" as includes *involuntary* abstinence from marriage, as *checks* indispensably arising out of the principle of population' (22).[18]

We consider now Malthus's reaction to Weyland given in an appendix to the 1817 *Essay*.[19] His main theme is that Weyland had added nothing substantive to his own position regarding 'the checks which practically keep down population to the level of the means of subsistence,' and had 'not given a single reason for the slow progress of population in the advanced stages of society, that does not clearly and incontrovertibly come under the heads of Moral Restraint, Vice, or Misery' (1817, III, 398).[20] There was only a difference in formal methodological procedure. He defended his own approach, which is to cite the *maximum* conceivable population-growth rate (as experienced in the United States) – the so-called natural tendency to increase – and then seek to explain the *lower* rates actually experienced in various countries and epochs in terms of 'the

18 On Malthusian 'moral restraint' see below, chapters 18: V and 19: IV. Weyland considered Malthus's recommendations to constitute a severe normative flaw (1816, Book III, ch. 6).

19 Weyland's book was alluded to by Trower in correspondence with Ricardo (1 July 1816): 'Have you seen Mr. Waylands [*sic*] Book on Population and Production, I hear it is intended as a refutation of Malthus' doctrines. I shall get it, as he is an able man, and the subject of the highest importance. It is a fortunate circumstance, that Mr. Malthus has not yet published the new edition of his work, as opportunity will now be afforded him of answering any arguments in Mr. Wayland's book that may require observation' (Ricardo, 1951–73, VII, 46). Ricardo himself was not impressed by the work: 'He has, I, think, not in the least succeeded in establishing his own doctrines in opposition to Malthus on the principle of population' (to Trower, 15 July; 48).

20 Cf: 'Mr. Weyland has not proved, or approached towards proving, that the *natural* tendency of population to increase is not unlimited; ... he has not advanced a single reason to make it appear probable that a thousand million would not be doubled in twenty-five years just as easily as a thousand, if moral restraint, vice and misery, were equally removed in both cases ...' (406).

difficulty which the mass of the people find in procuring an ample portion of the necessaries of life, which shows itself more immediately in some or other of the forms of moral restraint, vice and misery' (401).[21] Here we encounter the standard Malthusian view that the *relaxation* of food constraints permits the acceleration of population towards its maximum so that the notion of such maximum permanently retains its validity. Thus: 'Whenever the resources of any country increase so as to create a great demand for labour and give the lower classes of society a greater command over the necessaries of life, the population of such country, though it might have been stationary, or proceeding very slowly, begins immediately to make a start forward.'[22]

This perspective turns on the 'glaring facts' of constant sexual passion and constant prolificness of women during the 'progress of society,' and also on the fact that the United States was 'not particularly healthy.' If, therefore, the growth rate of European food supplies were to accelerate – playing upon the 'production and distribution of the means of subsistence,' *viz.* the real wage – then population growth rates might rise beyond (and even surpass) the American rate. On this view differential population-growth rates between countries and over time reflected differential growth rates of food supply: 'the varying weight of difficulties attending the maintenance of families, and the moral restraint, vice and misery which these differences necessarily generate, are the causes of the varying rates of increase observable in different countries' (402). Similarly: 'As long as it is a law of our nature that man cannot live without food, these differential rates of increase [of population] in different countries, are as absolutely and strictly *necessary* as the differences in the power of producing food in countries more or less exhausted' (405).

As noted, Malthus maintained that Weyland had added nothing to account for the checks that *in actuality* restrained population growth below its maximum. But this is far from the case. In Malthus's own analysis, the deceleration of population growth as the economy approaches 'exhaustion' is brought about by reductions in the corn wage which stimulate increased 'moral restraint, vice, and misery ...' This is reflected in the specific observations regarding the impact of variation in the 'command over the necessaries of life.' A contrast between the high English population-growth rate (despite the greater urbanization in England) contrasted with the slow

21 See also 412 (below, p. 203), where Malthus also justifies treating 'the *natural tendency* of population to increase ... as a given quantity,' and the 'actual increase' as regulated by the 'varying resources' which determine demand for labour.

22 There is a lack of precision here, indicated by a restatement involving 'necessaries *and conveniences*': thus the removal of 'pressure arising from the difficulty of procuring the necessaries and conveniences of life' relaxes the checks to early marriage and allows the maintenance of large families 'with perfect facility,' so that population growth accelerates.

expansions in various Continental countries, points in the same direction: 'What is it that in these countries [Norway, Sweden, Switzerland] indisposes people to marry, but the absolute hopelessness of being able to support their families? What is it that renders many more who do marry incapable of reproducing their own numbers, but the diseases generated by excessive poverty ... by an insufficient supply of the necessaries of life?' (411). It is low corn wages 'determined in the common way by the supply and the demand' that was responsible.[23] Thus decelerating food supply, by depressing the corn wage, generates the appropriate birth- and death-rate adjustments which reduce population growth. Now this is positively not the case for Weyland. This is not to say that the corn wage does not fall in the Weyland scheme; it does, as a necessary prerequisite for expanding food supplies. But that decline is not required to assure deceleration of population growth. It is true that the argument lacks a firm explanation for the rising ratio of manufacturing/agricultural population as a consequence of increasing land scarcity, which – together with the presumption that marriage and birth rates are typically lower in urban occupations and locations – constitutes the core of the argument (1816, 61–7, 83, 90). But the principle is firm enough. One may call the relative unhealthiness of towns or the pressures mitigating against marriage a form of 'misery and vice' – this is what Malthus does – but to do so does not answer Weyland's argument that population growth decelerates independently of the movement in the corn wage.

It is not certain, however, that Malthus appreciated that this was the key point of difference. At one juncture he phrases Weyland's contribution in a manner suggesting that he did not. At least he phrased Weyland's case *as if it was totally unrelated to decelerating food supplies*: 'The argument may be stated shortly thus; – that the natural division of labour arising from a very advanced state of society, particularly in countries where the land is rich, and great improvements have taken place in agriculture, might throw so large a portion of the people into towns, and engage so many in unhealthy occupations, that the immediate checks to population might be too powerful to be overcome even by an abundance of food' (1817, III, 406–7). This eventuality Malthus allowed, but as an *exception* not the rule. (In any event the depressing effects of town living on population constitute some form or other of 'moral restraint, vice or misery' and could be formally incorporated within the standard formula.) The fact is, however, that Weyland

23 He also asserts, it is true, that, if in Europe there was 'early marriage, ample means to maintain a family and healthy employments,' then population growth would expand to achieve (even surpass) the U.S. rate. By distinguishing 'early marriage' and 'healthy employments' from the 'means to maintain families' (the real wage), he is implicitly recognizing exogenous forces at play. However, these can be regarded as affecting the position of the population-growth function – shift parameters; ongoing variation in population growth occurs in response to variations in the real wage, given the population-growth function.

focused almost entirely on *diminishing returns* and the resultant *deceleration* of food supplies.

There is another reason for the possibility that the two were talking past each other. To appreciate it we must consider their alternative empirical estimates. As Malthus understood him, Weyland was asserting that Britain was 'within a hair's breadth' of the 'point of *non-reproduction*, at which ... the population *naturally* comes to a full stop before the means of subsistence cease to be progressive' (408). On the bases of empirical evidence regarding rapid population growth since the turn of the century, he proceeded to refute such contentions: 'But what has happened since? In spite of the enlargement of all our towns; in spite of the most rapid increase of manufactories, and of the proportion of people employed in them; in spite of the most extraordinary and unusual demands for the army and navy; in short, in spite of a state of things which, according to Mr. Weyland's theory, ought to have brought us long since to the point of *non-reproduction*, the population of the country has advanced at a rate more rapid than was ever known at any period of its history. During the ten years from 1800 to 1811, as I have mentioned in a former part of this work, the population of this country (even after making an allowance for the presumed deficiency of the returns in the first enumeration) increased at a rate which would double its numbers in fifty-five years' (408–9). Thus the facts *refuted* Weyland's view that 'as society advances, the increased indisposition to marriage and increased mortality in great towns and manufactories always overcome the principle of increase' or – quoting Weyland – that 'population, so far from having an inconvenient tendency uniformly to press against the means of subsistence, becomes by degrees very slow in overcoming those means.'[24]

Under the right circumstances – including sufficiently rapid agricultural progress and improved health – British population growth could achieve the maximum rate (doubling in twenty-five years) characterizing American growth at an earlier period: 'With regard to this country, as it is positively known that the rate of increase has changed from that which would double the population in 120 years, or more, to that which would double it in 55 years, under a great increase of towns and manufactures, I feel very little doubt that, if the resources of the country were so augmented and distributed, as that every man could marry at 18 or 20, with the certainty of being able to support the largest family, the population of the British Isles would go on increasing at a rate which would double the population in 25

24 We must keep in mind that Malthus was not disputing 'the increased indisposition to marriage.' That marriage and birth rates were declining was already clear to him in 1806 (1806, II, 536), and is reiterated in 1826: 'The augmented rate of increase in the population' occurred *despite* a falling birth rate, in consequence of an even sharper fall in mortality reflecting improved health standards (1986, *3*, 593n).

years. It appears, from our registers, that England is a healthier country than America. At the time that America was increasing with extraordinary rapidity, in some of the towns the deaths exceeded the births. In the English towns, with their present improvements, I do not think this would ever be the case, if all the lower classes could marry as soon as they pleased, and there was little or no premature mortality from the consequences of poverty' (59–60n). But even the going, lower, rate still made his point adequately: 'Whether the habits and customs of an old state could be so changed by an abundance of food, as to make it increase nearly like a new colony, is a question of mere curiosity. The argument only requires that a change from scanty to abundant means of supporting a family should occasion, in old states, a marked increase of population; and this, it is conceived, cannot possibly be denied.'[25]

The facts of rapid population growth thus proved 'incontrovertibly that the actual checks to population, even in the most improved countries, arise principally from an insufficiency of subsistence, and soon yield to increased resources, notwithstanding the increase of towns and manufactories' (410). This orientation left its mark on the statement of principle at the very outset of the *Essay*. In the 1803 edition, Malthus had allowed that 'population invariably increases where the means of subsistence increase, unless prevented by some very powerful and obvious checks' (1986, *2*, 20).[26] But in 1817 he significantly reduced this allowance: 'I have expressed myself in this cautious manner, because I believe there are some instances, where population does not keep up to the level of the means of subsistence. But these are extreme cases, and generally speaking, it might be said that ... [population] always increases where the means of subsistence increase' (1817, I, 34n). Malthus himself tells us (1817, III, 407) that it is the sort of position maintained by Weyland that he had in mind by the original qualification.[27]

Similarly, pointing to the rapid growth of population in England compared with Switzerland, Norway, and Sweden, despite the relatively extensive urbanization of the former, he noted: 'How is this to be reconciled with the doctrine that the progress of civilization and improvement is

25 A further statement in 1817 of this major theme will be found 1817, II, 80 (cited below, chapter 16, p. 799).

26 In the 1798 edition this qualification is absent (1986, *1*, 10).

27 Malthus's memory failed him here. The qualification as it appears in 1806 suggests he did not have British conditions in mind originally: 'I have expressed myself in this cautious manner, because I believe there are a few instances, such as the negroes in the West Indies, and one or two others, where population does not keep up to the level of the means of subsistence. But these are extreme cases; and generally speaking it might be said ... [that] Population always increases where the means of subsistence increase' (1806, I, 29n). In 1817 the illustration from what we would call 'underdeveloped' areas is simply removed.

always accompanied by a corresponding abatement in the natural tendency of population to increase?' (410–11). This, in fact, is unfair. England was undergoing a technological revolution. The circumstances did not reflect those of either his own model or that of Weyland.

Now Weyland, in fact, had also alluded to contemporary expansion of English population (attributing it to the 'artificial' stimulus of the Poor Laws) and a *yet more rapid increase in food supplies*; but he took this as proof of the 'gratuitous nature of the fears entertained concerning ... the tendency which [population] *naturally* has in such a society [where the 'most fertile spots have been long since occupied'] to exceed the limits of the food provided for its support' (1816, 129). There is indeed, formal support here for the generalization that population growth keeps within that of food supply. But the evidence was drawn from a period involving accelerated food and population, whereas Weyland's main concern related to *deceleration* of food and population. Malthus may not have realized what that main concern was. The fact remains that neither of the two focused upon the main technical contrast: whether, in the event of *decelerating* food production, the requisite deceleration of population growth occurs in response to wage reduction (Malthus's position) or is a built-in, quasi-automatic reaction occurring even without that stimulus (Weyland's position). Moreover, when Malthus does tangentially broach the issue, he seems to get Weyland's message wrong, thus pointing to the low real wages of Switzerland, Norway, and Sweden (compared with England): '[Is] it possible to know that in few or none of the countries of Europe the wages of labour, determined in the common way by the supply and the demand, can support in health large families; and yet assert that population does not press against the means of subsistence, and that "the evils of a redundant population can never be necessarily felt by a country till it is actually peopled up to the full capacity of its resources"' (1817, III, 412; citing Weyland, 1816, 123).[28] The fact is, however, that Weyland insisted further that in the stationary state 'the evils of a redundant population would not even then be necessarily felt.'

Setting aside the possibility of a failure of comprehension of his critic's position, Malthus was 'technically' on stronger ground, since Weyland confused diminishing returns and new technology, whereas (in this context at least) Malthus kept them appropriately apart. Given technology, for Malthus the prediction is one of reduced corn wages to assure the necessary deceleration of population growth. Yet we know that Malthus in 1817, both in the text and the appendix itself, introduces his *prudential wage path* as an alternative to declining corn wages, which shares with Weyland the common feature that a deceleration in population growth does not require the stimulus of a reduced corn wage (above, section III). Why then the

28 The quoted phrase is Malthus's own from earlier editions of the *Essay*.

strong objections to the latter's work? The answer seems to turn on the implication of Weyland's case that there need be no special encouragement of 'moral restraint,' considering the automatic forces at play which guarantee an appropriately decelerating population-growth rate. This emerges on several occasions in Malthus's appendix. Thus, on Weyland's supposition that population growth is automatically restrained, moral restraint would be 'useless and unnecessary' (407). Or regarding the low level of real wages in Europe: 'Can any man of reflection ... venture to state that there is no moral reason for repressing the inclination to early marriages, when it cannot be denied that the alternative of not repressing it must necessarily and unavoidably be premature mortality from excessive poverty?' (411). And directly addressing himself to Weyland's proposition regarding 'the natural tendency of population to keep within the power of the soil to afford it subsistence,' Malthus complained that Weyland alludes to the maintenance of good real wages 'in proportion as religion, morality, rational liberty and security of person and property approach the attainment of a perfect liberty,' *excluding moral or prudential restraint from marriage*: 'Among the moral duties, I certainly include a restraint upon the inclination to an early marriage when there is no reasonable prospect of maintenance for a family; and unless this species of virtuous self-denial be included in morality, I am quite at issue with Mr. Weyland; and so distinctly deny his proposition as to say that no degree of religion and morality, no degree of rational liberty and security of person and property, can, under the existing laws of nature, place the lower classes of society in a state of comfort and plenty' (414). Worse still was Weyland's implied justification of the Poor Laws: 'If population, instead of having a tendency to press against the means of subsistence, becomes by degrees very slow in overtaking them, Mr Weyland's inference that we ought to encourage the increase of the labouring classes by abundant parochial assistance to families, might perhaps be maintained. But if his premises be entirely wrong, while his conclusions are still acted upon, the consequence must be, that universal system of unnecessary pauperism and dependence which we now so much deplore [1826: a constantly increasing amount of unnecessary pauperism and dependence]' (416; 1986, *3*, 617). Finally, on Malthus's reading, Weyland 'substituted' for moral restraint 'the unhealthiness and mortality of towns and manufactories' (423), leading Malthus to condemn the apparent implication that improvement of towns was to be deprecated. To Malthus, on the contrary, the ongoing improvement in healthiness was to be welcomed, subject to appropriate reduction in the birth rate: 'If indeed such peculiar unhealthiness and mortality were the proper and natural check to the progress of population in the advanced stages of society, we should justly have reason to apprehend that, by improving the healthiness of our towns and manufactories, as we have done in England during the last twenty years, we might really defeat the designs of providence. And though I have too much respect for Mr.

Weyland to suppose that he would deprecate all attempts to diminish the mortality of towns, and render manufactories less destructive to the health of the children employed in them; yet certainly his principle lead to this conclusion, since his theory has been completely destroyed by those laudable efforts which have made the mortality of England – a country abounding in towns and manufactories, less than the mortality of Sweden – a country in a state almost purely agricultural' (424).

The allowance for a prudential wage path itself, however, does carry us far in Weyland's direction, with the distinction just alluded to that, for Malthus, the path requires external pressure encouraging a reduced birth rate, whereas, for Weyland, the process is supposedly automatic. Yet we also must face the fact that Malthus himself introduced into his text of 1817 *endogenous* pressures – the impact on taste patterns of rising corn relative to manufacturing prices – encouraging reduction in the birth rate (above, section IV). This recognition seems to undermine his objections to Weyland.

VII MANUFACTURING EXPANSION AND POPULATION GROWTH

Various formulations of 1817 suggest on first reading that increased demand for labour – and consequent population increase – is to be identified with expansion of *either* agriculture or manufactures: 'Mr. Weyland really appears to have dictated his book with his eyes blindfolded, and his ears stopped .... The very slightest glance at different countries of Europe shows with a force amounting to demonstration that to all practical purposes the *natural tendency* of population to increase may be considered as a given quantity; and that the actual increase is regulated by the varying resources of each country for the employment and maintenance of labour, in whatever stage of its progress it may be, whether it is agricultural or manufacturing, whether it has few or many towns' (1817, III, 412). But we know that Malthus adhered to his criticism of Smith for neglecting the principle that population growth turned on *agricultural* expansion (see above, p. 185). Presumably, then, the silent assumption is that expanded manufacturing activity generates population increase provided it is somehow realized in higher food output (and provided net urban mortality is not excessive).

A further passage added in 1817 regarding the population-growth rate in 1800–10 – a doubling in less than fifty-five years, 'quite extraordinary for a rich and well-peopled territory,' and one 'which in the nature of things cannot be permanent' (1817, II, 103) – contains a similar complexity. This rate of growth 'ha[d] been occasioned by the stimulus of a greatly-increased demand for labour, combined with a greatly-increased power of production, both in agriculture and manufactures.' Here we have allusion to aggregate demand as well as supply-side determinants of employment: 'These are the two elements necessary to form an effective encouragement to a rapid increase of population. A failure of either of these must immediately weaken the stimulus; and there is but too much reason to fear the failure of one of them at present' – an evident reference to a contemporary failure of aggregate demand.[29] But the record prior to the depression provided 'a striking illustration of the principle of population,' proving 'that in spite of great towns, manufacturing occupations, and the gradually-acquired habits of an opulent and luxuriant people, if the resources of a country will admit of a rapid increase, and if these resources are so advantageously distributed as to occasion a constantly-increasing demand for labour, the population will not fail to keep pace with them' (103–4).[30] One appreciates that the demand for labour rises with an increase in food supply whether that is achieved by agricultural extensions or new agricultural technology; how manufacturing technology exerts an influence is not clarified, but a positive effect on the agricultural surplus might have been intended (above, p. 194).

A flow of labour from the countryside to the towns is a further feature of contemporary English experience. This we have encountered in the 1798 edition, where Malthus wrote of an absolute decline in the agricultural workforce since 1688 (above, chapter 1, pp. 41–2). A transfer is again alluded to in 1803 and thereafter, with special reference to the high mortality rates and expanding labour demand in the towns: 'To fill up the void occasioned by this mortality in towns and answer all further demands for population, it is evident that a constant supply of recruits from the country is necessary; and this supply appears in fact to be always flowing from the redundant births of the country. Even in those towns where the births exceed the deaths, this effect is produced by the marriages of persons not born in the place' (1986, *2*, 243). At the same time Malthus dismissed concerns regarding the 'depopulation' of the rural areas, 'at least as long as the funds for the maintenance of agricultural labour remain unimpaired,' as indeed was the case: 'The [high] proportion of births, as well as the proportion of marriages [in the country], clearly proves, that, in spite of our increasing towns and manufactories, the demand on the country for people is by no means very pressing' (244). The rising population in the country allowed *some* net expansion of the

29 In the 1826 edition the reference to the dangerous consequences of a 'failure' of aggregate demand is deleted. The alteration reflects the resumption of the trend path (cf. 1986, *2*, 261).

30 The closing requirement for appropriate 'distribution' of the 'resources' reflects the position given in a note added to the opening statement to the *Essay* of basic propositions regarding the determinants of population increase: 'by an increase in the means of subsistence, is here meant such an increase as will enable the mass of the society to command more food. An increase might certainly take place, which in the actual state of a particular society would not be distributed to the lower classes, and consequently would give no stimulus to population' (1817, I, 34n).

agricultural workforce at the same time that it provided a source of labour for the expanding towns. The foregoing is retained throughout all editions.

An important note added in 1817 might be read as alluding to an *absolute decline* in the agricultural workforce owing to 'insufficiency of employment'; but, given the passage just cited, it more probably refers to a lack of agricultural employment relative to available labour supply. This note, which is attached to the proposition that an expanded rate of growth of food supplies would generate an expansion of population growth, raises some interpretive problems. Here, in an implicit criticism of Weyland's position that urban expansion depresses population growth, Malthus considers the precise role accorded the employment constraint: 'It may be thought that the effects here referred to as resulting from greatly increased resources, could not take place in a country where there were towns and manufactories; and that they are not consistent with what was said in a former part of this work, namely, that the ultimate check to population (the want of food) is never the immediate check, except in cases of actual famine' (1817, III, 59n). The defence that follows of the central proposition is, at first glance, inconsistent with what had been written of the positive stimulus to agriculture afforded by the growing towns: '*The great cause which fills towns and manufactories is an insufficiency of employment, and consequently of the means of support in the country*; and if each labourer, in the parish where he was born, could command food, clothing, and lodging for ten children, the population of the towns would soon bear but a small proportion to the proportion in the country. And if to this consideration we add that, in the case supposed, the proportion of births and marriages in towns would be greatly increased, and all the mortality arising from poverty almost entirely removed, I should by no means be surprised (after a short interval for the change of habits) at an increase of population, even in China, equal to that which is referred to in the text' (emphasis added). To attribute contemporary urban growth to '*insufficiency of employment' in farming* conflicts with the positive attraction of increasing investment in manufacturing discussed earlier in the chapter 'General Observations' (Book III, ch. 14), an attraction which assures the maintenance of the money wages of the expanding workforce, and thus provides a stimulus – in fact, a *necessary* stimulus – for agriculture: 'Now it is certain that, at no period, have the manufactures, commerce and colony trade of the country been in a state to absorb so much capital as during the twenty years ending with 1814. From the year 1764 to the peace of Amiens [1803], it is generally allowed that the commerce and manufactures of the country increased faster than its agriculture ... Since the peace of Amiens the state of its colonial monopoly and of its manufactures have been such as to demand an unusual quantity of capital ...' (1817, II, 497–8).[31] We also find the

31 Even in the first edition there is much emphasis on the pull of the towns, though in a

insertion into the 1817 edition of cases involving the maintenance of money wages, despite a rate of population growth faster than that of food, 'by the employment of the increasing population in manufactures' – implying demand pull (1817, III, 47). Conceivably the neglect of the positive pull of manufacturing in our present context reflects the circumstances of the postwar depression.[32]

There is also the contribution to population growth of improving urban health. The higher death rate in manufactures than in agriculture, especially a higher infant death rate, was an old theme appearing in 1798 (e.g., 1986, *1*, 29, 109) and maintained throughout all subsequent editions.[33] At the same time there was some evidence as early as 1803 of improving health standards in factories, Malthus citing J. Aikin (1795): 'Endeavours have been made, Dr. Aikin says, to remedy these evils, and in some factories they have been attended with success. An act of parliament has of late also passed on this subject [the Health and Morals of Apprentices Act of 1802], from which it is hoped, that much good will result' (1986, *3*, 444n).[34] In 1817 Malthus placed new emphasis on this improving trend, modifying the foregoing appropriately: 'Dr. Aikin says that endeavours have been made to remedy these evils, which in some factories have been attended with success. And it is very satisfactory to be able to add, that, since this account was written, the situation of the children employed in the cotton-mills has been further very essentially improved, partly by the interference of the legislature, and partly by the humane and liberal

---

criticism of artificial stimuli for manufacturing: 'The superior encouragement that has been given to the industry of the towns, and the consequent higher price that is paid for the labour of artificers, than for the labour of those employed in husbandry, are probably the reasons why so much soil in Europe remains uncultivated' (1986, *1*, 118).

32 In the 1826 edition (written in 1825) there is allusion to renewed prosperity 'during the last two or three years' in *both* agriculture and 'commerce' (1986, *3*, 377n).

33 Weyland (1816, 63n) used the 1806 version against Malthus. 'There certainly seems to be something in great towns, and even in moderate towns, peculiarly unfavourable to the very early stages of life; and the part of the community, on which the mortality principally falls, seems to indicate that it arises more from the closeness and foulness of the air which may be supposed to be unfavourable to the tender lungs of children, and the greater confinement which they almost ncessarily experience, than from the superior degree of luxury and debauchery usually and justly attributed to towns. A married pair with the best constitutions, who lead the most regular and quiet life, seldom find that their children enjoy the same health in towns as in the country' (1806, I, 462–3).

34 Cf. the reference to 'the increased healthiness observed of late years' (1806, II, 536). This may apply generally, and not only to urban areas. Yet in 1803 Malthus included 'great towns and manufactures, in which we can scarcely hope, and certainly not expect, to see any very material change,' as one of the forces which 'necessarily repress [the] full effects' of population increase (1986, *3*, 570), an observation remaining intact through 1826.

exertions of individuals' (1817, III, 16n). Again, the 'present improvements' of English towns is alluded to (461n), and turned against Weyland: 'If indeed such peculiar unhealthiness and mortality were the proper and natural check to the progress of population in the advanced stages of society, we should justly have reason to apprehend that, *by improving the healthiness of our towns and manufactories, as we have done in England during the last twenty years,* we might really defeat the designs of Providence. And though I have too much respect for Mr. Weyland to suppose that he would deprecate all attempts to diminish the mortality of towns, and render manufactories less destructive to the health of the children employed in them; yet certainly his principles lead to this conclusion, since his theory has been completely destroyed by those *laudable efforts which have made the mortality of England – a country abounding in towns and manufactories, less than the mortality of Sweden – a country in a state almost purely agricultural*' (above, pp. 202–3; emphasis added).

The foregoing suggests a number of propositions regarding contemporary events, and these clarify the problematic issues raised in this section: (1) sluggish growth of labour demand in the agricultural sector, but expanding food supplies at an accelerating rate, reflecting new technology; (2) accelerating demand for manufacturing labour, reflecting changing taste patterns and rising purchasing power, and growth in the urban relative to rural distribution of the expanding workforce; (3) expanding demand for manufacturing labour satisfied by a flow of labour from the country, and to some extent by 'internal' population growth with rising healthiness; (4) corn wages per capita steady at the least, but probably rising, *the higher food supply comprising the real counterpart of the increased demand for labour in urban centres.*

From all this we conclude that a condition for population expansion remained, as always in the *Essay*, expanded food supplies. At the same time we have confirmation of the 'revised' view (a withdrawal of the objections to Adam Smith) that net accumulation might occur in *manufacturing* and yet be in labour's interests – allowing high corn wages – *provided food is somehow made available.* One source of accelerating food supplies is new technology, which implies their availability prior to population growth. If that is so, we are faced with a somewhat different order from that given in some passages to which we now turn, where expanded food supplies are a response to a preceding expansion of demand for food on the part of manufacturing labour. Possibly both forces are envisaged as at play.

VIII THE ORDER OF PRECEDENCE OF FOOD SUPPLY AND POPULATION GROWTH, AND THE 'OSCILLATORY' PROCESS

After reading the 1817 edition of the *Essay on Population,* Ricardo wrote to Malthus, regarding the 'additional matter' of that 'excellent' and 'exceedingly clear' work, that there were only a few points of dissention, 'the chief difference' being 'whether food or population precedes' (letter of 21 October 1817; in Ricardo, 1951–73, VII, 201). This is evidently a major issue. Ricardo was frequently to criticize Malthus for identifying increased demand for labour with expansion of food supply, rather than conceiving expansion of food supply as a response to an actual (or expected) increase of demand for food on the part of growing families with real disposable income on hand. We have found that Malthus's position, as formulated in 1803 and 1806/7, according precedence to food over population (discussed above, chapter 1: XII) suggests, despite first appearance, that – as for Ricardo – high real wages generated by increased employment opportunities govern agricultural expansion in so far as the higher earning power is devoted to the maintenance of larger families. If this is so, then population growth and demand for food in fact precede expanded food output.

In the edition of 1817, the nature of the employment constraint is much amplified. Originally, as we have seen, it was maintained that 'according as the employment of the country is increasing, whether slowly or rapidly, ... wages will be such, as either to check or encourage early marriages; such, as to enable a labourer to support only two or three, or as many as five or six children' (above, chapter 1, p. 65). The precise sense of 'wages' is now said to raise practical complexities: 'the progress of population will be mainly regulated and limited by the real wages of labour ... [but] practically, the current wages of labour estimated in the necessaries of life do not always correctly represent the quantity of these necessaries which it is in the power of the lower classes to consume' (1817, III, 29; 'day labour' specified in 1826). For example, a corn-price increase in the face of sticky money wages may be counterbalanced by higher employment (especially higher piece-work opportunities) and by increased female and child labour so that real *family* earnings rise, with a positive effect on population growth: 'In all these cases the real earnings of the labouring classes throughout the year, estimated in food, are different from the apparent wages; but it will evidently be the average earnings of the families of the labouring classes throughout the year on which the encouragement to marriages, and the power of supporting children, will depend, and not merely the wages of day-labour estimated in food' (31). This explained 'why, in many instances, the progress of population does not appear to be regulated by what are usually called the real wages of labour; and why this progress may occasionally be greater, when the price of a day's labour will purchase rather less than the medium quantity of corn, than when it will purchase rather more.' As a prime example: during the two decades 1790–1811, the average day wage was below one peck of wheat, but population growth was faster than in the period 1735–55, despite a higher per-capita real wage, because of the greater employment opportunities available to working-class families in the later period: 'there was a much more rapid accumulation of capital, and a greater demand for labour; and though the continued rise of provisions still kept them rather ahead of wages, yet the fuller employment for every body that would work, the greater quantity of task-work done, the higher relative value of corn compared with manufactures, the increased use of potatoes, and the greater sums distributed in parish allowances, unquestionably gave to the lower classes of society the power of commanding a greater quantity of food, and will account for the more rapid increase of population in the latter period, in perfect consistency with the general principle' (32–3).

Once again, we recall Malthus's objection to Adam Smith for identifying capital accumulation with net increase in labour demand, since expansion in the luxury-goods sector does not *necessitate* agricultural growth, that is, wage-goods expansion (see above, chapter 1: VIII). Yet the picture drawn now, both theoretical and applied, is one of expanding employment opportunities (apparently quite general) providing labour with real command over increased food supplies, and stimulating expansion of the latter. It is equally striking that one reason offered for rapid population growth from 1790 to 1811 is 'the greater sums distributed in parish allowances.' Increased allowances are said to stimulate expanded agricultural output, though it had once been a firm principle that money-wage supplements are dissipated in increased competition for scarce food supplies (Malthus, 1800; see below, chapter 6: IV).

That expansions of agricultural output are a *response* to increased demand for the support of a rising population, despite a formal insistence on the 'precedence' of agriculture over population growth, is amply confirmed in an extremely important passage touching on the so-called *oscillatory* pattern of development: 'What is here said of the order of precedence with respect to agriculture and population, does not invalidate what was said in an earlier part of this work on the tendency to an oscillation or alternation in the increase of population and food in the natural course of their progress. In this progress *nothing is more usual than for the population to increase at certain periods faster than food*; indeed it is a part of the general principle that it should do so' (1817, III, 46–7; emphasis added).[35] It will be remarked that Malthus's paraphrase of the 'tendency to an oscillation or alternation' in the food–population relation refers to *growth rates* – population 'increas[ing] at certain periods *faster than food*' – although the original oscillatory passage refers to *absolute* increases.[36]

For our purposes here, there are two pertinent implications of the argument. First, increases in population growth relative to food are said to act as the *stimulus* to an acceleration of food supply; the process works by

35 The 'earlier part of [the] work' regarding oscillations has been discussed in chapter 1: IX, XII. The main passage at issue appeared already in 1798.

36 A deliberate change in weighting is discernible also in the original statement describing the low point. In 1798 this reads 'population is at a stand'; in 1803: 'population is nearly at a stand; and, in 1817: 'the progress of population is retarded' (see above, chapter 1, p. 63).

way of the upward pressure on the corn price exerted by increased expenditure on the part of the larger population, which pressure is all the more potent if the population expansion is absorbed in the manufacturing sector: 'and when the money wages of labour are prevented from falling by the employment of the increasing population in manufactures, the rise in the price of corn which the increased competition for it occasions is practically the most natural and frequent stimulus to agriculture' (47). This perspective on the mechanics of the growth process is consistent with Ricardo's, which envisages food supply as a response to prior, or at least expected, increases in demand on the part of a rising population.

The second feature to note is Malthus's insistence that all this does not negate the *priority* of food over population in the specific sense of an initial corn wage exceeding subsistence as a prerequisite for population expansion: 'But then it must be recollected that the great relative increase of population absolutely implies a previous increase of food at some time or other greater than the lowest wants of the people. Without this, the population could not possibly have increased.' The precedence of food over population in the sense of an excess of the per-capita corn wage over subsistence as a condition for any population growth is also suggested by a note attached to the text: 'According to the principle of population, the human race has a tendency to increase faster than food. It has therefore a constant tendency to people a country fully up to the limits of subsistence, but by the laws of nature it can never go beyond them, meaning, of course, by these limits, the lowest quantity of food which will maintain a stationary population. Population, therefore, can never, strictly speaking, precede food.' This expresses the tendency to excessive population in extreme terms. But in so far as Malthus is simply defining the *conditions of population growth*, the note must be read as a formal definition of a limiting case; population growth is precluded, setting out from a subsistence-wage level, unless there occurs a preliminary expansion of the food supply.

The precedence accorded food is generalized to 'any essential improvement in the condition of the labourer,' which implies an initial corn wage equal to subsistence. Here Malthus repeats the proposition that – setting out from an above-subsistence corn wage – the corn wage has a 'natural tendency' to decline, and he adds that it is to such decline that farmers respond: 'Universally, when the population of a country is for a longer or shorter time stationary, owing to the low corn wages of labour, a case which is not unfrequent, it is obvious that *nothing but a previous increase of food, or at least an increase of the portion awarded to the labourer, can enable the population again to proceed forward.* And, in the same manner, with a view to any essential improvement in the condition of the labourer, which is to give him a greater effective command over the means of comfortable subsistence, it is absolutely necessary that, *setting out from the lowest point, the increase of food must precede and be greater than the increase of population.* Strictly speaking then, as man cannot live without food, there can be no doubt that in the order of precedence food must take the lead; although when, from the state of cultivation and other causes, the average quantity of food awarded to the labourer is considerably more than sufficient to maintain a stationary population, *it is quite natural that the diminution of this quantity, from the tendency of population to increase, should be one of the most powerful and constant stimulants to agriculture*' (48–9; emphasis added).

The expansion of agriculture is here attributed to a *falling corn wage.* As we have seen, a few paragraphs earlier such expansion was related to *rising corn prices.* It seems legitimate to identify the two stimuli. And this is in fact confirmed by the paradoxical proposition that the higher the corn wage initially in consequence of strong 'prudential control' – in effect the higher the supply price of labour – the better the promise for agricultural expansion, since there is plentiful scope for a profit-rate increase in that sector via increase in the corn price *under pressure of rising demand*: 'It is worthy also of remark that on this account a stimulus to the increase of agriculture is much more easy when, from the prevalence of prudential restraint, or any other cause, the labourer is well paid; as in this case a rise in the price of corn, occasioned either by the increase of population or a foreign demand, will increase for a time the profits of the farmer, and often enable him to make permanent improvements; whereas, when the labourer is paid so scantily that his wages will not allow even of any temporary diminution without a diminution of population, the increase of cultivation and population must from the first be accompanied with a fall of profits. The prevalence of the preventive check to population and the good average wages of the labourer will rather promote than prevent that occasional increase and decrease of them, which as a stimulus seems to be favourable to the increase both of food and population' (49–50).

The 1817 version adds further to the original proposition of 1798 regarding sticky money wages – that 'it very rarely happens that the nominal price of labour universally falls' – in the oscillatory account (see above, chapter 1, p. 44). The elaboration fully confirms the stimulus afforded agriculture by demand emanating from an expanding manufacturing sector: 'A circumstance which has, perhaps, more than any other, contributed to conceal this oscillation from common view, is the difference between the nominal and real price of labour. It very rarely happens that the nominal price of labour universally falls; but we well know that it frequently remains the same, while the nominal price of provisions has been gradually rising. *This, indeed, will generally be the case, if the increase of manufactures and commerce be sufficient to employ the new labourers that are thrown into the market, and to prevent the increased supply from lowering the money-price. But an increased number of labourers receiving the same money-wages will necessarily, by their competition, increase the money-price of corn*' (1817, I, 31; emphasis added).[37] Should the expanded labour supply find no opportu-

37 The italicized section was added in 1817 to the original text.

nities in manufacturing or commerce, the money wage will be forced down by competition precluding expanded demand for corn. In effect, in this case, landlords and farmers refuse to expand corn production in exchange for labour services: 'If the new labourers thrown yearly into the market should find no employment but in agriculture, their competition might so lower the money-price of labour, as to prevent the increase of population from occasioning an effective demand for more corn; or, in other words, if the landlords and farmers could get nothing but an additional quantity of agricultural labour in exchange for any additional produce which they could raise, they might not be tempted to raise it.' It is thus to the higher demand for corn on the part of manufacturing labour acting on the price of corn that farmers respond. *Agricultural expansion requires a multisectoral system.*[38]

IX CONCLUDING NOTES: SOME INTERPRETIVE PROBLEMS

Since Malthus allowed that agricultural expansion (at least in some periods) turns on a preceding demand for corn emanating from a growing population (indeed, a growing manufacturing workforce) and rising corn prices, wherein lies the major difference with Weyland? Weyland, after all, had insisted on this very point: 'A *previous* increase of people is necessary to stimulate the community to a farther production of food; and consequently to the healthy advancement of a country in the career of strength and prosperity. It results from this proposition that the incipient pressure of population against the *actual* means of subsistence, or, more correctly speaking, the excess of population *just beyond the plentiful supply of the people's want,* instead of being the cause of most of the miseries of human life, is in fact (under the modifications just stated) the cause of all public happiness, industry, and prosperity' (1816, 22).[39] And in what consist Malthus's differences with Ricardo, who repeatedly insisted on the necessity for a prior increased demand for food (such as arises from expanding population) as stimulus for agricultural growth?

38 The impact of industrial instability on employment and population growth – already mentioned in 1803 – is further amplified: 'The cause of this sudden check to population was the failure of demand and of commercial credit which occurred at the commencement of the war [1792–4], and such a check could not have taken place in so sudden a manner without the most severe distress, occasioned by the sudden reduction of wages' (1817, III, 17–18). The unfavourable effect on population growth reinforces the notion of constraints working independently of the food supply.

39 Against this Malthus insisted in his appendix on the precedence of food (1817, III, 415–16). But he complained that he never asserted that population growth, if not preceded by food expansion, would imply *starvation*, but only that labour's condition 'would be deteriorated.' This might be a reference to the fall in the corn wage owing to a temporary excess of population growth discussed in the oscillatory account.

Setting aside these questions, a further word is called for on the relation between the oscillatory process and the land-based growth model. That the population-growth rate exceeds that of food is true only 'at certain periods'; presumably there are other periods when the food-growth rate takes the lead. This alternation must be contrasted with the notion of 'a previous increase of food at some time or other greater than the lowest wants of the people,' or that 'setting out from the lowest point, the increase in food must precede ... the increase of population' (above, p. 210), which refer to the general condition for population expansion – a *secular* proposition – rather than the precedence of the food-growth rate appearing as part of the *oscillatory* process. It is by no means certain that Malthus intended to superimpose a process of fluctuating corn wages in response to periodic deviations between the food- and population-growth rates onto that version of the growth model where the corn wage exceeds subsistence *throughout* the growth process, except in the ultimate stationary state. He himself did not carry out the exercise – not a word is said in the oscillatory context about increasing land scarcity – but an exercise combining the two perspectives on the growth process is invited, entailing wage and profit fluctuations about the downward trend.

It remains to note that the exposition of the growth model in the 1817 *Essay* neglects the 'indirect' effects of secular deterioration in agricultural productivity, effects that operate via population growth, and thus demand for manufactures. What might explain this contrast between the new *Essay* and the immediately preceding correspondence where those indirect effects are so conspicuous (cf. above, chapter 4: V)? Conceivably the form of the *Essay* – its origins in the earlier statements of 1798, 1803, 1806, and 1807 – dictated that the *direct* effect of land productivity on the profit and wage rates take centre stage, rather than concepts involving a denial of the Law of Markets. But more seems to be at stake, since the 'indirect effects' are no longer to be found in the correspondence following the 1817 *Essay* or in later formal publications, including the *Principles*. Malthus, it seems, had silently abandoned the earlier perspective.

II / VALUE, DISTRIBUTION, AND GROWTH

SIX

Price theory

I INTRODUCTION

This chapter and the next two deal with a number of issues raised in the historiography of Malthusian price theory. Schumpeter took an extreme view of the contrasts with Ricardian theory. He denied that cost prices were understood by Ricardo as reflecting equilibrium between demand and supply, that is, to be market-clearing prices, whereas Malthus went even beyond Say, 'nicely indicat[ing] the locus of cost of production, which "only determines the prices of commodities, as the payment of it is the necessary condition of their supply" (*Principles*, chapters 2, 3) – a turn of phrase that points far ahead toward Jevonian teaching' (1954, 602). Jevons (who made the famous complaint against Ricardo that he 'shunted the car of Economic science on to a wrong line – a line ... on which it was further urged towards confusion by his equally able and wrong-headed admirer, John Stuart Mill') himself wrote warmly of Malthus: 'There were Economists such as Malthus and Senior, who had a far better comprehension of the true doctrines (though not free from the Ricardian errors), but they were driven out of the field by the unity and influence of the Ricardo–Mill school' (1879, li–lii).[1] Myint ends up with a similar perspective by implying that the demand–supply explanation of long-run price was peculiar to Malthus: 'Malthus's interest in the short-run economics, as contrasted with

1 Cf. his *Lectures* of 1875: 'Senior is probably the soundest political economist that ever wrote, or taken with Malthus certainly' (1972–81, VI, 3); and correspondence: 'I have lately been reading Malthus' Principles of Political Economy and can recommend it to you as a book not sufficiently estimated as far as I can see' (to Foxwell, 31 October 1875; IV, 143).

Ricardo's long-run normal equilibrium, had a decisive influence on his choice of value theory. He concentrated on the market equilibrium and aimed at the condition that "the great law of demand and supply is called into action to determine what Adam Smith calls natural prices, as well as what he calls market prices" ... He relegated the normal cost theory to the background and maintained that "The cost of production itself only influences prices of these commodities as the payment of cost is the necessary condition of their continued supply to the extent of the effectual demand for them"' (1948, 35).

Paglin argued that, though the differences between Malthus and Ricardo were of a methodological rather than a substantive theoretical order, they had historiographical consequences leading to 'the modern theory of value': 'Malthus accepted a good deal of Ricardo's cost analysis but insisted on incorporating it into a supply and demand framework – thus complicating rather than simplifying the theory of prices ... We may merely note here that the details elaborated by Lauderdale and Malthus – utility, scarcity, supply and demand schedules – led to the modern theory of value, while the Ricardian simplifications led to clear-cut results in certain restricted classical distribution problems' (1961, 34). In a subsequent spelling-out of the case, however, Paglin also writes of a major *analytical* breakthrough by Malthus in accomplishing 'an integration of cost of production theory with supply and demand analysis, a step which anticipates Marshall's great synthesis three-quarters of a century later. It reveals Malthus as being a precursor of neoclassical economics rather than in opposition to it' (45–6).[2]

Our task will be to get a grip on the foregoing issues. In this chapter we look closely at Malthus's positive contribution to price analysis, with particular reference to demand considerations. This includes the role accorded 'utility' in exchange theory (sections II and III); and also the notion of demand 'intensity' – 'sacrifice in money' usually, in the sense of Marshallian demand price – in contrast to 'extent' of demand or quantity demanded at a given price, a contrast he believed made sense of the demand–supply determination of price (section IV). Malthus recognized the origins of this notion in the *Wealth of Nations* and claimed only to be spelling out its implications.

Section V raises a matter not to my knowledge hitherto recognized in the secondary literature – namely, *exclusion of corn from treatment in terms of demand and supply* on the grounds that the demand and supply sched-

2 Despite this latter perspective, Paglin nevertheless raises a question: 'If Malthus accepted cost of production as an important, though not the exclusive determinant of value, why was there such continuous disagreement with Ricardo? Why did not the lengthy correspondence produce at least some reconciliation of the two approaches?' (47–8). He surmises that the answer lies in Ricardo's concern to save his inverse wage–profit relation.

ules are *interdependent* in that special case, whereas pricing analysis requires *independence* of the schedules. And, in that special case, 'value-in-use,' in the physiological sense, provides the key, having in mind the corn–population relation. If ever Malthus laid serious claim to a typical concern with the 'short run' this analysis – further elaborated below, in chapter 8, on Malthus's 'physiocratic' heritage – would be there to haunt him. It is all the more difficult to appreciate, considering Malthus's own criticisms of the Smithian analysis of a corn-export bounty which charge Smith with excluding corn from treatment in terms of regular allocative principles.

Section VI turns to the cost dimension from a general perspective. Malthus remained under the same misapprehension regarding Ricardo as were the early neoclassicists (such as Jevons, Walras, and Wicksell) and the moderns (such as Arrow, Hicks, and Samuelson – not to speak of the Sraffians), attributing to him a 'one-legged' price theory. Nothing Ricardo could say caused him to abandon this misinterpretation, including Ricardo's repeated insistence: (1) that growth of population, and therefore of demand, must precede extensions of agriculture – usually in opposition to Malthus himself; (2) that corn was to be treated like any other commodity in applying demand–supply theory – again against Malthus; and (3), most generally, that he was arguing for the *primacy* of supply, not for supply as the sole consideration in pricing.

Sections VII and VIII consider Malthus's case against the Labour Theory, reflecting complexities attributable to *time* and *rent*. As for Malthus's insistence on the influence of *time* on 'the conditions of supply,' we are hard put to see where substantive differences with Ricardo lie as far as concerns the mere fact of deviations of relative values from relative labour inputs. On the other hand, essential contrasts between the two are raised by Malthus's insistence in the *Principles* upon *rent* as creating deviations of relative price from labour relativities, despite his celebrated adoption of the concept of a no-rent margin in 1815. In the second edition of the *Principles*, we find a weakening of objections to the no-rent cost margin.

My general conclusion is that there is little to justify designating Malthus as a 'Subjective Value' theorist in any sense that would not also apply to Ricardo. The contrast between Malthus's supply–demand focus and Ricardo's cost focus has been exaggerated. This perspective is further confirmed in section IX, where it is shown that J.B. Say – the 'utility' theorist *par excellence* – identified Malthus and Ricardo regarding value theory, and that Malthus accepted the identification.

But more is at stake. Differences between Ricardo and Malthus on costs emerge in the course of formal discussion of value *measurement*. The implications for price theory there emerging are considered below, in chapter 7.

II ON UTILITY

At the outset of his Value chapter in the *Principles*, Malthus dismisses 'value-in-use' as 'metaphorical' – descriptive of 'a clear [1836: and abundant] spring of water' or 'fine air' – and irrelevant to exchange value (1820, 51; 1836, 50).[3] There is a parallel here to Adam Smith's formulation of the paradox of value involving biological or physiological utility (1776/1937, 28); Malthus himself pointed out that water and air 'are [bodies] in the highest degree useful, and indeed essentially necessary to the life and happiness of the human race [1836: of human beings],' effectively extending the term 'value-in-use' to Smith's categories.[4] The important analytical point is that his dismissiveness regarding utility in the particular sense adopted no more gainsays his according demand an essential role in the determination of exchange values than it does Smith's.[5]

Even according to Schumpeter, Malthus – whose criticism of Ricardo's theory of value 'point[ed] in the direction of a utility theory' – lacked the notion of marginal utility, going straight to the supply and demand appara-

3 Cf. *The Measure of Value* and the independence of exchange value from value-in-use: 'It is generally allowed that the word value, in common language, has two different meanings; one, value in use, the other, value in exchange; the first expressing merely the usefulness of an object in supplying the most important wants of mankind, without reference to its power of commanding other objects in exchange; and the second expressing the power of commanding other objects in exchange, without reference to its usefulness in supplying the most important wants of mankind. It is obviously value in the last sense, not the first, with which the science of Political Economy is mainly concerned' (1823a/1986, 7, 181).

4 Broome (1991) finds that 'after Jevons's time the meaning of "utility" in economics is shifted. The word came to refer, not to the tendency of an object to produce good, but to the good an object produces ... "Utility" came to mean *good*' (1–2). But in fact both meanings can be found in Malthus. An example of the first appears in our text, and the second is given subsequently in the *Principles* (1820, 61, 62; 1836, 60), where value-in-use is defined as 'the intrinsic utility of an object.' It is doubtful whether we need seek specific implications intended by Malthus in his dual usage.

In his *Definitions* (1827) Malthus defined utility in the first sense as 'the quality of being serviceable or beneficial to mankind' (1827a/1986, *8*, 107). He adds that the 'utility of an object has generally been considered as proportioned to the necessity and real importance of these services and benefits.' This latter perspective was common usage (see Bowley, 1973, 142–3).

5 Schumpeter made the point that only Senior among the English classics 'realize[d] the possibilities of the utility approach to the phenomenon of economic value,' the others being 'content to turn away from "value-in-use" with a reference to the paradox of value that should not have been a paradox any more ... they did not follow up the utility clue because they did *not* see their way to using it effectively' (1954, 1054). This is a misleading statement, implying that the so-called paradox was inexplicable to Smith, Malthus, and Ricardo.

tus and concentrating entirely upon it (1954, 600).[6] George Stigler (1965, 78–9) does not mention Malthus among those who stated clearly the principle of diminishing marginal utility though they failed to apply it to economic problems (Lloyd, Senior, Jennings, Hearn); or among those who 'applied utility theory to economic events without explicitly developing the principle of diminishing marginal utility' (including Auguste Walras and Longfield).[7]

This view of Malthus is a fair one. After his brief allusion to physiological 'value-in-use,' he concentrates on the fundamentals of exchange theory. We shall find, in fact, that much of his analysis of the demand–price relationship eschews the *individual* in favour of the *market*, avoiding the typical utility problem. There is even a possibility that he positively *rejected* the principle of diminishing marginal utility: 'Stockings do not lose half their power of contributing to the comfort and convenience of the wearer, because by improved machinery they can be made at half their price, or their exchangeable value be reduced one half. It will be readily allowed that the man who has two pairs of stockings of the same quality instead of one pair, posesses as far as stockings are concerned, a double portion of the conveniences of life. Yet even in this case, he is not in all respects doubly rich. If, indeed, he means to use them himself, he really has twice as much wealth [1836: ... himself, he may have twice as much wealth, though this has been denied by some writers] ...' (1820, 338; 1836, 299–300).[8]

In all this, Malthus followed in Ricardo's footsteps, even to the extent of the chosen stockings example.[9] In fact, in the second edition, Malthus paid formal tribute to Ricardo as 'the first writer of note, who took pains to make a marked distinction between wealth and value [see Ricardo, 1951–73, I, 273]; and in this, he appears to me to have rendered an unquestionable service to the science of political economy' (1836, 303). The contrast between '*wealth*' and '*value*' for Ricardo reflected that between *total utility* and exchangeable value, the latter determined at the *margin* (1951–73, I, 275–6). This may well be true of Malthus, as the stockings illustration itself suggests. J.B. Say identified Ricardo and Malthus on the issue, as we shall see later, in section IX.

6 On Senior and marginal utility, see Bowley, 1973, 153–6.

7 Stigler mentions Dupuit and Gossen in addition to Bentham as elaborating the marginal-utility principle *and* applying it to economic problems. On Malthus's neglect of the diminishing-marginal-utility principle see also Myint, 1948, 35–6.

8 Smith (1951, 253) suggests that, by his reference in his second edition, Malthus may have been alluding to the anonymous author of *Observations on Certain Verbal Disputes* (1821), whose statement 'half the quantity we use of any article is generally *more* than half as intrinsically desireable, on the whole' (1821, 65) implies diminishing marginal utility.

9 'If by an improved machine I can, with the same quantity of labour, make two pairs of stockings instead of one, I in no way impair the *utility* of one pair of stockings, though I diminish their value' (1951–73, I, 280n).

A statement of the gains from trade (in Chapter VI: 'Wealth and Value') seems at first glance to belie this reading: 'The country would not have received lace and cambrics in exchange for its corn unless its wealth, or its necessaries, conveniences and luxuries taken together, had been increased by such exchanges; and this increase of wealth cannot possibly be measured in any other way than by the increase of value so occasioned, founded upon the circumstance that the commodities received are more wanted and held in higher esteem than those which were sent away' (1820, 339; 1836, 300).[10] But we must allow for terminological peculiarities. The 'increase in value' referred to here as the measure of an increase in wealth probably refers to *total* value – the total value of output in money of constant purchasing power, not value at the margin of output – serving as an *approximate* measure of the change in physical output. Thus the text immediately allows 'Wealth [1836: The wealth of a country] ... does not always increase in proportion to the increase in value' because 'an increase of value may sometimes take place under an actual diminution of the necessaries, conveniences and luxuries of life [1836: actual diminution of commodities]' (1820, 339; 1836, 301),[11] and conversely because value does not necessarily increase in proportion even when total output rises: 'neither does it increase in proportion to the mere quantity of what comes under the denomination of wealth, because the various articles of which this quantity is composed may not be so proportioned to the wants and powers of the society as to give them their proper value.'

All that distinguishes Ricardo and Malthus in the present context is usage of the term 'value' – for Ricardo it is consistently *per unit* value as determined at the margin, whereas for Malthus it is *total* value. But there is no substantive contrast as the 'stockings' case demonstrates – total utility doubles, though per-unit value halves. Certainly there is none regarding

10 A much earlier reference to subjective gains from trade will be found in 1811a/1986, 7, 39n.

11 Ricardo (*Note 194*) observed of the proposition that 'an increase of value may take place under an actual diminution of the necessaries, conveniences and luxuries of life': 'This is my opinion.' But without question, he had in mind *marginal* value. He found an earlier statement by Malthus which identified wealth and value to be inconsistent with the valid formulation as he understood it: 'This is my opinion but it is absolutely inconsistent with Mr. Malthus's theory. In [1820] page 60 he says "What we want further is some estimate of a kind which may be denominated real value in exchange implying the quantity of the necessaries and conveniences of life which those wages, incomes or commodities will enable the possessor of them to command." In the one passage we are told that value is in proportion to the abundance of necessaries and conveniences in the other we are assured that an increase of value may take place under an actual diminution of necessaries and conveniences' (1951–73, II, 297–8; cf. 33–4).

the subjective nature of the gains from trade (cf. Ricardo, 1951–73, I, 128, 131–4).[12]

III THE THEORY OF EXCHANGE

The *Principles* contains an attractive analysis of an exchange system. This Malthus prefaces in 1820 by noting that the phenomenon of exchange emerges only because the initial distribution of endowments diverges from the equilibrium distribution: 'Value in exchange is founded, as the term seems to imply, on the will and power to exchange one commodity for another. It does not depend merely upon the scarcity in which commodities exist, nor upon the inequality of their distribution; but upon the circumstance of their not being distributed according to the wills and powers of individuals, or in such quantities to each, as the wills and powers of individuals will enable them ultimately to effect by means of exchanges' (1820, 52). This impressive formulation of the basis for exchange is deleted in the 1836 version, but a further observation that exchange between two parties implies the existence of 'reciprocal demand' is retained (and extended to exchanges involving labour): 'Every exchange, therefore, must imply, not only the power and will to give some article in exchange for one more wanted, but a reciprocal demand in the party possessing the article wanted, for the article proposed to be exchanged for it' (1820, 53); 'every exchange must imply not only the power and will to give some object in exchange for one more wanted, but a reciprocal desire in the party possessing the commodity wanted, for the commodity or the labour proposed to be exchanged for it' (1836, 50–1). The purpose of the deletion and rewording is unclear, but it is doubtful whether any substantive alteration was intended.

The frame of reference seems to be 'Walrasian' pure exchange. But this view may have to be qualified, considering the intrusion of a production dimension: 'When this reciprocal demand [1836: desire] exists, the rate at which the exchange is made, or the portion of one commodity [1836: object] which is given for an assigned portion of the other, will depend upon the relative estimation in which they are held by the parties [1836: upon the estimation in which each is held by the parties concerned], founded on the desire to possess, and the difficulty or facility of procuring possession [1836: and the difficulty of procuring possession of it]' (1820, 53; 1836, 51). There is little elaboration of the production dimension except a hint, strengthened in the 1836 version, that individuals considering exchanges take account of production opportunities before proposing

12 The same also holds true of the requirements specified in the 1836 edition that commodities must suit the tastes of consumers if general effective demand is to be assured (1836, 301–3; cf. Ricardo, 1951–73, III, 108).

offers. This emerges in an observation regarding the wide disparity between 'the desires and powers of individuals,' which in 1836 reads: 'the desires of individuals, and their powers of producing, or purchasing.'

The substantive analysis proceeds by emphasizing the emergence of an 'average' rate of exchange between commodities generated in a competitive framework involving large numbers, that is, one founded on 'all the offers of bread, compared with all the offers of venison,' with a commendatory allusion to Turgot's notion (1770, Section XXXV) of (in Malthus's phrase) 'a current value of all commodities in frequent use' extending to the full complexity of cross-relationships (1820, 54; 1836, 51).[13] An addition of 1836 again reverts to production in asserting that the emerging equilibrium set of exchange rates reflects 'the estimation in which each of these several objects was ordinarily held by the society, being determined by the ordinary desires of individuals to possess it, and the ordinary difficulty of procuring possession of it' (1836, 51; a similar addition emerges again twice, 1836, 53, in the context of the commodity selected as money). It seems that, here, cost considerations enter, so to speak, into the determination of 'estimates,' confirming that the analysis retains its essential exchange character.

Ricardo objected in his *Note 9* to what he understood as a pure-exchange pricing model which neglected costs by focusing entirely on 'the wants of mankind, and the relative estimation in which they hold commodities': 'This would be true if men from various countries were to meet in a fair, with a variety of productions, and each with a separate commodity, undisturbed by the competition of any other seller. Commodities, under such circumstances, would be bought and sold according to the relative wants of those attending the fair – but when the wants of society are well known, when there are hundreds of competitors who are willing to satisfy those wants, on the condition only that they shall have the known and usual profits, there can be no such rule for regulating the value of commodities. In such a fair as I have supposed, a man might be willing to give a pound of gold, for a pound of iron, knowing the uses of the latter metal; but when competition freely operated, he could not give that value for iron, and why? because iron would infallibly sink to its cost of production – cost of production being the pivot about which all market price moves' (1951–73, II, 24–5). On my reading, however, Malthus originally set up an exchange model, not as a matter of principle to exclude cost considera-

13 Turgot's Section XXXV deals with measurement of *exchange* values. In principle any commodity would do, but the best are homogenous or standardized products: 'Men have ... been obliged to choose by preference, for their scale of comparison, commodities which, being more commonly in use and hence of a better known value, were more like one another so that in consequence their value had more relation to the number or the quantity than the quality' (1770/1963, 33). For Turgot's influence on Malthusian value theory see Groenewegen, 1983, 597, and Rashid, 1981, 75.

tions, but as a first approximation to a fuller exposition that would take account of them.

The analysis also served as a prologue to the rationalization – by a sort of conjectural history – of the emergence of the precious metals as medium of exchange, or 'representative and measure' of exchangeable or relative value, again with reference (in 1820) to Turgot (1770, Section XLI). Specifically, the metals overcame the problem of 'want of a reciprocal demand' on the part of individuals for specific goods, and without which it was unlikely that any 'general average valuation' between commodities could emerge in the first place; the existence of 'some commodity for which there is so general and consistent a demand, that it would scarcely ever be refused in exchange for what [any individual] wanted' was a necessary prerequisite, not only for *estimating* relative values, but for the actual *determination* of the competitive exchange ratios (1820, 54–5; 1836, 52).[14]

IV THE THEORY OF DEMAND

In his *Investigation of the Cause of the Present High Price of Provisions* (1800), Malthus applied Adam Smith's pricing model to the problem of parish allowances, representing market price as 'regulated' by the extent of excess demand at the natural price: 'Adam Smith has most justly stated, that the actual price at which a commodity is sold, is compounded of its natural price, the price at which it can be brought to market, allowing the usual profit in times of moderate plenty, and the proportion of the supply to the demand. When any commodity is scarce, its natural price is necessarily forgotten, and its actual price is regulated by the excess of the demand above the supply' (1986, 7, 7). Expounding the mechanisms, Malthus supposes an initial market-demand schedule for corn involving a ranking of the various *demand prices* of fifty individuals, each individual taking one unit of corn; there is no true choice–theoretic rationale at play. A reduction in total supply from fifty to forty units forces the price up to that level which permits only the top forty consumers to remain in the market. The new equilibrium price will reflect the demand price of the fortieth consumer: 'Let us suppose a commodity in great request by fifty people, but of which, from some failure in its production, there is only sufficient to supply forty. If the fortieth man from the top have two shillings which he can spend in this commodity, and the thirty nine above him, more, in various proportions, and the ten below, all less, the actual price of the

14 Malthus goes further in both editions by representing the emergence of an efficient medium of exchange as 'a most important step in the progress of society, [which tended] to facilitate exchanges and stimulate production ...' (1820, 58; 1836, 55). Here the argument extends beyond the framework of a pure exchange model.

article, according to the genuine principles of trade, will be two shillings. If more be asked, the whole will not be sold, because there are only forty who have as much as two shillings to spend in the article; and there is no reason for asking less, because the whole may be disposed of at that sum.' The effect of parish allowances (a cash grant of one shilling) is to raise the demand prices of the ten excluded consumers. This permits them to re-enter the market and offer (at least) two shillings. But the market price must rise to exclude ten consumers; and Malthus supposes it will increase at least 25 per cent. Malthus is in effect describing the impact of an outward twist of the demand schedule affecting the lower range only, rather than a parallel shift, for which reason the new market-clearing price rises by somewhat less than one shilling: 'Let us suppose, now, that somebody gives the ten poor men, who were excluded, a shilling apiece. The whole fifty can now offer two shillings, the price which was before asked. According to every genuine principle of fair trading, the commodity must immediately rise. If it do not, I would ask, upon what principle are ten, out of the fifty who are all able to offer two shillings, to be rejected? ... The two shillings of a poor man are just as good as the two shillings of a rich one; and, if we interfere to prevent the commodity from rising out of the reach of the poorest ten, whoever they may be, we must toss up, draw lots, raffle, or fight, to determine who are to be excluded ... [But] according to every acknowledged principle of commercial dealing, the price must be allowed to rise to that point which will put it beyond the power of ten out of the fifty to purchase. This point will, perhaps, be half a crown or more, which will now become the price of the commodity. Let another shilling apiece be given to the excluded ten: all will now be able to offer half a crown. The price must in consequence immediately rise to three shillings or more, and so on *toties quoties*' (7–8).[15]

The notion of a demand schedule reflecting *demand prices* was further

15 The excluded ten, it is further pointed out, need not be those originally excluded, since 'the richest of the ten first excluded, would probably be raised above the poorest of the first forty.' Smith (1951, 250) points out that Malthus's technical apparatus is equivalent to von Boehm-Bawerk's horse-market example (1890/1930), 203). He also notes that the same general argument, but without the device of an array of demanders, appears in the *Essay on Population* (1798/1986, *1*, 30-2). A formulation of demand–supply pricing involving demand prices is also given in *Observations on the Corn Laws* (1814): 'Every change in the prices of commodities, if left to find their natural level, is occasioned by some change, actual or expected, in the state of the demand or supply. The reason why the consumer pays a tax upon any manufactured commodity, or an advance in the price of any of its component parts, is because, if he cannot or will not pay this advance of price, the commodity will not be supplied in the same quantity as before; and the next year there will only be such a proportion in the market, as is accommodated to the number of persons who will consent to pay the tax' (1986, *7*, 90).

elaborated in the *Principles.*[16] Section II of the Value chapter commences with a definition of demand as 'the will combined with the power to purchase, and supply, [as] the production of commodities combined with the intention to sell them' (1820, 64).[17] This is elaborated in the second edition, with two variations, first, deflection of attention from a *production* to a *market* orientation: 'the demand for any sort of commodities may be defined to be, the will of persons to purchase them, combined with their general means of purchasing; and supply, the quantity of the commodities for sale, combined with the desire to sell them';[18] and second, the formal adoption of a measure of demand intensity in terms of *money sacrifice,* assuming money to have constant 'value': 'It is further evident, that when the use of the precious metals, as a medium of exchange and measure of value, has become general, and during those periods when their value is considered as remaining the same, the demand will be represented and measured by the sacrifice in money which the demanders are willing and able to make in order to satisfy their wants' (1836, 61–2).[19]

The concept of 'intensity of demand' in contrast to 'extent of demand' (quantity demanded at a given price) was, Malthus believed, required to explain prices. The general context is a defence of the 'law' of demand

16 Cf. the definition given in 1827: 'DEMAND IN REGARD TO ITS INTENSITY: The sacrifice which the demanders are able and willing to make in order to satisfy their wants. It is this species of demand alone, which, compared with the supply, determines prices and values' (1986, *8,* 112).

17 This definition, Ricardo remarked (*Note 13*), is not carried over by Malthus to his last chapter, 'Of the Progress of Wealth': 'In the last chapter, where he speaks of the pernicious consequences arising from a want of demand, he appears to me to forget that the power as well as the will to purchase is required. He says, that men will not demand because they prefer indolence to work; but they cannot produce if they will not work; and if they do not produce, they may have the will, but they want the other essential quality of demand; they want the power' (1951–73, II, 36–7).

18 A footnote is attached with a detail on expectations: 'There may be sometimes a comparatively small quantity of certain commodities ready for sale, but if a large supply is soon expected, the desire to sell will be great, and the prices low. On the other hand, there may be a comparatively large quantity of the commodities ready for sale, yet if a future scanty supply is looked forward to, the dealers will not be anxious for an immediate sale, and the prices may be high.'

19 Cf. 1836, 63: 'In the same manner, if while money is considered as of the same value, certain commodities, either from scarcity, or the greater cost of production become more difficult of acquisition, as they will certainly not be acquired except by those who are willing and able to sacrifice a greater amount of money in order to obtain them, such sacrifice, if made, must be considered as an evidence of greater intensity of demand.' A notion of sacrifice *in labour* emerges also in a special case: 'If a given number of commodities, attainable by labour alone, were to become more difficult of acquisition, as they would evidently not be obtained unless by means of increased exertion, we might surely [1836: merely] consider such increased exertion, if applied, as an evidence of a greater intensity of demand, or of a power and will to make a greater sacrifice in order to obtain them' (1820, 65; 1836, 63).

and supply, involving the *relation* of one to the other: 'the relative values of commodities [1836: the value of commodities] in money, or their prices, are determined by the relative demand [1836: the demand] for them, compared with the supply of them: and this law appears to be so general, that probably not a single instance of change of price can be found which may not be satisfactorily traced to some previous change in the causes which affect the demand or supply [1836: in the state of the demand or supply]. In examining the truth of this position we must constantly bear in mind the terms in which it is expressed; and recollect that, when prices are said to be determined by demand and supply, it is not meant that they are determined either by the demand alone or the supply alone, but by their relation to each other' (1820, 64–5; 1836, 62). A standard objection to those demand–supply explanations of price which involve *proportionality* between demand and supply is granted – namely, that the market always clears. This objection, Malthus pointed out, assumes that 'demand' refers to extent of demand, and was valid on that assumption, implying – so it would appear at first glance – a failure on his part to perceive a sense of equilibration involving correction of excess demand or supply: 'In one sense of the terms in which demand and supply have occasionally been used [1836: have been used], this position may be granted. The actual *extent* of the demand, compared with the actual *extent* of the supply, are always on an average proportioned to each other [1836: are always nearly equal to each other]. If the supply be ever so small, the extent of the effective demand [1836: *extent* of the demand] cannot be greater; and if the supply be ever so great, the extent of the demand, or the consumption, will either increase in proportion, or a part of it will become useless and cease to be produced [1836: the *extent* of the demand will in most cases increase in proportion to the fall of price occasioned by the desire to sell, and the consumption will finally equal the production]. It cannot, therefore, be in this sense that a change in the proportion of demand to supply affects prices [1836: takes place]; because in this sense demand and supply always bear [1836: bear nearly] the same relation to each other' (1820, 65; 1836, 62).[20] To make sense of equilibrium, an increase in demand had to be rendered as *an increase in demand price*. 'The greater is the degree of this will and power [1836: of this will and these means of purchasing] with regard to [1836: when directed to] any particular commodity, the greater or the more intense may be fairly [1836: 'fairly' omitted] said to be the demand for it,' which high intensity becomes manifest under appropriate supply (cost) conditions – implying a schedule of demand prices: 'But however great this will and power [1836: these means] may be among the purchasers [1836: demanders] of a commodity, none of them will be

20 The unitary-elastic assumption of the second edition is significant since, expenditure being constant, it precludes a measure of 'intensity' in terms of *total* outlay, Malthus normally dealing with *changing* intensity for a given product as supply varies.

disposed to give a high price for it, if they can obtain it at a low one; and as long as the abilities [1836: means] and competition of the sellers induce them [1836: continue] to bring the quantity wanted to market at a low price, the real [1836: whole] intensity of the demand will not show itself' (1820, 66; 1836, 63).[21]

Having established his categories, Malthus next accounts for an increase in the equilibrium price: (1) in terms of an *upward shift* in the demand curve (given supply) owing to an increase in 'the number or wants of its purchasers' (1820) or in 'the number, wants, and means of the demanders' (1836); and (2) in terms of a reduction in supply *given* the demand curve – and conversely for a fall in equilibrium price:

[It] may be said, that the giving a greater price for a commodity [1836: while the difficulty of obtaining money remains the same] absolutely and necessarily implies [1836: necessarily implies] a greater intensity of demand; and that the real question is, what are the causes which either call forth or render unnecessary the expression of this intensity of demand [1836: which determine the increase or diminution of this intensity of demand, which shows itself in a rise or fall of prices]? It has been justly stated, that the causes which tend to raise the price of any article estimated in some commodity named, and supposed for short periods not essentially to vary [1836: not essentially to vary in the difficulty of its production, or the state of its supply compared with the demand], are an increase in the number or wants of its purchasers [1836: the number, wants, and means of the demanders], or a deficiency in its supply; and the causes which lower the price are a diminution in the number or wants of its purchasers [1836: the number, wants, and means of the demanders], or an increased abundance in its supply. The first class of these causes is obviously calculated to call forth the expression of a greater intensity of demand, and the other of a less (1820, 66–7; 1836, 63–4).

Now it is remarkable that Malthus proceeded to deal with class-1 disturbances, involving a *shift* in the demand curve, in terms of an increased *quantity demanded* at the original price, the outcome of which is a rise in

21 This point reiterates an earlier proposition in Malthus's Section I (1820, 54, above, p. 225). In *Note 9* Ricardo had approved of the formulation, and the approval is reinforced in *Note 14* at the present juncture: 'I agree with Mr. Malthus [1820, 54], however great the demand for a commodity may be, its price will be finally regulated by the competition of the sellers, – it will settle at or about its natural price; that price, which, as Adam Smith observes, is necessary to give the current rate of wages to the workmen, and the current rate of profits to the capitalist. On a comparison of the uses of iron, and gold, the demanders might be both able and willing to give more for iron, than for gold; but they cannot; the competition of the sellers prevents it and sinks the value of both metals to their cost of production, to their natural price. – The market price of a commodity may from an unusual demand, or from a deficiency of supply, rise above its natural price, but this does not overturn the doctrine that the great regulator of price is cost of production' (1951–73, II, 38–9).

the (equilibrium) price which chokes off the excess quantity demanded on the part of at least some of the original purchasers. The original impression that Malthus failed to appreciate the equilibrium concept in a 'Walrasian' framework is belied by his extended analysis: 'If, for instance, a commodity which had been habitually demanded and consumed by a thousand purchasers were suddenly to be wanted by two thousand, it is clear that before this increased extent of demand could [1836: can] be supplied, some must go without what they wanted [1836: want]; and it is scarcely possible to suppose that the intensity of individual demand would not increase [1836: should not exist in such a degree] among a sufficient number of these two thousand purchasers [1836: demanders], to take off all the [1836: as to take off the whole of the] commodity produced at an increased price' (1820, 67; 1836, 64). Smith has argued convincingly on the basis of these texts that Malthus lacked profound interest in the *subjective aspects of demand* in the sense of individual consumer decision making: 'Having established the concepts of intensity and extent, Malthus was satisfied. He was too practical a person to go deeper than changes in the number, wants, or means of "purchasers" ... He emphasized the subjective side of demand in certain respects (intensity is a subjective concept) but he had no interest in analyzing what lay behind the intensity of demand' (1951, 252). Thus, Smith concludes, 'his propositions about the intensity of demand increasing as the quantity decreased were never explicitly applied to the individual. One gets the impression that Malthus thought of the individual as buying either his usual amount or not at all' (252–3).[22] This may be rather too strongly stated, but as an indication of the weight of emphasis it appears valid.

Shortly thereafter in the second edition, Malthus attaches a note observing that 'an increased intensity of demand' and 'increased extent of demand' often go together, and points to cases of increased intensity – an upward shift of the curve involving increased demand price – stimulating both output and *quantity demanded at the original price*: 'In fact, an increased intensity of demand, when not occasioned by an increased difficulty of production, is the greatest encouragement to an increase of produce and consumption' (1836, 69n). (Increased intensity of demand owing to higher cost involves *a movement along a given demand curve*, whereas the case at hand involves *a shift in the demand curve.*)

22 Some commentators, however, read Malthus's intensity concept as describing 'a person's willingness and ability to make a sacrifice in order to obtain something' (Bowley, 1973, 148). But Bowley conceded that the notion was better followed up by Longfield (143, 149f.; see also Bowley on Dupuit, 149). I surmise that, had Malthus explicitly considered the individual who adjusted quantity demanded to variations in price, he might have followed Ricardo's route involving income effects. The observation in *High Price of Provisions* (1800) that high prices lead to 'strict economy in all ranks of life' (1986, 7, 14) entails income constraints imposed on purchasers.

By comparing the two formulations, we can isolate the problem that troubled Malthus. To assume an increase in quantity demanded at the original equilibrium price does not assure a higher equilibrium price. Only if demand price rises; that is, some purchasers at least are prepared to make a larger sacrifice (at the margin) – in our terms, only *if the entire schedule of demand, not merely one point on it, rises* – will price rise.[23] None the less, the substantive point remains that his shifting demand schedule is expressed in both senses.[24]

We turn now to class-2 disturbances, involving a higher price emerging because of reduced supply, *given* the demand curve. The introductory 'in the same manner' cited below relates to the *increase in demand price* in both cases – in the former, on the higher demand curve, and now on the original demand curve: 'In the same manner, if a commodity were to be diminished one half in quantity, it is scarcely possible to suppose that a sufficient number of the former purchasers [1836: demanders] would not be both willing and able to take off the whole of the diminished quantity [1836: to take off the diminished quantity] at a higher price; but if they really would not or could not do this, the price could not rise' (1820, 67; 1836, 64).[25] The 1836 version adds an objection to West's position (1826,

23 Myint observes that Malthus missed the essential point of the principle of diminishing marginal utility when he regarded the 'extent' and the 'intensity' of demand as separate variables, each of which may change without involving a change in the other (1948, 36). But it is not clear whether Malthus believed strongly that the extent *could* increase with no increase in the intensity of demand – implying a *horizontal* demand curve, at least over a range – or whether his exposition was designed to demonstrate that a sensible demand–supply theory of price required the notion of a full-fledged *shift* of the demand curve to explain demand-induced price changes; that is, that the usual case would *not* involve horizontal demand curves. (Myint himself concedes that 1836, 69n, points in this direction.)

24 Blaug asserts that the distinction between a *shift* and a *movement* along a demand curve is implied by the 'extensive' vs 'intensive' dimensions (1985, 172). It is *not*. The intensity of demand is said by Malthus to rise along a *given* demand curve (as supply contracts) as well as on a higher demand curve (supply given). I do not appreciate Blaug's assertion that Malthus made no substantive use of his terminological clarification.

25 With the foregoing disturbances in mind, Smith observed correctly that 'Malthus's intensity is incapable of distinguishing price-determining from price-determined changes in demand. Probably because it applied to both cases he could not decide whether the intensity of demand was some latent price, to be called forth as needed' – this is the case of an outward shift involving increase in quantity demanded at the original price with its *consequence* in a higher equilibrium demand price – 'or whether it was simply a quantity susceptible of increase or decrease' (1951, 251). Nevertheless, I believe it would be going too far to assert that Malthus neglected the shift–movement contrast.

Smith also suggested that the anonymous author of *Observations on Certain Verbal Disputes* (1821), who took Malthus to task on precisely this issue, 'possessed a sense of the distinction between the price-determined and the price-determining that was unusually strong for this time' (253, regarding 1821, 65).

21–3) that *potential* demand is irrelevant: 'Sir Edward West seems to think, that a demand *in posse* cannot be called demand; but it does not appear to me that there is any impropriety in so applying the term; and it is quite certain that if there were not a greater intensity of demand *in posse* than *in esse*, no failure of supply could raise prices. In reality prices are determined by the demand *in posse* compared with the supply *in esse*' (1836, 64n).[26]

An impact on price of reduced supply would be generated by an exogenous deterioration in cost conditions. (Strictly, this extension is out of place in Section II of the chapter on Value, which deals with *market* not *cost* pricing, but the main concern is the character of the demand side.) Here Malthus elaborates in terms of differential demand elasticities – assuming that the cost price doubles – ranging from highly elastic (Malthus goes to extremes here and assumes that only a single buyer remains in the market at the higher price) to zero demand elasticity. The 'higher intensity' in the latter case entails a higher position on the vertical demand; the 'same extent' refers to an unchanged quantity demanded:

On the other hand, if the permanent cost of producing the commodity were doubled, it is evident that only such a quantity could be permanently produced [1836: brought to market] as would supply the wants of those who were able and willing [1836: both able and willing] to make a sacrifice for the attainment of their wishes equal to double the amount [1836: to double] of what they did before. The quantity of the commodity which would be brought to market under these circumstances might be extremely different. It might be reduced to the supply of a single individual, or might remain precisely the same as before ... In the latter case, there would be the same quantity supplied and the same quantity demanded [1836: there would be exactly the same quantity of the commodity supplied, and exactly the same effectual demand for it in regard to extent]; but there would be a much greater intensity of demand called forth [1836: the value brought to market in exchange for the commodity in question would have greatly increased]; and this may be fairly said to be a most important change in the relation between the supply and the demand of these commodities; because, without [1836: ... commodities. Without] the increased intensity of demand, which in this case takes place, the commodity would cease to be produced; that is, the failure of the supply would be contingent upon the failure of the power or will to make a greater sacrifice for the object sought. (67–8; 1836, 65)

26 Smith (1951, 250) argues that 'Malthus' resort to intensity of demand owed its validity not so much to any analytical superiority of intensity as such over the quantity-demanded concept as to the fact that his intensity was an *ex ante* concept in contrast with Ricardo's (and his own) *ex post* usage of 'extent.' It is not certain that the interpretation of Malthus's *extent of demand* as an *ex post* concept is valid considering the class-1 shifts discussed above.

Paglin has pointed out that, unlike Lauderdale, Malthus in his account of the relation between demand and costs failed to make explicit 'the range of variation of demand, the choice of combinations, open to the individual'; each individual either buys all or none at the higher price (Paglin, 1961, 46–7). This confirms the view that Malthus should *not* be classified among Subjective Value theorists.

Turning next to *reduced* equilibrium prices, we have cases where increased supply is disposed of by movement along a given demand curve, and cases involving downward shifts of the demand curve: 'Upon the same principles, if [1836: owing to an unusual supply] a commodity were to become much more abundant, compared with the former number of purchasers, this increased supply could not all be sold, unless the price were lowered. Each seller wishing to dispose of that part of the commodity which he possessed [1836 adds: under the fear of its remaining upon his hands] would go on lowering it till he had effected his object; and though the wills and powers [1836: means] of the old purchasers might remain undiminished, yet as the commodity could be obtained without the expression of the same intensity of demand as before, this demand would of course not then show itself. A similar effect would obviously take place from the consumers of a commodity requiring a less quantity of it' (1820, 68–9; 1836, 66).

As in the analysis of rising price, the present analysis also takes account of changes in cost price. Upon a reduction in costs *actual* supply normally expands because 'in almost all practical cases ... it rarely happens that a fall of price does not occasion an increased consumption,' Malthus without ado making use of extent of demand (1820, 69; 1836, 66–7). But in rare cases of zero demand elasticity, the fall in price occurs because of 'contingent' increase of supply: 'On the supposition, however, of the very rare case that a definite quantity only of the commodity was required, whatever might be its price, it is obvious that from the competition of the producers a greater quantity would be brought to market than could be consumed, till the price was reduced in proportion to the increased facility of production; and this excess [1836: this temporary excess] of supply would be always contingent on the circumstances of the price being at any time higher than the price which returns average profits. In this case of a fall of prices, as in the other of a rise of prices, the actual quantity of the commodity supplied and consumed may possibly, after a short struggle, be the same as before; yet it cannot be said that the demand is the same [1836: that no change has taken place in the demand]. It may indeed exist precisely [1836: latently] in the same degree, and the actual consumers of the commodity might be perfectly ready to give what they gave before rather than go without it; but such has been the alteration in the means of supply compared with the demand [1836: the former demand], that the competition of the producers renders the same intensity of demand [1836: renders the making of the same sacrifice] no longer necessary to effect the supply required; and not being necessary, it is of course not called forth [1836: not made], and the price falls' (1820, 69–70; 1836, 66–7).

To summarize Malthus's position: Equilibrium prices rise with changes in the 'demand–supply' relation which generate higher intensity of demand, thus allowing for special cases of zero demand elasticity where the extent of demand does not vary with price: 'It is evidently, therefore, not merely *extent* of actual demand, nor even the extent of actual demand compared with the extent of actual supply, which raises prices, but such a change in the relation between supply and demand as renders necessary the expression of a greater intensity of demand [1836 adds: or the offer of a greater *value* compared with the quantity supplied], in order either peaceably to divide any actual produce, or prevent the future produce of the same kind from failing' (1820, 71; 1836, 67). Similarly, lower prices result, not only with increased market supply assuming a negatively sloped demand curve, but to prevent 'contingent' excess supply should costs fall in the face of zero demand elasticity: 'And, in the same manner, it is not merely *extent* of actual supply, nor the extent of the actual supply compared with the actual demand [1836: compared with the extent of the actual demand (which are generally nearly equal)], that lowers prices, but such a change in the relation of the supply, compared with the demand, as renders a fall of price necessary, in order to take off a temporary abundance, or to prevent a constant excess of supply contingent upon a diminution in the cost of production, without a proportionate diminution in the price of the produce' (1820, 70–1; 1836, 67–8).

* * *

Malthus himself took credit only for the novel *term* 'intensity of demand.' In the second edition, he allowed that Adam Smith had long before recognized the major principle involved – the necessity for increased sacrifice on the part at least 'of some of the demanders' to assure a higher equilibrium price in the event of reduced supply. It is a contentious issue in the secondary literature whether Malthus's *intensity* refers to total expenditure or to demand price.[27] We have read it in the latter sense, and the

27 See in particular O'Brien for the position that Malthus 'apparently means ... the outlay rectangle formed by perpendiculars from the price and quantity axes to the demand curve' (1975, 105). The problem of interpretation is eased if we follow Smith (1951, 251–2n), who observes that from 1824 Malthus 'sometimes used the total amount spent for a quantity of a commodity as the measure of demand.' Cf. the following contrast in the *Definitions* (1827) between equilibrium in commodity and labour markets: 'It is not true, as stated by M. Say, that prices rise in the direct ratio of the *quantity* demanded, and the inverse ratio of the *quantity* supplied. They only vary in this way, when the demand is understood to mean the sacrifice which the demanders are able and willing to make, in order to supply themselves with what they want; which may be represented

present acknowledgment confirms that reading: 'Adam Smith says, that "when the quantity of any commodity which is brought to market falls short of the effectual demand, all those who are willing to pay the whole value of the rent, wages and profits, which must be paid in order to bring it thither, cannot be supplied with the quantity which they want. Rather than want it altogether some of them will be willing to give more." Now this willingness, on the part of some of the demanders, to make a greater sacrifice than before, in order to satisfy their wants, is what I have called a greater intensity of demand. As no increase of price can possibly take place, unless the commodity be of such a nature as to excite in a certain number of purchasers this species of demand, and as this species of demand must always be implied whenever we speak of demand and supply as determining prices, I have thought it ought to have a name' (1836, 65–6n). Paglin (1961, 46) asserted that demand intensity derived from Lauderdale, understanding the notion as 'a fairly close approximation to the idea of a demand schedule,' but said nothing on whether this constitutes a schedule of demand prices or demand quantities. Smith (1951, 251), correctly understanding 'intensity' as *demand price*, regarded Malthus as entirely original: 'Here, before James Mill we have a reinterpretation of the common phrase "the will and power to purchase" to make it mean the "intensity of demand," measured by the demand price. No other economist recognized explicitly that "demand" might have two measures, extent and intensity!' I can see no reason not to take Malthus's own perspective on his relationship to predecessors seriously.

Malthus insisted that his 'intensity of demand' must be distinguished from Smith's 'effectual demand' or quantity demanded at cost price. Demand intensity was applicable in all cases of supply variation, whether or not they related to changes in underlying cost conditions; and was required to rationalize the commonly stated *positive* relation between 'demand' and price: 'It is essentially different from effectual demand, which, as defined by Adam Smith, is the quantity wanted by those who are willing and able to pay the natural price; and this demand will of course generally be the greatest when the natural price is the least. But the increased intensity of demand, when actually called forth, uniformly implies an increased *value* offered, compared with the *quantity* of the commodity supplied, and is equally applicable to an article which is accidentally scarce, and one which has increased in its natural price. It is invariable and exclusively the intensity of demand, and not the effectual

in regard to price by the quantity of money ready to be employed in purchases in a market. When the demand for *labour* is spoken of, it can only relate to *extent*, and a greater demand can only signify a power of commanding a greater *quantity* of labour' (1986, *8*, 119).

demand, which is referred to, when it is said, and correctly, that the prices of commodities vary as the demand directly, and supply inversely.'[28]

The same disclaimer to originality is to be found in the 1820 version, though without reference to Smith. The notion of 'intensity' of demand or demand price reflected, Malthus believed, the common intention of users of the general demand–supply formula: 'If the terms demand and supply be understood and used in the way here described, there is no case of price, whether temporary or permanent, which they will not determine; and in every instance of bargain and sale it will be perfectly correct to say that the price [1836: prices of commodities] will depend upon the relation of the demand to the supply [1836 adds: or will vary as its demand (that is, the money offered) directly, and the supply inversely]. I wish it particularly to be observed that in this discussion I have not given any new meaning to the terms, demand and supply [1836: I have not given a meaning to the terms demand and supply different from that in which they have been most frequently applied before]. In the use which I have occasionally made [1836: the use which I have made] of the words *intense* and *intensity* as applied to demand, my sole purpose has been to explain the meaning which has hitherto always been attached to the term demand when it is said to raise prices' (1820, 71; 1836, 68). This formulation in terms of demand price overcame Ricardo's problem that there was no meaning to 'increased demand' if quantity demanded – *extent of demand* – did not rise, that 'the demand for a commodity cannot be said to increase, if no additional quantity of it be purchased or consumed' (1951–73, I, 382). '[It] is obvious,' Malthus responded, 'that it is not in the sense of mere extent of consumption that demand raises prices, because it is almost always when the prices are the lowest that the *extent* of consumption [1836: extent of demand and consumption] is the greatest. This, therefore, cannot be the meaning hitherto attached to the term, demand, when it is said to raise prices.'

In fact, Malthus proceeds, Ricardo himself had recognized the possibility of an increase in price occurring in circumstances where the quantity demanded actually *falls* – citing a case of excess demand at the original price (due to reduced supply) such that market price rises, which latter Malthus represents as a rise in demand *intensity*.[29] And he here repeated

28 Cf. also the *Definitions* (1827a/1986, *8*, 25). The fact remains that both Malthus and Smith assume that price does increase with an outward shift in the demand curve, whether it is described in terms of increased demand price at given quantities or increased quantity demanded at given prices.

29 A great deal of the debate was unnecessary, reflecting misunderstandings arising from differing terminology. This is strikingly illustrated in the context of the very case at hand, discussed in correspondence as early as 1814: 'I sometimes suspect that we do not attach the same meaning to the word demand. If corn rises in price, you perhaps attribute it to a greater demand, – I should call it a greater competition. The demand cannot I think be said to increase if the quantity consumed be diminished, altho much more money may be required to purchase the smaller than the large quantity' (Ricardo, 1951–73, VI, 129). Ricardo – who works in terms of total expenditure – is dealing with

that his intention was to interpret the demand-and-supply formula in a manner consistent with common usage, *including Ricardo's,* in other formulations: 'Mr. Ricardo, however, subsequently quotes Lord Lauderdale's statements respecting value [1951–73, I, 384], and allows them to be true, as applied to monopolized commodities for a limited period. He would allow, therefore, that the deficiency of any article in a market [1836: a deficiency in the usual quantity of an article] would occasion a great [1836: greater] demand for it, compared with the supply, and raise its price, although in this case less than usual of the article must be purchased by the consumers. Demand, in this sense, is obviously quite different from the sense in which Mr. Ricardo had before used the term' (1820, 71–2; 1836, 68–9). What follows in 1820 is elaborated in the 1836 version: 'The one implies extent of consumption, the other intensity of demand, or the will and power to make a greater sacrifice in order to obtain the object wanted. It is in this latter sense alone that demand raises prices' (1820, 72). 'The one is a demand in regard to extent, the increase of which implies a greater quantity of the commodity purchased; the other is demand in regard to intensity, the increase of which implies the will and power to make a greater sacrifice in order to obtain the object wanted. It is in this latter sense, I think, that the term is most frequently applied; at any rate, it is in this latter sense alone that demand raises prices. It is in the nature of things absolutely impossible that any demand, in regard to extent, should raise prices, unaccompanied by a will and power on the part of the demanders to make a greater sacrifice, in order to satisfy their wants' (1836, 69).

In closing his Section II, Malthus once more reiterated that his object was 'to shew that whenever we talk of demand and supply as influencing [1836: determining] prices, whether market or natural, the terms should [1836: must] always be understood in the sense in which Mr. Ricardo and every other person has hitherto understood them, when speaking of commodities bought and sold in a market.' He patently tries to avoid a suggestion of any deviation on his part from other authorities, including Ricardo. And it will be remarked that all Ricardo's notes on the 1820 version of Section II are friendly. Thus in his *Note 15*, as in *Note 9* and *Note 14*, he congratulated Malthus for the correct perspective on costs as ultimate determinant: 'Mr. Malthus here substantially admits, that it is not the relation of demand to supply, which finally and permanently regulates the price of commodities, but the cost of their production. On the other hand I do not deny, that in the progress of the rise or fall of commodities, there may be, what is usually termed, an increased demand, or an increased

---

an upward movement along a negatively sloped demand curve but refuses to use the term 'increase of demand.'

supply' (1951–73, II, 40–1; see also *Note 18* and *Note 19*). That he had no quarrel with the substance of Malthus's pricing analysis is of high doctrinal significance.

V THE LIMITATIONS OF DEMAND–SUPPLY ANALYSIS

Malthus, in the 1803 *Essay on Population*, accepted Smith's positive relation between the corn price and the money wage, and of the money wage on general prices. This sequence is spelled out, for example, in a warning regarding the contemporary transition of the economy from an 'agricultural' to a 'commercial' system: 'The competition of increasing commercial wealth, operating upon a supply of corn not increasing in the same proportion, must at all times greatly tend to raise the price of labour; but when scarce years are taken into the consideration, its effect in this way must ultimately be prodigious ... [If] we go on, as we have done lately, the price of labour and of provisions must soon increase in a manner out of all proportion to their price in the rest of Europe; and it is impossible that this should not ultimately check all our dealing with foreign powers, and give a fatal blow to our commerce and manufactures' (1986, *3*, 676).[30] The passage was revised in 1806, but retains the effect of an expanding manufacturing sector on the corn price and, via the money wage, on general prices (1806, II, 222). Similarly, 'corn being an article of the most absolute necessity, in comparison with which all others will be sacrificed, a deficiency of it must necessarily produce a much greater advance of price than a deficiency of any other kind of produce; and as the price of corn influences the price of so many other commodities, the evil effects of a deficiency will not only be more severe and more general, but more lasting, than the effects of a deficiency in any other commodity' (233).[31]

Ricardo was troubled by aspects of the 1803 formulation, presumably having in mind Malthus's Smithian analysis.[32] He also indicated unease with the 1803 chapter on bounties: 'Malthus is preparing a new edition of his Essay on Population for the press. He ought candidly to confess that he

30 The passage cited in our text imples that the rise in the corn price reflects pressure of demand from the manufacturing sector, and is responsible for the money-wage increase. But the ellipses contain a passage asserting that the corn price itself is 'regulated' by wages *and rent*: 'During the late scarcities, the price of labour has been continually rising – not to fall again; the rents of land have been everywhere advancing – not to fall again; and of course, the price of produce must rise – not to fall again; as, independently of a particular competition from scarcity, or the want of competition from plenty, its price is necessarily regulated by the wages of labour, and the rent of land ...'

31 The 1817 chapters constitute a complete restructuring of the text, from which the lengthy passage cited above is absent. But the notion of rent entering into the price of corn re-emerges, as on 1986, *3*, 386.

32 Ricardo wrote to Malthus (2 January 1816) that he had reservations regarding the two chapters on the agricultural and manufacturing systems in the 1803 edition, but was better satisfied with the revisions then under way in draft (1951–73, VII, 2).

has committed great errors in his chapters on the Agricultural and Mercantile systems, as well as in that on bounties' (to James Mill, 24 October 1815; 1951–73, VI, 314). In that chapter (1803, Book III, ch. 10), Malthus had taken Smith to task for his extreme proposition that the corn price governs general prices precisely and without lag; at the same time, he himself accepted that 'the money price of corn ... is undoubtedly by far the most powerful ingredient in regulating the price of labour, and of all other commodities' (1986, *3*, 383).

In the *Observations on the Effects of the Corn Laws* (1814), Malthus again considered Smith's extraordinary policy conclusion – that a corn-export bounty or corn-import restrictions are ineffectual as a stimulus to agriculture because of the exactly proportionate impact of the corn price on the money-wage rate, and thus on the prices of manufactured goods (Smith, 1776/1937, 476, 482). This Malthus denied: 'Nothing then can be more evident both from theory and experience, than that the price of corn does not immediately and generally regulate the prices of labour and all other commodities; and that the real price of corn is capable of varying for periods of sufficient length to give a decided stimulus or discouragement to agriculture' (1986, *7*, 94).[33]

Malthus objected to Smith in part on grounds of the empirical complexity of the wage basket, which alone undermined the notion of a *proportionate and rapid* response of the money wage to a rise in the corn price (89). Second, the deceleration in population growth required to ensure that the money wage indeed rises upon a corn-price increase is 'much slower and more painful' than the withdrawal of supply in commodity markets in the face of a corresponding disturbance such as a tax (90). But the most serious problem was that *the doctrine was wholly inconsistent with Smith's own allocation theory*, by implying the unresponsiveness of corn supply to changing demand: 'If we suppose, that the real price of corn is unchangeable, or not capable of experiencing a relative increase or decrease of value, compared with labour and other commodities, it will follow, that agriculture is at once excluded from the operation of that principle, so beautifully explained and illustrated by Dr Smith, by which capital flows from one employment to another, according to the various and necessarily fluctuating wants of society. It will follow, that the growth of corn has, at all times, and in all countries, proceeded with a uniform unvarying pace, occasioned only by the equable increase of agricultural capital, and can never have been accelerated, or retarded, by variations in demand. It will follow, that if a country happened to be either overstocked or understocked with corn, no motive of interest could exist for withdrawing capital from agriculture, in the one case, or adding to it in the other, and thus restoring the equilibrium between its different kinds of produce' (90–1).

33 Malthus immediately emphasized that any stimulus resulting from a specific intervention would be 'temporary,' considering the principle of profit-rate equalization.

The primary charge is, therefore, that Smith's analysis contravened his own allocative principles by its isolation of corn for special treatment (87). But as we shall now see, Malthus is himself open to precisely the same charge.

* * *

The 1815 pamphlet *Rent* imposes a remarkable and little-known constraint on the applicability of demand–supply analysis, involving a contrast between the demand for 'strict necessaries' and the demand for other goods. Only in the general category is there meaning to *demand independent of or external to supply; and here only the scarcity property applies.* By contrast, in the case of agriculture: 'The cause of the higher price of the necessaries of life above the cost of production, is to be found in their abundance, rather than their scarcity' (1815b/1986, 7, 121). The purported contrast – vehemently denied by Ricardo on the grounds that *relative scarcity is the general rule applicable to all cases* (1951–73, I, 405–6) – is of the first importance and should be considered in full: 'There is a radical difference in the cause of a demand for those objects which are strictly necessary to the support of human life, and a demand for all other commodities. In all other commodities the demand is exterior to, and independent of, the production itself; and in the case of a monopoly, whether natural or artificial, the excess of price is in proportion to the smallness of the supply compared with the demand, while this demand is comparatively unlimited. In the case of strict necessaries, the existence and increase of the demand, or of the number of demanders, must depend upon the existence and increase of these necessaries themselves; and the excess of their price above the cost of their production must depend upon, and is permanently limited by, the excess of their quantity above the quantity necessary to maintain the labour required to produce them; without which excess of quantity no demand could have existed, according to the laws of nature, for more than was necessary to support the producers.' On this view supply *precedes* population growth; Malthus in effect *applies Say's Law to food in a strong form – supply creates its own demand, and without lag.*[34]

34 In this Malthus was actually repeating a Smithian theme. For Smith distinguished between food-producing and materials-producing land, the former 'always' yielding a rent because, when food increases in supply, there follows a corresponding increase in population, and thus in the demand for food: 'As men, like all other animals, naturally multiply in proportion to the means of subsistence, food is always, more or less, in demand ...' (1776/1937, 146). Similarly, he distinguished between the effects of the discovery of new and efficient mines and new food-producing areas. In the former event, the price of the output may fall and force the original, poorer mines out of business; in this case the demand for output is a *datum.* But in the case of 'estates above the ground,' the increase in supply generates a shift in the demand curve, and accordingly 'the value of the most barren lands is not diminished by the neighbourhood of the most fertile' (173–4). An application of the general principle is made in Smith's analysis of the corn-export bounty (476). James Mill, in his early Smithian phase, rehearsed the entire case (1804, 23–4).

Given the contrast between food and other commodities, it is strange to find Malthus accepting as 'true' – albeit irrelevant – Buchanan's statement that 'the cause of the high price of raw produce is, that such price is required to proportion the consumption to the supply': 'It has been stated, in the new edition of the *Wealth of Nations*, that the cause of the high price of raw produce is, that such price is required to proportion the consumption to the supply [Buchanan ed., 1814, IV, 35]. This is also true, but it affords no solution of the point in question. We still want to know why the consumption and supply are such as to make the price so greatly exceed the cost of production, and the main cause is evidently the *fertility* of the earth in producing the necessaries of life. Diminish this plenty, diminish the fertility of the soil, and the excess will diminish; diminish it still further, and it will disappear. The cause of the high price of the necessaries of life above the cost of production, is to be found in their abundance, rather than their scarcity; and is not only essentially different from the high price occasioned by artificial monopolies, but from the high price of those peculiar products of the earth, not connected with food, which may be called natural and necessary monopolies.' The same can be said for the distinction between demand shifts in the face of upward-sloping (agriculture) and horizontal supply (industry) curves to be found in the pamphlet and also in the *Principles*: 'The difference between the price of corn and the price of manufactures, with regard to natural or necessary price, is this; that if the price of any manufacture were essentially [1836: equally] depressed, the whole manufacture would be entirely destroyed; whereas, if the price of corn were essentially depressed, the *quantity* of it only would be diminished. There would be some machinery in the country still capable of sending the commodity to market at the reduced price' (1815b/1986, 7, 133; 1820, 184; 1836, 178). Malthus evidently wanted to have his cake and eat it. What possible place can there be for a market-clearing equilibrium price if demand and supply are interdependent? Again, it is extraordinary to encounter Malthus's strong criticism of Adam Smith for extracting corn from the general demand– supply theory, considering his own practice.[35]

Malthus's texts of 1815 and 1820 both reiterate that land yielding specialty products rather than basic necessaries is to be treated within the category to which scarcity (rather than surplus) theory applied. The concept of a negatively sloped demand curve, Malthus points out, is in fact applicable only to cases where 'demand is exterior to, or independent of, the production itself.' Then only does contraction of supply raise price above costs, and conversely, in the opposite case; more complex cases involving an increase in demand concomitantly with a reduction in supply could also be appropriately treated:

35 See also the allocative analysis applied to the corn-export bounty in the *Essay on Population*, 1806, II, 253–7, 259–61 (removed in 1817).

The produce of certain vineyards in France, which, from the peculiarity of their soil and situation, exclusively yield wine of a certain flavour, is sold of course, at a price very far exceeding the cost of production [1836: including ordinary profits]. And this is owing to the greatness of the competition for such wine, compared with the scantiness of its supply; which confines the use of it to so small a number of persons, that they are able, and rather than go without it, willing, to give an excessively high price. But if the fertility of these lands were increased, so as very considerably to increase the produce, this produce might so fall in value as to diminish most essentially the excess of its price above the cost of production. While, on the other hand, if the vineyards were to become less productive, this excess might increase to almost any extent.

The obvious cause of these effects is, that in all monopolies, properly so called, whether natural or artificial [1820: in all common monopolies], the demand is exterior to, and independent of, the production itself. The number of persons who might have a taste for scarce wines, and would be desirous of entering into a competition for the purchase of them, might increase almost indefinitely, while the produce itself was decreasing; and its price, therefore, would have no other limit than the numbers, powers, and caprices, of the competitors for it. (1815b/1986, 7, 121–2; 1820, 146–7; 1836, 145–6)

This situation was ruled out in the case of corn: 'In the production of the necessaries of life, on the contrary, the demand is dependent upon the product itself; and the effects are, in consequence, widely different. In this case, it is physically impossible that [1836: beyond a certain narrow limit] the number of demanders should increase, while the quantity of produce diminishes, as the demanders [1820: can] only exist by means of this produce.'[36]

Malthus's perspective, we shall find, is scarcely carried through consistently. We shall have to face some major problems of interpretation when we come to cost-price analysis.

VI COST-PRICE ANALYSIS: GENERAL THEMES

In Section III of the Value chapter in the *Principles* (1820), formally devoted to cost pricing, Malthus went out of his way to emphasize that his 'system' differs from that of Ricardo, and this despite the earlier accommodating tone: 'It may be said, perhaps, that even according to the view given of demand and supply in the preceding section, the permanent prices of a great mass of commodities will be determined by the cost of their pro-

36 Ricardo points out in *Note 54* that 'the question is not about the number of demanders, but of the sacrifices they are willing to make to obtain the commodity demanded. On that must its value depend' (1951–73, II, 114). It is Ricardo who draws attention to the subjective dimension.

duction. This is true, if we include all the component parts of price stated by Adam Smith, though not if we consider only those stated by Mr. Ricardo [*Note 16*]. But, in reality, the two systems, one of which accounts for the prices of the great mass of commodities by the cost of their production, and the other accounts for the prices of all commodities, under all circumstances, permanent as well as temporary, by the relation of the demand to the supply, though they touch each other necessarily at a greater number of points, have an essentially different origin, and require, therefore, to be very carefully distinguished' (1820, 72–3).[37] The passage is shortened in the revised version (1836, 69–70) to end with 'Adam Smith,' thus suggesting a concern to avoid exaggerating perceived differences with Ricardo. But in both editions the text proceeds to distinguish between *cost systems* and the legitimate *demand–supply system*: 'In all the transactions of bargain and sale there is evidently a principle [1836: yet, still it is true that in all transactions of bargain and sale there is a principle] in constant operation, which can determine, and does actually determine, the prices of commodities, quite independently [1836: independently] of any considerations of cost, or of the quantity of labour and capital employed upon their production [1836: or of the ordinary wages, profits, and rent expended in their production]. And this is found to operate, not only permanently upon that class of commodities which may be considered as monopolies, but temporarily and immediately upon all commodities, and strikingly and pre-eminently so upon all sorts of raw produce' (1820, 73; 1836, 70). The 1820 version closes the case by remarking that the prices of corn or cattle could remain unchanged were new technology to reduce costs to zero: 'Provided no change were made in the quantity brought to market, and the society had the same wants and the same powers of purchasing, the prices of raw products would be the same as if they had cost the usual labour and expense to procure them.' Both versions conclude that, in the case of *agricultural* produce, market prices are determined on a principle 'quite distinct' from cost pricing: 'With regard, therefore, to a class of commodities of the greatest extent, it is acknowledged that the existing market prices are, at the moment they are fixed, determined upon a principle quite distinct [1836: a principle distinct] from the cost of production, and that these prices are in reality almost always different from what

37 Ricardo's *Note 16* clarifies and minimizes his own differences with Smith that pertained solely to the treatment of rent: 'By cost of production I invariably mean wage and profits, Adam Smith includes rent ... Twenty different loaves all selling for the same price may yield different portions of rent, but it is one only, that which yields no rent, which regulates the value of the rest, and which must be considered as the standard. In truth then in the cost of production of all agricultural produce there is no rent, for the value of that produced from the capital last employed yields a compensation for wages, and a compensation for profits of capital, but no compensation for rent. In this sense only do I differ from Adam Smith' (1951–73, II, 42–5).

they would have been, if this cost had regulated [1836: exclusively regulated] them' (1820, 74; 1836, 70).

This orientation may indicate the abandonment of any notion of long-run cost pricing in the agricultural case. But this is unlikely; the point seems to relate merely to the peculiar volatility of farm prices, a perspective bringing to mind a physiocratic preoccupation. Even in manufacturing, market prices (which 'more frequently coincide' with cost price) frequently diverge from costs; while costs – Malthus now adds – exert an influence on price only *via* supply: 'when we come to examine the subject more closely, we find that the cost of production itself only influences the prices of these commodities as the payment of this cost is the necessary condition of their continued supply [1836: in proportion to the extent of the effectual demand for them]' (1820, 74–5; 1836, 70).

The indirect influence of cost on price *via* supply is a theme Ricardo had emphasized repeatedly. Yet Malthus proceeds to elaborate at extraordinary length – as if his was an original formulation – the conclusion that 'the great principle [1836: law] of demand and supply is called into action to determine what Adam Smith calls natural prices as well as [1836: what he calls] market prices' (1820, 75; 1836, 71). In the elaboration, all distinction between agriculture and manufactures is lost from sight. The question to be addressed reduces to the effect of a change in costs on the demand–supply relation, and the conclusion is 'that the relation of the supply to the demand, either actual or contingent [1836: 'either actual or contingent' deleted], is the dominant principle in the determination of prices whether market or natural, and that the cost of production can do nothing but in subordination to it, that is, merely as this cost affects actually or contingently the relation [1836: as it affects the ordinary relation] which the supply bears to the demand' (1820, 76; 1836, 72).[38] Similarly: 'It does not, however, in any degree follow from what has been said, that labour and the costs of production [1836: that the costs of production] have not a most powerful effect upon prices. But the true way of considering these costs is, as the necessary condition of the supply of the objects wanted' (1820, 78; 1836, 73–4). Having set up a demand–supply framework to deflect attention from costs, *Malthus thus ends up with the Ricardian position.* Ricardo's reaction in *Note 19* implies just that: 'These positions, those which have preceded them and those which follow are not that I know of disputed by any body' (1951–73, II, 47). There were, in fact, no *substantive* differences regarding value theory between the two in this central regard.

A number of illustrations of the theme are then given, all far-fetched, leading to a misleading generalization: 'In fact, in every kind of bounty upon production, the same effects must necessarily take place; and just in

38 See above, p. 233, on 'contingent supply.'

proportion as such bounties tend to lower prices, they shew that prices depend upon the supply compared with the demand, and not upon the costs of production' (1820, 77; 1836, 73). A second 'illustration' is drawn from the monetary sphere: 'If an article which costs comparatively nothing in making [1836: comparatively nothing], though it performs one of the most important functions of gold [1836: the most important function], can be kept to the value of gold by being supplied in the same quantity, it is the clearest of all possible proofs that the value of gold itself no further depends upon the cost of its production, than as this cost influences its supply [1836: the supply compared with the demand], and that if the cost were to cease, provided the supply were not increased [1836: compared with the demand], the value of gold in this country would still remain the same' (1820, 77–8; 1836, 73).

Ricardo's *Note 20* agrees with Malthus on the economic principles involved, but points out that paper money constitutes a special case involving a monopoly constraining output to assure a value above costs (almost zero costs): 'I quite agree with Mr. Malthus observations in this paragraph, but he forgets that the issuers of paper money which has no value are in possession of a peculiar privilege. If every man might issue paper money in what quantity he pleased and which he was under no obligation to redeem how long would it have any value above its cost of production?' (1951–73, II, 48). More generally, he pinpoints precisely the weakness of Malthus's demonstration: 'Mr. Malthus mistakes the question – I do not say that the value of a commodity will always conform to its natural price without an additional supply, but I say that the cost of production regulates the supply, and therefore regulates the price' (48–9). Moreover, this was true 'only in cases where there is no monopoly, and every one is free to supply the commodities in such quantity as he chuses. All the instances brought forward by Mr. Malthus are either cases of close monopoly or cases where a part of the natural price is paid by other people, as in the instance of poor rates sinking the price of labour; or bounties on production sinking the value of the commodity raised, the producer being entitled to the bounty.'

As for the general perspective on cost price, Malthus duplicates the *Wealth of Nations*, although he preferred to render Smith's 'natural price' as 'necessary' price because 'the term necessary better expresses a reference to the conditions of supply' (1820, 83). Given the satisfaction of various conditions relating to the market for the three factors,[39] a state of

39 The context entails the 'conditions which must be fulfilled in order that any commodity should continue to be brought to market.' Malthus objects to Smith's representing profits as a 'deduction from the produce of labour' and landlords as 'loving to reap where they have never [1836: not] sown' (1820, 81; 1836, 76). He also takes issue with Smith's case for equilibrium wage differentials to reflect 'esteem' for talents; *scarcity* of talent is the key (1820, 79; 1836, 74).

general equilibrium emerges: 'The three conditions therefore above specified must, in every society, be necessarily fulfilled, in order to obtain the supply [1836: continued supply] of by far the greater part of the commodities which it wants; and the compensation which fulfils these conditions, or the price [1836: ordinary price] of any exchangeable commodity may be considered as consisting of three parts – that which pays the wages of the labourers employed in its production; that which pays the profits of capital [1836: including the advances to the labourers] by which such production has been facilitated; and that which pays the rent of land,[40] or the remuneration for the raw materials and food furnished by the landlord [1836: or the compensation for the use of those powers attached to the soil which are in the possession of the landlord]; – the price of each of these component parts being determined exactly by the same causes as those which determine the price of the whole' (1820, 82–3; 1836, 77).[41] Even the terminological objection to Smith's 'natural price' is abandoned in the second edition (see below, p. 262).

What is so difficult to appreciate is the generalisation of the standard long-run demand–supply apparatus to all products, *including corn*. For the application to corn neglects the interdependency of supply and demand which is said elsewhere to undermine the price mechanism in the case of that product (above, section V). Malthus seems to be inhabiting two worlds.

* * *

Hutches Trower recognized that Malthus, despite all his protestations regarding the primacy of demand–supply, in fact adopted a *cost* theory of long-run price. The differences between Ricardo and Malthus were purely terminological: 'I am at a loss to know why he considers these points, "as two systems, having an essentially different origin, and requiring to be carefully distinguished" [1820, 73] ... Nobody disputes that the prices are affected *immediately* by the relations between supply and demand, and he has not shewn, that they do not *ultimately* depend upon the cost of production. Adam Smith himself says "that the natural price is, as it were,

40 A note is attached here in the 1836 version (see below, pp. 262–3).

41 Ricardo's *Note 21* starts out in general agreement: 'In this account of necessary or natural price Mr. Malthus has in substance said the same as Adam Smith has done, in all which I fully agree ...' (1951–73, II, 52). As for the component elements of natural price being themselves determined by supply–demand he reserved judgement: 'We shall see how far these are influenced by supply and demand' (53). On my reading, Ricardo in fact applied demand–supply theory to the factor returns recognizing the interdependence of factor and commodity markets (Hollander, 1995b, Part III). But this is a hotly disputed proposition; for an alternative view, which sees here a major divide between Ricardo and Malthus, see Rashid, 1987, 287, 290.

the *central* price to which the prices of all commodities are continually gravitating"' (letter to Ricardo, 5 July 1820; in Ricardo, 1951–73, VIII, 201–2). Similarly: 'After all, it appears to me, that when the question is stripped of the ambiguities and misconceptions, which [Malthus] has mixed up with it, there is no very essential difference between you, at least with regard to *Principles*' (24 June 1821; 393). In his response to the first letter, Ricardo commended Trower: 'I am pleased ... with the observations you make on what [Malthus] has said respecting my doctrine, of price, being ultimately regulated by cost of production' (21 July; 207).

We turn briefly to the Malthus–Ricardo correspondence of 1820 after the appearance of the *Principles*.[42] Ricardo objected to the demand–supply formulations as inadequate in so far as it is *cost* that regulates supply: 'You say demand and supply regulates value – this, I think, is saying nothing, and for the reasons I have given in the beginning of this letter [276–7] – it is supply which regulates value – and supply is itself controlled by *comparative* cost of production' (9 October; 279). In reply Malthus objected to Ricardo's supposedly neglecting 'half of [his] subject' – the demand side, since in fact demand governed the agricultural cost margin. This criticism is striking because so often Malthus writes as if increased food *precedes* population, while Ricardo insists in his own *Principles* on the reverse. Ricardo's purported position is represented as reflecting a one-sided method: 'when you reject the consideration of demand and supply in the price of commodities and refer only to the means of supply, you appear to me to look only at the half of your subject. No wealth can exist unless the demand, or the estimation in which the commodity is held exceeds the cost of production: and with regard to a vast mass of commodities does not the demand actually determine the cost? How is the price of corn, and the quality of the last land taken into cultivation determined but by the state of the population and the demand' (26 October; 286). To this Ricardo responded by allowing readily the effect of demand on price in the case of an increasing-cost industry, but insisting none the less on the *primacy* of cost considerations: 'I shall not dispute another proposition in your letter "No wealth" you say "can exist unless the demand, or the estimation in which the commodity is held exceeds the cost of production." I have never disputed this. I do not dispute either the influence of demand on the price of corn and on the price of all other things, but supply follows close at its heels, and soon takes the power of regulating price in his own hands, and in regulating it he is determined by cost of production. I acknowledge the intervals on which you so exclusively dwell, but still they are only intervals' (24 November; 302). In my opinion, Ricardo's weighting reflects his predominant interest in the

42 Malthus noted at the outset that French readers 'agreed with [him] about value' (28 August; 225). But see section IX, below, on the Say–Malthus exchanges.

pattern of *long-run* equilibrium prices, a structure reflecting relative costs. In any event, it is clear – as Trower had insisted – that, on the general issue of cost pricing and its relation with demand and supply, nothing of substance separates Ricardo and Malthus.

The correspondence ends inconclusively, with Malthus insisting 'that a theory of exchangeable value which rejects rents, and considers labour almost exclusively, cannot be well founded' (27 November; 309). These issues are taken up below, in the next two sections.

VII THE CASE AGAINST THE LABOUR THEORY: TIME

Substantive issues relating to cost–price determination, as such, are dealt with in Section IV of the Value chapter, rejecting labour embodiment as measure of value. These may be appropriately attended to in the present chapter rather than the next.

There are differences both of form and of content between the 1820 and 1836 versions of Section IV on labour embodiment as measure. The 1836 version commences with a contrast between *causes* of value and *measurement* of value absent in 1820: 'The labour worked up in a commodity is the principal *cause* of its value, but it will appear ... that it is not a measure of it. The labour which a commodity will command is *not* the *cause* of its value, but it will appear ... to be the measure of it' (1836, 83n). And a twofold rationale is given for the quest for an appropriate measure. First, there is simply the objective of expressing relative values and profit, for which purpose money served adequately. More important, there is need for a device to distinguish the *source* of variation in exchange values: 'Nothing appears to me more essential, in an "Inquiry into the nature and causes of the Wealth of Nations," than to have the means of distinguishing between the rise of one commodity and the fall of another' (84n). (Malthus neglected to remark that this is precisely Ricardo's primary *desideratum.*) For this purpose money fails since its own 'intrinsic causes' of exchangeable value – the cost conditions pertaining to money itself – can vary (1836, 84). At this point (and here begins the 1820 version), Malthus objected that Adam Smith sometimes 'speaks of the value of a commodity as being determined [1836: measured] by the quantity of labour which its production has cost, and sometimes by the quantity of labour which it will command in exchange' (1820, 85; 1836, 84).[43] But in the second edition he goes a long way in withdrawing the criticism by admitting that *labour commanded* was 'most frequently' stressed by Smith, who 'practically' rejected labour embodiment (1836, 85). It was the use of labour embodiment 'by some distinguished modern writers' – obviously Ricardo – that justified an

43 The reference in 1820 to 'determined' is evidently an error.

elaborate criticism. And at stake was 'not merely what should be the definition and the measure of value in exchange, but a question of fact, whether the labour worked up in commodities either determines or measures the rate at which they exchange for each other ...' Even in the context of measurement, the *determination* of value had to be dealt with, which is why I raise the issue in the present chapter.

The case against a labour-embodied measure is developed at somewhat greater length in the 1820 than in the 1836 version. There it is rejected as 'radically defective' on two grounds. First, assuming provisionally a labour theory of *relative* price, an increase in labour embodied in the measure A would leave the A/B ratio unchanged in the event of a corresponding increase in the case of B; and 'there is at once an end of our being able to say with truth that all things become more or less valuable in proportion as more or less labour is employed in their production ... The exchangeable value of corn ... has certainly not altered in proportion to the additional quantity of labour which it has cost in its production' (1820, 86). That Ricardo's device of assuming a measure with *given* labour embodiment was designed precisely to overcome this problem is neglected.[44]

But Malthus went further and denied that a labour theory of relative value is applicable at all, whether in early or in advanced states.[45] The major problem is that of capital and *time*: 'But in fact there is scarcely any stage of society, however barbarous, where the cost of production is confined exclusively to labour. At a very early period, profits will be found to form an important part of this cost, and consequently to enter largely into the question of exchangeable value as a necessary condition of supply' (1820, 88). This theme is restated in 1836: 'in no stage of society with which we are acquainted' does labour embodied determine or measure rates of exchange. 'At a very early period profits will be found to enter largely into the question of exchangeable value as a necessary condition of the supply' (1836, 85). And in both versions *the time complication* is elaborated thus: 'To make even a bow and arrow, it is obviously necessary that the wood and reed should be properly dried and seasoned; and the time that these materials must necessarily be kept [1836: *the time* which these materials require to be kept] by the workman before his work is

44 Ricardo's *Note 22* insists on the legitimacy of talking of an increase in exchangeable value of corn and of money when more labour is embodied in both, such that their own terms of trade remain unchanged but the terms *vis-à-vis* all others alter: 'I see no inconsistency, in such case, in saying that corn, labour, and money have all altered in exchangeable value. I compare them with the value of sugar, iron, shoes, cloth, copper, &c. &c., and I find that they will exchange for more of all these things than before; where then can be the impropriety of saying that these three commodities have risen in value, altho they exchange for precisely the same quantity of each other as before?' (1951–73, II, 56).

45 In passing, Malthus again commends Turgot's 'rule' (see above, p. 225, regarding 1820, 54).

completed, introduces at once a new element into the computation of cost [1836: value]. We may estimate the labour employed in any sort of capital just upon the same principle as the labour employed in the immediate production of the commodity [1836: sentence omitted]. But the varying quickness of the returns is an entirely new element, which has nothing to do with the quantity of labour employed upon the capital, and yet, in every period of society, the earliest as well as the latest, [1836: it] is of the utmost importance in the determination of prices [1836: of exchangeable value]' (1820, 88; 1836, 85–6). The *time* complexity was in fact quantitatively great in simple states because of the characteristically high supply price of capital (1820, 89–90; 1836, 86–7). Subsequently, it is pointed out that, while in an advanced economy the typically lower profit rate reduced the quantitative significance for costs of the time phenomenon, the larger differences between commodities in fixed-capital usage increased deviations of cost price from labour inputs: 'In countries advanced in civilization, it is obvious that the same causes [1836: cause] of variation in the exchangeable value of commodities, independently of the labour which they may have cost [1836: independent of the labour which has been employed upon them], must prevail, as in the early periods of society, and as might be expected some others. Probably indeed the profits of stock will not be so high, and consequently neither the varying proportions of the fixed capitals, nor the slowness or quickness of the returns will produce the same proportionate difference on prices [1836: The profits of capital indeed are not so high, and consequently the slowness or quickness of the returns will not, as far as the rate of profits is concerned, produce the same proportionate difference of prices]; but to make up for this, the difference in the quantity of fixed capital employed is prodigious, and scarcely the same in any two commodities; and the difference in the returns of capital varies sometimes [1836: varies] from two or three days to two or three years [1836 adds: and in some cases many more]' (1820, 90–1; 1836, 88).

Ricardo's *Note 23* commends Malthus warmly for his analysis of the time complexity: 'In all the observations of Mr. Malthus on this subject I most fully concur. I have myself stated that in proportion as fixed capital was used; as that fixed capital was of a durable character; and *in proportion to the time which must elapse before commodities can be brought to market,* the general principle of the value of commodities being regulated by the quantity of labour necessary to their production, was modified; but I was of opinion, and still am of opinion, that in the relative variation of commodities, any other cause, but that of the quantity of labour required for production, was comparatively of very slight effect. Mr. Malthus remark that this cause operates in every stage of society is most just' (1951–73, II, 58–9; emphasis added).[46] But Malthus writes as if Ricardo was wholly

46 Ricardo formally identified the differential technological ratios with *time* differentials (1951–73, VIII, 180, 193).

unaware of the time complexity, for he proceeds to allow as a *separate* issue what is represented to be Ricardo's 'exception' to the labour theory – non-uniformity across industries in fixed capital/labour ratios: 'If to this cause of variation we add the exception noticed by Mr. Ricardo, arising from the greater or less proportion of fixed capital employed in different commodities, the effects of which would shew themselves in a very early period of savage life; it must be allowed that the rule which declares "that commodities never vary in value unless a greater or less quantity of labour be bestowed on their production," cannot possibly, as stated by Mr. Ricardo, be "of universal application in the early stages of society" [1951–73, I, 38]' (1820, 90).[47] This is replaced in 1836 by further elaboration of the *time* feature, again purportedly in opposition to Ricardo (1836, 87–8). If Malthus ever read *Note 23*, he had not absorbed its contents, insisting always on differentiating his own product.

In both editions Malthus refers positively to Ricardo's proposition – Ricardo had just refuted the wage-push theory of inflation on the grounds that economy-wide wage increases cannot raise general prices since wages rise in gold mining too – that 'every rise in wages ... or what is the same thing, every fall of profits, would lower the relative value of those commodities which were produced with a capital of a durable nature' (1951–73, I, 39); but he suggests a formal restatement: 'The proposition of Mr. Ricardo, which shews [1836: states] that a rise in the price of labour lowers the price of a large class of commodities, has undoubtedly a very paradoxical air, but it is nevertheless true; and the appearance of paradox would vanish if it were stated more naturally [1836: and correctly]' (1820, 91; 1836, 88). In introducing the proposed restatement – which focuses on the effect on relative prices of a reduced profit rate rather than an increased wage – Malthus reserved judgment on the identification of a *fall of profits* and a *rise of wages*: 'Mr. Ricardo would certainly allow that the effect he contemplates is produced by a fall of profits, which he thinks is synonymous with a rise of wages. It is not necessary here to enter into the question how far he is right in this respect; but [1836: Mr. Ricardo has allowed, that the effect he contemplated and attributed to a rise of wages is produced by a fall of profits, which he considers as the same thing; and] undoubtedly no one could have thought the proposition paradoxical, or even in the slightest degree improbable, if he had stated that a fall of profits would occasion a fall of price in those commodities, where from the quantity of fixed capital employed, the profits of that capital had before formed the principal ingredient in the cost of production. But this is what he has in substance said' (1820, 91–2; 1836, 88).[48] There were, however,

47 Malthus cites Ricardo's second edition of 1819. The third edition has 'when labour is almost exclusively employed in production' in place of 'in the early stages of society.'

48 In the manuscript revisions the reservation of judgment regarding the identification of a wage increase with a profit decline is reworded: 'They certainly accompany each

two objections: (1) that 'the effects arising from an opposite supposition, equally consistent with facts, have not been sufficiently considered by Mr. Ricardo' (1820, 92), an objection modified for the second edition to read: 'But the effects arising from an opposite supposition was not at first considered' (1836, 89); and (2) that 'the general result has been totally overlooked' (1820) reworded as 'the general result was overlooked' (1836). The criticisms allude to Ricardo's failure in 1817 and 1819 to allow that a wage increase generates a *rise* in some prices.[49]

A third class of commodities will be on the borderline: 'Wherever the line may be placed, it can embrace but a very small [1836: a small] class of objects; and upon a rise in the price of labour [1836: and fall of profits], all the rest will either fall or rise in price, although exactly the same quantity of labour continues to be employed upon them' (1820, 94–5; 1836, 90). In 1820, Malthus objected to Ricardo's adoption of commodities produced by labour alone in a one-year process as representative of such cases: 'The cases are extremely rare where the returns of a capital are delayed for a year, and yet no part of this capital is employed either in the purchase of materials or machinery; and in fact there seems to be no justifiable ground for pitching upon this peculiar case as precisely the one where, under any variation in the price of labour, the price of the commodity remains the same, and a rise or fall of wages is exactly compensated by a fall or rise of profits.'

The second edition adds a note to the main text reminding readers that

---

other; and it is not necessary at present to enter into the question of precedence ...' (Pullen, in Malthus, 1820/1989, II, 75). A sheet in the manuscript revisions (the intended location of which is uncertain, see Pullen, 66) represents the fall in the wage as a *consequence* of a rise in the profit rate.

49 Specifically: In the first two editions of the *Principles*, Ricardo asserted that an increase in the wage rate (fall in the profit rate) disturbed the price structure by *lowering* prices differentially (conversely, a fall in the wage rate might raise prices). But no prices could be raised by an increase in the wage rate (1951–73, I, 62–3).

Notwithstanding his earlier reservation of judgment, in his elaborations Malthus himself seems to identify a fall of profits with a rise in wages. Specifically, in the case of a class of commodities which involves 'the absence of fixed capital and the rapidity of the returns of the circulating capital' – in 1820, 'from a day to a year' – such that 'the proportion which the value of capital [in 1836 this becomes simply 'capital'] bears to the quantity of labour which it employs' is small, prices will rise 'upon a rise in the price [1836: the money price] of labour and fall of profits' (1820, 93; 1836, 90). Malthus applied this result in 1820 against Ricardo's position of 1817 and 1819: 'It is quite certain that merely because wages rise and profits fall, all that class of commodities (and it will be a large class) will rise in price, where, from the smallness of the capital employed, the fall of profits is in various degrees more than overbalanced by the rise of wages' (1820, 93–4). All this is omitted from the second edition. A manuscript revision which explains that cases of price increases upon a *fall* of the profit rate had 'been acknowledged by Mr. Ricardo in his third edition ...' (Pullen, in Malthus, 1820/1989, II, 77).

the criticisms thus far of Ricardo were made on Ricardo's own terms. Specifically, the result that, in nearly all cases, prices will either rise or fall with a change in distribution, notwithstanding unchanged labour input, followed only in terms of Ricardian 'money,' a measure Malthus himself did not accept: 'In this discussion, I have assumed money to be obtained in the way suggested by Mr. Ricardo; in which case the results will be as I have described, and as he has allowed in his third edition ...; but his money, as we shall see, is not so constituted as to be a proper measure of value. In reality *all* commodities obtained by the same quantity of labour fall with a fall of profits' (1836, 90n). That '*all* commodities obtained with the same quantity of labour fall with a fall of profits' follows only in terms of Malthus's own ideal measure – labour command, or a commodity produced without capital or by a 'timeless' process (as we shall see in the next chapter). But should all *other* commodities in the system require capital (or time) and entail identical technological characteristics (the same labour input over the same period), their *relative* prices would be unaffected by a change in the profit rate; that is, a change in distribution would leave their relative prices unaffected though all 'money' prices indeed fall – in this case proportionately. In usual cases, relativities would be disturbed, the more time-intensive the product, the greater the effect of the presumed profit-rate change. These *substantive* results are just as Ricardo had them, and one is led to ask: What distinguishes the two in substance? A full answer must await chapter 7, below.

The discussion in both editions comes to a provisional close with a strong rejection of the labour theory: 'What then becomes of the doctrine, that the exchangeable value of commodities is proportioned to the labour which has been employed upon them? Instead of their remaining of the same value while the same quantity of labour is employed upon them, it appears that, from well known causes of constant and universal operation, the prices of all commodities vary when the *price* of labour varies, with very few exceptions; and of what description of commodities these few exceptions consist, it is scarcely possible to say beforehand [1836: the prices of all commodities, with very few exceptions, vary with the variations in the rate and quantity of profits]' (1820, 95; 1836, 91).[50]

* * *

Ricardo's reaction to the foregoing analysis appears in four notes (*24*, *25*, *26*, and *27*). The first comments on Malthus's *acceptance* of the 'paradoxical' proposition whereby a rise in the wage reduces some prices, and his suggestion that the sense of paradox could be avoided by formally attributing the price movement to a fall in the profit rate. Ricardo quite

50 It may be significant that the distributional disturbance here posited is changed from a variation in the *wage rate* (1820) to a variation in the *profit rate* (1836).

rightly expressed surprise at Malthus's agreement in substance, considering his acceptance elsewhere of (the Smithian) notion of a positive effect of increasing wages on *all* prices without exception (1951–73, II, 60–1). It will also be recalled that Malthus had reserved judgment regarding the validity of *identifying* a wage-rate increase and a profit-rate decrease, though subsequently he seemed to accept it. Ricardo in his note insisted on such identification (providing a capsule statement of his own value-and-distribution position), and asserted that Malthus 'would find it difficult' to deny the inverse wage–profit theorem (61–2). More strongly, he again observed that Malthus apparently *accepted* the substance of this case, including the inverse relationship and the altered price structure (62–3). *Note 25* describes as a matter of 'inadvertence' his failure in 1817 and 1819 to recognize cases of a *positive* effect on prices of a *rise* in wages: 'I inadvertently omitted to consider the converse of my first proposition. Mr. Malthus is quite right in asserting that many commodities in which labour chiefly enters, and which can be quickly brought to market will rise, with a rise in the value of labour' (64).[51] *Note 26* reiterates, and with justice, that Malthus had effectively adopted all the essentials of Ricardian value-and-distribution doctrine, including at times Ricardo's measure of value (64–5). Finally, *Note 27* responds to Malthus's concluding challenge – 'What then becomes of the doctrine, that the exchangeable value of commodities is proportioned to the labour which has been employed upon them?' considering the disturbance to the structure of prices engendered by a change in distribution (above, p. 253). Ricardo admitted that his measure of exchange values, which operates accurately only if a strict labour theory applies, was 'not perfect' but believed the deviations to be 'slight,' whereas Malthus's 'silver' produced without any capital would not do at all: 'the imperfections on the score of variability which he himself attributes to it, are greater than any which he imputes to the one which I propose' (67).

VIII THE CASE AGAINST THE LABOUR THEORY: RENT

Although Malthus conceded that labour embodiment (indirect as well as direct) was 'the principal ingredient among the component parts of price' (1820, 107; cf. 1836, 83n), he devoted Section IV of the 1820 version (95–104) to an elaboration of a variety of sources of disproportionality between exchange rates and relative labour inputs apart from 'the different proportions of fixed capital employed, the different quickness of the returns of the circulating capital' – namely, 'the quantity of foreign commodities used in manufactures, the acknowledged effects of taxation,

51 McCulloch criticizes this *Note* in a letter of 22 January 1821; see also Ricardo's reply of 25 January, and McCulloch's next letter of 13 March. In this exchange Ricardo seems to retain the view that any increase in prices due to a wage increase is constrained (1951–73, VIII, 338–45).

and the almost universal prevalence of rent in the actual state of all improved countries ...' (104).[52] It is the complexity created by *rent* that receives nearly all the attention.

Malthus set out by asserting that, though the cost of the 'main vegetable food' resolves itself 'almost entirely into wages and profits,' rent still had to be allowed for in the supply price: 'though it follows that the price of corn is thus nearly independent of rent, yet as this price, so determined, does actually pay rent on the great mass of the lands of the country, it is evident that the payment of rent, or, what comes to the same thing, of such a price as will pay rent, is a necessary condition of the supply of the great mass of commodities' (1820, 96). This passage, which implies a contrast between marginal and average cost price, is hardly more than a formality since it does not gainsay that marginal costs do exclude rent. But that this is Malthus's position (weak though it is) is confirmed in a criticism of Ricardo on the grounds that to exclude rent from supply price on the *admitted* grounds that marginal costs exclude rent was linguistically inappropriate, and in fact contradictory: '*Allowing then that the price of the main vegetable food of an improving country is determined by the quantity of labour and capital employed to produce it under the most unfavourable circumstances*, yet if we allow, at the same time, that an equal value of produce is raised on rich land with little labour and capital, *we can hardly maintain, with any propriety of language, the general proposition that the quantity of labour realized in different commodities regulates their exchangeable value* [Ricardo, 1951–73, I, 5]. On account of the varieties of soil alone constant exchanges are taking place, which directly contradict the terms in which the proposition is expressed; and in whatever way rent may be regulated, it is obviously necessary to retain it as an ingredient in the costs of production in reference to the great mass of commodities; nor will the propriety of thus retaining it be affected by the circumstance, that the rent paid on commodities of the same description is variable, and in some few cases little or none' (97–8; emphasis added).[53] In case there should be any misunderstanding, Malthus repeats again that, *notwithstanding zero-rent land in the production of the 'main vegetable food,' rent must be included in supply price*: 'Under the full admission, therefore, just made, that the price of the main vegetable food of an improving agricultural country is, in reference to the whole quantity produced, a necessary price, and coincides with what is required to repay the labour and capital which is employed under the most unfavourable circumstances, and pays little or no rent, we still do not

52 Foreign imports, generally acknowledged to be priced independently of 'the quantity of labour and capital,' entered into manufacturing costs.

53 Malthus commended Adam Smith: 'Adam Smith distinctly allows that rent is a consequence, not a cause of price; but he evidently does not consider this admission as invalidating his general doctrine respecting the component parts of price. Nor in reality is it invalidated by this admission' (97).

seem justified in altering the component parts of price, or what I should be more disposed to call the necessary conditions of supply.'

The impression Ricardo obtained from all this is that, for Malthus, rent appears in supply price *even in the case of corn*, for in *Note 28* he refers to his earlier *Note 16*, which had explained the implications of the marginal principle (see above, note 37).[54] To my mind, Ricardo took Malthus too seriously, for, despite everything, Malthus still accepted that *marginal corn costs exclude rent*. Thus an autonomous reduction of rent would leave the cost price of corn unaffected, this in sharp contrast to the cost price of cattle, to which the no-rent marginal rule did not apply: 'And though with regard to the main food of the people it is true that, if rents were given up, an equal quantity of corn could not be produced at a less price; yet the same cannot be said of the cattle of the country. Of no portion of this species of food is the price resolvable into labour and capital alone' (99).

Let us look at an elaboration of this contrast between *corn* and *cattle*. Rent on corn land is said to differ widely from farm to farm and to be unrelated to the value of the crop; whereas, in the case of cattle, rent is 'proportioned to the value of the crop,' and a reduction in rent *would* lower cost price: 'All cattle pay rent, and in proportion to their value not very far from an equal rent. In this respect they are essentially different from corn. *By means of labour and dressing, a good crop of corn may be obtained from a poor soil*, and the rent paid may be quite trifling compared with the value of the crop; but in uncultivated [grazing] land the rent must be proportioned to the value of the crop, and, whether great or small per acre, must be a main ingredient in the price of the commodity produced. It may require more than an hundred acres in the highlands of Scotland to rear the same weight of mutton as might have been reared on five acres of good pasture; ... [but] the rent paid for the same quantity of mutton would be nearly the same. If this rent were greatly diminished, there cannot be a doubt that the same quantity of cattle might be produced in

54 Malthus extends the attack on the labour theory by attributing to 'monopoly' an explanation of some rent payments, as to urban land: 'But there are some parts of the land and of its products which have much more the character of a monopoly than the main food of an improving country; and it is universally acknowledged that the exchangeable value of commodities which are subjected either to strict or partial monopolies cannot be determined by the labour employed upon them. The exchangeable value of that vast mass of property in this country which consists of the houses in all its towns, is greatly affected by the strict monopoly of ground rents; and the necessity of paying these rents must affect the prices of almost all the goods fabricated in towns' (98–9).

Ricardo's *Note 29* objects to the last proposition: 'If the goods were not superior in quality, one does not see what inducement a buyer should have to purchase them in the dearer market' (1951–73, II, 69). The objection is unclear. He might have done better to argue that to allow 'monopoly' was irrelevant, given the supposed competitive framework, as he did in *Note 20* (see above, p. 245).

the market at much lower prices without any diminution of the profits or wages of any of the persons concerned; and consequently it is impossible to estimate the value of cattle by the quantity of labour and capital, and still less by the mere quantity of labour which has been expended upon them' (99–100; emphasis added).[55] Why the marginal-cost principle does not apply to cattle is unclear from this account, though we shall presently see that Malthus subsequently implies that cattle is subject to what he calls 'monopoly' analysis (below, p. 259).[56]

Ricardo's *Note 30* (1951–73, II, 70) insists on the *same* principle in all cases. It begins with the declaration that 'the value of cattle is regulated by the value of corn' – unfortunately without specifying how – and then generalizes the no-rent principle thus: '[If] therefore it be shewn that the corn which regulates the general value of that commodity, only affords wages and profits, cattle, obtained under the same circumstances, will yield no rent. I do not mean to say that corn raised or cattle fed on fertile land, pay no rent, only that some corn and some cattle yield no rent, and that this corn and cattle regulate the value of all other corn and cattle. If I manure a field, at some expence, and make it yield more grass, and fat an additional ox upon it, what portion of the price of that ox affords a rent? the value of the ox only replaces capital and its profits.' He in fact draws on Malthus's own *Inquiry into Rent* (1815b/1986, 7, 143), for the rule that a relinquishing by landlords of their rents leaves *marginal* cost price unaffected, applying it to both corn and cattle, though the pamphlet itself had not been explicit on that score.[57]

Malthus himself addressed the argument's turning on the possibility of alternative land use – which may be what Ricardo intended in his *Note 30* – that since the rent on cattle land is determined by the rent of corn land, and that is governed by the corn price itself turning on *marginal labour cost*, cattle prices are governed indirectly by the labour coefficient: 'It may possibly be said that although rent is unquestionably paid on all and every part of the cattle produced in this country; yet that the rent of uncultivated [grazing] land is determined by the price of cattle; that the price of cattle is determined by the cost of production on such good natural pastures or improved land as would yield a considerable rent if employed in raising corn, because the poor uncultivated lands of a populous country are never sufficient to produce all the animal food required; that the rents of the

55 The emphasized phrase allows for intensive cultivation in the case of corn alone, a characteristic that proves to be significant (below, p. 260). Grazing land seems to be represented as having no alternative use.

56 'Monopoly,' in the classical tradition, sometimes refers to an absolute constraint on aggregate output. This is possibly implicit in the paragraph just cited, where a regular upward-sloping supply schedule based on costs seems to be applied only to corn.

57 Ricardo was skating on thin ice; the no-rent principle breaks down in the case of multi-use land (see Hollander, 1991b, notes 4 and 7).

different qualities of land which must thus be devoted to the rearing of cattle depend upon the price of the main food of the country; and that the price of the main food of the country depends upon the labour and capital necessary to produce it on the worst land actually so employed' (1820, 100). This argument Malthus rejected: 'One of the links in this chain of dependence will not hold, and the connexion between cattle and labour is thus at once broken off. Though the price of the main food of a country depends upon the labour and capital necessary to produce it on the worst land in use; yet the rent of land ... is not regulated by the price of produce. Among the events of the most common occurrence in all nations, is an improvement in agriculture which leads to increased produce and increased population, and after a time to the cultivation of naturally poorer land, with the same price of produce, the same price of labour, and the same rate of profits. But in this case the rents of all the old lands in tillage must rise, and with them of course the rents of natural pastures and the price of cattle, without any change in the price of labour or any increased difficulty in producing the means of subsistence' (100–1). In the closing sentence Malthus accepts the alternative-cost principle running from corn to pasture (much as Adam Smith had done).[58] But his case is specious. It alters the terms of the debate by introducing a technical change which allows expansion to 'naturally' inferior land at no change in the corn price and, consequently, generates a rise in rent on 'the old land in *tillage*.' *Given* the production function, however, the rent of corn land *is* governed by marginal corn costs. It is simply that with technical improvement generating a downward shift of cost schedules – and *allowing for the long-run expansion of demand* – the same *marginal* cost conditions will be consistent with a higher rent.[59]

Malthus had closed by asserting that any increase in the rent of corn land raises 'the rents of natural pastures and the price of cattle.' This is extended: 'The statement just made applies to many other commodities, besides animal food. In the first place, it includes wool and raw hides, the materials of two most important manufactures, and applies directly to

58 The earlier case distinguishing cattle from corn seems to deny the possibility of alternative land use.

59 Ricardo addressed this issue in his *Note 31*: 'I can understand, that in consequence of improvements in agriculture, land of a worse quality may be cultivated, with a lower price of produce, than would have been cultivated if no such improvement had taken place; ... but with a lower price of corn – wages will be low, and profits will be high, and it is only because profits are higher that the worse land can be cultivated ... How great an error then it must be for Mr. Malthus to say, that with the same price of produce, the same price of labour, and *the same rate of profits*, naturally poorer land would be taken into cultivation' (1951–73, II, 72). Ricardo was wrong if he intended to imply that, *after the expansion*, corn would be at a lower price and profits would be higher than before. But his formulation is ambiguous in this regard.

timber and copse wood, both articles of great consequence' (1820, 101).[60] But the emphasis in what follows is not on opportunities for alternative land use such that the rent of corn land governs the rent of land applied to cattle. In fact, Malthus introduced a 'monopoly' perspective, or, rather, restated his main case in terms of monopoly. In this restatement corn land itself is said formally to fall in this category: 'If it be said that the doctrine which entirely rejects rent, and resolves the prices of all commodities into wages and profits, never refers to articles which have any connexion with monopoly, it may be answered, that this exception includes the great mass of the articles with which we are acquainted. The lands which afford the main supply of corn are evidently a species of monopoly, though subject to different laws and limits from common monopolies; and even the last land taken into cultivation for corn, if it has an owner, must pay the small rent which it would yield in natural pasture' (101–2). This, however, is a terminological formality, involving merely 'a species of monopoly' – unlike 'common monopolies' – doubtless referring to nothing more than private land ownership. Much more significant is the remainder of the passage, representing cattle prices as 'in the most direct manner' affected by monopoly. This is said to be a proposition 'just shewn,' resolving for us earlier problems of interpretation relating to the generalization that 'all cattle pay rent ...' (above, p. 256). The passage in question suggests that the case for rent in marginal costs of land-using products other than corn turns on 'monopoly' in the special sense of scarce land under pressure of demand such that rent emerges, even on the least productive plot ('the poorest land'), because of absolute constraints on output expansion: 'It has just been shewn that monopoly must in the most direct manner affect the price of cattle, the other great branch of human food; and with regard to the materials of clothing and lodging, there are very few that do not actually pay a rent, not only on the great mass of each kind, but on those which are grown on the poorest land actually employed for their production. To say that the prices of wool, leather, flax, and timber are determined by the cost of their production on the land which pays no rent, is to refer to a criterion which it is impossible to find. I believe it may be safely asserted that there is no portion of wool, leather, flax, and timber produced in this country which comes from land that can be so described' (102).

Although the passage seems to distinguish cattle from other land-using products (materials of clothing and lodging), Malthus had just *identified*

60 It is also extended in another sense: 'And secondly, there are some products, such as hops, for instance, which cannot be grown upon poor soils. Such products it is impossible to obtain without paying a rent; and if this rent varies, while the quantity of labour employed in the production of a given quantity of corn remains the same, there can be no ground whatever for asserting that the value of such products is regulated by labour.'

these products as falling under the same rule. And this is confirmed in the earlier passage contrasting cattle and corn, where the marginal principle entailing *intensive* use of land is applied *specifically to corn* ('By means of labour and dressing, a good crop of corn may be obtained from a poor soil ...'). In brief, 'monopoly' in the sense of absolute scarcity provides the key to agricultural products other than corn. And this is how Ricardo read Malthus, for in *Note 31* he protested that the no-rent cost principle does not turn on the existence of no-rent land since the intensive margin by itself ensured that 'rent is not a necessary component of price,' a principle *applied to all land-using products*: 'In the whole of this discussion Mr. Malthus forgets that the fact of rent not being a component part of price, does not depend on his proving that all lands actually taken in to cultivation do pay rent. If he could make out to every body's satisfaction, that there was no land in cultivation, for which a rent was not paid, he would be as far as before from settling the question that rent formed a component part of price. If I can employ more capital on my land, without paying any additional rent for so doing, I can raise some corn, some cattle, some hops and some of every other agricultural produce, into the value of which no rent will enter as a component part. It is the quantity so raised, and the price at which I can afford to sell it, which regulates the value of all other corn, cattle and hops, and till this is denied, and can be refuted, the proposition is in my opinion established, that rent is not a necessary constituent of price' (1951–73, II, 72–3). Ricardo again insists (as in *Note 30*) that in 1815 Malthus had recognized the valid approach: 'In his *Inquiry into the nature of rent* he has justly observed "It will always answer to any farmer who can command capital, to lay it out on his land, if the additional produce resulting from it will fully repay the profits of his stock, *although it yields nothing to his landlord*" ... This is unanswerable. Into the price of such additional produce no rent enters' (73).

Until this point Malthus had rejected the idea of cost price exclusive of rent in the case of land-using products *other than corn*, and insisted for this reason on deviations from any labour-input explanation of relative price. But he also asserted that the no-rent rule in the case of corn – where admittedly 'we come the nearest to it' – entailed 'a contradiction in terms,' repeating an earlier statement (above, p. 255) to the same effect: 'We cannot, therefore, get rid of rent in reference to the great mass of commodities. In the case where we come the nearest to it, namely, in the production of the main food of the country, the attempt to resolve the exchangeable value of all the different portions of this food into labour and profits alone, involves a contradiction in terms; and as no error seems to arise from considering rent as a component part of price, after we have properly explained its origin and progress, it appears to me essential, both to correctness of language and correctness of meaning, to say that the cost of producing any commodity is made up of all the wages, all the profits, and all the rent which in the actual circumstances of the society are necessary to bring that particular commodity to market in the quantity required; or, in other words, that the payment of these expenses is the necessary condition of its supply' (1820, 102–3). Again, Malthus seems to discern a 'contradiction' in the notion that price determined at the zero-rent margin covers average costs *inclusive* of rent.

Section IV closes in 1820 with the proposition that in so far as rent enters into price via materials costs, it appears as part of *capital* input. This line casts further light on the proposition that even *corn* cannot be said to follow the Ricardo labour rule: 'if rent enters into the raw materials of almost all manufactures, and of almost all capital, both fixed and circulating, the advance necessary to pay it will greatly affect the amount of capital employed, and combined with the almost infinite variety that must take place in the duration of these advances, will most essentially affect that part of price which resolves itself into profits ... [We] must acknowledge that even in the production of corn, where no direct rent is paid, its price must be affected by the rent involved in the fixed and circulating capital employed in cultivation' (103–4).[61]

Finally, while Malthus indicated a preference for a capital theory over a labour theory of price 'because the advances which are called capital generally include the other two' (103), he elected to stay with the threefold (Smithian) approach: 'The natural or necessary prices of commodities depend upon the amount of capital which has been employed upon them, together with the profits of such capital at the ordinary rate during the time that it has been employed. But as the amount of capital advanced consists of the amount of wages paid from the first to the last, together with the amount of rent paid either directly to the landlord or in the price of raw materials, the use of the three terms seems to be decidedly preferable, both as more correct, (rent being, in many cases, not an advance of capital,) and also as conveying more of the information that is wanted.'[62]

61 Ricardo's *Note 33* insists that 'a farmer who pays a high rent, requires no greater capital than one who pays a low rent. He pays a high rent not because he employs a more valuable capital, but because the same capital yields him a more valuable return. He pays it too, after he has sold the produce.' But for a recent insistence that interest is affected by rent, see Samuelson, 1991, 571n.

62 The 'capital' theory had been suggested by Torrens in 1818; see on this, Sraffa, in Ricardo, 1951–73, IV, 307. Ricardo's *Note 32* rejects a 'capital' theory of price: 'If equal capitals yielded commodities of nearly equal value, there might be some grounds for this argument; but as from a capital employed in valuable machinery, and steam engines, a commodity of a very different value is obtained than from a capital, of the same value, employed chiefly in the support of labour, it is at once obvious that the one term, thought to be the more correct by Mr. Malthus, would be the most incorrect that could be imagined' (1951–73, II, 74–5; 'and' is replaced by 'such as' in the copy sent to Trower on 26 November 1820; see Sraffa's note).

* * *

The complex argument involving rent as creating deviations from labour value is removed from the second edition. Could its removal mean that Malthus had abandoned his objections to zero-rent marginal costs in the case of 'most' agricultural produce? This seems unlikely since the Smithian three-factor cost approach appears in the 1836 version (see above, p. 246; indeed, an addition to Section III of the Value chapter withdraws the objections of 1820 to the term 'natural' price: 'It has sometimes been said that there is no such thing as natural price; but explained as Adam Smith has explained it, it is not only a very intelligible, but a very useful term ... To this price, which may fairly and usefully be called the natural, necessary, or ordinary price, the market prices are always tending. And this price determines the rate at which commodities usually exchange for each other' (1836, 78–9).[63] And that the Smithian cost-price principle extends to agriculture (despite market volatility, on which matter see above, p. 244) is also confirmed, in a reiteration of the distinction between cattle, the cost price of which might include a *substantial* rent component, and corn, where 'on the last land taken into cultivation ... rent is quite inconsiderable': 'So understood nothing can be more simple, or more generally applicable. The natural price of an acre of copse wood, or of a hundred sheep from the highlands of Scotland, which in a country generally well cultivated must be composed chiefly of rent, is as easily explicable as the natural price of corn on the last land taken into cultivation, where rent is quite inconsiderable' (79). Similarly: 'The natural price of those sorts of goods where a large proportion of fixed capital is employed, and the returns of the circulating capital are unusually slow, and where consequently the price must consist chiefly of profits, may be as satisfactorily accounted for as the price of a straw bonnet, or piece of Brussels lace. Where the materials are of scarcely any value, the capital required is quite inconsiderable, and the expense of production must consist almost entirely of labour.'

None the less, the deletions may indicate a weakening of the case against Ricardo. (Even in 1820 Malthus's objections, on his own admission, were weakest in the case of corn.) This is suggested by a note minimizing the rent component of (marginal) costs: 'Though it is quite true, as will appear in the next chapter, that rent has little effect in determining the prices of raw produce, yet, in almost all commodities, a part of the price is resolvable into rent. The reason is, that the same kinds of products

63 Malthus does not state who had said that 'there is no such thing as natural price,' though he probably intended J.B. Say. Say is mentioned (though deleted) in the manuscript revisions (Pullen, in Malthus, 1820/1989, II, 64). On Say's position see below, p. 265.

which sell for exactly the same prices, have a very different quantity and value of rent in them; but the greater is the value of the rent, the less is the value of the labour and profits; and therefore the varying value of rent in commodities has but little effect on their prices' (77n). So we end up after all, in the second edition, with rent having 'but little effect on ... prices.' There is also the striking fact that, in the *Measure of Value* of 1823 and in related papers of 1825 and 1827, Malthus proceeds entirely in terms of conditions of supply *excluding rent*, as we shall see later, in chapter 7.

IX MALTHUS AND J.B. SAY

In this section we consider Say's *Letters to Malthus* (1821) and Malthus's responses.[64] One might have expected Say and Malthus to see eye to eye, considering their *formal* demand–supply orientation. But this is far from the case; Say objected to Malthus's failing to generalize the utility perspective to production, holding up economic science as a result. The exchanges confirm the high degree of common ground between Ricardo and Malthus on price theory.

In his first letter, Say complained of a misrepresentation by Malthus, who had charged him, along with James Mill and Ricardo, for considering 'commodities as if they were so many mathematical figures, or arithmetical characters, the relations of which were to be compared, instead of articles of consumption, which must of course be referred to the numbers and wants of the consumers' (Say, 1821, 10, citing Malthus 1820, 354). He protested: 'I have repeated, in a great variety of forms, this idea, that the *value* of things (the *only* quality by which they become wealth) is founded on their utility; on the aptitude which they possess to satisfy our wants.'[65] This did not imply that, for Say, exchange values are demand-determined; Say cited his *Traité* (4th ed., II, 5) which distinguishes cases where utility is generated but at zero cost and zero exchange value, from cases where production costs are entailed, a contrast expressed as one between '*natural*' and '*social*' riches (1821, 11–12).[66] Say closes with the charge – which reads amusingly very much like Malthus on Ricardo – that Malthus appeared to represent labour as the sole 'sacrifice': 'does not this doctrine

64 According to Sraffa (in Ricardo, 1951–73, VIII, 249), a translation of the first of Say's *Letters* appeared in the *New Monthly Magazine* for September 1820, and the others in subsequent numbers. The translations were revised by John Richter and republished as a book (together with Say's *Catechism of Political Economy*) in 1821. (Another version appeared in *The Pamphleteer* 17/34 [1820], 289–346.)

65 This is not wholly fair to Malthus, who was concerned in this specific context with the issue of *aggregate* demand.

66 Only 'social riches' are subject to 'scientific' study since 'they alone are formed, distributed, and destroyed, according to laws which we are able to assign' (12). (See also 76–7, cited below.)

establish that our wants alone induce us to make the sacrifices by means of which we obtain productions? These sacrifices are the price which we pay to procure them; you, like Smith, call these sacrifices by the name of *labour*, an inadequate expression, for they are partly composed of the use derived from land and capital. I call them *productive services* ... You see that the existence of these revenues depends upon the production having an *exchangeable* value, which it can only have in consequence of the want which there is for such production in the actual state of society' (12–13).

Say also objected to Malthus's denial (1820, 35) that 'personal services [are] equally productive of wealth [as] the labour of merchants and manufactures.' Production, as such, Say insisted, involves the purchase of immaterial services; durability is not the issue in the creation of wealth or 'riches' (1821, 18–19n). This is extended to a rejection of Malthus's representation of the 'cornerstone' of the *Wealth of Nations* as the distinction between productive and unproductive labour, the former 'fixed in [a] material object' (Say, 20, referring to Malthus, 1820, 37). Rather, the lasting contribution of that work was its doctrine 'that the *exchangeable value* of things is the foundation of all riches.' Again, Say saw this as providing the scientific basis for political economy: 'From the publication of that important truth, political economy became a positive science; for the market-price of every thing is a determinate quantity of which the elements may be analysed, the causes assigned, the relations studied, and the consequences foreseen. Permit me, Sir, to say that to separate this essential character from the definition of wealth, is to plunge the science again into the depths of obscurity – to drive it back.'[67]

Also significant for us is *Letter V*, which formally treats the nature of 'wealth' or 'riches' – our income. Here Say again takes up Malthus's definition of 'riches' as 'all *material* objects which are necessary useful or agreeable to man' (1820, 28). Materiality was irrelevant for 'it is beyond the power of man, to add a single atom to the mass of matter of which the world is comprised' (1821, 76), Say reverting to the distinction between *natural riches*, which do not fall within the domain of economic science, and *social riches*, which do: 'Which then are the riches within the jurisdiction of that science? – Those which are susceptible of creation and destruction, of *more* and of *less*; and what I again ask, is this *more*, this *less*, but value?' And it is exchangeable value only that is intended, not the particular value an individual may set on an object as representing its utility to him: 'In order to constitute riches, the value must be *recognized*, not by the possessor merely, but by other persons. But what more irrefragable proof that its value is *recognized* can be given than that other

67 The first *Letter* ends with a rendering of Say's general perspective on production as *utility* creation, and on exchange (21–2). It may leave an impression that exchange rates *are* in some sense demand-determined, though that is positively not his position.

persons are ready to give for it a certain quantity of other things which are valuable' (77). Say did not appreciate how Malthus could exclude exchange value from his formal definition of 'wealth' or 'riches'; and he commended Adam Smith for formally abandoning 'value in use' and concerning himself entirely with 'value in exchange' (78).

Say proceeded to relate exchange value to production costs, but as part of a rejection of the orthodox 'natural price' concept: 'It is a necessary consequence, the price of every thing being its *exchangeable* value estimated in money, that there is no other price in political economy than *market price*: that that which *Smith* calls the *natural price*, is no more natural than any other; it is the cost of production; it is the market price of productive services.' Here, Say slips up. The orthodox market–natural distinction reflects the contrast between disequilibrium and equilibrium allocations of resources across industries. And Say's concern is also with equilibrium in the sense of resources satisfying the condition that a transfer elsewhere will not raise their net income. For example, in discussing the profits of the 'undertaker' – 'the reward of the labour and talents which he exerts in his business' – Say writes: 'He only continues this business while it produces such an income that he cannot expect a better in any other employment. He is one of the necessary producers, and his profits form part of the necessary charges of production' (34n). Say is dealing with 'natural' or 'necessary' price, whatever he calls it. His erroneous belief that he was avoiding the market–natural dichotomy reflects overenthusiasm for the doctrine relating to the earnings of 'productive services,' since it is true enough that the excess (or deficient) earnings of some or all of the productive services characterizing the deviation of the market from natural price can be formally represented as high (or low) 'cost,' if by cost we mean simply *actual* rather than *equilibrium* earnings.[68] The substantive fact remains that Smith, Say, Malthus, and Ricardo are on the same wavelength regarding 'natural' price.

Say, however, insisted on differentiating his product, *and put Ricardo together with Malthus in criticizing the latter's value theory*: 'I will not deny,' he wrote to Malthus, 'that you have, in Mr. Ricardo, a powerful and respectable ally. He is against you in the subject of *markets* [the aggregate-demand issue], and fights on your side in the question of *value*; but notwithstanding my connexion with him, and the reciprocal esteem we bear for each other, I have not hesitated to combat his arguments' (78–9).[69] The specific issue once again was Ricardo's distinction between *value* and *riches*

68 See the splendid statement in *Traité*, 4th ed., 1819, II, 507–8, cited by Ricardo with approval (1951–73, I, 282–3). See also a note in Say's handwriting attached to a letter from Ricardo to the effect that 'les services productifs' govern the *supply* side only (1951–73, IX, 172n).

69 The reference is to Say's notes to the French translation (1819) of Ricardo's *Principles* (1951–73, X, 374–5).

– which Malthus had commended (see above, p. 221) – reflected in the fact that reduced scarcity, with technical changes, reduces per-unit value, but increases total riches: 'Value ... essentially differs from riches, for value depends not on abundance, but on the difficulty or facility of production ...' This position, Say pointed out to Malthus, 'appears to accord perfectly with the opinions you maintain.' But he himself could not accept it, for 'riches are composed of the value of the things we possess, applying the word *value* to those values only which are recognized and exchangeable' – insisting again that such value only is 'capable of appreciation, capable of being *more* or *less*' (79–80). Here is a nice reversal of the traditional roles ascribed to Say and Ricardo in the textbooks. Say, it turns out, had no patience with the notion of riches as total utility because the latter is not subject to measurement by the rule of money prices, which alone is the concern of economic science. For him riches comprise a sum of exchange values. By contrast, Ricardo – and Malthus – set aside a separate place for 'riches.'

In elaborating his objection to any notion of 'riches' independently of exchange value, Say seems to narrow the gap between his own position and that of Ricardo and Malthus: 'You say that riches consists in the quantity of necessary and agreeable things we possess. I say so too; but these words, *quantity of things necessary and agreeable*, have a very vague and arbitrary meaning, unfit to enter into a perfect definition: I render them precise and clear by the idea of their *exchangeable value*. The condition of *utility* then is the being equal to another utility, which men are willing to give in exchange for that which you possess' (80). But he reiterates his objection to limiting riches only 'to objects which are *material*, necessary and agreeable': 'It is impossible for you to deny, that whatever has an exchangeable value makes part of our wealth. It is composed entirely of the productive powers which we possess; our lands, our capitals, and our personal faculties. Of these, land is alienable, but not consumable – capital is both alienable and consumable; while talents, though incapable of alienation, are consumable; they perish with those who possess them. From these funds, all the revenues upon which society subsists are derived; and (what may appear paradoxical, although it is perfectly true) all these revenues are *immaterial*; for they are derived from an immaterial quality – *utility*. The different kinds of utility are derived from our productive powers, and are comparable with each other by their value, which I have no need here to denominate *exchangeable*, because I can not recognize any value in political economy which is not exchangeable.'

The *Letters to Malthus* close by placing this perspective on 'wealth' or 'riches' into a framework reflecting Say's general conception of *production as an exchange process*. An increase in productive power such as Ricardo envisaged would increase the exchangeable value of the productive services in the sense that their command over goods (and services) rises, a greater command 'perfectly synonymous' with 'greater cheapness.' Say, therefore, after all, *accepts* the Ricardo – or rather the Ricardo–Malthus – position that technical progress does raise riches and lower value per unit: 'As to the difficulty raised by Mr. *Ricardo*,[70] that by improved processes a million of people might produce twice or thrice as much riches, without producing more values, it vanishes when we consider, as we ought, production as an exchange in which the *productive services* of labour, land, and capital is *given*, in order to *obtain* the *production*' (82). The elaboration that follows is unnecessarily complex, Say maintaining no more than that *costs and prices* fall per unit, with technical change, thus raising the *purchasing power* of some or all of the income recipients. The same theme will be found earlier, in reference to a demonstration in the *Traité* (4th ed., II, ch. 3) of the proposition that 'although wealth is an exchangeable value, the general wealth is increased by the low price of commodities and productions of all sorts' such as is generated by technical progress affecting all sectors (1821, 28–9). Say's point is that the productive services engaged in all the industries will earn greater real returns, reflecting the improved productivity: 'Productive services are increased in value in proportion as productions are increased in quantity, and diminished in price' (for which reason there is no lack of purchase power to absorb the increased output flow). This is also the reason 'why the reduction in the price of productions, by increasing the value of the productive funds of a nation [the sources of income] and of the income derived there from [wages, interest, and rent], augments the national wealth.'

This proposition is said to confound both Malthus and Ricardo: 'This demonstration, by the bye, completely overthrows an assertion of Mr. Malthus, *that cheapness is always (must be) at the expense of profits* [1820, 370], and consequently all the reasoning which he has built on this foundation. It is also fatal to all that part of Mr. Ricardo's doctrine, in which he flatters himself that he has proved, that the *costs of production,* and not the proportion of *supply* and *demand,* regulates the prices of goods. He identifies the *costs of production* with the *production* itself, whereas they are completely opposed to each other, and the former are diminished in proportion to the increase of the latter' (29n). The charge against Malthus relates to the supposed increase in real (commodity) wages, reflecting 'the abundance and cheapness of commodities,' which Malthus says 'must be at the expense of profits' (1820, 370). But this charge is misleading. Malthus was dealing specifically with the impact of *accumulation,* whereas Say generalizes the statement, which is unfair; in the event of technical improvement, an increase in the real wage may *coincide* with an increase in the profit rate. (The inverse wage–profit relation captures this characteris-

70 The 'difficulty raised by Mr. Ricardo' presumably relates to the passage in the first two editions of the *Principles* (1951–73, I, 287–8) regarding Say's formulation in the *Catéchisme.*

tic.) As for Say's remark relating to Ricardo on costs, it fails to recognize that Ricardo did *not* reject demand–supply theory by his according primacy to costs and supply. Moreover, the charge that he identified *costs* with *production* is groundless; for Ricardo, too, unit costs will halve if output doubles as a result of technical improvement.

* * *

In comments to Ricardo regarding Say's *Lettres*, Malthus continued to insist on distinguishing material goods from services and objected to Say's use of the term 'utility': 'I do not think it is a very able performance ... I cannot agree with him in making no distinction between services and products; in his strange and useless application of the term utility; in his opinions respecting the immateriality of revenues, and in his mode of reasoning ...' (25 September 1820; Ricardo, 1951–73, VIII, 259–60).[71] A year later the objection to Say on utility is reiterated again in correspondence with Ricardo, who had passed on to Malthus a long letter from Say dated 19 July 1820 'in vindication of his doctrine of value, utility &c.' (Ricardo to Malthus, 10 September 1821; IX, 63). Malthus responded critically to Say's letter: 'I have always thought his doctrine of utility an abuse of the natural meaning of the term ... At the same time, I should say, that as there is certainly no measure of utility, taken in the common acceptation of the term, and as a part of the article, how usefulsoever, may become quite useless if it be in excess above the demand, there is no other way of approximating towards an estimate of relative wealth, than by an estimate of relative value, formed by a comparison with the objects *least liable to variations* (but *not*, as Mr. Say says, merely with the "la plus ou moins grande quantité d'un autre produit *quelconque*"' (13 September 1821; 64).[72] This letter reveals a complete absence of the conception of marginal utility, let alone diminishing marginal utility. *Malthus could see no technical role for 'utility' in value formation.*

Malthus's adverse reaction to Say, particularly his complaint of an 'abusive' use of the term 'utility,' is reiterated in his *Quarterly Review* article of 1824 on McCulloch's version of Ricardian economics. He there commended McCulloch for distinguishing between *value* and *utility*, but protested at McCulloch's identification of his (Malthus's) position with that

71 Ricardo agreed in his letter of 9 October, 276, that 'M. Says letters to you are not very well done.' It emerges from the Say–Ricardo exchange of 1820–2 (see Ricardo, 1951–73, VIII–IX) that very little of substance separated those correspondents. Say recognized the primacy of costs in long-run price determination, however distinctively he expressed himself; while Ricardo nowhere rejected the demand dimension, though Say apparently misread him in this regard.

72 Malthus obviously had in mind his own labour-commanded measure when he objected that *any* commodity taken at random would not do.

of Say: 'The author ... notices the importance of making a proper distinction between value in exchange, and utility. In this we entirely agree with him and have always thought that M. Say, whose opinions seem chiefly to be alluded to, by applying *utility* in a sense altogether inconsistent with the common meaning of the term, has obscured a part of the subject which was sufficiently clear; we were not, however, aware that Mr. Malthus, whose name is coupled with that of M. Say, had fallen into a similar error. Our impression is, that he has adhered to the distinction stated by Adam Smith, which is plain and intelligible, and requires neither the rejection nor the alteration of common terms – changes which it is always desirable to avoid, unless really necessary' (1824a/1986, *7*, 258). Still, this charge against Say for obscuring the subject does not quite come to grips with the nature of the complaint. For that we turn to a chapter devoted to Say's use of the term 'utility' in the *Definitions* (1827).

The objection to Say is there formulated by reference to various general 'rules' for desirable definition. A definition must accord with what is understood in 'common conversation,' and also concord with 'the language of those who are considered as the best authorities in political economy' (1827a/1986, *8*, 14): 'Proceeding upon the principle, that nothing can be valuable which is not useful to some person or other, *he has strangely identified utility and value, and made the utility of a commodity proportionate to its value,* although the custom is universal of distinguishing between that which is useful and that which is merely high priced, of that which is calculated to satisfy the acknowledged and general wants of mankind, and that which may be only calculated to satisfy the capricious tastes of a few' (emphasis added). This is not a fair representation of Say's position. For it emerges from the Say–Ricardo exchange of 1820–2 that Say subscribed to a *cost* theory of long-run price – in fact, we have seen as much even in the *Letters to Malthus* themselves (above, p. 265). The relative prices thus emerging are proportionate to relative utility, or rather Say represents 'utility' as *synonymous* with value-in-exchange and in that limited sense only does he end up with a utility theory of value. And Malthus may have realized this, since later in the *Definitions* we find a formulation, using Say's terminology, of the cost determination of price: 'the effectual demand for commodities must on an average, be proportioned to the productive services set in motion to obtain them ...' (100), to which is appended a note that 'M. Say's comprehensive expression, "*services productifs*," includes profits and rent as well as labour.'[73]

Malthus further objected to Say's justification of a new term ('utility') to emphasize that by 'production' is never intended creation of new matter

73 Malthus's point here is to reiterate that, notwithstanding the multifold nature of 'cost,' 'it is certain that labour will accurately measure the value of the whole amount of these services.'

(see above, p. 264). This position, Malthus observed, was not held even by the Physiocrats, and certainly not by Smith (14).[74] In any event, it was superfluous for Say to maintain that *utility* is measured by exchange value 'when things are in their ordinary and natural state' – alluding to cost prices – since he also maintained that '*riches*' are proportional to value: 'And as M. Say observes, that when things are in their ordinary and natural state their value is the measure of their utility, while he had before affirmed that riches were in proportion to value [*Traité*, 4th ed., I, 2–4], it is difficult to conceive what beneficial purpose he could have in view in introducing the term utility thus made synonymous with value or riches' (15). Here, as on earlier occasions, we find a commendation of *Ricardo* for distinguishing riches and value, whereas Say 'introduces another term, utility, which as he applies it, can hardly be distinguished from either of the others.'[75]

Later in the *Definitions*, Malthus again complained of a confusing use of the term 'utility' by Say when he maintained (*Traité*, II, 506) 'that the price of an article is the measure of its utility, although it might be according to his own expression, *la chose la plus inutile*' (116). The science of political economy would benefit if the term retained its 'natural and ordinary meaning. All wealth is no doubt useful, but there are so very many immaterial, and some material objects which are highly useful, and yet not wealth, that there can be no excuse for confounding them.'[76]

There remains to note Malthus's reaction to Say's inclusion of services within the designation 'productive.' This is somewhat muted in 1827, compared with 1820 or 1821. In the course of defending the orthodox approach to the analysis of 'the causes of the wealth of nations' turning on a *materiality* requisite for 'wealth,' Malthus suggests that Say effectively took

74 As we have seen, Say objected to Malthus's use of the term 'riches' as *material* objects which are useful or agreeable to man, on the grounds that materiality is irrelevant to the 'production' of riches; moreover, 'riches,' to Say, are composed of exchangeable values, and these values (cost-determined) reflect or measure utility (see *Letter* V, in 1821; also *Letter* I).

75 Malthus also complained that Say, by neglecting Smith's contrast between value-in-use and value-in-exchange, had 'gone directly against ... the authority of Adam Smith, whom he himself considers as the main founder of the science.'

76 The same objection is raised against Storch. (On Storch, see Pullen, in Malthus, 1820/1989, II, 21.) Despite these objections, Malthus none the less defended Say against a charge by Bailey (1825) that Say had neglected the *relativity* dimension of value. Malthus cited Say's proposition that 'there is this difference between a real and a relative variation of price; that the former is a change of value arising from an alteration of the charges of production; the latter a change arising from an alteration in the ratio of value of one particular commodity to other commodities,' insisting that the real and relative values referred to 'other objects' (71). This formulation is none the less a little misleading since Malthus had in mind his own usage of the term '*real* value' (command over labour), whereas Say's sense (an index of input, apparently) is closer to Ricardo's.

the same position: 'The essential question in the definition of wealth is, whether or not it should be confined to material objects, and the reader is already apprised of my reasons for thinking that it should. Even M. Say, who admits "*les produits immatériels,*" allows, as I have before stated [46n] that the multiplication of them "*ne fait rien pour la richesse*"' (115).[77] Similarly, 'Storch, in his able *Cours d'Economie Politique,* though he justly lays great stress on what he calls *les biens internes,* with a view to civilization and the indirect production of wealth, confines the term *richesses* to *biens externes,* or material objects; and according to this meaning treats of the *Théorie de la Richesse Nationale* in the first, and far the largest, part of his work.'

In the second edition of his *Principles,* Malthus commended Say's position that the science of political economy arose from the possibility of quantification: 'Nothing can be more just than this. It is the main criterion to which, with a view to useful and practical conclusions, I should wish to refer' (1836, 29). But he turned it in his own favour. He himself pointed out that 'knowledge, talents, and personal qualities are capable of being accumulated' (28), but yet insisted on their exclusion from the definition of wealth on the grounds that they are *non-quantifiable.* In sum: 'If ... we wish, with M. Say, to make political economy a positive science, founded on experience, and capable of making known its results, we must be particularly careful in defining its principal term, to embrace only those objects, the increase or decrease of which is capable of being estimated; and the line which it seems most natural and useful to draw, is that which separates material from immaterial objects' (33). Malthus in all this is firmly in the orthodox classical tradition.

77 The earlier passage referred to is the following: 'both Mr. Ricardo and Mr. Mill, indeed, fully allow the distinction between productive and unproductive labour. M. Say, though he calls the labour of the menial servant productive, makes a distinction between the labour which is productive of *material* products and the labour which is productive of *immaterial* products. Of the latter products he says, "En favorisant leur multiplication, on ne fait rien pour la richesse, on ne fait que pour la consommation." – *Table Analytique* [of the *Traité*], liv. i, ch. 13. This is a most characteristic difference; and though I prefer the classification of Adam Smith, as more simple, I should allow that, on these principles, the causes of the wealth of nations may be clearly explained. But I own myself utterly at a loss to conceive how they can be explained, if all labour be considered as equally productive!'

SEVEN

Value measurement

I INTRODUCTION

Malthus's increasing concern with value measurement after 1820 indicates a preoccupation with the *cost* dimension, and provides further evidence of the inappropriateness of designating him a 'Subjective Theorist.' The topic is too important to be given short shrift, though its complexity has daunted many commentators.[1] Although it turns out that the debate was unprofitable, it is essential to see exactly why. We cannot ignore the fact that Malthus believed that he was making profoundly significant and innovative contributions to cost theory.

Malthus followed Smith in adopting a 'labour-commanded' measure of value and it is inviting to identify the two perspectives, as many have done, including Ricardo and Samuel Bailey. But it would be illegitimate to do so; the identity is a formal one only, and Malthus in his later writings went out of his way to distance himself from Smith. First, he came to question the role of the index as a measure of variations in general purchasing power and, second, to regard the index as reflecting accurately each commodity's supply conditions – its 'absolute' or 'intrinsic' value – including specifically labour embodied and profits rather than labour alone, and excluding rent.

It has been said that the role of the measure of value in classical theory

1 Cf. O'Brien: 'It should perhaps be mentioned that Malthus engaged in a long and unprofitable debate with Ricardo on the best measure of value ... Recounting this will only confuse the reader ...' (1975, 106). Also Blaug, 1985, 172, for a dismissive comment on the topic.

is: (1) to allow measurement of relative equilibrium prices; and (2) to assure constancy in the value of the total product in the face of changes in distribution (Costabile, 1983, 147). The first identified function can be fairly associated with Ricardo, but must be qualified in Malthus's case.[2] His original intention was to obtain an index of purchasing power. And while subsequently he found in labour commanded an index of 'intrinsic' costs, access to which – assuming the index to be valid – yields relative exchange rates, the absolute supply conditions of the *individual* products had a significance for Malthus which they did not have for Ricardo. There was in fact no substantive difference on the demand–supply mechanism as such, or its application to long-run cost pricing, or indeed on the *predominant* role of costs in long-run price determination, or – in the last resort – on the treatment of rent (rent is excluded from consideration in *The Measure of Value* and two papers of 1825 and 1827). The difference reflects, in essence, Malthus's preoccupation with the 'supply conditions' of individual commodities in terms of their absolute costs inclusive of dated-labour input, appropriate allowance made for *profits* on that input. His position reflects an insistence that *labour* is the true advance made by capitalists – a proposition hotly disputed by Ricardo – rendering absolute value a meaningful concept independent of other products. By contrast, Ricardo's concern with supply conditions focused on *relative* costs, and the contrasting impact of changes in technological and distributive data. Furthermore, while Malthus came to represent his labour-commanded measure – or its money proxy, gold produced by labour alone – as a perfectly accurate index of the absolute supply conditions of individual commodities, Ricardo abandoned his quest for a measure of absolute value.

Costabile (1983) offers a full-fledged Sraffian interpretation of Malthus's use of dated quantities of labour – Sraffa of *Production of Commodities* (1960) – an interpretation that is appealing, considering the 'sequence' analysis discernible in the profit-rate analysis found in the *Principles* (see below, chapter 10). And she gives Malthus excellent press regarding the theory of value: 'Malthus is usually regarded as an opponent of the labour theory of value, but in fact he was rather an opponent of Ricardo's statement that "the exchangeable value of these commodities [the reproducible commodities] or the rule which determines how much shall be given in exchange for another depends solely on comparative quantity of labour expended on each." Malthus considered labour embodied as the "cause" of value [1836, 32n]. He adhered to a theory of relative prices based on labour embodied, but in the only sense in which this can be made coherent, namely in the formulation obtained by reducing inputs to dated quantities of labour ... [For] the time distribution of the quantities of labour "embodied" in each commodity affects its price, through the amount of profits

2 The second function is considered in chapter 10.

which the latter must contain' (1983, 148–9). This is in one respect misleading. Malthus represented labour embodied as *one* – not *the* – 'cause' of value: 'In the vast majority of cases, there are other intrinsic causes of value, acting sometimes with great power, which increase the difficulty of obtaining the object desired, in addition to the labour actually employed' (1836, 92). In any event, Ricardo's perspective on *relative* price determination *is* perfectly 'coherent.'

The contrast between Malthus and Ricardo in this regard emerges in their respective treatment of corn pricing in the growth process. For Ricardo, the increase in (marginal) labour input raises the relative corn price; whether the secular fall in the profit rate has any further effect on prices will turn on the pattern of factor ratios across sectors. Malthus, with an eye on absolute value, focused on the cost prices of individual products *inclusive of the profit rate.* Thus the increase in labour embodiment in corn is *counteracted* by a fall in the profit rate; conceivably the absolute corn price might remain steady. The precise behaviour of the corn price may be approached from a different angle. In the simplest case involving a corn-wage basket, the value of the corn wage in terms of Malthus's measure is necessarily constant, whatever its physical magnitude or labour embodiment; accordingly, the corn price in terms of the measure varies inversely with the corn wage, a constant corn wage indicating a constant corn price. Although this outcome flows from the definition of value as labour commanded, Malthus insisted – notwithstanding Ricardo's complaints – that since the initial selection of labour commanded was not an arbitrary matter but was required by the nature of absolute value (labour embodied plus profits), the constant value of the wage basket was essentially a logical consequence of the nature of absolute value.

Sections II through IV of this chapter deal with aspects of Malthusian measurement in the *Principles* of 1820 – respectively, an initial preoccupation with a measure of general purchasing power, a criticism of Ricardo's labour-embodied measure, and a proposal for a *linked* corn–labour index. Section V is concerned with substantive changes to be found in the revised version of the *Principles*, amounting to the abandonment of concern with general purchasing power in favour of an index of a commodity's supply conditions. This new perspective, which is effectively Ricardo's – though the sense of 'supply conditions' differs – is also elaborated in the second of two little-known papers read before the Royal Society of Literature in 1825 and 1827. The revised positive contribution to value measurement in the second edition of the *Principles* is elaborated in section VI; and the greater detail to be found in *The Measure of Value* (1823b),[3] in section VII.

3 Our concern with *The Measure of Value* in this chapter relates specifically to supply conditions; implications in the pamphlet for distribution as such – particularly the inverse wage–profit relations (or the proportionality theorem) are taken up in chapter 10.

The two papers referred to above are considered in sections VIII and IX, with special reference to the treatment of the profit and wage rates, respectively. Section X places the valuation procedure in a growth context.

The rest of the chapter considers contemporary reactions to *The Measure of Value*, with particular reference to the proposed index of supply conditions. (Consideration of material pertinent to the theory of distribution is postponed until chapter 10.) Sections XI and XII summarize, respectively, an exchange with Ricardo regarding the pamphlet, and a more formal critique by J.S. Mill. Objections by Samuel Bailey are treated in section XIII. Malthus's *Definitions in Political Economy* (1827) provides an excellent summary statement of his position (section XIV).

II VALUE MEASUREMENT AND GENERAL PURCHASING POWER

Malthus accepted Adam Smith's position that, at any given time and place, money prices served adequately to provide appropriate stimuli to activity (1820, 59; 1836, 55). This is because, as amplified in the second edition, the 'variations which may take place in the value of money during the short period of a mercantile transaction will, in general, be so inconsiderable, that they may safely be neglected.' By contrast, 'at different periods and in different countries, [the money metals] are liable to great changes of value ... [C]onsequently given portions of them will, in many cases, express most imperfectly the difficulty of obtaining possession of the numerous objects for which they may be exchanged' (1836, 55–6).[4] Though the 'value of money' refers to *general* purchasing power, the formulation suggests the sense of command over commodities taken *individually*.

Nominal prices did not serve well in other respects in comparisons over time and space. This theme is elaborated in texts that diverge between 1820 and 1836 and have to be considered separately. As for 1820, we find explicit adherence to 'real value in exchange' in the sense of general purchasing power: 'What we want further is some estimate of a kind which may be denominated real value in exchange, implying the quantity of the necessaries and conveniences of life which ... wages, incomes, or commodities will enable the possessor of them to command. Without this knowledge, the nominal values above mentioned may lead us to the most erroneous conclusions; and in contradistinction to such values, which often imply

4 The 1836 version refers to the precious metals as functioning as a measure of value and as '*determining*' the rates of exchange between commodities, whereas this latter function is absent in 1820 (e.g. 1820, 54, 59; 1836, 52, 55). But apparently this modification does not imply a *theory* of relative price determination. Rather it reflects the more mundane point that, if apples and oranges are both expressed in dollar terms, then the apple/orange exchange rate is revealed. It does not account for the rate being what it is.

an increase or decrease of wealth merely in name, *the term real value in exchange seems to be just and appropriate, as implying an increase or decrease in the power of commanding real wealth, or the most substantial goods of life*' (1820, 60; emphasis added). Unfortunately, there existed no 'correct' measure of real exchange value since 'whatever article, or even mass of articles, we refer to, must itself be subject to change,' presumably a reference to changes in purchasing power resulting from changes in costs or demand conditions relating to the product or products in question. At best, an 'approximation' to the measure might be found.

Malthus objected to use of the term 'real' value to imply cost, and more specifically here to *labour embodiment* (an implicit criticism of Ricardo); apart from the sense of *value-in-use*, or the commodity's 'intrinsic capacities for satisfying the wants of mankind,' customary usage of the term 'value' implied some 'power of exchange' (61). And more specifically: 'If it do not refer to the power of an article in exchange for some one commodity named, such as money, it must refer to its power in exchange for 3 or 4, 5 or 6, 8 or 10 together, to the mass of commodities combined, *or to its power of commanding labour which most nearly represents this mass*' (61; emphasis added).[5] Labour command is thus represented as a matter of normal usage, and served well in making either international comparisons of 'wealth' or international and intertemporal comparisons of the 'value' (purchasing power) of the precious metals.

The complaint of a confusion on Ricardo's part between *cost* and *value* is repeated later in the chapter. Ricardo's measure failed in its intended role of providing an index of 'cost' of production. For cost and exchange value frequently diverged, as in the case where *all* commodities are subject to inferior technology: 'Cost and value are always essentially different. A commodity, the cost of which has doubled, may be worth in exchangeable value no more than before, if other commodities have likewise doubled' (131). Worse still, Ricardo's estimate of cost (unlike Smith's) related to only *part* of cost – the labour input: 'Wherever there are profits, (and the cases are very rare indeed in which there are none,) the value of a commodity in exchange for labour is uniformly greater than the labour which has been employed upon it' (131–2). Accordingly, the choice was 'between an imperfect measure of exchangeable value, and one that is necessarily and fundamentally erroneous' (132).

Malthus raised the possibility that Ricardo had no concern with exchange value, only with cost, that is, with measurement of the production

5 This is immediately modified: 'The most proper definition of real value in exchange, in contradistinction to nominal value in exchange, is, the power of commanding the necessaries and conveniences of life, *including labour*, as distinguished from the power of commanding the precious metals' (1820, 62; emphasis added). Malthus apparently intended to include *services* in the basket.

coefficients: 'If Mr. Ricardo says that by value, when he uses it alone, he does not mean exchangeable value, then he has certainly led us into a great error in many parts of his work; and has finally left us without substituting any measure of exchangeable value for the one to which he objects. There never was any difficulty in finding a measure of cost, or indeed of value, if we define it to be cost. The difficulty is, to find a measure of real value in exchange, in contradistinction to nominal value of price.' But this is difficult to understand. Did Malthus not realize that Ricardo did *not* seek a direct measure of changes in costs but rather an indirect measure *via a medium of exchange,* his 'gold' device? And that he proceeded by assuming a measure produced by *unchanged* technology? This in substance was Ricardo's own reactions in his *Note 11*: (1) If commodity X's command over various other commodities increases by 20 per cent while Y's command falls by 20 per cent, then – provided that the production conditions of those other commodities are unchanged – it could be presumed that X's 'real value,' in the sense of its labour input, had increased 20 per cent and Y's had decreased 20 per cent; (2) It would be convenient to measure changes in X's or Y's 'real value' by comparing its exchange rate against a single commodity ('gold') – rather than a class – assumed to be produced under unchanged cost conditions. Ricardo clearly meant by changes in the 'real value' of X changes in its purchasing power owing specifically to changes in its own technological cost conditions (1951–73, II, 32–3).

All this Ricardo saw as unobjectionable. Yet he did object when Malthus *arbitrarily* set up corn or labour as his standard, thus breaking his own definitional rules of propriety. The origin of this error Ricardo found to lie in a confusion between 'wealth' and 'value': 'Length can only be measured by length, capacity by capacity, and value by value. Mr. Malthus thinks that "the term real value in exchange seems to be just and appropriate as implying an increase or decrease in the power of commanding real wealth, or the most substantial goods of life" ... He does not say the power of commanding real value, but real wealth, he measures value by its power of commanding wealth' (33).[6] Specifically: 'Wealth is estimated by its utility to afford enjoyment to man; value is determined by facility or difficulty of production. The distinction is marked, and the greatest confusion arises from speaking of them as the same.'[7] We shall see below, in section V, that Malthus subsequently adopted Ricardo's perspective.

As for the charge that he had 'confounded' *cost* and *value,* Ricardo was

6 For Ricardo, X's command over other commodities was relevant *provided* these other commodities were produced at unchanged cost conditions; for then a change in the exchange rate indicated a change in X's 'real value' or 'difficulty of production.'

7 Strangely, Malthus had commended Ricardo's contrast between wealth (or riches) and value and J.B. Say had remarked on this common position (see above, chapter 6: IX).

unapologetic provided the *proportionality dimension* was respected (34–5). This is further elaborated in *Note 44*: 'Mr. M. as I have said before misunderstands me – I do not say a portion of its cost measures its exchangeable value – but I say its whole value will be *in proportion* to a portion of its cost, and I do not say this without allowing for modifications and exceptions – though I consider them of no great magnitude. Without misunderstanding me Mr. Malthus could never apply the following observation to my doctrine "Wherever there are profits, (and the cases are very rare indeed in which there are none) the value of a commodity in exchange for labour is uniformly greater than the labour which has been employed upon it"' (100–1).[8] Ricardo closed by turning Malthus's conclusion to his own advantage: 'The comparison between Mr. Malthus's proposed measure and the one which I have proposed is thus summed up "We have therefore to choose between an imperfect measure of exchangeable value, and one that is necessarily and fundamentally erroneous"' (102).[9]

We return to Malthus's case for labour commanded as the best proxy for general purchasing power over commodities taken individually. Adam Smith is acknowledged as having first adopted this categorization, although he was open to some small criticism: 'In speaking of the value of corn, he has sometimes left us in doubt whether he means value in use, or real value in exchange; and he sometimes ... confounds the cost of a commodity in labour with its value in commanding labour, which are essentially different' (1820, 63). But these errors were mere 'inadvertences': 'At the end of the third [*sic*] chapter of his first book he has explained value in use in the same manner as it has been explained here;[10] and in part of the succeeding chapter, *on the real and nominal price of commodities*, he has made exactly the same distinction between real and nominal value, the propriety of which, as it has been controverted, it has been my endeavour to establish.[11] To these distinctions he has, in the main, adhered; they properly belong to his system ...'

Section VI in 1820 deals formally with labour commanded 'as Measure

8 For Ricardo's position, see also 1951–73, I, 46–7.

9 Cf. *Note 27*, where Ricardo admits that his proposed measure of exchange values, which operates accurately only if a strict labour theory applies, is 'not perfect' but insists that the deviations 'are slight,' whereas Malthus's proposed measure would not do at all: 'the imperfections on the score of variability which he himself attributes to it, are greater than any which he imputes to the one which I propose' (67).

10 This should read 'the end of the fourth chapter': 'The word value ... has two different meanings, and sometimes expresses the utility of some particular object, and sometimes the power of purchasing other goods which the possession of that object conveys. The one may be called value in use, the other value in exchange' (1776/1937, 28).

11 '[Labour's] real price may be said to consist in the quantity of the necessaries and conveniences of life which are given for it; its nominal price, in the quantity of money' (1776/1937, 33).

of real Value in Exchange.'[12] Malthus selects labour commanded as the most appropriate, if not the ideal, measure: 'When we consider labour as a measure of value in the sense in which it is most frequently applied by Adam Smith, that is, when the value of an object is estimated by the quantity of labour of a given description ... which it can command, it will appear to be unquestionably the best of any one commodity, and to unite, more nearly than any other, the qualities of a real and nominal measure of exchangeable value. [1836: it will appear to be a measure essentially distinct from all others, and to approach as near to a standard measure, both of relative and of intrinsic value in exchange, as the nature of the subject will admit]' (1820, 118–19; 1836, 93–4).[13]

The full case is based on various 'general considerations,' not all of them very relevant or convincing, and removed from the second edition. First, a measuring device should be one 'most extensively the subject of exchange,' and labour filled the bill (119). Second, the labour commanded by a commodity X, so it is claimed, captures the effect of higher productivity across-the-board, even though relativities between a commodity X and any or all other commodities remain unchanged (119–20); but this is unclear since a *given* labour command by X would imply an *increased* command by X over general commodities in the event of general technical progress. Third, since 'the great stimulus to production' entails the power of commodities 'to command a greater quantity of labour than they have cost, we are actually led to consider this power of commanding labour as of the utmost importance in an estimate of the exchangeable value of commodities' (120). Though absent at this particular location from the second edition, this last rationale appears throughout subsequent developments. Ricardo's response is, therefore, of the first importance – namely, that the proposition held good 'in whatever medium you chuse to measure exchangeable value': 'Estimated in iron, sugar, coffee, a commodity has cost me a certain quantity of one of these articles – I will not produce it, unless it will exchange for more of that particular article. Estimated in labour, it has cost me a certain value, I will not produce it if it will not exchange for more. Estimated in quantity of labour, I will not produce it, if it will not command a greater quantity than has been employed in its production' (*Note 39*; 1951–73, II, 91).

A further reason for the choice – which does appear in 1836 – is that the labour price of commodities (like the money price) would reflect the relative exchange values of commodities in the same place and time, filling all the functions of a 'circulating medium' in reflecting 'nominal' changes in exchange rates irrespective of their origin (1820, 121–2; 1836, 94). The

12 Altered in Section V in the 1836 edition to read simply 'as Measure of Value in Exchange.'

13 The modifications of 1836 are dealt with below, in section VI.

passage closes in 1820 with reference to 'this great advantage' in favour of labour commanded, 'that it will serve to explain very accurately and usefully all variations of value, without reference to a circulating medium.' This latter assertion is absent in 1836, probably because there would be no point in adopting labour in place of money as measure of value at precisely the same time and place, as is actually conceded in 1820 as well as 1836 (1820, 122; 1836, 94–5). The case for labour commanded thus had to be strengthened.

Labour commanded had the advantage over all alternatives 'in the same place, and within short periods of time,' and this because labour was the most *stable* compared with any other single commodity, or even money, other commodities being subject to 'sudden changes in value' – purchasing power – owing to changes in demand and/or costs (1820, 123). Accordingly, it was safest for a merchant to estimate his net returns in labour terms (at least over a relatively short period): 'Day-labour, taking the average of summer and winter, is the most steady of all exchangeable articles; and the merchant who, in a foreign venture, the returns of which were slow, was sure of gaining fifteen per cent. estimated in labour, would be much more secure of finally gaining fifteen per cent. of real profits, than he, who could only be sure of gaining fifteen per cent. estimated in cloth, cotton, iron, or even money' (122–3).

At the same place, and 'within *short* periods of time,' labour commanded could in fact be said to serve as an 'accurate' measure of value. As for 'different places and distant periods,' it at least 'approache[d] the nearest of any one commodity' to an accurate measure (123). Here Adam Smith is taken to task for assuming, in his *Digression on Silver*, that the labour commanded by corn was *constant*, so that labour and corn were interchangeable as measures. This Malthus denied for the four-century period Smith considered (presumably because of fluctuations or varying trends in the corn wage),[14] but from 'century to century' Smith's procedures served adequately. This is a strange argument. Malthus sets out to prove that 'from century to century' *labour commanded* by X served better than any alternative measure of X's exchange value or purchasing power. In the course of the argument, he says of 'the real exchangeable value of *labour*' that it is best measured by labour's command *over corn*, and he maintains that commodity X's command over labour will best reflect its command over corn. In which case one wonders why corn is not selected as the measure directly.

The case proceeds with the allowance that the labour commanded by X will be *predominantly* governed by its labour embodiment – manufactured goods in particular being labour-intensive: 'With regard to the other necessaries and conveniences of life, they must in general be allowed to

14 For this same complaint in the second edition, see below, p. 298.

depend still more upon labour than corn, because in general more labour is employed upon them after they come from the soil' (123–4). But labour commanded captured *all* the diverse forces governing X's exchange value: 'The great pre-eminence of that measure of value, which consists in the quantity of labour which a commodity will command, over that which consists in the quantity of labour which has been actually employed about it, is, that while the latter involves merely one cause of exchangeable value, though in general the most considerable one; the former, in addition to this cause, involves all the different circumstances which influence the rates at which commodities are actually exchanged for each other' (124).[15]

Now Malthus conceded that the corn wage varies significantly across time and space. None the less, command over a given amount of labour in different countries or times would 'often' imply command over a given *quantum of wage goods, including both corn and manufactures*: 'Although in different countries and at distant periods, the same quantity of labour will command very different quantities of corn – the first necessary of life; yet in the progress of improvement and civilization it generally happens, that when labour commands the smallest quantity of food, it commands the greatest quantity of other commodities ...; so that when, in two countries, or in two periods differently advanced in improvement, two objects command the same quantity of labour, they will often command nearly the same quantity of the necessaries and conveniences of life, although they may command different quantities of corn' (125). This argument implies that the ultimate measure of X's value in exchange is *not* X's command over labour as such but its command over the general wage basket; yet Malthus concludes by focusing again on labour commanded: 'It must be allowed then that, of any one commodity, the quantity of common day-labour which any article will command, appears to approach the nearest to a measure of real value in exchange.' We must understand Malthus as taking the position that the labour commanded by X matters only proximately, and this because such command (and its variation) implies command over wage goods (varying in proportion). It is this latter that is ultimately intended by X's '*real* value in exchange.'[16] (And this would also explain the allusion to *labour's* real value in exchange.)

Section VI closes with the concession that labour commanded is only

15 This passage sets out by implying that the labour embodied in corn had played a part in the argument preceding this passage, whereas in fact the argument there turned specifically on the relatively constant labour commanded by corn. Presumably we should understand Malthus as maintaining implicitly in that earlier context that the command of corn over labour will be dictated in part by the labour embodied in corn, though less so than the case of manufactures. (This interpretation is confirmed 1820, 128; see below, p. 286).

16 Labour commanded would then not be an index of *general* purchasing power, but of purchasing power in a more limited sense.

the best among defective alternatives, and this in part because the corn wage is, after all, variable over time and space – since labour itself commands variable corn, X's command over labour says little of its command over corn, a reversion to the original emphasis on corn as 'the principal necessary of life,' ignoring the broader wage basket: 'But still, labour, like all other commodities, varies from its plenty or scarcity compared with the demand for it, and, at different times and in different countries, commands very different quantities of the first necessary of life; and further, from the different degrees of skill and of assistance from machinery with which labour is applied, the products of labour are not in proportion to the quantity exerted. Consequently, labour, in any sense in which the term can be applied, cannot be considered as an accurate and standard measure of real value in exchange' (125–6). X's command over labour does *not* after all yield an accurate indication of X's command over corn or over other commodities. But still it was the best index conceivable: 'If the labour which a commodity will command cannot be considered in this light, there is certainly no other quarter in which we can seek for such a measure with any prospect of success.'

To this closing theme of Section 6, Ricardo appended *Note 40*, which rubs in Malthus's concession that his labour-commanded measure lacked invariability: 'The reader is particularly requested to remark the character for invariability, which Mr. Malthus gives to the measure of real value, proposed by himself' (1951–73, II, 94). The earlier *Note 11* had also objected to Malthus's labour commanded on the grounds that labour is itself variable: 'Mr. Malthus justly complains of gold and silver as being variable commodities, and therefore not fit for a measure of real value, for times distant from each other. What we want is a standard measure of value which shall be itself invariable, and therefore shall accurately measure the variations of other things. And on what does Mr. Malthus fix as an approximation to this standard? The value of labour. A commodity shall be said to rise or fall accordingly as it can command more or less labour' (29). But Malthus himself 'acknowledge[d] that it is subject to the same contingencies and variation as all other things. Why then fix on it?[17] It may be very

17 See also *Note 38*: '"I object to your measure of value says Mr. Malthus because it is not so invariable as you represent it, – there are causes of variation which affect it for which you have not made due allowance." Who would not suppose then that when he proposed a measure of value he could propose one free from these objections? He does quite the contrary, he proposes a measure which is not only variable in itself, but is particularly variable, on account of its connection with other variable commodities, and in his reasons for chusing it gives several which have no reference to the subject, for nothing is to be considered in a measure of value but its invariability or its near approach to that character' (90–1).

Note 34 (on Malthus, 1820, 107) points out that, if corn alone requires double labour input, its exchangeable value relative to all other goods doubles, whereas for Malthus its value is unchanged, assuming a constant corn wage. But if labour can command

useful to ascertain from time to time the power of any given revenue to command labour, but why select a commodity that is confessedly variable for a standard measure of value?' (30).

III ON RICARDO'S MONEY MEASURE OF LABOUR EMBODIMENT

In Section V, 'Of Money, when uniform in its cost, considered as a Measure of Value' (1820, 108; omitted in the revised version), Malthus takes up Ricardo's money measure. He wished 'to consider how far the precious metals would be an accurate measure of the quantities of labour employed upon each commodity ... if it were really true that given quantities of the metals always required in their production the same quantity of labour' (108–9). He recognized the precious metals, even under actual, not ideal, conditions of production, to be an 'accurate measure of exchangeable value, at the same time and place' (109), but denied that the metals measured labour embodiment, even under Ricardo's ideal conditions, because 'the exchangeable value of commodities is scarcely ever proportioned to the quantity of labour employed upon them ...' There were various problems, all reflecting the standard complications undermining a labour theory.

Only in the case of commodities produced under the same technological characteristics as money – 'the same quantities of the two kinds of capital employed for the same time and in the same proportions' – would a change in distribution leave money prices unaffected. In the event of a wage increase, 'all commodities which still contained the same quantity of labour would alter in price, except those very few which were circumstanced exactly in the same manner with regard to the capitals by which they were produced as the precious metals' (110). These, of course, are propositions attributable to Ricardo himself, and Malthus might have acknowledged the fact.

An alternative would be Malthus's own ideal money produced by 'labour alone, without any advances above the food of a day' – silver picked up daily on the seashore (111).[18] But such money would not exchange one-for-one with a commodity requiring the same labour but some capital. And there was a further complexity pertaining to the growth process, entailing a fall

more manufactured wage goods, we have a situation where Malthus choses as his index *variable* labour: 'The proof that Mr. Malthus offers, that corn has not doubled in value, is, that it will not command so much of a thing, which has at the same time risen in value' (1951–73, II, 79).

18 Another alternative would be money requiring only advances of unskilled labour for a year (attributed in some contexts by Malthus to Ricardo). But here, too, a wage increase would generate changes to the price structure; and there would scarcely be any other commodities produced under similar conditions (110).

in both the corn wage and the profit rate. A fall in the corn wage implies higher corn command over labour, which – given the silver wage fixed by construction – necessitates an *increase* in the silver price of corn; while a fall in the profit rate would generate a *fall* in all money prices: 'A day's labour must always remain of the same money price, and corn could only rise as far as the diminution in the necessaries of the labourer would allow. Still, however, though the money price of the labourer could not rise, the rate of profits might fall; and on a fall in the rate of profits, every commodity would fall compared with money.' Relative money prices therefore were no indication of relative labour inputs in the course of growth.[19]

A variety of other complexities attached to real-world precious metals, including the small flow relative to stock causing long-term deviations of their market from their cost prices: 'The market prices of gold and silver depend upon the quantity of them in the market compared with the demand; and this quantity has been in part produced by the accumulation of hundreds of years, and is but slowly affected by the annual supply from the mines' (112). Malthus here recognized – we have seen above, in chapter 6, that this is not always the case – Ricardo's insistence on supply variation to assure the cost determination of price: 'It is justly stated by Mr. Ricardo [1951–73, I, 191–2] that the agreement of the market and natural prices of all commodities, depends at all times upon the facility with which the supply can be increased or diminished, and he particularly notices gold, or the precious metals, as among the commodities where this effect cannot be speedily produced.' But he turned the point in his own favour: 'Consequently if by great and sudden improvements in machinery, both in manufactures and agriculture, the facility of production were generally increased, and the wants of the population were supplied with much less labour, the value of the precious metals compared with commodities ought greatly to rise; but, as they could not in a short time be adequately diminished in quantity, the prices of commodities would cease to represent the quantity of labour employed upon them.'[20]

19 Ricardo's *Note 35* points out that nothing substantive had been added beyond Malthus's previous section (section IV) dealing formally with the labour theory: 'The objections made here to gold as a measure of value on the supposition that it always required the same quantity of labour to produce it are in substance the very same that were made in the last section to labour itself as a regulator of value. It was there shewn that commodities did not vary exactly in proportion to the quantity of labour which they required for their production: – it is now shown that they do not vary relatively to one particular commodity *exactly* in proportion to the quantity of labour required for the production of them, and the particular commodity' (1951–73, II, 82). Malthus's Section IV was discussed above, in our chapter 6: VII, VIII.

20 To all this Ricardo reacted in his *Note 36* by pointing to Malthus's confusion of ideal with real-world gold: 'It was never contended that gold under the present circumstances was a good measure of value, it was only hypothetically, and for the purpose of illustrating a principle, supposed that all the known causes of the variability of

This and related considerations led to the conclusion 'that no sort of regularity in the production of the precious metals ... can possibly render the money prices of commodities a correct measure of the quantity of labour which has been employed upon them, either in the same or different countries, or at the same or different periods' (117). But Malthus again reiterates his acceptance of money as a correct measure of the exchangeable value of commodities at the same time and place; his objections were to its use as a measure of labour embodied. Moreover, 'the less subject to variation are the modes of procuring [the precious metals], the more they will approach to a measure of exchangeable value at different times and in different places.' As for his own measure, it had some advantages, but (as mentioned above) it also failed to reflect relative labour embodiment in the case of commodities requiring some capital input: 'In the case supposed, money would certainly be of a uniform value. It would at all times both cost the same quantity of labour and command the same quantity; but we have seen that, in reference to those commodities where any sort of capital was used, their values, compared either with the precious metals or each other, could never be proportioned to the labour which they had cost' (118).

Strange to relate, Malthus by no means disdained to use Ricardo's measure involving a metal requiring capital as well as labour and assuming unchanged productivity. This fact emerges strikingly in *The Measure of Value* itself as we shall presently see (section IX). Possibly section V of the Value chapter in the *Principles* was omitted from the second edition for this very reason.

IV A PROPOSED LINKED CORN–LABOUR INDEX

Section VII, peculiar to the 1820 version, proposes a 'Mean between Corn and Labour' as 'Measure of Real Value in Exchange.' At the outset we have the definition of the real exchange value of *corn* as its command over 'labour and other commodities' (127).[21] And we also have the conclusion

gold, were removed. In the case supposed by Mr. Malthus, gold would not be brought to market in the same quantity as before, unless its market price was equal to, or exceeded, its natural price; the reduction of the quantity would slowly elevate its price' (1951–73, II, 82–3). He further protested: 'I said [cf. 1951–73, I, 87n1], "suppose all variations in the value of gold to cease, it would then be a good measure of value." I know they cannot cease – I know it is a metal liable to the same variations as other things and therefore not a good measure of value, but I beg you to suppose all causes of variation removed, that we may speak about the variations of other things in an unvarying measure without confusion. Am I answered by being told that gold is variable, and that I have omitted to mention some of the causes of its variation?'

21 Command by X over commodities *and labour* as conveying the sense of X's 'real value in exchange,' implies inclusion of services within the consumption basket. This applies also to 1820, 62; above, note 5.

that, 'from century to century as well as from year to year, a given quantity of corn appears to measure very imperfectly the quantity of necessaries, conveniences, and amusements of life, which *any particular commodity* will command in exchange' (127–8; emphasis added). Malthus thus questions whether the corn commanded by X measures X's real exchange value – its general purchasing power. Here labour does not enter into X's 'real value in exchange,' which is probably a slip. In any event, it is allowed that though 'a certain quantity of corn of a given quality, on account of its capacity of supporting a certain number of human beings, has always a definite and invariable value in use' (126) – an unhelpful conception unless the corn wage is fixed – its real value in exchange or its command over *commodities-in-general* varies considerably 'not only from year to year but from century to century' (126–7).[22] In an elaboration of this theme, reference is made to variations in the corn command over '*labour* and other commodities' (emphasis added).[23]

Adam Smith's notion of the labour commanded by X was also an unsatisfactory secular measure of X's real value in exchange, that is, in this case command by X *over other commodities, including corn ('wheat')* – 'the chief article in the general estimate of real value in exchange' (128). Here we find reference to the presumption of Section VI that the command by labour over manufactures would be steadier than its command over corn because into manufactures 'labour enters as a principal ingredient' (cf. above, pp. 280–1). Even so, the *characteristic variation in labour command over corn* was quantitatively sufficient to disqualify labour as an accurate measure of X's value in exchange relative to commodities-in-general, of which corn was a major component.

Neither X's command over corn alone nor its command over labour alone provided a satisfactory index of its general purchasing power. That is the crux of the matter. *But a joint measure might work*: 'No one commodity then, it appears, can justly be considered as a standard measure of real

22 Also its 'nominal' value in exchange, or its command over money.

On corn as a measure Ricardo remarks in his *Note 41*: 'This is also a measure proposed by Mr. Malthus, and the same account of its invariability is given, as he before gave of the invariability of labour' (1951–73, II, 95). This refers to Malthus's concession regarding labour's *variability* (see the sarcastic remark, above, p. 282).

23 For a secular example: 'In the reign of Henry VII, at the end of the 15th and beginning of the 16th centuries, it appears, from the statute price of labour and the average price of wheat, that half a bushel of this grain would purchase but little more than a day's common labour; and, of course, but a small quantity of those commodities in the production of which much labour is necessary. A century afterwards, in the latter part of the reign of Elizabeth, half a bushel of wheat would purchase three days' common labour, and, of course, a considerable quantity comparatively of those commodities on which labour is employed.' This implies a secular decline in both the corn wage and the corn price of manufactures; that is, the corn command over both labour and manufactures increased.

value in exchange; and such an estimate of the comparative prices of all commodities as would determine the command of any one in particular over the necessaries, conveniences, and amusements of life, including labour, would not only be too difficult and laborious for use, but generally quite impracticable. Two objects, however, might, in some cases, be a better measure of real value in exchange than one alone, and yet be sufficiently manageable for practical application' (126). The proposal that follows is for a linked corn–labour index. In the course of establishing the case, the objective of a measure to indicate a commodity's 'real value in exchange' in the sense of *general purchasing power* becomes yet clearer: 'When corn compared with labour is dear, labour compared with corn must necessarily be cheap. At the period that a given quantity of corn will command the greatest quantity of the necessaries, conveniences, and amusements of life, a given quantity of labour will always command the smallest quantity of such objects; and at the period when corn commands the smallest, labour will command the greatest quantity of them. If, then, we take a mean between the two, we shall evidently have a measure corrected by the contemporary variations of each in opposite directions, and likely to represent more nearly than either the same quantity of the necessaries, conveniences, and amusements of life, at the most distant periods, and under all the varying circumstances to which the progress of population and cultivation is subject' (128–9). The specific suggestion is to take as index one *peck of wheat* (average earnings per day) combined with *one day's labour* in equal proportions: 'Any commodity therefore which, at different periods, will purchase the same number of days' labour and of pecks of wheat, or parts of them, each taken in equal proportions, may be considered, upon this principle, as commanding pretty nearly the same quantity of the necessaries, conveniences, and amusements of life; and, consequently, as preserving pretty nearly its real value in exchange at different periods' (129).

Malthus allowed that, while X may command a *given* quantum of corn-cum-labour, this would *not* represent a given quantum of purchasing power over a basket including manufactures: 'The principal defect of the measure here proposed arises from the effect of capital, machinery and the division of labour in varying, in different countries and at different periods, the results of day-labour and the prices of manufactured commodities' (130). The objection is set aside on the grounds that 'these varying results no approximation hitherto suggested has ever pretended to estimate; and, in fact, they relate rather to riches than to exchangeable value, which, though nearly connected, are not always the same; and on this account, in an estimate of value, the cheapness arising from skill and machinery may without much error be neglected' (130–1).[24] This rationale is not easily

24 Ricardo supposes in *Note 43* that Malthus's closing observation suggesting the 'neglect'

comprehensible. Malthus's measure of (real) exchangeable value refers *precisely* to riches – that has been established at length throughout the chapter, and in the very section at hand.

Malthus's case of 1820 is summarized in the closing paragraphs of his chapter on Value, which addressed Ricardo's query in the *Principles*: 'Why should gold, or corn, or labour be the standard measure of value, more than coals or iron, more than cloth, soap, candles, and the other necessaries of the labourer? Why, in short, should any commodity, or all commodities together, be the standard, when such a standard is itself subject to fluctuations in value?' (1951–73, I, 275). In response, Malthus agreed that 'there is no question as to an accurate standard, which is justly considered as unattainable. But of all the articles given in exchange, labour is, beyond comparison, the largest and most important; and next to it stands corn. The reason, why corn should be preferred to coals or iron, is surely very intelligible' – presumably because corn is the main wage good and comprises a considerable fraction of the purchases of the largest income-earning class (1820, 132). And 'the reasons given in this section are, I trust, sufficient for preferring, in some cases, a mean between corn and labour to either of them taken separately. Where corn is not one of the articles to be measured, as in the case of an estimate of the value of the precious metals, or any particular commodity, a mean between corn and labour is certainly to be preferred to labour alone; but where corn is one of the main articles to be measured, as in an estimate of the exchangeable value of the whole produce of a country, the command of such produce over domestic and foreign labour is still the best criterion to which we can refer.' Malthus ends up with labour commanded only where our 'commodity X' is *corn itself* or where measurement of the entire national income is at stake. Otherwise, the mean measure was recommended. Though there was 'no question as to an accurate standard,' he could not see that Ricardo had provided a better solution.

Ricardo represented the Joint Index as a 'complete fallacy' (*Note 42*; 1951–73, II, 96).[25] The idea reflected the argument that corn and labour, though variable, 'always vary in different directions; if therefore I take a mean between the two, I shall probably obtain a measure approaching to the character of invariability.' But corn and labour did *not* vary in different

of 'cheapness arising from skill and machinery' was a simple error: 'What is this but saying that in an estimate of value it is of no importance what quantity of labour may be applied to the production of commodities? This I think must be an oversight for Mr. Malthus uniformly allows that the quantity of labour employed on commodities is the main cause of their value. How can it indeed be denied?' (1951–73, II, 100). Ricardo is correct to say that Malthus 'uniformly' recognized labour embodiment to be the main determinant of exchange value.

25 See also letter to Trower, 26 November 1820; 1951–73, VIII, 305–7.

directions: 'A country finds increasing difficulties in supplying the corn necessary for a continually augmenting population, and in consequence corn rises as compared with all other commodities. As corn rises, which forms so material an article of consumption to the labourer, though not the only one, labour also rises, but not so much as corn ... [It] is evident that they have both risen, though in different degrees, for they will both be more valuable estimated in all other commodities' (98–9).[26]

Ricardo expressed the hope that Malthus would 'see the expediency of relinquishing so imperfect, and so variable a standard' (96–7). As he pointed out in *Note 125* attached to the Rent chapter, Malthus in fact rarely applied the mean measure (1951–73, II, 206–7). In any event, possibly because of Ricardo's criticism, Malthus excised the proposal from the second edition.

V ABANDONMENT OF QUEST FOR AN INDEX OF PURCHASING POWER

The second edition of the *Principles* entails substantive changes in position.[27] Ricardo had taken his stand on measuring variations in the 'real value' of a commodity X by considering variations in its exchange rate against another commodity (or other commodities) known to be produced under unchanged cost conditions (his 'gold'); changes in X's real value automatically imply changes in its purchasing power but only those resulting from changes in its *own* production conditions. Malthus's second edition effectively adopts this approach by excluding those changes in X's purchasing power which reflect altered conditions '*extrinsic*' to X: 'There has been no more fruitful source of error in the very elements of political economy, than the not distinguishing between the power of purchasing generally, and the power of purchasing arising from intrinsic causes; and it is of the highest importance to be fully aware that, practically, when the rise or fall in the value of a commodity is referred to, its power of purchasing arising from extrinsic causes is always excluded' (1836, 60n).[28] The

26 Ricardo had also alluded to the one-way movement of corn and labour, albeit to different degrees, in *Note 34* (above, note 17). *Note 42* continues to rub in the main criticism by reference to Malthus himself: 'From Mr. Malthus argument in this place one would suppose that labour fell when corn rose, and consequently that with a given quantity of iron, leather, cloth &c. more labour could be obtained [to Trower: bestowed], the contrary is the fact, labour, as well as corn, rises as compared with these commodities. Mr. Malthus says so himself in page 125 "In the progress of improvement and civilization it generally happens, that when labour commands the smallest quantity of food, it commands the greatest quantity of other commodities" – what is this but saying that when a great quantity of other commodities is given for food, a greater [to Trower: a great] quantity of other things is also given for labour, or in other words that when food rises, labour rises?'

27 One cosmetic change is its avoidance of the term '*real* value in exchange.'

28 Malthus refers to Nassau Senior's definition of 'intrinsic' and 'extrinsic' causes acting

error alluded to here refers to the general Smithian definition of value-in-exchange simply in terms of the 'power of purchasing other goods, which the possession of that object conveys' (cited, 58n) – a position which Malthus neglects to mention he had himself originally adopted with due credit paid Smith (above, p. 278). The problem was that, because of the innumerable alterations in 'extrinsic causes,' there could exist no single commodity that could serve to measure the general purchasing power, say, of some given money income: 'Though it would certainly be desireable to have some measure of the power of purchasing the mass of commodities, or at least the principal necessaries and conveniences of life, as it would enable us to form an estimate of the wealth of those persons who were in possession of particular commodities, or of certain revenues in money, yet when we consider what such a measure implies, we must feel assured that no one object exists, or can be supposed to exist with such qualities as would fit it to become a standard measure of this kind' (57). Even were a measure attainable, it would reflect 'wealth' – evidently our real income is intended here – not 'value according to the most general use of the term' (58). Thus a commodity X that purchases a constant amount of A, B, C ... the costs, *and therefore the value*, of which are known to have fallen could not itself be said to be of unchanged value;[29] for the standard use of the term 'exchange value' in fact *excluded* from consideration variations attributable to extrinsic circumstances: 'The general power of purchasing, therefore, possessed by a particular commodity, cannot with any sort of propriety be considered as representing the variations in its exchangeable value, according to the most usual meaning attached to the term. The exchangeable value of a commodity can only be proportioned to its general power of purchasing so long as the commodities with which it is exchanged continue to be obtained with the same facility. But as it is known by experience that no considerable mass of commodities ever continues to be obtained with the same facility, it is observable that when we speak of the variations in the exchangeable value of a particular commodity, we refer almost invariably to its power of purchasing arising from intrinsic causes' (58–9).

---

upon commodity A's exchange rate relative to B, C ... (see Pullen, in Malthus, 1820/1989, II, 314); and continues: 'The causes which affect the desire to possess, and the difficulty of obtaining possession of any one commodity, may with propriety be denominated the *intrinsic* causes of its power of purchasing; because the more these causes increase, the greater power will the commodity possess of purchasing all those objects which continue to be obtained with the same facility. The causes which affect the desire to possess, and the difficulty of obtaining the possession of all the different commodities with which the first commodity might be exchanged, may with propriety be denominated the *extrinsic* causes of its power of purchasing' (1836, 57).

29 An example given here is revealing: (1) It takes as something like the norm cases of lower manufacturing costs and constant agricultural costs; and (2) defines costs to include *labour and profits* (58–9).

A comparison between editions of the summaries of 'three sorts of value' at the close of the section brings out the contrast. The first two are effectively unchanged: '1. Value in use; which may be defined to be the intrinsic utility of an object. 2. Nominal value in exchange [1836: or price]; which [1836: unless something else is specifically referred to] may be defined to be the value of commodities in [1836: estimated in] the precious metals' (1820, 62; 1836, 60). It is the third that is subject to revision; and the adoption of Ricardo's stance is clear, though Malthus does not formally acknowledge a debt. For all variations acting on commodities other than that whose exchange value is under investigation are excluded; moreover, while variations affecting the commodity in question relate to both long-run cost and demand conditions, the focus (as with Ricardo) is on the former. Thus in 1820: '3. Real value in exchange; which may be defined to be *the power of an object to command in exchange the necessaries and conveniences of life, including labour*' (1820, 62; emphasis added). And in 1836: '3. Intrinsic value in exchange, which may be defined to be the power of purchasing arising from intrinsic causes, in which sense, the value of an object is understood when nothing further is added. This definition is precisely equivalent to – The estimation in which a commodity is held, founded on the desire to possess, and the difficulty of obtaining possession of it; and accords entirely with the definition of the exchangeable value of a commodity, given in my work *On definitions in Political Economy*, namely, – The estimation in which a commodity is held at any place and time, determined in all cases by the state of the supply compared with the demand, and *ordinarily by the elementary cost of production*' (1836, 60; emphasis added).[30]

Subsequently, we encounter a further denial of the concept of general purchasing power and/or of any measure thereof. Even were one to conceive of a single commodity that represented 'the mass of all purchaseable commodities' – and this possibility is disallowed – the power

30 See also the following statements which appear later in the text: 'The definition of the value of a commodity at a particular place and time, is stated to be "the estimation in which it is held at that place and time, determined in all cases by the state of the supply compared with the demand, and, ordinarily, by the elementary costs of its production, which regulate that state;" or what comes to the same thing, its power of purchasing at that place and time, arising from intrinsic causes' (1836, 109). 'Recollecting then always, that I have not been inquiring for some object which approximates to a standard measure of value in exchange, on the supposition that the proper definition of the value of a commodity is its power of purchasing *generally*, but upon the supposition that the most usual, the most useful, and therefore the most correct interpretation of the term, is its power or purchasing *arising from intrinsic causes*, we may safely consider labour as the object which will answer the purpose required; and say, that the value of a commodity at any time, and at any place, may be measured by the quantity of the standard labour of that time and place, which it will exchange for or command' (110–11).

of commanding that commodity would fail to yield information regarding the purchasing power of particular incomes, because of the intrusion of commodities in the mass irrelevant for the particular consumer group with which one is interested (119–20). Clearly, Malthus had no conception of an index number utilizing an appropriately weighted basket for the purpose at hand. At the same time, it is also evident that measurement of general purchasing power is no longer the main purpose of the measure of value: 'It is obvious, therefore, that a measure representing the mass of commodities, or the general power of purchasing, even if attainable, which, however, is impossible, would not only, as formerly stated, fail entirely in reference to the main characteristic of value, but would be very unsatisfactory in the inquiries above mentioned. And in such cases we ought never to use the term value, or value in exchange by itself but add specifically the kind of articles, in the purchase of which the incomes would be chiefly spent' (120).[31]

* * *

The revised position of the posthumous *Principles* is amply confirmed in the second of two papers read before the Royal Society of Literature.[32] This paper (7 November 1827) maintains that by the *value* of a commodity is intended specifically the conditions of supply of that commodity, rather than *general purchasing* power: 'In this customary application of the term value, it is particularly worthy of remark, that we never consider the value of one commodity as affected by the causes which may operate upon another ...' (1827b/1986, 7, 317); similarly, 'practically, when we speak of the value of a commodity, we almost exclusively refer to the circumstances which affect its plenty or scarcity, to the conditions of the supply of the commodity itself, and not to those which affect others' (318).

This insistence on measurement of *value* – or on what in the second edition of the *Principles* is called 'intrinsic' supply conditions – as distinct from a measure of *wealth* is further reinforced by formal adoption of Ricardo's distinction between 'riches' and 'value,' a distinction Malthus had once rejected: 'When the same quantity of iron and broadcloth will command a greater quantity of the mass of all other commodities, the persons possessing this iron and broadcloth will be decidedly better off than before. But they will be better off, because they have the power of commanding a greater quantity of *wealth*, not because they have the power of commanding a greater quantity of value. I entirely agree with Mr. Ricardo' – Ricardo was writing here against Say (1951–73, I, 280–1) – 'that

31 But Malthus suggests no way of combining several different articles constituting 'the kind of articles' in question, such as wage goods.

32 The Society's *Transactions*, Vol. I, part 2 (1825–9), 74–81; in 1986, 7, 315–23.

if two sacks of wheat be of the value that one was before, the clothier who exchanges his cloth for them obtains the same value that he did, and no more, although he may obtain double the quantity of riches' (317–18). And he took issue with Smith: 'When Adam Smith says, that "every man is rich or poor according to the degree in which he can afford to enjoy the necessaries, conveniences, and amusements of human life," he gives a just description of *riches*; but when he goes on to say, that the man is rich or poor according to the quantity of labour which he can command, or which he can afford to purchase, he is no longer describing riches, but giving his own definition of value' (318). Ricardo (1951–73, I, 278) had 'most justly remarked, that if the mines were to become more productive, or velvets were manufactured with less labour, he would be able to command more of these species of riches, without being able to command more labour.'

The paper in fact closes on this theme: 'It has been a very general opinion among political economists, ever since the publication of Adam Smith's work, that from the very nature of value, so essentially different from length or weight, it cannot admit of a regular and definite measure. This opinion among political economists seems to have arisen from their not making a proper distinction between wealth and value' (322–3). Smith's 'first definition is a definition of wealth and of this there is certainly no measure. The second is a definition of value, and of this the very terms which he uses show that there *is* a measure.' Thus while Malthus accepted Adam Smith's labour-commanded index, he distinguished between their respective usages; Smith alone, he believed, took it as a measure of general purchasing power.

In a discussion of the term 'different values of the precious metals in different countries' (321), Malthus repeated his objection to 'value' in the sense of general purchasing power. And here he refers favourably to Ricardo's position (Ricardo, 1951–73, I, 377) that the 'value' of gold – in the sense of purchasing power – will differ, depending on which particular set of commodities is adopted in the exercise. And 'there is certainly no commodity, or set of commodities, which can with any degree of accuracy represent [the] mass,' that is, *all* the products in the system (322).

VI LABOUR COMMAND AS MEASURE OF ABSOLUTE SUPPLY CONDITIONS

In a refutation of the position – apparently Samuel Bailey's – that 'the term value of a commodity ought never to be used without at the same time specifying distinctly the article with which it is intended to be compared, and that any one article measures this value as well as any other,' Malthus in the second edition of the *Principles* observed that, were this indeed so, 'the term value becomes perfectly superfluous and useless' and should be discarded (1836, 121–2). The common meaning of the term, and the most useful, was 'the relation which commodities bear to the difficulty of obtaining them, or the estimation in which they are held at different times, and in different countries.' His concern was with the measurement of value in this sense – *absolute* rather than relative value.[33]

More specifically, by the 'main characteristic of value' alluded to in the second edition is intended 'the difficulty of getting possession' of a particular commodity (120n) – or the 'intrinsic causes.' And the labour-commanded measure of value indicated that difficulty and precisely those changes in the commodity's purchasing power reflecting the intrinsic causes at play. Although by 'difficulty' Malthus intended any changes in the demand and supply conditions pertinent to the commodity in question, it is the cost conditions that largely concerned him. Thus had Adam Smith 'limited his definition of the exchangeable value of a commodity to its power of purchasing arising from intrinsic causes, or the estimation in which it is held determined by the state of the supply compared with the demand, *and, ordinarily, by the elementary costs of its production,* which is unquestionably the sense in which he applies it himself, and in which it is most frequently applied by others, the measure he has proposed [labour commanded] would have been consistent with his definition, and both would have been just' (117–18; emphasis added).[34]

In all this, the repeated emphasis on 'intrinsic causes' is designed to overcome the problem that exchanges involving A (the commodity being measured) and other commodities, reflect in part changes in the 'values' of the other commodities, that is, changes in the demand and/or cost conditions pertinent to them rather than to A alone. These had to be excluded, and the presumption is that only the labour commanded by A solved the problem. This emerges most clearly in a criticism of Smith's procedures in line with that given in the essay of 1827, discussed above, in section V:

33 Cf. his insistance in the *Definitions* (1827) against Say on his own measure as an index of the supply conditions of each commodity taken individually: '*Def.* 5. Two articles are never exchanged with each other without a previous estimation being formed of the value of each, by a reference to the wants of mankind and the means of production. This general and most important relation to the means of production, and the labour which represents these means, seems to be quite forgotten by those who imagine that there is no relation implied when the value of a commodity is mentioned without specific reference to some other commodity' (1827a/1986, *8*, 116).

34 Money price or value expressed in money was for short periods an acceptable measure of the 'intrinsic causes' acting on a commodity, because of the valid presumption of no changes acting on the demand or supply of money: 'It cannot be too often repeated, that for short periods when the value of money is considered as nearly constant, we uniformly measure the variations of value, as well as the variations of price by money; and it is quite certain that money, under these circumstances, can only measure the variations in the value of a commodity arising from intrinsic causes, and has nothing to do with causes which are extrinsic' (119).

The specific reason, as it appears to me, why it has been generally supposed that there cannot be anything like a standard measure of value, is, that the principal founder of the *science* of political economy, Adam Smith, has given a definition of value in exchange [1776/1937, 28], not only different from that meaning in which it is practically, and most frequently, applied, but quite inconsistent with the specific measure of value which he has himself proposed. If by the value of an object in exchange, be meant, as Adam Smith has stated, the power of purchasing other goods which the possession of that object conveys, then, as it is quite certain that such power may increase from the facility of producing other goods as well as from the difficulty of producing the object in question, it is equally certain that here can be no measure of the value of such object; and that when in the same page he speaks of the real measure of this exchangeable value,and afterwards distinctly proposes the labour which a commodity will command as that measure, and enters upon an elaborate inquiry into the value of silver during the last four centuries, he proceeds upon a principle in the application of which he contradicts at every step his first definition. These contradictions were no doubt calculated to produce impressions unfavourable to the existence of a standard measure of value. Such at least were the impressions produced on myself. (117)

* * *

The new contention that labour commanded by X is the *ideal* index of X's 'intrinsic' value turns on the following argument. Where labour is the *only* factor, labour embodied and labour commanded coincide and there is no question that the latter then indicates the 'intrinsic value' of the commodity. This, however, could be generalized (for the 'proof' see below, pp. 297). This is what Malthus had in mind by the following summary in the present context: 'If we are entitled to assume, as I think we are, from what has been said in the preceding sections, that in the natural and ordinary state of things, a given quantity of standard labour applied to the production of any commodity, communicates to it a *given* value in exchange arising from intrinsic causes; and if by value in exchange, when nothing else is added to the term, we mean value in exchange arising from intrinsic causes, it follows, that, contrary to the usual impressions on the subject, there must be a measure of the values, of commodities however composed, and that measure can only be labour' (116–17).

As for the *practical application* of the proposed measure, there were no insurmountable difficulties; in fact, it had 'a prodigious superiority over the general power of purchasing, a measure which it is impossible practically to apply with any approach towards precision' (111). As we know, labour commanded is said to indicate 'intrinsic causes' acting on a commodity: 'But when we confine our view to the power of purchasing [possessed by some commodity] arising from intrinsic causes, we are able to measure the variations in this power, by the varying quantity of a specific object [namely, labour] for which it will exchange; and the practical application of this object is rendered easy, by referring to the money prices of commodities and labour.' Following Smith, allowance had to be made for differential wages; all labour units were to be reduced to multiples of common agricultural labour (116). Also following Smith, Malthus cautions of the care needed in obtaining an accurate estimate of the money wage to assure that what 'we take as the ordinary wages of any particular country or district are the whole of the natural and necessary conditions of the supply of labour' (114). If that were assured, 'we may fairly presume, that whether the quantity of money, or of necessaries paid to the labourer be great or small, the value of this quantity will be the same,' a reference to the constancy in the value – labour commanded – of the basket in money or in real terms, irrespective of its magnitude.[35]

* * *

The substantive difference between the 1820 version and the revised version in the *Principles* amounts to a *reinforcement* of the case for a labour-commanded index. In what follows we consider Malthus's new argument for labour commanded as the ideal index.

The issue in a new Section III introduced in the second edition is how to 'represent and measure' the 'effectual' demand for a product: 'An effectual demand for a commodity, is such a demand as will fulfil the natural and necessary conditions of the supply; or ... the sacrifice which the demanders must make in order to effectuate the continued supply of the commodity in the quantity required under the actual circumstances' (1836, 80). Though this is a general statement, the emphasis is on the demand price required to assure satisfaction of the 'natural and necessary' supply conditions. Money served adequately, provided its cost conditions are given, an invalid assumption over long periods; accordingly, 'if money varies essentially, as compared with the natural and necessary conditions of the supply of commodities, a given amount of money cannot possibly represent a given demand, or a given sacrifice.'

The solution was to use labour commanded, since 'the power of commanding a given quantity of labour of a given character, together with the will to advance it, represents a given demand' (82).[36] This statement is preceded by an elaborate attempt to *prove* the case. Assume first a com-

35 This latter alludes to the fact that the money or commodity wage commands a *given* quantum of labour, which command reflects the 'intrinsic' value in exchange of the basket.

36 This is qualified: 'It should be particularly observed, however, that this power is never possessed by the labourers themselves, but by those employers of labour who are both able and willing to pay the quantity of money or of commodities, whether great or small, which is necessary in the actual circumstances of the society to command the required quantity of labour' (82–3).

modity produced by labour alone: 'If the advance of a certain quantity of labour be the necessary condition of the supply of a particular commodity, then the money which will command such labour will represent the effectual demand for the commodity; that is, a demander able and willing to make such a sacrifice as will effectuate the supply' (80). Or more generally, 'the power of setting to work that quantity of labour, whether paid for by a larger or smaller quantity of produce or money, will be an effectual demand for it' (81). *Labour alone had that property*: 'There is no product of labour, which, applied directly, enters, as labour itself does, into the composition of all commodities that have value, and constitutes the *chief* element in the conditions of their supply. Consequently there is no *product* of labour which can represent the most important condition of the supply of all commodities, namely the quantity of labour absolutely necessary to their production; and we cannot say that a definite quantity of money, a definite quantity of corn, a definite quantity of cloth, or a definite quantity of any product of labour, subject, as they all are, to variations in their relation to labour, can continue to afford an effectual demand for that definite quantity of labour, without which the mass of commodities cannot by possibility be produced.'[37]

Should capital, land, and taxes be involved, the substance of the matter – so it is asserted – remained unchanged since it was possible to make an appropriate adjustment: 'But if, when commodities are selling at their natural prices, the quantity of labour directly applied to the production of a particular article were to absorb exactly one half, three fourths, or any definite proportion of the whole value, as the demand for this proportion, whatever it might be, the *half* we will suppose, might be represented and measured by an amount of labour equal in quantity and quality to that which had been actually employed upon the commodity, it is obvious that an equivalent to *double* the quantity of such labour would be an effectual demand for the whole article produced, involving profits, rent, taxes, or any other accession to the difficulty of bringing the commodity to market, besides that which is occasioned by the necessary quantity of labour to be advanced' (81–2). Similarly: 'As there is no object but labour which can represent and measure the demand for that aliquot of the value of a commodity which consists of immediate labour, it follows necessarily that there is no object but labour which can represent and measure the demand for the whole of a commodity, the value of which is made up of various ingredients besides labour.'[38]

37 As we show in chapter 10, Malthus none the less devised a corn-profit model. In the determination of the profit rate itself, a main rationale for the labour-commanded index gave way.

38 Malthus never justified adequately his case for his measure in the presence of scarce land. In his *Measure of Value*, we shall find (section VII), land is generally neglected.

Section V in the 1836 version reverts to the possible contention that labour commanded was no better than any other commodity as measure of relative values *at the same time and place* (above, p. 279). In 1820 Malthus had conceded this but had argued for the advantage of labour commanded when *different* periods were involved. This is also the case in 1836: 'This is no doubt true, if we take the same time precisely, and if we wish merely to know the relation of one commodity to some other or others in exchange; but the comparison utterly fails if we take different periods, and more especially if we refer to the main characteristic of the value of a commodity, namely, the difficulty of obtaining it, or the limitation of its supply compared with the demand' (95). But there is this difference between editions – it reflects the alteration in perspective between versions – that the concern is now with measurement of changes in the 'intrinsic' value of any commodity or changes in demand–supply conditions (supply conditions are in fact invariably the main issue) *pertinent solely and specifically to the commodity in question.*

To summarize the argument thus far: Ricardo's labour embodied failed as a measure of intrinsic value 'except in the rare case when labour alone is employed, and the produce is brought to market immediately. In the vast majority of cases, there are other intrinsic causes of value, acting sometimes with great power, which increase the difficulty of obtaining the object desired, in addition to the labour actually employed' (92). From this it followed 'that the quantity of labour actually employed in the production of commodities, answers neither of the two great objects of a measure of value. It neither measures the rate at which commodities exchange with each other at the same place and time, like money, nor does it measure the whole of the difficulty to be overcome, or the sacrifices to be made, in obtaining commodities at the same or different times, and in different countries, and enable us to say when two or more commodities have varied in relation to each other, in which, and to what extent in each, the variations have taken place' (92–3).

Malthus also objected to Garnier and Say for adopting *corn* rather than labour as measure of value, notwithstanding 'that corn not only varies greatly in the difficulty of obtaining it, from temporary abundance, or scarcity, but that very great alterations may take place for fifty or sixty years together in the same country, and in different countries, at different periods in the progress of cultivation, for a much longer period' (120–1). Adam Smith, too, in his 'Digression on Silver,' 'by referring most unaccountably to the prices of corn, instead of to the measure which he had himself proposed [labour commanded], has fallen into the very gross error of making the value of silver *rise* in the proportion of from two to three in the interval between the middle of the fourteenth, and the end of the fifteenth century, instead of *falling* in the proportion of from three to two, which would have been the just conclusion, if he had applied labour as his measure instead of corn,' for the 'same quantity of wheat ... instead of representing nearly the same quantity of labour from century to century, as intimated by Adam Smith, represented very little more than the half of that quantity, and his inference respecting the rise in the value of silver was quite reversed' (121).

* * *

Malthus's index assured a constant value of labour, in the sense of the *wages paid labour,* which fixed amount is shared between capital and labour. To that constancy we turn next.

It is an essential part of the case that (*pace* Ricardo) the measure is not undermined by variations in the real wage; it is always the value of produce that alters, never that of labour. This was true of the simplest case: 'The varying quantity of produce obtained by the same quantity of labour of a given character, where labour alone is concerned, while it implies great alterations in the value of a given portion of the produce, does not alter the value of a given quantity of labour' (99). And it extended to all cases: 'And it is equally true that the varying wages, whether in corn or money, paid to the labourer at different periods for labour of the same character, when this labour enters into the composition of commodities combined with profits, rent, taxes, or any other intrinsic causes of value, does not alter the value of the labour itself, or disqualify it from being used as a measure.' The case is extended to apply also to variations in the money wage over time; and also to geographic differentials in money wages (100–8). There were admittedly problems where 'the character of the labour is essentially different' geographically or temporally. Still the case for labour commanded as an index of 'limitation of supply compared with the demand' stood firm (108–9). An elaboration argues that the greater intensity of English than Indian labour in the production of muslins, ultimately reduces to the respective differential estimation of the *muslins,* not of *labour.*[39]

Needless to say, the constant 'value' of labour is a truism, given the definition of value as labour commanded. We shall see presently that *The Measure of Value* (1823) explores at length the significance of this truism (below, section VII). In the *Principles,* Malthus briefly touches on the matter in a discussion of the characteristic downward secular trend of the corn wage. '[It] is obvious,' he wrote, 'that the smaller quantity ... is obtained with just as much difficulty as the greater quantity ...' (1836, 115), alluding to the 'difficulty' of producing the variable corn basket, which difficulty he measured by labour commanded. Malthus here had in mind an *exact compensation* provided by a reduced profit rate, for the increased difficulty

39 This elaboration is probably a response to a criticism by Ricardo in his *Note 37* on the 1820 formulation (Ricardo, 1951–73, II, 86).

of producing the corn basket reflecting the higher labour input as 'cultivation is pushed upon poor land.'

The necessity to include profits – and, in the event of institutionally created land scarcity, other expenses – is confirmed in a discussion of special cases where, despite *natural* 'facility' of production, the commodity wage is low, not high: 'There are, however, instances where it may at first sight appear that what the labourer receives as wages is produced with facility, and yet the quantity he receives is very small; but it must always be recollected, that the labour actually employed in the production of wages, is never the sole element of their value. *Profits are universally another element, and in some cases, taxes and unnatural rents may raise the value of produce in an unusual proportion beyond the labour employed in its production*' (emphasis added). As in the standard case, the worker '[to] earn a very scanty support ... must make a great sacrifice; and a small quantity of produce thus becomes of great value, owing to the limitation of the supply compared with the demand, notwithstanding the real facility of production. Some parts of India have unquestionably at all times exemplified this state of things; and such instances form no exception to the general rule, that the value of the wages given to the labourer in any country can only be measured by the quantity of the ordinary labour of that country which he gives in exchange for them' (115–16). Because the 'sacrifice' required of the Indian labour (owing to artificial extractions) is as great in the earning of a small basket as it would be in that of a large, the small basket is of the same value as would be a large, which value is 'measured by' the quantity of Indian labour commanded.[40]

VII MEASUREMENT OF SUPPLY CONDITIONS, 1823

The substantive changes incorporated into the second version of the *Principles* are spelled out in much greater detail in *The Measure of Value* (1823). The book sets out by expressing the ideal – a commodity with properties that would allow it to act as a measure of general purchasing power, in the sense of its command over commodity A, B, C ... taken *individually*, rather than in our modern sense of a *general* index, for the command of any money income over such a product would indicate that income's purchasing power: 'That a correct measure of the power of purchasing generally, or of commanding such important commodities as the necessaries and conveniences of life, in whatever way such power might arise, would be very desirable, cannot for a moment be doubted, as it

40 The text continues by referring to money wages: 'But the Indian labourer receives a smaller quantity of money as well as of necessaries for his day's work; and this is because money also is very difficult of attainment in India, the manufactures sent abroad to purchase it, having cost a great mass of labour, profits, and rent.'

would at once enable us to form a just estimate and comparison of wages, salaries, and revenue, in all countries, and at all periods' (1823b/1986, 7, 181). The existence of such a comodity implied 'steadiness of value, not merely in one product, but in a great number,' and this was inconceivable.

The object of the inquiry was rather to discover 'whether there is any object, which, though it cannot measure the power of purchasing generally under the varying facilities of production and varying state of the demand and supply by which different commodities are affected, may be a correct measure of absolute and natural value as above described' (182). As defined shortly before, commodity A's 'absolute or natural value' refers to its value expressed in terms of some product X which itself is not subject to the range of disturbances that generate alteration in the X/A relationship – which is, of course, the Ricardian perspective. Now since Malthus focuses entirely on exchange-rate variations reflecting 'conditions of supply,' his inquiry effectively amounts to the properties of a measure of changes in A's *cost conditions*. Such a measure he finds to exist, not in any product X, but in *labour*; a doubling of A's command over labour reflecting an equivalent increase in A's production costs or 'conditions of supply.' Unlike Ricardo's commodity measure (gold), designed to capture changes in labour input, Malthus's was to serve as index of *total costs inclusive of profits*.

The Introduction (179–80) justifies devotion of a volume to the championship of *labour commanded* as measure of value on grounds of Adam Smith's lack of clarity and his inconsistency, specifically: (1) frequent confusion between labour embodied and labour commanded; (2) transfer to *corn* as measure in the historical treatment of the value of silver; and (3) assertions that the value of silver had risen in circumstances of *rising* money wages. Furthermore, general opinion was unconvinced of the merits of labour commanded as standard measure; indeed, the prevailing view was that no such standard could be found, 'in which opinion I concurred,' a reference to the *Principles* of 1820, which adopted labour commanded as the best among a range of imperfect measures. In 1823, Malthus makes his case on the grounds that this index is in fact *ideal* for his purposes, which include allowance for diminishing returns – a principle, he asserts, not recognized by Smith: 'Under these circumstances, having, by a process quite different from that of Adam Smith, and dependent on doctrines relating to gradations of soil, which were not noticed by him, arrived at the conclusion, that the labour which commodities will command may be considered as a standard measure of their natural and exchangeable value, I have thought myself justifiable in publishing my view of the subject in its present form' (180; see also 200–1, 211). More strongly still, labour commanded was the 'true' not merely a conventional measure: 'In my last work [1820], I thought that a mean between corn and labour might be a better measure of value than labour alone; but I am now convinced that I was wrong, and that labour alone is the true measure' (191n).[41] In this he differed from Ricardo, whose measure was merely a matter of convenience.

As mentioned, Malthus modified Adam Smith's natural prices by focusing on the margin of cultivation, or 'the natural conditions of the supply of commodities' entailing returns sufficient to pay wages and profits alone: 'it is now generally acknowledged that even the main vegetable food of an improving country, which is the foundation of wages, must necessarily be of the same value as that part of the produce which is almost exclusively resolvable into wages and profits, and pays very little rent' (182). Rent could, therefore, be abstracted from, at least as a first approximation: 'We cannot therefore essentially err in assuming for the present that the natural value of objects in their more simple forms is composed of labour and profits, and the effect of any portion of rent, or of other ingredients which are sometimes added to these elements, may be allowed for subsequently' (182–3). Indeed, favourable reference is made to Ricardo and James Mill: 'Mr. Ricardo, speaking of the commodities produced by the capitalist, says, "their whole value is divided into two portions only: one constitutes the profits of stock; the other the wages of labour" [1951–73, I, 110]. The language of Mr. Mill, in his *Elements of Political Economy*, is similar.'

The appropriate *money* proxy for labour commanded is silver or gold produced by labour alone by a process without a *time* dimension, such as metal picked up in an hour on the seashore.[42] Labour commanded and labour embodied then coincide, and (assuming constant labour productivity in silver) the money wage is invariable: 'Mr. Ricardo, by supposing gold to be produced always by a certain quantity of labour and *capital*, is compelled to acknowledge that his standard "would be a perfect measure of value for all things produced under the same circumstances precisely as itself, but for no others" [1951–73, I, 45]. This concession appears to me quite fatal. We want to measure the value of commodities under *all circumstances*, and it is only gold obtained exclusively by labour, or labour itself, which can do this [*Principles* 1820, 111 and 118]' (198n). Strange to relate, Malthus actually uses Ricardo's gold measure in *The Measure of Value* – doubtless because real-world metal is produced by a capital-using process (see especially, 1986, 7, 201, 203). Still his primary concern – at least through to page 61 of the pamphlet (1986, 7, 211)[43] – is with labour commanded as such, rather than its money proxy, and a 'Table illustrating

41 Moreover, since commodities exchanged in proportion to their labour command – labour input *plus* profit or dated labour – the measurement problem was eased by his index: 'The labour worked up in a commodity could not, in many cases, be ascertained without considerable difficulty; but the labour which it will command is always open and palpable' (207n).

42 An application in the *Principles* is discussed above, p. 283.

43 Here ends the substance of the book. The rest traces out various implications of the recommended measure.

the invariable Value of Labour and its Results' (199) entails *value* rather than *price* terms, avoiding all reference to the money index.

Reverting now to the substantive issue, 'the natural conditions' of commodity supply, we find a brief preliminary survey of long-run competitive exchange rates. Assuming that processes entail labour alone, the labour theory applies (183ff.). More complex processes are *time*-consuming, and then the labour theory breaks down, since 'the condition of the supply requires that a certain compensation be made in the final remuneration for the time which has elapsed from the period of the advances of the labour, to the period when the labourer, or capitalist, can be remunerated. This compensation, which equally applies to the formation of the capital, as to the products to be obtained by it, is the profit which must be paid on the advances of the labour, and is absolutely necessary to the encouragement of such advances' (184–5). Thus the exchange ratio between capital (time)-intensive and labour-intensive products would vary 'in the progress of society' – *a reduction in the profit rate is taken for granted here* – though relative labour inputs are unchanged (185). And the value of beef (a four- or five-year process) relative to corn (a one-year process) would fall more than 20 per cent, with a fall in the profit rate from 15 to 8 per cent though labour inputs are constant, because of the longer period of production in the former case.

Though Malthus recognized Ricardo's modifications to a labour theory, himself making claim for insisting on their quantitative significance, he ends up none the less allowing differential labour embodiment to be the *major* source of value differentials: 'The effects of slow or quick returns, and of the different proportions of fixed and circulating capitals, are distinctly allowed by Mr. Ricardo; but in his last edition, (the third [1951–73, I, 36] he has much underrated their amount. They are both theoretically and practically so considerable as entirely to destroy the position that commodities exchange with each other according to the quantity of labour which has been employed upon them; but no one that I am aware of has ever stated that the different quantity of labour employed on commodities is not a much more powerful source of difference of value' (186n).

All this suggests the *rejection* of a labour theory. But this is not quite where we end up. If to the labour embodiment in a commodity is added the profit on that labour (as measured in labour-commanded units), we then do obtain a total quantity of labour which *will* govern equilibrium exchange rates: '[If], with a view to the natural conditions of supply, we consider only the quantity of labour advanced, without reference to any other medium, we must of course estimate the profits in quantity of labour also, which will give us an amount of labour in proportion to which commodities will be found to exchange with each other, just in the same way as they would exchange with each other according to the quantity of labour employed on them, if labour had been the sole ingredient which had entered into their composition' (187).[44] The test of 'experience,' it is asserted, confirmed the proposition: 'when profits are calculated upon these advances, a quantity of labour is obtained, according to which it is found, by experience, that commodities do exchange with each other in the same country; and, further, that this quantity of labour not only expresses correctly their value in exchange with each other, but their absolute and natural value in reference to "the conditions of their supply"' (189–90). *But labour embodied supplemented by profits equals labour commanded; so that Malthus ends up with the proportionality of equilibrium exchange rates to labour commanded*: 'It appears, then, that in the same country, and at the same time, the exchangeable value of those commodities which can be resolved into labour and profits alone, would be accurately measured by the quantity of labour which would result from adding to the accumulated and immediate labour actually worked up in them the varying amount of the profits on all the advances estimated in labour. But this must necessarily be the same as the quantity of labour which they will command ...' (188).[45]

In a preliminary summary, Malthus maintained 'that the quantity of accumulated and immediate labour applied to their production, must, in all the less complex cases, form the advances on which profits may be correctly calculated' (189).[46] And we note also Malthus's favourable reference to the device – attributable to Robert Torrens (1818, 337) – of including residual fixed capital in the final product: 'When commodities are obtained by the assistance of a large proportion of fixed capital of a very durable nature, the advances are only consumed in part, and the whole produce of the accumulated and immediate labour employed must be considered as composed of the new produce obtained, together with

44 This is preceded by a statement that the calculation need not be in labour: 'If we had estimated the value of the labour advanced in money, or any other medium, we should of course estimate the profits in the same medium, and the natural price of the commodity estimated in such medium, would obviously be equal to the price of the accumulated and immediate labour expended on the commodity, together with the ordinary profits estimated upon such advances.'

45 To this he adds that ordinary money prices would reflect relative labour embodied to the extent that money is 'of a uniform value,' that is, has constant command over labour – that money wages are given: 'Where the precious metals may be considered for short periods as of a uniform value, the conformity of this measure with the proportions of money prices at which commodities would be exchanging all around us, might daily be brought to the test of experience and be established beyond the possibility of doubt.' This qualification implies that in making money calculations Malthus was assuming *constant money wages.*

46 Later he asserts that his analysis might also incorporate rent and taxes: 'Having obtained a measure of the value of commodities in their more simple forms, we may apply this measure to the ingredients which compose the most complicated productions, and estimate all the advances which consist of accumulatd profits, rents, tithes, and taxes in labour' (205).

the remainder of the fixed capital which is unconsumed' (1986, *7*, 186; cf. 207).[47]

A key feature of the entire argument is that *production decisions turn solely on absolute value as measured by a commodity's command over labour*; relative exchange rates between commodities were irrelevant: 'The conditions of the supply of commodities do not require that they should retain always the same relative values, but that each should retain its proper *natural* value, or the means of obtaining those objects which will continue to the producer the same power of production and accumulation' (189). And it was because the capitalist's advances consist in *labour* – not some product – that supply conditions are 'represented' solely by labour commanded: 'If the advances of capitalists consisted specifically in cloth, then these advances would always have the effect required in production; and as profits are calculated upon the advances necessary to production, whatever they may be, the quantity of cloth advanced, with the addition of the ordinary profits estimated also in quantity of cloth, would represent both the natural and relative value of the commodity. But the specific advances of capitalists do not consist of cloth, but of labour; and as no other object whatever can represent a given quantity of labour, it is obvious that labour stands quite alone in this respect, and that it is the quantity of *labour* which a commodity will command, and not the quantity of any other commodity, which can represent the conditions of its supply, or its natural value.'

Finally, we should again emphasize the necessarily constant value of the wage basket. Though this follows from the definition of value as labour commanded, Malthus provides an economic *rationale* for that constancy: 'As the quantity of labour required to produce [the wages] increases, either from difficulty or production or from the greater quantity of produce awarded to the labourer, all the value thus gained by labour is lost by profits ... Consequently, the value of the variable quantity of produce which, under different circumstances, forms the wages of a given number of men, being composed of the values of the two elements, labour and profits, varying as above described, must be constant' (196). It was 'precisely this necessary constancy in the natural value of the varying corn wages of labour, which renders the labour which a commodity will command, a standard measure both of its natural and exchangeable value' (201). Similarly: 'the value of the variable quantity of produce which, under different circumstances, forms the wages of a given number of men, being composed of the values of the two elements, labour and profits, varying as above described, must be constant, and may therefore, with propriety, be

47 See on this procedure Marx, *Capital, iii*, 213, and Sraffa, 1960, 94–5. Nothing is made of it by Malthus, since 'in reference to the separate value of the new produce, this will be the same as if to the labour actually worked up in such produce were added the profits of the whole capital advanced.'

proposed as a standard measure' (196). In fact, the wage basket itself might 'with propriety, be proposed as a standard measure.' Ricardo, he charged, by neglecting the so-called principle of compensation, had fallen into grave error: 'Whenever it is said that the "value of labour" rises in the progress of cultivation, a comparison is made between the value of a given quantity of labour at two different periods; and when it is added that wages rise in proportion to the quantity of labour required to produce them, objects are measured solely by the quantity of labour employed upon them, although the rate of profits may be totally different' (192n).

VIII SUPPLY CONDITIONS AND THE PROFIT RATE

The paper 'On the Measure of the Conditions Necessary to the Supply of Commodities' read to the Royal Society of Literature on 4 May 1825 summarizes *The Measure of Value.*[48] The emphasis is on the supply side; demand is accorded no formal role, the paper closing with the following remark: 'In this discussion I have purposely avoided using the term value ... [I]ndependently of value in use, which is readily understood, whenever we mean anything more by the term value, than the relation of the products of labour to each other at a given moment, we can only with any consistency mean that value which is the natural and necessary condition of their supply, and is adequate to reproduce them' (1825/1986, 7, 311). *Malthus was wholly at one with Ricardo on the primacy of supply conditions.*

The paper defends labour commanded, not as a rough and ready measure of value, but as the only conceivable accurate measure, and this despite years of criticism by Ricardo on grounds of the variability of labour itself. In fact, it is the stated purpose of the paper 'to show that the natural and necessary conditions of the supply of all commodities, not subject to a monopoly, are represented and measured by the labour which they will ordinarily, and on an average, command, and that no other object whatever can be substituted for labour, or can represent and measure the natural and necessary conditions of the supply of commodities' (301).[49]

The exercise proceeds on the assumption of zero-rent land so that no third factor complicates matters, the conditions of supply being those pertinent to the provision of labour and capital alone. All the objections to this procedure listed in the *Principles* of 1820 (see above, chapter 6: VIII) disappear from sight: 'The conditions of the supply of the whole quantity of agricultural products actually existing in any country, are, that the

48 The Society's *Transactions*, Vol. I, part 1 (1825–9), 171–80; in 1986, 7, 301–11

49 A note is attached explaining that '*the natural and necessary conditions of the supply of commodities* are precisely the same as *the natural and necessary costs of production*, when reduced to their simplest elements; but I have preferred the former expression, because the term *cost*, if not well guarded, is too apt to convey the idea of *money* expenditure.'

returns on the poorest land in cultivation should be adequate to pay the wages of the labour and the profits of the stock employed upon it; and as this land, or the last capital employed upon other land, yields little or no rent, while the produce obtained from lands that yield the highest rents will necessarily command exactly the same quantity of labour, it is obvious that rent, from the manner in which it enters into the composition of commodities, makes very little practical difference in the natural and necessary conditions of their supply, which will still be determined by the quantity of labour and profits necessary to produce them under the most unfavourable circumstances in which they continue to be brought to market' (307). Consequently, 'however various may be the ingredients of the capitals employed, or for however long or short a time they may be advanced, if we exclude rent and taxes, the conditions of the supply of commodities consist exclusively of the labour and profits necessary to their production and these two together are exactly represented by the quantity of labour which they will ordinarily and on average command.'[50]

The device of reducing capital to dated quantities of labour developed in *The Measure of Value* is nicely explained in the 1825 paper. Malthus starts from the simplest case of a timeless process, and thus zero profits, and works through to cases involving complex capital goods, the exercises designed to demonstrate that there exists no *product* that can be substituted for *labour* as measure of supply conditions. Thus, in the simplest process, involving the labour input alone, 'the only natural and necessary condition of the supply is the command of a day's labour. We cannot say that the conditions of the supply are the command of a certain quantity of cloth, iron, corn, or even money, unless we add that such quantity of cloth, iron, corn, or money, will command the necessary labour' (301). Here, 'the labour worked up in the commodity, and labour which it will command, are the same; and either may of course be taken as representing and measuring the condtions of the supply.' A second case involves the use of labour in time-consuming processes but without capital goods proper. The example devised is the production of simple tools themselves: 'Let us suppose that 20 days' labour, and 3 months' time were necessary for this purpose, it is quite obvious that when the articles were completed at the end of 3 months, they would be worth more in exchange, than the products of 20 days' labour brought to market immediately. If they were not, no person would produce them with a view to an exchange, and the conditions of their supply would not be fulfilled. The proportion in which they would be worth more in exchange, would depend upon their degree

50 This summary brings to mind various devices suggested by Longfield and J.S. Mill to assure the operation of the Ricardian inverse wage–profit relation even in complex capital-using processes. But, as will be seen below, Malthus does not seem to be concerned with the (economy-wide) determination of the profit rate.

of scarcity, compared with the products of the same quantity of labour brought to market immediately; and as the wages of the necessary labour were the only capital advanced, the rate of profits would be exactly measured by the excess of the labour for which they would exchange, when completed, above the quantity of labour which had been worked up in them' (302).

In this context Malthus writes as if the profit rate is both determined by and determines the excess of labour commanded over labour embodied: 'If when 20 days' labour had been worked up in them, they would exchange at the end of 3 months for 21 days' labour, profits would be 5 per cent for the quarter, or 20 per cent for the year; and vice versa, if profits were 20 per cent for the year, they would assuredly, on an average, exchange for 21 days' labour. In this case the labour worked up in the commodity, though the foundation, and by far the largest ingredient in the conditions of the supply, is not the sole ingredient; and without some additional remuneration for profits the commodity will not be supplied.' But in fact there is no explanation of why profits should be at 20 per cent per annum – *the profit rate is effectively taken as given.* Second, despite the reference to 'the *wages* of the necessary labour [as] the only capital advanced,' it is specifically 'the *labour* worked up in the commodity' that constitutes 'by far the largest ingredient in the conditions of supply.'

This emerges also in the passage that follows, representing labour commanded as an accurate measure of labour embodied plus profits combined, rather than of their individual contributions to costs: 'The labour which a commodity will ordinarily command, will not indeed, without other information, show the proportion in which the produce is divided between labour and profits, but it will always show the result of the two together. Thus, if tools of the kind above stated came to exchange for less labour, on an average, than before, though we should not be able to say whether this was owing to a saving of labour, or a fall of profits, or partly to the one, and partly to the other; yet we could infer with certainty, that the conditions of the supply had altered, and had been rendered more advantageous to the consumer' (303).

As in the simplest case nothing but labour would do as a measure of supply conditions. Were a *product* selected, a change in its exchange rate against 'tools' – whose value or supply conditions are being measured – might reflect a change in the supply conditions of that *measure* not of the tools: 'But, if we were to attempt to measure the conditions of the supply by any other object except labour, we could draw no such inference. If the tools would command a small quantity of beaver, deer, or peltry, this would be no proof that the conditions of the supply of the tools had altered, but might arise merely from its requiring more labour to obtain beaver, deer, or peltry.' This applies also to the use of *money* as a measure (306). Money could serve well only for short periods (308–9).

A third case involves the use of capital goods ('tools') in the production of a product ('timber'), and provides a fuller statement of the reduction of inputs to dated quantities of labour:

> It is evident, that the conditions of the supply of the timber, together with the tools, must be determined by the accumulated labour and profits worked up in the tools, added to the direct labour and profits required to cut down, prepare, and keep the timber. Let us suppose that this latter process requires in the same manner 20 days' labour, advanced on an average for 3 months; then omitting, for the sake of simplifying the calculation, the injury done to the tools; the conditions of the supply of the timber and tools together will be equal to 20 days' labour advanced for 6 months added to 20 days' labour advanced for 3 months. Twenty days' labour advanced for 6 months at two successive periods of 3 months each, if profits were 20 per cent per annum, would be 22 $\frac{5}{100}$ days, and 20 days' labour employed for 3 months would be 21 days' labour, equal together to 43 $\frac{5}{100}$. Now it is obvious, that this sum of labour and profits must be exactly the same as if we had estimated the conditions of the supply of the tools, or the accumulated labour and profits worked up in them, by the labour which they would command, and adding this labour to the labour employed in cutting down the timber, had considered the whole as advanced for 3 months. Thus the labour which the tools, when finished, would command, would be 21 days, which added to the 20 days would be 41 days; and 41 days advanced for 3 months would be equal to 43 $\frac{5}{100}$ days. (303–4)

The extended case also illustrated the complexity that different periods of production had to be reduced to a *uniform* period in order to 'determine' the profit rate (we still have to deal with the sense of 'determine'). This complexity is prefaced by a general formulation representing the profit rate in proportionate terms – a matter that will preoccupy us in chapter 10: 'In the case before adduced in which profits were considered as entering into the conditions of supply in their very simplest form, namely, that of mere labour advanced for a certain time, it was quite obvous that *the rate of profits must be determined by the excess of the labour for which the commodity would exchange after such time had elapsed, above the quantity of labour actually worked up in it*; or in other words, that the rate of profits must be determined by the proportion of the whole produce, which in a given period goes to repay the wages of the labour actually employed' (304; emphasis added). This proposition is said to be true of more complicated cases with appropriate adjustment: 'Thus in the last instance, we cannot determine the rate of profits by the proportion of the produce which goes to labour, if profits accumulate on one portion of the labour for 6 months, and on the other portion only for 3 months; but if for the first portion of labour with the profits upon it we substitute its equivalent, the labour which it will command, and suppose the whole labour advanced for the uniform period of 3 months, the conditions of the supply will not only be exactly the same as before stated, but the proportion which goes to labour will then determine the rate of profits. Thus, if we estimate the conditions of the supply of the tools by their value in immediate labour, which will be 21 days, and suppose that 41 days altogether are employed for 3 months, then if the tools and timber together will command 43 $\frac{5}{100}$ days' labour, it is a proof that the rate of profits is 5 per cent for the quarter, and 20 per cent for the year' (304–5).

Was this formulation designed to deal with *profit-rate determination*? The term 'determination' in the passage is inappropriate, for we are dealing with a single product. Malthus was writing loosely, intending rather *estimation*, with the profit rate (determined in some unspecified fashion) given to the industry, and was attempting to explain how complex processes involving different capital-investment periods can be reduced to the simplest case such that the profit rate (whatever it is) is still accurately recorded as the difference between total labour embodied and labour commanded.

The same issue re-emerges in the course of a yet more complex case involving capital-using processes. Here Malthus approaches the problem, first by assuming the profit-rate to be a *known* datum, and then as an alternative assumes it to be an *unknown*:

Let us now suppose that the tools and timber are applied to the making of a canoe which will take 200 days' labour, advanced on an average for a year; and if we also suppose, for the sake of simplifying the calculation, that the tools are worn out in the making of the canoe, we shall have three portions of labour and profits worked up in the canoe, that is 20 days' labour with a profit upon them for $1\frac{1}{4}$ years, and 200 days' labour with a profit on them for 1 year. And it is evident, that the amount of the conditions of the supply will be exactly the same whether we take these separate portions of labour and profits, and add them together, or substitute for the first two portions combined their equivalent in immediate labour [by the device of labour commanded], and consider the whole as employed for the uniform period of a year. Thus *supposing profits to be as before 20 per cent*, 20 days' labour advanced for 6 months at two separate periods, would, as before, be 22 $\frac{5}{100}$, which advanced again for a year would be 26 $\frac{46}{100}$; 20 days advanced for 3 months would be 21 days, which again advanced for a year would be 25 $\frac{20}{100}$; and 200 days advanced for 1 year would be 240 days. These added together make 291 $\frac{66}{100}$. Now if instead of adding the profits upon these portions of labour separately, we substitute for the two former with the profits upon them, their equivalents in immediate labour, we shall have as before 43 $\frac{5}{100}$ which added to the 200 days' labour directly employed, makes 243 $\frac{5}{100}$, and the profits upon these advances for 1 year will amount to exactly the same sum of labour, namely to 291 $\frac{66}{100}$ days; while, *on the supposition of our being ignorant of the rate of profits* it is obvious, that an estimate of all the advances, both accumulated and direct, in immediate labour, compared with the quantity of immediate labour for which the completed commodity will exchange, must express the proportion of the whole produce which in a given time goes to labour, and *show exactly the rate of profits.* (305–6; emphasis added)[51]

This formulation casts more light on our problem. Although profit-rate determination is an economy-wide consideration, in equilibrium all sectors will be generating the same return on capital so that, in principle, it should be possible to arrive at the general profit rate by investigating the labour embodied/labour commanded differential (assuming that all the appropriate adjustments to a uniform time period have been made) in any individual industry. In this sense the profit rate can be said to be 'determined' and not merely 'estimated' by the industry calculation. But we should still want to know why the differential between labour embodied and labour commanded emerging in any and all industries (taking them to be in their equilibrium state) was as it was and neither higher or lower.

There is a further piece of evidence to consider in this regard, and it might be decisive. It will be recalled that, while labour commanded is championed as an accurate measure of labour embodiment and profits combined, a change in labour commanded cannot serve to distinguish whether this is attributable to a change in the labour input *or in the profit rate* (above, p. 308). This caution regarding what a labour-commanded measure can and cannot do is repeated following an elaboration of the more-complex cases involving capital goods and materials, and this text confirms that appeal is made to an *externally* imposed profit rate.

After a strong statement of the zero-rent principle at both the extensive and intensive margins – strange to relate, reference is made to Adam Smith – Malthus summarizes his position: 'Consequently, in the most advanced stages of society, and in reference to the most complicated commodities, we have a very plain and simple measure of the conditions of their supply. If a commodity will in any country ordinarily and on an average exchange for a certain quantity of labour of that country, we may safely assume that such quantity of labour properly applied will reproduce the commodity; that is, will furnish the labour necessary to supply all the different portions of fixed and circulating capital, and all the immediate labour worked up in the production, together with such an additional quantity as will pay the ordinary profits of stock upon all the advances for

51 A note is attached allowing for the removal of the initial assumption that 'tools' are entirely used up, by the device of treating capital remaining as part of the final product: 'If the tools, or the fixed capital, be not worn out, which is the more frequent case, as the advances will then only be consumed in part, the whole produce of the accumulated and immediate labour employed must be considered as composed of the new produce obtained together with the remainder of the fixed capital, which remainder must be subtracted from the whole, in order to obtain the separate value of the new produce.'

the time that they have been advanced' (307). He then proceeds to the statement of concern to us here:

Now if a quantity of muslins of this description[52] were after a certain time to command on an average only 1,100 days' labour instead of 1,200, we could of course infer with certainty that the conditions of the supply had altered in favour of the consumer, though we could not at once say in which department the saving had taken place; whether in the quantity of immediate labour, owing to improved machinery or improved skill; whether in the quantity of labour required to purchase the raw materials, owing to lower freights and insurance, or cheaper production abroad; or whether in the quantity of labour representing profits, *owing to a general fall in the rate of profits.* Circumstances, however, might often point out to us where we were to look for the main part of the saving. If it were known for instance that improvements had been made in machinery, we should naturally expect to find that the amount of immediate labour had been essentially diminished; if it were understood that the foreign material had been produced with greater facility, or that freights, insurances, and duties had been essentialy decreased, we should expect to find a decided diminution in the labour required to purchase the raw cotton; *or if it were an acknowledged fact that the rate of profits had fallen,* we should immediately be led to look for a diminution in the labour representing profits both upon the advances of the different species of accumulated capital, and the advances of immediate labour. (308; emphasis added)

This formulation confirms that Malthus appealed to an 'external' explanation of profit-rate determination which might be applied to any particular industry. We shall return to this matter in chapter 10.

IX SUPPLY CONDITIONS AND THE LABOUR MARKET

One major issue remains to be discussed. Malthus raised the possible objection to the labour-commanded index that 'the quantity of labour might suddenly decrease or increase like any other commodity in which case it would not be a correct measure of the conditions of the supply'

52 The case in question is as follows: 'Thus if 600 yards of muslin of a certain quality would ordinarily command 1,200 days' labour, and such muslin were composed of three equal parts, one consisting of immediate labour, another of raw materials, and a third of the wear and tear of the machinery with the ordinary profits upon all the capital advanced by the last capitalist, it is plain that 400 days' labour would furnish all the immediate labour required; that 400 more would furnish all the labour necessary to produce the raw materials, or if *they* were foreign, the articles with which to purchase them, together with an adequate compensation for profits; and a third 400 would replace the labour consumed in the wear and tear of the machinery or fixed capital, and would further award to the capitalist the command of such an additional quantity of labour as would pay the ordinary rate of profits during the time that his whole capital was employed, and thus fulfil all the conditions of the supply.'

(1825/1986, 7, 309). He conceded that '[in] the case of a sudden scarcity and dearness of labour, the labour which a commodity made previously would command might not be sufficient to replace it,' but defended his position on the grounds that the disturbance 'could last but a very short time. Production cannot go on unless the labour necessary to produce the commodity can be put into motion, and some profit obtained by the capitalist. In the case supposed, goods and material capitals would be abundant compared with labour, and would sell for a time at a losing price; but this relative abundance would soon pass away, and when fresh labour came to be employed in producing new capitals and new goods, *these goods would necessarily be of sufficient value to replace the labour worked up in them, together with such an addition as would pay the new rate of profits,* and encourage the capitalist to proceed' (emphasis added).

The assertion that the abundance of goods and capital relative to labour would 'soon pass away' apparently refers, not to a corrective increase in labour supply which reduces the wage to its original level, but to a rise in money prices to accommodate the higher wage. This is implied by the statement that once the new production period is set in motion ('when fresh labour ...'), 'goods would necessarily be of sufficient value to replace the labour worked up in them ...,' such labour paid the new higher wage. After the accommodation of prices,[53] we end up with *unchanged* labour commanded. The labour-commanded index, therefore, fails to capture – Malthus perhaps would prefer one to say: *is not designed to capture* – those changes in supply conditions that reflect alterations in the labour market; only alterations in 'real' labour input are measured, and it is because these have not altered in the present case that labour commanded remains unchanged.[54] In effect, money-wage increases resulting from changes in 'real' labour-market conditions are treated on a par with purely nominal changes in the money wage resulting from a change in productivity in gold mining, that is, treated as a change in money *numéraire.* This amply confirms that Malthus's concern is labour input not wage costs in the analysis of value (see above, p. 308).

53 Malthus actually writes of the 'value' of the goods rising, which means their labour commanded rises. This is true in that the initial fall in labour commanded immediately following the money-wage rise, is ultimately corrected by the price increase the value of the goods rising to their original level.

54 It is true that the passage also alludes to a 'new profit rate' in the final adjustment. Possibly this is a reference to a *reduced* profit rate with the tighter labour market. The profit rate should not decline if firms can pass on their increased labour costs. Alternatively expressed, if labour embodied and commanded are both unchanged, the profit rate too is unchanged. If the profit rate is allowed to fall, then labour commanded should fall too, since the profit rate enters into supply conditions. The product price would not then fully compensate for the higher wage costs. This might be intended, but the brief reference to the 'new' profit rate gives us little to go on and, in the reverse case of a 'sudden' fall in the money wage, nothing is said of a 'new' profit rate.

In the reverse case of a 'sudden' *increase* in the labour supply, it is again clear that the final correction entails, *not* a reversal of the wage to its original level, but an adjustment of money costs involving now a fall in capital-goods prices:

On the other hand, in the case of a superabundance of labour from sudden importations, a commodity would command more labour than was necessary to replace it, though on *account of the accumulated labour in the capitals not having been affected by the new state of things, the power of producing the commodity would not be in proportion to the labour which it would command.* Thus supposing the extreme case of such a number of labourers being at once imported as suddenly to reduce the price of labour one half, it is obvious that all the commodities made before the fall in the price of labour would be scarce compared with the population, and would command much more labour than had been employed upon them, with the addition of ordinary profits; but neither would this state of things be of any duration. A considerable part of the additional number of labourers could not be employed on account of the scarcity of materials and machinery, while the remainder being set to work to supply this deficiency, *would very soon influence the quantity and prices of all capitals.* (310; emphasis added)[55]

Once more, when all adjustments have been completed, labour commanded can serve again in its function as a measure of value – in this particular case, a measure of unchanged dated labour and profit.

The measure was, in fact, specifically designed for *equilibrium* situations – 'the ordinary and natural state of things'; changes in the wage rate temporarily disturb the accuracy of the labour-commanded measure and are excluded: 'Till this [cost adjustment] had taken place, it is evident that the conditions of the supply would not be the natural and necessary conditions, the quantity of labour which a commodity would command would not be the ordinary and average quantity. Such cases, therefore, do not come within the pale of our proposition, which is, that the natural and necessary conditions of the supply of commodities not subject to any kind of monopoly are represented and measured by the labour which they will ordinarily and on an average command.' This proposition is said to correspond 'to that of Adam Smith respecting natural price, which states it to be that price which will pay the costs of production in the ordinary and natural state of things, and this proposition has never been considered as impugned by the accidental and temporary variations of the market prices of commodities, which are sometimes not sufficient and sometimes more than sufficient to reproduce them.'

Malthus himself obviously believed that no problems would be encoun-

55 No mention whatsoever is made of a change in the profit rate, suggesting that this was not seriously incorporated into the present analysis.

tered as far as concerns *secular movements of the wage.* Presumably such movements would be fully accommodated by prices in the manner outlined above.

* * *

The second paper for the Royal Society of Literature, read on 7 November 1827, formally sets out to elaborate the theme that (unless some exchange rate is specified) the term 'value' refers to *supply conditions* which are 'represented and measured' – not determined, one notes – by the labour 'ordinarily' commanded: 'On a former occasion [1825] I endeavored to show, that the quantity of common labour which a commodity will ordinarily command, represents and measures the ordinary conditions of its supply, or the natural and necessary costs of its production. It is now my object to show, that when the value of a commodity is mentioned without mentioning at the same time the article or articles in which it is to be estimated, it is generally understood to refer, and can only refer correctly, to the conditions of its supply, or the natural and necessary costs of its production' (1827b/1986, 7, 315).[56]

This paper, too, touches on the consequence for the labour-commanded measure of changes in the general wage rate. The specific problem relates to the effect of a fall in hours per workday in a particular industry. This disturbance is said to create no problem, the *worsening* of the conditions of supply of the product in question (linen) being appropriately reflected by the index: 'If, other things being the same, the people of a country at one time worked six hours, and at another twelve hours a day, it is obvious that, to produce the same quantity of linen goods, it would be necessary in the first case to pay the wages of double the number of labourers; the linen goods would be scarce, compared with the number of the producers;

56 As always the use of *money* as measure of a commodity's 'value' or production costs could be justified for only short periods when the cost of production of money – its own 'value' – was constant: 'Practically, it is certain that during periods of moderate extent we measure the values as well as the prices of commodities in the circulating medium, which we assume to be steady; and it will greatly assist our inquiry to ascertain what we are in the habit of considering as the characteristics of value, and the main causes of its rise or fall, while we are in possession of a measure which we are constantly applying, and consider as practically correct.' The money measurement of the 'value' of (say) cloth breaks down over *long periods* because of changes in the value (supply conditions) of the metal itself. Nor would a variety of other commodities mentioned serve to measure the 'value' of cloth, for their supply conditions worsen during the course of growth (318–19). The appropriate measure, the reader is led to conclude, *must* be labour commanded. Needless to say, if labour is not all of one kind, the wage structure is required to arrive at a common unit, and Malthus alludes favourably to this orthodox practice, at least over periods during which we consider money as remaining of the same value (316–17).

and the degree of value occasioned by the scarcity in the one case, and the relative plenty in the other, would be correctly estimated by the quantity of labour which ten yards of linen would ordinarily command in the first case, compared with the quantity of labour which it would ordinarily command in the second' (319).

How precisely will this outcome, so favourable for the measuring procedure, emerge? Malthus does not spell out the argument, but we can do it for him. As he maintains elsewhere, within any *given* period one may work with money wages and money prices. Now, in the case at hand, the hourly wage would be higher in period II than period I because of the reduction in the length of the workday; and since the number of hours required to produce cloth is unchanged over time, and since *each hour* must be paid a higher money wage, it follows that money wage costs per unit of output rise, assuring a higher price of linen. Now Malthus's result of an incease in labour commanded by linen is an optical illusion. It only occurs if the index is the *constant daily wage*. If we take the *higher hourly wage* – and it would seem most appropriate to do so – there will be *no* increase in labour commanded; the effective wage increase generates purely nominal change in the prices of goods. This latter result duplicates that obtained in the 1825 paper – namely, that once the system had settled down after a posited wage change, it would be found that prices have risen to reflect the higher money wage, implying no change in labour commanded. As we noted there (above, p. 313), the measure fails – or is not designed – to record the *worsened* conditions of supply indicated by higher wage costs per labour unit.

Malthus had more to say on the problem of a changing wage rate. The context is the earlier discussion of the wage structure, when we assume periods short enough to justify a *money* measure of production costs. He first observed that the *money price* of a commodity will accurately reflect increased labour productivity attributable to the use of machinery, though the money wage should be constant: 'if the introduction of machinery in any particular employment renders the labour in that employment much more efficient, without rendering it more difficult or requiring more skill; as the money price of such labour will continue the same, we invariably call its value the same. The goods, indeed, produced by such labour will be more plentiful compared with the number of producers, and consequently will be lower in price and value. But though the labour has thus become more efficient and productive, yet while its price remains unaltered, we consider its value as unaltered' (316). Although Malthus in this context was assuming constancy in the 'value' (production costs) of money and proceeds in terms of a money rather than a labour-commanded measure, a labour-commanded measure must always serve at least as well. And in fact the commodity will command less labour, since its price has fallen, while the money wage is said to be unchanged. *But what if the money wage were to rise?* The passage precludes increases in the money wage which reflect higher labour productivity; but what if the new technological circumstances render labour 'more difficult or requiring more skill,' thereby (as it were) raising the cost of producing labour? Will the labour-commanded index break down? Apparently it can still serve: There are two forces at play acting on the product price: (1) the higher output per *hour* of labour; (2) the increased *weighting* of each hour by the higher difficulty or skill requirements. On balance, the new technology would be installed only if (1) exceeded (2), so that a reduced commodity price is still the probable outcome reflecting some *net* improvement in supply conditions (a net cost reduction). And this is reflected in a reduced labour command, since the money wage rises.

But this is a special case involving a *reduced* commodity price with technical progress. Were we to assume an *exogenous* deterioration in actual or perceived working conditions, labourers coming to regard certain tasks with increased displeasure, the scarcity conditions of such labour, and therefore of its products, would be worsened, generating a *higher* money price of the product. Money reflects the worsened supply conditions. But since the money wage increases also, there is no assurance of an increased labour commanded, in which case the measure would fail. *This perspective confirms the original result that the labour-commanded index does not serve its designated task in conditions of fluctuating wages.*

X THE MEASURE IN A GROWTH CONTEXT

A major concern in *The Measure of Value* is to accommodate the allowance for the profit rate in the 'natural value' of any product. This concern is brought to bear in the growth context, Malthus assuming initially constant productivity in all sectors.[57] Upon an assumed profit-rate decline, the natural value (say, of cloth) falls *despite unchanged labour productivity*: 'With regard to those [commodities] which had continued to cost the same quantity of accumulated and immediate labour, we could not say that they were of the same value, unless we were prepared to assert that the value of commodities is determined solely by the labour employed upon them, not only when the rate of profits is the same but when it is totally different' (1823b/1986, 7, 192). The 'natural value' of corn – the table in *The Measure of Value* (see appendix to this chapter) is restricted entirely to corn, and corn alone enters the wage basket – like that of any other commodity, and assuming unchanged agricultural productivity, will also fall. Here there occurs no necessary change in the cloth/corn exchange rate.

57 Use of the labour-commanded index in a growth context must accommodate the requirement at each stage of a full price adjustment in commodity markets (above, p. 314).

But though the lower 'natural value' of a unit of corn will – again like that of any product – be reflected in lower labour commanded, the corn wage, whatever its magnitude, is necessarily of constant 'natural value,' always commanding a unit of labour. Given labour productivity, a fall in the profit rate reflects – 'as a self-evident truth' – a rise in the corn wage, but that higher basket remains of constant value, composed of the greater labour input in the larger basket compensated precisely by the reduced profit rate: 'If the increased reward of the labourer takes place without an increase of produce, this cannot happen without a fall of profits, as it is a self-evident truth, that given the quantity of the produce to be divided between labour and profits, the greater the portion of it which goes to labour the less will be left for profits. What then will be the result? It will appear that the value of the produce has fallen, and the value of wages, or of labour, will have remained the same. To obtain any given portion of the produce the same quantity of labour is necessary as before, but profits being diminished, the value of the produce is decreased; while this diminution of profits in reference to the value of wages is just counterbalanced by the increased quantity of labour necessary to procure the increased produce awarded to the labourer, leaving the value of labour the same as before' (197). Conversely, in the event of a fall in the corn wage, the natural value of a given quantity of corn *rises*, reflecting (1) the unchanged labour embodied plus (2) the higher profit rate; for the corn wage is of constant natural value, the higher profits exactly counterbalancing the lower labour embodied in the (smaller) corn basket: 'If instead of labourers being sent out of the country, labourers were imported, the result would be just opposite. A smaller quantity of produce would be awarded to the labourer and profits would rise. A given quantity of produce, which had been obtained by the same quantity of labour as before, would rise in value on account of the rise of profits, while this rise of profits, in reference to the wages of the labourer, would be balanced by the smaller quantity of labour necessary to obtain the diminished produce awarded to the labourer.'

In reviewing the foregoing exercises involving constant productivity, we should keep in mind that there are two ways at arriving at the 'natural value' of products: (1) calculating labour embodied in the process plus the profit on that labour – the supply conditions; and (2) calculating labour commanded which constitutes the *measure* of supply conditions. Analytically, it is more satisfying to proceed via the direct route (1), treating cloth and corn by the same procedure. But the same result emerges via route (2) – at least for corn, since by assumption cloth does not enter the wage basket. Thus, in the first case, where the lower profit rate reflects a higher corn wage, a larger basket is required to acquire a given amount of labour so that each unit of corn must fall in its labour-commanded value; in the second case, a smaller basket suffices to obtain given labour (the reason for the higher profit rate) so that each unit of corn must rise in its labour-commanded value. In both cases we achieve the result arrived at by route (1).

Assume now a *fall* in agricultural productivity, given the corn wage, and a corresponding fall in the profit rate. Cloth falls in its natural value relative to corn – it is subject only to a reduced profit rate, whereas corn is also subject to higher labour embodiment – and we predict a rise in the cloth/corn exchange rate.[58] But can one be more precise regarding the behaviour of *the natural value of corn*? It turns on the extent of the rise in labour embodiment relative to the fall in the profit rate. Since, on the present assumptions, the profit-rate decline reflects precisely the productivity deterioration, the two forces cancel, and the natural value per unit of corn is unchanged. This can be seen via route (2): Since the corn wage is constant, the same number of corn units are required to acquire a specific quantum of labour so that each unit remains of constant 'value' in terms of labour command.

The principle that 'natural value' incorporates profits is applied to all commodities *including the monetary metal* – provided money is produced with a time-consuming process. Falling agricultural productivity in the case of constant corn wages implies, we have just seen, a constant 'natural value' of corn, whereas cloth, and *money* too, are subject to falling 'natural values.' The money price as well as the cloth price of corn thus *rises*, as does the money wage: 'Supposing ... money always to require in its production the same quantity of labour and capital, it will regularly *fall* in value in the progress of cultivation and population; while labour being uniform in value will rise in money price, and the demand for corn increasing, compared with the demand for labour, the money price of corn will probably rise still more. But if the labourers were paid at all times exactly the same quantity of corn, (which, however, cannot be the case,) the value of corn, like the value of wages, would be constant and the variations of fertility would only show themselves in the enormous variations of profits' (201).[59]

A note critical of Ricardo spells out that '[it] is this rise in the money price of labour occasioned by the fall of profits, which Mr. Ricardo considers as that necessary rise in the *value* of labour on which he makes so much depend in his system; but if the foregoing reasoning be well founded, it follows that this rise is not a rise in the *value* of labour, but a fall in the value of money' (201n). In a summary of the distinguishing features of a fall in the value of the precious metals resulting from diminishing

58 This can be seen also by the following argument: If the 'natural value' of cloth falls because of given labour input–cum–lower profit, it must be that the labour commanded by a given cloth output also falls which can only be the case if the price of corn rises *relative* to that of cloth.

59 The *money* wage rises simply because the value of labour is constant and the value of the metal falls with the fall in profits.

agricultural returns or the so-called primary cause as distinct from purely monetary causes – 'the progressive cultivation of poorer land ... operating universally and necessarily on the precious metals in common with all other commodities, and raising or lowering them with regard to labour' – Malthus adds that the *structure* of manufacturing prices may alter: 'The marks which distinguish a fall in the value of the precious metals, arising from the primary cause, are, – a rise in the money price of raw produce and labour, without a general rise in the price of wrought commodities. All of them, indeed, as far as they are composed of raw produce, will have a tendency to rise; but, in a large class of commodites, this tendency to rise will be more than counterbalanced by the effect of the fall of profits. – Some therefore will rise, and some will fall, as I stated in my last work,[60] according to the nature of the capitals employed upon them, compared with those which produce money; and while the money prices of corn and labour very decidedly increase, the prices of commodities, taken on the average, may possibly remain not far from the same' (212).

We have assumed so far a given corn wage and reduced agricultural productivity. But in the normal course of growth, the corn wage *cannot* remain constant (see chapter 10: II). Since it necessarily declines, a given amount of corn commands more labour; that is, there occurs a 'real' increase in the natural value of corn per unit (not just a 'money' or 'nominal' increase), though labour (identified with the wage, and thus of constant natural value) as before rises only nominally: 'In the actual state of things, corn generally rises in the progress of cultivation, not only nominally, but really, as may be seen in the eighth column [see Appendix], while labour, it is evident, can only rise nominally' (202). This result also emerges by route (1): Since the effect of a higher labour input outweighs that of a lower profit rate – part of the incidence of diminishing returns is born by labourers in the reduced corn wage – the 'natural value' of corn per unit rises.

Following Malthusian principles, what occurs to the 'natural values' of metal or manufactures in the event of a decline in the corn-wage rate? Again we can approach the problem *either*: (1) by calculating their labour input plus profit; *or* (2) by estimating the labour commanded by a given amount of silver or cloth. But (2) would require preliminary knowledge of the appropriate relative prices, which we do not have. Only (1) is open to us. Now, by assumption, there is no change in their labour inputs, but the profit rate falls which indicates a lower 'natural value.' But the 'natural value' of corn rises, so that there is a relatively sharper increase in the money (and the cloth) price of corn than in the case of a constant corn wage.

In all of this Malthus has assumed *Ricardian gold* – a commodity pro-

60 The reference is to the *Principles* (1820), on which see above, chapter 6: VII.

duced with capital. For in terms of his own ideal money, a product of labour alone, labour commanded would be unaffected by a fall in the profit rate; that is, money wages are fixed by the productivity of mining. The rise in the 'natural value' of corn as the corn wage declines will, however, be captured in this case, too, by the variation in the money price of corn, which will reflect only the rise occurring on the corn side rather than that force in combination with a fall occurring on the money side: 'if money were obtained in the way in which its value would unquestionably be the most constant, all these variations would appear in the money prices of commodities, whenever the demand for labour varied; while the money price of a given quantity of labour would remain the same' (198).

XI THE RICARDO–MALTHUS EXCHANGE, 1823

A letter to Malthus dated 29 April 1823 contains Ricardo's initial response to *The Measure of Value*: 'After the most attentive consideration which I can give to your book, I cannot agree with you in considering labour, in the sense in which you use it, as a good measure of value' (Ricardo, 1951–73, IX, 280).[61] 'You may, if you please, arbitrarily select labour as a measure of value, and explain all the science of Political Economy by it, in the same way as any other man might select gold, or any other commodity, but you can no more connect it with a principle, or shew its invariability, than he could' (280–1). In arguing thus, Ricardo was conveying a point made in his own *Principles* directed there against Adam Smith – namely, that, whereas the labour embodied in a commodity 'is under many circumstances an invariable standard indicating correctly the variations of other things' – provided such embodiment is unchanged and assuming uniform factor proportions – labour commanded 'is subject to as many fluctuations as the commodities compared with it. Adam Smith, after most ably showing the insufficiency of a variable medium, such as gold and silver, for the purpose of determining the varying value of other things, has himself, by fixing on corn or labour, chosen a medium no less variable' (1951–73, I, 14). Labour embodied in a good could in principle be fixed, but labour commanded could not be fixed, given the fact that labour itself varies with altered conditions in the labour market; and, as he points out in the letter as well as the text, this applies to every commodity in the system, all varying independently against labour according to circumstances. The substance of Ricardo's primary objection relates, therefore, to Malthus's choice of 'a variable measure for an invariable standard. Who can say that a plague which should take off half our people would not alter the value of labour? We might indeed agree to transfer the variation to the commodities, and

61 This letter set off an exchange on value that lasted almost until Ricardo's death on 11 September.

to say that they had fallen and not that, labour had risen, but I can see no advantage in the change' (1951–73, IX, 282). Even should the corn wage be given, labour can still vary with an alteration in cost conditions in agriculture.

A further letter to Malthus (28 May) carries his objections a step further. In a now non-extant letter, to which Ricardo's was a reply, Malthus had alluded to the commodity ideally appropriate as measure – namely, shrimps or silver produced by labour alone in a process not requiring capital; since by construction the 'money' wage is constant, his ideal money becomes an exact proxy for labour command. Ricardo responded that such a measure serves adequately as index of 'absolute' value *only* if the commodities whose measurement is entailed are themselves also produced without capital, that is, in timeless processes: 'You contend that the shrimps and the silver, picked up by labour alone on the seashore, are accurate measures of the value of cloth ... You say "It is conceded that when labour alone is concerned in the production of commodities, and there is no question of time, both the absolute and exchangeable values of such commodities may be accurately measured by the quantity of labour employed upon them." Nothing can I think be more correct, and it is perfectly accordant with what I have been saying. Your mistake appears to me to be this, you shew us that under certain conditions a certain commodity would be a measure of absolute value, and then you apply it to cases where the conditions are not complied with, and suppose it to be a measure of absolute value in those cases also' (298–9).

By 'absolute value' Ricardo intended labour embodied (for a specific period) in contrast with Malthus's labour-cum-profits. Yet more than definition is at stake. Ricardo objected further that 'you ... deceive yourself when you think you prove your proposition, because your proof only amounts to this, that your measure is a good measure of exchangeable value, but not of absolute value' (299). This objection is clarified in a further letter (dated 13 July), where Ricardo admitted that his own measure failed to capture the labour coefficients of production of the product under investigation, whereas *both* measures – indeed, any product – served to indicate exchangeable value: 'My money measure would not measure the quantity of labour worked up in commodities. I have admitted it over and over again. I am also ready to admit that your money measure will measure exactly the quantity of labour and profits together of which commodities are composed, but so will my money measure. Neither of them will measure the quantity of labour alone worked up in commodites, but they will *both measure the quantity of labour and profits together of which commodities are composed*' (304; emphasis added).

The essential point in all this is that the *unattainable desideratum* was a measure that captures solely changes affecting the commodity being measured and not the measure. Any objection to Ricardian gold – which required capital as well as labour – on the grounds that it failed to capture such changes, applied with a vengeance to Malthusian money requiring labour alone. And Malthus also had no right to claim invariability for his money – so that the source of exchange-rate changes could be found in the commodity under measurement, not in the measure – merely because (by construction) the metal always commands a given amount of labour, and this notwithstanding real-wage variability (304–6).

Malthus's reply, dated *circa* 21 July, to Ricardo's letter of 13 July contains the essence of his position that a commodity produced with capital and labour would *not* do as a measure of the values of commodities that also require capital and labour – the precise reverse of Ricardo's position; the only conceivable measure was his own money proxy for labour commanded – namely, a product produced by labour alone.[62] The point here is that a fall in profits would leave *Ricardo's* gold price of cloth unchanged, while his own silver measure would indicate a fall in the cloth price, thus capturing an essential component of cloth's conditions of supply (306–7). As in *The Measure of Value* (1823b/1986, 7, 187, 189), the implications of the necessity to allow profits in natural value could be elucidated by comparing cases where profits must be paid with the case where labour alone is required, taking for granted that 'these profits can only be reckoned in labour because the advances consist only in labour' (307). This is said to lead 'incontestably' to the constancy of the 'natural and absolute value' of a given quantity of labour – an allusion to the constant value of the (possibly variable) *wages* per man (307–8). The letter reiterates the claim that the 'peculiar and preeminent fitness' of the measure in capturing variations in 'natural and absolute' value, that is, in costs, had been *proven.* There was nothing *arbitrary* about the selection (308). The table of the *Measure* was not even required, since all flowed 'intuitively,' including the constant value of labour during the course of 'progress,' an allusion to the constant labour commanded by the wage basket despite falling agricultural productivity. Here Malthus reads like Ricardo in that he represents the profit rate as varying inversely with labour's proportionate share, though this proposition is then used to *justify the constant value of the wage basket*: 'The other steps follow as strictly as any proposition in Euclid. The proof which may

62 This strong position is brought into sharp focus when compared with the following accommodating remark to Ricardo in 1818: 'I am surprised, with you that Major Torrens should puzzle himself so long with his peculiar objections to your measure of value. For myself, I own, I am quite satisfied with your own concessions; and if as you yourself acknowledge, taxation, foreign materials, and the different quantities of fixed and circulating capitals employed, all prevent the exchangeable value of commodities from being determined by the labour which they have cost in production, I should say, it followed that your theory was only true *caeteris paribus*, which might be equally said of the cost of the [foreign] materials. Given the wages of labour, the profits of stock, and the taxes, the exchangeable value of commodities will vary with the cost of the materials' (24 February 1818; in Ricardo, 1951–73, VII, 253).

be said almost to be of the class called intuitive is in reality complete without the table or the parts immediately connected with it. These parts merely supply a further confirmation of the truth by answering the following question. How comes it about that labour should remain of the same value in the progress of society, when it is known that it must require more labour to produce it? And the answer to this question is, that as profits depend upon the *proportion* of the whole produce which goes to labour, it must necessarily happen that the increase of value occasioned by the additional quantity of labour will be exactly counterbalanced by the diminution in the amount of profits, leaving the value of the labour the same' (308–9).

Malthus none the less admitted that his own constant value of the wage was not universally true. If between the time that labour is embodied in producing the corn wage and the payment of that corn wage there occurs an alteration in labour-market conditions – say, a sudden fall in population – the proposition that the labour embodied in the wage basket-cum-profits equalled the labour commanded by the wage basket breaks down: 'I however expressed myself without sufficient care, when I intimated that if any number of labourers were imported or exported the value of labour would remain the same. This will only be true after the supply comes to be affected by the increased or diminished number of labourers. If the corn obtained by 20 men be divided among ten, then the value of the wages of 10 men will be much less than the quantity of labour employed to produce them with the addition of profits, and vice versa' (309). However, he had covered himself in *The Measure of Value* (1823b/1986, 7, 195) itself by the condition that his proposition 'requires ... that the wages of the labourers who produce the wages to be advanced should be the same as the wages advanced; which will always be the case except in very violent and unnatural changes, and would be the case in the instances supposed after the first year' (1951–73, IX, 309). He was, in short, not dealing with disequilibrium states, as we concluded earlier (above, p. 314).

Ricardo found Malthus's admission that the value of labour may in certain circumstances be *variable* to be ruinous: 'By the concession which you make in your last letter you appear to give up your measure, for you say that "you expressed yourself without sufficient care, when you intimated that if any number of labourers were imported or exported the value of labour would remain the same." This is a large concession indeed, and I think entirely subverts your measure ...' (3 August; 320–1). Though the concession allowed only that constant labour value precluded changes in the corn-wage rate between the production and the payment of wage goods, Ricardo claimed that it undermined the whole scheme extending to secular analysis, having in mind wage changes reflecting prudential population control and the like. But the concession itself – 'If the corn obtained by 20 men be divided among ten, then the value of the wages of 10 men will be much less than the quantity of labour employed to produce them with the addition of profits' – was riddled with difficulties, since it assumed a given profit rate: 'What profits? They might have been 50 pct. You speak of profits in this place as if they were a fixed amount, and forget that they fall when wages rise' (321). In fact, the main proposition itself, that 'every commodity exchanges for two quantities of labour, one equal to the quantity actually worked up in it, another equal to the quantity which the profits will command,' was unacceptable (323). It treated the profit component as a sort of supplement to the initial labour embodiment independent of the wage paid that labour, neglecting the fact that the profit rate varied precisely because of changes in the value of labour between the time labour is embodied in the commodity and the time it comes to market (323–4). As for Malthus's so-called proof of the constant value of labour (that is, of the wage basket) despite secular increases in labour input in the basket, which ran in terms of the Ricardo-like *proportionality* theorem (above, pp. 323–4), that was a tissue of semantic non-sequiturs: 'We are enquiring about the meaning which should be attached to the words "increase of value" "diminution of value." You tell me that increase of value means an increased power of commanding labour: I deny that this definition is a correct one, because I deny the invariability of the standard measure you have chosen, and to prove its invariability you speak of the proportions in which the whole produce is divided, and that if wages have more profits have less; all which is true, but what connection do you prove between this proposition and the invariability in your measure of value?' (324).

Malthus replied on 11 August that his concession regarding fluctuations in labour supply which alter the wage between the production of the wage goods and their actual payment related to a special case such that a sudden fall in labour might generate negative profits. The analysis of *trend* remained unaffected. And in fact he withdrew his concession: 'You were ... inclined to draw much too large inferences from my concession than it would have warranted, *if I had adhered to it.* In fact it only supposed an exception in the case of a very violent and sudden change occurring in the interval between the time of the production of the food of the labourer, and the time of its being paid as wages, which would very rarely be so much as a year, and the effect of which would be quite at an end after that time had expired. The concession therefore would not apply either to any natural increase of population, or any retardation in the rate of it from prudence' (336; emphasis added).

The objection to his 'main proposition' on the grounds that, should the money wage rise with a higher corn price, profits will fall – that is, that profits fall because the value of labour has risen – Malthus rebuts, by arguing: (1) that Ricardo's higher money wage constituted nothing but a nominal fall in the value of money (a nice case of circular reasoning since it implicitly presumes labour commanded to be the measure); and (2) that the '*natural* and *correct* way of estimating profits' was by calculating the difference between labour embodied and labour commanded, avoiding use of a money estimates (338; see also 307, above p. 323). And from the circumstances that labour commanded provided an accurate index of the profit rate, followed the constant value of labour – that is, of the wage basket: 'But if we measure profits by the difference between the labour advanced and the labour which the commodity will command, and (excluding the variable article money) I would ask how we can estimate profits but upon the actual advances, which are acknowledged to be accumulated and immediate labour, then it appears to me to follow as clear as the sun, that if value as you say in the beginning of your letter is made up of labour and profits, the variable wages which command the same quantity of labour must be of the same value, *because* they will always have cost in their production the same quantity of labour, with the addition of the profits upon that labour' (338–9). Ricardo's error was to neglect the profit element in calculating the cost of producing the wage basket, with the result that a fall in labour productivity is recorded as an increase in the *value* of (say) a constant wage basket (339).[63] As always, he denied that he set out with a *definition* of what an 'invariable value of labour' consists in – it was the *conclusion*. He denied in effect that he had arbitrarily chosen labour commanded as measure so that the wage (possibly variable) has constant 'value' by definition; rather it *must* be of constant value by the pure logic of the case: 'The invariability of the value of labour is indeed my *conclusion*, but by no means the definition with which I set out' (340).

Ricardo leapt on Malthus's withdrawal of his admission that his mode of reasoning precluded wage fluctuations between production and payment of wages: 'It is a prudent step in you to withdraw your concession for I am sure that your theory could not stand with it' (15 August; 345). As for the main objection to the Ricardian measure of value – that, because it entailed a process requiring capital (and therefore involving profits), it failed to measure accurately changes in profits as they affect other commodities – the tables could be turned against Malthus's measure; for, if the Ricardo measure requiring both capital and labour failed to deal accurately with commodities produced with different capital/ labour ratios, then Malthus's requiring no capital must *a fortiori* fail. Here Ricardo once again allowed readily that his own measure – and all other conceivable measures – is imperfect, something Malthus no longer admitted regarding his own measure; the best to hope for was choice of a measure involving a capital/labour ratio similar to that of 'the greater number of commmodities' in the economy (346–7).

63 In fact the constancy for Ricardo of the *money* value of a commodity produced with the same factor ratios as money provided a precise parallel. There occurs no change in the money price because the profit rate compensated exactly for the wage variation (339–40).

That Malthus's measure did not have the supposed *universal* applicability attributed to it was proven by its inability to deal with the case of an *increase* in labour embodiment in a product (cloth) which none the less exchanges for *less* labour should the cloth wage rate rise – that is, is of lower 'value.' This sort of situation was precluded in the case of products such as Malthus's shrimps or gold produced without capital – for a deterioration in productivity in shrimping or mining is necessarily reflected in a fall in the shrimp or gold wage – but not in the general case (348–9).

Later remarks in the same letter reiterate Ricardo's insistance upon the *arbitrary* nature of any measure selected. Alternative measures will record profit (or their non-existence) differently, but there was no overwhelming reason for Malthus's choice (349–50). But in fact it was highly desirable to avoid a measure yielding a constant value of the wage, which from the labourer's perspective made little sense: 'The labourer, however, who lived by his labour, would find it difficult to be persuaded that his labour was of the same value at two periods, in one of which he had abundance of food and clothing, and in another he was absolutely starving for want. What he might think would certainly not affect the philosophy of the question, but it would be at least as good a reason against the measure you propose as that of the farmer in favor of it, when he found that he had no profits because he had no greater command of labour, although he might have more corn or more money' (350). And that the value of labour can alter[64] meant that the capitalist whose process yields £10 net on £100 could be represented as possessing an *increase* in value – and thus as having made a profit in money on his initial investment – although his £100 would now (one understands Ricardo intends the next round of production) command *less* labour than did the original £100 in the event that labour *rises*: 'You call every increase of value nominal which is not an increase in the measure you propose; – I do not object to your doing so, but those who do not agree with you in the propriety of adopting this measure may argue very consistently in saying they are possessed of more value when they have £110 than when they had £100, although the larger sum may not when it is realised command so much labour as the smaller sum did before, because they not only admit but contend that labour may rise and fall in value, and therefore in respect to labour he may be poorer although he possesses a greater value' (349–50). This same perspective is repeated at the very close of the correspondence (31 August). The point is there made that, even with Malthus's measure, and assuming that the labour commanded by a product exceeds its labour embodiment, there was, *pace* Malthus, no assurance that the process can continue profitably should the wage rate increase: 'I know that you will say that provided his produce is

64 Ricardo was here using the term to indicate a change in the commodity wage, but the argument would apply to changes in costs of producing a given commodity wage.

sure to command a certain quantity of labour he is sure of being able to reproduce, not so if he estimates in any other thing, because that thing and labour may have undergone a great relative alteration. But may not the real alteration be in the value of labour, and if he act on the presumption of its remaining at its then rate may he not be woefully mistaken, and be a loser instead of a gainer? Your argument always supposes labour to be of an uniform value, and if we yielded that point to you there would be no question between us. A manufacturer who uniformly used no other measure of value than that which you recommend would be as infallibly liable to great disappointments as he is now exposed to in the vulgar variable medium in which he is accustomed to estimate value' (381–2).

We return to the letter of 15 August. Ricardo, who obviously did not deny that the value of most commodities comprises labour and profits, could not fathom Malthus's insistence that 'the variable wages which command the same quantity of labour must be of the same value, *because* they will always cost in their production the same quantity of labour, with the addition of the profits upon that labour' (cited above, p. 326). The rationale offered for the fall in the value of corn with a rise in the corn wage – for Malthus a wage per labour unit of 8 qrs. implies a value in labour commanded of 0.125, and at 10 qrs. a value reduced to 0.1 – was unacceptable since there occurs no change in the labour input *per unit* of corn: 'I confess that I cannot see the connection of this conclusion with the premises ... Whatever you give to the labourer is made up of labour and profits, and therefore the value of labour is constant! This is your proposition. To me it wants every quality of clearness. I find that at one time I give a man 10 bushels of wheat for the same quantity of his labour for which at another time I give him 8 bushels: Wheat according to you falls in the proportion of 10 to 8: I ask, why? and your answer is because "as the positive value of the labour worked up in the wages increases, the positive value of the profits (the other component part of their whole value) diminishes exactly in the same degree." Now does this positive value refer to the same quantity of wheat? certainly not, but to two different quantities, to 10 bushels at one time to 8 at another' (350–1).[65]

The answer to this – on Malthus's terms (above, pp. 325–6) – would be that, despite constant labour input per unit of corn, the profit-rate decline (implied by the rise in the corn wage) must be allowed in estimating natural value or conditions of supply. It will be helpful to summarize the elements comprising Malthus's logic: (1) Supply conditions included an allowance for the profit rate as well labour embodied; (2) labour commanded can be shown to measure accurately supply conditions; (3) *therefore*, the value of *labour*, that is, the labour commanded *by the wage basket*,

65 The extract indicated by the ellipses at the outset of this passsage insists that to accept that value comprises labour and profits conceded nothing of substance to Malthus.

is constant so that any rise in the corn wage implies a fall in the per unit value of corn; (4) since by assumption agricultural productivity is unchanged, the lower value of corn must be attributable to a lower profit rate – the counterpart of the higher corn wage supposed. One must note that, though the constant value of the wage basket can be said to follow *definitionally* – value being defined as labour commanded – the choice of the measure was justified for Malthus at steps (1) and (2).

Ricardo, as we know, did not accept the argument. Malthus, he maintained, had failed to provide a satisfactory rationale for the necessary constancy of the value of the wage paid labour: 'I still think that the invariability of your measure is the *definition* with which you set out, and not the *conclusion* to which you arrive by any legitimate argument' (351–2). In fact, there *was* no accurate measure, and Malthus had merely selected one among *imperfect* measures – and selected unwisely by choosing an unrepresentative commodity requiring labour alone. All measures were necessarily imperfect, since the existence of non-uniform capital/labour ratios precluded accurate measurement of changes in the cost conditions of particular commodities; it was not the labour component that created the problem, he pointed out further, but the profits element, a reference to the effect of changes in distribution on relative value: 'My complaint against you is that you claim to have given us an accurate measure of value, and I object to your claim, not that I have succeeded and you have failed, but that we have both failed – *that there is not and cannot be an accurate measure of value,* and that the most that any man can do is to find out a measure of value applicable in a great many cases and not very far deviating from accuracy in many others ... [Y]our measure as well as mine will measure variations arising from more or less labour being required to produce commodities, but the difficulty is respecting the varying proportions which go to labour and profits. The alteration in these proportions alters the relative value of things in the degree that more or less of labour or profit enter into them, and *for these variations there has never been, and I think never will be any perfect measure of value*' (352; emphasis added).

In this passage, we find the key to the difference between the two perspectives. Their common concern is measurement of 'absolute value.' But all depends on the perception of this concept, and that perception differed between the correspondents without their being fully aware. In the foregoing passage, it is true that Ricardo seems to treat it in the same manner as Malthus to include labour *and profits*; but this is illusory, an illusion created by the fact that Malthus has set the agenda in his *Measure of Value*, obliging Ricardo to abide as far as possible within a Malthusian framework.[66] That Ricardo's own concept of 'absolute value' was *technologi-*

66 It is noteworthy that in his own *independent* writings Ricardo almost invariably works in terms of a change in the wage rate with profits treated as a (formal) residual, whereas in the present context he proceeds by direct reference to the profit rate.

cal, relating to labour input (and its time of investment) and excluding allowance for the profit rate, is clear from the fact that he points specifically to problems created by the effect on relative prices (in terms of any measure) of a change in the profit rate specifically in the event of *non-uniform* factor ratios. If his 'absolute value' included the profit rate, his case would have held up equally in the event of *uniform* factor proportions; any change in the profit rate leaving prices in terms of a measure similarly produced unaffected, disqualifying the measure as an index of changes in supply conditions inclusive of the profit rate.[67]

* * *

In a letter to McCulloch dated 21 August 1823, Ricardo repeated his position that 'we cannot have a perfect [measure] for there is no such thing in nature ... All we can do is to make the best choice amongst confessed imperfect measures' (361).[68] Malthus's measure would serve best only 'if the number of commodities produced by labour alone were the most numerous, but ... as the great mass of commodities is produced by the union of labour and capital for a certain length of time, I have nothing to amend in the choice I have made; I consider it a mean; Malthus's is at one extreme of the scale, old oak trees are at the other. In one there is nothing but labour, in the other there is nothing but accumulations of capital from profits with scarcely any labour whatever, and therefore they are both unfit measures of value.'

Malthus responded – in his last letter to Ricardo, dated 25 August – that there was 'no impropriety in saying with Adam Smith and myself that labour will *measure* not only that part of the whole value of the commodity which resolves itself into labour, but also that which resolves itself into profits ... [It] will measure both the quantity and the rate of profits accurately, and therefore will measure the value of an oak tree as well as of shrimps' (363).[69] Starting from the proposition accepted by all, that labour commanded measures the value of a product requiring labour

67 This is amply confirmed by reference to Ricardo's attempt to spell out formally the issues at exactly this time in his draft of 'Absolute and Exchangeable Value,' 1951–73, IV, 370: 'If then we constitued the shrimps [requiring labour alone in a timeless process] the measure of value of all things, cloth and wine [entailing time, and therefore advances on which profits are paid] would fall in such measure [with a change in distribution] altho' nothing had altered in respect to the circumstances of actual labour and advances [the period of production] under which all these commodities were produced.'

That the 'circumstances' under which commodities are produced (supply conditions) are *technological* does not, of course, mean that individual producers produce without reference to the profit rate.

68 Malthus was sent a copy by Ricardo; see Sraffa, in Ricardo, 1951–73, IX, 358n.

69 Cf. the letter to Ricardo, *ca* 21 July; 307 (above, p. 323).

alone, it would follow in the event of a change in technology necessitating for one such product an extension of the time of investment of labour to one year – and assuming a known annual profit rate of 10 per cent – that the value of such a product would rise to command eleven instead of the initial ten days' labour, reflecting the 10 per cent increase in the 'natural and absolute value' of that product (364). And he concluded: 'Apply this principle to the case of the cloth and wine which you have mentioned in the latter part of your letter, or the case of the oak tree, and you will find it answer in every instance, whatever may be the variations of profits, or the length of time required to bring the commodity to market, while in all these cases of great variations or great length of time, your measure according to your own concessions would be greatly inaccurate.' Malthus drove home his case by pointing to Ricardo's own remark to McCulloch (358) that, 'as soon as we are in possession of the knowledge of the circumstances which determine the value of commodities, we are enabled to say what is necessary to give us an invariable measure of value,' a remark which he read as confirming his own position since 'natural value' (or 'absolute value') included labour – and *all* advances could be reduced to labour – plus the profits on that labour: 'Now what can determine the natural and absolute value of commodities, but the natural and absolute conditions of their supply. Neither the advance of a certain quantity of corn nor even of a certain quantity of money will secure this supply unless they will command the requisite quantity of labour. Labour is the real advance in kind and the profits may be correctly estimated upon the advances whatever they may be. Consequently it appears to me that the circumstances which determine the natural value of commodities must be the quantity of labour advanced, accumulated and immediate, with the profits upon such labour for the time that it has been employed' (364–5). And only a product produced in a timeless process – 'if the quantity of labour so obtained be on an average the same as the quantity of labour which they will command' – constituted 'a steady measure of the circumstances which determine the value of commodities, or in other words an invariable measure of their value.' And he concluded by summarizing the outcome of his position that his selection was indeed an invariable measure: (1) That *only* his measure will reflect accurately changes in 'absolute value,' that is, supply conditions reflecting, not only changes in labour input, but a changing profit rate. (2) That this principle could be applied to *Ricardo's gold* (a commodity requiring capital as well as labour) since, if the profit rate falls, the value of such gold falls. (3) And that Ricardo erred by claiming that diminishing returns raises the value of a given corn-wage basket, because, although labour embodiment rises, allowances must be made for reduced profit; the 'value of wages' could not be treated as if it comprised labour alone, rather than labour and profit: 'Thinking my measure an invariable one, I am of opinion that it will shew the variations of yours occasioned by the varying rate of profits, and that when you suppose the value of labour to rise, it is really only a fall in the value of money; because when we refer to the circumstances which determine the value of commodities, we shall find that money must have fallen in value, on account of the profits required to produce it having fallen, while the labour has remained the same. When you say that the value of wages necessarily rises as poorer land is taken into cultivation, you consider the value of wages as if it were composed of the element of labour alone, and not of labour and profits' (365–6).

In his final letter on the measure of value of 31 August – he died a few days later – Ricardo readily accepted Malthus's position that 'labour will measure not only that part of the whole value of the commodity which resolves itself into labour, but also that which resolves itself into profits,' since this merely stated a 'fact'; but it was a fact 'true of every measure,' whereas what concerned Ricardo was an *invariable* measure of value or of supply conditions in the sense of the technical coefficients: 'But is not this true also of any variable measure you could fix on. Is it not true of Iron, Copper, lead, cloth, corn &c? The question is about an *invariable* measure of value, and your proof of invariability is that it will measure profits as well as labour, which every variable measure will also do' (380–1). Unfortunately, there existed no invariable measure, whereas *any measure captures the profit element in costs*: 'my measure is inaccurate ... not because it would not do every thing which you assert yours will do, but because I am not secure of its invariability' (381).[70] Thus, in Malthus's example: 'Shrimps are worth £10 in my money – it becomes necessary, we will suppose, in order to improve the shrimps to keep them one year, when profits are 10 pct., shrimps at the end of that time will be worth £11. They have gained a value of £1. Now where is the difference whether you value them in labour and say that at the first period they are worth 10 days labour and subsequently 11, or say that at the first period they are worth £10 and subsequently [£]11?' Malthus's presumption that labour and nothing else would do, since 'labour is the real advance in kind and the profits may be correctly estimated upon the advances whatever they may be' (above, p. 331), is denied: 'I am not sure that your language is accurate ... A farmer's capital consists of raw produce, and his real advances in kind are raw produce. His advances are worth and can command a certain quantity of labour undoubtedly, and his profits are nothing unless the produce he obtains will command more if he estimates both advances and profits in labour, but so it is in any other commodity in which he may value his advances and returns. Does it signify whether it be labour or any other

70 Cf. the earlier concession that his own measure failed to capture the labour coefficients of production of the product under investigation, whereas *both* measures – indeed, any product – served to indicate exchangeable value *including labour and profits*, or full cost price (13 July; 304, above, p. 322).

thing, provided there be no reason to suspect that it has altered in value?'[71] The conclusion of the argument is that Malthus's choice of labour required that labour itself be invariable in value, which it was not.

XII J.S. MILL ON *THE MEASURE OF VALUE*

According to Donald Winch, James Mill 'made critical notes, on Malthus's *Measure of Value*, but made no effort to get them published' (1966, 191).[72] The late Robert Fenn, however, considered the notes, which are in J.S. Mill's hand, to be the work of the younger Mill. These notes are cryptic and incomplete, but the author's position is apparently that to consider value in terms of *labour commanded* is arbitrary, since value entails an exchange rate against any or all things, including labour as one only among them. Malthus's proposition that the value of labour is *constant* – whatever the commodity wage may be – was a truism if value is arbitrarily defined as the labour commanded by the wage. The author was also unimpressed by the inverse wage–profit discussion in *The Measure of Value* – on which see chapter 10: IX – and the argument that selection of labour commanded as measure serves to convey that relation. This document, however, need not detain us, since its substance is incorporated in J.S. Mill's review of *The Measure of Value* for *The Morning Chronicle* of 5 September 1823. (Certainly the review sheds light on some of the opaque statements in the Commonplace Books.)

It is almost certain from its formulation that Mill had access to the Ricardo–Malthus correspondence in composing the review. It commences with a brilliant summary of the main proposition in *The Measure of Value*, particularly Malthus's belief that there exists an *ideal* measure of value, itself exempt from all sources of disturbance that act to disturb exchange rates, in contrast with 'received opinion ... that no such commodity is to be found': 'Such a measure Mr. Malthus thinks he has found in the quantity of labour which a commodity will purchase in the market. This, he says, is equal to the quantity of labour expended in its production, together with the ordinary profits' (Mill, 1823/1986, XXII, 51–2).

One objection is that *value* cannot be said to depend on labour and profits, though products are admittedly all shared between the labourer and the capitalist, setting rent aside in the standard fashion (52f.). Since the theory of value deals with exchange rates, a variation in the labour input in any product alters the structure of relative prices; but a variation

71 The outset of the passage implies corn input and corn output. But this can be accorded no analytical significance, as the remainder of the passage indicates.

72 In his Introduction to Ricardo's *Notes on the Measure of Value*, Porta (1992, x) repeats the opinion that the notes are by the elder Mill. These are to be found in J.S. Mill's Commonplace Book in the Mill–Taylor Collection (LSE), vol. 59, ff. 13–15. My late colleague Robert Fenn kindly provided me with his transcription of that material.

in the profit rate affects *all* products and leaves exchange rates unchanged except in special circumstances (an allusion to cases of non-uniform ratios), when the effect can be allowed 'as a modification' (53). 'But as a modification, it has been universally received among political economists, and is much more fully stated by Mr. Ricardo, the principal supporter of the old [labour] theory, than by Mr. Malthus or by any other opponent of that theory.' The notion 'that the value of the whole produce depends upon the proportion in which it is divided between the labourer and the capitalist' – implied by the proposition that value varies with profits – 'scarcely merits a serious refutation.'

Malthus's position that labour constitutes the *sole* accurate measure presumed that the capitalist's *advances* consist in labour, not in any product. This Mill denied: 'advances' do *not* comprise labour, but the 'food, clothing and lodging of the labourer.'[73] In any event it was 'immaterial whether the advances are in one commodity or in another. Whatever be the nature of the returns – be they in Corn, in Cloth, or in any other commodity, they must always be such as to repay the expences of production, together with the ordinary profits of stock; or, to use Mr. M.'s expression, they must include labour and profits. Labour, therefore, in this respect, possesses no advantage over any other commodity.'

There was the further problem that labour itself is subject to sources of variation which preclude it from serving as ideal measure – specifically changes in the commodity wage or the labour embodied in the commodity wage. Malthus's position that, though variable, the basket is necessarily of constant value is paraphrased thus by Mill: 'The reward of the labourer has been itself produced by labour, and its value, therefore, is resolvable into labour and profits'; accordingly, 'if the quantity of labour employed in producing [the real wage basket] be increased, profits must fall; if it be diminished, profits must rise, so as to leave the sum absolutely constant' (55). To this Mill gives the Ricardo-like reply that 'value does not depend upon the proportion in which the produce is divided between the labourer and the capitalist; it depends upon the demand and supply of the market, regulated and limited by cost of production.' Of *any* commodity in any amount it might be said that, if labour embodied in it rises so that a greater share of the commodity is paid as wages, a smaller share remains for profit, which in fact tells us nothing of the *value* of the product. In addition, Mill undermined the logic by devising a case where profits do *not* enter into production of the wage – where the wage is paid *ex post* – so that the notion of constant value of the wage breaks down.[74]

73 See Ricardo's correspondence of 1823 regarding 'advance in kind' for the same objection (above, p. 332).

74 Cf. comment 69a, p. 1151, in the Commonplace Book.

As for the table in *The Measure of Value*, that represented a highfalutin device which confused by its complexity. All it 'proved' was that 'the wages of a day's labour are always of the same value, because they are the wages of a day's labour' (57). Malthus, Mill concluded, had taken for granted as part of the proof what had to be proved: 'It is therefore evident that the whole of Mr. Malthus's argument is a begging of the question. His object is to prove that labour is an accurate measure of value, because the value of wages is invariable. But in order to prove this, he covertly assumes labour as the standard; and then, of course, he can easily prove that the wages of ten men, as compared with labour, are always of the same value because they can always purchase the labour of ten men. But although wages are invariable in value with repect to labour, they are not invariable with respect to commodities in general.'

Malthus stated in his *Measure of Value* that there was 'scarcely any of the science in which [his measure] will not tend to simplify and facilitate our inquiries' (1986, 7, 207).[75] But there is an *ad hoc* or assertive flavour to various implications drawn in his concluding elaborations, and Mill responded unfavourably. Thus the labour-commanded index records a secular rise in the 'value' of corn with a fall in the corn wage.[76] But on Malthus's empirical estimate the fall in the corn wage is shallow, so that the effect on rent of a rise in the value of corn would be correspondingly limited: 'On the subject of rents, such a standard would determine, among other things, that, as the increase in the *value* of corn is only measured by a decrease in the corn wages of labour, such increase of value is a very inconsiderable source of the increase of rents compared with improvements in agriculture ...' (1986, 7, 207).[77] Mill found this incomprehensible: 'It is difficult to trace the connexion between the premises and the condition of this argument' (1823/1986, XXII, 57). Adopting Ricardian

75 He admitted that he was adding little to the conclusions already reached in the *Principles* of 1820. The conclusion based on the constancy of the value of labour, he wrote, 'are almost exactly the same as the conclusions of the work. And the reason is, that although at that time I did not think that the labour which a commodity would command could, with propriety, be considered as a *standard* measure of value, yet I thought it the nearest approximation to a standard of any one object known, and consequently applied it, on almost all occasions, to correct the errors arising from the application of more variable measures. The conclusions, therefore, of my former and present reasonings were likely to be nearly the same, although the premises might now admit of further correction and illustration, and the conclusions might be pronounced with greater precision and certainty' (211).

76 Cf: 'In the actual state of things, corn generally rises in the progress of cultivation, not only nominally, but really ...' (202).

77 The argument is applied to the effect on the landlord of tithes: 'On the same principle that, if tithes do not fall mainly on the labourer, the acknowledged diminution in the *corn* rents of the landlord, occasioned by tithes, cannot be balanced by an increase of their value, and that, consequently, tithes must fall mainly on the landlord' (207–8).

usage, he insisted: (1) that 'there may be an increase in the value of corn, without any decrease in corn wages'; and (2) that the value of labour as well as corn rises secularly: 'When corn rises permanently in exchangeable value, the wages of labour almost uniformly rise along with it. The rise of wages is indeed less than that of corn, but it bears a very considerable proportion to it.' The essential point is his insistance upon the *variability* of the value of labour: 'The most important practical errors must therefore be the consequence of estimating the rise in corn by a comparison with labour, a commodity which always rises along with it.'[78]

The possibility of excess aggregate supply predominates among the implications drawn by Malthus from his measure to which Mill objected. This matter – and also implications for the inverse wage–profit or proportionate theorem – will be taken up in chapter 10.

XIII THE RESPONSE TO SAMUEL BAILEY

A chapter in Malthus's *Definitions in Political Economy* (1827) is devoted entirely to a defence of his *Measure of Value* against criticisms in Samuel Bailey's then anonymous *Dissertation on the Nature, Measure and Causes of Value* (1825). This chapter serves as a nice summary of Malthus's position.

Malthus found particularly objectionable the belief that 'the only use of a measure of value, in the sense of a medium of comparison, is between commodities existing at the same time,' no relation being conceivable between the value of commodities over time (1827a/1986, *8*, 75f., citing Bailey, 1825, 102f.). In fact, those who made such comparisons did so with two possible ends in mind: 'They obviously meant either to compare the esteem in which a commodity was held at one period with the esteem in which it was held at another, founded on the state of its supply compared with the demand, and ordinarily on its costs of production; or to compare the general power of purchasing which a commodity possessed at one period with its general power of purchasing at another period' (77; also 81). By this reference to 'esteem' Malthus did not intend 'utility'; esteem is indicated by the *cost price* of a commodity and it made sense to compare cost price in period t with cost price in period t+1, both expressed in terms of an invariable measure, or a commodity whose cost price – labour and profits – can be presumed *not* to have changed.[79] The presump-

78 He reacted similarly to the discussion of tithes: 'Another most important practical mistake. *Corn* rents indeed, are diminished by tithes. But if the exchangeable value of corn is raised, the landlord is indemnified. And although corn may not rise as compared with labour – and therefore, by Mr. Malthus, may be said not to have risen at all – there can be no doubt that, with reference to commodities in general, it has risen, and the landlord, consequently, is indemnified' (57–8).

79 There is a more extended discussion of 'esteem' in the subsequent chapter (95f.), but there, too, a substantive theory of demand is not at issue (see below, section XIV).

tion throughout is evidently that long-run prices can be assumed to rule.

Over short periods money served both possible functions well enough: 'If the money-price of corn has risen this year to double what it was in the last, I can infer, with almost absolute certainty, that corn is held in much higher estimation than it was. I can [also] be quite sure that ... it will command nearly double the quantity of all other commodities which are in their natural and ordinary state, and have not been essentially affected by the causes which have operated upon the price of corn' (77–8).[80] Subsequently, the notion of general purchasing power is elaborated. Notwithstanding the assertions in the *Dissertation on Value*, it was universally recognized 'that to estimate the relation of commodities, at different periods, in regard to their general power of purchasing, and particularly the power of purchasing labour, the main instrument of production, is a most important function ...; and that, for moderately short periods, money *does* perform this function with very tolerable accuracy. And for this specific reason; that, for moderately short periods, a given quantity of money will represent, more nearly than any other commodity, the general power of purchasing, and particularly the power of setting labour in motion, so vital to the capitalist' (79–80). The advantage of the precious metals in the short period derived 'from their great desirability, and the consequent uniformity of their supply in the market' (80). Estimates of profitability made in terms (say) of *corn* could be disastrously misleading: 'Hops, or corn ... will measure the relative values of commodities at the same time and place; but let the author or reader attempt to estimate the profits of a capitalist in hops or corn, by the excess of the value of his advances above the value of his returns so estimated, and he will soon be bewildered. If a very plentiful year of corn were to succeed to a comparatively scarce one, the farmer, estimating both his outgoings and incomings in the corn of each year, might appear to gain above fifty per cent, while, in reality, he might have lost, and might not be able, without trenching on his capital, to employ as many men on his farm as the year before.' At the same time, following Adam Smith, Malthus allowed that the precious metals will not serve over 'very long' periods.

A striking feature of the response to Bailey is *Malthus's defence of Ricardo.* His differences with Ricardo are represented as differences of detail, not of principle; and the defence is prologue to a justification of his own

80 As for general purchasing power, the relation was asymmetric. A variation in the money–corn exchange rate would not indicate that the general purchasing of *money* had changed: 'Broad, glaring, and incontrovertible facts show, that for short periods money *does* perform the function of measuring the variations in the general power of purchasing possessed by the corn; but that the corn does *not* measure the variations in the general power of purchasing possessed by the money' (78). This point is made against Bailey's position (1825, 117) that money would not 'be here discharging a particular function more than the other commodity' (also 81, regarding Bailey, 1825, 102).

measure. His primary concern at this stage was simply to undermine Bailey's contention that the Ricardo measurement procedure – entailing a commodity produced by a constant labour input – conflicted with the notion of *value in exchange*: '"Suppose," he observes, "that we had such a commodity as Mr. Ricardo requires for a standard; suppose, for instance, all commodities to be produced by labour alone, and silver to be produced by an invariable quantity of labour. In this case, silver would be, according to Mr. Ricardo, a perfect measure of value. But in what sense? What is the function performed? Silver, even if invariable in its producing labour, will tell us nothing of the value of other commodities. Their relations in value to silver, or their prices, must be ascertained in the usual way; and, when ascertained, we shall certainly know the values of commodities in relation to each other; but in all this, there is no assistance derived from the producing labour of silver being a constant quantity"' (82; citing Bailey, 1825, 122).

Malthus maintained in his defence of Ricardo that, given the foregoing assumptions, Ricardo's silver served better than real silver over secular periods as an index of general purchasing power than real-world silver; for it 'would be secured from that greatest source of variation in the general power of purchasing occasioned by the variation in its own producing labour; and an ounce of such silver would command much more nearly the same quantity of labour and commodities, for four or five hundred years together, than an ounce of silver derived from mines of greatly varying fertility.' The same held good of the function of a measure in indicating changes in 'estimation' over time of any given commodity – an allusion to cost price: '[Silver] would express at once the relative sacrifice which people were willing to make, in order to obtain such a commodity at ... different periods; the relative conditions of the supply, or elementary costs of production, of such commodity at these periods; and the proportion of the produce to the producer, or the relative state of the demand, as compared with the supply of such commodity at these different periods' (83). From an example that follows, it emerges again that, by 'esteem,' Malthus refers essentially to the *cost price* of the commodity in question, doubtless because its cost price reflected the conditions of supply in the sense – as he had just put it – of the 'sacrifice which people were willing to make in order to obtain it': 'It would not merely indicate, as the author states, in which of two commodities varying in relation to each other, at different periods, the variation had taken place [Bailey, 1825, 121]; but it would express the precise amount of the variation; that is, if it appeared by documents that the price of a yard of cloth of a certain quality four hundred years ago was twenty shillings, and its price at present was only ten shillings, it would follow, that the estimation in which it was held, or its value, had fallen one-half; because, as all commodities are, by the supposition, produced by labour alone, the sacrifice with which it could be obtained, the necessary conditions of its supply, or the elementary costs of its production, had diminished one-half.'[81]

Even accepting the labour-theory assumptions on which the Ricardo measure is based, there might occur changes in labour productivity throughout the economy, so that Ricardo's silver could admittedly not provide 'an *accurate* measure of the general power of purchasing,' that is, 'as the producing labour of many commodities may vary in the progess of society, it is quite impossible that the same quantity of any one object can, through successive periods, represent the same general power of purchasing' (83–4). This led Malthus to propose – in line of course with *The Measure of Value* and the revised *Principles* – that it were better 'to confine the term value of a commodity, when used generally, to the estimation in which it is held, determined by the state of the supply compared with the demand, and ordinarily by the elementary costs of production, rather than to its general power of purchasing' (84).[82] We shall see presently (below, p. 343) that Malthus's enthusiasm for a measure of changes in the cost conditions of a particular commodity, rather than changes in general purchasing power, was enhanced when it came to his *own* theory of cost-price determination.

Malthus commended Ricardo's device, albeit that it only served as a precise measure of purchasing power if no changes occurred in labour productivity in the case of commodities other than the one under investigation. One might yet refer to a doubling in X's 'value' when labour productivity in X halves, although X's general purchasing power would *not* double in the event of productivity changes in other products (85). Smith too was right, using his standard of labour commanded, to talk of a rise in the secular 'price' of cattle, though other commodities may rise simultaneously to an ever greater degree, reducing the general purchasing power of cattle.[83] Even Bailey, in dealing with 'the causes of value,' found himself obliged 'to estimate the causes affecting one commodity as distinct from the causes affecting another; although, according to his previous doctrine' – his formal insistance on relativities – 'the value of one com-

81 Malthus adds that variations of the Ricardian-money price of X would also show precisely variations of X's command over other commodities 'which had not altered in the conditions of their supply, or the elementary costs of production.'

82 Cf: 'It is universally acknowledged that there cannot be an accurate measure [of general purchasing power].'

83 There is an asymmetry in the commendations of Ricardo and Smith. Malthus refers to labour embodied as 'the sole *cause* of value' for Ricardo; but to labour commanded as *representing* costs for Smith. See also 86: 'On these grounds [the necessity of considering only the cost conditions of the 'purchasing' not the 'purchased' commodities], Mr. Ricardo, consistently with his peculiar theory, measures the varying values of commodities at different periods by their producing labour. And Adam Smith, consistently with his more just and applicable theory, measures the values of commodities at different periods by the labour which they will command.'

modity might be just as powerfully affected by causes operating upon another commodity as by causes operating upon itself.' Bailey had to concede 'that to confine the term value ... to the mere relation of any one commodity to any other, is to render it pre-eminently futile and useless' (86).

* * *

In all this Malthus drew on both Ricardo and Smith for support of the concept of *absolute value* – pre-eminently the cost conditions affecting a particular commodity – against Bailey's purely relativist position, although of course the absolute-value concept entails relativity in the use to which it is put. We come now to comments on Bailey's chapter 'On the Measure of Value Proposed by Mr. Malthus.'

Malthus pointed to the fallacy of three of its presumptions: (1) that 'unless labour always exchanges for the same quantity of other things, its value cannot be invariable, and, consequently, the very supposition of its being, at one and the same time, invariable, and capable of measuring the variations of other commodities, involves a contradiction' (Bailey, 1825, 140); (2) 'that to term anything immutable in value, amidst the fluctuations of other things, implies that its value at one time may be compared with its value at another time, without reference to any other commodity, which is absurd, value denoting a relation between two things at the same time'; and (3) 'that in no sense could an object of invariable value be of any peculiar service in the capacity of a measure.' Presumptions (2) and (3) were already shown to be unacceptable in Malthus's defence of Ricardo.[84] As for (1), Malthus pointed out that the implication was ludicrous – namely, that labour would be recorded as variable merely because of changes in its (formal) exchange rate even against non-wage goods: 'that the value of labour rises or falls as a given portion of it will exchange for a greater or less quantity of silk or any other commodity, however unconnected with the labourer's wants' (87).

With these preliminaries out of the way, Malthus came to a defence of his *Measure of Value* and its adoption of Smith's labour-commanded measure of value. As for its table, that was designed 'further to illustrate the subject, and bring into one view the results of different suppositions respecting the varying fertility of the soil and the varying quantity of corn paid to the labourer ...' (88). He rejected Bailey's objection to the constant

84 The objections to the latter two are readily summarized. Bailey implied by them what was patently untrue: 'Secondly, that the value of corn in one year cannot be compared with the value of corn in another, because value denotes only a relation between two things at the same time. And thirdly, that the comparative steadiness in the value of the precious metals, for short periods, is of no service to them in the capacity of a measure of value' (87).

value of labour under these varying circumstances, that 'in the same way any article might be proved to be of invariable value, for instance, ten yards of cloth. For whether we gave £5 or £10, for the ten yards, the sum given would always be equal in value to the cloth for which it was paid, or, in other words, of invariable value in relation to cloth. But that which is given for a thing of invariable value must itself be invariable, whence the ten yards of cloth must be of invariable value' (1825, 145). This involved 'either a most singular want of discrimination, or a purposed disregard of the premises on which the table is founded.' These premises, of course, relate to the determinants of *cost price*: 'that the natural and necessary conditions of the supply of the great mass of commodities, or, in other words, their elementary costs of production, are, the accumulated and immediate labour necessary to produce them, with the addition of the ordinary profits upon the whole advances for the time they have been advanced; and that the ordinary values of commodities at different periods, according to the most customary application of the term, are determined by the elementary costs of production at those periods, that is, by the labour and profits worked up in them.' From these premises it followed that *labour alone* served as measure since no *commodity* could be said to constitute 'the universal and the main instrument of production' or 'the natural and necessary condition of the supply of all commodities' or one of the 'elementary costs of production'; while no one had ever estimated the value of commodities over time 'by the different quantities of cloth and profits worked up in them.'[85] A note is attached protesting at the common charge that he had *arbitrarily* selected labour as measure (89n).

Malthus, furthermore, refuted Bailey's objection that the constant value of the wage irrespective of its quantitative magnitude or its 'elementary cost' reflected a mere truism – a criticism also made by Ricardo and the younger Mill. That constancy, he insisted, was rather a *deduction* from the preliminary proposition that the labour commanded by a unit of commodity X 'represented' precisely the embodied labour therein plus profits on these advances, that is, its elementary costs. In substance, Malthus sought first to justify his own version of the cost theory of value, and his position that labour commanded measures precisely such cost; and on this basis to give a substantive *interpretation* to the definitional constancy of the value of labour: 'It would, no doubt, be an absurd tautological truism merely to state, that the varying wages of a given quantity of labour will always command the same quantity of labour; but if it were previously shown that the quantity of labour which a commodity commands represents exactly the quantity of labour worked up in it, with the profits upon the advances, and does therefore really represent and measure those natural and neces-

85 In the 1823 correspondence Ricardo had of course objected that *commodities*, not labour, *are* in fact advanced (above, pp. 332–3).

sary conditions of the supply, those elementary costs of production which determine value; then the truism that the varying wages of a given quantity of labour always command the same quantity of labour, must necessarily involve the important truth, that the elementary costs of producing the varying wages of a given quantity of labour must always be the same' (89).[86]

Malthus did not reproduce the full demonstration in *The Measure of Value* that the labour commanded provides the precise measure of labour embodied plus profits.[87] But assuming that proof to hold good, it followed that the 'truistic' constancy of the value of (the labour commanded by) the wage, reflected the constant *sum* of labour embodied plus profits in the wage, such that any secular increase in the labour embodied in the wage would not – as Ricardo had it – imply that the wage was of higher value since that increase is precisely compensated by a reduced profit component: 'Mr. Ricardo had stated repeatedly, that the value of the wages of labour must necessarily rise in the progress of society. He builds, indeed, the whole foundation of his theory of profits on the rise and fall of the value of labour. The table shows that, if we estimate the value of wages by the labour worked up in them, that is, by one element of value, Mr. Ricardo is right, and the value of wages will really rise as poorer land is taken into cultivation; but that, if we estimate the value of wages by the labour and *profits* worked up in them, that is, by the two elementary ingredients of value, the value of wages will remain the same' (89–90).[88]

86 Cf. the following defence against the charge of tautology: 'It is obvious to any person inspecting the table, that the uniform numbers in the seventh column, illustrating the invariable value of the wages of a given number of men, might, with perfect certainty, have been stated without the intermediate steps; but if they had been so stated, no conclusion respecting the constancy of the value of such wages could have been drawn. The intermediate steps, which show that the value of the wages of ten men is there estimated by the causes which had been previously shown to determine the values of all commodities, can alone warrant the conclusion that the uniform numbers in the seventh column imply uniformity of value in the wages.'

87 That 'proof' starts out by positing the identity of labour embodied and commanded; and then modifies the situation by allowing for capital (or time) so that a profit element has been included, which implies an excess of labour commanded over labour embodied.

88 Given Malthus's objectives, it would have been preferable had he reworked his table. The table as it stands is misleading since it *commences* with a known profit rate and appears to build up to column 7 – the constant value of the wage. His true position – at least in the 1827 version – is that the profit rate emerges from the constancy of the wage. This is better conveyed by commencing with the constant value of the wage at (say) *unity* and then allowing for different labour inputs into the wage (owing to changes in the magnitude of the basket and/or changes in labour productivity) with profits yielded as the residual. This in contrast to Ricardo's procedure which sets *a day's labour as 'unity'* and derives profits as a residual varying inversely with the fraction of a day's labour embodied in the wage.

Malthus, moreover, had in mind a criticism of versions of cost price which entailed reference to 'labour and capital' rather than 'labour and profits.' Capital included both wage goods and real capital goods which are reducible to labour. In fact, 'excluding rent and taxes, the only elements concerned in regulating the value of commodities are labour and profits, including, of course, in such labour, the labour worked up in the raw materials, and that portion of the machinery worn out in the production; and including in the profits, the profits of the producers of the raw materials and machinery' (92). This perspective will explain numerous modifications made to the *Principles*.

* * *

Malthus proceeded to a bit of personal history in countering Bailey's charge that 'the table yields not a single new or important truth' (Bailey, 1825, 150). Allowing that the table *per se* did not yield any new truth, Malthus insisted that *The Measure of Value* as a whole – on which the table turned – certainly did, since 'the view I there took of the subject of value, and of the reasons for adopting labour as its measure, was, in many of its parts, quite new to me a year before the publication' (90).[89]

The first novelty claimed was recognition that labour commanded measured labour embodied–cum–profits, transforming an original concern with the index as *a measure of general purchasing power* to an appreciation of its efficacy as *a measure of production costs*: 'I had nowhere seen it stated, that the ordinary quantity of labour which a commodity will command must represent and measure the quantity of labour worked up in it, with the addition of profits ... I had before considered labour as the most general and the most important of all the objects given in exchange, and therefore, by far the best measure of the general power of purchasing of any one object; but after I became aware that, by representing the labour worked up in a commodity, with the profits, it represented the natural and necessary conditions of its supply, or the elementary costs of its production, its importance, as a measure, appeared to me very greatly increased.'[90]

Malthus also, of course, claimed originality for the proposition relating to the constant costs of producing the wage – costs determined like those of any product: 'Secondly; I had nowhere seen it stated that, however the fertility of the soil might vary, the elementary costs of producing the wages of a given quantity of labour must always necessarily be the same.' This alludes to the property required of a measure expressed in 1819 by

89 This makes sense of a remark by Ricardo (3 May 1823, 1951–73, IX, 287) regarding a *change* of position in 1823.

90 See also above, p. 339, regarding 1986, *8*, 83–4. The same theme emerges subsequently, 94–5.

Torrens, which Torrens believed were not fulfillable: 'Colonel Torrens, in adverting to a measure of value, says, "In the first place, exchangeable value is determined by the cost of production; and there is no commodity, the cost of producing which is not liable to perpetual fluctuation. In the second place, even if a commodity could be found which always required the same expenditure for its production, it would not, therefore, be of invariable exchangeable value, so as to serve as a standard for measuring the value of other things. Exchangeable value is determined, not by the absolute, but by the relative, cost of production"' (1819, 56; cited by Malthus, 91). Malthus thought of himself as meeting a challenge, provided that in dealing with variations in X's command over Y or Z, one held constant the 'causes' operating on X. (The *intrinsic* causes of the *Principles.*) But the cost conditions of producing the wage were necessarily constant, so that labour commanded constituted the sought-after 'X': 'In this case it is obvious that, according to Colonel Torrens, we should possess a measure of value if we could find an object the cost of producing which was always the same.' And it was shown in *The Measure of Value* 'that the conditions of the supply of labour, or the elementary costs of producing the corn wages of a given number of men, estimated just in the same way as we should estimate the elementary costs of producing cloth, linens, hardware, or any other commodity, must of necessity always remain the same.' These 'two necessary qualities of the labour which commodities will *ordinarily* command' – again we see Malthus's preoccupation with equilibrium or long-run positions – were 'practically new' to him, and made him 'view labour as a measure of value, so far approaching towards accuracy, considering the nature of the subject, that it might fairly be called a standard.'[91]

XIV A SUMMARY FORMULATION, 1827

We have seen that Malthus gave reasons in his *Definitions* for focusing on measurement of 'value' in the sense of production costs rather than general purchasing power. None the less, Chapter IX 'include[s] among the reasons for adopting labour as a measure of value, its qualities as a measure of the general power of purchasing,' since 'others may be of a different opinion' regarding the primary function of a measure (1827a/1986, *8*, 94–5). First, 'labour best represents an average of the general mass' of commodities: 'There is no commodity considered by society as wealth, for which labour is not, in the first instance, exchanged; there are very few for which it is not exchanged in great quantities: and this can be said of no other object, except labour, and the circulating medium which represents it. It is, at once, the first, the universal, and the

91 Chapter IX of the *Definitions* also contains a *mea culpa* (see below, p. 347).

most important object given in exchange for all commodities' (95). Second, there was an empirical reason to expect the general purchasing power of labour to be pretty constant over time since a reduction in the *corn* wage was balanced by an increase in the wage relative to *manufactures*: 'while there is one large class of commodities, such as raw products, which in the progress of society tends to rise as compared with labour, there is another large class of commodities, such as manufactured articles, which at the same time tends to fall; it may not be far from the truth to say, that the portion of the average mass of commodities which a given quantity of labour will command in the same country, during the course of some centuries, may not very essentially vary.' But though Malthus saw labour commanded as the most suitable index for 'those who may persevere in thinking that the best definition of value in exchange is the general power of purchasing,' he himself did not belong to that group and maintained rather 'that the variations in the exchangeable value of a commodity and the variations in its power of purchasing are not identical, and that a commodity increases in exchangeable value only when it will command a *greater value in exchange*, while its power of purchasing may increase merely because it will command a *greater quantity* of commodities which have confessedly fallen in value' (95–6).

Adopting labour commanded as measure of value was better justified on other grounds, which he proceeds to summarize in rather loose but assertive terms. Malthus again raised the notion of 'the esteem in which an object is held' as 'value, in its ultimate sense,' a position actually taken also by Bailey (96; for the discussion earlier in the *Definitions* see above, p. 336). This 'esteem,' *which attached to each commodity independently of any other*, could be measured only by labour commanded. Second, citing John Locke's demand–supply approach to the foundation of all value – presumably Locke, 1691, esp. 45–8, 63, 66–7 – Malthus asserted that '*the quantity of labour* which a commodity will *ordinarily* command, represents exactly the effectual demand for it; because it represents exactly the quantity of labour and profits united necessary to effect its supply; while the *actual* quantity of labour which a commodity will command when it differs from the *ordinary* quantity, represents the excess or defect of demand arising from temporary causes' (97). We are back then at the main proposition that *labour commanded provides a precise measure of long-run supply conditions.* Similarly, after giving a third rationalization in terms of labour commanded of a commodity as a measure of 'the sacrifice people are willing to make in order to obtain it' – a sort of Smithian conception – Malthus makes what he designates as a *fourth* case (though really it repeats the second) in terms of the argument for labour given in *The Measure of Value* involving value understood as 'on an average, determined by the natural and necessary conditions of their supply,' which reduces to measurement of 'the quantity of labour worked up in [a commodity] with the addition of profits' (98). Significant here is a criticism of Ricardo for being blind to this perspective: 'It was certainly a very remarkable fact, that when Mr. Ricardo chose the labour worked up in commodities "as, under many circumstances, an invariable standard," and rejected the labour which they would ordinarily purchase as subject to as many fluctuations as the commodities compared with it, he should not have seen that the labour which a commodity will ordinarily command, necessarily involves his own proposition, with that addition to it merely which can alone make it correct; and that it is precisely because the labour which a commodity will ordinarily command measures the labour actually worked up in it with the addition of profits, that it is justifiable to consider it as a measure of value. If then the ordinary value of a commodity be considered as determined by the natural and necessary conditions of its supply, it is certain that the labour which it will ordinarily command is alone the measure of these conditions' (98–9). A fifth reason for labour commanded again amounts to duplication. It restates the issue in terms of values as determined by 'the elementary costs of production,' which, 'excluding rents and taxes, are the labour and profits required to produce a commodity' (99), and asserts that 'commodities, which at two different periods in the same country would ordinarily command the same quantity of agricultural labour, might fairly be said to be equal to each other in their elementary costs of production, and, of course, in their values, if their values be determined by their elementary costs of production.'

In the course of elaborating a sixth reason for labour commanded,[92] Malthus asserts that 'the effectual demand for commodities must, on an average, be proportioned to the productive services set in motion to obtain them' (100). Here a note refers to J.B. Say's perspective on services, which, of course, includes rent: 'M. Say's comprehensive expression, "*Services productifs*", includes profits and rents as well as labour; but it is certain that labour will measure accurately the value of the whole amount of these services.' This was confirmed by an elaboration of the so-called proof of the accuracy of that index: 'if it be once allowed that when labour is exclusively concerned, the number of days' labour necessary to produce a commodity at any place and time represents the natural value of the commodity at that place and time, then, as it is quite certain that the value in exchange of any other commodity compared with the first, will be accurately in proportion to the respective quantities of the same kind of labour which they will command, it follows necessarily, that the value of the second commodity must always be in proportion to the quantity of labour it will command, however its value may have been affected by profits, rents, taxes, monopolies, or the accidental state of its supply

92 Formally, this reason turns on the 'value' of a commodity as proportioned to its supply compared with the number of its producers, which is difficult to appreciate.

compared with the demand' (100–1). To take this position is to reject the usual *exclusion* of rent from costs in making out the case for labour commanded.

Chapter IX closes with an admission of error for once maintaining against Adam Smith that because value – unlike length or weight – could not be expressed independently of time and place, 'it was not subject to "a regular and definite measure"' (103): 'I own that I was myself for a very long time of this opinion; but I am now perfectly convinced that I was wrong, and that Adam Smith was quite right in the prevailing view which he took of value, though he did not always strictly adhere to it' (103n). Malthus expanded his current position, emphasizing the now standard insistence that the essential rationale for labour commanded turned on the circumstance that labour was 'the great instrument of production,' doubtless alluding to the proposition that, when corrected by the profit rate, such labour embodied yielded labour commanded: 'I am also convinced that it would be a great improvement to the language of political economy, if, whenever the term value, or value in exchange, is mentioned without specific reference, it should always be understood to mean *value in exchange for labour, – the great instrument of production, and primary object given in exchange for everything that is wealth*; in the same manner as, when the price of a commodity is mentioned without specific reference, it is always understood to mean price in money – the universal medium of exchange, and practical measure of relative value' (emphasis added). He closed the summary notes by observing that his 'convictions' had 'acquired increase of strength the longer I have considered the subject.' These 'convictions' included a belief that his position illuminated the 'nature of demand' – a claim that doubtless reflects his innocuous notion that value as measured by labour commanded indicates a commodity's 'esteem' or 'sacrifice' or 'effectual demand' (above, pp. 336, 345) – and also provided the basis for 'a correct explanation of rents, profits and wages,' a grandiose claim indeed. Some of these implications had been spelled out at the close of *The Measure of Value*, and they are not further elaborated in the *Definitions*.

The original error alluded to in Malthus's confession involved in part a failure to distinguish properly between *wealth* (of which there was no measure) and *value* (of which there was), a weakness to be found in Smith himself: 'When [Smith] says, that a man is rich or poor according to the quantity of the necessaries, conveniences, and luxuries of life which he can command, he gives a most correct definition of wealth; but when he afterwards says, that he is rich or poor according to the quantity of labour which he can command, he evidently confounds wealth with value. The former is a definition of wealth; and of this, or of the general power of purchasing, which too much resembles it, there is no measure. The latter is his own definition or expression of real value; and of this the very terms which he uses show that there is a measure. The measure is distinctly expressed in the terms' (103).[93] This insistence on distinguishing carefully wealth from value reads very much like Ricardo, though of course their respective notions of 'value' differ.[94]

Malthus also maintained that erroneous conclusions had been drawn from the fact that 'a day's labour is not invariable either in regard to its intensity or time'; that is, *pace* Smith, that 'in different periods and in different countries, it is not really true ... that the labourer in working "lays down the same portion of his ease, his liberty, and his happiness"' (103–4). This Malthus allowed but none the less insisted that his case held firm: 'Because the labour of each place and time measures at that place and time the estimation in which a commodity is held, the state of its supply compared with the demand, the elementary costs of its production, the natural and necessary conditions of the supply, the proportion of the produce to the producers, &c. it must be considered as measuring, with a fair approach towards accuracy, the values of commodities at these places and times, so as to answer the question, – what was the value of broadcloth of a certain description in the time of Edward III in England? or, what is the value of money at present in China?' (104). Admittedly, the excellence of labour as measure would be enhanced were it the case that 'the labourer at different times and in different countries does ... always lay down the same portion of his ease, his liberty, and happiness'; still the advantage of using labour commanded as a measure was 'not essentially impaired': 'When commodities in different countries and at different times

93 In *The Measure of Value* itself, Malthus had pointed to the *close* relation between 'wealth' and 'value.' The best index of aggregate *wealth* would be provided by the measure of *value* or labour commanded: 'On the subject of the distinction between wealth and value, it would show, that though they are by no means the same, they are much more closely connected than they have of late been supposed to be; and that the best practical measures of the relative wealth of different countries would be the quantity of common labour which the value of the whole annual produce of each country would enable it to command at the actual price of the time, which in some countries might amount to above double the number of families actually employed, and in poor countries might not greatly exceed such number' (1986, 7, 208). This does not necessarily conflict with the position in 1827, since the passage refers only to 'the best practical,' not an *accurate*, measure of wealth.

94 Notwithstanding, we have just seen in the summary of his 'convictions' the claim that labour is 'the primary object given in exchange for everything that is *wealth*,' which is confusing. Subsequently, Malthus claimed – without formal justification, though doubtless with the various 'implications' of his device drawn in *The Measure of Value* at hand – that the definitions he selected reflected their 'superior practical utility ... in explaining the causes of the wealth of nations' (106), to which he attached a note reiterating the desirable sense to be given to the term 'value': 'It is specifically on this ground that I think the meaning of the term Wealth should be confined to material objects; that productive labour should be confined to that labour alone which is directly productive of wealth; and that value, or value in exchange, when no specific object is referred to, should mean value in exchange for the means of production, of which labour, the great instrument of production, is alone the representative.'

have been found to command the same quantity of the agricultural labour of each country and time, they may with propriety be said to have been held in the same estimation, and considered as of the same value' (105–6).

XV SUMMARY AND CONCLUSION

What, if anything, did Malthus accomplish by his procedures? Did he succeed in his corrections of Ricardo?

Ricardo may have once believed there was sense in the quest for an invariable measure of the *absolute* cost conditions of commodities, but he came ultimately to relinquish the idea. By contrast, Malthus came to see in labour commanded the perfect index of such 'intrinsic' costs. Ricardo's labour theory, as Malthus perceived it, excluded an allowance for profits, to counter which deficiency he proposed dated labour weighted by the profit rate. These costs, he maintained, are accurately recorded by labour commanded or its proxy, a commodity produced in a timeless process; labour commanded is not one of many possible *numéraires*, but the only *numéraire* which expresses precisely a commodity's supply conditions in this *absolute* sense. Behind this perspective lay the further conviction that labour (not a commodity or commodities) constitutes the sole true advance made by capitalists. In sharp contrast, we have Ricardo's perspective, which eschews absolutist connotations and works strictly with relativities. Labour input is the index Ricardo chose because – as a first approximation – *relative* labour input dictated *relative* cost prices. Furthermore, for Ricardo, commodities, not labour, comprise the 'real advance' by capitalists (above, pp. 332, 334).

The objection that Ricardo's labour theory made no allowance for profits was entirely misplaced: 'I have not said,' Ricardo protested in his *Principles*, that 'because one commodity has so much labour bestowed upon it as will cost £1000 and another so much as will cost £2000 that therefore one would be of the value of £1000 and the other of the value of £2000 but I have said that their value will be to each other as two to one, and that in those proportions they will be exchanged' (1951–73, I, 46–7). For Ricardo, supply conditions can be said to *exclude* profits since a *change* in the profit rate will not necessarily generate signals for capitalists to alter their activity pattern and disturb relativities. (We have encountered above, pp. 68–9, J.S. Mill's confirmation of this perspective.) Now an *ideal* measure of value would locate the industries where labour productivity had varied since relative cost prices are not disturbed by distributive changes. But such an ideal index Ricardo believed to be *unachievable* because in practice capital–labour ratios are non-uniform so that distributive changes *do* play on relativities.

By contrast, Malthus believed he had hit on the true index – an index of absolute value. Yet it is unclear why *absolute* value is at all significant, while his index has no particular advantage over Ricardo's in treating *relativities*, specifically the effects of changes in physical inputs and in distribution. For example, given the labour input, a fall in the profit rate reduces all (absolute) prices in terms of Malthus's money – silver produced in an 'instantaneous' process, which fixes the money wage or the labour commanded by silver – but uniformly in the case of uniform time periods of investment of labour between commodities (other than silver) and differentially in the case of differential time periods. Similarly, given the profit rate, a general fall in labour productivity leaves relativities unchanged, but a fall peculiar to a single product will effect its absolute costs alone, thus raising its relative price. But all these results are attained by Ricardo's procedures, and it is unclear what Malthus has gained.

In fact, Ricardo's procedures have the advantage of sharply distinguishing technological from distributive costs. Consider the case of corn subject to diminishing returns, where uniform factor ratios (time periods of investment of labour) pertain. For Ricardo, the price of corn rises no matter what may happen to the profit rate, since any variations of the latter is common to all products in the system (including Ricardian gold), leaving relativites unaffected. Malthus, for his part, insisted on a constant corn price – expressed in Malthusian money – should the rise in labour input be exactly counterbalanced by a fall in the profit rate. But this constancy in the absolute value of corn does not gainsay that the corn price of manufactures *does* rise – just as Ricardo has it – since manufacturing productivity is assumed unchanged so that absolute costs in manufacturing are affected solely by the reduced profit rate.

O'Brien remarks that Malthus, after his long debate with Ricardo on the best measure of value, finally decided 'that embodied labour was the best measure' (1975, 106). This is difficult to fathom. It is possible to take this position only if we identify Malthus with McCulloch, who treated profits as the wages of accumulated labour. But this, of course, we cannot do. For Malthus formerly rejected the labour theory in that extreme version (by McCulloch and James Mill) which reduces profits to labour: 'profits are altogether different from wages, and are regulated by quite different principles, as most justly stated by Adam Smith (Book 1, ch. 6). Such an assumption is so completely unphilosophical, so calculated to defeat all the useful purposes of a just nomenclature, and to create confusion in the ordinary language of political economy, that it cannot for a moment be admitted. We might just as correctly call rent labour' (1836, 91). A note distinguishes measurement from causation: 'We may measure the value which the element of profits gives to a commodity by labour, as I have said in another place [*The Measure of Value*]; but how we can say that more labour has been employed upon a commodity, merely because it must be kept longer before it is brought to market, is what I cannot understand.'

It remains to note that at every step of Malthus's analysis the profit rate is assumed known in the calculation of absolute costs, and thus of relative prices. Furthermore, the commodity wage is taken as a datum in the analysis; the concern is with dated quantities of labour. *In short: Distribution is perceived to be logically prior to pricing* – a Sraffian perspective. What then determines the profit rate for Malthus? There is strong evidence, which we shall bring in chapter 10, that it was envisaged as determined in purely physical terms as the ratio of net corn output to corn input, a physical ratio requiring knowledge of agricultural productivity and the corn wage. This profit rate is then used to calculate cost prices in the manufacturing sector. The contrast with Ricardo is stark; for Ricardo, it is the secular rise in the money-wage that provides the key, that rise playing on the profit rate in *all* sectors.

APPENDIX: 'TABLE ILLUSTRATING THE INVARIABLE VALUE OF LABOUR AND ITS RESULTS'

1. Quarters of Corn produced by Ten Men, or varying Fertility of the Soil	2. Yearly Corn Wages to each Labourer, determined by the Demand and Supply	3. Advances in Corn Wages, or variable Produce commanding the Labour of Ten Men	4. Rate of Profits under the foregoing Circumstances	5. Quantity of Labour required to produce the Wages of Ten Men under the foregoing Circumstances	6. Quantity of Profits on the Advances of Labour	7. Invariable Value of the Wages of a given Number of Men	8. Value of 100 Quarters of Corn under the varying Circumstances supposed	9. Value of the Product of the Labour of Ten Men under the Circumstances supposed
150 qrs	12 qrs	120 qrs	25 pr. Ct.	8	2	10	8.33	12.5
150	13	130	15.38	8.66	1.34	10	7.7	11.53
150	10	100	50	6.6	3.4	10	10	15
140	12	120	16.66	8.6	1.4	10	7.14	11.6
140	11	110	27.2	7.85	2.15	10	9.09	12.7
130	12	120	8.3	9.23	0.77	10	8.33	10.8
130	10	100	30	7.7	2.3	10	10	13
120	11	110	9	9.17	0.83	10	9.09	10.9
120	10	100	20	8.33	1.67	10	10	12
110	10	100	10	9.09	0.91	10	10	11
110	9	90	22.2	8.18	1.82	10	11.1	12.2
100	9	90	11.1	9	1	10	11.1	11.1
100	8	80	25	8	2	10	12.5	12.5
90	8	80	12.5	8.88	1.12	10	12.5	11.25

Source: *The Measure of Value*, 1823b/1986, 7, 199

EIGHT

Surplus vs scarcity: A physiocratic dimension

I INTRODUCTION

This chapter investigates an agricultural bias pervading T.R. Malthus's economics, pre-eminently manifested in the notion of a 'surplus' unique to agriculture. The question arises whether and to what extent the bias reflects a debt to the Physiocrats. That Malthus was aware in 1798 of the French literature, though possibly only at second hand, is clear; that by 1803 he had encountered it at first hand is also certain. I shall show that, though Malthus was sometimes critical – a prime example is his objection to the Single Tax proposal – it was because he regarded the French economists as failing to work out the full logic of their position. He in fact took the doctrine of a surplus peculiar to the agricultural sector farther than they did themselves, attempting to strengthen it at its weak points, as in value theory, and seeking to minimize doctrinal differences. The significance of the question of literal 'debt' is reduced, considering the *active* contribution made to what may be termed 'doctrinaire' physiocracy.

Section II defines the base from which Malthus set out. Although in 1798 he allowed that manufacturing contributes to national income, and apparently that it typically generates a surplus taking the form of profits, he yet defined agriculture as peculiarly productive on grounds of the 'real utility' of food production in its role as determinant of population growth. Here he envisaged himself as consistently spelling out the implications of that physiocratic definition of 'national wealth' which runs in terms of the '*gross* produce of the land.' I show next that in 1803 Malthus *withdrew* his allowances regarding manufacturing as generating original income, introducing the 'doctrinaire' or 'fundamentalist' or 'canonical' physiocratic position that manufacturing income constitutes a transfer payment made from income generated on the land. Further modifications of 1806 and 1807, however, entail rejection of the position that manufacturing does not generate original income – a return to 1798 (and Adam Smith). Yet Malthus still insisted on agriculture as the sole source of surplus, though this might in practice take the form of incomes other than land rent.

Complications created by sectoral interdependence are raised in section III. Particularly important are allowances for a dependency of the agricultural surplus on expenditures emanating from the manufacturing sector. Despite these qualifications the notion of a surplus unique to agriculture is confirmed in later editions of the *Essay* (section IV). A common opinion that Malthusian physiocracy is somewhat diluted in the 1817 version is rejected, considering a strong reiteration of the peculiar advantage supposedly attached to an economy whose national income includes rent as well as wages and profits.

Section V considers the rationalization for the surplus unique to agriculture. Since Chapter III of the *Principles* absorbs the 1815 pamphlet on Rent, we treat the two together. Malthus, we shall see, objected to the Single Tax proposal on the grounds that rents do not constitute entirely a disposable surplus. But he now also reinforces the canonical physiocratic proposition regarding a net value product in agriculture alone by the technical argument – already encountered above, in chapter 6: V – that supply of agricultural products creates its own demand, thereby assuring that when the output of food rises (as with higher agricultural productivity) the price of food remains roughly constant; that is, that a *physical* surplus assures a *value* surplus. Corn pricing is thus excluded from the usual case, where demand and supply conditions are independent. Issue is taken with the 'newer' writers Say, de Sismondi, Buchanan, and Ricardo, who applied a regular *scarcity* analysis to food, with the consequence that an increase in corn supply might well generate a reduction of the corn price. Malthus's case turned effectively on the assumption of very rapid population response to expansion of food supply. I conclude that the position of 1820 (and of 1815) constitutes a *reinforcement*, not a weakening, of the physiocratic dimension of Malthus's economics envisaged from the perspective of value theory.

Ricardo's reaction to the Malthusian analysis, focusing on land scarcity as the essential consideration in the analysis of rent, and Malthus's response are taken up in sections VI, VII, and VIII. We conclude that Malthus was in fact obliged to concede that rent as the return to land ownership indeed constituted a *transfer* payment out of incomes otherwise appearing in the form of wages or profits, but that he yet clung to appearances. The diminishing-returns complexity is further elaborated in section IX. That the principle posed a severe problem is reflected in two 'qualifications' in the *Principles.* The first denies that diminishing returns is the *sine qua non* of rent. Unfortunately for Malthus, this qualification effectively undermines the surplus approach by removing the price-theoretic support.

The second reiterates a position found in the *Observations* of 1814 which allows for positive rent at the margin of cultivation, considering the alternative use of land in an uncultivated state.

The question of Malthus's literal *debt* to the Physiocrates is discussed in section X; and the ultimate disintegration of Malthusian physiocracy in section XI.

II ON 'SURPLUS': THE *ESSAY ON POPULATION*

Agricultural bias emerges distinctly in the first *Essay on Population.* Malthus was, in fact, critical of the 'Economists' for not going far enough, insisting that, even were manufacturing to yield 'a clear rent,' that sector should be classified as 'unproductive,' at least relative to agriculture: 'They say, that labour employed upon land is productive, because the produce, over and above completely paying the labourer and the farmer, affords a clear rent to the landlord; and that the labour employed on a piece of lace is unproductive, because it merely replaces the provisions that the workman has consumed, and the stock of his employer, without affording any clear rent whatever. But supposing the value of the wrought lace to be such, as that besides paying in the most complete manner the workman and his employer, it could afford a clear rent to a third person; it appears to me, that in comparison with the labour employed upon land, it would be still as unproductive as ever' (1798/1986, *1*, 116). For though manufacturing activity admittedly added 'to the exchangeable value of [the] annual produce,' a transfer to agriculture of labour hitherto engaged on luxury production would involve an increase in 'productive' activity, in terms of 'real utility' or 'the mass of happiness in the society.'[1] This position held good even when labour after the transfer produces *less* food than it consumes, since the gross output of food rises compared with the original allocation (117–18). In brief: 'A capital employed upon land, may be unproductive to the individual that employs it, and yet be highly productive to the society. A capital employed in trade on the contrary, may be highly productive to the individual, and yet be almost totally unproductive to the society: and this is the reason why I should call manufacturing labour unproductive, in comparison of that which is employed in agri-

1 Thus two economies might grow at the *same* pace, yet with vastly different implications for labour: In the agricultural economy 'the poor would live in great plenty, and population would rapidly increase,' whereas in the commercial economy 'the poor would be comparatively little benefited, and consequently population would increase slowly' (114).

Malthus maintained, against Adam Smith, that foreign trade does not add much to 'wealth' precisely because it does not generate a significant increase of 'the internal funds for the maintenance of labour, and consequently, [adds] but little to the happiness of the greatest part of society' (118).

culture, and not for the reason given by the French Oeconomists ...'[2]

That Malthus offered his own justification of the productive–unproductive contrast in terms of the effect on food, and consequently on population, does not necessarily imply that he was unaware in 1798 that this latter relation was also recognized by the Physiocrats. His complaint was that the Physiocrats were inconsistent on their *own* terms involving 'wealth' defined as the 'gross produce of the land': 'Though according to the reasoning used by the French Oeconomists, the man employed in the manufacture of lace would, in this case [assuming a net revenue], seem to be a productive labourer; yet according to their definition of the wealth of a state, he ought not to be considered in that light. He will have added nothing to the gross produce of the land; he has consumed a portion of this gross produce, and has left a bit of lace in return; and though he may sell this bit of lace for three times the quantity of provisions that he consumed whilst he was making it, and thus be a very productive labourer with regard to himself; yet he cannot be considered as having added by his labour to any essential part of the riches of the state. The clear rent, therefore, that a certain produce can afford, after paying the expenses of procuring it, does not appear to be the sole criterion, by which to judge of the productiveness or unproductiveness to a state, of any particular species of labour' (116). All this alludes to the peculiar 'productivity' of agricultural activity with reference to its effect on population. We shall see (section VI) that Dupont de Nemours envisaged the *Essay* as paradigmatically physiocratic from just this perspective.

* * *

Malthus in 1798 thus considered agricultural activity as 'productive' (or relatively so), even in the absence of a net surplus or 'clear rent'; and manufacturing as 'unproductive' (or relatively so), even allowing for a net surplus, represented formally as excess of income over expenses relating to labour and capital. He allowed that manufactured wage-goods be treated like food: 'It seems in many respects improper, to exclude the clothing and lodging of a whole people from any part of their revenue. Much of it may, indeed, be of very trivial and unimportant value, in comparison with the food of the country; yet still it may be fairly considered as a part of its

2 Waterman (1991, 53) regards as a 'slip' the proposition that 'the wealth which supported ... two hundred thousand men, while they were producing silks and laces, would have been more usefully employed in supporting them, while they were producing [an] additional quantity of food' – even though the *per-capita* corn output falls short of the *per-capita* corn wage. To my mind, this is no slip. Malthus does *not* claim that in a private-property system such an outcome could ever materialize; this is in fact his point – private motivations may lead to a suboptimal outcome from the specific perspective of *gross* food output and total population.

revenue' (115). Adam Smith's general definition of national income covered this, and Malthus only objected 'where he seems to consider every increase of the revenue or stock of a society, as an increase of the funds for the maintenance of labour, and consequently, as tending always to ameliorate the condition of the poor.' For the identification of every increase of national revenue with an increase in labour demand was valid only from the perspective of the individual employer, whose (real) demand for labour indeed turned on his surplus stock or revenue, not from the perspective of society: '[It] will not be a real and effectual demand for the maintenance of an additional number of labourers, unless the whole, or at least a great part of this increase of the stock or revenue of the society, be convertible into a proportional quantity of provisions; and it will not be so convertible, where the increase has arisen merely from the produce of labour, and not from the produce of land. A distinction will in this case occur, between the number of hands which the stock of society could employ, and the number which its territory can maintain' (108).

It followed that net capital accumulation in the manufacturing sector, and therefore expansion of manufacturing output, might proceed apace with no positive effect upon the real-wages fund and labour demand. The impact of capital accumulation would be on money wages and food prices, not real wages: 'There would, notwithstanding, be a demand for labour, from the power which each manufacturer would possess, or at least think he possessed, of extending his old stock in trade, or of setting up new works. This demand would of course raise the price of labour; but if the yearly stock of provisions in the country was not increasing, this rise would soon turn out to be merely nominal, as the price of provisions must necessarily rise with it.'[3] The positive effect on food supplies of rising food prices is minimized, for transfers of capital into agriculture would occur but slowly, especially since the rise had been *preceded* by an increase in

3 Similarly: 'A great accession of work from manufactures, though it may raise the price of labour even more than an increasing demand for agricultural labour; yet, as in this case, the quantity of food in the country may not be proportionably increasing, the advantage to the poor will be but temporary, as the price of provisions must necessarily rise in proportion to the price of labour' (106). Food supplies might actually *fall* as the increasing demand for manufacturing labour attracted workers from the farms, although this outcome is set aside by the supposition that such a transfer would be 'compensated by improvements in the instruments of agriculture' (108). This allowance for new technology is not made merely to simplify the argument; technical change is represented as part and parcel of the 'normal' growth patterns. This emerges immediately in a reference to manufactures: 'Improvement in manufacturing machinery would of course take place,' acting (together with the larger manufacturing workforce drawn from agriculture) to expand manufacturing output. And this without 'giving the labouring poor a greater command over the necessaries and conveniences of life' – indeed even causing a net deterioration in well-being because of unhealthy conditions in the manufacturing centres and 'the greater uncertainty of manufacturing labour' (109).

money wages, which tends to depress activity (109). Food imports are also played down, for 'very high' food prices would be required 'to make an [appreciable] importation and distribution answer in large countries.' All in all, the expectation is of unchanged (even reduced) food supplies in consequence of non-agricultural expansion.

* * *

The conception of surplus as excess of income over expenses relating to labour and capital is modified or supplemented when it is allowed that profits on manufacturing or trading capital were frequently high enough to constitute a source of accumulation – a concept involving the character of *disposability*: 'It is, indeed, almost impossible, to see the great fortunes that are made in trade, and the liberality with which so many merchants live, and yet agree with the Economists, that manufacturers can only grow rich by depriving themselves of the funds destined for their support. In many branches of trade the profits are so great, as would allow of a clear rent to a third person: but as there is no third person in the case, and as all the profits centre in the master manufacturer, or merchant, he seems to have a fair chance of growing rich, without much privation; and we consequently see large fortunes acquired in trade by persons who have not been remarked for their parsimony' (117). The two classifications are not inconsistent, provided the first – surplus payment to a third party in excess of wage and profit expenses – is interpreted as an excess over 'expenses' incorporating *minimum* factor returns, thus containing no disposable element; with profits and wages assumed to be at their minima, the surplus or residual income will take the form of rent payment to the landlord (the 'third person'), and which (by implication) is alone disposable for accumulation. The second classification makes explicit the disposability criterion, and allows that *profit* too might constitute in part a surplus, in the sense of an income *disposable* for saving, even if no third party exists, as in manufacturing, where the land factor is supposedly inapplicable. Should the agricultural-profit rate exceed the minimum return, and thus contain a disposable element, the identification of surplus with rent fails. (For an elaboration, see below, p. 361.)

* * *

Malthus's objection to the physiocratic perspective on accumulation by manufacturers as a matter of abnormal deprivation does not suggest that he saw net returns in manufacturing to be merely apparent, constituting transfer payments out of agricultural income. That national income includes manufacturing (as with Adam Smith) is certain: 'The consumable commodities of silks, laces, trinkets, and expensive furniture, are undoubtedly a part of the revenue of the society ...' (118). This is no longer the case in the second edition (1803). There we discern the following physiocratic propositions: (1) that a surplus is generated *solely* by agriculture; and (2), and yet more strongly, that manufacturing income (in its entirety) entails a transfer payment. This can without question be described as 'fundamentalist' physiocracy. Indeed (1) alone would justify such a designation, since (2) was by no means universally maintained by the French economists (cf. Hollander, 1973, 83).[4]

As in 1798, Malthus points out in 1803 that the physiocratic criterion of productiveness turning on the ability to generate a surplus would oblige one to categorize manufacturing as 'productive' in the event that it generates a surplus, whereas the French economists seemed to want to avoid this conclusion (1986, *3*, 670–1). Again, manufactures were in fact 'essentially different' from agricultural produce, so that even were a surplus generated thereby, they should still be designated *unproductive*: 'The question respecting their productiveness or unproductiveness by no means depends entirely upon the largeness of the profits upon them, or upon their yielding or not yielding a clear rent' (671). But Malthus now adds, here turning away from Smith, that in any event manufacturing incomes constitute *transfer* earnings, not original incomes: 'But manufactures, strictly speaking, are no new production, no new creation, but merely a modification of an old one, and when sold must be paid for out of a revenue already in existence, and consequently the gain of the seller is the loss of the buyer. A revenue is transferred, but not created.'[5]

This perspective is elaborated in the following representation of the agricultural surplus as 'supporting' the service and manufacturing sectors, a strictly one-way dependency: 'If, in asserting the productiveness of the labour employed upon the land, we look only at the clear monied rent yielded to a certain number of proprietors, we undoubtedly consider the subject in a very contracted point of view. The quantity of the surplus produce of the cultivators is, indeed, measured by this clear rent; but its real value consists in its capability of supporting a certain number of people, or millions of people, according to its extent, all exempted from the labour of procuring their own food, and who may, therefore, either live without manual exertions, or employ themselves in modifying the raw produce of nature into the forms best suited to the gratification of man' (671–2).[6] In sharp contrast, 'a net monied revenue, arising from manufactures, of the same extent, and to the same number of individuals, would

4 Where appropriate I shall insert into the extracts from 1803 minor variations of 1806. Substantive modifications will be taken up subsequently.

5 And again: 'According to the system of the Economists' – if not always their form of expression – 'manufactures are an object on which revenue is spent, and not any part of the revenue itself' (673; 1806, II, 211).

6 The statement implicitly assumes wage and profit rates to be at their *minima*; otherwise, the surplus is *not* measured by the rent paid to land proprietors.

throw the country in which it existed into an absolute dependence upon the surplus produce of others; and if this foreign revenue could not be obtained, the clear monied rent, which we have supposed, would be absolutely of no value to the nation' (672). Yet more strongly, the enrichment of non-agricultural nations, like those of individuals, occurs by way of a transfer process: 'Land, in an enlarged view of the subject, is incontrovertibly the sole source of all riches; but when we take individuals or particular nations into our view, the state of the question is altered, as both nations and individuals may be enriched by a transfer of revenue without the creation of a new one.'

A particularly important passage spells out the peculiar role of the agricultural surplus. It makes the 'dependency' case quite generally; that is, 'whether the exchangeable value of the annual produce of the land and labour is the proper definition of the wealth of a country' – Adam Smith's approach, which treats manufacturing income as an original income – or 'whether merely the produce of the land, according to the French Economists, may not be a more correct definition' (670):[7] 'Whichever of these two definitions is adopted, as the best criterion of the wealth, power, and prosperity of a state, the great position [1806: the position] of the Economists will always remain true, that the surplus produce of the cultivators is the great fund which ultimately pays all those who are not employed upon the land. Throughout the whole world, the number of manufacturers, of proprietors, and of persons engaged in the various civil and military professions, must be exactly proportioned to this surplus produce, and cannot in the nature of things increase beyond it' (673; 1806, II, 208).[8]

* * *

Malthus cautioned in 1803 against drawing any parallel between monopoly profits and agricultural rent. Monopoly profits reflected only the 'mere monied revenue to an *individual*': 'As manufactures are not a new production, but the modification of an old one, the most natural and obvious way of estimating them is by the labour which this modification costs. At the same time, it may be doubted whether we can say positively that the price

7 Cf. the equivalent statement in 1798 specifying 'the gross produce of the land, according to the French Economists' (1986, *1*, 115). But in 1803 the definition of 'most of the Economists' is said to be 'the clear surplus produce of the land' rather than the *gross* produce (1986, *3*, 672).

8 This is troublesome. On the Smithian definition of national income, it cannot strictly be said that the agricultural surplus 'ultimately pays' the non-agricultural sector; this formulation applies only if we treat manufacturing income as a transfer. The retention of the passage in 1806 after Malthus had himself reverted to the Smithian definition is presumably an oversight. A modification in 1807 excises the expression 'ultimately pays' (see below, note 15).

of this labour, added to the price of the raw material, is exactly their real value. The ultimate value of everything, according to the general reasoning of the Economists, consists in being *propre à la jouissance.* In this view, some manufactures are of very high value; and in general they may be said to be worth to the purchaser what the purchaser will consent to give. In the actual state of things, from monopolies, from superior machinery, or other causes, they are generally sold at a price above what the Economists consider as their real worth; and with regard to a mere monied revenue to an individual, there is no apparent difference between a manufacture which yields very large profits and a piece of land which is farmed by the proprietor' (672).

Malthus deliberately downplayed any objections he had to make of the Physiocrats. They had understood the fundamental contrast between agriculture and manufactures. Their great weakness was to concentrate too much on the national surplus taking the specific form of *land rent*: 'I do not mean to say that the Economists do not fully comprehend the true distinction between the labour employed upon land, and the labour employed in manufactures, and really understand the value of the surplus produce of the cultivators, as totally distinct from the net monied revenue which it yields; but it appears to me that they have exposed themselves to be misunderstood, in their reasoning respecting the productiveness of land, and the unproductiveness of manufactures, by dwelling too much on the circumstance of a net rent to individuals' (672n). While '[in] an enlarged sense' – doubtless from an economy-wide perspective – 'it is certainly true, that land is the only source of net rent,' that national surplus, albeit generated solely in agriculture, could not be entirely represented by *rent.*

This objection is elaborated in a criticism of the celebrated Single Tax proposal. Interest recipients also shared in the net income: 'One of the principal errors of the French economists appears to be on the subject of taxation. *Admitting, as I shall be disposed to do, that the surplus produce of the land is the fund which pays everything besides the food of the cultivators*; yet it seems to be a mistake to suppose that the owners of the land are the sole proprietors of this surplus produce. It appears to me that every man who has realized a capital in money, on which he can live without labour, has virtually a mortgage on the land for a certain portion of the surplus produce' (675n; emphasis added). Malthus maintained the physiocratic notion that *taxation incidence falls solely on the agricultural surplus,* thereby supplementing the notion of surplus as net income *disposable for capital accumulation* (above, p. 358), but insisted on the empirical fact that surplus cannot be identified with land rent. And interest recipients might be taxed with no withdrawal of services resulting: 'those who live upon the interest of money, certainly pay a general tax in the same manner as the land-holders, and cannot throw it off from their shoulders, like those who live upon the profits of stock, or the wages of labour.' (Indeed, the incidence falls to some extent even on profits and wages, particularly 'professional' earnings 'for a very considerable time.') Precisely because landholders do not in practice receive all the surplus, it would be unjust to limit taxation to land rent: 'The real surplus produce of this country, or all the produce not actually consumed by the cultivators, is a very different thing, and should carefully be distinguished from the sum of the net rents of the landlords ....; a kind of mortgage is ultimately established on the land, by taxes and the progress of commercial wealth, and in this sense, all taxes certainly fall upon the land ... [But] though these taxes may still fall wholly on the land, they will not fall wholly on the landholders. It seems a little hard, therefore, in taxing surplus produce to make the landlords pay for what they do not receive.'

Surplus as disposable income from the perspective of *accumulation* need not coincide with surplus as disposable income from the perspective of *taxation.* They coincide only if we assume capitalists and labourers earn their minimum returns. As we have seen, both perspectives emerge in the texts. Conceivably, Malthus was implicitly utilizing this assumption, at least in the long run – in the short run (albeit 'for a very considerable time'), even profits may be taxed with no effect on capital supply; and Malthus's earlier allusions to savings by manufacturing capitalists out of profits might well refer to short-run earnings.

* * *

We return to the sharp contrast between industrial sectors. Both in 1803 and in 1806, Malthus draws the extraordinary physiocratic contrast between the effects on national profitability of corn and industrial exports: 'In the ordinary course of things, the exportation of raw produce is sufficiently profitable to the individuals concerned in it. But with regard to national profit, it possesses ... peculiar and eminent advantages above any other kind of export' (1986, *3*, 679; 1806, II, 231).[9] For 'raw produce, and more particularly corn, pays [1806: corn pays] from its own funds the expenses of procuring it, and the whole of what is sold is a clear national profit,' whereas only that part of the value of manufactured exports exceeding the 'value of subsistence' may be so included: 'If I set up a new manufacture, the person employed in it must be supported out of the funds of subsistence already existing in the country, the value of which must be deducted from the price for which the commodity is sold, before we can estimate the clear national profit; and of course, this profit can only be the profit of the master manufacturer and the exporting merchant [1806: 'and of course ... merchant' deleted]. But if I cultivate fresh land, or employ more men in

9 In 1806, Malthus adds various reasons explaining the 'national advantage' of agricultural exports, but the first remains as in 1803 (1806, II, 231).

the improvement of what was before cultivated, I increase the general funds of subsistence in the country. With a part of this increase I support all the additional persons employed, and the whole of the remainder which is exported and sold is a clear national gain; besides the advantage to the country of supporting an additional population equal to the additional number of persons so employed, without the slightest tendency to diminish the plenty of the rest' (679; 231–2).[10] Though Adam Smith had appreciated that the value of agricultural output 'bears a much greater proportion to the expense incurred in procuring it, than that of any other commodity whatever, and the national profit on its sale is in consequence greater' (678; 229), he forgot the rule when it came to foreign sales,[11] failing to allow for the subsistence absorbed in preparing manufactures for export.[12]

III ON SECTORAL INTERDEPENDENCE

We must keep in mind several allowances for sectoral interdependence in both 1803 and 1806/7. From Malthus's physiocratic perspective, focusing on the magnitude of surplus agricultural product, England appeared to be the 'richest' country in Europe relative to its land and population; and the ability to maintain a major non-agricultural sector flowed largely from *domestic* agriculture: 'And it is this great surplus produce in England, arising from her agriculture, which enables her to support such a vast body of manufacturers, such formidable fleets and armies, such a crowd of persons engaged in the liberal professions, and a proportion of the society living on money rents, very far beyond what has ever been known in any other country of the world' (1986, *3*, 674; 1806, II, 213). More specifically, an 'agricultural system' – as championed by the Physiocrats – was the only system that assured in the long run a healthy manufacturing sector by encouraging low materials costs, and thus raising international competitive-

10 This formulation suggests that the profit of the merchant and manufacturer *do* constitute net national income. But this is unlikely since, shortly before, the enrichment of non-agricultural nations was said to involve a *transfer* process (above, p. 360). A brief summary is more in line with that earlier statement: The exportation of farm produce merely 'replace[d] the subsistence that had been consumed in the manufacturing nation, together with the profits of the master manufacturer and merchant, which probably are not so great as the profits of the farmer and the merchant in the agricultural nation' (406). The 1806 deletion of 'the profit of the master manufacturer and the exporting merchant' may be intended to correct any dissonance.

11 Cf. 1776/1937, 642: 'The [trading and manufacturing country] exports what can subsist and accommodate but a very few, and imports the subsistence and accommodation of a great number. The other exports the accommodation and subsistence of a great number, and imports that of a very few only.'

12 Moreover, 'the actual state of the cultivation' and ability to maintain population would prove to be much greater *in the long run* in the corn-exporting country.

ness. Physiocratic terminology did less than justice to their own *valid* conceptions: 'According to the system of the Economists, manufactures are an object on which revenue is spent, and not any part of the revenue itself. But though from this description of manufactures, and the epithet sterile sometimes applied to them, they seem rather to be degraded by the terms of the Economists, it is a very great error to suppose that their system is really unfavourable to them. On the contrary, I am disposed to believe that it is the only system by which commerce and manufactures can prevail to a very great extent, without bringing with them, at the same time, the seeds of their own ruin' (673; 211–12). Historically, manufacturing economies had proved 'perfectly ephemeral beings, compared with those the basis of whose wealth has been agriculture.' Here too the idea that at the *national* level, revenue is generated only by agriculture emerges: 'It is in the nature of things, that a state which subsists upon a revenue furnished by other countries must be infinitely more exposed to all the accidents of time and chance than one which produces its own' (673; 212).[13]

There are also interdependencies involving an effect of manufacturing on agriculture. The first, strictly speaking of a non-physiocratic or even anti-physiocratic nature, is that manufactures provide a stimulus or motive for the expansion of the agricultural surplus, though with a warning against 'forcing manufactures' – as by the Navigation Acts – since agriculture is the leading sector in that 'the funds for the subsistence of the manufacturer must be advanced to him, before he can complete his work.' The second, that improved manufacturing technology raises the real purchasing power of the surplus, thereby adding 'virtually' to the real national income, is represented as consistent with the physiocratic system: 'Even upon this system, there is one point of view in which manufactures appear greatly to add to the riches of a state. The use of a revenue, according to the Economists, is to be spent; and a great part of it will of course be spent in manufactures. But if, by the judicious employment of manufacturing capital, these commodities grow considerably cheaper, the surplus produce becomes proportionably of so much greater value, and the real revenue of the nation is virtually increased' (673n; 211n).[14]

13 Malthus closed with the generalization that 'upon the whole ... our commerce has not done much for our agriculture; but ... our agriculture has done a great deal for our commerce [1806: that our commerce has not done so much for our agriculture as our agriculture has for our commerce]' (676; 220) – a nice instance of Malthus's fiddling at the margin with his texts. In 1807, he fiddled a bit more: 'It must be allowed, therefore, upon the whole, that our commerce has not done more for our agriculture, than our agriculture for our commerce' (1807, II, 144).

14 This is consistent with Adam Smith's representation of physiocracy: 'The industry of merchants, artificers, and manufacturers, though in its own nature altogether unproductive, yet contributes indirectly to increase the produce of the land. It increases the productive powers of productive labour, by leaving it at liberty to confine itself to its proper employment, the cultivation of land, and the plough goes frequently the easier

Malthus readily admitted (again in both 1803 and 1806) that 'no great surplus produce of agriculture could exist without [commerce and manufactures], and if it did exist, it would be comparatively of little value' (687n; 275n). None the less, commerce and manufactures were 'the ornaments and embellishments of the political structure rather than its foundations.' But this is wholly unconvincing since, as we shall see presently, Malthus relied on an increase in the demand for corn *from the manufacturing sector* to absorb all secular increases in the supply of corn. According 'priority' to agriculture is a mere formality.

IV AGRICULTURE AS SOLE SOURCE OF SURPLUS CONFIRMED

We come now to various modifications made in the third (1806) and fourth (1807) editions of the *Essay*. The passages in 1803 treating manufacturing earnings as a transfer payment rather than an original income (cited above, p. 359) are eliminated.[15] And in the edition of 1807 Malthus *formally* dissociated himself from the notion that manufacturing does not generate original income: 'This account of manufactures and revenue is not in my opinion correct; because, if we measure the revenue of the whole state by its whole consumption, or even by the consumption of those who live upon surplus produce, manufactures evidently form a considerable part of it; and the raw produce alone would not be an adequate representation either of its quantity or of its value' (1807, II, 135n).[16] Also

---

and the better by means of the labour of the man whose business is most remote from the plough' (1776/1937, 633–4).

Despite these allowances, Malthus hesitated in 1803 to accept Smith's designation of manufacturing as 'productive' activity, for he continues: 'There is no light, perhaps, in which we can view manufactures, where they appear to be so productive as in this; and if it do not completely justify Dr. Smith in calling manufacturing labour *productive* in the strict sense of that term; it fully warrants all the pains he has taken in explaining the nature and effects of commercial capital, and of the division of manufacturing labour.' This hesitation seems muted in the 1806 version: 'If this view of the subject do not, in the eyes of the Economists, completely justify Dr. Smith in calling manufacturing labour *productive*, it must fully warrant all the pains he has taken in explaining the nature and effects of commercial capital, and of the division of manufacturing labour.'

15 One generalization remains: 'Whichever of these two definitions is adopted, as the best criterion of the wealth, power, and prosperity of a state [the Smithian or the physiocratic], the position of the Economists will always remain true, that the surplus produce of the cultivators is the great fund which ultimately pays all those who are not employed on the land' (above, p. 360). But this is apparently an oversight, because in 1807 the passage is altered to read: 'Whichever of these two definitions is adopted as the best criterion of the wealth, power, and prosperity of a state, it must always be true that *the surplus produce of the cultivators measures and limits* the growth of that portion of the society which is not employed upon the land' (1807, II, 132; emphasis added).

16 He still recognized that, *even for the Physiocrats*, manufactures 'appear greatly to add to the riches of the state' because of the effect of manufacturing technology in raising the purchasing power of the agricultural surplus.

omitted in the 1806 revisions is the *defence* of the Physiocrats for essentially comprehending that 'the value of the surplus produce of the cultivators' is not identifiable with land rent, although they exposed themselves to a misunderstanding on that score (above, p. 361). In the context of the Single Tax doctrine (above, pp. 361–2) Malthus, by deleting in 1806 the phrase 'Admitting, *as I shall be disposed to do,*' withdrew his own acceptance of the position that 'the surplus produce of the land is the fund which pays everything besides the food of the cultivators,' which implied that non-agricultural incomes are received by way of transfer (1806, II, 217–18n). In 1807 the note in question is further altered to reinforce his objections to the concept of 'wealth' (read: *income*) as excluding manufactures: 'The great practical error of the Economists appears to be on the subject of taxation; and this error does not necessarily flow from their confined and inadequate definition of wealth, but is a false inference from their own premises. Admitting that the surplus produce of the land is the fund which pays everything besides the food of the cultivators; yet it seems to be a mistake to suppose that the owners of land are the sole proprietors of this surplus produce' (1807, II, 142n).

Malthus, however, reiterated that 'all taxes certainly fall upon the land' though 'not ... wholly on the landholders' (143n; see above, p. 362),[17] *confirming continued adherence to the sole source of surplus in agriculture,* albeit that the surplus in actuality takes the form, in part, of non-rent incomes, even in the manufacturing sector. The text of 1803 involving the modern notion of economic rent and *surplus as taxation capacity* (above, pp. 361–2) is elaborated: 'As consumers indeed it cannot be doubted, that even those who live upon the profits of stock and the wages of labour, particularly of professional labour, pay some taxes on necessaries for a very considerable time, and many on luxuries permanently; because the consumption of individuals, who possess large shares of the wealth which is paid in profits and wages, may be curtailed and turned into another channel, without impeding, in any degree, the continuance of the same quantity of stock or the production of the same quantity of labour' (1806, II, 218n; 1807, II, 142n). Finally, England continues to be represented as the 'richest' country in Europe, given the magnitude of its surplus agricultural produce; the

17 Malthus's review of Thomas Newenham (1808) for the *Edinburgh Review,* April 1809, contains a brief reiteration of his opposition to the Single Tax doctrine, yet support for a tax on rich Irish landlords: 'We are no advocates for the territorial tax of the Economists; but we certainly think, that the peculiar state of Ireland calls upon the Legislature, by every principle of justice and policy, to remove the burden of the partial and oppressive county rates, and the still heavier and more oppressive burden of tithes, from the poor tenantry, to the rich landlords. Such a measure would be an effective and permanent encouragement to agriculture; and would go further in allaying the discontents of Ireland, than anything short of complete emancipation, – which, at all events, it ought to accompany' (1809/1986, *4*, 65).

notion of *net* national revenue generated solely in agriculture remains implicit in the caution given regarding a manufacturing-based economy dependent on food imports; and we again find the distinction between the value of corn exports, which constitutes in its entirety a net addition to national income, and the value of manufacturing exports, from which must be deducted subsistence costs to obtain the 'clear national profit' (above, p. 362). In sum: *While the 'fundamentalist' notion of manufacturing income as a transfer payment was abandoned in 1806/1807, it remained Malthus's position that agriculture is the only source of surplus.*[18]

There is some evidence of further weakening. Agriculture as leading sector is retained, but in 1806 Malthus appears to dilute this position, and in 1807 possibly withdraw from it, at least on empirical grounds (above, note 13). Though the insistence against Smith that output might expand without benefit to labour is repeated in 1803 (1986, *3*, 438), and again in 1806 (II, 189), the objection is reduced by an allowance that, even given the food supply, expanded manufacturing output might raise the commodity wage: 'On the supposition of a physical impossibility of increasing the food of a country it is evident, that by improvements in machinery it might grow yearly richer in the exchangeable value of its manufacturing produce, but the labourer though he might be better clothed and lodged, would not be better fed' (1806, II, 192). Moreover, the assertion of 1803 – similar to that of 1798 (above, p. 357) – that an expansion of manufactures will not constitute 'a real and effectual fund for the maintenance of an additional number of labourers, unless the whole, or at least a great part of it, be convertible into an additional quantity of provisions; and it will not be so convertible where the increase has arisen merely from the produce of labour, and not from the produce of land' (1986, *3*, 694) is altered in 1807 to read: 'it may not be convertible' (1807, II, 114). And the term 'may' in 1806 replaces 'will' in 1803 in the basic distinction itself: 'a distinction may in this case occur between the number of hands which the stock of the society could employ, and the number its territory can maintain' (1806, II, 191).[19]

18 Two examination questions set by Malthus in 1808 seem to express Malthus's own position on our present issue: '9. How does it appear that Manufacturing Labour is productive of revenue and riches to a great amount, even though it be allowed that it does not yield a net rent? 10. What is the precise cause of Neat Rent, or disposable produce; and the reason why land generally yields a neat rent, and manufactures do not?' (Papers held in the Bodleian Library, Oxford, cited in Pullen, 1981b, 799n, 806–7n).

19 The changes reflect Malthus's reading of contemporary trends. In the 1798 version British experience since 1688 is used to illustrate the argument that even rapidexpansion of 'the annual produce' might be of *no advantage at all* to labour (1986, *1*, 110); whereas a weaker application of the principle is made in 1806 in the light of more recent experience: 'During the last ten or twelve years it cannot be doubted, that the annual produce of the land and labour of England has very rapidly increased, and in

* * *

In the 1817 version of the *Essay*, we again encounter the predominance of agriculture – reminiscent of the 1806 weighting (above, note 13) – whereby although 'commerce and manufactures are necessary to agriculture ... agriculture is still more necessary to commerce and manufactures' (1817, II, 396).[20] Agriculture as sole source of surplus again provides the key: 'It must ever be true that the surplus produce of the cultivators, taken in its most enlarged sense, measures and limits the growth of that part of the society which is not employed upon the land. Throughout the whole world the number of manufacturers, of merchants, of proprietors and of persons engaged in the various civil and military professions, must be exactly proportioned to this surplus produce, and cannot in the nature of things increase beyond it. If the earth had been so niggardly of her produce as to oblige all her inhabitants to labour for it, no manufactures or idle persons could ever have existed .... That quality of the earth by which it may be made to yield a much greater quantity of food, and of the materials of clothing and lodging, than is necessary to feed, clothe and lodge the persons employed in the cultivation of the soil ... is *the foundation of that surplus produce which peculiarly distinguishes the industry employed upon the land* (397–8; emphasis added). An elaboration confirms the national surplus to be the *excess of corn output over corn consumption in agriculture itself, which surplus might in part take the form of profits and wages*:[21] 'If in asserting the *peculiar productiveness of the labour employed upon the land*, we look only to the clear monied rent yielded to a certain number of proprietors, we undoubtedly consider the subject in a very contracted point of view. In the advanced stages of society, this rent forms indeed the most prominent portion of the surplus produce here meant; but it may exist equally in the shape of high wages and profits during the earlier periods of cultivation, when there is little or no rent. The labourer who earns a value equal to *fifteen quarters of corn* in the year may have only a family of three or four children, and not consume *in kind above five or six quarters*; and the owner

consequence the nominal wages of labour have greatly increased; but the real recompense of the labourer, though increased, has not increased in proportion' (1806, II, 202).

20 This is preceded by an empirical observation regarding the effect of mercantilist interference: 'America is perhaps the only modern instance of the fair operation of the agricultural system. In every part of Europe, and in most of its colonies in other parts of the world, formidable obstacles still exist to the employment of capital upon the land, arising from the remains of the feudal system. But these obstacles, which have essentially impeded cultivation, have been very far indeed from proportionably encouraging other branches of industry.'

21 Earlier definitions of surplus as excess of national income over 'expenses' can be accommodated provided the wage and profit rates are at their minima.

of the farming stock, which yields high profits, may consume but a very moderate proportion of them in food and raw materials. All the rest, whether in the shape of wages and profits, or of rents, *may be considered as a surplus produce of the soil* which affords the means of subsistence and materials of clothing and lodging to a certain number of people according to its extent, some of whom may live without manual exertions, and others employ themselves in modifying the raw materials obtained from the earth into the forms best suited to the gratification of man' (399–400; emphasis added).

As in earlier editions (above, p. 364) the *motive* for the production of the surplus turns on non-agricultural activity – scarcely a physiocratic notion.[22] None the less, the same priority is accorded the surplus produce, as in earlier versions: 'the funds for the subsistence of the manufacturer must be advanced to him before he can complete his work; and no step can be taken in any other sort of industry unless the cultivators obtain from the soil more than they themselves consume' (398; 1989, II, 30). I conclude that there occurred no further significant dilution of physiocratic content in 1817, such as has sometimes been discerned (cf. Winch, 1987, 61).[23]

V SURPLUS VS SCARCITY: THE PAMPHLETS OF 1815 AND THE *PRINCIPLES*

We consider next the rationalization of the surplus unique to agriculture to be found in Malthus's contribution to the pamphlet literature of 1815 and in his *Principles of Political Economy*. We should note, first, the clarification by Malthus in his *Inquiry into Rent* (1815), after establishing the course of 'rent' or the 'surplus produce from the land,' that by that designation he had intended 'the whole fund for the support of those who are not directly employed upon the land,' *including farmers' profits*, since 'profits are, in reality, a surplus ... in no respect proportioned (as intimated by the Economists) to the wants and necessities of the owners of capital' (1815b/1986, 7, 123n).[24] All this is consistent with the notion of surplus

22 See also: 'In a country in which manufactures and commerce flourish, the produce of the soil will always find a ready market at home; and such a market is peculiarly favourable to the progressive increase of capital' (421).

23 For all that, the chapter 'Of the Agricultural System' closed by conceding that labour's living standards need not be high in an agricultural economy (400–1). And in the chapter 'Of the Commercial System,' it is allowed that recent growth had been financed in part out of funds temporarily generated in manufacturing (405–6), though it is unclear what should be made of this insertion since accumulation by manufacturers had been recognized even in 1798 (above, p. 358).

24 On 29 December 1814 Malthus wrote to Ricardo that he was in the process of writing his pamphlet on Rent, which he hoped to publish (along with a third edition of his *Observations in the Corn Laws*) before the forthcoming meeting of Parliament (Ricardo,

given in the *Essay on Population* as an excess of corn output over 'internal' corn consumption, Malthus differing from the Physiocrats by his insistence that (agricultural) profits are included in that excess. The *all-inclusive* notion of surplus is represented as a Providential gift: 'Is it not ... a clear indication of a most inestimable quality in the soil, which God has bestowed on man – the quality of being able to maintain more person than are necessary to work it? *Is it not a part, and we shall see further on that it is an absolutely necessary part, of that surplus produce from the land, which has been justly stated to be the source of all power and enjoyment*; and without which, in fact, there would be no cities, no military or naval force, no arts, no learning, none of the finer manufactures, none of the conveniences and luxuries of foreign countries, and none of that cultivated and polished society, which not only elevates and dignifies individuals but which extends its beneficial influence through the whole mass of the people?' (122–3; emphasis added). But though the agricultural surplus includes profits in excess of some necessary minimum, the primary concern of the pamphlet was rent proper. Profits had to be separated out from rent because they 'take a different course in the progress of society.'[25]

The protectionist *Grounds of an Opinion* (1815) affirms that, pound for pound, the loss of agricultural capital and output is more damaging than a similar loss in other sectors: 'no loss, in proportion to its amount, affects the interest of the nation so deeply, and vitally, and is so difficult to recover, as the loss of agricultural capital and produce' (1815a/1986, 7, 165). This is an assertion. In what consists 'the interest of the nation' which is peculiarly reflected by the health of the agricultural sector? The same question emerges again in a discussion of the landowning class. Though landowners 'do not so actively contribute to the production of wealth, as either of the classes just noticed, there is no class in society whose interests are more nearly and intimately connected with the prosperity of the state' (167).[26] Here Malthus adopts Adam Smith's (physiocratic) proposition that 'no equal quantity of productive labour employed in

1951–73, VI, 167). The pamphlet commences with a statement of purpose. The topic was relevant 'on account of the discussions which are going on respecting the Corn Law, and the effects of rent on the price of raw produce, and the progress of agricultural improvement' (1986, 7, 115).

25 Inclusion of profits (in excess of the minimum) in the surplus defined in 1815, as in 1817, as excess of *corn* output over internal *corn* consumption is to treat profits as a *corn surplus*; and thus invites the concept of a rate of profit as a ratio of the corn surplus net of rent to the corn input, the so-called Sraffa rational reconstruction of *Ricardo*. That Malthus later developed this approach is argued below, in chapter 10.

26 Contrast the discussion of the benefits of lower prices under free trade for stockholders and fixed-income recipients: 'their interests are not so closely interwoven with the welfare of the state, as the classes already considered, particularly the labouring classes, and the landlords' (168).

manufactures can ever occasion so great a reproduction as in agriculture.' Again: 'If we suppose the rents of land taken throughout the kingdom to be one fourth of the gross produce, it is evident, that to purchase the same value of raw produce by means of manufactures [exports], would require one third more capital. Every five thousand pounds laid out on the land, not only repays the usual profits of stock, but generates an additional value, which goes to the landlord.' This '*additional value*' would be erased by a free corn trade – Malthus here recommends his *Rent* pamphlet – to the *national* detriment from the perspective of both consumption power and tax revenue: 'And this additional value is not a mere benefit to a particular individual, or set of individuals, but affords the most steady home demand for the manufactures of the country, the most effective fund for its financial support, and the largest disposable force for its army and navy' (167–8).

There are further considerations. It was necessary to recognize an unfavourable effect on manufacturing activity of a contracting agriculture since, with increased competition abroad under peace conditions, expanded foreign demand for home manufacturers could not be relied upon: it was 'peculiarly advisable to maintain unimpaired, if possible, the home market, and not to lose the demand occasioned by so much of the rents of lands, and of the profits and capital of farmers as must necessarily be destroyed by the check to our home produce' (166). Moreover, general price deflation engendered by a free corn trade would depress domestic activity (in Hume's fashion), even though manufacturing exports would doubtless increase to pay for food imports, leading to a 'physiocratic' or Spencian generalization that 'the quantity of a country's exports is a very uncertain criterion of its wealth. The quantity of produce permanently consumed at home is, perhaps, the most certain criterion of wealth to which we can refer.'

A typically physiocratic formulation focusing on the productivity contribution of land (presumably reflected in rent) appears in a query addressed at this period to Ricardo: 'Supposing two nations with the same population and wealth, and the same rate of profits; and one of them to be merely manufacturing and commercial, and the other mainly agricultural, would you not say, that the agricultural country would produce the given quantity of wealth and population with less labour, and would therefore have a greater mass of disposeable wealth, and could maintain larger fleets and armies?' (11 June 1815; in Ricardo, 1951–73, VI, 229–30).

Yet the allowance that agriculture is subject to diminishing returns distinguishes Malthus from the Physiocrats, and introduces a complexity. For Malthus conceded, even while he sings the praises of the 'additional value' constituting rent, that 'the last additions to the agricultural produce in an improving country are not attended with a large proportion of rent' (1986, 7, 168). It was 'precisely this circumstance that may make it answer to a rich country to import some of its corn, if it can be secure of obtaining an equable supply.' Nevertheless, he closes by insisting that, *in order to justify free trade in corn, the savings in resources must be sufficient to compensate for the loss of rent:* 'in all cases the importation of foreign corn must fail to answer nationally, if it is not so much cheaper than the corn that can be grown at home, as to equal both the profits and the rent of the grain which it displaces.' The logic of Malthus's argument is questionable – the notion of rent as an 'additional value' itself, but particularly when differential rent turning on diminishing returns is allowed.

* * *

Section I of the chapter 'Of the rent of land' in the *Principles* ('Of the Nature and Causes of Rent') repeats almost verbatim the position laid out early in the *Inquiry* (through to p. 17; in 1815b/1986, 7, 123).[27] This material includes the formal definition of rent as a residual – namely, 'that portion of the value of the whole produce which remains to the owner of the land, after all the outgoings belonging to its cultivation, of whatever kind, have been paid, including the profits of the capital employed, estimated according to the usual and ordinary rate of the profits of agricultural stock [1836: capital] at the time being' (1815b, 115–16; 1820, 134; 1836, 136).[28] The profit rate, like the wage rate, is thus taken to be a datum of the analysis, and the problem reduces to determining the excess of price over these known outgoings. In the *Inquiry*: 'The immediate cause of rent is obviously the excess of price above the cost of production at which raw produce sells in the market. The first object therefore which presents itself for inquiry, is the cause or causes of the high price of raw produce.' In the *Principles*: 'Rent then being the excess of price [1836: the excess of the value of the whole produce, or if estimated in money, the excess of the price of the whole produce,] above what is necessary to pay the wages of the labour and the profits of the capital employed in cultivation, the first object which presents itself for inquiry, is, the cause or causes of this excess of price.'[29] Malthus's concern is with the long run: 'It sometimes happens that, from accidental and temporary circumstances, the farmer pays more,

27 These pages possibly reflect earlier notes prepared for college lectures (Jacob Hollander, 1903, 3).

28 The 1815 pamphlet summarizes, at the very outset, the Smithian and physiocratic approaches: 'According to Adam Smith, [rent] is one of the three original sources of wealth, on which the three great divisions of society are supported. By the Economists it is so pre-eminently distinguished, that it is considered as exclusively entitled to the name of riches, and the sole fund which is capable of supporting the taxes of the state, and on which they ultimately fall' (115).

29 This definition is ambiguous. But, given the weight placed subsequently in the pamphlet on the marginal-cost principle of pricing – marginal cost including only wages and profits – it presumably should be read either as excess (per unit) of price (= mc) over average cost *at the margin*, or as excess of price over costs on *intramarginal* units.

or less, than this; but this is the point towards which the actual rents paid are constantly gravitating, and which is therefore always referred to when the term is used in a general sense.'

The definition is a prelude to criticism of Adam Smith, the Physiocrats,[30] and 'more modern writers' – Say (1814, 1817), de Sismondi (1803), and Buchanan (1814) – who are charged with considering rent (the concern is with *rent proper*) 'as too nearly resembling in its nature, and the law by which it is governed, the excess of price above the cost of production, which is the characteristic of a monopoly [1820: common monopoly]' (1815b, 116; 1820, 135; 1836, 136).[31]

Malthus allowed that in 'some parts' of the *Wealth of Nations* (Book I, ch. xi, and elsewhere) Smith took the correct position – more so than 'any other writer.' Yet even Smith had failed to explain 'the most essential cause of the high price of raw produce [1836: of the ordinary excess of the price of raw produce above its cost of production] with sufficient distinctness, though he often touches on it; and by applying occasionally the term monopoly to the rent of land, without stopping to mark its more radical peculiarities, he leaves the reader without a definite impression of the real difference between the cause of the high price of the necessaries of life, and of monopolized commodities [1836: the cause of this excess in the price of the necessaries of life, and in common monopolized commodities]' (1815b, 116; 1820, 135; 1836, 137). As for the Physiocrats, while accurate in 'some of their views' on the nature of rent, they had 'mixed them with so much error, and have drawn such preposterous and contradictory conclusions [1820, 1836: such unwarranted inferences] from them, that what is true of their doctrines has been obscured and lost in the mass of superincumbent error, and has in consequence produced little effect [1820, 1836: that what is true of their doctrines has produced little effect]' (1815b, 116–17; 1820, 136; 1836, 137]. The substantive complaint is the 'monopoly' implication of the Single Tax recommendation: 'The propriety of taxing exclusively the neat rents of the landlords, evidently depends upon their considering these rents as completely disposable, like that excess of price above the cost of production which distinguishes a common monopoly.' The posthumously published version is slightly more elaborate: 'Their great practical conclusion, namely, the propriety of taxing exclusively the neat rents of the landlords, evidently depends upon their considering these rents not only as completely disposable, like that excess of price above the cost of production, which distin-

30 'The Economists' (1815, 1820); 'the *Economists* of the school of M. Quesnay' (1836). Doubtless the alteration in 1836 is to indicate the wish to draw a line between more recent French economists, especially Say and de Sismondi, from the earlier eighteenth-century Quesnay group.

31 Malthus was using the term 'monopoly' to indicate an upward slope to competitive supply curves – in the limit zero elasticity; cf. Viner, 1958, 360, on this usage.

guishes a common monopoly, but also that every indirect tax operates as a deduction from neat rents in proportion to its amount.'

The objection here is much the same as that to be found earlier in the *Observations on the Corn Laws* – namely, that reducing rent by taxation endangered the rate of accumulation in land improvement. There he had expressed special concern with the dynamic consequences for 'the future improvement of land' of a reduced 'real' (relative) corn price, and he charged the Physiocrats with an essentially static orientation detrimental to growth of the food supply and population: 'It was a fatal mistake in the system of the Economists to consider merely production and reproduction, and *not the provision for an increasing population,* to which their territorial tax would have raised the most formidable obstacles' (1814/1986, 7, 97; emphasis added).[32] For though the 'motive' to expand is governed by 'the expected returns' on new capital investments, yet landlords must also be assured 'rent at least equal to the rent of the land in its former [uncultivated] state'; and while there typically existed a 'disposable surplus' on 'the greater part of the [already] improved lands,' any reduction in the corn price would necessarily impede expansion:

> But a diminution in the real price of corn is still more efficient, in preventing the future improvement of land, than in throwing land, which has been already improved, out of cultivation. In all progressive countries, the average price of corn is never higher than what is necessary to continue the average increase of produce. And though, in much the greater part of the improved lands of most countries, there is what the French economists call a disposable produce, that is, a portion which might be taken away without interfering with future production, yet, in reference to the whole of the actual produce and the rate at which it is increasing, there is no part of the price so disposable. In the employment of fresh capital upon the land to provide for the wants of an increasing population, whether this fresh capital be employed in bringing more land under the plough or in improving land already in cultivation, the main question always depends upon the expected returns of this capital; and no part of the gross profits can be diminished without diminishing the motive to this mode of employing it .... [If] the price of the produce will not leave a fair remuneration for the capital employed, according to the general rate of profits and a rent at least equal to the rent of the land in its former state, no sufficient motive can exist to undertake the projected improvement. (96–7)[33]

32 A further charge was made against Adam Smith for illegitimately excluding corn from treatment in terms of the standard-scarcity, or demand–supply, model (90–1). This criticism creates a severe anomaly since much of Malthus's own treatment of rent – above all, the argument in the 1815 *Rent* pamphlet and in the *Principles* that a *physical* surplus ensures a corresponding *value* surplus – turns on just such an exclusion.

33 A feature of this formulation is that the agricultural profit rate must relate to the *general* profit rate – there is no hint of it determining that general rate. This is the position taken earlier, yet more explicitly, in a criticism of Adam Smith for according corn spe-

Here in effect Malthus rejects the concept of no-rent land – his position resembles Marxian 'absolute' rent – though elsewhere he had allowed it of course. The notion of no-rent land introduces a serious technical challenge to physiocratic principles.[34] The allowance for rent at the margin, although it undermined physiocratic taxation policy, paradoxically strengthened the basic doctrine itself.[35]

We return to Malthus's reaction to 'modern writers.' In his discussion of de Sismondi, he objected to a note in *De la richesse commerciale* (1814) which takes the Physiocrats to task for *failing* to envisage rent as a transfer payment made possible by dint of landowners' 'privilège' and pressure of demand for food: 'In the excellent work of M. de Sismondi, *De la richesse commerciale* [1814, I, 49], he says, in a note on the subject of rent: "Cette partie de la rente foncière est celle que les Economistes ont décorée du nom du *produit net*, comme étant le seul fruit du travail qui ajoutât quelque chose à la richesse nationale. On pourroit, au contraire, soutenir contre eux, que c'est la seule partie du produit du travail, dont la valeur soit purement nominale, et n'ait rien de réelle: c'est en effet le résultat de l'augmentation de prix qu'obtient un vendeur en vertu de son privilège, sans que la chose vendue en vaille réellement davantage"' (1815b/1986, 7, 117; 1820, 136; 1836, 138).[36] The same was true of Adam Smith's editor, Buchanan, who took issue with the physiocratic perspective on the grounds that a relaxation of the scarcity constraint would allow a transfer of real income from landowners to the rest of the community. Buchanan in fact had gone further than any of the others in spelling out that, from the 'monopoly' perspective, rent was *not* 'a clear addition to the national wealth' but an imposition on the rest of society: 'while former writers,

---

cial treatment: 'It is, of course, only to a temporary encouragement or discouragement, that any commodity, where the competition is free, can be subjected. We may increase the capital employed either upon the land or in the cotton manufacture, but it is impossible permanently to raise the profits of farmers or particular manufacturers above the level of other profits; and, after the influx of a certain quantity of capital, they will necessarily be equalized. Corn, in this respect, is subjected to the same Laws as other commodities, and the difference between them is by no means so great as stated by Dr. Smith' (94). As we shall see in chapter 10, all this was later abandoned with the adoption of a corn-profit orientation.

34 Interestingly, the tendency to diminishing returns at the extensive agricultural margin is even to be found in the French literature; see Spengler, 1942, 198n, regarding Dupont de Nemours. Turgot has remarkable statements of the principle (Brewer, 1987; Hollander, 1987, 55).

35 The 1814 allowance for rent in marginal cost should not be read as a denial of diminishing returns and differential rent. These concepts are clearly intimated in a discussion of wartime experience and trade policy (96, 107–8). The differential rent principle and the no-rent margin make a (casual) appearance as early as 1806.

36 In 1836, Malthus adds a note commending de Sismondi's *Nouveaux Principes d'économie politique* (1818) for giving 'a different and more correct view of rent' (1836, 138n).

though they considered rent as governed [1836: governed entirely] by the laws of monopoly, were still of opinion that this monopoly in the case of land was necessary and useful, Mr. Buchanan sometimes speaks of it even as prejudicial, and as depriving the consumer of what it gives to the landlord' (1815b, 117–18; 1820, 137; 1836, 138–9).[37]

We are faced by an apparent difficulty. Malthus himself objected to the Physiocrats for adopting a monopoly or scarcity perspective on rent, but now objects to de Sismondi and Buchanan for their monopoly perspective on rent as opposed to the 'neat surplus' position they attributed to the Physiocrats. It is unclear how precisely Malthus read the Physiocrats, unless we envisage him (as we must) as rejecting only the supposed monopoly implication of the Single Tax proposal, rather than the position that rent represents a net creation of wealth and not a transfer due to land scarcity (or 'monopoly').

* * *

We come now to a reinforcement of the 'surplus' as opposed to the 'monopoly' perspective on rent. We recall the emphasis thus far on a *physical* corn surplus. This is now supplemented by the assurance that *value* surplus can look after itself. Thus in the *Principles* Malthus ascribed to the Physiocrats what he perceived as the valid proposition that 'the power of yielding rent' turns on the physical surplus – 'the fertility of the land ... yielding a surplus quantity of necessaries beyond the wants of the cultivators' – fully confirming the definition of 1817 – coupled with 'the peculiar quality belonging to the necessaries of life, when properly distributed, [which] tends strongly and constantly to give a value to this surplus by raising up a population to demand it' (1820, 144, 1836, 144).[38] Adam Smith, too, had maintained this position, at least 'in those passages of the *Wealth of Nations*, in which he approaches the nearest to the doctrines of the Economists [1836: to their doctrines]. But modern writers have in general been disposed to overlook them, and to consider rent as regulated upon the principles of a common monopoly, although the distinction is of great importance, and appears obvious and striking in almost any instance that we can assume [1836: take].' The insertion of the above passage in the *Principles implies formal adherence by Malthus to a central theme in physiocratic doctrine, and confirms that his earlier criticism related only to the Single Tax because of its (possibly unintended) implication that rent could be accounted for in terms of 'monopoly.'*

37 Malthus cited Buchanan, 1814, vol. IV, 134; vol. III, 212. For further criticism of Buchanan and de Sismondi, see 1815b, 122–3; 1820, 149–50; 1836, 147–8.

38 Malthus is quite clear (see below, p. 387) that the increased demand for corn emanates from the manufacturing sector, thus undermining seriously the priority accorded agriculture.

The technical contrast between the demand for 'strict necessaries' and the demand for other goods appears also in the *Inquiry into Rent.* Only in the general category is there meaning to *demand independent of or external to supply; and here only does the monopoly (or the scarcity) property apply.* In agriculture 'the cause of the higher price of the necessaries of life above the cost of production, is to be found in their abundance, rather than their scarcity' (1815b, 121).[39] Although this particular formulation is absent from the *Principles,* its substance is retained in a contrast between the effects of a reduction by 50 per cent in the productivity of the mines producing precious metals and of the land (1820, 145–6; 1836, 144–5);[40] and also in the analysis of the effect of a cheaper diet on rent, which involves the presumption that expansion of food supply generates its own demand via population growth, assuring the maintenance of food prices and rents (1820, 231; 1836, 211). The analysis is further confirmed in a reiteration, common to all three texts, that the concept of a negatively sloped demand curve applies only where 'demand is exterior to, or independent of, the production itself' (1815b, 122; 1820, 147; 1836, 145).

Malthus's contrast between speciality products and corn concludes in 1815 with the generalization that an increased supply of corn is the 'cause' of the excess of price over costs: 'The fertility of soil, and consequent abundance of produce from a certain quantity of land, which, in the former case, diminished the excess of price above the cost of production, is, in the present case, the specific "cause" of such excess; and the diminished fertility, which in the former case might increase the price to almost any excess above the cost of production, may be safely asserted to be the sole cause which could permanently maintain the necessaries of life at a price not exceeding the cost of production' (1815b, 122). This passage is deleted in 1820 (147), but there is no change in substantive position, considering a reformulation in its place of the contrast in terms of a physical corn surplus *as source of rent* – that is, rent potential – given the presumption that 'value' product can look after itself, provided the surplus is 'properly distributed': 'In all common monopolies, the price of the produce, and consequently the excess of price above the cost of production, may increase without any definite bounds. In the partial monopoly of the land which produces necessaries the price of the produce cannot by any possibility exceed the value of the labour which it can maintain; and the excess of its price above the cost of its production is subjected to a limit as impassable. [1836: In the partial monopoly of the land which produces necessaries the excess of their price above the cost

39 For the full statement see above, chapter 6, pp. 240–2.

40 In the former case, as population may be supposed unaffected, it was conceivable that rents, profits, and wages at the mines would be unaffected, and even rise; in the latter case, the consequence would be disastrous.

of production is subjected to an impassable limit.] This limit is the surplus of necessaries which the land can be made to yield beyond the lowest wants of the cultivators, and is strictly dependent upon the natural or acquired fertility of the soil. Increase this fertility, the limit will be enlarged, and the land may [1836: be made to] yield a high rent; diminish it, the limit will be contracted, and a high rent will become impossible; diminish it still further, the limit will coincide with the cost of production, and all rent will disappear' (1820, 148; 1836, 146–7).[41] All this is summed up with the strongest contrast between the *scarcity* approach to all goods other than necessaries and the *surplus* approach applicable to necessaries: 'In short, in the one case, the power [1836: *power*] of the produce to exceed in price the cost of production depends mainly [1836: depends] upon the degree of the monopoly [1836: and of the external demand]; in the other, it depends entirely upon the degree of fertility [1836: natural or acquired]. This is surely a broad and striking distinction' (1820, 148–9; 1836, 147).

To this conclusion Malthus attached a brief note: 'Yet this distinction does not appear to Mr. Ricardo to be well founded,' a reference to Ricardo's objections introduced into his *Principles* in 1819 (1951–73, I, 405). And he restated his objections to de Sismondi and Buchanan, reaching precisely the same conclusion regarding rent as in 1815:

> Is it possible, with M. de Sismondi, to regard rent as the sole produce of labour, which has a value purely nominal, and the mere result of that augmentation of price which a seller obtains in consequence of a peculiar privilege: or, with Mr. Buchanan, to consider it as no addition to the national wealth, but merely as a transfer of value, advantageous only to the landlords, and proportionably *injurious* to the consumers?
>
> Is it not, on the contrary, a clear indication [1836: Must we not, on the contrary, allow that rent is the natural result] of a most inestimable quality in the soil, which God has bestowed on man – the quality of being able to maintain more persons than are necessary to work it. *Is it not a part, and we shall see further on that it is an absolutely necessary part, of that [1836: general] surplus produce from the land, which has been justly stated to be the source of all power and enjoyment*; and without which, in fact, there would be no cities, no military or naval force, no arts, no learning, none of the finer manufactures, none of the conveniences and luxuries of foreign countries, and none of that cultivated and polished society, which not only elevates and dignifies individuals, but which extends its benefi-

41 The excess over 'the lowest wants of the cultivators' is stated in the immediately preceding paragraph thus: 'The exchangeable value of a given quantity of necessaries in commanding labour [1836: last three words deleted] always tends to approximate towards the value of the quantity of labour which it can maintain [1836: in such a manner as to support at least a stationary population], or in other words, to its value in use.'

cial influence through the whole mass of the people. (1820, 149–50; 1836, 147–8; emphasis added; *injurious* in original)

To conclude: The excess value return in the case of corn is attributed to the surplus physical produce – 'the surplus of necessaries ... beyond the lowest wants of the cultivators' – in that the former assures an increase of population external to agriculture and a corresponding increase in the demand for food. We are evidently still in the world of physiocracy.[42]

VI RICARDO'S OBJECTIONS: THE LAND-SCARCITY CONDITION

Ricardo objected strongly to Malthusian physiocracy, which he saw as clashing with other features of Malthus's economics. On reading the *Grounds of an Opinion,* he complained to Malthus, not of its protectionism as such, but of its faulty deductions from economic theory: 'you point out many inconveniences which we should suffer from the loss of agricultural capital, and from other causes; which would make it appear as if even economically you thought we ought to import corn – such is the approbation with which you quote from Adam Smith of the benefits of agriculture over commerce in increasing production, which I cannot help thinking is at variance with all your general doctrines' (13 February 1815; Ricardo, 1951–73, VI, 178).[43] In his *Essay on Profits* he pointed out that Malthus's

42 Indeed, we are witness to its *reinforcement* since the essential principle involved had apparently been rejected in 1806: 'On account of the tendency of population to increase in proportions to the means of subsistence, it has been supposed by some, that there will always be a sufficient demand at home for any quantity of corn which could be grown. But this is an error' (1806, II, 264n). The note allows only that a corn-price reduction would stimulate demand, as in the case of any other product: 'It is undoubtedly true, that if the farmers could gradually increase their growth of corn to any extent, and could sell it *sufficiently cheap,* that a population would arise at home to demand the whole of it. But in this case, the great increase of demand arises solely from the cheapness, and must therefore be totally of a different nature from such a demand as, in the actual circumstances of the country, would encourage an increased supply. If the makers of superfine broad cloths would sell their commodity for a shilling a year instead of a guinea, it cannot be doubted that the demand would increase more than ten fold; but the certainty of such an increase of demand, in such a case, would have no tendency whatever in the actual circumstances of any known country, to encourage the manufacture of broad cloths.'

43 Ricardo took strong exception for there were significant trade-policy implications at stake. In particular, there was no necessity to correct the welfare benefit of reduced corn prices for reduced rent, as Malthus maintained: 'I think too that rents are in no case a creation of wealth, they are always a part of the wealth already created, and are enjoyed necessarily, but not on that account less beneficially to the public interest, at the expense of the profits of stock. Viewing rents in this light it follows that I must withdraw the concession which I was inclined to make when you first stated the question "whether in importing corn at a cheaper price than we could grow it the whole difference of price was saved, or whether some abatement should not be made from

conception – his *physiocratic* conception – clashed with the *diminishing returns* perspective, whereby in early stages of development land is free: 'I cannot agree with Mr. Malthus in his approbation of the opinion of Adam Smith, "that no equal quantity of productive labour employed in manufactures, can *ever* occasion so great a re-production as in agriculture." I suppose that he must have overlooked the term ever in this passage, otherwise the opinion is more consistent with the doctrine of the Economists, than with those which he has maintained; as he has stated, and I think correctly, that in the first settling of a new country, and in every stage of its improvement, there is a portion of its capital employed on the land, for the profits of stock merely, and which yields no rent whatever. Productive labour employed on such land never does in fact afford so *great* a reproduction, as the same productive labour employed in manufactures' (1951–73, IV, 37–8). In fact, Malthus himself in the *Inquiry* had correctly taken issue with Adam Smith's agricultural bias when he observed that 'I cannot ... agree with him in thinking that all land which yields food must necessarily yield rent. The land [1836: covered with wood] which is successively taken into cultivation in improving countries [1836: in new colonies for the production of food], may only pay profits and labour. A fair profit on the stock employed, including, of course, the payment of labour, will always be a sufficient inducement to cultivate' (1815b/1986, 7, 116n; cf. 1820, 135n; 1836, 137n).[44] For Ricardo this was the correct view to take, and it should have led Malthus to reply that 'the same motives will also induce some to manufacture goods, and the profits of both in the same stages of society will be nearly the same.'[45]

As Ricardo clarified at length in the *Principles* (1817), agricultural rent was a reflection of *land scarcity*, not 'the advantages which the land possesses over every other source of useful produce, on account of the surplus

---

the advantage for the loss of rent?," as I now decidedly think that the whole difference of price would be gained without any deduction whatever' (6 February; 173). (The extant correspondence does not allude to the 'question' by Malthus or the 'concession' by Ricardo; it is likely that Ricardo referred to recent personal discussions.) Since no correction was required, 'the arguments ... of those who contend for a free trade in corn remain in their original full force, as rents are always withdrawn from the profits of stock.'

44 It is only late in the 1815 pamphlet (132f.) that we encounter a *formal* statement of the no-rent principle on marginal units of output, and the related principle that the corn price exceeds costs on intramarginal units. The statement in 116n may be an insertion into an earlier text.

45 Ricardo further complained in correspondence: 'You appear to me not quite consistent in admitting as you unequivocally do that the last portion of land cultivated, yields nothing more than the profits of stock – no rent, and yet to maintain that taxes on necessaries or on raw produce fall on the landlord and not on the consumer' (1951–73, VI, 173. Ricardo alluded to 1815b/1986, 7, 140–1).

which it yields in the form of rent.' This is not to say that he neglected a productivity requirement. His point is that should the hitherto free 'natural agents' utilized in manufacturing become scarce, a rent would be generated to *their* owners at the expense of other resource owners; conversely, if land scarcity were relaxed, the productivity advantage would flow to capitalists and labourers: 'Nothing is more common than to hear of the advantages which the land possesses over every other source of useful produce, on account of the surplus which it yields in the form of rent. Yet when land is most abundant, when most productive, and most fertile, it yields no rent; and it is only when its powers decay, and less is yielded in return for labour, that a share of the original produce of the more fertile portions is set apart for rent. It is singular that this quality in the land, which should have been noticed as an imperfection, compared with the natural agents by which manufactures are assisted, should have been pointed out as constituting its peculiar preeminence. If air, water, the elasticity of steam, and the pressure of the atmosphere, were of various qualities; if they could be appropriated, and each quality existed only in moderate abundance, they, as well as the land, would afford a rent, as the successive qualities were brought into use. With every worse quality employed, the value of the commodities in the manufacture of which they were used, would rise, because equal quantities of labour would be less productive. Man would do more by the sweat of his brow, and nature perform less; and the land would be no longer pre-eminent for its limited powers' (1951–73, I, 75). For Ricardo, then, rent 'adds nothing to the resources of a country, it does not enable it to maintain fleets and armies; for the country would have a greater disposable fund if its land were of better quality, and it could employ the same capital without generating a rent' (400). Accordingly, de Sismondi and Buchanan – *pace* Malthus – 'were correct when they considered rent as a value purely nominal, and as forming no addition to the national wealth, but merely as a transfer of value, advantageous only to the landlords, and proportionably injurious to the consumer.'

Ricardo also rejected Malthus's justification of a *value* surplus corresponding to the *physical* surplus involving the population principle. The demand–supply mechanism, he insisted, applied equally to *all* products: 'Mr. Malthus supposes that the rent on land yielding those peculiar products of the earth which may be called natural or necessary monopolies, is regulated by a principle essentially different from that which regulates the rent of land that yields the necessaries of life. He thinks that it is the scarcity of the products of the first which is the cause of a high rent, but that it is the abundance of the latter, which produces the same effect' (405). This distinction Ricardo rejected, 'for you would as surely raise the rent of land yielding scarce wines, as the rent of corn land, by increasing the abundance of its produce, if, at the same time, the demand for this peculiar commodity increased; and without a similar increase of demand, an abundant supply of corn would lower instead of raise the rent of corn land.' The fallacious contrast could in part be explained by the presumption that increased food supply preceded population growth and demand: 'Mr. Malthus appears to me to be too much inclined to think that population is only increased by the previous provision of food – "that it is food that creates its own demand" – that it is by first providing food, that encouragement is given to marriage, instead of considering that the general progress of population is affected by the increase of capital, the consequent demand for labour, and the rise of wages; and that the production of food is but the effect of that demand' (405–6).

VII MALTHUS AND LAND SCARCITY: THE RESPONSE TO RICARDO

Malthus in the *Principles* reacted strongly to Ricardo's adherence to the scarcity perspective of de Sismondi and Buchanan: 'It is extraordinary that Mr. Ricardo [1951–73, I, 400] should have sanctioned these statements of M. de Sismondi and Mr. Buchanan. Strictly, according to his own theory, the price of corn is always a natural or necessary price [1836: and, independent of agricultural improvements, the natural and necessary condition of an increased supply of product]. In what sense then can he agree with these writers in saying, that it is like that of a common monopoly, or advantageous only to the landlords, and proportionably *injurious* to the consumers?' (1820, 149n; 1836, 147n). Ricardo's position that agricultural rent reflects land scarcity, not 'the advantages which the land possesses over every other source of useful produce,' he rejected in terms of surplus as a gift of Providence: 'It seems rather extraordinary that the very great benefit which society derives from that surplus produce of the land which, in the progress of society, falls mainly to the landlord in the shape of rent, should not yet be fully understood and acknowledged. I have called this surplus a bountiful gift of Providence, and am most decidedly of opinion, that it fully deserves the appellation' (1820, 226; 1836, 207). He objected on the same grounds to J.B. Say's contrast between free natural agents and land scarcity (relative to demand), the latter envisaged as source of land rent: 'Heureusement personne n'a pu dire, le vent et le soleil m'appartiennent, et le service qu'ils rendent doit m'être payé' (*Traité*, 2d ed., 1814, II, 124). And though Say 'acknowledges that, for obvious reasons, property in land is necessary, yet he evidently considers rent as almost exclusively owing to such appropriation, and the external demand' (1815b/1986, 7, 117; 1820, 136; 1836, 138).[46]

46 A note of 1815 and 1820 commends the 'new and much improved edition [which] has lately been published, [and] which is highly worthy the attention of all those who take an interest in these subjects.' This general commendation is removed in the 1836 edition, and Malthus inserts instead a reinforcement of his objections to Say's position on rent: 'In his 5th edition [1826], vol. II, 346, he describes the subject anew, but he does not seize the right view of it. He still considers the price of the produce of land which occasions rent too much as the result of a common monopoly.'

Malthus felt obliged in the *Principles* to defend his notion of rent as a 'gift of Providence' against Ricardo. He insisted that we evaluate the gift 'in relation to the laws and constitution of our nature, and of the world in which we live' (1820, 228; 1836, 208). Specifically, given the ability of population to double itself every twenty-five years, assuming an adequate growth of food supply, it was Providential foresight to *check* the growth of food – in contrast to a profuse provision of air and water – *since space is limited*: 'It is not easy to conceive a more disastrous present – one more likely to plunge the human race in irrecoverable misery, than an unlimited facility of producing food in a limited space. A benevolent creator then, knowing the wants and necessities of his creatures, under the laws to which he had subjected them, could not, in mercy, have furnished the whole of the necessaries of life in the same plenty as air and water. This shews at once the reason why the former are limited in quantity, and the latter poured out in profusion.' The essential limitation imposed on the 'power of producing food' – by which is intended the requirement for expenditure of *effort* to obtain food – implied that 'the value of the actual quantity of land which [man] has received, *depends upon the small quantity of labour necessary to work it, compared with the number of persons which it will support; or, in other words, upon that specific surplus so much under-rated by Mr. Ricardo, which by the laws of nature terminates in rent*' (emphasis added). This justification of land as a unique generator of general *surplus* could not, Malthus proceeded, be generalized. The rent of land – here he takes 'rent' narrowly defined as measure of the surplus – was of a different order from any rent that might be generated in manufacturing by dint of the scarcity of 'natural agents.' Ricardo's identification was illegitimate in that the surplus attributable to land reflected *high productivity*; whereas the other reflected *low productivity*, and a transfer from labour to the owner of the natural agents: 'If manufactured commodities, by the gradations of machinery supposed by Mr. Ricardo, were to yield a rent, man, as he observes, would do more by the sweat of his brow; and supposing him still to obtain the same quantity of commodities, (which, however, he would not,) the increase of his labour would be in proportion to the greatness of the rent so created. But the surplus, which a given quantity of land yields in the shape of rent, is totally different. Instead of being a measure of the increase of labour, which is necessary altogether to produce the quantity of corn which the land can yield, it is finally an exact measure of the *relief* from labour in the production of food granted to him by a kind Providence' (1820, 229; 1836, 209–10).

An important explanatory note is attached to the hypothetical case of 'gradations' of natural agents in manufacturing. It reiterates the contrast between corn and all other goods – namely, that *the corn price alone can be taken as a datum upon an increase in labour productivity, and this because an increase in corn supply generates its own demand*, from which it followed that increased facility of production in agriculture implies a greater, not a lesser, surplus. This justification of the general case is misleading, for it starts out by supposing some sort of rising cost function in manufacturing – on a par with diminishing agricultural returns owing to increasingly inferior plots – and then transfers to new technology, rendering the inferior machines unnecessary, given demand: 'That is, supposing that gradations were towards worse machinery, some of which it was necessary to use [1836: as in the case of land], but not otherwise. *The reason why manufactures and necessaries will not admit of comparison with regard to rents is, that necessaries, with a limited territory, are always tending to the same exchangeable value, whether they have cost little or much labour*; but manufactures, if not subjected to an artificial monopoly, must fall [1836: in value] with the facility of producing them. We cannot therefore suppose the price to be given; but if we could, facility of production would, in both cases, be equally a measure of relief from labour' (1820, 229n; 1836, 209n; emphasis added).

Ricardo is also taken to task for his analysis in the *Principles* (1951–73, I, 403) of the hypothetical case of reduced fertility – namely, that in consequence of an increase in effective land scarcity, rents are forced upwards: 'Mr. Ricardo has supposed a case ... of a diminution of fertility of one-tenth, and he thinks that it would increase rents by pushing capital upon less fertile land. I think, on the contrary, that in any well cultivated country it could not fail to lower rents, by occasioning the withdrawing of capital from the poorest soils. If the last land before in use would do but little more than pay the necessary labour and a profit of 10 per cent upon the capital employed, a diminution of a tenth part of the gross produce would certainly render many poor soils no longer worth cultivating [1836: and would therefore reduce rent]' (1820, 145n; 1836, 144n). In a later section of the chapter on Rent, Malthus complained of a 'misunderstanding' by Ricardo on this score; he himself denied having drawn a positive relationship between fertility of land and rent without reference to other causes: 'Mr. Ricardo has quite misunderstood me, when he represents me as saying that rent immediately and necessarily rises or falls with the increased or diminished fertility of the land [1951–73, I, 404] .... [H]aving stated three causes as necessary to the production of rent, I could not possibly have meant to say that rent would vary always and exactly in proportion to one of them. I distinctly stated, indeed, that in the early periods of society [1836: in new colonies], the surplus produce from the land, or its fertility, appears but little in the shape of rent. Surely he has expressed himself most inadvertently while correcting me, by referring to the comparative scarcity of the most fertile land as the only cause of rent [403], although he has himself acknowledged, that without positive fertility, no rent can exist [404]. If the *most* fertile land of any country were still very poor, such country could yield but very little rent' (1820, 152; 1836, 152).[47] This is an

47 For his three causes, see below, p. 386.

unacceptable complaint. Malthus had been labouring away to prove that, unlike other 'machinery,' in the case of land alone – in so far as it produced necessaries – *rent rises with increased fertility.* The reason why rent rises with increased fertility (a physical dimension) is, as we know, that necessaries generate their own demand (and 'soon' into the bargain). This is his 'second cause' – that any increase in physical quantity is accompanied by a corresponding increase in value product; the two cannot diverge, a position Malthus attributed to the Physiocrats, as we have seen.

There is also a charge – an invalid charge – that Ricardo uncharacteristically set aside in his rent analysis the usual assumption of a '*natural*' (subsistence) wage which presumes rapid demographic adjustment, and concentrated on the immediate effect of new technology or the adoption of a cheaper diet in reducing the pressure on scarce land: 'It is a little singular, that Mr. Ricardo, who has, in general, kept his attention so steadily fixed on permanent and final results, as even to define the *natural* price of labour to be that price which would maintain a stationary population, although such a price cannot generally occur under moderately good governments, and in an ordinary state of things, for hundreds of years, has always, in treating of rent, adopted an opposite course, and referred almost entirely to temporary effects' (1820, 230; 1836, 210). On these grounds, runs the contention, Ricardo (1951–73, I, 333) had 'objected to Adam Smith [1776/1937, 159] for saying that, in rice countries a greater share of the produce would belong to the landlord than in corn countries, and that rents in this country would rise, if potatoes were to become the favourite vegetable food of the common people, instead of corn. Mr. Ricardo could not but allow, indeed he has allowed, that rents would be finally higher in both cases. But he immediately supposes that this change is put in execution at once, and refers to the temporary result of land being thrown out of cultivation. Even on this supposition however, all the lands which had been thrown up, would be cultivated again in a very much less time, than it would take to reduce the price of labour, in a natural state of things, to the maintenance only of a stationary population. And therefore, with a view to permanent and final results, which are the results which Mr. Ricardo has mainly [1836: principally] considered throughout his work, he ought to have allowed the truth of Adam Smith's statements.'

Malthus himself did not, in fact, accept that a transition to a cheaper diet would temporarily diminish rent. It was inappropriate to analyse the transition in terms of a once-and-for all shock to the system, given the typically slow character of any such change: 'But, in point of fact, there is very probability that not even a temporary fall of rent would take place. No nation ever has changed or ever will change the nature of its food all at once. The process, both in reference to the new system of cultivation to be adopted, and the new tastes to be generated, must necessarily be very slow. In the greater portion of Europe, it is probable, that a change from corn to rice could never take place; and where it could, it would require such great preparation for irrigation, *as to give ample time for an increase of population fully equal to the increased quantity of food produced*' (1820, 231; 1836, 211; emphasis added).

Here then once again emerges the typical presumption that expansion of food supply generates its own demand via population growth, assuring the maintenance of food prices and rents.[48] Indeed, 'though it must lead to great errors, not to distinguish very decidedly the temporary rates of wages from their final effects, it would lead to no such error to consider the temporary effect of the changes of food which have been referred to, as of the same kind with their final effects, that is, as tending always to raise rents' (1820, 232–3; 1836, 212). The case for rapid population increase relative to the expansion of food supply to assure the maintenance of prices is supported by case-studies of India and Ireland. And in the specific reference to Ireland will be found the further feature of a price floor created by the English market – a typically physiocratic perspective.

* * *

Yet despite everything a scarcity requirement is specified by Malthus. For he spelled out that 'the causes of the high price of raw produce [1820: the causes of the [1836: ordinary] excess of the price of raw produce above the costs of production] may be stated to be three' (1815b/1986, 7, 119; 1820, 139; 1836, 140). The first two were those already alluded to: 'First, and mainly, that quality of the earth [1836: soil], by which it can be made to yield a greater portion [1836: quantity] of the necessaries of life than is required for the maintenance of the persons employed on the land.' Second, 'that quality peculiar to the necessaries of life, of being able [1820: when properly distributed] to create their own demand, or to raise up a number of demanders in proportion to the quantity of necessaries produced.' The third was the 'comparative scarcity of the most fertile land [1820: 'The comparative scarcity of fertile land, either natural or artificial].' This third condition is elaborated thus: 'That there are some circumstances connected with rent, which have an affinity to a natural monopoly, will be readily allowed. The extent of the earth itself is limited, and cannot be enlarged by human demand. And the inequality of soils occasions, even at an early period of society, a comparative scarcity of the best lands; and so far [1820: this scarcity] is undoubtedly one of the causes of rent properly so called. On this account, perhaps, the term *partial monopoly* might be fairly applicable [1820: to it]. But the scarcity of land, thus implied, is by

48 The fact is, however, that Malthus elsewhere insists that food supply may increase or decrease without affecting population supply (see 1820, 241–2; and modifications in 1836, 217f.).

no means sufficient to produce the effects observed. And a more accurate investigation of the subject will shew us how essentially different [1820, how different] the high price of raw produce [1836: the ordinary excess of the price of raw produce above its cost of production] is, both in its nature and origin, and the laws by which it is governed, from the high price of a common monopoly' (emphasis in 1820, 1836).

It was the first characteristic that generated a physical surplus – the concern extends beyond rent proper – without which, however scarce land might be, 'neither rent, nor any essential surplus produce of the land in the form of high profits [1820: and high wages] could have existed' (1815b, 119; 1820, 140; 1836, 141). In the *Principles* the emphasis is, in fact, formally placed on the maximum rent *potential*, allowing that the surplus might take other forms than rent: 'On the other hand, it will be allowed, that in whatever way the produce of a given portion of land is divided, whether the whole is distributed to the labourers and capitalists, or a part is awarded to a landlord, the *power* of such land to yield rent is exactly proportioned to its [1836: natural or acquired] fertility, or to the general surplus which it can be made to produce beyond what is strictly necessary to support the labour and keep up the capital employed upon it.'

This physical potential, the 'foundation or main cause of all rent,' had to be supplemented since 'if the necessaries of life ... had not the property of creating an increase of demand proportioned to their increased quantity, such increased quantity would occasion a fall in their exchangeable value. However abundant might be the produce of a country, its population might remain stationary. And this abundance, without a proportionate demand and with a very high corn-price of labour, which would naturally take place under these circumstances, might reduce the price of raw produce, like the price of manufactures, to the cost of production' (1815b, 119–20). Or again: 'This surplus, necessary and important as it is, would not be sure of possessing a value which would enable it to command a proportionate quantity of labour and other commodities, if it had not a power of raising up a population to consume it, and, by the articles produced in return, of creating an effective demand for it' (1820, 141; 1836, 141). It is subsequently allowed – as 'so obviously true, as to be hardly worth stating' – that 'if land of the greatest fertility were in such excessive plenty compared with the population, that every man might help himself to as much as he wanted, there would be no rents or landlords properly so called' (1820, 206; 1836, 195); and similarly, if 'you could suppose the soil suddenly to be made so fertile, that a tenth part of the surface, and a tenth part of the labour now employed upon it, could more than support the present population, you would for some time considerably lower rent.'

There is a further significant allowance for the scarcity requirement; and though it appears only in 1815, it is in line with the argument thus far.

Malthus proceeds in all versions to elaborate the dependence of population growth upon a prior increase of the 'necessaries of life,' a dependence that rendered land 'fundamentally different from every other kind of machine.' He here drew on Smith's assertion that 'when food is provided, it is comparatively easy to find the necessary clothing and lodging'; furthermore, land also yields the requisite materials for other necessaries' (1815b, 120; 1820, 141–2; 1836, 141–2).[49] But he remarks in the pamphlet that, should cotton machinery have those qualities of land which permit it to yield 'food, clothing and lodging, in such proportions as to create an increase of population equal to the increased supply of these necessaries,' there would result a *rent* to such machinery – since 'the demand for the products of such improved machinery would continue in excess above the cost of production ....' And here is attached a most revealing note: 'I have supposed some check to the supply of the cotton machinery in this case. If there was no check whatever, the effects would show themselves in excessive profits and excessive wages, without an excess above the cost of production.' This note – as well as the imaginary case to which it is attached – is removed in 1820, but the supposed contrast between land and cotton machinery is elaborated – namely, that in the latter case alone increase of output eradicates the value product: 'After the new cotton machinery had been introduced into this country, a hundred yards of muslin of a certain quality would not probably command more labour than [1836: so much labour as] twenty-five yards would before; because the supply had increased faster [1836: in a greater degree] than the demand, and there was no longer a demand for the whole quantity produced at the

49 The following note attached to the text creates problems: 'It is, however, certain, that if either these materials be wanting, or the skill and capital necessary to work them up be prevented from forming, owing to the insecurity of property, or any other cause, the cultivators will soon slacken in their exertions, and the motives to accumulate and to increase their produce, will greatly diminish. But in this case there will be a very slack demand for labour; and, whatever may be the nominal cheapness of provisions, the labourer [1836: the whole body of labourers] will not really be able to command such a portion of the necessaries of life, including, of course, clothing, lodging, &c. as will occasion an increase of population.'

'Cultivators' reduce food production in the event of some impediment to the making-up of raw materials, presumable because of a lack of manufactured goods against which to exchange food; this would explain the 'nominal cheapness of provisions.' Food supplies and thus the demand for labour (and presumably the *corn wage*) will be reduced, which together with a low corn price implies low purchasing power over *other* necessaries – imagining the worker to be, so to speak, paid in corn. The trouble is that here population is said to respond, *not* to the corn wage as such, but to the *general* wage basket, 'including ... clothing, lodging, &c.' This is confirmed by the summary in the text: 'It is, therefore, strictly true, that land produces the necessaries of life – produces food, material, and labour, – produces the means by which, and by which alone, an increase of people may be brought into being, and supported.' So we end up after all with a different proposition from that with which we set out: population growth does *not* turn solely on the supply of food.

same price. But after great improvements in agriculture have been adopted upon a limited tract of land, a quarter of wheat will in a short time command just as much labour as before; because the increased produce, occasioned by the improvements in cultivation [1836: if properly distributed], is found to create a demand proportioned to the supply, which must still be limited; and the value of corn is thus prevented from falling like the value of muslin' (1820, 143–4; 1836, 143–4).

Where then do Malthus and Ricardo differ since Malthus too specifies a scarcity requirement? The answer would seem to lie in Malthus's primary concern with the *total surplus* or excess of corn output over internal (agricultural) consumption, and its *value* counterpart – the first accounted for by a Providential quality in land, the second by the population reaction to food, which assures appropriate demand. The third, or land-scarcity, condition accounts only for the surplus taking the specific form of rent narrowly defined. Were land free – recall the cotton-machinery example – 'the effects would show themselves in excessive profits and excessive wages ....' But those excessive returns too would have to be explained by the Providential surplus of corn output over minimum internal corn consumption, and by a corresponding value excess assured by population growth in response to any increase in the food supply. Malthus's concessions regarding the role of land scarcity effectively undermined his objections to those 'moderns,' including Ricardo, who insisted on rent as a transfer. But he disguised – or, better perhaps, hid from himself – this profound implication by stressing the alleged peculiar qualities attached to agriculture.

* * *

As we have seen, Ricardo's scarcity orientation disallowed any *analytical* distinction between sectors. This perspective is forcefully reiterated in a series of notes on Malthus's text. Malthus's first (net productivity) condition (above, p. 386) required only that land yields 'a greater value in return than the value of the labour expended on it' and this was 'true of every assumption in which man engages. If produce of all kinds did not fulfil those conditions it would not be produced' (*Note 47*; 1951–73, II, 106). The supplementary second condition was 'quite fallacious,' since it inverted the caused sequence: 'If Mr. Malthus had merely said that with the facility of providing food, population will rapidly increase, because food is one of the most important objects of consumption, it would be impossible to differ from him; but he invariably insists that the increase of population, does not depend on the means which we possess of providing for it, but rather which the people themselves have of providing for their offspring, but on the previous provision of food, which is laid up for them' (*Note 48* and *Note 51*; 107, 111). In any event, the intimate connection drawn between food and population *such that corn wages are constant* was illegitimate: 'but population and necessaries are not necessarily linked together so intimately – it is not difficult to conceive that with better education and improved habits, a day's labour may become much more valuable estimated even in what are now called the necessaries of the labourer' (*Note 56*; 115).

Ricardo was particularly insistent on the *identical* role played by 'external demand' in all cases: 'Here is an unfounded distinction. In the partial monopoly of the land, which produces necessaries, (says Mr. M.) such an excess of the value of the produce above the value of the labour, employed in obtaining it, can only be created by the qualities of the soil, – in the other case they are "created by external demand." The qualities of the soil can do nothing in either case without external demand. The rent of our most fertile lands is greater now than it was 100 years ago: Why? Because of the increase of external demand, compared with the facility of supplying it. The qualities of the soil were the same then as now, yet rent did not increase, till external demand increased' (*Note 55*; 114).

Scarcity theory undermined Malthus's attempted defence of rent as a 'gift of Providence' (above, p. 382): 'I repeat confidently that rent is owing to the limit which nature has set to her present, and not to the unbounded extent of it. If there had been no limits to fertility, if one capital after another had been equally productive, of produce, no rent could have been generated ...' (*Note 126*; 211). And he defended Say against Malthus (above, p. 382) in the same terms: 'Can any one doubt that if a person could appropriate to himself the wind and the sun, he would be able to commend a rent for the uses to be derived from them?' (*Note 45*; 104). He reacted similarly to the remark that rent is 'an exact measure of the *relief* from labour in the production of food' granted by Providence (above, p. 383): 'Mr. Malthus may call it so if he pleases, but would not the real relief be greater if the land were more fertile? Would not rent fall as the present became more liberal' (*Note 127*; 213). Moreover, it was wholly illegitimate to identify rent with the surplus: 'But is rent an exact measure of the relief from labour in the production of food? I deny it. The surplus produce is, but rent, and surplus produce, do not mean the same thing. The surplus produce in America, in proportion to the population, is greater than here. Is rent as high there? Mr. Malthus will not say it is. The surplus produce in America shews itself chiefly in profits and in high wages, and contributes much more to the general prosperity in that form, than if it appeared in the form of rent.'

Ricardo's answer to the criticism of his analysis of the hypothetical case of reduced fertility – namely, that in consequence of an increase in effective land scarcity rents are forced upwards (above, pp. 384–5) – is that this analysis – a deliberate strong case – assumed constant population and demand for food: 'To suppose the fertility of the land diminished one half, is a most extravagant supposition – I made it only to illustrate a principle. Mr. Malthus has misunderstood me – I fully acknowledge the interest which landlords have in the increased fertility of their land, and in improvements in agriculture, for they cannot fail ultimately to reap the benefit, all I contend for, is, that the immediate effects are injurious to them, and if the principle of population were not strong might be permanently injurious to them' (*Note 52*; 112–13). And *Note 59* responds to the charge (above p. 384) that he had 'misunderstood' Malthus: 'I certainly did misunderstand Mr. Malthus. He says he stated "three causes as necessary to the production of rent and he could not possibly have meant to say that rent should vary always and exactly in proportion to one of them." I should think that my inference that he did was the natural one if the other causes were at the time inoperative. One of the causes stated by Mr. Malthus as necessary to the production of rent is the comparative scarcity of the most fertile land. If he had said increase this comparative scarcity and rent will rise – I should have agreed with him, and here would have been one cause influencing rent without any interference from the other two. So when talking of what he calls another cause of rent, the fertility of the land, and the excess of its produce beyond what is necessary to support the labourers, employed on it, he said, "Diminish this plenty, diminish the fertility of the soil and the excess will disappear," – he did appear to me to identify the excess or surplus produce with rent, and he appeared to me to lead his readers to infer that rent arose and fell with the quantity of this surplus produce' (120–1). More generally, 'he appears to me by his language frequently to convey an impression to the mind of his reader that rent rises and falls with the rise and fall of the quantity of surplus produce beyond what is bestowed on the actual labourers. In [1820] page 228 Mr. Malthus says, "But if it be granted as it must be that a limitation in the power of producing food is obviously necessary to man confined to a limited space, then the value of the actual quantity of land which he has received depends upon the small quantity of labour necessary to work it compared with the number of persons which it will support or in other words, *upon that specific surplus so much underrated by Mr. Ricardo, which by the laws of nature terminates in rent*' (121). Ricardo quite rightly perceived Malthus's argument as a sort of rearguard action which in fact left the substance of the argument – the Providential basis – undefended.

VIII THE GROWTH CONTEXT

In the 1817 edition of the *Essay on Population,* Malthus maintained that, of two growing systems, both subject to falling returns to labour and capital, the agricultural economy had the advantage over the manufacturing economy in that its 'disposable income' remains relatively undiminished: 'It should ... be observed that in a state, the revenue of which consists solely in profits and wages, the diminution of profits and wages may greatly impair its disposable income. The increase in the amount of capital and in the number of labourers may in many cases not be sufficient to make up for the diminished rate of profits and wages. But where the revenue of the country consists of rents as well as profits and wages, a great part of what is lost in profits and wages is gained in rents, and the disposable income remains comparatively unimpaired' (1817, II, 425). This same notion is repeated in the *Principles*, Malthus now making use of Ricardo's propositions regarding the course of profits and wages: 'According to Mr. Ricardo, not only will each individual capital in the progress of society yield a continually diminishing revenue, but the whole amount of the revenue derived from the profits will be diminished [1836: Mr. Ricardo seems to think that the whole amount of the revenue derived from profits might be diminished in the progress of accumulation]; and there is no doubt [1836: and the probability I fear is] that the labourer will be obliged to employ a greater quantity of labour to produce that portion of his wages which must be spent in necessaries. Both these great classes of society, therefore, may be expected to have less power of giving leisure to themselves, or of commanding the labour of those who administer to the enjoyments [1836: and the intellectual improvement] of society, as contradistinguished from those who administer to its necessary wants' (1820, 237; 1836, 215–16). Rent, however, made up the shortfall: 'Among the inestimable advantages which belong to that quality in the land, which enables it to yield a considerable rent, it is not one of the least, that in the progress of society it affords the main security to man that nearly his whole time, or the time of nearly the whole society, shall not be employed in procuring mere necessaries .... [F]ortunately for mankind, the neat rent of the land, under a system of private property, can never be diminished by the progress of cultivation. Whatever proportion they may bear to the whole produce, the actual amount must always go on increasing, and will always afford a fund for the enjoyments and leisure of the society, sufficient to leaven and animate the whole mass.' Accordingly, 'that quality of land which, by the laws of our being, must terminate in rent, appears to be a boon most important to the happiness of mankind; and I am persuaded, that its value can only be underrated by those who still labour under some mistake, as to its nature, and its effects on society' (1820, 239; 1836, 217). Malthus sought to avoid the charge of a bias favouring a *specific* group of landlords: 'The benefit is attached to the soil ...,' and there were wide opportunities for ownership (1820, 237–8; 1836, 216–17).

Ricardo protested quite rightly that Malthus's representation of the secular rise in rent in the course of growth as a providential *boon* compensating for falling profits was unacceptable precisely because the rise in rent was at the expense of profit, the latter a part of the 'surplus' and not a 'clear gain': 'There is a surplus produce from the land from which profits and rents are taken. I am of opinion that the interests of society are best promoted by allowing the free importation of corn, the consequence of which is that the surplus produce from the land in cultivation at home will be divided in proportions more favorable to the farmer and capitalist, and less favorable to the landholder. Mr. Malthus appears to differ from me, but instead of shewing that society would be benefited by taking from the capitalist and giving to the landlord, he considers rent as a clear gain and accuses me of underrating its value because I am not willing to allow that the surplus produce increases or diminishes as rent rises or falls' (*Note 142*; 1951–73, II, 223). Malthus's perspective distorted his policy position: 'On my plan there will be no transfer neither from profits or wages to rent; prohibit importation and there will, while the actual produce will be less. "See the advantages of growing corn over importing it," says Mr. Malthus; "with the progress of capital, profits and wages will fall, but if you grow your own corn, you will have rents to compensate you for this loss." I answer, refuse to grow your own corn, and profits will not fall, and you will not want an inadequate compensation for a loss which you will not suffer' (*Note 141*; 1951–73, II, 222). The same position had been stated in the correspondence of 1818 in response to the 'question of the comparative advantage of employing capital in agriculture or in manufactures,' raised by Malthus in a no longer extant letter. The concept of rent as a net contribution to wealth generated only in agriculture failed to take account of the fact that the increase of real national income in the war years 1793–1813 (a period of effective protection) – which indeed reflected an increase of rent – would have been yet larger in the event of free trade, though it would then have appeared as *profit*:

If by wealth you mean, as I do, all those things which are desirable to man, wealth, I think, would be most effectually increased by allowing corn to be grown, or imported, as best suits those concerned in the trade. You say that in the one case the corn obtained would only be sufficient to support the workmen employed and *pay fully the profits of stock*; and in the other case it would pay in addition the increased amount of rent, and support an additional population proportioned to it. Now *if the profits of stock to be paid fully* in one case would be much greater both in value as defined by you, and in value, as defined by me than in the other, it is evident that the difference might not only equal the additional amount of rent, but exceed it. I contend that the profits of stock would be higher than this whole amount, if we consented to import corn; and therefore, although I will admit, that in the case supposed, our wealth has increased by the increase of rent, from 1793 to 1813, yet I would contend that if the trade had been free, and corn had been imported in preference to growing it, under the new and improved circumstances of agriculture, our wealth would have increased in a still greater ratio than it now has done. (24 June 1818; 1951–73, VII, 270–1)[50]

50 For Malthus, the experience of rising profits without reduction in wages – 'a matter of incontrovertible fact' – simultaneously with agricultural expansion and growth of national income in the form of rent, proved that 'rents are a creation not a transfer' from

IX THE DIMINISHING-RETURNS COMPLEXITY ELABORATED

Ricardo in 1815 had pointed to the conflict between the diminishing-returns conception in the *Inquiry into Rent*, whereby 'land which is successively taken into cultivation in improving countries may only pay profits and labour,' and the so-called *pre-eminence* of agriculture (above, pp. 379–80). This same issue arises in the *Principles* (1820), where in discussing definitions of 'productive labour' Malthus proposed tentatively that all labour – even service labour – be categorized as 'productive,' but to different degrees, upon which principle 'the labours of agriculture would, *generally speaking*' – not universally – 'be the most productive; because the produce of nearly all the land actually in use is not only of sufficient exchangeable value to pay the labourers employed upon it, but the profits of the stock advanced by the farmers, and the rents of the land let by the proprietors' (1820, 38; emphasis added).[51] This definitional approach 'would determine ... the natural pre-eminence of agriculture, which Adam Smith is obliged to explain afterwards, and, at the same time, shew the numerous cases where *an increase of manufacturing and mercantile labour would be more productive, both to the state and to individuals, than an increase of agriculture*; as in all cases where, from a greater demand for manufactured and mercantile products, compared with the produce of land, *the profits of manufacturing and mercantile capital were greater than both the rent and profits combined of labour employed upon new and less fertile land*' (39; emphasis added). This important qualification reflects the small rent (if any) generated on marginal land. The principle of diminishing returns was undermining the notion of a pre-eminent agriculture.[52]

---

profits (16 August; 279). In any event, the agricultural expansion would not have occurred had there been reliance on foreign corn: 'If [rents] have risen chiefly from improvements in agriculture occasioned by the direction of so much capital to the land in consequence of a high price [of] corn, is it not an increase of wealth which would not otherwise have been obtained?' Ricardo's response again allows an expansion of income in the form of rent but repeats that this involves a *transfer* from profits, which occurs only 'ultimately,' an evident reference to the situation after increase of population (20 August; 282–3).

51 Although the classification was not finally adopted, the substantive difference between sectors stands.

52 In the 1803 *Essay*, Malthus maintained that 'one of the principal ingredients in the price of British corn, is the high rent of land' which points away from comprehension of a no-rent margin at this early stage (1986, *3*, 683). This is absent in 1806. Similarly, a statement of 1803 that 'the price of produce ... is necessarily regulated by the wages of labour, and the rent of land' (1986, *3*, 676) is absent from the 1806 version. And in 1806 we have the generalization that 'universally, it is price that determines rent, not rent that determines price' (1806, II, 266). In that edition Malthus alludes to *differential rent*: 'land on which little labour has been bestowed, will generally yield a higher rent than that on which much has been bestowed ...' (267). Moreover, even the notion of a

* * *

Eltis has observed that Malthus 'set out a Physiocratic analysis with the modification that there were diminishing not constant returns in agriculture' (1984, 321). But the fact is that adopting diminishing returns is inconsistent with the physiocratic position. Several instances may be given of the problems Malthus created for himself.

There is, first, a wholly unfair attribution to his opponents – the so-called monopoly theorists – of support for the *legal* reduction of the corn price as a means to lower rent, since the high price of corn was disadvantageous to consumers and to no one's benefit except landholders: 'With regard to my own conviction, indeed, I feel no sort of doubt that if, under the impression that the high price of raw produce, which occasions rent, is as injurious [1836: And if, under the impression that the ordinary excess of the price of raw produce above the costs of production which occasions rent on the great mass of land is as injurious] to the consumer as it is advantageous to the landlord, a rich and improved nation were determined by law, to lower the price of produce, till no surplus in the shape of rent any where remained; it would inevitably throw not only all the poor

---

no-rent margin appears: 'If we take the clear surplus produce of the land, according to the Economists, in this case the funds for the maintenance of labour and the population may increase, without an increase of wealth, as in the instance of the cultivation of new lands, which will pay a profit but not a rent' (207); and with respect to the effect of increased foreign corn imports: 'Arable lands of a moderate quality would hardly pay the expense of cultivation. Rich soils alone would yield a rent' (226).

Prendergast has drawn attention to two articles by Malthus for the *Edinburgh Review* (1808 and 1809), claiming that the discussion of rent therein 'seems to indicate that Malthus had already gone some distance in the development of his theory [of differential rent]' (1987, 403), and to imply 'that further increases in produce could not be forthcoming except at a higher cost of production' (404). None the less, he 'had not yet arrived at the complete theory' involving 'the realization that corn in reference to the quantity actually produced is sold at its necessary price,' which is to be found in the *Observations* (1814). Prendergast explores the possible impact on Malthus of James Anderson.

Question 8 of the 1808 examination paper (above, note 18) asks: 'What is the sense in which the Economists understand the term *productive*? And how does it appear that this does not include even all the labour employed upon the land?' Precisely the same question appears in the Inverarity transcript of Malthus's lectures of 1830. His answer then is the following: 'The only labour which the Economists call "productive" is that which yields a neat rent but this sense of the word "productive" cannot be applied even to all the labour employed upon the land. In North America for instance the labourer might find it a sufficient inducement to cultivate land, which being before covered with wood yielded of itself a neat rent, if it will afford him reasonable profit without any neat rent. There are many coal mines which provided they yielded reasonable profits might be advantageously worked by the owner though they yielded no neat rent. This is the case with sea fisheries. Salmon fisheries sometimes however do yield a neat rent' (cited in Pullen, 1981b, 809).

land, but all, except the very best land, out of cultivation, and probably reduce its produce and population to less than one-tenth of their former amount' (1815b/1936, 7, 132; 1820, 182; 1836, 176).[53] These propositions are unconvincing. Obviously, assuming diminishing returns, a legal reduction in the corn price would bring about agricultural contraction and lower rent; Ricardo never disputed that. But Malthus claimed to derive from the implications of a legal reduction in the corn price support for his representation of rent as a 'neat surplus' rather than a transfer, and this he cannot do.[54]

In order to reinforce his case, Malthus contrasts agriculture and manufacturing, to the latter's disadvantage. Thus a reduced level of demand of sufficient magnitude would 'destroy' a (constant-cost) industry, whereas in agriculture – where 'machinery' takes the form of land of different gradations generating an upward-sloping supply curve – a downward shift in demand merely reduces output from marginal land: 'The difference between the price of corn and the price of manufactures, with regard to natural or necessary price, is this; that if the price of any manufacture were essentially depressed, the whole manufacture would be entirely destroyed; whereas, if the price of corn were essentially [1836: equally] depressed, the *quantity* of it would be diminished. There would be some machinery in the country still capable of sending the commodity to market at the reduced price ...' (1815b, 133; 1820, 184; 1836, 178). Conversely, in the case of an increase in demand: 'The most fertile [1836: and best situated] lands of a country, those which, like the best machinery in manufactures, yield the greatest products with the least labour and capital [1836: expenditure], are never found sufficient, [1820, 1836: *owing to the second main cause of rent before stated*], to supply the effective [1836: effectual] demand of an increasing population. The price of raw produce, therefore, naturally rises till it becomes sufficiently high to pay [1836: naturally increases till it answers to pay] the cost of raising it with inferior machines, and by a more expensive process; and, as there cannot be two prices for corn of the same quality, all the other machines, the working of which requires less capital [1836: expenditure] compared with the produce, must yield rents in proportion to their goodness' (1815b, 133–4; 1820, 185; 1836, 179; emphasis added). The text also briefly alludes to the *intensive* margin: 'Every extensive country may thus be considered as possessing a gradation of machines for the

53 This shows how small was the role Malthus accorded the diminishing-returns principle in the policy debate. For the argument no longer relates to the negative effect of reduced rent on the motive for *agricultural improvement*, as in the *Observations* (1814) or earlier in the *Rent* pamphlet itself. Rather the case proceeds along static lines – a reduced corn price would force marginal land out of use. The diminishing-returns principle thus adds nothing to the protectionist case apart from confirmation of the absolute contraction to agriculture that would result from free trade.

54 That indeed is Ricardo's complaint in *Notes 94* and *95*; 1951–73, II, 164–6.

production of corn and raw materials, including in this gradation not only all the various qualities of poor land, of which every large territory has generally an abundance, but the inferior machinery which may be said to be employed when good land is further and further forced for additional produce.' And the moral of it all was 'to shew at once the necessity of the actual [1836: existing] price of corn to the actual [1836: existing] produce, in the existing [1836: actual] state of most of the countries with which we are acquainted, and the different effect which would attend a great reduction in the price of any particular manufacture, and a great reduction in the price of raw produce.'

On the general principles involved, Ricardo expressed fulsome praise (*Note 98*; 1951–73, II, 169). But he was excessively generous, considering Malthus's insertion in 1820 that it is '*owing to the second main cause of rent before stated*' that the most fertile lands never suffice 'to supply the effective demand of an increasing population.' This second cause refers to 'that quality peculiar to the necessaries of life of being able ... to create their own demand, or to raise up a number of demanders in proportion to the quantity of necessaries produced,' which Ricardo of course rejected (above, section VII).

In all versions Malthus used the increasing-cost principle to argue that the corn price would be unchanged were landlords to *relinquish* rent, since price is determined at the no-rent margin: 'There is no just reason to believe, that if [1836: if, in the present state of this country] the lands [1820: landlords] were to give the whole of their rents to their tenants, corn would be more plentiful and cheaper [1836: in any marked degree cheaper]. If the view of the subject, taken in the preceding inquiry, be correct, the last additions made to our home produce are sold at [1820: at nearly] the cost of production and [1836: independently of agricultural improvements] the same quantity could not be produced from our own soil at a less price, even without rent [1836: at an essentially less price, even without rent, supposing the value of money to remain the same]. The effect of transferring all rents to tenants, would be merely the turning them into gentlemen [1836: landlords], and tempting them to cultivate their farms under the superintendence of careless and uninterested bailiffs, instead of the vigilant eye of a master, who is deterred from carelessness by the fear of ruin, and stimulated to exertion by the hope of a competence' (1815b, 57–8; 1820, 201–2; 1836, 191–2).

Ricardo approved this statement (1951–73, I, 74–5). But Malthus read much more into it than did Ricardo, representing it as confuting the objectionable 'monopoly' (scarcity) approach to corn pricing and rent maintained by the 'more modern' authors: 'the doctrine, that corn, in reference to the *quantity actually produced,* is sold at [1836: nearly] its necessary price like manufactures ... I consider ... as a truth of the highest [1820: of high] importance, which has been entirely overlooked by the Economists, by Adam Smith, and all those writers who have represented raw produce as selling always at a monopoly price' (1815b, 134; 1820, 191; 1836, 184; italics in 1815 version only). If the corn price is a 'necessary' price reflecting marginal costs under pressure of demand, and rent the outcome, any notion of the price of corn (and the return to land) arising from 'monopoly' – with the implication that rent constituted a transfer and was injurious to consumers – was unacceptable. Here Malthus was on shaky ground. The increasing-cost characteristic of agriculture, whereby the corn price (however high it may rise) is a *necessary* price to assure the requisite output, and rent the necessary result, entails standard competitive demand–supply analysis, the equilibrium price determined at the intersection of an upward-sloping supply curve and the *independent* demand curve. We have also seen (sections VII and VIII) that Malthus had to all intents and purposes admitted that rent *was* a scarcity payment, clinging, however, to his general notion of agricultural value surplus. Unfortunately, that notion turned on the *dependence* of the demand for corn on supply, which assured that an increase in supply did not depress the corn price. He had fallen into a logical trap – insisting upon the physiocratic view of rent as surplus while allowing the differential principle of rent. Malthus's theoretical position was, as Ricardo insisted, untenable.[55]

55 A lengthy note added in the 1836 edition charges Perronet Thompson (1826) with inconsistency for accepting the scarcity property underlying rent despite having accepted also the diminishing-returns property. Thompson was at one with Ricardo in identifying a single general principle as responsible for rent in all cases (1836, 148–9n).

There arises a serious question as to Malthus's genuine comprehension of Ricardo's position. On several occasions in his chapter on Rent, he asserts that, in the absence of agricultural improvement, there would be little prospect for increasing rent: 'But after all, the increase of rents which results from an increase in price occasioned solely by the greater quantity of labour and capital [1836: labour and other conditions of supply] necessary to produce corn on fresh land, is very much more limited than has been supposed' (1820, 208; 1836, 197). Similarly, any expansion of rents would be soon halted if such expansion was the consequence of 'an increase in price occasioned solely by the increased quantity of labour necessary to produce food' (1820, 209; 1836, 198). These, one might think, are without question references to expansion of population on to marginal land. But the fact is that, shortly after, Malthus makes a remark suggesting an amazing failure to comprehend the Ricardian position regarding rising rent with extensions to less productive areas. The text in question runs as follows: 'Mr. Ricardo, as I have before intimated takes [1836: appears to take] only one simple and confined view of the progress of rent. He considers it as occasioned solely by the increase of price, arising from the increased difficulty of production. But if rents in many countries may be doubled or tripled by improvements in agriculture, while in a few countries they could be raised a fourth or a fifth, and in some not a tenth, by the increase of price arising from the increased difficulty of production, must it not be acknowledged, that such a view of rent embraces only a very small part of the subject, and consequently that any general inferences from it must be utterly inapplicable to practice? (1820, 211–12; 1836, 200). So far so good; but attached is a most curious note: 'Mr. Ricardo always seems to assume, that increased difficulties thrown in the way of production will be overcome by increased price, and that the same quantity will be produced. But this

A similar anomaly emerges in elsewhere in the Rent chapter ('Of the Connexion between great comparative Wealth and a high comparative Price of raw Produce'). It starts off with a criticism of Smith for failing to deal adequately with the cost pricing of corn: 'Adam Smith has very clearly explained in what manner the progress of wealth and improvement tends to raise the price of cattle, poultry, the materials of clothing and lodging, the most useful minerals, &c. &c. compared with corn; but he has not entered into the explanation of the natural causes which tend to determine the price of corn. He has left the reader, indeed, to conclude, that he considers the price of corn as determined only by the state of the mines which at the time supply the circulating medium of the commercial world. But this is a cause obviously inadequate to account for the actual differences in the price of grain, observable in countries at no great distance from each other, and at nearly the same distance from the mines [1820: But this is a cause, which, though it may account for the high or low price of corn positively [1836: in reference to the whole of the commercial world], cannot account for the relative differences [1836: 'relative' omitted] in its price, in different countries, or compared with certain classes of commodities in the same country]' (1815b, 134; 1820, 192; 1836, 184–5). But Malthus had repeatedly *denied* the applicability of the usual tools of demand–supply analysis to the case of *corn*. Here, in objecting to Smith, he insists upon it.

* * *

That diminishing returns posed a severe problem for the surplus approach to rent is reflected in two qualification made in the *Principles*. It would seem that, having served the purpose of justifying rent as the consequence of 'necessary price,' the principle could be played down in order to emphasize the surplus dimension. The first qualification denies that diminishing

is an unwarranted assumption. Where is the increased price to come from? An increase of difficulty in the actual state of a country's resources will always tend to diminish produce' (1820, 212n). This note suggests that Malthus ascribes to Ricardo a view of increasing rent attributable to increased difficulty of production, which assumes a *given* level of activity; that is, the rising cost is unrelated to expansions of demand for corn requiring extensions and higher cost output; 'increased difficulty' occurs as an exogenous deterioration. If Malthus is taken seriously, it would seem that we must so read him in all other statements regarding the Ricardian position which represents rents as a *transfer* achieved by higher cost prices. Yet this cannot be. For sometimes in the Rent chapter, he represents the Ricardo view fairly, with emphasis on rising rents as cultivation is extended to *poorer* lands.

In the 1836 edition, Malthus's note is altered, but this version is equally difficult to understand: 'Mr. Ricardo always seems to assume, that increased difficulties thrown in the way of production will be overcome by increased price, and that the same quantity will be produced as would have been produced if no increased difficulty had occurred. But this is quite an unwarranted assumption' (1836, 200n).

returns is the *sine qua non* of rent; absolute land scarcity sufficed: 'We must not however draw too large inferences from this gradation of machinery on the land. It is what actually exists in almost all countries, and accounts very clearly for the origin and progress of rent, while land still remains in considerable plenty. But such a gradation is not strictly necessary, either to the original formation, or the subsequent regular rise of rents. All that is necessary to produce these effects, is the existence of the two first causes of rent formerly mentioned [above, p. 386], *with the addition of limited territory, or a scarcity of fertile land*' (1820, 186; 1836, 180; emphasis added). At this point it is asserted that the characteristic fall in wage and profit rates till stationariness will occur under these conditions, 'while the rents would be high, in proportion to the fertility of the soil': 'If all the land of such a [1836: this] country were precisely equal in quality, and all very rich [1836: and all as rich, as the best], there cannot be the slightest doubt, that after the whole of the land had been taken into cultivation, both the profits of stock, and the real wages of labour, would go on diminishing till profits had been reduced to what were [1836: was] necessary to keep up the actual capital, and the wages to what were [1836: was] necessary to keep up the actual population, while the rents would be high, just in proportion to the fertility of the soil [1836: just in proportions to the fertility of the soil natural or acquired, and the mass of rents very much greater than at present]' (1820, 187; 1836, 180). This is accompanied by an assurance once again that physical and value productivity coincide in the case of corn alone: 'Whatever may be the qualities of any commodity, it is well known that it can have no exchangeable value, if it exists in a great excess above the wants of those who are to use it. But such are the qualities of the necessaries of life that, *in a limited territory*, and under ordinary circumstances, they cannot [1836: if properly distributed] be permanently in excess' (emphasis added). Malthus adds that his argument would apply equally if limitation on the capital/land ratio were assumed: 'Nor would the effect be essentially different, if the quantity of stock [1836: the capital] which could be employed with advantage upon such fertile soil were extremely limited, so that no further capital [1836: outlay] were required for it than what was wanted for ploughing and sowing. Still there can be no doubt that capital and population might go on increasing in other employments, till they both came to a stand [1836: till both the profits of capital and the wages of labour had fallen as to come nearly to a stand], and rents had reached the limits prescribed by the powers of the soil, and the habits of the people' (1820, 187; 1836, 180–1).[56] This formulation implies a *constant* marginal

56 Malthus here took Ricardo to task for asserting differential land qualities and/or diminishing returns at the intensive margin as *necessary* conditions for rent: 'In these cases it is obvious that the rents are not regulated by the gradations of the soil, or the different products of capital on the same land ...' As usual the two were at cross purposes. For Ricardo allowed for the case of a vertical supply curve (1951–73, I, 250–1)).

product until a strictly defined capacity output, followed by a discontinuity, that is, a precipitous collapse to a level assuring zero growth of capital and population. Now, in this case, there will be a *physical* rent generated on land. But it is not at all clear what maintains the price of corn at a level which guarantees a *value* return to land; for since there is an absolute constraint on food output, the precondition for population growth and increasing demand for food is not satisfied. The second 'cause' of rent – the maintenance of the corn price – is inoperative.[57]

Second, Malthus in 1820 allows for rent *at the margin* – at least, at the extensive margin – to reflect the alternative opportunities available from use of land in its 'natural' or uncultivated state, a perspective contrasting with that of 1815 but reverting to the 1814 *Observations* (see above, p. 374).[58] The context is a formal restatement of the diminishing-returns principle:

From the preceding account of the progress of rent, it follows that the actual state of the natural rent of land is necessary to the actual produce [1836: the actual amount of the natural rent of land in the actual state of agricultural skill, is, with very little drawback, necessary to the actual produce]; and that the price of corn [1820, 1836: of produce], in every progressive country, must be just about equal to the cost of production on land of the poorest quality actually in use, [*1820, 1836: with the addition of the rent it would yield in its natural state*]; or to the cost of raising additional produce on old land, which [1820, 1836: additional produce] yields only the usual returns of agricultural stock [1836: capital] with little or no rent.

It is quite obvious that [1836: under the existing value of money] the price cannot be less; or such land would not be cultivated, nor such capital employed. Nor can it very much exceed this price, because the poor land progressively taken into cultivation yields at first little or no rent [*1820, 1836: because it will always answer to the landlord to continue letting poorer and poorer lands, as long as he can get any thing more than they will pay in their natural state*]; and because it will always answer to any farmer who can command capital, to lay it out on his land, if the additional produce resulting from it will fully repay the profits of his stock

57 Strange to relate, Malthus had *himself* recognized this problem in a note to the 1815 pamphlet deleted from the 1820 version: 'It will be observed, that I have said in a *progressive country*, that is, in a country which requires yearly the employment of a greater capital on the land, to support an increasing population. If there were no question about fresh capital, or an increase of people, and all the land were good, it would not then be true that corn must be sold at its necessary price. The actual price might be diminished; and if the rents of land were diminished in proportion, the cultivation might go on as before, and the same quantity be produced' (1986, 7, 135n).

58 The allowance for rent on marginal land ruled out the 'inference' from the theory of rent that agricultural contraction generates a rise in the profit rate proportional to the higher marginal product (1820, 188; 1836, 181). The conclusion is applied to free corn importation, thereby implicitly minimizing the prospective advantages therefrom.

[1836: capital], although it yields nothing to his landlord (1815b, 132–3; 1820, 183–4; 1836, 177–8; emphasis added)

The allowance in the *Principles* for rent at the margin is no casual matter. It is deliberately insisted on. Malthus felt it necessary to reconfirm his original (1815) position on the corn price as the 'necessary' price, *but with the new qualification in mind*: 'It will be observed, that the rents paid for what the land will produce in its natural state, though they make a most essential difference [1836: a difference] in the questions relating to profits and the component parts of price, in no respect invalidate [1836: do not invalidate] the important doctrine that, in progressive countries [1836: in countries] in their usual state with gradations of soil, corn is sold at [1836: nearly at] its natural or necessary price, that is, at the price necessary to bring the actual quantity to market. This price must on an average be at the least equal to the costs of its production on the worst land actually cultivated, *together with the rent of such land in its natural state*: because, if it falls in any degree below this, the cultivator of such land will not be able to pay the landlord so high a rent as he could obtained from the land without cultivation, and consequently the land will be left uncultivated, and the produce will be diminished' (1820, 190–1, 1836, 183–4; emphasis added).[59]

The 1820 and 1836 versions of the remaining text differs. The 1820 version insists without qualification on rent in costs: 'The rent of land in its natural state is therefore obviously so necessary a part of the price of all cultivated products, that, if it be not paid they will not come to market, and the real price actually paid for corn is, on an average, absolutely necessary to the production of the same quantity, or in the words before stated, corn, in reference to the whole quantity produced, is sold at its necessary price' (1820, 191). The 1836 version is somewhat equivocal, at least in the case of 'progressive countries': '*In progressive countries, however, this rent is trifling, and the price of corn is little more than is necessary to pay the wages of the labour and the profits of the capital required to obtain it.* But in the case of land being thrown out of cultivation under an abundance of capital and labour, the rent of the worst land cultivated for corn might by no means be trifling. Still however the actual price of the corn under the same value of money would be necessary to obtain the actual home supply, because if the farmers paid no rents, it would not answer them to produce corn which would not yield so profitable a return as the products of rough

59 See also the qualification that 'practically, the cases are very rare, where land is to be had by anybody who chooses to take it, and probably it is true, almost universally [1836: it is true, perhaps universally], that all appropriated land which yields food in its natural state [1836: *in its natural state*], always [1836: 'always' omitted] yields a rent, whether cultivated or uncultivated.'

pasture, or land in copse wood, or plantations' (1836, 184; emphasis added). In both editions the diminishing-returns principle drops from sight in the concluding section of the chapter on Rent of Land ('General Remarks on the Surplus Produce of the Land'). This suggests a wish to skirt the problem.[60]

X MALTHUS'S 'DEBT' TO THE PHYSIOCRATS

We have been concerned with characteristically 'physiocratic' concepts in Malthus's economics. There is no evidence that at the time of the first *Essay on Population* (1798) he had read any physiocratic literature in the original; his general references to the French economists may reflect second-hand familiarity, derived in part from Adam Smith. But the fact remains that in 1798 he sought to spell out the full implications of the physiocratic definition of '*national wealth*' involving the gross output of land, envisaging it to be in conflict with their own approach to *productivity* involving the *net* produce; agriculture was the pre-eminent sector because of its impact on population growth, and its superiority held good independently of the question of net product, even, indeed, if labourers transferred from manufacturing to agriculture consumed more food than they produced (above, section II).

For Semmel (1965, 534), the notion that the means of subsistence limit population was reached independently, since Malthus in 1798 was unaware of that particular notion in the French literature. He cited the Preface to the 1803 edition of the *Essay* as evidence. But actually that preface refers to *excessive* population growth relative to the growth of food as a notion to be found in a wide range of literature – including 'some of the French economists' as well as Plato and Aristotle in ancient times, 'occasionally' Montesquieu, and 'among our own writers ... Dr Franklin, Sir James Steuart, Mr Arthur Young, and Mr Townsend' – of which Malthus had originally been unaware (1803/1986, *2*, ii). It remains *possible* that the more general proposition relating population growth to food supply was derived originally in part from physiocratic sources, indirectly if not directly.[61] In any event, a powerful index of this 'physiocratic' dimension is provided by the reaction to the 1806 version of the doctrine by Dupont de Nemours

60 The 1824 article 'Political Economy' provides only a weak statement of the no-rent margin: 'we think, on the whole, that satisfactory reasons have been given why, in tracing the causes of exchangeable value, in reference to the most important commodities, rent may be considered as having only a very inconsiderable effect' (1986, *7*, 270).

61 Waterman denies any reliance by Malthus on the Physiocrats, suggesting Richard Paley as a likely source of anything apparently 'physiocratic' in Malthus (letter dated 1 February 1994). For a formal discussion of Paley's economics, including a 'quasi-Physiocratic emphasis on the strategic importance of agriculture,' see Waterman, 1996b. On Malthus and Paley, see also chapter 1, note 3, above.

(1817), the only Physiocrat to live long enough to comment on Malthus: 'Dans ce qu'il y a d'évidemment incontestable, l'ouvrage de M. *Malthus* est un long, mais savant et curieux commentaire de cette maxime des economistes Français: *La mesure de la subsistance est celle de la population*' (1817, 2).[62]

Two specific and favourable references by Malthus to the Physiocrats – to Dupont de Nemours and de Mirabeau – are given in the second edition. The first occurs in a note to a text controverting Smith's position against the Corn Laws on the grounds that any increase in the price of corn will be purely nominal: 'In the Physiocratie, by Dupont de Nemours,[63] it is proposed as a problem in political economy, to determine, whether an advance in the money price of corn is a real or only nominal advantage: and the question is resolved, I think justly, on the side of the reality of the advantage. Tom. ii' (1803, 458n/1986, *3*, 683n). The case in *Physiocratie* (which involves an application of the *tableau économique*) purports to demonstrate the real advantage to all classes including labour of a high corn price. The advantage to labour is elaborated by Quesnay in that work in terms of the approximately proportionate rise in the money wage upon a corn-price increase but lag in the prices of non-corn wage goods. And there is a considerable likelihood that Malthus had access to that case.[64]

The second reference (1803, 477/1986, *3*, 455n) is to *L'Ami des hommes*, specifically to an admission of an earlier error in representing 'population as the source of revenue' rather than the reverse: 'The author of L'Ami des Hommes, in a chapter on the effects of a decay of agriculture upon population, acknowledges that he had fallen into a fundamental error in considering population as the source of revenue; and that he was afterwards fully convinced that revenue was the source of population.[b]' (Note

62 Dupont de Nemours's *Examen du livre de M. Malthus sur le Principe de Population* includes a translation of four chapters in the 1806 edition of the *Essay* absent in P. and G. Prévost's translation of 1809. These chapters are Book III, Chapter VII, 'Of increasing Wealth as it affects the Condition of the Poor'; Chapter VIII, 'Of the Definitions of Wealth. Agricultural and Commercial Systems'; Chapter IX, 'Different Effects of the Agricultural and Commercial Systems'; Chapter X, 'Of Bounties on the Exportation of Corn.'

63 The title page actually has 'Recueil publié par Du Pont.' The substance of the work was by Quesnay.

64 But the Quesnay case is never alluded to formally in the *Essay*, and first appears (without attribution) in Malthus's pamphlets of 1814 and 1815. In *Grounds of an Opinion* (1815), a case for protection turns on the advantage to labour of high corn prices: 'I stated in the *Observations* [1986, *7*, 102–3], and more at large in the *Inquiry into Rent* [127], that under the same demand for labour, and the same consequent power of purchasing the means of subsistence, a high *money price* of corn would give the labourer a very great advantage in the purchase of the conveniences and luxuries of life' (162). The principle is less applicable to 'the very poorest of the society, and those who had the largest families,' since in those cases absolute necessaries absorb almost the entire budget.

'b' gives as reference: 'Tom. viii, 84. 12 mo. 9 vols. 1762.')[65] Malthus does not mention de Mirabeau by name (either because he was unaware of the identity of the anonymous author or because of discretion) and omits de Mirabeau's reference to 'un plus habile' (Quesnay) who corrected the error (see James, 1803/1989, II, 309). But evidently by 1803 he had encountered at first hand important samples of the French literature, including the food and population nexus.[66] The specific references to Dupont's *Physiocratie* and to *L'Ami des hommes* are removed in 1806. But since the relevant texts remained unaltered, there is no obvious analytical reason for the deletions, and presumably Malthus sought for political reasons to dissociate himself from the Physiocrats (James, 282).

There is, we have also seen, a *strengthening* of the 'physiocratic' orientation in the 1803 version, manifested: (1) in the representation of agricultural income alone as 'original'; and (2) in the insistence on surplus as generated in agriculture alone – even when as in subsequent editions of the *Essay* (1) is abandoned, (2) is retained – and the discussion of these features suggests firsthand familiarity (above, pp. 358–60). His specific reference to the physiocratic concept of 'the ultimate value of everything' as *'propre à la jouissance'* (above, p. 361) points to the same conclusion; as does also his specific reference to profits 'intimated by the Economists' to be 'proportioned ... to the wants and necessities of the owners of capital' (above, p. 369).

In reviewing the evidence of firsthand familiarity, I am not attempting to represent Malthus as slavish follower. On the contrary, we know he was frequently critical, especially regarding the Single Tax doctrine, which implied an identification of surplus with land rent narrowly defined. None the less, the essential fact remains that he accepted and sought to reinforce their agricultural bias, supplementing the notion of a *physical* surplus pertinent to agriculture by arguing for a corresponding *value* surplus. In fact, his support for agricultural protection to avoid loss or contraction of that surplus effectively transplanted into the then current circumstances involving Britain as net corn importer the same policy conclusions the Physio-

65 For a detailed discussion of the two references see Hollander, 1992b. Since the context involves the 'Tableau économique,' we may conclude that Malthus had access to this device, although he never adopted it as such. His familiarity with the *tableau* is further confirmed by a letter to Horner, 14 March 1815, pointing to the Economists' calculation 'that one third of the raw produce obtained by the farmer is advanced to the steril [*sic*] classes' (in Ricardo, 1951–73, VI, 187).

66 See Landry on Quesnay's ideas on population (1958, I, 11–49). Landry maintains that, despite certain ambiguous formulations made before 1757, Quesnay was never a 'populationist' in the sense of encouraging population increase by direct means independently of prior food expansion. In any event, he objected successfully to de Mirabeau's formulations in *L'Ami des hommes* (1757), which could be read in a populationist sense. (Landry maintains that in fact de Mirabeau too held that population growth, though desirable, should turn on prior land improvement.)

crats had earlier drawn, when France was a net corn exporter and free trade assured the world price as floor.

That Malthusian doctrine was *perceived* to be physiocratic by some contemporaries is evident from Dupont de Nemours's reaction in 1817 to the food–population linkage. In fact, he went much farther, for he described Malthus as 'encore plus profound et plus tenace que *Smith*' – evidently with the latter's 'Of the Agricultural Systems' in mind – 'sur les bons principes relatifs à l'administration de l'agriculture, des manufactures et du commerce ... et qui sait relever les erreurs de *Smith* même, lorsque celui-ci se trompe ou exagère' (1817, 30). Relevant too is the reaction of William Spence, who cited Malthus's statement in the *Essay* of 1803 that 'a revenue is transferred [by manufacturing], but not created' in defence of his own *Britain Independent of Commerce* (1808/1822, 152). But Spence – who believed that Malthus had adopted the main physiocratic tenets – added that 'the sentiment of this gentleman will be deemed of greater weight, when it is recollected, as I have before observed [129–30], that he is no blind admirer of the Economists; but admits that in some senses, manufactures may be said to create national wealth.' Malthus's assertion that 'the great position of the Economists will always remain true, that the surplus produce of the cultivators is the great fund which ultimately pays all those who are not employed upon the land' (above, p. 360) is similarly cited in his defence (130).[67]

XI SUMMARY AND CONCLUSION: THE DISINTEGRATION OF MALTHUSIAN PHYSIOCRACY

There was a physiocratic dimension – or at least a quasi-physiocratic dimension, since others also expressed agricultural bias – to Malthus's economics, more positive, specific, and lasting than usually suggested in the literature (cf. Meek, 1962; Semmel, 1965; Eltis, 1984; and Winch, 1987). Malthus possibly acquired his original knowledge of the French writings indirectly, but doctrinaire physiocracy is already clear in 1798, where the 'real utility' of national output is said to be increased by a transfer of labour from manufacturing to agriculture, even should *net* food production be reduced. It is the food–population link that most struck Dupont de Nemours, who actually envisaged the *Essay* as a commentary on Quesnay from this perspective. There are specific references to physiocratic texts in

67 In addition, Spence commended Malthus's criticisms of one aspect of physiocracy – 'the confined and erroneous conceptions of those, who, in contemplating the importance of the revenue derived from the land, restrict their view to the net money revenue received by the class of land-proprietors' (132).

An 1808 *Edinburgh Review* article strongly critical of Spence's physiocratic orientation is sometimes attributed to Malthus (Fetter, 1953, 246; Waterman, 1991, 227, 279). In fact it is almost certainly by Henry Brougham (see Hollander, 1996).

the 1803 *Essay* (by 1803 Malthus had at hand an extensive sample of original literature) and there we encounter doctrinaire physiocracy in its strongest form – namely, manufacturing sterility in the sense that manufacturing earnings are 'transfers' rather than original incomes: 'A revenue is transferred but not created.' Even though this extreme version of physiocracy is abandoned in 1806 and 1807, manufacturing sterility is retained in the weaker sense, attributing to agriculture alone a surplus-generating capacity. Although Malthus recognized savings from interest and profit in manufacturing and commerce, these apparent surplus incomes were none the less *derivative*; the Physiocrats had failed to realize that, while agriculture was indeed the sole source of surplus, part of it appeared in the form of industrial income.

In the *Inquiry into Rent* pamphlet (1815), Malthus further legitimized the fundamentalist physiocratic proposition regarding a unique surplus derived from agriculture by applying a sort of Law of Markets to corn, such that the physical surplus guarantees a value surplus. The criticism in the *Observations* (1814), and later in the *Principles*, of the Single Tax proposal reflects the concern that heavy taxation of rent will adversely affect growth, rather than a doctrinal objection. And the explicit allowance for diminishing returns in 1814/15 does not undermine the physiocratic bias, since even marginal land is said to yield rent. Moreover, the 'additional value' pertaining solely to agriculture; an old case – apparently originating with Quesnay – for a high corn price as advantageous to labour; and a warning against growth entailing the export of manufactures are reiterated in 1815. I conclude that through 1815 there is no weakening either of 'doctrinaire' or 'agrarian' physiocracy. Various alterations made to the fifth (1817) edition of the *Essay* also do not entail a 'dilution' of either variety. Finally, the reinforcement of doctrinaire physiocracy in 1815 in terms of value theory is reiterated in the *Principles*, and rent emerges strongly as a net creation of wealth.

Was Malthus originally *indebted* to the Physiocrats for the agricultural bias discussed in this paper, or was it a matter of parallelism? His knowledge of the French literature in 1798 was probably second-hand. But that he had become acquainted at first hand with the literature by 1803 is certain, and this reading seems to have left its mark. Moreover, he was envisaged as 'physiocratic' by William Spence and by Dupont de Nemours. But, most important of all, he reinforced the French doctrine, supplementing the notion of a physical (agricultural) surplus by the assurance of a corresponding value surplus.[68] The question of literal *debt* is secondary, considering the active contribution he made to doctrinaire physiocracy.

The longevity of Malthusian physiocracy is not in doubt. But there occurred a disintegration, which we shall now briefly document. In a letter

68 See chapter 6: V. Malthus was in effect following Adam Smith.

to Macvey Napier of 8 October 1821, Malthus compared the Ricardians, who had 'adopted a theory which will not stand the test of experience,' with the Physiocrats (B.L. Add. Mss 34, 612. f.453; see Conclusion: III). A similar identification appears in Malthus's celebrated *Quarterly Review* article of 1824: 'The system of the new school of political economy has always struck us as bearing a very remarkable resemblance to the system of the French economists ... Their systems were equally distinguished for their discordance with common notions, the apparent closeness of their reasoning, and the mathematical precision of their calculations and conclusions founded on their assumed data' (1824a/1986, *7*, 297). Here he gives as 'the specific error of the French economists ... the having taken so confined a view of wealth and its sources as not to include the results of manufacturing and mercantile industry'; fortunately, 'facts and experience [had] in the course of some years converted the economists of France from the erroneous and inapplicable theory of Quesnay to the just and more practical theory of Adam Smith.' Much the same complaint, again in a comparison with the Ricardians, appears in the *Principles* itself. The first chapter sets out by defining national income in Smith's fashion to include 'material objects which are necessary, useful or agreeable to mankind' (1820, 28; 1836, 32); and the final chapter objects to any definition limited to *net revenue* in the sense of 'disposable' income. Although his own (Smithian) definition '[did] not include the question of what may be called the amount of disposable produce, or the fund for taxation,' it was 'a much more correct definition of the wealth of a country than any that should refer to this disposable part alone [1836: in the sense understood, either by the French economists, who confine it to neat rent, or by Mr. Ricardo who confines it to rents and profits]' (1820, 424; 1836, 369). 'The Economists' had 'destroyed the practical utility of their works by referring exclusively to the net produce of the land';[69] while those who limited wealth to 'rents and profits, to the exclusion of wages' – a position attributed to Ricardo – 'commit[ted] an error exactly of the same kind though less in degree' (1820, 423; 1836, 368).[70] Wages in fact – he here includes even

69 Malthus at times – as in the 1824 extract – represented the French definition in terms of *gross rather than net agricultural output*. And in fact, a chapter in *Definitions of Political Economy* (1827) commences with the insistence that the term 'wealth' not be restricted 'either to gross raw produce, or the net raw produce,' and is entirely devoted to the objection that the Physiocrats excluded 'the results of manufacturing and mercantile industry' (1986, *8*, 9, 38).

70 In this context, it is noteworthy that Ricardo pointed to an ambiguity running through Malthus's *Principles*: 'When we meet we must agree upon the meaning to be attached to "a neat surplus from the land" – it may mean the whole material produce after deducting from it what is absolutely necessary to feed the men who obtained it, or it may mean the value of the produce which falls to the share of the capitalist, or to the share of the capitalist and landlord together ... This term neat produce is used ambiguously in your book ...' (24 November, 1820; 1951–73, VIII, 301). See also his *Note 127* (cited above, p. 390).

wages of service labour – accounted for most of national income and constituted *a significant source of expenditure, and also of taxation*: 'Those who live upon the wages of labour, unproductive as well as productive [1836: including of course those engaged in personal services,] receive and expend much the greater part of the annual produce, pay a very considerable sum in taxes for the maintenance of the government, and form by far the largest portion of its physical force. Under the prevalence of habits of prudence, the whole of this vast mass might be nearly as happy as the individuals of the other two classes, and probably a greater number of them, though not a greater proportion of them, happier.'

It is not clear whether all this should be represented as a truly *novel* attack on physiocracy. After all, the refusal to limit national income to the farm sector was an old story, and Malthus had long before insisted that others apart from landowners – interest recipients, and even capitalists and labourers – in part bore the burden of taxation and engaged in accumulation, if only in the short run. This insistence underlay his objection to the Single Tax proposal; the national surplus, albeit generated in agriculture, must not be identified with land rent. None the less, the reference to 'the prevalence of habits of prudence' in our present context is striking. For it implies that, with appropriate social attitudes and policy, the subsistence minimum could not be envisaged as the long-run norm; a *major* part of the national surplus – wherever its ultimate source – might permanently take the form of wages (even of service labour). If this is so, one is led to conclude that Malthus's primary policy concern – to encourage population control – was proving incompatible with physiocratic bias.[71]

Here we should note a new emphasis in the 1817 version of the *Essay on Population* on industry-biased growth, as typically characteristic of the later stages of economic development, reflecting growing land scarcity and an 'increasing taste for conveniences and luxuries' which tends to 'direct the greatest part of new capital to commerce and manufactures' (1817, III, 6), and along with it retraction of much of an earlier concern with such development from labour's perspective. To allow a natural tendency to *industry-biased* growth – and concede the possibility of improved living standards notwithstanding[72] – and yet to champion agricultural protection

71 I owe to Anthony Waterman the observation 'that the seemingly "fundamentalist physiocratic" theorem that "the number of manufacturers, of proprietors, and of persons engaged in the various civil and military professions, must be exactly proportioned to [the] surplus produce" [cited above, pp. 360, 368] contradicts Malthus's population theory. In particular, it destroys the possibility of treating the "subsistence" wage as a policy parameter' (letter dated 1 February 1994).

72 The novelty of the 1817 version is its recognition of the possibility of decelerating population growth relative to that of food so as to assure a rising corn wage (and thereby also higher command over non-food components of the basket), irrespective of the actual growth rate of food. Conceivably the corn wage may rise with prudential control, despite decelerating growth of food.

to assure balanced growth, implies a *reinforcement* of the physiocratic dimension, not its weakening. But as we shall see in chapter 17, Malthus over the period 1824–6 in fact came to *abandon* his protectionist position. This profound change reflected in large part a recognition that expanded *manufacturing* exports had mitigated the worst effects of the postwar depression, that is, that the manufacturing sector was proving itself, leading to an abandonment of an earlier case for unproductive consumption by landlords. Although there are earlier allusions to the significance of manufacturing in maintaining activity to the advantage of agriculture itself (above, section III), the theme is now underscored with particular reference to the growing empirical significance of the *export* sector; and it is no longer part of a protectionist case to assure sectoral balance despite a 'natural' trend to industrial supremacy, but rather part of a free-trade case justifying the imbalance. Possibly pertinent – though this is not definitive – is a suggestion of growing concern for British agricultural prospects, which also would imply an undermining of physiocratic bias.

Much of what is retained in the text of the *Principles* to appear in the posthumous 1836 edition reflects the surplus-oriented physiocratic theory outlined in the account above.[73] I conclude that Malthus could never shelve a powerful theoretical bias that governed his economics from the beginning. The fact that deletions of *protectionist* passages are more systematic suggests that dissatisfaction emanated initially from policy considerations, and that Malthus was unwilling or unable to return and totally reconstruct the theoretical framework. But of his discomfort there can be no doubt.

In documenting and rationalizing the apparent disintegration of Malthusian physiocracy, allowance should also be made for the charge against the French economists of downplaying, indeed of denying, the impact of *trade* in raising aggregate demand, a matter of increasing concern to him (1820, 441; 1836, 383; see chapter 2: VI). The informal Inverarity report of lectures given in 1830 is so hostile to the Physiocrats as to suggest that, by that date, Malthus had abandoned the entire system, though he failed to record such a thoroughgoing renunciation in the revisions to the *Principles*. He saw 'the fundamental error' of the economists to be their 'confined definition of wealth as well as their confined definition of the term *productive* which does not even include all the rude produce of the land,' an error leading to their neglect of 'the accumulation of capital and the better distribution and division of labour in the hands of what they call the sterile class' (Pullen, 1981b, 809). Other 'important errors and omissions' which 'render[ed] their works of comparatively little use' include neglect of the

73 For example, the Summary section to the 1820 chapter 'On Rent' elucidating the surplus-vs-scarcity approach, is reproduced in 1836 (1820, 226f.; 1836, 207f.; cited above, section VII).

advantages of manufactures and commerce; of the accumulation of capital in the sterile class; of the value super-added to the raw produce by the manufacturers; the benefit the raw produce derives from the extension of its market through its more transferable form; of the benefits of machinery and the better division of labour; the cheapness of commodities from the last two causes.'[74]

74 Of his discomfort on methodological grounds there can be no doubt. This theme – elaborated in our concluding chapter – turns on the letter to Macvey Napier of 1821, the *Quarterly Review* article of 1824, and the *Definitions* of 1827, as well as the Inverarity transcript in 1830.

NINE

Wages and employment

I INTRODUCTION

Malthus's growth model in its mature form emerges in the chapter 'Of the Wages of Labour' in the *Principles*, though full-fledged statements are given in the formal analysis of the profit rate and its secular trend in the chapter 'Of the Profits of Stock.' Our discussion follows the same order, the present chapter dealing with wages and employment with reference, respectively, to labour supply (section II) and labour demand (section III), the latter in the sense of society's aggregate labour requirements. While the discussion proceeds, following Malthus, on the provisional assumption that aggregate-demand problems may be set aside, the complication emerges none the less. We find in general that the analysis of labour demand – account taken of major variations between the two editions of the *Principles* – suffers from serious ambiguities regarding causation. Section IV considers the significance of family earnings for population growth.

II LABOUR SUPPLY: WAGES AND POPULATION GROWTH

Labour demand is portrayed in the *Principles* as a *monetary* demand rather than a matter of advanced wage goods, and money wages are said to be determined 'by the demand and supply of money, compared with the demand and supply of labour'; but supposing money 'to maintain nearly the same value,' the money wage is 'regulated by the variations in the demand compared with the supply of labour' (1820, 240–1).[1] Our first concern is with labour supply.

Labour supply is influenced by production 'costs,' but (as with commodity supply) costs are relevant only in so far as they govern supply conditions: 'The principle of demand and supply is the paramount regulator of the prices of labour, as well as of commodities, not only temporarily but permanently; and the costs of production affect these prices only as they are the necessary condition of the permanent supply of labour, or of commodities' (241).[2] Here Malthus (like Ricardo) takes Smith's position that aggregate demand for labour reflects the population-growth requirements of the economy, which can be taken as data as a first approximation. Labour supply accommodates itself to these 'requirements' in response to the money wages paid, given the prices of 'necessaries': 'It is as the condition of the supply, that the prices of the necessaries of life have so important an influence on the price of labour. A certain portion of these necessaries is required to enable the labourer to maintain a stationary population, a greater portion to maintain an increasing one; and consequently, whatever may be the prices of the necessaries of life, the money wages of the labourer must be such as to enable him to purchase these portions, or the supply cannot possibly take place in the quantity required.'[3] Instances where the money wage remains steady despite variation in wage-goods (corn) prices could be explained by a lagged effect of altered 'cost' conditions on labour supply: 'When, from a course of abundant seasons, or any cause which does not impair the capitals of the farmers, the price of corn falls for some time together, the cost of producing labour may be said to be diminished, but it is not found that the wages of labour fall; and for this obvious reason, that the reduced cost of production cannot, under sixteen or eighteen years, materially influence the *supply* of labour in the market. On the other hand, when the prices of corn rise from a succession of indifferent seasons, or any cause which leaves the demand for labour nearly the same as before, wages will not rise, because the same number of labourers remain in the market, and though the price of production has risen, the supply is not for some time affected by it' (241–2). Reduced food prices will, however, affect money wages, even in the absence of labour supply adjustment should labour demand conditions

1 Since the money wage is allowed to vary, the assumption that money is of constant 'value' must refer to value in the sense of general purchasing power (particularly command over wage goods) rather than command over labour.

2 Ricardo protested in *Note 143* (1951–73, II, 224–5) that this was a commonly held position, whereas Malthus suggested it required defence.

3 Cf. 'Adam Smith is practically quite correct, when he says, that "the money price of labour is necessarily regulated by two circumstances; the demand for labour; and the price of the necessaries and conveniences of life"' (1820, 243; 1836, 220).

be affected. Such indeed had been the case in the postwar years: 'The fall in the price of labour which took place in 1815 and 1816 was occasioned solely by the diminution of demand, arising from the losses of the farmers, and in no respect by the diminished cost of production' (242n).[4]

All of this is replaced in 1836 by a briefer statement of money-wage determination; but, as before, given the 'effectual demand' for labour, the money wage must be such as to assure an appropriate growth rate of labour supply. The statement reflects the proposition – to be elaborated in chapter 14: VI – whereby increased efficiency in the export industries generates a higher level of internal prices of commodities and labour: 'If the society can purchase a given quantity of money by commodities which require a smaller sacrifice of labour, profits, etc. to obtain them than is necessary to purchase or obtain the labour for which that money has before been usually exchanged, the money price of labour will rise. If either from the scarcity of money, or the plenty of labour, a *greater* sacrifice must be made to obtain the given quantity of money, the money price of labour will fall. And whatever may be the state of the effectual demand for labour, it is obvious that the money price of labour must, on an average, be so proportioned to the price of the funds for its maintenance, as to effectuate the desired supply' (1836, 218).[5] Here Malthus repeats the passage of 1820 regarding the prices of wage goods acting upon the money wage via labour supply adjustment – 'the condition of the supply.' And, as in 1820, he commends Smith's formulation regarding money-wage determination (see note 3).

At this point the 1836 version elaborates on corn-wage determination. A brief reference to corn-wage fluctuations is followed by an elaboration of 'more permanent' variations, in terms consistent with the basic growth model, with its downward trend path of the corn wage:

> The corn wages of labour are still more strikingly determined by the state of the demand and supply than money wages, on account of the variations in the quantity of corn being much greater in short periods than in the quantity of money. The great variations in the prices of corn in different seasons, while the money price of labour remains the same, are universally observed and acknowledged;

4 Elsewhere the postwar decline of money wages is partly attributed to labour supply adjustment, including a lagged population reaction to good wartime earnings, and also to demobilization (see chapter 12, p. 607).

5 The passage is preceded by a reminder that, though money and commodity wages vary, 'the average wages of a given number of common agricultural labourers ... are always of the same *value*,' in that 'they are always obtained in each country, and at all times, at the same elementary cost.' This refers to the assertion in the chapter on Measures of Value that, over space and time, 'sacrifice' in labour is constant. For example, in a spatial comparison, the American labourer 'evidently does not purchase what he obtains by a greater sacrifice than the English labourer. He does not give more for what he receives, but receives more for what he gives ...' (107).

but the variations of a more permanent kind in corn wages are sometimes not much less considerable. When the last land taken into cultivation in any country is fertile, and yet worked with some skill, there will be a large produce to divide between profits and wages, and it will depend upon the abundance of this produce and the manner in which it is divided, but chiefly on the former, whether the average corn wages are high or low. In the United States of America, for instance, the plenty and fertility of the land are such as to enable the farmers to pay their labourers as much as 18 or 20 quarters of wheat in the year, above double the quantity usually paid in the greatest part of Europe, and yet to retain good profits. But it is known that the labouring classes of a country can more than keep up their numbers when paid only 8 or 9 quarters in the year. The question therefore whether the labourer shall be paid, on an average, 8 or 18 quarters, or any intermediate quantity, must depend upon the demand and supply of corn compared with the demand and supply of labour; and it is obvious that the labourer could not, for many years together, receive the larger quantity in any country where corn was not essentially of low value, that is obtained with a small quantity of labour. (218–19)[6]

Although the main issue involves the division of the *physical* (corn) marginal product between capital and labour, the corn wage none the less entails a ratio of the corn price to the money wage – turning on 'the demand and supply for corn' compared with the demand and supply of labour' – rather than the literal advance of corn. The closing observation of the passage is particularly striking. It suggests a downward trend of the corn wage with

6 Malthus turns next to the general commodity wage, which he once more expresses with emphasis upon supply–demand:

> If instead of corn wages, or wages estimated in the prime necessary of life, we consider wages as consisting of the general necessaries and conveniences in which the money earnings of the labouring classes are usually spent, then if we suppose the agricultural labourer to be paid in the first instance in corn, his wages in necessaries and conveniences will depend partly upon the quantity of corn which he earns, and partly upon the value of that corn in exchange for the other necessaries of which he stands in need, such as clothing, housing, firing, soap, candles, leather, &c; the one depending on the varying supply of corn to labour, and the other on the varying supply of corn to the other commodities wanted. Usually wages estimated in general necessaries and conveniences are more steady than corn wages; because most of the articles besides corn, of which they are composed, are less affected by the seasons, and consequently more regular in their supply than corn; but if these articles are compared directly with labour instead of corn, the quantity of them which shall be given to the labourer will still depend not only upon the varying powers of labour in their production, but upon that ordinary state of the demand for them compared with the supply which, in any given condition of the productive powers of labour, determines the proportion of such necessaries which is awarded to the labourer. (219–20)

But this discussion seems to be of a formal or statistical rather than an analytical nature, unlike that relating to the corn wage, where a secular pattern emerges.

the higher level corresponding to a 'low [corn] value,' the latter reflecting *low labour input* – a wholly Ricardian concept of corn-price determination.

A criticism of Adam Smith, relevant to the aggregate labour market, is made in both editions. It relates to Smith's observation regarding China 'that if in such a country (that is, a country with stationary resources) wages had ever been more than sufficient to maintain the labourer, and enable him to bring up a family; the competition of the labourers and the interest of the masters, would soon reduce them to the lowest rate which is consistent with *common humanity*' (1820, 245–6; 1836, 222). 'Common humanity' was an irrelevant consideration since it affected neither labour demand nor labour supply conditions: 'But unfortunately, common humanity cannot alter the resources of a country [1836: the funds for the maintenance of labour]. While these are stationary, and the habits of the lower classes prompt them to supply a stationary population cheaply, the wages of labour will be scanty; but still they cannot fall below what is necessary, under the actual habits of the people, to keep up a stationary population; because, by the supposition, the resources of the country [1836: the funds for the maintenance of labour] are stationary, not increasing or declining; and consequently the principle of demand and supply would always interfere to prevent such wages as would either occasion an increase or diminution of people' (1820, 246; 1836, 223).[7]

* * *

To know the cost of producing wage goods and the requirements for a particular labour supply growth rate is, of course, insufficient unless we assume a given relationship between the real (corn) wage and the growth rate of labour supply; the analysis is incomplete without consideration of the determinants of 'the habits of the labouring classes,' or the position of the labour supply function. At the outset of section II in the chapter on Wages dealing with this matter, exception is taken to Ricardo's definition of the 'natural price of labour' as 'that price which is necessary to enable the labourers one with another to subsist, and to perpetuate their race, without either increase or diminution' (1820, 247; 1836, 223). The objection is to the term 'natural,' since that wage rate could only be expected

7 Malthus had earlier pointed out that the Smithian analysis of the wage *structure*, involving the principle of equalizing or compensating money-wage differentials, turns entirely on variation in relative labour supplies (1820, 243–4). He objected to Smith's inclusion of 'esteem' as a relevant consideration: 'It is not [1836: simply] the esteem of the dexterity and ingenuity referred to [1836 adds: or a disinterested wish to reward such skill], which raises the price of the commodity, but their scarcity and the consequent scarcity of the articles produced by them, compared with the demand' (1820, 357; 1836, 222). Ricardo's *Note 144* makes the same point (1951–73, II, 226). To my mind, Smith was fully aware of all this.

to rule in the stationary state – unless unlikely circumstances of secular stagnation are assumed. In normal circumstances the real wage *exceeds* the subsistence wage during the course of growth: 'This price I should really be disposed to call a most unnatural price; because in a natural state of things, that is, without great [1836: unnatural] impediments to the progress of wealth and population [1836: of accumulation], such a price could not generally occur for hundreds of years [1836: could not permanently occur in any country, till the cultivation of the soil, or the power of importation had been pushed as far as possible]. But if this price be really rare, and, in an ordinary state of things, at so great a distance [1836: at a great distance] in point of time, it must evidently lead to great errors to consider the market prices of labour as only temporary deviations above and below that fixed price, to which they will very soon return.' Here we have the common error of reading Ricardo as positing a subsistence wage during the course of growth about which the market wage fluctuates without lengthy deviation. For Malthus, the only meaningful definition of the 'natural or necessary' wage was rather (again citing Smith) 'that price which, in the actual circumstances of the society, is necessary to occasion an average supply of labourers, sufficient to meet the average [1836: effectual] demand' (1820, 247; 1836, 224). The 'market price' would then be defined as 'the actual price in the market, which from temporary causes is sometimes above, and sometimes below what is necessary to supply this average demand [1836: this demand].' Malthus is alluding to temporary fluctuations of the real wage about a secular path that tends towards the minimum, which is attained only in the far-distant stationary state. And in 1836 he expressly draws a parallel to the profit rate in line with this perspective: 'We might with almost as much propriety [as Ricardo's definition of the natural wage] define the natural rate of *profits* to be that rate which would just keep up the capital without increase or decrease. This is in fact the rate to which profits are constantly tending' (1836, 224n).

Malthus then explores the details of the determination of 'the condition of the labouring classes' (1820, 248; 1836, 224). Given the rate of increase of national 'resources' – in 1836 'the funds for the maintenance of labour' – the real wage will depend upon 'the habits of the people in respect of their food, clothing, and lodging,' that is, upon labour supply conditions; this takes us back to Smith's standard first approximation. Conversely, given the pattern of habits (dictating the rate of increase of labour supply), the real wage will be governed by the labour demand growth rate: 'If the habits of the people were to remain fixed, the power of marrying early, and of supporting a large family, would depend upon the rate at which the resources of the country [1836: funds for the maintenance of labour] and the demand for labour were increasing. And if the resources of the country [1836: these funds] were to remain fixed, the comforts of the lower classes of society would depend upon their habits, or the amount of those necessaries and conveniences, without which they would not consent to keep up their numbers [1836 to the required point].'[8] But in reality, both sets of growth rates are liable to variation. In fact there is an important allusion to an *interdependence* of the two sets – as in the 1817 *Essay on Population* (above, chapter 5: IV) – with 'habits' affected by demand-side variations: 'When the resources of a country [1836: funds for the maintenance of labour] are rapidly increasing, and the labourer commands a large portion of necessaries, it is to be expected that if he has the opportunity of exchanging his superfluous food for conveniences and comforts, he will acquire a taste for these conveniences, and his habits will be formed accordingly. On the other hand, it generally happens that, when the resources of a country [1836: funds for the maintenance of labour] become nearly stationary, such habits, if they ever have existed, are found to give way; and, before the population comes to a stop, the standard of comfort is essentially lowered ... From high wages [MR: high corn wages; 1836: high real wages],[9] or the power of commanding a large portion of the necessaries of life, two very different results may follow; one, that of a rapid increase of population, in which case the high wages are chiefly spent in the maintenance of large and frequent families; and the other, that of a decided improvement in the modes of subsistence, and the conveniences and comforts enjoyed, without a proportionate acceleration in the rate of increase' (1820, 248–50; 1836, 224–6).

This sort of interdependence is incorporated into the 'canonical' growth model, in that the secular decline in the growth rate of labour demand may bring with it a *degeneration* of habits which reinforces the fall of real (corn) wages.[10] This emerges in a discussion of international differentials between standards of comfort, according to which there correspond different levels of the real wage to similar growth rates of national 'resources' or, in 1836, of the 'funds for the maintenance of labour.' The context is a correction of Adam Smith's proposition that the inferior food of Scottish compared with English labourers 'is not the cause, but the effect, of the difference in their wages; though, by a strange misapprehension, I have frequently heard it represented as the cause' (1776/1937, 76): 'It must be allowed, however, that this correction of a common opinion is only partially just. The effect, in this case as in many others, certainly becomes in its turn a cause; and there is no doubt, that if the continuance of low wages for some time, should produce among the labourers of any country habits of marrying with the prospect only of a mere subsistence, such

8 This closing qualification of 1836 – 'to the required point' – confirms that the 'habits' in question define the position of the *entire* functional relation between the real wage and the population-growth rate, not merely the real wage at which population growth ceases.

9 High *corn* wages seem appropriate unless 'real' is understood to exclude 'conveniences and luxuries.' For the Manuscript Revision, see 1820/1989, II, 200.

10 This was also a Marxian conception, see Hollander, 1987, ch. 15.

habits, by supplying the quantity of labour required at a low rate, would become a constantly operating cause of low wages.'

There then follows an empirical account of alternative responses to initially high corn wages: (1) where the advantage is largely eradicated by a major increase in the rate of population growth; and (2) where the advantage is largely retained by stronger prudential control reflecting improved 'habits' (1820, 250–7; 1836, 226–31). In the latter case, population growth is prevented from 'keeping pace with the apparent [1836: *apparent*] command of the labourer over the means of subsistence' (1820, 257; 1836, 231), a formulation reminiscent of that given in the 1817 *Essay on Population.*

III LABOUR DEMAND

Section III of the Wages chapter elaborates upon labour demand from the perspective of its effect on population growth. Here is found a generalization that encapsulates the entire message of the *Essay on Population* – namely, that 'when the population of a country increases faster than usual [1836: for any time together], the labouring classes must have the command of a greater quantity of food than they had before possessed, or at least applied [1836: than they had before applied] to the maintenance of their families' (1820, 259; 1836, 233). Such increased command might be reflected in higher *per-capita* 'real wages' (1820) – higher '*corn* wages' in 1836; but an increase in aggregate corn wages might even be accompanied by a reduced *per-capita* corn wage, allowance made for greater employment opportunities generally, and increased labour participation rates of females and children. In fact, 'more of these causes' – referring to the latter – 'will be called into action by a rise of [corn] prices which sometimes lowers the command of a day's labour over the necessaries of life, than by a fall of prices which sometimes raises it [1836: which raises it]' (1820, 261, 1836, 234).[11] But in all cases 'the actual application of the greater quantity of food is ... necessary [1836: seems to be necessary] to the increase of population; and wherever such increase has taken place, some of these causes by which a greater quantity of food is procured, will always be in action, and may generally be traced' (1820, 260; 1836, 233).[12]

11 Malthus also refers to 'saving [by labour] in conveniences,' 'adopting a cheaper kind of food,' and 'parish allowances' (1820, 260; 1836, 233).

12 Malthus elaborated, with special reference to the United States and Ireland, England, and Scotland. As for the latter: 'The great increase of population of late years in England and Scotland has been owing to the power of the labouring classes to obtain a greater quantity of food, partly by temporary high wages in manufactures, partly by the increased use of potatoes, partly by increased task work and the increased employment of women and children, partly by increased parish allowances to families, and partly perhaps, (though I think but little taking the country throughout) by a saving in conveniences and luxuries [1836: and partly by the increased relative cheapness of manufactures and foreign commodities]' (1820, 260–1; 1836, 234).

At this juncture Malthus summarized his conclusion regarding labour demand: 'What is mainly necessary to a rapid increase of population is a great and continued demand for labour; and this is occasioned by and proportioned to, the rate at which the whole value of the capital and revenue of the country increases annually; because, the faster the value of the annual produce increases, the greater will be the power of purchasing fresh labour, and the more will be wanted each year' (1820, 261).[13] It is of the essence that labour demand is 'occasioned by and proportioned to,' but not identified with, the 'value of the annual produce.' (Earlier in his 1820 text Malthus had simply related labour demand to national 'resources' (e.g., above, p. 417); doubtless this latter expression should be read as synonymous with the 'value of the annual produce,' as in the current extract.) The 1836 version is more specific: 'What is essentially necessary to a rapid increase of population is a great and continued demand for labour; and this is proportioned to the rate of increase in the quantity and value of those funds, whether arising from capital or revenue, *which are actually employed in the maintenance of labour*' (1836, 234; emphasis added).

The change from labour demand as 'occasioned by and proportioned to' to labour demand merely as 'proportionate to' suggests a wish to avoid any *causative* notion. To appreciate the modification, we should keep in mind the problem at hand. Malthus sought a statistical proxy for 'labour demand' – society's requirement for labour – especially its growth rate. Variations in national income as proposed in 1820 would not do; but even variations in agricultural output provided an inadequate index, notwithstanding that higher labour requirements, to be 'effectual,' necessitate a larger flow of corn at labour's disposal. For the corn supply might rise, as with a series of excellent harvests, without a corresponding rise in society's labour requirements. (In such cases, employers would not be prepared to increase their labour forces, though employed workers might, of course, enjoy a higher *per-capita* corn wage.)[14] It could, however, be

13 Ricardo read this as a truism. For 'value according to Mr. Malthus depends on the quantity of necessaries and conveniences. His proposition then is "the population will increase with the demand for labour, and with the means of supporting the labourers" – a proposition that cannot be controverted' (*Note 148*, 1951–73, II, 234; cf. *Note 155*, 240). This is too harsh, since 'value' normally denotes for Malthus 'labour commanded.' His concern throughout the discussion of labour demand was that an output index is consistent with falling prices sufficient to lower total revenue (e.g., below, p. 427). An indication of rising labour demand would be rising total revenue, the money wage implicitly constant (or at least lagging behind), thus assuring rising labour command.

14 This can be translated using 'value' in terms of labour commanded. An expansion of corn may depress its money price per unit relative to the money wage so as to reduce the value of (the labour commanded by) the larger volume of corn compared with the original volume.

In one passage (1820, 257–8, 1836, 231–2; below, pp. 429–30) regarding employment opportunities in the broad sense – including 'task work' and female and child employment – we find the same emphasis on the value and quantity of raw produce as deter-

presumed that a recorded expansion of the food supply, the per-unit price maintained, does indicate a roughly corresponding increase in aggregate labour demand. In all this, there is no notion of literal advances of corn; the offer of wages by employers is in terms of *money*, which labourers spend on 'corn' at retail outlets. If then society's labour requirements (its demand for labour) rise, it may be presumed, so runs the argument, that the flow of corn output on the market will be higher to 'effectuate' such demand. Thus a statistical record of the latter provides an index of the former, there being no more direct measure.

* * *

The issues are further clarified in a critique of a proposition by John Barton (1817) relating to the effect of machinery.[15] The 1820 version proceeds in terms of aggregate labour demand varying – though not necessarily in a causal sense – with 'the value of the annual produce,' or with 'capital and revenue': 'It has been sometimes thought, that the demand for labour can only be in proportion to the increase of the circulating, not the fixed capital; and this is no doubt true in individual cases, but it is not necessary to make the distinction in reference to a whole nation; because where the substitution of fixed capital saves a great quantity of labour, which cannot be employed elsewhere, it diminishes the value of the annual produce, and retards the increase of the capital and revenue taken together' (1820, 261). The sequence, it will be noted, is *from* a technologically generated loss of employment opportunities (or reduction in labour demand) *to* a reduction in 'the value of the annual produce,' rather than the reverse. This suggests that, when Malthus posits the proportionality of society's labour requirements to national income, a causal sense was not intended, even in 1820. However, an elaboration – which reads much like the case of 'conversion' discussed in Ricardo's Chapter 31 – seems to reinstate the *dependence* of labour demand on the value of the national product:

If, for instance, a capitalist who had employed £20,000 in productive labour, and had been in the habit of selling his goods for £22,000, making a profit of 10 per cent, were to employ the same quantity of labour in the construction of a machine worth £20,000, which would enable him to carry on his business without labour in future, except as his machine might require repair, it is obvi-

minant of labour demand (and this in the 1820 version too). But that passage relates to 'the power of the cultivators' and is limited to demand for *agricultural* labour, whereas no such limitation is generally implied by other formulations of labour demand.

15 On Barton, see Hollander, 1979, 349–57.

ous that, during the first year, the same value of the annual produce and the same demand for labour would exist; but in the next year, as it would only be necessary for the capitalist, in order to obtain the same rate of profits as before, to sell his goods for a little more than £2,000 instead of £22,000, the value of the annual produce would fall, the capital would not be increased, and the revenue would be decidedly diminished; and *upon the principle that the demand for labour depends upon the rate at which the value of the general produce, or of the capital and revenue taken together, increases, the slackness of the demand for labour under such circumstances would be adequately accounted for.* (1820, 261–2; emphasis added)

Ruling out aggregate-demand problems, there was little to fear in practice: 'In general ... the use of fixed capital is favourable to the abundance of circulating capital; and if the market for products can be proportionately extended the whole value of the capital and revenue is greatly increased by it, and a great demand for labour created' (262). Again the notion of causality from the value of GNP to labour demand emerges.

This 'Ricardian' formulation is absent in the 1836 edition. In line with the systematic variation already alluded to, we find a subtle alteration of the implicit allusion to Barton which focuses now on proportionality of labour demand to the funds 'actually employed' in labour's maintenance: 'It has been generally considered, that the demand for labour is proportioned only to the circulating, not the fixed capital of a country. But in reality the demand for labour is not *proportioned* to the increase of capital in any shape; nor even, as I once thought, to the increase of the exchangeable value of the whole annual produce. It is proportioned only, as above stated, to the rate of increase in the quantity and value of those funds which are actually employed in the maintenance of labour' (1836, 234). This passage says nothing of *causality* or of the actual determinants of labour demand. In fact, an elaboration of the revised position – it replaces the 'Ricardo' example – emphasizes the dependence of labour demand on expenditure patterns with an eye to the potential danger of an expansion of the luxury sector at the expense of the (non-productive) service sector: 'These funds consist principally in the necessaries of life, or the means of commanding the food, clothing, lodging, and firing of the labouring classes of society. Now it is quite evident that if the capital of a society were directed in the most judicious and skilful manner to the production of these necessaries, and that the neat surplus above what was required for the maintenance of the person so employed, and of their employers, were spent in the maintenance of menial servants, soldiers, and sailors, all the demand for labour that the resources of such a country called out in the most effective manner would admit of, might exist, with little of that great mass of capital, which in most improved countries is employed in producing luxuries and superior conveniences. But if this be so, *it is obvious that capital, and even the exchangeable value of the whole produce may increase without any increase in the demand for labour*' (234–5; emphasis added).[16]

The case is carried further. Aggregate labour demand may even fall in the event of an excessive contraction of the service sector: 'If the circulating capital applied to the production of luxuries and conveniences employed only those persons who would otherwise be maintained as unproductive labourers by the surplus of necessaries, not only no addition is thereby made to the demand for labour, but if the persons before engaged in personal services were dismissed faster than they could be employed in the production of luxuries and superior conveniences a diminished demand for labour might take place under an increasing circulating capital' (235). This specific formulation is important as an indication of Malthus's general perspective on economic process. For it seems to confirm that he envisaged aggregate labour demand (society's labour requirement) as dependent on the expenditure pattern, especially expenditure out of surplus, each pattern dictating the flow of wage goods to effectuate the labour requirement in question.[17]

16 This proposition was a 'view of the subject ... stated by me about thirty years ago in the quarto edition of the Essay on Population, [1803] p. 421, and by Mr. Ricardo in his 3rd edition, [1821] p. 475. The reformulation is apparently an attempt to add greater precision to that of 1820, rather than a novel insight.

17 A summary statement raises some interpretative problems: 'if a large portion of the exchangeable value of the whole produce cannot be resolved into necessaries, it is clear that the whole produce may increase in exchangeable value without a greater value of the necessaries of life being actually employed in the maintenance of labour' (235). On first sight this suggests a need to take account of food imports. However, an elaboration in the Manuscript Revisions (absent in 1836) suggests otherwise:

> This will be made strikingly clear if we refer to any approximate calculations respecting the value of the whole produce for a manufacturing and mercantile country.
>
> Mr. Colquhoun estimated the value of the whole annual produce of the United Kingdom of Great Britain and Ireland in 1812 at 432 millions supporting 3,500,000 families and 17 millions of persons. If this value in money were converted into necessaries, at the average prices of the time, thus taking the full allowance of 60£ a year for each family as representing the wages of common labour, the whole of the new value created every year would be adequate to maintain more than double the actual population. It is obvious however that this value is not so convertible, that the half of it consists in the value of conveniences and luxuries consumed by the possessors of rents, profits, government annuities and by those classes of labourers who earn very much more than the wages of common labour, and consequently that the value of the funds directly appropriated to the maintenance of the labouring classes, or the demand for labour, cannot have increased in proportion to the value of the whole produce, and might have been as great with a very much less capital. (1820/1989, II, 205n)

The condition that 'a large portion of the exchangeable value of the whole produce ... [be] resolvable into necessaries' for an impact on labour demand seems – at least according to this Manuscript Revision note – to be nothing more than the proposition that since part of the national product corresponds to non-wage income expended on commodities of the type consumed by property- and landowners – and also (as J.S. Mill was later to put it) 'the elite amongst the working class' the excess of whose earnings

The evidence to this point is that, in his second edition, Malthus treated the so-called wage fund, not as the *determinant* of labour demand, but as an endogenous variable, the malleable result of a complex process in which labour demand (or society's labour requirement) is determined in part by final expenditure patterns. Yet this cannot be asserted with too much confidence. For the text elaborates on *stimuli to agricultural output* – rather than the determinants of labour demand as such, as might be expected in the context – and this suggests the more simplistic position. In the elaboration Malthus concedes that the earlier proposition whereby labour demand remains unchanged (even falls) should the service sector be contracted in favour of the manufacturing sector, while true, might be misleading from a secular perspective. Here he in effect applies the celebrated 'doctrine of proportions' in pointing to an optimum allocation of the surplus between luxuries and services *from the perspective of stimulus to agriculture*: 'But though it is unquestionably true that without the capital employed in luxuries and superior conveniences the same demand for labour might exist; yet practically, if the net revenue of a country could only be employed in the maintenance of menial servants and soldiers, there is every reason to think that the stimulus to production in modern states would be very greatly diminished, and that the cultivation of the soil would be carried on with the same kind of indolence and slackness as in the feudal times. On the other hand, if the whole of the surplus produce beyond what was required for the support of those who were employed in the production of necessaries could be spent in no other way than in the production and purchase of *material* luxuries and conveniences, if no menial servants could be kept to take care of houses, furniture, carriages, horses, etc. it is quite clear that the demand for material luxuries and conveniences would very soon abate, and the owners of land and capital would have very slender motives to employ them in the most productive manner' (235–6).

Malthus concluded, first, that it is 'the operation of both stimulants, under the most favourable proportions, which is likely to give the most effective encouragement even to the production of necessaries' (236);[18] and, second – in a major concession taking us back in effect to the 1820 version – that, although 'an increase in the value of the funds for the maintenance of labour is not strictly proportioned to the increase in the exchangeable value of the whole produce estimated in labour,' yet, 'in ordinary times, and when no great changes are taking place in the propor-

over the 'common' level is better reckoned in the non-wage category – not all the national product is in fact 'resolvable into necessaries.' All this adds little of substance to the main case.

18 Subsequently Malthus asserts that 'labour demand' in the manufacturing sector is 'steadier' than in the service sector.

tion of personal services to productive labour, an increase of such exchangeable value is generally followed by an increased demand for labour, since its ordinary and natural effect is to increase the value of the funds destined for the maintenance of labour.'[19]

The effective reversion to the 1820 position, including the suggestions of *causality* – with the now standard modification specifying 'the value of the funds for the maintenance of labour' – also appears in the optimistic position taken regarding technical change, or the adoption of 'fixed capital': 'Whenever the introduction of fixed capital has for a time the effect of diminishing the demand for labour, it will generally be found that the value of the whole annual produce is at the same time diminished: but in general the use of fixed capital is favourable to the abundance of circulating capital; and if the market for the products can be proportionally extended, the whole value of the capital and revenue of a state is greatly increased by it, as well as the value of the funds for the maintenance of labour, and a great demand for labour created' (236).[20]

A causal sequence emerges also in a discussion of 'fixed capital' in agriculture itself, found in both editions. An increase in the *value* of corn is assured provided corn output does not expand inordinately, a priviso that would be satisfied by the 'gradual' adoption of the new technology. There is a presumption, too, that the value of 'general produce' (manufacturing) would also rise.[21] In the first edition, the supposed increase in 'the exchangeable value of the general produce' is said to '*cause* a great demand for labour ...'; in the second – in line with the standard modification – it is specifically the increase in 'the value of the funds destined for the maintenance of labour' that will '*cause* a great demand for labour':

On the other hand, if, by the gradual introduction of a greater quantity of fixed

19 The closing phrase – 'funds *destined* for the maintenance of labour' – does not necessarily imply literal preaccumulations of wage goods or a primitive wage fund; the unfortunate expression may refer simply to the output of commodities of a kind typically consumed by labour.

20 The contemporary expansion of the cotton hardware and woollen industries is used to illustrate the positive effect on employment of the adoption of machinery. Unfortunately, the illustration demonstrates an increase in the 'value' of output and in employment only in those specific industries: 'The increase in the whole value of cotton products, since the introduction of the improved machinery, is known to be prodigious; and it cannot for a moment be doubted that [1836: both the circulating capital and] the demand for labour in the cotton business has [1836: have] very greatly increased during the last forty [1836: fifty] years. This is indeed sufficiently proved by the greatly increased population of Manchester, Glasgow, and the other towns where the cotton manufactures have most flourished. A similar increase of value, though not to the same extent, has taken place in our hardware, woollen, and other manufactures, and has been accompanied by an increasing demand for labour, notwithstanding the increasing use of fixed capital' (1820, 262–3; 1836, 236–7).

21 This expansion is not adequately justified; but there is perhaps a suggestion that it is made possible by labour released from the countryside.

capital, we could cultivate and dress our soil and carry the produce to market at a much less expense, we might increase our produce very greatly by the cultivation and improvement of all our waste lands [1836: and the improvement of all the land already in cultivation]; and if the substitution of this fixed capital were to take place in the only way in which we can suppose it practically to take place, that is, gradually, there is no reason to doubt that the value of raw produce would keep up nearly to its former level; and its greatly increased quantity, combined with the greater proportion of the people which might be employed in manufactures and commerce, *would unquestionably occasion a very great increase in the exchangeable value of the general produce and thus cause a great demand for labour* and a great addition to the population [1836: while it would occasion a very great increase in the exchangeable value of the general produce, *would increase at the same time the value of the funds destined for the maintenance of labour, and thus cause a great demand for labour* and a great addition to the population. (1820, 264; 1836, 237–8; emphasis added)[22]

Rapid agricultural innovation by raising corn output might, however, depress the demand for labour. The danger of technical change in exceptional cases – a theme of the final chapter of the *Principles* (see below, chapter 11: XIV) – is referred to at this juncture of the Wages chapter:

In general, therefore there is little [1836: There is no occasion therefore] to fear that the introduction of fixed capital, as it is likely to take place in practice, will diminish the effective demand for labour; indeed it is to this source that we are to look for the main cause of its future increase. At the same time, it is certainly true, as will be more fully stated in a subsequent part of this volume [1836: work], that if the substitution of fixed capital were to take place very rapidly, and before an adequate market could be found [1836: to take place much faster than an adequate market could be found] for the more abundant supplies derived from it and for the new products of the labour that had been thrown out of employ-

22 Regarding the agricultural sector, Malthus points to the fall in the value of necessaries in the event of an *abandonment* of 'fixed capital' – a fall in value accounted for by a fall in physical volume implying that the corn price does not rise sufficiently to compensate: 'Even in our agriculture, if the fixed capital of horses, which, from the quantity of produce they consume, is the most disadvantageous description of fixed capital, were disused, it is probable, that a great part of the land which now bears corn would be thrown out of cultivation. Land of a poor quality would never yield sufficient to pay the labour of cultivating with the spade, of bringing manure to distant fields in barrows, and of carrying the products of the earth to distant markets by the same sort of conveyance. *Under these circumstances, as there would be a great diminution [1836: a diminution] in the quantity of corn produced, there would be a great diminution [1836: a diminution] in the whole value of the produce,* and the demand for labour and the amount of the population would be greatly diminished [1836: and the value of the funds for the maintenance of labour would be diminished in proportion]' (1820, 263; 1836, 237; emphasis added).

ment, a slack demand for labour and great distress [1836: and distress] among the labouring classes of society would be universally felt.[23] But in this case the general produce, or the capital and revenue of the country taken together, would certainly fall in value [1836: but in this case the whole produce would fall in value], owing to a temporary excess of supply compared with the demand and would shew that the variations in this value, compared with the previous value paid in wages, are the main regulators of the power and will to employ labour [1836: closes at 'with the demand']. (1820, 264–5; 1836, 238)[24]

* * *

The remainder of Malthus's section III on labour demand further establishes the significance of 'value' in 'occasioning' an effective demand for labour. As usual, in 1820 it is the value of the whole produce, and in 1836 the value of the funds destined for labour's maintenance. Here the quantity dimension is emphasized on the grounds that increased value reflecting price alone is not condusive to *long-run* increase in labour demand: 'In the formation of the value of the whole produce of a country, a part depends upon price, and a part upon quantity [1836: In the formation of the value of the whole funds specifically destined for the maintenance of labour (the rate of the increase of which regulates the demand for labour) a part depends upon the value of a given portion of such funds, and a part upon their amount in kind, or in other words, a part depends upon their price, and a part upon their quantity]. That part which depends merely upon price is in its nature less durable and less effective than that which depends upon quantity. An increase of price with little or no increase of quantity [1836: has obvious limits, and] must be followed very soon in most cases by a nearly proportionate increase of [1836: money] wages; while the command of these increased money wages over the necessaries of life going on diminishing, the population must come to a stop, and no further rise of prices can occasion an effective demand for labour' (1820, 265; 1836, 238–9). Conversely, 'if the quantity of produce be increased so fast that the value of the whole diminishes from excessive supply, it may not command so much labour this year as it did in the last, and for a time there will be no demand [1836: a very slack demand] for workmen' (1820, 265–6; 1836, 239).

23 For Ricardo's important *Note 154* at this point clarifying his own position, see chapter 11, p. 583.

24 In this last observation (omitted in the 1836 version, which ends abruptly and seems incomplete), the comparison in question is opaque. Possibly Malthus intends to emphasize that it is a reduction (or increase) in the value of aggregate output *relative* to the value of the preceding wage bill that is crucial to employment decisions, not changes in the value of output *per se*. Yet this is the only occasion in the chapter on Wages where he expresses the matter in this way. See Ricardo's *Note 155*; 1951–73, II, 240.

In principle, good policy entailed a 'union' of the quantity and price dimensions, though the so-called doctrine of proportions raised practical problems. As for the first edition: 'It is obvious that the object which it is most desirable to attain is the union of the two. There is somewhere a happy medium, where, under the actual resources of a country, the increase of wealth and the demand for labour are a maximum; but this point cannot be ascertained. An increase of quantity with steady prices, or even slightly falling, is consistent with a considerable increase of the general value of produce, and may occasion a considerable demand for labour; but in the actual state of things, and in the way in which the precious metals are actually distributed, some increase of prices generally accompanies the most effective demand for produce and population. It is this increase both of quantity and price which most surely creates the greatest demand for labour, excites the greatest quantity of industry, and generally occasions the greatest increase of population' (1820, 266).

The 1836 version is altered in various respects. The first paragraph of the restatement asserts the desirability of expenditure on material wealth rather than services from the perspective of employment. The case involves an expansion of 'conveniences and comforts' (even if at reduced prices), which creates 'a more steady demand for labour' than would an expansion of services.[25] The paragraph also touches on the effect of reduced prices of *manufactured wage goods* in pushing out 'the limits of the effectual demand for labour': 'It is obvious that the object which it is most desirable to attain is the union of the two. There is somewhere a happy mean where, under the actual resources of a country, both the increase of wealth and the demand for labour may be a maximum. A taste for conveniences and comforts not only tends to create a more steady demand for labour, than a taste for personal services; but by cheapening manufactures and the products of foreign commerce, including many of the necessaries of the labouring classes, it actually enlarges the limits of the effectual demand for labour, and renders it for a longer time effective' (1836, 239). The second paragraph, in line with the established pattern of the 1836 version, rewords the issue of 'an increase in quantity with steady prices ...' to refer, not to general output (as may be understood by the 1820 version), but specifically to wage goods: 'An increase in the quantity of the funds for the maintenance of labour, with steady prices, or even slightly falling, may occasion a considerable demand for labour; but in the actual state of things, and in the way in which the precious metals are actually distributed, some increase of prices generally accompanies the most effective demand for produce and population. It is this increase both of quantity and price which most surely increases the *value* of the funds for maintenance of

25 Earlier statements regarding the service sector (1836, 234–5; above, pp. 422–3) contain no such evaluation.

labour, creates the greatest demand for labourers, excites the greatest quantity of industry, and generally occasions the greatest increase of population' (239–40).

On balance, we are obliged to conclude that, though some passages bear the interpretation offered earlier, whereby the value of the GNP (1820) or of wage goods (1836) merely provides an *index* of aggregate labour demand or the national labour requirement, other formulations suggest a stronger causal sequence, whereby labour demand is not merely 'proportioned to' but *dependent upon* either the value of the national product (1820) or the value of wage goods (1836). In either case, it remains true that an increase in society's labour requirement is rendered 'effectual' – generating an appropriate population response – only by an increased flow of *material* wage goods, pre-eminently corn.

A further complexity regarding labour demand emerges in the final chapter, 'Of the Progress of Wealth,' but in the first edition alone. It reflects the apparent difficulty that an expanded 'value' of aggregate output – 'value' indicating labour commanded – seems to be definitionally precluded in the case of a *given* population: 'With regard to labour I would observe that, when I speak of the value of the whole produce of a country being able to command more labour than before, I do not mean to refer specifically to a greater *number* of labourers, but to say that it could either purchase more at the old price, or pay the actual labourers higher; and such a state of things, with a population which cannot immediately be increased, always occasions that demand for labour, which so powerfully encourages the exertions of those who were before perhaps only half paid and half employed; and is at once the surest sign and most effective stimulus of increasing wealth. It is the natural consequence of the value of the produce estimated in labour increasing faster than the population, and forms the true and healthy encouragement to the further increase of numbers' (1820, 451–2). Here, too, we find the notion of an increased value of national income *occasioning* an increased demand for labour.

IV FAMILY EARNINGS AND FULL EMPLOYMENT

A high *per-capita* corn wage is not a *necessary* condition for rapid population growth; variation in the participation rate allows for an increase in total family corn earnings and provides a stimulus, notwithstanding a reduced *per-capita* corn wage (above, p. 419). That a high corn wage might not signal a requirement for correspondingly high population growth is elaborated in a discussion of a fall in the corn price relative to the money wage sufficient to depress total family earnings:

> It sometimes happens that wages are for a time rather higher than they ought to be in proportion to the demand for labour [1836: that corn wages are comparatively high without a proportionate demand for labour]. This is most likely to

take place when the price of raw produce has fallen in value [1836: the price of raw produce has fallen without a fall in the price of labour], so as to diminish the power of the cultivators to employ the same or an increasing number of labourers at the same price [1836: so as to disable the cultivators from employing the same quantity of labour as before]. If the fall be considerable, and not made up in value by increase of quantity, so many labourers will be thrown out of work that [money] wages, after a period of great distress, will generally be lowered in proportion. But if the fall be gradual, and partly made up in exchangeable value by increase of quantity, the money wages of labour will not necessarily sink; and the result will be merely a slack demand for labour, not sufficient perhaps to throw the actual labourers out of work but such as to prevent or diminish task work, to check the employment of women and children, and to give but little encouragement to the rising generation of labourers. In this case the quantity of the necessaries of life actually earned by the labourer and his family, may be really less than when, owing to a rise of prices, the daily pay of the labourer will command a smaller quantity of corn. The command of the labouring classes over the necessaries of life, though apparently greater, is really less in the former than in the latter case, and, upon all general principles, ought to produce less effect on the increase of population. (1820, 257–8; 1836, 231–2)

There is the further complexity that a high *per-capita* corn wage, if it entails unemployment, will *a fortiori* fail to stimulate population growth. This implication is elaborated in a concluding survey of the historical pattern of corn wages. The point is that a low corn price stimulates population growth only if the *aggregate* value of corn rises, such increase an assurance against unemployment – agricultural unemployment is specified in the second edition. As usual the formulation of 1820 runs in terms of 'the exchangeable value of the whole produce ... compared with labour,' whereas the 1836 version specifies 'the value of the funds for the maintenance of labour':

In considering the corn wages of labour in the course of this review, it has not been possible to make any distinction [1836: always to make a distinction] between the effects of a fall in the price of corn, and a rise in the price [1836: money price] of labour. In merely comparing the two objects with each other, the result is precisely similar; but their effects in the encouragement of population [1836: on the demand for labour and the encouragement of population] are sometimes very dissimilar [1836: dissimilar] ... There is no doubt that a great encouragement to an increase of population is consistent with a fall in the price of raw produce, because, notwithstanding this fall, the exchangeable value of the whole produce of the country may still be increasing compared with labour; but it may sometimes happen [1836: A great demand for labour is perfectly consistent with a fall in the price of raw produce, because, notwithstanding this fall, the whole *value* of the funds for the maintenance of labour may still be increasing; but it sometimes happens] that a fall in the price of raw produce is accompanied by a diminished power and will [1836: a diminished power on the part of the farmer] to employ labour; and in this case the demand for labour and the encouragement to population will not be in proportion to the apparent [1836: 'apparent' omitted] corn wages of labour. (1820, 288–9; 1836, 258)[26]

Both editions proceed to distinguish the effect on population growth of a rise in *per-capita* corn wage reflecting an increase in the money wage from a rise reflecting a fall in the corn price. Again, the corn wage as such was not an unambiguous index of population stimulus. Thus a higher corn wage which reflects a money-wage increase as a result of increased labour demand implies full employment in the broadest sense – including improved opportunities for family participation – and provides stimulus to population growth. By contrast, reduced corn prices in the face of a relatively sluggish money wage might entail a reduced 'capital of the farmer' (1820) or the 'value of the farmer's returns' (1836) and reduced family employment: 'If a [1836: the] labourer commands a peck instead of $\frac{3}{4}$ [1836: $\frac{5}{6}$] of a peck of wheat a day, in consequence of a rise of wages occasioned by a demand for labour, it is certain that all labourers may be employed who are willing and able to work [1836: in consequence of a rise of money wages, all the labourers who are willing and able to work may be employed,] and probably also their wives and children; but if he is able to command this additional quantity of wheat on account of a fall in the price of corn which diminishes the capital of the farmer [1836: value of the farmers' returns,] the advantage may be [1836: is] more apparent than real, and though labour for sometime may not nominally fall [1836: the price of labour may not nominally fall for some time,] yet as the demand for labour may be stationary, if not retrograde, its current price will not be

26 The 1836 version refers simply to the value of the funds for the maintenance of labour, *omitting* 'compared with labour,' which appears in 1820. The same omission will be found immediately below regarding 1820, 289–90, and 1836, 258–9. Yet labour command is referred to elsewhere in the 1836 version.

A passage added in the second edition refers to the contemporary agricultural depression – it must have been written soon after the first edition appeared – as entailing low demand for labour because of the negative effect on the *aggregate* value of necessaries exerted by low corn prices; *per-capita* corn wages were high, *but only for those employed*: 'It is certainly true ... that for some time, nearly perhaps ever since the war, the fully employed labourers have been able, in spite of the corn laws, to purchase a more than usual quantity of wheat. The specific evil of the present times in regard to agricultural labourers is, that from the low price of corn as compared with the price of labour and the other outgoings of the farmer, he is unable to farm with spirit, and the consequence is that a considerable number of men are unemployed except by the parish. Nothing can show more clearly that a brisk demand for labourers depends upon an increase of the funds for their maintenance, *without a proportionate fall in their value*' (1836, 252).

a certain criterion [1836: a criterion] of what might be earned by the united labours of a large family, or the increased exertions of the head of it in task work' (1820, 289–90; 1836, 258–9). [27] In sum: 'The same current corn wages will under different circumstances, have a different effect in the encouragement of population [1836: effect, both on the demand for labour, and the general condition of the labouring classes]' (1820, 290; 1836, 259).[28]

In a summary paragraph of 1820, Malthus reiterates that it is *family* command over 'the customary grain' that provides the index of population stimulus – obviously taking for granted full employment. However, in the event that the labourers exercise prudential control, this stimulus will not be activated. In fact, in an aside it is observed that high employment opportunities which reflect 'rapidly increasing resources' cannot be '*permanent*' – an allusion to land scarcity – rendering such constraint all the more essential: 'It appears then that, making a proper allowance for the varying value of other parts of the wages of labour besides food, the quantity of the customary grain which a labouring family can actually earn, is at once a measure of the encouragement to population and of the conditions of the labourer; while the money price of such wages is the best measure of the value of money as far as one commodity can go. But it is of the utmost importance always to bear in mind that a great command over the necessaries of life may be effected in two ways, either by rapidly increasing resources, or by the prudential habits of the labouring classes; and that as rapidly increasing resources are neither in the power of the poor to effect, nor can in the nature of things be permanent, the great

27 In 1836, an important footnote reads: 'Under all ordinary circumstances, more labour may be set in motion, before any increase of population has taken place.'

28 Malthus in 1836 adds in a note: 'This is frequently noticed in the Agricultural Report' (see House of Commons, Parliamentary Papers, 1833, v. *Agricultural Report*).

Some implifications are drawn with an eye on population stimulus from the fact that wheat is not always the main element in the wage basket:

> in estimating the corn wages of labour I have uniformly taken wheat, the dearest grain. I have taken one grain to the exclusion of other necessaries, because I wish to avoid complicating the subject [1836: in order to avoid complicating the subject]; and have chosen wheat because it is the main food of the greatest part of the population of England. But it is evident that at those periods, or in those countries, in which the main food of the people does not consist of wheat, the wheat wages that [1836: which] can be earned by a family will not form a just criterion of the encouragement given to population. Although the wheat wages might be very unequal at two different periods, or in two different countries, yet if in one case an inferior grain were habitually consumed, the encouragement to the population might be the same. The Irish labourer cannot command the support of so large a family upon wheat as the English [1836: as the English labourer], but he can command in general the support of a much larger [1836: of a larger] family upon the food on which he is accustomed to live; and consequently, population has increased much faster during the last century in Ireland than in England. (1820, 290; 1836, 259)

resource of the labouring classes for their happiness must be in those prudential habits which, if properly exercised, are capable of securing to the labourer a fair proportion of the necessaries and conveniences of life, from the earliest stage of society to the latest' (1820, 290–1).[29]

The summary is expanded in 1836. The restatement entails the now standard insistence on specifying labour demand (and, indirectly, population stimulus) in terms of the *value of the funds destined for labour's maintenance* rather than the *exchangeable value of the whole produce.* As in 1820 it also insists that appropriate allowance be made for necessaries other than corn (see note 28) and also for the state of employment with an eye to family earnings: 'It appears then, that in order to form a just estimate of the demand for labour, the encouragement to population, and the condition of the labourer, we must first consider the increase of the funds specifically destined for the maintenance of labour, instead either of the increase of wealth, the increase of capital, or the increase of the exchangeable value of the whole produce. Secondly, in estimating these funds we must consider their whole value, not merely their whole quantity, and make a proper allowance for those other parts of the wages of labour which do not consist of corn. And thirdly, in estimating the amount of food and necessaries earned by the labouring classes, which amount principally affects their condition, we must make a careful distinction between the earnings of a whole family, when employment is difficult to be found, and their earnings when there is a demand for more work to be done than there are hands to do it' (1836, 260). There follows, as in 1820, a reference to the implications of prudential control; increased real wages do not necessarily require a higher labour demand: 'It is further of the utmost importance always to bear in mind that a great command over the necessaries *and conveniences* of life may be effected in two ways, either by a *rapid increase in the quantity and value of the funds destined for the maintenance of labour, or by the prudential habits of the labouring classes*; and that as the former mode of improving their condition is neither in the power of the poor to carry into effect themselves, nor can in the nature of things be permanent, the great resource of the labouring classes for their happiness must be in those prudential habits which, if properly exercised, are capable of securing to them a fair proportion of the necessaries *and conveniences* of life, from the earliest stage of society to the latest' (emphasis added).

V SUMMARY AND CONCLUSION

The formal analysis of labour demand is ambiguous, the ambiguity created by the vague treatment of the notion of causality and by intrusion of

29 It will be noted that the higher wage basket with prudential control includes 'conveniences.'

concern with the value of final output – the problem of aggregate demand. The complexity is increased further by Malthus's frequent practice – which we encounter again in section IV of the next chapter – of reverting to a simple identification of labour demand with 'capital' in 1820 – or with a more mysterious 'capital and produce' in the second edition. Conceivably, this latter practice might have been found adequate for cases where the aggregate-demand issue is set aside by hypothesis for the purpose at hand. None the less, it is a disconcerting practice, considering the strong position that 'the demand for labour is not *proportioned* to the increase of capital in any shape' (cited above, p. 422).

TEN

Profit-rate analysis

I INTRODUCTION

This chapter opens with a major classical preoccupation – the effect of increasing land scarcity on the returns to labour and capital. Malthus's analysis 'Of the Profits of Capital' in his *Principles* provides one of the finest statements of the downward secular path of the corn wage and profit rates, as we show below, in section II. The model is further elaborated in section III, where we consider the formal transition to a mixed economy and the transmission from the agricultural to the manufacturing profit rate. We there demonstrate that Sraffa's famous interpretation of the early Ricardo (1951, xxxi; 1960, 93) applies in fact to T.R Malthus – the 'mature' Malthus of the *Principles* and thereafter. This entails the priority of distribution over pricing, with the profit rate determined in the wage-goods (corn) sector as a ratio of physically homogeneous output and input to which profit rates in other industries adjust by way of their terms of trade with corn.[1] Various criticisms of this interpretation are considered in section IV.

The sense of Malthus's adherence to a corn-profit model must be well

1 A corn-profit calculation requires technically that the wage basket comprise solely corn, or else changes in the relative prices of wage goods will affect the denominator in the corn profit-rate expression. To specify all values for the variables – the profit rate and prices – the wage must of course be known. Allowing for a declining secular corn wage, the falling profit rate still emerges in physical terms since the marginal product necessarily declines more rapidly that the wage. At each stage, the (lower) profit rate would in principle be applied to 'metal' and 'cloth,' dictating an appropriate reduction in their natural values, that is, a rise in the metal or cloth prices of corn. Such changes will not play further on the profit rate.

understood at the outset.[2] Malthus was aware that the profit rate is conventionally defined as a ratio of *values*. But though the general expression for the profit rate involves value terms, the *agricultural* profit rate is expressed in physical (corn) terms, and the rate thus determined carries over to manufacturing. Second, Malthus spelled out the assumptions required to permit proceeding in physical terms in agriculture; and he cautioned that, in application, the procedure might break down, even should both input and output be composed of the same physical substance. The evidence points: (1) to an *analytical* corn-profit model consciously spelled out – we are not concerned here with 'rational reconstruction' of the sort Sraffa engaged in – and (2) to limitations in application reflecting largely seasonal corn-price fluctuations.

Section V concerns a special case discussed in the 1820 version of the *Principles* involving manufacturing alone, which clarifies the evident intention to limit Smithian 'competition of capitals' solely to manufacturing. The second edition, too, has it that a manufacturing economy (even if it imports corn without impediment) *must* experience a falling rate of return, whereas an agricultural system could conceivably (via 'improvements') avoid that outcome.

The effect on the profit rate of fluctuations in the real wage is the subject of section VI. There, Malthus's inexplicable criticism of Ricardo for denying any such relation will be a special concern.

Malthus's championship in 1820 and thereafter of the Ricardian theorem on distribution running in proportionality terms is examined in sections VII–IX. There is evidence of growing support for the theorem in revisions made to the *Principles*, and also in *The Measure of Value* (1823) and in the *Quarterly Review* article of 1824. There is, of course, the fundamental difference over the Law of Markets, and that difference plays upon the alternative perspectives taken on the determination of the proportionate shares, and thus the profit rate. Section X elaborates on this feature, noting J.S. Mill's position in *The Morning Chronicle* that this difference does not flow, as Malthus believed, from the alternative measuring indexes.

A concluding section compares the propositions regarding sectoral interdependence encountered in the 1813–19 correspondence and other early formulations (above, Part I) with the 'mature' position. Acceptance of the Ricardian inverse wage–profit relation as a theorem regarding proportions is again shown to be reinforced, as is the lead role of agriculture following corn-profit logic, with the manufacturing rate of profit coming into line. Our case is based on the chapters in the *Principles* on

2 I reached this conclusion several years ago, basing it then solely on *The Measure of Value* (1823) and related correspondence: 'The determining role of agricultural profits and the solution to distribution prior to prices are Malthusian conceptions' (1979, 722). For a criticism of Sraffa's interpretation of Ricardo, see 162–3, 183–4, 685–6.

Wages and Profits supported by *The Measure of Value* (1823); a serious problem of interpretation is created by a section in the Rent chapter representing manufacturing as lead sector.

II THE SECULAR DECLINE OF THE PROFIT AND WAGE RATES

We turn first to section I of the profits chapter, entitled, in 1820, 'Of Profits as affected by the increasing Difficulty of procuring the Means of Subsistence' (the major component of 'advances'), and the corresponding material in section II of the 1836 version, entitled 'Of the Limiting Principle of Profits.'[3]

The profit rate is identified with 'the proportion which the difference between the value of the advances and the value of the commodity produced bears to the value of the advances,' and is said to vary with 'variations of the value of the advances compared with the value of the product' (1820, 294; cf. a similar formulation in 1836, 262–3).[4] The 'value of the advances' turns on agricultural productivity and the magnitude of the wage basket expressed in terms of 'necessaries': 'The two main causes which influence the means of supporting labour, are, first, the difficulty or facility of production on the land, by which a greater or less proportion of the value of the whole produce is capable of supporting the labourers employed; and secondly, the varying relation of the quantity of capital to the quantity of labour employed by it, by which more or less of the necessaries of life may go to each individual labourer' (1820, 294–5). Each is then considered in turn, and a variety of disturbing causes ruled out for clarity of exposition.[5] The formulation in the second edition is modified to focus explicitly on the agricultural margin, and it categorizes diminishing returns as the '*limiting* principle of profits' and variable real (corn)

3 In both editions the chapter commences with a definitional paragraph justifying use of the term 'capital' rather than 'stock,' capital constituting 'that particular part of ... [national] accumulated wealth, which is destined to be employed with a view to profit [1836: in the production and distribution of wealth]' (1820, 293; 1836, 262).

The first section of the 1836 version, on 'the Mode in which [profits] are estimated,' considers the inverse wage–profit relation.

4 In 1820 alone, 'advances' are said to be composed largely of 'the means of supporting labour.' Whether we should understand this as a deliberate reference to the pre-accumulation of wage goods by employers is questionable, in light of the earlier discussion of wages. The advances are themselves said in 1820 to be 'generally composed of accumulations which have previously cost in their production a certain quantity of wages, profit and rent, exclusive of the rent which, in the case of agricultural products, is paid directly' (1820, 293–4). This is simplified in 1836: 'these advances consist of accumulations generally made up of wages, rents, taxes, interest, and profits' (262).

5 For it is 'the combination of the two, and of others in addition to them, sometimes acting in conjunction and sometimes in opposition, which occasions in the progress of society those varied phenomena which it is not always easy to explain' (1820, 295).

wages as the '*regulating principle*': 'The two main causes which affect these proportions ['between the value of the advances necessary to production, and the value of the produce obtained'] are the productiveness, or unproductiveness of the last capitals employed upon the land, by which a smaller, or a greater proportion of the value of the produce is capable of supporting the labourers employed. This may be called the *limiting* principle of profits. And, secondly, the varying value of the produce of the same quantity of labour occasioned by the accidental or ordinary state of the demand and supply, by which a greater or smaller proportion of that produce falls to the share of the labourers employed. This may be called the *regulating* principle of profits; this second cause is constantly modifying the first, but it will be desirable to consider them separately' (1836, 271).

It will be noted that, in the 1820 version, Malthus refers to wages in the sense of 'the necessaries of life,' which may include non-agricultural goods, but in the later version, to a proportion of the 'produce,' a term which usually relates to agricultural output. We shall see shortly that in the course of expounding the downward trend path of secular wages under market pressures, Malthus systematically replaces the term 'real' wages, used in 1820, with 'corn' wages. In the event that, by 'necessaries' in 1820, *corn alone* was intended, then the modification would merely be designed to avoid misunderstanding, not to introduce a new conception. In the alternative case, the modification would have deeper implications. For the moment[6] we proceed on the assumption that, even in 1820, corn (agricultural necessaries) is intended or, if it is not, that at least the general downward trend path of the corn wage outlined below remains intact; and it is that path which is of interest since, at this stage, the argument relates to the agricultural sector.

The formulation of 1820 (even the revised version) is misleading since, as we shall shortly see, the 'greater or less proportion of the value of the whole produce ...' – let us assume the marginal produce is intended, as it certainly is in 1836 – actually *incorporates* allowance for a secular decline of the corn wage. This problem is overcome if we read 'variability of the wage' to refer specifically to *wage fluctuation*, not the downward trend. It is true that, in setting aside 'disturbing causes' in order to focus on the *first* force alone, Malthus assumes a constant corn wage, excluding *all* sources of wage variability, but this procedure was a matter of pedagogic simplification (very much in the manner of Ricardo), considering the subsequent restatement of the limiting principle, with its full allowance for the downward trend.

The first set of simplifying assumptions includes, then, expansion of capital and population at *constant* per-capita corn wages, given technology, under conditions of diminishing agricultural returns. Under these condi-

6 See below, p. 444, for an elaboration.

tions we have a steady decline in rate of profits: 'If the first cause operated singly, *and the wages of the individual labourer were always the same,* then supposing that the skill in agriculture were to remain unchanged, and that there were no means of obtaining corn from foreign countries, the rate of profits must regularly and without any interruption fall, as the society advanced, and as it became necessary to resort to inferior machines which required more labour to put in action' (1820, 295; emphasis added). 'If then we suppose the first cause to operate singly, *and the corn wages of the individual labourer to be always the same,* the whole skill in agriculture remained unchanged, and there were no taxes nor any means of obtaining corn from foreign countries, the rate of profits must regularly fall, as the society advanced, and as it became necessary to resort to inferior machines which required more labour to put in action' (1836, 271; emphasis added).

There is a complication. Malthus allows for rent even on marginal land, should it be necessary to compensate landowners for withdrawing such land from its 'uncultivated state.' Even after deducting such compensation, allowance had to be made for the rent component within advances: 'Some rent, though it may be trifling, is almost always paid in the materials of the farmers' capital'(1820, 296n). (The note is absent in 1836, but the 'almost entirely' of the text that follows presumably refers to this qualification.)[7] But possibly on quantitative grounds this was not seen to present a serious complication,[8] and Malthus proceeds blithely: 'After this payment was made, the remainder of the produce would be divided chiefly [1836: almost entirely] between the capitalist and the labourers, and it is evident that if the number of labourers necessary to obtain a given produce were continually increasing, *and the [1836: corn] wages of each labourer remained the same,* the portion destined to the payment of labour would be continually encroaching upon the portion destined to the payment of profits; and the rate of profits would of course continue regularly diminishing till, from the want of power or will to save, the progress of accumulation had ceased' (1820, 296; 1836, 272; emphasis added). In this case, 'the profits of agriculture would be in proportion to the fertility of the land taken into cultivation, or *to the amount of the produce obtained by a given quantity of labour*' (emphasis added) – the value dimension is absent. Furthermore, 'as profits in the same country tend to an equality, the general rate of profits would follow the same course'; or, as he later phrased it: 'the increased difficulty of procuring food from the soil' will lower the rate of profits on the land, and 'from the land this fall will extend to all other departments of in-

7 For Ricardo, the possible absence of 'no-rent' land creates no problems, considering the intensive margin. But for this reason he would have objected even to the 'trifling' element intimated. For his reaction in correspondence on learning of Malthus's denial of 'no-rent' land and of no-rent output, see chapter 4, pp. 170–1.

8 The complexity is played down only for agricultural *expansion*; contraction is another matter (1820, 183f.; 1836, 177f). There is an asymmetry to the model.

dustry' (1820, 335; 1836, 297). The precise process by which the general profit rate comes into line with the agricultural profit rate is elaborated subsequently, as we shall see in the next section.

It is striking that, though the formal expression for the profit rate involves *value* terms, the conclusion regarding the determination of the profit rate is expressed in *physical* units – specifically in agriculture it emerges – 'the amount of the produce obtained by a given quantity of labour.' A deliberate assumption is introduced to justify a profit ratio in *quantity* terms – namely, that of 'an equal demand for all the parts of the same produce': 'It is necessary to qualify the position in this way, because, with regard to the main products of agriculture, it might easily happen that all the parts were not of the same value. If a farmer cultivated his lands by means of domestics living in his house whom he found in food and clothing, his advances might always be nearly the same in quantity and of the same high value in use; but in the case of a glut from the shutting up of an accustomed market, or a season of unusual abundance, a part of the crop might be of no value either in use or exchange, and his profits could by no means be determined, by the excess of the *quantity* produced, above the advances necessary to produce it [1836: as before shewn, page 264]' (1820, 296n; 1836, 272n).[9] Although, in dealing formally with labour demand, a primary concern was to assure that expansion of physical corn output did not lose its value – for which reason the revised edition specifies, not physical necessaries, but the *value* of those necessaries as constituting labour demand (see chapter 9: III) – the problem is now set aside without ado in so far as concerns agriculture. As we shall see, the manufacturing sector is treated quite differently; there the downward pressure of supply on price is essential to the argument.

At this point we return to the assumed constancy of the corn wage. This assumption is nothing but an expository preliminary which had to be abandoned, not only as 'contrary to the actual state of things,' but as entailing a 'contradiction' (1820, 297; 1836, 272). The argument turns on the point that an initial real wage *at 'subsistence'* rules out population growth and agricultural expansion, whereas an initial wage *above subsistence*, which remains unchanged at that level, implies (given the function relating population growth to the real wage) an impossibility – namely, constant population growth despite the zero net capital accumulation characterizing the ultimate stationary state:

> The progress of population is almost exclusively regulated by the quantity of the necessaries of life actually awarded to the labourer; and if from the first he had no more than sufficient to keep up the actual population, the labouring classes could not increase, nor would there be any occasion for the progressive cultiva-

9 For the earlier text of 1836 alluded to, see below, pp. 456–7.

tion of poorer land. On the other hand, if the real [1836: corn] wages of labour were such as to admit of and encourage an [1836: a considerable] increase of population, and yet were always to remain the same, it would involve the contradiction of a continued increase of population [1836: at the same rate] after the accumulation of capital, and the means of supporting such an increase had entirely ceased.

We cannot then make the supposition of a *natural* and *constant* price of labour, at least if we mean by such a price, an unvarying quantity of the necessaries of life. And if we cannot fix the real price of labour, it must evidently vary with the progress of capital and revenue, and the demand for labour compared with the supply. [1836: We cannot then make the supposition of a *natural* and *constant* rate of corn wages. And if we cannot fix the wages of labour estimated in necessaries, they must evidently vary with the progress of the funds destined for the maintenance of labour, compared with the supply of labour.] (1820, 297; 1836, 272–3).

Again, one notes how Malthus uses the term 'funds destined for the maintenance of labour,' not the *value* of those funds. The focus is on the physical dimension, notwithstanding the formal analysis of labour demand.

The foregoing paragraph is a preliminary to an extended account of the *falling secular wage path*, an account divorced from that of *wage fluctuations about the trend*. For the analysis of the secular path appears within the section now under consideration, treating profits 'as affected by the increasing Difficulty of procuring the Means of Subsistence' (1820) or 'The Limiting Principle of Profits' (1836), whereas the treatment of wage fluctuations – the second main 'cause' affecting profits – is left for the next section, 'Of Profits as Affected by the Proportion which Capital bears to Labour' (1820) or 'The Regulating Principle of Profits' (1836). And in fact Malthus proceeds in the account of the falling wage trend by explicitly *excluding wage fluctuations* attributable to 'temporary accelerations or retardations' of the relative factor growth rates characterizing 'the actual state of things': 'We may however, if we please, suppose a uniform progress of capital and population, by which is not meant in the present case the same *rate* of progress permanently, which is impossible; but a uniform progress towards the greatest practicable amount, without temporary accelerations or retardations. And before we proceed to the actual state of things, it may be curious to consider in what manner profits would be affected under these circumstances' (1820, 297–8; 1836, 273).

In the full account – which is surely one of the best in the literature – it is explained that the incidence of diminishing returns cannot fall solely on labour. For the fall in the real (corn) wage, because of its effect on the population-growth rate, is constrained relative to that of the marginal product; accordingly, the effect of increasing land scarcity is to depress *both* the real wage and the profit rate until their respective minima, at which stage further expansion ceases.

The first paragraph in the account differs between editions: 'At the commencement of the cultivation of a fertile country by civilized colonists and whose rich land was in great plenty, a small portion only of the value of the produce would be paid in the form of rent. Nearly the whole would be divided between profits and wages; and the proportion which each would take, as far as it was influenced by the share of each individual labourer, must be determined by the demand and supply of capital compared with the demand and supply of labour' (1820, 298).[10] This is modified in 1836 to focus more explicitly on proportionate shares at the early stage; though absolute wages are high, proportionate wages may be low, thus assuring a high profit rate: 'At the commencement of the cultivation of a fertile country by civilized colonists, and while rich land was in great plenty, a small portion only of the value of the produce would be paid in the form of rent. The productiveness of labour being great, if nearly the whole were divided between wages and profits, the labourers might obtain a large quantity of produce, while a sufficient *proportion* of the whole might be left to yield large profits, and wages and profits would both be high at the same time.' A footnote attached to the second edition warns the reader 'that wages always refer to quantity, unless otherwise particularly expressed, and profit to proportion.' This seems to disclaim the notion that the profit varies inversely with *proportionate* wages; but the text proves otherwise,[11] for the full argument proceeds along the same lines in both versions, with the profit rate varying inversely with labour's *proportionate share* in the marginal product, which 'necessarily' rises despite the downward trend in the corn wage:

As the society continued to proceed [1836: increase], if the territory were limited, or the soil of different qualities, it is quite obvious that the productive powers of labour as applied to the cultivation of land must gradually diminish; and as a given quantity of capital and labour [1836: a given quantity of labour] would yield a smaller and smaller return, there would evidently be a less and less produce to be divided between labour and profits.

If, as the power of labour diminished, the physical wants of the labourer were also to diminish in the same proportion, then the same share [1836: *share*] of the whole produce might be left to the capitalist and the *rate* of profits would not necessarily fall. But the physical wants of the labourer remain always the same; and though in the progress of society, from the increasing scarcity of provisions compared with labour, these wants are in general less

10 In both this and the 1836 versions, there is allusion to 'value,' but it is not substantive, given that the problem as set up specifically relates to physical quantities. In fact, in the elaboration that follows we find the falling real wage expressed simply in terms of 'the increasing scarcity of provisions compared with labour.'

11 In fact the first section of the 1836 version elaborates on the proportionality theorem in unmistakable terms; see below, section VII.

fully supplied, and the real [1836: corn] wages of labour gradually fall; yet it is clear that there is a limit, and probably at no great distance, which cannot be passed. The command of a certain quantity of food is absolutely necessary to the labourer in order to support himself, and such a family as will maintain merely a stationary population. Consequently, if poorer land which required more labour were successively taken into cultivation, it would not be possible for the corn wages of each individual labourer to be diminished in proportion to the diminished product; a greater proportion [1836: *proportion*] of the whole would necessarily go to labour [1836: to pay the wages of labour]; and the rate of profits would continue regularly falling till the accumulation of capital had ceased.

Such would be the necessary course of profits and wages in the progressive accumulation of capital, as applied to the progressive cultivation of new and less fertile land, or the further improvement of what had before been cultivated; and on the supposition here made, the rate both of profits and of real [1836: corn] wages would be highest at first, and would regularly and gradually diminish together, till they both came to a stand at the same period, and the demand for an increase of produce ceased to be effective. (1820, 298–9; 1836, 273–4)[12]

It is appropriate to note Malthus's caution at the close of his final section, 'Remarks on Mr. Ricardo's Theory of Profits': 'But what would be the effects upon the profits of stock of any given increase of capital, or even of any given increase of the labour necessary to produce a certain quantity of corn, it would be quite impossible to say beforehand' (1820, 336; 1836, 298). But though there was no *a priori* way of specifying precisely the distribution of the incidence of diminishing returns, without question *both* the return of labour and capital tend downwards: 'In the case of a mere increase of capital, however large, it has appeared that circumstances might occur to prevent any fall of profits for a great length of time.[13] And, even in the case of an increase in the quantity of labour necessary to produce corn, it would depend entirely upon the principles of demand and supply and competition, whether the increase in the price of corn would be such as to throw almost the whole of the increased difficulty of production upon labour, or such as to throw almost the whole of it upon profits, or finally such as to divide the loss more equally in various propor-

12 Cf. a further comment in the second edition regarding the characteristic *decline* in the corn wage but *increased* proportionate wages with increasing land scarcity: 'In general where the facility of production is great, the labourer will obtain a large quantity of [necessaries], as in new colonies favourably circumstanced, and in the United States of America. On the other hand, where from the demand of a greatly increased population, cultivation is pushed upon poor land, and production is difficult, the labourer, though he may obtain a larger proportion of what he produces, will receive a smaller quantity of produce' (1836, 114–15).

13 See below, p. 451.

tions between them [1836: ... would be such as to throw *almost the whole* of the increased difficulty of production upon the labourer, or upon the capitalist, or again such as to divide the loss more equally between them, which is what generally happens].'

The message to be conveyed by all this is that 'no theory of profits ... can approach towards correctness, which attempts to get rid of the principle of demand and supply and competition.' Malthus shows not the slightest indication that Ricardo maintained the principle of the shared incidence of diminishing returns.[14] This matter will be taken up below, in section VI, dealing with the effect of real-wage fluctuations. There we show that, in his Rent chapter, Malthus briefly concedes some common ground (below, p. 475).

* * *

We must now consider Malthus's intentions by his systematic replacement of the term *real wage* by *corn wages* in the revised account.[15] As mentioned earlier (p. 438), no substantive analytical modification may have been intended, merely greater precision of exposition. This evaluation is reinforced by a passage involving trends appearing in 1820 alone – located inappropriately in the section on wage fluctuations – asserting that whether the initial conditions entail 'low or high *corn* wages,' net accumulation depresses the profit rate: 'If, in the early period of improvement, capital were scarce compared with labour, the wages of labour being on this account low, while the productive powers of labour, from the fertility of the land, were great, the proportion left for profits would necessarily be very considerable, and the rate of profits would be very high. In general, however, though capital may be said to be scarce in the early periods of cultivation, yet that particular portion of capital, which resolves itself into

14 Regrettably Mountifort Longfield (1834) neglected or failed to absorb Malthus's analysis – just as he neglected Ricardo's formulations – objecting as he did to the position that the profit rate is depressed by increasing land scarcity, considering the allowance that must be made for a declining wage: 'In the argument used to prove that the decreasing fertility of the soil is the great and necessary cause of a decline of profits, it is, I conceive, unwarrantably assumed, that the effect cannot be entirely borne by the labourer, and that therefore of necessity some part of it must fall upon capital. This necessity I cannot perceive. As population was advancing, the wages of labour must have been more than what would be necessary to the subsistence of the labourers, with such families as would keep up an unvarying population; they may sustain some reduction, and why not the entire amount of the reduction that has taken place in the returns made to labour and capital?' (184–5).

15 In the foregoing extract (1820, 336; 1836, 298) the corn price – presumably relative to the money wage – is the variable dictating the distribution of the effect of the decline in the physical corn product. Here, then, Malthus has set aside the (physiocratic) assumption used elsewhere that money wages rise in proportion to any given rise in the corn price, generating an *improvement* in real purchasing power.

food, is often plentiful compared with the population, and high profits and high real wages are found together. In the most natural state of things this is generally the case, though it is not so when capital is prematurely checked by extravagance, or other causes. But whether we set out from low or high corn wages, the diminution in the rate of profits, from the gradual increase of capital compared with labour, will remain undisturbed' (1820, 302–3).

We can rule out a recent interpretation of the replacement of *real wage* by *corn wage* (Gibbard, 1994) turning on the notion of a constant fixed-proportions wage basket comprising manufactures and corn, the corn wage declining as the arithmetic outcome of a rise in the corn price. After all, the revision does not affect the role accorded decelerating demand for labour. We cannot, in fact, positively exclude the possibility that Malthus came to insist on a *corn only* basket. We refer in the next section to evidence of the strengthening of a 'Sraffian' (corn-input, corn-output) dimension to profit-rate determination; the change in question might reflect this reinforcement by precluding a mixed wage basket. On the other hand, it would be presumptuous to take this for granted. And we shall explore the alternative possibility, that the predicted fall in the corn wage occurs even though it is *implicitly* assumed that part of labour's earnings are diverted to manufactures. What technical problems emerge when the issue is followed through on these lines?

In a corn-only version of growth constrained by increasing land scarcity, the fall in the corn wage is *necessarily* slower than that of the marginal product in agriculture, thereby raising the wage share of that marginal product and *depressing the profit rate.* With allowance for a mixed basket, this feature would have to be retained or else irreparable damage is done to the general argument. Assuming, then, the more complex case, the continual rise in the corn-manufactures terms of trade enables workers to acquire increasing amounts of manufactured wage goods for the surrender of given amounts of corn. Should the worker have a specific manufacturing-goods objective, the corn wage would fall more rapidly than in the pure-corn case, and still allow the purchase of that desired quantum under the improving terms of trade. Analytically, this implies that labour supply (population growth pre-eminently) turns, *not* on the corn wage – as in the basic assumption – but on a mixed wage. But the desire for manufactures can be treated as one of the *ceteris paribus* conditions; accordingly, when the corn price rises, labour-supply resistance to a given fall in the corn wage would be relaxed somewhat, so that the fall resulting from decelerating accumulation is *greater* than in the simple case. None the less, provided the decline falls short of that of the marginal product, this complication can be accommodated.

In the event that a given fall in the corn wage causes a *degeneration* of standards in the sense of a fall in the manufacturing requirement, labour-supply resistance would be further weakened, increasing the threat to the basic model; conversely, if the manufacturing requirement should rise, the threat is eased.[16] Now there is in fact support for such possibilities. In both the *Essay on Population* (1817) and the *Principles* itself, a role is accorded rising food prices relative to those of manufactures in the process of improving taste patterns (above, pp. 190, 418). In the limit, reductions in the corn wage might even be prevented – and an increase in manufacturing purchases allowed; and no damage would be done to the agricultural model in the sense that the corn-profit rate falls, indeed falls faster than in the simple case.[17]

III THE DETERMINING ROLE OF THE AGRICULTURAL PROFIT RATE: A 'CORN PROFIT' MODEL

We take up next the transmission from the *agricultural* to the *general* profit rate. The 1820 account involves the effect on manufacturing profits exerted by deteriorating terms of trade between manufacturing, on the one hand, and corn and labour, on the other: 'In the cultivation of land, the immediate and necessary diminution of profits appeared to be the increased quantity of labour necessary to obtain the same produce. In manufactures and commerce, it is the fall in the exchangeable value of the products of industry in these departments, *compared with corn and labour*' (1820, 300; emphasis added). An elaboration allows for real-cost (productivity) variations in the manufacturing sector, but asserts that, since the rates of exchange relative to corn (and labour) decline, the manufacturing profit rate is necessarily depressed: 'The cost of producing corn and labour continually increases from inevitable physical causes, while the cost of producing manufactures and articles of commerce sometimes diminishes, sometimes remains stationary, and at all events increases much slower than the cost of producing corn and labour. Upon every principle therefore of demand and supply, the exchangeable value of these latter objects must fall, compared with the value of labour. But if the exchangeable value of labour continues to rise, while the exchangeable value of manufactures either falls, remains the same, or rises in a much less degree, profits must continue to fall ....' The reference to 'corn and labour' might be read as indicating a *dual* input into manufacturing, labour not being further

16 Any such interdependence, however, creates the analytical difficulty that strictly 'corn' no longer designated by the y-axis.

17 In the absence of a mechanism entailing *strengthened* prudential control, is it conceivable that the fall in the corn wage might be so great as to prevent the fall in the agricultural profit rate? To my knowledge this issue was never formally addressed.

Ricardo, for his part, assumed that, with decelerating accumulation, the labourer 'will receive more money wages but his corn wage will be reduced; and not only his command over corn, but his general condition will be deteriorated, by his finding it more difficult to maintain the market rate of wages above their natural rate' (1951–73, I, 102). There is no indication that he perceived *any* potential complication related to the basic model with its reduction in the corn wage shallower than that of the marginal product.

decomposed. But there is every indication that labour itself is reduced to corn. The increasing 'cost of producing corn and labour' implies a higher cost of producing labour *via* the corn wage; and the rise in the 'exchangeable value of labour' can, in this context, only entail the effect of higher real corn costs. We may, therefore, restate the proposition in terms of a fall in manufacturing profits with a fall in the ratio of manufacturing to corn prices, corn comprising the 'advances' to labour and entering into manufacturing costs via the labour input. We have then, in Malthus, the approach made famous in Sraffa's rational reconstruction of Ricardo's 1814 observation: 'It is the profits of the farmer that regulate the profits of all other trades' (1951–73, VI, 104).

The 1836 version reiterates the main point at stake – that there are *two* sets of forces at play in profit-rate determination: 'In the cultivation of land, the cause of the *necessary* diminution of profits is the diminution in the quantity of produce obtained by the same quantity of labour' – a purely physical matter; '[in] manufactures and commerce, it is the fall in the exchangeable value of the same amount of produce' – a matter involving terms of trade (1836, 275). Here we must refer to a declaration in 1836 to the effect that 'corn, on account of its being the main support of the labourer, is the only object in the production of which a comparison may be instituted between the quantity advanced and the quantity produced' (265–6; see below, p. 457). It is this 'Sraffian' homogeneity of input and output that apparently provides the key.

A further elaboration spells out more fully than in 1820 that the fall in manufacturing prices occurs by way of output expansion in response to profit-rate differentials created by the initial fall in agricultural returns: 'The labour required to produce corn, has a constant tendency to increase from inevitable physical causes, while the labour required to produce manufactures and articles of commerce sometimes greatly diminishes, sometimes remains stationary, and at all events increases much slower than the labour required to produce corn. When, therefore, profits fall in agriculture it becomes obviously more advantageous to employ capital in manufactures and commerce than on the land; and capital will in consequence be so employed till a fall has taken place in manufactures and commercial products from their comparative abundance' (275). Here the Smithian notion of 'competition of capitals' applied specifically to manufactures is brought into play. An actual transfer of activity from agriculture to manufactures would imply contraction of the margin of cultivation; since nothing is said of this, conceivably Malthus intended only that *new* capital investments would flow predominantly to manufactures, eradicating differentials.[18] In this detail Malthus diverges from the pure corn-profit

18 Downward pressure on manufacturing prices and profits may also occur independently of an initial decline in the agricultural rate (see below, pp. 452–3, 483).

model, which says nothing of output variation in the achievement of profit-rate equality.

The final stage of the argument is rendered unneccessarily complex by the labour-commanded index: 'But it has been shown that the value of the same quantity of labour will always remain the same' – that is, that the *labour commanded* by the wage basket is constant – 'and it is evident that if the products fall in value [labour commanded], while the quantity of the labour or the value of the capital required to produce them, remain the same, profits must fall,' a fall that 'must necessarily go on, till profits in manufacturing and commerce have been reduced nearly to a level with those in agriculture.' Now if (as seems to be the case) 'the value of the capital ...' refers to the labour commanded by corn advances, we end up with the same proposition as in 1820 – mediated explicitly by the competition-of-capitals theorem – that the profit rate in manufactures is depressed by a fall in the terms of trade between manufactures and corn.[19]

* * *

Despite all this, the general profit rate was only 'limited by' – not *governed* by – agricultural productivity conditions, the latter imposing a *maximum* which the general profit rate can never exceed: 'Thus it appears that in the progress of improvement, as poorer and poorer land is taken into cultivation, the [1836: general] rate of profits must be limited by the powers of the soil last cultivated' (1820, 300; 1836, 275). But the general profit rate might be lower: 'If the last land taken into cultivation can only be made to yield [1836: will only yield] a certain excess of value above the value of the labour [1836: the lowest value of the capital] necessary to produce it, it is obvious that, upon the principles of competition [1836 omits: 'upon ... competition'], profits, generally, cannot possibly be higher than this excess will allow. In the ascending scale, this is a barrier which cannot be passed. But limitation is essentially different from regulation. In the descending scale [1836: while the land is still fertile], profits may be lower in any degree. There is here no controlling necessity which determines the rate of profits; and below the highest limit which the actual state of the land will allow, ample scope is left for the operation of other causes [1836: the operation of the regulating principle]' (1820, 300–1; 1836, 275–6).[20]

19 Any rise in the real costs of corn is transmitted to wages; the corn-labour rate is unchanged. We know that the trend of the corn wage is downward, but this is neglected here, where the sole concern is the relation between sectors.

20 This conclusion reverts to the opening definition of the profit rate as a ratio of *values* (above, p. 437). It is applied to agriculture despite the lengthy demonstration of the determination of the agricultural rate in *physical* terms. Possibly this inconsistency enters because the predominant concern is with the *general* rate.

The 'limiting' principle of profit-rate determination is discussed further in the final section of the chapter devoted to Ricardo's theory of profits. We shall focus on the interconnection between sectors to be found at the beginning and at the close of that section.

The opening exposition reiterates that the profit-rate trend is governed by diminishing returns – 'This continued accumulation of capital and increasing difficulty of procuring subsistence would unquestionably lower profits' (1820, 328; 1836, 293). The lower profit rate is said to determine the new set of equilibrium or cost prices in manufacturing (taking account of differential factor proportions) in that profits enter into manufacturing costs. In this account the corn price alone rises – falling agricultural productivity outweighing the lower profit rate – *the money wage remaining unchanged*: 'All commodities, in the production of which the same quantity of labour continued to be employed, but with the assistance of capitals of various kinds and amount, would fall in price, and just in proportion to the degree in which the price of the commodity had before been affected by profits; and with regard to corn, in the production of which more labour would be necessary, this article would rise in money price, notwithstanding the capital used to produce it [1836: 'notwithstanding ... it' omitted], just to that point which would so reduce corn wages as to render the population stationary [1836: as to retard the progress of population in proportion to the diminution of effectual demand]; and thus all the effects upon profits, attributed by Mr. Ricardo to a rise of money wages, would take place *while money wages and the value of money remained precisely the same*' (1820, 328; 1836, 293–4; emphasis added). In fact, the ideal money measure[21] is selected to that end in order to undermine (so Malthus believed) Ricardo's account, leaving his own as sole candidate: 'This supposition serves further to shew how very erroneous it must be to consider the fall of profits as synonymous with a rise of money wages, or to make the money price of labour the great regulator of the rate of profits [1836: sentence omitted]. It is obvious that, in this case, profits can only be regulated by the principle of competition, or of demand and supply, which would determine the degree in which the prices of commodities would fall; and their prices, compared with the uniform price of labour, would mainly regulate [1836: would regulate] the rate of profits.' That profits are 'regulated by the principle of competition, or of demand and supply,' suggests that it is the decline in manufacturing prices (in the face of a constant money wage) that actually governs the fall in the profit rate. But this is not the case. The secular fall in the profit rate is attributable to land scarcity, given which fall (and given the money wage) a set of equilibrium cost prices is generated throughout manufacturing incorporating that lower

21 Money is assumed 'to be procured by a uniform quantity of unassisted labour without any advances in the shape of capital beyond the necessaries of a single day' (1820, 327; 1836, 293).

profit rate. It might, however, be fair to suppose that by *regulation* in this passage Malthus intended 'brought into line with' the agricultural profit rate, a process requiring an increased supply of manufactures as in the original account (above, p. 447). The rendition reinforces but adds little to what was said before.

The final restatement again accords the agricultural profit rate the determining role – as a 'limiting principle' – governing the profit rate in other sectors: 'At all times indeed, and on every supposition, the great limiting principle which depends upon the increasing difficulty of procuring food from the soil, or on the still more general cause, a limitation of the population, in whatever way it may be occasioned, is ready to act; [1836: But in reference to the great limiting principle, which in his [Ricardo's] system is the only one which regulates profits, namely the increasing difficulty of procuring food from the soil, it merely in fact determines the *range* of possible profits; how high they may by possibility rise, and how low they may by possibility fall. It is indeed always ready to act;] and, if not overcome by countervailing facilities, will necessarily lower the rate of profits on the land, and from the land this fall will extend [1836: from which it will extend] to all other departments of industry' (1820, 334–5; 1836, 296–7). Malthus closes by insisting that 'even this great principle operates [1836: even then it always operates] according to the law of demand and supply and competition.' This might refer to the precise process by which manufacturing profit rates are brought into line with the lower agricultural profit rate described in the original statement. However, we have also seen that the same insistance on market process is encountered in the discussion of the incidence of diminishing returns (above, p. 443).

The text proceeds to restate the decline in the agricultural rate itself in price terms, diverging from the original account, which ran wholly in physical terms.[22] The conclusion, however, is back in line, again with

22 The argument is that a *constant* agricultural profit rate would require corn-price increases which fully compensate the deterioration in real-cost conditions, increases which are precluded. The constraints are said to reflect the 'intrinsic nature of necessaries, and of the soil from which they are procured.' An elaboration restates the process as involving an increase in labour embodied in corn relative to labour commanded: 'The specific reason why profits must fall as the land becomes more and more exhausted is, that from the intrinsic nature of necessaries, and of the soil from which they are procured, the demand for them and the price of them [1836: their price] cannot possibly go on increasing in proportion to the expense of producing them. The cost in labour of producing capital increases faster than the value of such capital when produced, or its efficiency in setting fresh labourers to work [1836: Though the value of a given quantity of produce rises on account of the increased quantity of labour required to obtain it, yet the value of the diminished produce of the *same* quantity of labour, or its efficiency in setting fresh labourers to work necessarily falls from the state of the demand and supply.] The boundary to the further value of and demand [1836: effectual demand] for corn, lies clear and distinct before us' (1820, 335; 1836, 297).

emphasis on the priority of the agricultural rate as a *limiting* determinant of the general profit rate, allowing scope for the operation of other forces – excess supply is specified in the 1836 version – which keep the general return below its potential: 'Putting importation out of the question, it is precisely when the produce of the last land taken into cultivation will but just replace the capital and support the population employed in cultivating it [that profits are] at their lowest theoretical limit. In their progress towards this point, the continued accumulation of capital will always have a *tendency* to lower them; and at no one period can they ever be higher than the state of the land, under all circumstances will admit. They may be lower, however, as was before stated, in any degree [1836: They may be much lower, however, as was before stated], from an abundant supply of capital compared with the demand for produce [1836: ... produce while the soil is still rich]; and practically they are very rarely so high as the actual state of the land combined with the smallest possible quantity of food awarded to the labourer would admit of [1836: and very rarely so low as not to allow the means of further accumulation]' (1820, 335; 1836, 297). It is not absolutely clear from this statement whether or not the effect on the profit rate of excess supply is limited to manufactures. It seems to be. But the question then arises how the agricultural rate comes into line, a matter left in abeyance.

* * *

In the section on 'Profits as affected by the Causes practically in operation' (Section III in 1820; Section IV in 1836), Malthus deals with potential countervailing pressures on the profit rate. Of these, technological change is the most significant (1820, 313–14; 1836, 282–3). In 1820, after raising two other disturbing causes acting positively on profits (increased effort and reductions in capital costs), Malthus summarizes his general position in a passage omitted in 1836 that is of considerable historiographical importance. This passage asserts: (1) that received doctrine related the profit rate 'principally' to 'competition of capital'; (2) that diminishing returns acted *directly to depress the agricultural profit rate*, which decline then extends to the non-agricultural sectors; (3) that this latter conception had been implicitly recognized in the *Essay on Population* and in the *Inquiry into Rent* (1815); and (4) that in practice, having in mind both the '*extremely slow*' pressure of land scarcity and the counteracting forces at play, and taking any considerable time span (any 'period of some length'), 'competition of capital' comes into its own:

The reader will be aware that the reason why, in treating of profits, I dwell so much on agricultural profits is, that the whole stress of the question rests upon this point. The argument against the usual view which has been taken of profits, as depending principally upon the competition of capital, is founded upon the

> physical necessity of a fall of profits in agriculture, arising from the increasing quantity of labour required to procure the same food; and it is certain that if the profits on land permanently fall from this or any other cause, profits in manufactures and commerce must fall too, as it is an acknowledged truth that in an improved and civilized country the profits of stock, with few and temporary exceptions which may be easily accounted for, must be nearly on a level in all the different branches of industry to which capital is applied.
>
> Now I am fully disposed to allow the truth of this argument, as applied to agricultural profits, and also its natural consequences on all profits. This truth is indeed necessarily involved both in the *Principle of Population* and in the theory of rent which I published separately in 1815. But I wish to shew, theoretically as well as practically, that powerful and certain as this cause is, in its final operation, so much so as to overwhelm every other; yet in the actual state of the world, its natural progress is not only extremely slow, but is so frequently counteracted and overcome by other causes as to leave very great play to the principle of the competition of capital; so that at any one period of some length in the last or following hundred years, it might most safely be asserted that profits had depended or would depend very much more upon the causes which had occasioned a comparatively scanty or abundant supply of capital than upon the natural fertility of the land last taken into cultivation. (1820, 316–17)

Again, Malthus neglects to specify whether increasing competition of capitals applies solely to manufactures, though that seems to be his position. It has a Smithian pedigree, and may reflect the physiocratic–Smithian notion that expanded food supply creates its own demand by generating population increase.

As mentioned, this last passage is absent in 1836, except for a brief summary statement of the essential consideration which focuses on the 'physical' dimension in agriculture: 'It appears then, that practically, and in the actual state of things, the physical necessity of a fall of profits in agriculture arising from the increasing quantity of labour required to produce the same quantity of food, may be so counteracted and overcome, for a considerable time by other causes, as to leave very great play to the influence of the competitions of capital' (1836, 284). The more extensive formulation of 1820 is, however, reiterated in substance at the close of the section under discussion in the 1820 version (with an important doctrinal reference to Adam Smith), and that later reformulation *does* appear in 1836. Malthus there points to the empirical significance of the disturbing causes, which often sufficed to counterbalance 'the effect of taking additional land into cultivation' such that 'in the actual state of most countries in the world' [1836: of many countries], or in their probable state for some centuries to come, we may fairly lay our account to their operation [1836: to such a result] when the occasion calls for them' (1820, 325; 1836, 288). The road was therefore open to the pressures exerted by 'the relative abundance or scarcity of capital' acting (so it is specified in 1836) on commodity – probably manufacturing – prices: 'But if this be so, [1836: and past experience justifies it] it follows, that in the actual state of things in most countries of the world, and within limited periods of moderate extent, the rate of profits will practically depend more upon the causes which affect the relative abundance or scarcity of capital [1836: and the demand for produce compared with the supply], than on the natural powers [1836: fertility] of the last land taken into cultivation. And consequently, to dwell on this latter point as the sole, or even the main cause which determines profits, must tend to the most erroneous conclusions' (1820, 325–6; 1836, 288–9).

Here Adam Smith is charged with neglecting land scarcity as a factor in profit-rate determination, but having erred less from a practical perspective than those (like Ricardo, of course) who focused 'almost exclusively' on land scarcity: 'Adam Smith, in stating the cause of the fall of profits, has omitted this point, and in so doing has omitted a most important consideration; but in dwelling solely upon the abundance and competition of capital, he is practically much nearer the truth, than those who dwell almost exclusively on the quality of the last land taken into cultivation.'[23] However, the possibility is raised in a note 'that Adam Smith, in speaking of the effects of accumulation and competition on profits, naturally means to refer to a limited territory, a limited population, and a limited demand; ... accumulation of capital under these circumstances involves every cause that can affect profits.'[24]

* * *

The 1820 version of the later chapter 'Of the Progress of Wealth' is of high relevance for us. There Malthus defended his position on aggregate demand against the possible objection by Ricardians that a low commodity wage resulting from 'want of demand' while good land resources are available necessarily implies a *high profit rate*: 'Perhaps it may be asked by those who have adoped Mr. Ricardo's view of profits what becomes of the division of that which is produced, when population is checked merely by want of demand? It is acknowledged that the powers of production have not begun to fail; yet, if labour produced largely and yet is ill paid, it will be said that profits must be high' (1820, 366). The response distinguishes between manufacturing and agriculture, the theory being 'perfectly simple' in the former case and 'not quite so simple' in the latter.

23 At this point the text of section III closes in 1820, but in 1836 the corresponding section (IV) proceeds to a further elaboration of the latter conclusion (below, pp. 485–6).

24 Conceivably Malthus had in mind the kind of analysis made in his own section on the Regulating Principle (1820, 304–5; 1836, 278) regarding a case where agricultural investment is ruled out *by hypothesis*, all investments flowing to the non-agricultural sector (below, note 56). But the meaning of the closing clause in this case is unclear.

As for manufacturing, the focus is on the *low price of manufactures relative to that of corn,* which depresses the manufacturing profit rate, although workers are by the hypothesis 'ill paid' in corn: 'It is obvious that in the production of any other commodities than necessaries, the theory is perfectly simple. From want of demand, such commodities may be very low in price, and a large portion of the whole value produced may go to the labourer, although in necessaries he may be ill paid, and his wages, both with regard to the quantity of food which he receives and the labour required to produce it, may be decidedly low' (1820, 366). Malthus adds that it would be an abuse of terminology to attribute the low profit rate to high *proportionate* wages (as the Ricardians might chose to do); the 'cause' was the 'fall of commodities,' that is, low manufacturing prices: 'If it be said, that on account of the large portion of the value of manufactured produce which on this supposition is absorbed by wages, it may be affirmed that the cause of the fall of profits is high wages, I should certainly protest against so manifest an abuse of words. The only justifiable ground for adopting a new term, or using an old one in a new sense, is, to convey more precise information to the reader; but to refer to high wages in this case, instead of to a fall of commodities, would be to proceed as if the specific intention of the writer were to keep his reader as much as possible in the dark as to the real state of things' (367).[25]

The agricultural sector posed a greater problem, and the difficulty flows from the characteristic corn-input, corn-output reasoning. Malthus sets out by referring to an 'acknowledgment' by Ricardo of limits to agricultural investment reflecting 'the limited wants of society, independently of the exhaustion of the soil.'[26] The difficulty involves the coincidence of a low agricultural profit rate and a high corn surplus relative to corn (wage) outlays; and this paradox is then explained by the circumstance that at least part of the corn output becomes *valueless*: 'In the case supposed ... there would be comparatively no population besides the agriculturists to make an effective demand for produce. Under such circumstances corn might be produced, which would lose the character and quality of wealth; and, as I before observed in a note [p. 296n], all the parts of the same produce, would not be of the same value ...; and from varying markets and varying crops, the profits of the farmer might be the lowest at the very time when, according to the division of the produce, it ought to be the highest, that is, when there was the greatest proportionate excess of produce above

25 Malthus, as we shall see, in fact accepted the inverse wage–profit relation (see section VII). The point at issue is what determines the proportionate breakdown.

26 This probably refers to Ricardo's acknowledgment that a more rapid rate of accumulation than population growth depresses the profit rate (1951–73, I, 292–3). A possible though less likely alternative is Ricardo's analysis of poor countries characterized by abundant fertile land, and yet stagnation, the remedy being 'to stimulate exertion, to create new wants and to implant new tastes' (100n).

what was paid to the labourer. The wages of the labourer cannot sink below a certain point, but a part of the produce, from excess to supply, may for a time be absolutely useless, and permanently it may so fall from competition as to yield only the lowest profits' (367–8).[27] The ellipses cover a reference to the possibility that *employed* farm labourers 'might be tolerably well fed, as is frequently the case, practically, in those countries where the labourers are fed by the farmers, but there would be little work or food for their grown-up sons,' to which is attached a note confirming the emphasis on the low value of the surplus corn: 'In Norway and Sweden, particularly the former, where the agricultural labourer either lives in the farmer's family or has a portion of land assigned to him in lieu of wages, he is in general pretty well fed, although there is but little demand for labour, and considerable competition for such employment. In countries so circumstanced (and there are many such all over the world) it is perfectly futile to attempt to estimate profits by the excess of the produce above what is consumed in obtaining it, when for this excess there may be often little or no market. All evidently depends upon the exchangeable value of the disposable produce.'[28]

Now where input and output comprise the same physical commodity, the profit rate ought logically to emerge independently of value in Sraffian fashion – value in the sense of the corn price of manufactures. Malthus, it is true, does refer here to 'the exchangeable value of the disposable produce.' But it is clear that he does not intend value in the sense of the corn price of manufactures; the analyses of the manufacturing and agricultural profit rates are asymmetrical. Consider the references to corn which is rendered '*absolutely useless*' from excess supply, or to corn for which there may be '*little or no market*' illustrated by Scandinavian experience; or to excessive agricultural extensions generating output which has *lost 'the character and quality of wealth,'* and the support called in from the discussion in the chapter on Profits of 'the case of a glut from the shutting up on an accustomed market, or a season of unusual abundance, [rendering] a part of the crop of *no value* either in use or exchange ...' It is such special circumstances involving zero value that undermined a corn-ratio explanation of the agricultural profit rate.

27 For the note referred to, see above, p. 440.

28 It is not clear that Malthus was certain of himself since he proceeds in the 1820 text to give a further justification of his position, which allows that farmers *might* obtain 'a fair profit,' but only on 'the small stock' still invested in agriculture, which, calculated on the total capital, implies a low profit rate: 'I would observe further, that if in consequence of a diminished demand for corn, the cultivators were to withdraw their capital so as better to proportion their supplies to the quantity that could be properly paid for; yet if they could not employ the capital they had withdrawn in any other way, which, according to the preceding supposition, they could not, it is certain that, though they might for a time make fair profits of the small stock which they still continued to employ in agriculture, the consequence to them as cultivators would be, to all intents and purposes, the same as if a general fall had taken place on all their capital' (368–9).

The valid conclusion seems to be that the 'Sraffian' corn-profit model was consciously adopted by Malthus, who was at the same time cautious when it came to application. The absence of the foregoing passages from the revised edition may indicate a lessening of his concerns. In fact, new material is added at the beginning of the chapter on Profits in that edition which provides a considerable strengthening of the corn-profit model. This is the case despite its initial insistence on 'estimating' the profit rate as a value rather than a physical ratio on the grounds that output and input comprise *different* commodities: 'Profits, as we all know, are practically estimated by the money prices of the products compared with the money prices of the advances; and as money for the short periods during which mercantile transactions last, is universally considered as measuring value and not quantity, it follows, that profits, as it has been stated, are always practically estimated by the values of the products compared with the values of the advances, and not by their relative quantities. It would be impossible indeed to compare them as to quantity, because the advances necessary to produce commodities, are never all of the same kind as the commodities produced; and when they are not the same, their *quantities* do not admit of a comparison. We cannot compare shoes or cloth with corn or labour in regard to quantity. It is of so much importance to be fully aware of the necessity of estimating both the advances and the returns of the capitals in *value* and not in *quantity*, that it may be worthwhile to illustrate the difference in the results of the two modes of proceeding' (1836, 263).[29]

It is striking to find Malthus asserting both that advances and output are *never* all of the same kind, and that *when* this is so – one would expect him to write '*since* this is so' – value calculations are required. But the fact is that he allows an exception, as we shall now show. *That exception is corn.* It is conceded that corn satisfies most closely the condition that input and output comprise the same commodity – 'there is not one [industry] in which so great a part of the advances is identical with the produce as in the cultivation of corn'; but even here calculation in terms of corn ratios misleads: 'Profits, as I have before stated, are always practically estimated by value, not quantity; and the real question is about the *price* of the

29 Cf. a note added at the close of the chapter: 'It has sometimes been said that profits depend entirely upon the productiveness of labour. If by productiveness of labour be meant what the words usually mean, and what they certainly ought to mean, namely the *quantity* of produce obtained by a given quantity of labour, every day's experience shews that the statement is quite unfounded. If the words be intended to mean productiveness of *value* then no doubt profits depend upon the productiveness of labour. This truth is involved in the very definition of profits, namely the excess of the value of the produce above the value of the advances, or of a given quantity of labour advanced. It is exactly what has been here inculcated, but the usual and correct meaning of terms must not be changed on particular occasions' (1836, 298n).

produce compared with the price of the advances, and not the excess of the returns in wheat above the advance in wheat' (264). In the simple example provided, it is presumed that the initial outlay is in money terms, which, given the initial corn price, represents a certain corn outlay;[30] but the profit rate – a ratio of values – will vary with the corn price, a poor harvest raising the price permitting the profit rate to remain unchanged despite a fall in corn output, and conversely in the case of a good harvest: 'if the profits of the cultivator were estimated by quantity they might vary between nothing and 45 per cent at the very time when estimated by price or value, as they always are practically, the cultivator was in each year making a regular profit of 20 per cent' (264–5).[31] Malthus closes the first substantive proposition of the new section by reiterating that, despite the *near homogeneity between the physical items constituting input and output in the case of corn,* the profit rate entails value, not physical ratios: 'Corn, on account of its being the main support of the labourer, is the *only object in the production of which a comparison may be instituted between the quantity advanced and the quantity produced*; yet even here we have found that the cause which determines profits is their relative values, and not their relative quantities' (265–6; emphasis added).

This seems at first glance to clash with the earlier formulations which accord a determining role to the agricultural profit rate (in the 'limiting' case) perceived in terms of physical corn ratios, with the manufacturing rates coming into line by way of a rise in the *relative* corn price. However, the objection to the corn-profit notion in our present context turns on

30 'The farmer practically pays his labourers in money. Let us suppose that this money, with the other money outgoings amounts to £200, that in the year in which the advance is made it will purchase 100 quarters of wheat, the price of wheat being £2 a quarter, and that the rate of profits is 20 per cent, in which case the return must be 120 quarters, or 20 per cent in quantity' (263–4).

31 In fact, the example was restricted by assuming unitary demand elasticity such that the variations assured a constant money value of the final product and an unchanged profit rate; a more realistic assumption would recognize the highly inelastic demand for corn. Reference is made to Tooke: 'It happens not very infrequently, that the rise in the price of agricultural produce greatly exceeds this. Mr. Tooke in his *Thoughts and details* ... 2nd ed. (1823), pp. 303, 305 supposes that, owing to a rise in the price of wheat from about 48s. a quarter to 75s. in 1795 and 1796, with a rise of other agricultural produce nearly in proportion, the farmers and landlords, after an allowance made for every probable deduction, must have divided between them a net additional profit of 12 to 14 millions per annum, and a still greater profit in 1800 and 1801' (265n).

Malthus also replies to potential critics of his argument: 'It may be said, perhaps, that these variations in the quantity of produce are only temporary, and that it is the average excess which is referred to, and not the variations of that excess occasioned by the season. It may be observed in answer, that, as it is universally allowed that the prices of the farmer's whole crop never rises in proportion to its abundance, and never falls in proportion to its deficiency, it is certain, that the average excess of value would not be the same as the average excess of produce' (265).

changes in the corn price between periods (t) and (t+1) owing to *harvest fluctuations*, an irrelevant matter in dealing with secular trends, and of a different order to the objection that input in agriculture is not entirely constituted of corn.[32] And there can be no doubt that agriculture and manufactures are treated differently, for in what follows Malthus precludes any conceivable possibility of proceeding in physical terms in the latter sectors specifically: 'In manufacturing and mercantile employments, there is no approach towards a possibility of comparing the advances with the products in regard to quantity' (266).[33] By contrast, as we have just seen, corn was 'the only object in the production of which a comparison may be instituted between the quantity advanced and the quantity produced.' And we have in fact encountered the assumption introduced in a note to *avoid* the complexity created by price fluctuations (above pp. 440, 454).

Further evidence for the corn-profit interpretation is to be found in *The Measure of Value* (1823). Its table (see appendix to chapter 7, above) proceeds solely in terms of *agricultural productivity and the corn wage*.[34] It might be said that this was a deliberate simplication to express 'self-evident' propositions, for example, that the profit rate necessarily falls with increased corn wages, given productivity: 'If the increased reward of the labourer takes place without an increase of produce, this cannot take place without a fall of profits, as it is a self-evident truth, that given the quantity of produce to be divided between labour and profits, the greater the portion of it which goes to labour the less will be left for profits' (1823b/1986, 7, 197). Conceivably a full-fledged treatment of the profit rate would have to take account of exchange values. But this does not in fact seem to be the case. Throughout the pamphlet Malthus assumed a given profit rate or a given change in the profit rate (187, 192–3, 201, 206, 212),

32 Skourtos (1991) has pointed out that de Sismondi (1827, 308) adopted the homogeneity postulate relating to agricultural input and output, and also raised the problem that the market values of corn input and of corn output may deviate.

33 The text proceeds to emphasize the effect on manufacturing prices of supply expansion, which eradicates any initial profit-rate increase attributable to physical expansion with new technology: 'However the powers of production in manufactures may increase, a nearly proportionate fall in the value of the produce determined by the state of the demand and supply prevents any permanent change in the division of produce, and consequently, leaves the capitalist in a short time with the same or nearly the same rate of profits. The workman receives a larger quantity of what he produces, but the same value; and his condition will be benefited, chiefly in proportion to the utility of the article to him as a consumer.'

34 Profit-rate determination in *The Measure of Value* turns *either* on the labour embodied in the corn wage – the 'backward' procedure – *or* (equivalently) on the labour commanded by the produce of ten men's labour, which is governed by productivity and the corn wage – the 'forward procedure.'

and recognized only a *one-way* relation, from distribution to relative values.[35]

IV THE CORN-PROFIT INTERPRETATION ELABORATED

Various criticisms have been addressed at the notion that Malthus perceived the profit rate as generated in agriculture, independently of value relationships, to which profit rates in other sectors come into line by adjustments of their terms of trade against corn. We shall address them in this section.

Costabile disagrees with my 'Sraffian' interpretation of Malthus on the following grounds: 'First of all, Malthus was the first to object to Ricardo's determination of the rate of profits in terms of corn in 1815; he refused the simplication of the one-sector models in the analysis of value and distribution' (1983, 152n). This observation is based on Malthus's early insistence against Ricardo's *Essay on Profits* that 'the real capital of the farmer which is advanced does not consist merely in raw produce but in ploughs waggons threshing machines &c: and in the tea sugar clothes &c: &c: used by his labourers' (Malthus to Horner, 14 March 1815; in Ricardo, 1951–73, VI, 187); similarly: 'In no case of production, is the produce exactly of the same nature as the capital advanced. Consequently we can never properly refer to a material rate of produce, independent of demand, and of the abundance or scarcity of capital' (to Ricardo, 5 August 1814, 117).[36] She asserts, moreover, that 'Malthus developed all his theory of profits in terms of value.' And she argues, third, that 'the device of reducing inputs to dated quantitites of labour would be pointless, if it is to be applied only to one-sector models. Malthus's corn-corn model in this example [of the table] was only a temporary simplifying device, which was perfectly justified since the main objective of the example was to illustrate the method of reduction to dated quantities of labour.'

Before dealing with these objections, a word is called for on Costabile's own interpretation. Costabile attributes to Malthus a Sraffa model – Sraffa of the *Production of Commodities* – in which the profit rate emerges in the wage sector as the solution to a set of simultaneous equations, given the real wage, commodity outputs, and technology (1983, 144, 156). On this view the value of capital itself depends on the profit rate: 'The rate of

35 For example, the exchange ratio between capital (time)-intensive and labour-intensive products would vary 'in the progress of society' – a reduction in the profit rate is taken for granted here – though relative labour inputs are unchanged. And the value of beef (a four- or five-year process, according to Adam Smith) relative to corn (a one-year process) would fall more than 20 per cent, with a fall in the profit rate from 15 to 8 per cent in the 'progress of society,' though the labour input is constant, because of the longer period of production in the former case (1823b/1986, 7, 185).

36 Costabile erroneously dates the second quote 1815 and implies it follows the first.

profits is determined as the ratio between the value of surplus product and the value of capital advanced. The latter value is determined on the basis of the device of reducing capital to dated labour' (153–4); 'capital advanced in the wage sector is constituted by commodities whose production requires time .... Hence the value of capital depends on the time which its production required, as a profit element must be charged on it for that time. It follows that the value of capital must depend on the rate of profits, which on the other hand is precisely our unknown. But this difficulty can be overcome by using Malthus' resolution of inputs in dated quantities of labour. Malthus did not apply this device in the specific example, in *The Measure of Value* [1823b/1986, 7, 195] we are referring to. But we are entitled to apply it, since Malthus, as we have shown, always calculated the value of inputs by this method' (155–6). This, then, is the main issue: Does the profit rate emerge in the wage-goods sector *independently of value* as a ratio between physically homogeneous products, to be carried over in establishing the 'natural values' of other commodities, each comprising the sum of dated quantities of labour (as I maintain), or does the determination of the profit rate itself require his value theory (as Costabile maintains)?

I turn now to Costabile's first observation, that Malthus, in his early reaction to Ricardo, *rejected* a single-sector approach to profits. Now this is not quite the case. His early concern was that a decrease in the corn price of cloth during the course of progress acts to reduce wages estimated in corn (if cloth is a wage good) with a positive effect on the *total* corn surplus, that is, on rent and profits combined, *not profits alone* (letters to Ricardo, 10 and 12 March 1815; in Ricardo, 1951–73, VI, 182–3, 185–6, and to Horner, 14 March 1815; 187), a point emphasized by Ricardo (4 April; 207).[37] Even so, what is said in 1815 need not still apply in 1820 and thereafter. The fact is that the *Principles* maintains conspicuously the dual notions: (1) that the profit rate as determined in agriculture governs the general profit rate specifically by way of the terms of trade between corn and manufactures (1820, 300; 1836, 275; above, pp. 446–7); and (2) that the decline in the agricultural profit rate with increasing land scarcity dictates a set of equilibrium cost prices throughout manufacturing (1820, 328; 1836, 293–4; cf. 1820, 334–5; 1836, 296–7; above pp. 449–50). (More generally, we find the proposition that 'the increasing difficulty of procuring food from the soil' will lower the rate of profits on the land, and 'from the land this fall will extend to all other departments of industry' (1820, 335; 1836, 297). Finally, while the treatment of the *actual* – as distinct from the *limiting* – profit rate entails increasing 'competition of capital' in manufacturing, the agricultural profit rate itself reflects 'the amount of the produce obtained by a given amount of labour,' the express assumption

37 Garegnani, in Caravale, 1991, I, 104, also errs in his interpretation in this regard.

being that there exists 'an equal demand for all the parts of the same [agricultural] produce' precisely in order to allow the determination of profits 'by the excess of the *quantity* produced, above the advances necessary to produce it' (above, p. 440).

There are certain additions to the second edition of the *Principles* which formally deny the possibility of making physical calculations in profit-rate determination (above, p. 457), but these do not vitiate the conclusion, since the problem does not relate to the relative corn/cloth price but to the possibility of differentials in the price of corn between periods (t) and (t + 1) owing to 'abundant' or 'deficient' crops, an irrelevant matter in dealing with secular trends. In fact there is evidence of an actual reinforcement of the corn-profit model after 1820 (above, p. 456). It is scarcely surprising, then, to find the determining role of the agricultural profit rate – in effect the solution to distribution prior to pricing – in *The Measure of Value*, which was written at the same time as many of the revisions to the *Principles*.

As for Costabile's further observations, I agree of course that Malthus places great weight on the device of reducing inputs to dated quantities of labour, and that the 1823 work extends beyond one-sector models. But this is recognized by my interpretation, which has the profit rate as determined in agriculture applied to establish the 'natural values' of *other* commodities, without itself requiring the value dimension for its determination.

Costabile candidly recognizes that Malthus did not specifically refer to his device of resolving inputs to dated quantities of labour in arriving at the value of capital, a device which she believes is required to obtain the profit rate (above, p. 460). Her assertion that 'we are entitled to apply it' since Malthus 'always calculated the value of inputs by this method' is a contentious one. There are indeed various statements by Malthus which apply the principle of compensation for the time labour is invested to 'the formation of capital' as well as to final products (e.g., 1823b/1986, 7, 184, and, with reference to fixed capital, 190–1, 207). But the question at issue is whether by this sort of extension Malthus specifically intended the system of Sraffa (1960) equations involving value of capital, from which emerges the profit rate as solution. That Malthus *intended* Sraffa's own model is something of an anachronism, one might think, whereas there is an alternative reading – that all the allowances in question relate to the establishment of the 'natural values' of commodities *other than corn*, in which procedure the profit rate is taken as a *datum* derived on the basis of the special case of corn where a physical ratio is possible.

I turn next to a second critic. Prendergast (1986, 188n) reads the second edition of the *Principles*, *not* as establishing the possibility of making a corn calculation, but, to the contrary, as insisting (even in the case of homogeneous input and output) on a value calculation. She suggests that this rejection of the estimation of profits by quantity may have been motivated by Torrens's objection to the formal definition in the 1820 *Principles* of the profit rate in terms of value ratios, on the grounds that profit is a surplus which would exist 'quite independently of value,' originating 'not in the interchange of commodities nor in the quality of value which wealth thereby acquires, but in the power of human industry to produce a greater quantity of the necessaries of life than is sufficient to support the labourers by whom it is carried on' (*The Traveller*, No. 6624, 26 April 1820).[38] That Malthus read Torrens I do not dispute.[39] But one cannot presume that he read him as proposing a corn output–input solution (which he himself rejected). Torrens in fact seems to have been making a more general point about the source of profits.[40]

Prendergast (187n) wishes to know how I relate the 1823 and 1814/15 correspondence (on which see above, pp. 459–60). The answer is twofold. Malthus's concern in the early correspondence was with a 'rate of produce' or total surplus including *rent*, but in 1823 with a rate of *profits*.[41] Second, the problem raised in the correspondence of a mixed wage basket is simply not raised in 1823 as an objection to the physical-ratio procedure. This is not to deny that Malthus frequently assumed a mixed wage basket; for he was concerned with the effect of changes in the relative prices of manufactured and agricultural wage goods on workers' welfare. None the less, in analysing the profit rate in the revised edition of the *Principles*, he

38 Cf. J.S. Mill's formulation of the same proposition introduced into the 4th edition (1857) of his *Principles*: 'We thus see that profit arises, not from the incidence of exchange, but from the productive power of labour; and the general profit of the country is always what the productive power of labour makes it, whether any exchange takes place or not ...' (1848/1965, II, 411).

39 Ricardo (4 May 1820) brought the *Traveller* reviews to Malthus's attention, claiming that 'as his arguments are on my side I of course think his criticisms just' (1951–73, VIII, 185). But this need not refer to the proposition that profit is a surplus which would exist 'quite independently of value.' There were other areas of agreement. Torrens had insisted that Ricardo appreciated (*pace* Malthus) that the profit rate is affected not only by the difficulty of production on the land, but also by the real rate of wages, and by improvements; and he could not understand how Malthus had imagined that he had refuted Ricardo in these regards. In a further review, he objected to Malthus's arguments for agricultural protection, and to Malthus's criticisms of Ricardo on rent (*The Traveller*, 1 May 1820). It is to Torrens's defence of his position in these regards that Ricardo may have referred. (For a summary of the reviews see Robbins, 1958, 282–3.)

40 In his continuation of the review of *The Principles* for *The Traveller* of 1 May 1820, Torrens extended to *rent* his denial that value is essential, making out a case that rent could exist even were institutions not of the exchange variety: 'Rent, like profit has its origin in the power of human industry to produce a greater quantity of wealth than is necessary to support the labour by which it is carried on; and may appear though there should be neither markets nor market prices, neither exchange nor exchangeable value.' It would exist 'in a state of society, in which there was no division of employment, and in which each capitalist engaged his labourers in the immediate production of the several articles he consumed ...' (see Robbins, 1958, 282–3).

41 However, the idea of 'national profits' inclusive of rent is sometimes found in later writings (see below, note 51).

intimates that the complexity of a mixed wage basket was not so great as to preclude a corn calculation (above, pp. 456–8). (Conceivably, his systematic replacement in the revised version of the *Principles* of the term '*real* wage' by '*corn* wage' in dealing with the secular trend of factor returns was explicitly intended to reflect this position.) He was apparently prepared to proceed for the purpose at hand *as if* corn alone entered the wage basket.[42]

Malthus, it appears, withdrew his strongly stated position of early 1814 that (as expressed by Ricardo) 'the profits of the farmer no more regulate the profits of other trades, than the profits of other trades regulate the profits of the farmer' (in Ricardo, 1951–73, VI, 104). However, if account is taken of his distinction between the 'regulating' and the 'limiting' determinants of the profit rate, the original position would still hold in modified form as pertaining to the former set, where there is full scope for the principle of competition of capitals with special reference to *manufacturing* and allowing for an influence on agriculture since profit rates tend to an equality. Similarly, his insistence on causality running *from* the profit rate *to* proportionate wages (below, p. 476) would pertain specifically to the 'regulating' sphere, where the profit rate is governed by aggregate demand–supply relations.[43]

There remains to note a circumstance that may lend some tangential support to the interpretation offered here. In a pamphlet of 1822 on profits and exchangeable value, John Cazenove – who was later to edit the second edition of Malthus's *Principles* – himself maintained the determining role of the agricultural profit rate: 'In regard to the profit which is derived from manufacturing and mercantile capital, it is governed by the returns of agricultural capital. It is plain that no one would employ a capital in trade, or manufactures, unless it yielded him a profit equal to what it would if employed on the land; and he cannot expect it to yield him much more, as the competition of capital will always ultimately reduce profits, in all the various departments of industry, to nearly the same level' (1822, 28–9). Now the agricultural rate itself is specifically defined in purely

42 Of course, wholly to abandon the complexity of a mixed wage basket – and other non-wage components of the capital stock – would undermine a wide range of Malthusian theory, including the criticism of Smith for his exact proportionality of corn and general prices, and his own allowances for deviations between the corn and the general commodity wage. In my opinion he set the complexity aside in specific contexts only.

43 I do not see how Prendergast can conclude that Malthus's (purported) rejection of a corn-profit calculation in the second edition on the grounds that to estimate profits by quantity neglects supply and demand 'seems to support Sraffa's conjecture regarding Ricardo's early theory of profits, that "the rational foundation of the principle of the determining role of profits in agriculture, is that in agriculture the same commodity, namely corn, forms both the capital and the product"' (189). What Malthus maintained in his second edition (or in 1823 or 1820) tells us nothing of what Ricardo maintained in 1815.

physical terms: 'The natural rate of profit ... is measured by the proportion which the surplus produce of the worst soil bears to that which is employed in its production' (29).[44] We are close to the notion of manufacturing profit rates coming into line by way of changes in the manufacturing terms of trade against corn, though Cazenove is not explicit on this detail. It is also pertinent for us that the section in question pays tribute to Malthus: 'Previously to the publication of Malthus's *Inquiry into the Nature and Origin of Rent* the question of profit seems to have been very imperfectly understood' (26).[45] Cazenove's position and commendation are suggestive of the interpretation offered here, though the corn-profit case is spelled out fully in 1820 rather than in the 1815 *Inquiry*.

V THE MANUFACTURING PROFIT RATE

In the course of amplifying the determining role of the agricultural-profit-rate principle, Malthus clarified the effect on manufacturing price of the profit-rate decline generated within agriculture (1820, 328; 1836, 293–4; above, p. 449). Specifically, since profits enter into costs, and the profit rate falls with diminishing returns, there will be a downward effect on cost prices, impinging differentially on commodities depending on capital intensity. Only the corn price rises – diminishing returns outweighing the reduced profit rate – and it is upon this increase (given the money wage) that Malthus relies to assure a decline in the corn wage until subsistence.

This analysis is a prologue in 1820 to an extended discussion of the effect on profits of falling *manufacturing* prices – deleted from the 1836 version: 'Mr. Ricardo never contemplates the fall of prices as occasioning a fall of profits, although practically in many cases, as well as on the preceding supposition, a fall of profits must be produced in this way' (1820, 328–9). Using the terms 'occasioning' and 'produced' implies that falling manufacturing prices cause the fall in profits. This is true only in a qualifed sense, since the 'occasioning' of the reduced profit was agricultural expansion on the 'preceding supposition'; the fall in manufacturing prices was the *outcome*, bringing manufacturing profit rates into line with the lower agricultural rate. The analysis that follows, by contrast, *supposes no domestic agricultural sector*, and here the decline in the profit rate is attributable to expansion of manufacturing – we are back in Smith's world of 'increasing competition of capitals.' The emphasis, however, is still on the fall in manufacturing price *relative to (foreign) corn*, which is consistent

44 Profit (like rent) had its source in 'the natural fertility of the earth, or its power of yielding more than is sufficient for the maintenance of those employed in its cultivation,' though (unlike rent) tended to fall secularly, since 'the surplus [net of rent] which remains after replacing the capital employed is smaller and smaller ...'

45 I owe both the reference to Cazenove and the corn-profit reading to Gordon (1985).

with the earlier more general analysis (above, pp. 446f.): 'as capital continued to be accumulated and employed in larger quantities on the exportable manufactures, such manufactures, upon the principles of demand and supply would in all probability fall in price. A larger portion of them must then be exchanged for a given portion of corn, and profits would necessarily fall' (329). The analysis might be allowed a Ricardian gloss, but this changed nothing: 'It is true that, under these circumstances, the labouring manufacturer must do more work for his support, and Mr. Ricardo would say that this is the legitimate cause of the fall of profits. In this I am quite willing to agree with him; but surely the specific cause, in this case, of more work being necessary to earn the same quantity of corn is the fall in the prices of the exportable manufactures with which it is purchased, and not a rise in the price of corn, which may remain exactly the same. The fall in these manufactures is the natural consequence of an increase of supply arising from an accumulation of capital more rapid than the extension of demand for its product; and that the fall of profits so occasioned depends entirely upon the principles of demand and supply will be acknowledged, if we acknowledge, as we certainly must do, that the opening a new market for manufactures in question would at once put an end to the fall of profits.'[46]

This analysis is further elaborated in an application to trade policy which sharply distinguishes between the consequences of increased manufacturing and of increased agricultural investment. A low corn price (and low money wages) resulting from easier corn imports cannot assure a generally high profit rate, and this because of the effect of increasing competition of capitals in manufacturing; on the other hand, expanded investment in domestic agriculture could be absorbed without depressing the general profit rate, should it entail 'permanent agricultural improvements.' Accordingly, had corn prices been kept low by free corn importation, and new accumulations directed largely to manufacturing, the profit rate would none the less have been reduced below its actual level: 'Upon the same principle, of considering the prices of commodities as constant, Mr. Ricardo is of opinion, that if the prices of our corn and labour were to fall, the profits of our foreign trade would rise in proportion. But what is it, I would ask, that is to fix the prices of commodities in foreign markets? – not merely the quantity of labour which has been employed upon them, because, as was noticed in a former chapter [pp. 95, 116], commodities will be found selling at the same price in foreign markets, which have cost very different quantities of labour. But if they are determined, as they certainly are, both on an average and at the moment, by supply and

46 In correspondence with Ricardo in 1815, Malthus had raised this question of the appropriate analysis of the profit rate in the absence of a domestic agricultural sector (see chapter 4, p. 139).

demand, what is to prevent a much larger supply, occasioned by the competition of capital thrown out of employment, from rapidly lowering prices, and with them reducing the rate of profits?' (330). The investments actually made in agricultural improvement during the quarter-century of effective protection, 1795–1820, had in fact *raised* the profit rate, whereas the profit rate would have been driven down had these been diverted to manufacturing: 'The millions which have been employed in permanent agricultural improvements have had no tendency whatever to lower profits; but if, in conjunction with a large portion of the common capital employed in domestic agriculture, they had been added to the already large capitals applied to the working up of exportable commodities, I can scarcely feel a doubt that the foreign markets would have been more than fully supplied; that the prices of commodities would have been such as to make the profits of stock quite low, and that there would have been both a greater mass of moveable capitals at a loss for employment, and a greater disposition in those capitals to emigrate than has actually taken place' (330–1).[47] Similarly: 'A country, which accumulates faster than its neighbours, might for hundreds of years still keep up its rate of profits, if it were successful in making permanent improvements on the land; but, if with the same rapidity of accumulation it were to depend chiefly on imported corn, its profits could scarcely fail to fall; and the fall would probably be occasioned, not by a rise in the bullion price of corn in the ports of Europe, but by a fall in the bullion price of the exports with which the corn was purchased by the country in question' (332–3).

The contemporary depression is found to substantiate the Malthusian analysis and correspondingly refute Ricardo's 'new' theory of profits. For the profit rate was low despite extremely low money wages: 'These statements appear to me to accord with the most correct theory of profits, and they certainly seem to be confirmed by experience .... [The] effect of falling prices in reducing profits is but too evident at the present moment. In the largest article of our exports, the wages of labour are now lower than they probably would be in an ordinary state of things if corn were at fifty shillings a quarter [i.e., even were corn price *lower* than those ruling]. If, according to the new theory of profits, the prices of our exports had remained the same, the master manufacturers would have been in a state of the most extraordinary prosperity, and the rapid accumulation of their capitals would soon have employed all the workmen that could have been found. But, instead of this, we hear of glutted markets, falling prices, and

47 Malthus adds in a note: 'Our present body of manufacturers, when they call for imported corn, think chiefly of the additional demand for their goods occasioned by the increased imports, and seem quite to forget the prodigious increase of supply which must be occasioned by the competition of so many more capitals and workmen in the same line of business.'

cotton goods selling at Kamschatka lower than the costs of production' (333).

In this context we find the famous complaint that Ricardo in his *Principles* had 'never laid any *stress* upon the influence of permanent improvements in agriculture on the profits of stock, although it is one of the most important considerations in the whole compass of Political Economy, as such improvements unquestionably open the largest *arena* for the employment of capital without a diminution of profits' (331).[48] For 'a very extensive territory' (even with poor-quality soil, provided it be 'capable of cultivation') might, 'by continued improvements in agriculture, admit of the employment of a vast mass of capital for hundreds of years, with little or no fall of profits,' whereas 'a small but fertile territory, being very soon filled with all the capital it could employ on the land, would be obliged to employ its further accumulations in the purchase of corn with falling manufactures; a state of things which might easily reduce profits to their lowest rate before one-third of the capital had been accumulated in the former case' (332). Ricardo protested at this in his *Note 191*: 'Once more I must say that I lay the very greatest stress upon the influence of permanent improvements in Agriculture. The passage quoted refers to a state of things when no improvements are taking place, and therefore the argument built upon it which supposes improvements has no foundation' (1951–73, II, 293).[49] But the difference between them evidently runs much deeper than this suggests. For Malthus, *manufacturing investment generates an increased flow of output for which the markets are constrained; agricultural investment allows expanded output with no such effects.* It is striking that Malthus allows for 'improvements' counteracting the profit-rate decline *solely in agriculture,* implying the odd assumption that industrial expansion occurs invariably with technology unchanged. Of greater theoretical significance is the application of the competition-of-capitals principle solely to manufactures. Why this should be so is not elaborated, but it presumably reflects the physiocratic–Smithian proposition that expanded food supplies create their own demand by generating population increase.

The conclusion drawn appears somewhat conciliatory, in that Malthus seems to allow in passing for the possibility of a falling profit rate owing in part at least to rising money wages. He had merely devised his special

48 His objection here was to Ricardo's observation in his *Principles* that 'however extensive a country may be, where the land is of a poor quality, and where the importation of food is prohibited, the most moderate accumulations of capital will be attended with great reductions in the rate of profit, and a rapid rise in rent; and on the contrary, a small but fertile country, particularly if it freely permits the importation of food, may accumulate a large stock of capital, without any great diminution in the rate of profits, or any great increase in the rent of land' (1951–73, I, 126).

49 This is the last substantive comment by Ricardo on chapter V, though he planned to extend his notes (cf. Sraffa in Ricardo, 1951–73, II, 295n).

example involving manufacturing alone to convey an alternative mechanism to Ricardo's, one where land scarcity is precluded by construction in order to focus solely on the effect on profits of reduced prices resulting from pressure of supply: 'It must be allowed then, that in contemplating the altered relation between labour and the produce obtained by it which occasions a fall of profits, we only take a view of half the question if we advert exclusively to a rise in the wages of labour without referring to a fall in the prices of commodities. Their effects on profits may be precisely the same; but the latter case, where there is no question respecting the state of the land, shows at once how much profits depend upon the prices of commodities, and upon the cause which determines these prices, namely the supply compared with the demand' (1820, 334). The foregoing conclusion scarcely follows. Profits might still turn on the real cost of producing wage goods via the money wage, even under the special conditions posited; and the rejection of the Law of Markets must be justified on independent grounds, not simply asserted.

The special case entailing an economy comprising manufacturing alone is absent in the 1836 version, though there is nothing to suggest a rejection of its major theme.[50] In both editions Malthus made the same point at the conclusion of the Rent chapter: 'The fertility of the land, either natural or acquired, may be said to be the only source of permanently high returns [1836: high national returns] for capital. If a country were exclusively manufacturing and commercial, and were to purchase all its corn at the market prices of Europe, it is absolutely impossible that the returns [1836: national returns] for its capital should for any great length of time be high' (1820, 234; 1836, 213).[51]

VI THE EFFECT OF REAL-WAGE FLUCTUATIONS[52]

We deal now with the effect on the profit rate of fluctuations in the real wage. Such fluctuations were 'capable of producing the very greatest effects; and on the supposition of adequate variations taking place between

50 In its place is an alternative attempt to controvert Ricardo on profits, based on the latter's index produced by a technology entailing the mean factor ratio.

51 The matter is complicated by the caution that 'the national profits on land [1836: the *national* profits or the increase of value to the nation obtained by the capitals employed on the land], must be considered as including rents as well as the common agricultural profits' (1820, 235n; 1836, 214n). This caution comes in a discussion of property-tax returns.

52 The consequences flowing from the 'other causes' (primarily *fluctuations* of the real wage) are covered in 1820 in Section II, 'Profits as affected by the Proportion which Capital Bears to Labour,' and in 1836 in section III, 'Of the Regulating Principle of Profits.'

the supplies of capital and the supplies of labour, all the same effects might be produced on profits as by the operation of the first cause [land scarcity], and in a much shorter time' (1820, 301). To simplify the analysis in 1820, labour demand deriving from 'revenue' (such as demand for menials) is set aside; and the possibility of inadequate aggregate demand is ruled out by hypothesis: 'I have stated in a former chapter, that the demand for labour does not depend upon capital alone, but upon capital and revenue together, or the value of the whole produce; but to illustrate the present *supposition*, it is only necessary to consider capital and labour. We may allow that no difficulty will occur with respect to demand' (301n).

The 1836 version is more complex: 'The second cause which affects profits, is the varying value of the produce of the same quantity of labour on the same value of capital, determined by the state of the demand and supply. This may be called the regulating principle of profits, as within the extreme limits prescribed by the state of the land, all the variations of profits whether temporary or durable, are regulated by it. Such variations in the value of produce are occasioned principally by the abundance or scantiness of capital, including the funds for the maintenance of labour, as compared with the labour which it employs' (1836, 276). Did Malthus intend a radical revision by this reformulation in terms of the 'varying value of the produce'? Probably not. The last sentence just cited seems to refer back to a 'wages fund,' as in 1820, conceiving its 'value' as varying along with that of 'produce' in general. And the paragraph following is similar to its counterpart in 1820, though again 'capital' is replaced by 'capital and produce': 'This is obviously a cause which, by awarding a greater or a smaller *proportion* of the produce to the labourer, must have a powerful influence on profits; and if considerable variations were to take place in the supplies of capital and produce and the supplies of labour, in a rich and unexhausted soil, the same effects might be produced on profits as by the operation of the first cause, and in a much shorter time' (275).[53]

While in reality both of the principal 'causes' acting on the profit rate are at play simultaneously, for expository purposes Malthus sets out in both editions by assuming an extreme case – capital accumulation *given* population, or at least with population growth artificially constrained behind that of capital: 'As capital at any time increases faster than labour [1836: As capital and produce increased faster than labour], the profits of capital will [1836: would] fall, and if a progressive increase of capital [1836: capital and produce] were to take place, while the population, by some hidden cause, were prevented from keeping pace with it, notwithstanding the fertility of the soil and the plenty of food, then profits would be gradually reduced, until, by successive reductions, the power and will to accumulate

53 On the new reference to *proportions*, see below, section VII.

had ceased to operate' (1820, 303; 1836, 277).[54] Under the conditions supposed, there would be upward pressure on real wages exerted by increasing demand for labour (1820, 303–4; 1836, 277). Rent would, by contrast, be constrained: 'According to the supposition, the progress of the population is retarded, and the number of labourers is limited, while land of considerable fertility remains uncultivated. The demand for fertile land therefore, compared with the supply, would be comparatively inconsiderable; and in reference to the whole of the national produce, the portion which would consist of rent would depend mainly upon the gradations of more fertile land that had been cultivated before the population had come to a stop, and upon the value of the produce to be derived from the land that was not cultivated' (1820, 303; 1836, 277).[55] The results flowing from this set of assumptions (and also a second set which relies on a falling profit rate in the manufacturing sector)[56] demonstrated 'that the increasing quantity of labour required for the successive cultivation of poorer land is not theoretically necessary to a fall of profits from the highest rate to the lowest' (1820, 305; 1836, 279).

That, of course, is the whole purpose of the exercise – to counter Ricardo's *supposed* position to the contrary; the downward trend path of the profit rate because of increasing land scarcity provided a misleading practical guide for the calculation of 'short term' profit-rate movements.

54 At the close of the passage cited in our text, the second version adds the supplementary consideration that the fall in the profit rate 'might take place rapidly, if a great proportion of those who are engaged in personal services were rapidly converted by saving into productive labourers.'

55 We note the presumption that rent appears even in marginal cost, reflecting foregone opportunity – the payment made for the use of land in an uncultivated state.

56 The alternative set of assumptions replaces the supposed constraint on population growth by an absolute constraint on land supply, all of it of the same (high) quality. Again, the trend of profits would be downward but the effect on rent and wages would differ:

> After all the land had been cultivated, and no more capital could be employed on it, there cannot be a doubt that rents would be extremely high and profits and wages very low. The competition of increasing capital in manufactures and commerce would reduce the rate of profits, while the principle of population would continue to augment the number of the labouring classes, till their corn wages were so low as to check their further increase. It is probable that, owing to the facility of production on the land [1836: the assumed fertility of all the soil] and the great proportion of persons employed [1836: persons which might be employed] in manufactures and commerce, the exports would be great and the value of money very low. The money price of corn and money wages would perhaps be as high as when their cost in labour [1836: as if the cost of the whole produce in labour] had been double or treble; rents would rise [1836: ... treble; food would then be a monopoly, rents would rise] to an extraordinary pitch [1836: height] without any assistance from poor lands, and the gradations of soil; and profits might fall to the point only just sufficient to keep up the actual capital without any additional labour being necessary to procure the food of the labourer. (1820, 304–5; 1836, 278)

We shall consider first the 1820 version: 'These periods, in which capital and population do not keep pace with each other, are evidently of sufficient extent to produce the most important results on the rate of profits, and to affect in the most essential manner the progress of national wealth' (1820, 307). And after an analogy with long-term bonds,[57] Malthus concluded: 'In the same manner, the natural and necessary tendency of profits to fall in the progress of society, owing to the increasing difficulty of procuring food, is a proposition which few will be disposed to controvert; but to attempt to estimate the rate of profits in any country by a reference to this cause alone, for ten, twenty, or even fifty years together, that is for periods of sufficient length to produce the most important effects on national prosperity, would inevitably lead to the greatest practical errors' (1820, 307–8). In the 1836 version the conclusion is formulated with the standard variation: 'These periods, in which population and produce do not keep pace with each other, are evidently of sufficient extent, essentially to alter the proportion which goes to pay the wages of labour; and consequently, to influence essentially the rate of profits. So entirely, indeed, does the rate of profits depend on the division of the produce, occasioned by the state of the supply and the demand, that in comparing two countries together, the rate of profits will sometimes be found the lowest in that country, in which the productiveness of labour on the land is the greatest' (1836, 280). The formal emphasis on proportionate shares in the second version is of high significance, as we shall see below, in section VII.

Malthus closes by reiterating that agricultural productivity, the first 'cause' in profit-rate determination, remained constantly at play: 'It is not meant to underrate the importance of that cause which has been almost exclusively considered by Mr. Ricardo [1836: which depends upon the diminishing productiveness of labour on the last land taken into cultivation].[58] It is indeed of such a nature as finally to overwhelm every other [1836: This cause is indeed of such a nature, that, if its action goes on, it must finally overwhelm every other. Yet, still an attempt to estimate the rate of profits in any country for ten or twenty years together by a reference to this cause alone, would lead to the greatest practical errors]' (1820, 312; 1836, 281). That trend was, however, gradual, indeed 'scarcely perceptible,' and variation of real wages (and other disturbances, including innovation, treated in Malthus's section III) might cause the profit rate to diverge from trend for up to a century: 'But though the principle here considered is finally of the very greatest power, yet its progress is extremely slow and gradual; and while it is proceeding with scarcely perceptible steps to its final destination, the second cause, particularly when combined with others which will be noticed in the next section [1836: 'particularly ...

57 The analogy has important methodological implications. See Conclusion, p. 985.
58 The removal after 1820 of the critical reference to Ricardo is discussed below, p. 473.

section' omitted], is producing effects which entirely overcome it, and often for twenty or thirty, or even 100 years together, make the rate of profits take a course absolutely different from what it ought to be according to the first cause' (1820, 312–13; 1836, 281–2).

The argument is also applied in a developmental context, Malthus introducing cases of *permanent* stagnation despite a high profit rate, and also of profit-rate differentials between countries extending hundreds of years in consequence of real-wage differentials, unrelated to agricultural productivity. Such differentials might operate 'for almost any length of time' (1820, 311); 'might operate most powerfully for a great length of time' (1836, 281). In the American case, because of the extent of the available land, 'the price [1836: the corn wages] of its labour may not essentially fall for hundreds of years [1836: a long term of years]; and the effects of a scanty but stationary capital on an overflowing but stationary population might last for ever' (1820, 311–12; 1836, 281).

* * *

Nowhere in the analysis of the trend paths of the factor returns (above, p. 444) did Malthus allow that Ricardo had also insisted on the shared incidence of diminishing returns between labour and capital; similarly, the Wages chapter attributes to Ricardo a theory of profits turning *solely* on agricultural productivity, with wages constant at an unnatural 'natural' level (above, chapter 9: II). And this line is again followed in the present analysis of the effect on profits of real-wage fluctuations. For Malthus complained that 'notwithstanding the utter inadequacy of this single cause [diminishing agricultural returns] to account for existing phenomena, Mr. Ricardo, in his very ingenious chapter on profits, has dwelt on no other' (1820, 308) – not only with respect to the wages assumption, but also with respect to value theory – thus committing a fundamental methodological error (308–9; see Conclusion, p. 967).[59] The summary proceeds to reject 'the conclusion at which Mr. Ricardo arrives in his chapter on profits, "that in all countries, and at all times, profits depend upon the quantity of labour required to produce necessaries for the labourer on that land, or with that capital which yields no rent"' (309). And here the apparent

59 Malthus here alludes to the labour theory and implies that his own analysis of the profit rate turns on various causes affecting the money value of commodities – an allusion to aggregate-demand considerations. But in fact the substance of his profit-rate analysis had not turned on these matters, but *solely* on pressures on the real wage. Thus a note at the outset of section II (1820) states explicitly: 'We may allow that no difficulty will occur with respect to demand' (1820, 301n; above, p. 469). And in his discussion of 'stationary capital' and a high profit rate, Malthus specifies that the supposed cause of stationariness is *not* 'want of demand,' but, on the contrary, 'great expenditure and want of saving habits' (309–10).

attribution of a constant trend of wages – and a neglect of fluctuations – is explicit. For Malthus elaborates: 'If by the necessaries of the labourer be meant, such wages as will just keep up the population, or what Mr. Ricardo calls the natural wages of labour, it is the same as saying that land of equal fertility will always yield the same profits – a proposition which must necessarily be untrue.' And if Ricardo intended the 'actual earnings, whatever they may be,' his analysis was 'incomplete' because it lacked an account of wage-rate determination: 'Even allowing that the exchangeable value of commodities is regulated by the quantity of labour that has been employed in their production, (which it has been shewn is not so,) little is done towards determining the rate of profits. It is merely a truism to say that if the value of commodities be divided between labour and profits, the greater is the share taken by one, the less will be left for the other; or in other words, that profits fall as labour rises, or rise as labour falls. We can know little of the laws which determine profits, unless, in addition to the causes which increase the price of necessaries, we explain the causes which award a larger or a smaller share of these necessaries to each labourer. And here it is obvious that we must have recourse to the great principles of demand and supply, or to that very principle of competition brought forward by Adam Smith, which Mr. Ricardo expressly rejects, or at least considers as of so temporary a nature as not to require attention in a general theory of profits' (310–11).[60]

Now all the passages just cited regarding Ricardo's supposed neglect of wage fluctuations as pertinent to the profit rate are absent from the second edition. There is, too, the deletion at the close of the section on the effect of wage fluctuations of the formal criticism of Ricardo for 'almost exclusively' considering the effect on profits of diminishing returns (above, p. 471). This might reflect a strategic decision to avoid focusing his account on Ricardo, rather than an actual retraction of the criticisms. But that some retraction was involved is suggested by a rephrasing of the simple declaration in 1820 at the outset of the section devoted specifically to Ricardian profit theory that, for Ricardo, 'profits are regulated by wages, and wages by the quality of the last land taken into cultivation' (326), to read: 'According to Mr. Ricardo profits are regulated by wages, and are high or low in proportion as wages are low or high ...' (1836, 291). This revision is quite general and allows for the effect of variable wages.

Ricardo himself objected to the original statements: 'I do not say that profits are regulated by wages, and wages by the quality of the last land taken into cultivation, for it is expressly the productiveness of that land which regulates profits if wages be supposed of a fixed value' (*Note 186*; 1951–73, II, 285). But wages were *not* a 'fixed value'; Ricardo had protested

60 On the apparently dismissive remark that the Ricardian proportionality theorem is 'merely a truism,' see also note 69, below.

in *Note 171* against the charge relating to constancy of the real wage: 'Mr. Malthus here brings a charge against me which he would find it very hard to prove. He has himself Page 294 section I of this chapter stated two causes for the fall of profits [above, p. 437]. I fully concur with him in thinking that profits never vary but from one or other of those causes. I however endeavored to show that they might be classed under one head, as in both cases the labourer received either a large, or a smaller proportion of the whole produce. If a larger I called his wages higher, if a smaller lower ... I have invariably insisted that high or low profits depended on low and high wages, how then can it be justly said of me that the only cause which I have recognized of high or low profits is the facility or difficulty of providing food for the labourer. I contend that I have also recognized the other cause, the relative amount of population to capital, which is another of the great regulators of wages' (264).[61] Again: 'I do not say that the labourers earnings will always be the same, but whatever they may be, profits will depend on the proportion which their value bears, to the whole value produced on the last land' (266). And he commented favourably on the initial statement relating to profit-rate determination: 'These 2 causes may both be classed under the name of high or low wages. Profits in fact depend on high or low wages, and on nothing else ... In all this Mr. Malthus and I appear to concur. Whenever the difficulty of production on the land is such that a greater proportion of the value of the whole produce is employed in supporting labour, I call wages high, for I measure value by these proportions ...' (*Note 161*; 252). More generally, he insisted that 'I maintain no other doctrine than that which has been well explained by Mr. Malthus in the 2 first sections of 5th chapter. His own statements are sometimes at variance with it, mine I believe never' (*Note 187*; 288).[62]

* * *

Malthus read the *Notes* on his *Principles*,[63] and conceivably Ricardo's objections induced him to alter his text – in which case Ricardo would have been pleasantly surprised.[64] Ricardo might have intended his expression

61 Cf. *Note 310* on the Progress chapter: 'Mr Malthus is greatly mistaken if he supposes that I contend profits must *always* be high while we have fertile land still in reserve. Profits will be low as I have said a hundred times if wages are high, and wages may be very high, with very abundant resources on land' (446–7).

62 Torrens, also, was surprised by Malthus's failure to recognize the allowances by Ricardo for an effect on the profit rate of variable wages (above, note 39).

63 See Ricardo to Trower, 2 March 1821: 'Mr. Malthus has now had my notes for 5 weeks' (1951–73, VIII, 349).

64 He wrote to McCulloch: 'Mr. Malthus's second edition will not appear for the present, he has had my notes ever since you returned them to me [January 1821], but I fear they have made very little impression on him' (25 April 1821; 1951–73, VIII, 373).

of accord to apply solely to the effect on the profit rate of wage *fluctuations* – not the falling *trend* – though this is unlikely, since at the close of the full-fledged analysis in Malthus's Section I, which covers the matter of joint incidence, Ricardo declared: 'I agree throughout this section with Mr. Malthus in principle, we only differ in our ideas of what constitutes a real measure of value' (*Note 164*; 258). But we cannot be sure that Malthus's retraction necessarily extended to allow for Ricardo's subscription to the joint incidence of diminishing returns. We must look farther afield to arrive at a conclusive answer.

The chapter on Rent very explicitly spells out the principle of shared incidence – in line with the 1815 statement, and in a note attached to a generalization regarding the fall in the profit rate on 'the lands first chosen' below those potentially available from extensions to 'inferior land,' Malthus concedes that there are *no differences other than linguistic ones* between himself and Ricardo on the proposition itself: 'When a given portion of labour and capital [1836: a given value of capital] yields smaller returns whether on new land or old, the loss is generally divided between the labourers and capitalists, and wages and profits fall at the same time. This is quite contrary to Mr. Ricardo's language. But the wages we refer to are totally different. He speaks of the cost [1836: mere labour cost] of producing the necessaries of the labourer; I speak of the necessaries themselves' (1820, 154n; 1836, 152n). Ricardo accepted all this in his *Note 61*: 'True the loss of *quantity* is generally divided between the labourers and capitalists, but we are not talking of quantity, we are talking of value,' and though the corn wage declines, the 'value' of the wage increases (1951–73, II, 124).[65]

In late correspondence with William Whewell, Malthus referred positively to Richard Jones's *Rent* (1831), but asserted that on one issue Jones went too far in his objections to Ricardo: 'I am very much obliged to you and Mr. Jones for a valuable work on the distribution of wealth, which I have lately received ... I am particularly gratified to find that he agrees with me on almost every point on which I differed from Mr. Ricardo – I am not sure however whether he has not gone beyond the truth in his unwillingness to admit the *tendency* of continued accumulation, and of the progress of population and cultivation to lower the rates of profits and corn wages on the land; ... If the progress of cultivation and population has no *tendency* to diminish corn wages, I do not see what cause should ever retard the rate

65 Yet in *The Measure of Value* (1823), Malthus observed against Ricardo that variations in the corn wage alone or in agricultural productivity alone fail to provide an indication of proportionate changes since either one might counteract the other (1823b/1986, 7, 195), failing to convey the notion that, in the course of regular growth, there occurs, for Ricardo, a *necessary increase* in the labour embodied in a *necessarily falling* corn wage, and accordingly an unambiguous rise in labour's proportionate share in the marginal product and a corresponding fall in the profit rate.

at which population is known to increase in the new colonies' (28 February 1831, TCL Add. Ms. c. 53[2]). This reference suggests that Malthus was defending the shared incidence of diminishing returns envisaged as a *Ricardian* proposition.[66]

VII THE INVERSE WAGE–PROFIT OR 'PROPORTIONALITY' THEOREM

The Wages chapter closes in 1820 with a reminder that it had dealt specifically with 'real' (commodity) and 'nominal' (money) wages, with an eye to 'the condition of the labourer, the encouragement to population, and the value of money, the three great points which chiefly demand our attention' (1820, 291). Ricardian wages – 'the value of labour as measured by the labour which has been expended in procuring the earnings of the labourer, or the cost in labour of the labourer's wages' – had been left in abeyance since 'such high or low wages serve only to determine the rate of profits, and their influence in this respect will be fully considered in the next chapter' (292). In the second edition 'Ricardian wages' are read as *proportionate* wages: 'I have said nothing of the rise or fall of wages according to the language adopted by Mr. Ricardo. Such wages, namely proportionate wages, only determine, or rather are determined by, the rate of profits, and will be considered in the next chapter [on Profits]' (1836, 260).

Now while the 1820 version is neutral regarding the Ricardo theorem expressed in terms of labour embodied in wages, the 1836 version formulates *and accepts* the theorem expressed in terms of proportions,[67] subject to the gloss that *'proportionate wages* determine, or rather *are determined by, the rate of profits.*' But it is doubtful whether the reformulation (we set aside for now the gloss)[68] indicates a massive change in perspective, since the analysis of the downward trend path of wage and profit rates proceeds in both versions in terms of proportions (1820, 299; 1836, 274, cited above, pp. 442–3).[69] There is, though, new support for the proportionality the-

66 But of this we cannot be absolutely sure since Jones himself repeatedly attributed to Ricardo a *constant* wage model with the incidence of land scarcity falling *solely* on the rate of profit (1831, 257f., 293, 302). At one point in this context, Jones extends his criticisms to Malthus, but only with regard to diminishing returns as such, not the matter of incidence: 'both Sir Edward [West] and Mr. Malthus ... shew an occasional disposition to take it for granted, that in the progress of agriculture, every additional portion of capital applied to the soils must produce a less return than that which proceeded it ...' (1831, 300).

67 For Ricardo, who uses a labour-embodied measure, the two are identical. For Malthus, they are not (see below, p. 480).

68 The direction of causality was alluded to above, p. 463. It will be elaborated further below, p. 483.

69 Some of the 1836 modifications emphasize 'proportionate wages' as the significant

orem in the second edition, where a section is added to the chapter 'Of the Nature of Profits, and the Mode in which they are Estimated,' carefully spelling out the inverse profit–wage theorem in proportionate terms, and defending the theorem against possible criticism of its cavalier treatment of the capital component.

The new section summarizes a long-standing allowance that estimation in money rather than labour-commanded terms is acceptable provided relatively short production periods are involved: 'it has been shown in the second chapter of this work, that the values of any commodities, or of the mass of commodities are always determined by the state of the supply compared with the demand; and that their values may be measured by the quantity of standard labour which they will command. It is also obvious from what has been said, that during the short periods which usually intervene between the advances of capital and the returns of produce, they may both be estimated correctly in money' (1836, 266). There follows the deduction – scarcely rigorous – that '[in] the employment of capital therefore, in any business, the advances, whether increasing or diminishing in value, may be known and measured beforehand, while the value of the product, and the proportion of that value which goes to replace the advances remains to be ascertained when the produce is sold.' This in turn leads to the main theme regarding profit-rate determination, which is rephrased in terms of a dependency of the profit rate on the *proportionate share of labour in the value of output*: 'The varying rate of profits therefore, in the production of every commodity depends upon the excess of its value when sold above the known value of the advances, determined in all cases by the state of the supply and the demand. This is a universal proposition, equally applicable whether profits are affected by temporary or by more permanent causes, whether the productive powers of labour are great or small, increasing, stationary, or diminishing. *And it will be found, that this proposition is essentially the same as the proposition which states, that profits depend upon the proportion of the value of the whole produce, which goes to pay the wages of the labour employed to obtain it*' (267; emphasis added). This was self-evident in the case where only 'immediate labour' and profits on immediate labour are involved, but other more complex cases are said to be reducible (on the basis of a rather cavalier assumption) to that simplest case – 'no case however complicated ... may not easily be solved in a similar manner' (268) – so that it remained 'strictly true' that 'profits depend on the proportion of the value of the

---

variable (above, p. 469), but there are also references in 1820 absent in 1836 (above, p. 444). Even the dismissive remark of 1820 regarding the proportionality theorem as truism by no means positively rejects it (1820, 310; above, p. 473).

produce which goes to pay the [immediate] labour which has been employed.'[70]

The suggested procedure provided a short-cut to an accurate estimate, avoiding the otherwise complex problem of breaking down advances between 'accumulated labour' and 'accumulated profits': 'When it is said that the profits depend upon the division of the produce between the labourer and the capitalist, it is not of course meant to exclude the labourers and capitalists who have furnished those large portions of the advances which do not consist of the wages of immediate labour; and we must either trace accurately the proportions of accumulated labour and accumulated profits in these advances, which it is not always easy to do, or adopt the mode above suggested, which gives at once the proportion of the produce which goes to pay the wages of the immediate labour employed. The result is exactly the same as if we had measured the whole advances in standard labour, and had estimated the rate of profits by the excess of the value of the produce above what was required to pay the wages of that quantity of labour' (268–9).

There is one further detail – the treatment of residual capital. In the examples thus far of the simplifying procedure (see preceding note) there is no allowance for 'the value of fixed capital' as such in advances – only wear and tear of fixed capital and interest on both fixed and circulating capitals are recognized. If such value *is* to be allowed for in advances, appropriate allowances must also be made in annual returns, although the formulation seems to imply that the best approach is to *exclude* the value of fixed capital from advances, and thus avoid the need to correct annual returns for residual capital: 'If we reckon the value of the fixed capital employed as a part of the advances, we must reckon the remaining value

70 The simplest case is said to be self-evident: 'The truth of this proposition is quite obvious in the cases where only immediate labour and the profits upon it are concerned. If £100 be expended in immediate labour, and the returns come in at the end of the year, and sell for £110, £120, or £130, it is evident that in each case the profits will be determined by the proportion of the value of the whole produce which is required to pay the labour employed.' Cases where the advances do not consist of labour alone are both dealt with on the (unjustified) assumption that 'the capitalist generally expects an equal profit on all parts of the capital which he advances.' In this case, if, for example, one-quarter of the total advances comprises wages of immediate labour, and the rest consists of 'accumulated labour and profits, with any additions which may arise from rents, taxes, or other outgoings' – this is then rephrased in the case of a farmer, as 'seed, keep of horses, wear and tear of his fixed capital, interest upon his fixed and circulating capitals, rent, tithes, taxes, etc.' – the calculation of the *overall* profit rate will be proportionate to the profit rate as calculated only on *immediate labour*. Assuming sales revenue of £2,400 and advances of £2,000: 'It is obvious that the value required to replace the advances being £2,000 the farmer's profits will be £400, or 20 per cent. And it is equally obvious that if we took one fourth of the value of the produce, namely £600, and compared it with the amount paid in the wages of immediate labour, the result would show exactly the same rate of profits.'

of such capital at the end of the year as a part of the annual returns. Without a correction of this kind it would appear that in those departments of industry in which the greatest quantity of fixed capital had been applied, the value of capital compared with the value of the produce had been the greatest, from which it would seem to follow that the rate of profits had been the lowest; but though the capitalist naturally considers the whole of what he employs in production as capital advanced; yet in reality his annual advances consist only of his circulating capital, the wear and tear of his fixed capital with the interest upon it, and the interest of that part of his circulating capital which consists of the money employed in making his annual payments as they are called for' (269–70).[71]

Strange to relate, in using data drawn from a real-life case[72] Malthus reckons not only annual advances, but also capital sunk in building and machinery, *without* making the correction just alluded to. And none the less he concludes with the problematic assertion that his case may be demonstrated thereby – namely, that 'the wages of the operatives or of the immediate labour employed in the production of the twist, form about one sixth of the [total] advances, and the comparison of these advances with one sixth of the value of the produce will clearly indicate the *rate* of profit upon the whole of the advances' (270). The resultant return is thus said to reflect the return on the entire capital, despite a failure to correct the returns for residual capital. It is difficult to appreciate Malthus's intentions here. In fact, the section closes with a reiteration that it is *annual* advances and returns that matter: 'In drawing the particular attention of the reader to the profits, which may be said to belong to the immediate labour employed in any production, it is by no means intended to propose a better mode of ascertaining profits than the ordinary one of comparing the annual money advances, with the annual money returns. The object is to show, that the two modes always accord (except in the rare case of a change in the price of labour or alteration in the value of money during the interval which elapses between the advances and the returns); and whether we take the most simple case, where the advances consist of immediate labour alone, or the most complex one, where but a small part only of the advances consists of immediate labour, it will always be found true that profits vary according to the proportion of the value of the whole produce which goes to pay the wages of the labour employed to obtain it.'

* * *

Malthus explicitly noted in the new first section that the distribution

71 On the inclusion of residual capital in final product, see chapter 7, pp. 304, 307.

72 He draws from a statement in the first *Report of the Factory Commissioners* (1833). For details see Pullen, in Malthus, 1820/1989, II, 224.

theorem – 'profits depend upon the proportion of the value of the whole produce, which goes to pay the wages of the labour employed to obtain it' – 'though rather differently worded, is Mr. Ricardo's proposition, but he has applied it incorrectly' (267n). This would be shown 'in a subsequent section,' a reference to the discussion of the inverse wage–profit relation in the final section, 'Remarks on Mr. Ricardo's Theory of Profits' (section IV in 1820; section V in 1836).

This final section commences in 1820 with the affirmation that 'according to Mr. Ricardo profits are regulated by wages, and wages by the quality of the last land taken into cultivation' (326; above p. 473). The criticism that follows focuses on Ricardo's measuring unit, which was designed to assure a constant value of the total to be divided between capital and labour: '[Ricardo's] theory of profits depends entirely upon the circumstance of the mass of commodities remaining at the same price, while money continues of the same value, whatever may be the variations in the price of labour. This uniformity in the value of wages and profits taken together is indeed assumed by Mr. Ricardo in all his calculations, from one end of his work to the other; and if it were true, we should certainly have an accurate rule which would determine the rate of profits upon any given rise or fall of money wages. But if it be not true, the whole theory falls to the ground. We can infer nothing respecting the rate of profits from a rise of money wages, if commodities, instead of remaining of the same price, are very variously affected, some rising, some falling, and a very small number indeed remaining stationary' (326–7). This assertion that, because commodity prices are differentially affected by money-wage variation, 'the money wages of labour cannot regulate the rate of profits,' is unconvincing since Ricardo's mean-proportions measure was designed precisely to deal with the issue.[73]

The rendition of Ricardo's position is rephrased in the second edition: 'According to Mr. Ricardo profits are regulated by wages, and are high or low in proportion as wages are low or high [1951–73, I, 110]; or as he has expressed himself more fully in another part of his chapter on profits: "In all countries, and at all times, profits depend upon the quantity of labour requisite to provide necessaries for the labourers on that land, or with that capital which yields no rent" [1951–73, I, 126]' (1836, 291).[74] The criticism that follows is more complex than the single paragraph in 1820, though it is consistent with it. It focuses, first, on an implicit assumption that advances consist only of the wages of direct labour: 'It is here understood, that

73 Malthus used the skimpy dismissal as a prelude to his own focus on the varying value of output relative to a constant value of labour input (below, p. 482).

74 The latter quote was given earlier in the chapter in the 1820 version (above, p. 472). Possibly Malthus reworded the passage in the light of Ricardo's *Note 186* (above, p. 473).

there are no other advances except those of wages; and, under these circumstances, the necessaries required to pay ten labourers must have required fewer than ten labourers to produce them, or there would have been no profits. It is further obvious that the profits upon the produce necessary to pay the wages of ten labourers must depend upon the difference between the whole produce, and that portion of it which is required to pay the number of labourers, whether nine, eight, seven, or any other proportion actually employed to produce the wages of the whole ten. Mr. Ricardo's proposition therefore will be found to be essentially the same as if he had said that profits are determined by the proportion of the produce which goes to pay the wages of the labour which obtained it. And so far this theory is quite correct' (292). (This is scarcely surprising, since he himself had adopted the method of obtaining the profit rate by reducing all cases to 'the most simple case, where the advances consist of immediate labour alone'; above, p. 479). But there were two additional – and invalid – assumptions made in 'application' and these, he believed, rendered '[the theory] as a whole essentially erroneous ... 1st. That the commodities which have cost in their production the same quantity of labour will on an average always be of the same value. And 2ndly. That the value of the same quantity of labour varies in proportion to the share of the produce which goes to pay the labourer; and the varying value of this labour being thus taken out of the *supposed* constant value of the produce obtained by them, the remainder determines the rate of profits.' It will be recalled that, in the first section of the 1836 version, Malthus had conceded that his version of the inverse wage–profit relation amounted to that of Ricardo, although the latter had 'applied it incorrectly' (above, p. 480). It is to the incorrect application that Malthus now alludes.

Formally basing himself on his own theory of value (see above, chapter 6), Malthus asserts that Ricardo's application undermined the entire theory by suggesting an erroneous sequence of causation. For (1), cost prices incorporate an allowance for profits, and thus vary with the profit rate, not labour alone (as if Ricardo did not know this): 'Commodities which have cost in their production the same quantity of labour, or the same value of capital, are subject to great variations of value, owing to the varying rate and varying quantity of profits which must be added to the quantity of accumulated and immediate labour employed upon them, in order to make up their value'; and (2), the value (Malthus's labour command) of the (variable) commodity wage is *constant*: 'However variable may be the *quantity* or proportion of produce awarded to each labourer, the value of that quantity or proportion will always be the same' (292–3). From this it followed 'that profits must be regulated upon a principle essentially different from that stated by Mr. Ricardo, and that instead of being determined by the varying value of a certain quantity of labour employed, compared with the given value of the commodity produced, they will be determined by the *varying* value of the commodity produced compared with the *given* value of the certain quantity of labour employed' (293).

The substance of this elaboration of the formal criticism of the labour theory of value – and the related criticism of Ricardo's measurement of labour's proportional share in terms of the money-wage rate – had in fact already been briefly taken up in 1820 (see above, pp. 473, 480). The final conclusion that it was necessary to focus in profit-rate analysis on the '*varying* value' of output relative to a '*given* value' of labour input, also reiterates the 1820 position. And to confirm his case in both editions, Malthus assumes a money measure produced solely by a day's labour, *which rules out any change in the money-wage rate*: 'This conclusion will appear still more strikingly true [1836: will appear strikingly obvious], if we adopt that supposition respecting the mode of procuring the precious metals which would certainly maintain them most strictly of the same value, that is, if we suppose them to be procured by a uniform quantity of unassisted labour without any advances in the shape of capital beyond the necessaries of a single day. That the precious metals would in this case retain, more completely than in any other, the same value, cannot be denied, as they would both cost and command the same quantity of labour [1836: as the quantity of labour actually employed in their production and the quantity of labour they would command would be the same]. But in this case, as was before stated, the money price of labour could never permanently rise [1836: must remain permanently the same]' (1820, 327; 1836, 293). The point at issue is that constancy of the money wage could not preclude an effect of increasing land scarcity on the profit rate: 'We cannot however for a moment imagine that this impossibility of a rise or fall in the money price of labour could in any respect impede or interrupt the natural career of profits. This continued accumulation of capital and increasing difficulty of procuring subsistence would unquestionably lower profits' (1820, 327–8; 1836, 293).[75]

That the foregoing conclusion held good despite constancy of the money wage Malthus believed showed Ricardo's mechanism to be falsified, failing to appreciate that Ricardian theory does *not* turn on the special measure of value (Hollander, 1979, 227–42). It is clear that Malthus was confusing measurement with substantive economic process. Even he, however, to his credit was troubled by the great weight placed on his own measure. *For he was prepared in the second edition to use Ricardo's mean-proportions money measure*, with a formal insistence only that the secular increase in the money wage which then emerges reflects a fall in the value

75 It will be recalled that the secular fall in the agricultural profit rate with diminishing returns depresses the returns to capital in all other industries, reducing their cost prices differentially. The corn price alone rises with the money wage constant throughout, assuming a money measure produced *without capital* (above, pp. 449, 464).

of money, not (as Ricardo believed) an increase in the value of labour: 'If however instead of supposing gold to be obtained by immediate labour alone in the way here stated, we suppose with Mr. Ricardo that it is obtained by fixed and circulating capitals in certain proportions, it will be found (as we have before intimated) that the state of prices and the rise of labour, contemplated by him in the progress of cultivation, are owing to a *fall* in the value of money, and not to a *rise* in the value of labour' (1836, 294).

I do not, however, maintain that the retention of the proportionality theorem assures the identity of the two systems. For there is the essential difference with Ricardo over the Law of Markets – Malthus's adherence to the Smithian notion of a falling profit rate in consequence of increased competition of capitals. That capital 'was increasing faster than the effectual demand for the produce at its former price' is a key feature of the argument, as we shall now see. (The priority accorded the agricultural profit rate discussed in our section III relates solely to the 'limiting' case, allowing scope for the operation of competition of capitals in reducing the general profit rate below the limit.)

We turn to the details of the analysis. Values are expressed in terms of Ricardo's measure, which assumes 'a country supplied with gold by a mine of its own, from which the same quantity of metal could always be obtained by the same quantity of labour with the same value of other capital' (295). In this case, the monetary metal among other commodities, falls in its 'value' – which for Malthus means value relative to labour; that is, *the money wage rises* – the fall reflecting the lower profit rate with increased competition of capitals, which becomes embedded in lower *cost* prices. The wage and profit movements are then expressed in proportionate terms: 'all those commodities which continued to be obtained by the same quantity of labour with the same value of other capital would fall in value from the abundance of the supply; and gold among the rest becoming more abundant, a different division of the produce would take place between the labourers and the capitalists; *a smaller proportion of it would go to pay profits, and a larger proportion to pay wages. Profits therefore would fall, and the money wages of labour would rise* ... But if the *rate of profits* has fallen the elementary costs of production have fallen. In this case, the conditions of the supply of a certain quantity of gold are the advance of the same quantity of labour, with the same value of other capital, as before *and a less* remuneration for profits. Consequently the elementary cost of gold to the purchaser is less than before' (295–6; first emphasis added).

The exposition is wanting in clarity, but it is pretty clear what is at stake. The essential point is that the rise in labour's proportionate share in output is represented as the *passive reflection* of the fall in the share going to capital with increased competition of capitals. And, as mentioned above, the money-wage increase in the case at hand involving Ricardo's measure is formally said to reflect, not an increase in the *value of labour*, but a fall in the *value of money*, or its costs of production, which like those of all commodities are reduced by the lower profit component: 'Mr. Ricardo considers [the rise in the money wages of labour] a rise in the *value* of labour, and has founded all his calculations in his chapters on rent, wages, and profits, on this assumption. If indeed the value of the produce of the same quantity of labour, or of labour and capital,[76] were to remain the same, which is what he supposes, then it would be quite true that if a larger proportion of this produce went to pay the wages of labour, the value of labour would rise. But if the value of the produce falls, then the circumstances of a larger proportion of the produce going to pay the wages of labour by no means implies that the value of labour has risen. It only implies that the labourer receives a larger quantity of an article which has fallen in value' (295).[77]

The essential difference between the two systems turns on Malthus's rejection of the Law of Markets – his Smithian perspective on the fall on profits. How one designates the money-wage increase in the analysis seems to be a matter of window-dressing, though this is not how Malthus represented it. For the point is made in closing that, if 'in the system of Mr.

76 Malthus adds a note on this detail: 'Mr. Ricardo often uses the terms *quantity of labour*, and *quantity of labour and capital*, to express the same thing. Generally, when on the subject of profits, he means the *quantity of labour and capital*, although it must be allowed that machinery and materials of different kinds cannot be estimated and compared by quantity. The true condensed expressions in regard to the advances on which profits are estimated must be (as it has appeared) either the *quantity of labour*, or the *value of the capital*. They are equivalent, and give the same results.'

77 These conclusions are carried over even when allowance is made for the rising labour cost of producing the wage basket: 'If it be said, as Mr. Ricardo says, that a greater quantity of labour is required to produce the corn which pays the wages of the labourer, this may be conceded; but as the proportionate fall of profits is found to have taken place, the diminution of the element of profits balances the increase of the element of labour, leaving the *value* of labour the same as before, while its increasing price is occasioned by the fall in the value of money' (296).

Now the constant 'value of labour' alludes to the labour commanded by the (real) wage paid labour: 'This balance necessarily takes place, as we have said, in the *elementary cost* of the varying wages of a given number of men, which always remains the same' (296n), referring to the proposition in the chapter on Measures of Value, whereby 'however variable may be the *quantity* or proportion of produce awarded to each labourer, the value of that quantity or proportion will always be the same' cited only a few pages earlier (above, p. 481; see also p. 448). As for the 'increasing price of labour,' that refers to the increasing *money wage*, but it is money of reduced value – and this even in the sense of reduced purchasing power: 'And that the value of money must have fallen is further evident from the conclusion of Mr. Ricardo himself, quite independently of the measure which I have applied to it. According to his theory the prices of manufactured commodities, which have not been produced by improved machinery, will, in the progress of cultivation, remain nearly the same, while labour and all raw products will rise. If therefore we measure the value of money by its general power of purchasing, its fall is decidedly established. Of a certain mass of objects it purchases a smaller quantity.'

Ricardo commodities obtained by the same quantity of labour *appear* to be of the same value, it is only because he has adopted as his measure a money, which from the nature of its composition as consisting in part of profits, necessarily varies with the variations in the value of the very commodities which it is intended to measure' (296).

* * *

A further elaboration in 1836 of the proportionality theorem and the order of causality appears at the close of the section on 'Causes practically in operation' following the discussion of the effect on the profit rate of 'the relative abundance or scarcity of capitals' common to both editions (above, pp. 451–3). That the profit-rate decline is reflected in an increase in 'the proportion of the *produce* ... required to replace the capital,' that is, an increase in the proportion going to labour, must not be understood as a causal relationship in the Ricardo manner. The cause of the profit-rate decline remains a reduced value of produce: 'If a capital of £100 be expended in producing 1,200 yards of calico, which sell for £120, profits will be 20 per cent. On the other hand, if they sell for £110, profits will be only 10 per cent; and whether they sell for £110 or £120 will be determined by the state of the supply compared with the demand. The money wages of labour and the value of money may remain the same; but a different proportion of the produce is required to replace the capital:[78] in the first case 1,000 yards are required, in the second nearly 1,100. It is evident however that the increase in the quantity of produce required to replace the capital is the *consequence*, not the *cause* of the fall of profits. The cause is the fall in the value of the produce of the same quantity of labour, or the same value of capital' (1836, 289–90). This is the case whatever happens to the *volume* of physical output. Here Malthus alludes in closing to agricultural productivity, but this seems to be an error, since the main illustration relates to *manufacturing*, considering the characteristic application of 'competition of capitals' to that sector alone: 'If instead of supposing that the same quantity of produce is obtained by the same value of capital, and sells at various prices, we suppose that the quantity produced and the prices at which it sells are both variable, which is the actual state of things, as profits depend upon *proportion* not quantity, it will be still true that profits will be determined by the proportion of the value of the produce which goes to replace the capital, whether the quantity remaining for profits be 100 yards or 400 yards, whether the labour employed on the land becomes less productive or more productive' (290).

At this point there appears a striking restatement of the proposition that

78 Here Malthus adds a note: 'The reader is aware of the corrections to be made for fixed capital,' an allusion to the argument discussed above, p. 478.

a lower profit rate resulting from 'competition' becomes embodied in the cost price. Again, the fall in the profit rate is identified with a rise in the *proportion* of the produce which 'replaces' capital: 'ordinary profits are one of the necessary conditions of the continued supply of commodities, and consequently one of the elements of their ordinary cost to the consumer; and this element is specifically determined by the ordinary state of the supply compared with the demand of the produce of the same value of capital. If the outlay of £100 for a year will obtain a produce which, on an average of ten or twelve years, sells for £120, the ordinary rate of profits will be 20 per cent. If at a future time the produce of the same value of outlay sells on an average during a similar period for £110, the ordinary rate of profits will be 10 per cent. The proportion of the produce which goes to replace the capital will in the latter case be 10/11 instead of 10/12, and it is obvious that this increased proportion of the same produce which is required to replace the capital, is specifically occasioned by a fall in the value of the produce of the same capital' (290–1). Profits, therefore, 'must always depend upon the different values of the produce of the same value of capital determined by the state of the supply, immediate or ordinary, compared with the demand' (291). Here Malthus returns to the labour-commanded measure and restates the proposition: 'And if labour be the measure of value, which I trust has been shown, this is the same as saying that profits are determined by the proportion of the value of the produce which goes to pay the labour which has obtained it; and it follows as a direct consequence that profits never fall but when the value of the produce of the same quantity of labour falls, and never rise but when the value of the produce of the same quantity of labour rises.'[79] The labour-commanded measure had, in fact, added nothing to the substantive proposition itself, but Malthus saw the matter otherwise.

VIII FURTHER EVIDENCE FOR THE PROPORTIONALITY THEOREM

That Malthus came to accept Ricardo's inverse wage–profit relation as a theorem regarding proportionate shares is confirmed in his *Quarterly Review* article for 1824: 'Of all the truths which Mr. Ricardo has established, one of the most useful and important is, that profits are determined by the

79 Here the editor (Cazenove) adds one of his eight notes: 'It is to be observed, that the various causes which practically affect profits, and which the author has enumerated in this section, are all reducible to one or the other of the two grand distinctions which are treated of in the two foregoing sections. For instance, agricultural improvements, or increased personal exertions on the part of the labourer, whereby a larger produce is obtained with the same amount of labour, clearly belong to what he has denominated the *limiting* principle of profits, whilst the various circumstances which affect the value of the same quantity of produce, the labour employed being also the same, belong to the *regulating* principle of profits. *Ed.*'

proportion of the whole produce which goes to labour. It is, indeed, a direct corollary from the proposition, that the value of commodities is resolvable into wages and profits; but its simplicity and apparent obviousness do not detract from its utility' (1824a/1986, 7, 276–7). Similarly: 'We fully agree with the author of the present treatise [McCulloch], that when it is said that profits depend on wages, they must not be understood to depend on wages estimated in money, in corn, or in any other commodity, but on proportional wages, that is, on the share of the commodities produced by the labourer, or of their value, which is given to the labourer' (287). His substantive criticisms related: (1) to Ricardo's supposed failure to determine the division, the inverse wage–profit relationship constituting 'only one important step in the theory of profits, which of course cannot be complete till we have ascertained the cause, which under all circumstances, regulates this proportion of the whole produce which goes to labour immediately and accumulated' (277); and (2) his position that his own doctrine relating to the role of aggregate demand stood up empirically better than the Ricardian emphasis upon the difficulty of production on the land in accounting for the (supposed) historical decline in the profit rate (295). Yet at the same time he accepted that the evidence accorded 'most perfectly with the more general proposition of Mr. Ricardo respecting profits, namely that they are determined by the proportion of the whole produce which goes to labour' (286).

Malthus's strengthened adherence to the proportionality theorem in the revised *Principles* is also confirmed in *The Measure of Value* (1823). In fact, the formulations of that essay frequently duplicate the revisions made to the text, providing us with their approximate dating. The common ground with Ricardo – indeed Ricardo's primacy – was remarked on by Malthus in a note attached to 'the general proposition, liable to no exception, that when the value of any produce can be resolved into labour and profits, then as the *proportion* of such produce which goes to labour increases, the proportion which goes to profits must decrease in the same degree, and as the *proportion* which goes to labour decreases, the proportion which goes to profits must increase in the same degree' (1823b/1986, 7, 194). The note constitutes an extraordinarily warm tribute to Ricardo's formulation of the inverse wage–profit relation as a proportionality theorem, though subject to two criticisms: (1) a failure to refer to the 'ultimate causes' of profit-rate variation, alluding to Ricardo's supposed neglect of the effect on profits of variable corn wages; and (2) a failure to deduce that *labour* – of course, the wage paid labour – *has constant value*: 'This proposition is essentially the same as that which is very clearly and ably expressed by Mr. Ricardo in his chapter on Profits [1951–73, 1,126], in the following terms: "in all countries and at all times profits depend on the quantity of labour requisite to provide necessaries for the labourers on that land, or with that capital which yields no rent;" a proposition which though incomplete in reference to the ultimate causes of the variations of profits, contains a most important truth. From this truth the legitimate deduction appears to me to be, the constant value of labour; but Mr. Ricardo has formed his system on a deduction exactly opposite to it. He has, however, in my opinion, amply compensated for the errors into which he may have fallen, by furnishing us, at the same time, not only with the means of their refutation, but the means of improving the science of Political Economy' (194n). We need only recall that, in the 1820 version of the *Principles*, the proportionality theorem was described dismissively as a 'truism' to realize that we are witness to a definite warming towards Ricardian theory.

The second criticism reflects Malthus's insistence on a constant value of labour, notwithstanding a decline in labour productivity, in contrast to Ricardo's rising value of labour under those conditions: 'It appears then that when the labourer continues to be paid the same corn wages, the value of the whole corn produce, or the value of each man's wages estimated in the usual way in labour and profits, must obviously remain constant, and that it must be most erroneous to infer that labour rises in value because it requires more labour in the progress of cultivation to produce the wages of 10 men or one man, if at the same time it requires such a diminished value of profits as exactly to balance it.' In this particular passage the corn wage itself is assumed constant, though, of course, the constancy of the value of the corn wage is quite general, as Adam Smith had recognized: 'I have entered at some length into the details which show the necessary constancy of the value of labour [of the wage paid a day's labour], on account of its great importance; but, in reality, it follows directly from the manner in which the natural value of commodities and of wages is estimated, that when the labourer earns a greater or a smaller quantity of money or necessaries, it is not the value of labour which varies, but, as Adam Smith says, "it is the goods which are cheap in the one case and dear in the other"' (196). Similarly, 'greater earnings of the labourer [are] occasioned, not by a rise in the value of labour, but by a fall in the value of the produce for which the labour was exchanged' (197).

Notwithstanding the impression to the contrary reflecting his objections to Ricardo's measuring device, Malthus thus accepted the proportionality theorem, and indeed the proposition that *the profit rate varies inversely with labour embodiment in the wage* whether changes in labour embodiment reflect a higher corn wage or reduced labour productivity – this, of course, assuming away provisionally the aggregate-demand problem. As always, he erred by supposing that Ricardo had neglected or denied the effect of variable wages.

IX FURTHER ELABORATIONS IN *THE MEASURE OF VALUE*

We have seen that the note in *The Measure of Value* commending Ricardo treats the inverse relation as a 'truth' from which followed the constant value of *labour* as a 'legitimate deduction.'[80] But in what follows the sequence is reversed, Malthus taking the constant value of labour as a point of departure and conceiving its breakdown between wages and profits as indicating precisely the corresponding proportionate breakdown in total output: 'if we refer to the variable quantity of produce which, under different circumstances, forms the wages of a given number of labourers, we shall find that *the variable quantity of labour required to obtain this produce will always exactly agree with the proportion of the whole produce which goes to labour*; because, however variable may be the amount of this produce, it will be divided into a number of parts equal to the number of labourers which it will command, and as the first set of labourers who produced these wages may be considered as having been paid at the same rate as the second set, whose labour the produce commands; it is obvious that if to obtain the produce which commands ten labourers, 6, 7, 8, or 9 labourers be required, the proportion of the [whole] produce which goes to labour, in these different cases, will be $\frac{6}{10}$, $\frac{7}{10}$, $\frac{8}{10}$, or $\frac{9}{10}$, leaving $\frac{4}{10}$, $\frac{3}{10}$, $\frac{2}{10}$, or $\frac{1}{10}$, for profits' (1823b/1986, 7, 195; emphasis added).[81] The same applies

80 This sequence is also to be found in correspondence with Ricardo explaining the constant value of labour despite falling agricultural productivity (*ca.* 21 July 1823, in Ricardo, 1951–73, IX, 308–9; cited in chapter 7, pp. 323–4). Ricardo himself found the 'proof' a tissue of semantic non-sequiturs (3 August 1823; 324).

81 The constancy of the value of labour is generalized to allow for complex cases in which the advances required to produce the wage basket 'which do not consist of wages' – materials and fixed capital – 'vary in different degree from wages' (205). This was because 'the exceptions ... to the general proposition that the labour which commodities will command may be considered as a standard measure of their value are only apparent, not real, and may all be consistently explained' (207). Allowing for *materials* advances in the production of wages as well as *wage* advances, it might appear that 'the profits of stock would not fall so much as if the same rise of corn wages had taken place, when all the advances had been in labour; so that 'profits not falling in proportion to the rise of labour, the value of labour would not continue the same' (206). But this was illusory: 'in all cases of this kind, there will be a less value of labour, which is equivalent to a less quantity of it employed to obtain the same produce; and a less quantity of labour altogether being consequently necessary to produce the food of the labourer, than if labour alone had been employed, the higher profits, or smaller diminution of the former profits, will only just be such as to maintain labour of a constant value.' Cases of 'fixed capital, of considerable duration' also created no difficulty, despite 'a probability that [such fixed capital] will alter in value in reference to the quantity of labour, and of profits estimated in labour, of which it was composed when first produced' (207). Malthus dismissed the problem in an extraordinarily cavalier fashion: 'after having advanced so far in establishing the labour which a commodity will command, as the measure of its value, we are entitled to consider the present value estimated in labour of any fixed capital which is about to be employed in production, as representing the quantity of accumulated labour actually so applied. It is further necessary, as before stated [p. 186], to reckon the remaining value of the fixed capital as a part of the produce resulting from the whole of the accumulated and immediate labour employed. When, however, these corrections have been made, all the cases in which fixed capital enters, which may be said to include the great mass of commodities, will be found to answer to the theory as accurately as the simplest case that can be stated.'

where there occur changes in the labour embodiment in a (given) corn wage.

The inverse relation – covering variable corn wages and varying productivity in the simplest case of advances consisting only of wages – is portrayed in the table accompanying the essay (above, p. 352, columns 5, 6, and 7): 'The first and most important truth illustrated in the table is, that, from the division of value into labour and profits, and the mode in which profits are always estimated, it follows necessarily, that the quantity of labour required to produce the wages of a given number of men, with the addition of the profits upon these advances estimated in labour, must always be exactly the same as the quantity of labour which the wages will command, and must together always make up the constant quantity which appears in the seventh column. But the quantity of labour required to produce the varying wages of ten men is, under the different circumstances supposed, very different, as appears in the fifth column; and it is obvious, that while the numbers in the fifth column vary, the numbers in the seventh column, or the quantity of labour and profits united, cannot be constant, unless, *as the quantity of labour required to produce the wages of ten men increases, the quantity of profits estimated in labour [column 6] diminishes exactly in the same degree*' (200; emphasis added). Malthus simply heads his column 6: 'Quantity of Profits on the Advances of labour,' whereas in the text just cited he refers to 'profits upon these advances *estimated* in labour.'[82] Now we have just seen that the labour input in corn wages is said to be proportionate to the share of the total product going to labour; that is, 'the variable quantity of labour required to obtain [the corn wages of a given number of labourers], will always exactly agree with the proportion of the whole produce which goes to labour.' Thus if the share of labour in the product of 150 is 120, or 80 per cent, it will be found that the labour input in the 120 wages paid to 10 men is 8 since with an output per man of 15 units, 8 men are required to produce 120 units.[83] But what of profits? We apparently need an amount in *labour commanded* since that is Malthus's estimating index[84] – not labour embodied (though the heading of column 6 is ambiguous and though column 5 *is* in labour embodied

82 See also: 'the quantity of labour required to produce the varying corn wages of the given number of men with the profits *estimated also in quantity of labour*'; or 'an exact balance of labour, and of profits *estimated in labour*, so as to yield always a constant quantity' (200; emphasis added).

83 Costabile's formal calculation of column 8 (1983, 151n), which emphasizes the time factor, seems justified by Malthus's express assumption that 'the first set of labourers who produce the wages are paid the same as the second set whose labour the produce commands' (195).

84 In calculating the 'natural value' of a given quantum of product, we add to labour embodiment an amount representing profits on that embodiment again *estimated* in labour (e.g., 187).

so that we would be summing labour embodied and labour commanded to obtain a constant labour command of 10). Although Malthus does not formally do so, this can in fact be obtained by calculating the corn wages required to produce the advances – namely, 96 units (wage per head at 12 and 8 men required to produce 120 units) leaving 24 units as profits, that is, a command over 2 men; or, since we are given the profit rate, estimating profits as 25 per cent x 96 = 24 units or command over 2.[85]

The inverse relation as formulated above – 'as the quantity of labour required to produce the wages of ten men increases, the quantity of profits, estimated in labour, diminishes exactly in the same degree' – *amounts to Ricardo's position regarding profit-rate determination, though arrived at by way of the labour-command index.* A second 'truth' is also pure Ricardo – namely, that, given productivity, the profit rate varies inversely with the corn wage, though it is always possible for a productivity increase to compensate (perhaps more than compensate) for a corn-wage increase: '2dly. It appears from the Table, that given the produce obtained by ten men, then as corn wages rise, the value of the produce will fall or command less labour; and the constant value of the advances in labour absorbing a larger proportion of the value of the produce, profits will fall in proportion. But when more is produced by the same number of persons, then unless the corn wages rise so high as exactly to balance it, the value of the whole produce is increased, and the rate of profits and corn wages may both rise at the same time. Thus while the produce is 130 quarters, as labour rises from ten to twelve quarters, profits fall in an opposite direction from 30 per cent. to 8.3 per cent.; but if we compare the wages of labour when the produce is 130 quarters, with the wages of labour when the produce is 150, it appears that labour may rise from twelve to thirteen quarters, at the same time that profits rise from 8.3 to 15.38' (201).[86]

Malthus took the opportunity to emphasize the quantitative significance of a rising corn wage relative to diminishing returns as a 'cause' of falling profits: 'A fourth result shown in the Table is, that the value of the corn obtained by ten men depends mainly upon the rate of profits, which again depends mainly upon the demand and supply of corn compared with labour [i.e., the corn wage]. If corn be in such demand, that notwithstanding the fertility of the soil, a small quantity of it comparatively will purchase the labour required, profits will be very high, and the value of the produce will greatly exceed the constant value of the wages of the labour

85 I rely here on Nakaya, 1985.

86 Malthus is here comparing columns 9 and 7 rather than 7 and 5. The proportionate shares are less obvious; but nothing is changed of substance – it is the same whether we take '10 units' (7) as our base and: (a) work 'backwards' to a quantity of labour embodied *in the wage* of 8 units (5) calculating a profit rate of (10 – 8)/8 = 25 per cent; or (b) work 'forward' to a quantity of labour commanded by the product calculating a profit rate of (12.5 – 10)/10 = 25 per cent.

advanced; but if the supply of corn be so great, compared with labour, that a large quantity of it is required to purchase the given quantity of labour, profits will be low, and the excess of the value of the produce above the constant value of the advances in wages will be considerable' (202). This quantitative evaluation[87] is based on the partial figures selected in the table, a selection which does not pretend to deal with the entire path of corn wages and the profit rate until a stationary state is achieved. Had Malthus done so he would have shown the *necessary fall* of the profit rate, notwithstanding a *necessary decline* in the corn wage, since the latter is constrained relative to the rate of decline in productivity – as he well knew (see above, section II).[88]

X OBJECTIONS TO THE LAW OF MARKETS

Malthus maintained in *The Measure of Value* that 'there was scarcely any of the science in which [his measure] will not tend to simplify and facilitate our inquiries' (1823b/1986, 7, 207). His opposition to the Law of Markets stands out in this context.

In the first place, an increasing 'value of corn' in terms of labour command, or a reduced corn wage, is beneficial to labour demand; conversely, a decreasing value of corn (an increase in the corn wage) may be prejudicial. This latter proposition is then reworded in terms of *excess commodity supply*, apparently alluding to a fall in general prices – not of corn alone – relative to the wage: 'On the subject of labour it would determine, that the increasing *value* of the funds destined for the maintenance of labour can alone occasion an increase in the demand for it, or the will and power to employ a greater number of labourers; and that it is consistent with theory, as well as general experience, that high corn wages, in proportion to the quantity of work done, should frequently occur with a very slack demand for labour; or, in other words, that when the value of the whole produce falls from excess of supply compared with the demand, it cannot have the power of setting the same number of labourers to work' (208). As for the theory of profits, his measure 'would show, that they are determined, not by the varying value of a given quantity of labour compared with the constant value of the commodities which it produces, but, as is more conformable to our experience, by the variable value of the

87 This happens to be precisely the opposite of Torrens's evaluation; cf. Torrens, 1819, 458.

88 The rise in the value (labour commanded) of corn over the full trend path reflects the higher embodiment of labour somewhat modified by the fall in the profit rate. In Malthus's partial table we do have the rise in the value of corn upon reductions in the corn wage, but this is accompanied by both increases and decreases in the profit rate, depending on the arbitrarily selected *relative* rates of decline of the corn wage and labour productivity.

commodities produced by a given quantity of labour, compared with the constant value of such labour; and that profits never, on any occasion, rise or fall, unless the value of the produce of a given quantity of labour rises or falls, either from the temporary or ordinary state of the demand and supply.'[89] This statement alludes to the second major outcome of the table (above, p. 491, regarding 1823b/1986, 7, 201), involving a comparison of columns 9 and 7. His proposition now is quite misleading. It introduces 'the state of demand and supply' as if its relevance had been *demonstrated*, whereas all he had shown in his table was a varying value of the produce in terms of its command over labour, given agricultural productivity and the corn wage.

What was Malthus attempting to do by this new formulation? (We bear in mind his agreement that the profit rate is a matter of proportionate shares.) He was evidently opening the door for the doctrine of the possibility of excess *general* commodity supply reducing revenues relative to costs, implying that no one who used Ricardo's measure of proportionate shares could allow for excess aggregate supply.[90] In point of fact, Ricardo rejected the phenomenon on the wholly independent grounds of Say's Law.

Malthus also had in mind particular or industry profits, asserting that such profits will be reduced in the event of excess *industry* supply – as if anyone had ever denied the proposition. The issue is raised in a later passage involving certain implications of his analysis: 'On the general subject of demand and supply, it would show that they must be restored to their universal empire, both in reference to the prices of commodities, and the dependence of the progress of wealth on the due proportion maintained between them' (209). In the subsequent discussion of the

89 See also *Principles*, 1836, 292–3, (cited above, p. 481), based on his own theory of value in his Chapter II. A similar contrast between his own and the Ricardian perspective is given in the *Quarterly Review*: 'The new school suppose that the mass of commodities obtained by the same quantity of labour remains always substantially of the same value, and that the variations of profits are determined by the variations in the value of this quantity of labour; while Adam Smith and Mr. Malthus suppose that the value of the same quantity of labour remains substantially the same, and that the variations of profits are determined by the variations in the value of the commodities produced by this same quantity of labour. In the one case, the varying value of labour is considered as the great moving principle in the progress of wealth; in the other, the varying value of the *produce* of labour' (1824a/1986, 7, 295).

90 This in fact also emerges earlier in a criticism of Torrens's 'capital' theory of value: 'Colonel Torrens, by representing capital under the form of certain quantities of cloth and corn, instead of value in labour, has precluded himself from the possibility of giving a just view either of value, profits, or effectual demand. An increase of cloth and corn from the same quantity of labour is of no avail whatever in increasing value, profits, or effectual demand, if this increased produce will not command so much labour as before, an event which is continually occurring, from deficiency of demand' (189n).

'general subject of demand and supply,' Malthus contrasted two versions of cost but insisted in both cases on the role of 'demand and supply' in determining the extent of profits: 'If the cost of a commodity be considered as composed exclusively of the actual advances of the capital required for its production, which seems to be the most natural and correct mode of viewing it,[91] then it is obvious, that as both the prices and values of commodities are proportioned to these advances, with the *addition* of profits very variable in their amount, neither of them can be determined by these advances alone, or by the costs of production so defined. We must therefore have recourse to demand and supply. And on the other hand, if profits be included in the costs of production, then, as it follows, from the constancy of the value of labour, that ordinary profits are determined by the ordinary demand compared with the ordinary supply of the products of the same quantity of labour, the certain conclusion must be, that demand and supply enter powerfully into the costs of production according to this latter definition, and that therefore their dominion as to prices and value is absolutely universal' (209–10). But again, when we look attentively at the matter, it emerges that nothing has been *demonstrated* regarding the role of demand–supply, even as far as concerns particular industries.

There is a further dimension to consider. It is the proposition in a note attached to the preceding text that excluding demand and supply, from costs implies *constant corn wages.* Malthus is here applying the expression 'demand and supply,' not to products in the normal sense, but to the determinants of the corn wage in the context of a corn model. This is indicated by references to the history of British corn wages and also to the United States, where agricultural productivity was so high in terms of corn output per capita that only enormous corn wages restrained the profit rate from rising to 100 per cent: 'In order to exclude demand and supply from the costs of production when ordinary profits are considered as making a part of them, it would be necessary to assume that the corn wages of labour are always the same, an assumption which would be quite unwarranted, not only in reference to short periods, but to periods of fifty or sixty years, as the history of corn wages in this country alone amply testifies (see ch. iv. sect. 4, of my Princ. of Pol. Econ. &c.); and what but the state of the demand and supply of corn, compared with labour, prevents profits in the United States from being 100 per cent.? The quantity of corn divided between the labourer and capitalist would be amply sufficient to

91 A note at this point reads: 'This is the view taken of it by Colonel Torrens in his *Production of Wealth,* which I think the just one; because it makes the proper distinction between cost and value, on which the great stimulus to production depends. But he has most unnecessarily and incorrectly given the same interpretation to *natural price,* which always includes profits.'

yield such profits, if the corn wages of labour were no higher than in England' (210n).[92]

* * *

We revert to the main issue. Nothing in *The Measure of Value* – neither the table nor the discussion surrounding it – demonstrates the dependency of the profit rate on aggregate demand–supply. On the contrary, the argument points to the central role played in profit-rate determination by the *corn wage* – which amounts on the 'backward-looking' scheme to the *labour embodied in the corn wage* (as with Ricardo) and on the 'forward-looking' scheme to a complex of the corn wage and the (physical) output of the labour for which the corn wage is paid (above, notes 34 and 86). Deficiency of aggregate demand is a matter of supplementary doctrine, the validity of which is simply asserted in *The Measure of Value.*

J.S. Mill, in his *Morning Chronicle* review (see chapter 7: XII), reacted as one might expect to the implication drawn by Malthus for 'the subject of labour' (above, p. 492): 'This is Mr. M.'s favourite doctrine of over-production ...' (Mill, 1823/1986, XXII, 58). And the case was 'unmeaning,' turning as it did on the phrase 'The value of the whole produce falls': 'What does this mean? The exchangeable value? No: for the *whole produce* can have no exchangeable value, as it is never, at least collectively, exchanged. Any other kind of value? But with no other kind have we any thing to do. By value, we uniformly mean exchangeable value. This is the only legitimate use of the term.' This specific criticism is unfair since Malthus evidently intended the value of the whole produce in terms of *labour.* But it is true that the focus of attention has been entirely altered since the substance of *The Measure of Value* dealt formally with the supply conditions pertinent to *individual* commodities, not aggregate supply.

92 The same expression was used earlier – the 'rate of profits ... depends mainly upon the demand and supply of corn compared with labour' – in a discussion concerning the effect on profits of *variations of the corn wage,* where Malthus again asserted that this demonstrates the significance of 'demand and supply': 'This shows how greatly the natural value of commodities depends upon the average state of the demand and supply, and completely confirms the position in my last work, that the only difference between natural and market prices is, that the former are regulated by the average and ordinary relations of the demand to the supply, and the latter, when they differ from the former, upon the accidental and extraordinary relations of the demand to the supply' (202). And again, in insisting that constant corn wages are not the norm, considering both 'temporary variations' and the variable *trend,* he expresses the latter in terms of 'the demand and supply of corn compared to labour': 'But in the progress of cultivation, the corn wages of labour do not continue the same, and corn must consequently be liable to great variation of value, both on account of temporary variations in the state of the supply compared with labour, and on account of the more permanent state of the demand and supply of corn compared with labour, owing to the increasing difficulty of production' (194).

The aggregate-demand issue arises also in Malthus's discussion of the implications of the labour-command measure for 'the general progress of wealth' (1823b/1986, 7, 210). Two situations adverse to continuous progress are considered: 'If commodities and the materials of capital increase faster than the effectual demand for them, profits fall prematurely, and the capitalists are ruined without a proportionate benefit to the labouring classes, because an increasing demand for labour cannot go on under such circumstances. If the value of commodities and the materials of capital increase for some time without an increase of their quantity, the labouring classes must soon be supported on the lowest amount of food on which they will consent to keep up their actual number; and the main part of the population would suffer severely without any proportionate benefit to the capitalists; *because the value of their capitals, measured by the labour which they can command, would shortly be incapable of further increase.* In either of these cases a decided check would be given to the progress of wealth ...' (emphasis added). In fact, a maximum growth rate required that 'the joint product of the capitalist and labourer, which the state of the land and the skill with which it is worked enable them to obtain, is so divided between them, that in the progress of cultivation and improvement any unnecessary or premature fall either of profits or corn wages is prevented.' And this implied, in turn, 'a proper proportion of the supply to the demand, that is ... an accumulation so proportioned to the actual consumption of produce by those who can make an effectual demand for it, as to occasion the greatest permanent annual increase in the value of the materials of capital.'

Mill – after asking of the putative premature fall in the profit rate: 'what has this to do with the measure of value?' – responded to all this by excluding the possibility of excess supply, leaving only the rise in the real wage as cause of a low profit rate: 'Why do profits fall prematurely? Because, from the increase of capital faster than labour, wages rise. There is no other cause which can lower profits. And yet, in the same breath, Mr. M. tells us, that there is no proportionate benefit to the labouring classes! If this case were to happen, the only consequence would be, that accumulation would cease to go on at this enormous rate, and would be continued only at the same rate with the increase of population. If Mr. M. confines to this case his doctrine of over-production, we may make the concession with perfect safety' (1823/1986, XXII, 59). It is true that in his first letter to Malthus regarding *The Measure of Value,* Ricardo himself had been much more accommodating: 'Allowing you your premises, I see very few instances in which I can quarrel with your conclusions. I agree with all you say concerning the glut of commodities; allow to you your measure and it is impossible to differ in the result' (29 April 1823; in Ricardo, 1951–73, IX, 283). But shortly before he had himself insisted that 'all the science of Political Economy' may be explained with either index (281). The 'Ricardian' response to Malthus seems rather to be that given by Mill.

Malthus himself certainly *believed* that his measure legitimized his rejection of Say's Law,[93] and this position is frequently found in the secondary literature.[94] He proceeded assertively regarding the implications for foreign trade, with an eye to that rejection, presuming again that his own position *depended* on his selected measure: 'On the subject of foreign trade, it would show that its universally acknowledged effect in giving a stimulus to production, generally, is mainly owing to its increasing the value of the produce of a country's labour by the extension of demand, before the value of its labour is increased by the increase of its quantity; and that the effect of every extension of demand, whether foreign or domestic, is always, as far as it goes, to increase the average rate of profits till this increase is counteracted by the further accumulation of capital' (1823a/1986, 7, 208–9).[95] This issue is elaborated in chapter 11: VI, X.

XI SUMMARY AND CONCLUSION

We found in chapter 4 that, by late 1819, Malthus – in correspondence with Ricardo – was accounting for the secular fall in the corn wage (and thus deceleration of population growth) in terms of an increasing labour/land ratio, and for the secular decline in the manufacturing profit rate, in terms of 'competition of capitals' or expanding aggregate supply relative to demand. For the reasons we suggested there – which include pressure from Ricardo – it is likely that Malthus did allow a *direct* effect of diminishing returns on the agricultural profit rate, though he often seemed loath

93 But at one point in *The Measure of Value* Malthus implies that use of his measure precludes aggregate-demand deficiency: 'On the subject of the accumulation of capital it would show that if the increase of capital be measured by the increase of its materials, such as corn, clothing, &c., then it is obvious that the supply of these materials may, by saving, increase so rapidly, compared with labour and the wants of the effective demanders, that with a greater quantity of materials the capitalist will neither have the power nor the will to set in motion the same quantity of labour, and that consequently the progress of wealth will be checked; but that if the increase of capital be measured, as it ought to be, by the increase of its power to command labour, then accumulation so limited cannot possibly go on too fast' (1823b/1986, 7, 209). This I find difficult to appreciate.

94 Cf. Costabile, 1983, 144–5; Costabile and Rowthorn, 1985, 421; Negishi, 1993, 119. It is revealing that, though the models ascribed to Malthus by Costabile and Rowthorn, on the one hand, and by Negishi, on the other, both insist upon the labour-commanded measure as essential, they are yet very different (see chapter 11, note 3). Moreover, we shall find that in fact Malthus himself frequently used a bullion-command measure (e.g. chapter 7, pp. 320–1; also chapter 11, pp. 534, 556).

Myint, 1948, ch. III, gives Malthus good press. But even on this account the possibility of excess saving seems to be recognized as an independent phenomenon (52).

95 A note reads: 'If profits rise in some departments without falling proportionally in others, the *average* rate of profits will have increased, although, from the difficulty of moving capital, the rate of profits in some employments may not have had time to rise before the stimulus to such rise comes to an end by a fresh increase of capital.' Once again he points to the demand side.

to admit it; to this rate the manufacturing rate conformed, and this by way of the *indirect* effect of increasing land scarcity acting on population growth, and consequently on the demand for manufactures. In this way land scarcity – in addition to the pressure of excess aggregate supply – contributes to the fall in the manufacturing rate. We also found evidence of Malthus's acceptance of the inverse wage–profit relation as a theorem regarding proportions, though he objected to the role played by Ricardo's money wage, a role dictated by the Ricardian measure of value.

In the present chapter we have found the acceptance of the proportionality theorem confirmed in the *Principles* – indeed there is evidence of increased support for it – and also strengthened adherence to a direct effect of agricultural productivity on the profit rate as well as on the corn wage. Malthus goes so far as to develop a corn-profit model for the agricultural profit rate, the manufacturing rate coming into line by relative-price variations mediated via the competition-of-capital process. The indirect effect of land scarcity on the manufacturing rate acting via decelerating population growth, and consequently demand for manufactures, is not, however, to be found in the *Principles* (though it is not explicitly excluded as one force at play).

All this turns on the analysis in the *Principles* in the chapters on Wages and Profits, with supporting evidence from *The Measure of Value* (1823) and the article for the *Quarterly Review* (1824). But section V of the Rent chapter – the context relates to the effect on the profit rate of agricultural contraction – raises some serious interpretative problems. In the first place, the agricultural profit rate – the rate on investments at the *intensive* margin is specified – is there said to be governed by the 'general' rate: 'With regard to the capital which the tenant may lay out on his farm in obtaining more produce without paying additional rent for it, the rate of its returns must obviously conform itself to the general rate of profits [1836, determined by other causes]' (1820, 189; 1836, 182). By the general rate is intended the rate in manufacturing, which would not rise with agricultural contraction. The 1820 version takes for granted a reduction in the money wage with agricultural contraction, which – in Smithian fashion – assures that manufacturing prices decline, though what precisely happens to the profit rate is unclear: 'If the prices of manufactured and mercantile commodities were to remain the same notwithstanding the fall of labour, profits would certainly be raised; but they would not remain the same, as was shewn in the preceding chapter.[96] The new prices of commodities and the new profits of stock would be determined upon principles of competition; and whatever the rate was, as so determined, capital would be taken from the land till this rate was attained. The profits of capital employed in the way just described must always follow and can never lead or

96 It is not clear where. Ricardo did not know (1951–73, II, 174).

regulate' (1820, 189–90). The 1836 version omits the foregoing explicit rationalization and merely asserts that the rate of return on marginal capital applications to land – it is unclear why the proposition is limited to the intensive margin – must conform to 'the general rate of the profits determined by other causes since it 'must always follow, but can never lead or regulate' (1836, 182–3).[97] Taken at face value, these strong statements *negate* the notion of the agricultural rate as lead sector. We are witness to something of a throwback to the early correspondence, with its heavy weighting of the manufacturing sector.[98]

Equally frustrating is Malthus's summary in both editions in the same context. The summary contrasts expansion where 'the last land taken into cultivation is rich' – where diminishing returns does *not* apply – and the profit rate is high, with a case involving contraction to land of higher productivity owing to easier corn importation: 'in the regular progress of a country towards general cultivation and improvement, and in a natural state of things, it may fairly be presumed, that *if the last land taken into cultivation be rich,* capital is scarce, and profits will then certainly be high; but if land be thrown out of cultivation on account of means being found of obtaining corn cheaper elsewhere, no such inference is justifiable. On the contrary, capital may be abundant, compared with the demand for corn and commodities, in which case and during the time that such abundance lasts, whatever may be the state of the land, profits must be low' (1820, 190; 1836, 183; emphasis added).[99] The proposition that expansion, assuming 'rich' land, proceeds at a high profit rate is thus rationalized in terms of *capital scarcity* rather than *agricultural productivity.* But Malthus merely asserts that capital will be 'scarce' and provides no justifica-

97 The revised version adds a forced rationalization for the notion that rents enter into costs despite the fact that no rent is paid at the *intensive* margin – namely, that marginal costs are higher than they would otherwise be were rent-free *extensions* possible: 'It is true that when the price of corn had settled itself, there would be some corn produced on the old cultivated land, the cost of producing which without rent would be just about equal to such a price. But it is quite certain that if instead of laying out so much additonal capital on the lands in tillage, the capitalists could have obtained the untilled land without rents, the price of corn would not have risen so high, or have required so much labour and other capital to produce the actual quantity; and consequently the rents of such lands clearly add to the price of corn, and form a part of the costs of production' (1836, 183).

98 We should, however, keep in mind that the problem arises in the context of a special issue involving: (1) agricultural contraction; and (2) variation specifically at the intensive margin.

99 'This is a distinction,' the 1820 text continues, 'of the greatest practical importance, which ... has been quite overlooked by Mr. Ricardo.' In the 1836 version the reference to Ricardo is omitted: 'These are all points of great practical consequence which have been much overlooked. The doctrine of the gradations of soils is a most important one, but in drawing practical conclusions from it, great care should be taken to apply it correctly.'

tion. The only rationalization I can think of is the mechanism of his pre-*Principles* correspondence involving the effect of land-scarcity conditions on population growth and the demand for manufactures. Specifically, 'rich' land assures a high demand relative to supply, that is, *capital scarcity* and a high manufacturing rate. In the case of agricultural *contraction* with easier corn imports, capital is released from agriculture and 'may be abundant compared with the demand for corn and commodities.'[100] The *temporary* nature of the depressing effect on the profit rate may also be significant. It lasts 'during the time that such abundance lasts' – leaving open the possibility that the 'state of the land' will *ultimately* act to regulate the profit rate.[101]

We return by way of summary to the measurement problem. Malthus's support for his labour-commanded measure of absolute value, or of dated labour input, is most conspicuous in the course of objections made to Ricardo's notion of a secular increase in *the value of the wage* – reflecting higher labour embodied in the wage basket. For Malthus, the value of the (corn) wage is necessarily *constant* no matter what the magnitude of the basket; Ricardo had neglected the so-called principle of compensation (1823b/1986, 7, 192n; chapter 7, p. 306). Malthus always denied that his result reflected the *arbitrary* definition of 'value' as labour commanded. Rather, since labour commanded could be shown to measure precisely absolute costs, the necessary constancy of the 'value' of the wage was an economically meaningful proposition.

But, in fact, Malthus had gained nothing by his procedures. Consider his treatment of a fall in the corn wage, agricultural productivity given. The smaller corn basket having the same 'value' as the larger, each unit of corn must have *risen* in 'value'; that is, its supply or cost conditions have worsened (and the 'esteem' in which it is held increased); but, since productivity is unchanged, this indicates a rise in the profit rate, and thus in the profit element within costs. Allow next for diminishing agricultural returns and assume a *constant* corn wage: By the latter assumption, the absolute value of corn per unit is constant, but real labour costs have increased, from which we may deduce that the profit rate must be lower to counteract precisely. In the event of a *falling* corn wage with expansion subject to diminishing agricultural returns, the value of (labour commanded by) corn per unit rises. This increase reflects the assumed higher labour embodiment which is only partially counteracted by a lower profit rate. Malthus's belief that he had undermined the Ricardian analysis of value and distribution by use of his labour-command measure of absolute value was, therefore, wishful thinking, since these same results are, of course,

100 The application of the 'competition of capitals' perspective to *corn* as well as manufactures ('commodities') is not typical.

101 Subject presumably to complications created by *rent* payments.

achieved in Ricardo's growth system. In the case of a *constant* corn wage, the incidence of diminishing returns falls wholly on the capitalists; in the case of a *falling* corn wage, it is shared between capital and labour. The only difference between the systems is that no causal role is accorded by Malthus to the money wage rate in the growth process in the derivation of these results, since it is fixed by construction.

That the results are precisely those that emerge in the Ricardian model is easily explained. At a formal or mathematical level, it makes no difference which *numéraire* is chosen. And this proves to be the case in this particularly important respect: that it is immaterial whether labour embodied or labour commanded is adopted as a *proportions-measuring* device. Ricardo, in effect, defined the value of output per man-hour as unity, so that the labour embodied in the wage per man-hour emerges as a fraction of unity, the residual constituting profits; Malthus defined the value of the wage per man-hour as unity, so that the labour required to produce that wage emerges as a fraction of unity and the residual constitutes profits. The inverse wage–profit relation as a theorem regarding proportions and all of Ricardo's substantive applications emerge using Malthus's device and *vice versa*. None the less, as both Ricardo and J.S. Mill insisted, there were positive *disadvantages* of working with the Malthusian measure. It was unhelpful – especially from the labourer's point of view – to envisage constancy of the value of labour despite changes in productivity conditions in the wage-goods sector, and worse still despite changes in the real (corn) wage reflecting changes in labour-market conditions.[102]

Finally, there is the 'implication' drawn for the Law of Markets from the labour-commanded measure. This altered the focus from its microeconomic concern with the supply conditions of particular commodities – the predominant concern throughout the body of *The Measure of Value* – to an aggregate perspective. The possibility of excess aggregate supply logically stands *independently* of Malthus's index – *vide* J.S. Mill's formulation of the problem of realization reflecting a failure of coordination between *ex ante* decisions to produce and to buy (1830) – and in fact his rejection of the Law of Markets can be found long before the case for the measuring index was established. But his enthusiasm for it certainly reflected a conviction that it did provide unrefutable confirmation of that rejection.

102 There was too Malthus's justification (discussed in chapter 7, p. 305) of his choice of *numéraire* on the grounds that supply conditions reflect specifically *labour* allowance made for time of embodiment and weighted by the profit rate. For Ricardo and J.S. Mill, labour as such is *not* the input individual capitalists are concerned with, while the profit rate can be measured by *any* of the products of the system.

III / EMPLOYMENT, AGGREGATE DEMAND, AND MONEY

ELEVEN

Sustainable growth: Accumulation and the aggregate-demand problem

I INTRODUCTION

The last and longest chapter in the *Principles* – 'On the Progress of Wealth'[1] – analyses the problem of constrained growth, notwithstanding high growth potential: 'There is scarcely any inquiry more curious, or, from its importance, more worthy of attention, than that which traces the causes which practically check the progress of wealth in different countries, and stop it, or make it proceed very slowly, while the power of production remains comparatively undiminished, or at least would furnish the means of a great and abundant increase of produce and population' (1820, 345; 1836, 309).[2] The issue at hand is distinguished from stationariness reflecting land scarcity. The focus was to be on aggregate-demand considerations: 'It has been fully stated and allowed, that a period of stagnation [1836: of comparative stagnation] must finally arrive in every country from the difficulty of procuring subsistence. But an indisposition to consume in large quantities the goods produced at home, and want of the means of advantageous barter may occasion, and [1836: But a deficiency of effectual demand] has often occasioned a similar stagnation at a very early period

1 In 1820 the full title is 'On the Immediate Causes of the Progress of Wealth,' reduced in 1836 to 'On the Progress of Wealth.'

2 The 'practical question ... what are the more immediate and effective stimulants in the continued creation and progress of wealth,' had its counterpart in the *Essay on Population*, which 'endeavoured to trace the causes which practically keep down the population of a country to the level of its actual supplies. It is now my object to shew what are the causes which chiefly influence these supplies, or call the powers of production forth into the shape of increasing wealth.' The 'practical question' is particularly well summarized in letters to Ricardo dated 7 and 16 July 1821 (see below, pp. 519–21).

[1836: an early period] of a nation's progress' (1820, 448; 1836, 388). But apart from stagnation at early stages of development, stagnation resulted also: (1) from failures of demand owing to a variety of circumstances peculiar to a relatively advanced economy, as in the postwar years; and (2) from *excessive* 'saving' – saving in the sense of investment.[3] The major concern in his chapter on Progress was with the second problem, and, more precisely, to define *the preconditions of sustainable output expansion.* The war period (1793–1813/14) provided a striking illustration of unparalleled sustainable growth, in that the creation of new capacity by 'saving' or 'accumulation' was in response to, and out of, initially increased profits. But should capitalists respond to high profits by expanding capacity too rapidly – and, specifically, finance accumulation by reducing (luxury) consumption – the result would be unused or underutilized capital, unemployment or underemployment of labour, and low profits. In effect, Malthus was elaborating the Smithian conception of increased 'competition of capitals' which entails a reduced profit rate and reduced commodity prices in consequence of expanded capacity; but he went much farther in seeking the means of avoiding such an outcome. (Unfortunately, too few cases are cited by Malthus to document the phenomenon of excessive accumulation.)[4] The present chapter, therefore, concerns stagnation

3 Mention should be made of cases of stagnation owing to 'great expenditure' which absorbs the surplus. (This is mentioned in the chapter 'Of the Profits of Capital' and is not central to the chapter on the 'Progress of Wealth.') For growth does require accumulation; it is *excessive* accumulation that is problematic: 'If for instance, in one country, with the last land taken into cultivation of a given fertility, capital were stationary, not from want of demand, but from great expenditure and the want of saving habits, it is certain that labour, after a time, would be paid very low, and profits would be very high' (1820, 309–10; absent in 1836). See also 1820, 373; 1836, 328–9 cited below, this chapter, p. 529.

4 The downward trend of interest and profit rates after *circa* 1750 despite the availability of cheap corn, thus excluding any explanation in terms of land scarcity, is cited: 'In the instance alluded to in a former chapter [1820, 318; 1836, 285], which occurred in this country in the middle of last century, there must have been a considerable difficulty in finding employment for capital, or the national creditors would rather have been paid off than have submitted to a reduction of interest from 4 per cent to $3\frac{1}{2}$, and afterwards to 3. And that this fall in the rate of interest and profits arose from a redundancy of capital and a want of demand for produce, rather than from the difficulty of production on the land, is fully evinced by the low price of corn at the time, and the very different state of interest and profits which has occurred since' (1820, 475–6; 1836, 405–6). As an added illustration: 'A similar instance took place in Italy in 1685, when, upon the Pope's reducing the interest of his debts from 4 to 3 per cent, the value of the principal rose afterwards to 112; and yet the Pope's territories have at no time been so cultivated as to occasion such a low rate of interest and profits from the difficulty of procuring the food of the labourer. Under a more favourable distribution of property, there cannot be a doubt that such a demand for produce, agricultural, manufacturing, and mercantile, might have been created, as to have prevented for many many years the interest of money from falling below 3 per cent. In both these cases, the demands of the landlords were added to those of the productive classes.'

generated by 'excessive' saving; stagnation pertinent to underdevelopment will also be taken up at the close. (The particular case of stagnation characterizing the postwar period is treated in the next, companion chapter.) In the course of these tasks we again encounter the major theoretical differences between the Malthusian and the Ricardian models turning on the legitimacy of the Law of Markets, for that law assured that expanded output with larger capacity was *necessarily* sustainable.[5]

We proceed as follows: section II establishes as a necessary preliminary Malthus's adherence to the Smithian productive–unproductive classification of labour with its view of 'wealth' as material product. We then turn in section III to the first of our substantive tasks. This entails the dual proposition that aggregate-demand constraints must prevent full use of larger capacity resulting from increased savings should such increase be financed by positively reduced consumption; and that correction of the excess would take the form of a contraction of activity impinging on the level of employment. The 'solution' to the problem of sustainable growth is also spelled out. Required is a *preliminary* increase in the 'value' of the national product – in terms of labour commanded, though a money measure is also countenanced – to allow expansion of capacity without reduction of consumption. The role played by consumption out of wages is given special attention in section IV. Malthus's perspective raises the issue of the precise determinants of saving, the subject-matter of our section V. Here we clarify that the problem of saving arises from an excessive reaction to initially high profits and would not normally be pertinent in periods of depression. Problems would arise only if capitalists

5 A word is in order on an extensive secondary literature. It is a matter of controversy whether or not Malthus in his growth-theorizing maintained the *ex ante* equality of savings and investment. Such equality is strongly denied by Costabile (1983, 161), by Eltis (1984, 179), by Costabile and Rowthorn (1985, 423), and by Waterman (1996a); it is insisted on by Negishi (1993). Though I do not engage in (formal) rational reconstruction, the evaluation of such exercises must turn on the validity of the attributions made in this essential regard. And it emerges throughout from my reading of the texts that Negishi's position is the more accurate in the growth context. (Malthus's interpretation of the postwar depression – which, as I show in chapter 12, does *not* turn on his growth analysis – is another matter; it allows conspicuously for divergence between savings and investment.) Negishi also seems to capture Malthus's position regarding the source of savings. Though Malthus recognized savings by classes other than the capitalists – landlords, rentiers, and even labour – it emerges that the problem of *excessive* saving turns largely on the behaviour of capitalists. Negishi's reconstruction, according to which only capitalists save, is therefore a helpful approximation.

I am also troubled by reconstructions – such as those mentioned above – in which the essence of Malthus's argument (the 'hard core') is formulated in terms of a one-sector model and a neglect of fixed capital; on my reading, one of Malthus's primary concerns was with a multisector economy, entailing both manufacturing and agriculture, in which real changes in capacity are of the essence. (But for a different perspective, see Waterman, 1995, 38.)

respond positively at such periods to inappropriate appeals for increased savings on grounds of 'patriotism.'

After outlining Malthus's formal difference with Ricardo on 'gluts' in sections VI and VII – the latter offering a micro-economic rationale for his objection – we return to the substance of Malthus's position as it relates to growth, specifically the means of assuring sustainable growth by initially raising the value of aggregate output. The role accorded trade in this regard is the subject-matter of section VIII; this is accompanied by a section which digresses to demonstrate Malthus's recognition of efficiency gains from trade, notwithstanding his objections to Ricardo's analysis. We return then to the main issue: section X concerns the problem of appropriate measurement, and XI the assurance of finance to maintain the higher level of money incomes generated by extended trade – the endogeneity of financial means.

Sections XII and XIII consider, respectively, property distribution – in effect a case for greater equality from the perspective of aggregate demand – and the role of 'unproductive consumption' – whether demand emanating from outside the productive sector is a *necessary* condition of successful growth. Malthus's rejection of 'new inventions' as a potential stimulus to sustainable growth, and objections to the Ricardian analysis of machinery, are taken up in section XIV. A related discussion of gross versus net revenue follows in section XV.

The bulk of this chapter relates to contemporary Britain and other advanced economies. Our final substantive section (XVI) is devoted to demand-side constraints in a developmental context.

II PRODUCTIVE AND UNPRODUCTIVE LABOUR

At the outset of the *Principles,* Malthus defended Adam Smith's distinction between 'productive' and 'unproductive' labour as essential to an understanding of the 'causes' of increasing national wealth (read: *income*) (1820, 30; 1836, 36).[6] The relation of productive labour to 'capital' is of two sorts. There is the conception of productive labour as that employed by capital rather than out of revenue, that is, labour engaged in (material) production by capitalists for purposes of profit rather than as a form of final consumption: 'In speaking ... and treating of capital, it seems quite [1836: highly] necessary to have some term for the kind of labour which it generally employs, in contradistinction to the kind of labour generally employed by revenue [1836: labour which in general is employed directly by revenue], in order to explain its nature and operation, and the causes of its increase [1836: the nature of productive labour, and its peculiar efficiency in causing the increase of wealth]' (1820, 31; 1836, 38). There is also a

6 As with Adam Smith, 'wealth' involves a flow, not a stock concept, with a counterpart in income generated in the course of producing (material) output.

narrower usage, that of labour *in the capital-goods sector.* For example, a brief assertion in 1820 that 'the cause of the different effects of produce employed as capital, and of produce consumed as revenue ... arises from the different kinds of labour maintained by each' (31), is elaborated in the later version to refer both to labour *employed by capital* in the production of material goods with a view to profit, and to the narrower sense of *capital-goods* labour: 'It is obvious, for instance, that it is only the productive labour of Adam Smith, which can keep up, restore, or increase, the material capital of a country. It is also this kind of labour alone, that is, the labour which is realized in the production, or increased value of material objects, which requires a considerable amount of capital for its continued employment; but that, for which there is an effectual demand, will generally be supplied, and the practical consequence is such as might naturally be expected. In those countries which abound in the number, and especially in the skill of their productive labourers, capital and wealth abound. In those where personal services predominate, capital and wealth are comparatively deficient' (1836, 36–7).

Service labour employed by capital with a view to profit admittedly created a classificatory problem but was quantitatively of little significance, except in the case of education: 'It is true, that what is called capital, is sometimes employed in the maintenance of labour, which is not called productive; as by the managers of theatrical exhibitions, and in the payment of the expenses of education. In regard to the first kind of expenditure, however, it would be excluded from coming under the head of capital, if capital were defined, as I have defined it, namely, that portion of the stock or material possessions of a country which is kept or employed with a view to profit in the production or distribution of wealth. But at all events, the amount of it is too inconsiderable to be allowed to interfere with a classification in other respects correct, and in the highest degree useful' (37).

As for educational workers, those engaged in vocational training could legitimately be fitted into the category, if only at one remove: 'In regard to the expense of education, it should be recollected that no small portion of it is employed in acquiring the skill necessary to the production and distribution of material objects, as in the case of most apprenticeships; and as the persons who have the means of teaching this skill, are themselves employed in this sort of production and distribution; and that the skill so acquired will finally be realized, according to its value on material objects, the capital so employed must clearly be considered as maintaining productive labour, in the most natural sense of the term. The same may be said of all that is, expended in the maintenance of those kinds of labour which, though they appear to have the same general character as personal services, are yet so necessary to the production and distribution of material objects, as to be estimated in the value of those objects when they reach the consumer.' General and professional educators would, however, be excluded, and legitimately so: 'In regard to the remaining expenditure in education, it will be excluded from coming under the denomination of capital, by the definition of capital above adverted to: and it may fairly be questioned whether the expenses of general education, and even, for the most part, the education for the learned professions, ought not properly to be considered as being paid from revenue rather than from capital. Practically they seem to be so considered' (37–8). But more generally the Smithian classification held up well on quantitative grounds: 'But in whatever light we view the expenditure upon these services, which are not realized upon any material products, it must be allowed that the great source of what is peculiarly called profits, and the great mass of what is usually called wealth, is directly derived from the employment of material capital in the maintenance of what Adam Smith has called productive labour' (38).

Most relevant for our present purposes is the defence in both editions of the distinction between productive and unproductive labour turning on the Smithian theme that *saving entails spending, not hoarding, but spending which results in additions to the real capital stock.* This implies the narrower definition: 'it is stated by Adam Smith, and it must be allowed to be stated justly [1836: omits 'and ... justly'], that the produce which is annually saved is as regularly consumed as that which is annually spent, but that it is consumed by a different set of people. If this be the case, and *if saving be allowed to be the immediate cause of the increase of capital*, it must be absolutely necessary, in all discussions [1836: it must be desirable in all questions] relating to the progress of wealth, to distinguish by some particular title a set of people who appear to act so important a part in accelerating this progress' (1820, 31–2; 1836, 38; emphasis added). Here Malthus states explicitly the *full-employment axiom* that 'almost all the lower classes of people of every society are employed in some way or other'; and that '[no] political economist of the present day can by saving mean mere hoarding; and beyond this contracted and inefficient proceeding, no use of the term, in reference to national wealth, can well be imagined, but that which must arise from a different application of what is saved, founded upon a real distinction between the different kinds of labour which may be maintained by it' (1820, 32, 1836, 38–9).[7]

Malthus pointed out in 1820 that 'it is not the question at present whether saving may or may not be carried too far (a point which will be considered in its proper place); but whether we can talk intelligibly of saving and accumulation, and discuss their effects on national wealth

7 The retention of these latter formulations implies that we cannot read much into the omission in the second edition of the commendation of Adam Smith's proposition 'that the produce which is annually saved is as regularly consumed as that which is annually spent.'

without allowing some distinction in the different kinds of labour' (33). It proves to be the narrower definition of productive labour – labour in the capital-goods sector – that Malthus actually adopts (in both editions) when he finally considers the issue of excessive saving (below, section III).

The second edition engages in a lengthy critique of a proposal to replace Smith's productive-unproductive classification of *labour* by one relating to *consumption.* This elaboration seeks the most effective approach to 'the nature of saving.' While the term 'saving' is unfortunately used by Malthus in the loose sense of 'an increase of wealth and capital,' the weight of the emphasis is none the less on saving in the sense of *additions to capital.*

A *utility-based classification* is immediately dismissed as irrelevant from the 'saving' perspective: 'If, as some affirm' – presumably a reference to J.B. Say – 'every person is a reproductive consumer who obtains for himself a value equal to that which he consumes, it is obvious that all menial servants kept for pomp or pleasure will be productive consumers; but it is quite impossible that a saving, or an increase of wealth and capital can result to any individual from the employment of a great number of such reproductive consumers' (1836, 39). Even the preferable sense of *present sacrifice for future benefit* would be problematic, again from the perspective of 'saving,' with special attention given to the notion of *additions to capital* (39–40). Any definition of 'productive consumption' that helped elucidate the meaning of saving reduced in fact to Smith's valid classification: 'It appears then upon examination, that the use of the term productive consumption will not enable us to explain what is most usually and most correctly meant by individual and national saving, unless when it is so defined as to mean the very same thing that Adam Smith means by the employment of productive labour' (40).

There is one other line taken in defence of Smith's classification peculiar to the second edition. Malthus makes the point that, though unproductive workers might themselves save and 'add to the national capital,' productive workers alone 'furnish a large surplus to that other most important class of society which lives upon the profits of capital' (40–1).[8] For unproductive labourers received their income as a form of transfer: 'It is equally true that any person who received a portion of wealth as a gift might save some of it, and add to the national capital.'[9]

8 In drawing this distinction Malthus reverts from the narrow to the broader categorization – from labour specifically in the capital-goods sector to labour employed in the capitalist sector.

9 Malthus raises the rhetorical question: 'If the labour of menial servants be as productive of wealth as the labour of manufacturers, why should not savings be employed in their maintenance, not only without being dissipated, but with a constant increase of value [1836: their amount]?' (1820, 32; 1836, 39). The 'dissipation' refers to the final consumption of services in contrast with employment that reproduces output with a

Though this formulation is peculiar to 1836, in both editions Malthus approved of the almost equivalent proposition implied in Adam Smith's balance of annual produce and consumption as determinant of 'the progressive, stationary, or declining state of a society' (1820, 34; 1836, 41): 'If in given periods the produce of a country exceeds its consumption [1836: exceeds in a certain degree the consumption of those employed in its production], the means of increasing its capital will be provided, its population will soon increase [1836: will increase], or the actual numbers will be better accommodated, and probably both.' But the balance turned on the productive–unproductive distinction: 'Without some such distinction we shall not be able to trace the causes why one nation is thriving and another is declining; and [1836: nor will] the superior riches of those countries where merchants and manufacturers abound, compared with those in which the retainers of a court and an overgrown aristocracy [1836: and of a feudal aristocracy] predominate, will not admit [1836: ... predominate, admit] of an intelligible explanation' (1820, 34; 1836, 41–2). In the second edition a further sentence is added underscoring the *materiality* dimension: 'To such an explanation it is absolutely necessary, that by the balance of production and consumption, we should mean the production and consumption of material objects: for, if all the gratifications derived from personal services were to be included in the term produce, it would be quite impossible either to estimate such a balance, or even to say what was to be understood by it.'

Although the foregoing passage is absent in 1820, that edition too proceeds to a historical account along wholly Smithian lines of the key role played by altered taste patterns from personal services to 'material conveniences and luxuries' in the transition from feudal dual-class relations of 'dependency' to a modern system with its strategic profit-earning middle class. The emphasis is on material products as both *requiring* and *generating* capital, the latter 'almost exclusively' deriving from the manufacturing and trading sectors (1820, 35; 1836, 42–3). A note is added in the 1836 version: 'There can hardly be a more important inquiry in political economy than that which traces the effects of different proportions of productive labour, and personal services in society; but this inquiry cannot be conducted without the application of different terms to these two different kinds of

profit. In 1820, Ganilh's objection to the classification is mentioned from this perspective: 'One of the most able impugners of the doctrine of Adam Smith respecting productive labour is Mr. Ganilh, in his valuable Work on the various Systems of Political Economy [1812]; but he appears to me to fail entirely, when he attempts to shew that savings are preserved instead of being destroyed, when consumed by the idle classes. I cannot understand in what sense it can be said that menial servants annually reproduce the capital by which they are fed. Book III. c. ii.' (1820, 33n). Why this objection to Ganilh is omitted in the 1836 version is unclear.

labour; and the distinction made by Adam Smith appears to me to be the simplest and the most convenient' (42n). But in both versions the conclusion is the same – that 'some distinction between the different kinds of labour, with reference to their different effects on national wealth, must be admitted to be not only useful but necessary' (1820, 35–6; 1836, 43).[10]

A further condition is laid down that the designation 'productive' labour, to be a useful one, required the production of what is 'susceptible of some sort of definite valuation' (1820, 45; 1836, 46). This valuation requirement excluded 'law' and 'moral precepts,' though both in a sense 'susceptible of accumulation': 'How is it possible to estimate them, or to say to what amount the country has been enriched by them? whereas [1836: On the other hand,] the labour which is the necessary condition of the supply of material objects is estimated in the price at which they are sold, and may fairly be presumed to add to the wealth of the country an amount at least equal to the value paid for such labour' (1820, 46; 1836, 46). But little was added by the new condition, since 'probably, with few or no exceptions, it is only the kind of labour which is realized upon material products [1836: the labour which is realized upon material products is the only kind] that is, at once susceptible of accumulation and definite valuation.'

Two criticisms of Germain Garnier's edition of the *Wealth of Nations* (1802) throw light on Malthus's intentions here. The first rejects the objection by Garnier to Smith's classification that it designates as 'productive' the labour of the instrument makers – the material instrument constituting riches or wealth – but excludes the labour of musicians (see Pullen, in Malthus, 1820/1989, II, 309). For Malthus, on the contrary, 'the utility of [the Smithian definitions] is immediately obvious from the facility of giving a definite valuation to the instruments, and the absolute impossibility of giving such a valuation to all the tunes which may be played upon them' (1820, 46; 1836, 47). Why a value cannot be given to 'the tunes' is left unstated. But the contention is a prologue to a rejection of Garnier's further identification of business and government clerks, on grounds of

10 The restriction of 'wealth' to material products is considered from the perspective of consumption as well as that of capital: 'Some degree of duration, and a consequent susceptibility of accumulation, seems to be essential to our usual conceptions of wealth, not only because produce of this kind seems to be alone capable of forming these accumulations which tend so much to facilitate future production, but because they alone [1836: they so essentially] contribute to increase that store reserved for consumption, which is [1836: the possession of which is] certainly one of the most distinguishing marks of riches compared with poverty ... [In] every case of productive labour, as explained by Adam Smith, there is always a period, though in some cases it may be very short, when either the stock destined to replace a capital, or the stock reserved for immediate consumption is distinctly augmented by it; and to this quality of adding to the national stock, the term, enriching or productive of riches seems to be peculiarly appropriate' (1820, 44–5; 1836, 45–6).

efficiency and *marketability* criteria, the former guaranteed by the latter, as it were: 'To this [identification], however, it may be replied, that in all business conducted with a view to the profit of individuals, it may fairly be presumed that there are no more clerks or labourers of any kind employed, nor with higher salaries, than necessary. But the same presumption cannot be justly entertained with regard to the business of government; and as the results of the labours of its servants are not brought to market, nor their salaries distributed with the same rigid attention to the exchangeable value of their services, no just criterion is afforded for determining this value' (1820, 47; 1836, 47).

This forced distinction evidently did not satisfy Malthus's editor, who made out the case against Garnier in terms of government salaries constituting *transfer* payments, not *original* earnings.[11] But Malthus himself did not apparently follow this line, since for him those government workers engaged in *material* products should in fact be designated 'productive,' subject to satisfaction of the efficiency condition: 'At the same time it may be remarked, that if a servant of government performs precisely the same kind of labour in the preparation or superintendance of material products as the servant of a merchant, he ought to be considered as a productive labourer, and one among the numerous instances which are always occurring of productive labourers, or labourers occasionally productive, to be found among those classes of society which, with regard to the great mass of their exertions, may with propriety be characterized as unproductive. This kind of exception must of course frequently happen, not only among the servants of government, but throughout the whole range of menial service, and in every other situation in society' (1820, 47; 1836, 47–8). No mention is made of marketability, but possibly this is taken for granted.

III THE PROBLEM OF SUSTAINABLE GROWTH

Accumulation envisaged as a potential stimulus to sustainable growth is the subject-matter of section III of the chapter 'On the Progress of Wealth.' Malthus insisted – *pace* Lauderdale (2d. ed., 1819) – that 'saving from the stock which might have been destined for immediate consumption, and adding it to that which is to yield a profit' (the 'conversion of revenue into capital') is a necessary condition for a 'permanent and continued increase

11 Cazenove added the following explanatory note emphasizing government salaries as transfers: 'The application of Adam Smith's distinction, is in this, as in most other cases, preeminently clear. The merchant's clerk increases his master's wealth. He adds a value to the subject on which his labour is bestowed, for if he did not, he would not be employed. The same thing cannot be said of the Government clerk; however useful or necessary his services may be, he contributes nothing to the funds from whence he derives his remuneration. He lives at the expense of his employers, the nation at large, and is paid out of a tax or duty, not out of profit or reproduction' (1836, 47n).

of wealth' (1820, 351–2; 1836, 314). Lauderdale 'appears to have gone as much too far in deprecating accumulation, as some other writers in recommending it. This tendency to extremes is exactly what I consider as the great source of error in political economy [1836: where so much depends on proportions].'

The issue is the non-sustainability of an increased growth rate of real national income – excluding, of course, services – if achieved by an increased rate of accumulation specifically financed by reduced consumption. For Malthus, any such program must *necessarily* fail, as both the motive and the ability to save (indicated by the profit rate) weaken, and this quite apart from increasing land or labour scarcity. The problem is set forth in three important but tricky passages:

> [1] It is undoubtedly possible by parsimony to devote at once a much larger share than usual of the produce of any country to the maintenance of productive labour; and [1836: suppose this to be done,] it is quite true that the labourers so employed are consumers as well as unproductive labourers [1836: those engaged in personal services]; and as far as the labourers are concerned, there would be no diminution of consumption or demand. But ... that the consumption and demand occasioned by the persons [1836: workmen] employed in productive labour can never alone [1836: *alone*] furnish a motive to the accumulation and employment of capital; and with regard to the capitalists themselves, together with the landlords and other rich persons, they have, by the supposition, agreed to be parsimonious, and by depriving themselves of their usual conveniences and luxuries to save from their revenue and add to their capital. Under these circumstances, I would ask, how it is possible to suppose that [1836: under these circumstances, it is impossible that] the increased quantity of commodities, obtained by the increased number of productive labourers, should find purchasers, without such a fall of price as would probably sink their value below the costs of production [1836: below that of the outlay], or, at least, very greatly diminish [1836: so reduce profits as very greatly to diminish] both the power and the will to save. (1820, 352–3; 1836, 315)

> [2] In the case supposed there would evidently be an unusual quantity of commodities of all kinds in the market, owing to the unproductive labourers of the country [1836: those who had been before engaged in personal services] having been converted, by the accumulation of capital, into productive labourers; while the number of labourers altogether being the same, and the power and will to purchase for consumption among landlords and capitalists being by supposition diminished, commodities would necessarily fall in value compared with labour, so as to lower profits almost to nothing [1836: very greatly to lower profits], and to check for a time further production. But this is precisely what is meant by the term glut, which, in this case, is evidently general not partial. (1820, 354; 1836, 316)

[3] It will be readily allowed that a new commodity thrown into the market, which, in proportion to the labour employed upon it, is of higher exchangeable value than usual, is precisely calculated to increase demand; because it implies, not a mere increase of quantity, but [1836: an increase of value owing to] a better adaptation of the produce to the tastes, wants and consumption of the society. But to fabricate or procure commodities of this kind is the grand difficulty; and they certainly do not naturally and necessarily follow an accumulation of capital and increase of commodities, most particularly when such accumulation and increase have been occasioned by economy of consumption, or a discouragement to the indulgence of those tastes and wants, which are the very elements of demand [1836: and of value]. (1820, 356; 1836, 318)

The apparent presumption (see passage 2) that labour is drawn into the productive sector from personal services suggests a savings process involving reduced demand for menials (hitherto employed out of revenue as a form of consumption) and transfer of those workers to the 'productive' sector – that sector producing (material) goods for profit. The displaced menials may still in fact be supported by the same flow of wage goods hitherto put at their disposal; but these wage goods now act as capital in that the workers maintained thereby are engaged in producing goods for sale on the market. The problem arises because of the failure of consumption to rise *pari passu* with the output forthcoming from the expanded 'capacity'; working-class purchasing power is unchanged despite the increase in aggregate output – there having simply occurred a transfer of labour between sectors – whereas capitalists' consumption is, by the initial assumption, reduced (cf. Hollander, 1969, 308; 1987, 250–1).

This interpretation, however, fails to take account of the explicit references to reduced expenditures by capitalists and landlords 'of their usual conveniences and luxuries' (passage 1); or a diminution in the 'power and will to purchase' (passage 2) or 'economy of consumption' (passage 3) – *all references to consumer goods, not services.*[12] This perspective suggests a preferable interpretation which avoids the notion of savings as involving a direct transfer of workers from services to the production of commodities. Rather, accumulation entails reduced expenditures on 'luxury' goods and increased expenditures on capital goods; and a corresponding switch of activity by part of the *luxury* workforce presumably still supported by the capital hitherto at its disposal. The outcome of this transition is an increased stock of capital goods that can be set in motion to raise the flow

12 Cf. also: 'The fortune of a country, though necessarily made more slowly, is made in the same way as the fortunes of individuals in trade are generally made – by *savings*, certainly; but by savings which are furnished from increased gains, and by no means involve a diminished expenditure on objects of luxury and enjoyment' (1820, 421; 1836, 367).

of final output – material output – only if appropriately provided by a complement of labour. Population growth would be a possible source; but an alternative source – one which Malthus apparently here had in mind – is the service sector. The end result of the savings process is thus not only larger capacity, in the sense of capital goods, but also an expanded productive labour force at the expense of service labour, satisfying the notion of a 'conversion' by accumulation of unproductive into productive labourers (passage 2), or that of a higher share of 'national produce' devoted to maintaining productive rather than unproductive labour (passage 1).[13]

On the first interpretation, workers are presumed to be maintained from a *wage fund.* On the second, they are treated like any other consumers, buying their goods at retail as the flow is forthcoming (passages 1 and 2).[14] A deficiency of purchasing power arises from the circumstance that demand for the expanded output emanating from the increased productive workforce cannot in and of itself suffice to render such production profitable[15] – this matter is elaborated in section IV – while the larger capacity had been built up by way of *reduced* consumer spending by capitalists and landlords.[16] The argument touches on the very nature of accumulation. At issue was the legitimacy of the Ricardian identification of 'the passion for accumulation' with that 'for expenditure' in their effects, 'the demand for food and clothing of the labourer, who is to be employed productively ... securing such a general demand for commodities and such a rate of profits for the capital employed in producing them, as will adequately call forth the powers of the soil, and the ingenuity of man in procuring the greatest quantity both of raw and manufactured product' (1820, 365–6; 1836, 325–6). In truth, whereas 'an adequate passion for consumption may fully keep up the proper proportion between supply and demand, whatever may be the powers of production ... a passion [1836: an inordinate passion] for accumulation must inevitably lead to a supply of commodities beyond what the structure and habits of such a society will permit to be [1836: profitably] consumed.' 'National savings,' as it is later phrased, 'considered as the means of increased production, is confined

13 Nothing is said about the precise manner in which labour is attracted from services to the capital-goods sector; one would wish to supplement the account in terms perhaps of an offer of higher wages.

14 This is already established in Malthus's previous section relating to population expansion as a potential source of demand (see below, section IV) and is alluded to in passage 1.

15 In the course of a criticism of the Ricardians on the theory of aggregate demand, Malthus attaches a note on the importance of money, confirming the payment of wages in money rather than directly in wage goods: 'Even the manufacturer would get on but slowly, if he were obliged to accumulate in kind all the wages of his workmen' (1820, 362n; 1836, 324n).

16 On this reading the expansion of 'capital' would entail real capital goods, structures, and materials rather than wage goods though Malthus does not *explicitly* specify this.

within much narrower limits than individual saving' (1820, 467; 1836, 401). For savings in the aggregate 'must necessarily be limited by the amount which can be advantageously employed in supplying the demand for produce; and to create the demand, there must be an adequate consumption [1836: adequate and effective consumption] either among the producers themselves or other classes of consumers' (1820, 467–8; 1836, 401).[17]

Adam Smith's famous assertion (1776/1937, 163–4) that consumption (demand other than that for food) has no limit, is found wanting. It was in fact limited by 'the countervailing luxury of indolence, or by the general desire of mankind to better their condition, and make a provision for a family saving; a principle which, as Adam Smith himself states, is on the whole stronger than the principle which prompts to expense [1776/1937, 324–5]' (1820, 468; 1836, 402). And the Ricardians are taken to task for denying any limit to saving (in the sense of realized investment) other than that imposed by land scarcity, particularly for denying the possibility of inadequate aggregate demand as a constraint on output expansion: 'Let a sufficient consumption always take place, whether by the producers or others, to keep up and increase most effectually [1836: omits 'most effectually'] the exchangeable value of the whole produce; and I am perfectly ready to allow that, to the employment of a national capital, increasing only at such a rate, there is no other limit than that which bounds the power of maintaining population. But it appears to me perfectly clear in theory, and universally confirmed by experience, that the employment of capital, too rapidly increased by parsimonious habits, may find a limit and, does, in fact, often find a limit [1836: that the employment of capital may, and in fact often does, find a limit] long before there is any real difficulty in procuring the means of subsistence; and that both capital and population may be at the same time, and for a period of great [1836: considerable] length, redundant, compared with the effective [1836: effectual] demand for produce' (1820, 469; 1836, 402).

Now the consequence of inadequate consumption – presumably in the absence of appropriate external supplements from the unproductive sector – is that 'capitalists cannot continue the same habits of saving. They must either consume more, or produce less' (1820, 466); or, in the second version: 'Nor could the capitalists in that case continue with effect the same habits of saving. The deficiency in the value of what they produced would necessarily make them either consume more, or produce less' (1836, 400–1). Unfortunately, the correction was in fact likely to take the form of a contraction in activity: 'When the mere pleasure of present expenditure, without the accompaniments of an improved local situation and an ad-

17 In the closing statement it is implied that an 'external demand' is not the *sine qua non* for successful saving (see below, section XIII).

vance in rank, is put in opposition to the continued labour of attending to business during the greatest part of the day, the probability is that a considerable body of them will be induced to prefer the latter alternative, and produce less. But if, in order to balance the demand and supply, a permanent diminution of production takes place, rather than an increase of consumption [1836: of effective consumption] the whole of the national wealth, which consists of what is produced and consumed and not of the excess of produce over consumption [1836: omits 'and ... consumption'] will be decidedly diminished' (1820, 466; 1836, 401). Moreover, accumulation financed by reduced consumption – and if 'pushed beyond a certain point'[18] – generates not only output that must be sold at a loss, but also unemployment: 'If, in the process of saving, all that was lost by the capitalist was gained by the labourer, the check to the progress of wealth would be but temporary, as stated by Mr. Ricardo; and the consequences need not be apprehended. But if the conversion of revenue into capital pushed beyond a certain point must, by diminishing the effectual demand for produce, throw the labouring classes out of employment, it is obvious that the adoption of parsimonious habits in too great a degree [1836: beyond a certain point,] may be accompanied by the most distressing effects at first, and by a marked depression of wealth and population permanently [1836: afterwards]' (1820, 369; 1836, 326).

In two crucially important letters to Ricardo – quoted enthusiastically by Keynes (1933, 141–4) – Malthus makes very clear indeed that his concern was to define the appropriate conditions for *sustainable* growth; that the main impediment to such growth was created by 'excessive' expansions of capacity that end in failure and generate unemployment; and that the degree of 'excess' was difficult to define, though it is said (unfortunately without elaboration) to turn partly on 'the fertility of the soil':

We see in almost every part of the world vast powers of production which are not put into action, and I explain this phenomenon by saying that from the want of a proper distribution of the actual produce adequate motives are not furnished to continued production. By inquiring into the immediate causes of the progress of wealth, I clearly mean to inquire mainly into motives. I dont at all wish to deny that some persons or others are entitled to consume all that is, produced; but the grand question is whether it is distributed in such a manner between the different parties concerned as to occasion the most effective demand for future produce: and I distinctly maintain that an attempt to accumulate very rapidly which necessarily implies a considerable diminution of unproductive consumption, by greatly impairing the usual motives to production must prematurely check the progress of wealth. This surely is the great *practical* question, and not whether we ought to call the sort of stagnation which would be

18 The implication of this and similar qualifications will be taken up presently.

thus occasioned a glut. That I hold to be a matter of very subordinate importance.

But if it be true that an attempt to accumulate very rapidly will occasion such a division between labour and profits as almost to destroy both the motive and the power of future accumulation and consequently the power of maintaining and employing an increasing population, must it not be acknowledged that such an attempt to accumulate, or that saving too much, may be really prejudicial to a country. Do look at my chapter again after this explanation. (7 July 1821; in Ricardo, 1951–73, IX, 10)

With regard to our present subject of discussion, it seems as if we should never thoroughly understand each other, and I almost despair of being ever able to explain myself, if you could read the two first paragraphs of the first section of my last chapter, and yet 'understand me to say that vast powers of production are put into action, and the result is unfavourable to the interests of mankind.'

I expressly say that it is my object to shew what are the causes which call forth the powers of production; and if I recommend a certain proportion of unproductive consumption, it is obvously and expressly with the sole view of furnishing the necessary motive to the greatest continued production. And I think still that this certain proportion of unproductive consumption varying according to the fertility of the soil, &c: is absolutely and indispensably necessary to call forth the resources of a country.

Surely I have nowhere said, as you seem to intimate, that people will continue to produce without a motive; because I expressly give as the reason for the scanty produce of the world, the want of sufficient motives to produce. Now among the motives to produce, one of the most essential certainly is that an adequate share of what is produced should belong to those who set all industry in motion. But you yourself allow that a great temporary saving, commencing when profits were sufficient to encourage it, might occasion such a division of the produce as would leave no motive to a further increase of production. And if a state of things in which for a time there is no motive to a further increase of production be not properly denominated a stagnation, I do not know what can be so called; particularly as this stagnation must inevitably throw the rising generation out of employment. We know from repeated experience that the money price of labour never falls till many workmen have been for some time out of work. And the question is, whether this stagnation of capital, and subsequent stagnation in the demand for labour arising from increased production without an adequate proportion of unproductive consumption on the part of the landlords and capitalists, could take place without prejudice to the country, without occasioning a less degree both of happiness and wealth than would have occurred if the unproductive consumption of the landlords and capitalists had been so proportioned to the natural surplus of the society as to have continued uninterrupted the motives to production, and prevented first an unnatural demand for labour, and then a necessary and sudden diminution of such demand.

> But if this be so, how can it be said with truth that parsimony, though it may be prejudicial to the producers cannot be prejudicial to the state; or that an increase of unproductive consumption among landlords and capitalists may not sometimes be the proper remedy for a state of things in which the motives to production fail. (16 July 1821; 20–1)

Malthus was clearly frustrated by Ricardo's apparent failure to appreciate that the problem at hand related to *unsustainable* expansions of capacity, and the conditions required to overcome that impediment.

* * *

The main problem is restated in the *Principles* in a criticism of a statement by Ricardo that a given quantum of wage goods will maintain the same numbers irrespective of the production cost of that quantum.[19] This Malthus denied on the general grounds that it neglected variations in the corn wage (1820, 418; 1836, 364). In the 1820 version the theme is illustrated by the case of a sudden increase in wage-goods production as a result either of technical progress *or of the 'conversion of revenue into capital'*[20] – that is, why we raise the point here – which results in a collapse of corn prices such that the expanded corn output is unable 'to set in motion' the same quantity of labour: 'There is not the slightest doubt that a given portion of necessaries would be quite unable to set in motion the same quantity of labour; and, if the exchangeable value of the produce should fall in a greater ratio than its quantity increases, (which may very easily happen,) then the same quantity of labour would not be set in motion by the increased quantity of necessaries, and the progress of wealth would receive a decided check.' This exposition is replaced in the 1836 version by a summary avoiding reference to the savings process: 'And the great variety of corn wages in different countries at the same time, and in the same country at different times, show most clearly that it is not the *quantity* of necessaries, but their *value* which determines their efficiency in setting labourers to work, and that whatever increases their value will at the same increase their efficiency, and whatever diminishes their value will diminish it.' A savings program illustrates a diminution in 'value' (labour commanded), and the removal of this specific illustration probably has no significant

19 'Mr. Ricardo, in his chapter on Value and Riches [1951–73, I, 279], has stated that "a certain quantity of clothes and provisions will maintain and employ the same number of men, and will therefore procure the same quantity of work to be done, whether they be produced by the labour of a hundred or of two hundred men; but they will be of twice the value, if two hundred have been employed in their production."'

20 On the version of the accumulation process adopted above, involving expanded *real capacity*, there will result an increased flow of output which presumably includes wage goods.

implication. Again, in 1820 alone, a similar 'check' to employment is said to result from 'a diminished demand for produce, owing to the decline of foreign commerce, or any other cause. Under these circumstances, both the quantity and value of produce would soon be diminished; and though labour, from the want of demand, would be very cheap, the capitalists would soon lose both the will and the power to employ it in the same quantity as before.' This latter observation is omitted entirely from the second edition, suggesting a quest for brevity. That there is no substantive change in position is confirmed by subsequent allusions to the savings problem common to both editions, as we shall now see.

The text in 1836 proceeds to extend from wage goods to 'luxuries' the proposition that it is *value*, not *quantity*, that matters for 'the efficiency of setting labourers to work': 'Nor is the remark less applicable to those articles which are denominated luxuries, than it is to the necessaries of life, for although such commodities do not in kind form any part of the funds which are destined for the maintenance of ordinary labour, yet an increase in their value gives to those who produce them a greater command over those funds, which form the most stimulus to an increase of their quantity' (1836, 364–5).[21] But both editions then come together to summarize the dilemma – *the inevitable failure of a growth process if financed by reduced consumption, yet the necessity for increased accumulation in the achievement of growth*: 'It has already been shewn that this value [1836: the value of the whole produce] cannot be maintained in the case of a rapid accumulation of capital occasioned by an actual and continued diminution in the expenditure and consumption of the higher classes of society in the form of revenue. Yet it will be most readily allowed that the saving from revenue to add to capital is an absolutely necessary step in the progress of wealth. How then is this saving to take place without producing the diminution of value apprehended' (1820, 419; 1836, 365).

Under certain conditions – initial deficiency of capital relative to demand – a *temporary* reduction in consumption might be essential; it is a *permanent* reduction in consumption that is, positively precluded as a source of funds for maintainable growth: 'All that I mean to say [1836: All that is, contended for] is, that no nation can *possibly* grow rich by an accumulation of capital, arising from a permanent diminution of consumption; because such accumulation being greatly beyond [1836: being beyond] what is wanted in order to supply the effective [1836: effectual]

21 This extract illustrates a terminological complexity. The expression 'funds destined for the maintenance of labour,' taken literally, seems to imply a wage fund, and is often read as such. But this is not the reading intended. Rather, Malthus refers simply to a category of goods typically purchased by labour alone. In the case at hand, the concern is with stocks of such wage goods held in inventory – whether by the producer, the merchant wholesaler, or the retailer – which, because of oversupply, could not be sold at profitable prices.

demand for produce, a part of it would very soon lose both its use and its value, and cease to possess the character of wealth' (1820, 369–70; 1836, 326–7). Again the dilemma is stark: 'Fully acknowledging that there is hardly a country in the four quarters of the globe where capital is not deficient, and in most of them very greatly deficient, compared with the territory and even the number of people; and fully allowing at the same time the extreme desirableness of an increase of capital, I should say that, where [1836: the state of] the demand for commodities was not such as to afford fair profits [1836: such as to afford much less than ordinary profits] to the producer, and the capitalists were at a loss where and how to employ their capitals to advantage, the saving from revenue to add still more to these capitals would only tend prematurely to diminish the motive to accumulation, and still further to distress the capitalists, with little increase of a wholesome and effective capital.' This observation might imply a problem specifically in conditions of actual excess capacity, with capitalists 'at a loss where and how to employ their capitals to advantage.'[22] But while the encouragement of accumulation would then certainly be inappropriate, the argument taken in full context is more general – *any* attempt to expand capital by a program involving reduced consumption must fail.

* * *

It is, we have seen, capital 'pushed beyond a certain point,' or 'parsimonious habits in too great a degree,' that creates the problem. By implication, a lesser degree of accumulation could proceed without encountering obstacles. That sustainable rate, it emerges, is one that avoids a positive reduction in consumption.

In approaching his problem Malthus pointed to 'a very striking and singular resemblance' between 'the laws which regulate the rate of profits and the progress of capital' and those 'which regulate the rate of wages and the progress of population' (1820, 370; 1836, 327). It would be equally erroneous for Malthus himself to deny the possibility of excessive population growth despite the availability of good land as it was for Ricardo to deny the possibility of excessive accumulation. He, for his part, had 'all along said, that population might be redundant, and greatly redundant, compared with the demand for it and the actual means of supporting it, although it might most properly be considered as deficient, and greatly

22 Malthus throughout had in mind contemporary recommendations for increased saving; cf. 1820, 375; 1836, 330: '[It] is equally vain, with a view to the permanent increase of wealth, to continue converting revenue into capital, where there is no adequate demand for the products of such capital, as to continue encouraging marriage and the birth rate of children without a demand for labour and an increase of the funds for its maintenance.'

deficient, compared with the extent of territory, and the powers of such territory to produce additional means of subsistence' (1820, 371–2; 1836, 328). But in that case, 'notwithstanding the acknowledged deficiency of population, and the obvious desirableness of having it greatly increased, it was useless and foolish directly to encourage the birth of more children, as the effect of such encouragement, without a demand for labour and the means of paying it properly, could only be increased misery and mortality with little or no final increase of population.' In 1820 he complained that 'though Mr. Ricardo has taken a very different course, I think that the same kind of reasoning ought to be applied to the rate of profits and the progress of capital' (1820, 372). This reference to Ricardo is absent from the 1836 version, but the substance remains. 'Required in both cases of deficient capital and deficient population, was an effective [1836: effectual] demand for commodities, that is, a demand by those who are able and willing to pay an adequate price for them,' an allusion (spelled out in the 1836 version) to an increase of demand 'prior to the increase of capital and population' (1820, 372–3; 1836, 328). Or as stated a little earlier: 'Parsimony, or the conversion of revenue into capital, may take place without any diminution of consumption, if the revenue increases first' (1820, 369n; 1836, 326n).[23]

The requisite *preliminary* increase in the exchangeable value of the (existing) national product, which increase provides the stimulus for expansion of general output, is further spelled out in a parallel drawn with 'individual cases,' where 'the power of producing particular commodities is called into action, in proportion to the effective [1836: intensity of effectual] demand for them; and the greatest stimulus to their production [1836: to their increase, independent of improved facilities of production,] is a high market price, or an increase of their exchangeable value, before more capital and labour have been employed upon them [1836: before a greater value of capital has been employed]. In the same manner, the greatest stimulus to the continued production of commodities, taken all together, is an increase in the exchangeable value of the whole mass, before more labour and capital have been employed upon them [1836:

23 Cf. a later formulation: required 'to call these powers [of production] fully into action' – by assuring (as it is put in 1836) an 'effectual and unchecked demand for all that is produced' – was 'such a distribution of produce, and such an adaptation of this produce to the wants of those who are to consume it as constantly to increase the exchangeable value of the whole mass' (1820, 413; 1836, 361).

In 1836, a link is recalled between wealth and value: 'In a former section, relating to the distinction between wealth and value, it was observed, that where wealth and value are perhaps most nearly connected, is in the general necessity of the latter as a stimulus to the production of the former. Unless the estimation in which an object is held, or the value which an individual, or the society places on it when obtained, adequately compensates the sacrifice which has been made to obtain it, such wealth will not be produced in future.'

before a greater value of capital has been employed upon them]' (1820, 414; 1836, 361). 'And this increase of value,' continues the 1820 version, 'is effected by such a distribution of the actual produce as is best adapted to gratify the existing wants of society, and to inspire new ones.' Similarly: 'General wealth, like particular portions of it, will always follow effective [1836: effectual] demand. Whenever there is a great demand for commodities, that is, whenever the exchangeable value of the whole mass will command more labour than usual at the same price [1836: whenever the whole mass will command a greater quantity of standard labour than before, without any greater value of capital having been required to produce them], there is the same kind of reason for expecting a general increase of commodities, as there is for expecting an increase of particular commodities when their market-price rise [1836: ... rise, without a corresponding rise in their money-cost of production]' (1820, 417; 1836, 363). Alternatively phrased, *only if profits are initially high will saving be sustainable*; for that 'is a sure sign that commodities are scarce, compared with the demand for them, that the wants of the society are clamorous for a supply, and that an increase in the means of production, by saving a considerable part of the new revenue created by the high profits, and adding it to capital, will be specifically and permanently beneficial' (1820, 467).[24]

This same theme is further elaborated in the course of rejection of de Sismondi's observation regarding 'the limit of accumulation,' that 'on ne fait jamais, après tout qu'échanger la totalité de la production de l'année contre la totalité de la production de l'année précédente [1819/1951, I, 113]' (1820, 420; 1836, 366).[25] Malthus was far more optimistic: 'If this were really the case, it would be difficult to say how the value of the national produce could ever be increased. But in fact a great increase of productions may immediately find an adequate market, and experience consequently a great increase of exchangeable value, if they are so well distributed and so well adapted to the tastes and wants of the society as to excite the desire of making an adequate sacrifice in order to procure and consume them' (1820, 420–1; 1836, 366). 'All increase of commodities,' the text proceeds in 1820, 'shews itself first in increased revenue; and as long as they increase in value as well as in quantity by being properly distributed and the consumption properly proportioned to the supply, it is obvious that a yearly saving may take place consistently with a yearly increase of revenue and a yearly increase of expenditure and demand'; and in the

24 The various omissions from the second version do not apparently reflect a substantive change of position.

25 J.S. Mill, however, identified the position of Malthus with that of de Sismondi (and also Chalmers), who, generalizing from the admissable case of one product, asserted erroneously that expansion of products in the aggregate is necessarily accompanied by a deficiency of purchasing power, thereby precluding sales at unchanged prices and profits (1848/1965, 571).

1836 version: 'In fact, such an increase of value always really takes place on occasion of an increased foreign demand for commodities; and unquestionably a similar increase of value would take place in the case of such a production and distribution of domestic commodities as better to suit the tastes and desires of the domestic consumers.' In conclusion: 'The fortune of a country, though necessarily made more slowly, is made in the same way as the fortunes of individuals in trade are generally made – by *savings*, certainly; but by savings which are furnished from increased gains, and by no means involve a diminished expenditure on objects of luxury and enjoyment' (1820, 421; 1836, 367).[26]

Malthus neglected to spell out explicitly whether by initially 'high profits' or 'increased gains' he intended increased *total* profits rather than an increased *rate of profits*. But it is my impression that these were seen to go hand in hand; at least there is nothing to suggest in this context that the two might move in different directions. Moreover, as we shall see in section V, the motive to save is related specifically to the profit rate.

IV ON WORKING-CLASS CONSUMPTION

The problem of sustainable growth is elaborated from the perspective of labour's consumption in a discussion of population increase as stimulus – namely, 'whether encouragements to population, or even the natural tendency of population to increase beyond the funds for [1836: funds destined for] its maintenance, so as to press hard against the limits of subsistence [1836 omits: 'so ... subsistence'] will, or will not, *alone* furnish an adequate stimulus to the increase of wealth' (1820, 351; 1836, 313–14; emphasis added).[27] This query is answered in the negative, because of the requirement for a demand for the additional output *beyond* that provided by the additional labourers employed: 'No productive labour will [1836: can] ever be in demand [1836: with a view to profit] unless the produce

26 Regarding the matter at hand, Malthus is a little more critical of de Sismondi in the 1836 version than in 1820: 'I agree with M. Sismondi in many [1836: in some] of his principles respecting consumption and demand; but I do not think that the view which he takes of the formation of national revenue, on which all increase of consumption and demand depends, is just ...' (1820, 420n; 1836, 366n).

27 Malthus refers to 'many writers [who] have been of opinion that an increase of population is the sole stimulus necessary to the increase of wealth, because population being the great source of consumption, must in their opinion necessarily keep up the demand for an increase of produce, which will naturally be followed by a continued increase of supply' (1820, 347; 1836, 311). He points out that this formulation is too loose, because 'to suppose an actual and permanent [1836: a great and continued] increase of population is to beg the question. We may as well suppose at once an increase of wealth; because an actual and permanent [1836; because such an] increase of population cannot take place without a proportionate or nearly proportionate increase of wealth' (1820, 350–1; 1836, 313). This sequence does not fit well with the frequent notion of food increase prior to population increase.

when obtained is of greater value than the labour which obtained it. No fresh hands can be employed in any sort of industry merely in consequence of the demand for its produce occasioned by the persons employed. No farmer will take the trouble of superintending the labour of ten additional men merely because his whole produce will then sell in the market at an advanced price just equal to what he had paid his additional labourers. There must be something in the previous state of the demand and supply of the commodity in question, or in its price, antecedent to and independently of the demand occasioned by the new labourers, in order to warrant the employment of an additional number of people in its produce' (1820, 348–9; 1836, 312). Allowing for the effect on wages exerted by population expansion did not change the situation. A real-wage decline 'beyond a point' would, of course, stop population growth, but even before this point was reached, 'it will probably happen that the increase of produce occasioned by the labour of the additional number of persons will have so lowered its value, as more than to counterbalance the fall of [money] wages, and thus to diminish instead of increase the profits of the capitalists, and the power and will to employ more labour.'[28] Thus downward pressure on prices exerted by increased commodity supply maintains real wages at too high a level to justify the increased employment. The issue will re-emerge in the analysis of the postwar depression (chapter 12: III).

As for empirical evidence, 'the only way, by which we can judge of the practical effect of population alone as a stimulus to wealth, is to refer to those countries where, from the excess of population above the funds applied to the maintenance of labour, the stimulus of want is the greatest. And if in these countries, which still have great powers of production, the progress of wealth is very slow, we have certainly all the evidence which experience can possibly give us, that population alone cannot create an effective demand for wealth.' References to Spain, Portugal, Poland, Hungary, Turkey, the whole of Asia and Africa, and most of America 'distinctly answer [the question] in the negative' (1820, 349–50; 1836, 313).

The problem of inadequate purchasing power arose even with allowance made for increased working-class consumption stimulated by the lower prices which accompany expanded output: 'On the supposition indeed of a *given* consumption, the accumulation of capital beyond a certain point must appear at once to be perfectly futile. But even taking into consider-

28 This latter proposition is expanded in 1836 thus: 'The increase of produce occasioned by the labour of the additional number of persons will have so lowered its value, and reduced profits, as to determine the capitalist to employ less labour. Though the producers of necessaries might certainly be able in this case to obtain the [real] funds required for the support of a greater number of labourers; yet if the effectual demand for necessaries were fully supplied, and an adequate taste for unproductive consumption, or personal services had not been established, no motive of interest could induce the producers to make an effectual demand for this greater number of labourers.'

ation the increased consumption likely to arise among the labouring classes from the abundance and cheapness of commodities, yet as this cheapness must be at the expense of profits, it is obvious that the limits to such an increase of capital from parsimony, as shall not be attended by a very rapid diminution of the motive to accumulate, are very narrow, and may very easily be passed' (1820, 370; deleted 1836). Malthus here engages in circular reasoning, since he assumes what he is purporting to prove – namely, that prices and profits do indeed decline with increased capacity.

Later in the chapter we find a restatement of the proposition that labour's consumption can never *of itself* suffice to stimulate expansion of output: 'It is indeed most important to observe that no power of consumption on the part of the labouring classes can ever, according to the common motives which influence mankind, *alone*, furnish an encouragement to the employment of capital. As I have before said, nobody [1836: No one will] will ever employ capital merely for the sake of the demand occasioned by those who work for him. Unless they produce an excess of value above what they consume, which he either wants himself in kind, or which he can advantageously exchange for something which he desires, either for present or future use, it is quite obvious that his capital will not be employed in maintaining them' (1820, 471–2; 1836, 404; emphasis added).

Supposing, however, a preliminary rise in value from elsewhere, consumption by labour then counts as an important source: 'When indeed this further value is created and affords a sufficient excitement to the saving and employment of stock [1836: of capital] then certainly the power of consumption possessed by the workmen will greatly add to the whole national demand, and make room for the employment of a much greater capital.' Malthus's intention seems to be to avoid any suggestion that demand by labour is in some sense insignificant. Wages, after all, constituted the major part of national income and must return to circulation by expenditure.[29] The problem essentially is that wages constituted a 'cost,' not only a revenue, element: 'But to those who are inclined to say that unproductive consumers cannot be necessary as a stimulus to the increase of wealth, if the productive classes do but consume a fair proportion of what they produce, I would observe that [1836: omits 'But to those ... I would observe that'] as [1836: But as] a great increase of consumption among the working classes must greatly increase the cost of production, it must lower profits, and diminish or destroy the motive to accumulate, before agriculture, manufactures, and commerce have reached any considerable degree of prosperity. If each labourer were actually to consume double the quantity of corn which he does at present, such a demand,

29 This seems to be confirmed by evidence given in 1827 to the Commons Select Committee on Emigration relating to the question whether low wages are favourable to activity (see chapter 17, p. 862).

instead of giving a stimulus to wealth, would probably [1836: unquestionably] throw a great quantity of land out of cultivation, and greatly diminish both internal and external commerce' (1820, 472–3; 1836, 405).[30] Even increased wages reflecting higher prudential control had a negative effect on profits: 'All such increased consumption, whether desirable or not on other grounds, must always have the specific effect of preventing the wealth and population of a country, under a system of private property, from being pushed so far, as it might have been, if the costs of production had not been so increased' (1820, 475; deleted 1836. See also 1820, 476–7; 1836, 406; cited below, p. 565). As we shall see in section VI, Ricardo fully allowed such a reduction in the profit rate but rightly denied that this constituted evidence of a 'glut.'

V ON THE DETERMINANTS OF SAVING

Successful accumulation required a high profit rate *prior* to increased saving, that profit rate generated by a demand for commodities 'by those who are able and willing to pay an adequate price for them' (above, p. 524). But would an initial increase in the profit rate necessarily call forth increased accumulation? Malthus insisted that accumulation *is* functionally related to the profit rate: 'Though high profits are not followed by an increase of capital, so certainly as high wages are by an increase of population, yet ... still it will not cease to be true that the natural and legitimate encouragement to the increase of capital is that increase of power and will to save which is held out by high [1836: by certain and steady] profits; and under circumstances in any degree similar, such increase of power and will to save must almost always be accompanied by a proportionate increase of capital' (1820, 373; 1836, 328–9). And this despite appearances to the contrary created by risk, which 'has precisely the same effect in diminishing the motive to accumulate and the reward of accumulation, as low profits.'

So far so good. But later in the chapter on the Progress of Wealth, the *norm* is said to be *excessive* accumulation in response to profit opportunities – excessive relative to the sustainable rate. Such behaviour would seem to

30 In the 1836 edition there is here attached an editorial note: 'The demand created by the productive labourer himself can never be an *adequate* demand, because it does not go to the full extent of what he produces. If it did, there would be no profit, consequently no motive to employ him. The very existence of a profit upon any commodity presupposes a demand *exterior* to that of the labour which has produced it.'

Waterman (1996b) points out that – unlike Mandeville (1732) – Paley (1785) was aware that the outcome of an increase in luxury is ambiguous, increasing demand, production, and population, on the one hand, reducing the supply of labour, on the other. It is clear that Malthus, at 1820, 472–3, was formulating this sort of problem. The issue emerges also in the *Essay on Population* (see below, chapter 17, p. 814).

deny the Ricardo–Senior *motive* to save governed by the return on capital in favour of a *passion* to save – closer to the Smith–Marx position – involving a 'greater tendency to parsimony than is consistent with the most effective encouragement to the growth of public wealth': 'With regard to the capitalists who are so engaged ['in production'], they have certainly the power of consuming their profits, or the revenue which they make by the employment of their capitals; and if they were to consume it, with the exception of what could be beneficially added to their capitals, so as to provide in the best way both for an increased production and increased consumption, there might be little occasion for unproductive consumers. But such consumption is not consistent with the actual habits of the generality of capitalists. The great object of their lives is to save a fortune, both because it is their duty to make a provision for their families, and because they cannot spend an income with so much comfort to themselves, while they are obliged perhaps to attend a counting house for seven or eight hours a day' (1820, 465; 1836, 399–400). The common assumption 'that the wants of mankind may be considered as at all times commensurate with their powers' is denied 'even in those cases where a fortune comes without trouble; and in reference to the great mass of capitalists, it is completely contradicted by experience. *Almost all merchants and manufacturers save, in prosperous times, much more rapidly than it would be possible for the national capital to increase, so as to keep up the value of the produce.* But if this be true of them as a body, taken one with another, it is quite obvious that, with their actual habits, they could not afford an adequate market to each other by exchanging their several products' (1820, 465–6; 1836, 399–400; emphasis added).[31]

In further elaborating his case Malthus charged Ricardo with representing saving as an end in itself: 'Even with regard to individuals, where this view of the subject is nearest the truth, it must be allowed that the final object in saving is expenditure and enjoyment. But, in reference to national wealth, it can never be considered either immediately or permanently in any other light than as a means' (1820, 466–7; 1836, 401).[32] This charge

31 Malthus here suggests that there is *some* rate of accumulation that might be achieved without the support of unproductive consumption: 'If [capitalists] were to consume [their revenue], with the exception of what could be beneficially added to their capitals, so as to provide in the best way both for an increased production and increased consumption, there might be little occasion for unproductive consumers.' This begs the main question: What is that rate of accumulation that can be maintained independently of an unproductive sector? It is presumably that rate that can be justified by a preliminary increase in aggregate value. (See section VI.)

32 In the 1820 version this is slightly qualified, possibly in response to Ricardo's 'Advertisement' inserted in his *Principles* of 1821: 'It may be true that, by the cheapness of commodities, and the consequent saving of expenditure in consumption, the same surplus of produce above consumption may be obtained as by a great rise of profits with an undiminished consumption; and, if saving were an end, the same end would be accomplished.'

is, at first sight, problematic since it is Malthus who represented capitalists as engaged in excessive accumulation under the impulse of various stimuli. But this can be explained by tracing through the consequences of such behaviour – namely, a fall in the profit rate and the other features of depression or stagnation, including unemployment and excess capacity. The problem of excessive accumulation motivated by a 'passion' to save is a problem pertinent specifically *to a period of high profits,* not one of low profits, and the collapse of profits brings with it the correction. In the 'long run,' so to speak, the motive provided by the profit rate predominates. (For this position in 1815 as applied to the war period 1794–1814, see below, chapter 12: II.)

That the profit rate constituted the appropriate index of demand for capital is amply confirmed in Malthus's section X on applications of theory: 'It is justly observed by Mr. Ricardo that "the farmer and manufacturer can no more live without profit than the labourer without wages. Their motive for accumulation will diminish with every diminution of profit, and will cease altogether when their profits are so low as not to afford them an adequate compensation for their trouble, and the risk which they must necessarily encounter in employing their capital productively" [1951–73, I, 122]. Mr. Ricardo applies this passage to the final and necessary fall of profits occasioned by the state of the land. I would apply it at all times, throughout all the variable periods which intervene between the first stage of cultivation and the last. *Whenever capital increases too fast, the motive to accumulation diminishes, and there will be a natural tendency to spend more and save less. When profits rise, the motive to accumulation will increase, and there will be a tendency to spend a smaller proportion of the gains, and to save a greater*' (1820, 515–16; 1836, 432–3; emphasis added).[33] Unfortunately, the adjustment was not a smooth one.

The increase in aggregate demand required to assure a preliminary rise in the profit rate introduces serious problems relating to motivation. In an implicit criticism of Ricardo, Malthus observed that 'it is a partial and narrow view of the subject, to consider only the propensity to spend what is actually possessed. It forms but a very small part of the question to determine that if a man has a hundred thousand a year, he will not decline the offer of ten thousand more; or to lay down generally that

33 At low profits, then, there will in normal circumstances be no problem of excessive accumulation. Malthus frequently warned against the ill-timed *encouragement* of saving by policy makers; and in the present context he pointed out that, if 'commodities are already so plentiful that an adequate portion of them is not [1836: profitably] consumed, the capital so saved, the office of which is still further to increase the plenty of commodities, and still further to lower already low profits can be comparatively of little use [1836: to save capital can only be still further to increase the plenty of commodities, and still further to lower already low profits, which can be comparatively of little use]' (1820, 467; 1836, 401).

mankind are never disposed to refuse the means of increased power and enjoyment' (1820, 469; 1836, 402–3). Rather, the problem related to effort supply: 'The main part of the question respecting the wants of mankind, relates to their power of calling forth the exertions necessary to acquire the means of expenditure. It is unquestionably true that wealth produces wants; but it is a still more important truth, that wants produce wealth. Each cause acts and reacts upon the other, but the order, both of precedence and of importance, is with the wants which stimulate to industry,' and it could not be taken for granted that such wants were 'always ready to second the physical powers of man' (1820, 469–70; 1836, 403). The problem of generating new wants and 'furnish[ing] fresh motives for industry' did not, as some believed, pertain only to underdeveloped economies: 'Even civilized and improved countries cannot afford to lose any of these motives. It is not the most pleasant employment to spend eight hours a day in a counting house. Nor will it be submitted to after the common necessaries and conveniences of life are attained, unless adequate motives are presented to the mind of the man of business. Among these motives is undoubtedly the desire of advancing his rank, and contending with the landlords in the enjoyment of leisure, as well as of foreign and domestic luxuries.' But 'the desire to realize a fortune as a permanent provision for a family' is said to constitute 'the most general motive for the continued exertions of those whose incomes depend upon their own skill and efforts' (1820, 471; 1836, 403–4). The effectiveness of such saving depends on consumption by *other* sectors of the economy, in the absence of which capitalists would be obliged to contract their own business activities: 'If, from the want of other consumers [1836: effective consumers], the capitalists were obliged to consume all that could not be advantageously added to the national capital [1836: under such circumstances] the motives which support them in their daily tasks must essentially be weakened, and the same powers of production would not be called forth.'

As stated here the problem posed involves the unwillingness on the part of businessmen to undertake entrepreneurial activity without sufficient motive. (Saving and business effort are conflated throughout the passage, with those engaged in saving presumed also to be engaged in business activity.) But this had surely not been the original issue; that, on the contrary, involved *excessive* attempts to accumulate when profits are favourable. However, the problem of assuring an adequate motive to save does not preclude the further problem that capitalists tend to engage in excessive attempts to save. The former relates to the requirements for ongoing sustainable expansions; the latter to a periodic predisposition to go too far.

VI THE 'GLUT' CONTROVERSY ELABORATED

In what follows we further elaborate Malthus's position by reference to his more formal attempt to isolate the source of his objections to the 'new doctrines' on profits of Say, James Mill, and Ricardo (1820, 355; 1836, 316). There is first the complaint that the Ricardians 'considered commodities as if they were so many mathematical figures, or arithmetical characters, the relations of which were to be compared, instead of articles of consumption, which must of course be referred to the numbers and wants of the consumers' (1820, 355; 1836, 316–17). Alternatively expressed, the New (Ricardian) School maintained that 'commodities being always exchanged for commodities, one half will furnish a market for the other half, and production being thus the sole source of demand, an excess in the supply of one article merely proves a deficiency in the supply of some other, and a general excess is impossible. M. Say ... has indeed gone so far as to state that the consumption of a commodity by taking it out of the market diminishes demand, and the production of a commodity proportionably increases it' (1820, 353; 1836, 315).[34] James Mill's version of the Law of Markets is drawn from his early reply to Spence, published in 1808, which 'has laid down very broadly the doctrine that commodities are only purchased by commodities and that one half of them must always furnish a market for the other half.' And the doctrine 'appears to be adopted in its fullest extent by the author of an able and useful article on the corn laws,' a reference to McCulloch's contribution in the *Supplement to the 6th Edition of the Encyclopaedia Britannica* (1824).

In the revised version Malthus states his objection in cryptic terms: 'These writers do not seem to be aware of what is unquestionably true, that demand is always determined by *value* and supply by *quantity*. Two bushels of wheat are double the quantity of one in regard to supply; but in numerous cases, two bushels will not make so great a demand as one bushel' (316n). This proposition, which rejects the concept of supply as a schedule of cost prices, notwithstanding the formal analysis of price determination, is also found in Malthus's 1823 review of Tooke (below, section VII). But this is not the tack taken in 1820; and even in the second edition it appears almost as an afterthought. The main line taken is to question the accuracy of the assumption that 'as a matter of fact ... commodities are always exchanged for commodities. The great [1836: An immense] mass of commodities is exchanged directly for labour, either productive or unproductive [1836: directly, either for productive labour, or personal services]; and it is quite obvious, that this mass of commodities, compared with the labour with which it is to be exchanged, may fall in value from a glut just as any one commodity falls in value from an excess of supply, compared either with labour or money' (1820, 354; 1836, 316). In an elaboration, Malthus seems to shift from the argument that a mass of commodities is *actually exchanged directly against labour*, to the mere *estimation against labour* – labour command: 'If commodities were only to

34 Say's position is given in his chapter 'Des Débouchés' (*Traité*, 2d ed., 1814, I, 144f.).

be compared and exchanged with each other, then indeed it would be true that, if they were all increased in their proper proportions to any extent, they would continue to bear among themselves the same relative value; but, if we compare them, as we certainly ought to do, [1836: with the means of producing them, and] with the numbers and wants of the consumers, then a great increase of produce with comparatively stationary numbers and [1836: or] with wants diminished by parsimony, must necessarily occasion a great fall of value estimated in labour, so that the same produce, though it might have *cost* the same quantity of labour as before, would no longer *command* the same quantity; and both the power of accumulation and the motive to accumulate would be strongly checked' (1820, 355; 1836, 317). But how far Malthus insisted on labour command specifically is unclear since he proceeds to refer also to a decline in aggregate value relative to bullion: 'It is asserted that effectual demand is nothing more than the offering of one commodity in exchange for another [1836: which has cost the same quantity of labour]. But is this all that is, necessary to effectual demand? Though each commodity may have cost the same quantity of labour and capital [1836: of labour] in its production, and they may be exactly equivalent to each other in exchange, yet why may not both be so plentiful as not to command more labour, or but very little more than they have cost [1836: than they have cost, that is, to yield no profit,] and in this case, would the demand for them be effectual? Would it be such as to encourage their continued production? Unquestionably not. Their relation to each other may not have changed; but their relation to the wants of the society, *their relation to bullion*, and their relation to domestic and foreign labour [1836: and their relation to labour], may have experienced a most important change' (1820, 355–6; 1836, 316; emphasis added).[35]

* * *

Thus far the case turned on the possibility of 'gluts' involving across-the-board expansion of output, commodities retaining 'their proper proportions.' This case is weakened when Malthus introduces disproportionate expansion of certain commodities (wage goods) in a note peculiar to the 1820 edition: 'Of all the opinions advanced by able and ingenious men, which I have ever met with, the opinion of M. Say, which states that "*un produit consommé ou détruit est un débouché fermé*" ... appears to me to be the most directly opposed to just theory, and the most uniformly contradicted by experience. Yet it directly follows from the new doctrine, that commod-

35 Here in the 1836 version appears an editorial note by Cazenove critical of Mill's *Elements* and Torrens's *Essay on Wealth*, both of which had used the term 'demand' in an unusual and unhelpful manner (1836, 317–19n).

ities are to be considered only in their relation to each other, not to the consumers. What, I would ask, would become of the demand for commodities, if all consumption except bread and water were suspended for the next half year? What an accumulation of commodditites! Quels *débouchés*! What a prodigious market would this event occasion!' (1820, 363–4n).[36]

This perspective is pertinent for the Malthus–Ricardo debate. Malthus recognized Ricardo's 'concession' that a more rapid rate of accumulation than population growth will reduce the profit rate by driving up the real wage, and this notwithstanding the availability of good land (1820, 356; 1836, 318);[37] but he attempted to turn the concession to his own advantage: 'I cannot quite [1836: I can by no means] agree with him,' he responded to Ricardo's assertion that the 'admission does not impugn the general principle.' On the contrary: 'Even if we suppose with Mr. Ricardo, what is not true, that an increase of population would certainly remedy the evil; yet as from the nature of a population an increase of labourers cannot be brought into the market, in consequence of a particular demand, till after the lapse of sixteen or eighteen years, and the conversion of revenue into capital [1836: by saving], may take place much more rapidly; a country is always liable to an increase [1836: in the quantity] of the funds for the maintenance of labour faster than the increase of population. But if, whenever this occurs, there may be a universal glut of commodities, how can it be maintained, as a general position, that capital is never redundant; and that because commodities may retain the same relative values, a glut can only be partial, not general?' (1820, 357; 1836, 319–20). In reacting thus, Malthus misrepresented Ricardo's position. Ricardo indeed allowed that, when accumulation involves an increase in basic foodstuffs (corn), there might result a glut. The Law of Markets did not then apply. But he always insisted that such an event would *not* occur: rather, accumulation would entail the increased production of those goods upon which labourers choose to expend their increased incomes – conveniences and luxuries in the case at hand of relatively slow population expansion (see Ricardo's letter to James Mill, 18 December 1821; in Ricardo, 1951–73, IX,

36 The removal of this note in 1836 has no substantive implications.

37 The concession referred to runs as follows: 'There is only one case, and that will be temporary, in which the accumulation of capital with a low price of food may be attended with a fall of profits; and that is, when the funds for the maintenance of labour increase much more rapidly than population; – wages will then be high, and profits low. If every man were to forgo the use of luxuries, and be intent only on accumulation, a quantity of necessaries might be produced, for which there could not be any immediate consumption. Of commodities so limited in number, there might undoubtedly be an universal glut, and consequently there might neither be demand for an additional quantity of such commodities, nor profits on the employment of more capital. If men ceased to consume, they would cease to produce. This admission does not impugn the general principle' (1951–73, I, 292–3).

131). In that event the profit rate indeed falls with the rise in the commodity wage, *but there is no glut.* Ricardo had conceded nothing.

* * *

A second major objection was to the failure of the Ricardians to take into account 'the influence of so general and important a principle in human nature, as indolence or the love of ease' (1820, 358; 1836, 320). For example, in the event of an increase in both agricultural and manufacturing productivity, there was no valid presumption that the (potentially) expanded outputs would be cleared by mutual exchange;[38] should farmers prefer increased *leisure* to increased real income, their low demand for luxuries would oblige a contraction of activity on the part of manufacturers: 'But in this intercourse of mutual gratifications ... [it] is taken for granted that luxuries are always preferred to indolence ... The effect of a preference of indolence to luxuries would evidently be to occasion a want of demand for the returns of the increased powers of production supposed, and to throw labourers out of employment. The cultivator, being now enabled to obtain the necessaries and conveniences to which he had been accustomed, with less toil and trouble, and his tastes for ribbons, lace and velvet not being fully formed, might be very likely to indulge himself in indolence, and employ less labour on the land; while the manufacturer, finding his velvets rather heavy of sale, would be led to discontinue their manufacture, and to fall almost necessarily into the same indolent system as the farmer' (1820, 358–9; 1836, 320–1). Malthus then appealed to history to demonstrate that 'an efficient taste for luxuries [1836: and conveniences], that is, such a taste as will properly stimulate industry, instead of being ready to appear at the moment it is required, is a plant of slow growth.' It was 'a most important error to take for granted, that mankind will produce and consume all that they have the power to produce and consume, and will never prefer indolence to the rewards of industry ...'[39] But here, too, there is a misrepresentation of Ricardo's position. Ricardo had never denied the possibility of a high demand for leisure. He insisted only: (1) that in the British environment it was not an issue; and (2) that in any event, increased *output* would not then be produced, precluding any problem of sales (1951–73, II, 315).[40]

38 The position to the contrary cited by Malthus is from Torrens, 1819, 471.

39 Allusions to the problem will be found in earlier correspondence: 'You seem to think that the wants and tastes of mankind are always ready for the supply; while I am most decidedly of opinion that few things are more difficult, than to inspire new tastes and wants, particularly out of old materials' (26 January 1817; in Ricardo, 1951–73, VII, 122; cf. 8 October 1816; 70).

40 There was no reason for Ricardo to deny that in the event of an exogenous increase in productivity across the board, such as Malthus posits, there would result excess capacity (of both capital and labour) if an appropriately high demand for leisure is assumed sufficient to outweigh the stimulus of low (real) prices.

With the matter of indolence still in mind, Malthus in the second edition supplemented the implications of generally increased productivity by a passage relating to increase of capacity by accumulation: 'It has been said, that it is specifically the deficiency of production on the part of the indolent, which occasions the want of demand for the products of the industrious; and that, if the idle were made to produce, the surplus would disappear. But this remark is evidently beside the question. The real question is, whether under the actual habits and tastes of the society, any number of persons who might be inclined to save and produce, if they suited their produce to these habits and tastes, would be secure of finding such a demand for all they could bring into the market as to prevent the possibility of what is called a glut, or a great fall of profits in a large mass of commodities. What might happen under different tastes and habits is entirely a different question' (1836, 321–2). An editorial note appears here by Cazenove, who was not satisfied with Malthus's response: 'This answer of the author will hardly be thought satisfactory. For if the allegation set up be a *true* one, it certainly falls within the limits of the question. The proper answer is, that it is *not a true* one. If the idle were to produce, it could only be by means of a larger accumulation, that is, of the conversion of more *revenue* into *capital*. But this, though it might make some alteration in the channels of demand, could not possibly increase the sum total of the demand.' But this is in fact Malthus's response in his next paragraph: 'It has also been said, that there is never an indisposition to consume, that the indisposition is to produce. Yet, what is the disposition of those master manufacturers, and merchants who produce very largely and consume sparingly? Is their will to purchase commodities for their consumption proportioned to their power? Does not the use which they make of their capital clearly show that their will is to produce, not to consume? And in fact, if there were not in every country some who were indisposed to consume to the value of what they produced, how could the national capital ever be increased?' This riposte reiterates the basic Malthusian problem of saving, namely, expansion of capacity by way of accumulation entailing a *positive reduction* in final expenditure by capitalists – though, of course, successful accumulation did require that consumption fall short of the value of output.

* * *

A third formal criticism of the Ricardians relates to the view that increased accumulation merely entails a switch from luxury consumption to a demand for wage goods and raw materials: 'A third very serious error of the writers above referred to, and practically the most important of the three, consists in supposing that accumulation ensures demand; or that the consumption of the labourers employed by those whose object is to save, will create such an effectual demand for commodities as to encourage a continued increase of produce. Mr. Ricardo observes [1951–73, I, 291], that "if £10,000 were given to a man having £100,000 per annum, he would not lock it up in a chest but would either increase his expenses by £10,000; employ it himself productively, or lend it to some other person for that purpose; in either case demand would be increased, although it would be for different objects. If he increased his expenses, his effectual demand might probably be for buildings, furniture, or some such enjoyment. If he employed his £10,000 productively, his effectual demand would be for food, clothing, and raw material, which might set new labourers to work; but still it would be *demand*" (1820, 359–60; 1836, 322).

Were it true that the difference between Ricardo and Malthus lay here, there would be evidence of severe mutual incomprehension. For the quoted passage from Ricardo involves the *process of saving*, whereas Malthus's predominant concern is its *outcome* – a larger capacity but inadequate purchasing power to absorb the increased flow of final goods at profitable prices. Moreover, the cited extract is a simplification of the full Ricardo position, according to which the saving process entails increased food production only to the extent that the demand for food by labour rises, which occurs only in the case of population expansion; it is ironic that in the present context Malthus abandons his usual reasonings in the *Essay on Population*, whereby food supply precedes population growth, to criticize Ricardo for what he perceived to be that same sequence. For he proceeds to deny the practical relevance of a process involving expansion of food, given the 'usual motives' governing accumulation: 'The usual motives for accumulation are ... either the future wealth and enjoyment of the individual who accumulates, or of those to whom he means to leave his property. And with these motives it could never answer to the possessor of land to employ nearly all the labour which the soil could support in cultivation; as by so doing he would necessarily destroy his neat rent, and render it impossible for him, without subsequently dismissing the greatest part of his workmen and occasioning the most dreadful distress, either to give himself the means of greater enjoyment at a future distant period, or to transmit such means to his posterity ... Nothing could justify such a conduct but a different motive for accumulation; that is, a desire to increase the population – not the love of wealth and enjoyment; and till such a change takes place in the passions and propensities of mankind, we may be quite sure that the landlords and cultivators will not go on employing labourers in this way' (1820, 360–1). The process, were it in fact set in motion, would be reversed; an inadequate stimulus to cultivation from the side of *expenditure* was a guarantee of permanent stagnation (361–3). The central argument is nicely summarized in the 1836 edition: 'Upon this principle it is supposed that if the richer portion of society were to forego their accustomed conveniences and luxuries with a view to accumulation, the only effect would be the direction of nearly the whole capital of the country to the production of necessaries, which would lead to a great increase of cultivation and population. But this is precisely the case in which Mr. Ricardo distinctly allows that there might be a universal glut; for there would undoubtedly be more necessaries produced than would be sufficient for the existing demand. This state of things could not, however, continue; since, owing to the fall which would take place, cultivation would be checked, and accumulation be arrested in its progress. It is therefore obvious that without an expenditure which will encourage commerce, manufactures, and personal services, the possessors of land will have no sufficient stimulus to cultivate well; and a country such as our own, which had been rich and populous, would, with too parsimonious habits, infallibly become poor and comparatively unpeopled' (1836, 323).[41]

As mentioned earlier (p. 535), Ricardo did not in fact admit by his so-called concession regarding gluts that a rate of accumulation involving increase of food production exceeding that of population would be the norm – the case was allowed for the sake of argument; rather the higher accumulation rate would be stifled as the commodity wage rose, workers enjoying their higher real incomes (at the expense of profits) in the form of luxuries and conveniences.

* * *

Malthus's 1823 review of Tooke's *High and Low Prices* represents the analysis there of the 'effect of quantity on price,' as effectively disproving Say's doctrine that 'all increase of demand depends upon increase of supply, and diminution of demand on diminution of supply' (1823a/1986, 7, 243). The principle itself affirmed

> that whenever there is a relative diminution of supply from whatever cause it may arise, it is immediately followed by a briskness of demand for the remaining produce, accompanied by a rise of prices and of profits which never fails to occasion a great stimulus to subsequent production. This process we have always been in the habit of considering as the great remedial law of nature in regard to production and consumption ... Whenever, within certain limits, a portion of the produce of a country has been diminished, by the seasons, by obstructions to importation, or by an increase in the proportion of unproductive consumption, not only does the power of setting fresh industry in motion remain unim-

41 This reasoning is elaborated in both editions in discussion of a case involving an across-the-board increase in savings on the part of farmers and manufacturers (1820, 363f.; 1836, 323f.).

As for the significance of manufacturing as a stimulus for the agricultural sector, we find it already referred to in the second edition of the *Essay on Population* (see chapter 8: III). It is a relationship also discussed by Mandeville and Paley (see Waterman, 1996b).

paired, but by the universal law of the effect of quantity upon price it is greatly increased. The farmer who, in consequence of a deficiency of his crops of one eighth, sells them for nearly a third more than the usual price before the money wages of labour have risen, is obviously able to set in motion a much greater quantity of industry than before. The specific funds destined for the maintenance of labour, though diminished in quantity, are by this happy provision of nature increased in their efficiency to recover the loss that has been sustained, and to increase the produce of the next year, while the labourers, although they unquestionably sustain some privation, are, in a considerable degree, recompensed by the great and general increase of employment. There is, in the language of Mr. Tooke, a burst of prosperity to the producing classes; and we should certainly add, without a *proportionate* diminution in the prosperity of the labouring classes. (242–3)

Say's error was to neglect or fail to weigh adequately the principle in question: 'As long as the increase of quantity increases the value of the funds specifically destined for the maintenance of labour, so long of course it increases effective demand, and gives a stimulus to production; ... But whenever this production so exceeds the actual state of the demand, whatever that may be, as to disable the producers from putting in motion the same quantity of industry as before, to that extent exactly is the effective demand for a further increase of produce diminished and the stimulus to the increase of wealth abated' (243–4).

That this observation pertained specifically to a particular product can be ruled out, though Tooke's 'principle' did apply to corn or cereals; Malthus's concern was *aggregate* supply and demand. This will be confirmed in our discussion of the analysis of the war years 1793–1813 (chapter 12: II). But it is also apparent in the course of a complaint that Tooke himself was unaware of the implication of his own logic and data, since 'in a note to the last *Part* of his work (Part IV, p. 5) he still declares his adherence to the doctrine of M. Say on supply and demand as explained by Mr. Mill in his *Elements of Political Economy*' (245). Specifically: 'To us it appears that Mr. Tooke has distinctly and luminously proved both by a correct train of reasoning, and what is of much more importance a constant appeal to a crowd of well-attested facts, that a small diminution in the proportion of the usual supplies of such a country as this, invariably calls forth a larger amount of currency and credit, and increases very decidedly the general demand for produce, or the power of devoting such a value to the purchase of the whole mass, as without the rise of prices occasioned by the deficiency, would command a much greater quantity; yet in the note above referred to he professes to believe that the aggregate of demand must always be equal to the aggregate supply, which if it means any thing beyond the very futile proposition, that all which is produced will sooner or later be consumed, must mean something directly opposed to the whole spirit and bent of his work.'

Malthus pretended that the offending note was a matter of 'inadvertence' and recommends Tooke to readers: 'We must however take leave to consider Mr. Tooke's work as better authority than this inadvertent declaration; and to this work we can confidentally refer the reader as containing the most satisfactory proofs of the ... proposition ... that when the supply of commodities is in some degree deficient compared with the demand, whether this arises from increase of demand, or diminution of supply, the state of trade is brisk, profits are high, and mercantile speculations are greatly encouraged; and on the other hand, when the supply is abundant compared with the demand, there is a period of comparative stagnation, with low profits and very little encouragement to mercantile speculation' (245–6; see also 239).[42]

VII THE ATTACK ON SAY'S LAW: A MICRO-ECONOMIC RATIONALE

Notwithstanding the obvious concern to establish the non-identity of *aggregate* demand and supply, a note in the review of Tooke critical of James Mill on the Law of Markets seems to wish to find a micro-economic rationale: 'The fallacy of Mr. Mill's argument depends entirely upon the effect of quantity on price and value. Mr. Mill says that the supply and demand of every individual are of necessity equal. But as supply is always estimated by quantity, and demand only by price and value; and as increase of quantity often diminishes price and value, it follows, according to all just theory, that so far from being always equal, they must of necessity be often very unequal, as we find by experience' (1823a/1986, 7, 245n). This theme also appears in the second edition of the *Principles* (above, p. 533). But what to make of it is unclear, since immediately thereafter it is allowed that supply too might be 'reckoned in value' without altering the conclusion: 'If it be said that reckoning both the demand and supply of commodities by value, they will then be equal; this may be allowed; but it is obvious that they may then both greatly fall in value compared with money and labour; and the will and power of capitalists to set industry in motion, which is the most general and important of all kinds of demand, may be decidedly diminished at the very time that the quantity of produce, however well proportioned each part may be to the other, is decidedly increased.'

Jacob Viner (1937, 197–8) gave Malthus no more than a passing grade for the passage in the review of Tooke. The question at hand in Viner's account is whether a fall in prices (owing to monetary contraction) can restrict production and, conversely, a rise in general prices increase production. He observes that these effects are ruled out by the Say–

42 Tooke, in the following year, rejected the implication drawn by Malthus (Arnon, 1991, 74; citing Tooke, 1824, 330n).

Mill–Ricardo doctrine 'that production, if properly directed, created the demand for its product, and that a general insufficiency of demand to absorb all of the possible output of industry was impossible.' Their doctrine, Viner posits, 'rests on concepts of "supply" and "demand" too physical and an implicit assumption of price and money-cost flexibility too unrealistic to serve adequately the purposes of analysis of short-run disturbances in a monetary economy.' A schedule concept of demand and supply would have revealed the fallacy: 'If "supply" and "demand" are interpreted, as they should be, not as simply quantities of commodities but, in the modern manner, as *schedules of quantities which would be produced or purchased, respectively, at specified schedules of prices*, it becomes easy to see that if money costs are inflexible the schedules of demand prices may fall more rapidly than the schedules of supply prices [upon money supply contraction], with a consequent reduction, not only in prices, but also in volume of sales, in output, in employment, in willingness of capitalists to invest, and in willingness of bankers to lend even if there were would-be borrowers.' As for Malthus, he 'was convinced that there was something wrong in the James Mill doctrine, including its Ricardian version,' but 'failed ... ever satisfactorily to expose the fallacy which underlay it, because he was himself insufficiently emancipated from the purely physical interpretation of "supply" and "demand."' None the less, in the passage from the Tooke review, 'confusing though it is ... he comes nearest to exposing this fallacy successfully.'[43] We have indeed seen that Malthus himself perceived of supply as *quantity*, despite his ambivalence regarding the significance of this characteristic for his case against the Ricardians.

Viner supposed that a convincing case against the Law of Markets would entail inflexible money costs. Malthus's position on the role of the money-wage rate has yet to be explored. Considering the attention accorded labour commanded, one would suppose that money-wage flexibility would assure correction of excess supply. Yet we shall see in the next chapter that this is far from the case.

VIII TRADE AND SUSTAINABLE GROWTH

In broad terms, the solution to the aggregate-demand problem is found in improved 'distribution.' A passage of 1836 clarifies that this is not a matter of assuring an appropriate allocation of activity, but rather one of increasing *aggregate demand relative to supply*: 'in dwelling on the importance of distribution as a main cause of the immediate progress of wealth, I by no means confine the terms to that process which in reference to commodi-

43 More impressive was the contribution of the Attwood brothers, 'who first explained in reasonably satisfactory fashion the dependence of the "demand and supply" of price theory on the state of the currency.'

ties in ordinary use, prevents cotton which are *not* wanted from being brought into the market, instead of woollens which *are* wanted. The persevering production of cottons, when very much larger profits might be made by producing woollens is too gross an error not to be soon corrected in any country, and least of all in such a country as this. The distribution, which I mean, is not so readily accomplished. It is that which effects the best adaptation of the supplies of produce, both in quantity and quality, to the actual tastes and wants of the consumers, and creates new tastes and wants by means of greater facilities of intercourse' (1836, 370–1). The problem is not minimized: 'To increase indeed, the proportion of the demand to the supply without a diminution of the produce is no easy task. We may know, that the opening of new channels of trade, and the extension of markets both at home and abroad will give us what we want; but these are objects which it is rarely in the power of people or a government to accomplish at will.'

One dimension to the solution is simply improved means of communication: 'If the means of distributing the produce of the country were still further facilitated and if the adaption of it to the wants, tastes and powers [1836: the wants and powers] of the consumers were more complete than at present, [1836: and better fitted to inspire new tastes,] there can be no doubt that a great increase in the value of the whole produce would follow [1836: first, in the shape of increased profits, and then of increased quantity, without a proportionate fall of value]' (1820, 414; 1836, 362). Experience had shown how improved transportation between London and the country, by extending demand, had raised 'the value of the whole produce, or the supplies of London and the country together,' thus motivating increased investment – the funds deriving in part from the 'temporary rise of profits' occasioned by this 'extension of demand.' Apart from this, the chief constituents are '1st, the division of landed property; 2dly, internal and external commerce; 3dly, the maintenance of unproductive consumers' or, in the 1836 version, 'the maintenance of an adequate proportion of the society employed in personal services, or otherwise entitled to make a demand for material products without contributing directly to their supply' (1820, 427; 1836, 372). The present section is devoted to the second of these constituents.

Malthusian theory maintains that improved or extended trading or exchange facilities raise the *aggregate value* of national product prior to, and thus stimulate, expansion. Here emerges with particular clarity the distinction between aggregate demand and aggregate supply, and a possible deviation between the two on a par with individual markets. In this context we see the imprint of Smith's doctrine of 'competition of capitals' alleviated by expanded trade opportunities. A word first on the origins of Malthus's position.

An early allusion to the gains from trade which seems to constitute an embryonic statement of the 1820 position by focusing on *demand* considerations will be found in Malthus's *Edinburgh Review* article of February 1811: 'Our opinion is, that, in all commercial transactions, both parties gain what, in the estimation of each, is decidedly more than an equivalent for what it has given; and that it is out of this excess, that the gains of the merchants concerned are taken, who, it appears to us, would be very badly off, and would be little disposed to continue their business, if what they imported were not worth more to the purchasers of it, and would consequently sell for more, than what had been exported' (1986, 7, 39n).[44] Malthus also maintained in a (non-extant) letter of summer 1813 that extensions of foreign trade since 1793 implied a rising profit rate and economic expansion (see chapter 12, pp. 586–7). Beyond this we have little to go on regarding origins, and we turn to the 1820 formulation.

The object of the exercise is to demonstrate that *sustainable growth entails growth financed by accumulation deriving from preliminary increases in the value of the national product.* This theme is elaborated first in a discussion of expanded *internal* trade: 'If two districts, one of which possessed a rich copper mine, and the other a rich tin mine, had always been separated by an impassable river or mountain, there can be no doubt that on the opening of a communication, a greater demand would take place, and a greater price be given both for tin and copper; and this greater price of both metals, *though it might only be temporary,* would alone go a great way towards furnishing the additional capital wanted to supply the additional demand; and the capitals of both districts, and the products of both mines, would be increased both in quantity and value to a degree which could not have taken place without this new distribution of the produce, or some event equivalent to it' (1820, 440–1; 1836, 383; emphasis added). Similarly: 'No country with a very confined market, internal as well as external, has ever been able to accumulate a large capital, because such a market prevents the formation of those wants and tastes, and that desire to consume, which are absolutely necessary to keep up the market prices of commodities, and to occasion an increasing demand for them, and for the capital which is to produce them [1836: ... commodities, and prevent the fall of profits]. The distribution of commodities occasioned by internal trade is the first step towards any considerable increase of wealth and capital; and if no exchanges could have taken place in this country, at a greater distance than five miles, it is probably that not a fifth part of our present capital could have been employed before the effective encouragement to accumulation and the further progress of wealth had [1836: nearly] ceased' (1820, 448; 1836, 388). And more generally: 'The whole produce of a nation may be said to have a market price in money and labour. When this market price is high, that is, when the prices of com-

44 There are also references in 1811 to 'gluts' of British manufactures in foreign markets engendered by excessive Bank of England financing of exports (see chapter 13, p. 651).

modities rise so as to command a greater excess of labour above what they had cost in production than before, while the same capital and number of people had been employed upon them, it is evident that more fresh labour will be set in motion every year, and the increase of wealth will be certain and rapid' (1820, 443; 1836, 384–5).[45]

The concession that the increased prices of commodities initially involved in extended trade 'might only be temporary' alludes to the effect of the *subsequent* expansion of activity financed from savings out of the initially increased profits. This is clarified in a subsequent observation that reduction in the unit prices of particular commodities with extended trade (or new technology) was compatible with a rising value of GNP, and even in the aggregate value of the specific commodities in question, an apparent allusion to cases of elastic demand: 'The reader will be fully aware that a great fall in the price of particular commodities, either from improved machinery or foreign commerce, is perfectly compatible with a continued and great increase, not only in the exchangeable value of the whole produce of the country, but even in the exchangeable value of the whole produce of these particular articles themselves. It has been repeatedly [1836: already] stated that the whole value of the cottons produced in this country has been prodigiously increased, notwithstanding the great fall in their price. The same may be said of the teas [1836: of teas, sugars, and many other articles,] although when they were first imported, the price per pound was [1836: their prices were] greatly higher than at present' (1820, 456–7; 1836, 394).

In 1820 the same optimistic result is extended to rare cases of zero demand elasticity: 'Even when the commodity is of such a nature as not to admit of an extension of the market for it from reduced price, which very rarely happens, yet the capital and labour, which in this case will be thrown out of employment, will generally, in enterprising and commercial countries, find other channels into which they may be directed, with such profit as to keep up, and often more than keep up, the value of the national income' (1820, 457). None the less, into this class of cases fell those 'few exceptions ... to the general and powerful tendency of foreign commerce, to raise the value of the national income; and whenever these exceptions do take place, that is, whenever the value of the national income is diminished, estimated even in money, a temporary distress from a defective distribution of the produce cannot fail to take place. If this diminished value be estimated in labour, the distress among the labouring classes, and check to the progress of wealth, will continue as long as the

45 Here emerges a further aspect of Malthus's case, the insistence on explicit allowance for a 'circulating medium,' without which the notion of the *value* of aggregate output was all but impossible to perceive. In particular, it would not do to proceed in terms of physical wage-fund reasoning (1820, 444; 1836, 385–6).

diminished value so estimated lasts; and if it could be proved that, under particular circumstances, any species of foreign trade tended permanently to diminish the power of the national produce in the command of domestic and foreign labour, such trade would certainly have the effect of checking permanently the progress of wealth and population' (457–8).[46]

Issue is taken with the Physiocrats for representing trade as essentially 'unproductive' – merely a matter of equalizing prices: 'The [1836: French] Economists, in their endeavours to prove the unproductive nature of trade, always insisted that the effect of it was merely to equalize prices, which were in some places too high and in others too low, but in their amount the same as they would be after the exchange had taken place' (1820, 441; 1836, 383). This was 'unfounded' and 'contradicted by incontravertible facts': 'Every exchange which takes place in a country, effects a distribution of its produce better adapted to the wants of the society. It is with regard to both parties concerned, an exchange of what is wanted less for what is wanted more, and must therefore raise the value of both the products' (1820, 440; 1836, 382–3). If trade 'did not tend to increase the value of the national produce, it would not be carried on. It is out of this increase that the merchants concerned are paid; and if some London goods are not more valued in Glasgow than in London, and some Glasgow goods more valued in London than in Glasgow, the merchants who exchange the articles in which these towns trade, would neither be doing themselves any good, nor anyone else ... The giving one article for another has nothing to do with effectual demand, unless the commodity received so far exceeds in value the labour employed on the commodity parted with, as to yield adequate profits to the capitalists concerned, and to give them both the power and the will to set fresh labour of work in the same trade' (1820, 441–2; 1836, 383–4).

The Malthusian perspective is especially illuminated by the contention that the increased value of national product derived from a given capital and labour force upon extended trading opportunities reflects, in its essentials, a greater psychic estimate of the imported than of the domestic produce and a willingness to undertake sacrifices in order to obtain it. The context is Malthus's response to the orthodox view 'that the industry of a country is measured by the extent of its capital, and that the manner in which this capital is employed, though it may make some difference to the enjoyment of its inhabitants, makes very little in the *value* of the national revenue.' This proposition was objectionable; and, much the same objection as that directed against the Physiocrats is made against Ricardo: 'This would be true on [the] supposition ... that the inhabitants could be persuaded to estimate their confined productions just as highly, to be as eager to obtain and consume them, and as willing to work hard for them, and

46 The postwar opening of trade illustrates the exceptional case. See chapter 12, p. 604.

to make great sacrifices for them, as for the commodities which they obtain from a distance. But are we at liberty to make such a supposition? It is specifically to overcome the want of eagerness to purchase domestic commodities that the merchant exchanges them for others more in request. Could we but so alter the wants and tastes of the people of Glasgow as to make them estimate as highly the profusion of cotton goods which they produce, as any articles which they could receive in return for them under a prosperous trade, we should hear no more of their distresses' (1820, 442–3; 1836, 384). In sum, while 'the quantity of productive industry maintained in a country is nearly proportioned to the quantity of capital employed ... the value of the revenue will be greater or less, according to the market prices of the commodities produced.'[47]

Foreign trade turned on the same principles: 'The motives which urge individuals to engage in foreign commerce are precisely the same as those which lead to the interchange of goods between the more distant parts of the same country, namely, an increase in the market price [1836: a desire to increase or keep up the market prices] of the local products; and the increase of profits thus made by the individual, or the prevention of that fall of profits which would have taken place if the capital had been employed at home, must be considered as a proportionate [1836: comparative] increase in the value of the national produce' (1820, 448–9; 1836, 388–9). In reaction to Ricardo's position that 'no extension of foreign trade will immediately increase the amount of value in a country, though it will very powerfully contribute to increase the mass of commodities, and therefore the sum of enjoyments' (1951–73, I, 127), Malthus declared: 'If the two first sentences in Mr. Ricardo's chapter on foreign trade were well founded, there would be no such intercourse between nations' (1820, 450n; 1836, 390n).[48]

IX ON THE EFFICIENCY GAINS FROM TRADE: A DIGRESSION

In this section we digress from the main theme of the chapter to consider the implications of Malthus's response to Ricardo on trade. His high opinion of the Ricardian analysis of the distribution of the precious metals involving a non-uniform value of money in international equilibrium is documented in chapter 14: VI. This evaluation applies specifically to the

47 The allowance that 'the quantity of productive industry ... is nearly proportioned to the quantity of capital employed' may be merely for the sake of argument, considering the denial of this relationship elsewhere.

48 The second sentence of Ricardo's chapter reads: 'As the value of all foreign goods is measured by the quantity of the produce of our land and labour, which is given in exchange for them, we should have no greater value, if by the discovery of new markets, we obtained double the quantity of foreign goods in exchange for a given quantity of ours.'

matter of specie distribution in Ricardo's chapter on Foreign Trade – the later part: 'I have always considered the first part of Mr. Ricardo's chapter (vii) on foreign trade as essentially erroneous' (1836, 129n). What are we to make of this declaration? Did Malthus positively reject the 'comparative cost' doctrine, despite the fact that Ricardo's specie-distribution analysis is designed to show that precisely the same pattern of trade emerges in a monetary as in a barter regime? Or did he object only to Ricardo's preoccupation with efficiency?[49]

There is one passage, also critical of Ricardo, which takes us some way towards an answer. Here Malthus rejects what he took to be Ricardo's *measure* of the gains from trade, on the grounds that the cost saving achieved by importing rather than by domestic production provided a grossly misleading overestimate in cases where the imported products could not be produced at home, or even where domestic production was possible but at enormous cost:

> Mr. Ricardo always views foreign trade in the light of means of obtaining *cheaper* commodities. But this is only looking to one half of its advantages, and I am strongly disposed to think, not the larger half. In our own commerce at least, this part of the trade is comparatively inconsiderable. The great mass of our imports consists of articles as to which there can be no kind of question about their comparative cheapness, as raised abroad or at home. If we could not import from foreign countries our silk, cotton and indigo, our tea, sugar, coffee and tobacco, our port, sherry, claret and champagne, our almonds, raisons [*sic*], oranges and lemons, our various spices and our various drugs, with many other articles peculiar to foreign climates, is is quite certain that we should not have them at all. To estimate the advantage derived from their importation by their cheapness, compared with the quantity of labour and capital [1836: other advances] which they would have cost, if we had attempted to raise them at home, would be perfectly preposterous. In reality, no such attempt would have been thought of. If we could by possibility have made fine claret at ten pounds a bottle, few or none would have drunk it; and the actual quantity of labour and capital [1836: advances] employed in obtaining these foreign commodities is at present beyond comparison greater than it would have been if we had not imported them. (1820, 461–2; 1836, 396–7)[50]

49 Malthus had written in 1820: 'Mr. Ricardo very justly states that, even on the supposition which he has made respecting the precious metals, the foreign exchange of commodities is not determined by the quantity of labour which they have relatively cost' (117n). This may not indicate support for the Comparative Cost doctrine, but merely satisfaction with Ricardo's concession that the labour theory breaks down under some circumstances. So the first part of Ricardo's chapter could not be *totally* objectionable.

Torrens's *Essay on the External Corn Trade* (1st ed., 1815) first states the principle of comparative advantage; for a summary of the literature regarding priorities, see O'Brien, 1988, 203–4.

50 Viner applauded Malthus's objection that not much sense could be made of changes in

The description of Ricardo's efficiency gains from trade in terms of 'obtaining *cheaper* commodities' or as involving the 'comparative cheapness [of imports], as raised abroad and at home' might possibly be read as an allusion to absolute advantage.[51] But however we read Malthus on this detail, it is clear that he did not positively reject efficiency improvement *via* trade of some order, such improvement accounting for *part* of the advantage.[52]

Malthus's recognition of efficiency gains emerges clearly in the *Principles* in various contexts. There is reference to an advantageous importation by countries of commodities 'which they either could not produce on their own soil or could obtain cheaper elsewhere' (1820, 112–13), which suggests an absolute-advantage perspective. An account of American growth, which appears in the same chapter (the Progress of Wealth) as the formal criticism of Ricardo on Trade, maintains that 'the rapid increase of the United States of America, taken as a whole, has undoubtedly been aided very greatly by foreign commerce, and particularly by [1836: and by] the power of selling raw produce, obtained with little labour, for European commodities which have cost much labour' [1836: of a kind which, if made at home, would have cost much labour] (1820, 428; 1836, 373). This is admittedly a loose statement, particularly in the 1820 version, but it seems in its corrected form to allude to particularly high agricultural (relative to manufactur-

---

'the *quantity* of our commodities' by means of trade in the event that the imported commodities could either not be produced at home or only at prohibitive cost (1937, 531). I can see no reason why Ricardo would have disputed this proposition.

51 The possibility that Malthus failed to recognize Ricardo's adherence to comparative costs, unlikely though it is, cannot be precluded *a priori*; there are many strange attributions in the literature to Ricardo on trade. For example, Torrens is reported as ascribing to 'the Ricardo school' the 'great maxim that as the value of a commodity in the home market depended on the cost – the labour – of production, so must it be in a foreign market. He would maintain, that though this principle was true of domestic policy, yet that it was not it that regulated the exchangeable value in a foreign market' (House of Commons, 3 July 1832, Hansard, *Parliamentary Debates*, 3d series, XIV, 19 , cited in Viner, 1937, 487n). Viner surmised that this ascription to Ricardo might reflect the circumstance that Torrens heard McCulloch explain the doctrine of comparative costs incorrectly, a surmise based on Mallett's account of a discussion at the Political Economy Club for 5 April 1832: 'The discussion at last ran into a question of value, what constituted value in exchange – and on this rock it split, and left us all at sea. McCulloch, boldly standing by Ricardo's doctrine, that equal quantities of labour are equal in value all over the world – and Torrens and Malthus treating it as a ridiculous notion' (*Minutes of Proceedings*, VI, 1921, 234; cited in Viner, 488n). There is too little to go on in this passage, but it scarcely suggests a fair reading of Ricardo, who in fact took Malthus to task for comparing 'a day's work of a South American or of a Hindu, with the day's work of an Englishman, or a Frenchman' (*Note 37*, in 1951–73, II, 86).

52 Rashid thus seems to go too far when he asserts (on the basis of 1836, 10–11, alone) that Malthus considered free trade beneficial but only between countries exchanging complementary products (1987, 286, 290).

ing) efficiency in the United States, leaving unstated the counterpart in particularly high efficiency in European manufacturing (relative to agricultural) productivity. The passage – at least as elaborated in the 1836 version – is not necessarily in conflict with the 'comparative advantage' principle.[53]

The discussion in the *Principles* of corn-import restrictions from the efficiency perspective is clouded by a 'physiocratic' bias. Restrictions proved advantageous 'whenever the demand for corn grown at home is such, that the profits of capitals employed on the new lands taken into cultivation, joined to the rents which they generate, form together greater returns in proportion to the stock employed, than the returns of the capitals engaged in commerce and manufactures; because, in this case, though foreign corn might be purchased, without these restrictions, at a cheaper money price than that at which it could be raised at home, it would not be purchased at so small an expense of capital and labour, which is the true proof of the advantageous employment of stock' (1820, 223). It is in this special case that the cheaper money price of imported relative to domestic corn does not reflect a lesser real input; one deduces that normally such a differential in money prices *would* indicate resource saving – 'the true proof of the advantageous employment of stock.'[54]

There are numerous other allusions elsewhere to the efficiency case for free trade. In 1813 Malthus opposed proposals for agricultural import restrictions on efficiency grounds – 'the wealth which you sacrifice to attain this particular object [self-sufficiency in food]' (letter to Horner, 16 June 1813; in Tucker, 1954, 331–2). In his *Observations on the Corn Laws* (1814), he expressed the efficiency case for free trade thus: 'The general principles of political economy teach us to buy all our commodities where we can have them the cheapest' (1986, 7, 98). In *Grounds of an Opinion* (1815),

53 Ricardo, with the 1820 wording at hand, complained in *Note 259*: 'It can be of no consequence to America, whether the commodities she obtains in return for her own, cost Europeans much, or little labour [;] all she is interested in, is that they shall have cost her less labour by purchasing them than by manufacturing them herself' (1951–73, II, 383).

Jacob Viner puts this note in perspective: 'This explicit statement that imports could be profitable even though the commodity imported could be produced at less cost at home than abroad was, it seems to me, the sole addition of consequence which the doctrine of comparative costs made to the eighteenth-century rule. Its chief service was to correct the previously prevalent error that under free trade all commodities would necessarily tend to be produced in the locations where their real costs of production were lowest' (1937, 441).

54 Indeed, Malthus adds in a note: 'If restrictions upon importation necessarily increased the quantity of labour and capital required to obtain corn, they could not of course be defended for a moment, with a view to wealth and productive power. But if by directing capital to the land they occasion permanent improvements, the whole question is changed.'

which opted for agricultural protection notwithstanding efficiency losses, we find a generalization regarding prospective trade patterns emphasizing the peculiar advantages of Europe compared with Britain: 'But if we look at the probable effects of returning peace to Europe, it is impossible to suppose that, even with a considerable diminution in the price of labour, we should not lose some markets on the continent, for those manufactures in which we have no peculiar advantage; while we have every reason to believe that in others, where our colonies, our navigation, our long credits, our coals, and our mines come in question, as well as our skill and capital, we shall retain our trade in spite of high wages' (1986, 7, 166). But here presumably (considering the dating) – and certainly in the 1814 passage – it is *absolute* advantage that Malthus intended.[55]

We should also have in mind Viner's observation that, while the classics 'revealed no great interest in the detailed explanation of the forces which determined the nature of the international specialization existing in their time ... they did not wholly ignore the question, and when they did touch on it their adherence to the doctrine of comparative costs did not prevent them from dealing with it on lines similar in essentials to those followed by Ohlin' (1937, 504). Evidence to this effect may be drawn from Ricardo and also from Malthus, expecially his analysis of relatively high English money wages or relatively low value of money (1836, 104–5, 106–7). These citations from the second edition, elaborating the principle of specie distribution already touched on in 1820, allude to the rationale for exportation in terms of relative productivity – 'the cheapness of our exportable commodities' in the British case, allowing the production of a larger quantity of exportable manufactures at a lower money price than (say) Holland; or the 'cheapness and abundance of her raw produce' in the American case – explained, in turn, at least in part by differential factor endowments.

All this, as Viner insisted, is in line with comparative-cost theorizing.[56]

55 A further statement in the same pamphlet alludes specifically to resource savings resulting from demand-elasticity considerations: 'It often happens that the high prices of a particular country may diminish the *quantity* of its exports without diminishing the *value of their amount* abroad; in which case its foreign trade is peculiarly advantageous, as it purchases the same amount of foreign commodities at a much less expense of labour and capital' (173).

56 Viner (1937, 505n) also cites *The Measure of Value*: 'It is evident ... that the values which determine what commodities shall be exported, and what imported, depend ... partly upon the quantity of labour employed in their production, partly upon the ordinary rates of profits in each country, and partly upon the value of money' (1823b/1986, 7, 47). See also: 'the money prices of commodities which regulate the ordinary rate at which different countries exchange their commodities with each other, will be determined partly by the quantity of labour employed upon them, partly by the ordinary rate of profits, and partly by the value of money' (203).

None the less, the fact is that Malthus did not formally state that doctrine.[57] And by his condemnation of the first part of Ricardo's Foreign Trade chapter, and by many passages suggesting absolute advantage, he gave an impression that he rejected it. And in this he would not have been alone; it is interesting that J.R. McCulloch, while accepting the Hume–Ricardo theory of the distribution of the precious metals, rejected the comparative-cost theory in favour of absolute advantage (O'Brien, 1970, 192f.; Thweatt, 1976, 229).

X TRADE: THE MEASUREMENT PROBLEM

One particular formulation of the role of trade attracted an important response from Ricardo. The formulation follows a criticism of Ricardo's preoccupation with the efficiency gains from trade; and it amply confirms Malthus's position that trade extensions initially raise the 'value' of the *original* material product in the aggregate – though lacking index numbers of output, Malthus found the latter concept difficult to define: 'We must evidently therefore estimate the advantage which we derive from such a trade upon a very different principle. This is the simple and obvious one often adverted to as the foundation of every act of barter, whether foreign or domestic, namely, the increased value which results from exchanging what is wanted less for what is wanted more. After we had, by our exports of home commodities, obtained in return all the foreign articles above-mentioned, we might be very much puzzled to say whether we had increased or decreased the *quantity* of our commodities, but we should feel quite certain that the new distribution of produce which had taken place, by giving us commodities much better suited to our wants and tastes than those which had been sent away, had decidedly increased the exchangeable value of our possessions, our means of enjoyment, and our wealth. Taking therefore a very different view of the effects of foreign commerce on exchangeable value from Mr. Ricardo, I should bring forward the extension of markets as being, in its general tendency, pre-eminently favourable to that increase of value and wealth which arises from distribution' (1820, 462; 1836, 397–8).[58] The *Definitions* (1827) also emphasizes Ricardo's diver-

57 Perhaps the closest *formal* statement is in his *Essay on Population*, 1826 (1986, *3*, 430n): 'When the money price of labour is high in any country, or, what is the same thing, when the value of money is low, nothing can prevent it from going out to find its level, but some *comparative advantages*, either natural or acquired, which enable such country to maintain the abundance of its exports, notwithstanding the high money price of its labour.'

58 See also Malthus, 1820, 450n; 1836, 390n: Were it true that 'no extension of foreign trade will immediately increase the amount of value in a country,' as Ricardo maintained, commercial 'intercourse between nations' would cease.

An early allusion to the gains from trade which seems to constitute an embryonic

gence from what is represented to be the standard perspective: 'Mr. Ricardo's very startling proposition respecting the effects of foreign trade, namely that "no extension of foreign trade will immediately increase the amount of *value* in a country," arises entirely from his using the term value in a different sense from that in which it had been used by his predecessors' (1827a/1986, *8*, 21).

Ricardo read this perspective – as it appeared in 1820 – as consistent with his own position, and protested in *Note 183* at the suggestion that Malthus was taking a different view. He himself had always insisted on an increase in *wealth* by way of trade, though admittedly not of *value*, considering his own use of terms: 'From what Mr. Malthus has himself said in respect to my opinions he must know that I as well as himself "should bring forward the extension of markets as being, in its general tendency, pre-eminently favorable to that increase of wealth which arises from distribution." Yet his language here would lead his reader to suppose otherwise. I should not say it would increase the value of such wealth because as the reader knows I measure value by a different medium from Mr. Malthus' (1951–73, II, 420–1). Here Ricardo had in mind his own statement in his *Principles* that, though trade does not increase the amount of 'value,' it does 'very powerfully contribute to increase the mass of commodities, and therefore the sum of enjoyments' (1951–73, I, 128). This tolerant attitude comes as a surprise, for whereas Malthus's increase in wealth reflects a higher exchangeable value of output attributable to *demand* considerations, thus contravening the Law of Markets in a major way, his own reflects higher real income attributable to *efficiency* considerations.[59]

That Ricardian 'value' was unaffected by trade Malthus found irrelevant,

statement of the 1820 position by focusing on *demand* considerations will be found in Malthus's *Edinburgh Review* article of February 1811: 'We trust that we shall not be suspected, because we disapprove of [Huskisson's] doctrine of equivalents, of adopting the old mercantile notion, that the profits of foreign trade are derived from a balance paid in the precious metals; which Mr. Huskisson very oddly seems to think is the alternative. Our opinion is, that, in all commercial transactions, both parties gain what, in the estimation of each, is decidedly more than an equivalent for what it has given; and that it is out of this excess, that the gains of the merchants concerned are taken, who, it appears to us, would be very badly off, and would be little disposed to continue their business, if what they imported were not worth more to the purchasers of it, and would consequently sell for more, than what had been exported' (1811a/1986, *7*, 39n).

59 This is not to deny that such increase of wealth would provide a new source for savings, but it is a source of a different order. Thus if two regions engage in trade with each other 'the advantage ... to both places is not [that] they have any increase of value, but with the same amount of value they are both able to consume and enjoy an increased quantity of commodities,' or 'if they should have no inclination to indulge themselves in the purchase of an additional quantity, they will have an increased means of making savings from their expenditure' (1951–73, II, 395). See also Ricardo's 1821 'Advertisement' (I, 8).

the important consideration for him being the increase in aggregate 'value' in the sense of command over 'money, labour and commodities,' and this for a sufficient time to have a positive effect on general activity: 'As it is so glaring and undeniable a fact that the returns from an unusually favourable trade will exchange for an unusual quantity of money, labour and domestic commodities; as this increased power of commanding money, labour and commodities is in reality what is meant by the merchant when he talks of the extension of the foreign market and a favourable trade, it appears to me that such a state of things which may, and often does last a sufficient time to produce the most important results, is alone, and at once, a decisive proof that the view of exchangeable value, which makes it depend exclusively upon the cost of production, is essentially incorrect, and utterly useless in solving the great phenomena which attend the progress of wealth' (1820, 449–50). The second version is identical apart from a reduction in the aggressive tone (1836, 389), and an additional summary statement that profits 'are always estimated by value, not by quantity. The specific object which the merchant has in view when he engages in foreign commerce, is to obtain returns for his capital of greater *value* than if he had employed it at home; and in all cases of a favourable foreign trade from extending markets, this is specifically what he obtains.'[60]

60 That 'a new foreign trade' raises Malthusian value is further supported in an argument identifying such trade with a subsidy, though the parallel is unconvincing since the case of trade entails an initially unchanged aggregate output (setting aside the measurement problem), and that of a subsidy involves an initial increase. 'I see no difference between a present from abroad, and the unusual profits of a new foreign trade, in their effects upon the wealth of a state. They are equally calculated to increase the wealth of the community, by an increase both of the quantity and *value* of the produce obtained' (1820, 451; 1836, 390). Specifically: 'If any foreign power were to send to a particular merchant commodities of a new description which would sell in the London market for fifty thousand pounds, the wealth of such merchant would be increased to that extent; and who, I would ask, would be the poorer for it? It is no doubt true that the purchasers of these commodities may be obliged to forego the use of some of the articles which they had before been in the habit of buying, and so far in some quarters may diminish demand [1836: demand may be diminished]; but, to counterbalance this diminution, the enriched merchant will become a purchaser of additional goods to the amount perhaps of the whole fifty thousand pounds, and thus prevent any general fall in the value of the native produce consumed in the country, while the value of the foreign produce so consumed has increased to the amount of the whole of the new produce imported.' A note qualifies the allowance for a possibly reduced demand 'in some quarters': 'This, however, will not necessarily happen. The greater temptation offered to consumption may induce some persons to spend what they otherwise would have saved, and in many cases the wealth of the country, instead of suffering by this change, will gain by it. The increased consumption, as far as it goes, will occasion an increase of market prices and profits, and this increase of profits will soon restore the capital which for a short time had been diverted from its destined office; and the country will be left with habits of greater consumption, and at the same time with proportionate means of supplying them [1836: ... its destined office].'

Issue is also taken with Ricardo's proposition that 'in all cases the demand for foreign and home commodities together, as far as regards value, is limited by the revenue and capital of the country. If one increases, the other must diminish' (1951–73, I, 130): 'According to my view of the subject, the national revenue, which consists of the sum of rents, profits, and wages, is at once decidedly increased [1836: *increased*] by the increased profits of the foreign merchant, without a proportionate diminution of revenue in any other quarter; whereas Mr. Ricardo is evidently of opinion that, though the abundance of commodities is increased, the revenue of the country, as far as regards value, remains the same [1836: *remains the same*]' (1820, 454; 1836, 392). The 'Ricardian' response[61] that foreign commerce will indeed raise aggregate 'value' (Ricardian value), but only if more labour comes, following expansion, to be embodied in aggregate output, was irrelevant; what mattered was expansion in the 'value' of – labour commanded by – the *original material national product* in consequence of new trading opportunities, an increase taking the form of increased profit: 'What I wish specifically to state is, that the natural tendency of foreign trade, as of all sorts of exchanges by which a distribution is effected better suited to the wants of society, is *immediately* to increase the value of that part of the national revenue which consists of profits, without any proportionate diminution elsewhere, and that it is precisely this *immediate* increase of national income arising from the exchange of what is of less value in the country, for what is of more value, that furnishes both the power and will to employ more labour, and occasions the animated demand for labour, produce and capital, which is a striking and almost universal accompaniment of successful foreign commerce' (1820, 460; 1836, 396).

Malthus in 1820 himself raised the possible objection that, assuming a *given* labour supply, any increase in labour commanded is precluded.[62] His response implies that the *money* value of output rises relative to the *money* wage taking the form of increased profits, which increase – by raising demand for labour – will, in fact, generate higher aggregate money wages entailing both higher wages per unit of labour and fuller employment of the given workforce, ultimately encouraging population growth (1820, 451–2; cited chapter 9, p. 429). Should the higher profits initially generated by trade be entirely transferred to labour via pressure on labour de-

61 'Mr. Ricardo will perhaps say, and say truly, that according to his own view of value, foreign commerce will increase it, as soon as more labour has been employed in the production of all the commodities taken together, which the country obtains; and that the plenty produced by foreign trade will naturally encourage this employment' (1820, 460; omitted in 1836).

62 This has its counterpart in a given (aggregate) value in the Ricardian labour-embodied scheme, assuming a constant labour force. In 1836 the objection and the defence do not appear (see 1836, 391). It is unclear why they are removed.

mand, this redistribution of course entails a fall in labour commanded to its original level, but it is no less true that there is a higher labour commanded *reckoned at the original wage.*

Viner objected to the apparent welfare implications flowing from the notion of gains from the trade as consisting in increased exchangeable value in the sense of *labour commanded* (though he said nothing to refute the positive analysis of the effect of trade in raising total monetary income): '[Malthus] reached the conclusion that foreign trade increases the sum of "labour command" in the following fashion: foreign trade, when it results in a new assortment of commodities available for use which is "better suited to the wants of society" than the pre-trade one, increases income in the form of profits without a proportionate decrease in other forms of income, and therefore increases the amount of money available for payment as wages, or the demand for labour; wages do not rise in proportion to the rise in total money income; therefore the new income constitutes a greater sum of "labour command" than the old one [1820, 460; 1836, 396]. Malthus would, therefore, presumably deny that there was gain from foreign trade if money wage rates rose relatively as much as total monetary income, so that there was no increase in "labour command." To measure gain by the increase in "labour command" without reference to the terms on which labour can be commanded is a fantastic procedure if labourers are recognized as constituting part of the population' (1937, 529).

It is not clear that this criticism is valid. As noted already, even should the higher profits be transferred entirely to labour, labour commanded rises when reckoned at the original wage rate. As for the observation that, in dealing with the gains from trade, Malthus intended *specifically* labour commanded by his exchangeable value, not value in terms of *money*, we should note that in his positive analysis Malthus frequently used both indexes interchangeably (see above, p. 534). Indeed, in a response given in the *Definitions* to Ricardo's denial that foreign-trade extensions can 'immediately increase the amount of value in a country,' we find the broader definition: 'If the value of foreign commodities imported be estimated in the way in which they had ever been estimated before, that is, either in the money, in the labour, or in the mass of commodities which they would command when brought home, then there cannot be the least doubt that the *immediate* effect of a prosperous venture which gives great profits to the merchants concerned would be to increase the amount of value in the country. The value of the returns compared with the value of the outgoings would, in this particular trade, be greater than usual; and it is quite certain, that this increase of value in one quarter would not necessarily be counterbalanced by a decrease of value in any other. Practically, indeed, nothing is more usual than a simultaneous rise in the value of the great mass of commodities from a prosperous trade, whether this value be estimated in money or in labour' (1827a/1986, *8*, 21).

On balance, it seems that Malthus was prepared to refer to bullion *tout court* 'for short periods,' on the grounds that rarely does 'any great increase or decrease in the bullion value of all commodities of a country take place, without an increase or decrease of demand for commodities, compared with the supply of them' (1820, 416; 1836, 363). But since it was conceivable for bullion prices to *fall* – and this over 'periods of some length' (1836) – while a country was experiencing 'an *increase* of wealth,' his preference was labour commanded. Thus in 1820: 'I shall refer generally to the labour, domestic and foreign, which the bullion price of the produce will command, or the sacrifices which people are willing and able to make of their own or other persons exertions in order to obtain it, as the best practical measure of that value that can be applied; and though undoubtedly not accurate, yet sufficiently so for the present purpose.'[63] In 1836 version is more pointed: 'When ... there is any doubt, in regard to a change in the value of money we must refer to that standard, the utility and comparative correctness of which I have endeavoured to establish; and in reference to which Adam Smith himself, says, "Labour, be it remembered, and not any particular commodity or set of commodities, is the real measure of the value of both silver and of all other commodities."'

In our present context, Malthus in fact recommends a two-stage procedure, taking account, first, of bullion prices and, then, of labour commanded as 'ultimate index, and this because changes in bullion value were indicative of changes in 'distribution':

It is scarcely possible for any essential change to take place in the value of the circulating medium of a country without occasioning an alteration in the distribution of its produce. The imprudent use of paper money must be allowed to be the principle cause of these changes. But even without a paper currency, or with one always maintaining the same value as bullion, every country is liable to changes in the value of its produce, compared with its money; and as such changes must have a great effect on the distribution of produce, partly temporary and partly permanent, a determination to reason on these subjects, without taking into account the effects of so powerful an agent, would be puposely to shut our eyes to the truth. Referring therefore ultimately to the command over labour, domestic and foreign [1836: over labour] as the best practical measure of the value of the whole produce, it will be useful to refer previously to its bullion value, in order to ascertain whether the distribution of the produce is

63 The *mean* measure was inappropriate in treating *national* wealth: 'As the best approximation to a measure of real value in exchange, in application to the commodities of different countries and different times, I before proposed a mean between corn and labour [Chapter II, Sect. VII]; and to this measure I should be disposed always to refer, when any commodities are to be estimated, with the exception of corn and labour themselves. But ... in speaking of national wealth, it is necessary to include the exchangeable value of food; and ... food cannot well be the measure of food ...'

such as to enable it to command labour in some proportion [1836: in proportion] to the increase of its quantity. If the bullion value of a country's products so increases as to command yearly an increased quantity of domestic and foreign labour [1836: of labour without a fall of profits,] we may feel pretty well assured that it is proceeding without check in wealth and prosperity. But, if there is merely an increase of commodities, it is impossible to say, without further inquiry, that they may not be so distributed as to retard, instead of promote, the progress [1836: further progress] of national wealth. (1820, 447–8; 1836, 387–8)

XI ON THE ENDOGENEITY OF FINANCIAL MEANS

In 1813 Malthus apparently relied on an automatic rise in monetary funds to support the higher aggregate value of the national product – and the higher profit rate – which he maintained was engendered by extended trade (above, section VIII). This is suggested by the wording of the argument to the contrary adopted by Ricardo in his side of the correspondence, which is all that is available to us. Thus in his letters of 10 and 17 August 1813, Ricardo insisted upon money-supply variation as *cause*, not *effect*, of an 'increased [nominal] value of commodities,' and this in objection to Malthus's position regarding the higher value of national product owing to extended trade (1951–73, VI, 93–4, 95).

In both editions of the *Principles*, Malthus formally addressed the possible objection that a higher aggregate value in *money* terms owing to 'a new foreign trade' is precluded should the money supply be *given* (incidentally confirming the continued significance of the money measure). As for 1820: 'It will be said perhaps that, neither the people nor the money of the country having been by supposition increased, the value of the whole produce estimated in labour or money cannot be increased' (1820, 451). In response, Malthus relied on an automatic 'accommodation' of the supply of money and/or its velocity in the circumstances posited, the rise in total money income occurring without inflation and depreciation of the currency: 'With regard to money, this most useful measure of value would perform its functions very indifferently, if it could in no respect accommodate itself to cases of this kind; and if the importation of a valuable commodity always proportionably reduced the price of the other parts of the national produce. But this is far from being the case, even if we do not suppose any fresh importation of the precious metals. The occurrence of such an event is precisely the period, when a greater velocity is given to the circulation of the money actually in use, and when fresh paper may be issued without a fall in the rate of foreign exchanges, or a rise in the price of bullion and of goods. One or other, or both of these resources will be applied, except in the most barbarous countries; and though undoubtedly, in the case of the importation of foreign commodities which come directly into competition with domestic goods, such goods will fall in price, and the producers of them be for a time rendered poorer, yet it will very rarely indeed happen that other goods not affected by such competition will fall in money value; and altogether no fall will take place in particular commodities sufficient to prevent a rise in the money price of the whole produce' (1820, 452–3). Malthus proceeded to allow, however, that it 'may naturally be expected that more money will be imported,' since 'a successful extension of foreign trade is exactly the state of things which most directly leads to the importation of bullion.'

In 1836 there is a brief statement of the objection: 'It may perhaps be thought that the *money* value of the whole produce cannot be increased without an importation of money' (1836, 391). As in 1820, the assurance is given that 'successful' trade extensions guaranteed an increase in the money supply or its effectiveness;[64] and in both editions the text elaborates on this outcome: 'For what is it that the merchant exporter specifically considers as a successful extension of foreign commerce in dealing with civilized nations? Undoubtedly, the power of selling his exports abroad for a greater value than usual, estimated in bullion; and of course, if the goods which he would import in return will not sell at home so much higher as to warrant their importation, a part of the whole of the returns will [1836: a part of the returns will finally] be imported in money. But if [1836: But if on the whole trade] only such an amount be imported as shall bear the same proportion to the returns in goods as the whole of the currency of the country does to the whole of its produce, it is obvious that no difficulty whatever can occur in the circulation of the commodities of the country at their former prices, with the single exception of those articles with which the foreign goods might directly enter into competition, which in this case would never be sufficient to prevent a general increase of the value in the whole produce' (1820, 453; 1836, 391–2).[65]

* * *

The passivity – or endogeneity – of finance is a key feature of Malthus's monetary writings in 1823. This must be placed in context. A so-called fundamental proposition elaborated in Malthus's *Quarterly Review* article on Tooke's *High and Low Prices* – the evidence for which he found in that work, though Tooke himself did not always realize it (above, p. 539) – relates to the effect on prices and profits of relative deficiency of (aggre-

64 An added note elsewhere in the 1836 version confirms this guarantee: 'Repeated experience appears to have shewn us that in the case of a brisk demand, no difficulty is ever found in furnishing the means of a considerable rise of prices in some classes of commodities, without any tendency to a fall in others' (1836, 128n).

65 Cazenove added his own editorial opinion that an increased level of prices does *not* require an increased money supply, having in mind variation in velocity. He misread Malthus, who throughout took account of the 'effectiveness of the money supply.' The concept of endogeneity of the money supply emerges early on in a letter of 28 November 1800 (see Keynes, 1933, 124n).

gate) supply: 'When the supply of commodities is in some degree deficient compared with the demand, whether this arises from the increase of demand, or the diminution of supply, the state of trade is brisk, profits are high, and mercantile speculations are greatly encouraged; and on the other hand, when the supply is abundant compared with the demand, there is a period of comparative stagnation, with low profits, and very little encouragement to mercantile speculation' (1823a/1986, 7, 227).[66] As we shall now see, it is via a sort of endogenous expansion in finance (and/or velocity) that the rise in general prices and profits induced by commodity-supply constraints relative to demand – evidently the concern is with the *aggregate* dimension – is made effective.

The case opens with a condemnation of Tooke for inexplicably asserting 'that war cannot operate in raising general prices through the medium of increased demand, *the quantity of money, and its rate of circulation continuing the same*' (cited 235). 'This,' Malthus protested, 'appears to us a most strange limitation, and if adhered to, would convert a very interesting practical inquiry into a barren discussion of a suppositious case which, perhaps, it would not be too much to say could never be realized.' Malthus thus represents the increase in finance required to support higher general prices as an *inevitable* consequence of (relative) supply deficiency – the pre-eminent example, and the empirical case at hand, being obstructions typical of wartime.

In elaborating his case Malthus phrases the main issue to read: Whether the wartime circumstances 'did really create an increase in demand as well as an obstruction of supply.' By this he intended a positive expansion of demand accompanied by the financial means required to give 'effect' to such expansion; it is this latter that Tooke precluded by his qualification: 'It is of the very nature of war, and of the obstructions which it occasions to supply, to influence the quantity of money in a country, and the rate of its circulation. And surely the proper inquiry for us, on the present occasion, is, *the fact*, whether the circumstances of the late war did really create an increase of demand as well as an obstruction to the supply, without precluding the natural means by which such a result would be effected' (236). Malthus saw no room to doubt 'the alterations in the proportion between the supply of commodities and the demand for them, during the last war, occasioned partly by obstructions to supply arising from the war, and partly from the unfavourableness of the seasons.' Any possible question related to the *demand* side: 'Our only question with Mr. Tooke, on this part of the subject, is, whether this state of the proportion between supply and demand does or does not occasion an increase of demand, which may properly be considered as positive as well as relative. This question, it appears to us, that the facts and general reasonings which he has brought forward clearly answer in the affirmative.'

66 There is brief mention of the same notion in *The Measure of Value* (1823b/1986, 7, 216).

The 'facts and reasonings' adduced by Tooke himself showed not only 'that a deficiency of supply of some important article compared with the average consumption, creates an increase of general demand, accompanied by a rise of prices; but *they point out distinctly how this rise of prices may take place, even without an increase either of Bank of England paper or money*' (237; emphasis added). It is by way of an 'invariable' expansion of currency and credit that the general price increase can be maintained (245; cited above, p. 540). These automatic increases in finance and in velocity of currency circulation figure large; their passivity was manifest in that there resulted therefrom no depreciation in the technical sense, that is, no 'necessary separation of the paper from the gold,' since prices rise in *gold* as well as in paper: 'Mr. Tooke, we repeat, has very happily explained how this is effected, by showing that a deficiency of supply calls forth at once an increased quantity of private paper and credit, without any necessary separation of the paper from the gold, thus making the gold conform itself in value to an increased quantity of currency divided among a diminished quantity of commodities. To this cause of the high prices of commodities occasioned by the sudden extension of private paper and credit, we should be strongly disposed to add a more rapid circulation of the currency, which, we believe, is the almost constant concomitant of what is called a brisk demand. And we cannot help considering these two causes combined as of very great power, and as affording the true explanation of events which would be otherwise unintelligible' (251).

The notion of an endogenous process whereby a higher level of prices attracts the requisite increase in finance seems to conflict with the standard Hume specie-flow mechanism to which Malthus also adhered. The supply of money is treated apparently both as *effect* and as *cause* of a higher price level. Now there is nothing to rule out mutual causality of this order. (Adam Smith had made much of it also in the monetary context (1776/1937, 185, 188–9). But Malthus may himself have sensed a problem. For in the Tooke review itself, he recognized 'limits' to monetary attraction (1823a/1986, 7, 251; see chapter 14, pp. 731–2). Limits are also defined in *The Measure of Value*, with the implication that, once reached, money outflow must occur: 'It is further established by experience, that a brisk or slack demand for commodities and labour, and particularly for corn, has a considerable effect on the value of gold. Such a demand not only occasions a more rapid circulation of money, and enables the same quantity to perform a greater number of transactions, but calls into action a greater quantity of credit and private paper, so that a general rise of bullion prices, including labour, seems to be at all times possible, even without any fresh importation of the precious metals; and the only practical limit to this rise, is the turn of the exchange, and the impossibility of maintaining the exchanges nearly at par beyond a certain elevation of labour and commodities' (1823b/1986, 7, 213). And similarly in the 1836 edition of the *Principles*: 'Repeated experience appears to have shewn us that in the case of a brisk demand, no difficulty is ever found in furnishing the means of a considerable rise of prices in some classes of commodities, without any tendency to a fall in others. Currency is always at hand. The important question is, whether the exchanges can be maintained under such prices; and we know too well that they have often risen higher than the exchanges would allow so as to keep paper and gold together' (1836, 128n).

XII DISTRIBUTION OF PROPERTY AND SUSTAINABLE GROWTH

We return to the initial 'cause' specified in the *Principles* as favouring increase of aggregate value (above, p. 543) – the division of landed property. Great inequality is said to be an impediment to the generation of a large market: 'Thirty or forty proprietors, with incomes answering to between one thousand and five thousand a year, would create a much more effective demand for wheaten bread, good meat, and manufactured produce [1836: effectual demand for the necessaries, conveniences, and luxuries of life,] than a single proprietor possessing a hundred thousand a year' (1820, 430; 1836, 374). It was not inconceivable 'for a nation with a comparatively small body of very rich proprietors, and a large body of very poor workmen, to push both the produce of the land and of manufactures to the greatest extent, that the resources and ingenuity of the country would admit.' But this supposed 'a passion among the rich for the consumption of manufactures, and the results of productive labour, much more excessive than has ever been witnessed in human society,' whereas 'practically it has always been found that the excessive wealth of the few is in no respect equivalent, with regard to effective [1836: effectual] demand, to the more moderate wealth of the many. A large body of manufacturers and merchants can only find a market for their commodities among a numerous class of consumers above the rank of mere workmen and labourers [1836: below the rank of the great proprietors of land]. And experience shows us that manufacturing wealth is at once the consequence of a better distribution of property, and the cause of further improvements in such distribution, by the increase in the proportion of the middle classes of society, which the growth of manufacturing and mercantile capital cannot fail to create' (1820, 431; 1836, 375).[67] The British 'middle classes' constituted a 'large class of effective demanders, who derive their power of purchasing from the various professions, from commerce, from manufactures, from wholesale and retail trade, from salaries of various kinds, and from the interest of public and private debts; and these demanders are likely, perhaps to acquire tastes more favourable to the encouragement of wealth than the owners of the small properties on the land' (1820, 436–7; 1836, 379).

67 See also the emphasis on a more egalitarian social structure appropriate for the generation of broad-based markets in an account of Irish potential (1820, 400–1; 1836, 350–1).

Too great a degree of equality, however, would prove an impediment on the supply side – an illustration of Malthus's famous doctrine of 'proportions': 'But though it be true that the division of landed property, and the diffusion of manufacturing and mercantile capital to a certain extent, are of the utmost importance to the increase of wealth; yet it is equally true that, beyond a certain extent, they would impede the progress of wealth as much as they had before accelerated it' (1820, 431; 1836, 375). The significance of the doctrine of proportions will be elaborated in our final chapter.

XIII 'UNPRODUCTIVE' CONSUMPTION

Section IX of the chapter 'Of the Progress of Wealth' considers the means of raising the exchangeable value of aggregate produce by way of demand emanating from *outside* the productive sector: 'The third main cause which tends to keep up and increase the value of produce by favouring its distribution is the employment of unproductive labour [1836: individuals in personal services,] or the maintenance of an adequate proportion of unproductive consumers [1836: consumers not directly productive of material objects]' (1820, 463; 1836, 398). Here reference is made to the original demonstration of Section III that, 'under a rapid accumulation of capital, or more properly speaking [1836: or in other words], a rapid conversion of unproductive [1836: persons engaged in personal services] into productive labour, the demand, compared with the supply of material products, would prematurely fall, and the motive to further accumulation be checked, before it was checked by the exhaustion of the land. It follows that, without supposing the productive classes to consume much more than they are found to do by experience, particularly when they are rapidly saving from revenue to add to their capitals, it is absolutely necessary [1836: it is necessary] that a country with great powers of production should possess a body of unproductive consumers [1836: consumers who are not themselves engaged in production].'[68]

A source of demand *external to the productive sector itself* was apparently not seen as a *sine qua non* of growth. One notes that the 1836 version of the foregoing passage no longer reads '*absolutely* necessary' in this respect, and the same sentence in both editions asserts that an external source of expenditure is required *unless* one 'suppos[es] the productive classes to consume much more than they are found to do by experience, particularly

68 Nothing in this formulation conflicts with the interpretation of the savings process offered earlier (above, section II), whereby landlords and capitalists cut their luxury spending in favour of accumulation – understood as spending on capital goods – with service labour drawn into the productive sector only at the next stage, when the new capacity must be manned. This version, it will be recalled, contrasts with a rather more naïve version involving a direct switch of service workers into the productive sector.

when they are rapidly saving from revenue to add to their capitals ...' This is confirmed when Malthus answers affirmatively the question whether 'there can be no occasion for unproductive consumers, if a consumption sufficient to keep up the value of the produce takes place among those who are engaged in production?' (1820, 464–5; 1836, 399); and further asserts that 'there might be little occasion for unproductive consumers' were capitalists to restrict their savings to 'what could be beneficially added to their capital' (cited above, p. 530).[69] The problem, however, was precisely that they tended to save at an *excessive* rate. It is this propensity to excess that necessitated 'a considerable class of other consumers, or the mercantile classes could not continue extending their concerns and realizing their profits' (1820, 466);[70] or as in 1836, 'a considerable class of persons who have both the will and power to consume more material wealth than they produce, or the mercantile classes could not continue profitably to produce so much more than they consume' (1836, 400).

Landlords' expenditures played the 'pre-eminent' role.[71] Here, implicitly, landlords are treated as 'unproductive,' and rent as a transfer, not an original income.[72] However, expenditure out of rent might not suffice: 'If the powers of production among capitalist are considerable, the consumption of the landlords, in addition to that of the capitalists themselves and of their workmen, may still be insufficient to keep up and increase the exchangeable value of the produce, that is, to make the increase of its quantity more than counterbalance the fall of its price' (1820, 466). The 1836 version deletes reference to 'considerable' powers of production, suggesting thereby the *inevitable* inadequacy of landlords' expenditure: 'If they were not assisted by the great mass of individuals engaged in personal services, whom they maintain, their own consumption would of itself be

69 See also a reference to the possibility that, were the 'people of Glasgow' sufficiently motivated to consume their own products, there would be no need for external trade (1820, 443; 1836, 384).

70 Marx was later to use the term 'realization' in the same sense.

71 Malthus inserts a fine 'physiocratic' flourish: 'In the fertility of the soil, in the powers of man to apply machinery as a substitute for labour, and in the motives to exertion under a system of private property, the great laws [1836: the laws] of nature have provided for the leisure [1836: or personal services] of a certain portion of society; and if this beneficent offer be not accepted by an adequate number of individuals, not only will a positive good, which might have been so attained, be lost, but the rest of the society, so far from being benefited by such self-denial, will be decidedly injured by it' (1820, 463–4; 1836, 398–9). See Waterman, 1996b, for Paley's quasi-physiocratic emphasis on the strategic importance of agriculture.

72 This is not always the case. For example, in the following passage rent is treated like wages and profits, as an *original* income: 'according to my view of the subject, the national revenue, which consists of the sum of rents, profits, and wages, is at once decidedly increased [1836: *increased*] by the increased profits of the foreign merchant, without a proportionate diminution of revenue in any other quarter' (1820, 454; 1836, 392; see above, p. 555). There is an ambiguity in this regard running through Malthus's writings.

insufficient to keep up and increase the value of the produce, and enable the increase of its quantity more than to counterbalance the fall of its price' (1836, 400). But even so there is a suggestion that under certain conditions expenditure by 'personal servants' may not be required: 'It may be thought perhaps that the landlords could not fail to supply any deficiency of demand and consumption among the producers, and that between them there would be little chance of any approach towards redundancy of capital. What might be the result of the most favourable distribution of landed property it is not easy to say from experience; but experience certainly tells us that, under the distribution of land which actually takes place in most of the countries in Europe, the demands of the landlords, added to those of the producers, have not always been found sufficient to prevent any difficulty in the employment of capital' (1820, 475; 1836, 405).

A summary statement of the problem confirms that inadequate consumption by capitalists and landlords reflected rather an 'empirical' matter – in contrast to that by labour, which had a 'theoretical' basis: 'But if the master producers, from the laudable desire they feel of bettering their condition, and providing for a family, do not consume sufficiently [1836: do not consume their revenue sufficiently] to give an adequate stimulus to the increase of wealth; if the working producers, by increasing their consumption, supposing them to have the means of so doing, would impede the growth of wealth more by diminishing the power of production, than they could encourage it by increasing the demand for produce; and if the expenditure of the landlords, in addition to the expenditure of the two preceding classes, be found insufficient to keep up and increase the value of that which is produced, where are we to look for the consumption required but among the unproductive labourers of Adam Smith?' (1820, 476–7; 1836, 406). In the 1820 version there is an explicit affirmation that the problem is indeed *not* inevitable: 'It has been repeatedly conceded, that the productive classes' – presumably capitalists are intended, and perhaps landlords – 'have the power of consuming all that they produce; and, if this power were adequately exercised, there might be no occasion, with a view to wealth, for unproductive consumers. But it is found by experience that, though there may be the power, there is not the will; and it is to supply this will that a body of unproductive consumers is necessary' (1820, 488–9).

While the existence of a class of unproductive labourers (or as in 1836, persons engaged in 'personal services,' including menials, statesmen, soldiers, judges and lawyers, doctors, and clergymen) detracted 'from the material production of a country, and its power of supporting an extended population,' yet on balance – subject to a qualification taken up shortly afterwards – they 'furnish[ed] fresh motives to production, and tend[ed] to push the wealth of a country further than it would go without them' (1820, 477; 1836, 407). For the '*possibility*' had been demonstrated (in the chapter 'On Profits' as well as the section on Accumulation in the chapter on the 'Progress of Wealth') of *redundant capital* – in the sense that 'the motive to accumulate may be checked or destroyed by want of effective demand long before it is checked by the difficulty of procuring the subsistence of the labourer' (1820, 478; 1836, 407); and it had also been shown (in the section at hand) that such possibility was a 'probable occurrence' – that is, that 'the actual habits and practice of the productive classes, in the most improved societies,' an obvious allusion to be *employing* class, 'do not lead them to consume as revenue [1836: to consume] so large a proportion of what they produce, even though assisted by the landlords, as to prevent their finding frequent difficulties in the employment of their capitals' (1820, 478; 1836, 407–8). From all this it followed that state, defence, health, and religious functionaries were 'necessary to call forth those exertions which are required to give full play to its physical resources.' But to this Malthus adds the 'probability' that 'the unproductive classes' – in 1836: 'those persons who are not employed in the production and distribution of material objects' – and who are 'paid voluntarily by individuals' – would be 'the most likely to be useful in exciting industry, and the least likely to be prejudicial by interfering with the costs of production. It may be presumed that a person will not take a menial servant, unless he can afford to pay him; and that he is as likely to be excited to industry by the prospect of this indulgence, as by the prospect of buying ribands and laces' (1820, 478–9; 1836, 408).[73]

In 1836 there appears a paragraph elaborating the function of menial service. That sector is represented as complementary to certain luxury outlays by 'the higher and middle classes,' thus encouraging the latter: 'It is also very important to observe, that menial servants are absolutely necessary to make the resources of the higher and middle classes of society efficient in the demand for material products. No persons possessing incomes above five hundred pounds a year, would be inclined to have such houses, furniture, clothes, carriages and horses, and such eatables and drinkables in their houses as they have at present, if they were obliged to sweep their own rooms, brush and wash their own furniture and clothes, clean their own carriages and horses, and had none but themselves to make a demand for eatables and drinkables' (1836, 408). And to this is added the basic function of services, whether 'menial or intellectual' – this of course is true also of 1820 – when paid voluntarily from revenue, that of raising aggregate expenditure on *material* products without adding to costs: 'And it is further to be remarked, that all personal services paid voluntarily, whether of a menial or intellectual kind, are essentially distinct

73 There is an unstated bias here against government provision, considering the 'cost' implications of taxation. The reference to 'voluntary payment' is intended to contrast with payment via the tax system.

from the labour necessary to production. They are paid from revenue, not from capital. They have no tendency to increase cost and lower profits. On the contrary, while they leave the cost of production, as far as regards the quantities of labour required to obtain any particular commodities the same as before, they increase profits by occasioning a more brisk demand for material products, as compared with the supply of them' (408–9).

The references to capital redundancy and to 'frequent' instances of 'difficulties in the employment of their capitals' because of excessive saving, suggest a problem of *unused capacity.* So too does the observation that capitalists tend to save too rapidly 'in prosperous times' (above, p. 530). Yet we must recall that the initial statement of the problem involved *slow growth,* that is, why capital accumulation tended to be relatively sluggish despite an abundance of natural resources, which implies, not *excessive,* but *inadequate,* accumulation. Possibly the reconciliation lies in the contrast between short-run and long-run perceptions – excessive capital accumulation may generate excess capacity; but with time the stock falls back to its original suboptimal level.

As for the qualification mentioned above regarding the *possibility* of adequate consumption by capitalists and landlords, that involves the so-called doctrine of proportions and had been touched on at the outset of Malthus's section IX (1820, 464; 1836, 399).[74] Here one notes the remark in that passage that a 'body of [unproductive] demanders' *may* be essential, indicating that under certain circumstances growth might proceed without it, and confirming that much of the problem was an empirical matter, not necessarily flowing from the nature of things.[75]

XIV 'NEW INVENTIONS' AND SUSTAINABLE GROWTH

Our concern thus far has been the problem of sustainable growth from the perspective of accumulation. We turn next to Malthus's rejection of 'fertility of the soil' and 'new inventions' as potential stimuli (Sections IV and V of his chapter on the 'Progress of Wealth').[76] Since, like accumulation, these 'tend to facilitate supply, without reference to demand, it is not probable that they should either separately or conjointly afford an adequate stimulus to the continued increase of wealth, which can only be kept up by a continued increase in the demand for commodities' [1836, omits:

74 For the full passage see the final chapter, p. 982.

75 Cf. letter to Ricardo of 26 October 1820: 'I ... fancy that I am fortified with new arguments to prove demonstratively that a neat revenue is absolutely impossible under the determination to employ the whole produce in the production of necessaries, and consequently if there is not an adequate taste for luxuries and conveniences, or unproductive labour, there must necessarily be a general glut' (Ricardo, 1951–73, VIII, 285).

76 Population increase as stimulus has been dealt with already, as part of the main issue (our section IV).

'which ... commodities']' (1820, 413; 1836, 360).[77] The land-fertility issue pertains in the main to secular stagnation in a development context, whereas new technology concerns, rather, modern economies, and carries further the story up to this point. We accordingly postpone discussion of the first issue to section XVI.

Labour-saving inventions are formally treated as *endogenous* and – at least 'in their more perfect form' – apparently a response to increasing land scarcity: 'Inventions to save labour seldom take place to any considerable extent, except when there is a decided demand for them. They are the natural products [1836: natural consequence] of improvement and civilization, and, in their more perfect forms, generally come in aid of the failing powers of production on the land. The fertility of the soil, being a gift of nature, exists whether it is wanted or not; and must often therefore exceed for many hundred years the power of fully using it. Inventions, which substitute machinery for manual exertions, being the result of the ingenuity of man, and called forth by his wants, will, as might be expected, seldom greatly exceed [1836: seldom exceed] those wants' (1820, 401–2; 1836, 351). This is a novel perspective. But, in what follows, innovation is effectively treated as if it were exogenous; there would otherwise be no rationale for the absolute cost reductions which are emphasized in the account. The discussion is particularly significant for the light thrown on Malthus's view of contemporary industrial development.

In the cotton industry the effect of machinery had been to reduce cost price and, considering an elastic demand both domestic and foreign, to increase *total* revenue expended, and also to expand absolute employment opportunities: 'When a machine is invented, which, by saving labour, will bring goods into the market at a much cheaper rate than before, the most usual effect is such an extension of the demand for the commodity, by its being brought within the power of a much greater number of purchasers, that the value of the whole mass of goods made by the new machinery greatly exceeds their former value; and, notwithstanding the saving of labour, more hands, instead of fewer, are required in the manufacture' (1820, 402; 1836, 352). In the case of zero demand elasticity – where the commodity 'is not of such a nature that its consumption can extend with its cheapness' – total expenditure will decline with cost-price reductions; nevertheless, the revenue saved is 'set free for the purchase of fresh com-

77 Similarly, both fertility and inventions 'come under the head of facilities of production; and in both cases a full use cannot be made of this facility, unless the power of supply which it furnishes be accompanied by an adequate extension of the market' (1820, 402; 1836, 351). Also: 'Like the fertility of land, the invention of good machinery confers a prodigious power of production. But neither of these great powers can be called fully into action, if the situation and circumstances, or the habits and tastes of the society prevent the opening of a sufficient market, and an adequate increase of consumption' (1820, 412–13; 1836, 360).

modities,' which 'encourages the employment of the vacant capitals in other directions,' an allusion to the capital and labour relinquished by the cost saving (1820, 403–4; 1836, 353). The extent of the benefit turned on circumstances.[78] The main problem raised here[79] is the likely 'loss' of capital and employment potential in the course of transfer: 'But in withdrawing capital [1836: a part of which must necessarily be fixed,] from one employment and placing it in another, there is almost always a considerable loss. [1836 adds: The uselessness of the old fixed capital would be at once a loss of revenue to the amount of the former interest and profits upon it.] Even if the whole of the remainder were directly employed, it would be less in amount. Though it might yield a greater produce, it would not command the same quantity of labour as before; [1836: Even if the whole of the remainder could be immediately employed, it would probably be less in value:] and, [1836: and on the whole] unless more menial servants were used, many persons would be thrown out of work and thus the power of the whole capital [1836: and revenue] to command the same quantity of labour would evidently depend upon the contingency of the vacant capitals being withdrawn undiminished [1836: *undiminished*] from their old occupations, and finding immediately equivalent employment in others' (1820, 404; 1836, 353–4). Here in 1836 there is an added sentence which implies a rather more *negative* view of the effect of machinery than in 1820: 'But this assumed facility of finding immediate employment for fresh capital in new occupations with undiminished profits, appears to me to be contradicted by general experience; and the supposition here made must be allowed to present a case essentially distinct from that where, as in most of our great manufactures, the extention of demand, owing to the cheapness occasioned by machinery, has greatly increased the whole value as well as the whole quantity of the produce.'

78 In a note at this point in 1836, Malthus protests at misreadings of his position on machinery: 'Considering the manner in which I have expressed myself here, it appears to me not a little extraordinary that I should sometimes have been classed with Mr. de Sismondi as an enemy to machinery. If the reader will direct his attention to what I have said, I think he must allow that it is hardly possible to say more with truth. To maintain that the *same extent* of benefit will result in all cases, and that there never can be the least difficulty in finding new employments for capital at the same profits, does appear to me, I own, an assertion equally contradicted by all just theory, and universal experience.' See also the objection in *both* editions to de Sismondi: 'I can by no means go with him in the fears which he expresses about machinery ...' (1820, 420n; 1836, 366n).

79 Malthus makes the preliminary point that 'this demand is not [1836: would not be] a new one, and, even when fully supplied, could only replace the diminution of capital and profits in one department, occasioned by the employment of so many ten thousands, instead of twenty thousands' (the latter a reference to innovation which allows capitalists to dispense with one-half their capital in the production of the same quantity of a particular article).

There were then in fact *two* problems: withdrawal of capital undiminished from old occupations and absorption of the released capital (and labour) into other ventures. With regard to the latter, all turned on motivation. The available capacity would be put to use only if the effort supply entailed was adequately rewarded – which might not be the case, especially in the absence of export markets suitable for expansion: 'If only an increase of domestic commodities could be obtained, there is every reason to fear that the exertions of industry would slacken ... [W]here the amount of the incomes [1836: revenues] of a country depend, in a considerable degree, upon the exertion of labour, activity and attention, there must be something in the commodities to be obtained sufficiently desirable to balance this exertion, or the exertion will cease. And experience amply shows, by the number of persons who daily leave off business, when they might certainly have continued to improve their fortunes, that most men place some limits, however variable, to the quantity of conveniences and luxuries which they will labour for, and that very few indeed would attend a counting house six or eight hours a day, in order to purchase commodities which have no other merit than the quantity of labour which has been employed upon them' (1820, 405; 1836, 354–5). All this was in response to the unattributed notion that 'when there is an income ready for the demand, it is impossible that there should be any difficulty in the employment of labour and capital to supply it, as the owner of such an income, rather than not spend it, would purchase a table or chair that had cost the labour of a hundred men for a year' – that is, at outrageous cost.

These principles are applied to the contemporary British case in an important formulation admitting that there was 'no magic in foreign markets' as such, since adequate motives to effort could conceivably be generated in a closed economy by the promise of domestically produced goods, though this was unlikely (1820, 411; 1836, 359).[80] The danger then was that capacity released by new technology would *not* be reabsorbed in the production of consumer goods, a danger compounded should the disturbance be accompanied by 'increased saving':

80 It is, however, allowed that 'when a great income has been created in a country, in the shape of a large mass of rents, profits and wages, a considerable resistance will be made to any essential fall in its value'; that is – following David Hume (1752/1955, 14) – that 'when by means of foreign trade, it has acquired the tastes necessary to give value to a great quantity of labour not employed upon actual necessaries, it may lose most of this trade, and yet continue great and powerful, on account of the extraordinary efforts which would be made by the spare capital and ingenuity of the country to refine home manufactures, in order to supply the tastes already formed, and the incomes already created' (1820, 406–7; 1836, 355–6). But there were limits to this allowance: 'But if we were to allow that the income [1836: revenue] of such a nation might, in this way, by possibility be maintained, there is little chance of its increasing; and it is almost certain that it would not have reached the same amount, without the market occasioned by foreign commerce.'

> If we could not export our cottons, it is quite certain that, though we might have the power, we should not have the will, to consume them all in kind at home [1836: to consume them all ourselves at such prices as would pay the producers. The quantity produced therefore would be very greatly diminished;] and the maintenance of our national wealth and revenue would depend entirely [1836: 'entirely' deleted] upon the circumstance whether the capital thrown out of the cotton trade could be so applied as to produce commodities which would be estimated as highly and consumed as eagerly as the foreign goods before imported. There is no magic in foreign markets. The final demand and consumption must always be at home; and if goods could be produced at home, which would excite people to work as many hours in the day, would communicate the same enjoyments, and create a consumption of the same *value*, foreign markets would be useless. We know however from experience, that very few countries are capable of producing commodities of the same efficacy, in this respect, as those which may be obtained by a trade to various climates and soils. Without such a trade, and with a great increase in the power of production, there is no inconsiderable danger that industry, consumption, and exchangeable value would diminish; and this danger would most unquestionably be realized if the cheapness of domestic commodities occasioned by machinery, were to lead to increased saving rather than to increased expenditure. (1820, 411–12; 1836, 359–60)

The foregoing was designed as a warning against minimizing the significance of aggregate demand. But since, in practice, there was no reason to expect a collapse of foreign outlets – rather the contrary – there was no cause to fear the adoption of machinery: 'But it is known that facilities of production have the strongest tendency to open markets, both at home and abroad. In the actual state therefore of most countries, there is little reason to apprehend any permanent evil from the introduction of machinery [1836: In the actual state of things therefore, there are great advantages to be looked forward to, and little reason to apprehend any permanent evil from the increase of machinery]. The presumption always is, that it will lead to a great extension of [1836: both of] wealth and value. But still we must allow that the pre-eminent advantages derived from the substitution of machinery for manual labour, depend upon the extension of the market for the commodities produced, and the increased stimulus given to consumption; and that, without this extension of market and increase of consumption, they must be in a great degree lost [1836: considerable degree diminished]' (1820, 413; 1836, 360).[81]

This position is in line with that earlier laid out in the discussion of the

81 For further discussion of applications to contemporary Britain, see chapter 12: II. The main theme is that, in the absence of foreign trade, it was unlikely that national income could have attained the level that had been achieved during the war years.

aggregate demand for labour – namely, that there was no reason to fear the adoption of machinery provided 'the market for products can be proportionately extended' (see chapter 9, p. 422). Ricardo was well aware that his own and Malthus's concerns with the potential dangers of machinery reflected opposing perspectives: 'Mr. Malthus's objection to machinery is that it adds so much to the gross produce of the country that the commodities produced cannot be consumed – that there is no demand for them: mine, on the contrary, is that the use of machinery often diminishes the quantity of gross produce, and although the inclination to consume is unlimited, the demand will be diminished, by the want of means of purchasing. Can any two doctrines be more different?' (letter to McCulloch, 18 June 1821; 1951–73, VIII, 387).[82] This difference is clearly implied in an important summary of his position by Malthus in the 1820 version, contrasting the alternative consequences of improved productivity. If unaccompanied by an appropriate 'distribution' and demand, they would be disastrous: 'If we were to suppose the powers of production in a rich and well-peopled country to be so increased that the whole of what it produced could be obtained by one third of the labour before applied, can there be a reasonable doubt that the principal difficulty would be to effect such a distribution of the produce, as to call forth these great powers of production? To consider the gift of such powers as an evil would indeed be most strange; but they would be an evil, and practically a great and grievous one, if the effect were to be an increase of the net product at the expense of the gross produce, and of the population' (1820, 482). If, however, 'a more favourable distribution of the abundant produce were to take place; if the more intelligent among the working classes were raised into overseers of works, clerks of various kinds, and retail dealers, while many who had been in these situations before, together with numerous others who had received a tolerable education, were entitled to an income from the general produce, and could live nearly at leisure upon their mortgages; what an improved structure of society would this state of things present; while the value of the gross produce, and the numbers of the people would be increasing with rapidity' (482–3).[83] And one can easily appreciate a comment on Robert Owen: 'The reader must already know, that I do not share in the apprehension of Mr. Owen about the permanent effects of machinery. But I am decidedly of opinion, that on this point he

82 Some interpretations of Ricardo err by supposing his problem to be the inability of workers displaced by machinery to find employment elsewhere (see Stigler, 1965, 196n). This reading implies that Ricardo was denying Say's Law.

83 Malthus cautioned 'that such a distribution of the produce could [not] be easily effected; but merely that, *with* such a distribution, the powers supposed would confer a prodigious benefit on the society, and *without* such a distribution, or such a change of tastes as would secure an equivalent consumption, the powers supposed might be worse than thrown away.'

has the best of the argument with those who think that accumulation ensures effective [1836: effectual] demand' (1820, 365n; 1836, 325n).[84]

XV ON GROSS AND NET REVENUE

The discussion of machinery, and the significance accorded improved 'distribution' in the maintenance and increase of aggregate value, afforded Malthus an opportunity to discourse on the matter of gross versus net revenue, and again to take issue with the Physiocrats for their sole concern with the 'net produce of the land,' and the (supposed) Ricardian exclusion of wages from 'wealth' (see above, chapter 8, p. 408). By insisting on the significance of *gross* revenue, he himself took the risk of appearing to disparage labour-saving technical progress: 'Perhaps it will be said, that to lay so much stress on disribution, and to measure demand by [1836: the increase of demand by the increase of] the exchangeable value of the whole produce, is to exalt the gross revenue at the expense of the neat revenue of a country, and to favour that system of cultivation and manufacturing which employs on each object the greatest number of hands' (1820, 422; 1836, 367). The merit of including wages in national income turned on labour's contributions to expenditure and to taxation capacity, and also could be justified from a *utility* perspective, wage-earners constituting 'the most important portion of the society': 'To dwell therefore mainly on the gross revenue of a country rather than on its neat revenue is in no respect to underrate the prodigious advantage derived from skill and machinery, but merely to give that importance to the value of the whole produce to which it is so justly entitled. No description of national wealth, which refers only to neat revenue, can ever be in any degree satisfactory ... Those who live upon the wages of labour, unproductive as well as productive [1836: including of course those engaged in personal services,] receive and expend much the greatest part of the annual produce, pay a very considerable sum in taxes for the maintenance of the government, and form by far the largest portion of its physical force. Under the prevalence of habits of prudence, the whole of this vast mass might be nearly as happy as the individuals of the other two classes, and probably a greater number of them, though not a greater proportion of them, happier' (1820, 422–3; 1836, 368).

84 On Owen, see Torrens, 1819. Torrens rejected – in terms of Say's Law – Owen's contention that 'the employment of machinery occasions the production of a greater quantity of commodities than the existing arrangements of society permit to be consumed' (469), a position identified with that of 'the celebrated M. de Sismondi.' The 'late glut of British goods in the markets of Europe and America, to which M. de Sismondi refers as a practical proof of his paradox, that poverty may be occasioned by the super-abundance of wealth' (474), is attributed to special circumstances. On Malthus's objections to de Sismondi on machinery, see note 78.

The position adopted by Malthus – implicit in the very definition of national wealth given at the outset of the *Principles*: 'the material objects which are necessary, useful, and agreeable to mankind' – had the apparent disadvantage of not specifying the '*disposable* produce,' but it was preferable to any definition turning *solely* on the latter: 'It will be readily allowed that this definition does not include the question of what may be called the amount of disposable produce, or the fund for taxation; but still I must consider it as [1836: it is nevertheless] a much more correct definition of the wealth of a country than any that should refer to this disposable part alone [1836: in the sense understood, either by the French economists, who confine it to net rent, or by Mr. Ricardo who confines it to rents and profits]. What should we say of the wealth of this country, if it were possible that its rents and profits could remain the same, while its population and produce were reduced two thirds? Certainly it would be much poorer according to the above definition; and [1836; and surely] there are not many that would dissent from such a conclusion' (1820, 423–4; 1836, 368–9). A definition of national wealth formally incorporating a measure of disposable surplus seemed inherently impossible: 'That it would be desirable, in a definition of national wealth, to include the consideration of disposable produce, as well as of actual quantity and value, cannot be doubted; but such a definition seems to be in its nature impossible, because in each individual case it must depend upon opinion, what increase of disposable produce should be accounted equivalent to a given diminution of gross produce' (1820, 424; 1836, 369). At the most, a qualitative allowance could be made, the statement to this effect reflecting a bias in favour of agriculture: 'We must content ourselves therefore with referring generally to the amount and value of national produce; and it may be subsequently stated as a separate, though very important consideration, that particular countries, with the same amount and value of produce, have a larger or smaller proportion of that produce disposable. In this respect, no doubt, a country with a fertile territory will have a prodigious advantage over those whose wealth depends almost entirely on manufactures. With the same population, the same rate of profits [1836: profits and wages], and the same amount and value of produce, the landed nation would have much the largest portion of its wealth disposable [1836: would have a much larger portion of its wealth disosable, or in other words, a larger proportion of its population might enjoy leisure, or be engaged in personal services without prejudice to its wealth]' (1820, 424–5; 1836, 369–70).

Malthus in all this was preoccupied by his reading of Ricardo's chapter 'On Gross and Net Revenue,' which he understood as focusing on net income such that a technological change permitting unchanged net but reduced gross revenue – that is, lower employment – would *not* be a national disadvantage. He perceived a larger gross produce, to the contrary, as advantageous because of the higher magnitude and because part of wage income is disposable: 'I can by no means agree with Mr. Ricardo, in his chapter *On Gross and Net Revenue.* I should not hesitate a moment in saying, that a country with a neat revenue from rents and profits, consisting of food and clothing for five millions of men, would be decidedly richer and more powerful, if such neat revenue were obtained from seven millions of men, rather that five, supposing them to be equally well supported. The whole produce would be greater; and the additional two millions of labourers would some of them unquestionably have a part of their wages disposable' (1820, 425–6n; 1836, 370n). To this Malthus added in the first edition: 'What is to become of the capital as well as the people in the case of such a change? It is obvious that a considerable portion of it must become redundant and useless.' The formulation suggests – at least in 1820 – a belief that Ricardo *condoned* the creation of mass unemployment.[85]

In both versions Malthus confirmed his approval of 'all saving of labour and inventions in machinery' on the same grounds as encountered in the formal discussions of Ricardo's chapter on Machinery: 'I quite agree with Mr. Ricardo ... in approving all saving of labour and inventions in machinery; but it is because I think that their tendency is to increase the gross produce and to make room for a larger population and a larger capital. If the saving of labour were to be accompanied by the effects stated in Mr. Ricardo's instance, I should agree with M. de Sismondi and Mr. Owen in deprecating it as a great misfortune.' Malthus took an optimistic view subject to the standard condition relating to aggregate demand: 'Fortunately, it happens but seldom that we have to determine the amount of advantage or disadvantage occasioned by the increase of the neat, at the expense of the gross revenue. The interest of individual capitalists uniformly prompts them to the saving of labour, in whatever business they are engaged; and both theory and experience combine to shew that their successful efforts in this direction, by increasing the powers of production, afford the means of increasing, in the greatest practicable degree, the amount and value of the gross produce, provided always that such a distribution and consumption of the increased supply of commodities takes place as constantly to increase their exchangeable value' (1820, 425–6; 1836, 370).

XVI SECULAR STAGNATION IN A DEVELOPMENT CONTEXT

Land fertility as such is rejected as a stimulus to growth. 'Fertility' merely defined potential or 'capability of wealth' (1820, 375; 1836, 331).[86] A 'rich

85 It is recognized in the 1836 edition that 'Mr. Ricardo, in his last edition, allows in a note that he has perhaps expressed himself too strongly on this subject, and that the labourer may have some portion of the net produce of the country; but he has not altered the text.' On the implications of the omission in the second edition, see Conclusion, p. 997.

86 In 1820, Malthus writes of fertility 'not affording an adequate stimulus to the continued increase of wealth'; this is amended to read in 1836, 'not affording with certainty ...'

and extensive' agricultural economy with low population density would remain undeveloped or grow slowly, supposing: (1) a deficient 'foreign vent for the raw produce'; and (2) that 'the commodities which contribute to the conveniences and luxuries of life were but little known,' whereas, by contrast, a desire for such commodities on the part of tenants would act as an 'incitement to call forth the resources of the land, and give encouragement to a rapid increase of population' (1820, 376–7; 1836, 332). Under the supposed conditions, to obtain even a large *physical* surplus of agricultural produce would involve a waste of 'time and attention in superintending the labour.' The landowner would in fact obtain a profit or rent from such land even 'in its uncultivated state.'[87] Accordingly, he 'would set a value ... upon his property, as a source of profit as well as of power and amusement; and though it was capable of yielding much more raw produce than he and his immediate dependents could consume, he would by no means be disposed to allow others to seize on it, and divide it at their pleasure,' though he 'would probably let out considerable portions of it for small rents.'[88]

The constraints are elaborated in an attempt to appreciate why the 'tendencies' to stagnation did not 'yield, at least in a considerable degree, to the more steady influence of self-interest' (1820, 390; 1836, 342). Again the problems are: (1) lack of foreign demand for domestic produce; and (2) lack of domestic manufacturing rendering employment of labour (by the landlords in this case) not worth the effort of superintendence: 'Among proprietors of this description, caprice and indolence might often prevent them [1836: prevent many] from cultivating their lands. Generally, however, it might be expected, that these tendencies would yield, at least in a considerable degree, to the more steady influence of self-interest. But a vicious division of territory prevents the motive of interest from operating so strongly as it ought to do in the extension of cultivation. Without sufficient foreign commerce to give value to the raw produce of the land; and before the general introduction of manufactures had opened channels for domestic industry, the demand of the great proprietors for labour

87 The landowners are represented as 'a small body of people ... possessed of a rich and extensive inland territory, divided into large proportions [1836: portions] and not favourably situated with respect to markets ...' (1820, 376; 1836, 331).

88 See also a case-study drawing on Humboldt on Spanish America: 'In the midst of an abundance of fertile land, it appears that the natives are often very scantily supplied with it. They would gladly cultivate portions of the extensive districts held by the great proprietors, and could not fail of thus deriving an ample subsistence for themselves and families; but in the actual state of the demand for produce in many parts of the country, and in the actual state of the ignorance and indolence of the natives, such tenants might not be able to pay a rent equal to what the land would yield in its uncultivated state, and in this case they would seldom be allowed to intrude upon such domains; and thus lands which might be capable of supporting thousands of people, may be left to support a few hundreds of cattle' (1820, 389–90; 1836, 341–2).

would be very soon supplied; and beyond this, the labouring classes would have nothing to give them for the use of their lands. Though the landholders might have ample power to support an extended population on their estates, the very slender increase of enjoyments, if any, which they might derive from it, would rarely be sufficient to overcome their natural indolence, or overbalance the possible inconveniences or trouble that might attend the proceeding' (1820, 390–1; 1836, 342).[89]

Ricardo's position that 'those who have food and necessaries at their disposal will not be long in want of workmen, who will put them in possession of some of the objects most useful and desirable to them' (cf. 1951–73, I, 292), was 'directly contradicted by experience' – the observed fact of secular stagnation entailing the use of raw produce largely in the support of 'idle retainers' (1820, 377; 1836, 332). In the first place, the establishment of domestic manufacturing was no simple matter – the land might be unsuitable for the requisite raw materials, and there would be an initial paucity of machinery, skill, and supervisory ability. But the major problem was one of motivation, so that though conceivably an individual labourer might with increased agricultural productivity devote more time to conveniences and luxuries, Malthus feared that increased leisure would be the preferred choice, the evidence suggesting that this possibility could not be dismissed, even in advanced economies (1820, 378–9, 1836, 333–4; see Conclusion, p. 968). Malthus goes further and asserts that it is 'the want of *necessaries* which mainly stimulates the labouring classes to produce luxuries; and were this stimulus removed or greatly weakened, so that the necessaries of life could be obtained with very little labour, instead of more time being devoted to the production of conveniences, there is every reason to think that less time would be so devoted.' The desire by labourers for conveniences and luxuries could not be relied upon: 'Few indeed and scanty would be the portion of conveniences and luxuries found in society, if those who are the main instruments of their production, had no stronger motives for their exertions than the desire of enjoying them.'[90]

The developmental problem was, in sum, to assure that 'if the means of maintaining labour be found, there can be no difficulty in making it

89 Encouragement of population growth was deadened by 'the original state of property, and the feudal customs and habits which it necessarily tends to generate,' for that state and those customs precluded the division of land to support prospective new families; and 'under these circumstances, if a comparative deficiency of commerce and manufactures, which great inequality of property tends rather to perpetuate than to correct, prevents the growth of that demand for labour and produce, which can alone remedy the discouragement to population occasioned by this inequality, it is obvious that Spanish America may remain for ages thinly peopled and poor, compared with her natural resources' (1820, 391; 1836, 343).

90 On all this Ricardo was in fact in accord (see below, section XVII).

produce objects of adequate value; or that when food can be obtained with facility, more time will be devoted to the production of conveniences and luxuries' (1820, 380; 1836, 334). These conditions cover both the overcoming of the technical or supply-side difficulties (insufficient or inappropriate raw materials and machinery, lack of supervisory skills), and of motivation, whether it be low effort supply on the part either of labour or of the landlord and capitalist/employer.[91]

Were it not for these constraints, it would be found that the high (average) product in those countries which are at 'an early period of cultivation, when only rich soils are worked,' would permit a low agricultural workforce relative to the total. But precisely because of the constraints in question there was found 'almost invariably a much larger proportion of the whole people employed on the land than in those countries where the increase of population has occasioned the necessity of resorting to poor soils; and less time instead of more time devoted to the production of conveniences and luxuries.' To illustrate, England, despite its relatively weak agricultural resources, had the smallest proportion of its workforce engaged in agriculture, a 'very extraordinary' fact which afforded 'striking proof how very dangerous it is, in political economy, to draw conclusions from the physical quality of the materials which are acted upon, without reference to the moral as well as physical qualities of the agents' (1820, 381; 1836, 335).[92] Conversely, highly productive land could even act *against* 'the growth of industry and skill' by adversely affecting motivation: 'If the facility of getting food creates habits of indolence, this indolence

91 Again drawing on Humboldt, Malthus points to exceptional agricultural activity in areas near newly established mines to prove the rule reflecting 'brisk' demand: 'When these are the effects of a really brisk demand for produce and labour, we cannot be at a loss for the main cause of the slow cultivation which has taken place over the greatest part of the country. Except in the neighbourhood of the mines and near the great towns, the effective demand for produce is not such as to induce the great proprietors to bring their immense tracts of land properly into cultivation: and the population, which, as we have seen, presses hard [1836: at times] against the limits of subsistence, evidently exceeds in general the demand for labour, or the number of persons which the country can employ with regularity and constancy in the actual state of its agriculture and manufactures' (1820, 389; 1836, 341). As for labour: 'That the indolence of the natives is greatly aggravated by their political situation, cannot for a moment be doubted; but that, in spite of this situation it yields in a great measure to the usual excitements is sufficiently proved by the rapid cultivation which takes place in the neighbourhood of a new mine, where an animated and effective demand is created for labour and produce' (1820, 388; 1836, 340–1).

92 Malthus cites Süssmilch (1798, iii, 60) for the urban–rural breakdown in various countries; and the 1811 census data (published in 1812) for the English case, summarizing thus in the second edition: 'the highest is that of three to seven, or three living in towns to seven in the country; whereas in England the proportion of those engaged in manufactures and commerce, and other employments not connected with the land, compared with those engaged in agriculture is as much as three to two.'

may make him prefer the luxury of doing little or nothing, to the luxury of possessing conveniences and comforts; and in this case, he may devote less time to the working for conveniences and comforts, and be more scantily provided with them than if he had been obliged to employ more industry in procuring food' (1820, 382; 1836, 336). Von Humboldt's study of New Spain (1811, III, 28) illustrated the theme 'that the extreme fertility of these countries, instead of affording an adequate stimulus to a rapid increase of wealth and population, has produced, under the actual circumstances in which they have been placed, a degree of indolence which has kept them poor and thinly peopled after the lapse of ages' (1820, 384; 1836, 337–8).

Malthus opined that the habits in question 'are not likely to change, except gradually and slowly under a course of powerful and effective stimulants. And while the extreme inequality of landed property continues, and no sufficient vent is found for the raw produce in foreign commerce, these stimulants will be furnished very slowly and inadequately' (1820, 388; 1836, 340). And he attributed the problem of stagnation and relatively slow growth in the Central American case principally to a 'want of consumers' of raw produce – 'that is, the want of power to sell the produce at such a price as will at once encourage good cultivation, and enable the farmers to give the landlords something which they want, for the use of their land' (1820, 392; 1836, 344) – clearly an allusion to manufactures. 'And nothing is so likely to prevent this price from being obtained, as any obstacles natural or artificial to internal and external commerce.' The developmental problem in New Spain, in brief, reflected 'want of demand,' not 'want of capital.'

Evidence from Ireland supplemented that from Spanish America. Characteristic of the Irish case was agricultural unemployment and underemployment and surplus labour, encouraging 'indolence': 'The prominent feature of Ireland is, the power which it possesses and actually exercises, of supporting a much greater population than it can employ, and the natural and necessary effect of this state of things, is the very general prevalence of habits of indolence. The landed proprietors and principal tenants being possessed of food and necessaries, or at least of the ready means of procuring them, have found workmen in abundance at their command; but these workmen not finding sufficient employment in the farms on which they had settled, have rarely been able to put their landlords in possession of the objects "most useful and most desirable" to them' (1820, 394; 1836, 345). There was some evidence that 'the most intelligent Irish landlords, influenced both by motives of humanity and interest, are now endeavouring to check the progress of that redundant population upon their estates, which while it generates an excessive degree of poverty and misery as well as indolence, seldom makes up to the employer, in the lowness of wages, for the additional number of hands which he is obliged to hire, or call upon for their appointed service in labour' (1820, 395;

1836, 345–6). The more progressive landlords realized that agricultural productivity would *rise* if the workforce were reduced, allowing the generation of a surplus for sale outside the agricultural sector: 'He is now generally aware that a smaller number of more industrious labourers would enable him to raise a larger produce for the consumption of towns and manufactures, and at the same time that they would thus contribute more largely to the general wealth of the country, would be in a more happy condition themselves, and enable him to derive a larger and more certain rent from his estates.' None the less, the general situation as things still stood proved that 'the possessors of food and necessaries in Ireland have not been able to obtain the objects most useful and desirable to them in return.'[93] This reflected the 'indolence' of Irish country-labourers; and 'whether this [arose] from there being really little for them to do in the actual state of things, or from a natural tendency to idleness, not to be overcome by ordinary stimulants,' the fact remained that the spare time available to them beyond that needed to obtain necessaries was not used to produce 'conveniences and luxuries' (1820, 395–6; 1836, 346).[94]

On the whole, Malthus looked to objective circumstances rather than 'a natural tendency to idleness' to account for the facts – very much in the manner of Adam Smith. Some of the difficulties are touched on in allusions to domestic manufacturing – particularly 'temptations to indolence' reflecting *inter alia* the difficulties in the way of acquiring the appropriate raw materials, given the low level of money earnings (1820, 397; 1836, 347). But as always, the primary problem was one of motivation: 'If the Irish peasant could find such a market for the result of his in-door occupations as would give him constant employment at a fair money price, his habits might soon change; but it may be doubted whether any large body of people in any country ever acquired regular and industrious habits, where they were unable to get regular and constant work, and when, to keep themselves constantly and beneficially employed, it was necessary to exercise a great degree of providence, energy, and self-command' (1820, 397–8; 1836, 348).

Lack of 'capital' is allowed as a contributing cause of Irish stagnation. But its increase would not alone solve the major problem – namely, inadequate demand for manufactured goods. In fact, premature output expansion must lead to failure of the program, considering limited domestic and foreign sales opportunities: 'An attempt to force a foreign market by means of capital, must necessarily occasion a premature fall of profits, and might,

93 This summary is omitted in 1836, but there is no substantive change of position.

94 In the 1836 version, a note cautions about careless use of labour commanded as measure of value: 'In applying labour as a rough measure of wealth, or in measuring value in Ireland we must remember ... that we must take the price of the labour which is actually, and with average constancy engaged, and not the price at which it may be occasionally offered by a half employed population.'

after great losses, be quite ineffectual; and with regard to the domestic demand, while the habits of the great mass of the people are such as they are at present, it must be quite inadequate to take off the products of any considerable mass of new capital' (1820, 398; 1836, 348).

The foregoing emphasis upon the necessity for a high demand for manufactures on the part of *labour* would conflict with the position elsewhere that such demand *alone* would not suffice (above, section IV), unless Malthus intended to be read with that qualification in mind. In any event, he elaborates at length on the requirement, with an eye to the currently prevalent low level of tastes attributable in part to the exceedingly *low* cost of a potato diet: 'In a country, where the necessary food is obtained with so little labour, and the population is still equal or nearly equal to the produce, it is perhaps impossible that the time not devoted to the production of food should create a proportionate quantity of wealth, without a very decided taste for conveniences and luxuries among the lower classes of society, and such a power of purchasing as would occasion an effective demand for them. But it is well known, that the taste of the Irish peasant for articles of this description is yet to be formed. His wants are few, and these wants he is in the habit of supplying principally at home. Owing to the cheapness of the potato, which forms the principal food of the lower classes of the people, his money wages are low; and the portion which remains, after providing absolute necessaries, will go but a very little way in the purchase of conveniences. All these circumstances are most unfavourable to the increase of wealth derived from manufactures destined for home consumption' (1820, 398–9; 1836, 348–9). Under these conditions premature increase in capital 'would certainly fail to yield such profits as would encourage its continued accumulation and application in the same way.' The conclusion derived from all this is 'that demand is quite as necessary to the increase of capital as the increase of capital is to demand. They mutually act upon and encourage each other, and neither of them can proceed with vigour if the other be left far behind.'

The evaluation of 'the actual state' of Ireland differs somewhat between editions. The allowance that 'one of the great wants of Ireland is capital' is altered to read: 'the greatest want' (1820, 398; 1836, 348). 'The check which the progress of her manufactures has received' is ascribed in the first to 'a want of demand rather than a want of capital,' whereas this is modified to read 'as much owing to a want of demand as a want of capital' (1820, 399; 1836, 349). There is then a somewhat reduced concern with demand-side compared with supply-side constraints. None the less, the continuation is the same in both versions: 'Her peculiar distress upon the termination of the late war had unquestionably this origin [a want of demand], whatever might have been the subsequent destruction of capital. And the great checks to her manufacturers formerly were the unjust and impolitic restrictions imposed by England which prevented, or circumscribed the demand for them' (1820, 400; 1836, 349).

An evaluation that stimulation of demand is the more difficult to assure appears in the 1820 version: 'When, however, a brisk demand for any manufacture has existed, few instances I believe have occurred of its being allowed to languish through the want of capital; though there is reason to think that advances of capital have been sometimes made, which have failed to create an adequate market.' This is replaced in 1836 by a paragraph pointing to 'a fatal deficiency in one of the greatest sources of prosperity, the perfect security of property,' which hindered the export of 'the redundant capital of England ... into Ireland with the best effect' (1836, 349–50). Correction of the deficiency 'could not fail to produce a great increase in the effectual demand for capital, as well as its supply,' whereas in going circumstances investment had 'sometimes been made with little beneficial result.' This negative evaluation is followed by a warning against large-scale agricultural investment by the state designed to generate employment, though a lesser role for government in the development process is allowed: 'A certain definite assistance in particular establishments, or in facilitating the communications between one part of the country and another, may be given by government with advantage; but any thing approaching to a forced supply of capital with a view to the general employment of the people in the extension of cultivation, would infallibily create an unnatural demand for labour which could not be maintained, would tend to paralyse individual efforts, and terminate in increased poverty and distress among the labouring classes.'

Malthus evidently had in mind in reaching this conclusion his original concern with the generation of markets. And a discussion common to both editions – though with security of property referred to only in the 1836 edition – points to a more equal social structure as appropriate for the generation of broad-based markets, at the same time as it warns against 'premature' investment:

> The state of Ireland in respect to the time and labour necessary to the production of her food is such, that her capabilities for manufacturing and commercial wealth are prodigious. If [1836: under a state of things where all kinds of property were secure] an improved system of agriculture were to raise the food and raw materials required for the population with the smallest quantity of labour necessary to do it in the best manner, and the remainder of the people, instead of loitering about upon the land, were engaged in manufactures and commerce carried on in great and flourishing towns, Ireland would be beyond comparison richer than England. This is what is wanted to give full scope to her great natural resources; and to attain this state of things an immense capital is undoubtedly required; but it can only be employed to advantage as it is gradually called for; and a premature supply of it would be much less beneficial and less permanent in its effects, than such a change in the tastes and habits of the lower classes of people and such an alteration in the mode of paying their labour as would give them both the will and the power to purchase domestic manufactures and

foreign commodities [1836: such an alteration in the mode of paying their labour and such an improvement in the structure of the whole society as would give both the lower and middle classes a greater will and power to purchase domestic manufactures and foreign commodities]. (1820, 400–1; 1836; 350–1).

To this is appended a note in 1836: 'There is nothing so favourable to effectual demand as a large proportion of the middle classes of society.'

XVII SUMMARY AND CONCLUSION

We have encountered in this chapter Malthus's repeated claims that he alone – in contrast with the New School of Ricardians – had taken account of the motives relating to effort supply and savings underlying economic expansion, and in so doing had hit upon the preconditions of sustainable growth. Doubtless he was justified in pointing out that the new orthodox did not concern themselves at any length with the 'generation of new wants,' taking for granted in advanced economies expansion of markets to absorb increased aggregate output. But Malthus went too far. Ricardo had never insisted that initial expansions of output were themselves guaranteed. This was his reaction to Malthus's concerns regarding machinery: 'Mr. Malthus's peculiar theory is that supplies may be so abundant, that they may not find a market. This is insisted on in various parts of his work. A very great facility of production, might, under certain circumstances, encourage a habit of indolence, and therefore might be a reason for commodities not being produced abundantly, but it can be no reason, when they are produced, for their not being exchanged against each other. We all like to buy and consume, the difficulty is in the production. One product is bought by another; every man will buy if he has a product to give in exchange, and does not value that higher than the commodity offered' (*Note 154*; 1951–73, II, 240). The constraint imposed by a high demand for leisure is conspicuous in Ricardo's investigation of secular stagnation despite abundant fertile land – as it was for Malthus – where the problem of endemic poverty (as in Poland, Ireland, and the South Seas) is attributed to 'the inactivity of the people,' the remedy for which being 'to stimulate exertion, to create new wants, and to implant new tastes' (1951–73, I, 99–100). In this context Ricardo describes what we would call a backward-bending labour-supply curve under going conditions of low aspiration such that any increase in the real wage reduces effort supply. Thus 'the remedy required in Ireland is a taste for other objects besides mere food. Any stimulus which should rouse the Irish to activity, which should induce them to dispose of their surplus time in procuring luxuries for themselves, instead of employing it in the most brutal pursuits, would tend more to the civilization and prosperity of their country than any other measures which would be recommended' (letter to Trower, 15 July 1816; 1951–73, VII, 49).

Much of what Malthus had to say regarding a requisite stimulus to wants and tastes was in line with all this. Ricardo's relative neglect of the issue was less a matter of principle than an empirical evaluation that the problems of low aspiration and high demand for leisure did not apply typically in advanced economies such as Britain, his main preoccupation. He specifically pointed out that Malthus's concerns were 'little applicable to countries with a dense population abounding in capital, skill, commerce and manufacturing industry, and with a taste for every enjoyment that nature, art or science will procure' (1951–73, II, 340–1).

Even so, for Ricardo any presumption regarding automatic expansion would be unjustified in advanced economies. Accumulation was in part motivated by the profit rate, and would therefore be choked off at low levels. Since this is also true for Malthus, one is led to ask where precisely the differences between the two systems would become manifest. The answer is that Malthus had in mind the consequences of accumulation at periods of *low* profits in response to ill-timed recommendations by policy makers. For Ricardo such accumulation (were it supposed to occur, for argument's sake) would be sustainable, whereas for Malthus such expansion would fail for a want of markets, and this because, given the initially low rate of profit presumed, the accumulation program would be financed by positive reductions in consumption rather than profits. Such 'forced' saving (investment) programs were *unsustainable*, generating excess capacity. More generally, increased capacity resulting from new technology may or may not be fully utilized: 'Like the fertility of land, the invention of good machinery confers a prodigious power of production. But neither of these great powers can be called fully into action, if the situation and circumstances, or the habits and tastes of the society prevent the opening of a sufficient market, and an adequate increase of consumption' (cited above, note 77). It could not be presumed, as Ricardo presumed, that the economy operates at (or perhaps rather fluctuates around) its production frontier.

We turn to the case of an initially high profit rate. For both Malthus and Ricardo, accumulation is stimulated. For Ricardo, the demand side is presumed to look after itself. Malthus too envisaged no problem were it not for an *excessive* response, again 'excessive' in the sense of accumulation financed by positive reductions in consumption and, therefore, unsustainable. Unfortunately, Malthus, who saw this as his key contribution, neglected to supply case-studies to illustrate the supposed phenomenon.

A fuller understanding of the issues at stake requires that we recall the function attributed by Malthus to new or extended trading opportunities. It was to generate an increase in the aggregate value of the initial aggregate 'output' (the latter difficult to measure since its composition is altered by trade), an increase manifested initially in a higher profit rate. (This increase is said to reflect a higher utility estimate, in the sense of willingness to undergo sacrifice, a perspective that justified in part use of a labour-commanded index.) In sharp contrast, for Ricardo there will be no effect on the profit rate unless of course the new trade relations entail cheaper imports of wage goods. It is true that for Ricardo, too, increased trade may be directly relevant for the growth process; but Malthus was sharply critical: 'Of the two ways in which capital may be accumulated, as stated by Mr. Ricardo in his chapter on foreign commerce, namely an *increase of revenue* from increased profits, or a *diminished expenditure* arising from cheap commodities [1951–73, I, 131–2], I believe [1836: it will be found that] the latter never has been, nor ever will be, experienced as an effective stimulus to the permanent continued production of increasing wealth' (1820, 459–60; 1836, 396; emphasis in 1836). This criticism is misplaced, since Ricardo did not intend by 'diminished expenditure' a *positive reduction* in consumption, but rather increased savings out of the increased real income reflecting efficiency gains. He made no claim here hostile to Malthus. Still there *is* the major difference that expanded trade for Ricardo exerts its effect on growth in this 'supply-side' manner; whereas for Malthus it plays on aggregate demand, manifested in the first instance as a high rate of profit.

It might seem that, by his presumption of a potential divorce between aggregate supply and demand, and his focus on the latter as a strategic variable, Malthus had at the least 'set the agenda' for what is popularly seen as the Keynesian Revolution. But the Malthus–Keynes nexus is a complicated one indeed (see Conclusion, section IX). Thus, in the next chapter, on macro-economic stabilization, which deals with 'short run' unemployment and excess capacity with particular reference to the postwar depression, we shall find that Malthus's predominant *secular* concerns make themselves felt. Increased investment is not seen as an alternative to increased consumption – the perspective of textbook 'Keynesianism' – precisely because investment might worsen *growth* prospects.

TWELVE

Macro-economic stabilization and applications

I INTRODUCTION

The theory of sustainable growth was applied to the interpretation of British experience over the two war decades 1793–1813, as we show in section II of this chapter. Conspicuous here is allowance for expanded capacity – reflecting in part new technology – a successful expansion because accompanied by the requisite growth of markets. By contrast, the postwar depression illustrated the theme that the mere existence of capacity was insufficient to assure its full use, let alone its expansion (section III). But though, in Malthus's estimate, Britain had undertaken a successful program of investment during the war itself, the postwar depression was attributed, not to further and unsuccessful attempts at saving in the sense of *excessive realized investment*, but rather to an 'exogenous' collapse of final demand generating leakages of savings from the income stream, excess capacity, and unemployment (see chapter 11, n5). The conspicuous feature here is the absence of automatic adjustment mechanisms assuring recovery from depression; downward money-wage flexibility was a necessary but not always a sufficient condition for recovery. In all this Malthus discerned his major difference with Ricardo on the depression. In section IV we consider Malthus's perception of the options available to alleviate the depression and set the stage for further sustainable expansion; constraints imposed by the large national debt play a central role in the discussion. A specific case for public works is considered in section V.

II ANALYSIS OF THE WARTIME EXPANSION

An early application of the theory of sustainable growth is found in the (non-extant) letter of summer 1813 in which Malthus apparently maintained that extensions of foreign trade since 1793 implied general economic expansion and a rising profit rate. This is easily reconstructed from the wording used by Ricardo in his extant response: 'I most readily allow that since the war, not only the nominal but the real value of our exports and imports has increased, – but I do not see how this admission will favour the view which you take of this subject ... Extensions of trade would ... swell the value of our exports and imports but does not prove a general increase of profits nor any material growth of prosperity' (10 August; in Ricardo, 1951–73, VI, 93). And again: 'That we have experienced a great increase of wealth and prosperity since the commencement of the war, I am amongst the foremost to believe; but it is not certain that such increase must have been attended by increased profits, or rather an increased rate of profits, for that is the question between us' (17 August; 94).[1] Considering its Smithian pedigree it is uncertain whether Malthus's theoretical position actually originated with his observation of wartime experience, but those observations at least provided for him apparent confirmation.

Throughout the full range of Malthus's later writings, the same theme emerges. As for the *Principles*, we may start with a general reiteration of the theory of effective (aggregate) demand and the broad claims made for it: 'The causes of an increase in the effective [1836: effectual] demand for particular commodities are of very easy explanation; but it has been considered, and with reason, as not very easy to explain the cause of that general briskness of demand which is sometimes so very sensibly felt throughout a whole country, and is so strikingly contrasted with the feeling which gives rise to the expression of trade being universally very dead. As the specific and immediate cause of this general increase of effective demand, I should decidedly point to such a distribution of the produce, and such an adaptation of it to the wants and tastes of the society as will give the money price for which it sells an increased command of domestic and foreign labour [1836: increased command of labour before more labour has been employed on its production]; and I am inclined to think that, if this test be applied to all the striking cases that have occurred, it will rarely or never be found to fail' (1820, 458; 1836, 394–5). The illustrations refer to recent American growth estimated in either bullion or labour, and British growth, 1793–1814, similarly estimated, both phenomena in part explained in terms of the effect of extended foreign commerce: 'It can as little be doubted that in this country, from 1793 to 1814, the whole exchangeable value of the produce, estimated either in domestic and foreign labour [1836: in labour],

1 Ricardo's statements differ on the question whether or not there occurred a 'material growth of prosperity' during the war.

or in bullion, was greatly augmented every year. In this increase of value, as well as riches, the extension of our foreign commerce has been considered, almost without a dissentient opinion, as a most powerful agent; and certainly till 1815, no appearances seemed to indicate, that the increasing value of our imports had the slightest tendency to diminish the value of our domestic produce. They both increased, and increased greatly, together, estimated either in bullion or labour' (1820, 459; 1836, 395).

Here then we encounter an illustration of the generally positive effect of expanded trade. Elsewhere in the *Principles* there are found more specific elaborations. In his discussion of the creation of excess capacity (capital and labour) in consequence of new technology, Malthus points to expansion of foreign markets as providing some assurance against the danger that such capacity might *not* be reabsorbed in the production of additional consumer goods (1820, 411f.; 1836, 359f.; see chapter 11, pp. 570f.); and he supports the theoretical principles by reference to contemporary Britain, where in the absence of foreign trade (and other sources of expanded demand) the real national income could not have attained the levels actually achieved:

Of this I think we shall be convinced, if, in our own country, we look at the quantity of goods which we export chiefly in consequence of our machinery, and consider the nature of the returns obtained for them. In the accounts of the year ended the 5th of January 1818, it appears that the exports of three articles alone in which machinery is used – cottons, woollen and hardware, including steel goods, &c. are valued above 29 millions. And among the most prominent articles of the imports of the same year, we find coffee, indigo, sugar, tea, silks, tobacco, wines, and cotton-wool, amounting in value all together to above 18 millions out of thirty! Now I would ask how we should have obtained these valuable imports, if the foreign markets for our cottons, woollens, and hardware had not been extended with the use of machinery? And further, where we could have found substitutes at home for such imports, which would have been likely to have produced the same effects, in stimulating the cultivation of the land, the accumulation of capital, and the increase of population? And when to these considerations we add the fortunes which have been made in these manufactures, the market for which has been continually extending, and continually requiring more capital and more people to be employed in them; and contrast with this state of things the constant necessity of looking out for new modes of employing the same capital and the same people, a portion of which would be thrown out of their old occupations by every new invention; – we must be convinced that the state of this country would have been totally different from what it is, and that it would not certainly have acquired the same income [1836: revenue] in rents, profits and wages, if the same ingenuity had been exercised in the invention of machinery, without the same extension of the market for the commodities produced. (1820, 407–8; 1836, 356–7)[2]

He goes yet further. The ability to undertake the war had turned on the technological progressiveness of the cotton, cloth, and hardware industries: 'In carrying on the late war, we were powerfully assisted by our steam engines, which enabled us to command a prodigious quantity of foreign produce and foreign labour' (1820, 409; 1836, 358). 'How,' he asks, 'would their efficacy have been weakened if we could not have exported our cottons, cloths and hardware?'

The expansion of Manchester, Glasgow, and Leeds reflected the use of machinery in the case of manufactures with elastic demands, and illustrated the main themes: 'This effect has been very strikingly exemplified in the cotton machinery of this country. The consumption of cotton goods has been so greatly extended both at home and abroad, on account of their cheapness, that the value of the whole of the cotton goods and twist now made exceeds, beyond comparison, their former value; while the rapidly increasing population of the towns of Manchester, Glasgow, &c. during the last thirty years, amply testifies that, with a few temporary exceptions, the demand for the labour concerned in the cotton manufactures, in spite of the machinery used, has been increasing very greatly' (1820, 402–3; 1836, 352). Similarly: 'In the actual state of things in this country, the population and wealth of Manchester, Glasgow, Leeds, &c. have been greatly increasing; because, on account of the extending demand for their goods, more people have been continually required to work them up; but if a much smaller number of people had been required, on account of a saving of labour from machinery, without an adequate extension of the market, it is obvious that these towns would have been comparatively poor, and thinly peopled [1836: would have been poorer and more thinly peopled]' (1820, 410; 1836, 358). It was inconceivable that equivalent markets could be found for cotton goods were the export outlets closed: 'Are there any plausible grounds whatever for stating that, if the twenty millions worth of cottons which we now export, were entirely stopped, either by successful foreign competition or positive prohibitions, we should have no difficulty in finding employment for our capital and labour equally advantageous to individuals in point of profit and equally enriching to the country with respect to the exchangeable value of its revenue?' (1820, 411; 1836, 359).

Foreign-trade extensions were not the only source of demand enumerated in the account of British secular experience. Referring to the last

2 Data for 1817 are referred to, though in fact at least the first half of that year was a period of depression. Here – and elsewhere, we shall find – Malthus implicitly plays down the postwar crisis as a temporary aberration when viewed in full secular context.

twenty-five years (in the 1836 version, to the 'last forty years'), Malthus stresses the 'very great additions' made to the national capital stock without 'diminished expenditure in the maintenance of unproductive labour' (1836: 'in the shape of revenue'), just as in the case of an individual merchant who 'during the acquisition of [a] fortune' simultaneously increases 'his expenditure in objects of luxury, enjoyment and liberality' (1820, 421; 1836, 367). This experience reflected new technology allowing agricultural expansion to 'poorer lands, without diminution of profits,' and expanded demand for manufactures: 'I have already shewn that the saving of labour, and the increase of skill, both in agriculture [1836: agricultural] and manufacturing industry, by enabling a country to push its cultivation over poorer lands, without diminution of profits, and to extend far and wide the markets for its manufactures, must tend to increase the exchangeable value of the whole; and there cannot be a doubt that in this country they must have been the main sources of that rapid and astonishing increase in the value of the national wealth, which has taken place during the last thirty or forty years' (1820, 422; 1836, 367–8).[3]

The discussion of property distribution also touches on the buoyancy of aggregate demand – or rather potential buoyancy considering, the depression – in contemporary Britain. The picture was a bright one, and this despite the law of primogeniture, it being 'generally acknowledged that the country, in its actual state and under its actual laws, presents a picture of greater wealth, especially when compared with its natural resources, than any large territorial state of modern times' (1820, 435; 1836, 378).[4] For by 'the natural extinction of some great families, and the natural imprudence of some others, but, above all, by the extraordinary growth of manufactures and commerce, the immense landed properties which formerly prevailed all over the country have been in a great degree broken down notwithstanding the law [1836: the right] of primogeniture.'[5] A

3 The reference to 'the last thirty or forty years' common to both editions implies a very loose periodization. Taking it as written in 1820, we are carried back to *circa* 1780–90. This would explain perhaps how Malthus can refer to agriculture as providing the main source of demand for manufactures despite the postwar agricultural depression; he had in mind the earlier years.

4 In the 1836 version the issue is stated as involving 'the abolition of the law of primogeniture, and the power of entail without any interference with testamentary dispositions.'

5 In fact, those few remaining great families served a positive function: 'And the few which remain may perhaps be of use in furnishing motives to the merchant and master manufacturer, to continue the exercise of their skill and powers till they have acquired large capitals, and are able to contend in wealth with the great landlords. If, from the abolition of the right [1836: law] of primogeniture, the landed fortunes were all very inconsiderable, it is not probable that there would be many large capitals among merchants; and, in this case, much productive power would unquestionably be lost' (1820, 435–6; 1836, 379).

'large body of ... the middle classes' had been firmly established, and constituted a 'large class of effective demanders, who derive their power of purchasing from the various professions, from commerce, from manufactures, from wholesale and retail trade, from salaries of various kinds, and from the interest of public and private debts; and these demanders are likely, perhaps to acquire tastes more favourable to the encouragement of wealth than the owners of the small properties on the land' (1820, 436–7; 1836, 379).

Wartime prosperity is also accounted for by war finance via government borrowing. The context is the relation of accumulation to the profit rate – the index of the power and will to save – government borrowing and expenditure having contributed to raising the profit rate, generating accumulation more than sufficient to compensate for capital losses during the war: 'One of the most striking instances of the truth of this remark, and a further proof of a singular resemblance in the laws that regulate the increase of capital and of population, is to be found in the rapidity with which the loss of capital is recovered during a war which does not interrupt commerce. *The loans to government convert capital into revenue, and increase demand at the same time that they at first diminish the means of supply. The necessary consequence must be an increase of profits.* This naturally increases both the power and the reward of accumulation; and if only the same habits of saving prevail among the capitalists as before, the recovery of the lost stock must be so rapid, just for the same kind of reason that the recovery of population is so rapid when by some cause or other, it has been suddenly destroyed [1836: ... is so rapid after some great mortality]' (1820, 373–4; 1836, 329–30; emphasis added).[6] Ricardo would find it

6 The effect on capital of the loans to government was negligible in *agriculture*: 'Capital is withdrawn only from those employments where it can best be spared. It is hardly ever withdrawn from agriculture. Nothing is more common, as I have stated in the chapter on rent, than increased profits, not only without any capital being withdrawn from the land, but under a continual addition to it.'

For further reference to 'recovery' from 'the prodigious destruction of capital by the government' during the 1792–1813 period, see 1820, 493; 1836, 416. Here a sharp distinction is made with a *net* loss of capital in 1813–15, and even more so in the postwar period: 'That a great loss of capital has lately been sustained, is unquestionable. During nearly the whole of the war, owing to the union of great powers of production with great [1836: a great effectual] consumption and demand, the prodigious destruction of capital by the government was much more than recovered. To doubt this would be to shut our eyes to the comparative state of the country in 1792 and 1813. The two last years of the war were, however, years of extraordinary expense, and being followed immediately by a period marked by a very unusual stagnation of [1836: effectual] demand, the destruction of capital which took place in those years was not probably recovered. But this stagnation itself was much more disastrous in its effects upon the national capital, and still more upon the national revenue, than any previous destruction of stock.' Similarly: 'It is acknowledged that the capital of this country compared with the population has been diminished since the war, partly by the unrecovered destruction which it sustained during

impossible to interpret this wartime experience: 'Mr. Ricardo's assumption of constant prices would make it absolutely impossible to account theoretically for things as they are. If capital were considered as not within the pale of demand and supply, the very familiar event of the rapid recovery of capital during a war [1836: omits 'during a war'] would be quite inexplicable.'[7] As for the parallel itself between capital and population: 'It is now fully acknowledged that it would be a gross error in the latter case [of population response to high wages], to imagine that, without the previous diminution of the population, the same rate of increase would still have taken place; because it is precisely the high wages occasioned by the demand for labour, which produce the effect of so rapid an increase of population. On the same principle it appears to me as gross an error to suppose that, without the previous loss of capital [1836: and an increased demand for produce] occasioned by the expenditure in question, capital should be as rapidly accumulated; because it is precisely the high profits of stock occasioned by the demand for commodities, and the consequent demand for the means of producing them, which at once give the power and the will to accumulate' (1820, 374–5; 1836, 330).

Inflationary injections of money played a secondary part in Malthus's interpretation of the wartime expansion, with an emphasis on forced savings rather than a direct stimulus to expenditure by monetary means, the process accounting in part for the 'rapid recovery of vast capital destroyed' (1820, 513; 1836, 430–1; see chapter 13, p. 674). The final section of the Wages chapter also refers to a favourable effect of inflation on labour demand (probably alluding to the forced-saving phenomenon): 'When a fall in the value of money [1836: an increase of currency] is accompanied, as it frequently is, by a rapid increase of capital, there is one reason, why, in the natural state of things, the price of labour should feel it more than other commodities. The encouragement given to population by such increase of resources could not appear with any effect [1836: any considerable effect] in the market under sixteen or eighteen years; and in the mean time [1836: before that time] the demand compared with the

---

the last two years of the contest, but [1836: and] still more by the sudden want of consumption and demand [1836: the want of demand], which occurred on its termination; how is the lost capital ever to be recovered, if we are not active in accumulation [1836: except by accumulation]? I am very far indeed from saying that we must not accumulate [1836: sentence omitted]. It is perfectly true that there is no other possible way of recovering our lost capital than by accumulation' (1820, 503–4; 1836, 424).

7 Further evidence for Malthus's case is drawn from American experience: 'The amount of capital employed on the land during the Revolutionary war, was prodigiously increased owing to the great increase of profits; and although many merchants and manufacturers were occasionally subjected to great losses, yet the high rate of profits generally seemed more than to balance them; and there cannot be a doubt of the increase both of mercantile and manufacturing capital.'

supply of labour would [1836: might] be greater than the demand compared with the supply of most other commodities' (1820, 287; 1836, 257).[8] The consequences of monetary injection are illustrated by reference to the war period, when there had occurred a major increase in the money wage, reflecting higher labour demand – though the effect on the corn wage was negated in southern England by the Poor Law institution: 'It is on this account, that in the fall in the value of money which took place from 1793 to 1814, and which was unquestionably accompanied by a great increase of capital, and a great demand for labour, I am strongly of the opinion [1836: there is strong reason to believe] that if the price of labour has not been kept down by artificial means, it would have risen higher in proportion than the average price of corn; and this opinion is fairly borne out by facts' (1820, 287–8; 1836, 257). In Scotland and some parts of the north of England, 'the rise of wages [1836: money wages] was in fact greater than the rise of corn, and ... the condition of the labourer till 1814 was decidedly improved, even in spite of the taxes, many of which certainly bore heavily on the conveniences and comforts of the labourer, though they affected but little his command over strict necessaries' (1820, 288; 1836, 258).[9]

The analysis of wartime events is conspicuous in the *Quarterly Review* article of 1823 on Tooke's *High and Low Prices.* We have already encountered Malthus's insistence there that wartime circumstances created not only a *relative* increase in demand reflecting obstructions to supply and poor seasons, but, more significantly, a *real* or positive expansion of demand accompanied by the monetary means required to give 'effect' to such expansion (1823a/1986, 7, 235–7; cited above, pp. 560–1). Malthus proceeded to elaborate the positive effects on agricultural income of a deficiency in farm supplies – reflecting the characteristic demand inelasticity for corn. He observed first that Tooke himself realized the implications of deficient harvests for agricultural prosperity over the war years, applying the principle of *the effect of quantity on price* to the state of agriculture from 1793 to 1812: '"The first great burst of prosperity," (he says) "clearly followed the deficient harvests of 1794 and 1795;" and he then calculates, with

8 A qualifying note appears in 1836: 'The increase of the funds for the maintenance of labour would however have some effect soon, by diminishing mortality, both among those rising to the age of puberty, and the full-grown labourers.'

The effect on the corn wage was not inevitable. The money wage might lag 'if any previous causes have given an extraordinary stimulus to the progress of population. In this case, though the resources of the country [1836: funds for the maintenance of labour] may be increasing fast, the population may be increasing faster, and the wages [1836: money wages] of labour will not rise in proportion to the fall in the value of money [1836: to the price of corn]' (1820, 286; 1836, 256).

9 Despite the foregoing accounts of buoyancy throughout the war, there is allusion in one of the two monetary papers of 1811 to depression 1809–11 for which the Bank was responsible. See chapter 13, p. 652.

much appearance of probability, that the rise in the price of corn occasioned by the deficiency of these two years, which was supposed to be about one-eighth, must have thrown into the hands of the agricultural interest in 1795 and 1796, when the prices were the highest, a clear profit of from 12 to 14 millions each year, or from 24 to 28 millions for the two years' (238). Assuming no compensatory reduction in manufacturing prices and incomes, such increase in agricultural prices and incomes must have constituted a *net* increase in aggregate demand at the original prices of 1793: 'Now unless it can be distinctly shown, that this enormous increase in the price and value of the grain of the country, was counterbalanced by a proportionate diminution in the price and value of other commodities, it follows incontestably, that there must have been a great positive increase of demand in reference to the actual mass of products, that is, such a demand as would have been effectual to the purchase of a larger mass of commodities than were consumed in 1793, on the supposition that they were sold at the same price' – a shift in demand curves, in our terms. Tooke did 'not attempt to show that there was any such counterbalancing fall of prices in the goods of the other producing classes'; there were, for example, 'no proofs whatever that the greater amount of currency expended on the corn diminished the amount of expenditure on foreign commodities.' In sum, the 'very great increase in the bullion price of corn, so far from diminishing proportionably the prices of other commodities, was not only accompanied by increased prices but by a greatly increased amount of the quantity consumed' (239). Malthus allowed that not all observed increases in consumption reflected increases in general demand, alluding in part to movements *along* rather than *shifts* of demand curves: 'A considerable increase of consumption may take place for some years together, not from what can with propriety be called an increase of demand, but from an overabundant supply occasioned either by the seasons, or by unbounded hopes and expectations relating to the employment of capital.' But taking 'a period of considerable length, and attend[ing] particularly to the rate at which the annual consumption increases, some judgement may no doubt be formed of the annual increase of effectual demand'; and 'tried by this criterion, we believe it will be found, by a reference to Mr. Tooke's and other documents, that the products of the land, the labour, and the capital of this country, *never in any period of our history increased for twenty-two years together with the same rapidity as in the twenty-two years from 1793 to 1814 inclusive*' (239–40; emphasis added).

As we know, Malthus complained that Tooke himself had denied the phenomenon: 'We are quite at a loss ... to understand on what grounds the great increase of consumption during the war is denied by Mr. Tooke' (241). In registering this complaint he supplemented the original cause responsible for the increase in aggregate demand – an initial supply deficiency pre-eminently of agricultural produce, considering the characteristic inelasticity of demand – by the 'conversion of capital into revenue,' a reference to the maintenance of the military evidently financed by loans and taxation: 'The conversion of capital into revenue which was taking place during the whole of the period must have powerfully co-operated with the seasons and the obstructions to importation, in occasioning a brisk consumption of all the produce brought to market, so as, with few and slight exceptions, to leave little on hand; and as it appears from all the documents which can be referred to that the yearly additions to this produce were unusually large, it follows necessarily that the consumption during the war was unusually great ... [W]hatever may have been the favourable or unfavourable changes which have taken place since the peace, the period, though very long for a crisis of distress and unnaturally low profits, is much too short to be compared with the period of the war' (241–2). Malthus repeats the striking conclusion that 'in no twenty-two years of our history of which we have authentic accounts has there ever been so rapid an increase of production and consumption, both in respect of quantity and value, as in the twenty-two years ending with 1814.'

The account of the war years 1793–1813 also emphasizes the 'extraordinary rapidity' of population growth, indicating that the money wage rose sufficiently to compensate for rising corn prices. In fact, we find implicit allusion to the proposition – Quesnay's proposition – that a proportionate increase in the money wage actually raised the real wage: 'Mr. Tooke has clearly shown that the effects of the seasons in raising prices may last for twenty years altogether, so as very greatly to increase the average price of corn; and it has already been stated as a matter of fact, that taking an average of the three years ending with 1792, and the three years ending with 1813, the bullion price of wheat rose from £2:12s.9d to £4:12s. [see 239]. Now, though it is well known that a year of scarcity or even two years, may pass over without a rise in the price of labour, yet when the rise of provisions is very considerable in itself, and extends over a considerable period, a rise in the money price of labour must follow, or the population will be quite unable to support itself, and the prices of corn must fall again from the destruction of the consumers. In the case immediately under our consideration, we well know that this alternative did not take place. On the contrary, the population increased with extraordinary rapidity, which necessarily implies such a rise in the money price of labour as, combined with more general employment, and other advantages in the purchase of clothing and foreign commodities, would enable the labouring classes to bring up larger families than before' (246).

III ANALYSIS OF THE POSTWAR DEPRESSION

Malthus denied 'that the distresses of the labouring classes since 1815' could be ascribed entirely 'to a deficient capital ... unable to employ all that are in want of work' (1820, 490; 1836, 413).[10] That an inadequate ratio of capital (even capital and revenue combined) to population compared with pre-1815 was admittedly a cause of 'very great distress' did not necessarily imply too little capital relative to 'the demand for it, and the demand for the commodities procured by it.' On the contrary, capital in the postwar years was *excessive* relative to demand. And this was a further and distinct cause of distress.[11]

Two cases are distinguished for illustration, the first involving a major reduction in the capital stock, and thus in aggregate output, assuming no 'other cause occurring of diminished demand' (demand 'for commodities' is inserted in the 1836 version). The outcome would be 'great distress among the working classes' – in 1836, also 'great inconveniences to consumers' – 'attended with great advantages to the remaining capitalists' (1820, 491; 1836, 414). Malthus did not have in mind the direct effect on the profit rate of low wages – Ricardo's perspective – but the favourable consequences of scarcity of commodities in general, *excess aggregate demand*, to which capitalists respond by saving from revenue. (For Ricardo, a fall in output as a result of a reduced capital stock would entail an equivalent fall in aggregate demand.) A high interest rate signalled a 'high demand for capital,' which in turn was a *derived* demand reflecting a high demand for final goods: 'Commodities, in general, would be scarce, and bear a high price on account of the deficiency in the means of producing them. Nothing would be so easy as to find a profitable employment for stock [1836: capital]; but it would by no means be easy to find stock [1836: capital] for the number of employments in which it was deficient; and consequently the rate of profits would be very high. In this state of things there would be an immediate and pressing demand for capital, on account of there being an immediate and pressing demand for commodities; and the obvious remedy would be, the supply of the demand in the only way in which it could take place, namely, by saving from revenue to add to capital. This supply of capital would ... take place just upon the same principle as a supply of population would follow a great destruction of people on the supposition of there being an immediate and pressing want of labour evinced by the high real wages given to the labourer' (1820, 491; 1836, 414–15).

10 Conceivably, Malthus had in mind Ricardo's position, as reported, for example, in Parliament: 'He conceived that the distress was chiefly to be ascribed to the inadequacy of the capital of the nation to carry on the operations of trade, manufacture, and commerce' – an inadequacy attributed to a low profit rate due to agricultural protection (24 December 1819; 1951–73, V, 38). However, misallocation reflecting the slow switch of resources from war to peace industries predominates in Ricardo's accounts (see Hollander, 1979, 535f.).

11 For Malthus's defence in the second edition (1836, 414n) against the charge of inconsistency, see Conclusion, p. 960.

An alternative course of events entailed a *fall* in the profit rate deriving from a failure of aggregate demand and the generation of *excess supply*: 'On the other hand, if the capital of the country were diminished by the failure of some branches of trade [1836: failure of demand in some large branches of trade], which had before been very prosperous, and absorbed a great quantity of stock ... the state of things, with the exception of the distresses of the poor, would be almost exactly reversed. The remaining capitalists would be in no respect benefited by events which had diminished capital [1836: the supply]. Commodities would be every where cheap. Capital would be seeking employment, but would not easily find it; and the profits of stock would be low' (1820, 491–2; 1836, 415). The current depression resembled the latter case.[12] To propose as its solution increased saving was wholly inappropriate since a 'demand for capital,' again a *derived* demand, was wanting: 'There would be no pressing and immediate demand for capital, because there would be no pressing and immediate demand for commodities; and, under these circumstances, the saving from revenue to add to capital, instead of affording the remedy required, would only aggravate the distresses of the capitalists, and fill the stream of capital which was flowing out of the country.' As is common with Malthus, he drew a close analogy with the artificial encouragement of population growth in inappropriate circumstances: 'But when profits are low and uncertain, when capitalists are quite a loss where they can safely employ their capitals, and when on these accounts capital is flowing out of the country; in short, when all the evidence which the nature of the subject admits, distinctly proves that there is no effective demand for capital at home, is it not contrary to the general principles of political economy, is it not a vain and fruitless opposition to that first, greatest, and most universal of all its principles, the principle of supply and demand, to recommend saving, and the conversion of more revenue into capital? Is it not just the same sort of things as to recommend marriage when people are starving and emigrating?' (1820, 495; 1836, 417–18).[13] It is not made absolutely clear here whether new savings undertaken under inappropriate conditions are supposedly translated into real investments, worsening the situation

12 In both editions Malthus refers to 'the present state of this country' (1820, 493; 1836, 416), adding in the second: 'This was written in 1820.'

13 Cf: 'The distresses of the capitalists would be aggravated, just upon the same principle as the distresses of the labouring classes would be aggravated if they were encouraged to marry and increase, after a considerable destruction of people, although accompanied by a still greater destruction of capital which had kept the wages of labour very low. There might certainly be a great deficiency of population, compared with the territory and powers of the country, and it might be very desirable that it should be greater, but if the wages of labour were still low, notwithstanding the diminution of people, to encourage the birth of more children would be to encourage misery and mortality rather than population' (1820, 492–3; 1836, 415).

because financed by absolutely reduced consumption (as in the analysis of sustainable growth), or whether new savings leak out. But the former interpretation is the appropriate one, as indicated on several other occasions where warnings are given against inappropriate savings programs – those financed by reduced consumption – which 'can only still further ... increase the plenty of commodities' (1820, 467, 1836, 401; see chapter 11, p. 531n31). Similarly: 'If instead of saving from increased profits, we save from diminished expenditure; if, at the very time that the supply of commodities compared with the demand for them, clearly admonishes us that the proportion of capital to revenue is already too great, we go on saving from our revenue to add still further to our capital, all general principles concur in shewing that we must of necessity be aggravating instead of alleviating our distress' (1820, 505; 1836, 425).

A number of important analytical issues are raised by the discussion of post-1815 conditions. There is first the relation between commodity and labour markets, which emerges at various junctures of the empirical account. Thus in a comment on the cause of unemployment *despite low money wages*, Malthus writes: '*Though labour is cheap*, there is neither the power nor the will to employ it all; because not only is the capital of the country diminished, compared with the number of the labourers, but, owing to the diminished revenues of the country, the commodities which those labourers would produce are not in such request as to ensure tolerable profits to the reduced capital' (1820, 495; 1836, 417; emphasis added). Demand for labour thus turns both on 'capital' and on final demand for commodities, the latter a sort of derived demand; apparently, the 'power to employ' reflects the former, whereas the 'will to employ' is governed by prospective final demand – though we should emphasize that Malthus is here concerned with aggregate demand, not demand for the products of any particular industry. As for the former, it is likely that Malthus intended to define a *technological* dependency of labour demand on capital, rather than a dependency in terms of preaccumulated agricultural produce.[14] The full account of contemporary events, involving a net reduction of 'national capital,' suggests the stock of material capital goods, excluding wage goods: 'That a great loss of capital has lately been sustained, is unquestionable. During nearly the whole of the war, owing to the union of great powers of production with great [1836: a great effectual] consumption and demand, the prodigious destruction of capital by the government was much more than recovered. To doubt this would be to shut our eyes to the comparative state of the country in 1792 and 1813. The two last years of the war were, however, years of extraordinary expense, and being

14 Formally, 'capital' is defined as 'that particular part of ... accumulated wealth, which is destined to be employed with a view of profit' which is quite general (1820, 293; 1836, 262).

followed immediately by a period marked by a very unusual stagnation of [1836: effectual] demand, the destruction of capital which took place in those years was not probably recovered. But this stagnation itself was much more disastrous in its effects upon the national capital, and still more upon the national revenue, than any previous destruction of stock' (1820, 493; 1836, 416).[15]

It will be especially noted that Malthus wrote of postwar unemployment *'though labour is cheap,'* given the lack of 'power and will to employ it all.' This alludes to *stagnation* (unemployment and excess capacity), a phenomenon referred to more explicitly earlier in Malthus's chapter. In that earlier account of the postwar years – we shall elaborate on it shortly – Malthus distinguished between the process of decline of final prices in the face of rigid or relatively rigid money wages and the final equilibrium when money wages had adjusted downwards: 'As long as this fall in the money price of produce continues to diminish the power of commanding domestic and foreign labour [1836: commanding labour], a great discouragement [1836: a discouragement] to production must obviously continue; and if, *after labour has adjusted itself to the new level of prices,* the permanent distribution of the produce and the permanent tastes and habits of the people should not be favourable to an adequate degree of [1836: effectual] consumption, the clearest principles of political economy show that the profits of stock might be lower for any length of time than the state of the land rendered necessary; and that the check to [1836: that the retarded rate of] production might be as *permanent* as the faulty distribution of the produce and the unfavourable tastes and habits which had occasioned it' (1820, 446–7; 1836, 387; emphasis added).[16] This state of stagnation, to repeat, is characterized not only by a reduced *power* to employ available labour because of a reduced real capital stock, but also by a reduced *will* because of 'diminished revenues' and therefore an inadequate aggregate demand for final produce. Noteworthy in this account is the emphasis on the coincidence of low wages and low profits – actual and potential – quite apart from the 'state of the land.'[17] Money-wage reductions are

15 Since there were huge farm surpluses in 1815 and 1816, it seems most likely that the reduction in capital stock excludes wage goods.

16 Viner read the passage as supporting the view that Malthus (like Wheatley, G.P. Scrope, and Western) 'appears to attribute the [postwar] decline of production resulting from a fall in prices to the lag of wages behind prices and the consequent destruction of the incentive to investment,' but finds his analysis to be 'much inferior to Thomas Attwood's' (1937, 187n). Viner seems to neglect the ultimate fall in the wage recognized by Malthus.

17 Cf. 1820, 512n: 'The profits of stock cannot be higher than the state of the land will allow, but they may be lower in any degree [see 300]. The great difference between Mr. Ricardo and me on this point is, that Mr. Ricardo thinks profits are *regulated* by the state of the land; I think they are only *limited* by it one way, and that if capital be abundant, compared with the demand for commodities, profits may be low in any degree, in

evidently *not* (or not in all circumstances) a sufficient condition for correction.

Malthus also took the opportunity to insist on distinguishing between different causes of *real*-wage increase: 'Mr. Ricardo always seems to think that it is quite the same to the labourer, whether he is able to command more of the necesaries of life by a rise in the money price of labour, or by a fall in the money price of provisions' (1820, 455–6; 1836, 393). In fact, a real-wage increase reflecting a collapse of corn prices entailed either *permanent* or – an allusion to the British case, it turns out – *temporary* stagnation: 'An increase in the wages of labour, both nominal and real, invariably implies [1836: An increase in the money wages of labour generally implies] such a distribution of the actual wealth as to give it an increasing value, to ensure full employment to all the labouring classes, and to create a demand for further produce, and for the capital which is to obtain it. In short, it is the infallible sign of health and prosperity. Whereas a general fall in the money price of necessaries often arises from so defective a distribution of the produce of the country, that the general amount of its value cannot be kept up; in which case, under the most favourable circumstances, a temporary period of want of employment and distress is unavoidable; and in many cases (as may be too frequently observed in surveying the different countries of the globe) this fall in the money price of necessaries is the accompaniment of permanent want of employment and the most abject poverty, in consequence of retrograde and permanently diminished wealth' (1820, 455–6; 1836, 394–5).

* * *

So much for the *state* of stagnation. What now of the *generation* of unemployment? There are three detailed analyses in the chapter 'Of the Progress of Wealth,' all referring to an initial collapse of corn prices in 1815–16. The first implies excellent harvests and raises the question of loss of employment despite an abundance of wage goods: 'From the harvest of 1815 to the harvest of 1816, there cannot be a doubt that the funds for the maintenance of labour in this country were unusually abundant. Corn was particularly plentiful, and no other necessaries were deficient; yet it is an acknowledged fact, that great numbers were thrown out of employment, partly from the want of power, and partly from the want of will to employ

spite of the fertility of the land.' This note does not appear in the 1836 edition (1836, 430). It is unclear why it was removed, but Ricardo had always protested that he had allowed for profit-rate variations with changes in labour-market conditions independently of agricultural productivity.

the same quantity of labour as before. How is this fact to be accounted for?' (1820, 444–5; 1836, 386).[18]

In attempting to answer the latter query, Malthus reminds his reader in 1820 of the observation on the previous page regarding the necessity to take account of 'a circulating medium,' for 'without such reference, the proof of a defective distribution' – an indirect allusion to a failure of demand – 'would be extremely difficult' (1820, 445; the 1836 version [386] simply asserts that it 'would certainly not be easy to explain [unemployment despite plentiful corn] without referring to a circulating medium.') And he protests that it is 'no use therefore to make suppositions about a great increase of produce, and, rejecting all reference to a circulating medium, to conclude that this great increase will be properly distributed and effectively consumed. It is a conclusion which we have no right whatever to make. We know, both from theory and experience, that if the whole produce falls in money value, the distribution must be such as to discourage production' (1820, 446).[19]

A preliminary word is therefore in order on the importance of money. One formulation of this theme appears in a note: 'Theoretical writers in political economy, from the fear of appearing to attach too much importance to money, have perhaps been too apt to throw it out of their consideration in their reasonings. It is an abstract truth that we want commodities, not money. But, in reality, no commodity for which it is possible to sell our goods at once, can be an adequate substitute for a circulating medium, and enable us in the same manner to provide for children, to purchase an estate, or to command labour and provisions a year or two hence. A circulating medium is absolutely necessary to any considerable saving; and even the manufacturer would get on but slowly, if he were obliged to accumulate in kind all the wages of his workmen. We cannot therefore be surprised at his wanting money rather than other goods; and, in civilized countries, we may be quite sure that if the farmer or manufacturer cannot sell his products so as to give him a profit estimated in money, his industry will immediately slacken' (1820, 361n; 1836, 324n). In conclusion: 'The circulating medium bears so important a part in the

18 On the unusually abundant farm supplies, see also 1820, 454–5; 1836, 392–3.
In *Grounds of an Opinion* we read of 'a change in the spirit of our legislative enactments relating to the admission of foreign corn' (1815a/1986, 7, 153), implying the effect of an actual, or at least an expected increase of imports. But domestic output itself was *low*. Characterizing the period was an 'unusual combination of low prices, and *scanty produce*' (154n; emphasis added); indeed, it had been 'impossible to forsee such a year as the present – such a combination, as a *very bad harvest*, and very low prices' (155n; emphasis added). Combining this account with that of the *Principles* we must suppose a reversal of harvest conditions in summer 1815. On this latter see Smart, 1910–17, I, 514.

19 The deletion of this passage in the second edition (see 1836, 387) is presumably cosmetic, the general argument remaining unchanged.

distribution of wealth, and the encouragement of industry, that to set it aside in our reasonings may often lead us wrong [1836: that it is hardly ever safe to set it aside in our reasonings, and all attempts at illustration, by supposing advances of a certain quantity of corn and clothing, instead of a certain quantity of money, which every year practically represents a variable quantity of corn, cannot fail to lead us wrong].'[20] The proposition that saving is undertaken in money, that wages are paid in money, and that profits are estimated in terms of money has high analytical potential. But to appreciate Malthus's precise intentions, we must attend to the context of the statement. In the 1820 version it is attached to an argument that, if the farm sector insists on producing a surplus of corn – engaging in excessive 'saving' in this particular sense – it would find the money value thereof so reduced as to preclude effective saving for the future on the part of farmers. In 1836 it is attached to the text which warns that, should farmers insist on 'saving' – again in the same sense of the term – instead of consuming luxuries, *manufacturers* would find their monetary proceeds inadequate, precluding saving on their part. In either event, we are not faced here with a proposition regarding *excess demand for money*, but one regarding a failure of mutual exchange attributable to excess 'saving,' with which no Ricardian would have objected.

A further reference to the importance of a 'circulating medium' – it is what concerns us now – alludes to the foregoing note: 'In the distribution of commodities, the circulating medium of every country bears a most important part; and, as I intimated before in a note, we are much more likely to obscure our reasonings than to render them clearer, by throwing it out of our consideration. It is not easy indeed, without reference to a circulating medium, to ascertain whether the commodities of a country are so distributed as to give them their proper value' (1820, 444; 1836, 385). This is related to the notion of the dependence of the value of aggregate output on a 'distribution' of commodities which 'best adapts them to the wants and tastes of society,' a high value implying a high excess of labour commanded over labour embodied. The passage continues to spell out the significance of the monetary dimension from this perspective, with reference to the illegitimacy of physical wage-fund reasoning: 'It may be said, perhaps, that if the funds for the maintenance of labour are at any time in unusual abundance, it may fairly be presumed that they will be able to command a more than usual quantity of labour. But they certainly will not be able to command more labour, nor even so much, if the distribution of them be defective; and in a country which has a circulating medium, the specific proof of the distribution being defective is, that the whole produce does not exchange for so large an amount of circulating medium

20 The 1836 criticism of corn–clothing calculations probably refers to Robert Torrens's standard practice.

as before, and that consequently the producers have been obliged to sell at a great diminution of money profits, or a positive money loss.' The significance of money in this context thus reflects the unacceptability of the notion of an offer of employment in terms of accumulated wage goods – Malthus's own perspective in other contexts; wage goods are sold on the open market.

* * *

With this in mind, we turn to the three main accounts of the postwar period given in the *Principles.* The first emphasizes that farm produce was sold at a severe loss, obliging farmers to reduce their (money) offers of employment. Once the reduction in agricultural prices had extended to those of manufactures (the precise linkage is clarified in the third passage), offers of industrial employment were perforce reduced. Despite a certain ambiguity regarding the purported behaviour of the money-wage rate in the clarifications introduced into the second edition, it appears that (relatively) rigid money wages played a part in the explanation of reduced demand for labour in both sectors. Increased employment capacity ('power') by fixed-income recipients hardly sufficed to compensate, especially given a lack of 'will' – a nice instance of what now is termed 'coordination failure':

But the moment we refer to a circulating medium, the theory of the fact observed becomes perfectly clear. It is acknowledged that there was a fall in the money value of the raw produce, to the amount of nearly one third. But if the farmer sold his produce for only two thirds of the price at which he had before sold it, [1836: while the money price of labour had not fallen,] it is evident that he would be quite unable to command the same quantity of labour, and to employ the same quantity of capital on his farm as he did the year before. And when afterwards a great fall of money price took place in all [1836: almost all] manufactured products, occasioned in a considerable degree by this previous fall of raw produce, it is as evident that [1836: if the price of labour had not fallen, or not in proportion, so large a quantity of produce would be required to pay the labourer that] the manufactures would be unable to command the labour of [1836: to employ] the same number of workmen as before. In the midst of the plenty of necessaries, these two important classes of society would really have their power of employing labour diminished, while all those who possessed fixed incomes would have their power of employing labour increased, with very little chance of an increase of will to extend their demand in proportion; and the general result would resemble the effects of that partial distribution of products which would arise from the interruption of accustomed communications. The same, or a greater [1836: the same] quantity of commodities might be produced for a short time; but the distribution not being such as to proportion the supply in each quarter to the demand, the whole would fall in exchangeable value, and a very decided [1836: a decided] check to production would be experienced in reference to the whole country. It follows, that the labouring classes of society may be thrown out of work in the midst of an abundance of necessaries, if these necessaries are not in the hands of those who are at the same time both able and willing to employ an adequate quantity of labour. (1820, 445–6; 1836, 386–7)[21]

A second passage treats the postwar events as an exceptional outcome of the reopening of trade, the exception proving the rule that expansion of trade opportunities normally has a positive effect on activity. The problem relates to cases of demand inelasticity. Such an exceptional case occurred with the postwar relaxation of trade constraints which brought with it a collapse of corn prices relative to labour,[22] generating unemployment, which required for correction an appropriate fall of the money wage:

It will readily be allowed that an increase in the *quantity* of commodities is one of the most desirable effects of foreign commerce; but I wish particularly to press on the attention of the reader than in almost all cases, another important effect accompanies it, expressly rejected by Mr. Ricardo [1951–73, I, 128],[23] namely an increase in the amount of exchangeable value. And that this latter effect is so necessary, in order to create a continued stimulus to productive industry, and keep up an abundant supply of commodities, that in the few cases in which it does not take place, a stagnation in the demand for labour is immediately perceptible, and the progress of wealth is checked. An extension of foreign commerce, according to the view which Mr. Ricardo takes of it, would, in my opinion, place us frequently in the situation in which this country was in the early part of 1816, when a sudden abundance and cheapness of corn and other commodities, from a great supply meeting a deficient demand, so diminished the value of the income of the country, that it could no longer command the same quantity of labour at the same price; the consequence of which was that, in the midst of plenty, thousands upon thousands [1836: thousands] were thrown out of employment – *a most painful but almost unavoidable preliminary to a fall in the money wages of labour, which it is obvious could alone enable the general income of the country to employ the same number of labourers as before, and, after a period of severe check to the increase of wealth, to recommence a progressive movement.* (1820, 454–5; 1836, 392–3; emphasis added)[24]

21 This closing phrase suggests the concept of wage-goods *advances*, but we must be cautious in giving it a literal reading in the light of Malthus's own apparent rejection of this perspective in the present general context.

22 On the inflow of foreign corn before the restrictions had been introduced and taken effect, see Smart, 1910–17, I, 445, 514.

23 The reference to Ricardo is omitted in the second edition.

24 Cf. also the comment relating to 1816: 'A mere abundance of commodities falling very

The impression from this passage is that downward flexibility of the money wage is both a necessary *and a sufficient* condition for recovery. But as we have seen this is not Malthus's position elsewhere (above, p. 599). A reconciliation would require that we read the present statement as abstracting from the obstruction to full recovery created by those 'permanent' changes in the 'distribution of the produce' and in 'tastes and habits' earlier alluded to which prevent full employment, even 'after labour has adjusted itself to the new level of prices.'[25]

At no stage is account taken of potentially negative consequences for demand of a fall in the money wage. In evidence given to a Commons Committee in 1827, Malthus warned that reduced wages would 'have a tendency to diminish the home trade' (see chapter 17, p. 862), but, regrettably, this position was not absorbed into the *Principles*.[26]

A third and yet more complete version of the downward trend from the full employment of the war years to a state of stagnation occurs in section X of the chapter on Progress, formally devoted to applications of theory to the postwar events. This approach is intimated in earlier correspondence with Ricardo. On 19 June 1815, Malthus alluded to 'the unavoidable evils attending a general fall of prices' (in Ricardo, 1951–73, VI, 231), and on 16 October to reports 'that all home trade was most exceedingly slack,' which he attributed to a collapse of demand for manufactures attributable to diminished agricultural incomes: 'Is it possible for above half the national income to fall very greatly in price, without affecting the demand and the other half. I confess I feel no doubt that the main cause of the present slackness of trade is the diminished incomes of the Landlords and Farmers. The actual produce of a country will always be sold, and the loss of the sellers will be the gain of the buyers; but it makes an infinite difference to a country whether its produce is sold at a price which will encourage production, or discourage it. During the period of a fall of prices it appears to me that all sorts of productions are prodigiously discouraged; and that at the end of 7 or 8 years of falling prices, or 7 or 8 years of rising prices, the state of a country will be most essentially different in point of wealth' (303). On 3 December 1817, he wrote of the low profits 'during

greatly in value compared with labour [1836: though it may be called an actual increase of wealth,] would obviously at first diminish the power of employing the same number of workmen, and a temporary glut and general deficiency of demand could not fail to ensue in labour, in produce, and in capital, attended with the usual distress which a glut must occasion [1836: must necessarily occasion]' (1820, 460–1; 1836, 396).

25 The problem is taken up more fully below, pp. 612f.

26 In his discussions of the consequences of increased parish allowances in the *High Price of Provisions* (1800/1986, 7, 9–13) and also in the *Essay on Population* (1798/1986, *1*, 30–1), Malthus did emphasize the inability to raise real wages by such grants because of the higher prices actually generated by increased spending by labourers.

the last two or three years,' asking: 'What destroyed so much agricultural capital, but low profits or rather no profits? and what occasioned so much distress among merchants and manufactures but a want of demand and fall of prices' (1951–73, VII, 214).[27]

Turning now to the formulation in the *Principles*, we have the initial fall in the prices of farm produce owing to oversupply; reduced demand for manufactures by landlords and farmers, reflecting their reduced revenues; and the collapse of manufacturing prices, unintended increase in inventories, and forced sales abroad. 'Sudden and extraordinary' monetary contraction exacerbated the situation: 'It commenced certainly with the extraordinary fall in the value of the raw produce of the land, to the amount, it is supposed [1836: it has been supposed], of nearly one third. When this fall had diminished the capitals of the farmers, and still more the revenues both of landlords and farmers, and of all those who were otherwise connected with the land, their power of purchasing manufactures and foreign products was of necessity greatly diminished. The failure of home demand filled the warehouses of the manufacturers with unsold goods, which urged them to export more largely at all risks. But this excessive exportation glutted all the foreign markets, and prevented the merchants from receiving adequate returns; while, from the diminution of the home revenues, aggravated by a sudden and extraordinary contraction of the currency, even the comparatively scanty returns obtained from abroad found a very insufficient domestic demand, and the profits and consequent expenditure of merchants and manufacturers were proportionably lowered' (1820, 493–4; 1836, 416–17).[28] In this particular account, monetary contraction is represented as an 'aggravating' force at play.[29] In

27 An addition (made in 1816) to the fifth edition of the *Essay on Population* simply attributes the collapse of cotton goods' prices to 'domestic competition': 'In the cotton trade of this country, which has extended itself so wonderfully during the last twenty-five years, very little effect has hitherto been produced by foreign competition. The very great fall which has taken place in the prices of cotton goods has been almost exclusively owing to domestic competition; and this competition has so glutted both the home and foreign markets, that the present capitals employed in the trade, notwithstanding the very peculiar advantages which they possess from the saving of labour, have ceased to possess any advantage whatever in the general rate of their profits' (1817, II, 405).

28 The loss of farmers' capital doubtless refers to real capital goods. The *Grounds of an Opinion* (1815) had referred to 'great increase of capital laid out upon the land' during the war and to 'great consequent extension of cultivation and improvement ... spirited improvement and *high farming*,' followed by a major fall in prices affecting 'one-fourth of the [agricultural] property' (1815a/1986, 7, 152–4). This certainly implies a loss of *real capital*.

29 The letter to Ricardo of 16 October 1815 confirms a concern with the contraction of output enduced by a reduced money supply: 'Pray has there been any account lately of the number of Bank of England notes in circulation. It has been said I understand that they have been much diminished lately, which is one great cause of the fall of prices. Is

an elaboration of the postwar fall in commodity prices and money wages in the second edition, the monetary contraction in the face of expanded output is given greater weight: 'It is well known that since the war which terminated in 1815, there has been a very great increase of produce and population in most of the countries of the commercial world, and from the necessity that has occurred of withdrawing a great part of the paper which was in circulation in these countries during the war, and the frequent failure of credit from overspeculation subsequently, there is reason to think that the great increase of produce and population has not been balanced by a proportionate increase of currency and credit; and under these circumstances a fall in the prices of produce and labour was inevitable' (1836, 134).[30]

One further feature of the depression is alluded to – the effect on wages of expanded labour supplies on the market following demobilization and ongoing population growth. Though this exerted downward pressure on the *money* wage rate, the 'value' of aggregate output (command over bullion, and ultimately over labour) none the less declined: 'While these unfavourable changes were taking place in rents and profits, the powerful stimulus which had been given to population during the war continued to pour in fresh supplies of labour, and, aided by [1836: the powerful stimulus which had been given to population by the continued demand for labour during the war, occasioned the pouring in of fresh supplies of labour, which aided by] the disbanded soldiers and sailors and the failure of demand arising from the losses of the farmers and merchants, reduced generally the wages of labour [1836: both wages and profits], and left the country with a generally diminished [1836: greatly diminished] capital and revenue; – not merely in proportion to the alteration of the value of the currency, but in reference to the bullion value of its produce, and the command of this bullion value over domestic and foreign labour [1836: over labour, at the price at which it was actually employed]' (1820, 494; 1836, 417). The end result was a rate of growth of population exceeding that of total output – not only that of 'demand for labour' – though total output was 'redundant' relative to aggregate demand: 'For the four or five

this so?' to which he adds that his information indicated 'that all home trade was exceedingly slack,' implying a causal link (1951–73, VI, 303). Ricardo replied to the contrary, that the note circulation had *increased* (17 October; 304); and insisted that it 'does not follow that because prices are low production will be discouraged.' Malthus then reworded his query: 'Pray do you not think that the currency as a whole is at present diminished' (30 October; 320).

30 In *The Measure of Value* (1823), Malthus mentions the role of money in the depression, but rather as an *indirect* effect of a preceding monetary expansion: 'as the increase of paper beyond what would circulate at par with gold gave facilities to production, and to the bringing of poor land into cultivation during the war, it has tended to increase the glut and low prices since the peace' (1823b/1986, 7, 220).

years since the war, on account of the change in the distribution of the national produce, and the want of [1836: effectual] consumption and demand occasioned by it, a decided check [1836: a check] has been given to [1836: the rate of] production, and the population, under its former impulse, has increased, not only faster than the demand for labour, but faster than the actual produce; yet this produce, though decidedly deficient [1836: though deficient], compared with the population, and compared with past times [1836: omits 'and compared with past times'] is redundant, compared with the effectual demand for it and the revenue which is to purchase it' (1820, 494–5; 1836, 417).

The fall in the money wage after 1815 had evidently proven an inadequate stimulus.[31] Conceivably a sharper fall would have sufficed; but such a reading would conflict with the statement of continued stagnation even 'after labour had adjusted itself to the new level of prices.'

The main alternative interpretation – Ricardo's temporary resource misallocation – is rejected as incompatible with the evidence, particularly with the pervasiveness of the depression and the absence of those potentially profitable industries presumed to exist in that account. In the course of this critique Malthus emphasized the phenomena of 'redundant' or 'floating' capital – money capital – and of savings which entail leakages from the income stream, notions which indicate excess demand for money[32] as counterpart to the excess commodity supply, reflected, as we saw earlier, in unintended inventory increase and forced exports: 'It may be said, perhaps, that the new cotton trade happens to be glutted; and it is a tenet of the new doctrine on profits and demand, that if one trade be overstocked with capital, it is a certain sign that some other trade is understocked. But where, I would ask, is there any considerable trade that is confessedly understocked, and where high profits have been long pleading in vain for additional capital? The war has now been at an end above four years; and though the removal of capital generally occasions some partial loss, yet it is seldom long in taking place, if it be tempted to remove by great demand and high profits; but if it be only discouraged from proceeding in its accustomed course by falling profits, while the profits in all other trade, owing to general low prices, are falling at the same time, though not perhaps precisely in the same degree, it is highly probable that its motions will be slow and hesitating' (1820, 333–4). Thus far the first edition alone. The same objection is, however, restated in both editions: 'That the transition from war to peace, of which so much has been said, is a main cause of the effects observed, will be readily allowed, but not as the operation is usually explained. It is generally said that there has not been time to

31 Again, the effect on demand of a lower money wage is neglected (above, p. 605).

32 See also references to 'the stream of capital which was flowing out of the country' (above, p. 597) and the 'emigration' of capital (below, p. 617).

transfer capital from the employments where it is redundant to those where it is deficient, and thus to restore the proper equilibrium. But I cannot bring myself to believe that this transfer can require [1836: such a transfer could hardly require] so much time as has now elapsed since the war; and again ask, [1836: I would ask] where are the understocked employments, which, according to this theory, ought to be numerous, and fully capable of absorbing all the redundant capital, which is confessedly glutting the markets of Europe in so many different branches of trade? It is well known by the owners of floating capital, that none such are now to be found; and if the transition in question is to account for what has happened, it must have produced some other effects besides that which arises from the difficulty of moving capital' (1820, 498–9; 1836, 420).[33]

Here too will be found a nice restatement of the attributed cause – namely, 'a great diminution of the whole amount of consumption and demand [1836: diminution of the demand compared with the supply of produce]. The necessary changes in the channels of trade would be effected in a year or two; but the general diminution of consumption and demand [1836: demand, compared with the supply] occasioned by the transition from such a war to a peace, may last for a very considerable time' (1820, 499; 1836, 420). What follows emphasizes the fall in aggregate demand with the cessation of government expenditure and amply confirms *the role of hoarding* in the new circumstances: 'The returned taxes, and the excess of individual gains above expenditure, which were so largely used as revenue during the war, are now in part, and probably in no inconsiderable part, saved. I cannot doubt, for instance, that in our own country very many persons have taken the opportunity of saving a part of their returned property tax ... This saving is quite natural and proper, and forms no just argument against the removal of the tax; but still it contributes to explain the cause of the diminished demand for commodities, compared with their supply since the war. If some of the principal governments concerned spent the taxes which they raised in a manner to create a greater and more certain demand for labour and commodities, particularly the former, than the present owner of them, and if this difference of expenditure be of a nature to last for some time, we cannot be surprised at the duration of the effects arising from the transition from war to peace' (1820, 499–500; 1836, 420).

There is, we conclude, ample evidence of Malthus's impressive appreciation of the non-identity of intended savings and intended investment

33 A similar charge against Ricardo was made by William Blake: 'By those who imagine consumption not to be a necessary ingredient of demand, and that in order to make a market for commodities, it is only necessary to produce more, these phenomena [of universal distress] offer problems not very easy of solution' (1823, 94; in Ricardo, 1951–73, IV, 352). Malthus was aware of Blake's *Observations*, but makes no reference to this common ground.

manifested in an excess demand for money to hold, and his approach to the depression in terms of this 'Keynesian' phenomenon. It is consistent with Malthus's account that the volume of saving should have been *less* in absolute terms during the depression than during the war – considering the reduction in output and income – accompanied, of course, by a yet greater reduction in real investment.

Jacob Viner also interpreted Malthus as attributing the depression to 'an increase in saving unaccompanied by a corresponding increase in investment,' and finding the remedy in increased private consumption, considering the absence of sufficient motive for investment under prevalent conditions (1937, 194n). Viner found William Ellis to be the only Ricardian 'who gave any attention to the fact that saving might have other motives than securing interest on current investment,' and 'showed some recognition that the "transmutation of savings into capital" was not an automatic and certain process' (104–5n). It should be noted, however, that Malthus later pointed out to Ricardo that Say himself recognized hoarding as a feature of contemporary European depressions: 'qu'il y a beaucoup d'épargnes qui ne se placent lorsque les emplois sont difficiles, ou qui étant placées se dissipent dans une production mal calculée' (citing *Lettres à M. Malthus*, 1820, 101), adding that this perspective 'does appear in the most marked manner to contradict both his, and your theory' (25 September 1820; in Ricardo, 1951–73, VIII, 260).

* * *

Malthus also rejected as contradicting the facts those interpretations of 'the low profits of stock, and the difficulty of finding employment for it' in the postwar period, turning on 'the cultivation of our poor soils, our restrictions upon commerce, and our weight of taxation' (1820, 495–6; 1836, 418). What required explanation was the contrast between the extraordinarily rapid growth rate during the war – despite use of marginal land, trade restrictions impeding corn imports, and high taxation – and the stagnation since 1815, despite a reversal of these obstacles, including increased corn imports: 'I find it very difficult to admit a theory of our distresses so inconsistent with the theory of our [1836: comparative] prosperity. While the greatest quantity of our poor lands were in cultivation; while there were more than usual restrictions upon our commerce, and very little corn was imported; and while taxation was at its height, the country confessedly increased in wealth with a rapidity never known before. Since some of our poorest lands have been thrown out of cultivation; since the peace has removed many of the restriction upon our commerce, and, notwithstanding our corn laws, we have imported a great quantity of corn; and since seventeen millions of taxes have been taken off from the people, we have experienced a degree of distress, the pressure of which has been almost intolerable [1836: the greatest degree of distress, both among capitalists and labourers.] ... [The] facts certainly shew that, whatever may be the future effect of the causes above alluded to in checking the progress of our wealth, we must look elsewhere for the immediate sources of our present distresses' (1820, 495–6; 1836, 418).

This is taken to its logical conclusion: 'How far our artificial system, and particularly the changes in the value of our currency operating upon a large national debt, may have aggravated the evils we have experienced, it would be extremely difficult to say. But I feel perfectly convinced that a very considerable portion of these evils might be experienced by a nation without poor land in cultivation, without taxes, and without any fresh restriction on trade' (1820, 496–7; 1836, 418–19). For a closed economy not subject to diminishing returns, without taxes and enjoying free internal trade, might yet experience low profits, low wages, and unemployment in consequence of an inappropriately high rate of accumulation: 'If, upon the principle laid down by M. Say ... the society were greatly and generally to slacken their consumption, and add to their capitals, there cannot be the least doubt, on the great principles [1836: on the principle] of demand and supply that the profits of capitalists would soon be reduced to nothing [1836: greatly reduced], though there were no poor land in cultivation; and the population would be thrown out of work and would be starving, although without a single tax, or any restrictions on trade.' (There is also a concept of an *optimum* rate of accumulation depending upon circumstances, in the case of the war, circumstances which permitted increase in wealth and population 'with considerable rapidity.') But we must exercise caution in relating this argument to postwar experience, as Malthus understood it, for *Britain did not then experience increased realized investment, but rather leakages of revenue.* His purpose in alluding to the sustainable-growth model was rather to emphasize that the availability in the immediate postwar period of a larger capital stock and productive workforce was no guarantee of increased output and income:

The state of Europe and America may perhaps be said, in some points, to resemble the case here supposed; and the stagnation which has been so generally felt and complained of since the war, appears to me inexplicable upon the principles of those who think that the power of production is the only element of wealth, and, who consequently infer that if the powers [1836: means] of production be increased, wealth will certainly increase in proportion. Now it is unquestionable that the powers [1836: means] of production were increased by the cessation of war, and that more people and more capital were ready to be employed in productive labour; but notwithstanding this obvious increase in the powers [1836: means] of production, we hear everywhere of difficulties and distresses, instead of ease and plenty. In the United States of America in particular, a country of extraordinary physical resources, the difficulties which have been experienced are very striking, and such certainly as could hardly have been expected. These difficulties, at least, cannot be attributed to the cultivation of poor land, restrictions upon commerce, and excess of taxation. Altogether the state of the commercial world, since the war, clearly shows that something else is necessary to the continued increase of wealth besides an increase in the power [1836: means] of producing. (1820, 498; 1836, 419–20)

While then the sustainable-growth model was not relevant in the postwar period, it served admirably to account for events in wartime Britain. For the precise effect of the postwar collapse of demand varied from economy to economy, and was particularly serious for economies such as the American and British, which during the war had experienced a positive expansion of capacity, and this *in response to high demand,* just as the model has it in accounting for successful accumulation: 'In those countries, where the pressure of the war found great powers of production, and seemed to create much greater [1836: to create greater]; where accumulation, instead of being checked, was accelerated, and where the vast consumption of commodities was followed by supplies which occasioned a more rapid increase of wealth than was ever known before [1836: than before], the effect of peace would be very different. In such countries it is natural to suppose that a great diminution of consumption and demand [1836: the demand compared with the supply], would decidedly check the progress of wealth, and occasion very general and severe distress, both to capitalists and the labouring classes. England and America come the nearest to the countries of this latter description. They suffered the least by the war, or rather were enriched by it, and they are now suffering the most by the peace' (1820, 501; 1836, 422).[34]

* * *

There are indications that Malthus perceived excess supply to be a temporary phenomenon: 'It is not of course meant to be said that a country with a large quantity of land, labour and capital has not the means of gradually recovering itself from any shock, however great, which it may

34 The effect of the postwar diminution of consumption was least in the case of 'those states which have suffered the most by the war ... In the countries where a great pressure has fallen upon moderate or scanty powers of production, it is hardly possible to suppose that their wealth should not have been stopped in its progress during the war, or perhaps rendered positively retrograde. Such countries must have found relief from that diminution of consumption [1836: from a state of things,] which now allows them to accumulate capital, without which no state can permanently increase in wealth' (1820, 500–1; 1836, 421–2). But Malthus gives no examples of countries whose capital stock was retarded by the war, and where diminished consumption after the war provided the means of successfully financing expansion of real capital. His allusion to them may have been hypothetical.

experience ...' (1820, 488). Again: 'Whenever the produce of a country estimated in the labour which it will command falls in value, [1836: while the same value of advances is continued,] it is evident that with it the power and will to purchase the same quantity of labour must be diminished, and the effective demand for an increase of produce must, *for a time*, be checked [1836: the power and will to set labourers to work will be diminished and the increase of produce must, *for a time*, be checked]' (1820, 417; 1836, 363–4; emphasis added). Similarly: 'A mere abundance of commodities falling very greatly in value compared with labour [1836: though it may be called an actual increase of wealth], would obviously at first diminish the power of employing the same number of workmen, and a *temporary* glut and general deficiency of demand could not fail to ensue in labour, in produce, and in capital, attended with the usual distress which a glut must [1836: must neccessarily] occasion' (1820, 460–1; 1836, 396; emphasis added). This formulation may imply that a fall in money wage would provide the required correction and – as he had expressed the matter a little earlier – permit the economy to 'recommence a progressive movement' (cited above, p. 604). But how much of this was wishful thinking? The fact is that the postwar years are also represented as an instance of stagnation, notwithstanding that 'labour is cheap' having 'adjusted itself to the new level of prices' (above, pp. 599, 608). In the policy context moreover (below, p. 620), it is made explicit that downward wage flexibility was an inadequate solution. All this raises questions: Did Malthus ever conclude that the depression had eased? If so, by what process – since money-wage adjustment would not suffice? And since even a 'temporary' depression might be too long, what role, if any, was allowed government?

A brief comment in the 1823 review of Tooke places the postwar period in context within a longer time span. It was 'much too short' to be given the same weight as the preceding two war decades of unprecedented growth: 'Whatever may have been the favourable or unfavourable changes which have taken place since the peace, the period though very long for a crisis of distress and unnaturally low profits, is much too short to be compared with the period of the war; and it may still most safely be said that in no twenty-two years of our history of which we have authentic accounts has there ever been so rapid an increase of production and consumption, both in respect of quantity and value, as in the twenty-two years ending with 1814' (1823a/1986, 7, 242). As Malthus read the evidence in 1823, the depression was still under way but constituted a deviation from trend. He in fact alluded to the *full thirty-year period 1793–1823* as indicative of his main demand-oriented perspective, again suggesting that the eight years since 1815 constituted a temporary aberration: 'We decidedly think indeed that, without allowing due weight to this principle [of the effect of quantity on price], the phenomena of the last hundred years, but more especially *the phenomena of the last thirty*, are absolutely inexplicable.

Certainly nothing but the union of a greatly increased activity of general demand, a greatly increased power of commanding labour, a great increase of encouragement to the use of machinery, and a great increase of profits, particularly in agriculture, all owing mainly to the peculiar state of the supply compared with the demand in a country of great resources and great ingenuity, could possibly have occasioned so rapid a recovery of the immense mass of capital consumed by the government during the war, and have given at the same time such a prodigious extension to almost every department of industry and improvement' (244; emphasis added).

There are indications, moreover, of a growing optimism in the 1820s regarding activity. In the second edition of the *Principles*, Malthus maintained that Ricardo had exaggerated the distinction between 'wealth' and 'value' – in Malthus's sense of labour commanded – since in practice they normally coincided: 'It may indeed safely be said that though wealth and value rarely go on together at an even pace; yet that when a just view is taken of the mass of value in any country, all the general causes of a permanent nature which are most effective in the production of wealth will be found also the most effective in the production of value; and in reference to the whole produce of a country, quantity seldom fails to increase value, *except in those temporary cases of a general glut*, in which it must be allowed that even the wealth of a country is far from being proportioned to the increased quantity of the commodities it has produced' (1836, 303–4; emphasis added).[35]

The *Quarterly Review* article, 'Political Economy' (1824), is rather more explicit. It confirms that, by that date, Malthus had recognized the onset of recovery, and thus answers one of our questions. It also becomes clear that money-wage adjustment was *not* perceived to have governed the recovery; it was rather a matter of expanded exports of British manufactures, reflecting in part, or at least coinciding with, trade liberalization: 'In the period which has elapsed since the return of peace, the difficulty of finding employment, particularly on the land, has been too notorious to require proof; and if, owing to the extraordinary stimulus given to the population by the previous demand for it, it still continues to increase with rapidity, yet there is reason to think that the present demand would not nearly have kept pace with the rate of increase, and that great distress would have been the consequence, if the happy opening of new and large channels of foreign commerce, combined with the improved views of our government in commercial legislation, had not prepared the way for a renewed demand for labour' (1824a/1986, 7, 287). The stimulatory role of

35 The assertion that some 'species of foreign trade tended permanently' to diminish aggregate value with the effect of 'checking permanently the progress of wealth and population' (cited above, chapter 11, p. 546) is absent from the 1836 version, also suggesting greater optimism in the light of later experience.

expanded British exports is amply confirmed in a letter to Thomas Chalmers of 1832, which alludes to high corn prices and high money wages as a result, somewhat as in the 1793–1813 period: 'It is owing to the abundance of [British] exports, derived from her skill machinery and capital, that money rents and the money prices of corn and labour are high, and that with a small quantity of English labour a large quantity of the products of foreign labour is purchased' (Thomas Chalmers Collection, CHA4.185.32).

IV THE POLICY PROBLEM DEFINED: A WEIGHING OF OPTIONS

In this and the following section we investigate Malthus's perception of the legitimate role of government in mitigation of depression. We must have in mind his rejection of social control over the savings rate in the account of secular stagnation characterizing underdeveloped economies, and this despite allowance that the constraints impeding progress did *not* respond 'to the more steady influence of self-interest' (1820, 390; 1836, 342; see chapter 11, p. 576).[36] This hands-off attitude applied also to advanced economies. Social control over the rate of accumulation was inappropriate, notwithstanding the problem of periodic excessive saving: 'Saving, as I have before said, is, in numerous instances, a most sacred private duty [e.g., 1820, 471; 1836, 403]. How far a just sense of this duty, together with the desire of bettering our condition so strongly implanted in the human breast, may sometimes, and in some states of society, occasion a greater tendency to parsimony than is consistent with the most effective encouragement to the growth of public wealth, it is difficult to say; but whether this tendency, if let alone, be ever too great or not, no one could think of interfering with it, even in its caprices. There is no reason, however, for giving an additional sanction to it, by calling it a public duty. The market for national capital will be supplied, like other markets, without the aid of patriotism. And in leaving the whole question of saving to the uninfluenced operation of individual interest and individual feelings, we shall best conform to that great principle of political economy laid down by Adam Smith, which teaches us a general maxim, liable to very few exceptions, that the wealth of nations is best secured by allowing every person, as long as he adheres to the rules of justice, to pursue his own interest in his own way' (1820, 517–18; 1836, 434). We should keep in mind that Malthus was highly critical of de Sismondi for 'the opinion which he holds respecting

36 Thus, in the second edition, with Irish underdevelopment in mind, he cautioned against 'any thing approaching to a forced supply of capital with a view to the general employment of the people ...,' and went no further than to admit the possible desirability of government providing 'certain definite assistance in particular establishments, or ... facilitating the communication between one part of the country and another' (1836, 350).

the necessity of a frequent interference on the part of government to protect individuals, and classes, from the consequences of competition' (1820, 420n; 1836, 366n).

This perspective may seem problematic. It is one thing to maintain a case for private decision making despite a *possibility* of excessive accumulation; it is another to make out such a case while recognizing a *characteristic tendency* on the part of capitalists to save 'in prosperous times' at too rapid a rate – a sort of built-in destabilization factor (see chapter 11: V). Despite the typical overreaction to high profits, the profit rate remained for Malthus the appropriate index of social demand for capital, since it ultimately predominates over other stimuli as motive to saving and could be relied on to correct deviations from a steady growth path: 'These tendencies, operating on individuals, direct them toward the just mean, which they would more frequently attain if they were not interrupted by bad laws or unwise exhortations ... [If], in reality, saving is a national benefit, or a national disadvantage, according to the circumstances of the period, surely it is a case of which individual interest needs not extraneous assistance' (1820, 516–17; 1836, 433). Again, the object here was to reject the representation of the saver as *necessarily* 'a friend of his country,' and those who spend as *ipso facto* 'failing in the duty of benefitting their country, and employing the labouring classes.' But 'beyond that, nothing was required'; for though the sustainable growth rate would indeed be higher were capitalists *not* to engage in bursts of unsustainable saving, intervention would worsen matters.[37]

And yet we shall see (section V) that Malthus *did* justify government intervention in dealing with the postwar depression, and considered stabilization policy, having in mind the inevitable presence of government in economic life, especially high wartime expenditure and its legacy in an unprecedented national debt. There is nothing patently contradictory in a willingness to countenance intervention in crisis conditions of severe and protracted unemployment, despite general rejection of social control over the savings rate.[38] Nevertheless, the focus, we shall now see, was on re-establishing the conditions conducive to a process of sustainable growth which itself would be undertaken by private initiative.

* * *

The postwar-policy problem, as Malthus saw it, was a complex one. Capa-

37 We have seen that Malthus also firmly rejected interference in the rate of application of 'machinery' (see chapter 11, p. 575).

38 In any event, we know that the postwar depression was not itself ascribed to an excessive rate of saving (investment), though it is true that one cannot be sure that the justification given for intervention would have been withdrawn in the event of a depression which *was* so brought on.

city, though excessive relative to current demand, was deficient relative to the long-term trend. For Malthus certainly accepted the social desirability of net accumulation, considering the 'destruction' of capital towards the end of the war and during the postwar contraction of activity: 'It is acknowledged that the capital of this country compared with the population has been diminished since the war, partly by the unrecovered destruction which it sustained during the last two years of the contest, but [1836: and] still more by the sudden want of consumption and demand [1836: the want of demand], which occurred on its termination; how is the lost capital ever to be recovered, if we are not active in accumulation [1836: except by accumulation]? I am very far indeed from saying that we must not accumulate [1836: sentence omitted]. It is perfectly true that there is no other possible way of recovering our lost capital than by accumulation' (1820, 503–4; 1836, 424).

In approaching the problem of re-establishing the conditions for renewed accumulation in conditions of excessive capital relative to demand, Malthus posited the satisfaction of certain prerequisites: '[If] a portion of our profits [*sic*. 1836: capital] be destroyed, and yet the profits of the remainder are low, and its employment attended with such frequent losses as joined to its tendency to emigrate [1836: and accompanied with frequent losses, and a tendency to emigrate], makes it stationary or even retrograde, surely the great general laws of demand and supply cannot more clearly show us that something else is wanted before we can accumulate with effect.'[39] What was wanted, in line with the basic model of sustainable growth, was a *prior* increase in the value of aggregate output: 'An increased national revenue, – an increase in the exchangeable value of the whole produce estimated in bullion, – and in the command of this bullion over domestic and foreign labour [1836: over labour]. When we have attained this, which can only be attained by increased and steady profits, we may then begin again to accumulate, and our accumulation will then be effectual' (1820, 505; 1836, 424–5). The requisite prior increase in value turned on 'the three causes, which, by favouring distribution, tend most to keep up and increase the exchangeable value of the whole produce ... the division of landed property, the extension of domestic and foreign trade, and the maintenance of unproductive labourers [1836: such a proportion of unproductive consumers as is best adapted to the powers of production]' (1820, 505–6; 1836, 425). And in conclusion: 'As soon as the capitalist can begin to save from steady and improving profits, instead

39 As usual we have the standard parallel with population: 'If population were ever so deficient in a state compared with its territory, yet, if the wages of labour still continued very scanty, and the people were emigrating, the great general laws of demand and supply would instruct us that some previous change in the state of things was necessary, before we ought to wish for an increased proportion of marriages, which in fact, under the actual circumstances, would not accomplish the object aimed at.'

of from diminished expenditure, that is, as soon as the national revenue, estimated in bullion, and in the command of this bullion over domestic and foreign labour [1836: over labour], begins yearly and steadily to increase, we may then begin safely and effectively to recover our lost capital by the usual process of saving a portion of our increased revenue to add to it' (1820, 512–13; 1836, 430).

Malthus did not minimize the difficulties of arriving at *specific* policy recommendations. The three strategic 'causes' favouring a solution to the problem of renewed growth – or, more accurately, in the first place favouring the generation of full employment – were 'much less within our immediate control than the common process of accumulation. If it were true that, in order to employ all that are out of work, and to create at the same time a sufficient market for what they produce, it is only necessary that a little more should be saved from the revenue and added to the capital of the country, I am fully persuaded that this species of charity would not want contributors, and that a change would soon be wrought in the condition of the labouring classes' (1820, 506; 1836, 425–6). But since 'an increase in the exchangeable value of the whole produce [is] the only cause which can restore a healthy and effective demand for labour it must be allowed that we may be at a loss with respect to the first steps which it would be advisable to take, in order to accomplish what we wish.'

Despite the practical difficulties impeding appropriate policy recommendations, Malthus insisted on spelling out the limited options available, if only to avoid *worsening* the situation by proceeding 'from ignorance.' As mentioned, it was desirable to achieve an increase in 'the exchangeable value of the whole produce' by extensions of trade; for 'this better distribution of the produce of the country, this better adaptation of it to the wants and tastes of the consumers, will at once give it a greater market value, and at once increase the national revenue, the rate of steady profits, and the wages of labour' (1820, 510; 1836, 429). But there were constraints on any program of trade liberalization. Customs revenue was required – 'While it is necessary to raise a large sum by taxation for the expenses of the government and the payment of the interest of the national debt, it would by no means be advisable to neglect so fair and fruitful a resource as the customs' (1820, 508; 1836, 427); and a slow repeal of trade restriction is in order.[40] None the less, the practical importance of this recommendation emerges strikingly in the 1824 article, where it is precisely to liberalized

40 With an eye on the silk trade, Malthus refers to Adam Smith's case (1776/1937, 435–6) favouring 'slow gradations' of repeal to avoid excessive disruption: 'The caution here given by Adam Smith certainly applies in a very marked manner to the silk trade: and, however desirable it may be (and it is so most unquestionably) to open trade with France, a sudden and incautious admission of a large quantity of French silks would tend to aggravate, instead of to relieve the present distresses of our working classes' (1820, 509; 1836, 428).

trade and expansion of export markets that the recovery is attributed (above, p. 614).

As for a more equal distribution of landed property, Malthus rejected abolition of the law of primogeniture as an immediate means 'to increase the exchangeable value of the national produce,' although there was 'no other way in which a different division of land could be effected, consistently with an adequate respect for the great fundamental law of property, on which all progress in civilization, improvement, and wealth, must ever depend' (1820, 507; 1836, 426). Its abolition, he warns, would do more harm than good on grounds established earlier, alluding to the obligation created by the law for younger sons 'to be the founders of their own fortune,' with beneficial consequences flowing from such reinforcement of the 'middle classes of society' – a class of 'demanders ... likely, perhaps to acquire tastes more favourable to the encouragement of wealth than the owners of small properties on the land' (1820, 436–7; 1836, 379).[41]

Given that sort of evaluation, it was also undesirable to attempt to pay off the national debt – possibly Malthus had Ricardo's celebrated proposal in mind here – since this would contribute to a weakening of the middle classes, with (so it is implied) adverse effects on the level of effective demand: 'But if the *distribution* of wealth to a certain extent be one of the main causes of its increase, while it is inadvisable directly to interfere with the present division of land in this country, it may justly become a question, whether the evils attendant on the national debt are not more than counterbalanced by the distribution of property and increase of the middle classes of society, which it must necessarily create; and whether by saving, in order to pay if off, we are not submitting to a painful sacrifice, which, if it attains its object, whatever other good it may effect, will leave us with a much less favourable distribution of wealth? By greatly reducing the national debt, it we are able to accomplish it, we may place ourselves perhaps in a more safe position, and this no doubt is an important [1836: a most important] consideration; but grievously will those be disappointed who think that, either by greatly reducing or at once destroying it, we can enrich ourselves, and employ all our labouring classes' (1820, 507; 1836, 426–7).[42]

41 There was also the 'higher consideration,' that the law assured the maintenance of an aristocracy and all that implied for the constitution: 'If then we set a value upon the British constitution; if we think that, whatever may be its theoretical imperfections, it has practically given a better government, and more liberty to a greater mass of people for a longer time than any which history records, it would be most unwise to venture upon such a change as would risk the whole structure, and throw us upon a wide sea of experiment, where the chances are so dreadfully against our attaining the object of our search' (1820, 437–8; 1836, 380).

42 By 'saving' to pay off the debt, Malthus presumably intends a sinking fund financed by taxation.

The third of the 'causes ... favouring distribution' related to unproductive consumption and brought into play the 'doctine of proportions.' There were no hard and fast rules: 'Yet to shew how much the wealth of nations depends upon the proportion of parts, [1836: Yet to shew how frequently the doctrine of proportions meets us at every turn, and how much the wealth of nations depends upon the relation of parts,] rather than in any positive rules respecting the advantages of productive or unproductive labour generally, [1836: the advantages of productive labour as compared with personal services,] it may be worth while to remind the reader that, though the employment of a certain number [1836: a number] of persons in menial service [1836: varying with the net revenue of the society,] is in every respect desirable, there could hardly be a taste more unfavourable to the progress of wealth than a strong preference for menial service [1836: and ill-accommodated followers] to material products (See ch. 1, 35)' (1820, 479; 1836, 409).

Malthus in fact leaves the allocation of activity between the productive and unproductive sector to private choice – this simply reflects his rejection of social control of savings – but he does tangentially raise the problem of the public sector and its finance: 'However, for the most part, [1836: We may, however safely] trust to the inclination of individuals in this respect; and it will be allowed generally, that there is little difficulty in reference to those classes which are supported voluntarily, though there may be much with regard to those which must be supported by taxation.' It was essentially the possibility of 'capital redundacy' – in contrast with the Ricardian view that full use of capacity is assured *assuming downward wage flexibility* – that created the policy dilemma: 'If there could be no sort of difficulty in finding employment for capital [1836: profitable employment for any amount of capital], provided the price of labour were sufficiently low [1836: provided labour were sufficiently abundant,] the way to national wealth, though it might not always be easy, would be quite straight, and our only object need be to save from revenue, and repress unproductive consumers. But, if it has appeared that the greatest powers of production are rendered comparatively useless without adequate [1836: without effectual] consumption, and that a proper distribution of the produce is as necessary to the continued increase of wealth as the means of producing it, it follows that, in cases of this kind, the question depends upon proportions' (1820, 481–2; 1836, 411).[43] This difficulty confirmed that it would be 'the height of rashness to determine, under all circumstances, that the

43 An explanatory note is added in 1836, which might have been inserted at countless places elsewhere in the text: 'By *effectual* consumption is meant, a consumption by those who are able and willing to pay such a price for produce, as will *effect* the continuation of its supply without a fall of profits not required by the state of the land.' This adds nothing not already known to the original formulation.

[1836: sudden] diminution of a national debt and the removal of taxation must necessarily tend to increase the national wealth, and provide employment for the labouring classes.' On a balance of considerations relating to British circumstances, a policy entailing in effect a transfer from the spending class of fundholders to landlords would be dangerous: 'Now the question is, whether [in] this country, in its actual state, with the great powers of production which it unquestionably possesses ... without such a body of unproductive consumers as those who live upon the interest of the national debt, the same stimulus would have been given to production, and the same powers would have been called forth.[44] Under the actual division of landed property which now takes place in this country, I feel no sort of doubt that the incomes which are received and spent by the national creditors are more favourable to the demand for the great mass of manufactured products, and tend much more to increase the happiness and intelligence of the whole society, than if they were returned to the landlords' (1820, 483–4).

That this passage is absent in the 1836 edition is inconsequential for the general conclusion, which, as we have seen, is stated earlier in that version too. Nevertheless, the 1820 text alone proceeds to a further extensive disquisition on the dangers of a sudden reduction in the national debt and in taxation, with its implied income transfer from fundholders to landlords and capitalists: 'It is the greatest mistake to suppose that the landlords and capitalists would either at once, or in a short time, be prepared for so great an additional consumption as such a change would require; and if they adopted the alternative suggested by Mr. Ricardo in a former instance, of saving, and lending their increased incomes, the evil would be aggravated tenfold. The new distribution of produce would diminish the demand for the results of productive labour; and if, in addition to this, more revenue were converted into capital, profits would fall to nothing, and a much greater quantity of capital would emigrate, or be destroyed at home, and a much greater number of persons would be starving for want of employment, than before the extinction of the debt' (1820, 486).[45] Under these conditions it 'would signify little to be able to export cheap goods. If the distribution of property at home were not such as to occasion an adequate power and will to purchase and consume the returns for these goods, the quantity of capital which could be employed in the foreign trade of consumption would be diminished instead of increased. Of this we may be convinced if we look to India, where low wages appear to be of little use in commerce, while there are no middle classes of society to

44 This is proceeded by a discussion of the hypothetical cases of increased capacity, unaccompanied and accompanied by appropriate 'distribution' (see chapter 11, p. 572).

45 Ricardo reacted in *Note 298*: 'I should think Mr. Malthus must be the only man in England who would expect such effects from such a cause' (1951–73, II, 435).

afford a market for any considerable quantity of foreign goods' (486–7). The landlords, 'not being inclined to an adequate consumption of the results of productive labour,' would admittedly increase their employment of menial servants; but it was doubtful that this 'should soon take place to a sufficient extent' (487). And if, in fact, they 'paid as much in wages to menial servants as they had before paid to the national creditors, could we for a moment compare the state of society which would ensue to that which had been destroyed?'

Malthus in all this was not positively championing the debt as an ideal. The problem was that of achieving a reduction without aggravating the depression: 'It is not of course meant to be said that a country with a large quantity of land, labour and capital has not the means of gradually recovering itself from any shock, however great, which it may experience; and after such an event, it might certainly place itself in a situation in which its property would be more secure than with a large national debt. All that I mean to say is, that it would pass through a period, probably of considerable duration, in which the diminution of effective demand from an unfavourable distribution of the produce would more than counterbalance the increased power of production occasioned by the relief from taxation' (488). Even after the adjustment, he adds, 'it may fairly be doubted whether finally it would attain a great degree of wealth, or call forth, as it ought, a great degree of skill in agriculture, manufactures, and commerce, without possessing, in some way or other, a large body of unproductive consumers, or supplying this deficiency by a much greater tendency to consume the results of productive labour than is generally observed to prevail in society.'

The 'evils of a great national debt' are spelled out in the first as well as the second edition. Though 'in many respects, it may be a useful instrument of distribution, it was 'a very cumbersome and very dangerous instrument' (1820, 484; 1836, 411). Apart from a sociopolitical consideration,[46] Malthus was concerned that the taxation required to finance the debt, 'if pushed to any considerable extent, can hardly fail of interfering with the powers of production.' This concern had been raised by Ricardo (1951–73, I, 247–8), and it is significant that Malthus too addressed supply-side considerations – the 'danger of impairing one element of wealth, while we are improving another.' There were also dangers flowing from

46 This involves 'the feeling which prevails so very generally among all those not immediately concerned in it, and consequently among the great mass of the population, that they would be immediately and greatly relieved by its extinction; and, whether this impression be well founded or not, it cannot exist without rendering such revenue [1836: the interest paid for it] in some degree insecure, and exposing a country to the risk of a great convulsion of property [1836: particularly as it prevents any economy of expenditure which is practicable, from affording such a relief from taxation, as will tell upon the feelings of the people].'

changes in purchasing power, a 'large' debt 'greatly aggravat[ing] the evils arising from changes in the value of money. When the currency falls in value, the annuitants, as owners of fixed incomes, are most unjustly deprived of their proper share of the national produce; when the currency rises in value, the pressure of the taxation necessary to pay the interest of the debt, may become suddenly so heavy as greatly to distress the productive classes; and this kind of sudden pressure must very much enhance the insecurity of property vested in public funds' (1820, 484–5; 1836, 412). None the less, as we have seen, it was inappropriate to take radical measures in current circumstances. The recommendation is the same in both editions, that 'it might [1836: would] be desirable slowly [1836: gradually] to diminish the debt, and [1836: and more especially] to discourage the growth of it in future, even though it were allowed that its past effects had been favourable to wealth, and that the advantageous distribution of produce which it had occasioned, had, under the actual circumstances, more than counterbalanced the obstructions which it might have given to commerce.'

In a note attached in 1820 regarding events the previous year, but retained in 1836, Malthus elaborated the requirement of stable prices in the face of a large national debt, and commended Ricardo's scheme to minimize the deflationary effect of a return to gold: 'In a country with a large public debt, there is no duty which ought to be held more sacred on the part of the administrators of the government than to prevent any variations of the currency beyond those which necessarily belong to the varying value of the precious metals. I am fully aware of the temporary advantages which may be derived from a fall in the value of money; and perhaps it may be true that a part of the distress during the last year, though I believe but a small part, was occasioned by the measure lately adopted, for the restoration of the currency to its just value. But some such measure was indispensably necessary; and Mr. Ricardo deserves the thanks of his country for having suggested one which has rendered the transition more easy than could reasonably have been expected.'

V GOVERNMENT EXPENDITURE AND FINANCE

In a criticism of predictions of national 'bankruptcy' in consequence of a higher national debt, Malthus seems to hint that loan-financed government expenditure was required in 1816: 'When Hume [1752/1955, 102] and Adam Smith [1776/1937, 882] prophesied that a little increase of national debt beyond the then amount of it, would probably occasion bankruptcy, the main cause of their error was the very natural one, of not being able to see the vast increase of productive power to which the nation would subsequently attain. An expenditure, which would have absolutely crushed the country in 1770, might be little more than what was necessary to call forth its prodigious powers of production in 1816' (1820, 502; 1836, 422–3).

But it is unlikely that Malthus was seriously proposing increased borrowing; after all, he had expressed a concern with the dangers attached to further increases in the national debt (above, section IV). My impression is that Malthus considered this 'Keynesian' solution to depression as effective, but could not bring himself to recommend it because of the longer-run consequences.

More to the point is a proposal for *tax-financed* public works as the most effective step immediately available to absorb the unemployed, to supplement increased private expenditures on 'unproductive' domestic projects and menial service. This was in opposition to recommendations actually to *reduce* unproductive consumption as a measure 'affording immediate relief to the labouring classes' (1820, 511; 1836, 429). Malthus here addresses what later came to be known as the 'Treasury View,' that increased government expenditure on public works would entail reduced private investment and therefore be of no avail. Reasoning in terms of his analysis of sustainable growth (see chapter 11: III), any transition from 'productive' to 'unproductive' expenditure would, he insists, have a stimulating effect: 'It is ... of importance to know that, in our endeavours to assist the working classes in a period like the present, it is desirable to employ them in unproductive labour, or at least in labour [1836: those kinds of labour] the results of which do not come for sale into the market, such as roads and public works. The objection to employing a large sum in this way, raised by taxes, would not be its tendency to diminish the capital employed in productive labour; because this, to a certain extent, is exactly what is wanted ... And altogether I should say, that the employment of the poor in roads and public works, and a tendency among landlords and persons of property to build, to improve and beautify their grounds, and to employ workmen and menial servants, are the means most within our power and most directly calculated to remedy the evils arising from that disturbance in the balance of produce and consumption, which has been occasioned by the sudden conversion of soldiers, sailors, and various other classes which the war employed, into productive labourers' (1820, 511–12; 1836, 429–30).[47] This perspective is amply confirmed by a brief but striking comment to Ricardo in January 1817: 'I am sorry to find from what you say that you do not feel yourself able to approach nearer to those opinions, which I still continue after repeated consideration to think correct. Everything that has occurred lately appears to favour my idea of the all powerful efficacy of demand, and to shew that [it] is very far indeed from depend-

47 Wages would have to be set low enough to discourage inappropriate labour-supply reactions; thus increased public expenditure 'might, perhaps, have the effect of concealing too much the failure of the national demand for labour, and prevent the population from gradually accommodating itself to a reduced demand. This however might be, in a considerable degree, corrected by the wages given.' (See also chapter 18, pp. 901–2.)

ing merely on supply. I quite agree with you in thinking that the funds raised for the support of the poor (though perhaps necessary at the moment) essentially interfere with other employments. But this opinion appears to me to accord with my view of the subject, more than with yours. According to you and Say, if people were willing to subscribe and convert their *revenue* into *capital*, there ought to be no difficulty, if the sole want is the want of supply; but in my view of the subject there ought to be a difficulty, from the want of a proportionate demand' (in Ricardo, 1951–73, XI, x–xi). The intrusion here of the sustainable-growth analysis seems inappropriate, considering the fact of *hoarding* clearly recognized in Malthus's account of stagnation (above, section III, p. 609). It is true that Malthus was writing in response to typical 'Treasury View' reasoning, and may have been reacting on those terms; but the fact remains that he does not explicitly argue on the 'Keynesian' grounds of a *net* increase in public-sector expenditure.

As we noted, Malthus excluded debt-financed expenditure, fearing the consequences of an increased *future* tax burden. And though he countenanced an immediate increase of taxation to finance the proposed expenditure, he was concerned by the prospect, and thus his recommendation is restrained. The problem, as is so common in Malthus's formulations, involves a balance of advantages – in this case, positive expenditure effects and motivational effects – against disadvantages. Thus, while unproductive labour (and 'those who live upon the interest of a national debt') 'ensure that [1836: that effective] consumption which is necessary to give the proper stimulus to production,' and while 'the desire to pay a tax, and yet enjoy the same means of gratification, must often operate to excite the exertions of industry quite as effectually as the desire to pay a lawyer or physician,' yet 'injudicious taxation might stop the increase of wealth at almost any period of its progress, early or late; and ... the most judicious taxation might ultimately be so heavy as to clog all the channels of foreign and domestic trade, and almost prevent the possibility of accumulation' (1820, 479–80; 1836, 409–10).[48] Much depended on circumstances. And he was sure that there were instances when tax-financed expenditures *had* provided a net stimulus: 'As great powers of production are neither likely to be called into action, or, when once in action, kept in activity without

48 The productivity of land would be one factor governing the outcome: 'The effect of obliging a cultivator of a certain portion of rich land to maintain two men and two horses for the state, might in some cases only induce him to cultivate more, and create more wealth than he otherwise would have done, while it might leave him personally as rich as before, and the nation richer; but if the same obligation were to be imposed on the cultivator of an equal quantity of poor land, the property might be rendered at once not worth working, and the desertion of it would be the natural consequence. An indiscriminate and heavy tax on gross produce might immediately scatter desolation over a country, capable, under a better system, of producing considerable wealth.'

great [1836: a great effective] consumption, I feel very little doubt that instances have practically occurred of national wealth being greatly [1836: decidedly] stimulated by the consumption of those who have been supported by taxes' (1820, 481; 1836, 410).

Despite the dangers inherent in the use of the tax system for macroeconomic objectives – his caution is enhanced in the second edition – it was at the least advisable to avoid a sudden reversion to a *lower* level of taxation and expenditure: 'Yet taxation is a stimulus so liable in every way to abuse, and it is so absolutely necessary for the general interests of society to consider private property as sacred, that one should be extremely cautious [1836: no one would think] of trusting to any government the means of making a different distribution of wealth, with a view to the general good. But when, either from necessity or error, a different distribution has taken place, and the evil, as far as it regards private property, has actually been committed, it would surely be most unwise [1836: it may not be wise] to attempt, at the expense of a great temporary sacrifice, a return [1836: a sudden return] to the former distribution, without very fully considering whether, if it were effected, it would be really advantageous; that is, whether, in the actual circumstances of the country, with reference to its powers of production, more would not be lost by the want of consumption [1836: effectual demand] than gained by the diminution of taxation' (1820, 480–1; 1836, 410–11; emphasis added).[49]

Basing himself on wartime and postwar experience – the fact that in 1816 a prodigious capacity built up over the two preceding decades was faced with a great and sudden diminution of expenditure (1820, 502; 1836, 423) – Malthus questioned 'the policy of raising the supplies of a long and expensive war within the year' (i.e., by taxation) though proposed 'by very able writers,'[50] precisely because, upon the 'restoration' of taxes, there would result 'stagnation' attributable to a failure of consumer spending: 'If this process were to last for any time, and the habits of the people were accommodated to this scale of public and private expenditure, it is scarcely possible to doubt that, at the end of the war, when so large a mass of taxes would at once be restored to the payers of them, the just balance of produce and consumption would be completely destroyed, and a period would ensue, longer or shorter, according to circumstances, in which a very great stagnation would be felt in every branch of productive industry,

49 Ricardo reacted sharply in *Note 297*: 'This argument in favour of taxation is quite consistent with Mr. Malthus' opinion of the advantages resulting from unproductive consumption. Mr. Malthus is a most powerful ally of the Chancellor of the Exchequer [Vansittart]' (1951–3, II, 433). Ricardo may have intended the Budget of June 1819, in which Vansittart moved new taxes to meet the charge of new loans (1951–73, V, 20).

50 These writers are not specified. Ricardo favoured war finance by taxation (1951–73, IV, 189).

attended by its usual concomitant general distress' (1820, 503; 1836, 423).[51] Here Malthus repeats his standard themes relating to motivation and the avoidance of a mechanistic perspective: 'The evil occasioned by imposing a tax is very rarely compensated by the taking it off. We should constantly keep in mind that the tendency to expenditure in individuals has most formidable antagonists in the love of indolence, and in the desire of saving, in order to better their condition and provide for a family; and that all theories founded upon the assumption that mankind always produce and consume as much as they have the power to produce and consume are founded upon a want of knowledge of the human character and of the motives by which it is usually influenced' (1820, 503; 1836, 423–4).[52]

Malthus feared he would be misunderstood.[53] That the sudden diminution of taxes in circumstances such as the postwar depression would be undesirable should not, he insisted, be read as a *general* case favouring taxation as an engine of growth. On the contrary: 'The just inference from it is, that taxes should never be imposed, nor to a greater amount, than the necessity of the case justifies, and particularly that every effort should be made, consistently with national honour and security to prevent a scale of expenditure so great that it cannot proceed without ruin, and cannot be stopped without distress' (1820, 519; 1836, 435).[54] It was 'obviously the duty of all governments, if they have any regard for the happiness of their subjects, to avoid all wars and excessive expenditure as far as it is possible; but if war be unavoidable, so to regulate the necessary expenditure as to occasion the least pressure upon the people during the contest, and the least convulsion in the state of the demand at the termination of it' (1820, 520; 1836, 436). As for the immediate problem – the depression – Malthus repeats that he opposed sudden contraction of taxation, and consequently of consumption: 'We may have good reason to lament that such taxation

51 All this assumes a 'rich' country, as he explains in an introduction to this comment: 'If the country were poor, such a system of taxation might completely keep down its efforts. It might every year positively diminish its capital, and render it every year more ruinous to furnish the same supplies; till the country would be obliged to submit to its enemies from the absolute inability of continuing to oppose them with effect. On the other hand, if the country were rich, and had great powers of production, which were likely to be still further called forth by the stimulus of a great [1836: effective] consumption, it might be able to pay the heavy taxes imposed upon it, out of its revenue, and yet find the means of adequate accumulation.'

52 Here, as is so often the case, there is some ambiguity as to whether the excessive saving alluded to relates to (unsustainable) investment or leakages from the expenditure stream.

53 Cf. Ricardo's *Note 297*, referred to in note 49.

54 Even though it is allowed that government spending can have a positive effect on growth, such growth would be 'unnatural,' taking account also of the inevitability of 'excessive borrowing,' presumably to supplement tax revenue.

and consumption should ever have taken place, and that so great an impetus, which could only be temporary, should have been given to the wealth and population of the country; but it is a very different question, what is the best remedy now that the evil is [1836: has been] incurred? ... [If] the country had been unfortunately subjected to the excitement of a long continuance of excessive expenditure, it surely must be against all analogy and all general principles, to look for the immediate remedy of it in a great and sudden contraction of consumption' (1820, 520–1; 1836, 436).[55] And he maintained that labour was mistaken in believing that lower taxation – or cheaper corn – would be of much help, given the low demand for its services: 'There is every reason to believe that the working classes of society would be severely injured by attaining the object which they seem so ardently to wish for ... [To] the working classes, no taking off of taxes, nor any degree of cheapness of corn, can compensate a want of demand for labour. If the general demand for labour fail, particularly if the failure be sudden, the labouring classes will be wretched in the midst of cheapness; if the demand for labour be considerable, they will be comparatively rich in the midst of dearness [1836: When there is no demand for labour, however low the price of food may be, the labouring classes can only obtain it by charity]' (1820, 521; 1836, 436–7).

The *Principles* closes by focusing on the problem of correcting faulty policy: 'To state these facts is not to favour taxes, but to give one of the strongest reasons against them; namely, that they are not only a great evil on their first imposition, but that the attempt to get rid of them afterwards, is often attended with fresh suffering. They are like those injudicious regulations of the mercantile system noticed by Adam Smith, which, though acknowledged to be pernicious, cannot be removed without producing a greater evil for an interval of considerable length' (1820, 521; 1836, 437).

VI SUMMARY AND CONCLUSION

Malthus's analysis of sustainable growth was *essentially* different from Ricardian (including here J.B. Say's) secular analysis. How far the potential divorce of aggregate supply and demand insisted on by Malthus in the secular context can be legitimately described in genuine Keynesian terms depends on one's perception of the primary concern of the *General Theory*

55 The 'analogy' reads thus: 'If the population had made a start during a few years of plenty, we should surely make great efforts to prevent, by importation [of corn], the misery which would be occasioned by the sudden return of average crops. If the human body had been subjected to a very powerful stimulus, we should surely be cautious not to remove it too suddenly.' It is not clear whether easier corn imports in this passage refer to an *actual* recommendation. Malthus did believe that population increase had been stimulated during the war; and yet he recommended the Corn Laws.

(see Conclusion, section IX). The problem of Malthus's 'Keynesian' *bona fides* emerges again in the present context relating to depression.

The non-identity of savings and investment and the allowance for excess commodity supply documented in this chapter may be said to have a 'Keynesian' flavour – at least Keynes of the textbooks. The problem is – as J.S. Mill was later to insist quite rightly in his famous 1830 paper 'The Influence of Consumption on Production' – that the orthodox position did not, except in extreme and irresponsible formulations, preclude as a matter of principle excess commodity supply reflecting excess demand for money to hold. On this issue, then, there was less of a divide between Malthus and the Ricardians or the Ricardians and Keynes than Malthus (and Keynes) believed.[56]

Setting aside this complexity we turn to matters of detail that distinguish the Malthusian and Keynesian perspectives. First, there is the approach taken to money-wage flexibility. Malthus understood the Ricardians as treating money-wage flexibility as a sufficient condition for recovery – or rather (excluding factor immobility) for the maintenance of full employment – whereas he himself in the *Principles* perceived it as a necessary but insufficient condition for recovery; the end of the depression for Britain reflected, not the money-wage reductions that had occurred, but 'the happy opening of new and large channels of exportation.' Keynes for his part did not treat money-wage reductions as a necessary condition for recovery. His concern was that labour as a whole might be unable to reduce its *real* wage by making revised *money* bargains, and this because money-wage reductions may set in motion countervailing depressant forces (1936, 269). Only in evidence of 1827 did Malthus caution against money-wage reductions from an expenditure perspective, reinforcing thereby the Keynes–Malthus linkage.

Second, the case made out by Malthus for public works turns on the prospective stimulus afforded by a transfer from 'productive' to 'unproductive' expenditure – not, as it was for Keynes, by a net injection of purchasing power. The model of sustainable growth intruded even into the analysis depression. This same feature is conspicuous in Malthus's position on monetary policy, a matter treated in the next chapter.

56 Cf. the remark by Becker and Baumol on Mill's paper: 'In reading it one is led to wonder why so much of the subsequent literature ... had to be written at all' (1952, 765).

THIRTEEN

Money and banking

I INTRODUCTION

Our concern in this chapter is with money and banking, particularly from a policy perspective, having in mind both the inflationary full-employment war years and the postwar depression. Malthus's early contribution to the so-called Bullionist literature is found in two *Edinburgh Review* articles – 'Depreciation of the Paper Currency' (February 1811) and 'Review of the Controversy respecting the High Price of Bullion' or, as it is often referred to, 'Pamphlets on the Bullion Question' (August 1811). In these articles he maintained the moderate position characterizing the Bullion Committee Report written under the chairmanship of Francis Horner.[1] Section II of this chapter summarizes Malthus's strongly argued case for a circulation comprising coin and convertible notes backed by an adequate gold reserve. We proceed in section III to the formal meaning he attached to the term 'depreciation' and his estimate of the extent of such depreciation dating from the 1797 suspension. Here we consider both the standard Bullionist conception of depreciation and also the more familiar conception running in terms of general purchasing power. Malthus's harsh condemnation of Bank of England policy is the subject-matter of section IV. His proposals,

1 Horner was instrumental in convincing Malthus to prepare the February article: 'I am very anxious to have the subject in his hands, and to engage him in the discussion, both because he agrees with me upon the fundamental principles of the doctrine, and because we have some differences, or rather difficulties which we try to solve differently, in some parts of the Theory. All I beg of you, though I have no right to ask anything, is not to let Milne [James Mill] lay his hands upon us' (Horner to Jeffrey, 3 December 1810; in Ricardo, 1951–73, III, 10).

which include a return to gold (here he silently duplicated the Ricardo recommendation) and acceptance of Ricardo's scheme for economizing gold, are also taken up. At this point, we extend the discussion of Malthus's 'Bullionism' to the 1815–16 years, drawing on the Ricardo–Malthus correspondence. A further issue in the controversy relates to the 'value' of bullion itself, defenders of the Bank claiming that it was bullion that rose in purchasing power, not paper that fell. This Malthus allowed in 1811, though only to an 'insignificant' degree. By 1820 he had changed his mind, insisting, to the contrary, on a *fall* in the value of bullion. This reinforced criticism of the Bank of England, noted with surprise by Ricardo, is the subject-matter of section V. Section VI considers the potential effect (as it emerges in 1811) on output and employment exerted by an increasing money supply and conversely the depressing effects owing to contractions, and the policy implications. Extensions of the analysis in the later *Principles* with applications to the postwar depression are also taken up.

The striking features that emerge are a minimization of the potential for counter-cyclical monetary policy, and an overwhelming concern to avoid inflationary experiments. Despite Malthus's rejection of the Law of Markets, he was as 'conservative' as Ricardo in these respects.

II THE CASE FOR GOLD

The essential characteristic of the metals that recommended them as standard measure is the small annual variations in their supply relative to the accumulated stock – 'the immense mass of the precious metals existing in the commercial world, and the small proportion which the annual supplies bear to this mass' (1811b/1986, 7, 61) – creating a presumption in favour of a stable value: 'One of the causes which peculiarly fits the precious metals for being used as a measure of value, is that the variations to which they are subject are comparatively slow and inconsiderable' (63).[2]

2 Cf: '[The] metals are indeed liable to change in their power of commanding the necessaries and conveniences of life; but the principal changes to which they are subject, depend upon causes so entirely beyond control, that the evils which he [the fixed-income recipient] may suffer from these changes must be considered as necessarily belonging to the kind of property which he possesses' (50). As late as the second edition of the *Principles* – after adoption of the ideal labour-commanded measure – we find the same theme: 'Money is beyond all question the most convenient practical measure of value; and while its relation to labour is known and constant, it fully answers the purpose required. It is, however, subject to variation like all other products; but this variation is for the most part so slow, that for short periods, as we have stated, its value has been considered as nearly constant' (1836, 122).

Ricardo too maintained that, though gold and silver were variable in their purchasing power, they still provided the most stable measure of value available; the variability attached to them was thus irrelevant to the bullionist case (*The High Price of Bullion*, 1951–73, III, 65n). On Ricardo's position – and that of Thornton, King, and Horner to the same effect – see Hollander, 1979, 414–21; Viner, 1937, 200–3.

But even in the event of variations in the value of the metal with demand and/or supply changes, the case held good for a convertible system satisfying the original *legal* value as the best means to assure relatively stable purchasing power of the currency. There is another advantage. In a comment on the unlikely case of a major increase in the 'real value' (purchasing power) of gold,[3] Malthus wrote strongly that to follow Bank policy on a paper standard was 'to preclude ourselves from the advantage which we have hitherto enjoyed, of possessing a measure of value common to other nations ...' (62). What could 'justify us in separating ourselves at once from the rest of the commercial world in relation to our measure of value, and resorting to an imaginary standard, which no foreign nations could acknowledge, and which might be subject, not only to all the variations which can be supposed to take place in gold, but to others beyond comparison more sudden and more extensive? .... And yet, on account of a supposed, though very improbable change, in the value of these metals at present, we propose, at once, to preclude ourselves from the advantage which we have hitherto enjoyed, of possessing a measure of value common to other nations, and to deprive ourselves entirely of the use of gold, and almost entirely of the use of silver, in our circulating medium' (61–2).

A metallic system allowed rapid and efficient settlement of international debts emanating from changes in demand and supply patterns of a *nonmonetary* nature (1811a/1986, 7, 27–8). Also much admired was the rapidity of adjustment under an international gold system following changes in the demand or supply of *gold* itself – though, as mentioned, these were likely to be of relatively minor significance. Viner has written that during the Bullionist period 'the adherents of a fixed metallic standard did not expressly claim as an advantage of such a standard that it was an international rather than a purely national standard,' with one exception – Malthus, who supported an international common standard, even if it entailed falling prices, although he 'did not give any reasons' (1937, 214–15). In point of fact, Malthus did give his justification for an international common standard; it turned on the rapidity of correction following disturbances to equilibrium: 'The precious metals are the currency of the commercial world; and whatever variations may take place in their value, either from a greater or less supply of them from the mines, or a greater or less use of them in commerce, it is clear, that all the nations which have a mutual intercourse with each other, must partake of them. If any have currencies, consisting partly of coin and partly of paper, convertible, at the will of the holder, into coin, it is equally clear, that this paper must partake in all the changes that affect the coin' (1811a/1986, 7, 37). Assuming 'a more abundant supply from the mines. – An influx of the precious metals

3 Some in 1811 were actually supposing an increase of 17 per cent over the preceding two years (see below, pp. 642–3).

would evidently take place, which, for a short time, would sink the market price of bullion below the mint price; but more bullion would be immediately converted into coin, and each bank would find that it might issue more of its notes without risk. The consequence would be, that the whole of the currency, retaining probably the same proportions of paper and coin, would be enlarged; the market price of bullion would quickly be raised to the mint price; the exchanges which had been very variable, would return to their usual state; and no other effect would be experienced, than a general rise of prices throughout the commercial world.'[4] In the reverse case of a reduced supply or increased demand, and supposing one nation's currency to be *inconvertible* – and assuming also little coin in circulation – 'that currency would not have the means of assimilating itself to the currencies of the nations with which it was connected' (38). It would be 'to all intents and purposes depreciated, when compared with gold and silver and the currencies of other countries, just as it would be from an original excess of paper issues; although, on the whole, taking paper and guineas together, the amount of the currency might not be increased by a single pound.'[5] The parallel with an initial disturbance involving excess paper issues is important, of course, since that is precisely the empirical case at issue.

At this introductory stage it is worth settling provisionally the question: What, in 1811, constituted for Malthus a state of international equilibrium – the equilibrium of the precious metals? As we shall see, the process of equilibrium is said to involve: (1) variations in the 'power of purchasing with the precious metals' engendered by metal flows; and (2) adjustments in the rate of exchange, which together restore the 'equilibrium of the precious metals' (25). *But does this equilibrium imply uniform metallic purchas-*

4 The context of the statement is a refutation of the contention that the pound was *not* depreciated but that gold itself had increased in value because of an unusually high world demand.

5 The logic is traced out thus: 'Now, if, in the case last supported, the paper of one of these countries were not convertible into coin, and very little specie remained in circulation, it is quite clear, that the currency would not have the means of assimilating itself to the currencies of the nations with which it was connected. The market price of bullion would rise very greatly above its mint price; all the gold which could be readily collected would be exported. But as this would be inconsiderable, and as the great mass of paper would remain undiminished, or perhaps be slightly increased, to supply the vacancies occasioned by the gold exported, the great excess of the market price of bullion above the mint price, and the very unfavourable exchanges, would become permanent ...' Malthus adds in conclusion: 'It is material to observe, that, under all possible variations in the value of the precious metals, whether they are increased in quantity tenfold, or diminished to one tenth, the defect or excess of the market price of the precious metals, compared with the mint price, always ceases as soon as the level is effected; and *nothing* but a depreciated currency *can* render gold in bullion permanently of greater value than gold in coin.' Presumably this latter remark turns on legal restrictions on melting of coin and other devices.

ing power between trading nations? Apparently so, since immediately preceding the above, Malthus had written of the reason why money flows are equilibrating rather than disequilibrating in just such terms: 'if we deny the application of these [demand and supply] principles to the currencies of different countries, it will be quite impossible to explain the reason why the wants of some countries do not absolutely exhaust them of the precious metals, and the desireable products of others overload them with bullion; – and why, instead of such a state of things, the precious metals are, on the whole, maintained in such proportions in the different countries of the commercial world, as, in reference to the commodities which form the subjects of their mutual intercourse, to be nearly of the same value in each' (23). Or again, he writes of equilibrium as involving 'the precious metals circulat[ing] as nearly as possible on a level' (26).[6] On this matter Malthus, like Ricardo, was to change his mind radically (see chapter 14: VI).

Malthus took Huskisson (1810) to task for maintaining that the essence of money is to possess 'intrinsic value,' and for asserting that 'the quality of being a *common measure* does not necessarily imply such value any more than the possession of a foot-rule implies the power of acquiring whatever it enables us to measure' (32). For Malthus, it is specifically because the metals are acceptable as a medium of exchange that they constitute what Huskisson called a 'universal equivalent,' and in that function resided their so-called intrinsic value, not in any minor function as plate and the like: 'We have no great objection to the term, *universal equivalent*, which Mr. Huskisson considers as the quality which most preeminently distinguishes the precious metals from all other commodities; but we doubt whether it advantageously supplies the place of the term *medium of exchange*, or *instruments of commerce*; because it is precisely on account of their being adopted by the common consent of society as the general medium of exchange, that they are received as a universal equivalent. Were it not for this consent, it is quite clear, that they would only be accepted as an equivalent for other commodities, of equal exchangeable value, by those who wished to make use of them as plate' (33).[7] Or again: 'It seems to us to have been

6 That *remittances* might engender gold movements even though a nation's bullion 'might have been precisely of the same value as those of the country into which they were now flowing' (24) is not in conflict with this definition of equilibrium since the equality has been *disturbed* by the change in the balance of payment – the change in national 'desires and wants' calling for a new equilibrium involving a smaller domestic bullion stock and a larger foreign bullion stock to assure a renewed equality of bullion purchasing power.

7 Malthus, however, withdrew his tolerance for the term 'universal equivalent' as applied to the metals, when he concluded: 'The precious metals, therefore, in our opinion, perform a more important part in society, and are more frequently called into action, as a measure of exchangeable value, than as a universal equivalent' (36).

confirmed by the evidence before the Bullion Committee ... that the quantity of the precious metals sold for home consumption in manufactures, is quite inconsiderable, compared with the quantity imported and exported by the bullion merchants' (46).

In the course of the discussion of Huskisson, we find an important observation regarding paper as proxy for the metal: 'One of the most important functions of the precious metals, is that of acting as a measure of value in exchanges; and if paper, or any other article possessing little or no intrinsic value, appears sometimes to usurp this important function, it is solely and exclusively on account of its constant reference to the intrinsic value of the precious metals' (33). Here 'intrinsic value' evidently refers to use of the metals as an exchange medium, rather than to their industrial or ornamental use, Malthus expressing the inconceivability that unbacked paper could usurp that function, considering the erosion of its general acceptability with inevitable excessive supply: 'Nor do we conceive it *possible*, that a paper currency could be established, and perform the part of measuring the exchangeable value of commodities, without imminent risk of the most tremendous convulsions of property, if there were not some article of intrinsic value in exchange, with which it was constantly compared; and which, therefore, and not the paper, would be the real measure of value.'

Further allusion is made to a demand for the metals reflecting, not their 'substance' (their industrial or ornamental use value), but their suitability as a medium of exchange, which once broadly recognized and accepted – that acceptability turning on the characteristic supply constraints – rendered every individual 'a dealer' in the metal, that is, one who deals like a professional dealer in any particular commodity without concern for its 'intrinsic uses' but with an eye to its purchasing power over 'other commodities' (34). But all this meant that paper could serve as proxy only if such paper is *convertible* into the precious metals: 'the very simple process of making every bank which issues notes, perform its promise of paying them in specie, at the option of the holder, under the penalty of complete loss of credit in case of failure, is known to be sufficient to effect a level of value between bank-notes and the precious metals; and precisely because, with regard to the precious metals, in their character of circulating medium, every man is a dealer, and wants them to sell – not to use' (35).[8]

Huskisson had himself stated that paper 'is valuable only as it stipulates the payment of a given quantity of gold or silver ... that money [metal] alone is the universal equivalent; paper currency [is] the representative of that money' (33).[9] But this went too far. It described a system of 100 per

8 In this formulation there is no hint of a demand for money to hold.

9 Cf: 'In fact, we believe, that the circumstances of our being chiefly dealers in the medium of exchange, not consumers of it, is the very foundation of all those systems of

cent gold banking as existed in pre-revolutionary Holland: 'In Holland, it was really true, that every bank credit represented a certain weight of coins, or of bullion of a known fineness; that no part of these coins or bullion was exported in consequence of the substitution of bank money for bullion; and that, if all the creditors of the bank required at once what those credits represented, the whole of the bullion and coins that had been deposited would be forthcoming at a moment's notice' (34). But Britain and most other countries sought to substitute 'a very cheap instrument for a very dear one' – this of course had been Adam Smith's position (1776/1937, 276) – and achieved such economizing by a fractional gold-reserve system, based on the assurance that all claims to gold will not normally have to be simultaneously met: 'The holder is in general satisfied, if he feels quite sure of always obtaining for his note a quantity of commodities *equal in value* to the quantity of the precious metals specified in it. This is, in fact, what, ninety nine times out of a hundred, he really wants; and what alone, in reference to the whole body of notes in circulation, the country possesses the means of effecting.'

Here Malthus again insisted on convertibility, *given the inconceivability of otherwise regulating supply*: 'It will be observed, that this circumstance does not, in any degree, tend to impeach the necessity of the obligation upon all bankers to pay their notes in specie, whenever they are called upon; as in no other way would it be *possible* so to regulate the quantity of bank notes, as *uniformly* and *certainly* to maintain them of the same value as coin' (35). It emerges that Malthus feared the inflationary consequences of paper issues divorced from a gold base on two main grounds: first, the loss of purchasing power, particularly to government creditors; and, second, *the depression in real activity that must be the end result notwithstanding initial real gains* (below, section VI).

III MEANING AND EXTENT OF A 'DEPRECIATED' CURRENCY, 1797–1811

Malthus in his first *Edinburgh Review* paper commended Robert Mushet (1810) and Ricardo's *High Price of Bullion* of 1810 for 'proving the actual depreciation of our [paper] currency, and in tracing it to its true cause,' Lord King (1803/1804) for his 'very clear and masterly view of the subject,' and Thornton (1802) for an 'uncommon combination of extensive knowledge of detail with just principles,' representing the impact on practice of these earlier writers as a positive one contributing to 'checking the progress of the evil' (1811a/1986, *1*, 21–2). But since 1809 the 'progress of depreciation' had again accelerated so that the new contributions of

paper currency, the great advantage of which consists in the substitution of a cheap for a dear instrument of commerce' (35).

Mushet and Ricardo were timely. The essence of the matter was well elucidated by Ricardo: 'He is, in our opinion, particularly entitled to praise for the manner in which he has laid down two most important doctrines – long known, indeed, and acknowledged by those who have maturely considered these subjects, but not unfrequently overlooked by others' (22). The analysis turned on the principles of *scarcity value* or 'the general principles of supply and demand ... the foundation on which the whole superstructure of political economy is built,' from which followed the 'grand doctrine ... that every kind of circulating medium, as well as every other kind of commodity is necessarily depreciated by excess, and raised in value by deficiency, compared with the demand, without reference either to confidence or intrinsic use ...' (22–3). A second aspect of the Ricardian doctrine is 'that excess and deficiency of currency are only *relative* terms; that the circulation of a country can never be superabundant, except in relation to other countries,' so that a worldwide expansion of paper currency would neither imply excess nor 'occasion the efflux of the precious metals.' Both features of Ricardian doctrine were required 'to explain what is meant by *excessive* issue of paper.'[10]

Malthus also shared the standard position of the Bullionists that the tests of 'excess' were the premium of bullion over paper – 'of all the symptoms of ... depreciation, there is none so completely unequivocal as an excess of the market price above the mint price of [the] metal ...' (43) – and an exchange rate below par, 'excess' understood as a volume of currency exceeding that which would have circulated had the metallic standard been in place (a hypothetical equilibrium) rather than an amount relative to some base period: 'There is certainly some objection to a positive limitation of the number of notes; because the only proper criteria of excess, is depreciation below the value of the precious metals, and not any particular amount of notes' (54);[11] or again: 'We entirely agree with those who are of opinion, that no positive conclusions are to be drawn respecting an excess of currency, from the mere quantity of notes in circulation, independently of other circumstances; and think, that the market price of bullion, and the state of exchanges, are the only certain criterions of depreciation' (1811b/1986, 7, 70; cf. 60–1). And he had high praise for Huskisson's proof of the actual depreciation of the currency in precisely

10 And also, Malthus adds, 'to comprehend the grand distinction, between the wants of the circulation, in order to maintain it on a level with bullion or the currencies of surrounding countries, – and the wants of private merchants, and of the government for the purpose of business, and national expenditure.' This alludes to the contrast between disturbances to international equilibrium of a monetary nature and those of a *real* nature, such as the necessity to settle a debt created by sudden imports or government subsidies to allies.

11 Cf. also in the same general context: 'From the fact of depreciation, we are quite sure there is at present excess [of notes], though it is impossible to say to what precise amount ...'

that sense of 'depreciation below the value of that metal which has long formed the effective legal tender of the realm, or below the currencies of the different nations of the commercial world ...' (1811a/1986, 7, 36). The '*fact*' of a redundant currency and the accuracy of the term 'depreciation' to describe the consequence is said to be 'beyond the possibility of doubt' (37).[12]

It remains to note that Malthus contrasted depreciation arising 'merely from excess' with depreciation reflecting 'want of confidence' in paper (51; cf. 65, cited below, p. 643). He allowed that this latter could explain the 'small rise [which] might possibly have taken place in gold' between 1808 and 1811 by inducing a 'greater use of [gold] in all mercantile transactions' (1811b/1986, 7, 65). Keynes (1933, 200) admired Marshall's exposition of 'the way in which distrust of a currency raises prices by diminishing the willingness of the public to hold stocks of it – a phenomenon to which recent events have now called everyone's attention.' He might well have cited Malthus.

* * *

We turn next to Malthus's account of the empirical and legal background, for some orders of magnitude regarding the problem and his broad periodization of events during the years 1797–1811. Though in defining depreciation Malthus had pointed to misleading conclusions from reference to statistics of note supply, this was so only 'independently of other circumstances' (1811b/1986, 7, 70). In what follows, variations in currency supply *are* taken into account but with appropriate care considering those circumstances.

1797 to the end of 1799: Expansion of bank notes by some 20 per cent without, however, generating depreciation. This is explained by various special considerations: 'When it is well known that a very great previous compression of the currency had taken place; when the demand for guineas arose from the practice of hoarding, and not from an unfavourable exchange; and when there was every reason to believe from the unusual quantity of gold collected by the Bank during these two years, that the addition to the notes in circulation was scarcely equal to the guineas which had been withdrawn' (66).

End of 1799 to mid-1802: Further expansion of notes by some 20 per cent, 'an addition coinciding very remarkably with the degree of depreciation which then took place,' and accompanied by a deteriorated exchange rate.

12 Further manifestations of excess as stated by Huskisson are accepted by Malthus, bearing in mind that legal arrangements forced a heavy guinea to pass for less than a light one and obliged sellers who obtained guineas to part with them for less than their true value.

Mid-1802 to the end of 1808: A period scarcely experiencing any expansion of note issue (some 2.5 per cent) while the paper price of gold remained at £4 an ounce – an unchanged degree of depreciation as measured by the excess of the market price over the mint price of the metal. (The data are largely drawn from the Appendix to the Bullion Report.) In 1803 notes in circulation actually declined, and 'the exchanges began to recover themselves' (67). Taking into account also the guineas that were withdrawn from circulation in 1800 and 1801, 'the period from 1802 to the end of 1808, afford[ed] as striking an illustration of the principles of the Bullion Committee, as any period that can be named either before or after the Restriction Bill.'[13]

End of 1808 to 1811: This is the period that most concerned Malthus, 'the great difference between the value of gold and paper [having] taken place since the latter end of the year 1808' (66). During these years, 'while the excess of the market price above the mint price of gold, and the unfavourable foreign exchanges, have very far exceeded all former experience, no less an addition has been made to the quantity of bank notes in circulation than one full third of their former amount – an addition equally exceeding all former experience.'[14] Or again: 'The paper issues of the Bank of England have, during the short space of the last three years, received an addition of more than one third of their amount in 1808 [based on Mushet] while, for the whole course of six years before, that is, from 1802 to the latter end of 1808, the average amount had been nearly stationary' (63). Malthus surmised that the mere fact of depreciation in the earlier years (1802–8), especially given the favourable exchange, had not exercised public opinion. The renewed concern after 1808 reflected a worsening rate of depreciation, albeit at a relatively steady pace, accompanied by a fluctuating and (both in 1809 and at the time of writing) an unfavourable exchange, those fluctuations attributed to 'mercantile' causes: 'We agree, therefore, entirely in opinion with the Report of the Bullion Committee, that the great and sudden depression of the exchange in the summer and autumn of 1809, is to be traced principally to mercantile causes. A depreciation of the currency to a certain degree, had existed for many years before; because, of all the symptoms of such depreciation, there is none so completely unequivocal as an excess of the market price above the mint price of that metal which is the standard measure of the

13 See also 21–2 regarding this period as one involving 'great ... prosperity of our commerce, owing to our peculiarly fortunate situation compared with the rest of Europe.' This situation 'having improved our foreign exchanges, the depreciation of our currency, which still existed in a certain degree, was no longer thought of; and the subject, as might be expected, was allowed to drop.'

14 Subsequently the periodization focuses more explicitly on the precise deviation of the market from the mint price of gold, and varying pressure to insist on payment in gold (76).

country, accompanied by a favourable state of foreign exchanges, which, we believe, took place for six years, from 1802 to 1808. But this depreciation, a considerable part of which was probably concealed from view by the favourable exchange, was not sufficient to excite alarm, till it operated in conjunction with an unfavorable one, occasioned by mercantile difficulties and great purchases; and till the restoration of the exchange in the usual way was prevented, by the impossibility of getting specie at the Bank, and the fresh issues of notes for mercantile speculations' (1811a/1986, 7, 43).

Loss of gold coin from circulation (see below, p. 646) is taken into account in a careful estimate of the contribution of notes to the net expansion of currency during the years 1808–11: 'According to Mr H. Thornton, most of our gold left us in 1801, and but little flowed into the country during the six years from 1802 to 1808. The probability, therefore, seems to be, that the notes under £5, added to the circulation by the Bank of England since 1808, have more than covered the quantity of guineas withdrawn during the last three years; and that a portion even of these notes – perhaps not an inconsiderable portion – ought to be looked upon as a permanent addition to the currency. But, to be quite sure that we do not err on our own side, in the estimate which we are about to make of the proportion in which our whole currency has been increased during the last three years, we will take only the notes above £5' (1811b/1986, 7, 69–70). Bank of England accounts presented to the Commons indicated that notes of £5 and above increased by some 30 per cent. Assuming a proportional increase in country bank issues and playing it safe, Malthus concluded 'that the increase of the whole circulation cannot be overstated at one fourth' (70). This immediately indicated the culprit responsible for the depreciated pound, allowance made for a larger volume of output and taxation: 'Now, we would ask, whether an increase of one fourth, in the short space of three years, is not sufficient to account for a depreciation of the currency in the same time, amounting to 17 per cent, or a little more than one sixth,[15] after making every allowance for the increased quantity of circulating medium that can be supposed to have been required by increased produce and increased taxation; – particulary when we recollect, that, during the six previous years of nearly equal taxation and expenditure, and much greater prosperity and produce, scarcely any perceptible addition was made to the amount of the circulation.' (The year 1811 entailed a 'convulsed state of the mercantile world' [81]. Elsewhere [71–2] it is specifically the export industries that are portrayed as depressed.)

A further event contributed to the renewed concern – one which

15 The market price of bullion is taken to be £4.14s per ounce (1,128 pence); the mint price is £3.17s.10½d (934 pence). If we measure the difference relative to the market price, we have (1128 – 934)/1128 = 17 per cent. These data draw on evidence to the Bullion Committee given by Aaron Goldsmid (61n).

apparently stimulated Malthus to write his August 1811 paper – namely, the resolution introduced into the House of Commons on 13 May that (paraphrasing Vansittart) 'the promissory notes of the Bank of England had hitherto been, and were at that time, held, in public estimation, to be equivalent to the legal coin of the realm, and generally accepted as such in all pecuniary transactions to which such coin was legally applicable' (60),[16] backed up a few weeks later by legal enforcement pursuant to the De Yonge judgment and Lord King's reaction to depreciation.[17] Such enforcement – represented as a step towards making the (depreciated) paper pound legal tender – contradicted the spirit of the resolution: 'When the last poor pleas of those who had maintained that a one pound Bank note and a shilling were equivalent to a guinea, was thus obviously and practically contradicted; – when, according to their own public acknowledgments, nothing but a law of a similar nature to one which might declare a shilling equivalent to a guinea, could any longer maintain the equivalency, in public estimation, of Bank notes, and the legal coin of the realm; it might have been expected, that whatever difference of opinion might prevail as to the measures necessary to be adopted in consequence of a depreciated currency, there could be none respecting the fact of the depreciation itself.' Similarly: 'By the late act, we have done nearly all that is possible, short of making bank notes a legal tender, to force the people of this country to consider bank notes and guineas as of equal value. And if this act should not be sufficient for the purpose, that is, if the public should obstinately persevere in giving the preference to that commodity, which, in any fair and open market, will sell for 20 per cent more than the other, the ulterior measure of making bank notes a legal tender, is openly and distinctly threatened. The immediate and avowed causes which, in the opinion of ministers, rendered this act, and the accompanying threat necessary, were, the conduct of a noble Lord respecting his rents, and the decision of the judges in the case of de Yonge' (75). Parliament in 1797, Malthus added, had permitted the recovery of debts in coin, and had certainly not intended to make a depreciated paper pound legal tender:

16 See Smart, 1910–17, I, 296f.

17 Lord King insisted that his tenants pay their rents in gold coin (see Feavearyear, 1963, 205). Malthus praised his action as a matter of constitutional right: 'We must say, therefore, that, whether with a view to the mere question of property, or that which probably might influence the noble Lord still more, a desire to make a practical protest against a system subversive of some of the most sacred and fundamental laws of his country, he could not have chosen a more happy time for another appeal to the good sense of the country and we really think that those who feel with the noble Baron on this subject, and on such fundamental and constitutional questions, are ready to say with the Barons of old, *Nolumus leges Angliae mutari*, must consider his as entitled to great praise for the manly and able manner in which he has conducted this appeal, both in his private and legislative capacity, undeterred by the clamours of ignorance and folly' (76–7). De Yonge similarly insisted on payment in full-weight guineas, and was upheld by the courts (see James, 1979, 210).

'In order ... effectually to protect the property of the subject from the chance of loss from a paper currency not immediately convertible into specie ... processes for recovering a debt in the legal coin of the realm were left open,' a fact that indicated 'the precise remedies which the Legislature intended should be taken, if at any time the currency really became depreciated, and the debtor proposed to pay his creditor in a medium decidedly of less value than that in which he had contracted to pay him' (77–8). The government had by its actions flouted the original intentions of the legislature and the interpretation of the laws of England by the judges, and sanctioned 'the degradation of the legal coin of the realm to whatever value in exchange a banking company may choose to give to their notes' (78).

* * *

The 17 per cent depreciation in 1808–11 relates specifically to the excess of the market over the mint price of gold. What, though, of depreciation in the sense of *reduced purchasing power*? Malthus refers to this dimension in the course of his contention that the problem related almost entirely to an excess issue of paper and not, as some were maintaining (see below, p. 645), to a higher value of *gold* – reduced bullion prices – reflecting a deficient supply of the metal relative to demand.[18] Two aspects of his proof involve some conception of *a level of prices* – indeed the 17 per cent figure is here applied to depreciation in precisely this sense – as if the differential market–mint price of gold were a sort of proxy: 'In the first place, if a rise in the price of gold, *compared with the mass of commodities* to the amount of 17 per cent, had taken place throughout Europe during the last three years, it is scarcely possible that such an event, so contrary to the

18 In his *Quarterly Review* article of 1823 on Tooke's *High and Low Prices* (1823), Malthus recommended that the term 'depreciation' should be exclusively confined 'to a deviation in defect from the standard which the coin or paper currency professes to represent; and denominate exclusively a *fall* or *rise* in the *value* of money or bullion any change which affects the standard itself, whether in any particular country, or generally. We cannot therefore agree with Mr. Tooke in his application of the term depreciation of money to a diminished value of the precious metals in the commercial world; and we were not a little surprised to find, that among his definitions there was no reference whatever to the alterations in the value of money and bullion in particular countries, alterations which have been acknowledged by all economists, and must be allowed to be especially connected with Mr. Tooke's subject' (1823a/1986, 7, 226). The issue remained relevant, since Tooke ascribed most British price movements to harvest fluctuations – except for those reflecting a difference between paper and bullion – whereas Malthus saw evidence of a considerable decrease in the value of bullion in Britain between 1793 and 1813, and a considerable rise thereafter.

Tooke seems to have adopted Malthus's distinctions in the second edition (see Arnon, 1991, 64).

general course of prices for many years past, should not have awakened a very marked degree of notice and attention among foreigners. Secondly, if the gold had left the paper, and not the paper the gold, as bank notes would then be of the same value, *compared with commodities*, as they were before, the paper prices of our goods of home consumption would have remained stationary, while a fall would have taken place in their bullion prices to the amount of 17 per cent' (62–3; emphasis added).[19] But, in point of fact, over the years 1808–11 bullion prices rose gradually in Europe, the 'value' there of the precious metals continuing a steady and gradual decline, whereas in Britain 'commodities of home growth and consumption' (other than those affected by the Continental blockade) 'such as wheat, butcher's meat, butter, &c. &c. have experienced a very marked rise [in their bullion prices], which, if not fully equal to 17 per cent, falls very little short of it' (63).

The latter formulation suggests that, while Malthus talks of value relative to 'the mass of commodities,' he does not have a strict statistical level of prices in mind – nor could he have, lacking indexation – but rather a sort of casual measure of purchasing power based on command over various *individual* commodities.[20] This notion of purchasing power is also suggested in an amplification of the allowance that 'a small rise might possibly have taken place in the price of gold 1808–11' with an increased demand for gold as currency 'occasioned by a general failure of confidence' in paper (65). This allowance, he proceeds, 'would contribute to account for those instances where some of our home commodities have not risen in

19 In addition, 'if the change had been confined to the gold, and the paper had retained its value [purchasing power], it is not probable that there should have been any very marked and unusual increase in the amount of bank notes during the three years in question' as in fact there had been.

20 On this issue, see also chapter 7, p. 275. According to Viner it would be anachronistic to attribute either to David Hume or to the later classics a notion of an equalization of the 'level of money' – Hume's term – between trading nations in the sense of 'purchasing power of money as against commodities in general, with some statistical average of prices as its reciprocal' (1937, 312). Viner clarifies what the classics had in mind in the international-adjustment context: '(1) When they speak of the value of money or of the level of prices without explicit qualification, they mean the array of prices, of both commodities and services, in all its particularity and without conscious implication of any kind of statistical average; (2) when they postulate a tendency for the uniformity of the value of money, or of prices, in different countries, they have reference only to particular identical commodities taken one at a time, and only to transportable commodities, and they claim such a tendency for uniformity only subject to allowance for transportation costs both for the commodities and for the specie; (3) where the monetary units are not the same, or where different standards are in use, they postulate uniformity in the prices of identical commodities only after conversion into a common currency unit at the prevailing rate of exchange; and they postulate uniform ratios between the prices of different transportable commodities in the currencies of the respective countries' (314).

price quite in the proportion of gold; and it should be recollected besides, that the effects of a depreciated currency are always rather slow in showing themselves, and are generally at first partial' (65–6). Here the notion of command over individual goods emerges.[21]

IV BANKING POLICY: BANK OF ENGLAND DEFENCE REFUTED

Before turning to Malthus's substantive refutation of the defence by Bank spokesmen, we note the standard Bullionist presumption that the major policy issue involved Bank of England notes, country issues varying in approximate proportion considering the self-interest of country bankers and their use of Bank notes as reserve: 'We cannot, indeed, without the most gross violation of all the principles of supply and demand, suppose it possible, that while bank notes and country notes are constantly interchangeable, any marked alteration in the proportion between currency and commodities could take place in the districts chiefly occupied by Bank of England notes, and not be accompanied by a similar alteration in the proportion between currency and commodities in the districts chiefly occupied by country notes. But this necessary equality in the proportion between currency and commodities throughout the country, before and after an increased issue of Bank of England notes, could not of course take place, unless such issue was followed by a proportionate increase of country bank paper' (1811b/1986, 7, 68–9). This case assumes unchanged areas of circulation which may occasionally be inappropriate. But 'as the instances in which the Bank of England notes enlarge their sphere of circulation, are confined almost exclusively to the failure of country banks, and are of course completely obvious, the principle may be considered as established on all ordinary occasions' (69).[22]

21 Another indication of the informal nature of the price level is indicated by the observation that though '[a] pound of gold might be said to measure the nominal value, or value in gold, of all the commodities in the country, by stating how many pounds they would exchange for at their market prices ... it does not follow, that the possessor of a pound of gold ... should be able to acquire *all* the articles of value with which it might be successively compared' (1811a/1986, 7, 33).

In his *Quarterly Review* article on Tooke, Malthus reveals his unfamiliarity or rejection of the notion of a level of prices as some form of statistical average; and he represents the idea of command over individual goods as 'clumsy' though apparently workable: 'If, rejecting any single criterion [of the value of bullion], or the combination of one or two, we proceed to compare an ounce of gold with all the comodities of the country in succession, though the measure would be a most clumsy one, and by no means well calculated to determine the degree of variation; yet we cannot doubt that the result would indicate a great fall in the value of bullion' (1823a/1986, 7, 248). However, in later texts a more formal notion of a price level may be intended, the second edition of the *Principles* referring to 'the general scale of English prices' (1836, 105) or 'a higher scale of money prices' (131); but we cannot be certain.

22 Malthus adds here that, 'of late years, indeed, the increased number of country banks, and their nearer approach to the metropolis, seem to imply, that the increase of

We turn now to more substantive issues. The anti-Bullionists denied that the paper pound was in fact depreciated: 'Strange to say, this fact has been still gravely denied both in and out of Parliament' (60). One aspect of the defence of the Bank of England turned on the contention – denied by Huskisson – that the high price of gold was 'not occasioned by the depreciation of [paper] currency, but by the unusual demand for gold abroad' (1811a/1986, 7, 37). Malthus formulated his own rejection. Unlike Huskisson, he allowed some increase in the 'value' of the precious metals on the Continent, that is, a general *fall* in bullion prices, discerning evidence for this in data before the Bullion Committee (38–9).[23] But he believed it to be 'inconsiderable,'[24] and – more important – irrelevant to appropriate banking policy, *which should be directed at the maintenance of the value of notes* vis-à-vis *the metal, whatever the 'value' (purchasing power) of the latter may be.* This course of action would be dictated by 'self-interest' in a convertible system, and should be directed by a sense of 'duty' in current conditions, given the 'discretion' allowed the Bank directors: 'But it appears to us to be extremely important to know, that the Bank directors cannot, with any degree of propriety, urge the argument of a great demand for gold on the continent, to justify the comparative depreciation of their notes. Whatever may be the variations in the value of the precious metals, their business is to regulate the issue of their notes, so as always to maintain them of the same value. To this course they would be forced, by considerations of personal interest, if the restriction bill had not passed; and, after its enactment, to this course they ought to be impelled, by a sense of their duty to the public, and a proper estimate of the high responsibility that must attach to a set of men, to whose discretion, during the continuance of this

---

country bank paper has been even greater, in proportion, than that of the paper of the Bank of England; and we cannot be wrong in assuming it to be at least as great.'

Thornton had earlier explained how country notes are kept in line by the required reserve of Bank of England notes; and he had also allowed that the proportion of country to Bank of England notes might vary with changes in the areas of circulation of the two sorts of notes and in the relative volumes of payments in the respective areas. On Thornton and later Bullionists (including Horner, King, Ricardo, and the Bullion Committee) who took this position, see Viner, 1937, 155–6.

23 This is accounted for by wartime disturbances to 'mercantile credit' and trade which 'occasioned the necessity of employing a greater quantity of the precious metals, in proportion to the number of exchanges to be transacted' – a reversion, as it were, to a 'less advanced period of civilization.' In his second paper Malthus summarizes thus: 'We allowed, in a former article on this subject, that a small rise might possibly have taken place in gold, during the last three years, from the greater use of it in all mercantile transactions; which might be occasioned by a general failure of confidence' (65).

24 This because of small annual supply variations relative to the total existing stock. Under these supply conditions, a 17 per cent variation in 'the real price of bullion,' that is, the purchasing power of the metals, 'seems certainly incredible.'

act, the entire regulation of the national currency is entrusted' (39). The same perspective is reiterated forcefully in the second paper of 1811, where, after insisting on the desirability of an international trading system based on gold, Malthus concludes with a statement of the appropriate policy regardless of whether any changes had occurred to the 'value' of the metals themselves: 'To us, therefore, it appears perfectly clear, that if such a change as we have just supposed had really taken place in the value of gold in Europe, it would be the obvious dictate of common sense and good policy to conform our notes to it, and to insist rigidly that the Bank should so regulate its issues, as to produce the same equality between bank notes and guineas, as it would be compelled to do, if the Restriction Bill had not passed' (1811b/1986, 7, 62).

But, having said this, Malthus proceeded to make out an empirical case that, in actuality, excessive paper issues constituted 'the main, and indeed almost sole, cause [of] the separation between guineas and bank notes.'[25] The empirical evidence – 'stationary bullion prices in other countries, a marked rise of paper prices at home, and an increased issue of notes equal to one third of their former amount' – coupled with the circumstance that variations in metal supply are 'comparatively slow and inconsiderable,' was proof positive that 'the paper had quitted the gold,' not the reverse (63–4).[26]

As for Bosanquet's defence of the Bank in his *Practical Observations* (1810), Malthus points to revealing concessions in the second edition. Bosanquet's original case had been that the high market price of gold and unfavourable exchange rate were temporary phenomena rather than evidence 'of a permanent depreciation of our currency below the legal tender of the realm, and the currencies of surrounding countries' (1811a/1986, 7, 40). The new concessions acknowledged 'that the gold contained in a guinea is now of more value than 21/40th parts of a two pound note, and, without any allusion to it as a temporary occurrence, propos[ed] an entirely new standard of value, from a comparison with which it appears that our currency is not depreciated!' In effect, Bosanquet

25 None the less, as we shall see, Malthus also believed that, during the 1809–11 period, the exchange deterioration was to be explained largely by *remittances*. His current concern is *solely* with those who contended that the premium of paper over gold was a result of a higher 'value' of gold, not a lower 'value' of paper.

26 Yet the notion of almost stationary bullion prices in Europe is not what emerges in a comment of 20 October 1811 to Ricardo on a manuscript by James Mill: 'A great deal of labour and time is used to prove that the value of gold is not higher in this country than on the continent; but the only supposition that can at all account for the present phenomena, independently of excessive issues, is an increased value of gold on the continent and not a greater value here, than abroad. The arguments of the author therefore on this point appear to me to be misdirected' (1951–73, VI, 62). On this view, since domestic bullion values were unchanged, the entire weight turns on the rise of paper prices.

was proposing *the Bank of England pound note as standard*: 'What this standard is, we are quite sure that our readers would never guess; and we cannot but consider it as one of the most curious instances of self-deception that we have ever met with, and a most unlucky specimen of the reasoning of practical men, that *the interest of £33.6s.8d. in the 3 per cent stocks*, should be gravely proposed as the standard measure of the value of our currency; that is, that *a one pound note of the Bank of England*, which is the interest of this sum, and the kind of currency in which it is paid, should be the criterion by which we are to judge of the depreciation of – *a one pound note of the Bank of England*!' Here Malthus gives an emotional warning of the consequences of a paper currency divorced from 'any commodity of *intrinsic worth*' and thus from all control over supply: 'Let the reader for a moment consider, in what a dreadfully critical state must the property and contracts of a country be placed, which has a paper currency not referable to *any commodity of intrinsic worth* for the correction of its quantity, and the maintenance of its value, and which might consequently sink, in the course of a few months, 50 or 100 per cent below the value of the precious metals, and deprive individuals of half their fortunes, and yet appear to be unchangeable. The moment we quit the precious metals as the constant standard of reference, there is no fancy so wild, respecting a paper circulation, which may not be indulged, and no limit to the degree of depreciation which may not in time be expected' (41).[27] An excessive paper issue, of course, was the inevitable result of relying on the 'integrity' of private self-interested individuals: 'In fact, what security have we, except in this integrity, that the Bank Directors may not agree to create and divide £24 millions in notes among them for their private fortunes? Or, to put a less strong, and not so improbable a case, what security have we that the Bank, when released from all obligation to keep their notes of the value of the precious metals, may not alter their mode of conducting business, and lend money for longer terms than they do at present, and on any fair personal security?'

Bosanquet's reference to the celebrated Real Bills doctrine of safe discounting – 'a recurrence of demand for notes by the *first class* of discounters; which he explains to be "those which the Directors distinguish as solid paper for real transactions"' – Malthus found disturbing. It suggested that 'there are other classes well known, and not always rejected at the Bank, which are probably distinguished as accommodation paper' (41–2). And, in fact, 'there are thousands and thousands of traders in the kingdom, who would eagerly seize the opportunity of borrowing capital on their personal security at 5 per cent; and the immense profits of the Bank,

27 It will be recalled (see above, pp. 634–5) that by 'intrinsic worth' Malthus does not intend manufacturing or other forms of use-value, but rather a universal acceptance of the metal as means of exchange.

in lending such sums, would beyond all comparison counterbalance the risk' (42). Yet, despite such irresponsible issues, 'a one pound note would be still worth the interest of £33. 6s. 8d. 3 per cents.' – that is, a pound note would be worth a pound note. Malthus had strong words for the Bank's appeal to the Real Bills rule, seeing it as no stronger than the original case for paper credit by John Law based on the security of land: 'In answer to the supposition, that they might be depreciated by excess of quantity, Mr Law observes [1750, 167], that "the commissioners giving out what sums are demanded, and taking back what sums are offered to be returned, this paper money will keep its value; and there will always be as much money as there is occasion or employment for, and no more." This we conceive, is precisely the language of the present Bank Directors; and they in no respect fall short of Mr Law in the grand mistake, of confounding the quantity of good security in the country, and the quantity of money which people may want to borrow at the legal interest, particularly during a time of mercantile speculation or distress, with the quantity necessary for the circulation, so as to keep it on a level with the precious metals, and the currencies of surrounding countries' (52–3).[28] It was fortunate that Bank policy was not in fact governed by *formal* adherence to 'The school of Mr Law,' but rather by non-theoretical principles reflecting 'a kind of practical routine,' and a residue of responsibility reflecting 'those wholesome times, when the Bank paid in specie, and was obliged to attend to the safety of its establishment' (53). This alone could explain why the excess issues had not been even greater. His warning related to the immediate future with the weakening of the beneficial influence of past responsible policy: 'If the Legislature, by declining to enforce the recommendation of the Committee, should relieve the Bank from all immediate prospect of a return to cash payments, the disorder in our currency which we have at present experienced, will be absolutely nothing, compared with that which we must then look forward to.'

The question of appropriate discounting is a major feature of the second paper of 1811. Here we must recall that the definition of 'depreciation' precluded appeal to the absolute quantity of notes in circulation to settle the question of 'excess.' But this provided an escape route for Bank supporters which had to be closed off: 'As the opposers of the Bullion Report have been very fond of insisting upon the small addition that has been made to the currency of late years, compared to the increased scale of our expenditure, we have thought it right to set this argument in what appears to us to be its true light' (1811b/1986, 7, 70–1). Malthus emphasizes here the experience of 1809–11 as compared with the stable years 1802–8: 'And when, instead of talking of the mere numerical increase of

28 In the parliamentary debates on the Bullion Report, Huskisson also compared the Bank position to that of John Law (see Fetter, 1965a, 43).

bank notes, compared with our prodigious expenditure and debt, we advert to the *proportion* in which the whole currency has been enlarged; and instead of spreading this numerical increase over fourteen years, we confine it to the periods in which the increase really took place; and, above all, when we advert to a period of six years of great taxation and expenditure, and great increase of the national debt, unaccompanied by any increase of Bank of England notes above £5, or any increase in the market price of gold; – the facts will appear to prove directly the reverse of what they are intended to prove and our only astonishment will be, that the rapid increase of currency which has taken place during the last three years, has not been accompanied by a still greater depreciation' (71).

One other theme emerges frequently – the almost complete absence of gold coin from circulation.[29] This is explained as the automatic consequence of the depreciated currency: 'That we must be so deprived, if we do not conform our bank notes to the value of gold bullion, cannot admit of a doubt. From whatever cause the separation between bank notes and gold has taken place, it is equally certain, that while a guinea will only pass for 21s. as currency, and will sell for 26s. or 27s. when melted, no guineas will appear in the circulation; and consequently, for whatever purposes we may want the precious metals, whether to discharge what is called an unfavourable balance of trade, or to pay our armies on the continent, while our paper currency is not of the value which it purports to be, our supply of them must always be most scanty and precarious' (62). To assure *any* metallic circulation required an open discount on paper, the formal establishment of two sets of prices, metallic and paper.[30] Anything else

29 Cf: 'Gold may be said to be already quite banished from our circulation; and nothing but the very extraordinary degraded state of our silver coin, and the high premium which is daily given even for this, in spite of the law, by bankers and merchange who want small change, could retain an ounce of it in circulation' (51–2). On the loss of gold coin see also 69. Malthus commended Mushet whose 'suggestions respecting a recoinage of silver, and the mode of preserving it from degradation, well deserve the attention of the government' (22).

30 Malthus explained why no such step had actually been taken: 'First, and chiefly, the law of the land, which, applied to the present unlooked for state of things, has the most singular and unjust operation; which forces a heavy guinea to pass for less than a light one, and would oblige any person who could obtain coin for his commodities, to forego all advantage from it, and part with it again for fifteen per cent. less than it was fairly worth.' Second, the self-interest of 'people in trade' making them unwilling 'if the depreciation of the currency arises merely from excess, and not from want of confidence, to alter, in any degree, a state of things, and a progression of prices, from which, as being sellers as well as buyers, they are known to receive considerable advantages.' Third, the awareness 'that the first person who was to ask two prices for his goods, would, as the law now stands, be considered as intending to make an illegal use of the coin which he might obtain, and would, in consequence, incur such odium, and deter so many customers, that the attempt would probably end in his ruin' (51).

That prices were expressed only in *pounds*, not in bullion, was a fact 'much insisted

(certainly legislation enforcing a one-to-one relation between notes and coin) would have deflationary effects, since all transactions below a pound were by coin, unless the Bank were to resort to issuing shilling notes: 'if the Bank Directors continue to conduct their establishment upon the principles which they have openly avowed before the Committee, we do not entertain the slightest doubt, that, in a short time, two prices *must* be established, or the country will be entirely deprived of the power of making its smaller payments ... We touch upon the period, when it will be no longer possible to avoid an open discount upon paper, without such a degree of embarrassment to commerce, as will much more than counterbalancing the late advantages which it has derived from a redundant currency. If our silver coin had approximated, in any tolerable degree, to its mint value, there is no doubt that it would long since have disappeared;[31] and all ranks of society would have joined in petitioning the Legislature, if it still thought the Bank unable to pay in specie, either to repeal the law which prohibits an open discount upon paper, or to enjoin the issuing of shilling notes' (1811a/1986, 7, 51–2). Here Malthus's harsh estimate of the Bank's policy emerges starkly – its mismanagement, flowing from self-interest, had created these 'disgraceful alternatives'; and the only honourable solution was a return to cash payments: 'And the question now is, whether the Bank Directors, by continuing to act upon their present principles, will submit to one of these two disgraceful alternatives, under the merited reproach of having created the necessity for them by their own mismanagement; or consent to tread back their steps, and return to payments in specie; which may unquestionably be done, without any other evil, either to themselves or their mercantile connexions, than that of foregoing an unfair advantage; which, as it ought never to have been possessed, ought, in honour and justice, as soon as possible to be relinquished' (52).

Repeatedly Malthus blamed Bank of England policies for generating a loss of the precious metals: 'if, even according to the concessions of those who oppose the Bullion Report, an excess of paper is in its nature calcu-

---

upon [by Bank apologists] as a decisive proof that there is no depreciation.' In reply, Malthus observed that were it the case that 'for all commodities in this country, two prices were established, one in bullion and one in paper, and if the paper price were fifteen or twenty per cent higher than the bullion price,' government employees and creditors could not be paid 'with the same nominal amount of a currency so obviously below the value of that which it contracted to pay them' (50; see also 60).

The point is made that to express prices in bullion would not effect the paper price of goods: 'The circumstances of there being no current bullion price of commodities, does not, in the slightest degree, tend to affect the prices in our actual currency. These prices would not be rendered higher by the establishment of another price which was lower ...' (50–1).

31 The allusion here is to the poor quality of the silver coinage.

lated to expel the precious metals from the circulation of the country where such excess exists, what pretence have we to complain of our inability to obtain gold? What pretence have we to attribute this inability to the untoward circumstances attending the state of the continent; when, under *any circumstances* the most favourable, the conduct which we have adopted could not fail to deprive us of all our guineas?' (1811b/1986, *1*, 71). Given the relatively closed European markets for British exports characteristic of the war years, yet heavy obligation to support allies, 'common sense and sound policy' called for the very opposite steps to those followed by the Bank, which assured, by its inappropriate discounting, a negligible gold reserve to meet remittances: 'In the first place, we conceive [good policy] would be, so to proportion our manufactures for foreign sale to the confined vent for them, as not to have immense quantities returned upon our hands, to involve our merchants in ruin; and, in the next place, to be very careful not to take any steps respecting our currency, which would tend to deprive us of the precious metals, and prevent the country from having a considerable store of them to resort to, and a steady supply of them coming in, whenever they were found to be the most convenient remittances for our foreign expenditure. Instead of this, however, what has actually been our conduct? By means of the profuse and unusual accommodations afforded by the Bank of England to our merchants, they have been encouraged, and enabled, to work an unusual quantity of manufactures, at high prices, for foreign sale, at the very time when the vent for them was unusually diminished; and, by means of the same profuse issues, all our gold has been driven from the circulation, and its return effectually prevented' (71–2). The consequence of the Bank encouragement of exports in the face of poor foreign markets in 1809–11 had been 'the most extensive failures in the mercantile world, and ... the most wide-spreading poverty and misery among the manufacturing classes, ever witnessed,' as well as grave difficulties in the way of supporting British armies abroad (72).

Defenders of the Bank were maintaining 'that the government will have a greater command of bullion for its foreign expenditure, if the domestic circulation be confined almost to paper.' Malthus allowed that the 'actual' gold reserve could never suffice 'to supply a continual foreign expenditure of any magnitude,' the function of a reserve being rather to meet 'any sudden demand occasioned by an unfavourable balance of payments.' The point he insisted on was that meeting a 'continued' need to make major transfers abroad required a different system entirely to that in operation: 'The means of this expenditure, if we suppose that bullion must form a part of it, can only be abundant, when, as fast as the precious metals are sent out in one quarter, a steady supply of them flows in from other quarters. But this, of course, can only happen, when bank notes and guineas are precisely of the same value; and when, instead of the scanty influx occasioned by the precarious and uncertain wants of Government, a large and steady demand for bullion, to maintain the accustomed circulation, produces its invariable concomitant, a large and steady supply' (72–3).

Here Malthus refers to yet a further and 'more fatal' error of those who championed the paper system – that it was essential for the support of government in wartime: 'That the profuse issues of the Bank of England, and the accommodations which the government receives from them in their general expenditure, form so essential a resource for carrying on the present expensive war, that our efforts would be immediately paralysed if this resource were to fail' (73). Government, he allowed, might obtain its resources by way of paper issues – he here set aside the morality of such devices – but only as a short-term means of indirect taxation; in the long term, such a policy (he is concerned largely with the 1809–11 period) only served to profit the Bank (see below, note 56). As for appeals to David Hume's case that paper issues had a *stimulatory* effect on activity, and warnings supposedly based on Hume's argument that a reduction in notes would have *deflationary* consequences, Malthus (as we shall see below, p. 672) lists a variety of qualifications put forward by Hume himself, which pointed to ultimate stagnation as a consequence of 'a profuse issue of bank paper,' a consequence that he feared was already under way (74–5).[32]

* * *

As for the solution, Malthus had little confidence in the Bank directors. For they might be inclined to keep in circulation so great a volume of paper as to render dangerous a return to gold – evidently the deflationary consequence – so that public support for the return would be weakened: 'We were, at first, inclined to approve of that recommendation of the Committee, to leave to the knowledge and discretion of the Bank Directors the mode of preparing themselves to resume their payments in cash at the time proposed. But it has been suggested, and the language and conduct of their friends have not sufficiently repelled the suspicion, that, under cover of this liberty, they might purposely keep the same, or a greater quantity of notes in circulation, with a view of compelling the legislature to continue the Restriction Act ...' (1811a/1986, 7, 53). Were this sort of behaviour an immanent danger, he would recommend the abolition of the Bank of England and its replacement by a system of competitive banking, as in the United States: 'We really think, that if any disposition of this kind should be discoverable in the Bank direction, it would be the bounden duty of the legislature to take immediate steps for *the establishment of one or*

32 A further defence of the Bank turned on the observation that an improvement of the exchage rate frequently was accompanied by an *increasing* note issue, leading the deputy-governor to insist that 'our foreign exchanges had no connection with the state of our currency.' For Malthus's reaction, see chapter 14, p. 685.

more other banks; and it cannot be doubted, that both the business of the government and of the public might be carried on, as in America, with equal convenience, and less chance of restriction acts, without the assistance, and very improper influence, of so overgrown an establishment as the Bank of England. It is, indeed, a monstrous deformity in the state, that an incorporated body of individuals should have the power of holding out a threat to the legislature, that if it does not persevere in sanctioning the nonfulfilment of their engagements, they would find the means of embarrassing and punishing the government and the public' (54). But this suspicion of the Bank's motive, Malthus opined – doubtless for effect – could not be 'seriously entertained,' although the directors had 'openly shown an unconquerable reluctance to acknowledge that there is any connection between the market price of bullion, and an excessive paper circulation.'

The solution was not, however, to dictate to the Bank 'a positive limitation of the number of notes' since excess was a hypothetical, not an actual quantum. Rather it was to require a slow contraction: 'But as, from the fact of depreciation, we are quite sure that there is at present excess, though it is impossible to say to what precise amount; perhaps, it might be the best mode of proceeding, in the present state of the knowledge and temper of the Bank Directors, to oblige them, every successive half year, to diminish the average quantity of their notes in circulation by half a million, and continue this diminution till the market price of bullion was restored to its mint price; and then the resumption of cash payments might take place with perfect safety and convenience, both to the Bank and the public; and the evil of any great and sudden diminution of the currency be completely avoided.' Malthus might have mentioned that this proposal had been made by Ricardo in *The High Price of Bullion* (1951–73, III, 94).

But things were looking grim. Far from the authorities being prone to reform, there was the new law of May 1811 effectively obliging the public to accept depreciated notes as *legal tender* at a rate equivalent to guineas (above, section III). This measure was perversely justified as a means of 'protecting the property of public creditor' (1811b/1986, 7, 78), though public creditors were precisely the class that suffered from inflation, all other groups being able to compensate themselves more or less; and there was imminent danger of risking an unprecedented dispoilation, all in the interest of 'twenty four individual merchants': 'Whether the currency becomes depreciated 40 or 50 per cent, or remains nearly stationary at 20 per cent; or whether, from the individual good conduct of the Directors, it recovers a part or the whole of its lost value; we do not hesitate to say, that in the whole course of English history no act can be pointed out which can be more properly designated by the term unconstitutional, or which more directly contradicts the general spirit of British legislation in the best times, than that which thus give up 20 millions worth of revenue belonging to British subjects, to be regulated in its value according to the will and pleasure of twenty four individual merchants, whose interests are in reality different from those of the owners of such revenue' (78–9).

The end result of the inflationary policy, if persisted in, especially if reinforced by this 'memorable act' of May 1811, was easy to forecast – 'failure of confidence' and depression (80; see below, p. 673). Even so, all was not lost. There remained some hope that the Bank directors might act as 'men of character and respectibility' and gradually withdraw notes from circulation. The gradual retraction – 'the grand point to be accomplished' – should also be accompanied by repeal of 'the late act for regulating public estimation,' thereby allowing 'the legal coin of the realm to circulate with paper at its real value in exchange' (80–1). To do so would be to assure the reappearance of guineas in circulation and a sound metallic basis for future contracts. And the open discount on paper would be a healthy preparation for its correction. Again Malthus emphasized the self-interested and antisocial perspective of the directors: 'We can readily understand why the Bank Directors, and perhaps the government, should object to this measure, as it would undoubtedly be a standing reproach to them, that any difference should remain, in public estimation, between guineas and bank notes; but that any of the other members of the state, who are not, or at least do not think themselves personally interested in the continuance of the present system, should contemplate such an event with fear, as a dangerous and alarming crisis, is what we cannot comprehend' (81).

The second paper closes with remarks on the gold reserve of the Bank required to allow a return to convertibility. Repeal of the forementioned act of May 1811 might alone suffice: 'With regard to the gold which ought gradually to be collected, to enable the Bank, after a moderate time, to resume its payments in specie, and render the cure complete, nothing would of course facilitate it so much, as the taking off the present bounty of 20 per cent on the melting or exportation of guineas; and we really think, that if the legal coin of the realm were allowed to pass for what it is worth, no great scarcity of it would long be felt, notwithstanding the present convulsed state of the mercantile world.' But if necessary, recourse could be made to Ricardo's 'valuable suggestion' – the so-called ingot scheme of economizing gold laid out in the Appendix to the fourth edition of *The High Price of Bullion*: 'This plan ... would preclude the necessity of providing, at first, such a quantity of gold as would be required to fill the smaller channels of circulation with guineas; and, while it was continued, would protect the Bank from the dangers to which it might be exposed, on the resumption of its payments in cash, – from the effects of small hoarding, or the pressing demand for guineas, or the failure of country banks' (82).[33] The reserve requirements would then be reduced

33 On 26 July 1811 Malthus had promised Ricardo that, 'if I should write again in the review, I will certainly mention your plan with the approbation which I think it deserves' (in Ricardo, 1951–73, VI, 41).

to 'a quantity of bullion as would be sufficient completely to secure it against an unfavourable balance of payments, occasioned either by its own imprudent issues, or the natural inequalities which must occasionally occur in the wants and supplies of different nations; which last cause can never be of serious magnitude and continuance, unless aggravated and prolonged by the former.' This conclusion reflects Malthus's contention that the so-called natural inequalities in international balances attributable to variations in 'wants and supplies' – an allusion to the problem of remittances – was not a serious one *unless accompanied by excess note issue* (see chapter 14: II). Whether Ricardo's scheme should be temporary or permanent is left open: 'How long such a plan should be allowed to continue, or whether it might be advantageously made permanent, would of course be the subject of future consideration. Its great object is to maintain, steadily, the bullion value of our paper currency, at a very small expense of the precious metals; and this object it seems calculated to answer.'

* * *

Malthus's position on the Bullionist issues re-emerges in his various pamphlets of 1814–15. In *Observations on the Effects of the Corn Laws* (1814), he avoided any final conclusion regarding the details of agricultural protection because of the 'very uncertain state of the currency' (1986, 7, 106). In the following year he records in *Grounds of an Opinion* (1815) a partial recovery of the pound relative to bullion, and this in part because of a fall in the value of bullion *vis-à-vis* European commodities in general (1815a/1986, 7, 154–5). The improvement in the bullion value of the pound had actually occurred despite *increased* Bank issues, which, in the current circumstances, were non-inflationary issues: 'I have very little doubt that the value of paper in this country has already risen, notwithstanding the increased issues of the Bank. These increased issues I attribute chiefly to the great failures which have taken place among country banks, and the very great purchases which have been made for the continental markets; and, under these circumstances, increased issues might take place, accompanied even by a rise of value' (155n). That full recovery had not yet been achieved reflected a value of bullion still too high (presumably compared with 1797): 'But the currency has not yet recovered itself. The real exchange, during the last year, must have been greatly in our favour, although the nominal exchange is considerably against us.[34] This shows, incontrovertibly, that our currency is still depreciated, in reference to the bullion currencies of the continent. A part, however, of this depreciation may still be owing to the value of bullion in Europe not having yet fallen to its former level.'

34 For the concepts 'real' and 'nominal' exchange rates, see chapter 14, p. 687.

The position that the recent Bank issues were non-inflationary was the subject of Torrens's celebrated charge against Malthus of characteristic inconsistency: 'When the controversy arose on the question of whether the difference between the value of our currency and of our coin was occasioned by an excessive issue of paper by the Bank, or by an extraordinary demand for the metals upon the continent, he was known to be a strenuous supporter of the former opinion; yet, in the 'Ground for an Opinion on the Policy of restricting the Importation of Foreign Corn,' (p. 9) he states his belief that the paper of this country has risen in value, notwithstanding the increased issues of the Bank' (1815, x–xi). This is a wholly unjustified complaint. Malthus in his 1811 statements had been quite clear that conditions might be such as to allow increased Bank of England issues without depressing their value (see above, note 32).

Torrens also complained of Malthus's 'very inaccurate and unphilosophical language ... [which] shews that he has not yet attained any accurate conceptions on the question of the currency.' He had in mind the statement that 'our currency is still depreciated in reference to the bullion currencies of the continent. A part, however, of this *depreciation* may still be owing to the value of *bullion* in Europe not having yet *fallen* to its former level.' For Torrens, 'when a difference exists between currency and bullion, if it has been produced by a fall in currency, there is depreciation; but when the difference is occasioned by bullion having risen, there is no depreciation. To say that currency is depreciated owing to bullion not having fallen to its level, is a confounding of terms' (xi, note). But the fact is that, for Malthus, deviations from par resulting from a high demand for gold abroad should also be a signal for note contraction; 'depreciation' was quite the appropriate term to use in describing a low pound–bullion rate reflecting an unduly high value of bullion (above, p. 645).

Ricardo in fact came to Malthus's defence against the charge of inconsistency relating to the currency: 'I think too that you have always held the opinion you now do that the difference between the value of gold and paper was partly owing to the rise of the value of gold. Is not [Torrens's] criticism very much strained as to the use of the word depreciation? But if he be right in all, the instances are much too few to justify his severe observation' (letter to Malthus, 27 March 1815; 1951–73, VI, 205). Similarly, on 'depreciation': 'I defended [in conversation with Torrens] the use of the word depreciation in the sense which you had used it' (letter to Malthus, 17 April 1815; 215). None the less, an interesting divergence of opinion with Ricardo emerges late in 1815 regarding banking policy. Ricardo recommended a purely paper circulation, and also the establishment of a state commission independent of political interference in place of the private Bank of England.[35] Malthus (who agreed that the Bank's

35 The latter recommendation appears in the following letter to Malthus: 'I think the Bank an unnecessary establishment getting rich by those profits which fairly belong to

profits were excessive) cautioned of the danger of real deflation engendered by attempts to maintain the value of paper *vis-à-vis* metal in the case of a purely paper circulation; a *mixed circulation* – not only adequate reserves – was essential, gold coins providing a supplementary source of metal supply where extraordinary demand for the metal arose. Accordingly, though currency in circulation might fall, only part rather than the entire circulation would be involved – a position very much in line with that of 1811: 'I quite agree with you in thinking that the Government ought to participate more largely in the profits of a paper circulation, but from the experience of the last 5 or 6 years I own I feel great doubts of the practicability of keeping a very large paper circulation on a level with the precious metals, without great and distressing variations in the whole quantity of currency. What has happened clearly proves that there may be a great demand for the precious metals in times of war and convulsion, on account of their superior convenience; and such a demand operating upon a country possessing a small quantity of them, must occasion either a great rise of price, or an extraordinary and most inconvenient diminution of currency. To keep a paper currency on a level with the precious metals without great fluctuations in the value of the currency, I fear we must have *hoards*, and a partial metallic circulation' (1 October 1815; in Ricardo, 1951–73, VI, 289).[36]

A formal statement of Ricardo's position regarding the advantage of a purely paper circulation was to appear the following year in his *Economical and Secure Currency* of 1816 (1951–73, IV, 55–8). Malthus commended the manuscript and recommended publication with qualification: 'I have read your manuscript with attention, and think it important and well worthy the attention of the public: but I doubt whether it is so well written in point of style and arrangement, as your two first pamphlets' (15 October 1816; 1951–73, VI, 298) – *The High Price of Bullion* of 1810 and *Reply to Bosanquet*

---

the public. I cannot help considering the issuing of paper money as a privilege which belongs exclusively to the state. – I regard it as a sort of seignorage, and I am convinced, if the principles of currency were rightly understood, that Commissioners might be appointed independent of all ministerial controul who should be the sole issuers of paper money, – by which I think a profit of from two to three millions might be secured to the public, at the same time that we should be protected from the abuses of the country Banks, who are the cause of much mischief all over the Kingdom' (10 September 1815; 1951–73, VI, 268).

36 A little later Malthus reconfirmed his agreement that 'the public ought to have some share in the enormous profits which the present paper system has allowed the Bank to make' (16 October 1815; 303).

Ricardo explained in a reply to a query by Malthus that he was not proposing 'retrospective' claims by the government on profits made in the past, but rather making proposals for the future: 'My views respecting the Bank are entirely prospective' (17 October; 304).

of 1811. But he repeated his main concern regarding the danger of deflationary note reductions: 'With regard to the matter I agree almost entirely with you, except that I do not think you have considered all the variations to which such a currency as you propose must be subject, particularly the great variation that is likely to arise from a sudden demand for bullion operating upon the scanty supply which is likely to take place upon your plan. If Mr. Vansittart wanted suddenly to send four million in specie to Spain, as he did one year, I cannot help thinking that it would occasion upon your system a most distressing diminution of currency ... [The] value of gold in this country at some periods during the Peninsular war [1808–13] was ten and fifteen per cent higher than at Amsterdam and Hamburgh; and I feel no doubt that, without very extraordinary stores in the Banks, the variations in the value of the precious metals would always be found the greatest, (from sudden demand) in those countries in which a paper currency was most universal. I have no doubt that the precious metals during the last ten years experienced less variation, (with regard to commodities) in France than in this country' (298–9).[37] On the other hand, Malthus warmly commended Ricardo's suggestion for the timing of dividend payments on government bonds to counteract 'the inconvenience to which trade and commerce are exposed by ... periodical distress for money' (cf. 1951–73, IV, 75): 'I am much pleased with your proposal for remedying the temporary distress for money in the market at certain seasons, and should think it would fully answer it.' And generally he approved of Ricardo's overall position condemning the privileges enjoyed by the private owners of the banks: 'You have made out your case about the bank very clearly; but I expect that the directors will stand upon their charter,' which in fact was to terminate only in 1833.

Ricardo took Malthus's opinion seriously, even as to style and organization, showing the letter to Grenfell,[38] and referring to it in correspondence with James Mill and Trower. To Mill he remarked: '[Malthus] agrees with almost all my matter, but thinks, as I think myself, that the performance is inferior *even* to my first two pamphlets' (24 October; 313). To Trower he wrote: '[Malthus's] opinion was not unfavourable to the matter, but was decidedly expressed respecting its inferiority of style and arrangement to my two first pamphlets' (29 October; 315). As for substance, Ricardo defended his scheme for a wholly paper circulation against Malthus's concerns by referring to the ease of obtaining gold for

37 On the question of the specific standard, Malthus added: 'I am not sure whether I should not myself propose silver instead [of] gold as a standard, to prevent the run upon the bank which might be occasioned by an alteration in the relative value of the two precious metals.'

38 Grenfell's reply to Ricardo opens with an ambiguous statement: 'I return Mr. Malthus's Letter, – what he says will I trust decide you to print and give the public the Benefit of your Reflexions on Currency and Bank Affairs' (17 October; 305).

shipment abroad during the Peninsular War, despite the absence of a metal coinage: 'I expected that you would not quite agree with my plan of abolishing the metals from circulation, but the grounds on which you object to it may I think be answered, and then your objections would I hope be removed. You fear that without a metallic circulation we could not on an emergency supply a large sum of bullion for the exigencies of the state. The fact is however against you for we have supplied large sums when the metals have been absolutely banished from circulation. This has been the case during the Pensinsular War' (300).[39] The deflationary consequences of reduced note issues designed to maintain the bullion value of the pound applied to *any* scheme involving convertibility; in any event, reserves were of course required on his own scheme, albeit reserves of uncoined metal: 'If indeed on my system the Bank could keep a less quantity of bullion in their coffers to answer the demands of the public, the objection would be well founded, but the only difference would be that in one case their hoards would consist wholly of coined gold and silver – in the other they would consist of the uncoined metals, – but on both systems, if the Bank paid their notes on demand, the currency must be equally reduced in quantity if gold and silver should become more valuable. That argument then may be used against a currency convertible at all, into specie or bullion, but does not apply to one more than the other' (17 October; 300–1).

Malthus for his part read the evidence differently, while applauding the principle of appeal to experience: 'You know I am always inclined to acknowledge the authority of experience, and I cannot help thinking that in the point to which you refer experience is against you' (30 October; 317). Specifically, though Britain had transmitted bullion during periods when paper alone circulated, systems with a mixed circulation experienced smaller fluctuations in the value of metal since they could satisfy unusual demands for the metal from the coinage and avoid contraction of the *entire* circulation: 'I allow most readily that the country *did* send the bullion, although it had none in circulation, but the demand for it and sending it under these circumstances, certainly produced very great fluctuations in its value: and what I mean to say is, that if the whole currency by being proportionably diminished had been made to experience the same fluctuations, the mercantile world [would] have been extremely distressed. I do not believe than any thing like the same fluctuations in the value of the precious metals took place during the course of the war at Hamburgh Amsterdam or in France. If you recollect in some of our inquiries it

39 Ricardo agreed with Malthus 'that on the whole silver would be better standard than gold, particularly if paper were used. All objections against its greater bulk would be removed.' Grenfell took a different line: 'I cannot agree with Mr. Malthus in preferring Silver to Gold as the Standard' (305).

appeared that the price of gold was at times considerably above ten per cent higher here than at Hamburgh, at one time I think above fifteen. I do not mean my observation to apply to your system as paying in *bullion* instead of *coin*; but to every system in which a sudden demand may come upon a country, possessing altogether but a small quantity of the precious metals' (317–18). On the appearance of Ricardo's pamphlet, he repeated his overall approval – that '[it] seems all to be very clear and good, and I should not wonder if it were very successful'; and also his single major concern – 'whether if there were no metallic circulation, there would not be occasionally great variations in the value of the precious metals, from a great demand' (9 February 1816; 1951–73, VII, 20).

A further issue relating to banking emerging in the 1815–16 correspondence confirms Malthus's deep suspicion of the government's motives. He suspected that 'if we don't pay in Specie now, we shall never do it' (letter to Ricardo, 28 April 1816; 30).[40] And he suspected a deliberate campaign to devalue the pound: 'In the present temper of the Country with regard to Currency, I should not wonder, if a fresh separation between gold and paper should take place, and the ministers should encourage it, as a preparation for an alteration in the coinage.'

V BULLIONISM REINFORCED: A RE-EVALUATION OF CHANGES IN THE VALUE OF BULLION

In the *Edinburgh Review* article for August 1811, Malthus conceded to the anti-Bullionists only an 'inconsiderable' increase in the value of precious metals or fall in bullion prices, confirming for him that 'the paper had quitted the gold' rather than the reverse (above, p. 646).[41] The value of bullion re-emerges in the *Principles*. There he maintained that the decades 1793–1813 actually experienced a *fall* in the domestic value of bullion, initiated by a rise in corn prices (1820, 170; 1836, 166). Ricardo reacted sharply in his *Note 85*, charging Malthus with undermining his original stance, which was to take a middle ground between the parties to the dispute: 'I have always understood that in the differences on the Bullion question Mr. Malthus took a middle course, and ascribed the apparent fall in the value of paper, partly to a real fall in the value of paper and partly to a real rise in the value of the medium (bullion) with which it was compared. He said, that the merchants were partly right, because the difference between bullion and paper was owing partly to a rise of bullion – the bullionists were also partly right because the difference was also owing to the fall of paper; now however, he tells us that the value of

40 In fact the Commons voted on 3 May 1816 to continue restriction for two years.

41 But there is some ambiguity created by the comment on James Mill (see above, note 26) distinguishing foreign and domestic bullion values – a rise in the former, no change in the latter.

bullion fell in this country, and therefore that the bullionists hardly pushed their argument so far as it would go' (1951–73, II, 150–1). This balanced position reflected, so Ricardo had believed, the sort of methodological position laid out at the outset of the *Principles*: 'How does he reconcile the opinion, given in this passage, to that expressed in Page 6 of the same work. "I have always thought that the late controversy on the bullion question presented a signal instance of this kind of error. Each party being possessed of a theory which would account for an unfavourable exchange and an excess of the market above the mint price of bullion, adhered to that single view of the question, which he had been accustomed to consider as correct; and scarcely one writer seemed willing to admit of the operation of both theories." Now what were the two theories. "Bullion has not varied said one party, and the variation in the price of gold has been owing to a fall of paper." "Paper has not varied" said the other party "and the variation of the price of gold has been owing to the rise in the value of gold." The truth lies between said Mr. Malthus; yet he now maintains not only that gold had not risen, as some of the bullionists, I think erroneously, contended, but he contends that it actually fell.'[42]

This retrospective account is not quite accurate, since Malthus in 1811 had allowed little in quantitative terms to the anti-Bullionists regarding bullion prices. His formal methodological stance did not then stop him from taking a position unambiguously hostile to the anti-Bullionists. But that his Bullionist stance was indeed subsequently reinforced, as Ricardo realized, is very clear from the elaborate insistence upon a *fall* in the value of bullion during the war years – a general *rise* in bullion prices – in both *The Measure of Value* (1823) and the *Quarterly Review* article on Tooke's *High and Low Prices* (1823).

At the close of his pamphlet Malthus undertook an interpretation of British monetary history since 1793. The war years were characterized by an upward trend in the profit rate. This trend in and of itself would, according to Malthusian price theory, raise the labour commanded by the precious metals – their value – by reducing the money wage rate (see the third result of the table; 1823b/1986, 7, 201).[43] But this tendency was in

42 The citation of Malthus's appeal for balance at the outset of the *Principles* was interpreted by Ricardo in his *Note 1* in the same way: 'Mr. Malthus must here allude to the dispute whether the alteration in the relative value of bullion and paper, was owing to a rise of bullion or to a fall of paper' (1951–73, II, 6). Ricardo added an important observation from his own perspective: 'The settling of this dispute was of no importance to the real question, for whichever party was right, it did not alter the fact, nor vary the degree, of the depreciation, and could not be settled satisfactorily, because there was no standard to which reference could be made to ascertain whether gold had risen or paper had fallen in value' (6–7).

43 It will be recalled from chapter 7, above, p. 319, that Malthus conceived of the profit rate as a 'cost' element, a rise in which would of itself generate an increase in prices including the 'price' of the monetary metal.

fact swamped by the effect on prices and wages of a higher demand for corn and labour: 'It cannot be doubted that the rate of interest and profits was comparatively high during the late war, and this high rate of profits would naturally have a tendency to lower the bullion price of labour; but this was more than counterbalanced by the tendency of a brisk demand for corn and labour to raise money prices generally, including labour, and the consequence was a fall, during the greatest part of the time, in the value of bullion' (213–14). Since the war the value of bullion had *risen*; in this case, the effect of a falling profit rate in raising the money wage was 'counterbalanced by the tendency of a slack demand for corn and labour to lower prices generally' (214). The consequence was 'a rise in the value of gold' in terms of labour, but 'a still greater rise in the value of the currency,' an allusion to a sharper fall in prices, and, of course, wages, in terms of paper.

Various empirical estimates are shown to reinforce the foregoing perspective. Here Malthus took strong issue with Tooke's proposition in *High and Low Prices* that the value of metal was unchanged during the war. Malthus pointed to Tooke's attribution of the increase in the corn prices and money wages during the war period to a series of poor seasons, and his denial that any part of this price trend could be ascribed (in Tooke's words) 'to alterations in the currency, beyond the degree indicated by the difference between paper and gold' (215).[44] That a series of scarce seasons raised the *bullion* price of labour itself necessarily implied for Malthus a fall in the 'natural value' of bullion.

This rather formal objection to Tooke is elaborated in the article for the *Quarterly Review*: 'We now proceed to consider the proofs which Mr. Tooke's work affords of the .... proposition .... that when periods of abundant or deficient supply are of considerable duration, which is found by experience to be frequently the case, they are necessarily accompanied by a fall or rise of the value of the precious metals in the country where they take place, according to any mode of estimating their value which has ever been considered as approximating to the truth' (1823a/1986, 7, 246). The formulation 'the proofs which Mr. Tooke's work affords' is deliberate. Malthus found that the data provided by Tooke, even some of his reasonings, supported his propositions. His complaint was that Tooke failed to reach the logical conclusions (cf. 227). The essence of the argument is that the bullion prices of commodities and labour increased appreciably in 1792–1813: 'Mr. Tooke has clearly shown that the effects of the seasons in raising prices may last for twenty years together, so as very

44 On the grounds, Tooke argued, that 'when, after a sufficient time has elapsed for the subsidence of the extraordinary effects of such an unusual succession of bad seasons, there is a restoration to a level even somewhat lower than that from which the rise is assumed to have taken place, and to have continued progressively.'

greatly to increase the average price of corn; and it has already been stated as a matter of fact, that taking an average of the three years ending with 1792, and the three years ending with 1813, the bullion price of wheat rose from £2.12s.9d to £4.12s. [see 239]. Now, though it is well known that a year of scarcity or even two years, may pass over without a rise in the price of labour, yet when the rise of provisions is very considerable in itself, and extends over a considerable period, a rise in the money price of labour must follow, or the population will be quite unable to support itself, and the prices of corn must fall again from the destruction of the consumers. In the case immediately under our consideration, we well know that this alternative did not take place. On the contrary, the population increased with extraordinary rapidity, which necessarily implies such a rise in the money price of labour as, combined with more general employment, and other advantages in the purchase of clothing and foreign commodities, would enable the labouring classes to bring up larger families than before' (246). 'We had then,' Malthus concluded, 'a great and general rise in the bullion price of corn and all sorts of provisions, a great and general rise in the bullion price of labour; and, with few exceptions, a general, though more variable rise in the bullion price of other commodities.' The question to answer therefore was 'whether this state of things does not necessarily involve *a fall in the value of bullion*, according to any intelligible meaning which has ever been attached to the terms; or any mode of estimating the value of the precious metals which has ever been considered as an approximation to the truth' (247).

On his own favoured measure – labour commanded – the value of bullion evidently declined during the war. After citing Smith's case for labour commanded,[45] Malthus modestly cites himself as authority: 'Owing to some obscurity in the enunciation of this doctrine in other passages, and still more to his not adhering to it steadily and consistently in other parts of his work,' Smith's measure 'was not generally adopted. Mr. Malthus has lately revived it, with new proofs of its correctness, in a pamphlet entitled, *The Measure of value stated and illustrated*; and as he does not seem likely to fall into the error of Adam Smith, in its application, it may be expected that it will receive a fair trial ... If, on these authorities, we should in the case before us take the labour which a commodity will command as the measure of its value, it will appear at once from the acknowledged rise in the bullion price of labour, that bullion had fallen

45 The passage cited reads: 'Labour, therefore, it appears evidently, is the only universal as well as the only accurate measure of value, or the only standard by which we can compare the values of different commodities at all times and all places. We cannot estimate, it is allowed, the real value of different commodities from century to century by the quantities of silver given for them. We cannot estimate it from year to year by the quantities of corn. By the quantities of labour we can with the greatest accuracy estimate it, both from century to century and from year to year' (1776/1937, 36–7).

just so much in value.'[46] Though Tooke's own data pointed to this conclusion, Tooke himself sought to avoid it, which fact Malthus found incomprehensible:

We are quite at a loss, therefore, to understand the grounds on which Mr. Tooke confines this fall and rise in the value of the whole currency, during the last thirty years, to the difference between paper and gold. He distinctly acknowledges the rise in the bullion price of corn, in the great mass of labour, and in numerous other articles, both domestic and foreign, during the war. He acknowledges also a state of prices directly opposite, since the termination of it. But he strangely supposes that the natural inference from these prices, in respect to the value of bullion, will be destroyed by his showing the specific causes of scarcity, freights, insurance, taxes, or, generally speaking, the obstructions to supply which occasioned these high prices, upon the principles of supply and demand. Now we are quite willing to agree with Mr. Tooke in all the causes of the high and low prices of the last thirty years, which he has summed up at the conclusion of his third part (pp. 83, 84). But we must strongly protest against his conclusion, that the statement of these causes 'leaves no ground for imputing to the alterations in our currency any effect beyond the difference between paper and gold.' Because the causes which he states are specifically those which, according to the principle of the effect of quantity on price, are calculated to raise bullion prices generally, or, in other words, to alter the value of bullion. (250–1)[47]

On the whole, Malthus played down the responsibility of Bank restriction for the wartime fall in the value of bullion and of the return to gold for the later rise – the changes in bullion values from 1793 to 1823 would have occurred in any event in circumstances of relative supply deficiency followed by relative supply excess: 'Though we are most decidedly of opinion that the facts and general reasonings of [Tooke's] work distinctly prove that the alterations in the value of the whole currency were considerably greater than the difference between paper and gold, yet we are equally convinced they do not prove that these alterations, beyond such difference, were occasioned by the Bank restriction and Mr. Peel's bill

46 None the less, the case for a fall in bullion value could be made in terms of any index – corn commanded; a mean between labour and corn – 'as was formerly suggested by Mr. Malthus' (in the *Principles* of 1820); labour embodied; 'all the commodities of the country in succession'; or 'the relative conditions of commodity supply, i.e., labour input plus profit' (165–7). In brief, 'according to any mode which has ever been adopted for estimating the value of commodities, whether we take one object, a few objects, all objects, the labour worked up in commodities, or the quantity of labour and profits, which is the necessary condition of their supply, the value of bullion must, on an average, have fallen considerably from 1792 to 1813, and by the same criterions it will appear that the value of bullion must have risen considerably since 1813' (167–8).

47 The precise process, adopted from Tooke, whereby supply deficiency acts to raise bullion prices, is discussed above, pp. 559–61, 593.

[1819]. The direct effects of these measures were obviously confined to the difference between paper and gold; and it would be exceedingly difficult to form any sort of estimate of their indirect effects' (253). As for the Bank restriction, 'the great rise of paper prices which it occasioned, by throwing a large proportion of the produce of the country into the hands of the productive classes would be likely so to increase the supply, as to prevent the rise of bullion prices from going so far as it otherwise would have done; and, altogether, these indirect effects must have been very trifling: there is every reason to believe, from the well ascertained power of the currency to increase in quantity and efficiency without separating from the standard, that if our paper had always been exchangeable for gold, we should still have seen a great rise of bullion prices during the war, and a great fall of them since.'[48] Similarly, *The Measure of Value* minimizes the responsibility of Bank restriction and of the return to cash payments for the variations in the value of bullion itself – 'the alterations in the value of the currency beyond the difference between bullion and paper' (1823b/1986, 7, 220). There would anyway have been 'considerable' variation: 'That the currency would have fallen very considerably under the circumstances of the last war, and risen very considerably under the circumstances which accompanied the peace, although paper had been kept on a par with gold, I cannot feel the least doubt.' He surmised that the excessive issue of paper exaggerated somewhat these movements: 'And probably the only difference has been, that as the increase of paper beyond what would circulate at par with gold gave facilities to production, and to the bringing of poor land into cultivation during the war, it has tended to increase the glut and low prices since the peace.'[49] Here is an

48 Malthus opined 'that if another war should occur some time hence, accompanied by an under supply of corn, high freights and insurance, a great increase of population, and greatly increasing exports, but without a Bank restriction act, and its necessary consequence, a bill like that of Mr. Peel, we must expect the same fluctuations in the value of bullion, and in bullion prices, as have distinguished the last thirty years.'

Malthus's position that Bank restriction and the return of gold were not responsible for changes in the value of currency beyond the difference between paper and gold is similar to that of the young Mill, who wrote in his 1823 review of Tooke that the possible effect on prices of Bank restriction and the return to gold had been 'settled long ago by general reasoning to the satisfaction of every thinking man' – namely, that restriction *per se* 'could raise prices by a percentage not exceeding the difference between the market and mint price of gold' (see Hollander, 1985, 487). But Mill did not apparently allow here for the possibility that indirectly, if not directly, the measures in question could at least in principle play on bullion prices (carrying paper prices with them).

49 The reference to 'the bringing of poor land into cultivation during the war' need not imply rising real costs. In the 1817 *Essay*, and in the *Principles*, new technology and improved skill are emphasized, allowing expansion during the war without real-cost increase. Cost increases during the war reflect impediments to an inflow of corn resulting from hostilities – 'the expense of freight, insurance, &c' (1820, 168; 1836, 164). Similarly, in the 1823 article on Tooke there is reference to 'high freights and insurance' (1823a/1986, 7, 253).

important assertion regarding: (1) the effect of money supply on real activity; (2) extensions to marginal land; (3) the postwar 'glut' – all matters which we take up elsewhere.

Yet more objectionable than Tooke's argument for an *unchanged* bullion value throughout the war period was the position of Blake (1823) – common to defenders of Bank of England policy – that the value of gold actually *increased* during the war: 'He proposes to prove that it was gold which rose, and not the paper which fell during the war, although he acknowledges as a matter of fact, that almost all prices, including labour, rose not only in paper but in gold' (216). Malthus did not, however, deny the fact of *fluctuations* in the price of gold during the war. He insisted only that 'on an average' the value of bullion fell: 'We say on an average, because there were unquestionably certain periods between 1809 and 1815, when the great demands of the government for its foreign expenditure, did really raise the price of gold in reference to its low preceding value. This is clearly shown by Mr. Blake in his late publication, and it is very much to be regretted, that he should have mixed up with so many interesting and important observations, a proposition so entirely untenable, as that the average value of gold should rise amidst the acknowledged average rise of the gold price of labour, and of all other commodities' (1823a/1986, 7, 250n).[50]

VI MONETARY POLICY

Malthus minimized the potential for monetary policy in the context of the postwar depression. Before proceeding to this matter, it is revealing to consider his position regarding the effect of money supply on economic activity as it emerged in his early papers for the *Edinburgh Review*. In particular, did he then envisage: (1) any positive effects on output and employment of an increasing money supply; and (2) any real deflationary effects resulting from contraction?

In the February 1811 paper, Malthus charged some of the protagonists in the contemporary debates – Ricardo pre-eminently – with a failure to appreciate what the 'merchant' knew well enough from experience, that an increase in the money supply *does* generate an increase in 'capital': 'There is yet another point, still more important, where the experience of the merchant will be apt to lead him to a conclusion quite different from that which is generally maintained by the writers in question. A merchant, or manufacturer, obtains a loan in paper from a bank; and, with this loan, he is able to command materials to work upon, tools to work with, and

50 In making his case against Tooke (and *a fortiori* against Blake) at the close of *The Measure of Value*, Malthus dealt separately with the Scottish and English data, the former being more reliable. The discussion is confusing since Malthus writes of a *fall* in the value of the currency (1812–23) where a rise is obviously intended.

wherewithal to pay the wages of labour; and yet, he is told that this transaction does not tend, in the slightest degree, to increase the capital of the country .... No writer that we are acquainted with, has ever seemed sufficiently aware of the influence which a different distribution of the circulating medium of a country must have on those accumulations which are destined to facilitate future productions; although it follows, as a direct consequence, from the most correct and legitimate view of capital that can be taken' (1811a/1986, 7, 46). Apparently, it is not the expansion of money *as such* that is referred to here, but an expansion involving 'a different distribution of the circulating medium,' in which case (in principle at least) such an altered distribution might occur with a constant (or even diminished) money supply. The text that follows in fact implies this. Whereas 'anything like an equal distribution of the circulating medium' would alter 'the proportion between capital and revenue ... to the disadvantage of capital,' should 'considerable portions of the currency [be] taken from the idle, and those who live upon fixed incomes, and transferred to farmers, manufacturers and merchants, – the proportion between capital and revenue would be greatly altered to the advantage of capital; and in a short time, the produce of the country would be greatly augmented' (47).[51]

This is a purely hypothetical case designed to establish a principle. But the point is that an altered *distribution* of the money supply does normally accompany an *expansion* of the money supply when achieved by way of lending to business. The consequence of such lending is a net expansion of 'capital,' though much less effectively than in the hypothetical case: 'Whenever, in the actual state of things, a fresh issue of notes comes into the hands of those who mean to employ them in the prosecution and extension of a profitable business, a difference in the distribution of the circulating medium takes place, similar in kind to that which has been last supposed; and produces similar, though of course comparatively inconsiderable effects, in altering the proportion between capital and revenue in favour of the former.' The term 'capital' is used in this last passage – and doubtless this is how Malthus read Adam Smith – as *loanable funds* available for business activity, rather than as real capital goods. This is confirmed immediately: 'The new notes go into the market, as so much additional

51 The reference to 'capital' and 'revenue' relates to Adam Smith's position (1776/1937, 315–16) that 'though the whole annual produce of the land and labour of every country is, no doubt, ultimately destined for supplying the consumption of its inhabitants, and for procuring a revenue to them; yet, when it first comes, either from the ground, or from the hands of the productive labourers, it naturally divides itself into two parts. One of them is, in the first place, destined for replacing a capital, and for renewing the materials, provisions and finished work, which had been withdrawn from a capital; the other for constituting a revenue ...,' which, Malthus adds, 'is destined to be spent without any view to reproduction.'

capital, to purchase what is necessary for the conduct of the concern.' The effect on real dimensions occurs subsequently, as we shall shortly see in discussing the so-called forced-saving process.[52]

Malthus felt obliged to emphasize both the significance of a *redistribution* of the money supply, rather than the increase as such, and the resultant effect on 'capital,' in the sense of loanable funds. In his restatement there is also an allusion to the effect of expanded note issues on the interest rate: 'It must always be recollected, that it is not the *quantity* of the circulating medium which produced the effect here described, but the *different distribution* of it. If a thousand millions of notes were added to the circulation, and distributed to the various classes of society exactly in the same proportions as before, neither the capital of the country, nor the facility of borrowing, would be in the slightest degree increased. But, on every fresh issue of notes, not only is the quantity of the circulating medium increased, but the distribution of the whole mass is altered. A larger proportion falls into the hands of those who consume and produce, and a smaller proportion into the hands of those who only consume. And as we have always considered capital as that portion of the national accumulations and annual produce, which is at the command of those who mean to employ it with a view to reproduction, we are bound to acknowledge, that an increased issue of notes tends to increase the national capital, and by an almost, though not strictly necessary consequence, to lower the rate of interest' (48). The fall in the interest rate alluded to here is not the result of an expanded real capital stock, but of increased loanable funds prior to such expansion. (This confirms that *profit-rate determination* was not yet an issue in 1811).

What, though, of the final effect on real activity? It is here that Malthus describes the phenomenon of forced saving, a reduction in consumption enforced by the loss of purchasing power attached to a given money income: 'The new notes go into the market, as so much additional capital, to purchase what is necessary for the conduct of the concern. But before the produce of the country has been increased, it is impossible for one person to have more of it, without diminishing the shares of some others.

52 For the history of the concept, see von Hayek, 1932, 1935, 18f.; Viner, 1937, 189–97; Robbins, 1968, 144–9; Hollander, 1979, 484–7.

Ricardo was later to concede that an increase in paper circulation might – though it 'seldom does' – redistribute real income from a non-saving to a saving group, that is, might 'facilitate the accumulation of capital in the hands of the capitalist; he having increased profits, while the labourer has diminished wages' (Lords Committee, *Report*, 26 March 1819; 1951–73, V, 446). In his Appendix to *The High Price of Bullion* (1951–73, III, 120–3), written in response to the February 1811 article for the *Edinburgh Review*, he seems to confuse Malthus's statement there of just this mechanism with the Forced Savings mechanism, possibly misled by the reference to fixed-income recipients in the passage cited above (1811a/1986, 7, 47), though all that Malthus intended was the presumption that such recipients are predominantly a consuming group.

This diminution is effected by the rise of prices, occasioned by the competition of the new notes, which puts it out of the power of those who are only buyers, and not sellers, to purchase as much of the annual produce as before: while all the industrious classes, all those that sell as well as buy, are, during the progressive rise of prices, making unusual profits; and, even when this progression stops, are left with the command of a greater portion of the annual produce than they possessed previous to the new issues' (47–8). On this view, the expansion of real capital occurs only 'during the progressive rise of prices.'[53]

Various disadvantages attached to this process. First, there is a danger of increased *speculative* ventures, a concern engendered by recent experience: 'It may perhaps fairly be questioned, whether the late unusual facility of obtaining discounts, though it has undoubtedly tended to increase the capital of the country, may not have given it so unsafe a direction, as to subject it to losses which may more than counterbalance its first gains; – whether, in short, it has not obliged some of the most respectable mercantile capitalists, who, in the way in which they were in the habit of carrying on their trade, scarcely ever failed of increasing the national accumulation, to yield the competition to a new and very different set of merchants, who may be said to gamble in trade, – who, in the hope of great profits, will risk any quantity of capital that they can command, – and in whose hands, therefore, the national accumulation is quite uncertain' (48). And there were *moral* concerns relating to individual welfare which outweighed any national advantage of achieving expansion by inflationary means: 'the grand and paramount objection to the stimulus which is applied to the productive powers of a country, by an excessive increase of currency, is, that it is accomplished at the expense of a manifest injustice. The observations we have made may afford a rational explanation of the facts, that countries are often increasing in riches amidst an increasing quantity of individual misery; that a rise of prices is generally found conjoined with public prosperity; and a fall of prices with national decline. But whatever phenomena they may assist to explain, they cannot alter the foundations of right and wrong, or give the slightest sanction to unjust transfers of property' (48–9).

The precise consequences of a fall in purchasing power by inflationary means is elaborated in the second of the two monetary papers. The loss

53 Ricardo, in the Appendix to *The High Price of Bullion*, pointed out that there was no assurance that low-saving groups alone would be affected by inflation (1951–73, III, 120–3).

For a further statement by Malthus implying forced saving, see his *Observations*: 'The discovery of the mines of America, during the time that it raised the price of corn between three or four times, did not nearly so much as double the price of labour; and, while it permanently diminished the power of all fixed incomes, it gave a prodigious increase of power to all landlords and capitalists' (1814/1986, 7, 93).

to individuals wrought by currency depreciation could be avoided by landowners, at least on the expiration of their leases; by labourers (including state employees) who 'must ultimately have their wages raised in proportion to the depreciation of that medium in which they are paid'; and certainly by 'the mercantile classes' – though in this case only 'as long as confidence remains unimpaired' (1811b/1986, 7, 78). It is the *public creditor* who suffers both immediately and ultimately from a depreciated currency. Yet the act of May 1811 – stipulating that bank notes are equivalent to guineas, though the market declared otherwise (above, pp. 641, 653) – was actually defended as a means of *protecting* the public creditor. This act concealed the loss inflicted, and allowed the government 'the pretence of saying, that the ruin which crushes the public creditors, while other classes find the means of escaping from it, is owing to a rise of profits, a rise of rents, and a rise of wages, and not to its true cause, a depreciated currency' (79).[54]

All this relates to monetary expansion in an *inconvertible* system. By contrast, 'when the paper currency of a country is regulated in such a manner as to maintain it of the same value as the precious metals, the evil which the possessor of a fixed income may still suffer from depreciation occasioned by banking, is so inconsiderable, and so strictly limited, as probably to be more than counterbalanced, even to him, by the advantage which the country derives from it' (1811a/1986, 7, 49). The process is represented as subject to rapid correction by a fall of prices to their original level upon output expansion: 'It is true, however, that, upon the issue of every fresh quantity of notes, prices rise sufficiently to send a quantity of coin out of the circulation, though not, certainly, a quantity equal in amount to the notes; and the currency is at first left greater in quantity, and consequently lower in value, compared with the commodities which it has to circulate, than before. But it frequently happens, we

54 Malthus added that it was desirable that the state allow debt repayment by the public in guineas rather than paper, even if it were to continue to pay its own debts in paper. For at least that would imply 'that the public dividends would not long continue to be paid in a depreciated currency.'

He also appended a personal comment. He himself held a modest number of government bonds: 'It seldom falls to the lot of a fraternity of reviewers to possess money in the stocks; but it is well known that we are richer than many of our brethren; and the report of our having accumulated above a hundred pounds in the three per cents (though we did not mean to boast of it) is really true. For this little nest egg, it may be supposed that we are proportionably anxious; and with a view to its safety, and the value of the yearly income we derive from it, what of all other things we should most like to see, is a fair and open discount upon paper, and a free circulation of guineas at their market price. We should then submit to our present diminution of income, in the full confidence that it would be temporary; and that when the injustice which the public creditor was suffering was daily and hourly brought before the view of the Legislature, a British Parliament would infallibly interfere to prevent it.'

conceive, that the beneficial employment of the coin set free, and the increased command of the produce transferred to the industrious classes by the increase of prices, gives such a stimulus to the productive powers of the country, that, in a short time, the balance between commodities and currency is restored, by the great multiplication of the former, – and prices return to their former level.'[55] It would appear, then, that in the original inconvertible case Malthus envisaged ongoing expansion of the money supply and ongoing erosion of the purchasing power of those on relatively fixed money incomes. It would otherwise be difficult to understand why, even under inconvertibility, prices should not fall to their previous level after output expansion. And his implicit point may actually be that such ongoing inflationary trends are precluded by convertibility.

There is also this 'moral' difference between the two cases, that price increases under convertibility, though detrimental to fixed-income recipients, cannot be reprobated. 'Injustice,' counteracting any beneficial effects on national output, is pertinent only where 'positive' depreciation takes place: 'Independently, however, of the chance of the prices of commodities being restored by the influence of increased capital, the possessor of a fixed income cannot consider himself as unjustly treated, while the currency in which his revenue is paid is maintained on a level with the precious metals. These metals are indeed liable to change in their power of commanding the necessaries and conveniences of life; but the principal changes to which they are subject, depend upon causes so entirely beyond control, that the evils which he may suffer from these changes must be considered as necessarily belonging to the kind of property which he possesses. And if his revenue continues to be paid in the same quantity of coin, or in paper of equal value, however he may occasionally complain of increased prices, he will not feel himself warranted in complaining of injustice. As long, therefore, as the currency of a country is maintained on a level with the precious metals, the increase of national capital, and of national industry, derived from banking establishments, is unaccompanied by any essential drawbacks; but as soon as a positive depreciation takes place, the injustice committed towards one portion of the society is so unquestionable, that, though it may be concealed for a time, it cannot, when known, admit of excuse' (50).[56]

55 Malthus interpreted the period 1751–9 in these terms and criticized Smith for 'carelessly, and without any inquiry about the fact' attributing price increases in the first years to bad harvests rather than note issues (cf. Smith, 1776/1937, 309). Malthus apparently understood Smith as excluding the possibility of an effect on the price level of increased note issues on the grounds that each additional note displaces, without price change, the equivalent value in metal, a common misreading (see Smith, 404).

56 In the August paper, Malthus focused also on note issues by way of Bank loans to government. This process is represented as, at best, a temporary means of transferring resources, but as inadequate as a means of financing the war, the real benefactors

The August paper steps back in a major way from the February allowance for a positive effect on activity: 'We are ... fully aware, that the transfer of property occasioned by a rise of prices, has a tendency to give a stimulus to industry. To this principle we gave its full weight in a former number ... But, independently of the great injustice of ever calling such a principle into action unnecessarily, the principle itself cannot safely be received without considerable limitation' (1811b/1986, 7, 74). For Malthus now points out that Hume himself (1752) had insisted that *any real benefit of inflation occurs only whilst it proceeds,* but since it is inconceivable that it could be allowed to proceed, depression *must* result: 'If those who have triumphantly brought forward the very just observations of Hume, on the good effects of an increasing circulating medium, had studied with attention the former part of the same admirable essay from which these observations are taken, they would have found, that, in the opinion of the author, the natural check to the continuance of great commercial prosperity in any one country, is the rise of corn and labour, necessarily occasioned by that prosperity itself; and that, for fear of accelerating the period of this check, he entertains great doubt of the benefit of banks, even without reference to any depreciation of their paper below the value of bullion. And when the same persons, in order to deprecate the return of the Bank to payments in specie, dilate with satisfaction on the poverty, beggary and sloth which are the consequences, according to Hume, of a decreasing circulating medium; let them read the whole essay, and then say whether it is not clearly Hume's opinon, that the most certain way of producing that povery, beggary and sloth which he describes, is a profuse issue of bank paper, – an intemperate use of an excessive stimulus, which, from its very nature, cannot admit of being continued' (74–5).[57]

Malthus goes yet farther by suggesting that, even were the inflation rate

---

being the Bank proprietors and debtors. The argument sets out by allowing that 'a paper circulation issued by a Government' constituted 'a system of *taxation* (for this is its true character) calculated to afford, for a short time, very powerful and effective resources ... But there never was, we conceive, so mistaken and puerile an imitation of it, as that of supporting the present profuse issues of the Bank, under the idea that they furnish similar resources to the Government for carrying on the present expensive contest' (73). Why the government does not benefit seems to involve unstated empirical considerations.

The text that follows focuses on the burden imposed on *individuals*: 'We are fully aware, that the system of indirect taxation to which we are now alluding, is of the nature of a transfer of property from one set of people to another, and not an actual consumption of it by the Government. But so are the taxes which are imposed for the purpose of paying the interest of the national debt. Yet these taxes occasion a very severe pressure upon individuals. And such a pressure as this, ought surely to be reserved to maintain a great national expenditure, and not be wantonly inflicted for the most trifling accommodations' (74).

57 This position was later maintained by J.S. Mill and, in our day, by Friedman (see Hollander, 1985, 552).

maintained, real deflationary consequences must follow – representing the depressed circumstances of 1811 as just such an outcome – although he provides inadequate explanation for this extension: 'We have increased the circulating medium at least one fourth during the last three years. Is it meant to be asserted, that we ought to go on at this rate, in order to avoid the check we so much dread? If we were to make the attempt, is it not certain, that the disease would overtake us even during the time that we were applying what we conceived to be the remedy? Has it not, in fact, already overtaken us? Is not that period, contemplated by Hume as so unfavourable to industry, already arrived? And do not our ruined merchants, our impoverished manufacturers, and the severe check that our capital and revenue have of late suffered, amply testify, that, even in the first application of the stimulus, it was administered in much too large a dose?' (75). Subsequently, there is some elaboration in a strong warning that continued excessive note issues – the act of May 1811 provided the stimulus for the warning – will end in 'a *failure of confidence*' and depression: 'One of the principal arguments urged in favour of the ever memorable act for making bank notes equivalent to guineas in public estimation, when they were not equivalent in the market, was, that however it might be lamented by some, that the measures which had led to the present state of our currency had ever been adopted, it was evidently impossible to retract, or even not to go on with them at present. This, it must be confessed, is a most fearful argument; and if it be really intended to go on in the same spirit which has marked the last three years, there are no limits to the degree of depreciation which may be expected. All that has yet happened is in exact conformity with the general principles which have been laid down on this subject by those who are called theorists; and the experience of the past enables us, with the utmost certainty, to predict, that an excessive issue of paper in England will be accompanied with precisely the same results which have invariable attended it in other countries, – with the same unavailing endeavours to prop the falling value of the paper – the same failure of confidence and check to all regular commercial dealings – and the same wide-wasting convulsion of private property' (80).[58] It is quite likely that the 'failure of confidence' reflects the warning given earlier regarding an increase in 'unsafe' speculative ventures which subjected the nation 'to losses which may more than counterbalance its first gains' (above, p. 669). Malthus in 1823 ascribed the postwar depression in part to the excessive wartime expansion of paper issues (above, p. 665), in effect confirming the principle of 1811.

As for the consequences of the hoped-for return to gold, we find warnings that delay would only create added difficulty: 'Of course, the

58 Cf. also the proposition that the 'mercantile classes' benefit from depreciation only 'as long as confidence remains unimpaired' (above, p. 670).

longer the term [of suspension] is protracted, and the greater is the previous depreciation of the currency, the greater will be the difficulty to the Bank, and the greater the hardship to the persons who benefit by the present system, of a return to the old one' (1811a/1986, 7, 53). Similarly, there was a 'moral certainty of rendering a return to a wholesome state of the circulation more and more difficult, the longer we continue the present system' (1811b/1986, 7, 75).[59] Malthus had in mind the real deflationary consequences of a return to gold; this is the import of his proposal to have the Bank contract its note supply slowly to assure that resumption could be undertaken 'with perfect safety and convenience, both to the Bank and the public; and the evil of any great and sudden diminution of the currency be completely avoided' (above, p. 653).

* * *

We turn now to what little there is in the *Principles* regarding the present issue. Despite his partial attribution of increased activity to money-supply increase during the war (see chapter 12, p. 542), Malthus did *not* recommend monetary injections as a solution to the postwar depression. On the contrary: The positive effect of a higher price level pertained only in conditions of excess demand: 'It is, I believe, the opinion of many persons, particularly among the mercantile classes, that nothing would so soon and so effectively increase the revenue and consumption of the country as a free issue of paper. But in holding this opinion, they have mistaken the nature of the great advantage which the national wealth may sometimes unquestionably derive from a fall in the value of the currency. The specific effect of this fall is to take away property from those who have fixed incomes, and give a greater command over the produce of the country to those who buy and sell. *When the state of the national expenditure is such that there is difficulty of supplying it, then whatever tends to throw a greater proportion of the produce into the hands of capitalists, as it must increase the power of production, must be just calculated to supply what is wanted*' (1820, 513; 1836, 430–1; emphasis added). This had indeed been the case during the war: 'Though the continuation of the act of restriction beyond the immediate necessity of the case, can hardly be considered in any other light than as an act of positive injustice towards the possessors of fixed incomes; yet I can feel very [1836: there is] little doubt that the fall in the value of money, and the facility of credit which it occasioned, acting in the way described, must have contributed greatly to that rapid recovery of vast capital destroyed, which, in the same degree, never probably occurred

59 There is also the specific concern that avoiding 'an open discount upon paper' – by legally obliging acceptance of a depreciated pound – would have severe deflationary consequences (51–2; see above, p. 650).

in the history of any nation before.' Malthus allowed that 'perhaps a sudden increase of currency and a new facility of borrowing, might under any circumstances, give a temporary stimulus to trade, but it would only be temporary' (1820, 514; 1836, 431). But any encouragement thus afforded investment[60] would actually worsen the situation by adding to the 'glut' of commodities – unless accompanied by government (or other forms of unproductive) spending: 'Without a large expenditure on the part of the government, and a frequent conversion of capital into revenue' – as in the war – 'the great powers of production acquired by the capitalists, operating upon the diminished power of purchasing possessed by the owners of fixed incomes, could not fail to occasion a still greater glut of commodities than is felt at present; and 'experience has sufficiently shown us, that paper cannot support prices under such circumstances.' Malthus thus applies his analysis of sustainable growth even to a period of unemployment and excess capacity; we are evidently not in a 'Keynesian' world, where increased investment acts as a net stimulus to activity equivalent to increased private or government consumption. Regrettably, Malthus failed to provide a detailed documentation of the 'experience' alluded to.

The case for the monetary stimulus of activity is thus minimal. Similarly, Malthus played down the responsibility of a reduced money supply for the postwar depression. As we have seen in chapter 12, its origin is ascribed to a collapse of farm prices *prior to* the collapse of the country banks – that had only exacerbated the crisis – and Malthus took the opportunity to appeal for a responsible control over paper on the lines later championed by the Currency school: 'In the history of our paper transactions, it will be found that the abundance or scantiness of currency has followed [1836: has generally followed] and aggravated high or low prices, but seldom or never led them; and it is of the utmost importance to recollect that, at the end of the war, the prices failed before the contraction of the currency began. It was, in fact, the failure of prices [1836: the prices of agricultural produce,] which destroyed the country banks, and showed us the frail foundations of which the excess of our paper currency rested. This sudden contraction no doubt aggravated very greatly the distresses of the merchants and of the country; and for this very reason we should use our utmost endeavours to avoid such an event in future; not, however, by vain efforts to keep up prices by forcible issues of paper, in defiance at once of the laws of justice and the great principles of supply and demand, but by the only effectual way, that of steadily maintaining our paper of the same value with the coin which it professes to represent, and subjecting it to no

60 Malthus did not elaborate on the precise nature of the temporary stimulus. Presumably he was ruling out forced saving, having just limited that process to an initial state of full employment.

other fluctuations than those which belong to the precious metals' (1820, 514–15; 1836, 431–2).[61]

VII SUMMARY AND CONCLUSION

The striking feature of Malthus's position on money and banking is its thoroughgoing 'conservatism.' Like Ricardo, he was a staunch defender of the gold standard – more so in that he objected to Ricardo's resumption scheme which would exclude gold coins from circulation, contributing to that unanimity of opinion on policy described as 'one of the most remarkable facets of nineteenth-century British economic doctrine' (Laidler, 1972, 169). Equally significant, considering the supposedly 'Keynesian' dimension to his economics, are the warnings that inflationary note issues would ultimately end in depression; his insistence that banking policy should be directed at maintaining the value of notes relative to the metal regardless of variation in the latter's general purchasing power – even should deviations be attributable to a high demand for gold abroad; and his disgust with the social irresponsibility of the Bank of England, leading him to contemplate the abolition of that institution in favour of the American system.

61 On Malthus's commendation of Ricardo's scheme for resumption, see chapter 12, p. 623.

FOURTEEN

Two issues in international monetary economics

I INTRODUCTION

This chapter continues the story of Malthus's Bullionism, with the focus now on international monetary economics, specifically the Transfer Problem and the Theory of International Prices. As background to the first issue, we establish in section II the positions of Thornton in *Paper Credit* (1802) and Ricardo in *The High Price of Bullion* (1810) on the effect of remittances, and then examine Malthus's position in the *Edinburgh Review* of February 1811, whereby, following Thornton, emergency corn importation or subsidies to allies generate a payment imbalance met by bullion, even though (*pace* Ricardo) there may be no currency redundancy. Ricardo's reaction in an Appendix to *The High Price of Bullion*, his continued insistence that gold flows only occur when money is the 'cheapest' export, is taken up in section III. In section IV we consider the subsequent Malthus–Ricardo correspondence, the striking feature of which is Ricardo's concession to Malthus that remittances *do* generate a trade imbalance which acts on the exchange and conceivably generates a metal outflow, that is, his abandonment of the original position that international debt created by non-monetary disturbance is met solely by commodity flows. Remaining analytical differences are also taken into account. In the end each correspondent stays with his own position on the question of whether currency redundancy constitutes the *sine qua non* for bullion movement. Section V provides a summary of the first topic, having in mind Jacob Viner's influential accounts (1924, 1937).

Throughout the analysis of the Transfer Problem, we find both Malthus and Ricardo assuming international equilibrium to imply uniformity in the value of money across trading nations. Subsequently, both protagonists abandoned this position. It will be helpful to have in mind from the outset a statement in the revised *Principles* that the effects of improved export efficiency on money value 'have never been sufficiently appreciated' (1836, 128), and crediting Ricardo (citing his 1821 edition) with the correct analysis of the distribution of the precious metals: 'Gold and silver having been chosen for the general medium of circulation, they are, by the competition of commerce distributed in such proportions amongst the different countries of the world, as to accommodate themselves to the natural traffic which would take place if no such metals existed, and the trade between countries were purely a trade of barter' (1951–73, I, 137). This 'just and important observation' turns on a higher equilibrium level of money wages in the economy with the more efficient export sector: 'This distribution is effected by the varying state of the exchanges. If one country possesses peculiar advantages in regard to its exportable commodities, its exchanges will for a time be steadily in its favour, and an influx of the precious metals will take place till the rise in the money price of labour balances the peculiar advantages, and a trade of barter is restored. On the other hand, if a country loses its advantages in regard to exportable commodities, it will lose a portion of its precious metals by an adverse exchange, and the fall of prices will continue till the reduced money prices of labour balances the disadvantages, and the trade of barter returns.'[1] Ricardo's own account of the differential is then reproduced, to explain 'why the prices of home commodities, and those of great bulk, though of comparatively small value, are, independently of other causes, higher in those countries where manufactures flourish' (128–9; citing 1951–73, I, 142). Malthus also lauded Ricardo's analysis of the effect on prices of an improvement in export efficiency, contrasted with an improvement in mining efficiency (1951–73, I, 146) as 'so just, and so well calculated to dispel some unfortunate prejudices which at present prevail, that I cannot resist the temptation of bringing it afresh before the public' (129). To this

1 A note is attached to the first case pertinent to the banking controversy. First, where paper circulates it may be possible to forgo a metallic influx and yet maintain a level of prices as if gold alone circulated. Second, paper issues can be relied on to maintain a higher price level 'in the case of a brisk demand.' Third, there is a caution that paper issues might create a deviation between gold and paper prices – presumably as in 1808–11: 'Practically in countries where a large part of the currency consists of paper, the actual influx of bullion is continually checked by an increased issue of bank notes and bills of exchange; but as long as there is no difference between paper and gold, the effect in lowering the value of money is precisely the same. Repeated experience appears to have shewn us that in the case of a brisk demand, no difficulty is ever found in furnishing the means of a considerable rise of prices in some classes of commodities, without any tendency to a fall in others. Currency is always at hand. The important question is, whether the exchanges can be maintained under such prices; and we know too well that they have often risen higher than the exchanges would allow so as to keep paper and gold together' (128n).

he attached a note: 'I have always considered the first part of Mr Ricardo's chapter (vii) on foreign trade as essentially erroneous; but the greater part of the chapter is not only new, but unquestionably true, and of the highest importance.' The problem, we shall find, is that Malthus also claims priority for the doctrine of non-uniformity of international equilibrium values in a statement given in the *Inquiry into Rent* (1815).

Section VI traces the development of this analysis of the so-called cost of obtaining the precious metals in Malthus's writings from 1811 on. Some brief empirical observations in the second edition of the *Principles* relating to changes in the value of money are considered in section VII.

II MALTHUS ON REMITTANCES AND THE EXCHANGE RATE: HIS INITIAL STATEMENT

Appreciation of Malthus's position on the mechanism of adjustment of international balances of indebtedness requires brief reference to Thornton's *Paper Credit* (1802) and Ricardo's *High Price of Bullion* (1810). Thornton had considered the case of harvest failure in a corn-exporting country entailing cessation of corn exports and the appearance of corn imports, the issue then being the processes whereby other exports are increased and/or imports decreased to assure balance; similarly, in the event of the granting of foreign loans, the issue involves the maintenance or re-establishment of trade balance by expansion of exports and/or contraction of imports to cover the amount of the loan. In both situations the trade imbalance would be met in gold should the foreign demand for home commodities not 'afford the prospect of a tempting or even of a tolerable price': 'At the time of a very unfavourable balance (produced, for example, through a failure of the harvest), a country has occasion for large supplies of corn from abroad: but ... the goods which the country having the unfavourable balance is able to furnish as means of cancelling its debt, are not in such demand abroad as to afford the prospect of a tempting or even of a tolerable price ... The country, therefore, which has the favourable balance, being, to a certain degree, eager for payment, but not in immediate want of all that supply of goods which would be necessary to pay the balance, prefers gold as part, at least, of the payment; for gold can always be turned to a more beneficial use than a very great overplus of any other commodity' (1802/1962, 151). A gold outflow could be prevented (so that the debt is discharged in commodities) only if domestic prices are sufficiently lowered: 'In order then to induce the country having the favourable balance to take all its payment in goods, and no part of it in gold, it would be requisite ... to render them excessively cheap.' Now Thornton did not necessarily recommend the note contraction required to bring about this result; on the countrary, 'it may be the true policy and duty of the bank to permit, for a time, and to a certain extent, the continuance of that unfavourable exchange, which causes gold to leave the country, and to be drawn from its own coffers ...' (152). Banking policy as such is irrelevant for us now; the point here is that a redundancy of currency can be said to *result from* the initial trade imbalance in the specific sense of 'an excess of paper ... above that very low and reduced quantity to which it is necessary that it should be brought down, in order to prevent the existence of an excess of the market price over the mint price of gold' (151). Such currency redundancy 'aris[ing] on the occasion of an unfavourable balance of trade, and at a time when there has been no extraordinary emission of notes, may fairly be considered as an excess created by that unfavourable balance' – though, he adds, 'it is one which a reduction in notes tends to cure.'

Ricardo responded critically in his *High Price of Bullion* (1810). He paraphrased Thornton thus: 'Mr. Thornton ... supposes that a very unfavourable balance of trade may be occasioned in this country by a bad harvest, and the consequent importation of corn; and that there maybe at the same time an unwillingness in the country to which we are indebted, to receive our goods in payment; the balance due to the foreign country must therefore be paid out of that part of our currency, consisting of coin, and that hence arises the demand for gold bullion and its increased price' (1951–73, III, 59–60). The problem was that Thornton has failed to explain 'why any unwillingness should exist in the foreign country to receive our goods in exchange for their corn' (61); for '[if] we consent to give coin in exchange for goods, it must be from choice, not necessity. We should not import more goods than we export, unless we had a redundancy of currency, which it therefore suits us to make part of our exports. The exportation of coin is caused by its cheapness, and is not the effect, but the cause of an unfavourable balance: we should not export it, if we did not send it to a better market, or if we had any commodity which we could export more profitably. It is a salutary remedy for a redundant currency; ... that the demand for it abroad arises only from the comparative deficiency of the currency in the importing country, which there causes its superior value.'[2]

By his formulation 'we should not import more goods than we export, unless we had a redundancy of currency,' Ricardo was not refusing to consider the Transfer Problem – namely, the finance of existing obligations in contrast to obligations yet to be made; he was dealing precisely with this problem and expressing his opinion that such debt already contracted would be discharged in commodities, not money – that emergency corn imports do not affect the balance of payments – unless money were for some reason 'cheap.' In the case of *subsidies* to a foreign power – which obviously falls into the category of existing obligations or debt already

2 In the third edition this position is underscored: 'the temptation to export money in exchange for goods, or what is termed an unfavourable balance of trade, never arises but from a redundant currency' (59).

contracted – he similarly insisted that a gold outflow will occur only if money is 'superabundant': 'If, which is a much stronger case, we agreed to pay a subsidy to a foreign power, money would not be exported whilst there were any goods which could more cheaply discharge the payment. The interest of individuals would render the exportation of the money unnecessary ... specie will be sent abroad to discharge a debt only when it is superabundant; only when it is the cheapest exportable commodity' (63).[3]

* * *

Malthus, in the *Edinburgh Review* for February 1811, commended Ricardo for 'proving the actual depreciation of our currency, and in tracing it to its true cause,' but took issue with his apparently *unicausal* explanation of exchange-rate determination, or 'partial view,' which recognized only the second of two primary forces at play: 'Independently of the wearing or the adulteration of the coin, the effects of which are readily intelligible, there are, we conceive, two causes, perfectly distinct in their origin, though nearly similar in their effects, by which the exchange is affected. The first, and the most ordinary, is the varying demand for different sorts of produce arising from the varying desires and necessities of the nations connected with each other by commerce. The second is a comparative redundancy or deficiency of currency, in whatever way it may be occasioned' (1811a/1986, 7, 24). Ricardo's error was that he attributed 'a favourable or unfavourable exchange *exclusively* to a redundant or deficient currency, and overlooks the varying desires and wants of different societies, as an original cause of a temporary excess of imports above exports, or exports above imports' (25). The Bullion Report itself was 'entirely free' of this error (44).[4] The exchange rate might thus deteriorate and bullion flow out in

3 Viner was not impressed by the Wheatley–Ricardo line: 'Wheatley and Ricardo ... were clearly wrong in their denial that extraordinary remittances would operate to depress the value of the English currency on the exchanges and in their insistance that in the absence of currency changes the demands of England and the rest of the world for each other's products would necessarily so immediately and completely adjust themselves to extraordinary remittances as to result under both a metallic and an inconvertible paper standard in the maintenance of equilibrium in the balance of payments without the aid of specie movements, changes in the relative level of prices in the two areas, or movements of the exchange rates' (1937, 142). And Viner points to a standard misattribution: 'Thornton and Malthus claimed, with Wheatley and Ricardo dissenting, that a ... change in relative prices would occur and would operate to restore equilibrium in the balance of payments when it had been disturbed by a crop failure or the remittance of a subsidy, and this ... came to receive wide acceptance under the erroneous designation of the Ricardian theory' (320).

4 See also chapter 13: V. This appeal for balance, illustrated by the bullion controversy, is repeated in the *Principles* (1820, 6–7; 1836, 5).

consequence of a balance-of-payments deficit created by extraordinary purchases abroad quite apart from initial currency expansion: 'If, for instance, in consequence of the sudden adoption of some foreign commodity into general use, or the sudden deficiency of some commodity of home growth, which must be supplied from abroad, the imports of a particular country should exceed its exports, the exchange might be turned greatly against it; and it might be obliged to make some of its payments in bullion, although, previous to the extraordinary imports occasioned by these new desires or new wants, both its bullion and its currency might have been precisely of the same value as those of the country into which they were now flowing' (24). In this case, bullion export would be 'the *effect of a balance of trade*, originating in causes which may exist without any relation whatever to redundancy or deficiency of currency.' Alternatively expressed: The transmission of bullion 'does not merely originate in redundancy of currency. It is not occasioned by its cheapness. It is not, as Mr Ricardo endeavours to persuade us, the cause of the unfavourable balance, instead of the effect. It is not merely a salutary remedy for a redundant currency' (26–7).

Here we are referred to Thornton's contrast between a relatively inelastic foreign demand for British goods – reference is made to potential 'gluts,' and possibly a technical sense of excess aggregate supply is intended – and an infinitely elastic demand for bullion: '[The transmission of bullion] is owing precisely to the cause mentioned by Mr Thornton – the unwillingness of the creditor nation to receive a great additional quantity of goods not wanted for immediate consumption, without being bribed to it by excessive cheapness; and its willingness to receive bullion – the currency of the commercial world – without any such bribe. It is unquestionably true, as stated by Mr Ricardo, that no nation will pay a debt in the precious metals, if it can do it cheaper by commodities; but the prices of commodities are liable to great depressions from a glut in the market; whereas the precious metals, on account of their having been constituted, by the universal consent of society, the general medium of exchange, and instrument of commerce, will pay a debt of the largest amount at its nominal estimation, according to the quantity of bullion contained in the respective currencies of the countries in question' (27).[5]

Speedy correction of disequilibrium is a major part of Malthus's case: 'An efflux ... of the precious metals, for instance, originating in the first cause [non-monetary disturbances to the balance of payments], could exist but a very short time, before it would produce a comparative deficiency in one country, and redundancy in the other; and, by the convertibility of

5 Elsewhere Malthus emphasized the Continental blockade as partly responsible for the difficulties in the way of exporting British manufactures, coupled with easy Bank loans to exporters encouraging excess supply (see chapter 13, p. 651).

bullion into coin, and coin into bullion, a proportional change in the bullion value of their respective currencies' (24). The full process involves increasing commodity exports attributable both to exchange depreciation and to the altered levels of domestic and foreign prices engendered by the preliminary gold outflow: 'The country, with a diminishing quantity of bullion, would evidently soon be limited in its powers of paying with the precious metals, while, at the same time, it would be encouraged to sell by the low bullion prices of its goods, and the foreign demand for them, occasioned by the fall in its bills. On the other hand, the country, with an increasing quantity of bullion, would have its power of purchasing with the precious metals increased, and its encouragement to sell diminished, by the advanced bullion prices of its goods, and the diminished foreign demand for them occasioned by the premium upon its bills. This state of things could not fail to have a speedy effect in changing the direction of the balance of payments, and in restoring that equilibrium of the precious metals, which had been for a time disturbed by the naturally unequal wants and necessities of the countries which trade with each other' (24–5).

These rapid corrections relative to a stable equilibrium were precisely what rendered an international gold standard so attractive (see chapter 13: II). Ricardo's position – as Malthus understood it – that the equilibrium distribution of metals once established can be disturbed *only* if (in Malthus's terms) 'either a new mine, or a new bank was opened;[6] or till some marked change had taken place in their relative prosperity' (27), conflicted with a valid conception of international equilibrium maintained by continuous corrective fluctuations in the exchange and bullion flows in the face of changes in mutual 'wants': 'We cannot doubt that the varying wants of these nations frequently subject them to unfavourable or favourable balances of payment, beyond what can be easily settled by bills: and that to settle these, and to carry on the various roundabout foreign trades of consumption, there ever has been, and always will be, a quantity of the precious metals in use destined to perform the same part with regard to the different nations connected with each other by commerce, which the currency of a particular country performs with regard to its distant provinces' (27–8). Even those (such as Huskisson) who acknowledged gold movements reflecting non-monetary disturbances to the balance of trade erred in supposing these transactions to be 'quite inconsiderable' (44). This quantitative estimate – approved by Ricardo in his *Reply to Bosanquet* (1951–73, III, 171n) – was firmly rejected (44–5).[7]

6 Ricardo assumed that gold coins as well as paper circulated, providing the source of bullion for export upon an increase in paper issues (see Hollander, 1979, 438–9).

7 Malthus focused not only on the continuous changes occuring in relative demand and supply for commodities disturbing the net international balance of a country and requiring correction, but also on the fact 'that most states, in their usual relations of commercial intercourse, have an almost constantly favourable exchange with some

Malthus could not appreciate Ricardo's denial that a state of international equilibrium – 'the precious metals circulat[ing] as nearly as possible on a level' (26) – might be disturbed by unusual importations of corn or the transmission of a large subsidy to an ally; why, that is, the subsidy recipient should immediately demand increased quantities of imports at going prices. For him, as for Thornton, there was no difficulty in understanding that the debt might *not* be discharged wholly in British goods, thus requiring gold exportation – though to some extent the fall in the exchange rate would encourage increased purchases: 'The unwillingness of the country to which the debt is owing, to receive in payment a great quantity of goods, beyond what it is in the habit of giving orders for, and consuming, stands much less in need of explanation, than that a bad harvest, or the necessity of paying a subsidy in one country, should be immediately and invariably accompanied by an unusual demand for muslins, hardware, and colonial produce in some other. We know indeed, that such a demand will to a certain degree exist, owing to the fall in the bills upon the debtor country, and the consequent opportunity of purchasing its commodities at a cheaper rate than usual. But if the debt for the corn or the subsidy be considerable, and require prompt payment, the bills on the debtor country will fall below the price of the transport of the precious metals. A part of the debt will be paid in these metals; and a part by the increased exports of commodities.'

Malthus also reviewed Blake (1810) favourably, in so far as he had avoided Ricardo's error by tracing 'the causes of the real exchange to the varying desires and necessities of different nations, which naturally make them sometimes debtors, and sometimes creditors, to the countries with which they deal, although their respective currencies may be in a state of the most perfect equality of value' (28).[8] But Blake had gone to the other extreme and maintained 'that an alteration in the amount of the currency of a country, without a corresponding alteration in its commodities, has no tendency to affect the real exchange, and to cause an exportation or importation of bullion' (29). Ricardo had been correct to assert that increased paper issues can raise the *bullion* prices of goods, *provided coin*

countries, and an almost constantly unfavourable one with others. And Dr A. Smith has justly observed, that bullion forms, in general, the most convenient medium for carrying on the various roundabout foreign trades of consumption which a country finds it necessary to engage in; and is, in consequence, greatly used for this purpose' (45).

8 The notion 'real' exchange rate is cited thus from Blake: 'The computed exchange varies from two causes totally distinct from each other. The first, arising from the abundance or scarcity of bills in the market, is the foundation of what may be called the *real* exchange; which depends upon the payments which a country has to make, compared with those it has to receive, and has no reference to the state of the currency. The second, arising from alterations in the value of the currency, is the foundation of what may be called the *nominal* exchange; which has no reference whatever to the state of debt and credit of the country.'

circulated: depress the exchange rate; and generate gold outflows: 'We are quite ready to agree with Mr Blake, that the *nominal* exchange, as far as it is *merely nominal*, has no tendency of this kind; but, we are firmly persuaded, with Mr Ricardo, that, as long as there is any quantity of coin to be displaced, and converted into bullion by increased issues of paper, so long will such increased issues continue to raise the bullion, as well as the nominal prices of commodities; that if the bullion prices of commodities be raised, what Mr Blake calls the real prices current will be raised; and the raising of the real prices current cannot fail to discourage the sale of home produce, and encourage the purchase of foreign produce, occasion a discount upon home bills, and premium on foreign bills, affect unfavourably the real exchange, and terminate in the exportation of bullion.' Malthus proposed 'to rank among the causes of the real exchange, not only the varying desires and necessities of different nations, but every such alteration in their currencies as tends to affect the bullion prices of commodities. The causes of the nominal exchange will then be all that part of every alteration in the currencies of different countries, which does not affect the bullion prices of commodities; and the computed exchange will of course be the result of both' (31).[9]

Malthus also objected to a defence of Bank of England policy by the deputy-governor to the effect that the foreign exchanges had nothing to do with currency, as evidenced by the fact that an 'improving exchange' frequently coincided with an increasing issue of notes, and a deterioration with note contraction (42). He could account for such movements in terms of his multicausal approach.[10] For example, improvements in the exchange might occur because of 'mercantile transactions' while there is ongoing pressure on the exchange in the opposite direction – steady but slow – created by excess paper issues: 'The real state of the case seems to be, that though the effects of a redundancy of currency upon the exchange are sure, they are slow, compared with the effects of those mercan-

9 Blake was also in error to assert that 'the bullion trade may be carried on between two countries while their real exchanges are at par' (29). In fact 'bullion cannot be purchased for importation without an excess of exports, and a consequent favourable exchange' (30). Essentially, 'Mr Blake seems to be quite unconscious of the grand difference between bullion and other commodities. The bullion prices of particular commodities may easily vary in such a manner, from plenty or scarcity, as to make it answer to import them when the exchange is at par, or even decidedly unfavourable. But how can the bullion prices of *bullion* experience such variations? The prices of that commodity, which is the general medium of exchange, can properly be said to vary only in reference to the sum of all other commodities; but a variation in the sum of all other commodities compared with bullion, cannot take place in any country which has a ready communication with others, without affecting the exchange. To us, therefore, it appears quite clear, that there are really no other variations in the prices at which bullion can be bought and sold for import or export, than those which appear in the exchange' (30–1).

10 Ricardo actually reacted in precisely the same way in 1819 (see Hollander, 1979, 459).

tile transactions not connected with the question of currency; and, while the former of these causes is proceeding in its operations with a steady and generally uniform pace, the more rapid movements of the latter are opposing, aggravating or modifying these operations in various ways, and producing all those complex, and seemingly inconsistent appearances, which are to be found in the computed exchange' (43).[11]

This perspective – which justified Malthus's designation as 'moderate bullionist' (Viner, 1937, 141–2) – is thrown into relief by comparison with a convertible system. In such a regime, variations in note issue act in an *equilibrating* fashion, an expansion of currency and a consequential rise in domestic prices accompanying the *favourable* exchange and helping correct it: 'If the Bank were paying in specie, the precise period when it could keep the greatest quantity of its notes in circulation, would be that in which the state of mercantile transactions was occasioning a current of payments in bullion into the country. The increased issue of notes, under such circumstances, would for a time be imperceptible; though its tendency would undoubtedly be to raise prices at home, and thus to shorten the duration of the favourable exchange; and, when it turned, to increase the strength of the current in the opposite direction' (1811a/1986, 7, 43). Conversely, an unfavourable exchange resulting from commercial dealings, would (under convertibility) be accompanied by a *contraction* of currency, putting downward pressure on domestic prices and acting as corrective: 'One of the certain effects of a really unfavourable exchange; and the precise cause which prevents the possibility of its permanence, is its tendency to raise the price of foreign commodities, and lower the price of home commodities; and an exchange to an amount here supposed, must, in a very moderate time, produce this effect in a considerable degree. We ought therefore to see a very marked fall in the price of our home produce, and a marked rise in the price of foreign commodities' (1811b/1986, 7, 64).

* * *

Malthus, of course, readily accepted Ricardo's view that 'redundancy or

11 Malthus later maintained that expansion of trade and consequential increase in the value of the national product would be supported by increased means of finance (see chapter 11: XI). In those circumstances 'fresh paper may be issued without a fall in the rate of foreign exchanges, or a rise in the price of bullion and of goods' (1820, 453–4). See also the review of Tooke (1823a/1986, 7, 251).

It has been surmised (Tucker, 1960, 325–8; Hollander, 1979, 113–16) that this position derives from 1811, where, as we have seen, Malthus refers to periods of *improving* exchange rates despite increased note issues. However, the 1811 and 1820 cases are not quite identical. Malthus is arguing in 1811 that expanded paper issues *do* generate a deteriorated exchange (and price increases) but at a relatively slow pace, which effects might be swamped by more volatile changes in the real trade balance. Even under convertibility (see the next section in our text) he asserts that increased note issue with inflows of bullion 'undoubtedly' generate internal price increases.

deficiency of currency' constituted one 'exciting *cause of the balance of trade* and payments, and of the exportation or the importation of bullion' (1811a/1986, 7, 24). Again: 'A similar effect would be produced upon the imports and exports, by the discovery of a new mine, or the increased issues of paper, as long as such issues continued to throw coin out of circulation. In these cases, the redundancy or deficiency of currency is the *cause* of an unfavourable or favourable balance of trade, an unfavourable or favourable course of the real exchanges, and the consequent exportation or importation of bullion' (25).[12] All this, however, is still on a theoretical plane. We must also determine Malthus's attribution of responsibility for the contemporary movements of the exchange rate – whether these were 'real' movements reflecting mercantile transactions or 'nominal' movements reflecting monetary fluctuations. It emerges that, in this empirical regard, Malthus was very close indeed to Ricardo. What required explanation was an exchange rate as much as 30 per cent against Britain. This order of magnitude could not conceivably reflect mercantile transactions, *unless* these were supplemented and reinforced by excess note issues which, by raising domestic prices – 'our home produce has experienced a marked advance in price, and our imported commodities are stationary' – prevented correction: 'All the circumstances attending the state of our currency, in relation to our foreign trade, will show that our unfavourable exchanges with the countries connected with France, are mainly nominal, and not real; if, indeed, we can so far admit the strange and improbable supposition of a real exchange of 30 per cent against us, as to think it worth examination ... Nothing, we conceive, could have produced effects so opposite to those which were to be expected, and of the duration and extent actually observed, except an issue of notes not only insufficient to prevent that compression of the currency, which is at once the natural effect and natural remedy of an unfavourable exchange, but greatly to enlarge the medium of circulation, at the very moment when circumstances required it to be contracted' (1811b/1986, 7, 64).[13] On the other hand, to declare that the deteriorated exchange rate was 'mainly nominal, not real,' that is, mainly attributable to domestic monetary expansion,

12 Malthus is here assuming a mixed currency of paper and coin, a theoretical case, since in the contemporary situation, there were scarcely any gold coins in circulation.

13 Additional evidence that the deteriorated exchange was largely a reflection of excess note issues relates to the circumstance that 'a very unfavourable real exchange with one country, or set of countries, is a very favourable exchange with others. This has been exemplified in the case of our great exports of silver to India and China, which, it is generally acknowledged, greatly contributed to render our exchanges with Europe more favourable than they otherwise would have been. We might expect therefore to see unusually favourable exchanges with all the countries not connected with France.' But in point of fact 'there is ... no one country with which the computed exchange, when correctly estimated, is favourable to us.'

The Jamaican exchange preoccupied Malthus in the 1811 correspondence. Ricardo contributed data which were used in the August review (1951–73, VI, 23, 31–3, 40–1).

might imply to careless readers that the initial causal force was necessarily monetary. This was not the case: 'We do not mean to say, that our late unfavourable exchanges have always exclusively *originated* in the increased issues of the Bank. On the contrary, we are inclined to believe, that, both at the end of the year 1799, and, still more strikingly, at the end of 1808, a greater and more sudden fall of the exchange took place, than could possibly be accounted for by the increase of notes that had been throw into circulation' (67). The deterioration might set in because of mercantile transactions and be reinforced – even 'rendered permanent' – by new bank issues. Here Malthus explained that demand for accommodation is likely to rise precisely when unfavourable exchanges prevail, and generate an excessively generous response by the Bank: 'The fact seems to be, that it is generally on occasion of an unfavourable state of the exchange, arising from the failure of crops, or from shocks to commercial intercourse and confidence, that the Bank is most beset with borrowers. Unfortunately, these applications for discounts, which merely imply an increasing desire of individual merchants to get money at five per cent; either to make foreign purchases; to supply funds which have been lost, or are slow in coming in; or to enter into new speculations on the failure of the old; are mistaken by the Bank for an indication, that the currency is insufficient for the purposes of trade; and the country is thus inundated with paper at the very moment when it ought to be diminished' (68). The Bank 'had not only issued notes to the amount of the guineas withdrawn, which alone would have prevented the return to a favourable exchange at its natural time; but issued them in such numbers, as greatly to increase the whole mass of the circulation, and, as a natural consequence, so to depreciate it, as to render our unfavourable exchanges necessarily permanent, and to expel all the gold from our circulation.'

Malthus thus emerges in policy matters very much in line with Ricardo. His insistence on allowing for the effect of business transactions or transfers on the exchange rate did not lead him to minimize the odium attached to inflationary note issues. He nicely summarized his position at the close of the second paper of 1811. The pressure on the national bullion reserve exerted by to an unfavourable balance reflecting 'the natural inequalities which must occasionally occur in the wants and supplies of different nations [would] never be of serious magnitude and continuance, unless aggravated and prolonged by [imprudent issues]' (82).

III RICARDO'S RESPONSE: THE APPENDIX TO *THE HIGH PRICE OF BULLION*

Ricardo responded to Malthus's first *Edinburgh Review* contribution in an appendix to the fourth edition of his *High Price of Bullion*, published early in April 1811. He there reiterated his position that transfers in payment of (existing) debt are made in commodities. Any gold outflow occurring in the event of a poor harvest is not in payment of the debt but a correction for the rise in general prices occasioned by the initial fall in transactions: 'England, in consequence of a bad harvest, would come under the case ... of a country having been deprived of a part of its commodities, and therefore requiring a diminished amount of circulating medium. The currency which was before equal to her payments would now become superabundant and relatively cheap ...; the exportation of this sum, therefore, would restore the value of her currency to the value of the currencies of other countries. Thus it appears to be satisfactorily proved that a bad harvest operates on the exchange in no other way than by causing the currency which was before at its just level to become redundant, and thus is the principle that an unfavourable exchange may always be traced to a relatively redundant currency most fully exemplified' (1951–73, III, 106–7).[14] Ricardo's gold movement merely maintains the original price levels of the two countries following the poor harvest; but the debt itself created by the import of corn would be settled in commodities.[15]

Did Ricardo provide any substantive rationale for debt discharge in commodities only, that is, for his denial that emergency corn imports or remittances affect the balance of payments? There is a suggestion of what he may have had in mind in a response to Malthus's charge that he had failed to justify the opinion 'that a bad harvest, or the necessity of paying a subsidy in one country, [is] immediately and invariably accompanied by an unusual demand for muslins, hardware, and colonial produce in some other' (cited above, p. 684). This he had 'not contended,' Ricardo insists, since 'the same effects would be produced if the country paying the subsidy, or suffering from a bad harvest, were to import less of other

14 Similarly, a later comparison with the effect on the exchanges of a positive change in money supply: 'that the same effect is produced, as I have already stated, by an abundant or deficient harvest, either in this country or in those countries with which we trade, or by any other addition or diminution to their real wealth, which by altering the relative proportion between commodities and money alter the value of the circulating medium' (118).

15 Viner refers to Ricardo's position as a concession to Malthus 'that when remittances were under way the currency in the remitting country would be in excess unless it were reduced in the proportion which the commodity export surplus constituted of the total stock of goods in that country, which still implied that the remittances could be effected under a convertible standard, or without depreciation of the currency under an inconvertible standard, without involving a relative fall in the level of prices in the remitting country' (1937, 140–1). Cf. also Viner, 1924, 195, on Ricardo's 'admission.' Viner there adds that, 'in the case of a subsidy, presumably, there would be ... a similar gold movement *after* the subsidy had begun to move out in the form of commodities, and for the same reason.'

Viner apparently perceived the excess money supply to reflect the lower level of transactions occasioned by *commodity* export. But this surely was not Ricardo's position, at least in the harvest case, which clearly entails excess money supply prior to any change other than the harvest deficiency.

commodities than it had before been accustomed to do' (110). A decade later, in correspondence, Ricardo referred both to a compensatory reduction in imports other than corn and to expanded exports, independently of exchange-rate variation: 'I doubt whether an unusual deficiency in the supply of corn "must always materially affect the state of debt and credit with foreign countries." If we import to a greater value, we shall also export to a greater value. If we import an unusual quantity of corn we are less able and willing to purchase the usual quantity of other foreign commodities. The exportation of commodities is supposed here to be caused by the previous effect on the exchange. I believe it to be caused by the unusual importation of foreign goods' (to McCulloch, 2 October 1819; 1951–73, VIII, 91). The logic for a compensatory reduction in imports is clear. But what of the supposed absolute increase of exports? According to the standard Ricardian theory of trade, the motive for exportation of any particular good is that its price abroad exceed that at home. Ricardo may here be presuming that increased domestic expenditure on corn not only reduces import demand by reducing expenditure on other goods but also stimulates exportation as domestic prices tend to fall. Of course, one cannot merely *presume* that this was his intention in the 1811 Appendix. What other evidence do we have? In informal Notes made in December 1810–January 1811 on Bentham's 'Sur les Prix,' there is a strong suggestion of reduced manufacturing prices as a concomitant of higher corn prices resulting from a poor harvest. Bentham had argued that (short-term) general price increases may be accounted for by poor harvests (and war) without money-supply increase. Ricardo pointed out that, if general prices were to rise, it could only be in consequence of a reduced volume of transactions implied by the short crops: 'If any rise in the price of commodities is caused in the way here supposed, it must be by diminishing the amount of commodities, which will make the money which circulates them relatively abundant.' But he then inserts an added sentence: 'But if it is the mass of prices of which the author speaks, he is mistaken because [when] one commodity rose in price another would fall' (1951–73, III, 300). Similarly: 'Is not the mass of prices the same after [corn] scarcity as before' (311). Ricardo here seems to deny *any* price-level increase, implying reduced manufacturing prices.

Jacob Viner found an alternative rationale in Ricardo's Appendix, albeit technically unconvincing (1924, 195, 198–9; 1937, 295–6). Let it be allowed that specie movements would in fact be set in motion. These movements will, after the once-and-for-all disturbance, be reversed; traders are, however, presumed to be able to identify such temporary gold flows and to refuse to engage in the wasteful effort involved in exporting and reimporting gold. This interpretation is based on the following passage from the Appendix: 'The ultimate result then of all this exportation and importation of money, is that one country will have imported one commodity in exchange for another, and the coin and bullion will in both countries have regained their natural level. Is it to be contended that these results would not be forseen, and the expence and trouble attending these needless operations effectually prevented, in a country where capital is abundant, where every possible economy in trade is practised, and where competition is pushed to its utmost limits? Is it conceivable that money should be sent abroad for the purpose merely of rendering it dear in this country and cheap in another, and by such means to ensure its return to us?' (1951–73, III, 103). Viner himself rejected this sort of argument – a sort of 'rational expectations' case – as a gross exaggeration of the extent to which individual traders can foresee whether a drain of gold will be temporary or not, or would find it in their interest to desist from engaging in gold exportation if the drain appears to be temporary.

To my mind, the extract from the Appendix does not constitute a rationalization of the opinion that transfers have no effect upon the balance of payments because they are taken care of in terms of goods immediately upon the temporary nature of the newly created debt being perceived by merchants. The argument merely constituted a *reductio ad absurdum* designed to demonstrate what Ricardo perceived as the illogicality of *Malthus's* position, namely, that money flows might occur in payment of an international debt even though money is not the cheapest exportable commodity – the notion (above, p. 682) that the creditor nation must be *bribed* to import commodities but not to import bullion: 'If,' Ricardo asked, 'the precious metals can be exported from a country in exchange for commodities, although they should be as dear in the exporting as in the importing country, what are the effects which will follow from such improvident exportation?' (101–2). By the same token, Ricardo was troubled by Malthus's assertion that the outflow of gold – despite the presumption that the domestic level of prices was not initially excessively high – would 'have a speedy effect in changing the direction of the balance of payments, and in restoring the equilibrium of the precious metals' (above, p. 683). The case was confused and made confusing by both denying and maintaining the equilibrating function of gold movement: 'Does it not follow from these admissions, that if the balance of trade may become unfavourable to a country, though its currency be not relatively superabundant, that there is no check against the exportation of its coin, whilst any amount of money remains in circulation; as the diminished sum, (by acquiring a new value,) will as readily and as effectually make the required payments as the larger sum did before? ... The observation that its diminished value in the importing country ... would make it revert again to the old channel, does not answer the objection When will this happen? and in exchange for what will it be returned?' (102–3). It is here that Ricardo pointed out that Malthus's sequence, which he read as implying, first, the export and, then, the reimport of gold, would in any event never occur because such movements would be 'foreseen' by merchants. What we may think of Ricardo's evaluation of merchants' perspicacity is irrelevant, *for it plays no part at all in his own argument, which is simply that 'the money never will be exported unless it is relatively redundant, as compared with other countries*'; or that if money flows out it is 'to *find* its level, not to *destroy* it' (105), as (he believed) Malthus's case implied.[16]

IV FURTHER ELABORATIONS IN CORRESPONDENCE

We turn now to the correspondence following the appearance of Ricardo's Appendix. Malthus was unconvinced: 'I have this moment been reading Mr Ricardo's observations on the Review, but remain quite unconvinced – indeed there is no point on which I feel more sure than the incorrectness of attributing the variations of the exchange exclusively to redundancy or deficiency of currency' (to Horner, 7 April 1811; in Ricardo, 1951–73, III, 12).[17] A letter of 16 June 1811, in which Malthus introduced himself, initiated the exchange with Ricardo. Here he repeats the position of his February article that, though the value of money should be *uniform* between trading nations, debts contracted because of an import surplus resulting from a bad harvest or foreign remittances might yet be paid off, at least partly in bullion: 'Many of the modern writers in political economy in their zeal to correct the absurd notions of the mercantile classes about the balance of trade have overlooked the real differences that exist be-

16 The charge against Malthus parallels a case against Thornton. Thornton had maintained that the outflow of specie (coin) created a 'void' in the money supply which may legitimately be filled by increased note issues to prevent deflation. To this Ricardo objected in the third edition of *The High Price of Bullion*: 'However great the scarcity of corn might be, the exportation of money would be limited by its increasing scarcity' (1951–73, III, 61).

At the same time we must keep in mind Ricardo's general empirical judgment that gold flows are in any event the exception rather than the rule: 'That the exchange is in a constant state of fluctuation with all countries I am not disposed to deny, but it does not generally vary to those limits at which remittances can be more advantageously made by means of bullion than by the purchase of bills' (109). Moreover, if gold flows do occur, the usual cause would be a monetary one rather than one arising during the liquidation of a debt: 'If "we acknowledge that bullion occasionally passes from one country to another, from causes connected with the exchange," we do not acknowledge that it would so pass till the exchanges had fallen to such limits as would make the exportation of bullion profitable, and I am of opinion that if it should so fall, it is in consequence of the cheapness and redundance of currency, which "would originate *almost entirely* in the fresh supplies which are yearly poured in from the mines of the New World"' (111–12; also *Reply to Bosanquet*, in 1951–73, III, 171n).

17 Horner replied: 'Ricardo's reply to your objections is not so well written, in point of clearness, as his usual style. I suspect that upon that dispute the truth lies between you, and that a mode of expressing and stating what takes place might be hit upon, to which you both assent.'

See Viner, 1924, 202, for the trend of opinion favouring the Thornton–Malthus line. In particular, Thomas Tooke, who much admired Malthus's *Edinburgh Review* contributions, wrote dismissively of Ricardo's Appendix.

tween the precious metals and other commodities, from the circumstance of their having been adopted as a medium of exchange' (1951–73, VI, 21). Its convenience as medium assured that bullion might be shipped in debt payment, although the local money supply showed 'no comparative redundancy' – using the term here to indicate uniformity in the 'value' or purchasing power of bullion over 'the mass of commodities' between trading nations;[18] the 'term redundancy is by no means allowable merely because bullion may be the most advantageous commodity to export.' This would occur in the event that commodity exports would not sell abroad at profitable prices considering costs of transportation and the 'danger of lowering the foreign market.' *And his position held good, even in the event of low domestic manufacturing prices*: 'At the very time that this [bullion] export takes place there may be other commodities in the country really redundant, that is selling at prices which do not yield average profits; and yet if from having already exported many of these commodities, or from any other cause, they do not bear a higher price, or only one or two percent higher in the foreign country, I imagine that from the greater expence of exporting bulky commodities, and the greater danger of lowering the foreign market, the preference would be given to bullion although in reference to the mass of commodities it might have exactly the same value in both countries, and there is of course no comparative redundancy' (21–2). The bullion flow occurs 'because something must go to pay the debt, and other commodities not being at the time in sufficient demand to pay the proper profits even with the assistance of the premium received on the bill, the medium of exchange is resorted to which is always in such demand as not to occasion a greater loss than the price of transport and perhaps coinage.' In fact, it was precisely the possibility of metallic flows to correct temporary trade disturbances that assured international equilibrium: 'Generally also, I cannot but be still of opinion that it must be the interest of different nations, occasionally to make use of their medium of exchange for foreign payments; and that it is much more natural and probable that an average level of the precious metals should be maintained, by a principle always ready to act in the correction of temporary fluctuations, than that no such temporary fluctuations should ever exist' (22–3).

Ricardo's reply is formally accommodating. He sought 'to remove the very few objections which prevent us from being precisely of the same opinion on the subject of money, and the laws which regulate its value in the countries which have constant commercial intercourse with each other' (18 June 1811; 23–4). But he proceeded by insisting on the identity be-

18 The letter thus confirms the notion of international equilibrium as one involving a *uniform* value of the precious metals – a matter on which both correspondents were later to change their minds.

tween bullion and all other commodities regarding 'its value and the laws which determine its exportation or importation' (24); the special uses of bullion as measure of value and medium of exchange did not affect the rules regulating trade in bullion: 'I have no doubt that on this point we should not differ; it remains therefore for you to shew why the new uses to which gold has been applied in consequence of its being adopted as the money of the world should exempt it from the general law of competition, and why it should not certainly and invariably (invariably only as that term is applied to other commodities) seek the most advantageous market' (25). While commending Malthus's usage of the term 'redundancy' (see above, pp. 681, 686–7), he again insisted that it was the *sole* cause of bullion exportation, though such redundancy could result from changes in Velocity and from changes on the Transactions side of the Quantity Equation, and not only – as Malthus had believed was his position (above, p. 683) – from 'either a new mine, or a new bank' or when 'some marked change has taken place in ... relative [national] prosperity': 'You admit that a relatively redundant currency may be and frequently is a cause of an unfavourable balance of trade but you contend that it is not the only cause. Now I so understanding the word, contend that it is the invariable cause. This relative redundancy may be produced as well by a diminution of goods as by an actual increase of money, (or which is the same thing by an increased economy in the use of it) in one country; or by an increased quantity of goods, or by a diminished amount of money in another. In either of these cases a redundancy of money is produced as effectually as if the mines had become more productive' (26). Currency redundancy was attributable to 'one cause, namely, a redundancy of currency produced in one of the ways above mentioned, and not to the demand for particular commodities,' an allusion to debt reflecting Britain's increased requirement for Continental corn.[19]

Here Ricardo raises the important distinction of his *High Price of Bullion* involving a corn importer's motive (above, p. 680). Malthus, he charged, had assumed the problem away by 'suppos[ing] the debt already contracted,' thus illigitimately dealing with effects, not causes: 'These demands [for particular commodities] are in my opinion regulated by the relative state of the currency, – they are not causes but effects. You appear to me not sufficiently to consider the circumstances which induce one country to contract a debt to another. In all the cases you bring forward you always suppose the debt already contracted, forgetting that I uniformly contend that it is the relative state of the currency which is the motive to the

19 But, according to the Appendix, a poor harvest *does* reduce transactions rendering the money supply excessive (above, p. 689). Conceivably, Ricardo intended in his letter to emphasize that any resultant money outflow merely corrects that excess but does *not* settle the debt.

contract itself. The corn, I say, will not be bought unless money be relatively redundant; you answer me by supposing it already bought and the question to be only concerning the payment' (26–7).

That Malthus 'suppose[d] the debt already contracted' might be read to imply that Ricardo himself refused to consider the Transfer Problem, namely, the finance of existing obligations in contrast to obligations yet to be made. But, as we contended earlier (p. 680), this is unlikely, since by the same token it would preclude the subsidy case. Rather, his complaint must have been that Malthus presumed an existing debt *contracted in terms of bullion,* and thereby reduced the problem to one of mechanics rather than of economic principle. For Ricardo, there could be no presumption that the debt would be contracted in bullion: 'A merchant will not contract a debt for corn to a foreign country unless he is fully convinced that he shall obtain for that corn more money than he contracts to pay for it, and if the commerce of the two countries were limited to these transactions it would as satisfactorily prove to me that money was redundant in one country as that corn was redundant in the other. It would prove too that nothing but money was redundant' (27).[20] Should some other merchant engage in sugar exportation – supposing sugar to be 'redundant' for whatever reason – the export of money for corn would be avoided: 'And I should say that sugar was the redundant commodity; and the exportation of sugar, the more redundant commodity, by diminishing the aggregate amount of commodities would raise the value of money, so that in a short time money would, if corn continued to be imported and sugar exported no longer be redundant even as compared with corn.'[21]

In reply Malthus wrote simply: 'I confess I cannot yet conceive that redundancy of currency is the sole motive for contracting a debt [in bullion], but we will discuss this point when we meet' (20 June; 28–9). The

20 See also *Reply to Bosanquet*: 'Mr Bosanquet speaks as if the nation collectively, as one body, imported corn and exported gold, and that it was compelled by hunger so to do, not reflecting that the importation of corn, even under the case supposed, is the act of individuals, and governed by the same motives as all other branches of trade. What is the degree of *compulsion* which is employed to make us receive corn from our enemy? I suppose no other than the want of that commodity which makes it an advantageous article of import; but if it be a voluntary, as it most certainly is, and not a compulsory bargain between the two nations, I do still maintain that gold would not, even if famine raged amongst us, be given to France in exchange for corn, unless the exportation of gold was attended with advantage to the exporter, unless he could sell corn in England for more gold than he was obliged to give for the purchase of it' (III, 207–8).

21 Malthus's allusion to the expence of 'bulky commodities' as explanation for bullion export (above, p. 693) was easily dealt with: 'Your observation is just concerning the extra expences attending the exportation of bulky commodities – but in all these discussions we must suppose these expences to make part of the price of the commodity; – our comparison is made on the prices at which the importer could afford to sell them and those prices necessarily include expences of every sort' (27–8).

meeting with Ricardo on 22 June failed to bring about a conciliation: 'Though perhaps we have approximated a little in our late conversations, I think, it seems, that we are not likely entirely to agree' (14 July; 33–4). Part of the problem was merely terminological, Malthus insisting on the term 'redundancy' solely to entail 'a comparative rise of prices, generally, without a tendency to lower the prices of any commodities; and never to a state of things where a rise in the prices of one set of commodities is *necessarily* accompanied by a fall in the price of others, as in the case of a scarcity of corn or of any necessary articles ... [T]hese two states of things which lead to two such different consequences ought to be differently designated' (14 July; 33–4, emphasis added).[22] The foreign debt engendered by corn imports may still be paid off in bullion though there is no redundancy, the insistence now on a *necessary* fall in the prices of manufactures in the event of corn scarcity reinforcing the position of 16 June, which had alluded only to the *possibility* that other commodities exist which sell 'at prices which do not yield average profits' (above, p. 693). For all that, debt settlement by gold export in the absence of genuine redundancy, he allowed, was not of great empirical relevance. Exchange-rate variation would usually suffice to encourage commodity exports: 'Hume, Smith, Huskisson and all the most respectable writers on these subjects have uniformly considered an unfavourable real exchange as tending strongly to correct itself before it arrives at the expence of transporting the precious metals; and I cannot help most decidedly agreeing with them. I do not see otherwise what would be the encouragement to the exportation of a greater quantity of manufactures during a war' (34). This was relevant to the debate, for 'no such encouragement would be given if, as you say, the variations in the rate of exchange always represent corresponding variations in the values of the currencies.'[23]

22 At this point Malthus commends Sir James Steuart's *Inquiry into the Principles of Political Oeconomy* (1767), Book II, ch. 18 ('Methods of Lowering the Price of Manufactures in order to make them vendible in foreign Markets'): 'Though I by no means agree with him in his general conclusions in that chapter; yet I think you will see there, what I mean by a comparative rise of prices not occasioned by a comparative redundancy of currency.' In this chapter Steuart lists various reasons for relatively high domestic prices endangering the trade balance, including the 'consideration of high profits' in manufactures; unbalanced expansion of manufacturing putting pressure on agricultural prices; disadvantageous natural conditions; and inferior technology (1966, 246–7). But the reference is presumably an aside; for the main issue of debt contraction and settlement does *not* entail a 'comparative rise of prices.'

Ricardo merely commented in his letter of 17 July: 'I shall not fail attentively to consider the chapters [*sic*] in Sir J. Steuarts work which you have mentioned' (40).

23 This issue had also been raised at the meeting of 22 June; see Ricardo's letter 23 June: 'After giving the subject which you yesterday mentioned due consideration, I cannot agree with you in opinion that the exchange will not accurately express the degree or depreciation which the currency may have experienced' (29–30).

Ricardo regretted that there was 'so little probability' of agreement (17 July; 35). He again insisted that a 'redundant' currency might be generated by a poor harvest, considering the net contraction on the Transactions side of the Quantity Equation, and this *despite* reduced manufacturing prices: 'Though it should be allowed that the rise in the price of one commodity, in the case of a scarcity of corn, should be accompanied with a fall in the price of all others, why should a redundancy of currency be impossible under such circumstances? The currency must, I apprehend, be considered as a whole and as such be compared with the whole of the commodities which it circulates. If then it be in a greater proportion to commodities after than before the scarce harvest, whilst no such alteration has taken place in the proportion between money and commodities abroad, it appears to me that no expression can more correctly describe such a state of things than a "relative redundancy of currency"' (35–6). He added, though, that 'not only money but every other commodity would become comparatively cheap as compared with corn, and would therefore be exported in return for the corn which would be in demand in this country.'

To allow that money is exported in part payment of the debt seems to abandon the position of the Appendix (see above, p. 688). But one cannot be sure. Ricardo's position is ambiguous. Did he or did he not accept that non-agricultural prices decline by his 'Though it should be allowed ...'? In a passage that follows, he seems specifically to attribute a fall in manufacturing prices to *Malthus*: 'You are of opinion ...,' but muddies the waters by adding 'Whether it would or would not do so is not material.' One would have thought it very material, since such a fall would reinforce his own case (above, p. 690). Indeed, he proceeds to assert just this – were Malthus correct, the debt would be paid entirely in manufactured goods: 'If however, I thought that the difference between us was as to the correct use of a word, I should immediately yield the point in dispute, but I am persuaded that we do not agree in the principle. You are of opinion that a bad harvest will raise the price of corn, but will lower in some degree the prices of other commodities. Whether it would or would not do so is not material; but if your opinion is correct then I say there would be no exportation of money because money would not be the cheapest exportable commodity. If before the deficient harvest money was at the same value in any two countries, that is to say all their exportable commodities without exception were at the same prices in both, then, according to your view of the question, after the scarcity the prices of all commodities would fall in the country where such scarcity occurred. Whilst then the prices were unequal in the two countries commodities only would be exported in exchange for corn, and there would be no question between us, because we differ as to the cause of the exportation of money' (37).[24] Malthus's

24 Equality of the value of the metals is defined by Ricardo in terms of *traded goods* ('exportables') specifically.

contention in the *Edinburgh Review* (above, p. 682) that manufactures may not be in sufficient demand abroad was unacceptable, given his own assumption that domestic manufacturing prices fall: 'You have indeed said that there may be a glut of commodities in the foreign market. What! a glut of commodities with a dearer price! impossible, – these two circumstances are incompatible. If the price of any commodity has been £20 in both countries and in consequence of the bad harvest it had been lowered to £15 in one of them, there could not be a glut of that commodity in the other country till it had there also fallen to £15' (38).

Ricardo allowed that a gold outflow might occur were money to become the cheapest export; but this would be the case only in the unlikely event that *all* manufacturing prices abroad are reduced. Here one again notes the emphasis on Malthus's supposition that manufacturing prices fall in England, suggesting that such is *not* his own assumption: 'Not only must the price of one commodity fall in the foreign market, but the prices of all (*because you suppose them all to have fallen in England*) before money could be exported in exchange for corn, and then I would allow that money would be exported, but even then it would be so only because it was more cheap on the whole, as compared with commodities, in the exporting country, and this I contend is the proof of its relative redundance' (emphasis added). Ricardo could not fathom why money would be exported should it be 'cheaper' with respect to corn but 'dearer' with respect to manufactures – why it would not be manufactures, the prices of which are *supposed* to have fallen domestically and relative to the foreign price, that are exported: 'You maintain that money is rendered cheap by a bad harvest as compared with corn only, but with all other commodities it is dearer than before, – and then what appears to me very inconsistent you insist that this commodity thus rendered scarce and dear will be exported, though before it had increased in value, it had no tendency to leave us, whilst too there are commodities which have undergone an opposite change, and which will nevertheless be obstinately retained by us. This is a mode of reasoning which I cannot reconcile' (38–9).

As for Malthus's reference to Hume, Smith, and Huskisson (above, p. 696), Ricardo readily allowed that a debt reflecting subsidies to a foreign ally or foreign payments made by the government would indeed lower the exchange, thereby encouraging commodity exports, but insisted 'that the exchange accurately measures the depreciation of the currency ... notwithstanding the high authorities against me' (39). He did not, however, 'contend that a convulsed state of the exchange, such as would be caused by a subsidy granted to a foreign power' – a disequilibrium state – 'would accurately measure the value of the currency, because a demand for bills arising from such a cause would not be in consequence of the natural commerce of the country. Such a demand would therefore have the effect of forcing the exports of commodities by means of the bounty which the exchange would afford.' But 'after the subsidy was paid the exchange would again accurately express the value of the currency. The same effects would follow, as in the case of a subsidy, from the foreign expenditures of Government. These have a natural tendency to create an unfavourable exchange, yet if the demand for bills is regular it is suprising how this bounty on exportation will be reduced by the competition amongst the exporters of commodities.'[25]

Now this gives reason for pause. Ricardo seems here quite happy to allow in the subsidy case that pressure *is* put on the exchange. It happens to be his belief that the relevant elasticities are such as to render it unlikely that the gold-export point is usually reached. But this is an empirical matter; in principle, metal would be exported should the subsidy be large enough. In any event, as soon as it is conceded that the exchanges are affected, the game is up, since the balance of payments must have been disturbed. Has there then occurred a surrender to Malthus, at least in the case of the subsidy? Apparently so. For, in his reply on 26 July, Malthus writes as if Ricardo had newly conceded an outflow of bullion in the specific case of a subsidy: 'In meditating on the subject of your letter of the 17th during my journey into Lincolnshire I think I seized more fully than I had hitherto done your view of the subject. Allowing as you now do that in the foreign expenditure of government, and the payment of a subsidy, bullion will be used in a greater proportion than other commodities on account of its being the currency of the commercial world and universally acceptable,[26] I should allow that in all other cases (at least if the contract made for goods were immediately fulfilled)' – presumably including poor harvests – 'bullion would be set in motion from its comparative redundancy according to your definition of redundancy' (41).

There are, however, complexities. The opening of Malthus's letter (40) also refers to a letter from Ricardo of 21 July, now wanting. It was perhaps in that letter that Ricardo explicitly conceded in the subsidy and government-expenditure cases that 'bullion will be used in a greater proportion than other commodities ...' (This is not the formulation in the extant letter of 17 July.) And there is Malthus's own agreement to relate bullion outflows to 'redundancy' in the sense of the term adopted by Ricardo – presumably involving a low general purchasing power.[27] But on

25 One notes also a further allowance that 'if such a state of things should permanently continue the exchange has no tendency to correct itself.' Ricardo was to alter his position regarding the *temporary* effect on the exchanges of a *once and for all* subsidy (below, pp. 701f).

26 Ricardo himself subsequently insists that bullion is used in *lesser* proportion than other commodities (below, pp. 703–4). Either Malthus misunderstood Ricardo, or Ricardo changed his mind.

27 He himself preferred a different terminology to express Ricardo's position – a *cheap* rather than a *redundant* currency: 'I still think that to express what you mean the term cheapness would be more correct ... The reason why I think the term cheapness of

20 October this latter is retracted: 'The more I have reflected on the subject of our late conversations the more I feel convinced that it is positively incorrect to state redundancy or cheapness of currency in any sense in which these terms can be fairly understood, as the sole cause of the variations of the exchange, and I feel myself compelled after the most careful and (as far as I can judge) the most impartial consideration of the subject to retain *my opinion that the precious metals move for other purposes than to restore the level of currency*' (62; emphasis added). This in effect is his unaccommodating reply to Ricardo's challenge that, should manufacturing prices decline in the event of a poor harvest – as Malthus believed was the case – the debt would be paid in manufactures, not the precious metals.

Ricardo in response again insisted that the exchanges are affected *only* by 'redundancy' – such that the (relative) domestic purchasing power of the currency is depresssed – that is, money at home is rendered 'cheap' – provided one did not interpret that concept too narrowly: 'I regret ... that you cannot bring yourself to subscribe to my doctrine respecting the exchange being influenced by no other causes but by the relation which the amount of currency bears to the uses for which it is required in the different nations of the earth. This may proceed from your interpreting my proposition somewhat too rigidly' (22 October 1811; 63). He insists that a nation never pays off its debt in gold unless gold is the 'cheapest' exportable commodity, in a specific allusion to the corn-import case: 'I wish to prove that if nations truly understood their own interest they would never export money from one country to another but on account of comparative redundancy ... It rests with you ... to prove that a case can exist where it may become the *interest* of a nation to pay a debt by the transmission of money rather than in any other mode, when money is not the cheapest exportable commodity, – when money (taking into account all expences

currency more correct than redundancy of currency may be explained by the following case which I have no doubt sometimes happens. In a general scarcity of corn a rich nation which can afford to give very high prices on such occasions purchases corn of a poor nation, although the comparative deficiency of corn may be greater in the poor nation than in the rich, and consequently it would be quite incorrect to say that the corn was exported [by the poor country] on account of a comparative redundancy. In my opinion currency is more wanted for *use* in a scarcity of corn than at other times; and according to our accustomed notions, one can hardly call a commodity redundant which is more wanted than usual; but still in reference to the mass of commodities currency is cheap, or rather as I should say home commodities are dear, and bullion goes in search of the cheaper commodities abroad' (41–2). But 'it would be still better to use the expression comparative cheapness of commodities abroad, than comparative cheapness of currency at home – particularly in all the cases where the variations have originated in the supplies of the commodities, and not in the supplies of the currencies.'

which may attend the exportation of different commodities as well as money) will not purchase more goods abroad than it will at home. You appear to me to have repeatedly admitted that it is the relative prices of commodities which regulates their exportation. Is it not then as certain that money will go to that country where the major part of goods are cheap, as that goods will go to any other country where the major part are dear. I say the major part because if the cheapness of one half of the exportable commodities be balanced by the dearness of the other half, in both countries, it is obvious that the commerce of such countries will be confined to the exchange of goods only' (63–4).[28] Only in the event of a *net* increase in the price level would gold be used in settlement – evidently if the exchange attains the gold-export point – thus correcting the initial deviation in metal value between trading partners: 'If in any country there exists a dearness of importable commodities *and no corresponding cheapness of exportable commodities* money in such country is above its natural level and must infallibly be exported in payment of the dear commodities, – but what does this state of things indicate but an excess of currency, and it may surely be correctly said that money is exported to restore the level not to destroy it' (65; emphasis added). But we are still left with the question: Assuming that the preceding describes Ricardo's own conception of the poor-harvest case – excluding any fall in domestic manufacturing prices – was he actually conceding *debt settlement* in money or was he merely reiterating the limited concession of the Appendix (above, p. 689) regarding gold outflows which merely re-establish the original money/goods ratio?

* * *

In a letter on 22 December 1811, Ricardo explicated and corrected certain notes, no longer extant, that he had personally given to Malthus on the latter's *Edinburgh Review* article of August. It will be recalled that, in an earlier letter, Ricardo had allowed pressure on the exchange in the *subsidy* case (above, p. 699). He now elaborates. The fall in the exchange rate stimulates the export of those goods requiring a 'trifling stimulus'; and the outflow of goods, and their importation abroad, implies increased domestic relative to foreign price levels, but 'in a degree to counterbalance' the

28 At the same time he alludes to an unwitting concession by Malthus, perhaps at a personal meeting: 'When you say that money will go abroad to pay a debt or a subsidy, or to buy corn, although it be not superabundant, but at the same time admit that it will speedily return and be exchanged for goods, you appear to me to concede all for which I contend, namely, that it would be the *interest* of both countries, when money is not superabundant in the one owing the debt, that the expence of exporting the money should be spared, because it will be followed by another useless expence – sending it back again' (64–5). This seems to reflect the complaint in the Appendix (above, p. 691).

exchange advantage: 'In my endeavors to trace the effects of a subsidy in forcing the exportation of commodities, I stated, if I recollect rightly that it would occasion, first, a demand for bills; secondly, an exportation of all those commodities the prices of which already differed so much, in the two countries, as to require only the trifling stimulus which the first fall in the exchange would afford; thirdly, a real alteration in the relative state of prices, viz a rise in the exporting and a fall in the importing country, – in a degree too to counterbalance the advantage from the unfavourable exchange' (73). *The debt, however, is apparently still not paid.* The last stage is 'a further fall of the exchange and a consequent exportation of an additional quantity of goods and then of money till the subsidy were paid. It appears, then, that if the subsidy were small it would be wholly paid by the exportation of commodities, as the fall in the exchange would be sufficient to encourage *their* exportation, but not sufficient to encourage the exportation of money' (73).

This final stage is asserted rather than explained. In particular, does the renewed fall in the exchange rate follow from the altered levels of prices at home and abroad, or is it independent, having in mind the preceding observation that the price changes merely 'counterbalance' the intermediate, unfavourable, exchange? What follows contributes to an answer. Apparently it is the change in the relative price levels that provides the key. For Ricardo proceeded to identify the effect on the price level of a poor harvest or a subsidy with that of a *positive* increase in the money supply, on the grounds that all three disturbances entail a fall in the value of money and a deteriorated exchange rate.[29]

We turn first to the template: 'I believe you admit, that in the case of an augmentation of 2 pct. to our currency, altho' it were wholly metallic, the prices of commodities would rise in this country 2 pct. above their former level, and that such rise being confined to this country alone it would check exportation and encourage importation; the consequence of which would be a demand for bills and a fall in the exchange. This rise of prices and fall of the exchange, proceeding from what you do not object to call a redundant currency, would not be temporary but permanent, unless it were corrected by a reduction of the amount of the currency here, or by some change in the relative amount of the currencies of other countries' (74). Since Malthus allowed all this, he should accept the same logic in the harvest and subsidy cases: 'Now as a bad harvest or the vote of a subsidy tend to produce the very same effects namely, a relative state of high prices at home, accompanied by an unfavourable exchange they

29 The identity may have to be qualified; see the following note regarding the harvest case and the subsidy.

admit only of the same cure, – and as in the case of an augmentation of currency the exchange would have no tendency to rise, neither would it in the case of a subsidy the unfavourable exchange being in both instances produced by a redundant currency, or in more popular language by a relative state of prices which renders the exportation of money most profitable. I have uniformly maintained that the money of the world is distributed amongst the different countries according to their commerce and payments, and that if in any country it should from any cause happen to exceed that proportion, the excess would infallibly be exported to be divided amongst the other countries' (74–5).

The identification of the harvest case with the subsidy suggests that Ricardo now allowed for the creation of an imbalance, even in the former case, and its correction via movement in the exchange.[30] Moreover, Ricardo now insisted – in contrast to the position stated on 17 July (above, p. 698) – that the unfavourable exchange in the event of excess currency, however generated, would not be self-corrective: 'If an excess of currency once occurs, an unfavourable exchange must continue till some alteration in the relative amount of currency. The circumstances which may occasion such an alteration are numerous, and are fully detailed in the papers which I left with you. To the precise agreement between the effects of an augmented currency and the effects of a subsidy I most particularly request your attention, as on such agreement depends the whole success of the argument which I am advancing in favour of *my opinion that an unfavourable exchange has no tendency to correct itself*' (75; emphasis added). The argument hinges on the observation that, when liquidation of a debt occurs in terms of both commodities and gold, the monetary outflow as a proportion of the original money supply will *necessarily* be less than the commodity outflow as a proportion of the original volume of commodities; the ratio between the ultimate gold stock and the volume of transactions is higher than in initial equilibrium, resulting in a correspondingly *higher* internal level of prices and permanently depressed exchanges in compensation: 'If the exportation of money were in the same proportion as the exportation of commodities, that is to say, supposing the commodities of a country to be equal to 100, and its money equal to 2, then if not less than one fiftieth of the exports in payment of the subsidy consisted of money, prices would after such payment be the same as before in both countries, and although

30 If this is not so, there would be this difference, that in the harvest case the domestic price level rises in consequence of the Transactions contraction implied by the poor harvest, which rise generates a fall in the exchange rate, and (possibly) a money outflow. These adjustments *per se* do not clear the original debt. In the case of the subsidy, the exchange-rate depreciation is the *first* impact, which leads to commodity export. It is this *induced* decline in Transaction that causes the price level to rise.

the exchange must have fallen to that limit at which exportation of money became profitable, it would immediately have a tendency to recover, and would shortly rise to par; but it is precisely because *less* than this proportion of money will be exported that the exchange will continue permanently unfavourable and will have no tendency to rise, more than it will have to fall' (73–4).[31]

Possible objections to the identification of a higher level of prices resulting from a positive money-supply increase with one resulting from a subsidy are then taken up. In all cases, Ricardo now insisted, correction of the exchanges *requires* an outflow of bullion: 'It may be urged that the relative state of high prices at home occasioned by an augmentation of currency is the natural effect of such a cause, but that this is not the case in a subsidy; that the exportation of commodities in payment of a subsidy is forced and that it will produce a glut in the foreign market, but that after the subsidy is paid and the necessity for the exportation shall cease prices will rise in the foreign market to their former rate. This however will not be true. Commodities may rise in a trifling degree abroad but cannot regain their former rate unless the exchange should also rise to par, but this it can never do whilst the demand for bills do not exceed the supply. Now as the prices of foreign commodities in the home market which could not have been supplied in the usual abundance during the operation of the subsidy when we had a large balance to pay, would fall, and would be in greater demand from the moment that our commodities would be received in exchange, the exportation of our goods would be balanced by the importation of foreign goods and the sellers of bills would neither exceed nor fall short of the purchasers' (75–6).[32]

31 Viner complained that 'Ricardo does not state the grounds on which he rests his assertion that the export of gold would be in relatively smaller proportions than the export of commodities' (1924, 201). He himself maintained that 'there can be little likelihood ... that commodity shipments in payment of a subsidy or a loan will affect the commodity side of the equation between commodities and money as much as the gold shipments will affect the money side. An increase in exports does not necessarily reduce the flow of commodities (and services) requiring mediation of their exchanges in the exporting country. In any case, even a huge subsidy is likely to be a small proportion of the total volume of commodities and services exchanged for money in the course of the year, whereas a relatively small fraction of the subsidy paid in gold may represent a large fraction of the total supply of gold of the exporting country' (201–2).

Why less than one-fiftieth of the exports takes the form of money is unclear. But if this should be the case, then the exchanges remain unfavourable, even after equilibrium has been re-established, *unless* money is exported. Malthus, by contrast, seemed to Ricardo to conceive of an automatic correction.

32 The letter closes with a wish to withdraw the original notes (see above, p. 701) on Malthus's August 1811 paper: 'These are the substance of the amendments which I wish to make to my paper, which is now so faulty that I shall be glad to have it returned to me. Have the goodness to bring it with you when you come to town.'

* * *

Malthus's reply to the long letter of 22 December reiterates his standard denial that bullion is exported only to 'restore' an initial disturbance to the value of money (above, p. 700). To make this case, he posits a subsidy which depresses the exchange rate to the gold-export point without generating sufficient commodity exports to settle the debt. Gold movements are then to be expected. If, however, these movements are prevented by note contraction, the remaining debts would be paid in commodities: 'If bullion only goes abroad to restore the level of currency, of course a compression of the paper at home would have the same effect, but suppose in a subsidy of 4 millions, 2 millions remained yet unpaid after the exchanges had fallen to the price of the transport of the precious metals, would you not, by compressing the currency instead of sending the bullion, force out commodities in order to pay the remaining debt which ought not naturally to have gone, to the obvious inconvenience of both nations' (1 January 1812; 78). This argument designed to prove that bullion flows occur for reasons other than restoration of balance in currency values is unclear.

Second, Malthus insisted that, in the case of a subsidy, the exchange would right itself, notwithstanding Ricardo's argument to the contrary: 'I most entirely approve of the first part of the paper you were so good as to leave with me; but notwithstanding your last explanation I am still of opinion that the exchange has a strong tendency to recover itself. In the [subsidy] case we were considering, it is true that our goods abroad would fall, but the foreign goods which we were in the habit of importing would remain at the same price, and it is not possible to conceive that the usual competition for bills to pay for these commodities, should not prodigiously slacken, when the means of payment were clogged with an unfavourable exchange of 3 per cent' (77).

Third, and most generally, Malthus rejected Ricardo's identification of the poor harvest and subsidy cases with a positive injection of money: 'You desire my particular attention to the resemblance between the effects of what I allow to be a redundancy of currency, and the granting of a subsidy or the purchase of large quantities of corn in a scarcity. I do attend, but cannot see the strong resemblances you speak of. In the one case there is a strong tendency to an immediate importation of commodities and exportation of bullion; and in the other case the immediate tendency is to an exportation of commodities. And even after the first effect is over, when there may be some apparent resemblance, yet upon a nearer view it fails. In the case of a real redundancy of currency all commodities are affected, and are rendered dearer at home and comparatively cheaper abroad; whereas in the other cases the prices of particular commodities alone, are affected, which I hold to be a most important difference' (77–8). The contrast raises new problems. It asserts that, in the case of debt, there is 'an immediate tendency to an exportation of commodites,' which seems to clash with the standard Thornton–Malthus view that debt will be met by *bullion*. The reference to the situation after the 'first effect' is unclear, but conceivably it relates to the situation after the export of commodities in payment of a subsidy, stimulated by the exchange-rate decline, where the domestic prices of those particular commodities rise; similarly, in the case of emergency corn imports, the fall of the exchange rate because of the imbalance stimulates some commodity export. The letter is too brief and hurried – 'I write in great haste and in the midst of company' (78) – to carry much weight. And in any event it may have been written for argument's sake, that is, to confute Ricardo on the latter's terms.

A final extant letter from Malthus dated 23 February 1812 reverts to *method*, particularly Ricardo's 'desire to simplify.' Here he reiterates his position of February 1811 (above, p. 681) that exchange-rate fluctuations may be generated by non-monetary disturbances; and that the exchange rate and its movements do *not* reflect – or do not solely reflect – relative money values, to which he adds that 'the exchange has a tendency to recover itself':

> I should like to see again the paper which you were so good as to read at Mr. Sharpe's, and indeed to look over the other once more.[33] I think however that I have seized pretty clearly your view of the subject; but after the fullest consideration that I can give it, I cannot quite agree with you. It really appears that a desire to simplify, which has often led away the most scientific men, has induced you to ascribe to one cause phenomena that properly belong to two, and not to give sufficient weight to the facts which (to me at least) appear to make against your doctrine. I confess I am still of opinion that these facts are not all satisfactorily explicable upon your principles; and I never look over the tables of exchange without being more and more confirmed in the truth of what I state in my first review [above, pp. 685–6], that 'though the effects of a redundancy of currency upon the exchange are *sure*, they are slow compared with the effects of those mercantile or political transactions, not connected with the question of currency and while the former of these causes is proceeding with a steady and generally uniform pace, the more rapid movements of the latter are opposing aggravating or modifying their operations in various ways, and producing all those complex and seemingly inconsistent appearances which are to be found in the computed exchange.' (82)

The criticism is curious since Malthus was fully aware of Ricardo's recognition of an effect on the exchange rate of non-monetary disturbances such as subsidies, and indeed attempted to use this very allowance against Ricardo's formal principle: 'With regard to the state of the ex-

33 For the first see Malthus to Ricardo (87–8); the second refers to the notes given to Malthus on the latter's August 1811 article.

change being a correct exponent of the relative value of different currencies, – surely such a position is inconsistent with the idea of a stimulus to exportation being given by an unfavourable exchange, a stimulus the effects of which you have yourself calculated upon as the chief reason why a subsidy would be paid with little or no necessity for the transport of the precious metals' (83).[34] In fact, he defined his difference with Ricardo regarding the subsidy case merely as one of the relative quantitative significance of gold and commodity movements, appealing to empirical proof to justify the heavier weighting of gold export: 'You think that in the payment of a subsidy more commodities will go in proportion than bullion.[35] I think, that if it be considerable, more bullion would go than had before been used to circulate the commodities sent. The decision of the point must depend upon whether it has been found in practice that a stimulus within the expence of the transport of the precious [metals], (or only for so short a time at that price, as to carry over a less than the usual proportion of the metals) is *sufficient* to pay a debt of 3 or 4 millions; or insufficient. If insufficient, then it is clear that more bullion would go in proportion than commodities; because no commodity that requires a greater stimulus than bullion could be sent while bullion was to be had at the mint price.' He pointed to the 'alarm which the Bank is known to feel on occasion of granting a subsidy' as showing 'unquestionably which way experience has decided.'

* * *

We have no extant documentation for the year 1812 except for one letter by Ricardo of 17 December written after numerous meetings with Malthus. He there allowed a substantial degree of agreement, but at least implicitly seems to reiterate his earlier position that a subsidy or other debt playing on the exchanges *requires* for correction a money outflow, which fact indicated that money is in excess, albeit an excess not *attributable* to positive monetary expansion: 'On many points connected with our old question we are I believe agreed, – though there is yet some difference between us ... I cannot help thinking that there is no unfavourable exchange which may not be corrected by a diminution in the amount of the currency, and I consider this to afford a proof that the currency must be redundant for a time at least. Whilst the exchange is unfavourable it is always accompanied though not always caused by an excess of currency' (17 December 1812;

34 He himself admitted to 'a little mistake' in his preceding letter of 1 January 1812, but still thought 'that the exchange has a tendency to recover itself. This very stimulus we are now speaking of is a proof.'

35 See above, p. 703. If in fact more commodities go, then the price level is *raised* after payment of the subsidy, necessitating further correction.

87–8). Following further meetings (and possibly correspondence), Ricardo again expressed a strong degree of agreement. Nothing separated them, apart from the *permanence* of the effect on the exchange rate of a subsidy or other debt; both agreed that money might flow out, though for Ricardo only 'as a last resort': 'You have clearly stated the point of difference now between us; I think we never so well understood each other before. There are some causes which operate on the exchange which are in their nature of transitory duration, – there are others which have a more permanent character. If we agree that a change of taste in one country for the commodities of the other, – and the transmission of a subsidy – will produce certain effects on the exchange, the only question between us is as to their duration. I am of opinion that they will operate for a very considerable time, and that in fact recourse is not had to bullion but as a last resort' (25 February 1813; 89).[36]

V THE TRANSFER PROBLEM: A SUMMARY

In his first formal statement on the Transfer Problem, Malthus relied on exchange depreciation and a reduced domestic price level following bullion export to assure re-establishment of equilibrium (above, pp. 682–3). Viner gave Malthus excellent press:

> Ricardo fails to show why or how the borrowing country's demand for the lending country's products will increase because of the loan so that it will take more commodities at the *same* prices. He fails to meet Malthus's argument that the borrowing country will not be willing to accept more of the lending country's goods at the *same* prices ... Malthus is undoubtedly right in claiming that a debt payable in gold can be liquidated in gold without discount [above, p. 693], whereas to pay it in commodities may require their sale at reduced prices. It follows, therefore, that the grant of a loan to a foreign country may, and ordinarily will, immediately create an unfavourable balance of payments and a redundancy in currency. Immediately thereafter the export of gold will begin – the effect, as Thornton and Malthus claim, and not the cause, as Ricardo claims,

36 One other issue appears in the extant correspondence. It relates to the 'law of value' as applied to money (Ricardo to Malthus, 22 March 1813; 90), but is important in our present context. There Ricardo wrote: 'In any point of view however I do not see how it bears materially on the question between us, namely whether the precious metals are frequently resorted to for the payment of debts between countries when no disturbance has taken place in the amount or proportion of the currency' (24 March; 92). But this remark is elusive. By excluding cases where changes occur in the *proportion* of the currency, it excludes the main disturbances originally under discussion, which Ricardo had interpreted as falling within such a rubric. If, however, this is not his intention, the statement confirms that one aspect of the difference between the correspondents is an empirical one.

of an insufficient export of goods and a consequent unfavourable balance of payments.

Similarly, in the case of the failure of the harvest, while prices remain at their former levels, imports and exports with the exception of grain will remain at their former levels. The cessation of grain exports will prevent imports and exports from balancing evenly. There will be, therefore, unfavourable balances of trade and of payments, which will be the cause and not the effect of an export of gold from the country whose harvest has failed. (1924, 197–8)

Viner may have been a little generous to Malthus. For in his elaboration in correspondence, Malthus insisted on domestic manufacturing prices *necessarily falling* upon a bad harvest, notwithstanding which fact there would still occur a fall in the exchanges and a bullion outflow (above, p. 696). And Viner may have been too harsh towards Ricardo, who in his Appendix did offer a rationale for his own position in the reduced demand for inputs other than corn and (possibly) in a stimulus to exports provided by a fall in manufacturing prices, and who in the subsequent correspondence pointed to the illogicality of Malthus's insistance on a gold outflow despite a necessary fall in manufacturing prices. Yet admittedly Ricardo is difficult to pin down. For, in the correspondence, he himself seems to deny any fall in manufacturing prices, though such a fall would greatly strengthen his own case (above, p. 697).

Where do we *finally* end up regarding the analysis of remittances? Viner represented Ricardo's side of the correspondence as a series of 'minor' concessions to Malthus (1937, 138–9).[37] The emphasis is on Ricardo's denial (above, pp. 703–4) that money outflows in payment of debt act on the relative price levels of the debtor and creditor nations to re-establish equilibrium in Hume-like fashion – his insistence that, to the contrary, an outflow would actually *raise* the domestic level of prices, causing 'permanent' deterioration of the exchange:

He gave a prominent place in the mechanism of adjustment of international balances to variations in the exchanges, and even maintained that an

37 Apart from these 'minor concessions,' Viner identified Ricardo's position with that of Wheatley (1803): 'To the argument that foreign remittances would under inconvertibility operate to depress the exchanges, Wheatley and Ricardo both replied that foreign remittances would have no effect on the exchanges whether under convertibility or inconvertibility; in both cases, they maintained, the demands of England and the rest of the world for each other's products would so adjust themselves automatically to the remittances that they would be transferred in goods without changes either in relative prices or in exchange rates. If under inconvertibility, therefore, there appeared a depreciation of sterling exchange, this was evidence of excess issue of currency. Ricardo later made some minor concessions to his critics, but Wheatley adhered rigidly to this doctrine to the end.'

unfavourable rate of exchange resulting from the necessity of paying a subsidy would tend to persist long after the subsidy had been fully paid. He admitted that the description he had given of the mechanism of adjustment of international balances was intended to apply only to a state of affairs in which all persons knew, actively sought, and were able to achieve, what was in the absence of 'friction' their best interest, and that under actual conditions the adjustment might work out somewhat differently. He still maintainted, however, that a shift in relative prices in subsidy-granting and subsidy-receiving countries, respectively, was not a part of the mechanism of adjustment of the commodity balance to the subsidy. He claimed that, if the fall in the exchange of the subsidy-granting country was not of itself sufficient to result in an increase in exports sufficient to pay the subsidy, and gold was therefore exported, the amount of gold exported would necessarily be a smaller proportion of the total stock of gold in the country than the proportion of the commodity exports sent in payment of the subsidy to the total stock of commodities. Prices in the subsidy-granting country would not fall, therefore, during the payment of the subsidy, and would be higher after payment had been completed than they were before. The exchange for this reason would continue permanently unfavourable to this country. (1924, 200–1)

Let us, however, recall Ricardo's original position in *The High Price of Bullion.* There he had maintained that the creation of international debt did not cause an imbalance since it would be paid in commodities. In the Appendix he allowed for a money outflow to correct for the redundancy created by a poor harvest, but made no allowance for a movement of the exchange rate as part of the payment of the debt itself (above, section III). The only rationale offered for payment in commodities we found to be the reduction in demand for imports other than corn, though this was only briefly stated, and there remained some doubt regarding reduced manufacturing prices as providing a stimulus to exports to meet the debt. To find, then, in the subsequent correspondence (section IV) the concession that, in fact, the exchanges are affected by debt is no *minor* adjustment, but a major concession to Malthus.

For all that, as Viner insisted, the full adjustment process did not follow a common line. And we must also recall Malthus's insistence to the end that trade imbalances are created though nothing had occurred to disturb the domestic relative to the foreign levels of prices. This position is actually reinforced in the correspondence, since it is reiterated notwithstanding the fall in industrial prices in the case of a poor harvest; there is no change in overall price level, yet gold flows may occur because of the status of gold as universal medium: 'The preference would be given to bullion although in reference to the mass of commodities it might have exactly the same value in both countries, and there is ... no comparative redundancy' (above, p. 693). Ricardo's response was twofold: he pointed out that were Malthus correct that manufacturing prices fall, there ought to be no bullion outflow. Yet surprisingly he did not press this line himself, but argued that all the cases under discussion could be said to entail currency redundancy (above, p. 702). This parallel Malthus refused to allow (p. 705).

We should emphasis in closing the confirmation of Malthus's common ground with Ricardo on banking policy encountered in chapter 13. I refer to the empirical judgment that inequalities in international balances resulting from changing trade patterns could not conceivably account for the magnitude of exchange-rate movement that had to be explained (above, p. 687). Excess note issue was the culprit.

VI ON THE COST OF OBTAINING THE PRECIOUS METALS[38]

In *The High Price of Bullion* (1810), Ricardo argued in terms of the uniformity in the value (purchasing power) of bullion across trading nations in equilibrium (1951–73, III, 52, 54, 56). In the *Principles* (1817), non-uniformity in the value of money is the rule, the differential in general purchasing power between countries reflecting differential purchasing power relative to labour and *non-traded* 'home commodities' (corn falls into this category). Special attention is paid to the effect of improved technology in the export sector: 'When any particular country excels in manufactures, so as to occasion an influx of money towards it, the value of money will be lower ... than in any other' (1951–73, I, 146). *Traded* commodities necessarily have the same money values, subject to transport costs and the like.[39]

In 1811 Malthus defined international equilibrium (the exchanges at par) as involving the precious metals 'circulat[ing] as nearly as possible on a level' (1811a/1986, 26); and yet more precisely, as circulating 'in such proportions in the different countries of the commercial world, as, *in reference to the commodities which form the subjects of their mutual intercourse,* to be nearly of the same value in each' (23; emphasis added). This would be consistent with non-uniformity in the 'value' of the precious metals in the sense of *general* purchasing power, or of command over corn (if corn is assumed to be a non-traded good), or of command over labour. But against this we must place the fact that, in the same text, Malthus posits a case where, prior to a real disturbance to the trade balance, 'bullion and ... currency might have been precisely at the same value' in the two trading partners (24). This latter position is further confirmed in a letter to Ricardo of 16 June 1811 (in Ricardo, 1951–73, VI, 21–2).

We turn to post-1811 sources, including the *Inquiry into Rent* (1815), the

38 I adopt the expression for the theory of international prices from Senior, 1830.

39 Conceivably, Ricardo even in 1810 had only traded commodities or exportables in mind, implicitly allowing for differentials over non-tradeables, including labour, but if this had been his intention from the outset, he failed to argue it through.

Principles (1820, 1836), and the two contributions of 1823 – *The Measure of Value* (1823) and the *Quarterly Review* contribution (1823) on Tooke's *High and Low Prices.* Here we find very explicit denials of the uniformity of the value of precious metals in international equilibrium. The context of the 1815 analysis is Adam Smith's position that a 'low value of gold and silver' – in the sense of corn commanded – 'is no proof of the wealth and flourishing state of the country, where it takes place' (1815b/1986, 7, 137; also 1820, 197; 1836, 1829).[40] Malthus denied all this. On the contrary, the low value of the metals – intending here the high price of corn, or more precisely of corn and labour – *was* an index of 'superiority of wealth': 'If we are to measure the value of the precious metals in different countries, and at different periods in the same country, by the price of corn and labour, which appears to me to be the nearest practical approximation that can be adopted (and in fact corn is the measure used by Adam Smith himself), it appears to me to follow, that in countries which have a frequent commercial intercourse with each other, which are nearly at the same distance from the mines, and are not essentially different in soil; there is no more certain sign, or more necessary consequence of superiority of wealth, than the low value of the precious metals, or the high price of raw produce' (1815b/1986, 7, 137–8).[41]

The relatively low value of the metals in a wealthy economy – the high money price of corn – is said to reflect diminishing agricultural returns in line with a charge that Smith (and the Physiocrats) had neglected the

40 According to Smith relatively rapid growth in any one country implies a rise in the corn price of gold or silver, or an *increase* in the 'value' of gold and silver. It is precisely this that attracts a flow of metals into the 'flourishing' country, a process which brings the trade balance into equilibrium; for 'as soon as that superiority [of value] ceases they [the metals] cease to go thither' (1776/1937, 217).

On occasion 'value' is used by Smith to refer to *general* purchasing power. Thus in his famous analysis of a corn-export bounty, he writes of the effect of a higher corn price on the prices of other agricultural produce and (via the wage) on manufactures: 'The real effect of the bounty is not so much to raise the real value of corn, as to degrade the real value of silver; or to make an equal quantity of it exchange for a smaller quantity, not only of corn, but of all other home-made commodities' (476).

41 There may be some crossed lines here. Smith was talking of a '*flourishing*' economy, that is, one with a relatively high growth rate, Malthus only of a *wealthy* country. But elsewhere Malthus talks interchangeably of a wealthy and rapidly growing economy.

The statement 'the economies are not essentially different in soil' evidently refers to agricultural production functions in their entirety, and does not assert identical 'actual' marginal products.

Considering the criticism of Smith, it is difficult to place the following commendatory statement in the 1836 version: 'Adam Smith has justly observed, that the natural effect of the increase of wealth is to raise the value of the precious metals; and it is quite certain that a great increase of produce and population, supposing the supplies of the precious metals, and all other circumstances affecting currency, to remain the same, would render bullion scarcer compared with the demand, and occasion the necessity of its being bought at a greater elementary cost' (1836, 133–4).

effect of increasing land scarcity on corn prices: 'Independently of irregularities in the currency of a country, and other temporary and accidental circumstances, the cause of the high comparative money price of corn is its high comparative real price' (135).[42] And in this context Malthus added a striking footnote *explicitly denying that the value of money tends to a uniform level* when the exchanges are at par. It involves a mechanical analogy to support the purported equilibrating process: 'This conclusion may appear to contradict the doctrine of the *level* of the precious metals. And so it does, if by *level* be meant level of value estimated in the usual way. I consider the doctrine, indeed, as quite unsupported by facts, and the comparison of the precious metals to water perfectly inaccurate. The precious metals are always tending to a state of rest, or such a state of things as to make their movement unnecessary. But when this state of rest has been nearly attained, and the exchanges of all countries are nearly at par, the value of the precious metals in different countries, estimated in corn and labour, or the mass of commodities, is very far indeed from being the same. To be convinced of this, it is only necessary to look at England, France, Poland, Russia, and India, when the exchanges are at par. That Adam Smith, who proposes labour as the true measure of value at all times and in all places, could look around him, and yet say that the precious metals were always the highest in value in the richest countries, has always appeared to me most unlike his usual attention to found his theories on facts' (138n).[43]

In the 1815 account, the non-uniform value of the precious metals between trading nations, in equilibrium, is said to reflect a differential in

42 In the event of *free trade in corn*, Malthus is clear that corn prices *do* tend to uniformity across trading nations: 'Let us now suppose the same countries to have the most perfect freedom of intercourse in corn, and the expenses of freight, &c. to be quite inconsiderable. And let us still suppose one of them to increase very greatly above the rest, in manufacturing capital and skill, in wealth and population. I should then say, that as the importation of corn would prevent any great difference in the price of raw produce [1836: in the prices of corn and labour], it would prevent any great difference in the quantity of capital laid out upon the land, and the quantity of corn obtained from it; that, consequently, the great increase of wealth could not take place without a great dependence on the other nations for corn [1836: a great importation of corn from other nations]; and that this dependence, under the circumstances supposed, would be the natural sign, and absolutely necessary consequence of the increased wealth and population of the country in question' (1815b/1986, 7, 136; 1820, 195–6; 1836, 187–8).

All this, however, is subject to transport costs which 'form a natural barrier to importation,' so that 'even the country which habitually depends upon foreign corn, must have the price of its raw produce considerably higher than the general level' (1815b/1986, 7, 136). Similarly, 'even upon the system of importation, in the actual state and situation of Europe, higher prices must accompany superior and increasing wealth' (138n).

43 It will be noted that Malthus slips between value as *command over corn and labour* and value as *purchasing power over 'the mass of commodities.'*

real corn costs. A differential money price of corn presupposes corn to be a non-traded good.[44] But there is no formal reference to the mechanism which assures that the value of money, in the sense of corn commanded, in economies with relatively efficient export sectors will be relatively low, though Malthus was later to claim precedence for such a mechanism (below, section VIII, p. 735). The text does refer to the circumstance of low manufacturing prices in the 'richest' economies, despite the high corn price and money wage, because of high efficiency (see chapter 3, pp. 106–7), but as an empirical matter only, and says nothing specifically relating to *exportables.* The case for precedence is, however, strengthened when account is taken of the correspondence with Ricardo (see letter dated 26 August 1815, cited chapter 4, p. 135).[45]

* * *

Section VI of the Rent chapter in the *Principles* is devoted to the determination of the *relative* corn price – relative both to domestic manufactures and to foreign corn. Yet despite this insistence on diminishing returns, Malthus accorded real differentials in corn costs a lesser empirical status in accounting for international variations in the corn price than differences in the value of the precious metals. This latter cannot refer to supply conditions relating to mining, since the complaint against Smith was precisely that he focused illegitimately on the 'state of the mines': 'These causes, in reference to the main effects observed [differential corn prices] seem to be two: 1. A difference in the value of the precious metals, in different countries under different circumstances. 2. A difference in the quantity of labour and capital necessary to produce corn. The first cause undoubtedly occasions the greatest portion of that inequality in the price of corn which is the most striking and prominent, particularly in countries at a considerable distance from each other' (1820, 193).[46] This weighting is expressed thus

44 In a letter to Ricardo at this time, Malthus was troubled by one empirical detail: 'Are you not surprised at the high money price of corn in America as well as the high money price of labour, with a currency convertible into specie' (16 July 1815; in Ricardo, 1951–73, VI, 236). Ricardo replied that 'if a free trade in corn were allowed with America I should not expect that the prices would differ more, here and there, than the expences and profits of sending it, – as it is' (presumably given corn-trade restrictions) 'I am surprised the price should be so high. A high money price of wages is I think quite natural' (30 July; 241).

45 Also relevant are the letters of 1 October and 22 December, cited above, chapter 4: V.

46 Ricardo's *Note 104* and *Note 105* accord no significance to differentials in the value of the precious metals since *all* commodities are affected by nominal changes: '[104] Nothing seems to me so unimportant as this cause. The value of money cannot alter, without affecting, in the same degree, the prices of all things; and provided we have the same quantity of all commodities, and that they bear the same relative value to each other, what can it signify what the value of money is' (1951–73, II, 180). This is

in 1836: 'The two principal causes of these effects [relating to corn-price differentials] are – 1. A difference in the value of the precious metals in different countries, in whatever way such difference may have arisen. 2. A difference in the elementary cost of producing a given quantity of corn. The principal causes of the differences in the value of money in different countries has already been stated in the last section of the preceding chapter;[47] and it is certain that they occasion the greatest portion of that inequality in the price of corn which is the most striking and prominent' (185).

In both versions the passage continues with some empirical observations. The determinants of the 'value of money' – setting aside differentials in the real costs of producing corn – are said in 1820 to be the relative 'demand for corn and labour' *and the relative abundance of 'exportable commodities'*: 'More than three-fourths of the prodigious difference between the price of corn in Bengal and England is probably occasioned by the

---

somewhat unfair. Malthus was not concerned with changes in the price level as such but with relative corn-price differentials, which he explains in terms of what appears to be a Ricardian-type analysis whereby export efficiency generates differentials in purchasing power of a common international medium over non-traded commodities and labour. And in fact Ricardo did not deny the operation of this cause: '[105] I agree with Mr Malthus in these two causes of the high price of corn, but while I deem the first unimportant, I attach the greatest consequence to the second; – the abundance of the most important commodity of all others, depends upon the judicious application of labour and capital to its production – my enquiry then is, in what way can we bestow these most judiciously in order to obtain an abundant supply of this chief necessary of life? and if I find that a given quantity of capital and labour, when applied to manufactures, will procure by means of barter a greater quantity of corn from abroad, than when applied to our own land, I decide in favour of that mode of obtaining it; and on the contrary, if labour and capital can be made more productive when directly applied to our own land, I am equally strenuous that no obstacle should be opposed to such an application of it' (180–1).

My impression is that Ricardo's coolness was merely an expression of unconcern with the entire issue of international corn-price differentials, his focus being rather on efficiency or welfare questions. But again we must emphasize that he does not dispute Malthus's analysis as such. In fact, he ends his *Note 105* by remarking: 'I am happy to say that I *agree* with Mr Malthus in everything he says in the remainder of this section'. And that, we shall see, covers Malthus's judgment that it is to the first cause – 'the abundance or deficiency of exportable commodities' – that should be attributed the *main* differences in the prices of corn in different countries, especially far-distant countries, and the analysis of the effect of export efficiency on prices. (The basic outcome of Ricardian analysis can be rationalized in terms of impediments to the movement of goods and services – including the heavy transport costs involved in transporting bulky commodities, which is very probably what Malthus had in mind by emphasizing the significance of distance.) I think, therefore, that it is fair to say that Ricardo understood the analysis as a rendition of his own theme in his Chapter VII.

47 The reference is to section VII: 'On the variations in the Value of Money in the same, and different Countries' (1836, 122–35).

difference in the value of money in the two countries; and far the greater part of the high price of corn in this country, compared with most of the states in Europe, is occasioned in the same way. The main causes which affect the precious metals in different countries, are the greater or smaller demand for corn and labour,[48] and *the abundance or deficiency of exportable commodities.* With great facility of production in particular branches of industry, or, in other words, an abundance of exportable commodities, corn and labour may be maintained at a very high comparative price; and in fact it is this high price specifically, which prevents the natural advantage attached to facility of production from being in a great degree lost by domestic competition, and practically renders the industry of all those nations, where corn and labour are high, peculiarly productive in the purchase of foreign commodities' (1820, 193–4; emphasis added). The second version is briefer. There is the same reference to Bengal and England, and an additional empirical observation: 'If the profits of stock in Flanders be nearly the same as in England (which I believe is the case), and the corn wages of labour rather lower than higher, it follows necessarily that the elementary cost of producing corn is nearly the same in both countries, and that the higher money price of corn in England is occasioned by the lower value of money, and not by the increased quantity of labour and other conditions of supply required to produce corn' (1836, 186). That nothing is said here about exportables is inconsequential, for Malthus was to expand on the effect of the export sector on the value of money, as we shall presently see.

An elaboration of the effect on the relative corn price of increasing land scarcity, given in the second edition, formally identifies the value of money with the reciprocal of the money wage. This emerges in the course of analytical exercises holding the 'value of money' constant:

The second cause of the high comparative price of corn is the high elementary cost of production [1836: the greater elementary cost of its production]. If we could suppose the value of money [1836: or the money wages of standard labour] to be the same in all countries, then the cause of the higher money price of corn in one country compared with another, would be the greater quantity of capital and labour, which must be employed to produce it [1836: the greater quantity of labour, and other conditions of the supply required to produce it]; and the reason why the price of corn would be higher, and continually rising [1836: would be high and tend to rise] in countries already rich, and still advancing in prosperity and population, would be to be found in the necessity of resorting constantly to poorer land [1836: the necessity of resorting to poorer

48 This is ambiguous. It may refer to *demand* pressures specifically, that is, even with unchanged cost conditions or to higher marginal *costs* assuming a higher level of demand for corn.

land, without proportional improvements to agriculture] – to machines which would require a greater expenditure to work them – and which would consequently occasion each fresh addition to the raw produce of the country to be purchased at a greater cost – in short, if would be found in the important truth that corn, in a *progressive country*, is sold at the price necessary to yield the actual supply; and that, as this supply becomes more and more difficult, the price must rise in proportion. (1820, 194; 1836, 186)

And in the second edition a revealing sentence is added to the text: 'On the supposition which we have made of the value of money being the same in different countries, the price of corn would rise *without being followed by rise in the money price of labour*' (emphasis added). Evidently the value of money is measured by *labour commanded*, so constancy of value must imply given money wages; here corn commanded falls away as index.

When we consider the text in the *Principles* corresponding to that of 1815 (1986, *7*, 137–8; above, p. 712) critical of Smith's proposition that the low value of the precious metals – now in the sense both of a high corn price and a high money wage – is no proof of relatively great wealth, we find in 1836 as in 1820 the reference to flourishing export industries (in 1836 agricultural and not only manufacturing).[49] Focusing on a single country tells us little because of the effect of money-supply conditions – the 'abundance of the mines' (1820, 197–8; 1836, 189); but by focusing on differentials between countries it was possible to infer that the corn price would be higher in the relatively wealthy country,[50] and this because of the relatively greater efficiency of its export sector:

If we are to measure [1836: estimate] the value of the precious metals in different countries and at different periods in the same country [1836: 'And ... country' omitted], by the price of corn, as proposed by [Adam Smith] himself [1836: by the measure which has has himself proposed], it appears to me that whether we consider the first or second cause which has been referred to in this section, there are few more certain signs of wealth than the high average price of raw produce. With the value of money uniform with respect to cost [1836: If

49 See also below, pp. 724–5, regarding the American export sector, which is specifically agriculture; and *The Measure of Value*: 'Generally the value of money is the lowest in the richest and most manufacturing countries; but this is not always the case; and a country which raises an abundance of raw produce at a small expense of labour and profits, while its money value is kept up by a ready sale for it in foreign markets, and a continued demand for labour, may have the value of its money very low, although it is not rich or manufacturing. This is the case with the United States of America ...' (1823b/1986, *7*, 203).

50 In 1820, this reads: 'taken relatively, or in comparison with the state of other countries, much may be inferred from it.' In 1836 this is modified: 'but taken relatively to other commodities and in comparison with the state of other countries at no great difference, and connected with each other, much may be inferred from it.'

the value of money were the same in all countries], then, independently of importation and improvements in agriculture, the wealth and population of a country would be proportioned to the high price of their corn [1836: the wealth and population of similar countries, though not the conditions of the labouring classes, would be proportioned to the high price of their corn]. And in the actual state of things, with great differences in the value of money, it may generally be presumed that those countries, which have the greatest abundance of exportable commodities, are either rich, or in the way rapidly to become rich. [1836: And in the actual state of things, with great differences in the value of money, arising from the incidental causes above noticed, as those countries not possessed of mines where the money prices of corn and labour are high must have had very flourishing manufactures, or an abundance of raw products fitted for exportation, such countries will generally be found either rich, or in the way rapidly to become rich.]

At this point, we find repeated in 1820 alone that note of 1815 (above, p. 713) specifically denying 'the doctrine of the *level* of the precious metals.' Why this note is absent from the 1836 version is unclear since the 'doctrine of the *level* of the precious metals' is rejected (and repeatedly so) in that edition.

* * *

The notion that money value is not 'on a level' emerges also in the course of an attempt in 1820 – absent in 1836 – to undermine Ricardo's gold measure of labour input, on the grounds that the precious metals themselves are subject to variations independently of their labour input. Malthus here refers to the role of the metals in foreign commerce: 'It would unquestionably answer to some countries possessing peculiar advantages in their exportable commodities, to buy their gold and silver abroad rather than procure them at home ... But if they could be imported by some countries from abroad with less labour than they could be obtained at home, it would answer to other countries to export them in exchange for commodities, which they either could not produce on their own soil, or could obtain cheaper elsewhere. And thus, in reference to the relative value of commodities both in different countries at the same period, and in the same country at different periods, it is obvious that *the prices in money might be subject to considerable variations, without being accompanied by any proportionate variations in the quantities of labour which they had cost*' (1820, 112–13; emphasis added).

This formulation is based on the unlikely assumption that *each* trading nation possesses mines requiring *given* labour input without capital; in a more realistic case, the first assumption would have to go, and an allowance for capital would be required. But even setting aside the effect of new mining discoveries, a variety of other sources of variation in the value of money precluded it from serving as an accurate measure 'in different countries and at different times, [of] the quantities of labour which commodities had cost' (114). For although 'the uniform fertility of the mines would not essentially alter the proportions in which the precious metals would be distributed to different countries,' yet 'the great differences, which are now known to take place in their value in different places, when compared with corn and labour, would probably continue nearly the same.' If this statement applies (as it probably does) to states of international equilibrium – *it would amply confirm that the value of money (purchasing power over corn and labour) is not 'on a level.'*

For Malthus's present purposes, this was not the main issue; rather, the differential in labour commanded (*Malthusian value*) indicated a differential in labour embodied (*Ricardian value*), corrected by a rough allowance for profits: 'According to all the accounts we have received of prices in Bengal, a given quantity of silver will there represent or command six or eight times more labour and provisions than in England. In all parts of the world articles of equal money prices exchange for each other. It will consequently happen that, in the commerce carried on between the two countries, the product of a day's English labour must exchange for the product of five or six days of Indian labour, after making a sufficient allowance for the difference of profits.'[51] This empirically based case is supplemented by a theoretical point: 'But if we are not fully satisfied with this kind of reference to experience, it is obvious that the same conclusion follows inevitably from theory. In those countries where the precious metals are necessarily purchased, no plausible reason can be assigned why the quantity of them should be in proportion to the difficulty of producing the articles with which they are purchased. When the English and Indian muslins appear in the German markets, their relative prices will be determined solely by their relative qualities, without the slightest reference to the very different quantities of human labour which they may have cost; and the circumstances that in the fabrication of the Indian muslins five or

51 Malthus denies that the high relative value of silver in India (low money prices of corn and low money wages) reflected a lag in the effect of the American discoveries relative to Europe – any initial differential effect attributable to 'incomplete communication' was by now 'at an end.'

Other examples – Russia, Poland, Germany, France, Flanders – also indicated differentials between countries in the purchasing power of silver over corn and labour. Since all countries were equally affected by the American discoveries, these *differentials* indicated – Malthus implicitly adjusts for the difference between labour commanded and labour embodied – 'how little dependence could be placed on a coincidence in different countries between the money prices of commodities and the quantities of labour which they had cost, even on the supposition that money was always obtained from the mines in America by the same quantity of labour and capital' (115). In brief, taking account of international trade, even ruling out variations in factor productivity in metal production did not assure that money prices reflected labour embodiment.

six times more labour has been employed than in the English, will not enable them to command greater returns of money to India' (115–16). In brief, the same money (metal) will be received by English and Indian cloth exporters to Germany per unit, independently of labour input.[52] Here Malthus seems to allow that a labour theory does work well enough *internally*; it breaks down in *international* exchange: 'And therefore, although the actual currency of an individual country, other circumstances being nearly equal, may be distributed among the different commodities bought and sold, according to the quantity of labour which they have severally cost, the supposition that the same sort of distribution would take place in different countries, involves a contradiction of the first principles of commercial intercourse' (116–17).[53]

Now the bulk of Ricardo's chapter VII, on international values, is concerned with *differentials* in money value internationally in the sense of differential purchasing power over corn and labour (supposedly 'home' commodities). Did Malthus not realize this? Yet the entire section at hand is directed *against Ricardo* as if the proposition was not central to the latter's position. This is Ricardo's reaction in his *Note 37*:

> I most distinctly admit that gold and silver may be of very different values in different countries, particularly if their value be measured by the quantity of corn and labour which they will command. I have indeed endeavored to shew [1951–73, I, 145] that this difference is owing to three causes; first, the expence attending the purchase of gold and silver, with bulky commodities, on account of the expence attending their conveyance to the markets where gold and silver are sold. Secondly, on account of the distance of the voyage which will still further enhance these expence. Thirdly the different rates of profit in different countries, owing to the unequal accumulations of capitals in proportion to the fertility of the land. If labour were much higher in Yorkshire, than in Gloucestershire, profits would be lower, and capital would by degrees be removed from the former to the latter place; so that each district would have that portion of the general capital which it could most beneficially employ; – not so between independent countries. Capital does not move from England to Poland, merely because labour is cheaper there; and for this reason, gold will be low in value compared with labour in one place, high in another. (1951–73, II, 86–7)[54]

52 Or rather, the money price paid in Germany for foreign cloth will reflect the *cheaper* source, for 'it is indeed universally allowed, that the power of purchasing foreign commodities of all kinds depends upon the relative cheapness, not the relative dearness, of the articles that can be exported.'

53 A note is attached at this point specifically on Ricardo: 'Mr Ricardo very justly states that, even on the supposition which he has made respecting the precious metals, the foreign interchange of commodities is not determined by the quantity of labour which they have relatively cost.' This alludes to Ricardo's analysis of comparative advantage.

54 Apart from this area of agreement, Malthus's exposition was faulty. For one thing, it

Sometime after 1820 Malthus removed the critique of Ricardo, while retaining the position shared with Ricardo, that the value of the precious metal does *not* tend to a common level. In fact, the second edition describes Ricardo's analysis of the distribution of the precious metals in the chapter on Foreign Trade as 'not only new, but unquestionably true, and of the highest importance' (see above, p. 679).[55]

* * *

For the substantive analysis of the distribution of the precious metals in the second edition we turn first to the section in Malthus's chapter II, 'Of the Labour which a Commodity will Command' (1820, section VI; 1836, section V), specifically to added material dealing with variations in money wages over time and with geographical differentials in money wages, designed to demonstrate the temporal and spatial variablility in the value of money.[56] Our concern now is with the geographic differential.[57]

---

identified 'labour' across countries, whereas correction for differential efficiency was required: 'I do not however agree with Mr Malthus' calculation in comparing a day's labour of one country, with a day's labour of another, we must take into consideration the different quantities of labour, which may be comprised under the general term of a day's labour. Mr Malthus has dwelt much on the disinclination to work, and on the indolence of labourers, in countries where food is obtained with the utmost facility, he surely then will not compare a day's work of a South American or of a Hindoo, with the day's work of an Englishman, or a Frenchman' (87). Furthermore, did 'Malthus really believe that there is five or six times *more labour* employed on Indian Muslins than on English? ... he surely does not reckon the labour bestowed on machines, such as steam Engines etc., on coals &c. &c.: Does not the labour on these constitute a part of the labour bestowed on the muslins?'

55 There is in the *Principles* at least one other specific reference to the doctrine in question: 'A fall in the value of money cannot ... be peculiar to one country without the posession of peculiar advantages in exportation ...' (1820, 172; 1836, 168).

56 On the details of the major replacement of text, see Pullen, in Malthus, 1820/1989, II, 94.

57 As for temporal variations, Malthus considers the five- or sixfold increase in money wages since the time of Edward III, remarking on this that 'no person I conceive imagines that the *value* of labour [presumably corn commanded, or even general purchasing power] has so risen' (1836, 100). Rather, 'we all know very well that the value of money has fallen.' He proceeds, assuming the 'character of labour to be unchanged' (touching here in effect on Ricardo's criticism in *Note 37*), to assert that this fall was accurately measured by the labour commanded by silver: 'if the labour has remained unchanged in its character, the conditions of the supply of a given quantity of silver, the elementary costs of its production, the average state of its supply as compared with the demand, or its power of purchasing at these different periods arising from intrinsic causes, will be exactly represented by the quantity of labour which the given quantity of silver will command at each period' (100–1). This formulation may seem circular, unless we understand the statement 'we all know ... that the value of money has fallen,' to refer to higher corn prices or even high prices' generally. (He does after all also refer to the metal's 'power of purchasing.') This fall in purchasing power is said to be accurately measured by the fall in labour commanded, that is, the rise in money wages.

As in 1820, a first principle is that 'money prices regulate the rate at which all actual exchanges are made' (1836, 101).[58] But 'the products of the same quantities of labour' – 'labour of the same character,' Malthus adds in the manner of Ricardo's qualification in *Note 37* – 'will, under different circumstances exchange for very different quantities of money.' And such a difference 'arises from the difference in the value of money, and not from the difference in the value of labour.' For the supply of money (and thus its value) in countries without mines is obtained *via* commodity exports, and export conditions may differ widely, though labour as such (in terms of energy and even skill) may be identical: 'Metallic money in all countries which have no mines of the precious metals, is only to be obtained by exportable commodities; and the soil, situation, and habits of some countries may occasion a comparatively scanty production of exports, although their labourers work with as much energy, and sometimes in regard to domestic commodities with as much skill, as the great mass of the labourers of those countries, where exportable commodities abound.'[59]

An amplification refers to Chinese labour as being no less 'effective' than British – at least, independent of machinery: 'From all the accounts we have of the Chinese settlers in different parts of the East, it appears that the labouring classes in China, are remarkable for their industry and energy, and even for their skill in making those domestic articles where superior machinery is not required. We cannot therefore justly say that Chinese labour, independent of machinery, or other particular advantages is not as effective as our own' (102). But Chinese *money* wages were notoriously low, which fact was attributable to the relatively insignificant export

58 See also: 'a Chinese commodity carried to Hamburgh would be sold at its China money price, with the addition of the freight, insurance, profits, &c. of the last voyage; and an English merchant purchasing Hamburgh and Chinese goods, would unquestionably estimate their relative values by their cost in money, without the least reference to the very different quantities of labour which had been employed in obtaining them; ... It is most justly observed by Adam Smith, that the merchant, in all his transactions, has only to consider money prices' (103; cf. 110).

59 Assuming two countries which do possess mines, the 'value in exchange' of the metals – identified here with their 'purchasing power' – would vary with differential fertility (or the differential use of 'machinery') in mining, the *more* fertile (or more progressive) the mine, the greater the metal supply relative to demand, with consequentally a higher level of money prices and higher money wages. And 'we should not hesitiate in saying that the difference in prices so occasioned, was owing to the difference in the value of money, not in the value of the labour' (101).

Malthus assumes here that 'the same quantity of labour of the same character' works the two mines; that is, 'the same sacrifice of physical force, supposing the profits and other circumstances in both countries to have been the same, had probably produced in one country double the quantity of silver which it had produced in the other' (101–2). This is difficult to appreciate – a greater fertility or technology implies *less* labour per unit or less sacrifice of physical force.

potential – relative to population and territory – constraining the source of money-supply inflows and thus assuring a relatively *high* value of money. Despite the American discoveries, Chinese prices had risen relatively little: 'Yet we well know that the money price of labour is extremely low in China, and this is obviously owing to the small amount of exports compared with the population, and the prodigious extent of territory, including a large part of Tartary, over which the precious metals which are imported into China will be necessarily spread, so as to throw the greatest imaginable obstacles in the way of a fall in their value; the consequence of which naturally is, that they have fallen comparatively but little in value since the discovery of the American mines ...'[60] The main conclusion is that 'under these circumstances it would surely be most preposterous to measure the value of Chinese labour in China by money' – which is variable in its value or purchasing power – 'instead of measuring the money by the labour' (102–3).[61] The latter, we are given to understand, is *constant* in its own value – assuming it is uniform in 'efficiency.' By this Malthus cannot have intended that labour's purchasing power over money (or corn or goods) is invariable; the 'value' of labour must here be understood in the sense of effort or energy expended. That at least seems to be where we end up.

Various examples are given of the supposed constancy of the value of 'labour.' The Dutch labourer was 'as strong, and works for the same number of hours in the day as the English labourer' (104). In agriculture he was 'peculiarly skilful,' and in many manufactures 'excelled' compared with his counterpart elsewhere in Europe. Here we see the notion of labour as involving energy, effort, and 'skill.' But despite the identity in

60 A further consequence is that 'the elementary cost of producing a pound of silver, the quantity of Chinese labour, profits, rent, &c. which must be worked up in the commodities exported to purchase it, are very much greater than in Europe.' This sequence is not crystal clear, but possibly the point is that, since Chinese *prices* are low, more is required in terms of *commodity* sales to acquire a given amount of silver. (The problem with this exposition is the fact that a reason for low Chinese prices is the relative unproductiveness or insignificance of the export sector.)

61 Malthus insists that, when the 'value of money' is spoken of, it relates to a particular economy and the labour of *that* economy: 'What alone can be correctly meant by the value of money, or of any other commodity *in China* is, the estimation in which such money is held in China, determined at all times by the state of the supply compared with the demand, and ordinarily by the elementary costs of its production in China, or what comes to the same thing, the value of money in China, is its power of purchasing in China, arising from intrinsic causes. And as it is obvious, that the quantity of Chinese labour which a pound of silver will command, must measure its power of purchasing in China, arising from intrinsic causes; it follows, that the value of money or of any other commodity in China, is measured by the quantity of Chinese labour which a given portion of it will command' (103–4). It will be noted that (Chinese) labour is the measure of the value of money (in China), the latter indentified with its power of purchasing in China' – an allusion to commodities in general (not just corn).

these respects of British and Dutch labour, British money wages were higher than Dutch, which could imply only a lower value of *money* in Britain, *ascribable to the effectiveness of British export industries*: 'Is this owing to the lower value of *labour* in the Netherlands, or the higher value of *money*? To the latter most assuredly; and the cause of it unquestionably is, that though the great mass of the labourers in the Netherlands may work with as much energy and skill as the great mass of English labourers; yet a certain proportion of the latter, assisted by superior machinery, more abundant capitals and cheaper fuel, are able to produce a large quantity of exportable manufactures at a lower money price than they can be produced in the Netherlands; which, together with some superiority in colonial products, enables England to maintain her exchanges, although she pays a higher money price for her labour, the difference in profits being inconsiderable' (104–5).[62]

Another illustration of the general theme is drawn from the United States case involving relatively high corn wages and money wages compared with England. The superiority in corn wages resided in 'the lower value of the corn, and not in the higher value of the labour' (106). The main issue, though, is the fact of money-wage differentials despite the identity of American and British labourers: 'But the American labourer is also paid higher in bullion, in the currency of the commercial world; and how comes it that bullion should be obtained with more facility in the United States than in England, when it is well known that the English labourer works for as many hours in the day, with as much strength, and with at least as much skill as the American labourer?' Again the explanation runs in terms of the high effectiveness of the American export sector, in this case the relative efficiency of agriculture (a variety of 'raw products' in addition to corn):

62 That the Corn Laws could account for most of the differential in British money prices – corn prices and general prices – and money wages over Continental price is denied, although it is allowed that repeal would lower money wages and 'the general scale of English prices.' The point is that it was the efficiency of the *export* industries that was the primary factor; without such advantages even the Corn Laws could not keep up British money prices: 'no possible corn laws could prevent the prices of our corn and labour from falling to the level of the rest of Europe, if we possessed no natural or artificial advantages in regard to our exportable commodities. Supposing the price of English common labour to be twenty-pence or two shillings, and of continental labour fourteen or sixteen-pence, each bearing the same relation in each country to manufacturing labour, with no more difference of profits than at present prevails, it is quite obvious, that without some peculiar advantages to balance the price of our labour, we could not *possibly* maintain our exchanges, and could not, in fact, export a single yard of cloth or calico, till the exchanges had continued against us a sufficient time to raise the value of money and lower the money prices of labour and corn to the level of the principal countries with which we were connected in commerce' (105).

> The lower value of money in England compared with the value of money in most of the states of Europe, has appeared to arise principally from the cheapness of our exportable manufactures, derived from our superior machinery, skill, and capital. The still lower value of money in the United States is occasioned by the cheapness and abundance of her raw products derived from the advantages of her soil, climate, and situation. Notwithstanding the scarcity of labour in the United States, it would be obviously impossible for the country to maintain the money price which she actually pays for her labour, if, in spite of such price, she were not able from her situation, and the state of her soil, to produce raw cotton, tobacco, corn, timber, &c. in large quantities at a lower money price than most of her competitors in the European markets. The state of the demand in these markets for corn, tends to raise the price of the American corn, which is exported towards the level of the money prices in Europe. The price of the American corn which is exported naturally raises the money price of American corn in general; and the very great demand for labour in America compared with corn, by awarding to the labourer a large quantity of it, necessarily makes the money wages of labour high; while the abundant exports of other raw products obtained with great facility, afford the means of maintaining the exchanges under so high a bullion price of labour.
>
> As a matter of unquestionable fact, the elementary cost of obtaining a pound of silver in the United States is less than in any country of Europe. A much smaller quantity of labour, of a character and quality hardly equal to that of England, is employed, with other outgoings estimated in the same kind of labour, to produce the articles which purchase it; and neither the difference in profits, nor the difference in the price of labour, is such as to counterbalance this facility of production, and prevent the abundance of exports. (106–7)

It is at first sight amazing to read of the 'scarcity of labour in the United States' or of 'the very great demand for labour in America compared with corn' assuring 'the labourer a large quantity of it,' in a general context designed *to prove that the value of American and British labour is uniform.* (Fortunately, Ricardo was already in the grave; for had he read this literally it surely would have killed him.) But it emerges once again that by the constant value of labour – or rather its international uniformity – Malthus refers to uniformity of *effort*, not of price in some sense: 'Unquestionably the American labourer is richer, and much better off than the English labourer. He obtains the command of a quantity of food more than sufficient to maintain the largest family; and from the high bullion price of his labour, he can afford in general to purchase a fair quantity both of home and foreign manufactured goods. But he evidently does not purchase what he obtains by a greater sacrifice than the English labourer. He does not give more for what he receives, but receives more for what he gives; and unless we mean to make *quantity* of products the measure of value which would lead us into the most absurd and inextricable difficulties, we must measure the value of what the labourer receives in the United

States by the labour which he gives for it. We must make the proper distinction between value and riches, and say that he is rich, not because he possesses a greater value to give in exchange for what he wants, but because what he wants, or the main articles which constitute his riches, are obtained with much more facility, and are really more abundant and cheaper than they are in Europe' (107–8).

The argument ends with a summary statement confirming, first, that where labour is identical across nations with respect to effort and duration, it serves as measure of value internationally; and, second, that though the value of money (or commodities) *differs* across nations, still the labour commanded by money (or by commodities) in each country measures its 'power of purchasing' – in a qualified sense – in that country: 'In those numerous cases, therefore, where the great mass of the day labour of different countries is of the same character in regard to physical strength and duration, such labour must be a measure of value exactly of the same kind as the labour of the same country at different periods. And while we avoid the gross error of confounding the value of money, or of any other commodity in another country, or in the general market of Europe, it will appear that the labour of each country for which any commodity will exchange, must measure its exchangeable value in that country, or its power of purchasing in that country arising from intrinsic causes' (108).[63]

In an addition appearing in the 1836 version of the chapter on Wages, Malthus specifies the determinants of the money-wage rate as the cost of obtaining the precious metals *and* the state of effectual demand for labour. As for the first: 'If the society can purchase a given quantity of money by commodites which require a smaller sacrifice of labour, profits, &c. to obtain them than is necessary to purchase or obtain the labour for which that money has before been usually exchanged, the money price of labour will rise. If either from the scarcity of money, or the plenty of labour, a *greater* sacrifice must be made to obtain the given quantity of money, the money price of labour will fall' (1836, 218). The first determinant had been considered earlier in Malthus's chapter II, section V, as we have seen (pp. 721f.). If the difficulty of obtaining money falls – either because of improvements to mining or easier exportation – the value of money falls; that is, the money wage rises. But now Malthus adds a further matter by his reference to 'plenty of labour' which he amplifies in a footnote: 'It must

63 Here and elsewhere, there is a qualification relating to a measure of purchasing power 'arising from intrinsic causes.' For the sense of the latter, see chapter 7: V.

The next issue raised is 'whether in different countries at the same period, where it is known that the character of the labour is essentially different [with respect to strength, skill, and duration], and in the same country at different periods, when it may be supposed that the character of the labour has changed, the proposed measure may still be considered as correct.' Here Malthus seems to deal with Ricardo's criticism in *Note 37* (see above, note 57).

always be recollected, that a plenty of labour, if that labour be employed, always tends to increase the competition for money, and raise its value.' The plenty of labour had not been referred to in section V as a determinant of the money wage.[64]

* * *

We turn next to the material specifically devoted in the 1836 version to 'Variations in the Value of Money in the Same, and different countries' (1836, 122–35; see above, note 47). Much of the substantive material of this section is identical with that in *The Measure of Value* (1823). We shall keep in mind both versions.

Malthus's discussion in the *Principles* of variations in the value of real-world money[65] distinguishes between two broad sets of causes for a secular tendency for the 'value of money' to decline, referring either to increase of corn prices and money wages with roughly constant manufacturing prices, or to increase of *all* prices. The former – a 'necessary tendency' – alludes to the general growth process; the second to 'incidental' monetary forces, including those engendered by the state of efficiency of the export sector. The following features will be noted regarding the growth process: (1) A decline in the profit rate with agricultural expansion; since prices are not in question at this first stage, there is implicit here further evidence of Malthus's corn-model reasoning. (2) An increase in the prices of agricultural produce, including corn (and of labour), reflecting diminishing agricultural returns. And (3) the presumed fall of profits countering higher material costs in *manufacturing*, though differentially depending on the capital structure of each of the industries compared with that of *money* (real-world money which requires a process utilizing capital). The argument implies that the metals are produced domestically:

With a view to distinguish the necessary tendency to a fall in the value of money occasioned by the accumulation of capital, the progress of cultivation, and the

64 The second determinant involves the real wage, and there labour-supply conditions are evidently pertinent following Smithian lines: 'And whatever may be the state of the effectual demand for labour, it is obvious that the money price of labour must, on an average, be so proportioned to the price of the funds for its maintenance, as to effectuate the desired supply. It is as the condition of the supply, that the prices of the necessaries of life have so important an influence on the price of labour. A certain portion of these necessaries is required to enable the labourer to maintain a stationary population, a greater portion to maintain an increasing one; and consequently, whatever may be the prices of the necessaries of life, the money wages of the labourer must be such as to enable him to purchase these portions, or the supply cannot take place in the quantity required.'

65 We set aside a preliminary discussion of the requirements for an *ideal* commodity measure of value, and turn to the variations in the value of *real world* money, though this is rather disconcerting, given a preliminary warning of the danger of using the same term – *gold* prices – in two senses, ideal and actual (1836, 124–5).

fall of profits, from the incidental fall occasioned by the varying fertility of the mines, and the possession of an abundance of exportable commodities, it might be useful to distinguish the differences in the value of money into two kinds: first, that which is occasioned by the high or low rate of profit, arising from the progress of capital and cultivation, and which may be denominated the necessary cause of the high or low value of money ...

The marks which distinguish a fall in the value of the precious metals, arising from what has been called the necessary cause, are, a rise in the money prices of corn, raw produce, and labour, without a general rise in the prices of wrought commodities. All of them, indeed, so far as they are composed of raw products, will have a tendency to rise; but in a large class of commodities, this tendency to rise will be much more than counterbalanced by the effect of the fall of profits. Some, therefore, will rise and some will fall according to the nature of the capitals employed upon them, compared with those which produce money; and while the money prices of corn and labour very decidedly increase, the prices of wrought commodities taken on an average, might possibly remain not far from the same. (1836, 126)

The corresponding text of 1823 is somewhat stricter since it is prefaced by the remark that the inquiry would relate to 'the causes which affect the value of the precious metals *as compared with labour*' (1823a/1986, 211; emphasis added).[66] But the substance is the same:

These causes are of two kinds: – first, those which occasion a high or low rate of profits, which, as connected with the progressive cultivation of poorer land, and operating universally and necessarily on the precious metals in common with all other commodities, and raising or lowering them with regard to labour, may be denominated the primary and necessary cause of the high or low value of metallic money ... The marks which distinguish a fall in the value of the precious metals, arising from the primary cause, are, – a rise in the money price of raw produce and labour, without a general rise in the price of wrought commodities. All of them, indeed, as far as they are composed of raw produce, will have a

66 This is a major theme of the pamphlet. International exchange rates, unlike domestic exchange rates, are not determined solely by relative labour input with the addition of profits. Rather, 'we know, from experience, that the commodities of different countries are actually exchanged ... according to their money prices at the time,' these money prices necessarily reflecting 'the different value of the precious metals in different countries,' which in turn are 'proportioned to the differences in the money prices of agricultural labour,' that is, to labour commanded (190). Here we find one of the clearest statements of the determinants of differentials in the value of money entailing export efficiency: 'The prodigious difference in the natural prices of two commodities in England and India, the natural values of which in each country were nearly the same, could only arise from a difference in the value of money occasioned by the very superior efficiency of English labour in the purchase of the precious metals, owing to the energy, skill, and situation of English labourers and capitalists, compared with those of India' (191).

tendency to rise; but, in a large class of commodities, this tendency to rise will be more than counterbalanced by the effect of the fall of profits. – Some therefore will rise, and some will fall, as I stated in my last work [1820, 91f.], according to the nature of the capitals employed upon them, compared with those which produce money; and while the money prices of corn and labour very decidedly increase, the prices of commodities, taken on the average, may possibly remain not far from the same. (211–12)

When it comes to the 'incidental' causes acting on the value of money, the assumption of domestic mining is silently dropped. In the event of causes 'occasioned by the varying fertility of the mines, the skill with which they are worked, the difficulty or facility of communication with them, and the deficiency or abundance of exportable commodities'[67] – *all* prices will rise more or less in proportion: 'On the other hand, when the value of money falls from the incidental causes above noticed, without a fall of profits, there will be a tendency to a proportionate rise of all commodities, as well as corn and labour, though in some cases it may take a considerable time before the proportionate rise of all objects are [*sic*] completed. This was remarked, at the time of the influx of the precious metals, from the discovery of the American mines, and also on the issue of an abundant paper currency, during the war which terminated in 1815' (1836, 127).[68] It is allowed that 'these two different kinds of causes will sometimes act in conjunction, and sometimes in opposition, and [1823b: so that] it may not always be easy to distinguish their separate effects; but as these effects have really a different origin, it is important [1823b: desirable] to keep them as separate as we can' (1823b/1986, 7, 212; 1836, 127).

The rough rule is posited that 'wherever a fall in the value of money takes place, without a fall in the rate of profits, an event which is generally open to observation, it is to be attributed to the incidental causes affecting the relations of money and labour, and not to that which is connected with the accumulation of capital, and the necessity of taking poorer land into cultivation, without improvements in agriculture' (1836, 127).[69] The

67 The 1823 version has a further instance of the 'secondary' and incidental category: 'And secondly, those which depend on the fertility and vicinity of the mines; the different efficiency of labour in different countries; the abundance or scarcity of exportable commodities and the state of the demand and supply of commodities and labour compared with money; which may be denominated the secondary and incidental causes of the high or low value of metallic money' (212).

68 Cf. 1823: 'On the other hand, when the value of metallic money falls, from the secondary causes above noticed, there will be a tendency to a proportionate rise of all commodities as well as of corn and labour, though in some cases it may take a considerable time before it is completely effected' (212).

69 The reference to 'incidental causes affecting the relations of money and labour' should not be read to imply that 'permanent' causes do *not* affect the money wage. They may well do, as was specified in 1836, 126 (above, p. 728).

'incidental' causes acting on the value of money are said to be 'much more powerful and prominant than those which take place in the progress of society, from the fall of profits.'[70] Similarly in 1823, most differentials in metal values between countries are said to reflect the so-called secondary causes: 'Of these two classes of causes the second produces much the greatest part of those differences in the value of metallic money, which are the most observable in different countries, and at different periods in the same country. If India and England had each of them mines of equal natural fertility, the superior efficiency of English labour, assisted by machinery, would extract a much greater quantity of metal from such mines; and the money price of labour might be three or four times higher, and the value of money three or four times lower in England than in India' (1823b/1986, 7, 212–13). As for differential export efficiencies, 'if [England] can prepare exportable commodities which are in demand abroad, with much less labour than other nations, she will be able to buy gold at a much lower natural value, and will continue to import it under favourable exchanges, till its value falls in proportion' (213). There is also the effect of variations in demand for corn, acting via an induced increase both in velocity of circulation and in credit, allowing money prices (including money wages) to rise even without increased gold importation. Again, Malthus maintains that the 'primary' cause is often swamped: 'The state of bullion prices in most of the countries of the commercial world make it evident, that the efficiency of labour, and the abundance of exportable commodities, are much more powerful in lowering the value of bullion in the countries where they prevail, than high profits in raising it; and the same appears to be true, in reference to an increased demand for corn and labour.'

The end result of all this is that the high ruling level of British corn prices and money wages reflected not so much the Corn Laws – though these had some effect (see also above, note 62) – but rather the efficiency of British manufacturing. Expressed alternatively, relatively high British corn prices did not indicate 'a high value of corn' but rather a low value of money: 'If this doctrine be true, and I most firmly believe it is, it appears that a rise in the money price of corn and labour is a necessary consequence of commercial prosperity; and though I would distinctly allow, that in reference to our own country at present the corn laws keep

The 1823 version reads: 'And, in general, whenever a fall in the value of money takes place, without a fall in the rate of profits, an event which is generally open to observation, it is to be attributed to incidental and secondary causes affecting the relations of money to labour, and not to that which is connected with the taking of poorer land into cultivating' (212).

70 This formulation is misleading. For a fall in the profit rate acts to *constrain* any rise in manufacturing prices, thereby dampening the overall impact of higher corn and raw material prices and higher money wages.

the prices of corn and labour higher than they would be, if things were left to take their natural course: yet still it is unquestionable, that the actual prices of corn and labour indicate a low value of money, and not a high value of corn, and that they operate in a totally different way from taxes on the labouring classes' (1836, 130). A subsequent empirical observation regarding current English and European conditions again places responsibility for the relatively high English corn price on 'a higher scale of money prices, or lower value of money,' reflected in a higher money wage – allowance made for price reductions in sectors subject to improved technology (including here the export sector): 'It is certainly true that the money wages of independent labour, notwithstanding their fall of late years, are higher in this country than in any other country in Europe, and there is every reason to believe that the English labourer with his money earnings can purchase as great a quantity of wheat as any European labourer of the same description. If this be so, it is a distinct proof that the higher price of corn in this country, as compared with the continent, is not at present owing to a greater difficulty of obtaining it, but to a higher scale of money prices, or lower value of money, which operates upon *all* commodities, though it is more than counterbalanced in that class of commodities where skill and superior machinery have most prevailed, and it is of these that our principal exports will naturally consist' (130–1).

We are back at the rule for distinguishing between categories of variation in the value of money – that relating to growth and that relating to monetary forces. The rule given earlier had turned on the behaviour of the *profit rate* (see above, p. 729) – should it be unchanged we cannot attribute a fall in the value of money to the growth process. Now the rule is extended to the behaviour of the *corn wage,* an apparent allusion to the expectation that, in the process of growth, the corn wage as well as the profit rate tends to decline.

* * *

There remains to note further material on the distribution of the precious metals. In evidence before the Select Committee on Artisans and Machinery, Malthus alluded to 'the difference in the value of money in each country, arising from the scarcity or abundance of exportable commodities, or the means of purchasing the precious metals with more or less labour' (House of Commons, Parliamentary Papers, 1824, V, 600). The review of Tooke's *High and Low Prices* refers to the role of the export industries in *maintaining* a high level of prices (or a low bullion value) during the 1793–1813 period; the general rise of prices reflecting wartime corn-import restrictions in the face of higher demand for corn from a growing population 'would be supported by the abundance and value of the exports' (1823a/1986, 7, 234). The theorem also contributed to define the 'limits' to the extent bullion prices can rise before the emergence of a deviation between paper and gold: 'The specific limit to them seems to be the turn of the exchange, and the impossibility of a country's maintaining its exports under an advance in the bullion price of labour, beyond what was balanced by peculiar skill and machinery, or the peculiar raw products which might be sold abroad at advanced bullion prices with little diminution of quantity' (251). An added note to the chapter 'Restrictions upon Importation' in the sixth (1826) edition of the *Essay on Population* expresses unconcern with the effect of protection on corn prices and money wages, since high manufacturing (export) productivity allows and assures a relatively high price level in international monetary equilibrium: 'No restrictions upon the importation of grain, however absurdly severe, could permanently maintain our corn and labour at a much higher price than in the rest of Europe, if such restrictions were essentially to interfere with the prosperity of our foreign commerce. When the money price of labour is high in any country, or, what is the same thing, when the value of money is low, nothing can prevent it from going out to find its level, but some comparative advantages, either natural or acquired, which enable such country to maintain the abundance of its exports, notwithstanding the high money price of its labour' (1986, *3*, 430n).[71] The doctrine emerges also in a letter to Thomas Chalmers of 1832: 'It is owing to the abundance of her exports, derived from her skill machinery and capital, that money rents and the money prices of corn and labour are high, and that with a small quantity of English labour a large quantity of the products of foreign labour is purchased' (Thomas Chalmers Collection, CHA4.185.32).

VII SOME EMPIRICAL OBSERVATIONS

Malthus, as we know, defined the change in the value of money by reference to the money wage. This is emphasized as a prelude to some important empirical observations in the second edition of the *Principles*: 'In all cases it is of the greatest use and importance to distinguish between a rise or fall in the value of money, and a rise or fall in the values of other commodities. As long as the varying prices of other commodities do not affect the money price of the standard labour in any country, we may consider the value of money as remaining the same, and attribute the relative variations between money and commodities to causes exclusively affecting the commodities, such as the cheapness of products arising from the improvements in machinery, or their dearness from an increased elementary cost of production' (1836, 131). If, however, 'the money price of the standard labour rises generally, it is a sign that the elementary cost of obtaining money has fallen, and that a smaller sum of labour, profits, rent, and taxes, is given to obtain a certain quantity of it'; and conversely in the case of a general fall in the money wage. That 'these effects ...

71 This argument had been made in the *Principles* (above, note 62).

frequently are produced by causes operating in the first instance on commodities' is illustrated by war and postwar experience. Unfortunately, the account is not plain-sailing.

The period 1795–1813 was characterized by rising corn prices and, in consequence, rising money wages: 'The raised price of corn, commencing with the year 1795, and continuing, with but few exceptions, till 1813, occasioned necessarily a rise in the money price of labour. Without such a rise, the conditions of the supply of the quantity of labour demanded would not have been fulfilled' (131–2). The peculiar efficiency of British manufactures permitted the maintenance of the relatively high British level of money wages with no exchange deterioration: 'The great relative superiority of our manufacturing industry at that time over the rest of Europe enabled us to maintain our exchanges under such a high money price of labour' (132). This high money wage *proved* the fact of a low 'elementary cost' of obtaining gold: 'While this high price continued in the standard labour of the country, with a price of manufacturing labour generally proportioned to it, it is hardly possible to deny that the elementary cost of obtaining bullion in this country was diminished, whatever might be the case in other countries, or whatever might be the costs of producing bullion at the mouths of the mines from which it was obtained. The fact that the quantity of manufactures which would purchase an ounce of gold would, under the circumstances supposed, purchase a smaller quantity of standard labour than usual, proves at once the fact, that the elements in the cost of obtaining gold in England, consisting of labour, profits, rents and taxes, were, taken altogether, less in value than before, or, in other words, that the elementary cost of obtaining gold in England had diminished.'

An account of the war that emphasizes constancy of the exchange rate seems strange, though less so if we bear in mind that the period extends beyond 1811. Also troublesome is the apparent representation of manufacturing prices as constant despite the rise in the corn-price and money-wage rate; for manufacturing prices are said to have been low enough, considering their peculiar efficiency, to 'maintain our exchanges.' We are in that case *not dealing with an account of general inflation,* although from Malthus's Bullionist perspective the war years had been invariably considered as such.

By contrast, the postwar period entailed a higher 'cost of obtaining gold.' This period did not experience a deterioration of industrial efficiency; efficiency had been maintained, but manufacturing prices had collapsed *below* cost. Here Malthus represents the higher cost of obtaining gold simply as a reflection of this fall in manufacturing prices or deterioration in the manufacturing terms of trade against gold: 'On the same principle it follows, that the cost of obtaining gold in England has since decidedly increased. Owing to the great fall in the prices of manufactured goods, a greater quantity of them is required to purchase a given quantity of gold – greater than in proportion to the cheapness arising from increased skill, and improvements in machinery. Consequently, such goods so exchanged for gold contain a greater value of English labour, profits, rents, and taxes; and the cost of obtaining gold in England has unquestionably increased' (132).[72] Shortly afterwards it is clarified that the mere fact of the lower cotton price of gold does not constitute evidence of a change in the value of the precious metals; all turned on the effect on the money wage: 'As long as the price of labour was not affected by these low prices of commodities, the elementary cost of obtaining the precious metals would not be increased. Although more cottons would be given for an ounce of gold, this would be merely giving a larger quantity of an article which had fallen in the cost of obtaining it, and the elementary cost of obtaining gold might remain the same; but as soon as the price of the standard labour began generally to fall, more labour must be given for the same quantity of silver, and the elementary cost of producing the precious metals would necessarily rise; and in the actual state of things it seems almost impossible to deny that such an increase of their value has really taken place' (134).

The second edition also provides a forecast. In Europe (and even in the United States), the relative effect of upward pressure on prices resulting from increased efficiency of the export industries would probably swamp that of diminishing returns: 'Even in such a country as the United States, where capital is scarce and profits are comparatively high, the fall of profits, which will certainly occur, in the progress of wealth and population, will probably be more than counterbalanced by the effect of a diminution in the facility of producing exportable commodities. And in reference to the fuller peopled countries of Europe, there is no room for such a fall of profits as can approach to the effects which have arisen, and may yet arise from the increased fertility of the mines; or the diminished quantity of labour, which in a particular country, owing to superior skill and machinery, is required to purchase the precious metals, while the cost of obtaining them at the mines of America, and the quantity imported into the whole of Europe remain nearly the same' (127). (The higher level of prices in the course of growth is ascribed misleadingly to the fall of profits.)

VIII INTERNATIONAL PRICES: A SUMMARY

We have found the doctrine of the non-uniformity of the equilibrium val-

72 The increasing the cost of obtaining bullion had been 'aggravated' by reductions in American gold supplies since 1810, though '[no] very satisfactory conclusion ... can be drawn respecting the cause of the late rise in the value of money in the greater part of Europe, and the United States of America, from the smallness of the defalcation in the mines, as compared with the whole mass of bullion in the world' (133). There follows a 'digression' to show that 'other causes ... are frequently more efficient in altering the value of the precious metals, especially in particular countries, than moderate changes in the state of their annual supply from the mines.'

ues of the precious metals between economies based on export-efficiency differentials clearly formulated in the *Principles* of 1820 and much amplified in both *The Measure of Value* (1823) and the second edition of the main text. In that edition Malthus applauded Ricardo's analysis as 'not only new, but unquestionably true, and of the highest importance' (above, p. 679). We should look more closely at what this commendation implies. By the designation 'new' Malthus apparently did not mean a novelty *attributable to Ricardo*; for he himself claimed precedence for the principle, referring to the note in his *Inquiry into Rent* of 1815 (cited above, p. 713), which 'appeared ... two years before the first edition of Mr Ricardo's work' (1836, 130n).[73] The same claim was made in a letter to Whewell: 'With regard to foreign trade and the level of the precious metals, I think you have correctly apprehended the doctrine of Ricardo on the subject which by the bye was mine, before it was his; and we used to have conversations on the subject after I had stated the general principle in a note to my pamphlet on rent 2 years before he published his work. You are aware I think from what you say latterly, that the effect alluded to does not depend *merely* on manufacturing skill, but on any causes which give to a particular country great relative advantages in its *exportable* commodities' (TCL Add. Ms. a.209[11]).

Was this a legitimate self-attribution? The fact is that the formulation of the non-uniformity of metallic values in the note to the *Inquiry* expresses the effect of differential agricultural productivities and lacks any formal discussion of the costs of 'producing' the metals in terms of the efficiency of the export industries. One might conclude that Malthus was engaged in retrospective wishful thinking.[74]

73 Again he reiterates that the Corn Laws are not responsible for a peculiarly high level of prices: 'In reality, the quantity of money in each country is determined by the quantity wanted to maintain its general exchanges at par; and the greater are the advantages of any country in regard to its exportable commodities, the more money will it retain, and the higher will be the price of its corn and labour, when its exchanges are at par. If England should lose her advantages in this respect, her corn and labour will fall to the level of the rest of Europe, in spite of any corn laws that could be imagined.'

74 Yet some allowance may be made for the stronger formulation given in the letter of 26 August 1815 (above, p. 714).

IV / SOME EMPIRICAL ESTIMATES

FIFTEEN

Agricultural productivity: Past and prospective

I INTRODUCTION

It is received doctrine that the expositions in 1815 by Malthus, Ricardo, West, and Torrens of the principle of diminishing returns were intimately related to contemporary circumstances. Cannan has written that 'the early nineteenth-century English economists deduced their doctrines, not from study of the works of their predecessors, but from the actual experience of England during the war' (1917, 117). Jacob Hollander observed similarly regarding Malthus's *Rent*: 'To what earlier influences [than the corn-law controversy of 1814], if any, is the genesis of the law of diminishing returns, as stated therein, referable? The general answer is, of course, to that extraordinary condition of British agriculture in the preceding decade, the conspicuous features of which – extension of cultivation and application of capital to land – were familiar to Malthus long before parliamentary blue-books gave them wide publicity' (1903, 4). And for an example from our own time: 'Each [of the four tracts] took as its starting point the relationship between high grain prices and the extension of cultivation to less fertile and less accessible land during the years of the Napoleonic Wars' (Blaug, 1985, 77).

While there is some validity to the foregoing generalization, we must, in Malthus's case at least, exercise caution. In the first place, there are already intimations of diminishing returns in the first *Essay on Population* (1798) and more so in the second and subsequent editions (see chapter 1). But these were, so to speak, either matters of principle or a reflection of North American condition. In the first four editions (1798, 1803, 1806, 1807) – as we show below, in section II – there are no intimations of a *practical* order relating to Britain of the productivity implications flowing from increasing land scarcity. It is only in correspondence (with Horner) of 1813, and then in his *Observations on the Effects of the Corn Laws* (1814), that we encounter diminishing returns as an *empirically relevant* phenomenon, the rise in corn prices since 1804 now attributed, at least in part, to increased domestic demand to which agricultural output responded at higher real cost (below, section III). The altered perspective preceded the evidence of recent extensions to higher-cost marginal land given before parliamentary committees,[1] though informal observation might have been relevant, for (as Cannan has observed) 'about the year 1813 there were two features in the economic condition of the country which could not fail to strike the most superficial observer – the high prices of corn and the improvement and extension of cultivation' (1917, 117; see also Hollander, 1903, 4, for emphasis on informal observation).

In section IV we show that, while the protectionist *Grounds of an Opinion* (1815) refers to the new parliamentary evidence, recent experience cannot be said in Malthus's case to have *generated* the diminishing-returns principle, but only to have *illustrated* it. (The same may be said of the differential-rent corollary of diminishing returns formulated in 1814 – below, p. 749 – since there are earlier intimations in the 1806 *Essay*.)

1 The Report ... on Petitions relating to the Corn Laws, House of Commons, 1814; the Report of the Lords Committees ... on the Growth, the Commerce and the Consumption of Grain, 1815. Smart provides an excellent summary of the report of the more important 1814 committee:

> they proceeded, first, to examine into the state of the growth of corn at home and the circumstances which affected the same, turning their attention to three points – (1) the recent extension and improvement of the agriculture of the United Kingdom; (2) the present expense of cultivation, 'including the rent'; (3) the price necessary to remunerate the grower. They dwelt accordingly on 'the very rapid and extensive progress' of the last twenty years – the great additional capitals applied, the conversion of inferior pasture into productive arable, the great reclamations and enclosures 'still in their infancy.' The great source of encouragement to this was the increasing population and growing opulence of the kingdom, but it was not to be concealed that these causes had been, 'incidentally but considerably,' aided by events which had checked importation during the war. The sudden removal of these impediments might prevent the enclosure and cultivation of great tracts of land still lying waste and unproductive, counteract the spirit of improvement in other quarters, and check its progress upon lands already under tillage. Within the same twenty years, money rents and the general expenses of management and cultivation had been doubled. In these circumstances, it was the opinion of most of the witnesses that 80/- per quarter was the lowest price which would afford the British grower an adequate remuneration. Indeed a higher price, stated by different witnesses from 84/- to 96/-, would be necessary as regards the 'cold clay or waste and inferior lands, on which wheat could not be grown but at an expense exceeding the average charge of its cultivation on better soils' and a considerable proportion of what was now raised on such lands. If such lands were withdrawn from tillage, they would for many years be of very little use as pasture, and the loss from such a change, as well to the occupiers as to the general stock of national subsistence, would be very great. (1910–17, I, 415–16)

Missing in the standard accounts is an estimate of the 'seriousness' of the land-scarcity problem. The *Grounds* – which takes account of recent wartime experience – portrays a prospect of, *at most,* a shallow rise in real costs with expansion in a closed economy in the light of new techological opportunities. In fact, there is even a reference to 'a chance' of future real-cost reduction. And this, we must emphasize, is *an evaluation based in part on 'experience,' as revealed in the recent parliamentary evidence.* The *Inquiry on Rent* turns out to be equally complex. Malthus sought to evaluate the historical and prospective manifestation of an analytical principle in practice. The evidence on which to arrive at a balanced estimate was mixed. And to his credit, he was honest enought to warn readers of the prospect of productivity decline in a protected economy. But he refused to exaggerate. The perspective of the pamphlets of 1815 – allowance for but minimization of the prospect of major productivity decline – is confirmed by the correspondence with Ricardo.

The fifth edition of the *Essay on Population* (1817) maintains the optimistic perspective on productivity of the previous editions. New technology is now unreservedly emphasized not only with respect to future prospects, but also regarding the interpretation of wartime events (section V). This requires explanation. That Malthus's protectionism coloured the new version is possible but unlikely since the optimistic stance was stronger in 1817 than in the formally protectionist *Grounds,* when it might have been expected. An alternative possibility is that sufficient time had passed to re-evaluate the original parliamentary evidence relating to wartime experience, particularly in the light of the postwar depression and the contraction of agriculture by the withdrawal of the *old* land areas rather than the new extensions made in the war. The '*chance*' on which Malthus did 'not insist' in 1815 now seems to have become an immediate *reality.* A third possibility – suggested in Waterman, 1991, 172–6 – is that Malthus was concerned to remove the 'dark hints' and 'melancholie hue' for which his *Essay* had been criticized by Sumner (1816).

Empirical estimates emerging in the *Principles* are considered in section VI. We show that the optimistic perspective is carried still farther than in 1817, downplaying prospective land scarcity based in part on the experience of the 1793–1813 war years. The great weight placed on new technology in the account of these decades is common to both editions.[2]

II EARLY FORMULATIONS, 1798–1806

As shown in chapter 1, the principle of diminishing returns (though not

2 Rashid (1981, 65) asserts simply that 'there is greater stress laid on agricultural improvements in the second edition' of the *Principles.* The story, however, is complex and differs somewhat between the chapters on rent and on profit.

its differential-rent implication) is apparent already in the 1798 *Essay*; but it was applied to the American case, not to contemporary Britain. As for Britain, Malthus alludes to a slow growth of population supported by a moderate expansion of agriculture, the latter reflecting 'the general improvements in husbandry' and a 'generally increased fertility of the soil' rather than a growing agricultural workforce (1986, *1*, 111–12). The positive effect on food supply of improved methods and organization had, however, been constrained by enclosures undertaken largely for *pasture*, which 'employ fewer hands and feed fewer mouths'; more specifically: 'I cannot help thinking, that the present great demand for butcher's meat of the best quality, and the quantity of good land that is in consequence annually employed to produce it, together with the great numbers of horses at present kept for pleasure, are the chief causes that have prevented the quantity of human food in this country from keeping pace with the generally increased fertility of the soil' (112). But 'a change of custom in these respects, would, I have little doubt, have a very sensible effect on the quantity of subsistence in the country, and consequently on its population.' Malthus actually asserted that the agricultural workforce had fallen absolutely as a result of reorganization and labour-displacing technology: 'The employment of much of the most fertile land in grazing, the improvements in agricultural implements, the increase of large farms, and particularly the diminution of the number of cottages throughout the kingdom, all concur to prove that there are not probably, so many persons employed in agricultural labour now, as at the period of the Revolution.' Land scarcity, as such, reflected in diminishing returns, thus plays no part in the 1798 account of actual British circumstances.[3]

There is one qualification to this generalization. Increasing land scarcity is alluded to in an application to the analysis of a supposedly higher British population growth rate *circa* 1600–50 compared with *circa* 1680–1750 (46–7; cited chapter 1, p. 32). But the fact remains that, despite this statement, Malthus did not perceive Britain in his own day as densely populated; it is expressly described as 'thinly inhabited,' or at least 'not ... extremely crowded and populous' (44). Moreover, the account based on increasing land scarcity is not the only account given in 1798 of earlier historical development. I refer to a striking declaration regarding the determinants of 'happiness' applied to England which asserts that – new colonies aside – a country's population/land ratio is *irrelevant* to the pace of growth of food supplies and the magnitude of real wages (51; cited chapter 1, p. 55). In the British and other European cases, living standards had remained at low and roughly constant levels for ages, with population increasing in response to expansions in food supply, reflecting the internal generation of novel technologies or higher motivation and the like.

3 Malthus also alludes to unbalanced development favouring industry (108f.).

We seem to be faced by a duality of perspective on historical development. But as we pointed out in chapter 1, Malthus had applied the land-scarcity analysis to seventeenth-century data circumspectly.[4] This particular analysis of the demographic data, though of theoretical importance, does not have much relevance for the appreciation of Malthus's considered view of English development.

* * *

The *High Price of Provisions* (1800) is concerned largely with the contemporary dearth of corn and its high price – higher than could be expected merely from the extent of the shortfall. The explanation offered turns on the upward pressures supposedly generated by the poor-relief system. At the very close of the pamphlet, however, there is reference to a secular lag of food production behind population growth – manifested in Britain's transition from net food exporter to net food importer – which is said to confirm the thesis of the *Essay*:

> It is a fact now generally acknowledged ... that of late years, even in the best seasons, we have not grown corn sufficient for our own consumption; whereas, twenty years ago, we were in the constant habit of exporting grain to a very considerable amount. Though we may suppose that the agriculture of the country has not been increasing, as it ought to have done, during this period; yet we cannot well imagine that it has gone backwards. To what then can we attribute the present inability in the country to support its inhabitants, but to the increase of population? I own that I cannot but consider the late severe pressures of distress on every deficiency in our crops, as a very strong exemplification of a principle which I endeavoured to explain in an essay published about two years ago ... It was considered by many who read it, merely as a specious argument, inapplicable to the present state of society; because it contradicted some preconceived opinions on these subjects. Two years of reflection have, however, served strongly to convince me of the truth of the principle there advanced, and of its being the real cause of the continued depression and poverty of the lower classes of society, of the total inadequacy of all the present establishments in their favour to relieve them, and of the periodical returns of such seasons of distress as we have of late experienced. (1986, 7, 17–18)

4 Malthus elaborated his qualification to that analysis thus: 'I say *ceteris paribus*, because the increase of the produce of any country will always very greatly depend on the spirit of industry that prevails, and the ways in which it is directed. The knowledge and habits of the people and other temporary causes, particularly the degree of civil liberty and equality existing at the time must always have great influence in exciting and directing this spirit' (47n).

Yet there is nothing here that necessarily implies diminishing returns in the technical sense of the term. The excessive population growth in question – considering the context of the pamphlet as a whole – is presumably attributed to the poor-relief system, confirming Malthus's belief in 1798 that the Poor Laws tended 'to increase population without increasing the food for its support,' thus putting upward pressure on food prices (1986, *1*, 33). In that context, we have shown in chapter 1, pp. 24–5, any land-scarcity constraints might be overcome, provided sufficient time is allowed for investment in land improvement to *overcome* rising real costs, thus permitting expansion with (at the least) no *fall* in productivity.[5]

* * *

The 1803 edition of the *Essay* provides further references to the high productivity of British agriculture, the recent census data indicating that 'the number of persons employed in agriculture is very unusually small in proportion to the actual produce' (1986, *3*, 674). If agricultural development was constrained it was because of 'undue encouragement' afforded manufactures – the Navigation Acts and the colonial trade monopoly – which had 'robbed [land] of much of the capital which would naturally have fallen to its share.' There are references to a rising corn price over the preceding two decades, but there is no suggestion that the upward trend reflected higher *real* costs with agricultural extensions. The rise reflected rather 'the abundance of commercial wealth' or 'the competition of monied wealth at home,' and, since such 'abundance' was accompanied by higher money wages, agriculture had been little stimulated: Farmers were 'justly afraid of growing too much corn, as a considerable loss will be sustained upon that part of it which is sold abroad; and a glut on the home market will universally make the price fall below the fair and proper recompense to the grower' (677). Land 'improvement' might follow from a 'redundancy of commercial capital,' but only 'slow and late,' once the return on capital had fallen to 3 per cent rather than the 5–6 per cent then available. Government competition for funds to finance the war acted as a further impediment – the crowding-out phenomenon: The National Debt of England, by 'absorbing the redundancy of commercial capital, and keeping up the rate of interest ... has prevented this capital from overflowing upon the soil' (675).

What of imported farm produce? Malthus played down its quantitative significance: 'Of late years indeed, the part of the society, not connected with agriculture, has unfortunately increased beyond this [farm] produce; but the average importation of corn, as yet, bears but a small proportion to that which is grown in the country, and consequently the power which

5 See below, pp. 766–7, for this perspective in 1817.

England [possesses] of supporting so vast a body of idle consumers must be attributed principally to the greatness of her surplus produce' (674). Malthus thus played down the absolute proportion of imports to domestic production, though he did recognize that imports were on the rise. And he had warnings for the future in the event of unbalanced growth favouring manufactures. He feared the stimulus that above-subsistence real wages would accord population growth in the face of an 'uncertain' long-run supply of foreign imports – though among the prospective impediments land scarcity abroad is conspicuously absent: 'When the commercial population of any country increases so much beyond the surplus produce of the cultivators, that the demand for imported corn is not easily supplied, and the price rises in proportion to the price of wages, no further increases of riches will have any tendency to give the labourer a greater command over the necessaries of life. In the progress of wealth, this will naturally take place; either from the largeness of the supply wanted; the increased distance from which it is brought, and consequently the increased expense of importation; the greater consumption of it in the countries in which it is usually purchased; or what must unavoidably happen, the necessity of a greater distance of inland carriage, in these countries. Such a nation, by increasing industry, and increasing ingenuity in the improvement of machinery, may still go on increasing the yearly quantity of its manufactured produce; but its funds for the maintenance of labour, and consequently its population, will be perfectly stationary. This point is the natural limit to the population of all commercial states' (696; cf. 451).

* * *

As for future domestic agricultural development, Malthus was optimistic in 1803, at least in the event of an 'enlightened system of agriculture' which would 'undoubtedly be able to produce food beyond the demands of the actual population' (687; see also 486, 488–9, discussed in chapter 18, p. 879). Malthus objected only to the 'prejudice' that any conceivable system can 'be made to keep pace with an unchecked population.' He even denied practical limits to growth in an 'enlightened' system: 'There is no apparent limit to the quantity of manufactures which might in time be supported in this way. There is no discoverable germ of decay in the system; and in theory, there is no reason to say, that it might not go on increasing in wealth and prosperity for thousands of years' (676).

The 1803 formulation goes farther and actually predicts *reduced* corn prices in consequence of the stimulus afforded output by a corn-export bounty. For Malthus insisted, against Smith, that a bounty provided an incentive to expansion, and thus generated lower prices: 'And if it is admitted, that the cultivation of corn is susceptible of being encouraged by a bounty like other commodities, it will scarcely fail to follow, that the greater plenty, occasioned by this encouragement, will in the long run lower the price' (685). The Smithian concern with an *increased* price level could therefore be turned on its head: 'And if the ultimate tendency of the bounty be clearly to lower the average price of corn in the home market, all Dr. Smith's just reasonings respecting the disadvantage of the cheapness of silver in any particular country or the dearness of all other commodities, return upon himself, and are applicable in favour of the corn laws, not against them.'

Despite the first impression, it is by no means certain that Malthus intended to assert *increasing* agricultural productivity by his prediction of a *reduced* corn price with expansion. What he may have intended is a contrast, clarified in the 1806 edition, between the 'direct' effects of a corn-export subsidy, which were to raise the domestic corn price, and its indirect effects, which were 'both to lower the average price, and to prevent the variations above and below that price' (1806, II, 259), the latter turning on a distinction between the 'growing' price of corn in normal years and an 'average' price over all years: 'When Dr. Smith asserted that a fall in the price of corn could not possibly happen in consequence of a bounty, he overlooked a distinction which it is necessary to make in this case between the growing price of corn in years of common plenty, and the average price of a period including years of scarcity ... Supposing the wages of labour to be regulated more frequently by the former than the latter price, which perhaps is the case, it will readily be allowed that the bounty could not lower the growing price, though it might very easily lower the average price of a long period, and I have no doubt whatever had this effect in a considerable degree during the first half of the last century' (261–2). This statement suggests that Malthus may *not* have had in mind diminishing (real) cost price in years of 'common plenty.'

The same contrast between 'direct' and 'indirect' effects is maintained also with respect to the general level of prices. The direct effect of the bounty is to raise general prices, but its indirect effects work to check inflationary pressures: 'The operation of the bounty on the value of silver is, in the same manner, in its direct effects to depreciate it, but its indirect effects may perhaps tend more powerfully to prevent it from falling. In the progress of wealth, when commerce outstrips agriculture, there is a constant tendency to a depreciation of silver, and a tendency to an opposite effect, when the balance leans to the side of agriculture' (262). The check to depreciation apparently operates by way of the effect of the restrained corn price on the money wage. As for contemporary Britain: 'That the rapid progress of commercial wealth combined with years of scarcity, has raised the nominal price of wages more than in any other country of Europe, will not be denied; and the natural consequence is, that silver is more depreciated here than in the rest of Europe' (263–4). But the long-term effect of the bounty would be to counteract this inflationary pressure: 'If the bounty has any effect in weakening this cause of depreciation, by preventing the average price of corn from being so much affected by the price of scarcity, the ultimate advantage which its indirect operation occasions, with regard to the value of silver, may more than counterbalance the present disadvantages of its direct operation' (264).

Although Malthus may not have based his case for a lower average corn price with agriculture expansion on any notion of *increasing* returns, there is also no hint of *diminishing* returns in the empirical accounts of 1803 or 1806. Similarly, when it comes to policy, the 1806 edition recommended intervention to encourage Britain's re-emergence as a net corn exporter – to be accomplished in two stages: first, corn-import restrictions and, subsequently, an export bounty (see chapter 17, pp. 814–15); and there is nothing in this program to suggest prospective real-cost increases.

III THE DIMINISHING-RETURNS PRINCIPLE APPLIED, 1813–1814

The diminishing-returns principle emerges clearly, to my knowledge, for the first time in Malthus's analyses of contemporary trends, in a letter to Francis Horner dated 16 June 1813 (see chapter 17, pp. 820–1). This letter states the case against agricultural import restriction on grounds of price stability as well as efficiency; corn prices were likely to be unstable in a closed economy, producing at a cost level above that of foreign producers: 'A little excess of supply not being relieved by exportations, on account of the general high prices of corn at home, I doubt if prices would be steady' (Tucker, 1954, 331). Here in 1813 we have the precise reverse of the position in the early editions of the *Essay on Population* regarding the level and stability of corn prices in a protected economy. While the altered perspective *preceded* the evidence of extensions to higher-cost marginal land during recent years given at parliamentary committees in 1814–15, less formal observation cannot be precluded, though it would at most be evidence *illustrating* the increasing-cost tendency that is involved.

We turn now to the *Observations* (1814) and its elaboration of the themes in the June 1813 letter. Though by this time the evidence given to the Select Committee on the Corn Laws set up in 1814 was available, on Malthus's own account he did not base his position on that evidence. A retrospective comment in *Grounds of an Opinion* (1815) implies that his 1814 position was a matter of 'general principle,' *confirmed* by the parliamentary evidence: 'In the *Observations on the Corn Laws* [1814/1986, 7, 96] I endeavoured to show that, according to the general principles of supply and demand, a considerable fall in the price of corn could not take place, without throwing much poor land out of cultivation, and effectually preventing, for a considerable time, all further improvements in agriculture, which have for their object an increase of produce. The general principles, on which I calculated upon these consequences, have been fully confirmed by the evidence brought before the two houses of Parliament; and the effects of a considerable fall in the price of corn, and of the expected continuance of low prices, have shown themselves in a very severe shock to the cultivation of the country and a great loss of agricultural capital' (152).[6]

Although Malthus in the *Observations* formally eschewed the application of 'general principles' (95),[7] since allowances were required in each case for 'the size, soil, facilities of culture, and demand for corn in the country in question,' he yet allowed a high probability of an inflow of imports into Britain in consequence of cost differentials: 'There is every reason to suppose, that even a large landed nation, abounding in a manufacturing population, and having cultivated all its good soil, might find it cheaper to purchase a considerable part of its corn in other countries, where the supply, compared with the demand, was more abundant. If the intercourse between the different parts of Europe were perfectly easy and perfectly free, it would be by no means natural that one country should be employing a great capital in the cultivation of poor lands, while at no great distance, lands comparatively rich were lying very ill cultivated from the want of an effectual demand. The progress of agricultural improvement ought naturally to proceed more equably.' Differentials of agricultural technology are admitted, but not to the extent of entirely overcoming productivity relativities of a more basic order: 'It is true indeed that the accumulation of capital, skill, and population in particular districts, might give some facilities of culture not possessed by poorer nations; but such facilities could not be expected to make up for great differences in the quality of the soil and the expenses of cultivation.'[8] This was *a fortiori* true with heavy pressure of demand from growing urban centres: 'And it is impossible to conceive that under very great inequalities in the demand for corn in different countries, occasioned by a very great difference in the accumulation of mercantile and manufacturing capital and in the number of large towns, an equalization of price could take place, without the transfer of a part of the general supply of Europe, from places where the demand was comparatively deficient, to those where it was comparatively excessive.'

6 This is also true of Edward West on his own account: 'The chief object of this essay is the publication of a principle in political economy, which occurred to me some years ago; and which appears to me to solve many difficulties in the science, which I am at a loss otherwise to explain ... On reading lately the reports of the corn committees, I found my opinion respecting the existence of this principle confirmed by many of the witnesses, whose evidence is there detailed ... The principle is simply this, that in the progress of the improvement of cultivation the raising of rude produce becomes progressively more expensive, or, in other words, the ratio of the net produce of land to its gross produce is continually diminishing' (1815/1903, 9). West's full account recognizes the *intensive* as well as the extensive margin (14). Malthus is less clear on this detail.

7 This version prints the first edition of 1814. I rely on Jacob Hollander's version of 1932 for the third edition of 1815.

8 See also below, pp. 754–5, 772, on the relative strengths of the opposing forces acting on productivity.

The economic arguments for Britain to adopt free trade are said to be overwhelming – it would 'in all ordinary cases not only secure a cheaper, but a more steady supply of grain' (100). Protection and domestic agricultural expansion could not assure a corn price 'within moderate bounds and to a certain degree steady,' since 'in our actual situation, it is only by keeping the price of corn up, very considerably above the average of the rest of Europe, that we can possibly be made to grow our own consumption' (99). Rising corn prices had assured 'a more than usual quantity of capital ... upon the land, as appears obviously to have been the case in this country during the last twenty years' (92). Indeed, the result of high grain prices after 1804–05 – attributable in part to the 1804 Corn Law but mainly to wartime impediments to importation from Europe and the United States – had been to assure that Britain 'was approaching to the growth of an independent supply' (100–1). But the near achievement of an independent supply was assured only under a structure of corn prices which exceeded that of Europe and the United States: 'The whole difference of price does not by any means arise solely from taxation ... [N]o inconsiderable part, is occasioned by the necessity of yearly cultivating and improving more poor land, to provide for the demands of an increasing population; which land must of course require more labour and dressing, and expense of all kinds in its cultivation. The growing price of corn therefore, independently of all taxation, is probably higher than in the rest of Europe' (107–8). This differential 'not only increases the sacrifice that must be made for an independent supply, but enhances the difficulty of framing a legislative provision to secure it' (108).

In this context, involving the probable consequences of a free-corn trade in the light of high-cost British agriculture, we find supportive contemporary illustration from the war period: 'During the five years from 1804 to 1808, both inclusive, the bullion price of corn was about seventy five shillings per quarter, yet, at this price, it answered to us better to import some portion of our supplies than to bring our land into such a state of cultivation as to grow our own consumption. We have already shown how slowly and partially the price of corn affects the price of labour and some of the other expenses of cultivation. Is it credible then that if by the freedom of importation the prices of corn were equalized, and reduced to about forty five or fifty shillings a quarter [ed. 3: about fifty-five a quarter], it could answer to us to go on improving our agriculture with our increasing population, or even to maintain our produce in its actual state?' (96; Jacob Hollander, 1932, 17–18). Here we find reference to the differential-rent property, in a denial 'that the effects of a fall in the price of corn on cultivation may be fully compensated by a diminution of rents': 'Rich land which yields a large net rent, may [indeed] be kept up in its actual state, notwithstanding a fall in the price of its produce ... But in poor land, the fund of rent will often be found quite insufficient for this purpose. There is a good deal of land in this country of such quality that the expenses of its cultivation, together with the outgoings of poor rates, tithes and taxes, will not allow the farmer to pay more than a fifth or sixth of the value of the whole produce in the shape of rent. If we were to suppose the prices of grain to fall from seventy five shillings to fifty shillings the quarter, the whole of such a rent would be absorbed, even ... making some allowance for a fall in the price of labour. The regular cultivation of such land for grain would of course be given up, and any sort of pasture, however scanty, would be more beneficial both to the landlord and farmer.'[9] It is unclear whether the empirical references to the differential-rent corollary served an illustrative or an originating role.[10]

* * *

An overview by Malthus in 1814 of the course of events during the eighteenth century involves generalizations pertinent to our concerns. I have in mind his account of Britain's transition after 1740 from net corn exporter to net corn importer, in terms of the stimulus which low corn prices relative to money wages afforded population growth while correspondingly discouraging domestic agriculture: 'The fall in the price of corn, from whatever cause it took place, which occurred towards the middle of the last century, accompanied as it was by a rise, rather than a fall in the price of labour, must have given a great relative check to the employment of capital upon the land, and a great relative stimulus to population; a state of things precisely calculated to produce the reaction afterwards experienced, and to convert us from an exporting to an importing nation' (1986, 7, 93). The matter cannot be left here, with the allusion to a fall in the corn price 'from whatever cause it took place.' Fortunately, the pamphlet clarifies that the 'only sacrifice' imposed by the corn-export bounty had been the initial

9 Thus, a fall in the corn price from the going rate to 45s. or 50s. that could be expected with an inflow from Poland and the United States, should there be a permanently open market, would constrain British agricultural growth, especially since wage and other costs would lag and fail to decline proportionately, even in the long-run.

Malthus (95) drew on Oddy (1805) for a Polish price at Danzig of 32s. a quarter. A note is added to the third edition: 'It appears by the evidence laid before Parliament that the bullion prices of wheat at Dantzic, during the four years ending with 1813, were not higher than this; but that when there is a free export, the prices are almost wholly regulated by the prices of this country' (Jacob Hollander, 1932, 36–7).

10 West derived differential rent from the diminishing-returns principle with reference to both margins (1815/1903, 38–9). Some evidence was provided in the reports of the Corn Committees: 'Thus in p. 41, of the Lords' Report, the witness says, that, "where estates are *in a very high cultivation*, the share of the gross produce obtained as rent by the landlord is less than where estates are more imperfectly cultivated." And this is the language of all the witnesses before the corn committee; they are unanimous in their opinion that where lands are in a high state of cultivation the rent bears a less ratio to the gross produce than where they are less expensively tilled' (25).

temporary rise in price, a process which 'operat[ing] as a stimulus to cultivation, terminated in a period of increased cheapness' (108). It is expansion owing to the subsidy that was responsible for the reduction in corn prices.

Did Malthus then intend long-run *decreasing* cost? This interpretation creates analytical difficulties. For the low corn prices in question are said to have been responsible for the 'reaction' – the conversion of Britain 'from an exporting to an importing nation' by checking agricultural investment while stimulating population growth. Assuming the allusion to be to decreasing costs, there would be no logical reason to expect a check to investment with growing population (since the low prices reflect reduced costs).[11] But that such a check was indeed Malthus's considered position is confirmed by a note added in the third (1815) edition of *Observations* attached to our initial passage: 'This is, in fact, the true argument against a bounty on the exportation of corn. If such a bounty be given in a country, in which the growing price of corn is as low as among its neighbours, I think it is certainly calculated, after going through a period of dearness, to produce a period of cheapness, upon the general principle stated by Adam Smith, that a great demand is very apt to produce a still greater supply. I am decidedly of opinion, that it had this effect in England during the second quarter of the last century. *But when this period of cheapness comes, it must necessarily give a proportionate check to agriculture, and encouragement to population, which, of course, prevents the cheapness from being permanent*' (Jacob Hollander, 1932, 36; emphasis added). It will be recalled that, in 1806, Malthus had asserted a downward trend in *average* prices in consequence of a bounty, notwithstanding apparently the absence of a downward trend in *growing* prices (above, p. 746). Conceivably he had something of the sort in mind here, although the generalization 'that a great demand is very apt to produce a still greater supply' does not seem to point in that direction. *In any event, the major difference with 1806 is that Malthus was now asserting that the reduced corn price resulting from a corn-export bounty would inevitably be reversed.*

It is in fact taken for granted in 1814–15 that events had rendered the old Smithian concern with the corn-export bounty a dead letter (1986, 7, 94). Not only had there occurred faster population growth in Britain since 1740 than in any other European country, but major structural changes entailing expansion of the middle classes had increased demand for 'the products of pasture' in even greater proportion than population increase and the demand for cereals (108). To render Britain again a net corn exporter would require so 'extensive' an export subsidy as to bring population growth to a halt – presumably by way of the effect on the home price of corn – and severely impede the manufacturing sector.

11 See below, note 42, for a similar problem in the 1817 *Essay*.

Here we should keep in mind that, already in 1806, Malthus had accorded the bounty a secondary order of importance; it was something for future consideration, the first priority being import restriction (above, p. 747). The position of 1814 was the next stage, reflecting: (1) a new theoretical insight, that the 'period of cheapness' resulting from a bounty generates shortages which *reverse* the downward price trend; and (2) new circumstances – namely, heavy competitive pressures deflecting land use from corn production, and rising population – and, of course, the upward trend in real costs creating a major discrepancy between British and Continental (and American) cost levels – under which conditions any bounty would have to be of unacceptable magnitude to be effective in deflecting output from the home market.

IV PRODUCTIVITY ESTIMATES, 1815

An allusion to rising real costs of corn occurs in a summary statement in *Grounds of an Opinion* (1815) recalling the *Observations*, where he had 'endeavoured to show that, according to the general principles of supply and demand, a considerable fall in the price of corn could not take place, without throwing much poor land out of cultivation, and effectually preventing, for a considerable time, all further improvements in agriculture, which have for their object an increase of produce' (cited above, p. 747). This is elaborated in an important new reference to experience since approximately 1795, and especially since 1808, brought out in evidence before Parliament – we must also keep in mind the comment regarding the *confirmation* of the 'general principles' laid down in 1814 by the 1815 parliamentary evidence – indicating expansion of agriculture by way of the 'high farming' encouraged by rising corn prices during a period of restricted importation: 'Whatever may be said of the peculiar interests and natural partialities of those who were called upon to give evidence upon this occasion, it is impossible not to be convinced, by the whole body of it taken together, that, during the last twenty years, and particularly during the last seven, there has been a great increase of capital laid out upon the land, and a great consequent extension of cultivation and improvement; that the system of spirited improvement and *high farming*, as it is technically called, has been principally encouraged by the progressive rise of prices owing in a considerable degree, to the difficulties thrown in the way of importation of foreign corn by the war' (1815a/1986, 7, 152–3). Prior to the extraordinary fall of corn prices in 1814–15, Britain had achieved greater self-sufficiency 'notwithstanding a great increase of population' (153).

But at the same time Malthus also emphasized that 'the evidence brought before the two houses of Parliament' pointed to a *high agricultural potential* to meet further population expansion: 'It is impossible not to be convinced ... that the land was still deficient in capital, and would admit of the employment of such an addition to its present amount, as would be competent to the full supply of a greatly increased population.' And in a further discussion of potentialities based on parliamentary evidence and also Sinclair's formal studies of agricultural productivity, he provided a strikingly optimistic account of British and Irish productivity subject only to the adoption of best existing technological and organizational practice. The argument commences with reference to 'the extraordinary improvements, and prodigious increase of produce that have taken place latterly in some districts, which, in point of natural soil, are not superior to others that are still yielding the most scanty and miserable crops. Most of the light soils of the kingdom might, with adequate capital and skill, be made to equal the improved parts of Norfolk; and the vast tracts of clay lands that are yet in a degraded state almost all over the kingdom, are susceptible of a degree of improvement, which it is by no means easy to fix, but which certainly offers a great prospective increase of produce' (160). He continued by allowing in fact for 'a chance' of real-cost reductions:

> There is even a chance (but on this I will not insist) of a diminution in the real price of corn owing to the extension of those great improvements, and that great economy and good management of labour, of which we have such intelligent accounts from Scotland. If these clay lands, by draining, and the plentiful application of lime and other manures, could be so far meliorated in quality as to admit of being worked by two horses and a single man, instead of three or four horses with a man and a boy, what a vast saving of labour and expense would at once be effected, at the same time that the crops would be prodigiously increased! And such an improvement may rationally be expected from what has really been accomplished in particular districts. In short, if merely the best modes of cultivation, now in use in some parts of Great Britain, were generally extended, and the whole country was brought to a level, in proportion to its natural advantages of soil and situation, by the further accumulation and more equable distribution of capital and skill; the quantity of additional produce would be immense, and would afford the means of subsistence to a very great increase of population. (160–1)

A note defining the 'real growing price of corn' alludes to diminishing marginal returns, given technology: 'By the real growing price of corn I mean the real quantity of labour and capital which has been employed to procure the last additions which have been made to the national produce. In every rich and improving country there is a natural and strong tendency to a constantly increasing price of raw produce, owing to the necessity of employing, progressively, land of an inferior quality.' But productivity tends downwards, notwithstanding new technology: 'This tendency may be partially counteracted by great improvements in cultivation, and economy of labour. See this subject treated in *An inquiry into the nature and progress of rent,* just published' (161n).

We must keep in mind the 'partial' counteraction of rising costs by new improvements, but all in all, considering the text as well as the note, there is little doubt that Malthus, basing his view in part on recent experience, *at most* conceived of a shallow prospective rise of real costs. This is no casual matter, for Malthus proceeded to an assurance that the British economy, if protected, would not be subject to any *serious* constraints as far as concerns growth. The context is a contrast between countries with 'small territory, and consisting chiefly of one or two large cities' and the British case, the former alone being dependent for expansion on imports: 'It is quite evident that the same alternative is not presented to Great Britain and Ireland, and that the united empire has ample means of increasing in wealth, population, and power, for a very long course of years, without being habitually dependent upon foreign supplies for the means of supporting its inhabitants. As we have clearly, therefore, our choice between two systems, under either of which we may certainly look forward to a progressive increase of population and power, it remains for us to consider in which way the greatest portion of wealth and happiness may be steadily secured to the largest mass of the people' (161–2). Here we have a splendid illustration of Malthus's utilitarianism.

To his credit, Malthus did not unfairly reinforce his protectionist proposals by emphasizing a prospective absolute *decline* in agricultural costs with domestic expansion. On the contrary: In a final summing-up of the pros and cons of alternative trade policies, he points to a prospect of secular *rising* corn prices and possible damage to the manufacturing sector in the event of restriction: 'If, on mature deliberation, we determine steadily to pursue a system of restrictions with regard to the trade in corn, *we must not be disturbed at a progressive rise in the price of grain* ... and we must not be disturbed at the occasional loss or diminution of a continental market for some our least peculiar manufactures, owing to the high price of our labour. Those who promise low prices upon the restrictive system, take an erroneous view of the causes which determine the prices of raw produce, and draw an incorrect inference from the experience of the first half of the last century. As I have stated in another place [*On Rent*], a nation which very greatly gets the start of its neighbours in riches, without any peculiar natural facilities for growing corn, must necessarily submit to one of these alternatives – *either a very high comparative price of grain, or a very great dependence upon other countries for it*' (172–3; emphasis added). But to focus on this caution alone is misleading. From the evidence given thus far it constitutes a 'worst-case' prospect.

* * *

In the theoretical *Inquiry into Rent* published in February 1815, Malthus gave his best-known statement of diminishing returns – and this includes a veiled allusion to the intensive margin – and differential rent (1815b/1986, 7, 133–4; see chapter 3, pp. 103–4). In this context he ascribed the contemporary high price of corn to its 'high comparative real price,' reflecting diminishing returns. None the less, various 'modifying' circumstances are allowed, including 'improvements in the modes of cultivation [and] the saving of labour on the land' and foreign trade. To treat innovation as a 'disturbing cause' implies recognition that the concept of diminishing returns is strictly applicable, *given technology*. Nevertheless, it is not treated quite like foreign trade, and this contrast implies that productivity decline predominates over time *notwithstanding new technology*; for only importation of foreign corn is said to 'do away, in a considerable degree, [with] the usual effects of great wealth on the price of corn' (135–6).[12]

These generalizations are said to apply to contemporary Europe 'with proper restrictions,' since in application of 'general principles' the particular circumstances of each case had to be considered (137; cf. the *Observations*, 95, cited above, p. 748). Allowance was necessary for transport costs which created international differentials in corn prices, and for differential soils, taxation, and technology. Thus a high relative corn price or heavy dependence on imports might reflect high taxation and poor soil, rather than 'great wealth and population'; conversely, impressive technology and good soil might permit a low corn price and independence, despite 'considerable wealth.' Nevertheless, Malthus stood by 'the general principles of the subject,' on grounds which distinguish between agriculture and industry. On this view the usual case is for marginal costs to rise absolutely, although the increase is less than it would be in the absence of new technology. This confirms that innovation is treated as a 'modifying' force that does not normally reverse the basic cost trend in agriculture. New technology does, on the other hand, assure a reduction in manufacturing prices (and this despite the disadvantage of rising corn prices and money wages).

As for the specific relevance of all this to British experience, we must have in mind the admission that in some *rare* cases new technology might prevent corn prices from rising, though Malthus does not give any example. And considering the generalization regarding the relatively high corn price in fast-advancing economies, it would seem that Britain constituted his primary case-study. This is confirmed by a summary statement at the close of the pamphlet which ascribes 'part ... and perhaps no inconsider-

12 In fact, it is subsequently conceded that, even with a free corn trade, the corn price would tend upward, presumably because *all* countries are expanding, albeit some faster than others: 'Even upon the system of importation, in the actual state and situation of the countries of Europe, higher prices must accompany superior and increasing wealth' (138n).

able part' of the high British corn price to land scarcity under pressure of 'wealth and population': 'I believe it to be the prevailing opinion, that the great expense of growing corn in this country is almost exclusively owing to the weight of taxation ...; [but] I think a part of this price, and perhaps no inconsiderable part, arises from a cause which lies deeper, and is in fact the necessary result of the great superiority of our wealth and population, compared with the quality of our natural soil and the extent of our territory. This is a cause which can only be essentially mitigated by the habitual importation of foreign corn, and a diminished cultivation of it at home. The policy of such a system has been discussed in another place; but, of course, every relief from taxation must, under any system, make the price of corn less high, and importation less necessary' (141).[13]

But there are interpretive problems. An analysis of recent British experience given earlier in the pamphlet has it that expanded agricultural investment since approximately 1794 was financed out of 'temporary' agricultural profits in consequence of 'improved modes of agriculture' supplemented by the rising corn price *unrelated to land scarcity* and accompanied by a lag in other cost items: 'Of the great additional quantity of capital employed upon the land in this country, during the last twenty years [1836: the twenty years, from 1792 to 1813], by far the greater part is supposed to have been generated on the soil, and not to have been brought from commerce or manufactures. And it was unquestionably the high profits of agricultural stock, occasioned by improvements in the modes of agriculture, and by the constant rise of prices, followed only slowly by a proportionate rise in the different branches of capital [1820: in the materials of the farmer's capital], that afforded the means of so rapid and so advantageous an accumulation' (128).[14] Malthus closed by reiterating that '[in] this case cultivation has been extended, and rents have risen,

13 A word here on a concern that rising corn prices, more precisely the compensatory money-wage increase, might discourage growth of labour demand given the effect on the prices of manufacturing exports. Contemporary growth rates were sufficiently rapid to render this concern academic: 'The peculiar evil to be apprehended is, that the high money price of labour may diminish the demand for it; and that it has this tendency will be readily allowed, particularly as it tends to increase the prices of exportable commodities. But repeated experience has shewn us that such tendencies are continually counter balanced, and more than counter balanced by other circumstances. As we have witnessed, in our own country, a greater and more rapid extension of foreign commerce, than perhaps was ever known, under the apparent disadvantage of a very great increase in the price of corn and labour, compared with the prices of surrounding countries' (139).

The essential points to emerge are: (1) confirmation of contemporary increase in the corn price and the money wage – at least relative to foreign countries; and (2) recognition of an unprecedented expansion of labour demand in the manufacturing sector, particularly exports.

14 On the modification to the 1815 text made in the *Principles* see below, section VI.

although one of the instruments of production, capital, has been dearer [1836: cultivation was extended, and rents rose, although one of the instruments of production, capital, was dearer].' Contemporary circumstances illustrated what Malthus had referred to as the 'temporary' effect on profits of rising corn prices and rising productivity, an effect that ultimately – 'at the expiration of the current leases' – is reflected in higher rents (127).

This perspective is further elaborated in a rationalization of the 'prodigious accumulation,' notwithstanding the 'vast annual destruction of stock' of the war period 1794–1814. It was investment by tenant farmers out of 'temporary high profits' that explained the expansion: 'Practically I should say, that when once a character of industry and economy has been established, temporary high profits are a more frequent and powerful source of accumulation, than either an increased spirit of saving, or any other cause that can be noted. It is the only cause which seems capable of accounting for the prodigious accumulation among individuals, which must have taken place in this country during the last twenty years, and which has left us with a greatly increased capital, notwithstanding our vast annual destruction of stock, for so long a period' (143–4).[15]

On this reading of wartime developments, major agricultural extension was consistent with an *upward* trend in the agricultural profit rate because of expanding foreign and domestic demand for farm produce acting on the corn price, accompanied by the adoption of cost-reducing technology.[16] *Falling agricultural productivity does not enter the picture.* But what then

15 Malthus here took issue with Smith: 'Adam Smith notices the bad effects of high profits on the habits of the capitalist. They may perhaps sometimes occasion extravagance; but generally, I should say, that extravagant habits were a more frequent cause of a scarcity of capital and high profits, than high profits of extravagant habits.'

16 Despite the confident statements regarding the source of agricultural capital, Malthus was to write to Arthur Young for confirmation: 'You would very much oblige me if you would give me your opinion on the following point. Whether the agricultural capital which has so much increased the produce of the country during the last 20 years, and raised the rent of land, independently of any change in the value of the currency, has been furnished *chiefly* by *tenants* or *landlords*? I wish much to ascertain this point, and know no person to whom I can apply with so fair a prospect of getting the information I want, as to you' (letter dated 6 February 1818; British Library Add. ms. 35, 133 f.187. The year of this letter is erroneously recorded as 1816 by Jacob Hollander, 1903, 50).

The response to Young's reply alludes only to confirmation that savings were generated within agriculture neglecting its source in rent or profit: 'I am happy to have it sanctioned by your opinion and superior authority. What you state agrees with the result of the observations I have occasionally had with persons who have attended to the progress of agricultural improvement of late years and I believe there can be no doubt that much the greater part of the capital that has been employed in these improvements, has been generated on the land, and been occasioned in no inconsiderable degree by the high prices' (letter dated 26 May; BM Add. ms. 35, 133 f.318).

In the 1817 edition of the *Essay on Population* Malthus focused on the generation of a surplus in the *cotton* industry as the source of rapid accumulation (1817, II, 406–7).

of the ascription in the same essay (above, pp. 755–6) of higher corn prices to increasing land scarcity? Conceivably the more optimistic account of productivity trends was formulated earlier, and not adequately reconciled with the change in perspective elsewhere in the pamphlet.[17] But of this we cannot be sure. In any event, the great weight placed on demand pressure and new technology is not necessarily inconsistent with *some* increase in marginal costs during the war; and certainly not inconsistent with a prospective secular upward trend. The correspondence with Ricardo casts light on the issue.

* * *

Ricardo in his letter of 17 August 1813 refers to Malthus's position that the general profit rate had *increased* over the war years 1793–1813 (Ricardo, 1951–73, VI, 94–5; for an elaboration, see chapter 2: II). That the profit rate has not declined over the two war decades – indeed that, at least for part of that period, it may have risen – he explained in terms of technical progress. Malthus did not apparently commit himself at this juncture to the question of agricultural productivity, one way or the other; his concern was the positive effect of *aggregate demand* on the profit rate. This fact emerges in a series of letters over the next years.

Two letters written late in 1814 (9 October, 23 November) refer to the increase in the profit rate from 1794 to 1814 as a *temporary* deviation from the trend – the trend dictated by the effect of agricultural productivity on the general profit rate – generated by extended foreign commerce (140–1, 153–5). From these formulations it is unclear whether or not Malthus perceived deteriorating agricultural productivity, notwithstanding which the profit rate increased with expanded demand; or whether he made some allowance for improved agricultural technology. A third letter late in 1814 refers to a low profit rate despite low corn prices from 1720 to 1750, 'while from 1793 to 1812 the interest of money and the profits of stock were high at the same time that the price of corn was becoming peculiarly dear,' the latter attributed to a 'prosperous commerce,' again without formal reference to diminishing returns (29 December; 168).

There is some clarification the following year. On 15 March 1815, Malthus described the 'last twenty years' as entailing 'poor land ... brought under cultivation by a rise of prices,' such that 'the whole capital on the land must have become more and more productive' (191–2).[18] This sur-

17 See Jacob Hollander, 1903, 3, regarding the genesis of the pamphlet. It was in preparation since 1807 and may have formed the nucleus of lectures on Adam Smith.

18 The remark turns on the table in Ricardo's *Essay on Profits*, 1951–73, IV, 17. On Malthus's reading, the expansion on to 'poor land' in the table occurs 'merely by the fall of profits' – not be a rise in the corn price – in which case 'corn will not necessarily rise.' The constancy of the corn price, notwithstanding diminishing returns, is explained below.

prising assertion regarding 'more productive' agricultural capital turns on a technical proposition that, notwithstanding diminishing *marginal* returns, there occurs a net expansion of the *total* corn surplus, taking account of intramarginal lands, as a result of the increase in the corn/manufactures price ratio. In any event, we have an indication that Malthus envisaged actual reductions in *marginal* productivity, though apparently the higher corn price itself reflected largely demand rather than cost pressure.[19] Here we keep in mind a distinction between rising P_c/P_m, owing to a fall in manufacturing profits and prices – we know this was not seen to be the case during the war – and rising P_c/P_m, owing *inter alia* to forces acting in P_c via demand, under which pressure 'fresh land may be taken into cultivation' – implying again diminishing returns (217; cited chapter 4, p. 129).[20]

In this same letter, moreover, the course of 'regular progress' is said to entail a falling general profit rate under pressure of supply in the manufacturing sector, but a *stationary* corn price.[21] Now it is confirmed shortly thereafter that this latter takes account of extensions to poorer land, the reduced profit rate *compensating* roughly for reduced productivity.[22] Malthus, therefore, apparently perceived diminishing returns over the war years, but with the higher corn price then experienced as attributable predominantly to demand, not cost, pressure. Those years were not envisaged as years of 'regular progress,' considering *rising*, not falling, manufac-

19 A further letter of 19 March also indicates that the case is not *limited* to a short-run or intermediate effect on the corn surplus owing to a higher demand-induced corn price; even following expansion and taking account of the higher real cost of marginal output – which governs the 'natural price' of corn – the total surplus on intramarginal land is said to rise (195).

It is, however, disturbing that Malthus found 'confirmation' for his case in 'the circumstances of a much smaller proportion of the population being employed on the land than formerly' (192) – which would suggest *increasing* productivity at the margin. This was, in fact, Ricardo's reaction to the whole case: 'If it be true that capital has become more and more productive on the land, it can I think only be accounted for on the supposition that great improvements have taken place in agriculture, and that wages have been kept moderate by the improvements in those manufactures which supply the poor with the necessaries on which a part of their wages are expended' (17 March 1815; 194). Malthus's alternative perspective might reflect the positive effect on the manufacturing sector flowing from the increased agricultural surplus.

20 On 19 and 24 March (195, 201) agricultural extensions are said to be stimulated by a falling corn wage; doubtless this is still intended here, though the emphasis is on a rising corn price as mechanism.

21 We recall the reference of 19 March (195) to higher real costs governing the 'natural price' of corn implying *rising* cost price; whereas in the present letter Malthus has it that the secular corn price is *constant*. Did he then change his position between 19 March and 18 April? Perhaps not. The first of the letters may refer only to the increased technical coefficients at the margin uncorrected for a falling profit rate.

22 See a reference on 1 October (291) to the period 1640–50 as one of deteriorating agricultural productivity and yet a low corn price because of a reduced profit rate.

turing prices and profits, and an even sharper rise in agricultural prices under pressure of demand such that P_c/P_m increased.

On 19 June 1815, Malthus allowed, after prodding from his correspondent, that a high corn price is desirable only if it does *not* reflect diminishing returns (231).[23] On 16 July, he reaffirmed that he did not 'consider a difficulty of producing desirable in itself,' but that 'a high corn price when not occasioned by such difficulty [was] a decided advantage,'[24] and 'at all times the best remedy for that difficulty of producing food, which in the progress of society is absolutely unavoidable' (236). Again, we have the notion of poorer land brought into cultivation by the stimulus of demand-induced higher corn prices. And what follows further confirms that just such a sequence was seen to characterize the 1794–1814 period: 'A great part of our high bullion prices [of corn and labour] is attributable to other causes, besides the barrenness of the land to be taken into cultivation,' an expression that seems to allow for some part of the higher corn price to be the result of lower agricultural productivity.[25]

As for the 'decided advantage,' without the high wartime prices of corn and labour relative to those of her trading partners, Britain would have been unable 'to subsidize Europe, and make such extraordinary exertions' – a proposition Ricardo hotly disputed.[26] What Malthus had in mind is elaborated on 26 August. It is a *permanent* differential in the prices of corn and labour relative to trading partners, which could be maintained only under conditions of peculiar productivity of the export sector – what

23 It is not absolutely clear that Malthus had *abandoned* his original notion of increased agricultural productivity, even under conditions of diminishing returns. He appears to have done so. But Ricardo reacted immediately that Malthus was inconsistent: 'you have said that the high price of corn and labour in this country at this time was an advantage, although it is universally allowed that high price is mainly owing to difficulty of production' (27 June; 234). This presumably refers to the war years, since the correspondents were writing at a time of depressed agriculture and *low* prices.

24 He listed as possible causes of a 'high relative price of corn': 'Division of labour in manufactures; machinery: Demand for corn abroad; Restriction on importations; Prosperous foreign commerce, &c:', apparently with the 1793–1813 period in mind.

25 Since it is throughout supposed that the general profit rate did not decline between 1793 and 1813, there would be no compensation for deteriorating agricultural productivity. Some corn-price increase from this source is to be expected.

26 Ricardo, as on 27 June, responded: 'A really high price of corn is always an evil; in this opinion I think you would concur because it is always occasioned by difficulty of production' (241). As for the wartime increase in the bullion price of corn: 'In our own case the high bullion price of corn is not wholly owing to the barrenness of the land to be taken into cultivation, but from whatever cause it has arisen it cannot I think have enabled us to grant greater subsidies than we should otherwise have done for subsidies as well as all services performed for us are paid for by the produce of the land and labour of the people of England. It surely is a palpable contradiction to say that our power of commanding services is increased whilst our productions with which those services are paid are diminished.'

Nassau Senior, later labelled a low 'cost of obtaining money' (see chapter 14: VI). Such permanent differentials would be precluded by 'the necessity of much more labour in the production of corn,' an allusion to high prices resulting from diminishing returns (255–6; cited chapter 4, p. 135).

There then follows a minimization of the consequence for agricultural costs of corn-import restrictions during the war – there had been only 'a very slight increase of the difficulty of raising corn,' amply confirming that wartime diminishing returns, though allowed, were not considered to have been a significant empirical issue. On the other hand, the restrictions had exerted an important *indirect* effect, that of preventing as great an inflow of resources into the manufacturing sector as otherwise would have occurred – a theme elaborated in the *Principles* (see below, pp. 780–1) – and thus countering increased 'competition of capitals,' to use Smith's term. This implies that the fall in export prices that was experienced reflected new industrial technology or 'facility of production' (256).[27] The emphasis then is on improved manufacturing, not deteriorating agricultural productivity during the 1794–1814 period, though some small deterioration is allowed.[28]

V PRODUCTIVITY ESTIMATES, 1817

The account of productivity trends emerging in the 1817 *Essay on Population* is strikingly optimistic, emphasizing the disturbing causes at play which accounted for an increase in the profit rate over the preceding two decades or so, despite prodigious accumulation and agricultural extensions: 'About the middle of the last century the interest of money was at 3 per cent; and we may conclude that the profits of stock were nearly in proportion. At that time, as far as can be collected from the births and marriages, the population was increasing, but slowly. From 1720 to 1750, a period of

27 Reduced manufacturing prices are desirable only when attributable to *efficiency* increase, not to increased 'competition.' For a much later confirmation, see *Principles*, 1836, 132.

28 We have a yet further minimization of the consequences of deteriorating agricultural productivity in the letter of 1 October referred to above, in note 22. Malthus there adds that the relative P_c/P_m could *not* rise 'very greatly' with diminishing returns, considering the effect of raw-material costs on manufacturing prices. And again there is a downplaying of diminishing productivity as a cause of permanent international differentials in the level of money wages: 'By the by surely we have been both wrong in thinking that in the progressive cultivation of poor land, the price of corn compared with manufactures would very greatly rise. I much question whether the natural and necessary rise of the raw materials will not in general be nearly in proportion to the additional labour employed on the land. In wool, leather, and flax, I have little doubt that this is the case. Is it possible that a difficulty in the production of corn, should, without the operation of any other peculiar cause, make the precious metals abundant and cheap in a country, and greatly raise the price of labour compared with other states. Surely with regard to money prices, we have attributed too much to difficulty of production' (291).

30 years, the increase is calculated to have been only about 900,000 on a population of 5,565,000. Since this period it cannot be doubted that the capital of the country has been prodigiously enlarged, and its cultivation very greatly extended; yet, during the last twenty years, we have seen the interest of money at above 5 per cent, with profits in proportion; and, from 1800 to 1811, an increase of population equal to 1,200,000 on 9,287,000, a rate of increase about two and a half times as great as at the former period' (1817, II, 440).

When precisely this striking passage was formulated is unclear. The reference to 'the last twenty years' during which the interest rate exceeded 5 per cent was conceivably inserted at the time of writing rather than publication; 1814 or thereabouts is a likely date for the passage, considering the fact that the profit rate declined during the postwar downturn. In any event, that the twenty-year period ending in 1814 was intended is confirmed in a similar passage in the chapter 'Of Corn Laws' (Book III, ch. 12) regarding the effect of new technology and other disturbing causes in reversing the downward pressure on the profit and wage rates. Here it emerges that Malthus's celebrated agricultural protectionism was dictated in part by his vision of buoyant prospects for ongoing accumulation and population growth at steady, even rising, wages and with no downward pressure on profits. He conceded a case for a free corn-import trade where an economy approached stationariness: 'If a nation be possessed of a territory, not only of sufficient extent to maintain under its actual cultivation a population adequate to a state of the first rank, but of sufficient unexhausted fertility to allow of a very great increase of population, such a circumstance would of course make the measure of restricting the importation of foreign corn more applicable to it. A country which, though fertile and populous, had been cultivated nearly to the utmost, would have no other means of increasing its population than by admission of foreign corn' (491). This was far from the case in contemporary England, considering the effect of new technology and the various other disturbing causes:

But the British isles shew at present no symptoms whatever of this species of exhaustion. The necessary accompaniments of a territory worked to the utmost are very low profits and extent [*sic*: should read 'interest'], a very slack demand for labour, low wages, and a stationary population ... Instead, however, of such symptoms, we have seen in this country, during the twenty years previous to 1814, a high rate of profits and interest, a very great demand for labour, good wages, and an increase of population more rapid, perhaps, than during any period of our history. The capitals which have been laid out in bringing new land into cultivation, or improving the old, must necessarily have yielded good returns, or, under the actual rate of general profits, they would not have been so employed: and although it is strictly true that, as a capital accumulates upon the land, its profits must ultimately diminish; yet owing to the increase of agricultural skill, and other causes noticed in a former chapter, these two effects of progressive cultivation [1826: these two events] do not by any means always keep pace with each other. Though they may finally unite and terminate the career of their progress together, they are often, during the course of their progress, separated for a considerable time, and at a considerable distance. (491–93)[29]

This perspective is placed in broader historical context. Relatively rapid industrialization over the period 1764–1803 had rendered Britain increasingly a corn-importing nation, a trend reversed by the subsequent wartime blockade: 'From the year 1764 to the peace of Amiens [1803], it is generally allowed that the commerce and manufactures of the country increased faster than its agriculture, and that it became gradually more and more dependent on foreign corn for its support. Since the peace of Amiens the state of its colonial monopoly and its manufactures has been such as to demand an unusual quantity of capital; and if the peculiar circumstances of the subsequent war, the high freights and insurance, and the decrees of Buonaparte, had not rendered the importation of foreign corn extremely difficult and expensive, we should at this moment, according to all general principles, have been in the habit of supporting a much larger portion of our population upon it, than at any former period of our history' (497–8). These circumstances had proven a blessing in disguise for otherwise 'very few or none of those great improvements would have taken place which may be said to have purchased fresh land for the state that no fall of price can destroy ... As it is, the practical restrictions thrown in the way of importing foreign corn during the war have forced our steam-engines and our colonial monopoly to cultivate our lands; and those very causes which, according to Adam Smith, tend to draw capital from agriculture, and would certainly have so drawn it if we could have continued to purchase foreign corn at the market prices of France and Holland, have been the means of giving such a spur to our agriculture, that it has not only kept pace with a very rapid increase of commerce and manufactures, but has recovered the distance at which it had for many years been left behind, and now marches with them abreast' (498–9). There is again a strong implication here of *increasing* or at the least *constant* long-run agricultural productivity.

It is subsequently clarified that the initial stimulus for output expansion was provided by high domestic corn prices. However, these were generated under pressure of demand and were subject to reversal; unlike the 1815

29 The 'two effects of progressive cultivation' refer presumably to agricultural expansion and low profits.

formulations, there is little to suggest even moderate secular cost increase at the margin: 'The war that succeeded to the peace of Amiens [1803] found us dependent upon foreign countries for a very considerable portion of our supplies of corn; and we now grow our own consumption, notwithstanding an unusual increase of population in the interval. This great and sudden change in the state of our agriculture could only have been effected by very high prices occasioned by an inadequate home supply and the great expense and difficulty of importing foreign corn' (500–1). A further passage suggests that, even after those prices subsequently declined, the investments remained profitable in that 'the same, or nearly the same, relations between the value of produce and the cost of production' applied, that is, in so far as production costs also declined: 'On account of the high money price of labour, and of the materials of agricultural capital, occasioned partly by direct and indirect taxation, and partly, or perhaps chiefly by the great prosperity of our foreign commerce, new lands cannot be brought into cultivation, nor great improvements made on the old, without a high money price of grain; but these lands, when they have been so brought into cultivation, or improved, have by no means turned out unproductive. The quantity and value of their produce have borne a full and fair proportion to the quantity of capital and labour employed upon them; and they were cultivated with great advantage both to individuals and the state, as long as the same, or nearly the same, relations between the value of produce and the cost of production, which prompted this cultivation, continued to exist' (493–4). At this point, we again find the case for agricultural protection given the *high* productivity of English and Scottish agriculture: 'In such a state of the soil, the British empire might unquestionably be able not only to support from its own agricultural resources its present population, but double, and in time, perhaps, even treble the number; and consequently a restriction upon the importation of foreign corn, which might be thought greatly objectionable in a country which had reached nearly the end of its resources, might appear in a very different light in a country capable of supporting from its own lands a very great increase of population' (494).

To all this we might add that, in a discussion of the implications of agricultural dependency by a manufacturing economy – the danger of a deterioration in the terms of trade – no emphasis is placed on diminishing returns abroad. The matter is indeed raised, but only to be deliberately played down as a relevant concern: 'It would come to the same thing, whether this inability to obtain an increasing quantity of food were occasioned by the advancing money price of corn, or the falling money price of manufactures. In either case the effect would be the same; and it is certain that this effect might take place in either way, from increasing competition and accumulation in the manufacturing nation, and the want of them in the agricultural, *long before any essential increase of difficulty had occurred in the production of corn*' (410; emphasis added).[30]

Finally, there is a letter to Ricardo, dated 3 December 1817, which insists on the *quantitative irrelevance of falling productivity in 'late years,'* ruling it out as an explanation of higher agricultural prices: 'I am strongly disposed to believe that for nearly the last century or at least for 80 or 90 years, no marked increase has taken place in the quantity of labour necessary to produce corn at home ... The increase of labour of growing corn has certainly had little or nothing to do with the increase in its price of late years' (3 December 1817; 1951–73, VII, 214–15).[31] A letter from Ricardo of 24 June 1818 alludes to 'new and improved circumstances' in agriculture from 1793 to 1813 – in particular abroad – very much as in his letter five years earlier (17 August 1813; above, p. 758). This was in response to a non-extant letter from Malthus which can be reconstructed from the Ricardo formulation; evidently Malthus had pointed to the 1793–1813 period, one of effective agricultural protection, as enjoying an increase of wealth in the form of rent otherwise unavailable. This Ricardo denied, since he viewed rent as a transfer from profits (270–1). Malthus's response attempts to turn the factual circumstances against Ricardo: 'You answered the question in my last letter just as I should have expected; and quite consistently with your general principles. But does it not follow as an unavoidable conclusion, that *if as a matter of incontrovertible fact, general profits have risen, and labour has not fallen, after the outlay of a great quantity of capital upon the land,* and a great increase of the national income from the increase of rents, then rents are a creation not a transfer' (16 August; 279, emphasis added). Moreover, the agricultural expansion would not have occurred in the event of reliance on foreign corn: 'If [rents] have risen chiefly from improvements in agriculture occasioned by the direction of so much capital to the land in consequence of a high price [of] corn, is it not an increase of wealth which would not otherwise have been obtained?'[32] Malthus evidently had in mind *domestic agricultural 'improvements'* (in contrast to Ricardo, who had focused on the potential British gain from foreign 'improvements'). Now in the 1815 correspondence Malthus had not emphasized new agricultural technology, and had allowed some deterioration – though 'very' slight – in real costs. He now goes a step farther, positively denying diminishing productivity from 1794 to 1814.

30 Cf. the 1803 argument (1986, *3*, 696), cited above, p. 745.

31 Since 1817 was a year of *low* corn prices, Malthus must have had in mind wartime increases.

32 It is interesting to compare the implicit case made out here for protection on grounds of the generation of rent, with the case to the contrary on efficiency grounds in the 1813 letter to Horner (above, p. 747).

* * *

These formulations of 1817 raise problems. The land scarcity–based growth model (the 'canonical' classical model) so brilliantly formulated in the 1817 edition (see chapter 5: III, IV) was apparently *not*, it follows from the foregoing account, a reflection of contemporary events. Yet, in 1814–15, the principle of diminishing returns is said to have been confirmed by wartime experience as revealed by the parliamentary evidence, albeit not to any great degree (above, sections III, IV). What, if anything, transpired between 1815 and 1817 to lead Malthus to a reorientation?

It will be recalled that in 1815 Malthus read the parliamentary evidence as recognizing high agricultural potential (above, pp. 752–3). The 1814 committee described the conversions of inferior pasture into productive arable, and the great reclamations and enclosures, as 'still in their infancy' (cited above, note 1); and Malthus himself in 1815 surmised that, 'if merely the best modes of cultivation, now in use in some parts of Great Britain, were generally extended,' there was a 'chance' – though not one he then 'insisted' on – that improved technology and skill might allow agricultural expansion at *reduced* real cost. Here he had in mind the great potential for further application of the wartime improvements on the 'light' soils; and even applications of the new methods to the 'vast tracts of clay lands that are yet in a degraded state ...' With the benefit of hindsight, we can say that Malthus was too optimistic regarding the long-term prospects for improvement of clay land, but his evaluation of prospects for the light soils was accurate enough. Now it was these lighter soils that were considered *high cost* areas in the 1814–15 evidence because of the high set-up costs attached to drainage, enclosure, internal roads, and similar investments. But once these investments had been met, current costs would be reduced, as proven by the postwar experience, since the postwar collapse of prices largely affected the clay areas utilizing original technology, whereas the ligher soils held their own.[33] From this perspective it would be fair to say that, while agricultural productivity might have fallen with expansion in the short run, this was not the case over a longer period, at least as far as the

33 For an excellent account of agricultural productivity, see Hueckel, 1981, 182f. The essential feature of the account of the 1793–1815 period is that the general expansion of corn occurred in part by extensions on the thin, light soils of chalk, limestone, or sand, which, to yield repeated crops, required new techniques and were suitable for such new 'mixed' or 'high-farming' techniques involving biological advances, particularly new root crops and cultivated grasses for feeding flocks (and thus generating manure) on arable land – techniques requiring heavy investment of capital and labour in enclosure, drainage, roads, etc. Expansion had also reflected the more intensive use on the heavy-clay lands of the old wheat–bean–fallow or two crop–fallow system – even at the expense of long-term soil exhaustion. These lands proved unamenable – even in the long run – to the new techniques because of drainage problems. The collapse of prices postwar affected the old areas more than the new, more-advanced extensions.

new areas are concerned; thus contraction upon a fall in demand was accommodated by the withdrawal of high-cost clay land *and greater concentration on the now low-cost light soils – 'low-cost' because of an upward shift of the production function.* Malthus, we have seen, himself pointed out in 1817 that lands 'when they have been brought into cultivation, or improved' – a costly procedure requiring a high corn price for their motivation and financing – 'have by no means turned out unproductive' (above, p. 764).[34] Future expansion might on this view be envisaged as likely to occur largely by expansion, at least on the light soils utilizing the new biologically based techniques of 'mixed' or 'high' farming, though Malthus was yet more optimistic in his high estimate of prospects for the application of these methods even to clay lands.[35]

This optimistic view of 1817 coloured even the evaluation of the war years. Yet at the same time, as we shall show in our discussion of Malthus's 'vision' of the population problem (chapter 16), there are references in 1817 – appearing also in 1826 – to an *ultimate* deceleration of population growth, attributable to land scarcity, although with no suggestion of any immediate manifestation. This may be supplemented by accounts which suggest that balanced growth (rather than manufacturing alone) would allow unlimited expansion, a notion also qualified in the light of the 'decreasing fertility of the new land taken into cultivation' (1817, II, 424–5). And Malthus proceeds to specify a variety of 'limits,' all based on diminishing returns, including an ultimate limit to population at which the subsistence wage equals the marginal product (430).[36] Even so, in all this

34 Modern evaluations indicate annual average percentage *increases* in 'total factor productivity,' *even during the war years* and, to a somewhat greater extent, postwar: 1790–1815, of +0.2; 1816–46, of +0.3 (Hueckel, 1981, 192).

35 See also: 'Land is practically almost always understocked with capital. This arises ... from the very nature of much of the soil of almost all large countries, which is such that the employment of a small capital upon it may be little productive, while the employment of a large capital in draining, or in changing the character of the soil by a sufficient quantity of natural and artificial manures, may be productive in a high degree' (1817, II, 435).

Early intimations of the prospect for overcoming the effect of land scarcity by time-consuming investment in land improvement appear in the first *Essay* (above, chapter 1: III). The chapter on Profits in the *Principles* also points towards this interpretation; below, p. 781.

36 See also Malthus, 1824: 'It may be expected, indeed, that in civilized and improved countries, the accumulation of capital, the division of labour, and the invention of machinery, will extend the bounds of production; but we know from experience, that the effect of these causes, which are quite astonishing in reference to some of the *conveniences* and *luxuries* of life, are very much less efficient in producing an increase of *food*' (1986, *4*, 198). Also: with unchecked population growth, the wage rate 'so far as it depends on the facility of procuring the means of subsistence, instead of being improved, would, in all probability, be deteriorated' (202). Similarly, in a comment to Senior of 23 March 1829: 'A retardation in the rate of increase [of population because

there is still no suggestion that such limits had any immediate relevance.[37]

The analysis of the corn-export bounty in the 1817 *Essay* is also suggestive. Despite the highly optimistic estimate of agricultural productivity, no unambiguous case is made for a bounty. As in the *Observations* (above, p. 751), Malthus denied that the ultimate effect of an export subsidy would be 'permanent' cheapness: 'But it has been urged further, that this increased production of corn must necessarily occasion permanent cheapness; and a period of considerable length, during the first sixty four years of the last century, while a bounty was in full operation in this country, has been advanced as a proof of it. In this conclusion, however, it may be reasonably suspected, that an effect, in its nature temporary, though it may be of some duration, has been mistaken for one which is permanent' (464). A permanent fall was precluded on the grounds that, while 'a great and indefinite demand' – and this is attributed to the bounty, having in mind foreign markets – 'is indeed generally found to produce a supply more than proportional to it' and thus 'unusual cheapness,'[38] nevertheless 'this cheapness, when it comes must in its turn check the production of the commodity; and this check, upon the same principle, is apt to continue longer than necessary, and again to occasion a return to higher prices.'[39] This argument implies an output and price cycle involving adjustments over several decades.

Let us now consider an amplification of the allowance for a fall in the corn price in consequence of the bounty: 'It is not therefore necessary, in order to object to the bounty, to say with Adam Smith that the fall in the price of corn which took place during the first half of the last century must have happened in spite of the bounty, and could not possibly have happened in consequence of it. We may allow, on the contrary, what I think we ought to allow according to all general principles, that the bounty, when granted under favourable circumstances, is really calculated, after going through a period of dearness to produce the surplus and the cheapness which its advocates promise ...' (470–1).[40] Attached to this passage is

---

of limits to subsistence] seems to be absolutely inevitable,' notwithstanding *all* positive forces acting on productivity (Senior, 1829, 70).

37 One rationale offered in 1817 for the expansion of the manufacturing sector relative to agriculture, since Elizabeth, is land scarcity (1817, III, 5–6).

38 As in 1814 Malthus relies on Smith.

39 The reversal of the price and output trend was inevitable, but in the British case it had been encouraged by an alteration in the Corn Laws in 1773 (420).

40 Malthus's case in 1817 presumed the bounty to be granted under 'favourable' circumstances: but 'if it be imposed under unfavourable circumstances; that is, if an attempt be made to force exportation by an adequate bounty at a time when the country does not fully grow its own consumption; it is obvious not only that the tax necessary for the purpose must be a very heavy one, but that the effect will be absolutely prejudicial to the population, and the surplus growth will be purchased by a sacrifice very far beyond its worth' (471–2).

a note, absent in earlier editions, pointing to historically increasing productivity, allowance made for improvement: 'As far as the bounty might tend to force the cultivation of poorer land, so far no doubt it would have a tendency to raise the price of corn; but we know from experience that the rise of price naturally occasioned in this way is continually counteracted by improvements in agriculture. As a matter of fact it must be allowed, that, during the period of the last century, when corn was falling [*ca* 1710–50], more land must have been taken into cultivation.'[41] Yet once again, despite all this, we end up with the position that 'according to the same general principles we must allow that this surplus and cheapness, from their operating at once as a check to produce and an encouragement to population, cannot be for any great length of time maintained' or 'produce permanent cheapness' (471).[42] There is an ultimate constraint.

VI EMPIRICAL ESTIMATES IN THE *PRINCIPLES*

Section VI of the chapter on Rent in the *Principles* is devoted to the 'Connexion between great comparative Wealth, and a high comparative Price of raw Produce.' Two 'causes' are isolated to account for a relatively high corn price in wealthy countries: '1. A difference in the value of the precious metals, in different countries under different circumstances [1836: in different countries, in whatever way such difference may have arisen]. 2. A difference in the quantity of labour and capital necessary to produce corn [1836: in the elementary cost of producing a given quantity of corn]'; and it is the first that 'undoubtedly occasions the greatest portion of that inequality in the price of corn, which is the most striking and prominent ... [F]ar the greater part of the high price of corn in this country, compared with [1836: its price in] most of the states in Europe, is occasioned in the same way' (1820, 193; 1836, 185–6).[43] Increase in real costs is thus

---

In the edition of 1803, too, Malthus criticized Smith's view that the corn price fell *despite* the export bounty since there was no way such a bounty can encourage agricultural output: 'If it be admitted,' he objected, 'that the cultivation of corn is susceptible of being encouraged by a bounty like other commodities, it will scarcely fail to follow, that the greater plenty occasioned by this encouragement, will in the long run lower the price' (1986, *3*, 685).

41 We have seen that in the 1803 and 1806 editions increasing productivity are (despite first appearance) apparently *not* part of the argument (above, section II).

42 The argument – as in the *Observations* – is technically unconvincing. For it is allowed that output increase is the cause of reduced unit costs or lower supply price (as with Marshall); to talk, then, of the reduced price discouraging output is to introduce inappropriately a 'Walrasian' mechanism of supply as a function of price. The optimistic tone on productivity is thus qualified when it came to an export bounty.

43 The analysis entails the proposition that it is the efficiency of the export industries that assure that 'corn and labour may be maintained at a very high comparative cost.'

played down empirically. And this orientation is manifest throughout the chapter.

A passage in section III of the chapter on Rent elaborates the cause of high corn prices between 1793 and 1814. The striking feature of the account is that, though Malthus refers to 'supply-side' considerations, *he says nothing of increasing land scarcity*: 'For some time before the war, which commenced in 1793, we had been in the habit of importing a certain quantity of foreign grain to supply our habitual consumption. The war naturally increased the expense of supply by increasing the expense of freight, insurance, &c.; and, joined to some bad seasons and the subsequent decrees of the French government, raised the price, at which wheat could be imported, in the quantity wanted to supply the demand, in a very extraordinary manner' (1820, 168; 1836, 164).[44] Another statement points explicitly to an increase in the profit rate between 1790 and 1813 as evidence against empirically diminishing productivity during the war: 'That the last land taken into cultivation in 1813 did not require more labour to work it than the last land improved in the year 1790, is incontrovertibly proved [1836: is proved] by the acknowledged fact that the rate of interest and profits was higher in the later period than the earlier ... [The] great drainings and permanent improvements, which were the effects of so powerful an encouragement to agriculture, have acted like the creation of fresh land, and have increased the real wealth and population of the country, without increasing the labour and difficulty of raising a given quantity of grain' (1820, 169–70; 1836, 165–6). In the same section, Malthus reiterates the point in a passage drawn from the *Inquiry into Rent* (see above, p. 756).[45]

Subsequently, in the 1820 version, Malthus denied that the Corn Laws had been responsible for high wartime corn prices: 'The high price of corn from 1798 to 1814 was occasioned by the war and the seasons – not by corn-laws; and ... a country with open ports may be subject to very great alternations of price in war and peace' (1820, 222n). Here there is no reference to higher real costs of production as a cause of higher corn prices, the emphasis being on poor harvests, with impediments to an inflow of corn resulting from hostilities. The obvious implication is that, setting aside seasonal complications and wartime costs, output might expand

44 It is doubtful whether Malthus intended to rule out demand pressure. But an editorial note by Cazenove gives this reading and objects: 'During the period alluded to, corn rose far beyond what was necessary to defray the increased expense of freight, insurance, &c., occasioned by the war. The *cause* of the rise was, therefore, *independent* of the increased cost of importation. It doubtless originated in the profuse expenditure of the state, and the increased activity of commercial and manufacturing activity at the time' (1836, 164). On this matter see Pullen, 1978, 289.

45 The 1836 version replaces 'during the last twenty years' by 'during the twenty years from 1793 to 1813.'

without rising costs. This implication is rationalized in 1820 in section IX of the Rent chapter in an extraordinary note – fully in line with the interpretation we offered of the 1817 evaluations (above, pp. 766f.) – maintaining that investment in permanent agricultural improvement should be viewed as a means of effectively adding to the land supply, thus assuring that cost price in terms of capital and labour embodied is actually *reduced* by import restrictions (1820, 223n).[46]

The note of 1820 positively denying that corn-import restriction was responsible for high corn prices in the period 1793–1814 (222n) is absent from the second edition.[47] But it is not clear that this entails a deliberate change of perspective, since attribution of responsibility to cost factors *unrelated to land scarcity* is retained. The note asserting cost reductions in the event of corn-import restrictions (223n) falls out with the various deletions from the second edition; and the removal of most of section IX includes a supposedly positive effect of corn-import restrictions on population growth (223–4). All this possibly hints at a more pessimistic outlook. Moreover, modifications to the statements pointing to profit-rate movements as evidence of the effect of new technology may indicate a change of empirical perspective. For the revised version implies that the profit rate had *tended downwards since 1813* after remaining roughly steady, despite major population expansion, for a century: 'The very great improvements in agriculture which have taken place in this country are clearly demonstrated by the profits of stock being as high now as they were nearly a hundred years ago [1836: *having been as high in 1813 as they were nearly a hundred years before*], when the land supported but little more than half of its present population [1836: half the population]. And the power of the necessaries of life, when properly distributed, to create their own demand is fully proved by the palpable fact, that the exchangeable value of corn in the command of labour and other commodities is, to say the least, undiminished [1836: was for many years before that period undiminished], notwithstanding the many and great improvements which have [1836: had] been successively introduced in cultivation [1836: into use], both by the introduction of better implements, and by an improved system [1836: a more skilful system] of managing the land' (1820, 165; 1836, 161; emphasis added).

But what weight should be put on this modification? In my view it reflects at most a perception of cyclical and postwar deviations from trend. For the theme that land improvement constitutes the major source of rent increase is retained, and here we find *enhanced* optimism regarding prospects for future technology: 'I should further say, that not only have

46 We shall elaborate on this perspective in chapter 17: VIII, on agricultural trade policy.

47 This falls in a major deletion of text – the substance of section IX in 1820 – involving a deviation of private and social returns to agricultural investment, with its policy implications.

improvements in agriculture never lowered rents, but that they have been hitherto, and may be expected to be in future, the *main* source of the inrease of rents, in almost all the countries with which we are acquainted ... [A]fter all, the increase of rents which results from an increase of price occasioned solely by the greater quantity of labour and capital [1836: labour and other conditions of supply] necessary to produce a given quantity of corn on fresh land, is very much more limited than has been supposed; and by a reference to most of the countries with which we are acquainted, it will be seen that, practically, improvements in agriculture and the saving of labour on the land, both have been, and may be expected in future to be, a much [1836: very much] more powerful source of increasing rents' (1820, 207–8; 1836, 196–7). And in this context, moreover, there is no hint of a reversal of the profit-rate trend since 1813: 'It has already been shewn, that for the very great increase of rents which have [1836: has] taken place in this country during nearly the last hundred years, we are mainly indebted to improvements in agriculture, as profits have rather risen than fallen, and little or nothing has been taken from the wages of families, if we include parish allowances, and the earnings of women and children. Consequently these rents must have been a creation from the skill and capital employed upon the land, and not a transfer from profits and wages, as they existed nearly a hundred years ago' (1820, 208–9; 1836, 197).

Despite all this, Malthus – drawing on the *Grounds* (1815) – proceeded to elaborate on the effect of diminishing returns on the corn price. And though he represented this only as a matter of 'general principle' (1820, 196; 1836, 188) he did assert in 1820 that technical improvement, albeit 'sometimes most powerful, and of very considerable duration,' 'cannot finally be sufficient to balance the necessity of applying to poorer land, or inferior machines' – in which respect 'raw produce is essentially different from manufactures' (1820, 197). Now a very long-run tendency to rising corn prices emanating from increasing land scarcity would not be inconsistent with a highly optimistic view of prospective cost conditions in the more immediate future, or indeed with a similarly rosy view of the past few decades. This would be consistent with the renditions of 1817. But what are we to make of the variation in the second edition, which represents falling productivity as a matter of *actual experience* rather than one of future prospect : 'We know from experience that [improvements] have not been sufficient to balance the effects of applying to poorer land, or inferior machines' (1836, 188)? If this refers to recent British experience – even if it is intended as a caution regarding the immediate future – it would clash seriously with the retention of the 'prediction' regarding future agricultural progress as the major source of rent. The fact that the only illustration given refers to corn 'obtained with less labour in the United States of America than in any European country' may suggest a very general proposition rather than one specifically pertinent to contemporary Britain. But if the revision did reflect growing pessimism regarding future prospects for the profit-rate trend based on recent experience, it is not carried through even in the Rent chapter. As for the Profits chapter, we shall show next that it retains fully the optimistic perspective of 1817 – increasing land scarcity was of no great prospective consequence.

* * *

The section 'Of Profits as affected by the Causes practically in operation' (Section III in 1820, IV in 1836) treats the effect on the profit rate – in the agricultural sector, in the first instance – of 'causes' other than land scarcity and wage variability. In the second edition, Malthus specifies that he has an eye on such 'disturbing' or 'modifying' causes, 'particularly in this country' (1836, 282). Agricultural improvement – new technology and increased effort – is emphasized in both editions: 'In the progressive cultivation of poorer land for instance, as capital and population increase, profits, according to the first cause, will regularly fall [1836: In the progressive cultivation of poor land, occasioned by the increase of capital and population, profits as far as they depend upon natural fertility, will regularly fall]; but if at the same time improvements in agriculture are taking place, they may certainly be such as, for a considerable period, not only to prevent profits from falling, but to allow of a considerable rise [1836: a rise] ... A second circumstance which would contribute to the same effect is, an increase of personal exertion among the labouring classes' (1820, 313–14; 1836, 282–3).[48] A 'third circumstance' acting positively on profits – 'the unequal rise of some parts of capital [1836: the farmer's capital], when the price of corn is raised by an increased demand' (1820, 315; 1836, 283) – refers to lags in the prices of domestic and imported materials, of other inputs and of wage goods behind the rise in the corn price.[49] The

48 In the first edition increased effort is related to increased earnings: 'This [increased] activity [per person] indeed, within certain limits, appears almost always to come forward when it is most called for, that is, when there is much work to be done without a full supply of persons to do it.' On this see Ricardo's *Note 172*: 'All these circumstances come under the general cause already noticed, namely the "proportion of the produce that is given to the labourer"' (1951–73, II, 272).

49 The case is specifically limited to corn-price increases that affect the 'value of money,' that is, raise the money wage: 'The rise of corn and labour at home will not proportionally raise the price of such products; and as far as these products form any portion of the farmer's capital this capital will be rendered more productive ... While the value of the farmer's produce rises, these articles will not rise in proportion, and consequently a given value of capital will yield a greater value of produce' (1820, 315–16). The second version restates the latter in proportionate terms: 'The rise of corn and labour at home will not proportionally raise the price of such products; and as far as these products together with taxes, form a part of the farmer's capital, a smaller proportion of the produce, owing to its increased value, will replace it' (1836, 284).

1836 version adds industrial innovation, which, by indirectly allowing reduced money wages, acts positively on the agricultural profit rate: 'A fourth circumstance, which favours a rise of profits is a fall in the prices of some important manufactures, as compared with corn, owing to improvements in machinery. This state of things always allows of some diminution in the corn wages of labour without a proportionate diminution of the comforts of the labourer: and if the money price of the farmer's produce increases without a proportionate increase in the price of labour, and in the materials of which his advances consist, his profits must necessarily rise' (1836, 284).

Our concern is with the empirical significance attributed to these 'modifying' or 'disturbing' causes. The prospective intervention of such disturbances led Malthus to declare that he 'should feel no doubt of ... an increase in the rate of profits in this country for twenty years together, at the beginning of the twentieth century, compared with the twenty years which are now coming on, provided this near period were a period of profound tranquillity and peace and abundant capital, and the future period were a period in which capital was scanty in proportion to the demand for it owing to a war, attended by the circumstances of an increasing trade and an increasing demand for agricultural produce similar to those which were experienced from 1793 to 1813' (1820, 325; 1836, 288–9).[50] The passage is somewhat ambiguous. It refers to a sharper prospective *rise* in the profit rate between 1900 and 1920 than in *circa* 1820–40, but it is unclear whether a rise in the profit rate was indeed expected in the 'twenty years ... now coming on.' What is certain is the emphasis on an *upward trend in the profit rate between 1793 and 1813*, reflecting the net impact of 'causes' which counteract diminishing agricultural returns. And this sets the stage for the main conclusion – that, if increasing land scarcity is indeed neutralized, the route is cleared for his own favourite hypothesis: 'But if this is so, [1836: and past experience justifies it,] it follows, that in the actual state of things in most countries of the world, and within limited periods of moderate extent, the rate of profits will practically depend more upon the causes which affect the relative abundance or scarcity of capital, [1836: and the demand for produce compared with the supply,] than on the fertility [1836: than on the natural powers] of the last land taken into cultivation. And consequently, to dwell on this

50 Ricardo (*Note 184*) commented: 'What a number of conditions! the only one of importance is the abundance or scarcity of capital compared with the demand for it, which is saying in other words that if in the beginning of the twentieth century the comparative quantity of capital and labour should be such that the labourers should not be able to command so large a proportion of the produce obtained on the last land profits will then be higher. On these conditions there is no denying the conclusion. Whether they will be so or not must depend on improvements in Agriculture – or on the permission of law to import corn without restrictions from other countries' (1951–73, II, 284).

latter point as the sole, or even the main cause which determines profits, must lead to the most erroneous conclusions. Adam Smith, in stating the cause of the fall of profits, has omitted this point, and in so doing has omitted a most important consideration; but in dwelling solely upon the abundance and competition of capital, he is practically much nearer the truth than those who dwell almost exclusively on the quality of the last land taken into cultivation' (1820, 325–6; 1836, 289).[51]

A more elaborate account of current circumstances emerges a little earlier in the same chapter. It follows an assertion in 1820 that, in practice, and for 'any period of some length,' profits depend 'very much more upon the causes which had occasioned a comparatively scanty or abundant supply of capital than upon the natural fertility of the land last taken into cultivation' (1820, 317); or, in the second edition, that 'practically, and in the actual state of things, the physical necessity of a fall of profits in agriculture arising from the increasing quantity of labour required to produce the same quantity of food, may be so counteracted and overcome, for a considerable time by other causes, as to leave very great play to the influence of the competition of capitals' (1836, 284).

Now, in the first version, Malthus refers to 'obvious and incontrovertible' facts pointing to the foregoing conclusion, some of which had 'been stated in the preceding section' (1820, 318). But that section had dealt with wage fluctuations and their effect on the profit rate, whereas the introductory statement just cited apparently relates to 'competition of capitals' in *commodity* markets. And in fact, in the second version, the allusion to the 'preceding section' is absent: 'The facts which support this conclusion are numerous and incontrovertible. It may be said, indeed, with truth that the different rates of profits during periods of peace and war, which are observed to take place in all countries, are chiefly attributable to the abundance or scarcity of capital and produce compared with the demand, and not to the varying productiveness of labour on the land' (1836, 284–5) – which doubtless refers to commodity-market pressures. In any event, the specific set of facts now considered relates to the historical pattern of the profit or interest rate in Great Britain: (1) *1727–1757*: 'Excluding then the period of war [the war of the Austrian Succession, 1740–8], we have here a period of twenty-two years, during which the general rate of interest was between $3\frac{1}{2}$ and 3 per cent' (1820, 318; 1836, 285).[52] The acceptance by creditors of a low interest paid on government

51 A note withdraws some of the criticism of Smith: 'It ought to be allowed that Adam Smith, in speaking of the effects of accumulation and competition on profits, naturally means to refer to a limited territory, a limited population, and a limited demand; but accumulation of capital under these circumstances involves every cause that can affect profits' (1820, 326n; 1836, 289n).

52 Malthus drew on George Chalmers (1st ed., 1782). See Pullen, in Malthus, 1820/1989, II, 422, for data regarding Chalmers and the period Malthus intended.

bonds for so considerable a period was 'a most decisive proof of a great difficulty in the means of employing capital profitably, and consequently, a most decisive proof of a low rate of profits' (1820, 318–19; 1836, 285).[53] (2) *1793–1813*:[54] Following several decades (since 1727) entailing 'a great accumulation of capital ... and an unusual quantity of new land ... brought into cultivation,' the average market rate of interest over the war decades was none the less somewhat above 5 per cent. And considering the 'extraordinary rapidity with which capital was recovered, after it had been destroyed,' it could be presumed that the *profit* rate 'was quite in proportion to this high rate of interest.' Further evidence is brought from Arthur Young to indicate 'an increase in the profits of capital employed upon the land' (1820, 319–20; 1836, 285–6).

In the 1820 version, Malthus concluded that the 'different rates of interest and profits in the two periods here noticed are diametrically opposed to the theory of profits founded on the natural quality of the last land taken into cultivation. The facts, which are incontrovertible, not only cannot be accounted for upon this theory, but in reference to it, either exclusively or mainly, they ought to be directly the reverse of what they are found to be in reality' (320). This passage is absent from the second edition, but in both the argument points to evidence controverting the position that the profit rate is uniquely governed by diminishing agricultural productivity: 'The nature of these facts, and the state of things under which they took place, (in the one case, in a state of peace with a slack demand for agricultural products [1836: for capital and produce], and in the other, a state of war with an unusual demand for these products [1836:

53 Cf. also the following comment on the downward trend of interest and profit rates after *cira* 1750, despite the availability of cheap corn, thus excluding any explanation in terms of land scarcity: 'In the instance ... which occurred in this country in the middle of last century, there must have been a considerable difficulty in finding employment for capital, or the national creditors would rather have been paid off than have submitted to a reduction of interest from 4 per cent to $3\frac{1}{2}$, and afterwards to 3. And that this fall in the rate of interest and profits arose from a redundancy of capital and a want of demand for produce, rather than from the difficulty of production on the land, is fully evinced by the low price of corn at the time, and the very different state of interest and profits which has occurred since' (1820, 475–6; 1836, 405–6).

As an added illustration: 'A similiar instance took place in Italy in 1685, when, upon the Pope's reducing the interest of his debts from 4 to 3 per cent, the value of the principal rose afterwards to 112; and yet the Pope's territories have at no time been so cultivated as to occasion such a low rate of interest and profits from the difficulty of procuring the food of the labourer. Under a more favourable distribution of property, there cannot be a doubt that such a demand for produce, agricultural, manufacturing, and mercantile, might have been created, as to have prevented for many, many years the interest of money from falling below 3 per cent. In both these cases, the demands of the landlords were added to those of the productive classes.'

54 The twenty-year period Malthus alludes to is not explicit here, but subsequently it becomes clear that 1793–1813 is intended.

for both,]) obviously and clearly point to the *relative* redundancy or deficiency of capital, as, according to every probability, connected with them [1836: ... of capital and produce as their cause]' (1820, 320; 1836, 286).[55] In both editions, the preferred hypothesis involves the effect of capital redundancy or deficiency (see Conclusion, V).

We turn now to the details of the period 1727–57:

In the first period of the two which have been noticed, it is known that the price of corn had fallen, but [1836: and] that the wages of labour had not only not fallen in proportion, but had been considered by some authorities as having risen ...[56] Allowing, however, even a stationary price of labour, with a falling price of corn [1836: not arising from improvements], and the fall of agricultural profits is at once accounted for. Such a state of prices might alone be much more than sufficient to counteract the effects arising from the circumstance of pretty good land being yet uncultivated. When we add, that the other outgoings belonging to the farmers' capital, such a leather, iron, timber, &c. &c., are supposed to have risen while his main produce [1836: the price of his main produce] was falling, we can be at no loss to account for a low rate of agricultural profits, notwithstanding the unexhausted state of the country. And as to the low rate of mercantile and manufacturing profits, that would be accounted for at once by the proportion of capital to labour [1836: by the increase of mercantile and manufactured products compared with the demand for them, and their consequent diminished prices in relation to labour]. (1820, 321–2; 1836, 287–8)[57]

55 What is intended by the alteration from a change in intensity of demand for '*agricultural products*' to one for '*capital and produce*' will emerge shortly. Ricardo, of course, found the notion 'relative redundancy of capital' antithetical unless understood as a reference to labour-market pressures: 'What does Mr. Malthus mean by relative redundancy of capital? I do not like the term; but waiving that objection, under every increase of capital, if population increases still faster, and labour falls, population is redundant as compared with capital; and if population increases at a slower rate than capital, capital is relatively redundant to population. This is again another way of stating that profits will be high or low, according as wages are low or high' (*Note 178*; 1951–73, II, 277).

56 Malthus refers to Smith and Young: 'Adam Smith states the fall of corn and the rise of labour during the first sixty-four years of the last century as a sort of established fact; but Arthur Young, in his very useful inquiries into the prices of corn and labour published in his Annals of Agriculture, seems to think with some reason [1836: 'with some reason' omitted], that the fact is not well authenticated, and is besides a little [1836: 'besides a little' omitted] inconsistent with the apparently slack demand for labour and produce and comparatively slow progress of population, which took place during the period in question.'

57 Ricardo accepted the analysis in so far only as it implied attribution of the falling profit rate to an increase in the corn wage: 'Whatever Mr. Malthus may call it this is a high price of labour, because by his own shewing it is an increased proportion of the produce obtained from the last land which is awarded to the labourer. He is particularly bound to call such wages high, because he measures value by quantity, and he tells us the labourer will have an increased quantity of corn, which he calls increased real

This is not a happy analysis. There is the characteristic duality of approach towards agricultural and manufacturing profits, and a failure to account adequately for each. Thus there is no explicit explanation of the behaviour of corn prices, money wages, and other outlays to which 'the fall' in the agricultural profit rate is attributed, despite 'the unexhausted state of the country.' (The low corn price might be the result of the 'slack demand for agricultural products' alluded to shortly before – but *why* the slack demand?) Malthus then provides (in 1820) a different account to explain the low manufacturing rate – 'the proportion of capital to labour.' Taken literally, this implies *labour scarcity* directly reflected in the market for labour. But the alteration in 1836 points to 'the increase of mercantile and manufactured products compared with the demand for them' – pressure in *commodity* markets or Smithian 'competition of capitals.' This suggests that the earlier change from 'a slack demand for agricultural produce' to 'a slack demand for capital and produce' reflects a generalization of the effect of low demand to incorporate both farming and manufactured products. Now this was the position in 1820 as well; and the only remaining question is whether in 1820 Malthus also intended pressures operating by way of the labour market. We shall shortly see what the remaining text yields in this regard.

Turning now to the second period, 1793–1813. In the 1820 version, Malthus introduces his analysis by remarking that 'it is probable that all the circumstances noticed in this section concurred to give room for the operation of that principle which depends upon the proportion of capital to labour' (1820, 322). Here Malthus again seeks to demonstrate the empirical irrelevance of increasing land scarcity, leaving only one explanatory hypothesis.

Malthus first emphasized the neutralization of diminishing returns by agricultural improvements and increased effort supply: 'In the first place, there can be no doubt of the improvements in agriculture which were going forwards during these twenty years, both in reference to the general management of the land and the instruments which are connected with cultivation, or which in any way tend to facilitate the bringing of raw produce to market. 2dly, the increasing practice of task-work during these twenty years, together with the increasing employment of women and children, unquestionably occasioned a great increase of personal exertion; and more work was done by the same number of persons and families than

---

wages. Profits then fall because wages rise – circumstances have made the position of the labourer favourable to him. Labour is under supplied compared with capital' (*Note 179*; 1951–73, II, 278–9). As for the manufacturing rate: 'If money wages were higher than before, that would account for a fall in mercantile profits.' This is standard Ricardian analysis.

before' (1820, 322; 1836, 288).[58] Malthus proceeded in 1820 to a *third* cause at play – a rising corn price but a less-than-proportionate increase in money wages and other cost items: 'The third cause, which had a very considerable effect, much more indeed than is generally attributed to it, was a rise in the money price of corn without a proportionate rise in mercantile and manufacturing produce. This state of things always allows of some diminution in the corn wages of labour without a proportionate diminution of the comforts of the labourer; and if the money price of the farmer's produce increases without a proportionate increase in the price of labour and of the materials of which his capital consists, this capital becomes more productive and his profits must necessarily rise' (323).[59] This latter 'cause'[60] had been mentioned in the analysis of the period 1727–57, when it operated in the reverse direction – corn prices declining in the face of a less-than-proportionate decline in money costs.

After summarizing the effects of his three causes, Malthus again confirmed that he did not intend downward labour-market pressure by his allusion to the room created for 'the operation of that principle which depends upon the proportion of capital to labour': 'All the causes just noticed are of a nature to increase the productive powers both of labour and capital; and if ... they are of sufficient force to overcome the effect of taking poorer land into cultivation, the rate of profits may rise consistently even with an increase in the real wages of labour.' And an increase in real wages (taking account of family earnings and piece work) had actually occurred: 'In the case in question, though it is generally supposed that the money wages of labour did not rise in proportion to the rise in the price of provisions; yet I cannot help thinking, both from the acknowledged demand for labour and the rapid increase of population, that, partly owing to parish assistance and the more extended use of potatoes, and partly to

58 The adoption of new technology and increased task-work are attributed to 'the circumstances of the time' – namely, 'the high price of corn, which encouraged the employment of more capital upon the land with the most effective modes of applying it, and by the increasing demand for labour, owing to the number of men wanted in the army and navy at the same time that more than ever were wanted in agriculture and manufactures' (322–3). It will be recalled that effort supply is represented in 1820 as a positive function of the real wage (above, note 48). This alone tells us that by change in the proportion of capital to labour as responsible for the profit-rate increase Malthus could not have intended a downward labour-market movement.

59 The 1836 version retains a version of this 'third' cause, and adds a fourth (above, p. 774) which is evidently based on this passage. But that involved manufacturing innovation.

60 Ricardo objected: 'Now this is one of the occasions when it appears to me that Mr. Malthus comes to a wrong conclusion by mixing the two measures of value – corn value – and money price' (*Note 181*; 1951–73, II, 281). See also *Note 180* on the first two 'causes' (280).

task-work and the increased employment of women and children, the labouring classes had on an average an increased command over the necessaries of life. I am inclined to think, therefore, that the increased rate of profits from 1793 to 1813 did not arise so much from the diminished quantity of agricultural produce given to the labourer's family, as from the increase in the amount of agricultural produce obtained by the same number of families' (323–4). As for marginal productivity: 'I have no doubt that, as I stated in the chapter on rent, the capital employed upon the last land taken into cultivation in 1813 was more productive than the capital employed upon the last land taken into cultivation in 1727; and it appears to me that the causes which have been mentioned are sufficient to acount for it theoretically, and to make such an event appear not only possible, but probable, and likely to be of frequent recurrence' (324).

The section closes by holding out great promise for the future, particularly in an economy dependent on domestic food supplies. This optimism turns on the presumption that agricultural technology is encouraged by 'a great demand for corn of home growth'; that a high demand for labour (that is, high real wages) would stimulate effort; and that increasing wealth generates upward pressure on the corn price (and a lesser increase in other commodities) – all experienced during the war years (324–5). On balance, 'the probabilities of an increase in the productive powers of labour sufficient to counterbalance the effect of taking additional land into cultivation are so strong, that ... in the actual state of most countries in the world, it is then probable that *for some centuries to come*, we may fairly lay our account to their operations when the occasion calls for it' (325; emphasis added).[61]

An important formulation in the 1820 version of the *Principles* – 'Remarks on Mr. Ricardo's Theory of Profits' – gives one of the clearest rationalizations in the whole range of Malthus's writings of the level of the profit rate between 1795 and 1820. The theme – encountered above, in chapter 10: V – is that the devotion of available capital to manufacturing exports, as in an open system, would have depressed the profit rate by dint of increased 'competition of capital' or excess supply.[62] This sequence of

61 Ricardo did not object to the optimistic tone regarding technology, insisting only that prospects for innovation would be as good in an open economy: 'Under a system of free importation, there would be a sufficient demand for corn of home growth to encourage improvements in Agriculture' (*Note 182*; 1951–73, II, 283). As for the effect of 'a rising price of corn owing to an increase of wealth,' he objected on price-theoretic grounds: 'If this is not occasioned by an increased cost of production, why should it operate on corn more than on other things. If it did not, either corn would not rise, or there would be a proportionate rise of other commodities, and then the whole might be referred to a fall in the value of money – which produces no effects on profits.'

62 The theme that agricultural investment diminishes the pressure exerted by 'competition of capitals' in manufacturing appears in the 1815 correspondence (above, p. 761).

events had been avoided by protection that had assured the attraction of capital to agriculture, taking the form of investment in land improvement: 'If the price of corn during the last twenty-five years could have been kept at about fifty shillings the quarter, and the increasing capital of the country had chiefly been applied to the working up of exportable commodities for the purchase of foreign corn, I am strongly disposed to believe that the profits of stock would have been lower instead of higher. The millions which have been employed in permanent agricultural improvements have had no tendency whatever to lower profits' (1820, 330–1).[63] To the contrary: 'The millions of capital which have been expended in drainings, and in the roads and canals for the conveyance of agricultural products, have tended rather to raise than lower profits; and millions and millions may yet be employed with the same advantageous effect' (330n). For it was an 'unquestionable fact' that agricultural profits were 'higher in 1813 than they were about eighty years before, although in the interval millions and millions of accumulated capital had been employed on the soil' (333). Again: 'Nothing is more common, as I have stated in the Chapter on Rent, than increased profits, not only without capital being withdrawn from the land, but under a continual addition to it' (1820, 374n; 1836, 329n).[64] As for the future, Malthus reiterated that new technology might assure ongoing growth for 'hundreds of years' in an economy chiefly dependent on home supplies of food, whereas a growth program based on manufactures was likely to be stifled prematurely (332–3).[65]

The formal discussion of the historical behaviour of the profit rate, and its rationalization, are much reduced in the second version. But this revised text serves to remove our initial problem at one stroke by specifying that it is upward commodity-market, not downward labour-market pressures, that are intended in the analysis of the war years: 'From 1793 to 1813 it is probable that all the circumstances noticed in this section concurred to give room for that principle which depends upon the demand compared with the supply of capital' (1836, 288; compare the 1820 version, cited above, p. 778). It also restates the 'causes' then at play – improved productivity and effort supply – and mentions the effect of a rise in the relative money price of corn and of improved *manufacturing* technology. As in 1820, Malthus proceeded to his forecast of the likely state of affairs in the beginning of the twentieth century, repeating both his practical emphasis on 'causes which affect the relative abundance or scarcity of capital' and his commendation of Smith for focusing upon this feature (above, pp. 774–5).

63 Corn prices fluctuated around the 50s. level in prewar years and remained well above that level, in some years even double, until 1820 (see Mitchell, 1962, 488).

64 This perspective lends support for our interpretation of the optimism of the 1817 *Essay on Population* (above, p. 766).

65 Cf. the same general notion in the *Essay* of 1817 (II, 424–5), cited above, p. 767.

* * *

Further indications of trends in agricultural productivity emerge elsewhere in the *Principles.* In his chapter 'Of the Progress of Wealth,' Malthus implies no deterioration whatsoever; rather he focuses on increased skill and labour-saving technology: 'I have already shewn that the saving of labour and the increase of skill, both in agriculture [1836: agricultural] and manufacturing industry ... enable a country to push its cultivation over poorer lands, without diminution of profits' (1820, 422; 1836, 367). Evidently the 'poorer' lands could be cultivated without real cost increase, given more productive techniques. Such agricultural improvements, which extended 'far and wide the markets for ... manufactures' and tended 'to increase the exchangeable value of the whole,' are represented as 'the main sources of that rapid and astonishing increase in the value of the national wealth, that has taken place during the last thirty or forty years.'[66] And it was increase in skill that accounted for the 'very extraordinary' fact that England, despite relatively weak agricultural resources, had the smallest proportion of its workforce engaged in agriculture: 'One of the great landed nations of Europe, and indeed of the world, England, with only one or two exceptions, [1836: with hardly an exception,] is supposed to have pushed its cultivation the farthest; and though the natural qualities of its whole soil by no means stand very high in the scale of comparative richness, there is a smaller proportion of the people employed in agriculture, and a greater proportion employed in the production of conveniences and luxuries, or living on monied incomes, than in any other agricultural country of the world' (1820, 380; 1836, 334–5).

There is one addition in the second edition that casts further light on contemporary productivity trends. It relates to the cost of obtaining money and asserts categorically that the high ruling level of British corn prices and money wages reflected, not so much the Corn Laws, but rather the efficiency of British manufacturing; or, expressed alternatively, that high British corn prices did not indicate 'a high value of corn,' but rather a low value of money: 'If this doctrine be true, and I most firmly believe it is, it appears that a rise in the money price of corn and labour is a necessary consequence of commercial prosperity; and though I would distinctly allow, that in reference to our own country at present the corn laws keep

66 Taking 1820 as the base, this implies ongoing growth since approximately 1780 or 1790, which is loose, regarding both the years prior to 1790 and the postwar-depression years. Subsequently, in the course of a denial that land quality is of primary importance in explaining the contrasting experiences in the period 1793–1813 and post-1815, Malthus specifies that the first period witnessed 'the greatest quantity of *our poor lands ... in cultivation*' followed by a period in which 'some of our *poorest lands have been thrown out of cultivation*' (1820, 495–6; 1836, 418; emphasis added). The reference to an expansion to 'poor land' should be read in the same manner as the passage in our text.

the prices of corn and labour higher than they would be, if things were left to take their natural course: yet still it is unquestionable, that the actual prices of corn and labour indicate a low value of money, and not a high value of corn, and that they operate in a totally different way from taxes on the labouring classes' (1836, 130). A subsequent observation regarding current English and European conditions places the responsibility for the relatively high English corn price on 'a higher scale of money prices, or lower value of money' reflected in a higher money wage – allowance made for price reductions in sectors subject to improved technology (including here the export sector) – and *not 'a greater difficulty of obtaining it'*: 'It is certainly true that the money wages of independent labour, notwithstanding their fall of late years, are higher in this country than in any other country in Europe, and there is every reason to believe that the English labourer with his money earnings can purchase as great a quantity of wheat as any European labourer of the same description' (130–1). And the conclusion is quite unambiguous: 'If this be so, it is a distinct proof that the higher price of corn in this country, as compared with the continent, in not at present owing to a greater difficulty of obtaining it, but to a higher scale of money prices, or lower value of money, which operates upon *all* commodities, though it is more than counterbalanced in that class of commodities where skill and superior machinery have most prevailed, and it is of these that our principal exports will naturally consist.' This is precisely the theme encountered in the chapter on Rent in both versions (above, pp. 769f.).

VII SUMMARY AND CONCLUSION

The 1820 and the posthumous versions of the *Principles* both emphasize an increasing rate of return on capital over the war years attributable *inter alia* to higher productivity and effort supply, in effect denying the increasing-cost allowances made in the *Observations* and *Grounds of an Opinion*. Taking the *Principles* as a whole, we can discern no revision of the optimism expressed in the 1817 – and the 1826 – *Essay on Population* regarding *prospective* productivity increase. Only in the second edition of the chapter on Rent are there possibly new doubts, but these are not sustained or carried through. For these reasons Malthus's new recognition in the 1820s that Britain's future prosperity turned on industry-led growth (see chapter 17: IX) cannot be attributed with any confidence to a growing concern with prospective agricultural productivity.

SIXTEEN

Demographic trends: The population problem

I INTRODUCTION

In his presidential address to the American Economic Association, Gary Becker alludes to Malthus's 'great contribution,' represented as including: (1) diminishing returns to increases in employment 'when land and other capital are fixed'; (2) population growth positively related to the wage, the lower population growth at low wages turning on reduced birth rates (the preventive check) and increased death rates (the positive check); and (3) a long-run equilibrium wage at which population is constant at a level determined by the production function (1988, 1–2). Becker emphasizes the stability of the equilibrium wage in the face of disturbances. A catastrophic reduction in population size (e.g., the Black Death) and, consequently, a wage increase will be followed by positive population growth which restores both the wage and the population size to their respective equilibrium levels. In the event of increases in the amount of usable land, population size will become permanently higher, with the wage ultimately reduced to its original long-run level. Becker represents Malthus as reaching 'much more pessimistic conclusions about the long-term economic prospects of the average family' than, for example, Godwin and Condorcet, who had maintained that the economic position of mankind will continue to improve over time. Events were 'not kind to the theory' for, in fact, 'fertility eventually fell sharply rather than rose as wage rates and per capita incomes continued to advance during much of the nineteenth and twentieth centuries in the United States, Western Europe, and Japan' (2–3).

E.A. Wrigley also maintains that Malthus failed to appreciate future trends anticipated by changes already under way in his own time. While it was rational for him on the basis of recent history to link food-price rises with population growth and to fear the effect of rapid population growth, that pattern did not continue. Over the period 1781–1806 the (cumulative) rate of population growth exceeded 1 per cent annually, with food-price increases approximately 2.25 per cent; for the period 1801–26, with the population growth rate averaging nearly 1.5 per cent, food prices remained on average pretty stable and actually fell on average over the period 1816–36 (1983, 116–17). Similarly, the historical relationship indicated that, at higher rates of population growth, real wages fell increasingly sharply; but again 'very soon after Malthus turned his mind to this question, the pattern which he detected, and which he thought to be permanently imprinted on the socio-economic system, abruptly disappeared. Exceptionally high population growth rates proved consonant with rising real wages after 1800' (119).

In his authoratative textbook, Mark Blaug asserts that Malthus in 1803 showed little awareness of the striking acceleration of population growth: 'In the second edition of the *Essay* in 1803, he took notice of the census of 1801 but barely examined its findings, and he showed no awareness that he was living in a time of population growth without precedent in European history' (1985, 68). He further asserts that Malthus 'seriously underestimated' the declining mortality rate: 'Malthus himself emphasized birth and marriage rates and even in the later editions of the *Essay* he seriously underestimated the fall in the death rate that had taken place. It is not so much that he got the facts wrong, for even now we cannot agree what the facts were, but rather that he never clearly grasped, or even took much interest in, the nature of the population explosion that gave such prominence to his views.'

I shall demonstrate in this chapter that the foregoing evaluations of Malthus's perspective or 'vision' of the population problem are seriously wanting. The rapid acceleration of population growth revealed by the census data was greatly emphasized – so much so that one wonders what version of the *Essay* Professor Blaug had at hand; and it was accounted for in terms of falling death rates, sufficiently effective to outweigh the effect of declining marriage and birth rates. Moreover, Malthus sought to rationalize these demographic trends in economic terms. His land-based theory can be said to have been refuted by evidence of reduced fertility and mortality rates and the continuous advance of wages and per-capita incomes only if we insist on freezing the position of the labour-supply growth function and also holding technology constant or, at the most, subject to discrete improvements which (because the labour-supply relation is unchanged) implies a return to the original equilibrium wage. This is precisely what Becker does; and it is what he attributes to Malthus, or perhaps only to Malthus's theory. In an aside he does concede that 'the Malthusian model [like the neoclassical] can equally well postulate exogenous progress to "explain" persistent growth' (1988, 3; see also Eltis, 1985;

Costabile and Rowthorn, 1985). But this is the point: this is how the model was indeed used by Malthus.

Our argument proceeds as follows: Section II contrasts the first essay of 1798 with that of 1803 in their differing perspectives on contemporary population growth. The first essay explains a supposedly slow population growth rate in terms of the slow growth of food supplies. Thereafter Malthus attempted to account for rapid and accelerating population growth. The rationalization in 1803 runs in terms of *falling mortality, not rising fertility*; for the preventive check is much emphasized. Most significant is Malthus's attribution of improved prudential habits to the acceleration of economic activity and good wages. 'Excessive' population growth is not the problem either in the first or in the later editions of the *Essay*.

Accelerating population growth with no reduction in the real wage (even possibly an increase) turns ultimately on the rapid accumulation of agricultural wage goods. The source of increasing food supplies – the subject matter of chapter 15: II – is summarized in section III. High agricultural productivity despite 'mercantilist' intervention, supplemented somewhat by imports, provides the key; thus no strategic role is accorded increasing land scarcity in the argument. One aspect of the contemporary or empirical 'population problem' – taking account of the pervasive optimism of Malthus's pronouncements – is summarized in section IV. It is simply that population growth must, except in the rare circumstances pertaining to new colonies, be restrained below its *maximum potential* to assure against falling standards, a problem that exists even under conditions of rapidly accelerating food supply. Section V deals with applications of the population principle made in the 1817 and 1826 versions of the *Essay*. The picture once again is one of rapid population growth, which, because it reflects 'prodigious' accumulation, is consistent with constant, and even rising, real wages (and no decline in the profit rate), notwithstanding agricultural extensions. The great role allowed ongoing new technology remains the striking feature of the analysis. The last substantive section elaborates on Malthus's endogenization of 'prudential' population control in terms of the relative increase of food prices to those of manufactured goods.

Whether Malthus's own estimate and interpretation of contemporary population trends – the concern of this chapter – is in line with present-day historical scholarship is a worthwhile question. There seems, in fact, some new consensus that, as far as concerns early-nineteenth-century population growth, the effect of the *birth rate* takes precedence over mortality: 'From 1700 to 1739, population grew at an average annual rate of 0.3 per cent; from 1800 to 1839, it grew at 1.45 per cent. The new estimates from the Cambridge Group assign a clearly dominant role to the birth rate, which accounts for about 70 per cent of the increase in population growth rates. If the birth rate had remained unchanged, the declines in the death rate would have boosted annual growth rates to about 0.7 per cent per year in the early nineteenth century, a significant increase but far short of the actual' (Lee and Schofield, 1981, 31). According to Wrigley, increasing fertility contributed some two and a half times as much as falling mortality to the rise in the population between 1670–89 and 1810–29; while increasing fertility reflects higher nuptuality, that is, earlier marriage and lesser celibacy by women, rather than increased children per marriage (1983a, 130–1). If all this is so, then Malthus was wrong to put so much weight on falling mortality from the mid-eighteenth century through the early 1800s. He was far more 'optimistic' than is apparently justified – a pleasing irony, considering his reputation.

II MALTHUS ON CONTEMPORARY POPULATION GROWTH, 1798 AND 1803

It is not unusual for commentators to understand the 1798 *Essay* as bearing the message 'that population was actually and invariably increasing faster than subsistence and that this was the reason for the misery involved' (Schumpeter, 1954, 579; cited above, chapter 1, pp. 13–14). This is a questionable reading. It is not *actual* but maximum or *potential* population growth that exceeds the growth of subsistence. The 'principal states of modern Europe' were in fact experiencing slow population growth, Malthus maintained in 1798: 'Instead of doubling their numbers every twenty-five years, they require three or four hundred years, or more, for that purpose' (1986, *1*, 26; see also 110, regarding 'very slow' English population growth). The reason for the short-fall of actual behind potential growth turns, of course, on the operation of the preventive and positive checks, the wage acting in an *equilibrating* fashion to assure that population growth keeps in line with (in the present case) a slowly growing food supply by acting appropriately on birth and death rates.

The major European states (England and France) were not even subject to the problem of temporary excessive population growth characterizing Brandenburgh and Magdeburgh (44f.). The data regarding birth and death rates indicated that population 'has accommodated itself very nearly to the average produce of each country,' so that periodic plagues 'to repress what is redundant' were not a feature of the recent record (47). It is the effect of low real wages which discourages population growth and assures that it stays in line with the growth of food supplies in the course of regular secular expansion. Conversely, an acceleration of food production, by raising real wages, would encourage an appropriate population increase (49–50).

The slow growth of Britain's food supply is not, it should be noted, explained in terms of proximity to the stationary state. Britain was a country 'not extremely crowded and populous' and, in the absence of faulty policies favouring manufactures, 'might undoubtedly have been more populous than at present, and yet not be more encumbered by its population' (118). That the food supply appropriate for working-class consumption had been growing only slowly, despite an increased potential for agricultural expansion created by reorganization and new technology, was explained by mercantilist interferences and also diversions of capital to satisfy rising upper-class demands (110). The English problem, as Malthus saw it, was to raise the growth rate of agricultural output and rely on population growth to respond to higher real wages. Direct encouragement of the birth rate (extensions of the Poor Laws and the various idealistic proposals of the day) promised disaster by giving free rein to the ever-existing potential of population to expand faster than food supplies (49–50). Population growth could look after itself. And though there were limits to what could be achieved by this program, deriving from the constrained possibilities for agricultural growth in an 'old settled' country, this was scarcely a practical concern, and there is certainly no suggestion that the higher real wages that were attainable by agricultural growth would be effaced by *excessive* increases in labour supply. Without the institutional encouragement of population, labour supply would rise, at most, at a rate corresponding to that of labour demand. This theme, we shall find, is carried over to all later editions of the *Essay*.

* * *

The 1803 version places greater emphasis upon the preventive (as distinct from the positive) check in the accounts of modern history.[1] At various points will be found references to that check where none existed in 1798 (1986, *2*, 313, cf. *1*, 48; *2*, 314n, cf. *1*, 51–2). Most striking is an entirely new passage representing delayed marriage as 'the most powerful of the checks, which in modern Europe keep down the population to the level of the means of subsistence' (*2*, 315).

Malthus was ill-advised to retain in 1803 the original frame of reference (the first two chapters of 1798), with its general presumption that population growth must be constrained within the limits imposed by a *slowly* growing food supply. Evidence of the higher effectiveness of the prudential check would contribute to explain a slowly growing population. But the same evidence has a totally different implication at a time of *rapid* population growth; reduced nuptuality (and a reduced birth rate) obviously does not serve to explain that phenomenon.

A revised picture of population growth was brought to light by the census data made available between editions, as Malthus himself stresses. In 1798 he had estimated British population ('this island') at 7 million (*1*, 12) when it was in fact closer to the 10.9 million reported by the 1801

1 Even in 1798, however, Malthus had expounded on the widespread practice of the preventive check across all strata of society (1986, *1*, 26-8).

census – some 56 per cent greater.[2] The census data also revealed that the English population had been increasing steadily since the 1740s, and at an accelerating rate. (In fact, it reached the highest level it was ever to attain in the early 1820s.) Such a rate of growth, given evidence of increasing prudence, could be rationalized only in terms of reduced mortality: 'If this sketch of the state of society in England be near the truth, it will be allowed that the preventive check to population operates with considerable force throughout all the classes of the community. And this observation is further confirmed by the abstracts from the registers returned in consequence of the late Population Act. The results of these abstracts show, that the annual marriages in England and Wales are to the whole population as 1 to $123\frac{1}{5}$, a smaller proportion of marriages than obtains in any of the countries which have been examined, except Norway and Switzerland. In the earlier part of the last century, Dr. Short [1750, 265] estimated this proportion at about 1 to 115. It is probable that this calculation was then correct; and the present diminution in the proportion of marriages, notwithstanding an increase of population more rapid than formerly, owing to the more rapid progress of commerce and agriculture, is partly a cause, and partly a consequence, of the diminished mortality observed of late years' (*2*, 238).[3] Similarly: 'It would appear, by the present proportion of marriages, that the more rapid increase of population, supposed to have taken place since the year 1780, has arisen more from the diminution of deaths, than from the increase of births' (244n). It is the infantile death rate, in particular, that had been reduced by 'the acknowledged greater healthiness of the latter part of the century, compared with the middle of it' (247).

Some of Malthus's observations regarding the diminution of mortality are striking, as also is his denial of any pressure emanating from births (despite the Poor Laws): 'Indeed, it seems to be nearly ascertained that both these causes [the habits of the people with respect to prudence and cleanliness, or in natural healthiness of situation], which tend to diminish mortality, operate in this country to a considerable degree. The small proportion of annual marriages before mentioned indicates that habits of prudence, extremely favourable to happiness, prevail through a large part of the community, in spite of the poor laws; and it appears from the clearest evidence, that the generality of our country parishes are very

2 In 1803 the base population figure used in illustrating the geometric and arithmetic progressions is 11 million in place of the original 7 million (1986, *2*, 12). For details of the inaccurate estimates brought to light by the census, see 236f.

3 The allusion to the preventive check in the first sentence of this passage appears also in 1798 (1986, *1*, 28; see above, note 1), but this check is in 1803 no longer said to characterize 'all old states.' This change reflects the fact that at centre stage now is population growth 'more rapid than formerly.' England could not technically be classed as an 'old state.'

healthy' (240). Still we must keep a sense of proportion. Malthus was not describing a Garden of Eden. There are references to a high mortality rate among children in the manufacturing towns, and to a slow growth rate of labour demand (239), which would seem to clash with the emphasis on a decline in the mortality rate and accelerating progress of national income. Unless, that is, and this presumably is the solution, we read Malthus as pointing to mortality rates that remain absolutely high, though tending downwards, and – while recognizing the fact of rapid accumulation – as denying the ability of labour demand to keep pace with an 'unrestricted' growth rate of population, or to permit high-enough real wages to maintain a 'large family.'

* * *

Malthus, as we have just seen, considered 'the present diminution in the proportion of marriages' to be both *cause* and *consequence* of 'the diminished mortality observed of late years.' A decline in the marriage rate as cause of reduced mortality may relate to improved infant care in smaller families (cf. 247). A fall in the mortality rate thus induced is, however, unlikely to be responsible for any major net rise in the population growth rate, since the depressing and stimulating pressures acting on population will roughly cancel out. Exogenous reduction in mortality is a more likely cause. And – in contrast to the first edition (e.g., 1986, *1*, 110) – there are indeed numerous references to increased healthiness, particularly of the great manufacturing towns: 'In the observations on the results of the Population Act it is remarked that the average duration of life in England appears to have increased in the proportion of 117 to 100, since the year 1780. So great a change, in so short a time, if true, would be a most striking phenomenon ... [As] the increase of population since 1780 is incontrovertible, and the present mortality extraordinarily small, I should ... be disposed to believe, that much the greater part of the effect is to be attributed to increased healthiness' (245). Similarly: '[There] is good reason to believe, that not only London, but the other towns in England, and probably also country villages, were at the time of these calculations [Price, 1783] less healthy than at present ... [The] returns pursuant to the Population Act, even after allowing for great omissions in the burials, exhibit in all our provincial towns, and in the country, a degree of healthiness much greater than had before been calculated' (242). But as remarked above, we must not go overboard. There was no intention to deny a characteristically higher infantile death rate in 'great, and even in moderate' towns than in the country.

What now requires attention is the reverse sequence posited: the effect of falling mortality in discouraging marriage, and of rising mortality in encouraging marriage: 'A great mortality ... will necessarily produce a great frequency of marriage' (193); or again: A 'greater mortality naturally produces a greater proportion of births' (204).[4] Now, at least in principle, a lower death rate will discourage nuptuality should the fall in the death rate increase labour supply and reduce real wages. And elsewhere Malthus follows up this line: 'In this country, it is not to be doubted that the proportion of marriages has become smaller since the improvement of our towns, the less frequent returns of epidemics, and the adoption of habits of greater cleanliness' (*3*, 571). Here reference is made to a fall in the marriage rate in Britain during the severe scarcities of 1800 and 1801 – years of declining real wages – leading to a generalization which extends the principle to periods of falling real wages resulting from a declining mortality rate: 'The same motives which prevented many people from marrying during such a period, would operate precisely in the same way, if, in future, the additional number of children reared to manhood from the introduction of the cowpox, were to be such as to crowd all employments, lower the price of labour, and make it more difficult to support a family.'

Unfortunately, this could scarcely be what Malthus had in mind when he ascribed the (long-term) fall in the English marriage rate to 'the diminished mortality observed of late years' (above, p. 789). For if we approach the linkage along these lines, there would be reason to expect *falling* real wages to characterize contemporary population growth (extending beyond the years of 'shortage' 1800 and 1801). Yet the accelerating population growth rate is ascribed to 'the more rapid progress of commerce and agriculture,' which suggests that economic growth positively encouraged the decline in the mortality rate by raising real wages, or at least provided scope for an exogenous decline in mortality to act positively on population without depressing real wage, and therefore the marriage rate. In one interesting passage added in 1803, Malthus alludes to 'a more equable distribution of the products of the soil' – which certainly suggests higher real wages – as contributing to a weakening of the positive check, along with apparently exogenous improvements in national health attributable in part to cleaner towns: 'War, the predominant check to the population of savage nations, has certainly abated, even including the late unhappy revolutionary contests; and since the prevalence of a greater degree of personal cleanliness, of better modes of clearing and building towns, and of a more equable distribution of the products of the soil from improving knowledge in political economy, plagues, violent diseases and famines have been certainly mitigated, and have become less frequent' (*2*, 315).[5]

4 In a recent account of Malthusian economic–demographic interaction much is made of the effect of a lower birth rate in reducing the death rate, but nothing is said of the reverse relationship (Lee and Loschky, 1987, 729).

5 Cf. also on the healthier towns *3*, 496; 'Dr. Heberden [1801, 35] draws a striking picture of the favourable change observed in the health of the people of England since this period' – a reference to 'the extinction of the plague; and justly attributes it to the

Malthus's precise intentions in linking reduced nuptuality to reduced mortality remains, therefore, an open question as far as it pertains to contemporary Britain. But this is not the entire picture. In 1803 he inserted the proposition that nuptuality need not rise with an acceleration of economic activity. For *rapid economic growth might itself generate improved prudential habits*, a most important contribution to demographic theory (196; cited chapter 5, p. 191). The improved degree of prudence in turn would reduce the mortality rate (196–7). Now 'improving cultivation and trade,' improved 'habits with respect to prudence and cleanliness,' and the fact that population growth reflected 'diminished mortality, instead of an increased number of births,' characterized contemporary Britain, on Malthus's own estimate. This suggests that our passage – though it appears in a chapter dealing with checks to population in central Europe – pertains in part to the British case.[6] Higher British earnings did not, in that case, generate a higher marriage rate, and indirectly contributed to the reduced mortality rate.

III CONTEMPORARY AND PROSPECTIVE AGRICULTURAL DEVELOPMENT: A SUMMARY

As we have shown in chapter 15: II, land scarcity, and consequently rising real costs, make no appearance in the account of contemporary and prospective agricultural development given in the *Essay on Population*. It is a major theme of the second edition, as of the first, that agricultural expansion was hindered by ill-considered governmental encouragement of commerce and manufacturing. Having in mind that the real demand for labour turned mainly on agricultural produce, the observed acceleration of population growth must then have been accounted for by improved technology or imports. Malthus himself (see above, p. 789) refers to the 'more rapid progress' of agriculture (as well as commerce), so there can

---

improvements which have gradually taken place, not only in London but in all great towns; and in the manner of living throughout the kingdom, particularly with respect to cleanliness and ventilation.' These improvements could not have had their desirable effect, Malthus adds, 'if they had not been accompanied by an increase of the preventive check,' an increase stimulated in part by 'the spirit of cleanliness and better mode of living' – a sort of virtuous circle.

6 Elsewhere, the principle is stated quite generally thus: 'If, indeed, it be allowed that in every society, not in the state of a new colony, some powerful check to population must prevail; and if it be observed, that a taste for the comforts and conveniences of life will prevent people from marrying under the certainty of being deprived of these advantages; it must be allowed that we can hardly expect to find any check to marriage so little prejudicial to the happiness and virtue of society as the general prevalence of such a taste; and consequently that the spread of luxury in this sense of the term, is practically desirable, and one of the best means of raising that standard of wretchedness, alluded to in the eighth chapter of this book' (*3*, 566–7).

be no doubt of his ascription of the acceleration to the former – in fact, almost entirely so, since imports are played down. The artificial constraints on agricultural development had been used in 1798 (1986, *1*, 108f.) to account for *slow* population growth, whereas the issue in 1803 was *accelerating* population growth. These checks to agriculture must therefore now be understood in a relative, not absolute, sense.

We should also have in mind the striking observation that 'from a review of the state of society in former periods, compared with the present ... the evils resulting from the principle of population have rather diminished than increased'[7] – which implies reduced misery, that is, higher real wages – and could be expected to diminish further with increasing prudential control (*3*, 575). And in this context, Malthus even goes so far as to assert the irrelevance of absolute population size for the wage: 'The increase of absolute population, which will of course take place, will evidently tend but little to weaken this expectation, as every thing depends upon the relative proportions between population and food, and not on the absolute number of people. In the former part of this work, it appeared, that the countries which possessed the fewest people often suffered the most from the effects of the principle of population; and it can scarcely be doubted that, taking Europe throughout, fewer famines, and fewer diseases arising from want have prevailed in the last century than in those which preceded it' (see also chapter 5, p. 192). Similarly, regarding the magnitude of the average product: 'Corn countries are more populous than pasture countries, and rice countries more populous than corn countries. But their happiness does not depend either upon their being thinly or fully inhabited, upon their poverty or their riches, their youth or their age; but on the proportion which the population and the food bear to each other. This proportion is generally the most favourable in new colonies, where the knowledge and industry of an old state operate on the fertile unappropriated land of a new one. In other cases the youth or the age of a state is not, in this respect, of great importance. It is probable that the food of Great Britain is divided in more liberal shares to her inhabitants at the present period, than it was 2,000, 3,000 or 4,000 years ago. And it has appeared that the poor and thinly inhabited tracts of the Scotch Highlands are more distressed by a redundant population than the most populous part of Europe' (*2*, 314). This differs from the corresponding formulation of 1798 in asserting an actual secular *increase* in per-capita product rather than mere constancy (*1*, 51).

IV THE POPULATION PROBLEM

Let us now seek to get a grip upon the basic issue as formulated in 1803.

7 And this 'even under the disadvantage of an almost total ignorance of their real cause.'

In what consists the 'problem' of population, if, as we have shown, *excess* population growth relative to food is not the problem in a system avoiding dependence upon foreign corn supplies with the danger that posed of providing an unreliable stimulus to population growth? The denial of a population problem in this sense is the same in 1803 as in 1798, with one difference: In 1798 Malthus explained the *slow* growth of population by reference to the slow growth of food supplies, whereas in 1803 (with the census results of 1801 at hand) his attention was on the newly discovered fact of *accelerating* population growth, which he accounted for by *reduced mortality* owing in part to exogenous improvements in health,[8] in part to accelerating domestic food supplies and, to a limited degree, imports.

All this applies under normal conditions. There are special cases of forced population growth. The occurrence of epidemics illustrates some cause at play generating *unusually* rapid population growth relative to food, and is a possibility, 'though the country, absolutely considered, may not be extremely crowded or populous' (1986, *1*, 44; cf. *2*, 303), indicating that this matter is not of a secular order. There is also the question of secular excess population growth, with a depressing effect upon earnings, but specifically in the case of institutional arrangements encouraging population growth (*3*, 319).

But if, in normal circumstances, and from a secular perspective, excess population growth was not the issue, what is the sense of the *immediacy* of the problem upon which Malthus repeatedly focused? The answer turns on the maximum *capacity* of population to grow at a rate exceeding the maximum capacity of food, the former in fact represented as higher in 1803 than in 1798.[9] This is nicely put in 1803 in a statement wherein Malthus disclaims concern with ultimate stationariness. The issue is whether corn could be increased at a rate equal to the 'natural' (maximum conceivable) growth rate of population. Since it could not, there is continuous need for the operation of checks (positive and/or preventive). In this sense the 'principle of population' poses a *permanent* problem, not one for some future period: 'With regard to the principle of population, it is never the question whether a country will produce any more but whether it may be made to produce a sufficiency to keep pace with an unchecked increase of people. In China, the question is not, whether a certain additional quantity of rice might be raised by improved culture; but whether such an addition could be expected during the next twenty five years, as would be sufficient to support an additional 300 millions of people. And in this

8 It will be recalled that reduced mortality was also related to the reduced marriage rate (above, p. 789).

9 Thus regarding North America, Malthus added in 1803 with new census figures available: 'The period of doubling from procreation must have been considerably less than twenty five years' (*2*, 306; cf. *1*, 40–1).

country, it is not the question whether, by cultivating all our commons, we could raise considerably more corn than at present; but whether we could raise sufficient for a population of 20 millions in the next twenty five years, and 40 millions in the next fifty years' (460).

This, of course, is not a statement of *actual* population doubling every twenty-five years that must necessarily be restricted, but of its potential. The problem of population therefore existed even under conditions of accelerating food production, since population growth still had to be restrained below its maximum. And, in fact, somewhat paradoxically, the newly recognized acceleration of population growth served to vindicate the initial position of 1798: 'That the checks which have been mentioned are the true [1826: immediate] causes of the slow increase of population, and that *the checks result principally from an insufficiency of subsistence,* will be evident from the comparatively rapid increase which has invariably taken place, whenever, by some sudden enlargement in the means of subsistence, these checks have in any considerable degree been removed' (*2*, 304; emphasis added).[10]

* * *

There is, we have demonstrated, ample evidence of a highly optimistic evaluation in 1803 of the course of wages, and this without deceleration of population growth – subject, however, to the adoption of appropriate agricultural policies. Yet this outlook negates the entire notion of an arithmetic ratio,[11] with its implication of a decelerating domestic growth rate of food. And this may have been too much for Malthus. The fact is that land scarcity ultimately imposing a decelerating growth rate of food does make an appearance in an allusion to the likely *temporary* nature of the current high growth rate of 'the resources of this country' – the expectation is a deceleration setting in *within some three or four decades* – with implications for population growth: 'We now suppose that the proportion of births to deaths is above 13 to 10; but if we were to assume this proportion as a criterion by which to estimate the increase of population for the next thirty or forty years, we should probably fall into a very gross error. The effects of the late scarcities [1801–2] are strongly marked, in the returns of the *Population Act,* by a decrease of births, and an increase of burials, and should such seasons frequently recur, they would soon destroy the great excess of births which has been observed during the last twenty

10 That the preventive check (including moral restraint) reflects the 'insufficiency of subsistence' is expressed elsewhere as 'an infrequency of the marriage union from the fear of a family ...' (315n).

11 When Malthus formulated his arithmetic ratio, he took policy measures into account, as well as new technology (e.g., *1*, 12; *2*, 11).

years; and indeed we cannot reasonably suppose that the resources of this country should increase for any long continuance with such rapidity as to allow of a permanent proportion of births to deaths as 13 to 10, unless indeed this proportion were principally caused by great foreign drains' (246).[12] Doubtless, it is the ultimate prospect of land scarcity that underlies the forecast. But, even so, there is no suggestion that increasing land scarcity was currently manifest, dictating an actual deceleration of population growth. It is a prospective decline to which Malthus alludes.[13]

An apparent difficulty with the second *Essay* is the tension between the facts of rapid population growth at constant or even rising wages, and the theoretical framework. One solution to the problem is implied by the remark that the current growth rate of population must be temporary and unlikely to continue for more than three or four decades. Yet this is highly impressionistic and informal – 'we cannot reasonably suppose that the resources of this country should increase for any long continuance with such rapidity ...' But the fact is that accelerating population growth with rising wages was clearly recognized. And it could be easily accommodated. Focusing upon the principle that population growth must be checked below its maximum capacity by the lesser growth rate of food, whatever that might be, acceleration of the latter (domestic and/or imported) relaxes the requisite constraints on the former and permits a corresponding acceleration. And we have also seen that that is precisely how Malthus states the matter in response to the facts revealed by the 1801 census (above, p. 794). The evidence was used to support his basic theme regarding the checks to population imposed by the *relatively* slow growth of food – relative, that is, to the maximum *potential* accorded population growth.

V POSTWAR EVALUATIONS

Malthus's perspective in 1817 on contemporary development represented Britain as a 'combined' system of manufacturing and agriculture (see chapter 5: II). New technology in cotton manufacture had generated a surplus which had sufficed to finance rapid accumulation (and thus labour demand) over a quarter-century; and while the cotton profit rate had been reduced to the general level, that level itself had been maintained, unlike the purely theoretical case of a country 'engaged principally in manufactures.' Two counteracting forces to what otherwise would be a downward profit rate are specified: (1) 'the extent of [English] lands'; and (2) 'the large arena for the employment of an increasing capital' – an allusion to

12 The allusion to 'drains' is to deaths occurring abroad.

13 We cannot be certain that Malthus was allowing in his forecast for appropriate policies; the allusion to increasing land scarcity may assume the current system of intervention favouring manufactures and trade.

expanding markets for manufactured goods in the colonies (1817, II, 406–7). Increasing land scarcity does not figure in Malthus's account of contemporary English trends; on the contrary, the profit rate had been *maintained* by the extent of available land. Here one recalls the concern in 1803 (above, chapter 15, p. 745) that, if current import trends continued, England would lose its character as an agriculturally based economy. Evidently we are witness to an abandonment of the preoccupation with excessive food imports. The new view was written in 1816, after the protective Corn Law legislation; but Malthus was describing a pattern extending back a quarter-century, not a few months.

The contemporary events illustrated the operation of counteracting forces. For the 'canonical' growth model based on diminishing returns yields a rationalization for the slow (almost stationary) growth of population and of capital at a low profit rate, a rate near the minimum at which net saving ceases. But the English experience of 'prodigious' capital accumulation, and acceleration of population growth with a rising profit rate, notwithstanding major agricultural extensions, had to be understood in terms of those disturbing causes which countered 'the *tendency* of a continually increasing capital and extending cultivation ... to occasion a progressive fall both of profits and wages' (439). The altered circumstances had transformed the British economy (see chapter 15: V). Instead of the 'symptoms' characterizing a country constrained by land scarcity, Britain showed all the characteristics of rapid growth: 'A country which, though fertile and populous, had been cultivated nearly to the utmost, would have no other means of increasing its population than by the admission of foreign corn. But the British isles shew at present no symptoms whatever of this species of exhaustion ... *[We] have seen in this country, during the twenty years previous to 1814, a high rate of profits and interest, a very great demand for labour, good wages, and an increase of population more rapid, perhaps, than during any period of our history*' (491–2; emphasis added).[14] So potent in fact is the role accorded new technology that, in discussing the corn-export bounty, Malthus greatly diluted the notion even of a *tendency* to diminishing returns, asserting against Smith 'that the bounty, when granted under favourable circumstances, is really calculated, after going through a period of dearness, to produce the surplus and the cheapness which it advocates promise,' adding that '[as] a matter of fact it must be allowed, that, during the period of the last century when corn was falling, more land must have been taken into cultivation' (470–1; see chapter 15, p. 768).

This perspective thus governs the interpretation of the wartime experi-

14 Cf. a further reference to contemporary England: 'A country with an extensive and rich territory, the cultivation of which is stimulated by improvements in agriculture, manufactures, and foreign commerce, has such various and abundant resources, that it is extremely difficult to say when they will reach their limits' (441).

ence. Relatively rapid industrialization over the period 1764–1803 (the end of the Seven Years War to the peace of Amiens) had rendered Britain increasingly a corn-importing nation (497–8).[15] The subsequent blockade and the necessity to rely on domestic resources reversed this trend, with resultant productivity gains in agriculture. There is a strong implication here of, at the very least, *constant* (long-run) agricultural productivity.

* * *

In the light of the 1817 productivity estimates, Malthus's vision of contemporary demographic trends requires further discussion. In 1803 he had stated: 'It would appear, by the present proportion of marriages, that the more rapid increase of population, supposed to have taken place since the year 1780, has arisen more from the diminution of deaths than the increase of the births' (1986, *2*, 244n; see above, p. 789). This is removed in 1806. In its place there is inserted a reference to 'the absolutely stationary number of deaths during the last twenty years, notwithstanding a considerable increase of births ...' (1806, I, 466–7). But this statement still implies a falling *rate* of mortality. And indeed almost immediately Malthus implicitly reaffirms the primary role of reduced mortality in accounting for the population explosion: 'As the increase of population since 1780 is incontrovertible, and the present mortality extraordinarily small, I should ... be disposed to believe that the greater part of the effect [the 'most striking' increase in life span since 1780] is to be attributed to increased healthiness' (469; for the almost identical version given in 1803, see above, p. 790).[16] In 1817, the altered reference of 1806 is deleted entirely; but the passage regarding the 'incontrovertible' population increase and the 'extraordinarily small' mortality is, however, retained (1817, II, 65), and in fact the word 'much' (removed temporarily in 1806) is reinserted in the conclusion: 'I should ... be disposed to believe, that much the greater part of the effect [expanded life span] is to be attributed to increased healthiness.' The position of 1803 regarding the source of the contemporary

15 'After 1764, the wealth and manufacturing population of Great Britain increased more rapidly than those of her neighbours' (469–70).

16 In 1806, too, Malthus observed that 'the increased healthiness observed of late years could not possibly have taken place without [the] accompanying circumstance' of delayed marriage (1806, II, 536), a reference to the special necessity for a reduced birth rate during a period of falling mortality.

In his *Letter to Whitbread* (1807), Malthus warned of the consequences of an irresponsible extension of the Poor Law system – having in mind that it is physically impossible for the natural and acquired resources of any country long to support an unrestricted population: 'we should soon see a most unfavourable change take place in the *present small mortality which we justly consider as one of the great tests of our national happiness*; and a large proportion of deaths would invariably accompany the large proportion of births' (1807b/1986, *4*, 15; emphasis added).

population increase in reduced mortality is thus confirmed, and indeed reinforced, in 1817.

Consider now Malthus's reaction to the 1811 census results indicating rapid population growth with no downward pressure on real wages: 'The returns of the Population Act in 1811 undoubtedly presented extraordinary results. They shewed a greatly accelerated rate of progress, and a greatly improved healthiness of the people, notwithstanding the increase of the towns and the increased proportion of the population engaged in manufacturing employments. They thus furnished another striking instance of the readiness with which population starts forward, under almost any weight, when the resources of a country are rapidly increasing' (80). Again: 'What has already taken place is a striking illustration of the principle of population, and a proof that in spite of great towns, manufacturing occupations, and the gradually-acquired habits of an opulent and luxuriant people, if the resources of a country will admit of a rapid increase, and if these resources are so advantageously distributed as to occasion a constantly-increasing demand for labour, the population will not fail to keep pace with them' (103–4). The experience of accelerating population growth is thus again taken as evidence of the theme that population growth is constrained below its maximum physiological level by the *relatively* sluggish expansion of 'resources' (real food supply); a relaxation of this constraint allows population growth to rise towards its full potential. The validation of this theme was all the more impressive given the expansion of urban centres and a rising proportion of the workforce engaged in manufactures (and, one should add, despite activation of the 'preventive' check).

Here we should recall (see chapter 5, p. 198) the reaction in the 1817 edition to Weyland's conclusion (1816) that high agricultural productivity reflecting rich resources and improved technology 'might throw so large a portion of the people into towns, and engage so many in unhealthy occupations, that the immediate checks to population might be too powerful to be overcome even by an abundance of food' (1817, III, 406–7). Malthus objected, taking issue with Weyland's 'calculations to shew the extreme difficulty with which the births of the country supply the demand of the towns and manufactories,' such that Britain was 'within a hair's breadth of that formidable point of *non-reproduction*, at which, according to Mr. Weyland, the population *naturally* comes to a full stop before the means of subsistence cease to be progressive' – a stationary state despite abundance of food (408). Weyland's data, he maintained, were twenty years outdated; despite rapid urban development, the population had 'increased at a rate which would double its numbers in fifty-five years' (408–9). The evidence provided 'a full and complete refutation of the doctrine, that, as society advances, the increased indisposition to marriage and increased mortality in great towns and manufactories, always overcome the principle of increase ...'; and it proved 'incontrovertibly that the actual checks to population, even in the most improved countries, arise principally from an insufficiency of subsistence, and soon yield to increased resources, notwithstanding the increase of towns and manufactories' (410).[17]

The new data of course presented a challenge, for they indicated an *acceleration* of population growth in an old-settled country where a *deceleration* was to be expected. Specifically, evidence available at the beginning of the century indicated a population growth rate amounting to a doubling in eighty-three and one-half years; the 1811 census figures raised the estimate to a doubling in fifty-five years: 'This is a rate of progress which in a rich and well-peopled country might reasonably be expected to diminish rather than to increase. But instead of any such diminution it appears that as far as 1810 it had been considerably accelerated' (1817, II, 81).[18] Or again, even the lowest of alternative birth rate/death rate ratios then under debate was 'quite extraordinary for a rich and well-peopled territory ... [W]ere it to continue, [it] would ... double the number of inhabitants in less than fifty-five years' (103). This rate of increase, however, and by implication its prerequisite – a rapidly increasing food supply – could not be 'permanent': 'This is a rate of increase, which in the nature of things cannot be permanent. It has been occasioned by the stimulus of a greatly-increased demand for labour, combined with a greatly-increased power of production, both in agriculture and manufactures. These are the two elements which form the most effective encouragement to a rapid increase of population.' Malthus thus contemplated ultimate deceleration of food supplies, and consequently of population. But not seriously: *Its onset would not occur for some three or four decades* (245–6).[19]

The postwar depression years left their impression, but long-term optimism shines through. Malthus in 1817 blamed the 'distresses' in part on the high population growth rate in the face of a *temporary* downturn in accumulation. The problem was envisaged as a temporary one, first, because some deceleration of population growth might be expected considering the current circumstances of agricultural scarcity similar to those of 1800–1, but, more significantly, because of the expected re-establishment of the high trend path of capital accumulation: 'The great

17 See also 414–15, where Malthus refers to his reply to Weyland in the last chapter of Book III 'added in the present edition,' a reference to 59–60n.

18 In the 1806 edition, after a reference to a doubling in eighty-three and one-half years, Malthus added: 'and as we cannot suppose that the country could admit of more than a quadrupled population in the next hundred and sixty-six years, we may safely say that its resources will not allow of a permanent rate of increase greater than that which is taking place at present' (1806, II, 535). This is unchanged in 1817, but altered in 1826 to read: 'a permanent rate of increase greater than that which was then taking place' (see 1986, *3*, 593, for the final version).

19 Malthus repeats the passage from 1803 to this effect (above, pp. 795–6). As early as 1806 (I, 470), he removed an 1803 note regarding the 'late scarcities' of 1800–1 and their effect on birth and death rates (1986, *3*, 246n), indicating that he considered those years to be aberrations.

object to be kept in view, is to support the people through their present distresses, in the hope (and I trust a just one) of better times. The difficulty is without doubt considerably aggravated by the prodigious stimulus which has been given to the population of the country of late years, the effects of which cannot suddenly subside. But it will be seen probably, when the next returns of the population are made, that the marriages and births have diminished, and the deaths increased in a still greater degree than in 1800 and 1801; and the continuance of this effect to a certain degree for a few years will retard the progress of the population, and combined with the increasing wants of Europe and America from their increasing riches, and the adaptation of the supply of commodities at home to the new distribution of wealth occasioned by the alteration of the circulating medium, will again give life and energy to all our mercantile and agricultural transactions, and *restore the labouring classes to full employment and good wages*' (359; emphasis added). Apparently, 'full employment and good wages' are envisaged as the secular norm.

There was, however, one feature of the record that troubled Malthus. In the 1817 edition we find reference to a somewhat *lower* corn wage on average in the years 1790–1811 compared with 1735–55 (1817, III, 32). This seems to have come as a surprise, and recourse is made to the important theme that the average wage of day labour may conceal the true picture; for what mattered in analysing population was the 'average earnings of the families of the labouring classes throughout the year': 'An attention to this very essential point will explain the reason why, in many instances, the progress of population does not appear to be regulated by what are usually called the real wages of labour; and why this progress may occasionally be greater, when the price of a day's labour will purchase rather less than the medium quantity of corn, than when it will purchase rather more.' Over the years 1790–1811 'there was a more rapid accumulation of capital, and a greater demand for labour; and though the continued rise of provisions still kept them rather ahead of wages, yet the fuller employment for every body that would work, the greater quantity of task-work done, the higher relative value of corn compared with manufactures, the increased use of potatoes, and the greater sums distributed in parish allowances, unquestionably gave to the lower classes of society the power of commanding a greater quantity of food, and will account for the more rapid increase of population in the latter period, in perfect consistency with the general principle' (32–3).

* * *

We have seen that while Malthus had written in 1806 that a faster rate of population increase than that implied by a doubling every eighty-three and one-half years could not be expected, he was obliged in 1817 to concede otherwise (above, note 18). This reinforced the notion of rapid population growth as a consequence of rapid economic expansion, including domestic agricultural output, reflecting pre-eminently new technology. When we come to the edition of 1826, the last issued by Malthus himself, the accelerating population trend is again much emphasized. With the results of the census of 1821 in hand – 1801–11, 13.3 per cent increase, or doubling in fifty-five years; 1810–21, 15.6 per cent increase, or doubling in forty-eight years – Malthus declaimed regarding 'a most extraordinary rate of increase, considering the actual population compared with its territory, and the number of its great towns and manufactories' (1986, *2*, 263).

We also note that Malthus's expectation in 1817 of renewed 'full employment and good wages' is now said to have been 'to a considerable degree' confirmed (*3*, 377n). This outcome reflected not a relative constraint on population growth by way of reduced marriage and birth rates – labour-supply constraints – but the rapid expansion of labour demand. In fact Malthus alludes to *too rapid* a population expansion impeding a total recovery: 'This has, in a considerable degree, taken place, but it has been owing rather to the latter causes noticed than to the former. It appeared, by the returns of 1821, that the scarce years of 1817 and 1818 had but a slight effect in diminishing the number of marriages and births, compared with the effect of the great proportion of plentiful years in increasing them; so that the population proceeded with great rapidity during the ten years ending with 1820. But this great increase of the population has prevented the labouring classes from being so fully employed as might have been expected from the prosperity of commerce and agriculture during the last two or three years.' Considered in isolation this latter paragraph might seem to imply a substantive change in position, since so much had been made in earlier editions of a *secular reduction* in the marriage and birth rates, the rapid population growth turning on reduced mortality. But we should not make too much of the passage, for in all other contexts the original weighting is retained; and, moreover, a new note is added to the original 1806 Appendix which reinforces that weighting: 'It appears from the three returns of the Population Act, in 1801, 1811, and 1821, that the proportion of marriages has been diminishing with the increasing health of the country, notwithstanding the augmented rate of increase in the population' (593n). There was then no reversal in the last edition of the earlier estimates. They were indeed in one respect reinforced. For the loose prediction given in 1806 and 1817 of decelerating growth of food supplies, and therefore of population within some three or four decades, *is extended to a full century* (*2*, 246), and this despite *acceleration* of the population growth rate revealed by the third census. The prediction was, so to speak, academic.

VI MORE ON PRUDENCE

It will be recalled from chapter 5: IV that Malthus did not treat increasing prudential control solely as a matter of exogenous change in habits (stimulated perhaps by education or propaganda programs), but rather to some extent as endogenous to the growth process. We there saw that reference in 1803 to increased wages stimulating improved prudential control by generating 'more of a decent and proper pride' is supplemented in the 1817 *Essay*. There a role is accorded rising food prices *relative* to those of manufactures in the process of changing taste patterns, a process which encouraging inward shifts of the labour growth curve, thereby checking, and even preventing, reductions in the corn wage and allowing increases in the commodity basket.

The foregoing mechanism would apply to the case of decelerating growth in consequence of diminishing agricultural returns, which entails *absolute* increases in the real corn price; Malthus makes it clear that deceleration of accumulation need not depress the corn wage in the event of appropriate prudential control – such control induced in part by a fall in the corn price of manufactures. Indeed, 'strictly speaking, the good or bad condition of the poor is not *necessarily* connected with any particular stage in the progress of society to its full complement of wealth' (chapter 5, p. 192). Although, as the present chapter has demonstrated, new technology had rendered increasing land scarcity irrelevant as a feature of contemporary British conditions, the general case might still apply in so far as P_c/P_m increases with *relatively large reductions in the price of manufactures.* Moreover, Malthus did not deny that the corn price had recently increased, but only that its rise reflected falling agricultural productivity.[20]

VII SUMMARY

From 1803 Malthus attempted to account for the newly recognized phenomenon of rapidly accelerating population. The active ingredient, on his reading, was not the birth rate but declining mortality, both exogenous and in response to higher real wages, the latter reflecting ongoing improvements in technology. 'Prudential control' was increasingly effective and to some extent endogenous to the growth process by dint of relationships linking working-class tastes for comfort: (1) to rising real wages; and (2) to increases in food prices relative to those of manufactures. The land scarcity–based growth model was thus not used, as is so often supposed, in exercises involving discrete improvements and unchanged labour-supply conditions, such that the outcome entails a return to the original equilibri-

20 Cf. letter to Ricardo, 3 December 1817; in Ricardo, 1951–73, VII, 214–15: 'I am strongly disposed to believe, that for nearly the last century or at least for 80 or 90 years, no marked increase has taken place in the quantity of labour necessary to produce corn at home ... The increase in the labour of growing corn has certainly had little or nothing to do with the increase in its price of late years.'

um wage. Rather the supposition was one of ongoing outward movements of the marginal product curve sufficient to accommodate unprecedented population growth – the net effect of the reduction in both mortality and birth rates was to displace *outwards* the wage population growth curve – without pressure on the real wage.

The *Essay on Population* reveals, moreover, high optimism regarding *future* rapid population growth consistently with the maintenance of high real wages. In 1803 and 1817 the prediction of ultimate deceleration is applied to some three or four decades ahead, and in 1826 to a full century ahead. And from 1798 to 1826 no concern is expressed regarding *excessive* population growth, assuming avoidance of the artificial depression of domestic agriculture and the artificial encouragement of population.

V / TRADE POLICY AND SOCIAL WELFARE

SEVENTEEN

Agricultural protection

I INTRODUCTION

Lionel Robbins wrote of the English classical economists as the 'intellectual spearhead' of the general movement for freeing spontaneous enterprise and energies (1952, 19). To this generalization he attached a note regarding Malthus: 'It may be thought that an exception in this respect should be made for Malthus, who, as it is well known, was not in favour of the free importation of corn. But too much should not be made of this exception. In general, Malthus was at one with the Classical Economists, in wishing an extensive removal of the barriers to trade.' What motivated the exception?[1] We are not told. This chapter documents a finding that removes the apparent anomaly – namely, the finding that Malthus withdrew his support for the prohibitory Corn Laws.[2]

To my knowledge, Malthus's new position is nowhere mentioned in the

1 A revealing formulation is provided in a letter from Malthus to Macvey Napier, dated 27 September 1821: 'I am not disposed to be offended at differences of opinion, particularly on such a subject as the Corn Laws, which, if justifiable, must be allowed to be an exception to the general rule of Political Economy' (Macvey Napier Papers, British Library, Add. Mss. 34, 612, f. 445).

2 The 1815 Corn Law, originally supported by Malthus, entailed *absolute prohibition* of foreign wheat when the domestic price fell short of 80s. per quarter, and free importation at prices exceeding 80s. In 1822 a new Corn Law reverted to an earlier sliding-scale system, with 70s. as the prohibition limit and duties varying inversely with the domestic price at prices above 70s. The sliding-scale system did not come into effect until 1828. (See appendix B.)

The sectoral distribution of the gainful labour force of Great Britain over the period that concerns us is given in appendix A.

secondary literature.[3] It has, it is true, long been recognized that Malthus suffered pangs of conscience because of his protectionism.[4] William Empson, in his obituary article of January 1837 – a combined review of the *Principles* (1836) and memoir – provides a graphic account:

[Malthus] was quite aware of the risk which his reputation was running by the course of argument he pursued on that occasion [1815]. He said that he well knew that nothing he had ever written had injured it so much. On the whole, too (to use his favourite summing up), he was not on this occasion as sure as usual of the soundness of the judgement which he had pronounced. He continued to think that the friends of truth and fair dealing had received considerable provocation by the one-sided manner, as well as by the insolence of personal imputations with which the discussion had been conducted against the landlords. He deemed it highly useful that inflammatory declamation should be met by cool argument – that both sides of the question should be heard with patience, and unreasonable expectations, one by one, exposed. There are invidious duties which it demands a certain spirit to discharge. Of these, he felt it to be one, to

3 I have consulted the following modern works and found no recognition of Malthus's transformation: Blaug, 1958, 1985; Bonar, 1924; Dorfman, 1989; Flinn, 1983; H. Scott Gordon, 1971; Barry Gordon, 1979; Grampp, 1960, 1965; Hilton, 1977; James, 1979; (but see below, p. 885, regarding 1832–3); Langer, 1987; O'Brien, 1975; Petersen, 1979; Pullen, 1987a; Rashid, 1988; Robbins, 1952; Semmel, 1963, 1965; Tucker, 1960; Winch, 1987 (but see note 4, below). Objections to my case will be found in Pullen, 1995, and my response in Hollander, 1995a.

In her variorum edition of the *Essay*, Patricia James makes no mention of the change, and cites editorially only the existence of the new note (in Malthus, 1803/1989, II, 74). Pullen refers to the note in his variorum edition of the *Principles*, but does not mention the change in question (in Malthus 1820/1986, II, 393).

Vamplew, 1986, 130, positively denies any change in position: 'Although most other political economists shared Ricardo's opinion that Malthus was preaching "dangerous heresy," he continued to hold his favourable view towards agricultural protection as can be seen from his *Essay on the Principle of Population* (1826) and the posthumously published *Principles of Political Economy* (1836). Similarly, Grampp refers to 'the defense of the Corn Laws in the last edition of the *Essay on Population*' (1956, 933).

4 Winch has written regarding the Corn Law of 1815 that Malthus was 'not entirely happy with the result,' and relates his concern to the riots of 1815: 'It may also be worth pointing out ... that while Malthus was, so to speak, on the winning side in 1815 – a protective Corn Law was passed, though not necessarily for the reasons given by Malthus – he was not entirely happy with the result. A familiar pattern of popular unrest accompanied the passage of the Bill, and these events clearly shook the moderate politician in Malthus so much that he concluded that the people should not have a divisive measure imposed upon them. Again, the conclusion of his science of politics took precedence over his principles of political economy, but it was characteristic of Malthus that he continued to suffer agonies of conscience throughout his life for the part he may have played in undermining the general principle of non-intervention to which he was deeply attached' (1987, 73–4).

put people upon their guard – that they were not to expect from the repeal of Corn Laws, advantages of a kind which no repeal of measures of this nature could possibly confer. This duty he never regretted that he had performed. But his general principles in favour of freedom of trade were so absolute, that, at times, doubts came over him, whether any exception ought to be admitted. It follows, that he was far from continuing always equally satisfied that the necessity of the particular exception, which he had argued, in behalf of restrictions upon the importation of corn was sufficiently made out. (1837/1963, 258–9)

But there is nothing here – and nothing in Otter's famous memoir (1836) – recognizing an actual *abandonment* of support for the Corn Laws.

Two related strands characterize Malthus's support of agricultural protection as a matter of principle until the early 1820s. One is the agricultural-surplus framework characteristic of physiocracy; the other is the case for balanced growth, implying self-sufficiency in food, even in an economy 'naturally' inclined towards an industrial bias.[5] Other arguments are made, but they are of a practical nature rather than matters of principle. A note to the 1826 *Essay on Population* suggests a formal transition to the free-trade program designed by Ricardo to assure competitive resource allocation, albeit that the outcome would entail industry-biased development, and reduced rental incomes. Earlier evidence of the transition can be found in 1824, and possibly even 1823, and is discernible in the revisions to the *Principles* and correspondence. It reflected, I shall argue, Malthus's positive response to the government's new program of dismantling mercantilist industrial and commercial policies, including manufacturing tariffs – the Huskisson reforms; the possibility of global free trade was not to be threatened by 'so large an exception' as afforded by the Corn Laws, though their abandonment would result in a relative decline of the domestic agricultural sector. This new rejection of balanced growth and self-sufficiency in food in favour of industry-based growth reflected also a recognition that expanded exportation of manufactured goods was essential to the maintenance of general activity. This lesson, learned in the postwar period, undermined the physiocratic notion (as expressed in 1815) that 'the quantity of a country's exports is a very uncertain criterion of its wealth' (below, p. 834), and more generally the case for balanced growth to counter pressures emanating from Smithian 'increasing competition of capitals.' The episode adds credence to Malthus's claim (in 1815) that his protectionism was not designed to defend the class interests of landowners, but reflected his perception of the national interest – a perception requiring modification with the beginning of the end of the old commercial system.

5 For an emphasis on 'sectoral balance,' see Winch, 1987, ch. 5.

To lay the groundwork for the transition and for its rationale, we take up in section II the original case for protection in earlier editions of the *Essay* (those of 1803 and 1806), with particular reference to Malthus's opposition to 'commercial systems.' The static efficiency gains of free trade were not at issue. Rather the object of agricultural protectionism – in 1803 by way of a corn-export bounty, and in 1806 with greater attention to import restriction – was to assure 'security, independence, and permanent prosperity,' even at the cost of a slight deceleration of growth. It is the presumption here that the faster expansion of manufacturing relative to domestic agriculture exacerbates the problem of seasonal instability, and puts upward pressure on the level of money costs to the ultimate disadvantage of manufacturing itself. There was also a danger to national negotiating power of reliance on imported food. Moreover, to rely on imports was foolhardy because of the prospective transition of agriculturally based economies to mixed systems and the drying up of foreign surpluses for export.

The diminishing-returns principle emerges in 1803 during the course of a warning against easier agricultural imports – marginal areas would have to be withdrawn. The same principle, we show in section III, was used to the contrary effect in a letter to Horner in June 1813 and again in the *Observations on the Effects of the Corn Laws* (1814). A case made out for agricultural tariffs is shown to be designed as corrective for 'mercantilist' resource misallocation, rather than as protection. The pamphlet recognizes that protection would not assure greater corn-price stability – this because of a British cost structure out of line with that of foreign sources of supply – and implied a level of prices that would prove ruinous to manufacturing, in consequence of high corn costs, and thus of high money wages. We show in sections IV and V that these concerns are carried over to the 1815 protectionist pamphlet *Grounds of an Opinion*, but they are now overridden by other considerations: concern with the effect of an inflow of cheap foreign corn on the level of activity, with an eye to the 'justice' accorded various income recipients. Though the policy recommendation turns on Malthusian doctrine, it might still be said to entail short-run expediency rather than principle – the timing for free trade was wrong. This is certainly the case of a security argument, considering French corn-export restrictions. But there is also Malthus's 'agricultural bias' to consider, for this too played a significant role in his protectionism in 1815, as Ricardo complained (section VI).

Malthus's opposition to 'commercial systems' in the 1817 edition of the *Essay on Population* – this provides the context of the note that concerns us – is the topic of section VII, particularly concern with depressed manufacturing prices (and profits) in a commercial system in consequence of increasing 'competition of capitals' – Adam Smith's preoccupation. There were, so it is asserted, no such limits in a mixed system. Intervention was thus justified (as in the early editions of the *Essay*) to prevent growth favouring manufactures and dependent on imported corn that would characterize a freely operating system. Again there is a questioning of the reliability of a long-term supply of imported corn as foreign agricultural economies diversify. There were also sociological disadvantages attached to an excessively large manufacturing sector. And Malthus reverted to the position that free trade did not guarantee corn-price stability, considering French intervention in the corn-export trade and British 'mercantilist' intervention.

The opinion is afloat that the 1817 edition entails a dilution of physiocratic content (chapter 8, pp. 368–9). But an emphasis on 'balanced growth' cannot in itself be taken to reflect a weakening of physiocratic orientation, considering an explicit downplaying of commerce newly introduced in this fifth edition – including a reference to Bishop Berkeley's 'wall of brass' – as well as the reiteration of the peculiar advantage to an economy whose national income includes rent as well as wages and profit – the 'agricultural bias' of 1815. The recommendation for balance should also be evaluated in the light of a new recognition in 1817 of a 'natural tendency' towards *industry*-biased growth. A call for balance under these circumstances is a call to prevent increasing dependence on foreign food supplies, precisely what one would expect from a physiocratic stance.

The case for agricultural protection emerging in the *Principles* of 1820 is reinforced by a supposed deviation of the social from the private return to capital investment in agriculture (section VIII). This is supplemented by the argument that a manufacturing system depends, in an international context, on low money costs, and therefore upon the depression of wages, to the detriment of labour. We are back to the 1803 and 1806 cases, where a disproportionate growth of manufactures threatens international competitiveness by putting *upward* pressure on prices – pressure, we are warned in 1820, that can be counteracted only by policies hostile to labour. Conversely, in a mixed system, prudential population control – and the relatively high real wages resulting – could be more easily accommodated.

The absence from the posthumous second edition of the principal arguments for protection, and other indications of the new position (including the note of 1826), are documented in section IX. We then finally take up the rationale for the policy transition of 1826. This we trace in part to Malthus's approval of Huskisson's trade reforms, promising (provided Britain abandoned her agricultural protectionism) 'universal' free trade. But a reorientation of principle is also involved – a renunciation of the case for balanced growth and self-sufficiency in food in favour of industry-based growth, the Ricardian position. This may be explained in part on grounds of the dependence of *general* activity on the export industries and in part on grounds of the theorem whereby the level of prices is determined by the productivity of the export industries. Various other considerations, including the role played by an apparent dilution of

Malthus's 'physiocracy' in the transition – the notion of the peculiar productivity of agriculture – are also taken into account.

The *volte face* went unnoticed by most of Malthus's contemporaries.[6] Our Conclusion addresses his failure to correct the oversight of those who were unaware of the change.

II EARLY OPPOSITION TO 'COMMERCIAL SYSTEMS': 1803, 1806

A denial in 1803 and 1806 of any practical limits of growth in an 'enlightened' agricultural system implies support for *imbalance* favouring agriculture: 'There is no discernible germ of decay in the system'; all the problems generated in a 'commercial society' could be avoided in a country which 'in average years, grows more corn than it consumes, and is in the habit of exporting a part of it,' so that the corn price and the money wage can never rise much above those of foreign competitors (1803/1986, *3*, 676; 1806, II, 221–2). It was Malthus's lament that Britain had 'stepped out of the agricultural system into a state, in which the commercial system clearly predominates; and there is reason to fear, that even our commerce and manufactures will ultimately feel the disadvantage of the change.' Although the transition from net corn exporter to net corn importer has occurred 'only within the last twenty or thirty years,' the country had 'already felt some of its inconveniences; and if we persevere in it, its evil consequences may by no means be a matter of remote speculation' (688n; 276n). To reverse the transition by means of a corn-export bounty was 'worth the experiment, as the continuance of our national greatness, and commercial prosperity, seem absolutely to depend upon it [1806: as the permanence of our national prosperity may depend upon it]' (685; 268).[7] All of this, of course, constitutes a refutation of the Smithian view that government intervention in the corn market is to no avail.

Concern with the encouragement granted manufacturing by mercantilist intervention played a major part in the formal case favouring agricultural protection. In these terms Malthus defended his own self-declared reputation as 'liberal' free-trader against any possible misunderstanding. In the absence of intervention favouring manufactures, there was no reason to expect 'that the commercial part of the society would have increased beyond the surplus produce of the cultivators' (679; 235). But 'the high profits of commerce from monopolies, and other peculiar encouragements, [had] altered [the] natural course of things; and the body politic is in an

6 It certainly went unnoticed by Marx, who represented Malthus as a '*bought advocate*' of the landed aristocracy, who 'wants bourgeois production in so far as it is not revolutionary, in so far as it is not a historical force, but merely creates a broader and more convenient material basis for the "old society"' (cited in Meek, 1953, 122–3, 157).

7 The last modification suggests a lesser concern with the problem.

artificial, and in some degree, diseased state, with one of its principal members out of proportion to the rest.' As for himself, '[no] person can well be more averse to medicine in the animal economy, or a system of expedients in political economy ...; but in the present state of the country, something of the kind may be necessary to prevent greater evils. It is a matter of very little comparative importance, whether we are fully supplied with broadcloth, linens, and muslin, or even with tea, sugar, and coffee; and no rational politician therefore, would think of proposing a bounty upon such commodities. But it is certainly a matter of the very highest importance, whether we are fully supplied with food; and if a bounty would produce such a supply, the most liberal political economist might be justified in proposing it; considering food as a commodity distinct from all others, and pre-eminently valuable' (680; 235–6).

These declarations suggest that pro-agricultural intervention would *not* have been justified in the event of a 'natural' bias emerging which favoured manufactures. This is implied even in the following extract, which opens with the strong statement that the 'nature of things has, indeed, stamped upon corn a peculiar value ... [a] remark, made by Dr. Smith [1937, 482] for another purpose, [which] may fairly be applied to justify the exception of this commodity from the objections against bounties in general' (686; 272). Assuming universal free trade, 'one should undoubtedly feel the greatest reluctance in proposing any interruption to such a system of general liberty; and indeed, under such circumstances, agriculture would not need peculiar encouragements. But under the present universal prevalence of the commercial system, with all its different expedients of encouragement and restraint, it is folly to except from our attention the great manufacture of corn which supports all the rest. The high duties paid on the importation of foreign manufactures, are so direct an encouragement to the manufacturing part of the society, that nothing but some encouragement of the same kind, operating with the same force, can place the manufacturers and cultivators of this country on a fair footing. Any system of encouragement, therefore, which might be found necessary for the commerce of grain, would evidently be owing to the prior encouragements which had been given to manufactures' (686–7; 272–3).[8]

Taking Malthus at his word, in the present context we would be obliged to conclude that he favoured intervention only as a second-best solution: 'If all [trades] be free, I have nothing to say; but if we protect and encourage, it seems to be folly not to encourage that production, which of all

8 Here a contrast is drawn between the woollen industry and corn, which is absent from the 1806 edition: 'We consider the woollen manufacture of England as of the first importance, and protect and encourage it with peculiar care; but can any thinking man compare its influence on the strength and prosperity of the state, with the manufacture of corn, the scarcity or failure of which, will involve in it the failure of the favourite manufacture itself.'

others is the most important and valuable' (687; 273).[9] Yet the fact is that at the close of the chapter on corn-export bounties the danger of excessive growth of manufactures is reiterated quite generally, that is, independently of artificial stimuli, in an application of the celebrated 'doctrine of proportions.' 'If from the increasing riches of the commercial part of any nation and the consequently increasing demands for the products of pasture, more lands were daily laid down to grass, and more corn imported from other countries, the unavoidable consequence seems to be, that the increasing prosperity of these countries, which their exportations of corn would contribute to accelerate, must ultimately destroy the population and power of the countries which had fostered them ... [A]llowing with the moderns, all the advantages of luxury, and when it falls short of actual vice, they are certainly great; there seems to be a point, beyond which it must necessarily become prejudicial to a state, and bring with it the seeds of weakness and decay. This point is, when it is pushed so far, as to trench on the funds necessary for its support, and to become an impediment instead of an encouragement to agriculture' (687n; 274n). The character of agriculture's 'pre-eminence' or 'peculiar value' suggests that, despite his formal disclaimers, Malthus *would* have proposed intervention favouring agriculture even in an otherwise freely operating system.

* * *

In 1806 Malthus repeated the 1803 appeal to try the experiment of turning Britain from an importing to an exporting country.[10] But a bounty was no longer the first priority. Rather an extended case is made for *corn-import restriction* as the immediate requirement: 'In a nation which never imported corn except in a scarcity, commerce could never get the start of agricul-

9 He allowed (at least in 1803) that in some circumstances encouragement of *manufactures* would be in order: 'It has been before observed, that, if from the beginning every kind of trade had been left to find its own level, agriculture would probably never have wanted any particular support; but when once this general and desirable liberty has been infringed, it seems to be clearly our interest to attend principally to those parts of the political structure, which in the actual circumstances of the country appear to be comparatively the weakest; and, upon this principle, we should be justified in giving particular encouragement to manufactures in such countries as Poland, and the southern parts of Siberia, and the same kind of encouragement to agriculture, in England' (688).

10 A note refers to recent (1804) legislation: 'Since this was first written [1803], a new system of corn laws has been established by the legislature, but it is not so powerful in its operation as that of 1688 and 1700. The new laws tend strongly to encourage the growth of an independent supply of corn, but not so strongly the production of an excess. An independent supply however is certainly the first and most important object.' It is difficult to appreciate this note. The 1804 Corn Laws did not comprise a 'new system' but a (stricter) version of that adopted in 1791. See appendix B on the details of this and other Corn Law legislation.

ture; and restrictive laws on importation, as far as they go, tend to give a relative discouragement to manufactures, and a relative encouragement to agriculture' (1806, II, 257–8). Import restrictions are recommended, even if they should mean a slight deceleration of growth, in the interest of greater 'security, independence, and permanent prosperity' – in effect, self-sufficiency in food: 'If without diminishing manufactures, they were merely to determine a greater part of the future annual accumulation to fall on the land, the effect would undoubtedly be in the highest degree desirable; but even allowing that the present very rapid march of wealth in general were to suffer a slight relaxation in its progress, if there be any foundation whatever for the alarms that have of late been expressed respecting the advantageous employment of so rapidly increasing a capital, we might surely be willing to sacrifice a small portion of present riches, in order to attain a greater degree of security, independence, and permanent prosperity' (258–9).[11]

What then were the precise 'evils of an importing system'? There are several 'objective' considerations. One purpose of the proposed generation of a corn-export surplus by way of a corn-export subsidy was to alleviate the recurrent seasonal problem ('scarcity') in a dependent economy: 'It is impossible always to be secure of having enough, if we have not, in general, too much; and the habitual exportation of corn, seems to be the only practicable mode of laying by a store of sufficient magnitude to answer the emergencies, that are to be expected' (1803/1986, *3*, 679).[12] (An elaborate version of the theme is given in 1806, II, 233–4.) Subsequently it is applied to the case of a nation, 'possessed of a large territory, [which] is unavoidably subject to this uncertainty in its means of subsistence, when the commercial part of its population is either equal to, or has increased beyond, the surplus produce of its cultivators' (1803/1986, *3*, 696; 1806, II, 199–200).

There is also a secular concern. Increase in demand for corn relative to supply, reflecting manufacturing expansion at a faster rate than agriculture, implied upward pressure on the corn price, and thus on the money wage, with potentially serious implications for the international competi-

11 A historical note is attached to the text regarding the potential of import restrictions, implying the weakness of Smith's position: 'If the operation of the corn laws, as they were established in 1700, had continued uninterrupted, I cannot bring myself to believe, that we should be now in the habit of importing so much corn as we do at present. Putting the bounty on exportation out of the question, the restrictive laws on importation alone would have made it impossible. The demand for British corn would, for the last 30 years, have been both greater and more uniform than it has been; and it is contrary to every principle of supply and demand to suppose, that this would not have occasioned a greater growth. Dr. Smith's argument clearly proves too much, which is as bad as proving too little' (257–8n).

12 And in addition there is the advantage to *manufactures* of a 'steady and comparatively low price of provisions.'

tiveness of manufacturing itself. The effect of a rising corn price on the money wage is further reinforced by 'scarce seasons' – unavoidable in the 'present system' – having in mind downward wage rigidity. Rising wages in turn play back on corn costs, again reinforcing the upward trend of food and materials prices. The ultimate threat is to the competitiveness of the export industries, on the (Smithian) grounds that manufacturing-cost prices are governed by money-wage costs (676; 222).

These characteristic problems of a 'commercial society' could be avoided in a country running a corn-export surplus: 'When a country, in average years, grows more corn than it consumes, and is in the habit of exporting a part of it, its price, and the price of labour as depending on it, can never rise in any very extraordinary degree above [1806: ... a part of it, those great variations of price which from the competition of commercial wealth often produce lasting effects, cannot occur to the same extent. The wages of labour can never rise very much above] the common price, in other commercial countries; and under such circumstances, England would have nothing to fear from the fullest, and most open competition. The increasing prosperity of other countries, would open to her a more extensive market for her commodities, and give additional spirit to all her commercial transactions' (677; 224–5). Here Malthus distinguishes the differential effect of a high corn price, depending on its source: 'The high price of corn and of rude produce in general, as far as it is occasioned by the freest competition among the nations of Europe, is a very great advantage, and is the best possible encouragement to agriculture.' But 'when occasioned merely by the competition of monied wealth at home' – an allusion to manufacturing bias – 'its effect is totally [1806: 'totally' omitted] different. In the one case, a great encouragement is given to production in general, and the more is produced, the better. In the other case, the produce is necessarily confined to the home consumption. The cultivators are justly afraid of growing too much corn, as a considerable loss will be sustained upon that part of it which is sold abroad; and a glut in the home market will universally make the price fall below the fair and proper recompense of the grower. It is impossible that a country, under such circumstances, should not be subject to great and frequent variations in the price of corn ...' There is even a denial of *practical limits* to growth in an 'enlightened' agricultural system: 'There is no apparent limit to the quantity of manufactures which might in time be supported in this way. The increasing wealth of a country in such a state, seems to be out of reach of all common accidents. There is no discoverable germ of decay in the system; and in theory, there is not reason to say, that it might not go on increasing in wealth and prosperity for thousands of years' (676; 221).[13]

13 Malthus objected only to the 'prejudice' that any system could 'keep pace with an unchecked population' (687; 276).

As for agricultural dependency, the ultimate concern was the danger to national negotiating power: 'If we proceed in our present course, let us but for a moment reflect on the probable consequences. There cannot be a doubt, that, in the course of a few years, we shall draw from America, and the nations bordering on the Baltic, as much as 2 million quarters of wheat, besides other corn, the support of above 2 millions of people. If, under these circumstances, any commercial discussion, or other dispute, were to arise with these nations, with what a weight of power they would negotiate!' (685; 268–9). The danger was acute in the case of Britain, 'whose commercial ambition is peculiarly calculated to excite a general jealousy,' which might induce foreign nations to act 'contrary to their own interest.'

* * *

In 1803 Malthus admitted that the danger of unbalanced growth favouring manufactures was for the future – 'some twenty years hence' – because of the impressiveness of British manufacturing technology (her 'capital, skill, machinery, and establishments, [being] in their full vigour') and the temporary wartime damage to foreign competitors. High money wages had still not eroded Britain's competitive edge; but this could not continue forever 'with the prices of provisions and of labour still going on increasing' (1986, *3*, 676–7).[14] Subsequently (in a passage retained in 1806), the effectiveness of the empirical rule relating to the 'decay' of a commercial nation dependent on food imports is further diluted. England was a probable exception in the short run, by which is intended apparently *two or three centuries*: 'I am not now speaking of the next twenty or thirty years, but of the next two or three hundred. And though we are little in the habit of looking so far forwards, yet it may be questioned, whether we have a right knowingly to adopt [1806: whether we are not bound in duty to make some exertions to avoid] a system which must necessarily terminate in the weakness and decline of our posterity' (688n; 1806, II, 275–6n). Needless to say, this renders academic the problem of excessive reliance on imported food, a fact that Malthus more or less concedes: 'But whether we make any practical application of such a discussion or not, it is curious to contemplate the causes of those reverses in the fates of empires, which so frequently changed the face of the world in past times, and may be expected to produce similar, though perhaps not such violent changes in the future.'

14 Reference is made in 1803 to Adam Smith (1776/1937, 564–5), who had referred to merchants' complaints of high British wages to the detriment of exports.

* * *

Since there was benefit to manufactures from 'the steady and comparatively low price of provisions and of labour' (1986, *3*, 679), Malthus – turning devil's advocate – formally addressed the advisability of *encouraging* corn imports as a means of checking the money wage. This proposal he rejected in both 1803 and 1806 on the empirical grounds of downward nominal wage rigidity, carrying with it the ruination of domestic arable farming, at least in marginal areas: 'Experience warrants us in saying, that, from political fears, or other causes, the fall in the price of labour would be uncertain; but the ruin of our agriculture would be certain [1806: Experience warrants us in saying, that the fall in the price of labour would be slow and uncertain, but the decline of our agriculture would be certain]. The British grower of corn could not, in his own markets, stand the competition of the foreign grower, in average years. We should be daily thrown more and more into a dependence upon other countries for our support. [1806: sentence omitted.] Arable lands of a moderate quality would not pay the expense of cultivation. Rich soils alone would yield a rent. Round all our towns, the appearances would be the same as usual; but in the interior of the country, half of the lands would be neglected, and almost universally, where it was practicable, pasture would take place of tillage' (677; 1806, II, 226).

The damage to agriculture would have severe implications for the economy as a whole and for population growth, continues the 1803 version: 'How dreadfully precarious would our commerce and manufactures, and even our very existence be, under such circumstances!' It could hardly be expected that a century should elapse without seeing our population repressed within the limits of our scanty cultivation; and suffering the same melancholy reverse, as the once flourishing population of Spain.'[15] This might seem to be largely rhetorical: Why should population be 'repressed' if foreign corn is available? But this is the crux of the matter. A steady inflow of foreign corn could *not* be presupposed. Malthus proceeds to illustrate by supposing that European countries with large territories

15 Possibly the undesirable consequences for commerce and manufactures were seen to flow from the reduction of home demand emanating in agriculture. Malthus is not explicit.

Elsewhere in 1803 a further case against free importation is elaborated: 'Even supposing, that either by glutting the home market with British corn, or by the importation of foreign corn, duty free, we could succeed in lowering the wages of labour, the expenses of the British farmer in raising corn and bringing it to market, would not be lowered in proportion' (683). Here Malthus had in mind high rent and taxes: 'A fall in the wages of labour could not proportionally affect the price at which British corn could be brought to market; and the British farmer would labour under a very considerable disadvantage in a competition with the farmers of America and the shores of the Baltic, where these two ingredients of price are comparatively trifling' (683–4).

suitable for agriculture (Britain, France, Germany, and Prussia) were to encourage manufacturing at the expense of domestic agriculture, relying on food imports from Russia and America. The rising European demands for food could not adequately be met for long, given population pressure on food supplies in Russia and America and the 'gradual establishment' of manufacturing in those countries. The European countries would learn from experience what it meant to rely on foreign sources of food supply. The statement – which has a strong physiocratic flavour – draws a sharp contrast between growth programs based on agriculture and manufacturing: 'From these causes and the necessity of drawing a part of such vast supplies of corn from a much greater distance inland, and loaded perhaps with the expense of land carriage, the price would ultimately rise so extravagantly high, that the poor manufacturers would be totally unable to pay it, and want and famine would convince them too late of the precarious and subordinate nature of their wealth. They would learn by painful experience, that, though agriculture may flourish considerably, and give plenty and happiness to great numbers, without many manufactures; yet, that manufactures cannot stir a single step, without their agricultural paymasters, either at home or abroad; and that therefore it is the height of folly and imprudence, to have these paymasters at a great distance, with different interests, and their payments precarious, instead of at home, with the same interests and their payments always ready and certain' (1986, *3*, 678).[16]

The 1806 version is less apocalyptical, Malthus writing there of a re-establishment of equilibrium after the predicted contraction of domestic agriculture: 'This state of things would continue, till the equilibrium was restored, either by the fall of British rent and wages, or an advance in the price of foreign corn, or, what is more probable, by the union of both causes ... During this period even her commerce and manufactures would be in a most precarious state; and circumstances by no means improbable in the present state of Europe might reduce her population within the limits of her reduced cultivation' (1806, II, 226–7). As in 1803, Malthus warns against reliance upon foreign agricultural export surpluses, because these are likely to dry up with expansion abroad, and be subject to politically motivated obstructions (228–9).

In both versions of the *Essay*, Malthus's reservations regarding a growth program based on food imports, turned in part on the stimulus to population growth afforded by rising demand for labour (the emphasis is on the relaxation of the preventive check) but entailing unreliable sources of food supply: 'if a demand for labour continue increasing with some rapidity, although the supply of food be uncertain, on account of variable seasons

16 It will be remarked that increasing land scarcity abroad is conspicuously absent from the prospective impediments to food imports (696).

and a dependence on other countries, the population will evidently go on, till it is positively checked by famine or the diseases arising from severe want' (1986, *3*, 451; 1806, II, 280–1).

There is an amusing if perverse side to Malthus's early protectionism. To depend on foreign sources of food supply, Malthus observed at one point in 1803 (absent in 1806), would in fact be to wish for the *constrained* development of those foreign countries: 'Nothing can be so hateful to a liberal mind, as the idea of being placed in a situation in which the growing prosperity of your neighbours will be the signal of your own approaching ruin. Yet this would be the situation of the principal countries of Europe, if they depended chiefly upon Russia and America, or any other nations for their corn' (1986, *3*, 678). It was therefore desirable to avoid dependence on foreign food supply wherever possible – and 'a country possessed of a considerable territory' was in the fortunate position of being able to do so. Now Malthus recommended an export surplus in corn. It is strange to encounter the dilemma 'to a liberal mind' resolved by deliberately running a corn-export surplus which encourages an artificially created dependency on the part of trading partners. In any event, the problem of international relations, we shall see, was resolved in the 1820s by precisely the reverse argument implied by the case for the abolition of the Corn Laws.

III THE 'FREE TRADE' POSITION IN 1813–1814

William Smart observed regarding the Corn Law debates of 1813 and 1814 that 'what perhaps strikes one most ... is the entire ignoring of the tendency of land produce to diminishing returns and of the law of rent. These now cardinal principles of economic science were only definitely formulated in [1815]' (1910–17, I, 457). This is positively not true of Malthus, who in his remarkable letter to Horner of 16 June 1813 (see chapter 2, p. 72) stated the efficiency advantages of free trade, specifically taking account of diminishing returns. In fact, we have seen (above, p. 818) that even the early *Essay on Population* allows for diminishing returns (and alludes to differential rent). But there it does so as part of a case for *protection*, warning of the damaging effect on agriculture of freer corn importation.

The letter to Horner sets out by insisting that 'an increase in the relative demand for domestic corn must generate an increase in the relative supply on the basis of some of the most fundamental principles of Political Economy' (in Tucker, 1954, 331); and conversely: 'If there were no corn laws whatever I am decidedly of opinion that our general wealth would increase more rapidly, but I think that we should not so nearly grow our own consumption as at present. If Europe were like one large nation with regard to importation and exportation, its cultivation would proceed like the cultivation of a large nation; and it could never answer to bring *indiffer-*

ent land under tillage in one district, till the *good* lands in other districts, from which there was an easy communication, were first cultivated. England in reference to Europe may be considered as a large manufacturing district, with the natural tendency of such a district to import a considerable part of its corn, though with a power of growing it, if forced.' This is only a more detailed formulation of what appears in the *Essay*. But when it comes to policy, Malthus seemingly now abandons the protectionist case: 'In using this force, there is reason to believe that we shall check our manufactures more than we shall increase our agriculture, and this it appears to me forms the true argument against the system; an argument surely of great weight although we allow that an independent supply is practical by such means.' Furthermore, prices were likely to be unstable in a closed economy producing at a cost level above that of foreign producers: 'A little excess of supply not being relieved by exportations, on account of the general high prices of corn at home, I doubt if prices would be steady.' In this respect, too, Malthus had apparently reversed himself, since in the early editions of the *Essay* the corn-export bounty was said to dampen price volatility.

The 1813 letter is difficult to appreciate, considering its location between the formal protectionism in the earlier *Essay* of 1806 and 1807 and the later *Grounds* (1815).[17] But conceivably it does not indicate Malthus's

17 The letter of 16 June is also problematic in that it relates the case for a free corn trade to the diminishing-returns phenomenon, though Britain is represented throughout by Malthus as having been subject to continued improvement in agricultural technology during the war period.

Strange to relate, two years later, after Malthus had stated his support for the Corn Bill of 1815, it was Horner who objected on precisely the efficiency grounds specified by Malthus in June 1813. He evidently had not absorbed Malthus's diminishing-returns lesson of 1813, for he represents the principle as a *novelty* appearing in Malthus's two pamphlets of 1815 – *Grounds of an Opinion* and *Inquiry into Rent* – with the policy application attributable to himself:

> I have to thank you for sending me your two new publications upon the corn question, which I have read, and am still reading. You will think me very hardened, but I must own that my old faith is not shaken by your reasonings; on the contrary, I am even so perverse, as to think I have discovered, among your ingenious deductions respecting rent, some fresh and cogent arguments in favour of a free corn trade for this country; by which I always mean, as free a trade as we can secure by our own good sense, however it may be impaired by the deficiency of our neighbours in that qualification. If the consequence of 'high farming' and curious cultivation be a progressive rise of the price of produce, an importation of partial supplies from countries, which by a ruder agriculture can furnish it cheaper, seems the provision laid by nature for checking too exclusive an employment of capital upon the land least fit for culture. It would be a palpable sacrifice of the end to the means, if, for the sake of extending our most finished husbandry to every sterile ridge that can be forced to yield something, we impose upon the whole body of the people extravagant prices for the necessaries of life. Nor do I see, upon your peculiar principles, what other result there would be, if Dartmoor and Blackstone Edge were laid out in terraces of garden-ground, but a population always in some peril of being starved, if their rulers will not let them eat the superfluity of their neighbours. (12 June 1815; 1853, II, 222–3)

position at that time in its entirety. It is important to have in mind in this regard the fact that the *Observations* (1814), which summarizes the pros and cons of agricultural protection without final commitment, takes account of the considerations raised in the letter. In that pamphlet Malthus allowed that agricultural protection could *not* assure a corn price 'within moderate bounds and to a certain degree steady,' since 'in our actual situation, it is only by keeping the price of corn up, very considerably above the average of the rest of Europe, that we can possibly be made to grow our own consumption' (1986, 7, 99). For Britain's cost 'advantage' – at the margin – lay with manufacturing, in part because of diminishing agricultural returns and in part because of differential taxation placing agricultural costs out of line with those of Europe and the United States (107–8). There were also absolute 'facilities' in manufacturing. The possibility of stimulating 'a large average surplus' by export subsidies had to be abandoned, given the cost structures of Britain and the Continent. But in that case 'very high duties upon importation, operating alone' were dangerous.[18] Once domestic expansion has been encouraged by 'steady high prices,' a particularly good harvest would generate massive price reductions (108–9). Should this decline discourage domestic agriculture, there would follow increased domestic prices and renewed importation when the price increase surpassed the appropriate limit – a nice instance of a price cobweb. The potentially damaging effect of a high agricultural-cost structure on British *manufacturing* competitiveness is also taken into account: 'The more strongly the natural state of the country directs it to the purchase of foreign corn, the higher must be the protecting duty or the price of importation, in order to secure an independent supply; and the greater consequently will be the relative disadvantage which we shall suffer in our commerce with other countries. This drawback may, it is certain, ultimately be so great as to counterbalance the effects of our extraordinary skill, capital and machinery' (105). Britain during the war had more than held her own in manufacturing, despite high corn prices and money wages, because her advanced technology had been protected against foreign imitation in wartime; but the prospect was a contraction of international commerce playing back on agriculture itself (105–6). Apart from the question of the price level, there is also recognition that, since trade is

18 A positive case that might be made for a corn-export bounty – albeit forced – was totally inapplicable to corn-import restrictions: 'A bounty upon exportation in one country, may be considered, in some degree, as a bounty upon production in Europe; and if the growing price of corn in the country where the bounty is granted be not higher than in others, such a premium might obviously after a time have some tendency to create a temporary abundance of corn and a consequent fall in its price. But restrictions upon importation cannot have the slightest tendency of this kind. Their whole effect is to stint the supply of the general market, and to raise, not to lower, the price of corn' (99).

essentially *barter*, permitting agricultural imports would be to the advantage of manufacturing by way of expanded exports: 'As all trade is ultimately a trade of barter and the power of purchasing cannot be permanently extended without an extension of the power of selling, the foreign countries which supplied us with corn would evidently have their power of purchasing our commodities increased, and would thus contribute more effectually to our commercial and manufacturing prosperity' (99).

So far we have, in effect, a detailed elaboration of the 1813 letter. There are also arguments for some intervention. But these include a case for *corrective* duties, not for protection, Malthus expressing his approval of Adam Smith's proposal for countervailing tariffs on products (including corn) subject to local taxes: 'If the whole of the difference in the expense of raising corn in this country and in the corn countries of Europe was occasioned by taxation, and the precise amount of that taxation as affecting corn, could be clearly ascertained; the simple and obvious way of restoring things to their natural level and enabling us to grow corn, as in a state of perfect freedom, would be to lay precisely the same amount of tax on imported corn [2d ed.: in the same proportion] and grant the same amount in a bounty upon exportation. Dr. Smith observes, that when the necessities of a state have obliged it to lay a tax upon a home commodity, a duty of equal amount upon the same kind of commodity when imported from abroad, only tends to restore the level of industry which had necessarily been disturbed by the tax' (1814/1986, 7, 107).[19] This, however, did not amount to a practical proposal, since current monetary instability precluded any specification of appropriate tariff rates.

Agricultural protection to compensate for duties granted manufactures is also justified: 'By protecting duties of various kinds, an unnatural quantity of capital is directed towards manufactures and commerce and taken from the land; and while, on account of these duties [landholders and farmers] are obliged to purchase both home-made and foreign goods at a kind of monopoly price, they would be obliged to sell their own at the price of the most enlarged competition. It may fairly indeed be said, that to restore the freedom of the corn trade, while protecting duties on various other commodities are allowed, is not really to restore things to their natural level, but to depress the cultivation of the land below other kinds of industry' (103–4). Malthus conceded that 'it might still be a national advantage to purchase corn where it could be had the cheapest,' possibly alluding to the enhancement of international competitiveness in

19 Smith's observation runs as follows: 'When a tax is laid at home upon any produce of domestic industry, it is reasonable that an equal tax should be imposed upon the like produce of foreign industry, thus leaving the competition between foreign and domestic industry after the tax, as nearly as possible, upon the same footing as before it' (1776/1937, 431–2). See 1937, 835–6, for Smith's legitimization of drawbacks on exports. See Jacob Hollander, 1932, 35, for the modification in the second edition.

consequence of a low level of money wages. But the concession is qualified in that property owners would not be treated with 'impartial justice' in the event of free trade.[20]

The outcome of all this is that, taking the 1814 pamphlet as a whole, *Malthus does not emerge as a protectionist*; his recommendations justifying intervention are designed to correct either for distorting internal taxation or for distorting tariffs.[21] When the letter to Horner of June 1813 is read in the light of the *Observations*, Malthus emerges as an opponent of the Corn Laws in the event that all sectors are treated equally, although he desisted from committing himself to a formal recommendation. If this is so, there emerges a contrast with the early *Essay*, where agricultural protection was justified as a matter of principle to prevent any industrial bias, albeit a 'natural' one.

20 A reworking of the passage in the second edition emphasizes the inability of capital displaced from agriculture, in the event of free trade, to transfer to the manufacturing sector: 'By protecting duties, drawbacks and taxes on almost all foreign commodities, capital is prevented from leaving those trades, the prices of the products of which have been increased by domestic taxation [Malthus intended the peculiar burden of taxation imposed on agriculture]: while if the ports were thrown open to the free admission of foreign corn, agriculture would be exposed to the loss of capital, occasioned by the competition of foreigners, who not being burdened by the same weight of taxation, would possess the most obvious advantages in the contest with our home growers. It may fairly indeed be said, that to restore the freedom of the corn trade, under these circumstances, is not really to restore things to their natural level, but to depress the cultivation of the land below its natural proportion to other kinds of industry' (Jacob Hollander, 1932, 35).

21 Ricardo questioned the legitimacy of the general argument in a letter to Malthus, 13 January 1815: 'I cannot help thinking that Lord Lauderdale was mistaken (and I believe you hold the same opinion as him) in supposing [1814, 8–9] the farmer to lie under a particular disadvantage from not having the monopoly of the home market, whilst so many other trades were enjoying that benefit. You will agree that the monopoly of the home market is eventually of no great advantage to the trade on which it is conferred. It is true that it raises the price of the commodity by shutting out foreign competition but this is equally injurious to all consumers, and presses no more on the farmer than on other trades. If monopolies tend to raise the price of labour, the inconvenience must be suffered by all who employ labour, and will therefore not be particularly injurious to the farmer or landlord. If all the monopolies of the home market were immediately abolished, there would be at least as much disposition to import corn; – if so they do not interfere with the natural course of the corn trade. Lord Lauderdale with his opinion of the effect of monopolies is I think quite consistent in recommending a duty on the importation of corn' (1951–73, VI, 169–70).

Similarly, J.S. Mill – who championed Ricardo's countervailing duty of 1822 (below, note 65 – also denied that the existence of protection for certain manufactured products justified the protection of agriculture, notwithstanding that the manufacturing industries in question were artificially enlarged (1825a/1967, IV, 66). Such a case would imply that as soon as *any* single industry gains protection, similar protection should be granted all other industries (agriculture is not distinguished from any other industry); it also implied that the profit rate, in the protected industry exceeds the general profit rate, which, assuming competition, could not be substantiated.

IV THE CASE FOR PROTECTION, 1815: AGGREGATE ACTIVITY, CLASS DISTRIBUTION, AND SECURITY

In a résumé of alternative trade policies in *Grounds of an Opinion* (1815), Malthus repeats the secular prospect – assuming restriction – of rising corn prices and resultant increases in money wages and prices to the detriment of manufacturing exports: 'If, upon mature deliberation, we determine to open our ports to the free admission of foreign grain, we must not be disturbed at the depressed state, and diminished produce of our home cultivation ... On the other hand, if, on mature deliberation, we determine steadily to pursue a system of restrictions with regard to trade in corn, we must not be disturbed at a progressive rise in the price of grain ... and we must not be disturbed at the occasional loss or diminution of a continental market for some of our least peculiar manufactures, owing to the high price of our labour' (1986, 7, 172–3). In 1815 he was prepared to take the risk. There were other overriding considerations, to which we now turn.

1 Aggregate activity

Malthus's support for protection in *Grounds* turns in part upon new factual circumstances, including the 'improved state of our exchanges, and the fall in the price of bullion,' which reduced the uncertainty regarding the appropriate degree of protection (152) – a problem raised in 1814. Although the pound had stabilized, Malthus expected 'a rise in the value of paper on a return to cash payments, and some general fall of prices quite unconnected with any regulations respecting the corn trade' (155), and warned that such deflation should not be reinforced by downward pressure on prices resulting from corn-trade liberalization. Even were import regulations to be ultimately abandoned, temporary regulations would be in order (155, 171). In the deflationary circumstances to be expected, a free corn trade was wholly inappropriate, even if desirable in principle.[22]

22 Ricardo, too, maintained the inappropriateness of removing corn protection at a time of general depression – a clear recognition of the conflict between short-term and long-term policy measures (13 October 1819; 1951–73, VIII, 103). In fact in 1822 he proposed 'at this moment of distress ... to give the monopoly of the home market to the British grower, till corn reaches seventy shillings per quarter' and a duty of 20s. per quarter when the home price exceeded 70s. (IV, 263–4; V, 172–3).

In his *Principles* (1817), Ricardo actually recommended, as a general rule of policy, the imposition of protective duties after a period of war and trade disruption, though for a limited period and to be reduced over time. A guarantee of such a policy stabilized long-term expectations of farmers during crisis periods: 'Notwithstanding ... that it would be more productive of wealth to the country, at whatever sacrifice of capital it might be done, to allow the importation of cheap corn, it would, perhaps, be advisable to charge it with a duty for a few years' (I, 268). For a similar proposal see McCulloch's 'Corn Laws and Trade' (*Encyclopaedia Britannica*, III, 363), to which Ricardo referred in the second edition of the *Principles* (1819/1951–73, I, 267n).

Malthus elaborated on the likely effect of agricultural deflation (following trade liberalization) on general income, drawing on David Hume's celebrated position: 'With regard to this great majority [of capitalists], it is impossible that they should not feel very widely and severely the diminution of their nominal capital by the fall of prices. We know the magic effect upon industry of a rise of prices. It has been noticed by Hume, and witnessed by every person who has attended to subjects of this kind. And the effects of a fall are proportionately depressing. Even the foreign trade will not escape its influence, though here it may be counterbalanced by a real increase of demand. But, in the internal trade, not only will the full effect of this deadening weight be experienced, but there is reason to fear that it may be accompanied with an actual diminution of home demand ... In this case, the whole of the internal trade must severely suffer, and the wealth and enjoyments of the country be decidedly diminished' (166).[23] Should the disturbance be temporary, there is still the temporary loss of 'happiness' to consider: 'Even if the manufacturing towns should ultimately increase, in proportion to the losses of the country, of which there is great reason to doubt, the transfer of wealth and population will be slow, painful, and unfavourable to happiness' (167; also 163).

2 *Class distribution*

This general Humean perspective is further reinforced by a passage from the *Observations*, referring to the error of treating reductions in general prices (increases in 'the values of corn or silver') as a matter of indifference, when in fact they generated 'both temporary and lasting effects, which have a most powerful influence on the distribution of property' (168).[24] This was *a fortiori* so in the presence of a *national debt*, which alone altered the framework appropriate for the treatment of the trade issue: 'I own it appears to me that the necessary effect of a change in the measure of value on the weight of a large national debt is alone sufficient to make the question fundamentally different from that of a simple question about a free or restricted trade; and, that to consider it merely in this light, and to draw our conclusions accordingly, is to expect the same results from premises which have essentially changed their nature' (171).[25] This generalization turns on an analysis of falling prices with respect to *class* gains and losses, temporally considered. For the wartime

23 It is a fall in the prices of home goods that assures the increased exports – diverted from home consumption – to pay for increased corn imports.

24 The distributional effects in fact relate to income ('produce') as well as wealth ('property'); see 169.

25 Cf. the case against inappropriate applications of 'general principles' (158; below, note 29).

inflation, as far as induced by increase of paper money, had (so it is asserted) stimulated industry and accumulation by counteracting the 'prodigious' burdens of the national debt, thus benefiting the 'industrious classes' at the expense of stockholders (169).

But a fall in general prices with reduced corn prices would imply an '*unfair*' advantage to stockholders: 'If the price of corn were now to fall to 50 shillings a quarter, and labour and other commodities nearly in proportion, there can be no doubt that the stockholders would be benefited unfairly at the expense of the wealth and prosperity of the whole country.'[26] Even 'extraordinary generosity' towards stockholders in the form of the real increase in the interest paid on government loans generated by a falling price level would be unobjectionable were it not for the 'intolerable' burden imposed on the economy; workers and the 'industrious middle orders' as well as the 'higher orders' would find their nominal incomes positively reduced 50 per cent (on Malthus's assumption regarding the effect of free trade) and be faced by the same nominal, and thus an increased real burden of taxation (170). In fact, continued repayment of 'present interest' (running at some £40 million annually) would be 'absolutely' impossible (to the detriment of the stockholders themselves).[27] In an overall summary of all the issues, Malthus concludes: 'From this review of the manner in which the different classes of society will be affected by the opening of our ports, I think it appears clearly, that very much the largest mass of the people, and particularly of the industrious orders of the state, will be more injured than benefited by the measure' (171).[28] As for the matter of 'justice' towards the stockholders, that could be assured by a corn price of 80s. 'since the whole of the loans made during the war just terminated, will on average, be paid at an inter-

26 The 'unfairness' seems to reflect partly the small relative size of the stockholding and fixed-income class (168). The nominal interest rate had also increased since the loans had been contracted (171).

27 This perspective Ricardo opposed: 'Your observations on the advantages, (and therefore on the injustice to other classes) which the stockholder would reap from a low price of corn are I think very correct, – but I do not think these objections should stand in the way of the general good. They the stockholders have at different periods suffered much, and if the sinking fund be now appropriated to other services another striking injustice will be added to the long list' (13 February 1815; 1951–73, VI, 178).

28 McCulloch wrote effusively: 'To make any additions to what Mr. Malthus has here so ably stated, would be altogether superfluous' (1816, 201). Ricardo objected sharply to McCulloch regarding the effect on activity and tax capacity of a reduced value of agricultural product: 'You may say the whole will not be equally productive as before and that therefore more taxes must be raised to pay the interest of the National Debt. You may repeat the quotation from Mr. Malthus of which you avail yourself page 198, but Mr. Malthus does not satisfy me – I am persuaded he is wrong, though to shew his error would require more space than I now can allow myself. I firmly believe that if corn fell from 80 to 60s. the ability of the people to pay taxes would be increased instead of diminished' (4 December 1816; 1951–73, VI, 104).

est very much higher than they were contracted for,' thus compensating for reduced purchasing power.

3 The national-security case

There was also a security case for protection. New parliamentary evidence indicated severe loss of agricultural capital in consequence of poor domestic harvests combined with low corn prices, the latter reflecting a massive inflow of French corn (1986, 7, 152, 154, 155n3). Here Malthus alludes to the position in the *Observations* (1986, 7, 96) that a considerable fall in the corn price must throw 'much poor land out of cultivation' and prevent, 'for a considerable time, all further improvements in agriculture, which have for their object an increase of produce' (152). The loss would be particularly great considering the major extensions since about 1808 – 'the system of spirited improvement and high farming' – induced by high corn prices and wartime constraints on importation. At the same time, new French regulations governing corn exportation precluded reliance on a regular inflow of agricultural imports and threatened *greater* volatility of prices under 'free trade' than under a system with some protection. Although Malthus stood by the argument of the *Observations* that a truly free trade régime would assure 'not only a cheaper, but a more steady supply of grain' than under protection (155–6) – again, in the latter respect, contrasting with the *Essay on Population* – the issue was, he insisted, in fact *not* free trade versus protection: 'In expressing this distinct opinion on the effects of a free trade in corn, I certainly meant to refer to a trade *really free* – that is, a trade by which a nation would be entitled to its share of the produce of the commercial world, according to its means of purchasing, whether that produce were plentiful or scanty. In this sense I adhere strictly to the opinion I then gave; but, since that period, an event has occurred which has shown, in the clearest manner, that it is entirely out of our power, even in time of peace, to obtain a free trade in corn, or an approximation towards it, whatever may be our wishes on the subject' (156).[29] This insistence on assuring that 'general principles' are not ap-

29 Regarding the principle of true free trade contrasting with the case where imports from the Continent would be checked by foreign controls, Malthus elaborates: 'Such a species of commerce in grain shakes the foundations, and alters entirely the data on which the general principles of free trade are established. For what do these principles say? They say, and say most justly, that if every nation were to devote itself particularly to those kinds of industry and produce, to which its soil, climate, situation, capital, and skill, were best suited, and were then *freely to exchange* these products with each other, it would be the most certain and efficacious mode, not only of advancing the wealth and prosperity of the whole body of the commercial republic with the quickest pace, but of giving to each individual nation of the body the full and perfect use of all its resources' (158).

plied irresponsibly is very strongly formulated in the pamphlet: 'I am very far indeed from meaning to insinuate, that if we cannot have the most perfect freedom of trade, we should have none; or that a great nation must immediately alter its commercial policy, whenever any of the countries with which it deals passes laws inconsistent with the principles of freedom. But I protest most entirely against the doctrine, that we are to pursue our general principles without ever looking to see if they are applicable to the case before us; and that in politics and political economy, we are to go straight forward, as we certainly ought to do in morals, without any reference to the conduct and proceedings of others' (158). In fact, 'it is not in the power of any single nation to secure the freedom of the foreign trade in corn. To accomplish this, the concurrence of many others is necessary; and this concurrence, the fears and jealousies so universally prevalent about the means of subsistence, almost invariably prevent' (159).

The true choice was between a bogus 'free trade' subject to French export control precluding an inflow from the Continent during 'scarce years,'[30] and a restrictive system designed to render Britain 'in average years, nearly independent of foreign supplies' (158). Malthus concluded that the latter arrangement would 'more effectually conduce to the wealth and prosperity of the country, and of by far the greatest mass of the inhabitants, than the opening of our ports for the free admission of foreign corn, in the actual state of Europe' (160). The enormous loss of agricultural capital with the inflow of French corn in 1814 was proof of the potential volatility of foreign supply. By contrast, the 'very great' increase of domestic output over the period *circa* 1807–11 had assured against severe distress in 1812, a year of poor harvest, despite minimal imports because of hostilities (153).

The new French legislation reduced the reliability of foreign supplies, even in peacetime. *Genuine* free trade promised not only cheaper corn, but greater stability, than did protection – for protection implied a general level of corn prices above the European level, such that a peculiarly good harvest could be cleared only with a major price reduction; but the French regulations introduced an even more serious source of instability – namely, restriction on exports to Britain when French harvests were only moderate-

30 Malthus considered France to be the major potential source of supply: 'There can be no doubt that, if our ports were open, our principal supplies of grain would come from France; and that, in all years of common plenty in that country, we should import more largely from it than from the Baltic' (157). See also the statement that France was the country 'which, in all common years, will furnish us with a large proportion of our supplies' (164). It is interesting that wartime France had issued an order in 1804 *permitting* corn exports to assure against injury to her agriculture (Smart, 1910–17, I, 94). Malthus admits to that, but describes the orders as reflecting 'special licenses, granted for purposes of revenue'; were it not for the revenue requirements of France they would not have been granted (1986, 7, 156n).

ly poor (157–8).[31] The 'conclusion from theory,' that price fluctuations would be greater under *so-called free trade* than under 'the most determined system of prohibitions' (158), was (Malthus claimed) confirmed by a century of experience (164).

Malthus here repeated a theme of 1806,[32] that government intervention in the corn trade could not be justified as a device to protect farmers and landlords: 'In future, we should endeavour, if possible, to avoid all discussions about the necessity of *protecting* the British farmer, and securing to him a *fair living profit.* Such language may perhaps be allowable in a crisis like the present. But certainly the legislature has nothing to do with securing to any classes of its subjects a particular rate of profits in their different trades. This is not the province of a government; and it is unfortunate that any language should be used which may convey such an impression, and make people believe that their rulers ought to listen to the accounts of their gains and losses' (173). Its role was rather to assure national self-sufficiency in corn in normal years – a role accorded on similar grounds to the Navigation Acts: 'But a government may certainly see sufficient reasons for wishing to secure an independent supply of grain. This is a definite, and may be a desirable, object, of the same nature as the Navigation Act; and it is much to be wished, that this object, and not the interest of farmers and landlords, should be the ostensible, as well as the real, end which we have in view, in all our inquiries and proceedings relating to the trade in corn' (173–4).[33]

V THE CASE FOR PROTECTION, 1815: A 'UTILITARIAN' OVERVIEW

The foregoing case for protection might be stated in utilitarian terms –

31 Malthus warned *a fortiori* of the dangers of reliance on foreign sources of supply in wartime (164).

32 'In discussing the policy of a bounty on the exportation of corn, it should be premised, that the private interests of the farmers and proprietors should never enter the question. The sole object of our consideration ought to be the permanent interest of the consumer, in the character of which is comprehended the whole nation' (1806, II, 237). 'The object of the nation in the corn laws is not the increase of the profits of the farmers, or the rents of the landlords, but the determination of a greater quantity of national capital to the land, and the consequent increase of supply' (252). In his 'free trade' letter to Horner of 16 June 1813 (above, p. 820) Malthus also insisted that 'one never ought to hear a word about the interests of landlords and farmers.'

33 Cf. the recommendation to avoid any formulation of the issue involving 'the losses and profits of farmers, and the present condition of landholders compared with the past,' though it 'may be necessary, perhaps, to make inquiries of this kind, with a view to ulterior objects' (153). Nevertheless, Malthus defended farmers against the charge of 'rash speculation' in undertaking major expansion, since the peace was 'most unexpected.'

there was a threat to the 'happiness' of the masses in a system which depended, in average years, on foreign sources of supply subject to interruption. Malthus himself provided a specific utilitarian calculus – close to Adam Smith's – which considers the labouring classes as 'the foundation on which the whole fabric rests; and, from their numbers, unquestionably of the greatest weight, in any estimate of national happiness' (1986, 7, 162). He stated the quantitative weighting in very strong terms: 'If I were convinced, that to open our ports, would be permanently to improve the condition of the labouring classes of society, I should consider the question as at once determined in favour of such a measure.'

There is no difference in utilitarian method as such between Malthus and Ricardo, but their evaluations of the effect of free trade on labour's welfare – based on their respective economic models – are strikingly different. Here we must have in mind that, for Malthus, as for the Physiocrats, high corn prices were positively desirable from labour's perspective: 'I stated in the *Observations* [1986, 7, 102–3] and more at large in the *Inquiry into rents* [138–9], that under the same demand for labour, and the same consequent power of purchasing the means of subsistence, a high *money price* of corn would give the labourer a very great advantage in the purchase of the conveniences and luxuries of life. The effect of this high money price would not, of course, be so marked among the very poorest of the society, and those who had the largest families; because so very great a part of their earnings must be employed in absolute necessaries. But to all those above the very poorest, the advantage of wages resulting from a price of eighty shillings a quarter for wheat, compared with fifty or sixty, would in the purchase of tea, sugar, cotton, linens, soap, candles, and many other articles, be such as to make their condition decidedly superior.'

There was also the greater *stability* of corn prices in a protected system compared with any system of 'free' trade practically achievable, as shown above. Furthermore, while the depressing effect on labour's welfare of 'free trade' – once again the presumption is that it cannot be *genuine free trade* – by way of lower corn prices and instability might admittedly be counterbalanced by a sufficient net increase in demand for manufacturing labour, this outcome would be 'slow and difficult,' considering the prospective 'sudden and decisive' loss of agricultural employment: 'Our commerce and manufactures, therefore, must increase very considerably before they can restore the demand for labour already lost; and a moderate increase beyond this will scarcely make up for the disadvantage of a low money price of wages' (163). In summary: 'On the labouring classes, therefore, the effects of opening our ports for the free importation of foreign corn, will be greatly to lower their wages, and to subject them to much greater fluctuations of price. And, in this state of things, it will require a much greater increase in the demand for labour, than there is in any rational ground for expecting, to compensate to the labourer the advantages which he loses in the high money wages of labour, and the steadier and less fluctuating price of corn' (164–5).[34]

The capitalists constituted 'the next most important class of society,' presumably in terms of absolute number. One-half were farmers or dependent immediately on the farm sector. They would suffer from free trade, though Malthus concedes that this is so only in the short run: 'Not that the profits of farmers will not recover themselves, after a certain period, and be as great, or perhaps greater, than they were before; but this cannot take place till after a great loss of agricultural capital, or the removal of it into the channels of commerce and manufactures' (165). Against this must be balanced the benefit to capitalists directly engaged in foreign trade. (Malthus neglects the workforce thus engaged, having already dealt with labour as a whole.) It is allowed that, in principle, the efficiency gains from trade entail a major expansion of foreign commerce, including a *net* expansion of manufactured goods made available to the *domestic* market. However, in practice 'to increase effectively this quantity of produce, after the severe check sustained by agriculture, it is necessary that commerce should make a very powerful start,' and, *given European restrictions against British export industries*, it was probable that – despite lower money wages – the financing of increased corn imports by increased manufacturing exports would have to be supplemented by reductions in imports other than corn: 'It is by no means impossible that we shall be obliged to pay for our foreign corn, by importing less of other commodities, as well as by exporting more of our manufactures.' Or again: 'There may be the same or even a greater quantity of corn consumed in the country, but a smaller quantity of manufactures and colonial produce; and our foreign corn may be purchased in part by commodities which were before consumed at home' (166). In this case, of course, the efficiency gains – represented as providing a degree of 'compensation' for the otherwise severe losses of agricultural capital (165) – would be reduced. That capitalists immediately engaged in foreign trade benefit is, however, taken for granted; and here emerges again the utility calculus: 'As those, however, form but a very small portion of the class of persons living on the profits of stock, in point of number, and not probably above a seventh or eighth in point of property, their interests cannot be allowed to weight against the interests of so very large a majority.'

VI 'AGRICULTURAL BIAS,' 1815

As we have seen in chapter 8, p. 379, Ricardo complained, not of Malthus's

34 There is a further problem reflecting the effect on manufacturing of a depressed agriculture from the perspective of aggregate demand. On this issue, see above, p. 825, and also below, pp. 833–4.

protectionism as such in *Grounds of an Opinion*, but of his subscription to the notion of 'the benefits of agriculture over commerce in increasing production,' which clashed with both the scarcity and the diminishing-returns perspectives adopted elsewhere. Is there any justification for Ricardo's charge?

We have thus far traced Malthus's protectionism in *Grounds* in part to objective concerns: (1) for 'security' in the light of new French export regulations; and (2) for the effect of a reduced price level on *overall activity* directly and also via alterations in distribution, especially in the light of the national debt. Part of the protectionist position can be accounted for by new monetary circumstances permitting a better-informed specification of the appropriate limit price below which duties were to be imposed. And part reflects the current agricultural depression, and the unrealistically large expansion of manufacturing that would be necessary to absorb even the current unemployed. Even in the 'objective' pamphlet of 1814 there is concern with 'mercantilist' interventions (above, section III). None of this can be said to indicate agricultural bias as such.

There is, however, considerable justification for Ricardo's charge. For, the loss of agricultural capital and output is said in the *Grounds* to be, pound for pound, more damaging than a loss in other sectors, a reflection of the 'additional value' peculiar to the agricultural sector (chapter 8, p. 370). This additional value would be erased by a free corn trade – Malthus here recommends his *Rent* pamphlet – to the *national* detriment from the perspective of both consumption power and tax revenue: 'And this additional value is not a mere benefit to a particular individual, or set of individuals, but affords the most steady home demand for the manufactures of the country, the most effective fund for its financial support, and the largest disposable force for its army and navy' (1986, 7, 167–8). This is the dimension to the protectionist case to which Ricardo objected so strongly (13 February 1815; 1951–73, VI, 177–8). True enough, Malthus conceded that 'the last additions to the agricultural produce in an improving country are not attended with a large proportion of rent' (168); indeed, 'it is precisely this circumstance that may make it answer to a rich country to import some of its corn, if it can be secure of obtaining an equable supply.' None the less, he closed by insisting that 'in all cases the importation of foreign corn must fail to answer nationally, if it is not so much cheaper than the corn that can be grown at home, as to equal both the profits and the rent of the grain which it displaces.' In order to justify free trade in corn, the savings in resources must be sufficient to compensate for the loss of rent.

We have made allowance for various 'objective' supplementary considerations. The compensatory expansion of manufactures required to absorb displaced agricultural workers in the event of free trade would be 'slow and difficult.' It was also necessary to allow for the negative effect on manufacturing activity of a depressed agriculture from the perspective of aggregate demand. Assuming increased competition abroad under peace conditions, expanded foreign demand for home manufactures could not be relied upon, so that it was 'peculiarly advisable to maintain unimpaired, if possible, the home market, and not to lose the demand occasioned by so much of the rents of land, and of the profits and capital of farmers as must necessarily be destroyed by the check to our home product' (166). Yet even here a physiocratic generalization emerges: 'The quantity of a country's exports is a very uncertain criterion of its wealth. The quantity of produce permanently consumed at home is, perhaps, the most certain criterion of wealth to which we can refer.'

We may now return to the letter to Horner in June 1813 and the *Observations* of 1814 (above, section III). Those documents – in fact, large parts of the *Grounds* itself – can be read as championing free agricultural trade in principle, but not in practice, given the general obstructions to domestic and foreign trade in place. But the element of 'agricultural bias' in the *Grounds* alters the picture, since an optimal allocation for Malthus entailed a larger agricultural sector than for Ricardo, implying the need for a degree of intervention to assure it, and this certainly played some part in his support of the 1815 legislation – Ricardo's complaint in substance. When we come to the fifth edition of the *Essay on Population*, we find the case for protection as a matter of principle strengthened in an elaboration and modification of the position developed in the early editions.

VII BALANCED GROWTH AND PROTECTIONISM, 1817

The point is made in the chapter 'Of the Agricultural System' in the 1817 edition of the *Essay on Population* that 'landed' nations are bound ultimately to develop a manufacturing sector – Malthus alludes approvingly to both Smith and the Physiocrats – which would be well founded precisely because of their agricultural base and would permit the undermining of any 'purely commercial state' (1817, II, 411–12; cited chapter 5, p. 177). The implication that advantages attached to a mixed economy and balanced growth is developed in two chapters – 'Of Commercial Systems' and 'Of Systems of Agriculture and Commerce Combined.'

The former, which concerns objections to the 'commercial system,' does not elaborate upon upward pressure on corn prices and money wages to the detriment of manufactures – whether, as in 1803/1806, because of demand pressure emanating from the manufacturing sector or, as in 1814, from a real-cost perspective. (There is in fact evidence of a *denial* in 1817 of any upward trend of real costs.) Rather, the danger to manufacturing activity arises from the prospect of falling (manufacturing) prices. As will also be recalled from chapter 5, pp. 176–7, Malthus in the 1817 chapter denied that population growth in a manufacturing-based economy might proceed unchecked until the lands of its agriculturally based trading partners were 'fully cultivated' (402), a denial that in effect reinforced the significance of *domestic* agriculture for the maintenance of a healthy manufacturing sector elaborated in earlier editions. Two sources of premature deceleration and ultimate stationariness existed in a dependent manufacturing economy. The first is traced to foreign competition and the undermining of the manufacturing nation's competitive edge (411–12), a perspective that merely reiterates the argument of 1803 and 1806. In addition there is also increasing *domestic* competition (405–7). The logic for a falling *general or economy-wide* profit rate with increased competition is not spelled out, but the general perspective suggests Adam Smith's 'competition of capitals.'

As for Malthus's support for a 'union of the agricultural and commercial systems' (441), already apparent in 1803 and much elaborated in 1817, we need review the material only briefly. A mixed system is protected against the potentially severe consequence of increasing foreign competition in export markets – namely, actual retrogression – though there would be some slackening of the growth rate (423–4). A domestic agricultural sector also lowered the risk of increasing domestic competition in manufacturing.[35] In brief, increasing Smithian 'competition of capitals' can be avoided by *balanced growth.* Thus an economy 'with resources in land' can expand regardless of 'the state and progress of other countries' in agricultural development (426–7). A diversified economy, though 'surrounded by Bishop Berkeley's wall of brass,' might indeed expand *without limit,* though at a slower pace than if it would specialize and engage in foreign commerce (427).[36]

While a domestic agricultural sector is represented as essential to manufacturing, the converse is true as well. From a historical-development perspective, the successful transfer from feudalism required a flourishing manufacturing sector, a proposition developed in the earlier chapter, 'Of the Agricultural System' (391). More to the point is the reference to a ready market at home for agricultural produce, which is

35 While the corn/manufacturing price ratio rises – here there is specific allusion to diminishing returns – the *aggregate* value (command over corn) of manufactures will not decline (424–5).

36 The caution regarding distant prospects for U.S. diversification threatening British sales was, however, qualified: 'According to all general principles, it will finally answer to most landed nations, both to manufacture for themselves, and to conduct their own commerce. That raw cottons should be shipped in America, carried some thousands of miles to another country, unshipped there, to be manufactured and shipped again for the American market, is a state of things which cannot be permanent. That it may last for some time, there can be no doubt; and I am very far from meaning to insinuate that an advantage, while it lasts, should not be used, merely because it will not continue forever. But if the advantage be in its nature temporary, it is surely prudent to have this in view, and to use in such a way that when it ceases it may not have been productive, on the whole, of more evil than good' (428).

'peculiarly favourable to the progressive increase of capital' (401).[37]

* * *

With these preliminary considerations in mind, we turn to the formal case for corn-import restriction of 1817 as laid out in the chapter 'Of Corn Laws: Restrictions upon Importation' – the very chapter that contains the 1826 note retracting protectionism.[38]

The chapter commences by recognizing various 'reasonable' *objections* to corn-import restriction – including efficiency losses, population restraint, and the discouragement of manufacturing exports: 'A country, with landed resources, which determines never to import corn but when the price indicates an approach towards a scarcity, will necessarily, in average years, supply its own wants. Though we may reasonably therefore object to restrictions upon the importation of foreign corn, on the grounds of their tending to prevent the most profitable employment of the national capital and industry, to check population, and to discourage the export of our manufactures; yet we cannot deny their tendency to encourage the growth of corn at home, and to procure and maintain an independent supply' (475–6). And the chapter closes by reiterating that deviations from a 'perfect freedom of trade' had to be justified; for that object 'should always be considered as the great general rule. And when any deviations from it are proposed, those who propose them are bound clearly to make out the exception' (507).

The question facing Britain reduced to the *desirability* of an interventionist policy: 'whether a balance between the agricultural and commercial classes of society, which would not take place naturally, ought, under certain circumstances, to be maintained artificially' (477); or, more specifically, whether it was politic 'artificially to maintain a more equal balance between the agricultural and commercial classes by restricting the importation of foreign corn, and making agriculture keep pace with manufactures' (484). It was not a matter of creating an *imbalance* favouring agriculture, but of preventing Britain's 'natural' tendency towards a 'commercial society' dependent upon foreign corn.

Malthus commences his case by repeating the central argument against 'commercial systems' in 1803, 1806, and 1817 itself, in the context of proposals for Europe to devote itself entirely to manufactures in exchange for American corn. Even were such a trade pattern the natural outcome in the absence of controls, the manufacturing economies would ultimately

37 Elsewhere in the 1817 *Essay* will be found evidence of an abandonment of various concerns with industry-biased growth – including welfare concerns from labour's perspective (below, p. 863).

38 For an overview of this chapter, see Pullen, in Malthus, 1820/1989, II, 392–3.

suffer when the Americans themselves took up manufactures (as they inevitably would), and restricted their corn exports: 'It is an unquestionable truth that it must answer to every territorial state, in its natural progress to wealth, to manufacture for itself, unless the countries from which it had purchased its manufactures possess some advantages peculiar to them besides capital and skill. But when upon this principle America began to withdraw its corn from Europe, and the agricultural exertions of Europe were inadequate to make up for the deficiency, it would certainly be felt that the temporary advantages of a greater degree of wealth and population (supposing them to have been really attained) had been very dearly purchased by a long period of retrograde movements and misery' (483). The presumption is that each 'landed' country will, with population growth, divert increasing fractions of its agricultural output to internal requirements, reducing correspondingly its corn exports: 'If a nation possesses a large territory consisting of land of an average quality, it may without difficulty support from its own soil a population fully sufficient to maintain its rank in wealth and power among the countries with which it has relations either of commerce or of war. Territories of a certain extent must ultimately in the main support their own population. As each exporting country approaches towards that complement of wealth and population to which it is naturally tending, it will gradually withdraw the corn which for a time it had spared to its more manufacturing and commercial neighbours, and leave them to subsist on their own resources' (481). The trade in corn was thus a distinctly *non-permanent* trade, to be viewed as no more than a means of balancing temporary requirements, not as a trade upon which could be based the international division of labour: 'An extensive foreign trade in corn beyond what arises from the variableness of the seasons in different countries is rather a temporary and incidental trade, depending chiefly upon the different stages of improvement which different countries may have reached, and on other accidental circumstances, than a trade which is in its nature permanent, and the stimulus to which will remain in the progress of society unabated' (482). Corn is contrasted with 'the peculiar products of each soil and climate' which are *permanent* objects of trade: 'The peculiar products of each soil and climate are objects of foreign trade, which can never, under any circumstances, fail. But food is not a peculiar product; and the country which produces it in the greatest abundance may, according to the laws which govern the progress of population, have nothing to spare for others.'

Malthus was aware that the foregoing considerations were of a distinctly long-run nature, and supplemented his interventionist case by the more 'immediate effects that attend a great predominance of a manufacturing population, such as increased unhealthiness, increased turbulence, increased fluctuations in the price of corn, and increased variableness in the wages of labour' (484), concluding that, on balance, 'it may not appear impolitic artificially to maintain a more equal balance between the agricultural and commercial classes by restricting the importation of foreign corn, and making agriculture keep pace with manufactures.'

There was also the question of short-run output stability. Malthus pointed out that, in the event of differential variability between nations, free trade would enhance instability in the (naturally) less variable nation – doubtless he had in mind that the increasing *average* stability is at the expense of the naturally less-variable nation such as Britain was supposed to be (486–7). This increased instability with free trade would be reinforced when the less stable partner 'is allowed to inundate the other with its crops when they are abundant,' while – alluding here to French export controls, a major theme in 1815 – 'it reserves to itself the privilege of retaining them in a period of slight scarcity, when its commercial neighbour happens to be in greatest want' (491). These two considerations alone 'essentially change[d] the premises on which the question of a free importation, as applicable to a particular state, must rest.' The issue is conveniently summarized thus: 'Countries are very different in the degree of variableness to which their annual supplies are subject; and though it is unquestionably true that if all were nearly equal in this respect, and the trade in corn *really* free, the steadiness of price in a particular state would increase with an increase in the number of the nations connected with it by the commerce of grain; yet it by no means follows that the same conclusion will hold good when the premises are essentially different; that is, when some of the countries taken into the circle of trade are subject to very great comparative variations in their supplies of grain, and when this defect is aggravated by the acknowledged want of real freedom in the foreign trade of corn' (484–5).

There is a related source of instability. British government intervention favouring manufactures had, in practice, been effectively countered by wartime impediments to corn imports – agriculture 'now marched with [manufactures] abreast' (499). Indeed, the rate of agricultural growth during the war had been somewhat *too* rapid – forced by 'very high prices occasioned by an inadequate home supply and the great expense and difficulty of importing foreign corn' (501).[39] Such unnatural acceleration threatened a glut of the market on a return to peacetime conditions (as in 1815): 'But the rapidity with which this change has been effected must necessarily create a glut in the market as soon as the home growth of corn became fully equal or a little in excess above the home consumption; and, aided only by a small foreign importation, must inevitably occasion a very sudden fall of prices.' Corn-import restrictions were thus required not only

39 Reference is made to evidence before the House of Lords (1814–15) that 'the freight and insurance alone on a quarter of corn were greater by 48 shillings in 1811 than in 1814. Without any artificial interference then, it appears that war alone may occasion unavoidably a prodigious increase of price.'

to assure ongoing agricultural investment – with funds derived from the non-agricultural sector (in the Smithian manner) – but also to avoid future instability in the event of dislocations created by war: 'A country which so restricts the importations of foreign corn as on an average to grow its own supplies, and to import merely in periods of scarcity, is not only certain of spreading every invention in manufactures and every peculiar advantage it may possess from its colonies or general commerce on the land, and thus of fixing them to the spot and rescuing them from accidents; but is necessarily exempt from those violent and distressing convulsions of property which almost unavoidably arise from the coincidence of a general war, and an insufficient home supply of corn' (502–3). The danger of a free corn trade was that a sudden collapse of prices after a period of war and effectively restricted importation would check 'future improvement,' inviting a repetition of the cycle. Here Malthus reverts to the concerns of 1815 (above, pp. 826–8) regarding the debt burden: 'We should certainly not grow a sufficiency at home to keep pace with our increasing population; and at the end of ten or twelve years we might be found by a new war in the same state that we were at the commencement of the present. We should then have the same career of high prices to pass through, the same excessive stimulus to agriculture followed by the same sudden and depressing check to it, and the same enormous loans borrowed with the price of wheat at 90 or 100 shillings a quarter, and the monied incomes of the landholders and industrious classes of society nearly in proportion, to be paid when wheat is at 50 or 60 shillings a quarter, and the incomes of the landlords and industrious classes of society greatly reduced – a state of things which cannot take place without an excessive aggravation of the difficulty of paying taxes, and particularly that invariable monied amount which pays the interest of the national debt' (501–2).[40] All this could be avoided if in *normal* circumstances domestic production sufficed for all except exceptional requirements.

It is allowed that, with a free corn trade, the absolute size and rate of growth of population would be greater than with reliance on domestic agriculture, but the cost was too high namely – here is a nice summary of the main objections to a 'commercial system' – 'a greater degree of uncertainty in its supplies of corn, greater fluctuations in the wages of labour, greater unhealthiness and immorality owing to a larger proportion of the population being employed in manufactories, and a greater chance of long

40 This illustrated a more general theme: 'There is a tendency to an alternation in the rate of the progress of agriculture and manufactures in the same manner as there is a tendency to an alternation in the rate of the progress of food and population. In periods of peace and uninterrupted trade, these alternations, though not favourable to the happiness and quiet of society, may take place without producing material evil; but the intervention of war is always liable to give them a force and rapidity that must unavoidably produce a convulsion in the state of property' (432).

and depressing retrograde movements occasioned by the natural progress of those countries from which corn had been imported' (495–6). Malthus downplayed the price instability frequently attributed to a *protected* economy – the magnitude of the corn-price decline required to expand exports abroad in the event of a glut: 'a nation with an ample capital' would find little difficulty carrying over any surpluses to future years (504). (Here Malthus abandoned the position of 1814; see above, p. 822) A worse source of instability was that occasioned by a flood of imports. And in any event those nations 'which habitually grow their own supplies' would lessen the magnitude of price increases in years of general scarcity, thus diminishing the potential range of variability (505). On balance, 'the range of variation will be the least under such a system of restriction as, without preventing importation when prices are high, will secure in ordinary years a growth equal to the consumption' (505–6).[41]

It is precisely at this point that Malthus inserts into the 1826 edition his note which maintains that, notwithstanding the greater stability of prices under protection, he did *not* favour protection, and this because of its 'unsocial tendency' – the damage caused to the 'interests of the commercial world in general' – a tendency which was actually 'increased rather than diminished by the numbers which may suffer from scarcity at the same time' (below, p. 851). But the concern to avoid the 'unsocial tendency' generated by protection evidently outweighed not only the greater instability attributed to an open system, but also the other disadvantages said in the text to flow from an economy reliant, even in normal years, upon foreign imports of corn – namely, the long-term unreliability of foreign corn supplies, and thus the danger of basing the international division of labour on the exchange of manufactures for corn, and the undesirable social and moral characteristics as well as the danger of premature stationariness attached to a predominantly manufacturing economy.

* * *

Malthus's long-standing concern with the encouragement granted manufacturing under the mercantilist 'commercial system' also emerges in the chapter 'Of Corn Laws: Restrictions upon Importation.' As usual, the doctrine of proportions is implicitly at play: 'The happiness of a society is, after all, the legitimate end even of its wealth, power, and population. It is certainly true that with a view to the structure of society most favourable to this happiness, and an adequate stimulus to the production of wealth from the soil, a very considerable admixture of commercial and manufacturing population with the agricultural is absolutely necessary; but there is

41 Nowhere in the chapter is deteriorating agricultural productivity taken into account. Rather, the contrary. And that agricultural prospects were promising reinforced the case for protection (see below, p. 864).

no argument so frequently and obviously fallacious as that which infers that what is good to a certain extent is good to any extent; and though it will be most readily admitted that, in a large landed nation, the evils which belong to the manufacturing and commercial system are much more than counterbalanced by its advantages, as long as it is supported by agriculture; yet, in reference to the effect of the excess which is not so supported, it may fairly be doubted whether the evils do not decidedly predominate' (496). Here Adam Smith's position is cited, that 'the capital which is acquired to any country by commerce and manufactures is all a very uncertain and precarious possession, till some part of it has been secured and realized in the cultivation and improvement of its lands' (1776/1937, 395); and he paraphrases Smith's view that the 'monopoly of the colony trade, by raising the rate of mercantile profit, discourages the improvement of the soil, and retards the natural increase of that great original source of revenue – the rent of land' (cf. 1776/1937, 577). Finally, we find brief mention of the necessity to correct for distortions created by taxation: 'It is further to be observed that, independently of more direct regulations, taxation alone produces a system of discouragements and encouragements which essentially interferes with the natural relations of commodities to each other; and as there is no hope of abolishing taxation, it may sometimes be only by a further interference that these natural relations can be restored' (1817, II, 506–7).

The implications of the case for balanced growth are enhanced by the appearance of a new emphasis in 1817 (Book III, Ch. XIII: 'Of Increasing Wealth, as it affects the Condition of the Poor') on industry-biased growth as typically characteristic of the later stages of economic development, reflecting growing land scarcity and an 'increasing taste for conveniences and luxuries,' both of which tend to 'direct the greatest part of this new capital to commerce and manufactures' (1817, III, 6),[42] and along with it retraction of much of an earlier concern with such development from labour's perspective.[43] Despite the perceived 'natural' tendency to *industry-*

42 Gilbert (1980, 93) notes that Malthus in 1817 and thereafter had no further need to make arbitrary assumptions involving abstract economies accumulating capital solely in manufacturing.

43 The context is a familiar one, Adam Smith's notion that the demand for labour varies with 'wealth' and Malthus's insistence that this is so only in so far as 'wealth' reflects wage-goods production (identified roughly with food). That manufactured goods (luxuries) might increase with *no* expansion of food, and thus fail to stimulate any population growth, is a limiting case; while the usual case entails only a lag of food supply (and population growth) behind the increase of wealth: 'In the usual progress of improvement, the increase of wealth and capital is rarely accompanied with a proportionately increased power of supporting an additional number of labourers' (4), a lag (noted by Smith) that parallels more-or-less that of agriculture behind general activity. That 'the funds for the maintenance of labour do not necessarily increase with the increase of wealth, and very rarely increase in *proportion* to it' (2), was developed in the earlier editions, but in 1817 Malthus emphasized rather more diminishing returns as rationale (5f.).

biased growth – and allowance for the possibility of improved standards for labour notwithstanding – Malthus championed agricultural protection *to assure balanced growth.* Malthus's physiocratic orientation is to that extent reinforced rather than weakened, unless we attribute his protectionism *entirely* to a concern with mercantilist stimuli accorded manufactures or to reasons of state, rather than interpret is as a matter of economic principle.

VIII THE CASE FOR INTERVENTION, 1820

The case for agricultural protection on principle given in the *Grounds* is further reinforced in Section IX of the Rent chapter in the *Principles* (1820), 'Of the Connexion of the Interests of the Landlord and of the State in Countries which import Corn.' Here Malthus rejected Adam Smith's position – as he paraphrased it – 'that the freest importation of corn and raw produce cannot injure the farmers and landlords' (1776/1937, 428), as 'unquestionably too strong' (1820, 217–18). Indeed, the loss of rent by easier importation would 'in some cases which are likely to occur, not be counterbalanced by proportionate advantages to the state,' as already demonstrated in the chapter on Corn Laws in the 1817 edition of the *Essay*, to which readers are referred. And to this he now adds a new argument for protection based on the circumstance that the profit rate on agricultural investment does not indicate the full social benefit – 'the only considerable case where practically, and as the business is really conducted, the interest of the individual and of the state are not proportioned to each other' (218). This circumstance reflected the fact that most agricultural investments were undertaken by tenant farmers not landowners: 'If land were always considered as a merchantable instrument, bought and sold merely with a view to the profit which might be made of it, and worked exclusively by the proprietors, every increase of value and power which the instrument might acquire from being used and improved, would naturally enter into the computation in deciding whether a capital might be more profitably employed on land, or in commerce and manufactures; and the advantage to the state, from the employment of such capital, would in general be proportioned in both cases to the advantage gained by individuals ...' (218–19). But, since 'a very large part of the improvements which have taken place on the soil, has been derived from the capital, skill and industry of tenants, no truth can be more distinct and incontrovertible than that the advantage which such individuals have derived from a capital employed in agriculture, compared with a capital employed in commerce and manufactures, cannot have been proportioned to the advantages derived by the country; or, in other words, that the interests of individuals in the employment of capital, have not in this case been identified with the interest of the state' (219–20).

The social return from agricultural investment thus exceeds the private return in the form of profits, the net gain to the state appearing as rent:

'The rent and profits together are the real measure of the wealth derived by the country from the capital so employed' (221). The principle of net social gain is then applied to wartime development, restrictions on corn imports having then encouraged socially desirable investments which otherwise would not have been made: 'If then during the war no obstacles had occurred to the importation of foreign corn, and the profits of agriculture had in consequence been only ten per cent while the profits of commerce and manufactures were twelve, the capital of the country would of course have flowed towards commerce and manufactures; and measuring the interest of the state, as usual, by the interest of individuals, this would have been a more advantageous direction of it, in the proportion of twelve to ten. But, if the view of the subject just taken be correct, instead of a beneficial direction of it to a profit of twelve per cent from a profit of ten per cent as measured by the interests of the individuals concerned, it might have been a disadvantageous direction of it to a profit of only twelve per cent from a profit of fourteen per cent as measured by the interest of the state.[44] It is obvious therefore that the natural restrictions upon the importation of foreign corn during the war, by forcibly raising the profits of domestic cultivation may have directed the capital of the country into a channel more advantageous than that into which it would otherwise have flowed, and instead of impeding the progress of wealth and population, as at first one should certainly have expected, may have decidedly and essentially promoted it' (222–3). The application is then generalized: 'And this, in fact, such restrictions not only may, but must do, whenever the demand for corn grown at home is such, that *the profits of capitals employed on the new lands taken into cultivation, joined to the rents which they generate, form together greater returns in proportion to the stock employed, than the returns of the capitals engaged in commerce and manufactures*; because, in this case, though foreign corn might be purchased, without these restrictions, at a cheaper money price than that at which it could be raised at home, it would not be purchased at so small an expense of capital and labour, which is the true proof of the advantageous employment of stock' (223; emphasis added).[45] The allowance that, though the

44 Ricardo rejected all this: 'Here again the estimate is made of money profits, but I require that in both instances the money profits should be reduced into the power of commanding labour and commodities. I do not want to know what value we could have obtained in the two cases, but what riches we might have got, – what means of happiness to the community!' (*Note 120*; 1951–73, II, 203).

45 Ricardo objected: 'True if estimated in corn returns, and not in money returns. The only question of importance, in fact, is, whether we could buy our corn at home or abroad at the least expense of capital and labour – and we are to judge of this only by a comparison of the quantity we can import with a given capital and the quantity we can grow with an equal amount of capital. It is by quantity and not by money value that we must judge. We may make anything of a high money value, by rendering it scarce' (*Note 121*; 204).

domestic 'money price' of corn should be raised by import restriction, the cost in terms of 'capital and labour' is none the less reduced doubtless mirrors the corn output constituting *rent* that had to be taken into account.[46]

This seems to be an extraordinary application. The notion of a deviation between the social and the private return on agricultural investment which justified intervention to encourage increased agricultural investment – with the appropriate estimate in calculating the return per £100 of new investment involving *the sum of rent and profit* in contrast to profit alone in manufacturing – goes far beyond any recommendation by Smith, even at his most 'physiocratic.' But a note attached to the closing proposition casts more light on Malthus's intentions. This note maintains that investment in permanent agricultural improvement should be viewed as a means of effectively adding to the land supply. And we have the assertion that the cost price (in terms of capital and labour) is *reduced* by import restrictions: 'If restrictions upon importation necessarily increased the quantity of labour and capital required to obtain corn they could not of course be defended for a moment,[47] with a view to wealth and productive power. But if by directing capital to the land they occasion permanent improvements, the whole question is changed. Permanent improvements in agriculture are like the acquisition of additional land' (223n).

Malthus did not, therefore, have in mind simple extensions to increasingly less productive land in the standard classical fashion, but improvement in the sense of clearances rendering new areas fit for tillage.[48] The real cost per unit of corn in terms of capital and labour, runs the argument, does not rise. And this, Malthus further deduced, implied faster economic growth – and faster population growth – in a protected economy: 'But if the progress of wealth has been rather accelerated than retarded by

46 This seems to be confirmed by the reference cited below to 'the greater quantity of raw produce that has been purchased by a given quantity of capital and labour at home, than could have been purchased by the same quantity of capital and labour from abroad.' However, there is a problem: The fact is that Malthus also eschewed concern with real output – concentrating rather on the 'rate of profits and real value in exchange.'

47 Ricardo leaped upon Malthus's admission that, if import restrictions indeed 'necessarily increased the quantity of labour and capital required to obtain corn,' he would oppose them, to point out in *Note 122*: 'It is only because they do so, that are attacked. Can any man doubt of their having this effect?' Regarding non-economic grounds for protection he added: 'I confess on those other grounds the arguments in favour of restrictions have very little solidity in my view of the subject' (II, 205).

48 Eltis makes the interesting point that this is the sort of argument that *Quesnay* might have given to subsequent criticisms based on the notion of a no-rent margin: 'He would only have conceded the relevance of Ricardo's theory to a country where there was no need for farmers to invest at the margin of cultivation in any way that improved their farms in the course of their leases' (1984, 66).

such restrictions upon the importation of foreign corn, on account of the greater quantity of raw produce that has been purchased by a given quantity of capital and labour at home, than could have been purchased by the same quantity of capital and labour from abroad,[49] it is quite obvious that the population must have been accelerated rather than retarded; and certainly the unusually rapid increase of population which is known to have taken place during the last ten or fifteen years of the war, so much beyond the average of the century, tends strongly to confirm this conclusion' (223–4). Here we have a major deviation from earlier positions which assumed that protection would cause some deceleration in national-income and population growth rates.[50]

Malthus closed his Section IX by reiterating that, since the interests of the state and the landlords may coincide in the special case at hand, restrictions on corn imports – as distinct from all other products – were justified: 'This consideration, combined with those before adverted to, may make it at least a matter of doubt, whether even in the case of restrictions upon the importation of foreign corn, the interest of the state may not sometimes be the same as that of the landlords. But no such doubt exists respecting a restriction upon the importation of other commodities' (225).

Thus far we have considered the chapter on Rent. In his chapter on Profits, Malthus expressed optimism regarding prospects for technological progress – *particularly in a regime of agricultural protection* – writing of such prospects in terms of 'centuries to come' (324–5), a position we have encountered in chapter 15, p. 780, on empirical estimates. And he envisaged a prospect of ongoing economic growth based on domestic corn supplies 'for hundreds of years' with no fall in the profit rate (332), in contrast with premature stagnation in the event of a growth program based on manufactures and involving corn imports: 'A country, which accumulates faster than its neighbours, might for hundreds of years still keep up its rate of profits, if it were successful in making permanent improvements on the land; but, if with the same rapidity of accumulation it were to depend chiefly on imported corn, its profits could scarcely fail to fall; and the fall would probably be occasioned, not by a rise in the bullion price of corn in the ports of Europe, but by a fall in the bullion price of the exports with which the corn was purchased by the country in question' (332–3).[51] 'Our present body of manufacturers,' he complained, 'when they call for imported corn, think chiefly of the additional demand for their goods occasioned by the increased imports, and seem quite to forget the prodi-

49 Ricardo's *Note 123* reads simply: 'Grant this indeed, and the conclusion follows.' But of course he refused to grant it.

50 In his letter to Horner, 16 June 1813 (above, p. 820), Malthus refers to faster population growth under free trade.

51 This is the same general notion as in 1817 (II, 424–5), cited chapter 5, p. 181.

gious increase of supply which must be occasioned by the competition of so many capitals and workmen in the same line of business' (331n). And the note touching on permanent land improvements in a protected economy (above, p. 844) closes with an allusion to the danger for industry-biased growth in contemporary circumstances: 'Even however, if they had no effect of this kind, they might be desirable on other grounds yet more important. Late events must make us contemplate with no small alarm a great increase in the *proportion* of our manufacturing population, both with reference to the happiness and to the liberty of our country' (223n).[52]

IX MALTHUS'S NEW POSITION: THE EVIDENCE

A total reconsideration of the merits of agricultural protection is suggested by a comparison of the first and second editions of the *Principles*. We must proceed with caution, since Malthus died suddenly 'before he had completed the whole of the alterations which he had in contemplation, and while he was yet occupied in correcting and improving the latter parts of the work' (Otter, 1836, xi). Pullen, discussing the fact that alterations between editions in the later parts of the *Principles* are less extensive than those in the early parts, offers a possible explanation that, if valid, reinforces our case, as we shall see – namely, that Malthus 'had intended to proceed systematically from beginning to end of the *Principles*, but did not have time to complete the alterations before his death,' which 'would mean that the views expressed in the latter, less-corrected part of the *Principles* are not necessarily Malthus's final views' (Pullen, in Malthus, 1820/1989, I, lxv). Some of the alterations might possibly have been by the editor, John Cazenove (Pullen, I, lxi–lxiv; and II, 371, 394). But the extent of the excisions of the protectionist passages of 1820 do *not* suggest an editor's hand.[53] It is inconceivable to me that Cazenove would have undertaken a *silent* rewriting of the text. Conversely, had he been responsible for the excisions, he would presumably have proceeded systematically and not neglected a protectionist passage remaining at the end of the book.

The most striking alteration from our perspective is the removal of the material in Section IX of the chapter on Rent, involving a supposed excess of social over private return to agricultural investment and a case for protection based upon it (above, section VIII). Included in the deletion is a summary of the case in the chapter 'Of Corn Laws: Restrictions upon Importation' in the 1817 *Essay* whereby the loss sustained by the landlord

52 A contrast between agricultural and manufacturing economies – possibly relevant for protection – emphasizing that only in the latter is there downward pressure on wages with an eye to export markets, will be taken up shortly (below, pp. 848–9). It appears also in the second edition.

53 There are eight notes in the *Principles* with specific indications of an editorial addition. None of these is relevant for our present topic.

from free trade would not usually be 'counterbalanced' by a proportionate gain to the state (1820, 218). Removed, too, is the note justifying agricultural protection on the dual grounds: (1) that investment in permanent agricultural improvements constitutes a means of effectively adding to the land supply; and (2) that there had occurred an 'alarming' increase in 'the *proportion* of our manufacturing population' (223n). A further excision is a note warning of the glutted markets likely to result if British capital were devoted largely to manufacturing (331n). Absent, too, is the relevant text asserting that '[a] country which accumulates faster than its neighbours, might for hundreds of years still keep up its rate of profits, if it were successful in making permanent improvements on the land' (332); the policy conclusion flowing from this perspective that a growth program turning on manufacturing and involving corn imports was bound to be stifled prematurely; and the application of these principles to contemporary Britain.

We found also that, in the *Principles* of 1820, Malthus went farther and related agricultural technology to a 'great home demand for corn [which] must tend greatly to encourage improvements in agriculture' (324). In a replacement passage Malthus added prospective *industrial* technology to his reasons for optimism, and deleted the formal attribution of improved agricultural technology to a high demand for food (although he retained a reference to the positive effect on the profit rate of 'a rise in the price of corn from increased demand'): 'If to these two causes of the increased productiveness of the powers of labour [agricultural improvements and increased effort] we add a fall in the prices of manufactures from improved machinery, and a rise in the price of corn from increased demand, unaccompanied by a proportionate rise of most foreign, and many home commodities, the effect of taking poorer land into cultivation is so likely to be counterbalanced under such circumstances, that in the actual state of many countries, or in their probable state for some centuries to come, we may fairly lay our account to such a result when the occasion calls for it' (1836, 288).[54]

The second edition leaves unchanged a statement, at the very end of the book, about agricultural protection as the exception to the general free-trade rule: 'There can be little doubt that our commerce has been much impaired by unnecessary restraints, and that much benefit might be derived from the removal of them ... [T]here seems to be no reason for the absolute prohibition of any commodities whatever; and there is little doubt that, upon this principle, a much greater freedom might be given to foreign commerce, at the same time that a larger revenue might be derived from the customs. *I have already stated, in more places than one, why,*

54 A summary paragraph alluding to the positive effect on profits (as in 1793–1813) of 'an increasing demand for agricultural produce' is retained (1820, 325; 1836, 288–9).

under all the circumstances of the case, I think it desirable that we should permanently grow nearly our own consumption of corn. But I see no sufficient cause why we should permanently prefer the wines of Portugal and the silks of London to the wines and silks of France' (1820, 508; 1836, 427; emphasis added).[55] What weight should be given to the retention of the protectionist exception? I would say, little when placed in the balance against the extensive and systematic deletions made earlier in the *Principles* – here one must remember that the new edition was never fully revised by Malthus and that alterations between editions are less extensive in later parts of the book. And there is also evidence of the rejection of agricultural protection in Malthus's *Quarterly Review* article of 1824, a note in the 1826 *Essay on Population* and in three letters of 1829–33, matters elaborated in the next section.

Before proceeding, there remains one further complexity requiring attention. It relates to the advantage attributed to states possessing 'a fertile soil,' that they are 'not obliged to pay much attention to that most distressing and disheartening of all cries to every man of humanity – the cry of the master manufacturers and merchants for low wages, to enable them to find a market for their exports. If a country can only be rich by running a successful race for low wages, I should be disposed to say at once, perish such riches! But, though a nation which purchases the main part of its food from foreigners, is condemned to this hard alternative, it is not so with the possessors of fertile land' (1820, 235–6; 1836, 214–15).[56] Prudential population control, Malthus further observed, might be disastrous in an economy dependent on manufacturing exports: 'A small sacrifice of produce, that is, the not pushing cultivation too far [1836: without agricultural improvements], would, with prudential habits among the poor, enable it to maintain the whole of a large population in wealth and plenty. Prudential habits [1836: with regard to marriage carried to a considerable extent], among the labouring classes of a country mainly depending upon manufactures and commerce, might ruin [1836: injure] it. In a country of fertile land, such habits would be the greatest of all conceivable blessings' (1820, 236–7; 1836, 215).[57] This does not constitute a *formal* case for agri-

55 The ellipses cover a case for revenue tariffs (below, note 64).

56 The passage is difficult to appreciate, considering Malthus's adherence to the international monetary proposition whereby the equilibrium level of corn prices and money wages is determined by the efficiency of the export industries (see chapter 14: VI).

57 A note is attached to the recommendation for prudential habits to avoid 'pushing cultivation too far': 'Under similar circumstances, with respect to capital, skill, &c. [1836: to agricultural skills, &c.], it is obvious that land of the same degree of barrenness could not be cultivated, if by the prevalence of prudential habits the labourers were well [1836: very well] paid; but to forego the small increase of produce and population arising from the cultivation of such land, would, in a large and fertile territory, be a slight and imperceptible sacrifice, while the happiness which would result from it to the great mass of the population, would be beyond all price.'

cultural protection – it spells out only a 'most desirable benefit belonging to a fertile soil.' None the less, we may have here an implicit case for protection pertinent to contemporary policy. For it is asserted that such a country could reap the benefits of international commerce even if its exports were limited to its 'peculiar' products, this presumably a reference to highly specialized products safe from foreign competition: 'The peculiar products [1836: and manufactures] of a country, though never probably sufficient to enable it to import a large proportion of its food as well as of its conveniences and luxuries, will generally be sufficient to give full spirit and energy to all its commercial dealings, both at home and abroad' (1820, 236; 1836, 215). Even so, there is a striking variation between editions. In 1820 alone did Malthus caution that his justification of the export of 'peculiar products' did not cover the cotton and silk industries: 'Cottons are no more a peculiar product of this country than silks: and woe will, I fear, befal us, greater than ever we have yet experienced, if the prosperity of our cotton trade should become necessary to purchase the food, of any considerable body of our people!' (1820, 236n). This striking note is omitted from the second edition.

* * *

When exactly the changes in the *Principles* were made is unclear. However, the *Quarterly Review* article of 1824 on Ricardian political economy intimates a change of attitude. Malthus there reiterated Smith's physiocratic position that 'the capital employed in agriculture in proportion to the quantity of labour it puts in motion, adds a *much greater value* to the annual produce of the land and labour of the country, to the real wealth and *revenue* of its inhabitants, than any equal capital employed in manufacturers' (1986, 7, 267), but added that the 'superior importance of food and raw materials' does *not* justify agricultural bias in legislation: 'It does not follow, nor is it considered as a consequence by Adam Smith, that any forced encouragement should be given to agriculture,' for this 'would probably defeat the very end in view.' And he made explicit reference to 'the happy opening of new and large channels of foreign commerce, combined with the improved view of our government in commercial legislation' – the Huskisson reforms – which had prevented 'great distress' and assured 'a renewed demand for labour' (287).

That these remarks must be taken seriously is confirmed by the note to the chapter 'Of Corn Laws: Restrictions upon Importation' in the sixth edition of the *Essay on Population*, a work ready for the press by late 1825.[58] This note refers to articles on the Corn Laws in the 1824 *Supple-*

58 The 'Advertisement' is dated 2 January 1826. The footnote itself is introduced by '1825.' Henceforth, in referring to the change of 1826, we should have in mind that the alteration was actually made the previous year (probably sometime after April).

ment to the *Encyclopaedia Britannica* and in the April 1825 *Westminster Review* – by J.R. McCulloch and J.S. Mill, respectively – maintaining that a free corn trade assured against major price fluctuations. This Malthus denied,[59] drawing on Tooke's study of British prices (1823) – which in turn relied on Lowe (1822) – indicating a commonality of good and bad seasons across European trading nations (even extending to North America) (1826/1986, *3*, 435n). But he was not swayed and concluded that, considering the interests of the commercial world as a whole, a free corn trade was nevertheless desirable. This universal concern he had rejected in the 1817 *Essay* on the grounds that it was 'visionary,' considering the potency of nationalist sentiment: 'One objection however to systems of restriction must always remain. They are essentially unsocial. I certainly think that, in reference to the interests of a particular state, a restriction upon the importation of foreign corn may sometimes be advantageous; but I feel still more certain that in reference to the interests of Europe in general the most perfect freedom of trade in corn, as well as in every other commodity, would be the most advantageous. Such a perfect freedom, however, could hardly fail to be followed by a more free and equal distribution of capital, which, though it would greatly advance the riches and happiness of Europe, would unquestionably render some parts of it poorer and less populous than they are at present; and there is little reason to expect that individual states will ever consent to sacrifice the wealth within their own confines to the wealth of the world' (436).[60] This earlier statement is repeated in the 1826 text, but the added note takes a wholly

59 In 1815 Malthus had allowed that *genuine* free trade minimized price fluctuations; his fear was that, considering French legislation restricting corn exports, this was ruled out with destabilizing consequences (1986, *7*, 157–8; above, p. 829).

60 In fact we find pointers in this direction as early as 1806: 'According to the general principles of political economy, it cannot be doubted, that it is for the interest of the civilized world that each nation should purchase its commodities wherever they can be had the cheapest. According to these principles, it is rather desirable that some obstacles should exist to the excessive accumulation of wealth in any particular county, and that rich nations should be tempted to purchase their corn of poorer nations, as by these means the wealth of the civilized world will not only be more rapidly increased but more equably diffused' (1806, II, 237–8).

But these general principles had to give way to 'local interests and political relations,' especially to assure the health of domestic agriculture: 'It is evident, however, that local interests and political relations may modify the application of these general principles; and in a country with a territory fit for the production of corn, an independent, and at the same time a more equable supply of this necessary of life, may be an object of such importance as to warrant a deviation from them. It is undoubtedly true, that every thing will ultimately find its level, but this level is sometimes effected in a very harsh manner. England may export corn a hundred years hence without the assistance of a bounty; but this is much more likely to happen from the destruction of her manufactures, than from the increase of her agriculture; and a policy which, in so important a point may tend to soften the harsh corrections of general laws, seems to be justifiable.'

internationalist perspective, implying that the experiment was, after all, worth trying. The appropriate policy was one that did not 'impeach the principles of free trade': 'I am very far however from meaning to say that the circumstances of different countries having often an abundance or deficiency of corn at the same time, though it must prevent the possibility of steady prices, is a decisive reason against the abolition or alteration of the corn laws. The most powerful of all the arguments against restrictions is their unsocial tendency, and the acknowledged injury which they must do to the interests of the commercial world in general. The weight of this argument is increased rather than diminished by the numbers which may suffer from scarcity at the same time. And at a period when our ministers are most laudably setting an example of a more liberal system of commercial policy, it would be greatly desirable that foreign nations should not have so marked an exception as our present corn laws to cast in our teeth. A duty on importation not too high, and a bounty nearly such as was recommended by Mr. Ricardo, would probably be best suited to our present situation, and best secure steady prices. A duty on foreign corn would resemble the duties laid by other countries on our manufactures as objects of taxation, and would not in the same manner impeach the principles of free trade' (436n). A final statement at the close of the note makes explicit that the specification of the pros and cons of the Corn Laws in the chapter was not designed as a 'protest' *against* their abolition or change: 'But whatever system we may adopt, it is essential to a sound determination, and highly useful in preventing disappointments, that all the arguments both for and against corn laws should be thoroughly and impartially considered; and it is because on a calm, and, as far as I can judge, an impartial review of the arguments of this chapter, they still appear to me of weight sufficient to deserve such consideration, and *not as a kind of protest against the abolition or change of the corn laws*, that I republish them in another edition' (emphasis added). And it is indeed true that in the body of the chapter Malthus had stated that the balanced-growth policy 'may be purchased too dear' and could not be recommended as a hard-and-fast rule (424). The stage had already been set for a renunciation of the case for balanced growth – with the requisite agricultural protection – in the new circumstances that Britain encountered.

The note is in some respects unclear. Better to discern Malthus's intentions we should elaborate on the Ricardo scheme alluded to, a scheme for a 'substantially free trade in corn,' as Ricardo himself phrased it in *Protection to Agriculture* (1822/1951–73, IV, 266).[61] The proposal entails a countervailing duty on corn imports to correct for differential taxation imposed on British farmers relative to British manufacturers, and an appropriate drawback on exports: 'With a view to the real interest of the consumer, in

61 Ricardo's plan was overwhelmingly rejected by the House of Commons (cf. V, 203).

which the interests of the whole community are, and ever must be, included, whenever any peculiar tax falls on the produce of any one commodity, from the effects of which all other producers are exempted, a countervailing duty to that amount, but no more, should on every just principle be imposed on the importation of such commodity; and further, that a drawback should be allowed, to the same amount also on the exportation of the like commodity. If, before any taxation, the remunerating price of wheat was 60s. per quarter, both in England and on the Continent, and in consequence of the imposition of a tax, such as tithes, falling exclusively on the farmer, and not on any other producer, wheat was raised in England to 70s., a duty of 10s. should be also imposed on the importation of foreign corn. This tax on foreign corn, and on home corn also, should be drawn back on exportation' (1951–73, IV, 243).[62] Ricardo was careful to distinguish his proposed drawback from a regular export subsidy (243–4). And he reiterated that the purpose of the recommendation was *to assure, not to distort,* competitive resource allocation: 'The duty which I have here proposed, is the only legitimate countervailing duty, which neither offers inducements to capital to quit a trade, in which for us it is the most beneficially employed, nor holds out any temptations to employ an undue proportion of capital in a trade to which it would not otherwise have been destined. The course of trade would be left precisely on the same footing as if we were wholly an untaxed country, and every person was at liberty to employ his capital and skill in the way he should think most beneficial to himself.'[63]

62 This is qualified somewhat since Ricardo actually allowed a drawback lower than the duty: 'A duty of 10s. per quarter, on importation, to which I wish to approach, is, I am sure, rather too high as a countervailing duty for the peculiar taxes which are imposed on the corn grower, over and above those which are imposed on the other classes of producers in the country; but I would rather err on the side of a liberal allowance than of a scanty one; and it is for this reason that I do not propose to allow a drawback quite equal to the duty. As far as the producer of corn was concerned, when the duty had fallen to 10s., the trade would, to him, have all the advantages of a free trade, within the trifling amount of 3s. per quarter' (264).

63 Robert Torrens claimed priority for the scheme and similarly justified it on free-trade grounds: 'It was stated in the first edition of this work [1815] that when a tax is imposed on any domestic article, a duty of equal amount should be imposed on the importation of the similar foreign article, and a bounty, also of equal amount, should be granted on the exportation of the other. This was considered, in the first instance, as a somewhat startling proposition, and as one savouring, not of the enlightened doctrines of free trade, but rather of the exploded system of legislative restriction and encouragement. The principle, however, was adopted by Mr. Ricardo, in his valuable Treatise on the Protection of Agriculture, who explained and enforced it with his usual ability. It is now generally admitted that this principle, instead of being opposed to the doctrine of free trade, is part and parcel of that doctrine, inasmuch as it tends to restore that natural equilibrium between the different branches of industry, which equilibrium taxation occasionally disturbs' (Torrens, 1826, vi–vii; on Torrens's original formulation of 1815, see Robbins, 1958, 268).

Malthus's case in the note for a 'duty on importation not too high, and a bounty nearly such as was recommended by Mr. Ricardo' is ambiguous, for it might be understood as implying that only the 'bounty' was to be of the Ricardian variety, not the duty. But against this reading stands the fact that Ricardo's 'bounty' is a partial drawback of a duty to be imposed on imported corn justified by the differential domestic taxation of corn relative to manufactures, and as such is part of a policy package. In brief, support for the Ricardo drawback on its own is not meaningful and would scarcely merit the special designation it is accorded by Malthus. This is all the more true since, as early as 1814, he had accepted, at least in principle, the case for drawbacks in his positive references to Smith's proposal for countervailing tariffs (above, p. 823).[64]

The essential message of the note lies in its proposal to replace the 1815 prohibitory system by one *designed not to 'impeach the principles of free trade.'* And I conclude that if, as seems to be the case, Malthus's allusions in 1826 are to the entire Ricardo policy package, what is involved is not an extension to agriculture of the case for a countervailing tariff of the Smithian sort – the 1814 suggestion now treated as both desirable and practicable – but the Ricardo plan involving a tariff and drawback turning on the differential taxation of corn.[65] Clearly, much more is involved than a

64 The last sentence in the cited note is also ambiguous, but the comparison with *foreign* duties which 'would not in the same manner impeach the principles of free trade' might refer to *revenue* tariffs – tariffs imposed 'as objects of taxation' (although European countries were in fact increasingly adopting *protective* legislation). The *Principles*, at the close, makes a case for revenue taxes thus: 'While it is necessary to raise a large sum by taxation for the expenses of the government and payment of the interest of the national debt, it would by no means be advisable to neglect so fair and fruitful a resource as the customs' (1820, 508; 1836, 427). Malthus then proceeds to the *Smithian* case: 'In regulating these taxes, it is also natural that those foreign commodities should be taxed the highest, which are either of the same kind as the native commodities which have been taxed, or such as, for special reasons of health, happiness, or safety, it is desirable to grow largely at home.' But we must recall what was said regarding the state of the revisions made to the later chapters of the text.

The desirability of correcting for distortions created by taxation is also briefly mentioned at the close of the 1817/1826 chapter on agricultural import restrictions in the *Essay on Population* without specifying the exact nature of such correction (see above, p. 841).

65 Malthus may have been reminded of Ricardo's scheme by Mill's 1825 article, to which he refers in the note. McCulloch (1824b), too, had championed the Ricardo scheme, and Mill drew on this account in elaborating the case that 'the agriculturalists are not entitled to a countervailing duty, unless they can show that they are more heavily taxed than other classes of producers; nor ought the duty even then to exceed the difference between the burdens of the agriculturists and those of others. The reason is, that if all commodities of home production are taxed exactly alike, even without countervailing duties, it is the same thing, with respect to trade, as if they were not taxed at all ...' (1825a/1967, IV, 68). There were also frequent references in Parliament to the Ricardo plan (e.g., Lethbridge, 5 March 1824, House of Commons, Parliamentary Debates, N.S., *10*, 747–9; Thompson, 3 February 1825, *12*, 48–51).

simple recommendation to lower an existing tariff. The uncertain tone of the text in question – the reference to a duty 'not too high' and a bounty 'nearly such' as recommended by Ricardo – seems to reflect the work of a typically slow and laborious writer.[66] It is when we consider all the evidence together that a clear picture emerges of the significance of the change in question.

* * *

The evidence extends beyond formal texts to correspondence. The transformation is confirmed in three letters, one to Nassau Senior, dated 31 March 1829; the second to Thomas Chalmers, dated 6 March 1832; and the third to Jane Marcet, dated 22 January 1833. The first relates to the proposition that an increase in real wages following agricultural improvement or the relaxation of corn-import restrictions will prove to be temporary unless accompanied by an improved degree of prudential population control. The point for us is Malthus's position that such increase was none the less desirable:

> In the same manner I must allow that it follows from my principles, that if by a free trade, corn were obtained much cheaper, and a labouring family could really command a much larger quantity of it, population would unquestionably increase with greater rapidity than before, so as to reduce the increased corn wages; and that the final condition of the labouring classes would not depend on this change which had taken place in the law, but upon the greater or less prevalence of the moral checks to population after the peculiar stimulus to its increase had subsided; and repeated experience has shown that the facility of obtaining food at one period is not *necessarily* connected with the formation of more general habits of prudence subsequently.
>
> It does not by any means follow from these principles, that we should not use our utmost endeavour to make two ears of wheat grow where one grew before, or to improve our commercial code by freeing it from restraints. An increase of population is in itself a very decided advantage, if it be not accompanied by an increased *proportion* of vice and misery. And the period during which the pressure of population is lightened, though it may not be of long duration, is a period of comparative ease, and ought by no means to be thrown out of our consideration. (in Senior, 1829, 84–5)

The letter to Chalmers reads simply: 'I quite agree with you in regard to the moral advantage of repealing the corn laws' (Thomas Chalmers Collec-

66 See the comment by Tribe at the History of Economic Thought Society meetings (1992, 23).

tion, CHA4.185.32). James cites this remark, noting that it 'might have surprised Malthus's contemporaries' (1979, 433). Indeed so – unless they had read and remembered the 1824 article, the alterations to the *Principles*, and the note in the 1826 edition of the *Essay*.

The third letter of the early 1830s, to Marcet, relates to her *John Hopkins's Notions on Political Economy* (1833) and contains the following passage: 'If I were obliged to find any fault, I should say that you have presented in rather too brilliant and unshaded colours the advantages which would accrue from the abolition of the Corn Laws, so as to excite expectations which cannot be realized. *In the actual state of the redundancy of labour in this country, it appears to me scarcely possible to conceive that the money wages of labour will not fall nearly in proportion to the price of corn, and the labourers be greatly disappointed.* It will no doubt give a stimulus to foreign trade; but it must for a considerable time aggravate the redundancy of labour in country parishes; and during the process of the change, there will probably be more thrown out of work than in any other case of the restrictions of the freedom of trade, on account of the largeness of the concerns. It will also tend to raise the value of money and increase the pressure of the national debt. *Still I am for the removal of the restrictions,* though not without fear of the consequences' (Polkinghorn, 1986, 845). The dangers of a free corn trade alluded to here are partly of a transitional nature. What the apparently longer-term 'consequences' to be feared were it is difficult to say, but Malthus might have had in mind the implications of a reduced price level mentioned in the penultimate sentence. In any event, he closes by calling for 'the removal of the restrictions.'

Finally, we call attention to the startling fact that in his *Measure of Value* (1823), prior to the recovery of agricultural prices, Malthus showed marked impatience with the pretensions of the landlords – their proposals in that year to adjust contracts to their own benefit and at the expense of fundholders – which is unlike anything written by Malthus earlier,[67] and as sharp as anything ever said by Ricardo: 'But whatever may have been the pressure on the owners of land since the peace, they cannot have the slightest plea for an attempt to indemnify themselves at the expense of the public creditor. In the turns of the wheel of fortune, all parties should have fair play; no class of persons can be justified in endeavouring to lift themselves up by using unfair and dishonourable means to pull others down; and least of all ought such means to be thought of by the landlords of this country, who, whatever inconveniences they may have suffered latterly, have unquestionably altogether benefited much more largely from the alterations in the value of the currency, than the very persons who in

67 Critical remarks in the *Principles* (1820, 429), regarding 'a most unequal and vicious division of landed property' do not explicitly specify contemporary Britain.

their opinion should be made to relieve them from their embarrassments' (1986, 7, 220–1).[68] All this indicates a change in *mood* on Malthus's part that might be said to set the stage for the subsequent change in policy; by 1823, Malthus was beginning to see eye to eye with Ricardo.[69] The criticism of landlords in 1823 and the subsequent transition in policy are all the more significant considering the fact that many landlords felt threatened by any move to liberalize the Corn Laws – including the more liberal scheme of 1822[70] – and continued throughout the 1820s and 1830s to call for the maintenance and increase of protection in order to defend the 'constitution.'[71]

X THE RATIONALE FOR THE POLICY TRANSITION

We turn to consider *why* the transition to free trade. The primary question is whether the new perspective implied the abandonment of the original arguments favouring protection or only their reduced weighting against the often-recognized disadvantages of protection – domestic efficiency

68 Malthus evidently had in mind pressure in 1823 by landlords for the (so-called) 'equitable adjustment of contracts.' This includes Cobbett's petition involving *inter alia* 'equitable adjustment with regard to the public debt, and also with regard to all debts and contracts between man and man, suspension for one year of all distraints for rent, all process for tithes, and all processes arising out of mortgage, bond, annuity, or other contract affecting house or land' (Smart, 1910–17, II, 1910, 136); Stanhope's proposal in the House of Lords to cut interest on the national debt (136–7); and Lord Titchfield's call for adjustment of contracts on grounds of justice to the aristocracy who had borrowed when prices were high (139–40). Similar proposals in the Commons were made by Western, whose motion was defeated (141).

69 Ricardo was a member of the select committee appointed in March 1821 to consider the agricultural depression. Its report was not, however, ready for consideration during that session. A revived Agricultural Committee reported again in 1822. The tone of the two reports differed substantially. The first 'supported in principle a free trade in corn, but the landlords on the committee had succeeded in adding a number of protectionist recommendations. The Report of 1822 was much more definitely protectionist' (Sraffa, in Ricardo, 1951–73, IV, 203–4). But even before the report was read to the committee by the chairman (25 March), Ricardo was pessimistic in the light of the pressure from the 'country gentlemen, who form themselves into a compact body determined to yield no point which has the least semblance to diminished protection' (letter to McCulloch, 25 March 1822; 1951–73, IX, 180). His immediate reaction to the report was to write the pamphlet *On Protection to Agriculture*, which appeared shortly thereafter.

70 In April 1825 the government let some bonded corn onto the market, and a bill of May 1825 released all corn warehoused in England before 1822, at a duty of 10s., as against the 17s. stipulated by the (still inoperative) 1822 legislations (Hilton, 1977, 272). This was denounced by the House of Lords as the thin end of the wedge (B. Gordon, 1979, 55).

71 Fetter, 1980, 41; Hilton, 271. However, Barnes writes of a growing moderation on the part of landowners (1930, 186); and Hilton also alludes to a 'change of mood' (127–32, 140).

losses, check to population growth, and discouragement of manufactures (above, p. 836) – in the light of new theoretical and empirical considerations. I shall focus first on the 1826 note, and then look farther afield.

As will be recalled, that note refers to the contemporary period as one 'when our ministers are most laudably setting an example [to the world] of a more liberal system of commercial policy'; foreign nations should not be allowed 'so marked an exception as our present corn laws to cast in our teeth' (above, p. 851). Malthus evidently approved of the first breaches in the old 'commercial system' and saw the Corn Laws as an impediment to bringing foreign countries into line.[72] The note is not simply a reaffirmation that, from a cosmopolitan viewpoint, free trade in corn was desirable; it implies, rather, an estimate that, given the new British policy, global free trade involving the full range of products was no longer a pipedream – *indeed, liberalization of corn imports would provide a potent weapon for its achievement.*[73]

What of the net cost to *Britain* of the abandonment of agricultural protection? The original case for protection turned partly on grounds of increased *instability* of output in a free-trade regime, considering (in part)

72 The first formal amendments to the Navigation Acts were introduced in Parliament in 1822, followed by more extensive reforms in 1823 (especially the Reciprocity of Duties Bill). A free trade budget in 1824 reduced protective duties on a wide variety of goods, and removed the linen-export bounty, restrictions on the export of British wool, and various prohibitions on the use of foreign silk goods (Smart, 1910–17, II, 192–226). The Chancellor of the Exchequer (F.J. Robinson) made the point that to allow exceptions was to impede the whole trend: 'Whenever a foreign state imposed a new duty on any of our manufactures, the Government was immediately assailed by letters from all quarters asking them to make representations and remonstrances. How could they do so, when the answer was inevitably a *tu quoque*?' (cited 198). A second free-trade budget of 1825 reduced protective duties on *inter alia* cottons, woollens, linens, paper and books, and iron; and again the case was made (by Huskisson) that Britain should set a good example: 'Let foreign countries see our Chancellor year after year largely remitting public burdens, and at the same time exhibiting a prosperous Exchequer, still flowing to the same perennial level, and he had no doubt that, when they had contemplated for a few years longer the happy consequences, their eyes would be opened, and they would imitate our present rather than adopt our cast-off system of restrictions and prohibitions' (282–3).

At precisely this time J.S. Mill was making the same case, that 'the mutual support which every monopoly lends to every other, is one of the strongest reasons why they should all be destroyed' (1825a/1967, IV, 66).

73 In 1824 Malthus reacted similarly to the freeing of machinery exportation from controls in evidence given to the Commons Select Committee on Artisans and Machinery, 10 May (House of Commons, Parliamentary Papers, V, 600): '[Q]: Is it your opinion that the relaxation of the old commercial jealousy, and the establishment of free trade would be an advantage to this country? – [A]: Yes. [Q]: Do you not conceive that the allowance of the exportation of English machinery, would have the effect of inducing other countries to establish a free trade? – [A]: I think that such would be its tendency, and that is a very proper reason for relaxing these laws.'

'those violent and distressing convulsions of property which almost unavoidably arise from the coincidence of a general war, and an insufficient home supply of corn' (above p. 839). Conceivably the newly recognized possibility of global free trade – to which end it was hoped the abandonment of the Corn Laws would contribute – was seen as decreasing the probability of such disruptions.[74] The prospect of reductions of French corn-export restrictions in response to the new British policy might also be enhanced, thereby reducing the problem of instability, and more broadly that of 'security' so much emphasized in 1815 (above, pp. 828–30).[75] But this is speculative. In fact Malthus explicitly reiterated in his note his expectation of *greater* instability with free trade than with protection,[76]

74 J.S. Mill was to take the matter very seriously: 'It is commerce which is rapidly rendering wars obsolete, by strengthening and multiplying the personal interests which are in natural opposition to it. And it may be said without exaggeration that the great extent and rapid increase of international trade, in being the principal guarantee of the peace of the world, is the great permanent security for the uninterrupted progress of the ideas, the institutions, and the character of the human race' (1848/1965, III, 594).

75 This would have been naïve. For French regulations governing corn exports were further confirmed in 1822: 'La nouvelle Loi [1822] statua ensuite que l'exportation des grains serait suspendue ... lorsque les blés indigènes y auraient dépassé de deux francs le prix fixé comme limite pour l'importation des blés étrangers ... [La] Loi fixait d'une manière définitive la barrière a l'exportation des blés indigènes, elle restreignait la faculté d'importation des blés étrangers, et dans le cas, enfin, où elle continuait d'autoriser cette importation, elle augmentait tout les droits dont la legislation antérieure l'avait déjà grevée' (Gouraud, 1854, II, 184–5). More generally, Smart observes that 'just as Great Britain was relaxing her restrictive system, other countries were about to make it more difficult for her by introducing the principles she had discarded' (Smart, 1910–17, II, 112). Crouzet writes that 'most European countries (France, Austria, and Russia in particular) had since 1815 adopted a resolutely protectionist policy (there has sometimes been talk of a "Second Continental Blockade")' (1982, 123–4). And similarly, Clough (1964) writes of the establishment between 1814 and 1826 of an 'ultra-protective tariff system ... which continued in force with but little change until the Second Empire' (96).

I cannot say whether Malthus was convinced by critics such as Horner, who in 1815 had played down the quantitative significance of potential French supplies. Horner protested in a letter of 12 February: 'This affirmation is not founded upon the parliamentary evidence, which bears the contrary way' (1853, II, 223).

In 1826 there appeared William Jacob's *Report on the Trade in Corn and on the Agriculture of the North of Europe* (dated 21 February 1826, delivered to the Commons, 20 April 1826, House of Commons, Parliamentary Debates, N.S., *15*, 400–89), one theme of which was that British protection caused a contraction of European cultivation. This was attacked by agriculturalists as the opinion of a convert to liberalism designed to put at ease fears regarding a dependency on foreign sources of supply. There were intimations of this theme in a speech by W.Whitmore, 28 April 1825, *13*, 252f. (See also Whitmore's speech of 18 April 1826 drawing on the still untabled report, *16*, 318f.)

76 Malthus opens his note of 1826 by stating that the commonality of harvest fluctuation across Europe, which prevented the possibility of steady prices under free trade, was *not* 'a decisive reason against the abolition or alteration of the corn laws' (above, p. 851). Now Huskisson and the government had been induced by the evidence of common

although we also recall that the Ricardo scheme was expected at least to reduce the problem, and that might have carried some weight in the new balance. But if the problem of stability still remained a concern, it was one that was outweighed by the benefits of free trade.

There can be little doubt about the destiny of that part of the original case for the Corn Laws turning on the need to counter 'mercantilist' regulations, including manufacturing protection (above, p. 840). In so far as the new governmental program included a reduction of *industrial* tariffs (above, note 72), this particular dimension would have been rendered increasingly obsolete. Even so, this consideration would not account for the transition in its entirety, since the full protectionist case related to the prevention of an otherwise 'natural' tendency towards a preponderance of manufacturing.

An important dimension to Malthus's positive response to the new government policy emerges in his 1824 *Quarterly Review* article on Ricardian economics. There he allowed that expansion of foreign markets for British *manufactures* had mitigated the worst effects of the postwar depression by drawing labour from the agricultural sector: 'In the period which has elapsed since the return of peace, the difficulty of finding employment, particularly on the land, has been too notorious to require proof; and if, owing to the extraordinary stimulus given to the population by the previous demand for it, it still continues to increase with rapidity, yet there is reason to think that the present demand would not nearly have kept pace with the rate of increase, and that great distress would have been the consequence, if the happy opening of new and large channels of foreign commerce, combined with the improved views of our government in commercial legislation, had not prepared the way for a renewed demand for labour' (1986, 7, 287). It is particularly relevant, considering the 1826 note, that the expansion of foreign markets is in part ascribed to the 'improved views of our government in commercial legislation.' The empirical significance of *manufactures* from the perspective of aggregate activity reinforces the case for free trade since expanded markets could

---

climatic conditions and seasonal correspondence positively to warn *against protection and the resultant discouragement of secular agricultural expansion abroad,* since sporadic inflows of corn during scarce years could not be relied upon (see Hilton, 1977, 110–17). Malthus had already in 1817 recognized the problem of periodic *general* European scarcity which might discourage foreign producers from shipping food to Britain, drawing on evidence before the 1814 Commons Committee on the Corn Laws (1817, II, 450–1). But in 1817 he had used these purported facts to make a case for a corn-export bounty to assure that home production would suffice for *normal* requirements so that the extraordinary requirements of poor seasons could be more easily met by imports, despite general scarcity. In the 1826 note, in sharp contrast, the very same facts are said *not* to justify protectionism – the conclusion reached by Huskisson, though without specifying Huskisson's grounds.

scarcely be relied upon with agriculture 'so marked an exception' to a general free-trade program. The protectionist case of 1815 had turned in part on the unrealistically large expansions of manufacturing required to absorb even the agricultural workers who were unemployed in 1815 (above, p. 831). By the mid-1820s, the manufacturing sector was proving itself adequate in that respect.[77] Actually, even when making his case for agricultural protection in 1815 (above, p. 825) and in the 1817 essay (above, p. 836), Malthus had included the discouragement of manufactures among the *costs* of such a policy. This concern becomes decisive in 1824.

There is a related matter – the classical proposition that the relatively high manufacturing (export) productivity of a particular trading nation allows and assures that nation a higher price level in international monetary equilibrium. This proposition would put paid to the original concern – that of 1803, 1806, and 1814 (it does not appear in 1817) – with the undermining of competitiveness in consequence of a higher price level generated by a disparate expansion of manufactures. The causal sequence is reversed; general prices are high because of high export efficiency. We have encountered Malthus's subscription to that position in our account of international monetary economics (chapter 14: VI); it appears, we there found, in a note added in 1826 to the very chapter 'Restrictions upon Importation' which has preoccupied us (1986, *3*, 430n).[78]

The question arises whether the newly emphasized danger to aggregate activity arising from impediments to manufacturing exports reflected only the circumstances of the early 1820s,[79] Malthus still maintaining that balanced growth was essential to reduce the force of increased competition of capital characterizing an industrial economy since export sales of home manufactures could *not* ultimately be relied upon (above, pp. 836f.). The

77 This sort of consideration might also have undermined the concern in 1815 with price deflation – and its implications for the debt burden – in consequence of free agricultural trade (above, p. 826).

78 The doctrine will also be found in an addition to the second edition of the *Principles* (1836, 104–5) – it is only hinted at in 1820 (compare 1820, 198, and 1836, 189; see Pullen, II, 182); in evidence of 1824 before the Select Committee on Artisans and Machinery (House of Commons, Parliamentary Papers, V, 600); in the review of Tooke's *High and Low Prices* (1823a/1986, *7*, 153); and in the letter to Chalmers of 6 March 1832 (see below, p. 861).

79 Malthus describes the Ricardo free-trade scheme as the 'best suited to our present situation.' This might allude specifically to circumstances with an eye on manufacturing expansion, implying that the free-trade proposal was designed to deal with an immediate employment problem. But the description might equally refer to more permanent considerations, as the note taken as a whole and other considerations discussed below suggest.

There was some evidence already in 1823 of 'the passing away of agricultural distress' (Smart, 1910–17, II, 134).

1824 formulation rejecting intervention suggests strongly abandonment of that concern (above, p. 849).

* * *

Let us now recall the original protectionist position in *Grounds of an Opinion* (1815), and its affirmation that, pound for pound, the loss of agricultural capital and output is more damaging than a similar loss in other sectors from the perspective of both consumption power and tax revenue (above, p. 833). The emphasis in 1824 on expenditure derived from export sales and the rejection of pro-agricultural intervention implies the abandonment of the case for unproductive consumption by landlords. In this regard, the Malthus–Chalmers correspondence is highly revealing. For in the same letter to Chalmers of 6 March 1832 in which he wrote of his support for Corn Law repeal (above, p. 854), Malthus also defended industrial exports as essential to national wealth and power (alluding in part to the advantages of a high level of money rents and prices), and questioned the quantitative significance of aggregate demand exerted by the 'dependents upon the landlords' compared with that exerted by capitalists and traders: 'Have you not pushed too far the doctrine of the non-importance of foreign commerce? In the 29th section of your synoptical view you allow that the superior influence of Great Britain over other nations in distant parts is due to her exports.[80] Without these therefore she would be less powerful, and I should certainly add less wealthy, though she might still be as strong in defensive war. It is owing to the abundance of her exports, derived from her skill machinery and capital, that money rents and the money prices of corn and labour are high, and that with a small quantity of English labour a large quantity of the products of foreign labour is purchased. The demand for useful and beneficial personal services is limited; and after all these have been fully paid, would it not be an impoverishing and very disadvantageous exchange to substitute for the rich capitalists and comfortable and independent traders living upon the profits of stock, a body of dependents upon the landlords?' (Thomas Chalmers Collection, CHA4.185.32).[81] Similarly, in a letter of 16 February

80 Chalmers, 1832, 564: '29. That the superior influence of Britain over other nations in distant parts, is due to her exports; and that if, instead of her lighter manufactures, she had to export raw produce, her power in offensive war would be lessened, while she might continue as strong in defensive war as before; and that, therefore, the balance of power is a topic of needless and misplaced anxiety on the part of British statesmen.'

81 In an earlier letter to Chalmers of 1827, and subsequently in 1833, the case for 'manufacturing prosperity' is also reiterated; but it is not made explicit that expanded *exports* are intended: 'I agree with you in much of what you say about the wealth derived from manufactures, but I think ... you have pushed your principle too far. I feel strongly persuaded that without our manufacturing prosperity, we should not have had the

1833 to Chalmers, Malthus wrote: 'Do not manufactures and commerce increase the *Revenue* of a country, and *enlarge* the *returning power*? I own I cannot but think that if the taste for luxuries and superior conveniences were at an end, the cultivation of the land would be essentially deteriorated, – at least under the present division of landed property. How could the actual number of labourers have an adequate demand for the produce of the soil, if commerce and manufactures were greatly to be diminished? What numbers would be out of work! What constant calls for an extension of Poor Laws, and of all public and private charities!!' (CHA4.210.5). This is much the same point that Malthus had already made in 1824.[82]

There were indeed earlier allusions, even in 1815, to the significance of manufacturing, *including the export sector*, for the maintenance of activity to the advantage of agriculture itself (cf. *Inquiry into Rent*, 1815b/1986, 7, 130). But now this theme is reiterated forcefully with an eye to the growing significance of the export sector; and it is no longer part of a protectionist case to assure sectoral balance in an economy 'naturally' becoming predominantly industrial, but rather *part of a free-trade case justifying such imbalances.*

In his evidence before the Commons Select Committee on Emigration on 5 May 1827, Malthus commented thus on the view that low wages are favourable to trade and commerce: 'In one respect it is, and in one respect not; it may enable the capitalist to work up his commodities cheaper, and to extend his foreign trade, but it certainly will have a tendency to diminish the home trade, and I think the home trade much more important than the foreign' (House of Commons, Parliamentary Papers, 1827, Vol. V, 317, Question 3285). This seems to suggest no change whatsoever in Malthus's original 'physiocratic' stance.[83] However, Malthus was con-

same disposable population, and certainly not the same power of commanding the labour, the provisions, and the armies of Europe. We might have driven Buonaparte from this country if he had invaded us, but we could not have driven him out of Spain' (18 January 1827; CHA4.80.19).

82 It is pertinent that the free-trade position outlined in Chalmers's *Political Economy*, which Malthus applauded, also emphasizes the desirability of an expanded manufacturing sector – a consideration which implied increased agricultural imports: 'The limit of our imports determines the limit of our exports; so that when the one trade comes to its *ne plus ultra*, the other must also be brought to a dead stand. They mutually limit and determine each other. So that the advantage to our export commerce, from a further enlargement of our imports, opening, as it would, a fuller and freer exportation, and telling most favourably for this great branch of trade upon the foreign exchanges, is really one of the most urgent forces that is now operating on the side of an unrestricted corn trade' (1832, 524).

83 In fact, Pullen compares the statement with a much earlier comment in an 1808 review of William Spence (often mistakenly attributed to Malthus) that 'the internal commerce of a country is of infinitely greater consequence than its external' (1989, xix). Equally, it might be compared with a similar formulation of 1815, cited above, p. 834.

cerned here to emphasize that 'the extent of the effectual demand for the manufactures and commodities consumed at home, depends essentially upon the good condition of the labouring classes' (p. 317, Question 3282).[84] His comment compares the positive effect on demand of expanded exports via wage reductions with the fall in domestic demand entailed by wage reductions, a theme foreign to earlier formulations, with their emphasis on the advantage of high expenditure out of *rent.* And his new position is wholly in line with the change apparent in the *Essay on Population* from the earlier editions, where workers were not seen to benefit from expansion of manufactured output, to the later editions, which allow a significant weight to manufactures in the working-class budget (see Gilbert, 1980).

That Malthus came to modify his agricultural bias requires further attention. The problem is that, despite the various omissions from the second edition of the *Principles* (above, section IX), there was no wholesale and consistent rejection of physiocratic doctrine (see chapter 8). But it is fair to say that there occurred a *dilution* of the physiocratic component to Malthus's thought, even if it is not adequately reflected in the *Principles.*[85] The causal sequence may, however, have been the reverse – the undermining of agricultural protectionism on the various grounds documented in this chapter obliging a continuous questioning of physiocratic perceptions. In all likelihood, the sequences were mutually reinforcing.

More generally, from the viewpoint of labour's welfare, there is evidence of a new emphasis discernible in the 1817 *Essay* on industry-biased growth as typically characteristic of the later stages of economic development, and, along with it, the retraction of much of an earlier concern with such growth from *labour's* perspective (see above, p. 841). The evidence given in this chapter points to the implications for trade policy of this orientation. Gilbert hesitates to see this transition as indicating Malthus's 'evolution ... from an apologist for *agricultural* interests to a an apologist for *industrial* interests'; there is nothing, he writes, 'like the pro-industrial bias or sympathy so transparent in Ricardo or other "mainstream" British classicists'; it was a matter rather of 'a more balanced view of industrial and agricultural growth as potential contributors to working class welfare' (1980, 95). The issue of 'apologetics' seems out of place. But it does appear, from the evidence provided in this chapter, that Malthus had in fact thrown in his lot with the Ricardians.

84 Moreover, on a utilitarian calculus, the 'general condition' of the labourers was 'the most important of all' (p. 317, Question 3281) – the standard classical position.

85 Or for that matter in 1824. Thus we have the restatement of the formal physiocratic position regarding surplus in the 1824 review (above, p. 849). But we have also seen that a case for pro-agricultural intervention is positively denied.

* * *

Can Malthus's new policy position be explained to a degree by increasing pessimism regarding British agricultural prospects? As we have seen in chapter 15, p. 762, Malthus justified corn-import restriction in the 1817 *Essay* (repeated in 1826) in part because of buoyant prospects for ongoing accumulation and population growth at steady – even rising – real wages and without pressure on the profit rate; matters would be different where an economy approached stationariness: 'In such a state of the soil, the British empire might unquestionably be able not only to support from its own agricultural resources its present population, but double, and in time, perhaps, even treble the number; and consequently a restriction upon the importation of foreign corn, which might be thought greatly objectionable in a country which had reached nearly the end of its resources, might appear in a very different light in a country capable of supporting from its own lands a very great increase in population' (1817, II, 494). Hilton has suggested that the doctrine of rent and diminishing returns 'could explain the government's move away from autarchy and protection in 1821' (1977, 121–2); more strongly, diminishing returns 'permeated' Huskisson's free-trade report, having in mind the periodic need for upward adjustment of the protection price (119). Now this latter consideration had indeed been specified by Malthus in 1814 as one objection to the proposed Corn Bill (1986, 7, 107–8). When he made out his protectionist case in 1815, he took account of other, overriding arguments. These arguments by the mid-1820s were in the course of becoming obsolete. But is there evidence that, with the waining of those other concerns, Malthus *formally* reinstated the principle of diminishing returns as a major part of the case for free trade?

Were we to focus solely on the *Essay on Population*, this possibility would not be strong. For the 1826 edition is as optimistic regarding secular prospects as were the earlier editions; indeed, loose predictions made in 1806 and 1807 of a deceleration of food supply setting in within some three or four decades are extended in 1826 to a full century ahead (see above, p. 802). However, several of the revisions for the second edition of the *Principles* (above, section IX) suggest a different story. These include the removal: (1) of the justification for protection on the grounds that permanent agricultural improvements effectively add to the land supply, and related statements (applied to Britain) regarding prospective agricultural-based growth proceeding for 'hundreds of years' without decline in the profit rate; and (2) of the proposition that 'a great demand for corn of home growth must tend greatly to encourage improvements in agriculture.' It may seem from this that, in approaching the new attitude towards industry-based growth, some allowance should be made for a re-evaluation of agricultural prospects – a re-evaluation which would imply the further undermining of physiocratic bias. Yet this conclusion must be stated with caution. Our full account in chapter 15 shows that the revisions to the chapter on Rent yield no consistent pattern, while the subsequent chapters, on Profits and on the Progress of Wealth, reveal no changes at all.

* * *

A moral dimension might be relevant in our exploration. For Chalmers, that dimension outweighed any political dangers inherent in dependence on foreign food supplies, entailing avoidance of 'the certain and urgent evil of a dissatisfied population; who feel, and perhaps with justice too, as if defrauded of their rights, by the compulsory restraints of the legislature on the importation of food' (1832, 533–4), or again: 'Let the freedom of this trade be restored perfectly, though progressively – that government may withdraw itself from the obnoxious attitude of appearing to stand in the way of the people's subsistence. Let this semblance of hostility between the governors and the governed be for ever obliterated; for, however insignificant the material, the moral benefit that would ensue is incalculable' (539).[86] As we know Malthus approved of this perspective in 1832 (above, p. 854). Whether it was a consideration in 1824–6 is an open possibility, for he implicitly raised the question of morality in 1823 in his sharp objections to the proposal by landlords to adjust contracts to their own benefit (above, pp. 855–6).[87]

One final matter may be mentioned by way of hypothesis. We have seen in part I that, throughout the 1815–16 period – especially in correspondence – Malthus was expressing the view that agricultural protection would act to stimulate the profit rate and consequently growth (paradoxical as it might seem). In the *Principles* this line is absent, and in fact replaced by a sort of corn-model analysis. This theoretical transition might conceivably be relevant to the policy transformation.

86 Whether the real advantage to labour would be a permanent one depended on the practice of prudential population control.

87 A word here regarding the suggestion by Winch that Malthus's 'unhappiness' with the results of the 1815 Corn Law reflected the unrest accompanying the passage of the bill (above, note 4). The fact is that the *rioting* of 1815 did not dissuade Malthus; he saw this as a matter of principle. On the March 1815 London riots, Ricardo had written to Malthus: 'The opposition to the bill is more formidable than I expected ... I regret that the people should have proceeded to acts of riot and outrage' (9 March 1815; 1951–73, VI, 180). Malthus responded: 'The riots of course should not be regarded' (10 March; 183). He did, on the other hand, allow that 'a neglect of such numerous petitions may in many respects be a bad precedent.' Again, this time to Horner on 14 March 1815: 'I remain firm in my opinion as to the Policy of some Restrictions, but tho I would not yield to the mob, I should be disposed to yield to the prodigious weight of Petitions, and let the people have their way' (188; see also a letter to John Murray, 8 March 1815, Murray Archives). The numerous petitions in 1825 (see, e.g., House of Commons, Parliamentary Debates, N.S., *13*: 25 April, 142–9, 150–62; 26 April, 165–70, 171; 28 April, 247–9, 249–98) might well have exerted some influence.

XI SUMMARY AND CONCLUSION

Malthus's transition to free agricultural trade constitutes his positive response to the government's new liberal trade program with its promise of major expansion of British manufacturing exports – assuming the removal of barriers to corn imports – and his recognition of a contemporary absorption into the industrial sector of surplus agricultural capital and labour. The new liberal policy also undermined that part of his original concern with industry structure reflecting artificial stimuli accorded manufactures.

More is in question than a change of perception regarding the state of the contemporary economy, although growing concern with land scarcity may have played a role in addition to the alteration in government policy. For much of Malthus's original protectionism reflected 'agricultural bias,' including a concern to prevent the disproportionate expansion of industry, even in a freely operating system. A fundamental reorientation of analytical perspective seems to be involved – renunciation of the case for balanced growth in favour of industry-based growth, and growing dissatisfaction with physiocratic conceptions, including the dependency of expenditure levels on the magnitude of rental incomes.

That Malthus championed free trade solely on the cosmopolitan grounds of international morality may also be dismissed. Although the note of 1826 argues for free trade in terms of net *universal* advantage, the specifics of the case suggest that Malthus also envisaged prospective net advantages for Britain. He may not have abandoned entirely his secular concern with the reliability of foreign sources of food supply, but this was now given a sufficiently low weight to be outweighed by the advantages of new openings in the more immediate future for British manufacturing exports, in conjunction with the long-recognized efficiency advantages of free trade.

Malthus conveyed his new position to at least three of his contemporaries (Senior, Chalmers, and Marcet); it is they who apparently did not spread the word. Moreover, his 1824 article is clear enough, as are his 1823 charges against landowners. It is the fault of reader if they did not get the message or chose not to broadcast it. But it remains true that the note of 1826 is scarcely a conspicuous location to spell out his new position, especially since the text to which it is attached remained unchanged. Since no one apparently referred to his renunciation of agricultural protection, why did not Malthus correct the oversight of his contemporaries? Was it perhaps so trifling a change that it could be left quiescent?[88] Or could Torrens have been mistaken in saying of Malthus that he 'possesse[d], in a very eminent degree, a spirit of candour and a love of truth' (1815, xi); or Ricardo, when he wrote of Malthus that 'a more candid or better man nowhere exists,' whose 'erroneous opinions respecting the expediency of

88 I owe these questions to the late George Stigler.

a free trade in corn ... are honest conscientious opinions' (13 October 1819; 1951–73, VIII, 101)? After all, several notable parliamentary figures did convert regarding the merits of the 1815 act and in many cases made no bones about it (see appendix C).

There is perhaps a hint of a lessening of concern with the policy question. For the problem 'whether a balance between the agricultural and commercial classes of society, which would not take place naturally, ought, under certain circumstances, to be maintained artificially' was described in 1817 as 'the most important practical question in the whole compass of political economy'; whereas this is modified in 1826 to read simply 'a most important practical question' (1986, *3*, 424). This, however, does not carry us all the way, since the change in policy itself seems to reflect, or at least parallel, a deeper analytical reorientation.

The problem, I suggest, must be approached in terms of Malthus's failure to complete the second edition of the *Principles*, for had he himself published the revised version – and explicitly pointed out the deletions of protectionist passages – the new view could not possibly have remained a public secret. In the event, the second edition evinced little interest, and the nature and import of the revisions have been camouflaged by the lack of a variorum edition. The only major notice was that by Empson for the *Edinburgh Review* (1837), and he missed entirely the import of the changes documented in this chapter: 'In substance and in doctrine, it contains the principles of Political Economy taught by Mr. Malthus' (1837/1963, 234). This is simply misleading. If my case is well made out, Malthus's procrastination may reflect his need to absorb the full implications of the theoretical and policy reorientation, a problem not faced by the politicians. And more than the usual courage would have been required to undertake a concerted campaign to spread the word.[89] For after 1815 Malthus was all but blacklisted by the *Edinburgh Review* because of his prohibitionism, and he was obliged to turn to the ultra-Tory *Quarterly Review.* Had he announced his new position with a fanfare, he would in all likelihood have been subject to virulent charges of treachery.[90] His unwillingness to go farther than he did to broadcast his new position is not difficult to appreciate in these terms.[91]

89 For other possible explanations of the delay in completing the new edition, see Pullen, 1989, lix–lx, lxviii–lxix.

90 Fetter provides the context: '*Blackwood's*, attacking the Tories when they appeared to have been influenced in 1826 by the free trade teachings of the economists, said: "The man [Huskisson] who yesterday could not number his own toes has been magically transmuted by Political Economy and Philosophy into a statesman of the first order" ... The *Quarterly*, after it became clear that political economists were almost unanimous in opposition to the Corn Laws, left no doubt that its opinion of them agreed with *Blackwood's.* Robert Southey wrote [1831, 277]: "No professors, even in the subtlest ages of scholastic philosophy, were ever more successful in muddying what they found clear, and perplexing what is itself intelligible"' (1965b, 431).

91 A final consideration regarding Malthus's intellectual honesty is taken up in Conclusion: VIII.

APPENDIX A: SIZE, SECTOR DISTRIBUTION OF THE GAINFUL LABOUR FORCE, AND LABOUR-PARTICIPATION RATIOS, GREAT BRITAIN, 1780–1851

Date	Size of labour force (millions)	Agriculture, forestry, and fishing (%)	Manufacturing, mining, and industry (%)	Trade and transport (%)	Domestic and personal (%)	Public, professional, & all other (%)	Labour participation ratio (%)
1780	4.0	–	–	–	–	–	–
1801	4.8	35.9	29.7	11.1	11.5	11.8	45.7
1811	5.5	33.0	30.2	11.6	11.8	13.3	45.8
1821	6.2	28.4	38.4	12.1	12.7	8.5	44.0
1831	7.2	24.6	40.8	12.4	12.6	9.5	44.2
1841	8.4	22.2	40.5	14.2	14.5	8.5	45.4
1851	9.7	21.7	42.9	15.8	13.0	6.7	46.6

Source: Tranter, 1981, 206

APPENDIX B: DIGEST OF MAJOR CORN LAWS[1]

1660	Import:	Above 44s.	Nominal duty of 4d. per quarter of wheat
		Below 44s.	Duty of 2s.
	Export:	Above 40s.	Prohibited
		Below 40s.	Permitted subject to nominal duty of 1s.

1663 Often referred to as first 'protective' Corn Law

	Import:	Above 48s	Nominal duty of 4d.
		Below 48s.	Duty of 5/4
	Export:	Above 48s.	Prohibited
		Below 48s.	Nominal duty of 1s.

1670 'An Act for the Improvement of Tillage.' Increased protection; introduction of sliding-scale principle. Exportation permitted regardless of prices.

	Import:	Above 80s.	Nominal duty of 4d.
		53/4 to 80s.	Duty of 8s.
		Below 53/4	Duty of 16s.
	Export:	Above 48s.	Nominal duty of 1s.
		Below 48s.	Free

1 Appendix B is drawn from Smart, 1910–17; Barnes, 1930; Fay, 1932; Gras, 1915; and Customs Blue Book, 1897. All prices refer specifically to wheat.

1673 Inauguration of export bounty; 'experimental,' in operation for about five years. (No mention of this act in Customs Blue Book, 1897, pp. 229–30.)

Import:	As 1670	
Export:	Above 48s.	Nominal duty of 1s.
	Below 48s.	Bounty of 5s.

1689 Reintroduction of export bounty system based on 1673. Frequently cited as 'first' corn bounty act in English history.

1700 Nominal duty on exportation to cease.

1747–73 Import rates periodically augmented after 1689 The rates ruling from 1747 to 1773 were:

Above 80s.	Duty of 1s. 4d.
53/4 to 80s.	Duty of 9s.
44s to 53/4	Duty of 17s.
Below 44s.	Duty of 22s.

1773 Effective 1774. Liberalization. Adam Smith remarked on this (Burke's) law (introduced by Thomas Pownall): 'With all its imperfections ... it is the best which the interests, prejudices, and temper of the times would admit of.'

Import:	Above 48s.	Nominal duty of 6d.
	44s. to 48s.	Duty of 17s.
	Below 44s.	Duty of 22s.
Export:	Above 44s.	Prohibited
	Below 44s.	Bounty of 5s.

1791 Increased protection; practically ineffectual after 1793.

Import:	Above 54s.	Nominal duty of 6d.
	50s. to 54s.	Duty of 2/6
	Below 50s.	Duty of 24/3
Export:	Above 46s.	Prohibited
	44 to 46s.	Free without bounty
	Below 44s.	Bounty of 5s.

1804 Increased protection; practically ineffectual

Import:	Above 66s.	Nominal duty of 7½d.
	63s to 66s.	Duty of 3s. 1½d.
	Below 63s.	Duty of 30s. 3¾d.

Export:	Above 54s.	Prohibited
	48s. to 54s.	Free without bounty
	Below 48s.	Bounty of 5s.

1814 All export bounties and restrictions repealed.

1815 New policy of absolute prohibition up to a fixed price level, and duty-free freedom of importation above that level.

Above 80s.	Free
Below 80s.	Prohibited

1822 Never operative. The 1822 scale of import duties was not to go into operation until the wheat price reached 80s., which it did not do during the period that the Act remained in force.

Above 85s.	Duty of 1s.
80–85s.	Duty of 5s.
70–80s.	Duty of 12s.
Below 70s.	Prohibited

1828 Abandonment of absolute protection up to a certain price; return to a sliding-scale of import duties.

Above 73s.	Duty of 1s.
72–73s.	Duty of 2s. 8d.
71–72s.	Duty of 6s. 8d.
70–71s.	Duty of 10s. 8d.
69–70s.	Duty of 13s. 8d.
68–69s.	Duty of 16s. 8d.
67–68s.	Duty of 18s. 8d.
66–67s.	Duty of 20s. 8d.[2]

1842 Major tariff reductions throughout the scale. Duty of 20s. at prices below 51s.

1846 Repeal. Fully effective 1849. A registration duty of 1s. lasted till 1869.

2 66s. was the 'pivot' price, i.e., the duty set against that price was the protection farmers were considered entitled to in 'normal' years. For each price reduction of 1s. from 66s. the duty increased by 1s. (Customs Blue Book, 1897, p. 247). For a critical contemporary account of the general principles, see J.S. Mill, 1827/1967.

APPENDIX C: HUSKISSON AND OTHERS AND THE ABANDONMENT OF AGRICULTURAL PROTECTION

Tucker (1978, 11) discerns a degree of hesitation regarding the abandonment of agricultural protection in Huskisson's public pronouncements absent from his anonymously published *Essays on Political Economy* (1830). As president of the Board of Trade, he pleaded for the appropriate moment, in the light of a depressed agriculture (26 February 1823; House of Commons, Parliamentary Debates, N.S., *8*, 278), and for time (17 June 1825, *13*, 1245–6). On 17 April 1826 he made out a case for free trade in corn on grounds of reduced tariffs on cottons (*15*, 342–51). In his first free-trade budget, he emphasized the quantitative significance of cotton exports in defending his new policy, and alluded to the encouragement afforded agriculture by the buoyancy of industrial activity (8 March 1824, *10*, 800, 803–7). On this feature of government policy – relating the fortunes of agriculture to that of commerce – see Hilton, 1977, 150. On Huskisson as a free trader, see also Smart, 1910–17, II, 289–90; and on Huskisson's alteration of position, see Allington, 1977.

Alexander Baring refers to Huskisson and to the Chancellor of the Exchequer (F.J. Robinson) as changing their positions on the 1815 system (18 March 1824, *10*, 1221, 1222–3, 1229–30; 28 April 1825, *13*, 288–98). One MP referred to Robinson as a 'deserter' (*10*, 1230–1).

In the debate of 8 March 1827, in reply to Brougham's question whether Lord Liverpool and the Chancellor had changed their minds, the Chancellor – who quotes from Lord Liverpool's address in 1815 on British national interests – replied that indeed he had (*16*, 1041–3). In the same debate, Sir Robert Peel justified his own change of heart (1064–9). The Earl of Darnley, speaking in the House of Lords, 11 May 1826, is paraphrased thus: 'what might be good in 1815, was not therefore good in 1826' (*15*, 1082–3). Sir Henry Parnell – a strong champion of prohibition in 1815 – called for full-fledged free trade in 1825 (25 March, *12*, 1229–32; 17 June, *13*, 1222–42) and elaborated further on his change of mind on 9 March 1827, *16*, 1101–5. Semmel (1970, 138) refers to Parnell's 'conversion' in 1827, but neglects the 1825 statements.

Henry Brougham changed his mind on the Corn Laws in 1826 – 'The present system was never intended as a final arrangement' – but he called for the replacement of effective import prohibition by a protective duty (*15*, 367; see Sockwell, 1994, 41).

The government was frequently charged with inconsistency for not acting vigorously to abolish the Corn Laws, considering its broader free-trade objectives (e.g., Baring, 8 March 1824, *10*, 814–15; 18 March 1824, *10*, 1222–3; 25 March 1825, *12*, 1226; Whitmore, 28 April 1825, *13*, 249–98; Ellice, 5 March 1824, *10*, 738–9; 9 February 1826, *14*, 156–7; Burdett, 6 March 1826, *14*, 1113–9). Parnell, in his June 1825 speech, maintained that the schedules were 'wholly at variance with the principles of "open competition" laid down.'

EIGHTEEN

Social reform and the role of government

I INTRODUCTION

Marx identified the Malthusian population doctrine with the 'iron law of wages' and read it as precluding social improvement under any form of institutional arrangement, whether capitalist or socialist (see Baumol, 1983, 306). The notion of an infinitely elastic labour supply at an exogenous wage is alive and well even in the non-Marxian literature, leading to the obvious question: 'Why did [Malthus] devote so much effort in the *Principles* to analysing the causes of economic progress, if any increase in material wealth is soon to be overtaken by an increase of population which reduces the average standard of living back to the subsistence level?' (Pullen, 1981a, 53) In some instances a spectrum of Malthusian doctrines is recognized, with Malthus himself located at various points along it from the 'hard' to the 'soft' end (Hutchison, 1978, 73), and his abandonment of the hard-line version – the adoption of a *psychological* in place of a *physiological* long-run labour supply curve – identified in the second edition of the *Essay on Population* (cf. Robbins, 1952, 77; for an early version see J.S. Mill 1848/1965, III, 753). But even so, the hard-line version is said to be analytically essential both for the construction of the 'canonical' classical growth model and for providing that model with any meaningful empirical content (e.g., Schumpeter, 1954, 569, 580; Blaug, 1958, 111, 120–1; Sowell, 1962; Stigler, 1965; Hutchison, 71; Blaug, 1985, 71; Stigler, 1981).

The notion that hard-line Malthusianism is essential to classical growth theory is very much mistaken. Only in the absence of prudential restraint is the corn-wage path inevitably downwards, assuming land scarcity, whereas the practice of prudential restraint permits progress towards the stationary state at a constant, even rising, per-capita wage. The rather derogatory reaction in the secondary literature to Malthus's allowances for prudential behaviour reflects a failure to appreciate the dynamic nature of his model-building – a tendency to interpret his growth-oriented perspective with the use of static tools (the standard wage, population coordinates), coupled with an unfortunate presumption that specific historical prediction provides the *raison d'être* for model-building in economics, which neglects its role of providing a classificatory framework for purposes of policy recommendation, a procedure tracing out, not what *will* happen, but what *can* happen under alternative reaction patterns. (In some cases, this latter is compounded by a word-minded confusion of Malthusian positive and normative economics.)

The first object of this chapter is to consider Malthus's specific policy objectives – namely, both 'high' wages and an increasing population, and the arguments supporting their compatibility (section II). Here we recall from Part I a restraint on the population growth rate apart from, or in addition to, decreasing productivity resulting from permanent land scarcity – namely, the requirement for time-consuming investment to render land fit for cultivation. Account was thus to be taken of the *time* dimension in defining productivity; a doubling of population, which may involve a falling marginal product if accomplished in ten years, can be attained with a lesser reduction if twenty years are allowed. The necessity for preliminary preparation suggests that, even should land scarcity not yet be manifest, the system runs into a form of temporary diminishing returns, and *a fortiori* over the stretch involving declining marginal productivity.

One outcome of the modification is that – failing land improvement – at each absolute population size the maximum population growth rate consistent with a given corn wage falls short of the potential rate. Second, the stationary state is reached at a lower population, although *with time* and allowing for the appropriate land improvements, the maximum level can be achieved. Now the policy objective discussed in Section II (a 'large' population at 'high' wages) turns critically on the notion of preparatory land improvement. For a given population size, assuming it to be desirable, otherwise possible only at low wages, may be achieved under more favourable conditions allowing for the foregoing type of improvement. Such improvement, it turns out, is most likely to occur *where the age distribution of population favours a high proportion of healthy adults* and is precluded by too rapid population expansion. From this perspective, population control becomes a measure to raise productivity, and thus allow for *future* expansion of population, which would not be necessarily at the cost of reduced wages.

In section III we expand on the sense of Malthus's 'pessimism.' The conclusion reached in chapter 16 regarding the contemporary 'population problem' will be recalled – namely, that even under conditions of accelerating food supplies – such as was manifest in recent experience – constraint of population growth below its maximum potential was essential to assure against a depression of living standards, a constraint which was consistent with an acceleration of population growth. Our concern now is specifically with social policy, and in this context we find Malthus (quite reasonably) adopting a more conservative or cautionary stance, which, despite the experience of impressive technological progress, presumes increasing land scarcity and the need for time-consuming land improvements. Under these circumstances there was a need for an appropriate *deceleration* of the rate of population growth to assure against a fall in living standards. But even this is far removed from any prediction of inevitable deterioration.

What follows in the present chapter expands on Malthus's reformism. That Malthus was not the 'reactionary' he is often made out to be has been convincingly argued by Levy (1978; see also 1996), who bases his case on statements indicating that Malthus came ultimately to recognise a trade-off between the 'misery' deriving from early marriage and large families, and the 'vice' attached to delayed marriage, and considered the latter as the lesser of two evils. In fact, already in 1798 he had intimated a deliberate preference for prudence – albeit accompanied by vice – as an alternative to misery, though not as clearly as in later editions. Furthermore, since (as Levy points out) Malthus was never to put great faith in 'moral restraint' – delayed marriage and abstinence from sexual relations – the somewhat greater optimism regarding future prospects in later editions is largely unrelated to the allowance for moral restraint strictly defined. These matters are dealt with in sections IV and V. The former touches on Malthus's allowance in 1798 for a psychological supply price of labour, his preference on moral ground for prudence (though implying vice) over poverty, and his rather high hopes for prudential behaviour and for high wages in a private-property system. The latter shows the transition from the first *Essay* to involve a reinforcement, not a new statement, of the preference for prudence over poverty, with the moral cost–benefit calculation now very clearly spelled out.

Thereafter I take up the more general issue of the role of government in economic activity. The stage is set in section VI by reference to various generalities laid down in the Introduction of the *Principles* warning against adherence – even formal adherence – to unqualified *laissez-faire.* But to discern Malthus's own position on particulars we must return to the *Essay.* Section VII expands on labour policy, pointing to a higher degree of interventionism in later versions compared with the 1798 *Essay*, including the extraordinarily 'un-Malthusian' case for family allowances under favourable conditions. Malthus's reformist perspective is then placed in a broader intellectual framework, involving issues relating to social control, including religion and education. Himmelfarb (1984, 122) paints too dark a picture when she insists of the later editions that 'Malthus, himself, even while delivering those tidings [regarding moral restraint], was unable to throw off the "melancholy" induced by the law of population. The revision of his thesis was only partial and hypothetical. Moral restraint was an addendum to misery and vice; it supplemented but did not supersede them. And it supplemented them not in the present but in some remote and problematic future.'

Examination of the specifics of Malthus's recommendations confirms a secular utilitarian perspective. The same holds true of Malthus's case for a more equal income distribution (section VIII). This utilitarian dimension will be carried over to chapter 19, where we elaborate on Malthus's theodicy and its economic implications.

Throughout I shall indicate the edition in which each passage on which I base my case first appears. This exercise reveals that Malthus's insistence not to push hard-line policy conclusions too far, intimated even in 1798, was well established by 1803. Our story is thus not one of a belated mellowing.

II POLICY OBJECTIVES: 'HIGH' WAGES AND POPULATION GROWTH

Marx's famous charge that Malthus 'condemned the worker to death from starvation, and to celibacy' (1862–3/1968, II, 119) is a parody. Malthus himself gave the reply to this charge in 1803 and all later editions: 'This prudential restraint, if it were generally adopted, by narrowing the supply of labour in the market, would, in the natural course of things, soon raise its price. This period of delayed gratification would be passed in saving the earnings which were above the wants of a single man, and in acquiring habits of sobriety, industry and economy, which would enable him, in a few years, to enter into the matrimonial contract without fear of its consequences. The operation of the preventive check in this way, by constantly keeping the population within the limits of the food, though constantly following its increase, would give a real value to the rise of wages ...' (1986, *3*, 475). 'The object of those who really wish to better the condition of the lower classes of society, must be to raise the relative proportion between the price of labour and the price of provisions, so as to enable the labourer to command a larger share of the necessaries and comforts of life. We have hitherto principally attempted to attain this end by encouraging the married poor, and consequently increasing the number of labourers, and overstocking the market with a commodity, which we still say that we wish to be dear ... It is really time now to try something else' (485–6).

Reduction of the birth rate was the key to increased wages, and one of the desirable consequences of the improved conditions would be reduced mortality. Exogenous improvements in health, including vaccination, which cut the mortality rate, were championed, subject to a compensatory reduction in the birth rate to prevent an excessive growth rate of population. In 1806 Malthus introduced a protest against blatant misinterpretations of his position on this matter:

In many parts of the Essay I have dwelt much on the advantage of rearing the requisite population from the smallest number of births. I have stated expressly, that a decrease of mortality of all ages is what we ought chiefly to aim at; and as the best criterion of happiness and good government, instead of the largeness of the proportion of births, which was the usual mode of judging, I have proposed the smallness of the proportion dying under the age of puberty. Conscious that I have never intentionally deviated from these principles, I might well be rather surprised to hear that I had been considered by some as the enemy to the introduction of the vaccine inoculation, which is calculated to attain the very end which I have uniformly considered as so desirable. I have indeed intimated what I still continue most firmly to believe, that if the resources of the country would not permanently admit of a greatly accelerated rate of increase in the population (and whether they would or would not, must certainly depend upon other causes besides the number of lives saved by the vaccine inoculation), one or two things would happen, either an increased mortality of some other diseases, or a diminution in the proportion of births. But I have expressed my conviction that the latter effect would take place; and therefore consistently with the opinions which I have always maintained, I ought to be, and am, one of the warmest friends to the introduction of the cow-pox. In making every exertion which I think likely to be effectual, to increase the comforts and diminish the mortality of the poor, I act in the most exact conformity to my principles. (1806, II, 513–15)

From 1803 on Malthus downplayed fears that wage increases achieved by prudential restraints on labour supply would damage competitiveness in foreign markets: 'If at some future period any approach should be made towards the more general prevalence of prudential habits with respect to marriage among the poor, from which alone any permanent and general improvement of their condition can arise, I do not think that the narrowest politician need be alarmed at it, from the fear of its occasioning such an advance in the price of labour as will enable our commercial competitors to undersell us in foreign markets' (1986, *3*, 568).[1] Malthus here presumes the abolition of the poor-relief system, and consequently both a higher efficiency of labour (once freed of the nefarious consequences of that system) and a lower tax burden. More important, there would be savings of resources otherwise lost in supporting children 'who die prematurely, from the consequences of poverty,' and the average price of food would be reduced 'from the demand being less frequently above the supply.'

1 See, however, Pullen, 1982, 276n, regarding the rather more qualified position of the *Principles*: 'Prudential habits with regard to marriage carried to a considerable extent, among the labouring classes of a country mainly dependent upon manufactures and commerce, might injure it.' This position was cited by Marx, 1965, I, 634. Any such concerns would be reduced when reference is made to 'the cost of producing the precious metals.

It would, however, be an error to suggest that Malthus favoured a stationary state (even at high wages) as the ideal. He certainly wanted 'a market rather understocked with labour' (488), but not 'in such a degree as to affect the wealth and prosperity of the country,' an allusion to aggregative indexes. It was 'of the very utmost importance to the happiness of mankind, that they should not increase too fast' (472) – not that population should be stationary. For, as he explained in 1806, he favoured growth of population at 'high' wages: 'It is an utter misconception of my argument to infer that I am an enemy to population. I am only an enemy to vice and misery, and consequently to that unfavourable proportion between population and food which produces these evils. But this unfavourable proportion has no necessary connection with the quantity of absolute population which a country may contain. On the contrary, it is more frequently found in countries which are very thinly peopled, than in those which are populous' (1806, II, 507–8). His critics had failed to appreciate that the proposed program of checks to the birth rate, designed to avoid 'poverty and premature mortality,' was consistent with population expansion, and had erroneously supposed 'that the *ultimate* object of my work is to check population, as if anything could be more desirable than the most rapid increase of population unaccompanied by vice and misery. But of course my ultimate object is to diminish vice and misery, and any checks to population which may have been suggested, are solely as means to accomplish this end. To a rational being, the prudential check to population ought to be considered as equally natural with the check from poverty and premature mortality which these gentlemen [his critics] seem to think so entirely sufficient and satisfactory; and it will readily occur to the intelligent reader, that one class of checks may be substituted for another, not only without essentially diminishing the population of a country, but even under a constantly progressive increase of it' (515–16).

What of the internal consistency of the *desiderata* alluded to in the foregoing passage? The key to higher standards, as we know, is a reduction in the birth rate by way of postponed marriage; and such a program would be consistent with achieving population increase, assuming a reduced *mortality* rate: 'Two or three years in the average age of marriage, by lengthening each generation, and tending, in a small degree, both to diminish the prolifickness of marriages, and the number of born living to be married, may make a considerable difference in the rate of increase, and be adequate to allow for a considerably diminished mortality' (536–7; see also chapter 1, p. 60). Moreover, the potential for productivity increase (attributable *inter alia* to land improvement) is greater in the case of a population comprising a high proportion of healthy adults; the program, by altering the age distribution, would result ultimately in the creation of 'fresh resources' for the support of population growth under relatively favourable circumstances: 'Without a diminished proportion of births, we cannot attain any *permanent* improvement in the health and happiness of the mass of the people, and cannot secure that description of population, which, by containing a larger share of adults, is best calculated to create fresh resources, and consequently to encourage a continued increase of efficient population' (550; see chapter 1, p. 61).[2]

A strong confirmation of the significance of the quality of human capital is provided by a warning given in the *Letter to Samuel Whitbread* (1807) against any careless extension of the Poor Laws which would remove the stimulus to prudence: 'as it is physically impossible for the natural and acquired resources of any country long to support an unrestricted population, we should soon see a most unfavourable change take place in the present small mortality, which we justly consider as one of the great tests of our national happiness; and a large proportion of deaths would invariably accompany the large proportion of births. The births however might still exceed the deaths, *the population might still be increasing, but the character of it would be greatly changed; it would consist of a much larger proportion of persons not capable of adding by their exertions to the resources of the state*; each generation would pass away in a more rapid succession; and the greatness of the mortality would sufficiently indicate the misery of the state of the society' (1807b/1986, *4*, 15; emphasis added). Schumpeter must have been unaware of these texts when he charged Malthus with failing 'to discuss any effects of his moral restraint other than the effect on numbers – for example, effects on the quality of the population, or on schemes for motivation' (1954, 580).

The immediate policy implications are unambiguous. An increase in population size that is otherwise achievable only at low wages might with patience be attained with no deterioration. And as Malthus expressed it in 1806, 'there is no man who has the slightest feeling for the happiness of the most numerous class of society, or has even just views of policy on the subject, who would not rather choose that the requisite population should be obtained by such a price of labour, combined with such habits, as would occasion a very small mortality, than from a great proportion of births, of which comparatively few would reach manhood' (1806, II, 551–2n). It is clear that increased population increase was an objective; that the means to that end were either a high birth rate accompanied by low wages and high mortality, or a low birth rate accompanied by high wages and low mortality; and that Malthus unambiguously championed the latter alternative.

2 In this context we find some fine examples of a utility calculus: 'A young person saved from death is more likely to contribute to the creation of fresh resources than another birth. It is a great loss of labour and food to begin over again. And universally it is true, that under similar circumstances, that article will come the cheapest to market which is accompanied by fewest failures' (1806, II, 514n; 1803/1986, *3*, 582). 'Every loss of a child from the consequences of poverty, must evidently be preceded and accompanied by great misery to individuals; and, in a public view, every child that dies under ten years of age, is a loss to the nation of all that had been expended in its subsistence till that period' (1986, *3*, 565).

Various references to an increase in food supplies prior to an increase in population can be appreciated in these terms. Productivity increase reflecting investment in agricultural improvement is what Malthus apparently had in mind in 1803: 'We are not ... to relax our efforts in increasing the quantity of provisions; but to combine another effort with it, that of keeping the population, when once it had been overtaken, at such a distance behind as to effect the relative proportion which we desire; and thus unite the two grand desiderata, a great actual population, and a state of society in which squalid poverty and dependence are comparatively but little known; two objects which are far from being incompatible' (1986, *3*, 486). 'One objection that may be made to this plan [reduced population growth rate under conditions favourable to agricultural investment], is the diminution of population that it would cause. It is to be considered, however, that this diminution is merely relative; and when once this relative diminution has been effected, by keeping the population stationary, while the supply of food has increased, it might then start afresh, and continue increasing for ages, with the increase of food, maintaining always the same relative proportion to it. I can easily conceive that this country, with a proper direction of the national industry might, in the course of some centuries, contain two or three times its present population, and yet every man in the kingdom be much better fed and clothed that he is at present. While the springs of industry continue in vigour, and a sufficient part of that industry is directed to agriculture, we need be under no apprehensions of a deficient population ...' (488–9).

These statements are so 'optimistic' as to suggest that population increase can be *indefinitely* maintained at constant wages, provided its *rate of increase* is suitably restrained. In that case stationary states will at most constitute temporary breathing stops. But in all likelihood this does not constitute Malthus's considered opinion. At the outset of the *Essay* he had clarified that an *unlimited* potential to the expansion of food supplies was an unrealizable supposition; and this clarification is emphasized in the 1806 edition: 'I have allowed the produce of the earth to be unlimited which is certainly going too far' (1806, II, 516–17).[3] In terms of our reconstruction, the potential for land preparation tends to weaken; even allowing for clearing, draining, hedging, and so forth – activities that cannot strictly be classified as 'technical change' – 'diminishing returns' cannot be entirely avoided. But exogenous technological change – reflecting new knowledge – must also be taken into account; and it appears that the constrained rate of increase of food supplies allowed for improvements of this kind too, so that falling agricultural productivity amounts to an

3 Cf: 'Of the possibility of increasing very considerably the effective population of this country, I have expressed myself in some parts of my work more sanguinely, perhaps, than, experience would warrant' (1806, II, 516; 1986, *3*, 583).

empirical proposition incorporating all forces playing favourably and unfavourably on efficiency. Ultimately, then, growth must cease. Malthus certainly favoured population expansion, but he believed there to be absolute limits. It was his objective to assure that, in the stationary state, wages should be high. But 'ultimate' stationariness was a far-distant prospect; in the meantime population might grow without a fall in wages, provided its rate of increase was appropriately limited.

III ON MALTHUS'S 'PESSIMISM'

Malthus's 'pessimism' is considerably constrained on our reading. It amounts to the proposition that, in the absence of prudential or moral checks to the growth rate of population, average living standards must 'ultimately' fall. In this limited sense both the effect of land scarcity and the need for time-consuming land improvements are continuously making themselves felt. Second, the checks, to a degree, have their source in an awareness of this consequence. It has been held that Malthus neglected entirely 'the possibility that people may inhibit their reproductive powers for reasons totally unconnected with any foresight of difficulties in providing subsistence for children' (Flew, 1970, 37). Though this assertion is stated rather too strongly (in so far as Malthus appreciated that some men merely sought to avoid family responsibility), yet in this sense, too, population pressure would always be constantly felt – in the upper classes, fear of a 'fall in station'; and, in the lower, fear of actual poverty.

These notions of population pressure are, however, not to be equated with actual population pressure in a literal sense of the term. Malthus in 1803 unfortunately retained the remark that 'there are few states in which there is not a constant effort in the population to increase beyond the means of subsistence. This constant effort as constantly tends to subject the lower classes of society to distress, and to prevent any great permanent amelioration of their condition' (1986, *3*, 17).[4] But on his own terms a 'tendency' is not to be understood as a 'prediction' (see below, section IX). Similarly, he was asking for trouble by introducing a reference in 1817 to a 'natural tendency of population to increase beyond the powers of the earth to produce food for it' (1817, III, 412), when he himself was pointing out the solution, and at times emphasizing the actual significance of the checks to the birth rate, even under unfavourable circumstances: 'Universally, the practice of mankind on the subject of marriage has been much superior to their theories; and however frequent may have been the declamations on the duty of entering into this state, and the advantage of

4 In the first *Essay*, the formulation was stronger: 'Yet in all societies, even those that are the most vicious, the tendency to a virtuous attachment is so strong, that there is a constant effort towards an increase of population. This constant effort ...' (1986, *1*, 14).

early unions to prevent vice, each individual has practically found it necessary to consider of the means of supporting a family, before he ventured to take so important a step. That great *vis medicatrix reipublicae*, the desire of bettering our condition, and the fear of making it worse, has been constantly in action, and has been constantly directing people into the right road, in spite of all the declamations which tended to lead them aside. Owing to this powerful spring of health in every state, which is nothing more than an inference from the general course of the laws of nature, irresistibly forced on each man's attention, the prudential check to marriage has increased in Europe; and it cannot be unreasonable to conclude that it will still make further advances' (1803/1986, *3*, 571). The full implication of the reference to 'declarations which tended to lead them aside' can be appreciated only if we have in mind Church doctrine regarding marriage as a remedy for fornication, based on St Paul's 1 Corinthians: 7, formulated in the *Book of Common Prayer*, and read at the marriage ceremony (Levy, 1992). Malthus's deflection of the religious case will be elaborated below, pp. 907–8.

Paradoxically, even Malthus's 'pessimism' has an optimistic side to it, for it is precisely the 'tendency' of population to increase, in the sense of the desire for marriage and procreation, that assures the necessary motivation for (aggregate) expansion. For 'the desire of the means of subsistence would be comparatively confined in its effects, and would fail of producing that general activity so necessary to the improvement of the human faculties, were it not for the strong and universal effort of population, to increase with greater rapidity than its supplies' (1803/1986, *3*, 471). Thus, while population 'should not increase too fast ... it does not appear, that the object to be accomplished would admit of any very considerable diminution in the desire of marriage. It is clearly the duty of each individual not to marry till he has a prospect of supporting his children; but it is at the same time to be wished, that he should retain undiminished his desire of marriage, in order that he may exert himself to realize this prospect, and be stimulated to make provision for the support of greater numbers' (472).

IV THE FIRST (1798) *ESSAY*: PRUDENCE VS POVERTY

Malthus's original objective in writing his *Essay* was, of course, to counter various utopian reformers. A system of perfect equality – without private property and the marriage institution whereby couples bear the cost of raising their own children[5] (more generally a system governed by 'benevolence' rather than 'self-interest') – would inevitably fail in consequence of

5 Cf. Levy, 1978, 272: 'In order to explain the decision to marry, the classics [following Smith] argued, we must explain the costs of children, since in a world without effective mechanical contraception children will regularly follow marriage.'

population pressure on scarce land (1986, *1*, 67–8; see chapter 1: III). Failure of the experiment would lead to the re-establishment of a private-property system and the reinstitution of marriage, institutions which 'make every man provide for his own children,' thereby 'operat[ing] in some respect, as a measure and guide, in the increase of population; as it might be expected that no man would bring beings into the world, for whom he could not find the means of support' (72). In all this Malthus made no serious attempt to consider prospects for population control under communal arrangements; unlike Godwin, he took for granted that people would not act with an eye to the social consequences of their private behaviour (Levy, 1978, 279). None the less, rejection of utopian communism was not based upon the supposed *inevitability* of population pressure, as Marx represented the matter, but its supposed inevitability in the absence of an institutional framework which gives free rein to private calculation. (Even this abstracts from legal restraints; see below, p. 910.) Prudential behaviour, in brief, was a cultural variable, the advantage lying with the private-property system – assuming always that it is allowed to function effectively. And precisely for this reason Malthus castigated the contemporary Poor Laws as an ill-thought-out stimulus to early marriage (1986, *1*, 32f.).

A famous passage referring to 'reason' which asks man 'whether he may not bring beings into the world, for whom he cannot provide the means of subsistence' appears already in the first *Essay* (14). In fact, the operation of the preventive check characterized in varying degrees all classes in contemporary England (26). Delay of marriage in the highest rank was in order to prevent the expected reduction in 'fancied pleasures' that marriage and children would entail, and in that of gentlemen to prevent a fall in social rank occasioned by the costs of raising a family. 'The sons of tradesmen and farmers' were exhorted not to marry until able to support a family. As for the labourer: 'The labourer who earns eighteen pence a day, and lives with some degree of comfort as a single man, will hesitate a little before he divides that pittance among four or five, which seems to be but just sufficient for one. Harder fare and harder labour he would submit to, for the sake of living with the woman that he loves; but he must feel conscious, if he thinks at all, that, should he have a large family, and any ill luck whatever, no degree of frugality, no possible exertion of his manual strength, could preserve him from the heart-rending sensation of seeing his children starve, or of forfeiting his independence, and being obliged to the parish for their support' (27). There were yet stronger impediments in the case of the single unproductive labourer (menial servant), given the alternatives of high earnings and easy work that would have to be forgone: 'By much the greater part, therefore, deterred by [an] uninviting view of their future situation, content themselves with remaining single where they are' (28). Malthus was, moreover, very conscious of differences in cultural standards within the working class of the same country and at the same period – clear evidence of a psychological minimum-supply price amenable to influence – and even emphasized the difficulty of lowering standards: 'In the different states of Europe there must be some variations in the proportion between the number of inhabitants, and the quantity of food consumed, arising from the different habits of living that prevail in each state. The labourers of the south of England are so accustomed to eat fine wheaten bread, they will suffer themselves to be half starved, before they will submit to live like the Scotch peasants. They might perhaps in time, by the constant operation of the hard law of necessity, be reduced to live even like the lower Chinese: and the country would then, with the same quantity of food, support a greater population. But to effect this must always be a most difficult, and every friend to humanity will hope, an abortive attempt' (49).

And now to the principal point for us. By 'prudence' we are to understand delayed marriage, probably *accompanied by vice*: 'The effects ... of these [preventive] restraints upon marriage are but too conspicuous in the consequent vices that are produced in almost every part of the world; vices, that are continually involving both sexes in inextricable unhappiness' (28). Similarly, prudential considerations 'are calculated to prevent, and certainly do prevent, a very great number in all civilized nations from pursuing the dictate of nature in an early attachment to one woman. And this restraint almost necessarily, though not absolutely so, produces vice' (14). Yet notwithstanding, in the course of his case against the outdoor-relief system, Malthus intimated a preference for prudence as a necessary evil for the sake of avoiding misery: 'Every obstacle in the way of marriage must undoubtedly be considered a species of unhappiness. But as from the laws of our nature some check to population must exist, it is better that it should be checked from a foresight of the difficulties attending a family, and the fear of dependent poverty, than that it should be encouraged, only to be repressed afterwards by want and sickness' (35). It may always be said that Malthus was specifically expressing a choice for delayed marriage over marriage at an early age (despite the concomitant vice) when early marriage is *artificially encouraged*, but did not commit himself when the choice was between delay of marriage (vice) and early marriage (misery) in a freely operating system. But considering the very explicit statements regarding the trade-off between vice and misery in later editions (below, pp. 887f.), one suspects that his position in 1798 was not thus limited.

More important, there are strong indications to this effect in the 1798 *Essay* itself, in Malthus's repeated championship of improved living standards, the maintenance of which almost necessarily entails the exercise of a higher degree of prudence – having in mind the near certainty that this restraint 'produces vice.' The choice of prudence over poverty is thus implicit in Malthus's rejection of the 'common complaint among master manufacturers that high wages ruin all their workmen,' on the grounds that these men would 'save a part of their high wages for the future support of their families, instead of spending it in drunkenness and dissipation, if they did not rely on parish assistance for support in case of accidents' (34). Various 'palliatives' suggested by Malthus, including agricultural subsidies or 'premiums' and the encouragement of tillage relative to grazing, were designed to 'furnish the market with an increasing quantity of healthy work, and [which] at the same time, by augmenting the produce of the country, would raise the comparative price of labour, and ameliorate the condition of the labourer' (37). And a complaint against Godwin is that he failed to consider the potential of reforms beneficial to labour – apparently permanently so – within the private-property system: 'Perhaps there is no possible way in which wealth could, in general, be employed so beneficially to a state, and particularly to the lower orders of it, as by improving and rendering productive that land, which to a farmer would not answer the expense of cultivation. Had Mr. Godwin exerted his energetic eloquence in painting the superior worth and usefulness of the character who employed the poor in this way, to him who employed them in narrow luxuries, every enlightened man must have applauded his efforts. The increasing demand for agricultural labour must always tend to better the condition of the poor; and if the accession of work be of this kind, so far is it from being true, that the poor would be obliged to work ten hours, for the same price, that they before worked eight, that the very reverse would be the fact; and a labourer might then support his wife and family as well as by the labour of six hours, as he could before by the labour of eight' (106).

Malthus did not, however, carry through with a far-reaching interventionist program.[6] Apart from foreign-trade policy, it was by and large 'the generous system of perfect liberty adopted by Dr. Adam Smith and the French economists' that he relied upon (102n), for much was expected merely from the correction of faulty institutions.[7] There is, it is true, the denial that living standards would be raised to any major degree: 'The principal argument against the perfectibility of man and society remains whole and unimpaired from any thing that [Godwin] has advanced. And as far as I can trust my own judgement, this argument appears to be conclusive, not only against the perfectibility of man, in the enlarged sense in which Mr. Godwin understands the term, but against any very marked and striking change for the better, in the form and structure of general society; by which I mean, any great and decided amelioration in the condition of the lower classes of mankind, the most numerous, and,

6 For an elaboration, see below, section VII.

7 For example, improved mobility with abolition of the poor laws would allow transfer 'wherever there was a prospect of a greater plenty of work, and a higher price for labour' (37).

consequently, in a general view of the subject, the most important part of the human race' (98; cf. also 36–7). But what precisely is intended by a 'great and decided' improvement? In this context it is one similar to recent North American standards: 'Were I to live a thousand years, and the laws of nature to remain the same, I should little fear, or rather little hope, a contradiction from experience, in asserting, that no possible sacrifices or exertions of the rich, in a country which had been long inhabited, could for any time place the lower classes of the community in a situation equal, with regard to circumstances, to the situation of the common people, about thirty years ago, in the northern states of America.' There is still considerable scope for improvement within these limits. Comparison with the American case indicates a related sense in which 'major' improvement is ruled out – namely, the impossibility of maintaining high standards without any concern whatsoever for the rate of population growth: 'The lower classes of people in Europe may, at some future period, be much better instructed than they are at present; they may be taught to employ the little spare time they have in many better ways than at the alehouse; they may live under better and more equal laws than they have ever hitherto done, perhaps, in any country; and I even conceive it possible, though not probable, that they may have more leisure; but it is not in the nature of things, that they can be awarded such a quantity of money or subsistence, as will allow them all to marry early, in the full confidence that they shall be able to provide with ease for a numerous family.'

The denial of the possibility of any 'major' improvement in earnings may also be better appreciated by reference to the potential for a diminution of the 'passion between the sexes' (76). Godwin put his faith in the potentialities for intellectual improvement sufficient to weaken sexual passion, whereas Malthus thought him a dreamer, since 'no observable progress whatever has hitherto been made' (78), and prospects were bleak under the best of circumstances: 'Allowing, as I should be inclined to do ..., that great intellectual exertions tend to diminish the empire of this passion over man; it is evident that the mass of mankind must be improved more highly than the brightest ornaments of the species at present, before any difference can take place sufficient sensibly to affect population. I would by no means suppose that the mass of mankind has reached its term of improvement; but the principal argument of this essay tends to place in a strong point of view, the improbability, that the lower classes of people in any country, should ever be sufficiently free from want and labour, to obtain any high degree of intellectual improvement.' But to assert that the wage rate could never rise sufficiently to allow a 'sensible' diminution in sexual passion is not to deny more modest increases in living standards – increases, of course, which could only be maintained by the exercise of prudence, notwithstanding that prudence 'almost necessarily ... produces vice.'

V THE TRANSITION FROM 1798: THE MORAL CALCULUS ELABORATED

By 'moral restraint' – the check to population growth formally introduced in the second edition of (1803) – was intended the restraint from marriage 'which is not followed by irregular gratifications' (1986, *2*, 16).[8] Malthus himself pointed to the new check and its practical implications in the famous Preface to the second edition: 'Throughout the whole of the present work, I have so far differed in principle from the former, as to suppose the action of another check to population possible, which does not strictly come under the head either of vice or misery; and, in the latter part, I have endeavoured to soften some of the harshest conclusions of the first essay. In doing this, I hope I have not violated the principles of just reasoning; nor expressed any opinion respecting the probable improvement of society, in which I am not borne out by the experience of the past. To those who shall still think that any check to population whatever, would be worse than the evils which it would relieve, the conclusions of the former essay will remain in full force; and if we adopt this opinion, we shall be compelled to acknowledge that the poverty and misery that prevail among the lower classes of society are absolutely irremediable' (iii).[9]

This statement, which has done much to stamp the first *Essay* as a thoroughly depressing document, is misleading. Malthus had *not* shown in 1798 that 'the poverty and misery that prevail among the lower classes of society are absolutely irremediable' – only that they are so in the absence of prudence. And he had from the outset recommended delay of marriage despite the 'vicious' consequences. Equally important, the implications of 'moral restraint' must not be exaggerated. As David Levy has observed, 'the addition in the later editions of the possibility of moral restraint – the possibility of a chaste life outside of marriage – is not important for the positive economics,' since Malthus did not believe that the period before marriage would be spent chastely (1978, 280; cf. Coats, 1971, 163).

8 Cf. the explanatory note added in 1806 in response to criticism: 'It will be observed, that I here use the term *moral* in its most confined sense. By moral restraint I would be understood to mean a restraint from marriage, from prudential motives, with a conduct strictly moral during the period of this restraint; and I have never intentionally deviated from this sense. When I have wished to consider the restraint from marriage unconnected with its consequences, I have either called it prudential restraint, or a part of the preventive check, of which indeed it forms the principal branch' (1806, I, 19–20n; 1986, *2*, 16n).

James, 1979, 68–9, suggests there are hints of 'moral restraint' in Malthus's correspondence of 1798. The allowance in the first *Essay* itself that delayed marriage produces vice but 'not absolutely so' (above, p. 883) implies the notion of moral restraint. For an earlier observation to this effect see Fetter, 1898, 161. But Fetter went too far when he asserted that Malthus *emphasized* the restraint; it is largely prudential control that he then had in mind.

9 For an interesting discussion of 'What is moral restraint?' see Eversley, 1959, 244–9.

It is true enough that 'in economic theory a behavioural change that alters one of the parameters of a system in equilibrium is of interest solely because of its effect upon the value of that parameter. Whether that change is ethically good, bad or neutral is irrelevant to the new equilibrium values of the dependent variables' (Waterman, 1991, 137–8). But the point at the issue for us is precisely whether Malthus saw in his moral restraint an *effective* reinforcement of delayed marriage. *He did not*: 'In my review of the different stages of society,' Malthus added in 1806, 'I have been accused of not allowing sufficient weight in the prevention of population to moral restraint; but when the confined sense of the term, which I have here explained, is adverted to, I am fearful that I shall not be found to have erred much in this respect. I should be very glad to believe myself mistaken' (1806, I, 20n). Malthus doubted whether moral restraint would be generally practised. But while he regretted the 'evils and unhappiness, particularly to the female sex, arising from promiscuous intercourse,' so that it was impossible 'for any person, who acknowledges the principle of utility as the great foundation of morals, to escape the conclusion, that moral restraint, till we are in a condition to support a family, is the strict line of duty,' he added that 'few ... can be less sanguine in their expectations of any great change in the general conduct of men on this subject than I am' (1803/1986, *3*, 482; but see 572, below, p. 889, for an apparently more optimistic view).

To have allowed much weight in practice to 'moral restraint' would have been to concede too much to Godwin, and this Malthus did not do, despite the Preface of 1803.[10] Even in the absence of moral restraint, runs the clear message, prudential delay of marriage was to be welcomed. Now the reason for this position is that misery also entails vice; on a balance of moral costs and benefits, prudence with 'irregular gratification' was preferable. Malthus, in brief, 'tolerated immoral restraint as the lesser of two evils' (Levy, 1978, 280). We shall review the evidence. Consider first the remarkable account introduced in 1803 of the 'vices' attached to poverty. These include crime:

10 Southey (1803, 299), early on, read the new essay as a weakening of the case against Godwin. More recently, Stigler also maintained that 'Malthus, capitulated, while still claiming victory ... Given the possible – though in Malthus' opinion the improbable – efficacy of moral restraint, Godwin had carried this issue' (1965, 165). Waterman argues that, for Malthus, perfectibility is impossible without private-property institutions, for which reason nothing was conceded to Godwin (1991, 140–3). But in this context Waterman seems to confound simple 'prudence' with moral restraint. For Malthus, private-property institutions, including the marriage relation, play on 'prudential' behaviour, not 'moral' behaviour. (On this issue, see Levy, 1996, n 32.) It is noteworthy, though, that Godwin himself believed that 'virtue' *would* prevail in his utopian society alone (Godwin, 1801, 72).

To the general prevalence of indigence, and the extraordinary encouragements which we afford in this country to a total want of foresight and prudence among the common people, is to be attributed the principal part[11] of those continual depredations on property, and other more atrocious crimes, which drive us to the painful resource of such a number of executions. According to Mr. Colquhoun, above twenty thousand miserable individuals of various classes, rise up every morning without knowing how or by what means they are to be supported during the passing day, or where, in many instances, they are to lodge on the succeeding night. It is by these unhappy persons that the principal depredations on the public are committed; and, supposing but few of them to be married, and driven to these acts from the necessity of supporting their children; yet still it will not cease to be true, that the too great frequency of marriage among the poorest classes of society is one of the principal causes of the temptations to these crimes. A considerable part of these unhappy wretches will probably be found to be the offspring of such marriages, educated in workhouses where every vice is propagated, or bred up at home in filth and rags, with an utter ignorance of every moral obligation. A still greater part perhaps consists of persons, who, being unable for some time to get employment owing to the full supply of labour, have been urged to these extremities by their temporary wants; and having thus lost their characters, are rejected even when their labour may be wanted, by the well-founded caution of civil society. (1986, *3*, 490)

Also included under 'vice' is the degradation of young girls: 'squalid poverty, particularly when joined with idleness, is a state the most unfavourable to chastity that can well be conceived. The passion is as strong, or nearly so, as in other situations; and every restraint on it from personal respect, or a sense of morality, is generally removed. There is a degree of squalid poverty, in which, if a girl was brought up, I should say that her being really modest at twenty was an absolute miracle. Those persons must have extraordinary minds indeed, and such as are not usually formed under similar circumstances, who can continue to respect themselves, when no other person whatever respects them. If the children thus brought up were even to marry at twenty, it is probable that they would have passed some years in vicious habits, before that period' (491–2).

There follows a strong warning of the consequences of 'the vice of promiscuous intercourse' attached to mere prudence: 'If the prevalence of the preventive check to population in a sufficient degree were to remove many of those diseases, which now afflict us, yet be accompanied by a considerable increase of the vice of promiscuous intercourse, it is probable that the disorders and unhappiness, the physical and moral evils arising from this vice, would increase in strength and degree, and, admonishing

11 The 1986 edition fails to catch the true 1803 rendition, here writing 'a considerable part,' which is in fact the version introduced in 1807 (1807, II, 277).

us severely of our error, would point to the only line of conduct approved by nature, reason and religion, abstinence from marriage till we can support our children, and chastity till that period arrives' (495). Yet, notwithstanding, weighing the alternatives leads to an unambiguous conclusion: 'I should be most extremely sorry to say any thing which could either directly or remotely be construed unfavourably to the cause of virtue: but I certainly cannot think that the vices which relate to the sex, are the only vices which are to be considered in a moral question; or that they are even the greatest and the most degrading to the human character ... [T]here are other vices, the effects of which are still more pernicious; and there are other situations, which lead more certainly to moral offenses than the refraining from marriage. Powerful as may be the temptations to a breach of chastity, I am inclined to think that they are impotent, in comparison of the temptations arising from continued distress. A large class of women, and many men, I have no doubt, pass a considerable part of their lives in moral restraint; but I believe there will be found very few, who pass through the ordeal of squalid and hopeless poverty, or even of long continued embarrassed circumstances, without a considerable moral degradation of character' (489). The same estimate emerges in a comment on an observed increase in checks to marriage in contemporary Europe – Norway, Switzerland, as well as England and Scotland: 'Experience ... seems to teach us, that it is possible for moral and physical causes to counteract the effects that might at first be expected from an increase of the preventive check; but allowing all the weight to these effects which is in any degree probable, it may be safely asserted, that the diminution of the vices arising from indigence, would fully counterbalance them; and that all the advantages of diminished mortality, and superior comforts, which would certainly result from an increase of the preventive check, may be placed entirely on the side of the gains to the cause of happiness and virtue' (572). And similarly in a reply (introduced in 1806) to Arthur Young's criticism that Malthus had assumed 'perfect chastity in the single state':[12] 'Perfect virtue is indeed absolutely necessary to enable men to avoid *all* the moral and physical evils which depend upon his own conduct; but who ever expected perfect virtue upon earth? I have said what I conceive to be strictly true, that it is our duty to defer marriage till we can feed our children, and that it is also our duty not to indulge ourselves in vicious gratifications; but I have never said that I expected either, much less both, of these duties to be completely fulfilled ... Whatever I may have said in drawing a picture *professedly* visionary, for the sake of illustration, in the practical application of my principles I have taken man as he is, with all his imperfections on his head. And thus viewing him, and knowing that some

12 'On the application of the principles of population, to the question of assigning land to cottagers,' *Annals of Agriculture* 41/239 (1804), 208–31.

checks to population must exist, I have not the slightest hesitation in saying, that the prudential check to marriage is better than premature mortality. And in this decision I feel myself completely justified by experience' (1806, II, 537–8). That the emphasis, in practice, is on 'prudence' not 'moral restraint' emerges also in the *Encyclopaedia Britannica* article 'Population': 'The delay of marriage, owing to the difficulty of providing for a family, when the degree of irregularity to which it may lead cannot be ascertained, may be usefully called the prudential restraint on marriage and population. And this will be found to be the chief mode in which the preventive check practically operates' (1824b/1986, *4*, 204). Malthus was on the defensive against critics who believed he considered vice or misery to be unavoidable. But this criticism was justified precisely because moral restraint, in Malthus's view, could *not* be much relied upon.[13]

VI PROLOGUE TO THE THEORY OF ECONOMIC POLICY: THE *PRINCIPLES*

The foregoing discussion has turned on various implications for social policy to be found in the *Essay on Population*. In this section I bring attention to broader generalizations regarding the role of government appearing in the *Principles*.

A central theme of the methodological Introduction is that failure to formalize the *exceptions* to 'general rules' might undermine the reputation of economic theory. This is illustrated (in 1820) by the general rule of governmental non-interference: 'It is, for instance, one of the general rules in political economy, that governments should not interfere in the direction of capital and industry, but leave every person, so long as he obeys the laws of justice, to pursue his own interest in his own way, as the best security for the constant and equable supply of the national wants. Though to this rule they allow that exceptions may possibly occur; yet thinking that the danger from the officious meddling of governments is so much greater than any which could arise from the neglect of such exceptions, they would be inclined to make the rule universal. In this, however, I cannot agree. Though I should most readily allow that altogether more evil is likely to arise from governing too much, than from a tendency to the other extreme; yet, still, if the consequences of not attending to these exceptions were of sufficient magnitude and frequency to be conspicuous to the public, I should be decidedly of opinion, that the cause of general principles was much more likely to lose than to gain by concealment' (1820, 13–14).

The illustration from the case of non-interference of the need to admit

13 Allowing 'promiscuity' as an alternative to the misery and vice of poverty is inconsistent with a *global* rejection of mechanical contraception. This matter is taken up in chapter 19, pp. 935, 944–5.

exceptions to general rules, is removed from the second edition. But another passage with a similar message is retained and too much should not be made of the omission: 'It is obviously ... impossible for a government strictly to let things take their natural course; and to recommend such a line of conduct, without limitations and exceptions, could not fail to bring disgrace upon general principles, as totally inapplicable to practice' (1820, 20; 1836, 16). Moreover, the position 'that altogether more evil is likely to arise from governing too much, than from a tendency to the other extreme' is implicit in a passage common to both versions on the necessity for 'science' and 'professional knowledge' in approaching the problem of legitimate intervention: 'It may, however, safely be asserted, that a propensity to govern too much is a certain indication of ignorance and rashness. The ablest physicians are the most sparing in the use of medicine, and the most inclined to trust to the healing power of nature. The statesman, in like manner, who knows the most of his business, will be the most unwilling to interrupt the natural direction of industry and capital. But both are occasionally called upon to interfere, and the more science they respectively possess, the more judiciously will they do it; nor will the acknowledged propriety of interfering but little supersede, in any degree, the use of the most extensive professional knowledge in both cases' (1820, 20–1; 1836, 16). There was, then, apparently no change in the presumption against excessive interference, though not against interference as such.

Malthus leaves the specifics of his own position open, which is to be expected in the context, concerning himself rather with generalizations relating to some characteristic difficulties facing policy makers. While there was a 'universally acknowledged' role for the state – perhaps Malthus had in mind Smith's famous generalizations – 'and though the line appears to be drawn with tolerable precision, when it is considered generally ... when we come to particulars, doubts may arise, and certainly in many instances have arisen, as to the subjects to be included in this classification. To what extent education and the support of the poor should be public concerns? What share the Government should take in the construction and maintenance of roads, canals, public docks? What course it should adopt with regard to colonization and emigration, and in the support of forts and establishments in foreign countries? On all these questions, and many others, there may be differences of opinion; and on all these questions the sovereign and his ministers are called upon to decide' (1820, 18–19; 1836, 14–15).

The practical difficulties of judgment were compounded when it came to the repeal of existing legislation 'formed at a period comparatively unenlightened': 'But to see fully the amount of partial evil arising from present change, and the extent of general good to be effected by it, so as to warrant active interference, requires no inconsiderable share of knowledge and judgement' (1820, 19) – this is absent from the 1836 version;

'while to remain inactive under such circumstances, can only be justified by a conviction, founded on the best grounds, that in any specific change contemplated, taken in all its consequences, the balance of evil will preponderate' – a utilitarian conception (1820, 19; 1836, 15). The deletion from the second edition of the requirement for caution before proceeding to reform is probably of little significance, although that version continues with a further passage that focuses on a different sort of caution: 'To proceed straight forward in the rigid application of general principles without any reference to the difficulties created by the existing laws of the country, and its actual situation and circumstances, might plunge it into such complicated distress, as not only to excite the public indignation against the authors of such measures, but to bring permanent discredit upon the principles which had prompted them.'[14]

Malthus closed by pointing to the necessity of taxation which also rendered 'letting things alone' academic. The problem was to assure 'the least possible prejudice to the prosperity of the state, and the happiness of individuals' (1820, 19; 1836, 15). And here sound theory was essential.

VII LABOUR POLICY AND SOCIAL CONTROL

For a more specific picture Malthus's actual position on the role of government, we return to the *Essay*.[15] As we noted earlier, though some allowance was made for agricultural subsidies in 1798, this sort of intervention is scarcely conspicuous (above, p. 884). The impression that Malthus played down the potential of *direct* intervention with an eye to agricultural expansion – though he did not absolutely exclude it – is further confirmed by an addition of 1806: 'To restore our independence, and build our national greatness and commercial prosperity on the sure foundation of agriculture, it is evidently not sufficient, to propose premiums for tillage, to cultivate this or that waste, or even to pass a general inclosure bill, though these are all excellent as far as they go' (1806, II, 270–1).[16] The general perspective in this regard is nicely summarized in the following statement of 1803, which is carried over to all later editions: 'It is not probable that any country with a large territory should ever be completely cultivated: and I am inclined to think that we often draw very inconsiderate conclusions against the industry and government of states from the appearance of uncultivated lands in them. It seems to be the clear and express

14 This is illustrated from the national debt: 'Measures calculated to terminate in a rise in the value of money might be little felt in a country without a national debt; but with a large money amount to be paid annually to public creditors, they might occasion a distribution of property most unfavourable to production.'

15 For the rejection of social control over the savings rate both in advanced and underdeveloped economies, see chapter 12, p. 615.

16 The text proceeds to champion an appropriate system of Corn Laws.

duty of every government to remove all obstacles and give every facility to the enclosure and cultivation of land; but when this has been done, the rest must be left to the operation of individual interest; and upon this principle it cannot be expected that any new land should be brought into cultivation, the manure and the labour necessary for which might be employed to greater advantage on the improvement of land already in cultivation; and this is a case which will very frequently occur' (1803/1986, *3*, 458).

In 1803 and the later editions of the *Essay*, as in 1798, the emphasis is on private property, the marriage institution, and self-interest generally as providing the key to progress with an eye to working-class standards: 'That the principal and most permanent cause of poverty, has little or no [1806: direct] relation to forms of government, or the unequal division of property,' followed 'from the principle of population' (574; 1806, II, 498). But again there is also the insistence that this should not be read as a case against the feasibility of improvement and reform, including a more equable income distribution, albeit within a class-structured society – that 'gradual and progressive improvement in human society, which, before the late wild speculations on the subject, was the object of rational expectation' (575). The principle of population was not to be treated as a barrier to 'improvement': 'The structure of society, in its great features, will probably always remain unchanged. We have every reason to believe, that it will always consist of a class of proprietors and a class of labourers; but the condition of each, and the proportion which they bear to each other, may be so altered, as greatly to improve the harmony and beauty of the whole. It would indeed be a melancholy reflection that, while the views of physical science are daily enlarging, so as scarcely to be bounded by the most distant horizon, the science of moral and political philosophy should be confined within such narrow limits, or at best be so feeble in its influence, as to be unable to counteract the increasing obstacles to human happiness arising from the progress of population. But however formidable these obstacles may have appeared in some parts of this work, it is hoped that the general result of the inquiry is such, as not to make us give up the cause of the improvement of human society in despair. The partial good which seems to be attainable is worthy of all our exertions; is sufficient to direct our efforts, and animate our prospects' (575–6).

A word is required here on Malthus's political perspective. Repeatedly he states his fear that, if workers are unaware of the root cause of poverty and have unrealistic expectations awakened as to what can be done for them by society, their disappointment would be such as to explode in anarchic violence, only to be crushed by despotic governments supported even by those who would be sympathetic to reform: 'The pressure of distress on the lower classes of people, with the habit of attributing this distress to their rulers, appears to me to be the rock of defence, the castle, the guardian spirit of despotism. It affords to the tyrant that fatal and unanswerable plea of necessity ... While any dissatisfied man of talents has power to persuade the lower classes of people, that all their poverty and distress arise solely from the iniquity of the government ... it is evident that the seeds of fresh discontents and fresh revolutions are continually sowing ... Are we to be surprised, that, under such circumstances, the majority of well disposed people, finding that a government, with proper restrictions was unable to support itself against the revolutionary spirit, and weary and exhausted with perpetual change, to which they could see no end, should give up the struggle in despair, and throw themselves into the arms of the first power which can afford them protection against the horrors of anarchy' (500–1). In short, the 'habit of expecting too much, and the irritation occasioned by disappointments, continually give a wrong direction to ... efforts in favour of liberty, and constantly tend to defeat the accomplishments of those gradual reforms in government, and that slow melioration of the condition of the lower classes of society, which are really attainable' (1806, II, 390–1). The failure to appreciate the root cause of poverty merely 'paralyzed the exertions of the best friends of liberty; and those salutary reforms which are acknowledged to be necessary in order to repair the breaches of time, and improve the fabric of our constitution, are thus rendered much more difficult, and consequently much less probable' (1817, III, 173).[17]

As for appropriate steps, while there was little a government could do assuming 'an unrestricted increase of population' – a fundamental qualification, as we shall see – 'yet its influence is great in giving the best direction to those checks which in some form or other must necessarily take place' (1806, II, 388–9). A new allowance for 'the effect of good government in diminishing poverty' is spelled out in the Advertisement to the 1806 edition (I, vi). The allusion is in part to the strengthening of prudential habits by assuring 'perfect security of property,' but also to extension of the franchise: 'If ... the representative system, by securing to the lower classes of society a more equal and liberal mode of treatment from their superiors, gives to each individual a greater personal respectability, and a greater fear of personal degradation, it is evident that it will powerfully cooperate with the security of property in animating the exertions of industry, and in generating habits of prudence, and thus more powerfully tend to increase the riches and prosperity of the lower classes of the community, than if the same laws had existed under a despotism' (II, 390). The point here is that the contribution by labourers to legislation would raise their self-esteem, with widespread effects of a desirable kind.

17 Winch, 1987, 51, observes that 'Malthus's diagnosis of the way in which popular discontent, mob violence and despotism were connected draws on contemporary events and on classical commonplaces supplemented by Hume's ideas on the possible euthanasia ... of the British Constitution in absolute monarchy.'

An important role is allowed for government in education; Malthus rejected out of hand the objection 'to a system of national education in England ... that the common people would be put in a capacity to read such works as those of Paine' (1803/1986, *3*, 527; see also 1807b/1986, *4*, 17). That the social return to educational investment exceeds the private return is a central feature of the position introduced in 1803: 'Much might be expected from a better and more general system of education. Everything that can be done in this way has indeed a very peculiar value; because education is one of those advantages, which not only all may share without interfering with each other, but the raising of one person may actually contribute to the raising of others. If, for instance, a man by education acquires that decent kind of pride, and those juster habits of thinking, which will prevent him from burdening society with a family of children which he cannot support, his conduct, as far as an individual instance can go, tends evidently to improve the condition of his fellow labourers; and a contrary conduct from ignorance, would tend as evidently to depress it' (562–3). The best hopes, Malthus concluded, was an educational scheme such as that proposed by Adam Smith – in part state-financed – but including in the curriculum 'the frequent explanation of the real state of the lower classes of society, as affected by the principle of population, and their consequent dependence on themselves, for the chief part of their happiness, or misery' (525). 'I cannot help looking forward to a very decided improvement in the habits and temper of the lower classes, when their real situation has been clearly explained to them' (1806, II, 549).

In the absence of an appropriate educational program, other desirable schemes designed to reduce the *mortality* rate must inevitably fail. But those schemes, when thus accompanied, could be justified by the principle of population correctly understood: 'It may be said, however, that any plan of generally improving the cottages of the poor, or of enabling more of them to keep cows, would evidently give them the power of rearing a greater number of children, and, by thus encouraging population, violate the principles which I have endeavoured to establish. But if I have been successful in making the reader comprehend the principal bent of this work, he will be aware that the precise reason why I think that more children ought not to be born than the country can support is, that the greatest possible number of those that are born may be supported. We cannot, in the nature of things, assist the poor, in any way, without enabling them to rear up to manhood a greater number of their children' (565). The dilemma is resolved if 'we can impress these children with the idea, that, to possess the same advantages as their parents, they must defer marriage till they have a fair prospect of being able to maintain a family. And it must be candidly confessed that, if we cannot do this, all our former efforts will have been thrown away ... [A] diminution of mortality at present will be balanced by an increased mortality in future; and the improvement of their condition in one place will proportionally depress it in another' (565–6). It is implied in various formulations that the educational program is likely to be most effective when the rising generation has had some experience of comfort: 'No experiment respecting a provision for the poor can be said to be complete till succeeding generations have arisen,' appropriately governed by prudential motives (1806, II, 540).

The best-known of Malthus's proposals relates, of course, to the abolition of the contemporary poor-relief system; these, more than anything, have stamped him with illiberality towards labour.[18] Thus in 1803 he denied – against Thomas Paine (1791) – a right to subsistence: 'A man who is born into a world already possessed, if he cannot get subsistence from his parents on whom he has a just demand, and if the society do not want his labour, has no claim of *right* to the smallest portion of food, and, in fact, has no business to be where he is. At nature's mighty feast here is no vacant cover for him. She tells him to be gone, and will quickly execute her own orders, if he do not work upon the compassion of some of her guests' (697). In later editions this graphic formulation is absent, but the substantive point, as repeated elsewhere, always against Paine, remains: 'No person has any claim of right on society for subsistence, if his labour will not [1806: fairly] purchase it ...' (505; 1806, II, 382).

Malthus's position in its essence is that the guarantee of 'indiscriminate charity' worsened the very problem it was designed to solve: 'It may be distinctly stated to be an *absolute impossibility* that all the different classes of society should be both well paid and fully employed, if the supply of labour on the whole exceed the demand; and as the poor-laws tend in the most marked manner to make the supply of labour exceed the demand for it, their effect must be, either to lower universally all wages, or, if some are kept up artificially, to throw great numbers of workmen out of employment, and thus constantly to increase the poverty and distress of the labouring classes of society' (1817, II, 371). Similarly, 'the sole reason why I say the poor have no claim of *right* to support is the physical impossibility of relieving this progressive population' (1806, II, 531). Indeed, were it not for the artificial generation of an infinite demand for labour, the problem of poverty would involve solely the current poor and he would have no objections: 'If all could be completely relieved, and poverty banished from the country, even at the expense of three-fourths of the fortunes of the rich, I would be the last to say a single syllable against relieving all,

18 An early summary of Malthus's objections to the Poor Laws is given in the first essay, Chapter V: Wage supplements merely drive up the prices of (agricultural) wage goods, held to be in relatively inelastic supply, to the cost of independent labourers; they tend to increase population 'in some measure [creating] the poor which they maintain'; they encourage irresponsibility and idleness; and they reduce labour mobility (1798/1986, *1*, 29–38). See also 'Plan of the gradual abolition of the poor laws proposed' (1803/1986, *3*, 514–23).

and making the degree of distress alone the measure of our bounty' (1803/1986, *3*, 535; see also 1807b/1986, *4*, 9). The problem, as formulated in an objection to Robert Owen's communal scheme (1816) was, therefore: 'How to provide for those who are in want, in such a manner as to prevent a continual increase of their numbers, and of the proportion which they bear to the whole society' (1817, III, 258; see also II, 274–86). Here we have a nice application of the 'greatest happiness' rule, a rule – Malthus implies – that makes little sense, allowing for open-ended population increase irrespective of *per capita* income and distribution.

The characteristic Malthusian dilemma[19] appears also in the discussion of other policy measures. Even self-financed pension, health, and unemployment-insurance schemes (as distinct from state poor-relief), though desirable, would fail if contributions were based on a specific family size of, say, two children with *open-ended* benefits: 'Such a mode of distribution implies a power of supporting a rapidly increasing and unlimited population on a limited territory, and must therefore terminate in aggravated poverty,' for no conceivable scheme 'can possibly place the labouring classes of society in such a state as to enable them to marry generally at the same age in an old and fully peopled country as they may do with perfect safety and advantage in a new one' (271–2).

Similarly, improvement of cottages were desirable, provided the program was intelligently designed to avoid exacerbating population pressure: 'I cannot help thinking also, that something might be done towards bettering

19 In some respect the 'dilemma' was more apparent than real, at least in the absence of Whitbread's proposed extensions (see below, p. 900). For Malthus in fact conceded early on that the mechanics of the outdoor-relief system counteracted 'their first obvious tendency to increase population ... I have little doubt that it is almost exclusively owing to these counteracting causes, that we have been able to persevere in this system so long, and that the condition of the poor has not been so much injured by it as might have been expected' (1803/1986, *3*, 563n). See also the allowance in 1806: 'The obvious tendency of the poor laws is certainly to encourage marriage, but a closer attention to all their indirect as well as direct effects, may make it a matter of doubt to what extent they really do this. They clearly tend, in their general operation, to discourage sobriety and economy, to encourage idleness and the desertion of children, and to put virtue and vice more on a level than they otherwise would be; but I will not presume to say positively that they tend to encourage population' (1806, II, 547). To this he appended in 1807: 'The most favourable light, in which the poor laws can possibly be placed, is to say, that under all the circumstances, with which they have been accompanied, they do not [much] encourage marriage; and undoubtedly the returns of the Population Act seem to warrant the assertion. Should this be true, some of the objections which have been urged in the Essay against the poor laws will of course be removed; but I wish to press on the attention of the reader, that they will in that case be removed in strict conformity to the general principles of the work, and in a manner to confirm, rather than to invalidate, the main position which it has attempted to establish' ('much' added in 1817).

These qualifications have implications for modern statistical testing of Malthus's position on the demographic impact of the old Poor Law (cf. Blaug, 1963; Huzel, 1969, 1980).

the situation of the poor by a general improvement of their cottages, if care were taken, at the same time, not to make them so large as to allow of two families settling in them; and not to increase their number faster than the demand for labour required. Perhaps one of the most salutary and least pernicious checks to the frequency of early marriages in this country is the difficulty of procuring a cottage, and the laudable habits which prompt a labourer rather to defer his marriage some years in the expectation of a vacancy, than to content himself with a wretched mud cabin, like those in Ireland' (1803/1986, *3*, 563). Land and cow grants were approached in the same manner: 'Even the cow system, upon a more confined plan, might not be open to objection. With any view of making it a substitute for the poor laws, and of giving labourers a right to demand land and cows in proportion to their families; or of taking the common people from the consumption of wheat, and feeding them on milk and potatoes; it appears to me, I confess, truly preposterous: but if it were so ordered as merely to provide a comfortable situation for the better and more industrious class of labourers, and to supply at the same time a very important want among the poor in general, that of milk for their children, I think that it would be extremely beneficial, and might be made a very powerful incitement to habits of industry, economy, and prudence.' Malthus's concern to achieve just the right balance is clear: 'One should undoubtedly be extremely unwilling not to make as much use as possible of that known stimulus to industry and economy, the desire of, and attachment to, property: but it should be recollected that the good effects of this stimulus show themselves principally when this property is to be procured or preserved by personal exertions; and that they are by no means so general under other circumstances. If any idle man with a family could demand and obtain a cow and some land, I should expect to see both very often neglected' (564).

The need to assure against transitional hardship is reflected in Malthus's concern with the mechanics of Poor Law abolition: 'According to this plan all that are already married, and even all that are engaged to marry during the course of the year, and all their children would be relieved as usual; and only those who marry subsequently, and who of course may be supposed to have made better provision for contingencies would be out of the pale of relief' (1806, II, 530). None the less, the point remains that once abolition of poor relief had been achieved, private charity would have to take responsibility for relief cases. As for illegitimate children, the state had a responsibility to punish parents for desertion or intentional ill-treatment, but was not responsible for the abandoned children themselves: 'The infant is, comparatively speaking, of no value to the society, as others will immediately supply its place. Its principal value is on account of its being the object of one of the most delightful passions in human nature – parental affection. But if this value be disregarded, by those who are alone in a capacity to feel it, the society cannot be called upon to put itself in their place ...' (1803/1986, *3*, 517). Again, it is private charity that would have to be relied upon. But in all this it must not be forgotten that, under the going system of parish adoption, the infantile death rate was atrocious. Moreover, Malthus believed both that fathers would behave more responsibly under his proposal (518), and that private charity could be relied upon: 'If this system were pursued, we need be under no apprehensions whatever, that the number of persons in extreme want would be beyond the power and the will of the benevolent to supply. The sphere for the exercise of private charity would, I am confident, be less than it is at present; and the only difficulty would be, to restrain the hand of benevolence from assisting those in distress in so liberal a manner as to encourage indolence and want of foresight in others' (517).

These pronouncements all relate to individual cases of poverty resulting from irresponsible marriages. What of cyclical unemployment? Government, we are told in 1806, had 'but little power in 'the direct and immediate relief of poverty' (1806, II, 388), and he later advised, in alluding to the distress of 1817, that workers be encouraged 'to bear an unavoidable pressure with patience' (1817, III, 172). None the less, the problem of short-run unemployment greatly troubled him. And he introduced as early as 1803 a major qualification – based on a temporal utility calculus – that removes any hint of the irresponsible application of the population principle to immediate questions of policy: 'The general principles on these subjects ought not to be pushed too far, though they should always be kept in view; ... and many cases may occur, in which the good resulting from the relief of the present distress, may more than overbalance the evil to be apprehended from the remote consequence. All relief in instances of distress, not arising from idle and improvident habits, clearly comes under this description; and in general it may be observed, that it is only that kind of systematic and certain relief, on which the poor can confidently depend, whatever may be their conduct, that violates general principles, in such a manner, as to make it clear that the general consequence is worse than the particular evil' (1803/1986, *3*, 562). The principle of population provided guidelines only, not a pretext for extreme *laissez-faire*. Also relevant is a sort of 'Benthamite' calculation involving the differential weighing of consequences according to propinquity and relative certainty. The fact that various alternatives to poor relief, such as land-renting schemes, might fail ultimately, even if temporarily successful – unless accompanied by appropriate educational measure designed to affect the new generation – 'should by no means deter us from making such experiments, when present good is to be obtained by them, and a future overbalance of evil not justly to be apprehended. It should only make us less rash in drawing our inferences' (1806, II, 541).

Malthus added the further point in 1806 that, if the decision were made to retain a system of Poor Laws, knowledge of the principle of population might allow the removal of the worst disadvantages (552). Here we have a further hint regarding his probable attitude to the kind of system introduced in 1834.[20] A main concern, of course, was that the guarantee of wage supplements – the current 'Speenhamland' system often gave further grants per child, at least after the first two – would encourage young men to marry earlier than they would otherwise do, thus countering the encouragement of prudence, or delay of marriage, till, with the savings made in the interval, a couple could support the smaller number of children that could then be expected. The consequence of such excessive population growth would be to depress the market wage – in fact, farmers preferred to pay lower than market wages, knowing that the difference would be made up from the rates paid partly by others than themselves (*Letter to Samuel Whitbread,* 1807b/1986, *4,* 10, 16). The problem would be exacerbated, Malthus feared, by implementation of Whitbread's amendments, which would extend the burden of the rates to all property and also empower parishes to build cottages for the poor (10–11, 13). None the less, Malthus clarified that, if the 'tendency' to depress the 'independent labourer' could be avoided, he would not oppose a system of poor relief; he proposed rather its 'confinement' to assure a balance of advantage: 'To make the advantages of a system of poor laws counterbalance its disadvantages, it seems to be necessary that they should be so confined in their operation, as not to depress the wages of labour below what is sufficient for the support of the *average* number of children that might be expected from each marriage. If they extended no further than this, every man in marrying might have a fair and rational hope, that by industry and good conduct, he might be able to continue independent; and if this hope failed merely through the largeness of his family, he would not be much degraded either in his own eyes or those of his fellow labourers' (15).[21]

The focus upon the *proportion* which those in want 'bear to the whole society' (above, p. 897) is particularly significant in this context. Although Malthus's initial concerns were awakened by reports of rapid increases in

20 Grampp questions whether Malthus's actual effect on that legislation was as great as is usually supposed (1974, 202–3).

21 Even in 1798 Malthus recognized the need for indoor relief in extreme cases, and implied support for the principle of 'lesser eligibility' incorporated later in the 1834 legislation (1798/1986, *1,* 37). His further allowances (above, note 19) similarly suggest a balanced position. See also Malthus, 1824b/1986, *4,* 238: 'To what extent assistance may be given even by law to the poorer classes of society when in distress, without defeating the great object of the law of property ... depends mainly upon the feelings and habits of the labouring classes of society, and can only be determined by experience. If it be generally considered as so discreditable to receive parochial relief, that great exertions are made to avoid it, and few or none marry with a certain prospect of being obliged to have recourse to it, there is no doubt that those who were really in distress might be adequately assisted, with little danger of a constantly increasing proportion of paupers; and in that case a great good would be attained without any proportionate evil to counter-balance it.'

the poor rates and the prospect of 'an extraordinary proportion of paupers in the society' (1803/1986, *3*, 514), he none the less insisted on a careful weighing of the pros and cons of poor relief, provided that an increase in the proportion in question could be avoided:

If we could be secure, that, though the number of the dependent poor might increase with the increasing population, yet that their *proportion* to it would remain the same; and if this proportion were not so great as very materially to affect the whole body, the question would at once assume a different form. It would still be true however that the poor laws even in such a state would have a tendency to depress the independent labourer, to weaken in some degree the springs of industry and good conduct, and to put virtue and vice more on a level than they would be in the natural course of things; but as in all human institutions it is impossible to avoid some disadvantages, it might fairly be urged that the certain relief of the aged and the helpless, of those who had met with misfortunes which no common prudence could have avoided, and of those who had a greater number of children than they could be expected to foresee, would more than counterbalance those inconveniences, and that the good would preponderate over the evil. (1807b/1986, *4*, 14–15)

Along these balanced lines Malthus added in 1806 an important qualification to an earlier case for non-intervention in the event of a poor harvest, specifically alluding in his Advertisement to the addition of an observation 'on the policy as well as duty of assisting the poor through temporary seasons of distress' (1806, I, v–vi) – 'policy' alluding to the need to cushion workers from temporary adverse pressures in order to avoid inappropriate population effects: 'We must not forget that both humanity and true policy imperiously require, that we should give every assistance to the poor on these occasions that the nature of the case will admit. If provisions were to continue at the price of scarcity, the wages of labour must necessarily rise, or sickness and famine would quickly diminish the number of labourers, and the supply of labour being unequal to the demand, its price would soon rise in a still greater proportion than the price of provisions. But even one or two years of scarcity, if the poor were left entirely to shift for themselves, might produce some effect of this kind, and consequently it is our interest as well as our duty to give them temporary aid in such seasons of distress. It is on such occasions that every cheap substitute for bread, and every mode of economizing food should be resorted to. Nor should we be too ready to complain of that high price of corn which by encouraging importation increases the supply' (II, 169–70).

These statements are to be taken seriously. Thus Malthus allowed public works as an appropriate step in some cases of short-term unemployment (e.g., letter to Ricardo, 11 January 1817 [above, pp. 624–5]). But there was always a danger that, where a problem of *secular* excess labour supply existed, public works might complicate the long-term solution. The severe dilemma is well expressed thus: 'It is probable that the poor might be employed more than they have hitherto been, in a way to be advantageous to their habits and morals, without being prejudicial in other respects ... [But in] no conceivable case can the forced employment of the poor, though managed in the most judicious manner, have any direct tendency to proportion more accurately the supply of labour to the natural demand for it. And without great care and caution it is obvious that it may have a pernicious effect of an opposite kind. When, for instance, from deficient demand or deficient capital, labour has a strong tendency to fall, if we keep it up to its usual price by creating an artificial demand by public subscriptions or advances from the government, we evidently prevent the population of the country from adjusting itself gradually to its diminished resources, and act much in the same manner as those, who would prevent the price of corn from rising in a scarcity, which must necessarily terminate in increased distress' (1817, III, 273–4).[22] As mentioned, this was not a global rejection of public works, only an appeal for caution and awareness of all possible outcomes: 'Without then meaning to object to all plans for employing the poor, some of which, at certain times and with proper restrictions, may be useful as temporary measures, it is of great importance, in order to prevent ineffectual efforts and continued disappointments, to be fully aware that the permanent remedy which we are seeking cannot possibly come from this quarter.' Were the public-works scheme 'such as to co-operate with the lessons of Nature and Providence, and to encourage and promote habits of prudence and foresight, essential and permanent benefit may be expected from it: if it has no tendency of this kind, it may possibly still be good as a temporary measure, and on other accounts, but we may be quite certain that it does not apply to the source of the specific evil for which we are seeking a remedy' (275).

A further solution to (short-term) unemployment, where excess labour supply reflects a lagging population response to a preceding stimulus that has proven temporary, was seen to lie in emigration, although again 'with any view of making room for an unrestricted increase of population, emigration is perfectly inadequate' (1803/1986, *3*, 353). It was 'the duty and interest of governments to facilitate emigration,' though they could not legitimately oblige it' (1806, II, 535n). And Malthus observed in 1817 with the postwar depression in mind: 'If, for instance, from a combination of external and internal causes, a very great stimulus should be given to the population of a country for ten or twelve years together, and it should

22 The possible 'pernicious' effect is focused on in evidence given to the Select Committee on Emigration (5 May 1827). Here Malthus maintained that public works 'relieves [labour] for a short time, but leaves them afterwards in a condition worse than before'; this was so because '[it] has a tendency to induce them to marry earlier, and it enables them at first to support their children; but when the work ceases, they are left in a more destitute condition than before' (House of Commons, 1827, 321).

then comparatively cease, it is clear that labour will continue flowing into the market, with almost undiminished rapidity, while the means of employing and paying it have been essentially contracted. It is precisely under these circumstances that emigration is most useful as a temporary relief; and it is in these circumstances that Great Britain finds herself placed at present ... The only real relief in such a case [as in 1816 and 1817] is emigration; and the subject at the present moment is well worthy the attention of the government, both as a matter of humanity and policy' (1817, II, 305). Early in 1827 – the revival from the commercial crisis of 1826 would not yet have been under way – he wrote to Wilmot-Horton: 'My general opinions on the subject of Emigration are well known and I certainly think that the present is one of the occasions in which Government might advantageously give every facility for the purpose; but I have not attended to the details, in regard to the best practical means of affecting the object ...' (7 January 1827).[23]

Assuring *permanent* benefit required, of course, that any 'void' created by emigration should not be entirely filled up. Writing again to Wilmot Horton regarding the latter's scheme entailing government-aided emigration (Horton, 1830) he expressed this concern, while none the less indicating his support: 'Could you indeed accomplish it, in an entirely unobjectionable manner, you would in my opinion be the greatest benefactor to the human race that has yet appeared. It would be securing at once, and permanently, good wages to all who were able and willing to work, allowing still for a continual increase of population. But though it would be a contradiction to all theory and all past experience to deny the strong tendency of population to recover lost numbers, and the extreme difficulty of keeping the labouring classes from increasing beyond the effectual demand for labour, yet I think that both policy and humanity require that we make every practical effort to improve their condition; and I feel no doubt that your plan of emigration would essentially contribute to this most desirable end, by affording undoubted present relief, and the best chance which offers itself of the means of permanent improvement' (9 June 1830). I do not see from this correspondence that Malthus 'was no great enthusiast for emigration' (James, 1979, 396; also O Gráda, 1984, 87). On the contrary. And on 22 February he confirmed that, whatever the long-run prospects for adequate population control, '[at] all events there is the immediate temporary relief, which is a consideration not to be put out of the question.'

23 This letter and the others quoted below are the property of Derbyshire County Council and are held in the council's Record Office, Matlock (DRO D3155). They are not printed in Ghosh, 1963.

Wilmot-Horton's plan entailed government loans to parishes or individuals. Malthus warned of problems regarding finance: 'I do not object to your mode of providing for the expense, though the little I have is in the funds; but I fear that in the present temper of Parliament and the country, if any surplus revenue can be dispensed with, the clamour will be for relief from taxation' (22 February 1830).

One can best appreciate Malthus's position by supposing the general practice of prudential restraint – a situation in which 'low' family size (which incidentally Malthus thought of as about six children) is the rule. With the removal of population pressure, the practical approach to policy is transformed. Public works, emigration, insurance schemes now come fully into their own. But, most striking of all, a case could even be made for family allowances to help those who had more children than they could be expected to foresee – a position first formulated in 1803. As for the initial framework assumed: 'If the lowest classes of society were ... diminished, and the middle classes increased, each labourer might indulge a more rational hope of rising by diligence and exertion into a better station; the rewards of industry and virtue would be increased in number; human society would appear to consist of fewer blanks and more prizes; and the sum of social happiness would be evidently augmented. To indulge, however, in any distant views of this kind, unaccompanied by the evils usually attendant on a stationary or decreasing demand for labour, we must suppose the general prevalence of such prudential habits among the poor, as would prevent them from marrying, when the actual price of labour, joined to what they might have saved in their single state, would not give them the prospect of being able to support a wife and six children without assistance. And in every point of view, such a degree of prudential restraint [would be extremely beneficial; and][24] would produce a very striking amelioration in the condition of the lower classes of people' (1803/1986, *3*, 567–8). Malthus allowed 'that even this degree of prudence might not always avail, as when a man marries he cannot tell what number of children he shall have, and many have more than six,' but did 'not think that any evil would result from making a certain allowance to every child above this number; not with a view of rewarding a man for his large family, but merely of relieving him from a species of distress which it would be unreasonable in us to expect that he should calculate upon. And with this view, the relief should be merely such as to place him exactly in the same situation as if he had six children. Montesquieu disapproves of an edict of Louis XIV, which gave certain pensions to those who had ten and twelve children, as being of no use in encouraging population. For the very reason that he disapproves of it, I should think that some law of the kind might be adopted without danger, and might relieve particular individuals from a very pressing and unlooked for distress, without operating in any respect as an encouragement to marriage' (568).[25]

Malthus's reformist perspective shines through in late correspondence.

24 The 1986 version neglects to provide the bracketed phrase. It was deleted from the 1807 version (1807, II, 410).

25 One might think that this passage refers to a permanent stationary state; but the notion of an average family size of six children is then remarkable.

Supposing an initial state of stationariness, agricultural improvement (or the relaxation of corn-import restrictions) will lead to higher wages, which would prove unmaintainable – unless, of course, accompanied by an improved degree of prudential restraint. Yet even in its absence he made a case for the temporary improvement: 'It does not by any means follow from these principles, that we should not use our utmost endeavours to make two ears of wheat grow where one grew before, or to improve our commercial code by freeing it from restraints. An increase of population is in itself a decided advantage, if it be not accompanied by an increased *proportion* of vice and misery. And the period during which the pressure of population is lightened, though it may not be of long duration, is a period of comparative ease, and ought by no means to be thrown out of our consideration' (31 March 1829; in Senior, 1829, 85).[26] In this respect the reformist orientation is more striking even than that of J.S. Mill, who later argued that, unless the effect of tariff reform or technological change could be rendered of permanent advantage to labour, there was little point to them. In fact, Malthus believed 'that the experience of such a period may sometimes operate in giving to the labouring-classes a taste for such a mode of living as will tend to increase their prudential habits' as was required to render the improvement permanent (in Senior, 85–6). In the light of all this, he was asking for trouble by referring as late as 1830 (as in 1798) to prospects for ample wages at full employment as a rare phenomenon (1824b/1986, *4*, 201; republished in 1830). This position, it must again be emphasized, held good, not as a universal prediction, but subject to the presumption of an unchecked growth rate of population (202) – precisely the situation his proposals sought to avoid.

* * *

Malthus's championship of 'high' wages and a low mortality rate needs no further amplification.[27] But the evidence of his 'reformist' status should

26 See above, p. 854. See also his concern in the *Essay on Population* with the short-run benefits, above, p. 899. Other examples are found in chapter 17, p. 826. Similarly, in the *Principles* we find a concern with cyclical fluctuations from this perspective: 'Theoretical writers are apt, in their calculations, to overlook these intervals; but eight or ten years, recurring not infrequently, are serious spaces in human life. They amount to a serious sum of happiness or misery, according as they are prosperous or adverse, and leave the country in a very different state at their termination. In prosperous times the mercantile classes often realize fortunes, which go far towards securing them against the future; but unfortunately the working classes, though they share in the general prosperity, do not share [1836: in it] so largely as in the general adversity. They may suffer the greatest distress in a period of low wages, but cannot be adequately compensated by a period of high wages. To them fluctuations must always bring more evil than good' (1820, 521–2; 1836, 437).

27 It might though be added that, in the 1826 edition of his *Essay*, Malthus commended

be seen within a broader intellectual context. As for his position on the Constitution, we find in his *Principles* that he opposed the abolition of primogeniture and the consequent break-up of great estates on 'higher considerations ... than those which relate to mere wealth' (1820, 437; 1836, 380). For the British constitution was 'mainly due to a landed aristocracy'; and 'if we think that, whatever may be its theoretical imperfections, it has practically given a better government, and more liberty to a greater mass of people for a longer time than any which history records, it would be most unwise to venture upon any such change as would risk the whole structure, and throw us upon a wide sea of experiment, where the chances are so dreadfully against our attaining the object of our search' (1820, 437–8; 1836, 380).[28] The second edition, however, recognizes the extension of the franchise (presumably the 1832 Reform Act); *and it is allowed that, though perhaps premature, it might turn out for the best*: 'This was written in 1820. Imperious circumstances have since brought on a reform of a more sudden and extensive nature than prudence would have perhaps suggested, if the time and the circumstances could have been commanded. Yet it must be allowed, that all which has been done, is to bring the practical working of the constitution nearer to its theory. And there is every reason to believe, that a great majority of the middle classes of society, among whom the elective franchise has been principally extended, must soon see that their own interests, and the interests and happiness of those who are dependent upon them, will be most essentially injured by any proceedings which tend to encourage turbulence and shake the security of property. If they become adequately sensible of this most unquestionable truth, and act accordingly, there is no doubt that the removal of those unsightly blots, of those handles, which, with a fair show of reason, might at any time be laid hold of to excite discontents and to

---

recent factory legislation for improving the working conditions of children in cotton mills (1986, *3*, 444n).

For further emphasis on Malthus's reformist orientation, see Bonar, 1924, 319–54; Penrose, 1957; Spengler, 1960 [1945]; James, 1979, 109, 369–76, 388–406, 432–3, 449f.; Petersen, 1979, 48, 218–39; Dupâquier, 1983; and Himmelfarb, 1984, 119–22.

28 On Malthus as a 'Country,' or 'old-fashioned,' or 'moderate' Whig, hostile to executive encroachments, and to excessively large standing armies, and reliant on country gentlemen to resist corruption and defend liberty, see Winch, 1983, 75–7. Winch, 1987, 48–5, provides various indexes of Malthus's Whig credentials. See also Waterman, 1991, 26: 'Though a priest of the established church, Malthus was writing [in 1798] from within a whig tradition of social theory ...' (Waterman, 196–204, provides a useful classification of contemporary idealogies.) Bonar observed that 'the details of [Malthus's] views on the State and government are those of an advanced Whig of the school of Fox and Grey. His adherence to Adam Smith did not prevent him from departing from "*laissez faire*" even more than his master' (1924, 208). Otter referred to Malthus as 'a firm, consistent, and decided Whig, the earnest advocate of salutary improvements and reforms, but strongly and sincerely attached to the institutions of his country, and fearful of all wanton experiment and innovations' (1836, li).

stir up the people, will place the British constitution upon a much broader and more solid base than ever' (1836, 380n).

Malthus's opposition to nationalist (neo-mercantilist) arguments for a large population at low wages stands out unambiguously. That national strength required a large population he agreed, but it was 'as to the mode of obtaining a vigorous and efficient population' that he differed from others championing a large population (1806, II, 509). The military draft, moreover, would have to be filled by drawing labour from high-paying alternatives: 'We cannot obtain incompatible objects; if we possess the advantage of being able to keep nearly all our people constantly employed either in agriculture or commerce, we cannot expect to retain the opposite advantage of their being always at leisure, and willing to enlist for a very small sum. But we may rest perfectly assured, that while we have the efficient population, we shall never want men to fill our armies if we propose to them adequate motives' (581–2). There is even a suggestion that prospects for peace would be enhanced if governments had to pay well for their soldiers: 'The ambition of princes would want instruments of destruction, if the distress of the lower classes of people did not drive them under their standards. A recruiting serjeant always prays for a bad harvest and a want of employment, or, in other words, a redundant population' (1803/1986, *3*, 478–9). The advantages of good earnings extend to the improvement of national defence capacity – in effect a reversal of the Smithian proposition that 'defence is more important than opulence' to read: *opulence, provided labour benefits sufficiently, encourages defence*; for 'where every family possessed the necessaries of life in plenty, and a decent portion of its comforts and conveniences, there could not exist that hope of change, or at best that melancholy and disheartening indifference to it, which sometimes prompts the lower classes of people to say, "Let what will come, we cannot be worse off than we are now"' (480).[29] One also notes Malthus's complaint that, while labourers had it in their own hands to assure rising standards, the state had done its best to thwart the message: '[The labourer] has always been told, that to raise up subjects for his king and country is a very meritorious act. He has done this act, and yet is suffering for it. He naturally thinks that he is suffering for righteousness sake; and it cannot but strike him as most extremely unjust and cruel in his king and country, to allow him thus to suffer, in return for giving them what they are continually declaring that they particularly want' (484). The education program viewed from this perspective is radical indeed.

Equally striking is Malthus's deflection of the religious argument in favour of a high population which traditionally involved the encourage-

29 All of this points directly to a common view shared by Malthus, Godwin, Paine, and Cobbett, including a dislike of standing armies and of overbearing government measures against sedition (Bonar, 1924, 338).

ment of early marriages and large families (above, p. 881; see also chapter 19, p. 944). And his reaction to the French Revolution is also revealing, for it was by no means hostile. His recognition of the upward wage trend in France since 1789 points directly to the possibility of reform – in this case the abolition of various feudal institutions – as a means to increased personal responsibility, and indirectly to a reduced birth rate: 'The improved condition of the labouring classes in France since the revolution has been accompanied by a greatly diminished proportion of births, which has had its natural and necessary effect in giving to these classes a greater share of the produce of the country, and has kept up the advantage arising from the sale of the church lands and other national domains, which would otherwise have been lost in a short time. The effect of the revolution in France has been, to make every person depend more upon himself and less upon others. The labouring classes are therefore become more industrious, more saving and more prudent in marriage than formerly; and it is quite certain that without these effects the revolution would have done nothing for them' (1817, II, 378–9). This passage is of the first importance since those writers to whom Malthus was responding in 1798 had been 'infected with the enthusiasm of the French Revolution' (Fetter, 1898, 154).[30]

Consistent with the reformist perspective of the foregoing passage is Malthus's critical view of 'feudal' society, which incidentally adds to the evidence that Malthus was no sycophantic apologist of the landlord class: 'The profits of stock are that source of revenue from which the middle classes are chiefly maintained; and the increase of capital, which is both the cause and effect of increasing riches, may be said to be the efficient cause of the emancipation of the great body of society from a dependence on the landlords. In a country of limited extent, consisting of fertile land divided into large properties, as long as the capital remains inconsiderable, the structure of society is most unfavourable to liberty and good government. This was exactly the state of Europe in the feudal times. The landlords could in no way spend their incomes than by maintaining a great

30 On Malthus and the French Revolution see also Bonar, 1924, 336–7: 'It had been said that he cannot be justly described as being a reactionary; and, in truth, besides being a critic of Godwin and of Condorcet, he is influenced to some extent by the same ideas that influenced them. The *Essay on Population* is coloured throughout by a tacit or open reference to the Rights of Man, a watchword borrowed from France by the American Republic, to be restored again at the Revolution ... His economical antecedents and his political views bound him to the French Revolution.' Elie Halévy observed 'that Malthus's influence was first felt by the liberal section of opinion, since he only differed from the theorists of indefinite progress by adopting a more moderate interpretation of their own theory' (1955, 245). Also Spengler, 1960 [1945], 378: 'Malthus differed from Godwin and Condorcet regarding values and ends, democratic and otherwise, in terms of detail far more than in terms of generality.' Spengler's article casts much light on the matter of this section; esp. 385–7. See, too, Waterman, 1991, 26.

number of followers; and it was by the growth of capital in all the employments to which it is directed that the pernicious power of the landlords was destroyed, and their dependent followers were turned into merchants, manufacturers, tradesmen, farmers, and independent labourers; – a change of prodigious advantage to the great body of society, including the labouring classes' (1817, III, 21–2).

A final word regarding Malthus's objections to contemporary 'communist' schemes. Population growth, he believed, perhaps naïvely, could only be adequately controlled in a system of private property under the rule of self-interest, where each individual was 'responsible for the maintenance of his own children' and 'subjected to the natural inconveniences and difficulties arising from the indulgence of his inclinations [in too early marriage] and to no other whatever' (1817, II, 284).[31] Similarly: 'The happiness of the whole is to be the result of the happiness of individuals, and to begin first with them. No co-operation is required. Every step tells. He who performs his duty faithfully will reap the full fruits of it, whatever may be the number of others who fail. This duty is express, and intelligible to the humblest capacity. It is merely, that he is not to bring beings into the world for whom he cannot find the means of support. When once this subject is cleared from the obscurity thrown over it by parochial laws and private benevolence, every man must feel the strongest conviction of such an obligation ... It is clearly his interest, and will tend greatly to promote his happiness, to defer marrying, till by industry and economy he is in a capacity to support the children that he may reasonably expect from his marriage' (1803/1986, *3*, 483). Radical institutional change would not *in itself* provide the answer to low standards of living, for excessive population growth would still have to be avoided: 'The misery and vice arising from the pressure of the population too hard against the limits of subsistence, and the misery and vice arising from promiscuous intercourse, may be considered as the Scylla and Charybdis of human life. That it is possible for each individual to steer clear of both these rocks is certainly true ...; but that these rocks do not form a difficulty independent of human institutions, no person with any knowledge of the subject can venture to assert' (1806, II, 553n).

Malthus apparently neglects the 'free-rider' problem. Even assuming the success of an education program inculcating the principle that the wage depends on checks to the marriage rate, each self-interested individual has a motive to marry young – accepting the basic assumption of a desire for marriage and procreation – if he believes others will behave responsibly and delay marriage, thereby raising or maintaining the wage. It is not the case that the responsible individual will 'reap the full fruits' of his good behaviour 'whatever may be the number of others who fail,' since his

31 This holds apparently presuming an adequate educational program (above, p. 895).

expectations of future earnings may be ruined by irresponsible behaviour by others. (J.S. Mill was to take this problem seriously.)[32]

The utilitarian perspective on social organization – the evaluation of institutions only by their consequences rather then as 'good' or 'bad' *per se* – may be illustrated by Malthus's case against communism. He admitted that 'the greatest production of food which the powers of the earth would admit cannot possibly take place under a system of private property' (1817, III, 413; also 1824b/1986, *4*, 199). The key to his objections to 'systems of equality and community of goods' – he here had in mind Robert Owen (1816), not only Godwin's scheme, which, lacking a state, was essentially anarchical – is that self-interested calculations regarding age of marriage are precluded and would have to be replaced by legal restraints involving rigorous enforcement and punishment of an 'unnatural, immoral, or cruel' order (1817, II, 285). It was, in fact, his 'greatest objection to a system of equality and the system of the poor-laws (two systems which, however different in their outset, are of a nature calculated to produce the same results) ... that the society in which they are effectively carried into execution, will ultimately be reduced to the miserable alternative of choosing between universal want and the enactment of *direct* laws against marriage' (368–9). Poverty, in brief, was not *inevitable* under communism any more than under capitalism; Malthusianism was not a universalist doctrine regarding the non-improvability of mankind, as Marx maintained – and as Malthus himself suggested in the 'theological' chapters of 1798 (see chapter 19: II). But any solution in a communist society – in 1798 Malthus predicted the collapse of communist systems – would entail unacceptable constraints on personal freedom. Legal restraints might have seemed less objectionable to him if countenanced by public opinion, as J.S. Mill later maintained. But of this we cannot be sure.

As for the private-property system, individuals were to be free to marry, even without a prospect of maintaining a family, for although 'an immoral act, yet it is not one which society can justly take upon itself to prevent or punish; because the punishment provided for it by the laws of nature falls directly and most severely upon the individual who commits the act, and through him, only remotely and feebly, on the society' (1803/1986, *3*, 516). This perspective is difficult to appreciate since it seems to play down the *social* implications of irresponsible private behaviour, whereas the general

32 An early statement of the free-rider problem in relation to Malthus is by Lloyd, 1833. Waterman, 1991, 141f., offers an interpretation of our present text in terms of 'target income' which avoids the free-rider problem. It is certainly true that Malthus championed savings banks as 'the best' proposal, in principle, 'to effect a permanent improvement in the condition of the lower classes of society,' by encouraging responsible planning by each individual (1817, III, 275). The problem, however, remains: whether – because of *general* responsibility – the individual's target income can be achieved despite his own irresponsible behaviour.

utilitarian argument suggests that self-interested evaluations are acceptable in so far as they assure the greatest good. One can perhaps make sense of the position if we suppose that irresponsibility was taken by Malthus as the probable exception.[33]

A related problem emerges when we contrast the utility-based arguments for moral restraint and for discrimination in private charity (above, p. 896). The former – taking into account an appropriate time span – is said usually to involve a surplus of net *private* as well as *social* happiness, whereas the latter seems to require private decisions based wholly on the social impact. The road is opened wide by this second application for social control to assure the desirable outcome should private decision making prove deficient in terms of the 'greatest happiness' criterion. Malthus does not seem to have taken the plunge, possibly because the current forms of intervention were pernicious and had still to be removed – that was the first task. And the problem was, in any event, an academic one (pp. 898–9).

VIII INCOME DISTRIBUTION

We turn now to income distribution as such, specifically Malthus's own qualification to the 'principal argument' of his 1798 essay pointing to 'the necessity of a class of proprietors, and a class of labourers' (1986, *1*, 102n). His qualification denied 'that the present great inequality of property, is either necessary or useful to society. On the contrary, it must certainly be considered as an evil, and every institution that promotes it is essentially bad and impolitic.' Similarly: 'Though in every civilized state, a class of proprietors and a class of labourers must exist; yet one permanent advantage would always result from a nearer equalization of property. The greater the number of proprietors, the smaller must be the number of

33 Cf. Bonar, 1924, 213: 'It has been said that Malthus was Utilitarian, but not Utilitarian enough; he should have kept more constantly before him the Greatest Happiness of the Greatest Number. But Malthus was a Utilitarian of the old school; the greatest happiness of the great body of the people seemed to him to be best secured by the devotion of the individual members of it, each to his own permanent and real happiness.' See also 227–8, regarding the relation between the Greatest Happiness principle and individual happiness: 'The only course open to the older Utilitarians would have been to have shown that the individuals best secures his own happiness by securing that of his fellows; but that is not shown by Bentham, who in fact rather takes his maxim for granted than proves it in any way. Even if they had taken this course, there would have been a difficulty. If each man is his own best judge, how can another (Bentham or any other legislator) judge for him. The simple statement of any individual, that he for his part did not find his happiness in the general good, would be unanswerable. It could only be answered on principles that go beyond the older Utilitarianism, with its principle of individual infallibility. It can only be answered when we recognize that the individual's pleasures or pains are no criterion even of his own good, and that there is an ideal of human life which is none of the individual's fixing.'

labourers: a greater part of society would be in the happy state of possessing property; and a smaller part in the unhappy state of possessing no property other than their labour' (121). The desirability of a more equal income distribution is reiterated in 1803, as we saw earlier (above, p. 893), with something of an aesthetic rationale in terms of the improved 'harmony and beauty' of society (1986, *3*, 575–6). But more than that was intended.

Malthus first reiterated the case for some degree of inequality: 'It has been generally found that the middle parts of society are most favourable to virtuous and industrious habits, and to the growth of all kinds of talents. But it is evident that all cannot be in the middle. Superior and inferior parts are in the nature of things absolutely necessary; and not only necessary, but strikingly beneficial. If no man could hope to rise, or fear to fall in society; if industry did not bring with it its reward, and indolence its punishment; we could not expect to see that animated activity in bettering our condition, which now forms the master-spring of public prosperity' (567). But he then allowed that in the current circumstances greater equality was justified: 'Our best-grounded expectations of an increase in the happiness of the mass of human society are founded in the prospect of an increase in the relative proportions of the middle parts.'[34] This case relates to those 'virtuous and industrious habits' characteristic of the middle classes. Furthermore, with a large middle class – and also assuming a diminution by way of population control of those employed 'in severe toil' – the prospects for advance would be more conspicuous and inviting: 'If the lowest classes of society were thus diminished, and the middle classes increased, each labourer might indulge a more rational hope of rising by diligence and exertion into a better station; the rewards of industry and virtue would be increased in number; human society would appear to consist of fewer blanks and more prizes; and the sum of social happiness would be evidently augmented.'

The utilitarian case for higher wages is also conspicuous in the *Principles*. After emphasizing the quantitative superiority of the labouring class, Malthus proceeds: 'Under the prevalence of habits of prudence, the whole of this vast mass might be nearly as happy as the individuals of the other two classes, and probably a greater number of them, though not a greater proportion of them, happier' (1820, 423; 1836, 368). Similarly: 'It is most desirable that the labouring classes should be well paid, for a much more important reason than any that can relate to wealth; namely the happiness of the great mass of society' (1820, 472; 1836, 405).

The implications for 'wealth' of higher wages and more generally of greater equality are discussed above, in chapter 11, 'Sustainable Growth' (pp. 526–9, 561–2). Here we note only the rejection of Paley's case favour-

34 See also his reaction to the 1832 Reform Act (above, p. 906).

ing inequality – 'that the condition most favourable to the population of a country, and at the same time to its general happiness, is, "that of a laborious frugal people ministering to the demands of an opulent, luxurious nation"' (1803/1986, *3*, 566). This position Malthus denied, having in mind both national wealth and national happiness and the high likelihood of instability with a narrowly based luxury-producing sector: 'Such a form of society has not, it must be confessed, an inviting aspect. Nothing but the conviction of its being absolutely necessary could reconcile us to the idea of ten millions of people condemned to incessant toil, and to the privation of everything but absolute necessaries, in order to minister to the excessive luxuries of the other million. But the fact is, that such a form of society is by no means necessary. It is by no means necessary, that the rich should be excessively luxurious, in order to support the manufactures of a country; or that the poor should be deprived of all luxuries, in order to make them sufficiently numerous. The best, and in every point of view the most advantageous manufactures in this country, are those which are consumed by the great body of the people. The manufactures which are confined exclusively to the rich are not only trivial, on account of the comparative smallness of their quantity; but are further liable to the great disadvantage of producing much occasional misery among those employed in them, from changes of fashion. It is the spread of luxury therefore among the mass of the people, and not an excess of it in a few, that seems to be most advantageous, both with regard to national wealth and national happiness; and what Dr. Paley considers as the true evil and proper danger of luxury, I should be disposed to consider as its true good, and peculiar advantage.'[35] The fact that Paley is a major source of Malthus's utilitarianism (see below, chapter 19) does not efface a profound difference between them regarding the conception of the greatest-good formula. It is precisely

35 There is no hint here of an anti-industrial tone. But this does not gainsay Malthus's early opposition to 'commercial systems' (see chapter 17: II).

Malthus refers in a note to an apparent change in Paley's position between *Moral Philosophy* (1785) and *Natural Theology* (1803) and draws a significant deduction regarding, so to speak, the optimal degree of luxury diffusion: 'From a passage in Paley's *Natural theology*, I am inclined to think that subsequent reflection induced him to modify some of his former ideas on the subject of population. He states most justly that mankind will in every country breed up to a certain point of distress [*Natural theology* 1803, 339]. If this be allowed, that country will evidently be the happiest, where the degree of distress at this point is the least; and consequently, if the spread of luxury, by producing the check sooner, tend to diminish this degree of distress, it is certainly desirable' (1803/1986, *3*, 566n).

The principle of population – Paley refers to Malthus's arithmetic and geometric rates – is, however, said by Paley to imply the impossibility 'to people a country with inhabitants who shall be all in easy circumstances,' leading to a justification of 'the distinctions of civil life' (*Natural Theology*, 340–1). Paley scarcely drew the same conclusion regarding income distribution as Malthus. His message was to be taken up by Sumner, 1816 (see Waterman, 1983, 204–5; 1991, 160–70).

these details that matter in practical policy applications of the general rule.

IX CONCLUSION

There is little excuse for charging Malthus with spawning a dismal doctrine. The thrust of Malthus's welfare position points to an increased degree of appropriation of the national surplus by labour. It is significant that his utilitarianism turns on the well-being of the *median* member of society, bearing as this does a more democratic flavour than one based simply on the *mean.*

Senior appended to his *Two Lectures on Population* (1829) a correspondence between himself and Malthus in which he candidly admitted to having misread the *Essay on Population* and publicly apologized for having ascribed to Malthus a denial of 'the possibility of permanent improvement,' a 'caricature' which he hoped would 'gradually wear away' (Senior, 1829, 55–7, 81, 88–9). As Senior originally understood the *Essay,* it conveyed the message that a temporary increase in wages will inevitably be cancelled in consequence of population pressure – a view he rejected: The problem of population pressure was 'likely to diminish in the progress of improvement' as tastes become more sophisticated; indeed, the experience of high wages would in all probability generate the elevation of tastes (minimum standards) required to render any improvement permanent (Senior, 35; cf. 74–5). This was in fact Malthus's own position (as he explained to Senior in conversation). For the misreading, Senior blamed Malthus's form of expression: 'I was misled by your use of the word "*tendency.*" I supposed you to believe, that the desire of marriage, which tends to increase Population, is a stronger principle, or, in other words, a principle more efficacious in its results than the desire of bettering our condition, which tends to increase subsistence; and, consequently, that in an old country, with a people so fully supplied with necessaries as to make it possible for population to increase in a greater ratio than food, such an increase would, in the absence of disturbing causes, be a more probable event than the opposite event; namely, than an increase of subsistence in a greater ratio than that of population. I believe that I was led into this error principally by the conduct of all those writers who, since the appearance of your work, have written on Population. The multitudes who have followed, and a few who have endeavoured to oppose you, have all assumed this to be your opinion. And yet when I recur to your writings, I see how inconsistent it is with your uniform statement, that the pressure upon subsistence is almost always the most severe in the rudest states of society, where the population is the least dense, and the means of procuring subsistence, supposing they were employed, would be the greatest in proportion to that population' (56–7).

Malthus explained that his formulation had been designed to impress the message that the solution to low wages or the maintenance of improved wages lay in population control (71–2). But he admitted that he would have been more careful had he been aware of the danger of misinterpretation (60). All he intended was the notion 'that population was always ready, and inclined, to increase faster than food, if the checks which repressed it were removed' (61) – whereupon Senior again pointed out that 'many, perhaps the majority of your readers, adopt the proposition without the qualification,' believing 'that the expansive power of population is a source of evil incapable not only of being subdued, but even of being mitigated' (79). The attribution to Malthus of the notion that reform was to no purpose had given political economy a bad name and was the regrettable outcome of the misunderstanding which Senior hoped would be cleared away once and for all: 'Undoubtedly these opinions are not fair inferences from your work; they are, indeed, directly opposed to the spirit of the greater part of it; but I think they must be considered as having been occasioned by a misconception of your reasoning. They are prevalent now: before the appearance of your writings, they were never hinted at. I trust, however, that, unsupported as they are by your authority, they will gradually wear away; and I anticipate from their disappearance not merely the extinguishment of an error, but the removal of an obstacle to the diffusion of political knowledge' (81–2).[36] Little could the correspondents have expected that the old saw would be repeatedly resuscitated.[37]

The more general question of the legitimate role allowed government, we have also seen, was approached by Malthus in a well-balanced manner. There was an initial presumption favouring *laissez-faire*, but the 'exceptions' had to be explicitly and conspicuously debated to defend the reputation of economic principles' (above, section VI). Some of Malthus's allowances for government are surprisingly 'liberal,' his evaluations varying with the immediacy and potency of the 'population problem.' But we must also recall from chapter 12 (p. 615) a denial of any role for government in regulating *the rate of savings*, despite all his concerns with instability reflecting deficient aggregate demand. Though this might seem to conflict with his own appeal in the Introduction to the *Principles* to avoid extreme positions on policy, such criticism would be somewhat anachronistic,

36 Cf. McCulloch: 'Malthus ... did not lay sufficient stress on the influence of the circumstances under which population is placed, and of the prudential considerations which they invariably bring along with them, in determining the rate of increase; and they have been all but overlooked by several of his followers. Hence the theory of population gave rise for a while to the most unreasonable fears and unfounded conclusions ... But the principle of increase is not the bugbear, the invincible obstacle to all real improvement, supposed by those who put forth such statements' (1864, 174–5).

37 Stigler (1965, 172) understood Senior in an 'ironic' sense. Such a reading of Senior's published remarks seems unjustified, but cannot be wholly excluded considering a most critical comment regarding Malthus made privately to a correspondent (see Conclusion, p. 994).

implying as it does the ability of contemporary governments to intervene in an appropriate and timely fashion. Malthus's positive allowances for intervention as far as concerns aggregate activity were rather of a remedial nature, and included emigration, public works, and poor relief; for the rest, with cyclical instability specifically in mind, and 'with a view to the happiness of the great mass of society, it should be our object, as far as possible, to maintain peace, and an equable expenditure' (1820, 522; 1836, 437).

NINETEEN

Utilitarianism in a theological context

I INTRODUCTION

Whether Malthus was a 'Utilitarian' is still a debated issue. D.P. O'Brien, for example, maintains that 'only the two Mills, part from Bentham himself, were really Utilitarians' (1975, 25). Against this we have the view of Lord Robbins: 'The principle that the test of policy is to be its effect on human happiness ... is common to all the English Classical Economists. We get the picture badly out of focus if we conceive that reliance on the principle of utility was confined to Bentham and his immediate circle' (1952, 177). The justice of Robbins's perspective has been demonstrated in chapter 18 with specific reference to the population problem. A related issue is considered in this chapter: the role of Malthus's theodicy in establishing him as a 'theological' utilitarian.

The final two chapters of the first edition of the *Essay on Population* (1798) treat the compatibility of the 'disheartening' outcome of the population principle with a beneficent deity. The theodicy in these chapters, it has been argued, 'though often treated as an embarrassing and detachable part of the *Essay* ... contains essential clues to the form of theological utilitarianism which underlies Malthus's moral philosophy' (Winch, 1987, 18–19). The removal of these concluding chapters in the later editions should not be misinterpreted: 'It is a mistake to believe that Malthus abandoned the brand of theological utilitarianism contained in his earlier theodicy in order to become a more secular social theorist; there was no conflict between Malthus the Christian "moral" philosopher and Malthus the scientist. The retention of the categories of vice and virtue, alongside, indeed attached to, pain and happiness, testify to their continuing importance. Indeed, an understanding of what precisely was 'moral' about moral restraint requires constant reference to the methodological standpoint of the theological utilitarian, for whom the greatest surplus of virtue and happiness over vice and misery was the supreme criterion for judging the worth of individual actions and social outcomes' (37).[1]

I do not deny a 'moral' dimension to Malthus's utilitarianism, though the same holds true with respect to Bentham and Mill. But my analysis supports Lord Robbins's position that Malthus's explanation of 'disharmonies' by reference to Divine Wisdom is 'extraneous to analysis' and without influence on the theory of policy (1952, 28n).[2] More strongly, the last two chapters in the 1798 essay turn out to be an embarrassment, and the apologia for a benevolent Deity is radically altered in later editions.

Whether Malthus envisaged a net balance of temporal good, taking into account *this* world considered across time and space, is not absolutely clear from the theological chapters. But it is clear that what temporal good is envisaged is there unrelated to the magnitude of labour's *per-capita* income; aggregate population takes centre stage. And from his universalist perspective, Malthus represented the 'distress' characterizing the specific case of 'old settled countries' – such as Britain – as a *partial* evil that is overwhelmingly outweighed when full allowance is made for the purely spiritual dimension (and possibly outweighed, one should add, even on a universal-

1 Cf. Winch, 1983: 'It is well known that Malthus modified his position in the second *Essay* by emphasising the preventive check of moral restraint; he also withdrew some of his more heterodox theological speculations. Nevertheless, neither the natural theology nor the moral categories of vice and virtue disappears when the *Essay* became a more academic treatise in demography' (70). Winch (1993) restates his case but, in my opinion, without adequately weighing the available evidence (see below, note 31). See also Pullen, 1981, on the theological basis for Malthus's approach to the population issue: 'In all editions of the *Essay* there are aspects of Malthus' theory of population which are unintelligible or contradictory if they are divorced from his theological ideas ... For example, having argued that population pressure leads to misery and vice, it would seem illogical for him to state that population growth per se is desirable. One would have expected him to advocate zero population growth. But within his theological system there is no contradiction, because he believed that it is the will of the Creator that the earth should be filled and because he saw the constant and universal pressure of population as a necessary and desirable stimulus for growth of mind' (53).

2 See, too, Rashid, 1984, 137, who disputes Pullen's claim that Malthus's theodicy is integral to Malthus's thinking: 'Malthus attached importance to his theory of mind, but only as a mode of reconciling us to the goodness of God and not because it added to the logical or factual acceptability of his theory.' Also Bonar, 1924, 38f. who considered the theodicy to be materially insignificant for the principle of population. Even Winch, who insists on the continued significance of the theological dimension in the second and subsequent editions, allows that 'the significance of all this for Malthus's views on politics and the science of political economy should not be exaggerated,' for he debated with economists 'without decisive recourse to theodicy' (71). Similarly, Waterman emphasizes 'moral restraint' as an essentially theological concept, but also recognizes that 'the specification "moral restraint" as a species of the preventive check makes no difference whatsoever to the body of "economic analysis" ...' (1991, 136, 144–50).

ist temporal view). This may satisfy theologians, but it clashes with the first *Essay* as a whole where, when dealing with the specifics of the British case, the magnitude of labour's *per-capita* income is the central policy concern, and suggestions are made for the mitigation of poverty through social and private action.

The *Essay* closes, it is true, with a protestation that the theological message is not one of 'despair,' since the quantity of 'evil' varies with activity or indolence. This might appear to open the door for improvement in living standards. But the theme is stated at the same universalist level as the rest of the chapter rather than with any eye to the specifics of any particular case. And in any event Malthus felt constrained, as we shall see, to reiterate that evil could never 'be removed from the world' and that any variation in its weight with activity is designed Providentially to 'keep alive a constant *expectation* of throwing it off,' which seems to withdraw much of the initial allowance, unless (and this may indeed be the case) it relates specifically to *individual* instances of improvement.

There is in addition a problem emerging in the body of the *Essay* but conspicuously absent from the last two chapters – that any reduction in misery entails, in practice, vice, casting doubt on the benevolence of the Deity. It is this problem, brought to Malthus's attention by critics of the first *Essay*, that led him to introduce the matter of 'moral restraint,' though (as will be recalled from chapter 18: V) he believed it to be empirically irrelevant. A theological dimension thus certainly remains in 1803 and thereafter – the mere fact that the two concluding chapters of 1798 disappear as such is of no consequence. Indeed, it is fair to say that the defence of the Deity is reinforced – though only if limited to an ideal rather than the real world, considering the practical insignificance of restraint. Even so, its substance differs from that of 1798. First, there is no longer any emphasis on the training of mind for a *future* existence, the most characteristic feature of the 1798 theodicy;[3] indeed there is considerable evidence that Malthus (perhaps as early as 1806) abandoned his unorthodox position. Second, the case for a reduction of poverty is now formally and conspicuously represented as a 'moral' issue, so that the theological problem is no longer to explain 'distress' but to explain the need for 'painful' checks to *avoid* distress.

Malthus also addressed the moral implications of the practical trade-off between vice and misery. But he approached practical policy issues in the manner of a social reformer, basing his recommendations on 'secular' utilitarian calculations; his taking account of 'vice' and 'virtue' does not gainsay this orientation, for the central feature of the theodicy of 1798 (training of mind for a 'superior' state of happiness) no longer plays a

3 A notion of training or 'improvement' of the mind remains which counteracts 'indolence' (below, pp. 930–1), but without the same weight on a *future* existence.

significant role. As for specifics, he was as much opposed to Church and State pressures towards a large population regardless of the consequences for living standards as he was to 'communist schemes' threatening the same outcome.[4] J.S. Mill adopted precisely this orientation: 'This great [Malthusian] doctrine, originally brought forward as an argument against the indefinite improvability of human affairs, we [the Philosophical Radicals] took up with ardent zeal in the contrary sense, as indicating the sole means of realizing that improvability by securing full employment at high wages to the whole labouring population through a voluntary restriction of the increase of their numbers' (1873/1981, I, 108). This comment on the 'original' doctrine is fair only if said of the theological chapters since, elsewhere in the first *Essay*, Malthus had pointed to the solution. But at least Mill recognized that a positive reformist attitude had ultimately been adopted by Malthus himself: 'Few writers have done more than himself, in the subsequent editions, to promote ... juster and more hopeful anticipations' (1848/1965, III, 753).[5]

Section II, below, is devoted to the theological chapters of the 1798 version and the tension between them and the body of the work. Section III elaborates on the implicit secular or utilitarian orientation of the first *Essay* manifested particularly in the recommendation of prudential control, despite the inevitability of 'vice.' The following section considers moral restraint within a utilitarian framework, and demonstrates Malthus's continued efforts in 1803 and thereafter – despite the omission of the formal chapters on theology – to reconcile dogma and utility, a process

4 It is still common enough to read of Malthus's 'conservatism.' See, for example, Sowell, 1962, 268, 1974, 28; Taylor, 1960, 147.

This matter is treated ambiguously in Winch's account (1983, 70–1). Winch maintains that 'neither the natural theology nor the moral categories of vice and virtue disappeared when the *Essay* became a more academic treatise on demography,' and that Malthus extended his criticism of utopian planners to include Robert Owen. 'It would seem, therefore, that Malthus takes his place in a long tradition of Anglican apologetics for inequality and poverty,' differentiating him 'from more secular devotees of political economy.' But at the same time we are told not to exaggerate all this when it comes to political economy: 'Malthus's population doctrine proved capable of being absorbed into political economy, with or without its natural theology overtones.' By thus using the passive voice – and alluding to the applications made of the doctrine by others (Dugald Stewart and J.S. Mill) – Winch seems to imply that Malthus himself in the *Essay on Population* falls into the apologetic school of divines.

5 For Mill's reading of the first essay as 'pessimistic,' see also 1879/1967, V, 728, and the comment on Hamilton's *Philosophy* (1865/1979, IX, 109–10). Mill in 1859 protested against Edwin Chadwick's 'slur on Malthus' (1972, XV, 590).

Others, outside the sphere of the Philosophical Radicals, also pointed to the reformist orientation of the *Essay on Population*. As we have seen in chapter 18: IX, Nassau Senior publicly apologized to Malthus for having lectured on population under a false impression of his position (a 'caricature') and hoped that the misconceptions 'unsupported as they are by your authority ... will gradually wear away.'

involving effectively the undermining of the theological foundation. Section V carries this theme further, from the perspective of prudential control *tout court* as justified in terms of a net balance of social utility, very much in line with the procedures of the secular utilitarians. The desirability of population expansion from a utility perspective, sharply contrasting with the standard religious case, is discussed in section VI; the argument is shown to open the door even to the justification of a stationary state in some circumstances. There are, it emerges, two theological stances – one emphasizing the *ideal* solution to the danger of potential population pressure; the other taking mankind as it is in *fact*, and arriving at a different set of recommendations. The concluding section summarizes the reasons for the decision to delete the theological chapters.

II THE THEOLOGICAL CHAPTERS OF THE FIRST *ESSAY*

The last two chapters of the 1798 *Essay* are designed to 'vindicate the ways of God to man' in the light of 'the constant pressure of distress on man from the difficulty of subsistence' (1986, 1, 122).[6] Malthus proceeded, as in an earlier footnote, to make a case envisaging this world as 'a mighty process for the creation and formation of mind' from matter, in the course of which 'many vessels will necessarily come out of this great furnace in wrong shapes. These will be broken and thrown aside as useless; while those vessels whose forms are full of truth, grace, and loveliness, will be wafted into happier situations, nearer the presence of the mighty maker' (88n).[7] This conception contrasts with a view of the world as a 'state of

6 Malthus approached his problem from the standpoint of natural theology, rejecting reliance upon the supernatural, revelation, or scriptural authority: 'it seems absolutely necessary, that we should reason from nature up to nature's God, and not presume to reason from God to nature' (350). Malthus does not always live up to this objective, often identified with that of Paley. Paley, too, however, pointed in his *Moral and Political Philosophy* to 'two methods of coming at the will of God on any point: 'I. By his express declarations, when they are to be had; and which must be sought for in Scripture. II. By what we can discover of his designs and disposition from his works, or, as we usually call it, the light of nature' (1st ed., 1785, 54). Moreover, the work is replete with scriptural reference. This is true *inter alia* of the case favouring retribution in the next world (41). Paley also proceeded by assertion. Thus the affirmative answer to the question 'Will there be after this life, any distribution of rewards and punishments at all? ... the foundation, upon which the whole fabric rests, must in this treatise be taken for granted' (53–4).

7 Bonar (1924, 35, 323f.) traces the influence of Abraham Tucker's *Light of Nature Pursued* (see also Waterman 1983, 196–200; 1991, 101–6). Malthus himself made explicit reference to John Locke for the general emphasis on the 'endeavour to avoid pain' as a stimulus to exertion, to which he adds his theme that exertion is a prerequisite for creation of mind (1986, *1*, 125–6). For other possible sources – the English empirical school and English Neoplatonism – see Harvey-Phillips, 1984, 598–9.

The notion of formation of mind is repeatedly restated in one form or other. There

trial, and school of virtue, preparatory to a superior state of happiness,' since that implied 'a previously formed existence, that does not agree with the appearance of man in infancy' (122–3).[8] The essential difference is between the tribulations of existence constituting a course of *training* – Malthus's position; and one of *probation* or testing or trial – Paley's view (see especially 131). Punishment is the consequence of failure on this latter view, whereas the former entails no question of future punishment, but rather 'merely condemning to their original insensibility those beings, that, by the operation of general laws, had not been formed with qualities suited to a purer state of happiness.'

There remains some doubt whether Malthus conceived a net balance of purely *temporal* good when he summarized by asserting that 'vice' and 'misery' are aspects of the 'infinite variety of nature' and 'admirably adapted to further the high purpose of the creation, and to produce the greatest possible quantity of good' (132). There is, it is true, an effect of general and constant laws of nature on mind, and thus on temporal activity of all kinds: 'the industry and foresight of the husbandman; the indefatigable ingenuity of the artificer; the skilful researches of the physician, and anatomist; and the watchful observation, and patient investigation of the natural philosopher' (126–7). But the weight of concentration is overwhelmingly on activity resulting in aggregative expansion of numbers – not increase in per-capita income; here lies the Providential design regarding population: 'As the reasons ... for the constancy of the laws of nature, seem, even to our understandings, obvious and striking; if we return to the principle of population, and consider man as he really is, inert, sluggish, and averse from labour, unless compelled by necessity ... we may pronounce, with certainty, that the world would not have been peopled, but

---

is in the first of the two chapters, for example, reference to the impressions and excitements of this world acting to awaken man's 'sluggish existence ... into a capacity of superior enjoyment' (124), to increase 'acuteness of intellect' (125), and to 'rouse man into action and form his mind to reason' (126). This is reiterated and applied in the second of the chapters: 'When the mind has been awakened into activity by the passions, and the wants of the body, intellectual wants arise; and the desire of knowledge, and the impatience under ignorance, form a new and important class of excitements' (131–2). Thus the apparently negative aspects of existence 'furnish endless motives to intellectual activity and exertion,' and the *effort* to understand 'invigorates and improves the thinking faculty' and provides 'stimulants to mental exertion' (133–4). Fully and effortlessly to understand God's plan would 'tend to repress further exertion, and to dampen the soaring wings of intellect' (134).

8 The view that human life constitutes a state of probation or trial was advanced by Butler and Paley (though it goes back to Origen, third century) and taken up by Sumner in 1816 (see Waterman, 1983, 198, 205–6; 1991, 65, 160–70). There is no *formal* discussion of this perspective in *Principles of Moral and Political Philosophy*. A convenient statement will be found in Paley's posthumously published 'Sermons on Several Subjects' (1850).

for the superiority of the power of population to the means of subsistence ... It keeps the inhabitants of the earth always fully up to the level of the means of subsistence; and is constantly acting upon man as a powerful stimulus, urging him to the further cultivation of the earth, and to enable it, consequently, to support a more extended population. But it is impossible that this law can operate, and produce the effects apparently intended by the supreme Being, without occasioning partial evil. Unless the principle of population were to be altered, according to the circumstances of each separate country ...; it is evident, that the same principle, which, seconded by industry, will people a fertile region in a few years, must produce distress in countries that have been long inhabited' (127). Malthus asserted at one point that 'life is generally speaking, a blessing independent of a future state' (136). But the argument of the foregoing passage – which does not specify *why* larger population size is desirable apart from a presumed Divine intention – proceeds at so general a level as to allow representation of the 'distress in countries that have been long inhabited' as nothing but a '*partial evil*' to be expected in any universalist environment subject to general laws of nature. Any temporal balance of good need not pertain to a specific region such as Great Britain. Moreover, even a universal balance of good does not incorporate the effect on happiness of high living standards.

We must also have in mind the primary concern, which is training of the mind for the *next* world. Within that broad theological frame of reference, it is easy to appreciate why *motive* matters: 'If the scriptural denunciations of eternal punishment were brought home with the same certainty to every man's mind, as that the night will follow the day, this one vast and gloomy idea would take such full possession of the human faculties, as to leave no room for any other conceptions: the external actions of men would be all nearly alike; virtuous conduct would be no indication of virtuous disposition; vice and virtue would be blended together in one common mass; and, though the all-seeing eye of God might distinguish them, they must necessarily make the same impressions on man, who can judge only from external appearances. Under such a dispensation, it is difficult to conceive how human beings could be formed to a detestation of moral evil, and a love and admiration of God, and of moral excellence' (134–5). It is thus in a world of uncertainty alone that one is justified in assuming that virtuous behaviour reflects virtuous motive, and conversely in the case of vicious behaviour, making it possible to learn to detest 'moral evil' (an idea to be found in Paley's *Natural Theology*, as is clarified in Waterman, 1992, 131–2). And 'moral evil is absolutely necessary to the production of moral excellence' precisely because it generates abhorrence in others (131).

This orientation implies that any scope for moral improvement applies to *individuals*, not to entire national groupings. The same seems to be true of a reduction in physical misery. For 'sorrows and distresses' are said to be necessary to excite sentiments of humanity, 'social sympathy,' 'Christian virtues' and to provide opportunities for the 'ample exertion of benevolence' (130). This theme requires further attention, considering a caution given at the very close of the *Essay*: 'Evil exists in the world, not to create despair, but activity. We are not patiently to submit to it, but to exert ourselves to avoid it' (137). The effort to overcome evil is in fact represented as a 'duty': 'It is not only the interest but the duty of every individual, to use his utmost efforts to remove evil from himself, and from as large a circle as he can influence; and the more he exercises himself in this duty, the more wisely he directs his efforts, and the more successful these efforts are; the more he will probably improve and exalt his own mind, and the more completely does he appear to fulfil the will of his Creator.' The denial that the proposed solution to the problem of evil implies an absence of scope for improvement is elaborated thus: 'The idea that the impressions and excitements of this world are the instruments with which the Supreme Being forms matter into mind; and that the necessity of constant exertion to avoid evil, and to pursue good, is the principal spring of these impressions and excitements, seems to smooth many of the difficulties that occur in a contemplation of human life; and appears to me, to give a satisfactory reason for the existence of natural and moral evil; and, consequently, for that part of both, and it certainly is not a very small part, which arises from the principle of population. But, though upon this supposition, it seems highly improbable, that evil should ever be removed from the world; yet it is evident, that this impression would not answer the apparent purpose of the Creator; it would not act so powerfully as an excitement to exertion, if the quantity of it did not diminish or increase, with the activity or the indolence of man. The continual variations in the weight, and in the distribution of this pressure, keep alive a constant expectation of throwing it off.' We again have here a universalist perspective, rendering it unclear whether Malthus intended a balance of temporal good in any *particular* country, including his own. And at the end of the passage he seems to withdraw much of the implicit allowance for improvement – unless we read him as recognizing only the possibility of *individuals* successfully rising above the mass.

To summarize the 'solution' proposed for the theological problem: On a universal level independent of time and space, there is said to be a net balance even of temporal good ('life is, generally speaking a blessing independent of a future state'). But the 'good' in question is unrelated to the level of per-capita income; and Malthus leaves open the possibility that, considering any specific region, particularly an old-settled country such as Britain, population pressure generates actual 'distress,' albeit a 'partial' evil in the broader context encompassing spiritual training for the next world. Within that broad context Malthus considered that the 'partial pain ... inflicted by the supreme Creator, while he is forming numberless beings to a capacity of the highest enjoyments, is but as the dust of the balance in comparison of the happiness that is communicated' (136). The positive case closes with the assertion that 'we have every reason to think, that there is no more evil in the world, than what is absolutely necessary as one of the ingredients of the mighty process.'

As noted, it is in the closing paragraphs of the *Essay* that we find the warning against 'despair.' This suggests a certain unease with the substantive defence of the Deity in the light of 'the constant pressure of distress on man from the difficulty of subsistence.' The temporal improvement allowed relates to both a diminution of 'natural' and 'moral' evil, that is, of poverty and vice. But there is an unfortunate vagueness about the allowance since it is not clarified whether such improvement is applicable to Britain and how precisely it would be achieved. The problem reflects to some extent a more basic ambiguity – whether the Providential ordinance relates to a *potentially* or an *actually* excessive growth rate of population relative to that of food; only if the problem is one of potentiality can it be avoided. On balance, we have suggested, Malthus's appeal against despair seems to open the door to *individual* rather than *collective* improvement; the problem remains one of actual population pressure in old-settled states.

It is only in the body of the first *Essay* that one finds the solution to the problem of poverty at the national level in the specific British case – it amounts, of course, to prudential control. However, prudential control entails vice, so that there emerges a trade-off between misery and vice. Malthus's defence of the Deity is thus already in difficulty in 1798. Apparently Malthus did not realize this when he published his apologia, but it was immediately brought to his attention by critics. It was this newly appreciated theological difficulty that led him to introduce moral restraint as an alternative to misery and vice, as we shall see in section IV.

* * *

Before proceeding we might consider the subsequent history of Malthus's theological position. Pullen argues the case that Malthus was persuaded to omit the two theological chapters because of their unorthodoxy – the denial of life as a state of trial or testing or probation, the notion of conditional immortality and the rejection of original sin – but did not retract his original views (1981a, 48, 50).[9] Waterman, on the other hand,

9 There is some indication to this effect in a letter dated 1 March 1799 to the *Monthly Magazine* touching on the projected rewriting of the *Essay*: 'As the subject of the two last chapters is not necessarily connected with it, I shall, in deference to the opinion of some friends whose judgments I respect, omit them' (cited in Rashid, 1984, 137). Moreover, in the Preface to the 1803 edition – though removed in 1806 – Malthus wrote: 'I should hope that there are some parts of it [the first essay], not reprinted in this, which may still have their use; as they were rejected, not because I thought them all of less value than what has been inserted, but because they did not suit the different plan of treating the subject which I had adopted' (1803/1986, *2*, ii).

maintains that Malthus finally adopted Paley's (and Sumner's) position, which considers this world to be a state of 'probation' or trial, providing challenges that invite improving solutions extending to the introduction of 'moral restraint' itself (1983, 205–6; 1991, 146–7, 172; see also Harvey-Phillips, 1984). And this latter view seems convincing.[10] The significance of the abandonment of the original theodicy in favour of Paley's is, we shall find, suggestive of a more 'mundane' treatment of the benevolence of God.[11] Certainly Malthus's original position is centred on training for the *next* world.

III A UTILITY CALCULUS, 1798

We have seen from a passage in the theological chapters of the first *Essay* that, for Malthus, motive mattered in the classification of virtuous behaviour (above, p. 923). More specifically: 'Our ideas of virtue and vice are not, perhaps, very accurate and well defined; but few, I think, would call an action really virtuous, which was performed simply and solely from the

10 The evidence includes the removal of the 1803 Preface referring to continued adherence to the original theology; and (more positively) a passage in the 1817 Appendix, following favourable reference to Sumner (1816) commencing: 'I have always considered the principle of population as a law peculiarly suited to a state of discipline and trial' (1817, III, 426). Taken literally this passage is a blatant untruth, for Malthus originally strongly denied the notion of life 'as a state of discipline *and trial*.' (Malthus also alludes to a 'competent tribunal' which induced him to expunge materials, apart from the two theological chapters, 'which have been thought too harsh, and not sufficiently indulgent to the weaknesses of human nature, and the feelings of Christian charity.')

There is also the conclusion to the article 'Population' (1824). Here Malthus raises the original issue of the 1798 theological chapters: 'It has been thought that a tendency in mankind to increase, beyond the greatest possible increase of food which could be produced in a limited space, impeaches the goodness of the Deity, and is inconsistent with the letter and spirit of the Scriptures' (1824b/1986, *4*, 239). In the brief defence of the Deity that follows, there is not a whisper of the original 1798 position regarding creation of mind but rather the assertion that 'it is almost universally acknowledged, that both the letter and spirit of revelation represent this world as a state of moral discipline and probation.'

I owe to A.M.C. Waterman the reminder that James Mill objected on purely secular grounds to Malthus's theology, viewing it as confused (in Ricardo, 1951–73, VII, 212n).

11 The categories may, however, have been breaking down for all parties. It is striking that the notion of life as a state of trial or probation as discussed by Paley in *Natural Theology* – where it is attributed to Rousseau (see Paley, 1803, 357) – seems to absorb Malthus's original theological position and put it to similar use. Thus the trials and tribulations of life 'all serve for the *formation* of character: for, when we speak of a state of trial, it must be remembered, that characters are not only tried, or proved, or detected, but that they are generated also and *formed*, by circumstances' (355). Moreover, this is asserted with an eye to 'a future state': 'A future state alone rectifies all disorders; and if it can be shewn that the appearance of disorder is consistent with the uses of life, as a preparatory state, or that in some respects it promotes these uses, then, so far as this hypothesis may be accepted, the ground of the difficulty is done away.'

dread of a very great punishment, or the expectation of a very great reward' – an allusion to 'future' punishment and reward contained in scripture (1986, *1*, 135). This perhaps constitutes an implicit criticism of Paley. For Paley maintained not only that 'actions are to be estimated by their tendency to promote happiness. – Whatever is expedient, is right. – It is the utility of any moral rule alone which constitutes the obligation to it' (1785, 61); but also that virtue differed from prudence only in allowing for the consequences in the next world as well as this: 'In the one case, we consider what we shall get or lose in this world; in the other case, we consider also what we shall get or lose in the world to come' (53).[12]

It is all the more interesting to encounter in the body of the first *Essay* a utilitarian perspective on moral behaviour – involving, incidentally, a version of the psychological principle of satiety – and one that seems to run in terms of temporal consequences alone: 'Intemperance in every enjoyment defeats its own purpose. A walk in the finest day, through the most beautiful country, if pursued too far, ends in pain and fatigue. The most wholesome and invigorating food, eaten with an unrestrained appetite, produces weakness, instead of strength. Even intellectual pleasures, though certainly less liable than others to satiety, pursued with too little intermission, debilitate the body, and impair the vigour of the mind. To

12 On this see Stephen, 1900, I, 161. Stephen observed that 'Paley's conception of the Deity is, in fact, coincident with Bentham's conception of the sovereign. He is simply an invisible sovereign, operating by tremendous sanction' (II, 358; cf. III, 309).

Jacob Viner points out that the later Cambridge revolt led by William Whewell against Paley's *Principles* 'was in part due to the fact that except for its addition of pleasures and pains in the future life to the pleasure–pain calculus, it was a close counterpart of Bentham's completely irreligious hedonic utilitarianism' (1972, 74). In his early criticism of Bentham, Mill objected to the narrowness of Bentham's philosophy as implying a view of morality akin to 'the doctrine of expediency as professed by Paley' (1833/1969, X, 7).

To be fair to Paley we must keep in mind a qualification to the generalization: 'Actions in the abstract are right or wrong, according to their *tendency*; the agent is virtuous or vicious, accordingly to his *design*. Thus, if the question be, Whether relieving common beggars be right or wrong? we inquire into the *tendency* of such a conduct to the public advantage or inconvenience. If the question be, Whether a man remarkable for this sort of bounty is to be esteemed virtuous for that reason? we inquire into his *design*, whether his liberality sprang from charity or from ostentation? It is evident that our concern is with actions in the abstract' (1785, 61n). It is not wholly clear on this view how to classify charity undertaken from fear of 'future' consequences or expectation of 'future' reward, but apparently the agent's good design might be thus dictated without loss of virtue. It is this that Malthus disputed.

J.S. Mill came to Paley's defence against a misreading by Sedgwick: 'Paley held, with other Christians, that our place hereafter would be determined by our degree of moral perfection; that is, by the balance, not of our good and evil deeds, which depend on opportunity and temptation, but of our good and evil dispositions; by the intensity and continuity of our *will* to do good' (1835/1969, X, 70). However, Mill also emphasized the role for Paley of 'simple self-interest as the motive, of virtue' (1852/1969, X, 170).

argue against the reality of these pleasures from their abuse, seems to be hardly just. Morality, according to Mr. Godwin [1796, I, 73], is a calculation of consequences, or, as Archdeacon Paley very justly expresses it, the will of God, as collected from general expediency [cf. 1785, 423]. According to either of these definitions, a sensual pleasure, not attended with the probability of unhappy consequences, does not offend against the laws of morality: and if it be pursued with such a degree of temperance, as to leave the most ample room for intellectual attainments, it must undoubtedly add to the sum of pleasurable sensations in life' (77). There was then nothing immoral attached to a sensual pleasure if unattended with the probability of unhappy consequences.

This perspective seems to govern an implicit secular utility calculus running through the first *Essay*, one purpose of which was to define the set of institutions which reduces the force of the population problem. That the criterion implicitly adopted is that of utility in the sense of a balance of *temporal* (though not necessarily *material*) happiness emerges most clearly from the dual propositions that 'prudential' population control 'almost necessarily, though not absolutely so, produces vice' (14), and – as we saw in chapter 18 (p. 883) – that 'vice' itself generates unhappiness – defined in purely temporal terms: 'The effects ... of these [preventive] restraints upon marriage are but too conspicuous in the consequent vices that are produced in almost every part of the world; vices, that are continually involving both sexes in inextricable unhappiness' (28). More strongly, a case against the outdoor poor-relief system intimates the toleration of prudence as a necessary evil for the sake of avoiding misery – the toleration of vice on a net balance of consequence: 'Every obstacle in the way of marriage must undoubtedly be considered a species of unhappiness. But as from the laws of our nature some check to population must exist, it is better that it should be checked from a foresight of the difficulties attending a family, and the fear of dependent poverty, than that it should be encouraged, only to be repressed afterwards by want and sickness' (35).

The implicit secular orientation of Malthus's position requires elaboration. An anonymous critic of the first *Essay* wrote that 'without intending it, however, we think the author, in this essay, has furnished the best apology for prostitution, that has ever been written' (*Analytical Review* 28, 124).[13] The point is that Malthus, by dealing with the social problem in the body of his 1798 *Essay* in terms of man 'as he is,' was adopting a position conflicting with the theological viewpoint of the last two chapters,

13 The same point has been made in the account by Flew, which refers to an 'embarrassing implication' for Malthus of his original statement: 'In so far as the sum of (the relevant sorts of) vice and misery provides a necessary check and in so far as such vice and misery are alternatives, it follows that to indulge in (any relevant form of) vice must be to reduce misery' (1970, 48).

where there is no hint of any trade-off, but merely the tangential suggestion that *both* 'natural' and 'moral evil' (misery and vice) can be reduced – and this apparently, we have found, only in individual cases.

Flew remarks that the 'unnoticed moral of the *First Essay* is very similar to the notorious paradox of Mandeville's *Fable of the bees*: "private vices, public benefits"' (1970, 48). Similar charges were made in Malthus's lifetime (although not necessarily in our specific context), and Malthus later denied them: 'Let me not be supposed to give the slightest sanction to the system of morals inculcated in the *Fable of the Bees*, a system which I consider as absolutely false, and directly contrary to the just definition of virtue' (1806, II, 523n). But what Malthus was here defending is only the general proposition that by the individual's pursuit 'as his primary object, [of] his own safety and happiness, and the safety and happiness of those immediately connected with him ... the most ignorant are led to promote the general happiness, an end which they would have totally failed to attain, if the moving principle of their conduct had been benevolence' (522–3). He did not have his implicit allowance for 'vice' in mind in this context. That allowance does, in fact, carry the Mandeville message, and clashes with the theological chapters.

When Malthus became conscious of the clash is an interesting question. In a letter to the *Monthly Magazine*, dated 1 March 1799 (though dealing with war rather than sex), he strongly denied that he had ever intended to justify vice as an alternative to misery: 'In whatever light we view the situation of man, on earth, he can never be justified in recurring to vice in order to avoid misery. To bear the unavoidable evils of life with unyielding integrity is the highest test of our virtue; to attempt to escape them by vicious means is the great proof of our weakness, and of our unfitness for a superior state' (cited Rashid, 1984, 136). This particular letter reflects the theological position of the last two chapters.[14] Malthus was apparently not yet willing to face the implication of his own observations in the body of the text.[15]

Malthus pointed to the intended implications of 'moral restraint,' or postponement of marriage not followed by 'irregular gratifications,' in the Preface to the second edition (see chapter 18, p. 886). This statement, which stamped the first *Essay* as a depressing document, is unfortunate since Malthus's demonstration in the body of that version that poverty and misery are 'absolutely irremediable' held good only *in the absence of prudential behaviour*. And from the outset – again in the body of the essay rather

14 Though there is this difference, that the final clause hints at the 'state of discipline and trial' rejected in the first *Essay*, but later adopted.

15 The theological chapters are unrepresentative in another respect. It is reported that as early as 1796 Malthus rejected, in opposition to Paley, the criterion of happiness in terms of population size; *increasing* population – clearly a reflection of good living standards – was the objective (see below, section VI).

than in the theological chapters – he had recommended delay of marriage despite the 'vicious' consequences.[16]

IV MORAL RESTRAINT AND UTILITARIANISM

Far from the theological concerns of Malthus diminishing between the first and second editions, the introduction of moral restraint evidently constitutes an attempt to reinforce the theological defence. Allusions to the training of 'mind' and character – the substance of the expunged theological chapters – re-emerge in 1803 in Book IV, on the obligation to practise the 'virtue' of moral restraint; various beneficial social effects to be expected therefrom; possible objections; and warnings against its avoidance. But the emphasis on preparation for the next world is lacking, and there other major differences between the two versions; Malthus, in 1803 and thereafter, effectively pulled the theological carpet from under his own feet.

The first chapter of Book IV sets out the issue by focusing on that proposition of 1798 implying a trade-off of vice against misery (1798/1986, *1*, 35; see above, p. 883). 'This idea will admit of being pursued further' (1803/1986, *3*, 465). As noted earlier, *this proposition does not appear in the original theological chapters*, which contain no hint of a trade-off (above, p. 925). Malthus evidently realized that those chapters had to be recast. That some sort of check is inevitable is represented, as in 1798, as a 'law of nature.' But the theological emphasis is now upon the *avoidance* of excess population growth 'with the least possible prejudice to the virtue and happiness of human society'; it is no longer to explain (and justify) 'the constant pressure of distress,' but rather to explain (and justify) the necessity for checks and, at one remove, the source of that necessity, namely, sexual passion – represented against Godwin to be the 'most powerful and general of our desires' after that for food (468). Alternatively stated, Malthus *qua theologian* set himself the task in 1803 of accounting for the Deity's creation of man as a being driven by a desire that necessitates (painful) control, displacing the emphasis entirely from a disheartening outcome of the population principle defined *in terms of actual poverty*.

We turn to the details of the argument regarding sexual passion – and the consequent 'tendency' for population growth to exceed that of food. This passion is represented (much as in the 1798 theological chapters) as *necessary* to the Divine purposes of assuring: (1) the 'replenishing' of the earth; and (2) 'the formation and improvement of the human mind' by

16 There are, it is true, strong statements in 1798: 'Necessity, that imperious all-pervading law of nature,' was such that 'the race of man cannot, by any efforts of reason, escape from it' (1986, *1*, 9). But since the necessary consequences of the law of nature is said to be misery *and vice*, there is the implication even here of a trade-off. The bleak statement may perhaps be explained as a reflection of the 'growth-of-mind' theodicy, which required the spur of necessity (see Harvey-Phillips, 1984, 596; Waterman, 1991, 108).

counteracting 'indolence.' The potential for 'evil' resulting from *general* or *uniform* laws is also allowed – an allusion to excess population growth in conditions of land scarcity. But there is this major difference between 1803 and the 1798 theological chapters – a new, very positive solution to the problem of poverty: 'It is however, a law, exactly similar in its great features to all the other laws of nature. It is strong and general, and apparently would not admit of any very considerable diminution, without being inadequate to its object; the evils arising from it are incidental to those necessary qualities of strength and generality; and these evils are capable of being very greatly mitigated and rendered comparatively light by human energy and virtue. We cannot but conceive that it is an object of the Creator, that the earth should be replenished [at least to a considerable degree];[17] and it appears to me clear, that this could not be effected without a tendency in population to increase faster than food; and as, with the present law of increase, the peopling of the earth does not proceed very rapidly, we have undoubtedly some reason to believe, that this law is not too powerful for its apparent object ... [We] have reason to think that it is more conducive to the formation and improvement of the human mind, that the law should be uniform, and the evils incidental to it, under certain circumstances, be left to be mitigated or removed by man himself. His duties in this case vary with his situation; he is thus kept more alive to the consequences of his actions; and his faculties have evidently greater play and opportunity of improvement, than if the evil were removed by a perpetual change of the law according to circumstances' (471–2). That misery was avoidable, and this without corresponding increase in vice, is thus the central theological theme of 1803, and often repeated: '[If], in addition to that general activity and direction of our industry put in motion by these laws [of nature], we further consider that the incidental evils arising from them are constantly directing our attention to the proper check to population, moral restraint; and if it appear that, by a strict obedience to the duties pointed out to us by the light of nature and reason, and confirmed and sanctioned by revelation, these evils may be avoided, the objection will, I trust, be removed, and all apparent imputation on the goodness of the Deity be done away' (474). 'As it appears therefore, that it is in the power of each individual to avoid all the evil consequences to himself and society resulting from the principle of population, by the practice of a virtue clearly dictated to him by the light of nature, and expressly enjoined in revealed religion; and as we have reason to think, that the exercise of this virtue to a certain degree would tend rather to increase than diminish individual happiness; we can have no reason to impeach the justice of the Deity, because his general laws make this virtue necessary, and punish our offenses against it by the evils atten-

17 The qualification in parenthesis was deleted in the 1806 edition (II, 315).

dant upon vice, and the pains that accompany the various forms of premature death' (480). On this view, natural and moral evil, including poverty, could be appreciated as the avoidable consequence of inadequate self-control – with an eye always to the balance of happiness: 'Natural and moral evil seem to be the instruments employed by the Deity in admonishing us to avoid any mode of conduct which is not suited to our being, and will consequently injure our happiness ... [If] we heed not this admonition, we justly incur the penalty of our disobedience, and our sufferings operate as a warning to others' (465–6).

* * *

Malthus's defence of the Deity is intimately bound up with the notion of utility as the foundation of morals.[18] The utilitarian rule is stated thus by Malthus:

> As animals, or till we know their consequences, our only business is to follow these dictates of nature; but, as reasonable beings, we are under the strongest obligations to attend to their consequences; and if they be evil to ourselves or others, we may justly consider it as an indication, that such a mode of indulging these passions is not suited to our state or conformable to the will of God. As moral agents, therefore, it is clearly our duty to restrain their indulgence in these particular directions; and by thus carefully examining the consequences of our natural passions, and frequently bringing them to the test of utility, gradually to acquire a habit of gratifying them only in that way, which, being unattended with evil, will clearly add to the sum of human happiness and fulfil the apparent purpose of the Creator.
>
> Though utility, therefore, can never be the immediate excitement to the gratification of any passion, it is the test by which alone we can know [1817: independently of the revealed will of God], whether it ought or ought not to be indulged; and is therefore the surest foundation of all morality [1817: the surest criterion of moral rules] which can be collected from the light of nature. All the moral codes, which have inculcated the subjection of the passions to reason,

18 Paley's *Moral and Political Philosophy* is cited in support: 'The method of coming at the will of God, concerning any action, by the light of nature, is to enquire into the tendency of the action to promote or diminish the general happiness. And this rule proceeds upon the presumption, that God Almighty wills and wishes the happiness of his creatures; and consequently, that those actions, which promote that will and wish, must be agreeable to him; and the contrary' (1785, 56–7). This perspective, Malthus observed, implied that the Christian religion was adaptable 'to a more improved state of human society,' in so far as 'it places our duties respecting marriage and the procreation of children in a different light from that in which they were before beheld' (1803/1986, *3*, 479).

have been, as I conceive, really built upon this foundation, whether the promulgators of them were aware of it or not. (531; 1817, III, 214–15)[19]

There is, however, a crucial difference between Malthus and Paley to keep in mind. For Malthus, the utilitarian rule pointed to moral restraint: 'There are perhaps few actions that tend so directly to diminish the general happiness, as to marry without the means of supporting children. He who commits this act, therefore, clearly offends against the will of God; and having become a burden on the society in which he lives, and plunged himself and family into a situation, in which virtuous habits are preserved with more difficulty than in any other, he appears to have violated his duty to his neighbours and to himself, and thus to have listened to the voice of passion in opposition to his higher obligations' (479–80). 'Judging merely from the light of nature, if we feel convinced of the misery arising from a redundant population on the one hand, and of the evils and unhappiness, particularly to the female sex, arising from promiscuous intercourse, on the other, I do not see how it is possible for any person who acknowledges the principle of utility as the great foundation of morals [1817: the great criterion of moral rules], to escape the conclusion, that moral restraint, till we are in a condition to support a family, is the strict line of duty; and when revelation is taken into the question, this duty undoubtedly receives very powerful confirmation' (482; 1817, III, 102–3).[20] But *this was not the conclusion reached by Paley* (1785, 592–3), who, to Malthus's distress – somewhat exaggerated, since in fact Paley assumed the limits to be nowhere in sight (see note 37, below) – recommended state encouragement of population expansion in conditions of increasing land scarcity: 'The particular end in view in this case appears to be absolutely criminal. We wish to force people into marriage, when from the acknowledged scarcity of subsistence they will have little chance of being able to support their children. We might as well force people into the water who are unable to swim. In both cases we rashly tempt providence. Nor have we more reason to believe that a miracle will be worked to save us from the misery and mortality resulting from our conduct in the one case than in the other' (485).

Malthus also drew on Paley's later work, *Natural Theology* (1803 [1802],

19 James, (1979, 119–20), points out that a correspondent in the *Christian Observer* for September 1805 ('Unus,' possibly Thomas Gisborne) objected to the principle of Expediency enunciated in this passage (as well as to the reason given – involving consequences – for defining an action as vicious, below, p. 940). The modifications to the text of 1817 may have been made by Malthus in response to this criticism, as suggested by James, though James erred in dating the modification 1806.

20 The notion that the source of morality resides in social utility is applied also to the case of private charity in a warning against the exercise of 'indiscriminate' benevolence. For benevolence and sex are both 'natural passions, which are excited by their appropriate objects, and to the gratification of which we are prompted by the pleasurable sensations which accompany them' (531).

344),[21] in championing from the utilitarian perspective the regulation – not the extinction – of the passions: 'Our virtue ... as reasonable beings, evidently consists in educing from the general materials, which the Creator has placed under our guidance, the greatest sum of human happiness; and as all our the natural impulses are abstractly considered good, and only to be distinguished by their consequences, a strict attention to these consequences, and the regulation of our conduct conformably to them, must be considered as our principal duty' (1803/1986, *3*, 471). It is precisely because the passions 'could not be generally weakened or diminished, without injuring our happiness' that their control rather than their extinction was required (467). In this context too we find *utility represented as the source of morality* (and law) in the course of an analogy drawn with hunger: 'The act of the hungry man who satisfies his appetite by taking a loaf from the shelf of another, is in no respect to be distinguished from the act of him who does the same thing with a loaf of his own, but by its consequences. From the consideration of these consequences, we feel the most perfect conviction, that, if people were not prevented from gratifying their natural desires with the loaves in the possession of others, that the number of loaves would universally diminish. This experience is the foundation of the laws relating to property, and of the distinctions of virtue and vice, in the gratification of desires otherwise perfectly the same. If the pleasure arising from the gratification of these propensities were universally diminished in vividness, violations of property would become less frequent; but this advantage would be greatly overbalanced by the narrowing of the sources of enjoyment. The diminution in the quantity of all those productions, which contribute to human gratification, would be much greater in proportion than the diminution of thefts; and the loss of general happiness on the one side would be beyond comparison greater than the gain to happiness on the other' (467–8). This same concept of a net balance of happiness is generalized to sex and all the passions: 'Few or none of them will admit of being greatly diminished, without narrowing the sources of good, more powerfully than the sources of evil. And the reason seems to be obvious. They are, in fact, the materials of all our pleasures, as well as of all our pains; of all our happiness, as well as of all our misery; of all our virtues, as well as of all our vices. It must therefore be regulation and direction that are wanted, not diminution or extinction' (470).

As for sexual passion, Malthus goes out of his way to list the sources of positive happiness flowing therefrom when 'taken in an enlarged sense' (468).[22] Thus 'the formation and steady pursuit of some plan of life in-

21 My references to this work will be to the American edition of 1803. The original appeared in 1802, and this is important, since the 'moral restraint' of Malthus's second edition, it has been argued, depends on it (Waterman, 1991, 147–8; see above, p. 926).

22 Here again (see above, p. 930) his target is Godwin, who played down the 'attendant circumstances' attached to physical sex.

volving the prospect of companionship and children is represented as 'one of the most permanent sources of happiness' (469); the 'bond of conjugal affection' had a 'most powerful tendency to soften and meliorate the human character, and keep it more alive to all the kindlier emotions of benevolence and pity'; and, furthermore, when the passion faces 'obstacles ... in the way of very early and universal gratification,' there is a resultant positive effect on 'gentleness, kindness, and suavity of manners,' that is, on 'the formation and improvement of character' (469–70). All in all, though some evil results from the passion between the sexes – or rather from its 'irregular gratification' – on a *balance* of considerations, the net advantage was overwhelming.

Adding in the widespread practice of moral restraint, the outlook becomes bright indeed, both from the perspective of living standards and from that of 'the female character':

> If, for the sake of illustration, we might be permitted to draw a picture of society, in which each individual endeavoured to attain happiness by the strict fulfilment of those duties, which the most enlightened of the ancient philosophers deduced from the laws of nature, and which have been directly taught, and received such powerful sanctions in the moral code of Christianity, it would present a very different scene from that which we now contemplate. Every act, which was prompted by the desire of immediate gratification, but which threatened an ultimate overbalance of pain, would be considered as a breach of duty; and consequently no man, whose earnings were only sufficient to maintain two children, would put himself in a situation in which he might have to maintain four or five, however he might be prompted to it by the passion of love ...
>
> The interval between the age of puberty and the period at which each individual might venture on marriage must, according to the supposition, be passed in strict chastity; because the law of chastity cannot be violated without producing evil. The effect of anything like a promiscuous intercourse, which prevents the birth of children, is evidently to weaken the best affections of the heart, and in a very marked manner to degrade the female character. And any other intercourse would, without improper arts, bring as many children into the society as marriage, with a much greater probability of their becoming a burden to it. (474–5)

Sexual continence before marriage was thus the ideal, and this because promiscuity produced evil, including a weakening of 'affection' and a degradation of 'the female character.' This would be so, assuming the practice of birth control or 'improper arts' – though in its absence there would be the same problems, and worse, which flow from early marriage and poverty. As expressed a little later, 'moral restraint' was 'the strict line of duty,' since promiscuity generated 'evils and unhappiness, particularly to the female sex' (482), that is, some form or other of character degeneration, and probably also sexually transmitted diseases. This is further confirmed by various amplifications regarding 'the vice of promiscuous intercourse' resulting from mere prudence, which includes both 'moral' and 'physical' evils (495; see chapter 18, pp. 888–9).

* * *

The formal defence of the Deity in 1803 thus extends far beyond 1798. But there is reason to doubt whether Malthus continued to draw upon the *original* theological chapters of 1798 in defining his brand of utilitarianism. For one thing, it is characteristic of the later editions that training of the mind for the 'future state' or 'state of superior enjoyment,' though mentioned, does not receive anything like the same attention it is accorded in 1798; while the source of virtue in a calculation of consequences is said to be common to 'heathen' as well as Christian moralists: 'The difficulty of moral restraint will perhaps be objected to this doctrine. To him who does not acknowledge the authority of the Christian religion, I have only to say that, after the more careful investigation, this virtue appears to be absolutely necessary, in order to avoid certain evils which would otherwise result from the general laws of nature. According to his own principles, it is his duty to pursue the greatest good consistent with these laws; and not to fail in this important end, and produce an overbalance of misery by a partial obedience to some of the dictates of nature, while he neglects others. The path of virtue, though it be the only path which leads to permanent happiness, has always been represented by the heathen moralists as of difficult ascent' (477–8). Appeal to the Scriptures regarding the nature of the individual's 'duty' is secondary to the main argument for pre-marital continence – the net balance of social good (including moral tone or character) resulting therefrom.[23]

At the same time it would be misleading to pretend that Malthus's utilitarianism as applied to moral restraint is wholly plain sailing. An explanatory note attached to the term 'moral restraint' in 1806 suggests appeal to some absolute code: 'It will be observed, that I here use the term *moral* in its most confined sense. By moral restraint I would be understood to mean a restraint from marriage, from prudential motives, with a conduct strictly moral during the period of this restraint; and I have never intentionally deviated from this sense. When I have wished to consider the restraint from marriage unconnected with its consequences, I have either called it prudential restraint, or a part of the preventive check, of which indeed it forms the principal branch' (1806, I, 19–20n).[24] As Sir Leslie

23 A view of happiness which includes character or moral tone does not, of course, of itself necessarily imply a 'theological' perspective.

24 Bonar, however, sees no problem here: 'The adjective "moral" does not imply that the motives are the highest possible. The adjective is applied not so much to the motive of the action as to the action itself, from whatever motives proceeding; and in the mouth of a Utilitarian this language is not unphilosophical. Moral restraint, in the pages of

Stephen observed, the term 'vice' is occasionally used in the *Essay* not as 'productive' of misery, but as 'an alternative to misery; and yet something bad in itself. Is this consistent with [Malthus's] Utilitarianism?' (1900, II, 158).[25]

This problem is best approached directly by reference to Malthus's unwillingness to categorize illicit sex as 'misery' rather than 'vice.' 'Misery' was an inappropriate term for actions which in individual cases generated a balance even of long-run happiness (with an eye to *this*, not the next, life in contrast to the perspective of 1798). The 'viciousness' of promiscuity was defined relative to its '*general tendency*' to reduce individual happiness, and thus the happiness of society: 'As the general consequence of vice is misery, and as this consequence is the precise reason why an action is termed vicious, it may appear that the term misery alone would be here sufficient, and that it is superfluous to use both. But the rejection of the term vice would introduce a considerable confusion into our language and ideas. We want it particularly to distinguish that class of action, the general tendency of which is to produce misery, but which, in their immediate or individual effects, may produce perhaps exactly the contrary. The gratification of all our passions in its immediate effect is happiness, not misery; and, in individual instances, even the remote consequences (at least in this life) come under the same denomination. I have little doubt that there have been some irregular connexions with women, which have added to the happiness of both parties, and have injured no one. These individual actions, therefore, cannot come under the head of misery. But they are still evidently vicious, because an action is so denominated, the general tendency of which is to produce misery, whatever may be its individual effect; and no person can doubt the general tendency of an illicit intercourse between the sexes, to injure the happiness of society' (1803/1986, *2*, 16–17n).[26]

Malthus failed to make explicit that no stigma attaches to the behaviour of individual couples engaged in 'irregular connexions' where a net balance of happiness could be expected for that couple without injury to

Malthus, means simply continence; it is an abstinence from marriage followed by no irregularities' (1924, 53).

25 Thus certain 'viscious' practices of the South Sea Islanders result in a lesser need for other population checks (famine) and are pleasurable *per se* and ought, on a neutral view, be considered beneficial; and the rejection of birth control, which would limit population without causing 'misery,' seems not to be consistent. Malthus, Stephen opines, 'wishes to avoid the imputation of sanctioning such practices, and therefore condemns them by his moral check; but it would be hard to prove that he was consistent in condemning them.'

26 Although Malthus neglected in the foregoing passage to define the 'injury' to the 'happiness of society,' he presumably intended character degeneration and disease (as in other contexts discussed above), since increased poverty cannot be the issue.

other parties.[27] And the fact is that he stepped back from that conclusion. For in 1817 he altered the third sentence justifying the term 'vice' to read: 'We want it particularly to distinguish those actions, the general tendency of which is to produce misery, and which are therefore prohibited by the commands of the Creator, and the precepts of the moralist, although, in their immediate or individual effects, they may produce perhaps exactly the contrary' (1817, I, 23–4n). Here then we find an appeal to biblical injunction. Similarly: 'There are perhaps few actions that tend so directly to diminish the general happiness, as to marry without the means of supporting children. He who commits this act, therefore, clearly offends against the will of God ...' (above, p. 993). However, it is noteworthy that such injunctions are not represented as *independent*; rather, the Creator condemns certain acts *because* they tend to generate net social disutility. This perspective is implicit in Paley's dictum, approved by Malthus, that the 'method of coming at the will of God ... by the light of nature, is to enquire into the tendency of the action to promote or diminish the general happiness' (see above, note 18). To this extent dogma and utility can proceed hand in hand, and Stephen's problem is avoided.[28]

In other contexts, too, this gloss seems to be intended, as in the reference to 'a strict obedience to the duties pointed out to us by the light of nature and reason, and confirmed and sanctioned by revelation,' or to 'the practice of a virtue clearly dictated ... by the light of nature, and expressly enjoined in revealed religion' (cited above, p. 931). And we find the proposition that those private acts 'the general tendency of which is to produce misery' are to be classed as *vicious*, deliberately altered in 1817 to incorporate this perspective: 'An action is so denominated, which violates an express precept, founded upon its general tendency to produce misery' (24n).[29]

27 Contrast this with the statement of 1799, cited above, p. 929. That statement, dealing with a refusal to legitimize *war*, creates a problem from a strictly utilitarian viewpoint; one could envisage circumstances in which war might be justified as an alternative to poverty (see Rashid, 1984, 137–8).

28 Even in those cases where the command of God seems to be given independent status, it would not do to exaggerate the problem. Bentham, after all, represented the ultimate task of government to be the encouragement of socially desirable behaviour with conspicuous allowance made for 'men's moral, religious, sympathetic, and anti-pathetic sensibilities' (1789, 68). And J.S. Mill defended Paley along these lines against a charge by Sedgwick: 'To say that if we adopt the principle of utility, we cannot admit religion as a sanction for it, or cannot attach importance to religious motives or feelings [is] simply false' (1835/1969, X, 69).

29 That Malthus was, however, troubled by the general issue seems to be implied by the changes in terminology referred to above, p. 932, specifically the replacement in 1817 of the term 'foundation of all morality' by 'criterion of moral rules' in the representation of utility, and the insertion of the qualification 'independently of the revealed will of God.'

V PRUDENTIAL CONTROL AND UTILITARIANISM

As we emphasized in chapter 18: V, Malthus did not believe that the premarital period could be spent chastely. Yet the small likelihood of any extensive adoption of the ideal solution ('moral restraint'), Malthus insisted, did not detract from the theological defence of the Deity: 'He who publishes a moral code, or system of duties, however firmly he may be convinced of the strong obligation on each individual strictly to conform to it, has never the folly to imagine that it will be universally or even generally practised ... I allowed myself to suppose the universal prevalence of this virtue ... that I might endeavour to remove any imputation on the goodness of the Deity, by showing, that the evils arising from the principle of population were exactly of the same nature as the generality of other evils which excite fewer complaints; that they were increased by human ignorance and indolence, and diminished by human knowledge and virtue; and on the supposition that each individual strictly fulfilled his duty, would be almost totally removed; and this without any general diminution of those sources of pleasure, arising from the regulated indulgence of the passions, which have been justly considered as the principal ingredients of human happiness' (1803/1986, *3*, 482–3). In the Appendix of 1817, Malthus insisted again that he was doing his duty by introducing the *ideal* solution, 'whether the remedy be ... adequate or inadequate' (see below, note 32).

Here it is illuminating to consider a charge by Robert Torrens (1815, viii–x) against Malthus of a blatant inconsistency in introducing moral restraint, despite his criticisms of Godwin and Condorcet. This criticism is, in one major respect, unjustified. Torrens failed to note Malthus's own defence in 1803 against such complaints – that his position differed in principle from that of the idealists by its emphasis on *self-interest* (subject to appropriate institutions) rather than on *benevolence*: 'It is not required of us to act from motives to which we are unaccustomed; to pursue a general good, which we may not distinctly comprehend, or the effect of which may be weakened by distance and diffusion. The happiness of the whole is to be the result of the happiness of individuals, and to begin first with them. No co-operation is required. Every step tells. He who performs his duty faithfully will reap the full fruits of it, whatever may be the number of others who fail. This duty is express, and intelligible to the humblest capacity. It is merely, that he is not to bring beings into the world, for whom he cannot find the means of support' (1803/1986, *3*, 483).

Malthus could, however, be held to account had he proposed a solution to the population problem which he realized would not be widely adopted. He himself admitted as much when he pointed a finger at 'visionary' writers: 'If it will answer any purpose of illustration, I see no harm in drawing the picture of a society, in which each individual is supposed strictly to fulfil his duties; nor does a writer appear to be justly liable to the imputation of being visionary, unless he make such universal or general obedience necessary to the practical utility of his system, and to that degree of moderate and partial improvement, which is all that can rationally be expected from the most complete knowledge of our duties.' If, however, people see their self-interest to lie not in moral restraint but in mere 'prudence,' we are left with the practical choice between 'vice,' or premarital sexual activity, with its unwelcome social consequences (see above, pp. 935–6), and 'misery.' Malthus, to his credit, recognized this and, taking the world as it is, carried on to justify prudential population control on effectively *neutral* utilitarian grounds – notwithstanding that this line clashes with the theological defence of the Deity turning upon ideal behaviour. We have already elaborated on the net balance of social utility deriving from population control with an eye to *reality* (chapter 18: V),[30] a calculus, it will be recalled, taking account of the 'vices' attached to poverty, and including theft and murder – and their punishment envisaged as a 'painful' act or disutility – and the degradation of young persons (490–2).[31] A consequence of excessive population growth is thus an inevitable degradation of character, unless one has recourse to prudential control, *albeit involving premarital sex*, since the damage (even to character) is thereby lessened (489). It is pertinent, too, that the reduction of the misery attached to poverty is itself defined as a moral problem: 'And, with regard to the necessity of this celibacy in countries that have been long peopled, or our obligation not to marry till we have a fair prospect of being able to support our children it will appear to deserve the attention of the moralist, if it can be proved that an attention to this obligation is of more effect in the prevention of misery, than all the other virtues combined' (473). Similarly: 'Can any man of reflection,' Malthus asked in 1817, 'venture to state that there is no moral reason for repressing the inclination to early marriages; when it cannot be denied that the alternative of not repressing it must necessarily and unavoidably be premature mortality from excessive poverty?' (1817, III, 411).

To claim, as Malthus does at one point (see above, p. 937), that illicit intercourse is to be classed as 'vicious' because (viewed as a tendency, not necessarily in individual cases) it injures 'the happiness of society,' loses all substance once it is allowed that such behaviour generates a *net* balance of social happiness via its reduction of poverty and the vicious consequences of poverty. Malthus went yet further in 1806 by his insistence that he had 'taken man as he is' in arriving at 'practical applications' of his principle

30 The desirable political and military consequences ascribed to the widespread practice of moral restraint would follow from prudential control *tout court*, and must be included in the utility calculus (chapter 18, pp. 905f.).

31 Winch's strictures on the argument of this chapter (1993) would be more convincing had he taken this position into account.

of population, that his was no visionary concept of man: 'Thus viewing him and knowing that some checks to populations must exist, I have not the slightest hesitation in saying, that the prudential check to marriage is better than premature mortality' (1806, II, 537–8).[32]

Malthus recognized that the elements allowed into the utility calculus is always a matter of personal judgment (1803/1986, *2*, iii, cited chapter 18, p. 886).[33] Doubtless the precise constituents of 'morality' differ somewhat between Malthus and Mill or Bentham (as they do between the latter two).[34] But the characteristic theodicy of 1798 – its concept of 'the mighty process for the creation and formation of mind' to fit it for 'happier situation, nearer the presence of the mighty maker' – is played down even within the course of the defence of the Deity; and moreover is wholly irrelevant to the utilitarian calculus adopted in the actual treatment of particular social issues, which eschews the ideal. In fact, we go further. Malthus introduced a purely secular orientation by the two allowances discussed above. First, the concession that, in individual cases, 'irregular' sexual relationships might generate 'happiness' to both parties with injury to nobody (above, p. 937); such behaviour is termed 'vicious' only because of its *general* tendency to individual, and thus social unhappiness. This is far from a theological perspective, though Malthus struggled to avoid the

32 Malthus, however, insisted that he had done his duty by pointing to the *ideal* solution 'whether the remedy be ... adequate or inadequate': 'I have not considered the evils of vice and misery arising from a redundant population as unavoidable, and incapable of being diminished. On the contrary I have pointed out a mode by which these evils may be removed or mitigated by removing or mitigating their cause. I have endeavoured to shew that this may be done consistently with human vice and happiness. I have never considered any possible increase of population as evil, except as far as it might increase the proportion of vice and misery. Vice and misery, and these alone, are the evils which it has been my great object to contend against. I have expressly proposed moral restraint as their rational and proper remedy; and whether the remedy be good or bad, adequate or inadequate, the proposal itself, and the stress which I have laid upon it, is an incontrovertible proof that I never can have considered vice and misery as themselves remedies' (1817, III, 391–2).

33 As J.S. Mill was to point out, the greatest happiness principle did not in itself yield rules of just behaviour, especially if allowance is made for the consequences of actions for character, that is, the effects of action 'upon [an individual's] susceptibilities of pleasures or pain, upon the general direction of his thoughts, feelings, and imagination ...' (1835/1969, X, 56). All in all, there was 'as much difference in the moral judgements of different persons, as there is in their views of human nature, and of the formation of character' (67), so that 'clear and comprehensive views of education and human culture must ... precede, and form the basis of, a philosophy of morals' (56). Thus a utilitarian perspective necessarily turns on some conception or other of 'morality' drawn from an external source defining 'right' or 'true human feeling.' This had been Bentham's position as well, and one which Mill had in his early reaction from Bentham originally disputed (cf. Hollander, 1985, 617f.).

34 As will also be recalled from chapter 18, VIII, the fact that Malthus's utilitarianism drew on Paley must not cloud their differences on the constituents of the greatest-good formula.

implication. And yet more important, is the balancing of moral costs and benefits which led Malthus to countenance simple prudence as the lesser evil. This attitude is a direct invitation to abandon entirely the 'ideal' solution posited for the existence of evil.[35]

Although Malthus had introduced 'moral restraint' in response to critics of the first *Essay* (above, p. 925), the alteration did not have a mollifying effect, as is clear from the savage criticism to which he was subjected after the second and later editions (e.g., Jarrold, 1806; Hazlitt, 1807; Weyland, 1816; Ravenstone, 1821). This is particularly understandable when we keep in mind Malthus's effective rejection of moral restraint as a *practical* solution. (See on this issue Levy 1996; also on reactions to the second and later essays, James, 1979, 109–115, 116–26; Waterman, 1991, ch. 4; Bonar, 1924, Book IV.)

There are then two theological Malthuses at work, one proposing the ideal solution to the problem of the threat of poverty created by potential population pressure;[36] and the other taking the world, warts and all, and arriving at a wholly different set of recommendations. In the latter guise, there is nothing to distinguish Malthus from the secular utilitarians. It remains only to note a revealing disclaimer of any right to interfere in the event of an increase in vice with increased prudential control: 'If, on contemplating the increase of vice which might contingently follow an attempt to inculcate the duty of moral restraint, and the increase of misery that must necessarily follow the attempts to encourage marriage and population, we come to the conclusion, not to interfere in any respect, but to leave every man to his own free choice, and responsible only to God for the evil which he does in either way; this is all I contend for; I would on no account do more; but I contend, that at present we are very far from doing this' (1803/1986, *3*, 497–8).

VI MORE ON THE DESIRABILITY OF POPULATION EXPANSION

Paley interpreted the 'greatest happiness' rule as implying a case for large numbers: 'The happiness of a people is made up of the happiness of single persons; and the quantity of it can only be augmented by increasing the

35 Our conclusion may be contrasted with that of Eversley, 1959, 248–9: The preventive checks which reduce fertility 'may be divided into good, bad, and indifferent checks. The good one is moral restraint, i.e. restraint from marriage with virtuous conduct, and out of regard for the well-being of society, as well as one's own advantage. The bad one is self-seeking prudential restraint from marriage with loose sexual conduct. The indifferent one is prudential restraint mostly for selfish reasons, with an occasional human lapse presumably permitted.'

36 Malthus often reverted to the ideal. Thus moral restraint is represented in 1824 (and repeated 1830) as 'the only mode of keeping population on a level with the means of subsistence, which is perfectly consistent with virtue and happiness' (1986, *4*, 203).

number of the percipients, or the pleasures of their perceptions' (1785, 587–8).[37] An early objection by Malthus (along typically Smithian lines) appears in the unprinted pamphlet *The Crisis*, written in 1796: 'On the subject of population I cannot agree with Archdeacon Paley, who says, that the quantity of happiness in any country is best measured by the number of people. Increasing population is the most certain possible sign of the happiness and prosperity of the state; but the actual population may be only a sign of the happiness that is past' (cited by Empson, 1837, in Semmel, 1963, 244).[38] As we have seen in chapter 18: II, increasing population – not a large population as such – was desirable, although only in so far as such increase implied a response to good standards, and would not dictate reduced standards at higher absolute population sizes.[39] In the third edition of 1806, Malthus protested strongly against misrepresentations of his position (1806, II, 507–8). His program of checks to the birth rate was consistent with population expansion, and critics had erroneously supposed his object was to check population, 'as if anything could be more desirable than the most rapid increase of population unaccompanied by vice and misery' (515–16). The consistency of the *desiderata* of 'high' wages and population growth turns, it will be recalled, on the greater potential for productivity increase in the case of a population with a high proportion

37 Paley in fact wrote in somewhat qualified fashion: 'within certain limits ... it may be affirmed, I think, with certainty, that the quantity of happiness produced in any given district (the object of which all the endeavours of public wisdom should be directed,) *so far* depends upon the number of inhabitants, that, in comparing adjoining periods in the same country, the collective happiness will be nearly in the exact proportion of the numbers, that is, twice the number of inhabitants will produce double the quantity of happiness.' Land scarcity, however, was not a practical issue for Paley: 'The fertility of the ground, in temporate regions, is capable of being improved by cultivation to an extent which is unknown' (590).

Bentham was also to qualify his utility-based case for population increase: 'Increase of population is desirable, as being an increase of – 1. The beings susceptible of *enjoyment*; 2. The beings capable of being employed as *instruments of defence*. It results of course from the encrease of the means of subsistence, and *cannot be carried beyond them*' (1801–4/1954, III, 361).

38 Empson reported that Malthus subsequently regarded Paley and Pitt as 'the two converts of whom he was most proud.' For Paley's apparent 'conversion,' see chapter 18, note 35.

39 Malthus's famous statement that, without Poor Laws, 'though there might have been a few more instances of very severe distress, the aggregate mass of happiness among the common people would have been much greater than it is at present' (1803/1986, *3*, 368), imples that a *smaller* population at good average wages is preferable on utility grounds to a larger population at poor average wages. Thus it is not apparent that he countenanced growth of population (and therefore higher population at any time) when accompanied by *reduced* standards. Bonar's evaluation (1924, 333) therefore goes too far: 'Malthus desired the great numbers as well as the great happiness, and was indeed quite naturally led by his theological views to prefer a little happiness for each of many individuals to a great deal for each of a few.'

of healthy adults, Malthus expecting that the initial restriction of population growth, by altering the age distribution, would 'create fresh resources, and consequently ... encourage a continued increase of efficient population' under relatively favourable circumstances (550).

Malthus's concern with an expanded population reflects in part the notion that God intended the replenishment of the earth.[40] But this must be read with the Malthusian gloss, which deviates radically from the standard religious argument in favour of a high population by way of early marriage and large families: 'I believe that it is the intention of the Creator that the earth should be replenished; but certainly with a healthy, virtuous, and happy population, not an unhealthy, vicious, and miserable one. And if in endeavouring to obey the command to increase and multiply, we people it only with beings of this latter description, and suffer accordingly, we have no right to impeach the justice of the command, but our irrational mode of executing it' (509). But once we allow for a reduced population growth rate with an eye to the living standards of the masses, the door is wide open to justify *slow* population growth, albeit *formally* satisfying the biblical injunction, the degree of rapidity to be recommended – and the amount of 'vice' that is acceptable – entirely a matter of circumstance and subjective judgment as to appropriate living standards. As for circumstance we need only take the extreme case to see how far the theological component is diluted. J.S. Mill, unlike Malthus, formally championed stationariness, even when expanding population is not at the cost of reduced wages, on grounds of women's interests (letter dated 8 April 1852; 1972, XIV, 88–9) and amenity (1848/1965, III, 756);[41] but Malthus did allow in 1817 that, in limiting circumstances, stationariness would be *essential* (1817, III, 12–13; cited chapter 5, pp. 187–8). Evidently, the absolute magnitude of population corresponding to a stationary state will be lower with than without prudential control, and the injunction to 'replenish' the earth is to that degree lessened; yet notwithstanding this fact, Malthus championed prudence. Since for him (as well as such followers as Thomas Chalmers) population growth in certain conditions was undesirable, we cannot accept the argument for the continued significance of the original theological dimension (above, pp. 917–18).

* * *

These themes lead us back to the birth-control issue (see above, p. 935). Allowing 'promiscuity' as an alternative to the misery and the vice of

40 See Pullen, 1981, 42; Spengler, 1960, 379, 385.

41 Mill did, however, recognize the case for a large population relative to that of neighbours from the perspective of defence (755). How far Mill's case for a 'stationary state' was a matter of day-dreaming is discussed in Hollander, 1994a.

poverty, as Malthus did, is inconsistent with a *global* rejection of mechanical contraception. It is, one deduces, the practice of birth control by married couples that Malthus had largely in mind by his celebrated denunciation of mechanical contraception as 'immoral.' This conclusion is reinforced in 1817 by reference to the disincentive effects supposedly attached to the practice: 'I have never adverted to the check suggested by Condorcet without the most marked disapprobation. Indeed I should always particularly reprobate any artificial and unnatural modes of checking population, both on account of their immorality and their tendency to remove a necessary stimulus to industry. If it were possible *for each married couple* to limit by a wish the number of their children, there is certainly reason to fear that the indolence of the human race would be very greatly increased; and that neither the population of individual countries, nor of the whole earth, would ever reach its natural and proper extent. But the restraints which I have recommended are quite of a different character. They are not only pointed out by reason and sanctioned by religion, but tend in the most marked manner to stimulate industry. It is not easy to conceive a more powerful encouragement to exertion and good conduct than the looking forward to marriage as a state peculiarly desirable: but only to be enjoyed in comfort, by the acquisition of habits of industry, economy and prudence' (1817, III, 393–4; emphasis added).[42] It is clear that Malthus continued to reason as if the child-bearing decision is, *and should be*, entailed by the marriage decision, and this in part on grounds of 'morality' in some absolute sense, independently of the social consequences. There were, therefore, limits to his reformist utilitarian perspective. Yet the *logic* of his own allowances pointed directly to the obvious conclusion – that drawn by the Philosophical Radicals; for once it is allowed: (1) that 'vice' can be justified on a utilitarian balance; and (2) that there are circumstances where even stationariness of population is required, it is impossible to rule out generalized birth control as one means to achieve the end, especially since – as Francis Place pointed out – birth control would permit both early marriage and good standards, and a reduction in prostitution (Place, 1822/1930, 176–7).[43] Social utility would then dictate such practices by married couples, as (Malthus himself allowed) it did for the unmarried.

42 Cf. the earlier proposition that the desire for marriage and procreation acts as stimulus to effort (chapter 18, p. 881). On this 'paradox' in the context of Malthus's optimistic theology, see Pullen, 1981, 51–2; Grampp, 1974, 298; Winch, 1993, 250.

43 Place acknowledged the connection with Malthus and gave him a sympathetic reading: 'Mr. Malthus seems to shrink from discussing the propriety of preventing conception, not so much it may be supposed from the abhorrence which he or any reasonable man can have to the practice, as from the possible fear of encountering the prejudices of others ...' (173).

VII SUMMARY AND CONCLUSION

We have confirmed that the theological chapters of 1798 are – as Lord Robbins insisted – extraneous to policy. This is so even in the first edition, and *a fortiori* so in later editions. That these chapters proved an embarrassment is in fact apparent from the Senior–Malthus correspondence of 1829. As we saw in chapter 18, p. 915, Malthus rejected Senior's original attribution to him of the view that reform was to no purpose; he had intended only to convey that the solution to low wages, or the permanent maintenance of improved wages, lay in population control, since 'population was always ready, and inclined, to increase faster than food, if the checks which repressed it were removed' – whereupon Senior pointed out that 'many, perhaps the majority of your readers, adopt the proposition without the qualification,' believing 'that the expansive power of population is a source of evil incapable not only of being subdued, but even of being mitigated.' Writing two chapters expressly designed to 'vindicate the ways of God to Man,' having in mind the 'constant pressure of distress' could only have misled readers in just the manner Senior complained of. In sum: The theological chapters worked on a presumption of *actual* population pressure, whereas Malthus had in mind elsewhere in his first edition, and throughout the later editions, *potential* population pressure.

There is a further issue not taken up formally in this chapter but of high relevance – the fact that comparison of the 1798 and later editions reveals a completely changed 'vision' of the population problem (see chapter 16). The empirical issue originally, as far as concerns contemporary Britain, was a supposedly low population growth rate accounted for proximately by low wages, in turn attributable to sluggish agricultural progress.[44] In 1803 and thereafter, the picture was transformed in the light of information revealed by the censuses of 1801, 1811, and 1821. Now the problem was to explain accelerating population growth at steady (and even rising) real wages. The explanation offered turned on reductions in mortality rates – not increases in marriage and birth rates – in conditions of, and in part attributable to, rapid growth of national income and capital accumulation. The 'vision' was a *bright* not a *dismal* one, for 'the evils resulting from the principle of population have rather diminished than increased, even under the disadvantage of an almost total ignorance of their real cause' (1803/1986, *3*, 575).[45] The original theological problem had thus been entirely superannuated by events; and the revised

44 This, it will be recalled from chapter 1, pp. 38–9, 41–2, by no means reflects unimpressive technology but the diversion of resources from agriculture under pressure of high luxury consumption and government interference.

45 Even in 1798, the empirical problem in Britain is *not* represented as one of excess population growth. Rather, low real wages reflected remediable impediments to agricultural growth. Strictly, then, the theological chapters were unnecessary, even in 1798.

theological problem of the need for the 'painful' check of chastity before marriage was merely *theoretical*, considering the ongoing acceleration of national product, or, at worst, a problem for some distant future.

The empirical dimension alone would account for the removal of the theological chapters. But there may be other reasons, including the abandonment of the theodicy there outlined, reflected in the contrast between God's grand spiritual end or purpose of 1798 extending *beyond* this world, and thus assuring an overwhelming net balance of good, and the *mundane* ends of material existence – namely, the replenishment of the earth and the cultivation of the soil (Harvey-Phillips, 1984, 603).[46] Our study has also confirmed that, in so far as concerns actual demographic policy in the *Essay on Population*, Malthus effectively eschewed theological considerations. His utilitarianism in these contexts is almost entirely earthbound.

Rashid, too, maintains that Malthus changed to Paley's view of life as a 'state of trial'; and he attempts to rationalize the adoption thus: 'As the inescapably sombre implications of his population theory sank into his daily thought, Malthus felt increasingly more comfortable with a theology that emphasized life on earth as a state of trial; for according to Malthus's early beliefs 'there was no penalty in the hereafter for failing to improve oneself. One simply returned to dust. Orthodoxy, on the other hand, promised positive pain to those who failed to adhere; as such, orthodoxy provided more incentive to accept the moral restraint ... [It] was Malthus the utilitarian population theorist that determined the beliefs of Malthus the theologian' (1984, 138). For my part, I dispute the notion of 'inescapably sombre implications' flowing from the population theory – the evidence is to the contrary. Malthus may have changed his theological view, but Rashid's rationalization is not convincing.[47]

As for the continued defence of the Deity in 1803 and thereafter, we have shown how, to the extent he based himself on *ideal* behaviour involving abstinence before marriage, Malthus the pure theologian clashes with Malthus the theologian–social scientist, taking account of *actual* human behaviour. In may be said that the two perspectives might be reconciled by an education program inculcating the desirability of moral restraint. But this is not Malthus's approach. Education for him was to convey the significance of prudential population control; there is no emphasis upon the inculcation, via a state-funded program, of the obligation of single people to practise continence on 'moral' grounds, except in so far as such behaviour is favourable to individual, and therefore (it is implied) social

46 This 'mundane' perspective Harvey-Phillips represents as Paley's view. This is fair enough, for Paley seems to aver to a balance of happiness in *this* world (cf. 1785, Book II, ch. V: 'The Divine Benevolence'). Yet we must not forget that, for Paley, moral behaviour allows for fear of punishment and hope of reward after death (above, section II).

47 For further evidence pointing to this conclusion, see Pullen, 1987b.

utility. To the extent that premarital sexual activity could be shown to generate a lesser net balance of social unhappiness than poverty, he tolerated such activity – and this *on moral grounds.*

Our analysis points to the proximity in practice between Malthus and J.S. Mill in their applications of the utilitarian rule. There are certainly differences of detail, but so too are there differences between Malthus and Paley. As social reformers Malthus and Mill stand side by side. In fact they are close to an extraordinary degree. Thus Malthus's insistence, in the light of increasing land scarcity, on a deceleration of population growth with an eye to the maintenance of real wages points the way to the notion, usually identified with Mill, of stationariness at high standards, and this despite formal obeisance to the biblical injunction regarding population expansion.

The one area where Malthus lags behind Mill is that of birth control by married couples – though Mill, too, was hesitant to make his position public in the *Principles* – and here it is, we have found, that a certain inconsistency emerges. There is also the problem that Malthus did not adequately attend to the social implications of irresponsible private behaviour. But all in all, the perspective on utilitarianism for Malthus as well as Mill reflects hostility to the upper-class, military, and Church ideology that rejected population control. That Malthus, unlike Mill, presumed the likely permanence of a class-based society is less significant than it appears at first glance, since his case was not based on natural law or any such appeal, but on a utilitarian calculus of the greatest happiness order, with labour's interests rated highest. Similarly, their respective attitudes to communism turn on this sort of calculation. And, as we have also seen, Malthus, like Mill and against Paley, argued strongly for greater equality.[48]

48 Mill's hostile comments on Paley's use of the utility rule in defence of 'accredited doctrines' is pertinent here (1852/1969, X,173).

CONCLUSION

I INTRODUCTION

Reactions to Malthus's procedures were reviewed at the outset of this investigation. They range across the spectrum, from the attribution to him of a peculiarly inductive method to the discernment of the typically deductive procedures of the Ricardians – even extending to the charge by Horner that he practised what later came to be designated the 'Ricardian Vice.' This Conclusion draws on the foregoing chapters to provide a summary statement of Malthusian method.

We establish first (section II) Malthus's own strong formal case for deductive theory; we also review his actual practice, involving a predilection for long-run equilibrium analysis which extends beyond value and growth theory to 'sustainable growth' and stabilization. Yet, despite the common ground with Ricardo, the main target in the *Principles* was Ricardo: 'It has been my wish to avoid giving to my work a controversial air. Yet to free it entirely from controversy, while one of my professed objects is to discuss controverted opinions, and to try their truth by a reference to an enlarged experience, is obviously not possible. There is one modern work, in particular, of very high reputation, some of the fundamental principles of which have appeared to me, after the most mature deliberation, to be erroneous; and I should not have done justice to the ability with which it is written, to the high authority of the writer, and the interests of the science of which it treats, if it had not specifically engaged a considerable portion of my attention. I allude to Mr. Ricardo's work, *On the Principles of Political Economy and Taxation*' (1820, 22–3; 1836, 18). Section III spells out the formal critique of Ricardian theory, the complaint against exessively simplified models and inappropriate application, but certainly not against deductive theory as such. We then show in section IV that there are lesser-known charges of irresponsibility that Malthus addressed against Adam Smith, culminating in a harsh rationalization of Smith's extreme application of corn-pricing analysis to the corn export subsidy, effectively charging Smith with the practice of the 'Ricardian Vice.'

Malthus was sometimes as critical of the Physiocrats as he was of Ricardo, but the fact is that he played the same game. Indeed, it seems fair to say that, till late in the day, he was entrapped by the physiocratic surplus concept (the superior productivity of agriculture). This theoretical perspective Malthus reinforced by his application of the Law of Markets to corn via the population mechanism, thereby fixing its price and the corn wage – an application entailing long-term analysis with a vengeance. All his objections to Smith regarding this dimension to his corn-price analysis can be turned against Malthus himself.

Malthus's perspectives on theory confirmation and on the general purpose of theory are considered in section V. Again similarities with Ricardo's position come to light. The sense of Malthus's 'doctrine of proportions,' and of his famous representation of political economy as more like morals and politics than mathematics, are taken up together in section VI. These perspectives are shown to concern 'uncertainties' that must be taken into account by policy makers – uncertainties flowing predominantly from Malthus's complex macro-economic position – which disallow general or universally applicable policy directives. But this by no means implies a rejection of deductive theorizing or, indeed, a denial of the potential for the use of mathematics in analysis.

Section VII addresses the familiar complaint against Malthus of 'inconsistency.' It is true enough that Malthus failed to develop a full-fledged 'system.' But this was the ideal, and he was aware of the deficiency. The most conspicuous and serious instances of inconsistency we have encountered are the simultaneous adoption of the *scarcity* and *surplus* perspectives; Malthus was caught in a theoretical trap imposed by his subscription to 'physiocratic' doctrine. There is also the related clash between the notion of Say's Law applied to food – the proportionate response of population to increases of food – which implies a constant corn wage, and the representation of the wage as policy parameter. Yet apart from these instances – serious though they are – the charges against him when looked at with the specifics of each case at hand have been overdone. Unfortunately, he left himself wide open for misunderstanding because of his love of paradox, argument, and provocation, as well as a certain carelessness in the use of terms, all beautifully demonstrated by Grampp (1974) and amply confirmed in this study.

This leads me to an issue never far from the surface in Malthus criticism – his intellectual candour. The story in section VIII, which attempts to account for the general *impression* of a profound chasm between Ricardian and Malthusian procedures, is one, in part, of Malthus's 'misrepresentation' of the Ricardian position. There is, though, no necessity to have recourse to the charge of intellectual dishonesty, since he did not disguise those misrepresentations from Ricardo himself. But I do find it troublesome that he failed to appreciate Ricardian method – though in the end he did come to correct some of the misinterpretation; and I am unable to account for the fact that Malthus seemed to be unaware that he himself was 'guilty' of many of the failings of method and substantive doctrine he attributed to others. His criticisms of Adam Smith can often be turned against himself; and much the same applies to those addressed at Ricardo, most specifically the long-run orientation.

I provide a final summing-up in section IX, and here return to the Keynes–Malthus relation.

II MALTHUS'S POSITIVE CASE FOR DEDUCTIVE THEORY AND HIS PRACTICE

We shall now establish Malthus's own strong case for theory appearing in the *Essay* of 1803 and all later editions in the chapter 'Of the necessity of general principles on this subject.' It must have been overlooked by those who believe Malthus neglected to state his methodological principles (cf. Blaug, 1980, 56), or who insist on Malthus as 'inductivist':

> It has been observed by Hume, that of all sciences there is none where first appearances are more deceitful than in politics [1752/1955, 3–4]. The remark is undoubtedly very just, and is most peculiarly applicable to that department of the science, which relates to the modes of improving the condition of the lower classes of society.
>
> We are continually hearing declamation against theory and theorists, by men who pride themselves upon the distinction of being practical. It must be acknowledged that bad theories are very bad things, and the authors of them useless and sometimes pernicious members of society. But these advocates of practice do not seem to be aware that they themselves very often come under this description, and that a great part of them may be classed among the most mischievous theorists of their time. When a man faithfully relates any facts, which have come within the scope of his own observations, however confined it may have been, he undoubtedly adds to the sum of general knowledge, and confers a benefit on society. But when from this confined experience, from the management of his own little farm, or the details of the workhouse in his neighbourhood, he draws a general inference, as is frequently the case, he then at once erects himself into a theorist; and is the more dangerous, because, experience being the only just foundation for theory, people are often caught merely by the sound of the word, and do not stop to make the distinction between that partial experience which, on such subjects, is no foundation whatever for a just theory, and that general experience, on which alone a just theory can be founded. (1986, *3*, 558)

There follows a mocking contrast between 'the theorist who calls himself practical, and the genuine theorist': 'There are perhaps few subjects on which human ingenuity has been more exerted than the endeavour to meliorate the condition of the poor; and there is certainly no subject in which it has so completely failed. The question between the theorist who calls himself practical, and the genuine theorist, is, whether this should prompt us to look into all the holes and corners of workhouses, and content ourselves with mulcting the parish officers for their waste of cheese parings and candle ends, and with distributing more soups and potatoes; or to recur to general principles, which show us at once the cause of the failure, and prove that the system has been from the beginning radically erroneous. There is no subject to which general principles have been so seldom applied; and yet, in the whole compass of human knowledge, I doubt if there be one in which it is so dangerous to lose sight of them; because the partial and immediate effects of a particular mode of giving assistance are so often directly opposite to the general and permanent effects' (558–9).

In the course of justifying the benefits of *formal* allowance for exceptions to general rules in his Introduction to the *Principles*, Malthus provided a further potent defence of theoretical analysis: 'There are some eminent persons so strongly attached to the received general rule [1836: the general rules] of political economy, that, though they are aware that in practice some exceptions to them may occasionally occur; yet they do not think it wise and politic to notice them, for fear of directing the public attention too much and too frequently to exceptions, and thus weakening the force and utility of the general rule' (1820, 13; 1836, 10). The statement does not relate specifically to the 'doctrine of proportions' or the problem of optima. Malthus illustrated, rather, by reference in 1820 to exceptions to the general rule of the desirability of *laissez-faire*; and in 1836 to exceptions to the positive effect on growth of expanded trade (see chapter 18: VI). *A policy of silence regarding exceptions in fact had the opposite impact on the reputation of economic theory than that intended.* Malthus was concerned to defend that reputation, and made out a very strong case for 'theories and general principles,' subject to the qualifications insisted upon:

Nothing can tend so strongly to bring theories and general principles into discredit as the occurrence of consequences, from particular measures [1836: premises], which have not been foreseen. Though in reality such an event forms no just objection to theory, in the general and proper sense of the term; yet it forms a most valid objection to the specific theory in question, as proving it in some way or other wrong; and with the mass of mankind this will pass for an impeachment of general principles and of the knowledge or good faith of those who are in the habit of inculcating them. It appears to me, I confess, that the most perfect sincerity, together with the greatest degree of accuracy attainable, founded upon the most comprehensive view of all the circumstances of the case, are necessary *to give that credit and circulation to general principles which is so desirable.* And no views of temporary advantage, nor, what is more likely to operate, the fear of destroying the simplicity of a general rule, should ever tempt us to deviate from the strict line of truth, or to conceal or overlook any circumstances that may interfere with the universality of the principle. (1820, 14–15; 1836, 11–12; emphasis added)

In the second edition – concerned specifically with exceptions to the stimulatory effect on a country's wealth of 'the increasing wealth and prosperity of surrounding states' – this statement is further strengthened, again with an eye to preserving the good reputation of theory: 'It is not favourable to the science of political economy, that the same persons who have been laying down a rule as universal should be obliged to found their explanations of most important existing phenomena on the exceptions to it. It is surely much better that such a rule should be laid down at first with its limitations' (1836, 10). Reisman sees this statement as 'an attack on dogmatic thinkers who fail to see the limitations of a proposition until they are forced into an unexpected suspension of *ceteris paribus*' (1990, 3). This is not quite the point. The exceptions are supposedly *known* to the theorist. Malthus's concern is to protect the good reputation of economic theory with the public by assuring that the known exceptions are clearly stated along with the general rule.

It is scarcely surprising, given this position, that Malthus refused to join Richard Jones in his campaign to discredit deductive theory (see above, pp. 475–6). He allowed a wide role for definitions as starting hypotheses in economics; he defended the principle of diminishing returns as an explanation of rent; and he charged Jones with neglecting 'the most important parts of the subject' namely, 'the progress of rent in new colonies' and the Ricardian case of 'farmer's rents in the most improved states of Europe' – and for going 'beyond the truth in his unwillingness to admit the tendency of continued accumulation, and of the progress of population and cultivation to lower the rates of profits and corn wages on the land' (letter to Whewell, 28 February 1831; TCL Add. Ms. c. 53[2]; de Marchi and Sturges, 1973, 386). In the *Principles* he actually referred to 'the separation of rents, as a kind of fixture upon lands of a certain quality,' as '*a law as invariable as the action of the principle of gravity*' (cited chapter 3, note 10) – a formulation surely worthy of James Mill! And, to Whewell, he expressed his concern that the anti-Ricardo campaign had gone too far: 'I am much gratified by the opinions of such judges as Mr. Jones and yourself in regard to what I may have done in Political Economy. I confess I felt that when I almost stood alone in my difference with Mr. Ricardo and was compared to Dr. Priestly amidst the new discoveries of chemistry, it would not finally be so. But I was hardly prepared to expect that in so short a time as has since elapsed, one of the questions in the political economy club should be "Whether any of the principles *first* advanced in Mr. Ricardo's work are now acknowledged to be correct?" My apprehension at present is that the tide is setting too strong against him; and I even think that Mr. Jones is carried a little out of the right course by it. In his zeal to show that Mr. Ricardo is quite wrong, which he certainly is, in dwelling upon the diminished returns of agricultural capital as the sole cause of increasing rents, he seems inclined to deny the undoubted truth of the natural tendency to such diminished returns in a *limited sphere*, unless prevented by improvements in agriculture or manufactures' (31 May 1833, TCL Add. Ms. a.209[11]; de Marchi and Sturges, 391). And he even took Ricardo to task for inadequate logic, revealing his own perspective: 'The grand difficulty as you justly observe is in regard to the postulates; but it is still a matter of very great importance to be secure that no error creeps into the subsequent reasonings, and it must be allowed that Ricardo did not always draw correct conclusions from his premises.'

Significantly, in the *Principles*, Malthus envisaged a *single general principle* to account for all the rent varieties distinguished by Jones: 'This view of the subject includes all the different kinds of rent referred to by Mr. Jones, in his late valuable account of the state of rents, and the various modes of paying labour in different parts of the world. Whether the labourer is paid in money, in produce, or by a portion of land which he is to work himself with a part of his labour, while he gives the other part to his lord, the foundation of rent is exactly the same, depending always upon the value of the excess of what the whole of the lord's land produces, above that which under the actual circumstances is received by the cultivators, and the amount of rent which can be received from a given extent of land will rise according to all the different degrees of fertility above that which will only support the actual cultivators' (1836, 153–4n).

Even in the context of the Bullionist debate, where deep methodological contrasts are so often discerned, we find that Malthus and Ricardo were on the same wavelength. Both appealed to 'experience,' though they read the evidence differently; and Malthus as well as Ricardo appealed to theory-based general principles. Recall his striking warning in 1811 against excessive note issues: 'If it is really intended to go on in the same spirit which has marked the last three years, there are no limits to the degree of depreciation which may be expected. *All that has yet happened is in exact conformity with the general principles which have been laid down on this subject by those who are called theorists*; and the experience of the past enables us, with the utmost certainty, to predict, that an excessive issue of paper in England will be accompanied with precisely the same results which have invariably attended it in other countries ...' (above, chapter 13, p. 673; emphasis added).

The Introduction to the *Principles* clarifies more formally that the *ideal* was the establishment of generally accepted principles, and that appeal could be made to 'experts' and agreed-upon criteria of evaluation. Some progress had indeed been made since the subject had been 'raised into a science by the works of the Economists [1836: French Economists] and of

Adam Smith': 'Happily for the interests of the science and its usefulness to society, the Economists and Adam Smith entirely agreed on some of those great general principles which lead to the most important practical conclusions; such as the freedom of trade, and the leaving every person, while he adheres to the rules of justice, to pursue his own interest in his own way, together with some others: and unquestionably their agreement on these principles affords the strongest presumption of their truth' (1820, 2–3; 1836, 2). It is revealing to find an apparently universal presumption in favour of free enterprise, since the matter is absent from the discussion that follows of the 'great differences of opinion' that still remained: 'All the main propositions of the science have been examined, and the events which have since occurred, tending either to illustrate or confute them, have been repeatedly discussed. The result of this examination and discussion seems to be, that on some very important points there are still great differences of opinion. Among these, perhaps, may be reckoned – The definitions of wealth and of productive labour – The nature and measures of value – The nature and extent of the principles of demand and supply – The origin and progress of rent – The causes which determine the wages of labour and the profit of stock – The causes which practically retard and limit the progress of wealth – The level of the precious metals in different countries – The principles of taxation, &c' (1820, 3–4; 1836, 3). The list includes theoretical issues, the solution of which was 'obviously necessary to the improvement of the science' as well as the generation of 'practical rules': 'On all these points, and many others among the numerous subjects which belong to political economy, differences have prevailed among persons whose opinions are entitled to attention. Some of these questions are to a certain degree theoretical; and the solution of them, though obviously necessary to the improvement of the science, might not essentially affect its practical rules; but others are of such a nature, that the determination of them one way or the other will necessarily influence the conduct both of individuals and of governments; and their correct determination therefore must be a matter of the highest practical importance.'[1] And though agreement could never be universal, considering the nature of political economy – presumably contrasting with mathematics – it could be reached by a majority of those deemed to be 'competent judges': 'In a science such as that of political economy, it is not to be expected that an *universal* assent should be obtained in all its important propositions; but,

1 As for 'practical rules,' Malthus followed Ricardo's line in emphasizing the necessity for a sound body of theory to deal with taxation in particular, though his own *Principles* does not formally attend to applied public finance, as does Ricardo's: 'It depends entirely upon the general laws which regulate the wages of labour, the profits of stock, the rent of land, exchangeable value, the currencies of different countries, the production and distribution of wealth, &c. &c. whether any existing system of taxation be the best, or whether it might be altered for the better' (1820, 20; 1836, 16).

in order to give them their proper weight and justify their being acted upon, it is extremely desirable, indeed almost necessary, that a considerable *majority* of those who, from their attention to the subject, are considered by the public as likely to be the most competent judges, should agree in the truth of them.'

That Malthus in the *Principles* made no claim to having formulated a general system was evidently not a matter of 'Baconian' principle. He after all paid tribute to the *Wealth of Nations* as the best 'systematic treatise' available (1820, 5; 1836, 4). It was not, however, definitive, and he hoped for a restatement by a process involving logical refinement and empirical testing; in the interim, it was better that 'the different subjects which admit of doubt should be treated separately': 'The present period ... seems to be unpropitious to the publication of a new systematic treatise on political economy. The treatise which we already possess is still of the very highest value; and till a more general agreement shall be found to take place, both with respect to the controverted points of Adam Smith's work, and the nature and extent of the additions to it, which the more advanced stage of the science has rendered necessary, it is obviously more advisable that the different subjects which admit of doubt should be treated separately. When these discussions have been for some time before the public, and a sufficient opportunity has been given, by the collision of different opinions and an appeal to experience, to separate what is true from what is false, the different parts may then be combined into a consistent whole, and may be expected to carry with it such weight and authority as to produce the most useful practical results.'[2] This procedure was a matter of strategy. The ideal is clear; he did not oppose 'system building' but *premature* system building.

Malthus had hopes for the future resolution of remaining differences, though this would require appropriate absorption of new empirical materials: 'The last twenty or thirty years have ... been marked by a train of events of a most extraordinary kind; and there has hardly yet been time so to arrange and examine them as to see to what extent they confirm or invalidate the received principles of the science to which they relate.' But he wrote scathingly of writers who 'call themselves practical': 'Among those writers who have treated the subject scientifically, there is not perhaps, at the present moment, so general an agreement as would be desirable to give effect to their conclusions; and the writers who peculiarly call themselves practical, either draw no general inferences, or are so much influenced by narrow, partial, and sometimes interested views, that no reliance can be placed on them for the establishment of general rules' (1820, 4–5; 1836, 3–4). And subsequently, he repeated his opposition to the 'more practical opponents' of the 'scientific writers on political economy' who

2 On this passage, see Pullen, 1989, xxxvi.

'draw too hasty inferences from a frequent appeal to partial facts' (cited below, p. 965).

There can then be no doubt of his formal rejection of simple-minded induction from purely empirical relations; Malthus sought a strong theoretical basis for any interpretation of the facts. As a conspicuous example, the higher profit rate in the period 1793–1813 than in 1727–57 had been urged against the land-scarcity approach as an adequate body of theory (see chapter 15: VI). But it remained to consider 'whether the circumstances which have been stated in this section [relative capital redundancy or deficiency] are sufficient to account theoretically for such a free operation of this principle, notwithstanding the progressive accumulation of capital, and the progressive cultivation of fresh land, as to allow of low profits at an earlier period of this progress and high [1836: higher] profits at a later period. At all events, the facts must be accounted for, as they are so broad and glaring, and others of the same kind are in reality of such frequent recurrence, that I cannot but consider them [1836: that they must be considered] as at once decisive against any theory of profits which is inconsistent with them' (1820, 320–1; 1836, 286–7). In both editions the 'relative redundancy of deficiency of capital' (or 'of capital and produce') is the favoured hypothesis to account for an increase in the profit rate notwithstanding 'the progressive cultivation of fresh land.' It is noteworthy also that his satisfaction with the *theoretical* explanation allowed greater confidence in approaching future prospects: 'It appears to me that the causes which have been mentioned are sufficient to account for [the pattern] theoretically, and to make such an event appear not only possible, but probable, and likely to be of frequent recurrence' (1820, 324). A conspicuous formulation of the concern for theory as such emerges in the discussion of international differences in value: 'But if we are not fully satisfied with this kind of reference to experience, it is obvious that the same conclusion follows inevitably from theory. In those countries where the precious metals are necessarily purchased, no plausible reason can be assigned why the quantity of them should be in proportion to the difficulty of producing the articles with which they are purchased' (1820, 115–16; see chapter 14, pp. 718–19). Malthus also represented his position on the Corn Laws as far as it involved diminishing returns and 'the laws of supply and demand' as a matter of 'general principle' confirmed by the parliamentary evidence (see chapter 15, pp. 747, 752).[3]

Malthus's methodological position thus by no means constitutes a condemnation of deductive theory in favour of 'induction.' His general recommendations point rather to the construction of models based upon

3 The problem here is that the general principle of diminishing return is sometimes defined, given technology, and sometimes with allowance made for technical improvement (see chapter 15: VI). This matter will be taken up shortly.

sound general principles – 'realistic' axioms reflecting 'general experience' – for use in responsible applications. And significantly, despite the concern with application, we find in the Introduction to the *Principles* an eloquent appeal for 'the improvement,' indeed for the 'completion,' of the science based on 'just principles,' and this – in line with mathematics and the natural sciences – *even if there should be no immediate practical advantages.* The context is a complaint against those who 'do not look with a favourable eye on new and further inquiries, particularly if they do not see at once clearly and distinctly to what beneficial effects they lead, [an] indisposition to innovation, even in science, [which] may possibly have its use, by tending to check crude and premature theories; but ... if carried too far ... strikes at the root of all improvement' (1820, 15; 1836, 12). Again, he here had in mind developments since the 1790s: 'It is impossible to observe the great events of the last twenty-five years in their relation to subjects belonging to political economy, and sit down satisfied with what has been already done in the science. But if the science be manifestly incomplete, and yet of the highest importance, it would surely be most unwise to restrain inquiry, conducted upon just principles, even where the immediate practical utility of it was not visible. In mathematics, chemistry, and every branch of natural philosophy, how many are the inquiries necessary to their improvement and completion, which, taken separately, do not appear to lead to any specifically advantageous purpose! How many useful inventions, and how much valuable and improving knowledge would have been lost, if a rational curiosity and a mere love of information had not generally been allowed to be a sufficient motive for the search after truth!' (1820, 15–16; 1836, 12–13). Even pure theoretical inquiry thus had its place, though the *practical* return on progress in economics Malthus believed to be potentially very great: 'I should not, therefore, consider it as by any means conclusive against further inquiries in political economy, if they would not always bear the rigid application of the test of *cui bono?* But such, in fact, is the nature of the science, so intimately is it connected with the business of mankind, that I really believe more of its propositions will bear this test than those of any other department of human knowledge' (1820, 16; 1836, 13). It was 'unquestionably desirable, therefore, both with a view to the improvement and completion of the science, and the practical advantages which may be expected from it, that such inquiries should be pursued; and no common difficulty or obscurity should be allowed to deter those who have leisure and ability for such researches' (1820, 16–17; 1836, 13).

* * *

Despite a recurring theme of multicausality and the practical consequences of its neglect, Malthus also subscribed to 'the admirable rule of Newton, not to admit more causes than are necessary to the solution of the phenomenon we are considering,' and insisted 'that those which really are necessary must be admitted' (1820, 7; 1836, 5–6). This was the nature of scientific progress: 'Before the shrine of truth, as discovered by facts and experience, the fairest theories and the most beautiful classifications must fall. The chemist of thirty years ago may be allowed to regret, that new discoveries in the science should disturb and confound his previous systems and arrangements; but he is not entitled to the name [1836: rank] of philosopher, if he does not give them up without a struggle, as soon as the experiments which refute them are fully established' (1820, 7; 1836, 6).[4]

It is clearly refutation in favour of an *alternative* theory that is intended. Simplification and generalization were 'the desirable and legitimate object of genuine philosophy, wherever it can be effected consistently with truth' (1820, 6; 1836, 5). Indeed, Malthus recognized the danger in his quest to avoid oversimplified explanations, of arriving at a theory that was 'both complex and incorrect': 'One of the specific objects of the present work is to prepare the general rules [1836: some of the most important rules] of political economy for practical application, by a frequent reference to experience, and by taking as comprehensive a view as I can [1836: by endeavouring to take a comprehensive view] of all the causes that concur in the production of particular phenomena. I am sufficiently aware, that in this mode of conducting inquiry, there is a chance [1836: In this mode of conducting inquiry, there is, no doubt, a chance] of falling into errors of an opposite kind to those which arise from a tendency to simplification. Certain appearances, which are merely co-existent and incidental, may be mistaken for causes; and a theory formed upon this mistake will unite the double disadvantage of being both complex and incorrect' (1820, 21; 1836, 16–17). But forewarned was forearmed: 'Aware, however, of my liability to this error on the one side, and to the error of not referring sufficiently to experience on the other, my aim will be to pursue, as far as I am able, a just mean between the two extremes, and to approach, as near I can, to the great object of my research – the truth' (1820, 22; 1836, 17).

This quest for balance – to the end of achieving a body of soundly based theory – is further elaborated in an insistence upon consistency with 'general experience' while admitting the need to avoid appeal to 'isolated facts': 'The tendency to premature generalization occasions also in some of the principal writers on political economy, an unwillingness to bring their theories to the test of experience. I should be the last person to lay an undue stress upon isolated facts, or to think that a consistent theory, which would account for the great mass of phenomena observable, was

4 The reference is probably to Joseph Priestley (see Pullen, in Malthus, 1820/1989, II, 289). Ironically, the same charge in the same terms was made against Malthus himself, as we shall see below, p. 990.

immediately invalidated by a few discordant appearances, the reality and the bearing of which, there might not have been an opportunity of fully examining. But certainly no theory can have any pretension to be accepted as correct, which is inconsistent with general experience. Such inconsistency appears to be at once a full and sufficient reason for its rejection' (1820, 10; 1836, 8). One again notes the objective of achieving a body of *true* or *correct* and *complete* theory, with high explanatory ability and consequent reliability in future application. A theory inconsistent with 'general experience' 'must be either radically false, or essentially incomplete; and in either case it can neither be adopted as a satisfactory solution of existing phenomena, nor acted upon with any degree of safety for the future' (1820, 11; 1836, 8). The type of experience intended can be inferred from an illustration taken from population theory: 'The first business of philosophy is to account for things as they are; and till our theories will do this, they ought not to be the ground of any practical conclusion. I should never have had that steady and unshaken confidence in the theory of population which I have invariably felt, if it had not appeared to me to be confirmed, in the most remarkable manner, by the state of society as it actually exists in every country with which we are acquainted. To this test I appealed in laying it down; and a frequent appeal to this sort of experience is pre-eminently necessary in most of the subjects of political economy, where various and complicated causes are often in operation, the presence of which can only be ascertained in this way' (1820, 11; 1836, 8–9).

Malthus certainly frequently leaves an impression that he was engaged in a methodological revolt against Ricardo, insisting on an *inherently* different approach. Most conspicuous is his condemnation of 'theoretical' writers in a protest against the denial of the possibility of redundancy of capital and labour: 'It is a contradiction in terms, to say that labour is redundant compared with capital, and that capital is at the same time redundant compared with labour: – but it is no contradiction in terms to say that both labourers and capital may be redundant, compared with the means of employing them profitably. I have never maintained the former position, though I have been charged with so doing; but the latter has been so fully established by experience, that I am surprised at the pertinacity with which theoretical writers continue to refuse their assent to it' (1836, 414n).[5] It would be excusable, though unjustified, were this response read as a condemnation of theory as such rather than of theory based on empirically invalid axioms generating results incapable of explaining the conspicuous phenomena of unemployment and excess capacity. Similarly, the sort of complaint against 'some of the ablest writers' in neglecting 'facts and experience' to be found in the reaction to Tooke in 1823 might be understood as an attack on deductive theory as such: 'This

5 Ricardo had accused Malthus of 'contradiction' (Ricardo, 1951–73, II, 9; VIII, 185).

mode of treating his subject we consider as peculiarly judicious. At all times an extensive collection of facts relative to the interchange of the various commodities of the commercial world ... cannot but be of great importance to the science of political economy; but it is more particularly required at the present moment, when it must be acknowledged that *some of our ablest writers in this science have been deficient in that constant reference to facts and experience, on which alone it can be safely founded or further improved*' (1823a/1986, *7*, 225; emphasis added). But as the close of this extract clarifies, the appeal was not for the abandonment of deductive theory but for *improved* model building based on realistic axioms.

* * *

We have thus far been concerned with Malthus's formal pronouncements on method. The positive case made out for deductive theory is confirmed by his practice. Here we shall summarize some salient features.

Weyland (as we know from the Introduction, p. 6) was not fooled, as some commentators have been, into perceiving the *Essay on Population* as a work turning on empirico-historical procedures. The common notion of a major methological transition between the 1798 and later revisions has been overdone; the 1803 and the later editions also set out with the same sort of exercise in Euclidian geometry entailing self-evident axioms and irrefutable conclusions. Recall Malthus's explanation introduced in 1806 that he had not written a volume to prove the axioms, which were evidently acceptable as soon as stated (see chapter 1, p. 57); and there is a prefatory assurance introduced in 1803 and repeated thereafter that while he had taken pains to assure the accuracy of 'the facts and calculations' reported, should 'any of them nevertheless turn out to be false, the reader will see that they will not materially affect the general tenour [1807: scope] of the reasoning' (1986, *3*, iv; 1807, II, x). The structure of the work and its policy applications focus on a maximum conceivable permanent growth rate of population predicated upon a presumed maximum conceivable growth rate of food, and on the checks on population growth below the maximum imposed by actual growth of food. As Malthus explained to Senior in 1829, his purpose was to demonstrate 'that population was always ready, and inclined, to increase faster than food, if the checks which repressed it were removed' (above, chapter 18, p. 915) – that there was the *potential* for excessive population growth. The vast bulk of the empirical work introduced in 1803 – it transformed the 'look' of the *Essay* – was directed only at illustrating the checks actually at play over time and space which in practice constrain the growth of population. Thus it was that, in 1798, population (so he then believed) was growing slowly because of the checks imposed by the (supposedly) slow growth of the food supply; thereafter, the picture was transformed as the food supply expanded rapidly and the population growth rate followed suit as the checks were relaxed. And in this context we find some of Malthus's most strongly stated formulations: 'The following proposition may be said to be capable of mathematical demonstration. In a country, the resources of which will not permanently admit of an increase of population more rapid than the existing rate, no improvement in the condition of the people, which would tend to diminish mortality, could *possibly* take place without being accompanied by a smaller proportion of births, supposing of course no particular increase of emigration ...' (see chapter 1, p. 59). Indeed, he considered it essential to insert a chapter, 'Of the necessity of general principles on this subject [of population],' which commences with the insistance on theory following Hume (above, p. 951).

In other contexts, too, Malthus took pride in his analytical contributions – witness, for example, his claims to priority for the analysis of the cost of acquiring the precious metals (see chapter 14: VIII); and his enthusiasm for such 'paradoxical' theorems as that relating to the advantage to labour of a high corn price (see chapter 4: IV). He was equally proud of the demonstration of the necessarily constant 'value of labour,' representing the proof in *The Measure of Value* as following from the axioms 'as strictly as any proposition in Euclid' (chapter 7, p. 323). Conspicuous analytical constructs include the endogenization of prudential population control and the brilliant exposition of the prospect of stationariness at high real wages (chapter 5: IV), Sraffian-type price theory (chapter 7: I), and the corn-profit model (chapter 10: III).

Exercises in pure theory constitute a high proportion of Malthus's efforts in the *Principles.* And as we have demonstrated in Part II, neither Malthus's insistance on a demand–supply approach to price nor his charge that Ricardo's long-run theorizing was of little practical relevance precluded him from devoting himself almost entirely to reinforcing the *long-run supply or cost* dimension – he saw no technical role for 'utility' in value formation – and devising an appropriate measure of supply conditions. J.B. Say, we have shown (chapter 6: IX), identified Malthus with Ricardo regarding value theory, and Malthus accepted the identification.

As for the measurement device – designed specifically for long-run equilibrium states (see chapter 7: IX) – Malthus in fact made stronger claims than did Ricardo. Ricardo's concern was to obtain an index of supply conditions in the technological sense of labour input, or rather labour input over time – 'time' representing the capital component. Were an ideal measure available, an increase in marginal labour input in agriculture would raise the gold price of corn, and any distributive change that might occur would leave relative prices unaffected. Time and again, he reiterated that, though 'absolute cost prices' include an allowance for profit, *relative* prices are not necessarily affected by a change in distribution; expressed equivalently, resource allocation may be unaffected by a change in distribution. The desideratum was precluded, he readily admitted, by the fact that the measure and the product in question will usually be differentially affected by changes in distribution, and changes in cost prices would be recorded unrelated to the technical coefficients. Malthus, by contrast, sought an index to capture changes in both labour input and the profit rate, or of 'absolute value' in the strict sense. He himself admitted that his money measure – produced by labour alone, without a time component – could not distinguish between the impact on costs of changes in technological input and changes in the profit rate, but it captured their combined impact on either element, given the other. Thus, *given* the inputs into both the money measure and the commodity measured, a fall in the profit rate would be precisely reflected by a fall in the money price of the commodity. This is the case because, when the profit rate varies, the silver measure is unaffected in its *absolute* cost. Only other (capital-using) products are affected, among them Ricardo's measure (involving capital), which varies with every variation in the profit rate.

From the Ricardian perspective this procedure involved selection of a measure at the extreme end of the spectrum; a worse choice could not be imagined. A fall in the profit rate would certainly be reflected in a change in the value of capital-using products expressed in Malthusian money. One may think of it as a rise of the wage rate which affects Malthusian money more than it affects a capital-using product, thus lowering its money value, and lowering it to a greater extent the greater its capital intensity. But, by the same token, it was useless as a measure of labour input since it could not distinguish between alterations in labour input and alterations in the profit rate. Thus it is that Ricardo admitted there to be no ideal measure, whereas Malthus insisted that there was. Since their *desiderata* differed, the two differed in their estimates of what was possible. But it is Malthus, not Ricardo, who makes the claim for an *accurate* measure of absolute value, working entirely in terms of long-run equilibrium in the course of his elaboration.

With respect to growth theory, we have recorded in Parts I and II some elegant statements of the simultaneous decline in the corn-wage and profit rates turning on a land scarcity–based growth model – the 'canonical' model. Certainly there is the insistence on accounting for profit-rate and wage-rate movements unrelated to increasing land scarcity in terms of Smithian 'competition of capitals'; but the story, we have found, is one of attempted reconciliation of the two perspectives, and in the end it is Malthus who hits upon a Sraffa-type approach to profit-rate determination involving corn input–corn output reasoning generating an agricultural rate to which the manufacturing rate must conform. A nicer case of long-run equilibrium analysis it is difficult to imagine.

As a further illustration of the present theme, the analysis of sustainable growth (above, chapter 11) is concerned with the conditions of long-term expansion. That was the main preoccupation. The matter of stabilization (chapter 12), important though it is, was secondary, as evidenced by the fact that the analysis of sustainable growth stands sentinel – we shall return to this matter in our final summing up – and because Malthus came increasingly to see the postwar years as something of an aberration (chapter 12: III).

* * *

A word on the empirical dimension to Malthus's economics. As mentioned above, the mass of materials added in 1803 and thereafter to the *Essay on Population* was largely 'illustrative,' and there were those (such as Weyland) who refused to read this as genuine induction. In other important contexts, too, the quality of the empirical dimension was questioned. As for agricultural protection, Horner wrote to Malthus critically regarding one of the main planks of the case for protection: 'Why do you say, [1815a/1986, 7, 164; see chapter 12, note 30] that "in all common years, France will furnish us with a large proportion of our supplies?" This affirmation is not founded upon the parliamentary evidence, which bears the contrary way' (12 February 1815; in Horner, 1853, II, 226). And he proceeded to an extraordinarily detailed criticism of Malthus's use of current and historical data, including the empirical case in support of the proposition that corn-price fluctuations would be exaggerated under (bogus) free trade compared with import prohibition (226–7). This challenge to Malthus on the latter's home ground – insistence on respect for the *evidence* – is potentially of high significance. But Malthus in his reply, written in haste, conceded nothing of substance.[6]

It also remains to note that Malthus did not pretend to intimate knowledge of the corn trade to permit detailed suggestions regarding the precise mechanism of restriction (1986, 7, 173). But he accepted the limit price of 80s. per quarter to be the generally recognized price that 'in the actual state of things ... would prevent our cultivation from falling back, and perhaps allow it to be progressive.' This latter is a rather weak statement, given the highly optimistic evaluation of prospects under protection in the closing paragraph of the pamphlet: 'I firmly believe that, in the actual state of Europe, and under the actual circumstances of our present situation, it is our wisest policy to grow our own average supply of corn; and, in so doing, I feel persuaded that the country has ample resources for a great and continued increase of population, of power, of wealth, and of happiness' (174).

III THE FORMAL CRITIQUE OF RICARDIAN THEORY

We have established Malthus's positive case for deductive theory and his

6 I am grateful to Professor Kenneth Bourne for providing me with the reply, dated 16 February 1815, since published in Horner, 1994, 820–2.

own 'long-run' procedures. Even in the course of the sometimes sharply worded criticism of the 'New School,' it emerges that his objections were specifically directed against what he perceived to be: (1) excessively simplified models; and (2) inappropriate applications, but *not* against deductive theory as such.

An early statement of Malthus's perceived differences with Ricardo regarding method will be found in the letter dated 23 February 1812 (chapter 14, p. 706). Movements of the exchange rate might be generated by non-monetary disturbance, and did not solely reflect relative money values, runs Malthus's contention, whereas '[it] really appears that a desire to simplify, which has often led away the most scientific men, has induced you to ascribe to one cause phenomena that properly belongs to two, and not to give sufficient weight to the facts which (to me at least) appear to make against your doctrine' (in Ricardo, 1951–73, VI, 82). As explained years later and more formally in the Introduction to the *Principles*, his complaint against contemporary 'scientific writers' was that they engaged in 'a precipitate attempt to simplify and generalize,' and failed to test theory against experience, though (as we know from section II) he is equally critical of the 'practical opponents' of theory: 'The principal cause of error, and of the differences which prevail at present among the scientific writers on political economy, appears to me to be a precipitate attempt to simplify and generalize; and while their more practical opponents draw too hasty inferences from a frequent appeal to partial facts, these writers run into a contrary extreme, and do not sufficiently try their theories by a reference to that enlarged and comprehensive experience which, on so complicated a subject, can alone establish their truth and utility' (1820, 5–6; 1836, 4–5). The tendency of 'minds of a certain cast' to simplify and generalize had led to crude and premature theories – this 'in almost every science with which we are acquainted' (1820, 6; 1836, 5). In political economy, specifically, 'the desire to simplify has occasioned an unwillingness to acknowledge the operation of more causes than one in the production of particular effects; and if one cause would account for a considerable portion of a certain class of phenomena, the whole has been ascribed to it without sufficient attention to the facts, which would not admit of being so solved.' Again, the Bullionist controversy regarding the cause of the unfavourable exchange and the excess of the market over the mint price of bullion illustrated the propensity towards monocausal interpretations, for 'scarcely one writer seemed willing to admit of the operation of both theories, the combination of which, sometimes acting in conjunction and sometimes in opposition, could alone adequately account for the variable and compli-cated phenomena observable' (1820, 6–7; 1836, 5).

The letter to Macvey Napier dated 8 October 1821 amplifies the complaint (see chapter 8, p. 408). Here Malthus compares the Ricardians (McCulloch and Mill) – who had 'adopted a theory which will not stand the test of experience' – with the Physiocrats: 'Their system takes a partial view of the subject, like the system of the French Economists; and like that system, after having drawn into its vortex a great number of very clever men, it will be unable to support itself against the testimony of obvious facts, and the weight of those theories, which though less simple and captivating, are more just on account of embracing more of the causes which are in actual operation in all economical results' (B.L. Add. Mss 34, 612 f.453).[7] The *Quarterly Review* attack on the New Political Economy (1824) elaborates further on this same methodological theme and mind-set of its practitioners: 'The system of the new school of political economy has always struck us as bearing a very remarkable resemblance to the system of the French economists. Their founders were equally men of the most unquestionable genius; of the highest honour and integrity, and of the most simple, modest and amiable manners. Their systems were equally distinguished for their discordance with common notions, the apparent closeness of their reasonings, and the mathematical precision of their calculations and conclusions founded on their assumed data. These qualities in the systems and their founders, together with the desire so often felt by readers of moderate abilities of being thought to understand what is considered by competent judges as difficult, increased the number of their devoted followers in such a degree, that in France it included almost all the able men who were inclined to attend to such subjects, and in England a very large proportion of them' (1824a/1986, *7*, 297). 'The specific error of the new school in England' – so runs the charge – 'is the having taken so confined a view of *value* as not to include the results of demand and supply, and the relative abundance and competition of capital.'

This latter position has been encountered conspicuously in our chapter 10, on profit-rate determination. There we found reference to the same purported failing – that 'notwithstanding the utter inadequacy of this single cause [diminishing agricultural returns] to account for existing phenomena, Mr. Ricardo, in his very ingenious chapter on profits has dwelt on no other' (above, p. 472), thus committing a fundamental methodological error. The criticism is expressed in terms of a striking mechanical analogy, a perspective that amply confirms that the case does not involve an attack on theory *per se*:

> If the premises were all such as he has supposed them to be, that is, if no other cause operated on profits than the increasing difficulty of procuring the food of the labourer, and no other cause affected the exchangeable and money value

7 Malthus probably intended his objection that the Physiocrats excluded 'the results of manufacturing and mercantile industry' from 'wealth,' a complaint that is the subject-matter of a chapter in *Definitions in Political Economy*, commencing with the insistence that the term 'wealth' not be restricted 'either to the gross raw produce, or the net raw produce' (1827a/1986, *8*, 9, 38). This objection is also spelled out in 1824, and in the Invararity report of 1830.

of commodities than the quantity of labour which they had cost in production, the conclusion which he has drawn would be just, and the rate of profits would certainly be regulated in the way which he has described. But, since in the actual state of things the premises are most essentially different from those which he has supposed; since another most powerful cause operates upon profits, as I have endeavoured to shew in the present section [on wage fluctuations]; and since the exchangeable value of commodities is not determined by the labour they have cost, as I endeavoured to shew in a former chapter, the conclusion drawn by Mr. Ricardo must necessarily contradict experience; not slightly, and for short periods, as the market prices of some articles occasionally differ from the natural or necessary price, properly explained; but obviously and broadly, and for periods of such extent, that to overlook them, would not be merely like overlooking the resistance of the air to a falling body, but like overlooking the change of direction given to a ball by a second impulse acting at a different angle from the first. (308–9)

The summary proceeds to reject 'the conclusion at which Mr. Ricardo arrives in his chapter on profits, "that in all countries, and at all times, profits depend upon the quantity of labour required to produce necessaries for the labour on that land, or with that capital which yields no rent"' (309). (The validity of this and other charges is considered below, section VIII.)

Malthus's sharp criticisms of Thomas Tooke (above, chapter 11, p. 540) are relevant here. The context relates to the complaint that Tooke (1823) had declared his adherence to Say's Law of Markets, despite its failure to account for 'past phenomena': 'As we have always been of the opinion ... that the sole use of political economy is its application to practice, and that no theories are entitled to confidence in reference to the future, which will not give a satisfactory solution of past phenomena, we were disposed to hail Mr. Tooke's work as specifically calculated to set aside a theory which is directly contradicted by the most general experience, and as far as it has prevailed has wrested the science of political economy from its only just and safe foundation. What then was our disappointment to find that, although Mr. Tooke has written in such a way as, we trust, will convince others, he does not seem to be convinced himself! In a note to the last part of his work (iv, p. 5) he still declares his adherence to the doctrine of M. Say on supply and demand as explained by Mr. Mill in his *Elements of Political Economy*' (1823a/1986, *7*, 244–5). Tooke 'professes to believe that the aggregate of demand must always be equal to the aggregate supply,' though he himself had 'distinctly and luminously proved [the contrary] both by a correct train of reasoning, and what is of much more importance a constant appeal to a crowd of well-attested facts' (245).

On this formulation, confidence in a theory for future application to practice lies in its explanatory record. And it has emerged from the methodological criticisms of both the New (Ricardo) School and the Physiocrats that explanatory power will be enhanced if the model itself captures accurately empirical reality, a characteristically complex reality; the 'realistic' specification of axioms or 'general principles' is thus represented as a precondition for success.

Also pertinent is Malthus's complaint (see chapter 11, p. 577) against the supposed neglect by Ricardo of evidence pointing to increased demand for leisure following higher agricultural productivity. The purported neglect undermined the prediction whereby 'the greater ... the facility of procuring food, the more abundantly will the people be supplied with conveniences and luxuries,' and illustrated a broader failure: 'One among the many rash and false conclusions which are often made from the want of due attention to the change which the application of a proposition may make in the premises on which it rests [1836: often made in the application of a proposition without due attention to all the parts of the premises on which it rests]. In the present case, all depends upon the supposition of a given degree of industry and skill, and the means of employing them [1836: and the encouragement to employ them]. But if, after the necessaries of life were obtained, the workman should consider indolence as a greater luxury than those which he was likely to procure by further labour, the proposition would at once cease to be true. And as a matter of fact, confirmed by all the accounts we have of nations, in the different stages of their progress, it must be allowed that this choice seems to be very general in the early periods of society and by no means uncommon in the most improved states' (1820, 378–9; 1836, 333–4).

The characteristic complexity of valid economic models generated severe problems in the quest for responsible application. The so-called doctrine of proportions (see section VI) encapsulates some of these difficulties, especially in contexts involving the aggregative demand–supply relation. But the concern was widespread. As a conspicuous example, it will be recalled (chapter 17, p. 828) that the case for agricultural protection was made out in 1815 in part on the grounds that the alternative was not genuine free trade, which fact entirely altered the recommendation: 'I protest most entirely against the doctrine, that we are to pursue our general principles without ever looking to see if they are applicable to the case before us; and that in politics and political economy, we are to go straight forward, as we certainly ought to do in morals, without any reference to the conduct and proceedings of others' (1986, 7, 158). Similarly, the existence of a heavy national debt made the question 'fundamentally different from that of a simple question about a free or restricted trade' (171). To consider it thus was 'to expect the same results from premises which have essentially changed their nature.'

Malthus, furthermore, insisted on the inappropriateness in many instances of drawing practical conclusions from exercises in comparative statics. For example, the problem should not be phrased as the consequences for rent of sudden improvements in fertility (1820, 206–7; 1836,

195–6), or of changes in diet, given population (1820, 231; 1836, 211). Similarly, regarding the effect of 'machinery' (chapter 9: III; chapter 11: XIV). Such changes occur gradually during the course of ongoing growth. Again, this perspective is represented as contrasting with Ricardo's.

Did Malthus practise what he preached in insisting that allowance be made in application for special circumstances that modify general principles? (We have reviewed his own general theoretical orientation in section II.) The fact is that several of his applications are more 'extreme' than Ricardo's. This applies to his application of wage-fund theorizing to deny the efficacy of workers' combinations (1817, III, 371), Ricardo objecting both to the analysis and to the application (1951–73, VII, 203). Similarly, there is the application of the doctrine to Poor Law policy, Malthus focusing on the constraints imposed by the food supply and Ricardo refusing to place any weight on such constraints on grounds of an elastic response of food to higher demand (1951–73, VII, 3, 202).

IV METHODOLOGICAL OBJECTIONS TO ADAM SMITH

While it is true that Malthus's primary target was Ricardo, the fact neglected by so many commentators is that Adam Smith was also subject to objections on similar methodological grounds.[8] We should here have in mind that criticisms of Smith's procedures on grounds of hasty application of deductions drawn from incomprehensive models – procedures in our day designated the 'Ricardo Vice' – were common enough amongst Malthus's contemporaries. Sir Edward West, for example, complained that 'the opinion that the demand for labour is regulated solely by the amount of capital, has originated in a mode of reasoning very much used by Dr. Smith, which frequently furnishes very beautiful illustrations, often gives a clue to important conclusions, and is always a very excellent test of the truth of our inductions, but which from an incautious use of it has led perhaps to more false conclusions in the science than any other cause. I mean the reasoning from an assumed state of society and facts, and considering what the effects of the known or supposed principles of human nature would be in a state of society such as never existed' (1826, 80). John Rae complained of Smith's excessive system-building: Smith 'has himself in all his speculations, adopted the explanatory and systematizing form of

8 Cf. Blaug, 1980, 58: 'Malthus had severe misgivings about Ricardo's methodology, particularly about Ricardo's habit of directing exclusive attention to the long-run equilibrium implications of economic forces, and he suspected, although he was never able clearly to express it, that there was in Smith an inductive method that was diametrically opposed to Ricardo's deductive approach.' The remainder of Blaug's statement on Malthus holds good: 'In practice, however, Malthus's style of reasoning was identical to that of Ricardo and their wide disagreement on questions of value and the possibility of, "general gluts" involved no substantive differences in methodology.'

philosophizing, instead of the scientific and inductive ... [His] object being every where to build common facts and familiar observations into a system, not to inquire into the causes or real laws from which they spring, he takes these things for fundamental principles which would present themselves to the inductive inquirer as phenomena, the principles of which his manner of philosophizing would call on him to investigate' (1834/1965, II, 334–5).

There were those who warmly approved of Smithian system building, James Mill conspicuous among them. Mill had nothing but praise for Smith's system-building propensity. His general evaluation is brought out in a contrast drawn in 1806 between Smith and Sir James Steuart: 'The general principles of Political Economy seem to become more obscure in his hands than they were before ... there is no combination of principles in his volumes which can be called a system at all ... Dr. Smith reared the study to the dignity of a science. He explained the real sources of wealth, which till his time had been so grossly misunderstood; and conferred as great a benefit upon Political Economy, as was conferred on Astronomy by those philosophers who first confuted the perplexed doctrine of the cycles and epicycles, and established the simple principles of the Copernican system' (1806, 231–2). Mill's commendation is all the more important since his reviews are replete with criticisms of those he considered insufficiently speculative. As for detail, Mill's wholly Smithian analysis of the corn-export bounty is particularly revealing. Appreciation of Smith's case against the bounty turned upon 'a single principle ... that the nature of the farmer's business is altogether different ... from all other trades' (1804, 23–4). In this context, we meet the typically uncompromising phraseology that characterizes all of Mill's writings: 'No proposition is better established than this, that the multiplication of the human species is always in proportion to the means of subsistence,' the consequence of which was that 'the production of corn creates the market for corn.' Conversely, 'to send away any part of the regular produce of the country' – a consequence of the bounty – 'however rapidly that produce may be increasing, is just to cut short a proportional part of the natural population of the country.' And we have the full-fledged Smithian analysis of the consequence of the bounty on general prices by way of the effect upon money wages: 'We must next advert to the view which Dr. Smith has exhibited of this subject, a view which any one can affect to treat lightly only from not understanding it. No proposition is established more thoroughly to the conviction of those who have studied the scientific principles of political economy than this; that the money price of corn, regulates the money price of every thing else .... Nothing then can be more incontrovertible than the proposition of Smith, that "the real effect of the bounty is not so much to raise the real value of corn, as to degrade the real value of silver; or to make an equal quantity of it exchange for a smaller quantity, not only of corn, but of all other commodities"' (36–8). The important feature of all this is Mill's *approval* of the Smithian analysis including some very strong assumptions: (1) the simplified concept of 'corn' as a shorthand for worker's subsistence; and (2) the population doctrine used to assure constancy of the corn wage. Also conspicuous is the neglect of time lags, or disequilibria.

Others saw things in a wholly different light. De Sismondi compared Smith's view of political economy as 'une science d'expérience' with Ricardo's speculations (1827/1951, I, 69–70). Longfield observed of Smith that he 'appears not to have possessed much taste or capacity for long or subtle trains of reasoning. The "Wealth of Nations" is written with very little attention to system, and this circumstance has probably tended to increase its utility. It prevented any error from infecting the entire work. An erroneous principle would not lead the author far astray' (1834/1971, 262).[9]

Where did Malthus stand? In the *Principles* he paid tribute to the *Wealth of Nations* as the best 'systematic treatise' available and 'still of the very highest value' (1820, 5; 1836, 4).[10] He pointed out – certainly with the aggregate-demand issue in mind – that 'many of the doctrines of Adam Smith, which had been considered as settled, have lately been called in question by writers entitled to great attention; but they have often failed, as it appears to me, to make good their objections; and in all such cases I have thought it desirable to examine anew, with reference to such objections, the grounds on which his doctrines are founded' (1820, 22; 1836, 17–18). In 1824 he wrote of the conversion of French economists to 'the juster and more practical theory of Adam Smith' and expressed his hopes for the future in Britain: 'Facts and experiences have, in the course of some years, gradually converted the economists of France from the erroneous and inapplicable theory of Quesnay to the juster and more practical theory of Adam Smith; and as we are fully convinced that an error equally fundamental and important is involved in the system of the new school in England as in that of the French economists, we cannot but hope and expect that similar causes will, in time, produce in our own country similar effects in the correction of error and the establishment of truth' (1986, 7, 297). And it is here that he criticized the Ricardian New School for altering Smith's theories 'upon mere speculation; and not because they do not accord with facts and experience' (258).

The commendation of Smith in the contrast with the Physiocrats refers to his extension of national income to include the industrial sector (see chapter 8, p. 408); and the objection to the Ricardians in the same context

9 The context is Longfield's rejection of diminishing agricultural returns as the 'cause' of a secularly falling profit rate.

10 Malthus charged Smith with inconsistency regarding value measurement, notwithstanding his status as 'principal founder of the *science* of political economy,' having in mind the definition of value-in-exchange as general purchasing power (see chapter 7, p. 295).

is to their rejection of the Smithian notion of 'competition of capitals' as conflicting with the Law of Markets. The Ricardians had simply abandoned, on (spurious) logical grounds, the 'correct theory of profits' – Malthus's own term (see chapter 10, p. 466) – confirmed *inter alia* by the buoyant war years and the postwar depression. Much of his energy went into an attempt to reinforce Smithian doctrine.

But this is far from the whole story. First, the *Wealth of Nations* also provided illustrations of the danger of arriving at 'complex' but 'incorrect' theory (above, p. 959), because of erroneous and careless inductions from the data 'not warranted by general principles' (1820, 21; 1836, 16). The example given involves Smith's apparent subscription at one point to *increasing* agricultural returns, and the notion that corn imports cannot 'interfere with home growth'; Malthus's appeal to *sound general principles* in so central a context is striking:

I am inclined to think that Adam Smith occasionally fell into this error, and drew inferences [1836: Adam Smith has occasionally fallen into this error, and drawn inferences] from actual appearances, not warranted by general principles. From the low price of wheat, for instance, during the first half of the last century, he seems to infer [1836: have inferred] that wheat is generally cheaper in rich than in poor countries; and from the small quantity of corn actually imported during that period, even in the scarcest years, he infers [1836: has inferred] generally, that the quantity imported can never be such as to interfere with the home growth. The actual state of things at a subsequent period, and particularly during the last twenty-five years, has sufficiently shown that these appearances were merely incidental; that a very rich country may have its corn extremely dear, as we should naturally expect; and that importation in England has amounted to more than 1/10 instead of 1/571 [1836: 1/517] part of the crop raised in the country; and may therefore, essentially [1836: to a considerable extent] interfere with the home growth. (1820, 21–2; 16–17)[11]

A related complaint emerges in 1815 – namely, Smith's failure to appreciate that in equilibrium – when a 'state of rest has been nearly attained' and the exchanges are at par – the precious metals are *not* on a level: 'That Adam Smith, who proposes labour as the true measure of value at all times and in all places, could look around him, and yet say that the precious metals were always the highest in value in the richest countries,

11 Malthus, however, believed that Smith's omission was less serious than that of the Ricardians: 'In dwelling solely upon the abundance and competition of capital, he is practically much nearer the truth than those who dwell almost exclusively on the quality of the last land taken into cultivation' (see above, pp. 453, 775). But we have also seen that he could never make up his mind as to whether Smith had or had not recognized the diminishing-returns principle, attaching a note conceding an *implicit* allowance for the phenomenon.

has always appeared to me most unlike his usual attention to found his theories on facts' (1815b/1986, *7*, 138n; see chapter 14, p. 713).

As early as 1811, Malthus had taken Smith to task for a careless interpretation of Scottish experience of the 1750s. (For the background to this, see chapter 13:VI). He himself followed Hume in attributing an initial expansion of output to the stimulus of temporary price increases resulting from a net increase in the money supply, and the subsequent fall in prices to output expansion such as 'to restore [the quantity of commodities] ... to a level with the increased currency':

> In 1751 and 1752, when Hume published his Political Discourses, and soon after the great multiplication of paper money in Scotland, there was a very sensible rise in the price of provisions; and this was naturally, and probably justly, attributed by him, in part, to the abundance of paper. In 1759, when the paper currency had probably not been diminished, Dr. Smith notices a different state of prices; and observes that, for a long period, provisions had never been cheaper. The dearness at the time that Hume wrote, he attributes carelessly, and without any inquiry about the fact, to the badness of the seasons; and intimates, that it could not be occasioned by the multiplication of paper money. The probability, however, seems to be, that the high prices of 1751 and 1752 were influenced by the paper, – as we do not see how it is possible for the substitution of paper for coin to take place, without an increase of prices; but that the new stimulus given to industry to this increase of capital, had so increased the quantity of commodities in the interval between 1752 and 1759, as to restore them to a level with the increased currency. (1811a/1986, *7*, 49)

The charges against Smith extend further still. Malthus took a harsh line towards Smith regarding the effect of changes in the corn price, upon which turned the remarkable Smithian conclusion that government intervention in the corn trade would be to no avail. In the second edition of his *Essay on Population*, Malthus added a chapter entitled 'Of Bounties on the Exportation of Corn,' taking exception to Smith's extreme formulation, including his neglect of lagged relationships. A rise in the price of corn occasioned by the export subsidy *would* affect the agricultural profit rate, since money wages and general prices do not rise in proportion: 'The money price of corn, in a particular country, is undoubtedly by far the most powerful ingredient in regulating the price of labour, and of all other commodities; but it is not the sole ingredient. Many parts of the raw produce of land, though affected by the price of corn, do not, by any means, rise and fall exactly in proportion to this price. When great improvements in manufacturing machinery have taken place in any country, the part of the expence arising from the wages of labour will bear a comparatively small proportion to the whole value of the wrought commodity, and consequently, the price of it, though affected by the price of corn, will not be affected proportionally' (1803/1986, *3*, 683). Even assuming a *proportionate* rise in the money wage rate, taxes and rents – which are assumed here to enter costs – will be roughly constant, so that agricultural profitability must rise (684). Similar reasoning was applied to the short-run effects of freer corn importation. Here the fall in the price of corn has disastrous effects on profitability, since, in consequence of relatively constant rental and tax charges, in addition to sticky money wages, costs do not fall proportionately. These considerations could not be neglected in practical policy applications: 'When great and numerous taxes on consumption exist in any country, those who live by the wages of labour must always receive wherewithall to pay them, at least all those upon necessaries, such as soap, candles, leather, salt, &c. A fall in the price of corn, therefore, though it would decrease that part of the wages of labour which resolves itself into food, evidently, would not decrease the whole in the same proportion. And besides these, and other limitations which might be named, the experienced difficulty of lowering wages when once they have been raised, should be taken into consideration before the position can be practically applied.' In an earlier chapter Malthus had expressed the fear that easy corn importation would drive down the corn price, but not the money wage: 'Experience warrants us in saying, that, from political fears, or other causes, the fall in the price of labour would be uncertain; but the ruin of our agriculture would be certain' (677).

Again, in the *Observations* (1814): 'Nothing ... can be more evident both from theory and experience, than that the price of corn does not immediately and generally regulate the prices of labour and all other commodities; and that the real price of corn is capable of varying for periods of sufficient length to give a decided stimulus or discouragement to agriculture' (see chapter 6, p. 239). This critical evaluation turned both on the failure of Smith to take account of the empirical complexity of the wage basket and of lagged relations, and on internal or logical inconsistency – namely, the extraction of corn from standard allocation theory. In fact, Malthus asserted that Smith realized that corn could *not* be treated as an exception to the allocative generalizations applicable to all other commodities, and deliberately fudged: 'That no such exception exists with regard to corn, is implied in all the general reasonings of the *Wealth of Nations*. Dr. Smith evidently felt this; and wherever, in consequence, he does not shift the question from the exchangeable value of corn to its physical properties, he speaks with an unusual want of precision and qualifies his positions by the expressions *much*, and *in any considerable degree*' (1814/1986, 7, 91). This is a severe charge indeed, though (as we have shown in chapter 6, p. 240) Malthus himself is open to precisely the same charge by his application of the Law of Markets to food, which entails the strict interdependence of demand and supply curves.[12]

12 But Malthus himself was inconsistent in this regard; see chapter 6, p. 246; also 3, p. 104; 8, p. 398; 11, p. 538.

Smith had responded with 'hauteur' to similar criticisms made by Anderson in 1777, suggesting the absence of any valid defence (Hollander, 1979, 41–2; also 1987, 322–3, and Dow, 1984). We must ask whether, so far as concerns Smith, it suffices to leave the matter there, or whether we should seek further for an account of his peculiar position. Malthus himself did go farther. He suggested that Smith was carried away by the attraction of pet theoretical notions, specifically 'his habit of considering labour as the standard measure of value, and corn as the measure of labour'; these measures, if accurate, together implied that given quantities of corn 'on an average of a few years, at all times and in all countries, purchase the same quantity of labour and of the necessaries and conveniences of life' (1814/1986, 7, 92–3). That 'neither labour nor any other commodity can be an accurate measure of real value in exchange, is now considered as one of the most incontrovertible doctrines of political economy; and indeed follows as a necessary consequence, from the very definition of value in exchange.'[13] And the variability of the corn wage 'from year to year ... century to century ... and for ten, twenty, and thirty years together' was an established fact of economic life.[14] If this is supposed to constitute an ultimate explanation of Smith's position, it will scarcely do; it merely pushes the question a step back, since Smith himself frequently emphasized the variability of the corn wage. But for us here the important point is that criticisms one usually thinks of as directed at Ricardo are also applied to Smith, and at key junctures.

One further striking illustration of Malthus's methodological objections to the *Wealth of Nations*, emerges below, in section VI. In championing a systematic allowance for 'limitations and exceptions' in formulating general economic principles, a requirement imposed by the characteristic 'doctrine of proportions,' the putative *illegitimate* procedure is illustrated by reference to *Smith's* – not Ricardo's – propositions that 'capitals are increased by parsimony' and that 'every frugal man is a public benefactor.'

V ON VERIFICATION, PREDICTION, AND DISTURBING CAUSES: THE USES OF ECONOMIC THEORY

To this point, it has appeared that the test for valid theory turned on its explanatory power or consistency with 'general experience' (above, pp. 959f.). This leads us to the problem of 'disturbing causes.' In considering this problem, it proves helpful to have in mind an evaluation of the

13 Malthus, of course, later withdrew all this and reinstated labour commanded – as an *ideal* measure into the bargain – so that all the criticism addressed at Smith can be returned to sender.

14 The complaint against Smith's assumption in his Digression on Silver of a constant long-run corn wage is conspicuous in the *Principles* (1820, 123; 1836, 121; see above, chapter 7, pp. 280, 298–9).

classical view on theory 'verification' offered by Mark Blaug: 'Over and over again, in Senior, in Mill, in Cairnes, and even in Jevons, we have found the notion that "verification" is not a testing of economic theories to see whether they are true or false, but only a method of establishing the boundaries of application of theories deemed to be obviously true: one verifies in order to discover whether "disturbing causes" can account for the discrepancies between stubborn facts and theoretically valid reasons; if they do, the theory has been wrongly applied, but the theory itself is still true. The question of whether there is any way of showing a theory to be false is never even contemplated' (1980, 81). No mention is made here of Malthus. Where did Malthus stand on these matters?

From what we have seen already, Malthus did countenance, at least in principle, the isolation and rejection of 'false' theories, evaluating theory in terms of its explanatory power. This formal allowance is seen in practice throughout the impressive analysis of the postwar depression (see chapter 12), where he makes an excellent case for his own over Ricardo's explanatory hypothesis. And it is confirmed in the following passage, which takes account of failures of theory – revealed by failures of prediction – resulting not only from 'specific misapplication' but also from 'general inapplicability' and logical error: 'A theory may appear to be correct, and may really be correct under given premises; it may further *appear* that these premises are the same as those under which the theory is about to be applied; but a difference, which might before have been unobserved, may shew itself in the difference of the results from those which were expected; and the theory may justly be considered as failing, whether this failure arises from an *original error in its formation*, or from its general inapplicability, or specific misapplication, to actual circumstances' (1820, 11; 1836, 9; emphasis added). It is very clear that he perceived the Law of Markets – and any exclusive version of agricultural profit-rate analysis – as invalid in part because of 'original error': 'The new school suppose that the mass of commodities obtained by the same quantity of labour remains always substantially of the same value, and that the variations of profits are determined by the variations in the value of this same quantity of labour; while Adam Smith and Mr Malthus suppose that the value of the same quantity of labour remains substantially the same, and that the variations of profits are determined by the variations in the value of the commodities produced by this same quantity of labour. In the one case, the varying value of labour is considered as the great moving principle in the progress of wealth; in the other, the varying value of the *produce* of labour. The difference is most distinct and important. And as political economy, according to the first description of it in the present treatise, "is not a science of speculation, but of fact and experiment," the specific question is, which of the two views here stated best explains the broad and established facts of which we have had experience' (1824a/1986, 7, 295).

Malthus had the better of Ricardo in accounting for the post-1815 depression. It is, however, regrettable and surprising that he failed to provide specific illustrations of the central theme of his analysis of sustainable growth – that 'almost all merchants and manufacturers save, in prosperous times, much more rapidly than it would be possible for the national capital to increase, so as to keep up the value of the produce' (see chapter 11, pp. 530, 584). It is also true that, on one conspicuous occasion, Malthus explicitly expressed his confidence in his analysis, despite admitted difficulty in providing confirmatory evidence. I refer to the oscillatory pattern of growth, which Malthus allowed 'will not be remarked by superficial observers; and it may be difficult even for the most penetrating mind to calculate its period' (cited chapter 1, p. 44; see also p. 63). Malthus – like Adam Smith and Ricardo – found inductive procedures as a means of discerning cause–effect relations sterile; and in the present case there were too many counteracting forces 'concealing' the oscillations, which 'no reflecting man who considers the subject deeply can well doubt.' *More generally, he recognized a characteristic resilience of theory against refutation.* This is clear from his insistence on recognizing modifications, limitations, and exceptions to any general rule or proposition (above, section II); and it emerges also in a further criticism of 'the tendency to simplify and generalize': 'The same tendency ... produces a still greater disinclination to allow of modifications, limitations, and exceptions to any rule or proposition, than to admit the operation of more causes than one. Nothing indeed is so unsatisfactory, and gives so unscientific and unmasterly an air to a proposition as to be obliged to make admissions of this kind; yet ... there are many important propositions in political economy which absolutely require limitations and exceptions' (1820, 7–8; 1836, 6). Here Malthus summarizes with the observation that the complexity introduced by *multi-causality* – and also by *mutual cause–effect relations* – supplemented by the problem of 'limitations and exceptions' to any general proposition, accounted for 'frequent' failures of prediction: 'It may be confidently stated that the frequent combination of complicated causes, the actions and reactions of cause and effect on each other, and the necessity of limitations and exceptions in a considerable number of important propositions, form the main difficulties of the science, and occasion those frequent mistakes which it must be allowed are made in the prediction of results' (1820, 8; 1836, 6).[15] 'Mistakes in prediction,' one is led to believe, *need* not imply

15 An important instance is provided by Malthus's early objections to a defence of Bank of England policy on the grounds that the foreign exchanges had nothing to do with currency, since an 'improving exchange' frequently coincided with an increasing issue of notes, and a deterioration with note contraction (1811a/1986, 7, 42; see above, chapter 14, p. 685). Improvements in the exchange might occur because of 'mercantile transactions' despite pressure on the exchange in the opposite direction created by excess paper issues. Ricardo reacted in precisely the same way in 1819 (see Hollander, 1979, 459).

error in the theory itself. And the problem of evaluating the verdict is not minimized: 'Where unforseen causes may possibly be in operation, and the causes that are foreseen are liable to great variations in their strength and efficacy, an accurate yet comprehensive attention to facts is necessary, both to prevent the multiplication of erroneous theories, and to confirm and sanction those that are just' (1820, 11–12; 1836, 9).

That 'failure' of prediction need not be definitive requires further illustration. There is allusion to the generation of specific forecasts as one of the practical purposes of theoretical analysis – namely, '[to] trace distinctly the operations of that circle of causes and effects in political economy which are acting and re-acting on each other, so as to foresee their results, and lay down general rules' (1820, 16; 1836, 13). But 'forecasting' does not take centre stage, since '[in] many cases ... it may not be possible to predict results with certainty, on account of the complication of the causes in action, the different degrees of strength and efficacy with which they may operate, and the number of unforeseen circumstances which are likely to interfere' (1820, 17; 1836, 13). The role of theory is rather to allow the classification of alternative outcomes depending on circumstances: 'But it is surely knowledge of the highest importance to be able to draw a line, with tolerable precision, between those cases where the expected results are certain, and those where they are doubtful; and further to be able satisfactorily to explain, in the latter case, the reasons of such uncertainty.' For, 'to know what can be done, and how to do it, is, beyond a doubt, the most valuable species of information.' Also important, theory defined what is ruled out: 'The next to it is, to know what cannot be done, and why we cannot do it. The first enables us to attain a positive good, to increase our powers, and augment our happiness: the second saves us from the evil of fruitless attempts, and the loss and misery occasioned by perpetual failure' (1820, 17; 1836, 13–14). All this is very much in line with Ricardo's perspective as is clear from his treatment of the Corn Law issue (see Hollander, 1979, ch. 11).

Let us consider Malthus's use of population theory from this perspective. The population expansion under way was, as we know from chapter 16, attributed to a fall in the *mortality* rate more than sufficient to compensate for an increase in the preventive checks – namely, a decline in the marriage and birth rates. The evidence, he insisted against Weyland, proved 'incontrovertibly that the actual checks to population, even in the most improved countries, arise principally from an insufficiency of subsistence, and soon yield to increased resources, notwithstanding the increase of towns and manufactories ...' (see above, chapter 5, p. 200): or again 'Mr. Weyland really appears to have dictated his book with his eyes blindfolded, and his ears stopped ... The very slightest glance at different countries of Europe shows with a force amounting to demonstration that to all practical purposes the *natural tendency* of population to increase may be considered a given quantity; and that the actual increase is regulated by the varying resources of each country for the employment and maintenance of labour, in whatever stage of its progress it may be, whether it is agricultural or manufacturing, whether it has few or many towns' (cited chapter 5, p. 203). But what would have constituted a 'refutation'? Had there been no positive population response to a relaxation of the food constraint, one might suppose. Yet if this could be accounted for by a sufficiently marked fall in the birth rate to outweigh the fall in mortality – and it will be recalled that Malthus *rationalized* improved prudence not only in terms of exogenous changes in prudential control, but as an endogenous variable involving the pressure exerted by a relative increase in corn prices (chapter 5: IV) – the model would be protected, and legitimately so. It is certain that Malthus did not see the contemporary upward trend in the real wage as in any way refuting his population doctrine. That doctrine served his primary purpose, which was to warn against policies or institutions that positively encouraged population growth, thereby liberating or encouraging the 'tendency' towards excess population growth.[16]

This line of argument extends to the land scarcity–based growth or 'canonical' model itself. The evidence adduced by Malthus for the period 1793–1815 pointed to the significance of technical progress in preventing a rise in the real cost of producing food (see chapter 15: V, VI), and he made much of prospective productivity increase. Yet he did not abandon the land-scarcity model, and himself elaborated on the downward trend in the corn wage and profit rate, notwithstanding the *actual* upward trend of both, at least until the postwar depression. The procedure might seem irresponsible unless – as seems also to be the case for Ricardo – the primary purpose of model-building was seen to provide a framework for policy, indicating what can happen, rather than a technical organon designed to generate specific historical predictions.[17] For all that, there are to be found loose 'predictions' of the course of events several decades, even a century ahead, in consequence of increasing land scarcity; and Malthus's statements of diminishing agricultural returns we have found to be *stronger* than Ricardo's, incorporating as they often do improvement in technology (see, e.g., chapter 3, p. 105; 15, p. 748).[18]

16 Poor relief was a conspicuous concern. Other illustrations are provided by our discussion of Malthus on emigration and public works (chapter 18: VII). He was warning of the *potential* danger emanating from excessive population growth in reaction to improved standards which had to be considered in devising social policy, not positively predicting such an outcome.

17 For an illustration of this orientation see above, section II, on the implications of the analysis entailed in interpreting the profit-rate differential in the periods 1793–1813 and 1727–57.

18 But here again there is no consistency of practice; see chapter 5, p. 194.

VI THE 'DOCTRINE OF PROPORTIONS': POLITICAL ECONOMY AND MATHEMATICS

Two important examples illustrate the necessity to allow for 'limitations and exceptions' to general rules (above, section II), one relating to *savings* and the other to *property distribution*, both with respect to economic growth. As for the first, Malthus had in mind Smith's general proposition – this provides further illustration of Malthus's concern with Smithian strong statements – 'that capitals are increased by parsimony,' 'that every frugal man is a public benefactor' (1776/1937, 321, 324) or that increase of wealth depends upon the balance of produce above consumption: 'That these propositions are true to a great extent is perfectly unquestionable. No considerable and continued increase of wealth could possibly take place without that degree of frugality which occasions, annually, the conversion of some revenue into capital, and creates a balance of produce above consumption' (1820, 8; 1836, 6). The 'limitation' of the Smithian propositions – that they were 'not true to an indefinite extent' – reflected the fact that 'the principle of saving, pushed to excess, would destroy the motive to production.' In brief: 'If consumption exceed production, the capital of the country must be diminished, and its wealth must be gradually destroyed from its want of power to produce; if production be in a great excess above consumption, the motive to accumulate and produce must cease from the want of will to consume [1836: from the want of an effectual demand in those who have the principal means of purchasing]. The two extremes are obvious; and it follows that there must be some intermediate point, though the resources of political economy may not be able to ascertain it, where, taking into consideration both the power to produce and the will to consume, the encouragement to the increase of wealth is the greatest' (1820, 9; 1836, 7). Malthus alludes here to the so-called Doctrine of Proportions.[19]

A second example of the necessity for allowing 'limitations and exceptions' to general rules, and one which also involves the problem of

19 Ricardo protested in his *Note 2* that there was no dispute regarding the requirement for capital accumulation if growth is to proceed, and also none regarding the possibility that the motive to accumulate may weaken (1951–73, II, 8–9). But he realized that the main issue was not reduced 'motive' as such, but such a reduction that reflects specifically Malthusian non-sustainable growth entailing excess commodity supply, excess capacity, and unemployment rather than the labour scarcity that he, Ricardo, so readily allowed: 'Mr. Malthus will be found to maintain not only the opinion, which is just, that the profits of the capitalist will be diminished by an increase of productions under the circumstances supposed; but also the opinion which is wholly inconsistent with it that the wages of the labourer will be likewise reduced' (9). To him, Malthus's position was incomprehensible: 'Productions altogether are increased, a selection may be freely made what those productions shall be, and yet neither the capitalist nor the labourer shall be benefited by them, altho they must be awarded to one or other of them.'

defining optimal positions, involves the ideal division of property from the perspective of growth: 'There is here ... a point as well as in the other instance, though we may not know how to place it, where the division of property is best suited to the actual circumstances of the society, and calculated to give the best stimulus to production and to the increase of wealth and population' (1820, 9–10; 1836, 7–8). It followed then 'that no general rule can be laid down respecting the advantage to be derived from saving, or the division of property, without limitations and exceptions.' Moreover, the problem of defining 'optima' – the characteristic that 'the most advantageous mean cannot be marked' – meant that 'effects may be produced by an unnoticed approximation to this middle point, which are attributed to other causes, and lead to false conclusions.'

The significance of property distribution for economic growth is much elaborated in the *Principles* with this complexity in mind (see above, chapter 11: XII).[20] While a greater degree of equality was advisable from the perspective of aggregate demand, 'beyond a certain extent' – and considered from the supply side – the effect would be damaging. In general terms, 'there is a certain elevation at which the projectile will go the farthest; but if it be directed either higher or lower, it will fall short (1820, 431–2; 1836, 375). In the case at hand: 'With a comparatively small proportion of rich proprietors, who would prefer menial service [1836: menial servants, retainers] and territorial influence to an excessive quantity of manufactured and mercantile products, the power [1836: among capitalists] of supplying the results of productive labour would be much greater than the will to consume them, and the progress of wealth would be checked by the want of effective [1836: effectual] demand. With an excessive proportion of small proprietors both of land and capital, all great improvements on the land, all great enterprises in commerce and manufactures, and all the wonders [1836: most of the wonders] described by Adam Smith, as resulting from the division of labour, would be at an end; and the progress of wealth would be checked by a failure in the powers of supply' (1820, 432; 1836, 375–6). Malthus was somewhat more specific: 'If the demand be great, independently of the land, a slight diminution in the power of production may turn the scale, and any change which is unfavourable to accumulation, enterprise, and the division of labour, will be unfavourable to the progress of wealth. But if the country be ill situated for foreign commerce, and its tastes, habits, and internal communications be such as not to encourage an active home trade nothing can occasion

20 An early instance of the approach is to be found on the *Essay on Population*: 'allowing, with the moderns, all the advantages of luxury, and when they fall short of actual vice, they are certainly great; there seems to be a point, beyond which it must necessarily become prejudicial to a state, and bring with it the seeds of weakness and decay' (1803/1986, *3*, 687n; 1806, II, 274n).

an adequate demand for produce, but an easy subdivision of landed property ...' (1820, 439–40; 1836, 382).

A related instance involves the magnitude of the 'unproductive' sector from the perspective of growth (chapter 11: XIII). The problem is spelled out at the outset of Section IX of the chapter on Progress: 'What the proportion is between the productive and unproductive classes of a society, [1836: the productive labourers and those engaged in personal services,] which affords the greatest encouragement to the continued increase of wealth, it has before been said that the resources of political economy are unequal to determine. It must depend upon a great variety of circumstances, particularly upon the fertility of the soil and the progress of invention in machinery. A fertile soil and an ingenious people can not only support a considerable proportion of unproductive consumers without injury [1836: support without injury a considerable proportion of consumers not directly productive of material wealth,] but may absolutely require such a body of demanders, in order to give effect to their [1836: the] powers of production. While, with a poor soil and a people of little ingenuity, an attempt to support such a body would throw land out of cultivation, and lead infallibly to impoverishment and ruin'(1820, 464; 1836, 399). In addition: 'Another cause, which makes it impossible to say what proportion of the unproductive to the productive classes [1836: what proportion of consumers directly productive to those not directly productive] is most favourable to the increase of wealth, is the difference in the degree of consumption which may prevail among the producers themselves.' And a statement regarding the role of 'the unproductive classes' in terms of the 'doctrine of proportions' closes Malthus's Section IX: 'Their specific use in encouraging wealth is, to maintain such a balance between produce and consumption as to give the greatest exchangeable value to the results of the national industry. [1836: On the whole it may be observed, that the specific use of a body of unproductive consumers, is to give encouragement to wealth by maintaining a balance between produce and consumption as will give the greatest exchangeable value to the results of national industry.] If unproductive labour [1836: such consumers] were to predominate, the comparatively small quantity of material products brought to market would keep down the value of the whole produce, from the deficiency of quantity. If [1836: If, on the other hand,] the productive classes were in excess, the value of the whole produce would fall from excess of supply. It is obviously [1836: There is therefore] a certain proportion between the two which will yield the greatest value, and command [1836: and command for a continuance] the greatest quantity of domestic and foreign labour [1836: of labour]; ...' (1820, 489; 1836, 412–13).

The foregoing perspective governed Malthus's approach to the national debt (see above, chapter 13: V). The positive effect on aggregate demand of the growth of the national debt in the past had exceeded the negative effect from the supply side; there was no such assurance for the future. But

Malthus did offer evaluations of the relevant circumstances, in the present instance specifying that, notwithstanding his concern with the taxation burden of financing the debt in the peculiar conditions faced by Britain, repayment (such as Ricardo recommended) would entail unacceptable dangers of demand contraction.

The doctrine of proportions is generalized: 'It will be found, I believe, true that all the great results in political economy, respecting wealth, depend upon proportions,' though there is no part of the whole subject, where the efficacy of proportions in the production of wealth is so strikingly exemplified, as in the division of landed and other property' (1820, 432–3; 1836, 376). The 1836 version generalizes further: 'It is not, however, in political economy alone that so much depends upon proportions, but throughout the whole range of nature and art.' In both versions responsibility for *failures of prediction* is attributed in part to neglect of the characteristic: 'it is from overlooking this most important truth, that so many errors have prevailed in the prediction of consequences; that nations have sometimes been enriched when it was expected that they would be impoverished, and impoverished when it was expected that they would be enriched; and that such contradictory opinions have occasionally prevailed respecting the most effective encouragements to the increase of wealth.' (A note in the second edition illustrates from the predictions made during the war 'of the abundant wealth which would be the immediate result of the peace.') The characteristic problem of 'proportions' introduced 'a kind of uncertainty over the science of political economy' (1820, 515; 1836, 432). But if 'the doctrine should be found, upon sufficient examination, to be true; if it adequately accounts for things as they are, and explains consistently why frequent mistakes have been made respecting the future, it will be allowed that such objectors are answered. We cannot make a science more certain by our wishes or opinions; but we may obviously make it much more uncertain in its application, by believing it to be what it is not.'

Malthus deserves credit for his attempts to specify where possible the outcome of the balance in specific cases. None the less, in one major respect the problem of proportions seems to have paralysed him. For a primary practical outcome of the perspective in the context of sustainable growth is that *savings decisions must be left to the free market*: 'Saving ... is, in numerous instances, a most sacred private duty,' but whether the rate of accumulation 'if let alone, be ever too great or not, no one could think of interfering with it, even in its caprices' (1820, 517; 1836, 434; see chapter 12, p. 615). Malthus, in fact, has replaced Smith's clear-cut rule that increased savings is a national benefit by another unambiguous rule – that of *laissez-faire* with respect to accumulation. It comes as something of an anti-climax. (See further, below, p. 1003.)

* * *

Malthus, we have just seen, allowed that the problem of 'proportions' introduced 'a kind of uncertainty over the science of political economy.' In the same context, at the close of the *Principles* (1820, 518; 1836, 434), he reiterated almost verbatim the famous declaration of the Introduction, that 'the science of political economy bears a nearer resemblance to the science of morals and politics, than to that of mathematics':

> It has been said, and perhaps with truth, that the conclusions of Political Economy partake more of the certainty of the stricter sciences than those of most of the other branches of human knowledge. Yet we should fall into a serious error if we were to suppose that any propositions, the practical results of which depend upon the agency of so variable a being as man, and the qualities of so variable a compound as the soil, can ever admit of the same kinds of proof, or lead to the same certain conclusions, as those which relate to figure and number. There are indeed in political economy great general principles, to which exceptions are of the most rare occurrence, and prominent land-marks which may almost always be depended upon as safe guides; but even these, when examined, will be found to resemble in most particulars the great general rules in morals and politics founded upon the known passions and propensities of human nature: and whether we advert to the qualities of man, or of the earth he is destined to cultivate, we shall be compelled to acknowledge, that the science of political economy bears a nearer resemblance to the science of morals and politics than to that of mathematics. (1820, 1–2; 1836, 1)

The emphasis here is on the difficulties of proof in economics and, above all, the uncertainty of its conclusions compared with 'the stricter sciences.' This confirms the outcome of our preceding sections, that the main message Malthus intended to convey by his striking formulations was that, characteristically, economics did not typically generate general and universally applicable practical rules, particularly rules pertaining to policy, a restriction that flowed in part from the allowance that had to be made for aggregate-demand in addition to aggregate-supply constraints.

The problem reflects the complexity of economics, though at no time did Malthus cast aspersions on deductive theorizing as such. Indeed, the fact is that Malthus did not even object to the use of mathematical tools in economic theory. He was, of course, engaged in formulating behavioural and technological relations and theorems of various sorts, as is so apparent in the treatment of growth; he was evidently comfortable with mathematical formulas, especially in the demographic context;[21] and he relished mechanical analogies. A striking instance is the reservoir analogy used in support of the geometric and arithmetic ratios (see chapter 1, p. 31). A

21 Cf. 1986, *2*, 256 regarding a 'general formula for estimating the population of a country at any distance from a certain period, under given circumstances of births and mortality,' citing Bridge (1810).

second is that between the downward trend of the profit rate attributable to increasing land scarcity, and the value of long-term annuities (see chapter 10, p. 471). Thus even his objections to Ricardo's (supposed) neglect of all other considerations are formulated mathematically: 'The value of the government long annuities has a natural and inevitable [1836: constant] tendency to diminish as they approach nearer and nearer to the end of the term for which they were granted [1836: approach towards the term for which they were granted] ... [But] it would be a most erroneous calculation to estimate the value of this kind of stock solely by the number of years which it would have to run [1836: sentence omitted]. It is well known that out of the comparatively short term of ninety years, so large a proportion as twenty has sometimes elapsed, not only without any diminution, but with an actual increase of [1836: their] value' (1820, 307–8; 1836, 281).[22] This same perspecitve is also encountered in the mechanical analogy brought to counter Ricardo's supposedly monocausal theory of the profit rate (above, pp. 966–7).

All this might be considered in the nature of circumstantial evidence. But, Malthus himself confirms this reading, for he wrote to Whewell upon receipt of the latter's *Mathematical Exposition of Some Doctrines of Political Economy* (1829): 'I think ... that you have arrived at pretty just conclusions, and am inclined to infer from what I have seen, that mathematical calculations may in some cases be introduced with advantage into the science of Political Economy particularly with a view to determine the different *degrees* in which certain objects are affected, under different hypotheses' (TCL Add. Ms. a.209[10]; de Marchi and Sturges, 1973, 387). But, as for practice, the true problem was one of *estimation*: 'The grand difficulty, however, with a view to practicability, is the getting data to work with, sufficiently near the truth, such as can be stated distinctly in mathematical language. In many cases where one should wish to come to definite conclusions I should fear this was quite impracticable.'[23]

Moreover, a conceptual mathematical maximization procedure was at play in specifying, at least in principle, appropriate policy: 'I have long thought that there are many of the results in political economy which have some resemblance to the problems de maximis et minimis, such as the

22 In 1836 this passage continues in an elaboration of the bond analogy. That elaboration occurs in 1820 later in the section. The substance is the same: 'To recur to the illustration already used – as the Long Annuities approach nearer and nearer to the term at which they expire, their value must necessarily so diminish, on this account alone, that no demand arising from plenty of money could possibly keep up their value' (1820, 312); 'when, however, they approach near to the term at which they expire, they must necessarily so diminish in value on this account alone, that no demand arising from plenty of money could possibly keep up their price' (1836, 281).

23 Jevons was more optimistic, referring to 'the long course of scientific progress [when] a sufficient supply of suitable statistics has been at length obtained' (1879, 148).

most favourable division of landed property, neither too great nor too small; and the most advantageous proportions (with a view to the permanent increase of wealth) in which the whole produce of capital should be divided between the capitalists and the labourers.' Here, then, Malthus recognized that his 'principle of proportions' itself invited the optimization procedures of the calculus, though he could 'not see how such propositions could be put into the proper language for a fluxional solution, varying as the results must do with the fertility of the soils and the productiveness of capital.'

It follows from all this that the denial of a parallel between political economy and mathematics (and insistence on its resemblance with 'morals and politics') not only does not imply rejection of mathematics in economic theory, but, to the contrary, sees mathematics – more specifically the calculus – as (potentially) the appropriate procedure in dealing with the 'principle of proportions.' The statement sought only to convey a denial of simple, generally applicable, rules of thumb, such as those flowing from theoretical structures which allowed only for supply-side constraints.

A word regarding Ricardo's reaction to Malthus's published statement on the contrast between economics and mathematics: 'Another of his great mistakes,' he wrote to James Mill, 'is I think this; Political Economy he says is not a strict science like the mathematics ...' (1 January 1821; 1951–73, VIII, 331). Ricardo proceeded to complain that 'therefore he thinks he may use words in a vague way, sometimes attaching one meaning to them, sometimes another and quite different. No proposition can be more absurd.' Precisely what Ricardo intended is unclear.[24] There is some validity to Ricardo's charge regarding loose use of terminology, but it scarcely reflects accurately the formal constrast with mathematics, since Malthus did not in fact deny a role for mathematics in economics.

VII THE CHARGE OF 'INCONSISTENCY' AND RELATED MATTERS

The 'doctrine of proportions' cannot be adduced in exoneration of the criticisms that have been levelled against Malthus on grounds of consistency, though we readily allow that his task was particularly onerous.[25] It

24 The objection apparently turns on Say's Law: 'In all those cases where [in discussion] he has advanced one proposition in which he says he differs with you, Say and me, and has actually endeavoured to prove another, which we should not dispute, he appears to me to hold the proposition which he does prove to be identical with the one not proved; the error therefore is in his language, he appears to me not to be aware of the import of the words which he uses – they convey a totally different meaning to his mind, and to mine!'

25 There is, however, considerable justification for Pullen's observation that the accusations of 'muddled thinking' appear to have been exaggerated and unjustified, because Malthus's critics have been unaware of, or have not properly recognized, his doctrine of proportions (1982, 270).

is primarily the denial of, and attempt to disprove, Say's Law in the industrial sector that introduces the peculiar complexity absent from Ricardo's system – not the demand–supply approach to price or variable corn wages in the growth context, both of which were insisted upon by Ricardo. The problem Malthus faced was exacerbated by the need to combine his allowance for potential deviations between aggregate demand and supply with the land-scarcity approach to the agricultural sector – the 'canonical' perspective. He certainly struggled with the differential treatment of the two sectors for years, as we saw in Part I, reaching some kind of resolution in the *Principles* in the corn-profit model (chapter 10: III, IV). Whatever one may think of this resolution, the fact is that it makes no appearance in the formal analysis of sustainable growth undertaken in the chapter on Progress, which proceeds largely by simply setting the 'canonical' issues aside (see chapter 11).[26] Nevertheless, we must avoid the conclusion that Malthus proceeded *on principle* without attention to 'system' and the desirability of achieving a consistent unity (see above, section II). If there are logical inconsistencies and loose ends, they must be frankly recognized as weaknesses, whereas too often failures of reconciliation have been justified as inherent in a peculiar methodology represented as preferable to Ricardo's.

Malthus was himself dissatisfied with his *Principles.* The delayed publication, the revisions commenced before the ink was dry, the failure to complete the second edition – all are indicative. Some simple data establish the initial hesitancy. On 12 October 1817, Malthus first intimated to Ricardo his planned volume: 'I am meditating another volume but hardly know what to call it' (in Ricardo, 1951–73, VII, 194); and again on 3 December: 'I am meditating a volume as I believe I have told you, and I want to answer you, without giving my work a controversial air. Can you tell me how to manage this' (215). (Ricardo understood the request as relating to an appropriate title and to matters of organization, not substance, and left it to Malthus; 16 December, 222.) On 30 March 1818, he reported to Prévost on his work, mentioning that 'in this I shall advert frequently to Mr. Ricardo's work' (II, vii). In the second half of 1818, he read parts of the manuscript to Ricardo (VII, 284, 372); but he complained on 16 August that his progress was slow (279), and again on 21 October: 'I am going on with my volume, though slowly, and with more interruptions than I intended or expected. I boggle ever at the title; and it is not till after some delay and difficulty, that I have at length determined upon

26 To that extent it would be correct to say that 'land scarcity and diminishing returns are ... not integrated with "effective demand" into a coherent model' (Waterman, 1996b). Malthus's letter to Ricardo of 16 July 1821 contains an illusive comment relating 'the fertility of the soil' with the degree of 'unproductive consumption' required to assure sustainable growth (cited chapter 11, pp. 519–21).

"The Principles of Political Economy considered, with a view to their practical application" ... But though I have at length determined on what I am going to write about, I doubt whether I shall finish this spring' (312). An announcement in fact appeared on 10 November 1818 in the *Monthly Literary Advertiser* that this title was in press (329n). In December 1818, Ricardo reported to Trower, and to James Mill, Malthus's intimation to him that the book would not appear till the end of 1819 (370, 376). As we remarked at the outset of this book, the delay, Ricardo believed, reflected in part 'doubts which he cannot help entertaining of the correctness of his opinions.'

Nearly a year later, Malthus was still struggling to complete the manuscript, and himself explained the delay by lack of confidence, confirming Ricardo's suspicions,[27] and by the disparate periods of composition: 'I have been saying in my introduction, that my work has been delayed by my respect for your authority, and the fear that I must have overlooked some essential points either in your view of the subject or in my own. But though I have been lately finishing the beginning, I have by no means arrived at the end. I think I have a fourth or fifth to write yet; and having composed the different parts at different times and not in their natural order, I have still much to put out and put in, before it will be fit to send to the press. I can hardly expect to be out before February or March' (10 September 1819; VIII, 65–66; see also Malthus, 1820, 24, for the final formulation).[28] It is clear that Malthus was troubled by his own deficiency in system building – *vide* the comment on 'natural order.' The process of revision began almost immediately after the appearance of the volume early in April 1820 and is alluded to as early as 26 October: 'I am preparing a new edition and shall be glad of any corrections and suggestions which you will give both in reference to those parts which relate to you, and many others'(to Ricardo; VIII, 285). The revisions were never fully completed.

* * *

Malthus's own admission that he had not managed to develop a 'system' in his *Principles*, that the different chapters had been composed at different

27 Malthus from the start expressed concern not to offend Ricardo, as is clear from the following comment on a detail in his first *Edinburgh Review* article: 'I was sorry to find a small monosyllable put into the [February 1811] article either by Jeffrey or by accident, which made a considerable alteration in the sense, and may have offended Mr. Ricardo in some degree justly. I had said "We do not think these facts are all satisfactorily explicable upon the principles of Mr. Ricardo alone," – it is printed *at all*, and makes a good deal of difference' (to Horner, 7 April 1811; in Ricardo, 1951–73, III, 12).

28 Early in November 1819, the *Monthly Literary Advisor* announced the *Principles* as forthcoming shortly (VIII, 138), and the book finally appeared early in April 1820.

times and were inadequately collated, coupled with his hesitancy and doubt lends some circumstantial support for the validity of the charge of inconsistency levelled against him. Here, we follow up this and related charges, extending our investigation quite generally.

We start with Ricardo's primary objection to the protectionist case in *Grounds of an Opinion.* Ricardo complained, not of the protectionism as such: 'You are avowedly for restrictions on importation; of that I do not complain. It is not easy to estimate justly the dangers to which we may be exposed ... It is a most difficult point to calculate these dangers at their fair value'; his objection was rather to Malthus's appeal to principles *inconsistent* with the theory of allocation adopted elsewhere: 'in an economical view, altho' you have here and there allowed that we might be benefited by importing cheap, rather than by growing dear – you point out many inconveniences which we should suffer from the loss of agricultural capital, and from other causes; *which would make it appear as if even economically you thought we ought [not] to import corn,* – such is the approbation with which you quote from Adam Smith of the benefits of agriculture over commerce in increasing production, and which I cannot help thinking, is at variance with all your general doctrines' (letter dated 13 February 1815; 1951–73, VI, 177–8; emphasis added).

This reaction to the *Grounds* – it also applies at least to the 1820 edition of the *Principles* – that the case for protection reflected in part the analytical notion of superior agricultural productivity and was 'at variance with all [Malthus's] general doctrines' is perfectly valid. And it is difficult to appreciate how it was that Malthus took Adam Smith severely to task for extracting corn from the usual demand–supply mechanism (above, p. 974), while he himself did the very same. Moreover, the rationale for the distinct character of corn turned on an immediate population reaction to increased supplies of corn – again this is to be found in the *Wealth of Nations* and was much admired by James Mill (see above, p. 970) – which is at variance with the claim of the superiority of a method that allows for *short-run* and *lagged* reactions. The problem is further compounded by the adoption of the scarcity approach implicit in the diminishing-returns conception while singing the praises of the agricultural surplus (see chapter 8: VII–IX). *Inconsistencies reflecting the simultaneous subscription to conflicting paradigms – scarcity-oriented versus surplus-oriented paradigms – thus pervade Malthus's economics* (as to some degree they affect the *Wealth of Nations,* considering Smith's agricultural bias), though it is to Malthus's credit that he ultimately came to abandon much of the physiocratic perspective.

Mention should be made here of Ricardo's frustration at Malthus's rejection in 1820 of the notion of no-rent marginal produce – despite his elaboration of the phenomenon in 1814/15 (see chapter 4, pp. 170–1); and, we should add, despite its subsequent reappearance in the discussion of the inverse wage–profit relation, and throughout *The Measure of Value* (see chapter 6: VIII; 7: VIII; 8: IX). Other valid charges relate to his failure to stay consistently with his own preferred measure of value (chapter 4: note 91). There is a switching back and forth regarding the priority of food and population (chapter 5: IX), though the application of the Law of Markets to food turned crucially on the priority of food. Most serious is the fact that the notion of a proportionate response of population to food undermines the treatment of the wage as a policy parameter (see chapter 8: XI). And there are the contradictory approaches to labour demand documented in chapter 9.

Robert Torrens formulated the complaint with an alteration of emphasis. He represented Malthus as 'appear[ing] as the ingenious opponent of the new theory of profit, which may be traced by a process of reasoning, self-evident in all its steps, from those discoveries respecting the nature and origin of rent which he himself has made' (1821, xii–xiii); and – looked at from the reverse angle – appearing (like Priestley) 'as the pertinacious champion of the theories which the facts established by himself had so largely contributed to overthrow' (xiii).[29] To read Malthus – as Torrens did – as positively *rejecting* the land scarcity–based growth model is unjustified, as we have made abundantly clear throughout this work, but it is true that he worked with concepts opposed to it.

Torrens's complaint illustrates the 1815 charge of characteristic inconsistency (see the Introduction, pp. 6–7). Other aspects of his objection are less convincing. First, he found that Malthus used the population principle – derived in fact from Wallace – to confute Godwin and Condorcet on the grounds that, were moral restraint practised (as a feature of the perfectibility of man), it would be undermined by population pressure; and then proceeded to admit that population growth might be checked by moral restraint (1815, ix). This is a false charge, since it neglects the different institutions in the two cases – communism versus private property, including marriage – with their differential behavioural patterns (see chapter 19, p. 939). Second, he pointed to Malthus's support of corn-export bounties in the *Essay on Population*, whereas the 1814 *Observation* 'states the impossibility of England's becoming an exporting country' (x). Again, this is an invalid objection; Malthus is clear that empirical conditions had altered since the early 1800s (see chapter 15, pp. 751–2). The third illustration involves the Bullion controversy (x–xi). Malthus in 1810–11 had ascribed the deviation of the value of paper from coin to an excessive issue of paper rather than to an extraordinary increase in the Continental demand for the metal; in *Grounds of an Opinion* (1815), he maintained that paper had since risen in value despite increased note supply (and attributed part of the remaining differential to a high bullion value in Europe). (See chapter

29 Pullen (in Malthus, 1820/1989, II, 289) points to the irony of Torrens's comparison since Malthus himself had been critical of Priestley (see above, note 4).

13, p. 655) But Torrens neglected to allow for Malthus's specification of the circumstances ruling in 1815 – changes in *ceteris paribus* conditions, including failure of country banks – such that 'increased issues might take place, accompanied even by a rise of value.'[30]

Francis Horner was upset at what he perceived to be the support now seemingly afforded by Malthus to the anti-Bullionists by a re-evaluation of the wartime experience: 'how I grudge my adversaries on the bullion question the lift you have given them. Surely your corn zeal lessened too much in your eyes, for the moment, the magnitude of that evil' (12 February 1815; 1853, II, 228). Malthus in reply insisted that a 'much greater part of the [wartime] difference between bullion and paper was occasioned by commercial causes and a peculiar demand for the precious metals, than was supposed by the Bullionists in general ...' (16 February).[31] His uncompromising response insists on a sound factual basis for theory; and reflects favourably on his own intellectual independence: 'If I have given our adversaries a lift on the bullion question, I really cannot help it. My object is the truth; and I should think myself a very bad theorist, and quite unworthy to be attended to if I did not keep myself always open to the lessons of experience. I consider what has happened since the Bank Restrictions as a very curious and instructive series of facts, tending to throw great light on the theory of paper money and the causes that effect [*sic*] the price of bullion.'

Ricardo came to Malthus's defence in 1815 against the charge of inconsistency by Horner as far as it relates to the monetary issue, recalling that Malthus had 'always held the opinion ... that the difference between the value of gold and paper was partly owing to the rise of gold' (27 March 1815; 1951–73, VI, 205). He was less tolerant when Malthus in 1820 maintained that there had occurred an actual *fall* in the domestic value of bullion between 1793 and 1813, thus adding to the responsibility of the Bank (above, chapter 13, p. 660); for Ricardo had in mind the opinion given by Malthus himself in the Introduction to his *Principles* that *both* of the current theories accounting for an unfavourable exchange were valid, the truth lying *between* the parties to the dispute – illustrating the preference for multicausal approaches. Ricardo thus charged Malthus with failing

30 Malthus himself complained of the charges in a letter to Ricardo: 'Do you know whether Torrens is much read. I think he has treated me unjustly in the preface and that the instances of inconsistency which he produces, even if established, would by no means warrent his sweeping accusation' (24 March 1815; in Ricardo, 1951–73, VI, 201). Ricardo agreed: 'I am decidedly of opinion that Torrens has treated you unjustly in his remarks in the preface to his book. But if he be right in all, the instances are much too few to justify his severe observation' (27 March; 205).

31 Horner, 1994, 822.

to live up to his own rules. But the fact is that, even in 1811, Malthus had reacted as forcefully as Ricardo himself against the Bank of England, representing the anti-inflation case as soundly based on valid theoretical principles (above, p. 954); very little had been allowed the Bank defenders. And with the passage of time an even stronger anti-Bullionist diagnosis seemed appropriate. This does not necessarily undermine a *general* presumption in favour of multicausality.[32] (It is true, though, that the illustration in the Introduction is misleading.)

Malthus's reputation for inconsistency in part reflects the fact that his protectionist position of 1815 was seen as a novelty conflicting with an earlier free-trade position. Empson reported in 1837 that Malthus had been aware of the risk to his reputation created by his support for the Corn Laws in 1815 (in Semmel, 1963, 258). An example of the reaction at that time is Francis Horner's letter to Murray: 'The most important convert the landholders have got is Malthus, who has now declared himself in favour of their [Corn] Bill; and, to be sure, there is not a better or more informed judgment, and it is the single authority which staggers me' (30 January 1815; in 1853, II, 221–2).[33] More generally, as James has written: 'To the astonishment and consternation of his friends, Malthus's "Opinion" was that the importation of grain should be restricted, on the lines proposed by the government. It says much for all concerned that Malthus's outrageous heresy and disloyalty – for so it was regarded – did not affect his private friendships. Jeffrey, however, would never ask him again to contribute to the *Edinburgh Review,* except for an article on Population in 1821' (James, 1979, 259).

But *why* the astonishment and consternation? Malthus had expressed his protectionist sentiments distinctly in the second, third, and fourth editions of the *Essay on Population,* supporting the corn-export bounty in 1803 and import restraints in 1806. Was his earlier position unknown? This cannot be. And in fact Horner's letter continues: 'But those who have looked closely into his philosophy will admit that there is always a leaning in favour of the efficacy of laws; and his early bias was for corn laws in particular. It was a great effort of candour, in truth, to suspend his decision upon this particular measure so long' (Horner, 1853, II, 222). Conceivably, the earlier position had been out of sight long enough to be generally out of mind, a state of limbo that would have been reinforced by the extraordinarily balanced tone of the *Observations* in 1814 – although it is true that

32 It remains true, after all, that Malthus insisted on the validity of Thornton's case for exchange-rate variations reflecting non-monetary disturbances. Unfortunately, his own complaint against Ricardo's 'desire to simplify' is much exaggerated, since Ricardo, as we have shown, also allowed for the effect of non-monetary disturbances on the exchanges, a fact of which Malthus was well aware.

33 Malthus's *Grounds* appeared on 10 February. Horner must have seen the manuscript.

Malthus himself there recalled his position among the protectionists against Adam Smith at an earlier stage (1986, 7, 188). Possibly, considering his references to Malthus as a 'convert' who favoured '*their Bill*' and '*this particular measure*,' Horner's consternation turned on the support given what (except in starvation conditions) amounted to total import prohibition rather than some modest tariff.

But there is a complexity – Malthus's letter to Horner of 16 June 1813 (above, pp. 72, 820). This letter implies support for a free corn trade – at least in principle – taking account of diminishing returns: 'England in reference to Europe may be considered as a large manufacturing district, with the natural tendency of such a district to import a considerable part of its corn, though with the power of growing it, if forced. In using this force, there is reason to believe that we shall check our manufactures, more than we shall increase our agriculture, and this it appears to me forms the true argument against the [corn law] system; an argument of great weight though we allow that an independent supply is practical by such means' (Tucker, 1954, 332). And we have seen that the *Observations* limits any potential advantages from protection to tariffs designed as correction for existing distortions. *Malthus, in 1813–14, thus emerges, at least in private, as free-trader in contrast with his public protectionism of 1806–7.* That Horner had the letter of June 1813 in mind is by no means certain,[34] but a possible change in orientation by Malthus must be allowed.

As we have shown in chapter 17, (pp. 828–30), part of the protectionist case of 1815 turned on the perceived circumstance that the alternative was not free trade, considering actual and potential French export regulations. Genuine free trade was not an option, a position still consistent with abandonment of the early protectionism as a matter of principle in favour of a free-trade position. Against this, however, there is the long-standing notion of the superior productivity of agriculture, which ought to mitigate against a free corn trade. The 1813 letter thus remains problematic. But it is true that changing circumstances played some part in the chopping and changing; the alterations of position need not be entirely represented as a matter of inconsistency. And the subsequent story (fully documented in chapter 17) falls into line. Malthus's abandonment of agricultural protectionism in the 1820s follows from further perceived changes in the economic climate now promising genuine free trade, coupled, though, with a dilution of physiocratic bias, including the superior productivity of agriculture (and the case for balanced growth),

34 There is some reason to doubt it. In writing to Malthus (12 February 1815) he objected to the *Grounds* and the *Inquiry* for failing to draw the obvious policy conclusions from the principle of diminishing returns, and represented the principle itself as a novel contribution by Malthus, and the policy application as a novel contribution by *himself* (1853, II, 222–3). He had apparently forgotten the 1813 letter from Malthus.

under pressure both of superior logic and experience of industry as lead sector.

A word on the population issue. Senior, it will be recalled, publicly admitted his misunderstanding of Malthus's use of the word 'tendency' to preclude the possibility of improvements in living standards; he had been 'led into this error principally by the conduct of all those writers who, since the appearance of your work, have written on Population. The multitudes who have followed, and the few who have endeavoured to oppose you, have all assumed this to be your opinion' (1829, 35, 56–7; see chapter 18, p. 914).[35] Yet even Senior politely hints that Malthus had to take some responsibility for the misreading, since the harsh pronouncements commonly drawn regarding living standards were, 'before the appearance of your writings ... never hinted at' (81). And, in private correspondence he was far less accommodating: 'Mr. Malthus has not I think very clearly expressed his opinion – but if you ... will look at his correspondence with me you will find that he nearly abandoned or rather disavowed the doctrine that population has a uniform tendency (in the sense of probability) to exceed subsistence' (in Mallet, 1921, 305). Senior is here skating close to the assertion that Malthus had *altered* his position, which – were it true – would support Torrens's complaint. But that would be too harsh; Malthus was expressing a long-standing methodological stance, as we have argued in section V.

VIII THE RICARDO-MALTHUS RELATION REVIEWED

We must now seek to appreciate how the impression has been created of a profound divorce between Ricardian and Malthusian procedures when none exists. There is, in the first place, the valid complaint by Ricardo of Malthus's misunderstandings and misrepresentations of his position – that Malthus in his *Principles* had, though 'without intending it, misrepresented me in many particulars' (see Introduction, p. 6). Malthus was well aware of Ricardo's complaint, as is clear from a letter of 26 October 1820 (in Ricardo, 1951–73, VIII, 285). In response, Ricardo remarked: 'I am quite sure that you are the last man who would mistake an adversary, knowingly, yet I find in your book some allusions to opinions which you represent as mine and which I do not really hold. In one or two cases you I think furnish the proof that you have misapprehended me, for you represent my

35 Malthus confirmed this characteristic: 'It is quite true as Mr. Jones observes that I have been unfortunate in my followers. I trust he is aware that the general and practical conclusions which I have myself drawn from my principles both on population and rent, have by no means the gloomy aspects given to them by many of my readers' (Malthus to Whewell, 23 February 1831; William Whewell Papers, Trinity College, Cambridge, Add. Ms. c. 53^2).

doctrine one way in one place, and another way in another' (24 November 1820; 301).

Several conspicuous instances upset Ricardo, with good reason. One relates to the effect of real-wage variation on the profit rate; another to the demand dimension in price determination. These two cases demonstrated for Malthus an unsatisfactory methodological orientation – the penchant for monocausality – which reduced the practical relevance of theory. The first we illustrate from Malthus's reaction to the *Essay on Profits* (1815): 'A writer may, to be sure, make any hypothesis he pleases; but if he supposes what is not true practically, he precludes himself from drawing any practical inference from his hypothesis. In your essay on profits you suppose the real wages of labour constant; but as they vary with every alteration in the prices of commodities, (while they remain nominally the same) and in reality are as variable as profits, there is no chance of your inferences being just as applied to the actual state of things' (26 January 1817; in Ricardo, 1951–73, VII, 122). Similarly, regarding Ricardo's *Principles*: 'To attempt to estimate the rate of profits in any country by a reference to this cause alone [diminishing agricultural returns], for ten, twenty, or even fifty years together, that is for periods of sufficient length to produce the most important effects on national prosperity, would inevitably lead to the greatest practical errors. Yet notwithstanding the utter inadequacy of this single cause to account for existing phenomena, Mr. Ricardo in his very ingenious chapter on profits, has dwelt on no other' (1820, 308; see chapter 10, p. 472); or again, the facts were 'diametrically opposed to the theory of profits founded on the natural quality of the last land taken into cultivation' (1820, 320; see chapter 15, p. 776). Ricardo immediately protested: 'Mr. Malthus here brings a charge against me which he would find it very difficult to prove. He has himself Page 294 Section I of this Chapter stated his causes for the fall of profits' – agricultural productivity and variable corn wages: 'I fully concur with him in thinking that profits never vary but from one or other of those causes' (*Note 171*; 1951–73, II, 264). As for the second formulation, he could scarcely contain himself: 'This is disingenuous. Who has advanced a "theory of profits founded on the natural quality of the last land taken into cultivation." The theory is that profits depend on the productiveness of the last land taken into cultivation, whether that productiveness be owing to the natural quality of the land, or the economy and skill with which labour may be applied to it. Profits are increased, either by diminishing the quantity of labour bestowed on the last land which yields a given produce, or by increasing the produce with a given quantity of labour. Mr. Malthus will I am sure not say that I have ever denied this principle – he will not say that I have not distinctly advanced it' (*Note 177*, 276–7).

Malthus's errors regarding Ricardo are troublesome. But fortunately it seems that he came ultimately to correct at least some of them (see chapter 10, p. 473). For the second edition leaves unattributed the view that 'an attempt to estimate the rate of profits in any country for ten or twenty years together by a reference to this cause alone, would lead to the greatest practical errors' (1836, 281), and abandons the alternative formulation (286).[36]

The second instance of 'misrepresentation' relates to value theory. We may approach this matter by reference to a touching letter from Malthus: 'I want more particularly to talk to you about those parts of the subject where you think I have misconceived and mistaken you. You know I would not do it intentionally; but I think there may be some parts where the words will fairly bear out my construction, and yet you may not have intended to be so understood, in which case I may not be so much to blame ... [W]hen you reject the consideration of demand and supply in the price of commodities and refer only to the means of supply, you appear to me to look only at the half of your subject. No wealth can exist unless the demand, or the estimation in which the commodity is held exceeds the cost of production: and with regard to a vast mass of commodities does not the demand actually determine the cost?' (26 October 1820; in Ricardo, 1951–73, VIII, 285). Ricardo immediately protested: 'I have never disputed this' (24 November; 302). And again he explained his position, in this case the weight placed on production costs as the determinant of supply conditions in the face of changes in demand: 'I do not dispute either the influence of demand on the price of corn and on the price of other things, but supply follows close on its heels, and soon takes the power of regulating price in his own hands, and in regulating it he is determined by cost of production. I acknowledge the intervals on which you so exclusively dwell, but still they are only intervals.' All this was in line with his *Principles*, where Ricardo had spelled out the process of long-run cost determination of the corn price, assuming increases of demand in the face both of constant-cost and increasing-cost conditions (1951–73, I, 163). I suspect Ricardo's forms of expression designed to convey the 'primacy' of supply was responsible for part of the misunderstanding (see Hollander, 1991). But the fact that on at least one occasion in 1820 Malthus stated the Ricardian position fairly – recognizing the insistence on supply variation to assure cost determination of price (see chapter 7, p. 284) – raises the unfortunate possibility that he might sometimes have been playing games. (See above, pp. 475–6, where Malthus may be *defending* Ricardo against Jones on the matter of the shared incidence of diminishing agricultural returns, notwithstanding his common ascription to Ricardo of constant wages in the course of growth.)

A third instance of 'misrepresentation' that sorely troubled Ricardo

36 Similar criticisms directed at Ricardo at 1820, 190 and 312, are left unascribed at 1836, 183 and 281. See also a letter dated 25 September 1820, where Malthus recognizes Ricardo's allowance of a fall in the profit rate 'temporarily from the improved condition of the labouring classes' (in Ricardo, 1951–73, VIII, 260).

relates to his chapter 'On Gross and Net Revenue' (above, chapter 11, pp. 574–5). Malthus read this chapter as arguing that a national advantage resulted from obtaining a given net income with a smaller workforce, notwithstanding a massive loss of employment. Ricardo protested that his sole objective was to argue that no social gain flowed from generating a given net revenue (of £5 million) by means of more rather than fewer men, having in mind specifically the magnitude of net revenue with an eye to national 'power': 'The employing a greater number of men would enable us neither to add a man to our army and navy, nor to contribute one guinea more in taxes' (1951–73, II, 381). He had no intention of recommending a policy involving actual creation of massive unemployment: 'Mr. Malthus supposes 7 million not to be required – that is changing my proposition not refuting it. M. Say has also remarked on this passage, and although I had carefully guarded myself, by the observation, that I was only answering Adam Smith's argument respecting the power of paying taxes &c., and was not considering what was undoubtedly on any other occasion most worthy of consideration, the happiness of so many human being, yet he speaks as if this consideration was wholly unimportant in my estimation. I assure him he has done me injustice ...' (382).[37] Malthus may have been induced to modify his text for the second edition as a result of this complaint (see above, chapter 11, 575).

Even honest errors of interpretation would not preclude a propensity on Malthus's part to exaggerate the distinctiveness of his own methodology (above, section III). His case for realistic axioms was made out against Ricardo with little justification. Ricardo, after all, insisted that his behavioural assumptions would be inappropriate in an investigation of underdeveloped economies, and that in such cases policy deductions derived from a land scarcity–based theory would be irrelevant, indeed dangerous. And his case for the Law of Markets itself turned specifically on behaviour patterns pertinent to a specific time and space–bound reality. Similarly, Malthus's warnings (see above, pp. 968–9) against basing policy conclusions directly upon exercises in comparative statics – as in the analysis of technological improvements – were misdirected. The strategy of Ricardo's analysis of the consequences for employment of machinery in his Chapter 31 was clarified by Ricardo himself in terms fully consistent with Malthus's position: 'The statement which I have made will not, I hope, lead to the inference that machinery should not be encouraged. To elucidate the principle, I have been supposing, that improved machinery is *suddenly* discovered, and extensively used; but the truth is, that these discoveries are gradual, and rather operate in determining the employment of the capital which is saved and accumulated, than in diverting capital from its actual employment' (1951–73, I, 395). This reflects precisely the confessedly

37 See further on Malthus's misrepresentation, Hollander, 1979, 364–5, 367.

limited scope of the propositions derived in the *Principles* expressed in a famous letter of 4 May 1820: 'Our differences may in some respects ... be ascribed to your considering my book as more practical than I intended it to be. My object was to elucidate principles, and to do so I imagined strong cases that I might shew the operation of those principles. I never thought for example that practically any improvements take place on the land which would at once double the produce, but to shew what the effects of improvement would be undisturbed by any other operating cause, I supposed an improvement to that extent to be adopted, and I think I have reasoned correctly from such premises' (1951–73, VIII, 184).

Ricardo's famous lament of 1815 that 'we so materially differ' may also have given an impression of a deep divide: 'If I am too theoretical which I really believe is the case, – you I think are too practical. There are so many combinations, – so many operating causes in Political Economy, that there is a great danger in appealing to experience in favour of a particular doctrine, unless we are sure that all the causes of variation are seen and their effects are duly estimated' (7 October 1815; 1951–73, VI, 295). But Ricardo must have been fooled by Malthus's continual lip-service to 'experience' when in fact he was as deductive as Ricardo, and justified model-building on precisely the same grounds.

Ricardo, in fact, attempted to meet Malthus halfway as far as concerned their methodological priorities. He had earlier pointed out when analysing the outcome of given changes in conditions that he, unlike Malthus, typically concerned himself with the long-run effects, though conceding that ideally both short-run and long-run effects had to be considered: 'It appears to me that one great cause of our difference in opinion, on the subject we have so often discussed, is that you have always in mind the immediate and temporary effects of particular changes – whereas I put these imediate and temporary effects quite aside, and fix my whole attention on the permanent state of things which will result from them. Perhaps you estimate these temporary effects too highly, whilst I am too much disposed to undervalue them. To manage the subject quite right they should be carefully distinguished and mentioned, and the due effects ascribed to each' (24 January 1817; in Ricardo, 1951–73, VII, 120). This celebrated contrast starts out in stark and exclusive terms, but ends as a differential weighting of preoccupation. And this latter seems valid. The fact is that Ricardo did concern himself with the short-run effects of given disturbances – it was, after all, Ricardo who proposed a procedure for avoiding too sudden a return to gold (extending even to making out a possible case for devaluation), and who recommended the gradual repeal of the Corn Laws.

As for Malthus, he agreed with Ricardo that 'one cause of our difference in opinion is that which you mention' (26 January 1817; 121). But the fact is that he, too, proceeded with long-run analysis (see above, section II), a striking example involving the extraction of corn from treatment in terms of allocation theory on the grounds that supply and demand are in that case interdependent, considering the (immediate) effect of increased food on population growth, a reinforcement of physiocratic analysis – it is a procedure Adam Smith also followed on occasion – with profoundly important policy implications. It was, therefore, both self-righteous and unjustified to continue his remark: 'I certainly am disposed to refer frequently to things as they are, as the only way of making one's writing practically useful to society, and I think also the only way of being secure from falling into the errors of the taylors of Laputa, and by a slight mistake at the outset arrive at conclusions the most distant from the truth' (121–2). I have no intention to denigrate in general Malthus's concern with responsible application, surprising as appear to be the applications of the corn-pricing and wage-fund analyses (above, p. 969). There are impressive cases of caution, as in application of the 'Sraffian' corn-profit analysis (see chapter 10, pp. 436, 457–8). It is the contrast with Ricardo, insisted upon by Malthus to his own credit, that is too sharply drawn.

In Malthus's concern to convey the possibility of non-sustainable growth, we have *the* major analytical difference with Ricardo. And this was certainly on his mind in the letter of 26 January 1817. There is, first, an insistence 'that the progress of society consists of irregular movements, and that to omit the consideration of causes which for eight or ten years will give a great *stimulus* to production and population, or a great *check* to them, is to omit the causes of the wealth and poverty of nations – the grand object of all enquiries in Political Economy ... We see in all the countries around us, and in our own particularly, periods of greater and less prosperity and sometimes of adversity, but *never* the uniform progress which you seem alone to contemplate' (122). There is something to this – though we know that J.S. Mill succeeded brilliantly in allowing for cyclical fluctuations in real income. Unfortunately, Malthus then proceeded to elaborate on 'the still more specific and fundamental cause of our difference,' Ricardo's presumption that 'the wants and tastes of mankind are always ready for the supply,' whereas in fact 'few things are more difficult, than to inspire new tastes and wants .... [P]ractically the actual check to produce and population arises more from want of stimulus than want of power to produce' (122–3). The fact, however, is that Ricardo allowed much of this in 'underdeveloped' economies, though not in contemporary Britain; and it is by no means clear that Malthus's model proved superior in application to long-run trends.

Whereas Ricardo sought to minimize his purely methodological differences with Malthus, representing them as no more than different weightings of concern, on one occasion he defined what seems an irreconcilable contrast regarding the scope of the science. It was the contrast that so much struck Keynes (see Introduction, p. 8). Malthus had taken for granted the long-standing concern of economists to be with 'the nature and causes of wealth' (25 September 1820; 1951–73, VIII, 261). This

Ricardo denied: 'Political Economy you think is an enquiry into the nature and causes of wealth – I think it should rather be called an enquiry into the laws which determine the division of the produce of industry amongst the classes who concur in its formation. No law can be laid down respecting quantity, but a tolerably correct one can be laid down respecting proportions. Every day I am more satisfied that the former enquiry is vain and delusive, and the latter only the true objects of the science' (9 October; 278–9). Malthus responded sharply: 'With regard to your new definition of the objects of Political Economy, I own it appears to me very confined; and if it be just, I should say that political economy would be at once converted from a science which I have always considered as the most practically useful in the whole circle, into one which would merely serve to gratify curiosity' (26 October; 286).

It is regrettable that Ricardo failed to specify his precise intentions. But presumably he did *not* mean that the analysis of 'wealth' as such was 'vain and delusive.' This was certainly not the case in the letter of 23 February 1816.[38] And, more technically, the profit–rent division plays on the savings rate and the growth rate of the economy in so far as savings propensities differ between classes, while the profit–wage breakdown is equally significant from the perspective of the causes and consequences of growth. Similarly, the analysis of machinery reflects a concern with wealth. In a letter to Malthus of 28 September 1821 this is fully confirmed: 'Mankind are only interested in making labour productive, in the enjoyment of abundance, and in a good distribution of the produce obtained by capital and industry' (1951–73, IX, 83). This more catholic perspective on scope seems an accurate statement of Ricardo's actual procedures. Reading back into his original statement of 9 October 1820, it is conceivable that he was denying the possibility of making predictions regarding wealth – 'No law can be laid down respecting quantity' – considering the unpredictable intervention of new technology, but not insisting on the literal abandonment of 'the nature and causes of wealth' as a legitimate scientific concern. But Malthus seems to have understood it in the latter sense and reacted understandably.

* * *

Waterman maintains, from the theological context, that though 'in attack' Malthus 'was an admirable, indeed exemplary, controversialist, courteous,

38 'I hope you have quite determined to extend your new edition [of the *Essay on Population*] to another volume, and that you are now making great progress in it. I wish much to see a regular and connected statement of your opinions on what I deem the most difficult, and perhaps the most important topic of Political Economy, namely the progress of a country in wealth and the laws by which the increasing produce is distributed' (1951–73, VII, 24).

magnanimous, and fair-minded; in retreat he was less gracious, correcting logical slips by minimal, unadvertised amendments, and camouflaging retraction by a verbal smokescreen' (1991, 147; see also 138; 1987, 269). Now there is something to this since retractions of his criticisms against Ricardo in the second edition are indeed 'minimal' and 'unadvertised amendments.' Thus the accusation that the possibility of low profits despite high agricultural productivity reflected 'a distinction of the greatest practical importance, which ... has been quite overlooked by Mr. Ricardo' (1820, 190) is replaced in the second edition by a more accommodating observation: 'These are all points of great practical consequence which have been much overlooked. The doctrine of the gradations of soils is a most important one, but in drawing practical conclusions from it, great care should be taken to apply it correctly' (1836, 183). And as already indicated (above, p. 995), in the second edition Malthus silently withdrew his unjustified criticism that Ricardo had failed to allow for the effect on profits of variable real wages.

But this is not the whole picture by any means. That the 'misrepresentations' of Ricardo's position were largely honest errors is suggested by Malthus's personal regard for Ricardo: 'I never loved any body out of my own family so much. Our interchange of opinions was so unreserved, and the object after which we were both enquiring was so entirely the truth, and nothing else, that I cannot but think we sooner or later must have agreed' (reported by Empson, 1837, 499; in Semmel, 1963, 261). There are also the generous tributes he himself *publicly* paid Ricardo. On so central a policy issue as the return to gold, he declared in 1820 that 'Mr. Ricardo deserves the thanks of his country for having suggested [a measure] which has rendered the transition more easy than could reasonably have been expected' (see chapter 12, p. 623; similarly in 1811, see chapter 13, p. 654). By his distinction between *value* and *wealth,* he had rendered 'an unquestionable service to the science of political economy' (chapter 6, p. 221; see also p. 292). Regarding the inverse wage–profit relation, he wrote: 'Of all the truths which Mr. Ricardo has established, one of the most useful and important is that profits are determined by the proportion of the whole produce which goes to labour'; Ricardo's contribution had in fact furnished 'the means of improving the science of Political Economy' (chapter 10, pp. 486–8). That his own doctrine relating to the role of aggregate demand stood up empirically better than the Ricardian emphasis upon the difficulty of production on the land in accounting for a (supposed) historical decline in the profit rate did not gainsay that the evidence accorded 'most perfectly with the more general proposition of Mr. Ricardo respecting profits, namely that they are determined by the proportion of the whole produce which goes to labour.' It will be recalled, too, that Malthus defended Ricardo against Jones (above, pp. 953–4) and against Bailey, representing his own differences with Ricardo on value measurement as a matter of detail rather than of principle (chapter 7, pp. 337f.).

Waterman's perspective would carry us some way towards understanding the quiet manner in which Malthus announced his transformation on commercial policy in the 1820s. But there is no need to have recourse to this sort of rationale. After all, he had set the stage in very explicit terms for the change in the crucial note itself, and explained the retention of the original text in the new edition (see chapter 17, p. 851).[39] As for the original position in the protectionist pamphlet of 1815, it is greatly to his credit that he did not unfairly reinforce the recommendation by suggesting prospective increasing returns; he candidly spelled out the probable costs (see chapter 15, 754). Interestingly, Ricardo at that time took this view: 'a more candid or better man nowhere exists,' whose 'erroneous opinions respecting the expediency of a free trade in corn ... are honest opinions' (13 October 1819; see above, pp. 866–7).[40] He even let his high regard for Malthus's 'characteristic candour' emerge in the *Principles* itself (I, 398).

A closing remark is in order on Malthus's policy recommendations regarding population control. Horner remarked in 1804 to Jeffrey that Malthus 'is a man in conversation of good sense, great candour, and liberality; the last is a rare qualification for an English clergyman ...' (cited in Fetter, 1957, 10). Our chapter 18 has fully confirmed the validity of this evaluation; his policy position was extraordinarily progressive and, in the circumstances, courageous. This episode reinforces confidence in the interpretation we have offered regarding the abandonment of protectionism.

IX A FINAL SUMMING-UP: MALTHUS, THE CLASSICS, AND KEYNES

Lord Robbins opined that Malthus's role in building up the system of classical thought is 'a matter likely to arouse much more controversy than the answer to a similar question in the case of the other great classical economists,' though Robbins himself had little doubt of a profound contribution as far as regards 'the central traditions of the theory of value and distribution,' including here the theory of population in a land-scarcity context (1970, 86, 89) – Samuelson's 'canonical' model. There is indeed

39 Salim Rashid takes a very different view: 'I believe your substantive conclusion. Malthus did change his mind. But the evidence you present will be unconvincing to anyone who considers Malthus to be a scholar – perhaps you do too! However, I have long believed Malthus to have possessed a devious and even dishonest streak. He did change his mind but lacked the honesty to say so outright. Anyway, that is my jaundiced view' (letter to the author, cited with permission, dated 8 March 1991).

40 There was also a positive side to Torrens's complaint of inconsistency documented in our Introduction: 'If these fluctuating and contradictory opinions, however, do not indicate that, in the science of political economy, Mr. Malthus has attained any very clear conclusions, or arrived at any certain conceptions, they at least must serve to convince us that he possesses in a very eminent degree, a spirit of candour and a love of truth' (1815, xi).

much common ground in this domain once we silence the noise emanating from the misunderstandings between himself and Ricardo and the exaggerated representation of his own procedures as methodologically distinct. At the same time, I would not ignore the differences of detail in their respective cost theories of value; and there are the 'physiocratic' agricultural-surplus and the corn-profit constructs, which complicate the picture.

As for monetary theory – the matter of the Bullionist debates – that the main difference between Ricardo and Malthus was a matter of 'focus,' not analysis (Robbins, 90), seems a fair evaluation. In fact, we have seen that Malthus exerted some considerable influence on Ricardo in this domain (chapter 14, 710). The problem of placing Malthus in the classical fold is, admittedly, troublesome regarding aggregate equilibrium. To my mind this problem does not pertain to Malthus's allowances for excess capacity as such, notwithstanding the impressive quality of his analysis of the postwar depression; Ricardo's concern to avoid deflation in returning to gold, and, in particular, J.S. Mill's position on the influence of consumption on production in the 1830s make that clear.[41] It is in the secular realm that any notion of a common 'classical system' seems to break down. Yet even here there are several considerations that narrow, though by no means bridge, the gap. First, the extensions made to Smith's 'competition of capitals' relate most specifically to the industrial sector; the Law of Markets was still applied to corn, and the agricultural sector was treated in land-scarcity terms. Second, while the problem for Malthus related to the danger of excessive accumulation – excessive because financed from reduced consumption rather than from increased profits – in so far as accumulation is motivated by the profit rate, as Malthus (taking the long view) believed was the case in advanced economies, there normally would *not* occur non-sustainable accumulation. As we know (above, p. 983) he, in fact, refused to countenance governmental interference with the savings rate; the profit motive in that particular regard was sacrosanct; similarly, he relied on 'the interest of individual capitalists' with respect to the rate of adoption of 'machinery' (chapter 11, 575). Though he opposed debt repayment and the encouragement of increased saving during depression, his thoroughgoing 'conservatism' – his Friedmanesque stance – regarding the gold standard, fear of inflation, and perspective on counter-cyclical monetary policy have all been documented (chapter 13). The *practical* implications of his position are, in brief, surprisingly orthodox. And the lack of novel policy recommendations – along with the extreme complexity of the analytical problem Malthus set for himself – may well account for

41 There is, though, this important difference, that Mill allowed for self-corrective mechanisms to explain the temporary nature of depression, whereas Malthus had in mind permanent disequilibrium depending for correction on exogenous stimuli.

that long-term victory of the Ricardian paradigm so greatly regretted by Keynes. From this perspective – and also regarding his position on the rate of return as the social index of the appropriate savings rate (above, p. 983) – there is considerable merit to Negishi's observation that so 'classical' does Malthus appear at times in the *Principles* that he 'is not so much an underconsumptionist as a supply sider' (1989, 138–9, also 143–7; and 1993, 116).

The Malthus–Keynes nexus is complex. Malthus might seem at least to have 'set the agenda' for what is popularly seen as the Keynesian Revolution with its focus on aggregate demand as a strategic variable. But, as we have argued (chapter 11, p. 585; 12, pp. 628–9), the details of the analysis of macro-stabilization do not point in this direction. What of Keynes's own perspective on the linkage? His extraordinary tribute of 1933 (see Introduction, pp. 7–9) turned on the section in the *Principles* concerning 'distribution occasioned by unproductive consumers,' which he found to contain 'a masterly expositon of the conditions which determine the *optimum* of saving in the actual economic system in which we live' (1933, 145). He cited two specific passages (1820, 495, 512) as 'the best economic analysis ever written of the events of 1815–20' (146). And the 'whole problem of the balance between Saving and Investment had been posed in the *Preface* [*sic*] ... ' (146–7, citing 1820, 8–9). He also refers to Malthus's 'complete comprehension of the effects of excessive saving on output *via* its effects on profits' (141).[42] Since all this appeared in 1933, it is unlikely that Keynes intended to suggest Malthus's ideas as precursor of those in the *General Theory*.[43] Rutherford (1987) raises this point and suggests that Keynes had in mind *The Treatise on Money*; and he finds indeed a 'close correspondence.' Patinkin maintains to the contrary that Keynes 'had already achieved a full understanding' of the theory of effective demand by 1933 (1982, 23). But the fact is that, in his essay Keynes did not *focus* on effective demand as such, even complaining that Malthus had described it 'none too clearly' (above, p. 8). And in the *General Theory*, where the focus is more specifically on the aggregate-demand function, he repeats the complaint, observing that Malthus had failed to provide an adequate 'alternative construction' to Ricardo's: 'The idea that we can safely neglect

42 Yet, strangely, despite all this, he also conceded that Malthus's comprehension was 'intuitive' and that he had expressed himself 'none too clearly' (122).

There was one more specific criticism – Malthus's 'over-looking entirely the part played by the rate of interest. Twenty years ago I should have retorted to Malthus that the state of affairs he envisages could not occur unless the rate of interest has first fallen to zero. Malthus perceived, as often, what was true; but it is essential to a complete comprehension of why it is true, to explain how an excess of frugality does not bring with it a decline to zero in the rate of interest' (147–8).

43 Moreover, the Malthus letters of July 1821, cited at length by Keynes (above chapter 11, pp. 519–21), identify *ex ante* savings and investment.

the aggregate demand function is fundamental to Ricardian economics, which underlie what we have been taught for more than a century. Malthus, indeed, has vehemently opposed Ricardo's doctrine that it was impossible for effective demand to be deficient; but vainly. For, since Malthus was unable to explain clearly (apart from an appeal to the facts of common observation) how and why effective demand could be deficient or excessive, he failed to furnish an alternative construction; and Ricardo conquered England as completely as the Holy Inquisition conquered Spain' (1936, 32). It is my impression that, at the most, Keynes derived only a general sort of 'inspiration' from Malthus on effective demand, but nothing substantive.

As explained, a strong Malthus–Keynes link with respect to 'short-run' demand deficiency does not seem convincing. There is, however, an interpretation of the *General Theory* which finds its predominant concern to be with output fluctuations about a level below the achievable or optimum rate given by the production frontier, that level constituting a permanent shortfall of output attributable proximately to a capital stock below its achievable level, and suggesting appropriate institutional changes to assure investment decisions 'based on long views' (Meltzer, 1988, 133, 317–19). Were this indeed Keynes's primary concern – some might see this as closer to a post-Keynesian perspective (see O'Brien, 1975, 230) – then Malthus would have provided at least a prologue to it by his insistence that the *secular* performance of the economy is not governed solely by the locus of its production frontier, and also by his effort to define the conditions for sustainable growth. But whatever the parallels with Keynesian economics might be, it is here that one encounters Malthus's most striking contribution, and – as mentioned – Malthus stands apart from the New School, though on policy there remains a surprising degree of common ground.

In addition to his concern with 'sustainable growth,' which sets Malthus apart, there is his support for the 1815 Corn Bill. Possibly the finest tribute to Ricardo – albeit a 'silent' one – is the fact that, in the end, Malthus abandoned agricultural protectionism and much of its theoretical physiocratic underpinning, accepting the Ricardian vision of Britain's future as a mixed economy fuelled by the industrial sector. With this step a common 'classical' position was profoundly enhanced.

APPENDIX: MALTHUS AND KEYNES: SOME RECENT SECONDARY LITERATURE

Kates (1994) has recently attempted to demonstrate that 'Keynes developed a theory of fluctuations in aggregate demand to explain fluctuations in output and employment due to the influence on him of the writings of Thomas Robert Malthus which Keynes was reading in October and November, 1932 [in the course of] updating his essay on Malthus for inclusion in *Essays in Biography*' – that 'had Keynes not read Malthus, he almost certainly would never have written a book attacking Say's Law or attributing recessions and depressions to failure of effective demand' (10–11). Or again: 'Keynes discovered the idea of effective demand by reading Malthus' (12). Such a claim, Kates points out (10f.), has never been made in the literature, with two qualifications relating to the work of O'Leary (1942) and Klein (1966); others perceived Keynes as arriving at his position independently and finding *ex post* support in Malthus. As for the two exceptions, Kates notes that, while O'Leary saw an influence, he himself conceded that 'it is impossible to say to what extent' (12). And Klein was 'ambiguous about the extent to which Malthus influenced Keynes,' and 'cannot... be interpreted as saying that Keynes discovered the idea of effective demand by reading Malthus.'

While I do not wish to undermine Kates's claim to originality, it seems to me that Klein was not quite as ambiguous as Kates maintains:

> In many cases it is impossible to say whether or not any earlier writers could have had any direct influence on the development of Keynes' ideas. It may be that he always developed his ideas independently, and then pointed out others who have previously expressed similar ideas. But in one instance, we can be reasonably sure that Keynes derived a profound inspiration. T.R. Malthus, a respectable and highly competent economist, was openly admired by Keynes, and, at a time when the revolution was about to be executed. In his *Essays in Biography*, finished by February, 1933, Keynes paid great tribute to Malthus and particularly noted the latter's discussion of effective demand. As was mentioned in a previous chapter, the break between Keynes and his contemporaries can be likened in many ways to the dispute which occurred after the Napoleonic Wars between Malthus and Ricardo. The issues in each case were essentially the same. Malthus and, later, Keynes wanted to replace Say's Law with a theory of effective demand. There can be little doubt that Keynes was aware of this historical similarity and must have profited much from a perusal of the early literature. (Klein, 1966, 125)

Kates is then closer to Klein than Kates allows. Klein is not merely claiming Malthus as an 'anticipator,' but as having been 'a profound inspiration,' specifically with regard to the discussion of effective demand. Kates mentions this but grudgingly. There is also Klein's statement (not mentioned) that, 'while we shall never probably know how much stimulation Keynes received from many of his anticipators, we can be quite sure that he drew much from Malthus, whom he openly admired' (44).

I would not put so much weight on Klein were it not for the fact that Kates himself is 'ambiguous about the extent to which Malthus influenced Keynes.' He has a section titled 'The Overlap between Malthus and Keynes' to establish 'how close Malthus and Keynes were ... just how similar their arguments are,' and draws the implication that this cannot be a matter of *chance*: 'There is an extraordinary degree of overlap if both Keynes and Malthus actually reached the same conclusions independently' (12–13). But the *specifics* of Malthus's case are never properly dealt with; and also lacking is a detailed account of exactly what Keynes thought he was getting from Malthus (the materials on 17–18 are insufficiently precise). This deficiency is underscored by the position adopted near the close: 'That Malthus had a different theory of "effective demand" than Keynes would ultimately develop is not really germane' (18). If Kates cannot show that Malthus inspired the specific arguments used by Keynes in the *General Theory*, then his initial claims are much diluted; even accepting that Keynes introduced effective demand only after reading the Malthus–Ricardo correspondence and Malthus's *Principles* (1820) – this demonstration constitutes the bulk of Kates's paper – if what he got from Malthus was a perspective that differed from his own, then the debt is not clear-cut. The ambiguity charged against Klein is thus just as applicable against Kates; in fact, Kates invites the charge. Similarly, the point made against O'Leary can equally be made against Kates.

With this in mind I turn to the treatment accorded Rutherford (1987). As mentioned, Kates fails to be sufficiently specific regarding Malthus's argument; Rutherford provided a detailed account, and he envisaged a link between the *Treatise on Money* and Malthus. Kates mentions this in note 8 but fails to realize its significance. For Rutherford drew a different conclusion from the *timing* of Keynes's *Essay* relative to his reading of Malthus: 'Too little attention has been paid to the timing of the claims Keynes made for Malthus. The critical references to the principle of effective demand were added to the Essay on Malthus in 1933, suggesting that it is with the economics of the *Treatise* that we should make our comparison' (1987, 188). Now Kates himself mentions in the text to which the Rutherford's note is attached: 'The fact that Keynes had previously had his own saving-investment apparatus and believed in public sector stimulus would have made the Malthusian addition of effective demand attractive to him' (18–19). Surely this implies a much more subtle debt than that stated at the outset.

REFERENCES

I WORKS BY THOMAS ROBERT MALTHUS

Books and pamphlets

Works = *The Works of Thomas Robert Malthus.* Ed. E.A. Wrigley and D. Souden (8 vols.). London 1986

1798. *An Essay on the Principle of Population.* 1st ed., London; Facsimile ed., London 1926. Also in *Works, 1*

1800. *An Investigation of the Cause of the present High Price of Provisions.* 1st ed., London. In *Works, 7*, 5–18

1803. *An Essay on the Principle of Population.* 2d ed. London. In *Works, 2–3*

1806. *An Essay on the Principle of Population.* 3d ed. (2 vols.). London

1807a. *An Essay on the Principle of Population.* 4th ed. (2 vols.). London

1807b. *A Letter to Samuel Whitbread on his Proposed bill, for the Amendment of the Poor Laws.* 1st ed., London. In *Works, 4*, 5–19

1814. *Observations on the Effects of the Corn Laws.* 1st ed., London. In *Works, 7*, 87–109

1815a. *The Grounds of an Opinion on the Policy of Restricting the Importation of Foreign Corn.* 1st ed., London. In *Works, 7*, 151–74

1815b. *An Inquiry into the Nature and Progress of Rent.* 1st ed., London. In *Works, 7*, 115–45

1817. *An Essay on the Principle of Population.* 5th ed. (3 vols.). London

1820. *Principles of Political Economy.* 1st ed., London. Ed. J. Pullen (2 vols.). Cambridge 1989

1823b. *The Measure of Value Stated and Illustrated.* 1st ed., London. In *Works, 7*, 179–221

1826. *An Essay on the Principle of Population.* 6th ed. (2 vols.). London. In *Works, 2–3*

1827a. *Definitions in Political Economy.* 1st ed., London. In *Works, 8*
1836. *Principles of Political Economy* (posthumously published). 2d ed., London. [In *Works, 5–6*]
1966. *The Travel Diaries of T.R. Malthus.* Ed. P. James. Cambridge
1989. *An Essay on the Principle of Population.* Ed. P. James (2 vols.). Cambridge

Journal articles, and others

1809. 'Review of Thomas Newenham.' *Edinburgh Review* 14/27 (April), 151–70. In *Works, 4,* 47–67
1811a. 'Depreciation of Paper Currency.' *Edinburgh Review* 17/34 (February), 339–72. In *Works, 7,* 21–56
1811b. 'Pamphlets on the Bullion Question.' *Edinburgh Review.* 18/36 (August), 448–70. In *Works, 7,* 57–82
1823a. 'High and Low Prices.' *Quarterly Review* 29/57 (April), 214–39. In *Works, 7,* 225–53
1824a. 'Political Economy.' *Quarterly Review* 30/60, 297–334. In *Works, 7,* 257–97
1824b. 'Population.' *Supplement to the 4th, 5th and 6th editions of the Encyclopaedia Britannica,* VI, Edinburgh, April, 307–33. In *Works, 4,* 179–243
1825. 'On the Measure of the Conditions Necessary to the Supply of Commodities.' *Transactions of the Royal Society of Literature,* I, part 1, 1825–1829, 171–80. In *Works, 7,* 301–11
1827b. 'On the meaning which is most usually and most correctly attached to the term Value of a Commodity.' Transactions of the *Royal Society of Literature,* I, part 2, 1825–29, 74–81. In *Works, 7,* 313–23
1966. *The Travel Diaries of Thomas Robert Malthus.* Ed. P. James. Cambridge

II OTHER PRIMARY WORKS

Aikin, John. 1795. *A Description of the Country from thirty to forty Miles round Manchester.* London
Anderson, James. 1777. *Observations on the Means of Exciting a Spirit of National Industry.* Edinburgh
– 1801. *A Calm Investigation of the Circumstances that have led to the Present Scarcity of Grain in Britain.* London
[Anon]. 1798. Review of Malthus, 1798. *Analytical Review* 28/2 (August), 119–25
[Anon]. 1821. *Observations on Certain Verbal Disputes in Political Economy.* London
Bailey, Samuel. 1825. *A Critical Dissertation on the Nature, Measure and Causes of Value.* London
Barton, John. 1817. *Observations on the Circumstances Which Influence the Condition of the Labouring Classes of Society.* London

Bentham, Jeremy. 1789. *An Introduction to the Principles of Morals and Legislation.* 1st ed., London. Ed. J.H. Burns and H.L.A. Hart. London 1970

– 1801–4. ['Method and Leading Features of an Institute of Political Economy.'] In *Jeremy Bentham's Economic Writings,* ed. W. Stark, III, 305–80. London 1954

Blake, William. 1810. *Observations on the Principles which Regulate the Course of Exchange.* London

– 1823. *Observations on the Effects Produced by the Expenditure of Government during the Restriction of Cash Payments.* London

Bosanquet, Charles. 1810. *Practical Observations on the Report of the Bullion Committee.* London

Bridge, Bewick. 1810. *Lectures on the Elements of Algebra.* London

Buchanan, David. 1814. *Observations on the Subjects Treated of in Dr. Smith's Inquiry into the Nature and Causes of the Wealth of Nations.* 1st ed., Edinburgh and London

Carlyle, Thomas. 1849. 'Occasional Discourse on the Negro Question.' *Fraser's Magazine,* 40 (December), 670–9

Cazenove, J. 1822. *Considerations on the Accumulation of Capital and its Effects on Exchangeable Value.* London

Chalmers, George. 1782. *An Estimate of the Comparative Strength of Great Britain during the present and four preceding reigns.* 1st ed., London

Chalmers, Thomas. 1832. *On Political Economy.* Glasgow

Commons, John. (1934) *Institutional Economics: Its Place in Political Economy.* New York

de Sismondi, J.C.L. Simonde. 1803. *De la richesse commerciale, ou principes d'économie politique appliqués à la legislation du commerce.* (2 vols.). Geneva

– 1818. *Nouveaux principes d'économie politique.* 1st ed., Geneva; 2d ed., Paris 1827. Ed. G. Sotiroff, Geneva 1951

Dupont de Nemours, P.S. 1768. *Physiocratie.* Leiden

– 1817. *Examen du livre de M. Malthus sur le Principe de Population.* Philadelphia

[Empson, William]. 1837. 'Life, Writings and Character of Mr. Malthus.' *Edinburgh Review* 64/130, Article IX (January) 469–506. In *Occasional Papers of T.R. Malthus,* ed. B. Semmel, 231–68. New York 1963

Ganilh, Charles. 1812. *An Inquiry into the Various Systems of Political Economy.* Trans. D. Boileau, London

Godwin, William. 1796. *Enquiry Concerning Political Justice.* 2d. ed. (2 vols.). London

– 1801. *Thoughts occasioned by the perusal of Dr. Parr's Spital sermon ... being a reply to the attacks of ... the author of an Essay on Population and others.* London

[Hazlitt, William]. 1807. *A Reply to the 'Essay on Population' by the Rev. T.R. Malthus.* London

Heberden, William. 1801. *Observations on the Increase and Decrease of Different Diseases and particularly the Plague,* London
Horner, Francis. 1853. *Memoirs and Correspondence.* Ed. Leonard Horner (2 vols.). London
– 1994. *The Horner Papers: Selections from the Letters and Miscellaneous Writings of Francis Horner, M.P., 1795–1817.* Ed. Kenneth Bourne and W.B. Taylor. Edinburgh
Horton, R.J. Wilmot. 1830. *The Causes and Remedies of Pauperism in the United Kingdom considered.* London
Hume, David. 1752. *Political Discourse.* 1st ed., Edinburgh. In E. Rotwein, ed., *David Hume: Writings on Economics.* London 1955
Huskisson, William. 1810. *The Question concerning the Depreciation of our Currency stated and examined.* London and Edinburgh
– 1830. *Essays on Political Economy.* London
Jacob, William. 1826. *Report on the trade in Foreign Corn, and on the Agriculture of the North of Europe.* (Ordered to be printed by the House of Commons.) London
Jarrold, Thomas. 1806. *Dissertations on Man, Philosophical, Physiological and Political, in Answer to Mr. Malthus's Essay.* London
Jevons, W.S. 1879. *Theory of Political Economy.* 2d ed., London
– 1972–81. *Papers and Correspondence.* Ed. R.D.C. Black (7 vols.). London
Jones, Richard. 1831. *An Essay on the Distribution of Wealth.* London
Keynes, J.M. 1936. *The General Theory of Employment, Interest and Money.* 1st ed., London
King, Lord. 1803. *Thoughts on the Restrictions of Payments in Specie at the Banks of England and Ireland.* London. (2d ed. 1804, entitled *Thoughts on the Effects of the Bank Restriction*)
Lauderdale, James Maitland, Earl of. 1814. *A Letter on the Corn Laws.* London and Edinburgh
– 1819. *An Inquiry into the Nature and Origin of Public Wealth.* 2d ed., Edinburgh
Law, John. 1750. *Money and Trade considered, with a Proposal for supplying the Nation with Money* [1705]. Glasgow
Locke, John. 1691. *Some Considerations of the Consequences of the Lowering of Interest and Raising the Value of Money.* London
Longfield, Mountifort. 1834. *Lectures on Political Economy.* 1st ed., Dublin. In *The Economic Writings of Montifort Longfield.* New York, 1971
Lowe, Joseph. 1822. *The Present State of England, in regard to Agriculture, Trade and Finance.* London
Lloyd, W.F. 1833. *Two Lectures on the Checks to Population.* Oxford
McCulloch, J.R. 1816. *Essay on the Question of Reducing the Interest on the National Debt.* Edinburgh
– 1823. 'Political Economy.' *Supplement to the 4th, 5th and 6th editions of the Encyclopaedia Britannica,* VI, April, 216–78
– 1824a. 'Corn Laws and Corn Trade.' *Supplement to the 6th edition of the Encyclopaedia Britannica,* III, 342–73

– 1824b. 'Price of Foreign Corn – Abolition of the Corn-Laws.' *Edinburgh Review* 41/81 (October), 55–78
– 1864. *The Principles of Political Economy.* 5th ed., Edinburgh
Mandeville, Bernard. 1732. *The Fable of the Bees; or Private Vices, Publick Benefits.* 6th ed. Ed. F.B. Kaye, Oxford 1924
Marcet, Jane. 1833. *John Hopkins's Notions on Political Economy.* Boston
Marshall, Alfred. 1920. *Principles of Economics.* 8th ed., London
Marx, Karl. 1867–94. *Capital.* I. Moscow 1965; III, Moscow 1962
– 1862–3. *Theories of Surplus Value.* II, Moscow 1968
Mill, James. 1804. *An Essay on the Impolicy of Bounty on the Exportation of Corn.* London
– 1806. 'Sir James Stewart's "Collected Works."' *Literary Journal* I, 2d Series, March, 225–35
– 1821. *Elements of Political Economy.* 1st ed., London
Mill, J.S. 1823. 'Malthus's Measure of Value.' *Morning Chronicle,* 5 September, 2. In *Collected Works,* XXII, 51–60. Toronto 1986
– 1825a. 'The Corn Laws.' *Westminster Review* 3 (April), 394–420. In *Collected Works,* IV. 45–70. Toronto 1967
– 1825b. 'The Quarterly Review on Political Economy.' *Westminster Review* 3 (January), 213–32. In *Collected Works,* IV, 23–43. Toronto 1967
– 1827. 'The New Corn Law.' *Westminster Review* 7 (January), 169–86. In *Collected Works,* IV, 141–59. Toronto 1967
– 1830. 'Of the Influence of Consumption on Production.' In *Essays on Some Unsettled Questions in Political Economy.* London 1844. In *Collected Works,* IV, 262–79. Toronto 1967
– 1833. 'Remarks on Bentham's Philosophy.' In *England and the English,* ed. E.L. Bulwer, II, 321–44. London. In *Collected Works,* X, 3–18. Toronto 1969
– 1835. 'Sedgwick's Discourse.' *London Review* 1 (July), 341–71. In *Collected Works,* X, 31–74. Toronto 1969
– 1848. *Principles of Political Economy.* 1st ed., London; 7th ed., London, 1871. In *Collected Works,* II–III. Toronto 1965
– 1852. 'Whewell on Moral Philosophy.' *Westminster and Foreign Quarterly Review* 58 (October), 349–85. In *Collected Works,* X, 175–201. Toronto 1969
– 1865. *An Examination of Sir William Hamilton's Philosophy.* 1st ed., London; 4th ed., London, 1872. In *Collected Works,* IX, Toronto 1979
– 1873. *Autobiography.* 1st ed., London. In *Collected Works,* I, 1–290. Toronto 1981
– 1879. 'Chapters on Socialism.' *Forthnightly Review,* n.s. 25 (February), 217–37; (March), 373–82; (April), 513–30 (posthumously published). In *Collected Works,* V, 705–53. Toronto 1967
– 1972. *The Later Letters, 1849–1873. Collected Works,* XIV–XVII, Toronto
– Commonplace Book, Mill-Taylor Collection, London School of Economics

Mirabeau, V.R. 1762–4. *L'Ami des hommes, ou, traite de la population.* 5th ed. (9 vols.). Paris

Mushet, Robert. 1810. *An Enquiry into the Effects Produced on the National Currency and Rates of Exchange by the Bank Rectriction Bill.* London

Newenham, Thomas. 1808. *A View of the Natural, Political and Commercial Circumstances of Ireland.* London

Oddy, Joshua Jepson. 1805. *European Commerce, showing New and Secure Channels of Trade with the Continent.* London

[Otter, William]. 1836. 'Memoir of Robert Malthus.' In Malthus, *Principles of Political Economy,* 2d ed., xiii–liv. London

Owen, Robert. 1816. *A new view of society; or, essays on the principle and the formation of the human character.* 2d ed., London and Edinburgh

Paine, Thomas. 1791. *Rights of man: being an answer to Mr. Burke's attack on the French Revolution.* London and Dublin

Paley, William. 1785. *The Principles of Moral and Political Philosophy.* 1st ed., London

– 1802. *Natural Theology, or Evidences of the Existence and Attributes of the Deity.* 1st ed., London; 2d ed., London 1803

– 1850. 'Sermons on Several Subjects,' No. XXXIII, *The Works of William Paley D.D.* (posthumously published). 599–601. Philadelphia

Place, F. 1822. *Illustrations and Proofs of the Principle of Population.* London 1822; London 1930; New York 1967

Political Economy Club. 1921. *Centenary Volume.* London

Price, Richard. 1783. *Observations on Reversionary Payments, on Schemes for Providing Annuities for Widows, and for Persons in Old Age.* 4th ed., London

Rae, John. 1834. *Statement of Some New Principles on the Subject of Political Economy.* 1st ed., Boston. In R. Warren James, ed., *John Rae: Political Economist,* Toronto 1965

Ravenstone, Piercy [Richard Puller]. 1821. *A Few Doubts ... on the Subjects of Population and Political Economy.* London

Ricardo, David. 1951–1973. *The Works and Correspondence of David Ricardo.* Ed. P. Sraffa (11 vols.). Cambridge

Say, J.B. 1803. *Traité d'économie politique.* 1st ed., Paris; 2d ed., 1814; 4th ed., 1819; 5th ed., 1826

– 1821. *Letters to Mr. Malthus on Several Subjects of political Economy and on the Cause of the Stagnation of Commerce.* London

Senior, Nassau. 1829. *Two Lectures on population ... to which is added, a Correspondence Between the Author and the Rev. T.R. Malthus.* London

– 1830. *Three Lectures on the Cost of Obtaining Money, and on Some Effects of Private and Government Paper Money.* London

Short, Thomas. 1750. *New Observations on Town and Country Bills of Mortality.* London

Sinclair, John. 1812. *An Account of the Systems of Husbandry adopted in the more improved Districts of Scotland.* 1st ed., Edinburgh and London; 3d ed., 1814

Smith, Adam. 1776. *An Inquiry into the Nature and Causes of the Wealth of Nations.* London. Modern Library ed., ed. E. Cannan, New York 1937

– 1802. *Recherches sur la nature et les causes de la richesse des nations.* Trans. Germain Garnier (5 vols.). Paris

– 1814. *Inquiry into the Nature and Causes of the Wealth of Nations.* 3 vols. 1st ed., ed. David Buchanan. Edinburgh and London

[Southey, Robert.] 1803. 'Malthus's Essay on Population,' *Annual Review and History of Literature; for 1803*, 2, 292–301 [1804]

– 1831. 'Moral and Political State of the British Empire,' *Quarterly Review* 44/87 (January), 261–317

Spence, William. 1807. *Britain Independent of Commerce.* 1st ed., London; 2d ed., 1808. In *Tracts on Political Economy.* London 1822; New York 1933

Steuart, Sir James. 1767. *An Inquiry into the Principles of Political Oeconomy.* 1st ed., Dublin (3 vols.). Ed. A.S. Skinner, Chicago 1966

Sumner, John Bird. 1816. *A Treatise on the Records of the Creation and on the Moral Attributes of the Creator.* (2 vols.). London

Süssmilch, Johann Peter. 1741. *Die goettlliche Ordnung in den veraenderungen des menschlichen Geschlechts.* 1st ed., Berlin; (3 vols.) Berlin 1798

Thompson, T. Perronet. 1826. *The True Theory of Rent in Opposition to Mr. Ricardo and Others.* London

Thornton, Henry. 1802. *An Enquiry into the Nature and Effects of the Paper Credit of Great Britain.* 1st ed., London. Ed. F.A. von Hayek, London 1939, 1962

Todhunter, I. 1876. *William Whewell, D.D.: An Account of His Writings, with Selections from his Literary and Scientific Correspondence.* (2 vols.). London

Tooke, Thomas. 1823. *Thoughts and Details on the High and Low Prices of the Thirty Years, 1793–1822.* 1st ed., London; 2d ed., London 1824

Torrens, Robert. 1815. *An Essay on the External Corn Trade.* 1st ed., London; 3d ed., London 1826

– 1818. 'Strictures on Mr. Ricardo's Doctrine respecting Value,' *Edinburgh Magazine*, October, 335–8

– 1819. 'Mr. Owen's Plans for Relieving the National Distress.' *Edinburgh Review* 32/64 (October), 453–77

– 1821. *An Essay on the Production of Wealth.* 1st ed., London. New York 1965

Tucker, Abraham. 1763–78. *Light of Nature Pursued.* (5 vols.). London

Turgot, A.R.J. 1770. *Reflexion sur la Formation et Distribution des Richesses.* Paris

von Boehm-Bawerk, E. 1890. *Capital and Interest.* Trans. William Smart, London 1930

von Humboldt, Friedrich Heinrich Alexander. 1811. *Essai politique sur le royaume de la Nouvelle Espagne* (5 vols.). Paris

Wallace, Robert. 1753. *Dissertation on the Numbers of Mankind in Ancient and Modern Times.* Edinburgh

West, Sir Edward. 1815. *Essay on the Application of Capital to Land.* 1st ed., London. Ed. J. Hollander, Baltimore 1903
– 1826. *Price of Corn and Wages of Labour.* London
Weyland, John. 1816. *The Principles of Population and Production.* London
Whewell, William. 1829. *Mathematical Exposition of Some Doctrines of Political Economy.* London
Young, Arthur. 1801. *An Inquiry into the Propriety of applying Wastes to the Better Maintenance and Support of the Poor.* London
– 1804. 'On the Application of the Principles of Population to the Question of assigning Land to Cottagers.' *Annals of Agriculture,* 41/239, 208–31
– 1812. 'An Enquiry into the Progressive Value of Money. *Annals of Agriculture* 46/270, [65]–135

III PARLIAMENTARY DOCUMENTS

Customs Tariffs of the United Kingdom from 1800 to 1897 [c. 8706]. London
House of Commons, Parliamentary Debates. Various years
House of Commons, Parliamentary Papers. 1801. *Abstract of Answers and Returns under Act for taking Account of Population of Great Britain.* (140) IV. [1801 census]
– 1812. *Abstract of Answers and Returns under Act for taking Account of Great Britain.* (316, 3n) XI. [1811 census]
– 1824. *Sixth Report from the Select Committee on Artisans and Machinery* (51) V. Malthus's evidence, 10 May, 598–601
– 1827. *Third Report from the Select Committee on Emigration.* (550) V. Malthus's evidence, 5 May, 311–27
– 1833. *First Report of the Factories Inquiry Commission.* (450) XX

IV MANUSCRIPT COLLECTIONS

Thomas Chalmers Collection. New College, Edinburgh
Mill–Taylor Collection. London School of Economics, London
John Murray Archives, 50 Albermarle Street, London
MacVey Napier Papers. British Library, London
William Whewell Papers. Trinity College, Cambridge
Wilmot-Horton Correspondence, Derbyshire Record Office, Matlock
Arthur Young Papers. British Library, London

V SECONDARY WORKS RELATING TO MALTHUS

Bonar, J. 1924. *Malthus and His Work.* 2d ed. London
– 1926. 'Notes on Malthus's First Essay.' In Malthus, 1798 Facscimile ed., i–xxvii. London

Costabile, L. 1983. 'Natural Prices, Market Prices and Effective Demand in Malthus.' *Australian Economic Papers* 22, 144–70

Costabile, L., and B. Rowthorn. 1985. 'Malthus's Theory of Wages and Growth.' *Economic Journal* 91, 418–37

de Marchi, N.B., and R.P. Sturges. 1973. 'Malthus and Ricardo's Inductivist Critics: Four Letters to William Whewell.' *Economica* 40 (November), 379–93

Dooley, Peter C. 1988. 'Malthus on Long Swings: The General Case.' *Canadian Journal of Economics* 21 (February), 200–5

Dorfman, R. 1989. 'Thomas Robert Malthus and David Ricardo.' *Journal of Economic Perspectives* 3 (Summer), 153–64

Dupâquier, J. 1983. 'Preface.' In *Malthus Past and Present*, ed. J. Dupâquier, A. Fauve-Chamoux, and E. Grebenik, vii–xiii. London and New York

Fetter, F.A. 1898. 'The Essay of Malthus: A Centennial Review.' *Yale Review* 7 (August), 153–67

Flew, A. 1970. 'Introduction.' In Malthus, *Essay on the Principle of Population*, 7–56. Harmondsworth

Flinn, M.W. 1983. 'Malthus and his Time.' In *Malthus Past and Present*, ed. J. Dupâquier, A. Fauve-Chamoux, and E. Grebenik, 85–96. London and New York

Ghosh, R.M. 1963. 'Malthus on Emigration and Colonization: Letters to Wilmot-Horton.' *Economica* 30 (February), 45–62

Gilbert, G. 1980. 'Economic Growth and the Poor in Malthus' *Essay on Population.*' *History of Political Economy* 12/1, (Spring), 83–96

Gordon, B. 1985. 'John Cazenove (1788–1879): Critic of Ricardo, Friend and Editor of Malthus.' Working Paper, Third HETSA Conference held at La Trobe University, Melbourne, May

Grampp, W.D. 1956. 'Malthus on Money Wages and Welfare.' *American Economic Review* 46/5 (December), 924–36

– 1974. 'Malthus and His Contemporaries.' *History of Political Economy* 6/3 (Fall), 278–304

Hartwick, John M. 1988. 'Robert Wallace and Malthus and the Ratios,' *History of Political Economy* 20/3 (Fall), 357–80

Harvey-Phillips, M.B. 1984. 'Malthus's Theodicy: The Intellectual Background to his Contribution to Political Economy.' *History of Political Economy* 16/4 (Winter), 591–608

Hollander, Jacob H. 1903. 'Introduction.' In Malthus, *An Inquiry into the Nature and Progress of Rent*, Baltimore

– 1932. 'Introduction.' In Malthus, *Observations on the Effects of the Corn Laws.* 1st ed., London 1814; 2d ed., London 1814; 3rd ed., London 1815. Baltimore

Hollander, Samuel. 1969. 'Malthus and the Post-Napoleonic Depression.' *History of Political Economy* 1/2 (Fall), 306–35

– 1986. 'On Malthus's Population Principle and Social Reform.' *History of Political Economy* 18/2 (Summer), 187–235
– 1992a. 'Malthus's Abandonment of Agricultural Protectionism: A Discovery in the History of Economic Thought. *American Economic Review* 82/3 (June), 650–9
– 1992b. 'On Malthus's Physiocratic References.' *History of Political Economy* 24/2 (Spring), 369–80
– 1995a. 'More on Malthus and Agricultural Protection.' *History of Political Economy* 27/3 (Fall), 531–8
James, Patricia. 1979. *Population Malthus: His Life and Times.* London
Kates, S. 1994. 'The Malthusian Origins of the *General Theory*.' *History of Economics Review* 21 (Winter), 10–20
Keynes, J.M. 1933. 'Robert Malthus: The First of the Cambridge Economists.' In *Essays in Biography*, 95–149, London
Lee, Maw Lin, and David Loschky. 1987. 'Malthusian Population Oscillations.' *Economic Journal* 97 (September), 727–39
Levy, D. 1978. 'Some Normative Aspects of the Malthusian Controversy.' *History of Political Economy* 10/2 (Summer), 271–85
– 1996. 'Malthusian vs. Christianity: The Moral Challenge to God's Existence.' Ms.
Meek, R.L. 1953. *Marx and Engels on Malthus.* London
Nakaya, Toshihiro. 1985. 'Theoretical Structure and Character of Malthus' *Measure of Value*.' Society of Economics, Nanzan University, Working Paper Series no. 2
Negishi, T. 1989. *History of Economic Theory.* Amsterdam
– 1993. 'A Smithian-Growth Model and Malthus's Optimal Propensity to Save.' *European Journal of the History of Economic Thought* 1/1 (Autumn), 115–27
O Gráda, C. 1984. 'Malthus and the Pre-Famine Economy.' In *Economists and the Irish Economy*, ed. A.E. Murphy, 75–95. Dublin
O'Leary, James J. 1942. 'Malthus and Keynes.' *Journal of Political Economy* 50 (December), 901–19
Paglin, Morton I. 1961. *Malthus and Lauderdale: The Anti-Ricardian Tradition.* New York
Penrose, E.F. 1957. 'Malthus and the Underdeveloped Areas.' *Economic Journal* 67 (March), 219–39
Petersen, W. 1979. *Malthus.* Cambridge, MA
Polkinghorn, B.A. 1986. 'An Unpublished Letter from Malthus to Jane Marcet, January 22, 1833.' *American Economic Review* 76/4 (September) 845–7
Porta, Pier Luigi. 1992. 'Introduction.' In *David Ricardo: Notes on Malthus's 'Measure of Value,'* ed. Pier Luigi Porta, ix–xxi. Cambridge
Prendergast, Renee. 1986. 'Malthus's Discussion of the Corn-Ratio Theory of Profits.' *Cambridge Journal of Economics* 10/2 (June), 187–9
– 1987. 'James Anderson's Political Economy – His Influence on Smith

and Malthus.' *Scottish Journal of Political Economy* 34 (November), 388–409

Pullen, John M. 1978. 'The Editor of the Second Edition of T.R. Malthus' *Principles of Political Economy*.' *History of Political Economy*, 10/2 (Summer), 286–97

– 1981a. 'Malthus's Theological Ideas and Their Influence on His Principle of Population.' *History of Political Economy* 13/1 (Spring), 39–54

– 1981b. 'Notes from Malthus: The Inverarity Manuscript.' *History of Political Economy* 13/4 (Winter), 794–811

– 1982. 'Malthus on the Doctrine of Proportions and the Concept of the Optimum.' *Australian Economic Papers* 21, 270–85

– 1987a. 'Malthus, Thomas Robert.' In *The New Palgrave: A Dictionary of Economics*, ed. J. Eatwell, M. Milgate, and P. Newman, III, 280–5. London

– 1987b. 'Some New Information on the Rev. T.R. Malthus,' *History of Political Economy* 19/1 (Spring), 127–40

– 1989. 'Introduction.' In T.R. Malthus, *Principles of Political Economy*, xv–xix. Cambridge

– 1995. 'Malthus on Agricultural Protection: An Alternative View.' *History of Political Economy* 27/3 (Fall), 517–30

Pullen, John M., and J.C. Baldry. 1988. 'Malthus' Production Function,' *The History of Economic Thought Society of Australia Bulletin* 10 (Summer), 10–23

Rashid, S. 1981. 'Malthus' *Principles* and British Economic Thought, 1820–1835.' *History of Political Economy* 13/1 (Spring), 55–79

– 1984. 'Malthus' Theology: An Overlooked Letter and Some Comments.' *History of Political Economy* 16/1 (Spring), 135–8

– 1987. 'Malthus and Classical Economics.' In *The New Palgrave: A Dictionary of Economics*, ed. J. Eatwell, M. Milgate, and P. Newman, III, 285–90. London

– 1988. 'Recent Literature on Malthus.' In W.O. Thweatt, ed., *Classical Political Economy*, 53–84. Boston

Reisman, David. 1990. 'The Cambridge Malthus.' *History of Economic Thought Newsletter* 45 (Autumn), 1–4

Rutherford, R.P. 1987. 'Malthus and Keynes.' *Oxford Economic Papers* 39/1 (March), 175–89

Semmel, B. 1963. 'Introductory Essay: Malthus and the Reviews.' In *Occasional Papers of T.R. Malthus*, ed. B. Semmel, 3–29. New York

– 1965. 'Malthus: Physiocracy and the Commercial System.' *Economic History Review* 17/3, 522–35

Sowell, T. 1962. 'Malthus and the Utilitarians.' *Canadian Journal of Economics and Political Science* 28/2 (May), 268–74

Spengler, J.J. 1942. *French Predecessors of Malthus.* Durham, NC

– 1960 [1945]. 'Malthus's Total Population Theory: A Restatement and Reappraisal.' In *Essays in Economic Thought: Aristotle to Marshall*, ed. J.J. Spengler and W.R. Allen, 349–406. Chicago 1960

Tribe, Keith. 1993. 'Comment to Hollander (1992[a]).' *History of Economic Thought Newsletter* 50 (Spring), 23

Vamplew, W. 1986. 'Malthus and the Corn Laws.' In *Malthus and His Time*, ed. M. Turner, 129–39. London

Waterman, A.M.C. 1983. 'Malthus as a Theologian: The First Essay and the Relation between Political Economy and Christian Theology.' In *Malthus Past and Present*, ed. J. Dupâquier, A. Fauve-Chamoux, and E. Grebenik, 198–209. London and New York

– 1987. 'On the Malthusian Theory of Long Swings.' *Canadian Journal of Economics* 20 (May), 257–70

– 1991. *Revolution, Economics, and Religion: Christian Political Economy, 1798–1833*. Cambridge

– 1992. 'Analysis and ideology in Malthus's *Essay on Population.*' *Australian Economic Papers* 31 (June), 203–17

– 1995. 'Peasants, Population and Progress in Malthus and Chalmers.' In *The Peasant in Economic Thought*, ed. E. Forget and R.A. Lobdell, 31–53. Aldershot

– 1996a. 'On Modelling Malthus's Growth Theory.' Unpublished manuscript

Winch, D. 1983. 'Higher Maxims: Happiness versus Wealth in Malthus and Ricardo.' In *That Nobele Science of Politics*, ed. S. Collini, D. Winch, and J. Burrow, 63–90. Cambridge

– 1987. *Malthus*. Oxford

– 1993. 'Robert Malthus: Christian Moral Scientist, Arch-Demoralizer, or Implicit Secular Utilitarian?' *Utilitas* 5/2 (November), 239–54

Wrigley, Edward A. 1983b. 'Malthus's Model of a Pre-industrial Economy.' In *Malthus Past and Present*, ed. J. Dupâquier, A. Fauve-Chamoux, and E. Grebenik, 111–24. London and New York

V OTHER SECONDARY WORKS

Allington, Nigel. 1977. Review of Huskisson (1830). In *History of Economic Thought Newsletter* 18 (Spring), 23–8

Arnon, Arie. 1991. *Thomas Tooke: Pioneer of Monetary Theory*. Aldershot

Baumol, W.J. 1983. 'Marx and the Iron Law of Wages.' *American Economic Review* 83/2 (May), 303–8

Becker, G.S., and W.J. Baumol. 1952. 'The Classical Monetary Theory: The Outcome of the Discussion.' *Economica*, 19 (November), 355–96. In *Essays in Economic Thought: Aristotle to Marshall*, ed. J.J. Spengler and W.R. Allen, 753–72. Chicago 1960

Blaug, Mark. 1985. *Ricardian Economics: A Historical Study*. New Haven, CT

Bowley, Marian. 1973. *Studies in the History of Economic Theory before 1870*. London

Brewer, A. 1987. 'Turgot: Founder of Classical Economics.' *Economica* 54 (November) 417–28

Cannan, Edwin. 1917. *A History of the Theories of Production and Distribution in English Political Economy from 1776 to 1848.* 3d ed., London
Coats, A.W. 1971. 'The Classical Economists and the Labourer.' In *The Classical Economists and Economic Policy,* ed. A.W. Coats, 144–79. London
Dow, A. 1984. 'The Hauteur of Adam Smith: An Unpublished Letter from James Anderson of Monkshill.' *Scottish Journal of Political Economy* 31/3, 284–5
Eltis, Walter. 1984. *The Classical Theory of Economic Growth.* London
– 1985. 'Ricardo on Machinery and Technological Unemployment.' In *The Legacy of Ricardo,* ed. G.A. Caravale, 257–84. London
Faccarello, G. 1982. 'Sraffa versus Ricardo: The Historical Irrelevance of the "Corn-Profit" Model.' *Economy and Society* 11 (May), 122–37
Fetter, F.W. 1957. 'Introduction.' In *The Economic Writings of Francis Horner in the 'Edinburgh Review,'* 1–22. New York
– 1965a. *Development of British Monetary Orthodoxy, 1797–1875.* Cambridge, MA
– 1965b. 'Economic Controversy in the British Reviews, 1802–1850.' *Economica* 32 (November), 424–37
– 1980. *The Economist in Parliament.* Durham, NC
Gibbard, Keith. 1994. 'Hollander's Textual Interpretation of Ricardian Growth Theory: A Reconsideration.' *History of Political Economy* 26/3 (Fall), 465–86
Gordon, B. 1970. *Economic Doctrine and Tory Liberalism, 1824–1830.* London
Gordon, H. Scott. 1971. 'The Ideology of Laissez-Faire.' In *The Classical Economists and Economic Policy,* ed. A.W. Coats, 180–205. London
Grampp, W.D. 1960. *The Manchester School of Economics.* Stanford
– 1965. *Economic Liberalism. II: The Classical View.* New York
Groenewegen, P.D. 1983. 'Turgot's Place in the History of Economic Thought: A Bicentenary Estimate.' *History of Political Economy* 15/4 (Winter), 585–616
Himmelfarb, G. 1984. *The Idea of Poverty: England in the Early Industrial Age.* New York
Hollander, Samuel. 1973. *The Economics of Adam Smith.* Toronto
– 1979. *The Economics of David Ricardo.* Toronto
– 1985. *The Economics of John Stuart Mill.* Oxford
– 1987. *Classical Economics.* Oxford
– 1991b. 'On the Endogeneity of the Margin and Related Issues in Ricardian Economics.' *Journal of the History of Economic Thought* 13/2 (Fall), 159–74
– 1994a. 'Economic Theory and Policy: An Introduction to John Stuart Mill's Political Economy. In *Economic Thought and Political Theory,* ed. D. Reisman, 63–101. Boston
– 1994b. 'On the Textual Interpretation of Ricardian Growth Theory:

The "New View" Confirmed (Again).' *History of Political Economy* 26/3 (Fall), 487–500
– 1995b. *Ricardo – The New View.* London
Keynes, J.M. 1933. 'Alfred Marshall.' In *Essays in Biography,* 150–66. London
Laidler, D. 1972. 'Thomas Tooke on Monetary Reform.' In *Essays in Honour of Lord Robbins,* ed. M. Peston and B. Corry, 168–86. London
Landry, A. 1958. 'Les Idées de Quesnay sur la population.' In *François Quesnay et la Physiocratie,* ed. A. Sauvy, I, 11–49. Paris
Langer, G.F. 1987. *The Coming of Age of Political Economy, 1815–1825.* New York
Levy, D. 1976. 'Ricardo and the Iron Law: A Correction of the Record.' *History of Political Economy* 8/2 (Summer) 235–52
Meek, R.L. 1962. *The Economics of Physiocracy.* London
O'Brien, D.P. 1970. *J.R. McCulloch: A Study in Classical Economics.* London
– 1975. *The Classical Economists.* Oxford
– 1988. 'Classical Reassessments.' In W.O. Thweatt, ed., *Classical Political Economy,* 179–220. Boston
Peach, T. 1988. 'David Ricardo: A Review of Some Interpretative Issues.' In *Classical Political Economy,* ed. W.O. Thweatt, 103–31. Boston
Robbins, L.C. 1952. *The Theory of Economic Policy in English Classical Political Economy.* London
– 1958. *Robert Torrens and the Evolution of Classical Economics.* London
– 1968. *The Theory of Economic Development in the History of Economic Thought.* London
Samuelson, P.A. 1978. 'The Canonical Classical Model of Political Economy.' *Journal of Economic Literature* 16 (December), 1415–34
– 1991. 'Sraffa's Other Leg.' *Economic Journal* 101 (May), 570–4
Semmel, B. 1970. *The Rise of Free Trade Imperialism: Classical Political Economy, the Empire of Free Trade and Imperialism.* Cambridge
Skourtos, M.S. 1991. 'Corn Models in the Classical Tradition: P. Sraffa Considered Historically.' *Cambridge Journal of Economics* 15/2 (June), 215–28
Smith, V.E. 1951. 'The Classicists' Use of Demand.' *Journal of Political Economy* 59 (June), 242–57
Sockwell, W.D. 1994. *Popularizing Classical Economics: Henry Brougham and William Ellis.* New York
Sowell, T. 1974. *Classical Economics Reconsidered.* Princeton, NJ
Sraffa, Piero. 1951. 'Introduction.' In Ricardo, *Works and Correspondence,* I, xiii–lxii
Stigler, G.J. 1965. *Essays in the History of Economics,* Chicago
– 1981. 'Review of Hollander, *The Economics of David Ricardo.*' *Journal of Economic Literature* 19 (March), 100–2
Thweatt, William O. 1976. 'James Mill and the Early Development of Comparative Advantage.' *History of Political Economy* 8/2 (Summer), 207–34

Tucker, G.S.L. 1954. 'The Origin of Ricardo's Theory of Profits.' *Economica* 21 (November), 320–33
– 1960. *Progress and Profits in British Economic Thought: 1650–1850*. Cambridge
– 1978. *The Political Economy of William Huskisson*. Research Report no. 46, University of Newcastle, NSW
von Hayek, F.A. 1932. 'A Note on the Development of the Doctrine of "Forced Savings."' *Quarterly Journal of Economics* 47 (November), 123–33
Waterman, A.M.C. 1996b. 'Why Keynes Thought that William Paley Was the First of the Cambridge Economists.' *Cambridge Journal of Economics*. In press
Winch, D., ed. 1966. *James Mill: Selected Economic Writings*. Edinburgh and London

VII GENERAL ECONOMIC THEORY AND ITS HISTORY

Becker, G.S. 1988. 'Family Economics and Macro Behavior.' *American Economic Review* 78 (March), 1–13
Blaug, Mark. 1980. *The Methodology of Economics or How Economists Explain*. Cambridge
– 1985. *Economic Theory in Retrospect*. 4th ed., Cambridge
Broome, John. 1991. *Weighing Goods: Equality, Uncertainty and Time*. Cambridge, MA
Garegnani, P. 1991. 'The Labour Theory of Value: "Detour" or Technical Advance.' In *Marx and Modern Economic Analysis*, ed. G.A. Caravale, I, 97–118. Aldershot
Hodgson, Geoffrey M. 1993. *Economics and Evolution: Bringing Life Back into Economics*. Oxford
Hutchison, T.W. 1978. *On Revolutions and Progress in Economic Knowledge*. Cambridge
Klein, Lawrence R. 1966. *The Keynesian Revolution*, 2d ed. New York
Lloyd, P.J. 1969. 'Elementary Geometric/Arithmetic Series and Early Production Theory.' *Journal of Political Economy* 77 (January/February), 21–34
Meltzer, Allan H. 1988. *Keynes's Monetary Theory: A Different Interpretation*. Cambridge
Myint, H. 1948. *Theories of Welfare Economics*. London
Patinkin, D. 1982. *Anticipations of the General Theory? And Other Essays on Keynes*. Chicago
Robbins, L.C. 1970. *The Evolution of Modern Economic Theory*. London
Schumpeter, J.A. 1954. *History of Economic Analysis*. New York
Sraffa, Piero. 1960. *Production of Commodities by Means of Commodities*. Cambridge
Taylor, O.H. 1960. *A History of Economic Thought*. New York

Viner, Jacob. 1924. *Canada's Balance of International Indebtedness, 1900–1913*. Cambridge, MA
– 1937. *Studies in the Theory of International Trade.* New York
– 1958. *The Long View and the Short.* Glencoe, IL
von Hayek, F.A. 1935. *Prices and Production,* 2d ed. London

VIII BIBLIOGRAPHICAL WORKS

Fetter, F.W. 1953. 'The Authorship of Economic Articles in the *Edinburgh Review,* 1802–47. *Journal of Political Economy* 61 (June), 232–59
Hollander, Samuel. 1991a. 'New Editions of Malthus.' *Utilitas* 3/2 (November), 303–10
– 1992b. 'On Malthus's Physiocratic References.' *History of Political Economy* 24/2 (Summer), 369–80
– 1996. 'On the Authorship of "Spence on Commerce" in the *Edinburgh Review,* 1808.' *Victorian Periodicals Review* 29/4 (Winter), 315–29

IX WORKS ON ECONOMIC, POLITICAL, AND SOCIAL HISTORY

Barnes, D.G. 1930. *A History of the English Corn Laws: 1660–1846.* London
Blaug, Mark. 1963. 'The Myth of the Old Poor Law and the Making of the New.' *Journal of Economic History*' 23/2 (June), 151–84
Clough, S.B. 1964. *France: A History of National Economies, 1789–1939.* New York
Crouzet, F. 1982. *The Victorian Economy.* New York
Eversley, D.E.C. 1959. *Social Theories of Fertility and the Malthusian Debate.* Oxford
Fay, C.R. 1932. *The Corn Laws and Social England.* Cambridge
Feavearyear, Albert. 1963. *The Pound Sterling: A History of English Money,* 2d, ed., Oxford
Gouraud, C. 1854. *Histoire de la politique commerciale de la France,* 2 vols. Paris
Gras, N.S.B. 1915. *The Evolution of the English Corn Market.* Cambridge
Halévy, E. 1955. *The Growth of Philosophic Radicalism.* Trans. Mary Morris. Boston
Hilton, Boyd. 1977. *Corn, Cash, Commerce: The Economic Policies of the Tory Governments, 1815–1830.* Oxford
Hueckel, Glenn. 1981. 'Agriculture during Industrialization.' In *The Economic History of Britain since 1700,* ed. R. Floud and D. McCloskey, I: *1700–1860,* 182–203. Cambridge
Huzel, J.P. 1969. 'Malthus, the Poor Law, and the Population in Early Nineteenth-Century England.' *Economic History Review* 22/3 (December), 430–52
– 1980. 'The Demographic Impact of the Old Poor Law: More Reflexions on Malthus.' *Economic History Review* 33/3 (August), 367–81

Lee, R.D., and R.S. Schofield. 1981. 'British Population in the Eighteenth Century.' In *The Economic History of Britain since 1700*, ed. R. Floud and D. McCloskey, I: *1700–1860*, 17–35. Cambridge

Mitchell, B.R. 1962. *Abstract of British Historical Statistics.* Cambridge

Smart, William. 1910–17. *Economic Annals of the Nineteenth Century* (2 vols.). London

Stephen, L. 1900. *The English Utilitarians* (3 vols). London

Tranter, N.L. 1981. 'The Labour Supply, 1780–1860.' In *The Economic History of Britain since 1700*, ed. R. Floud and D. McCloskey, I: *1700–1860*, 204–26. Cambridge

Viner, J. 1972. *The Role of Providence in the Social Order.* Philadelphia

Wrigley, E.A. 1983a. 'The Growth of Population in Eighteenth-Century England: A Conundrum Resolved.' *Past and Present* 98 (February), 121–50

GENERAL INDEX

Abbreviations: Throughout the index the following abbreviations are used in subheadings:

M.	= Malthus
R.	= Ricardo
Essay	= *Essay on Population*
Principles	= *Principles of Political Economy*

INDEX TO CORRESPONDENCE

Abbreviations: Throughout the index the following abbreviations are used in subheadings:

M. = Malthus
R. = Ricardo

MALTHUS'S CORRESPONDENCE